# BOOKS | À LA CARTE EDITION

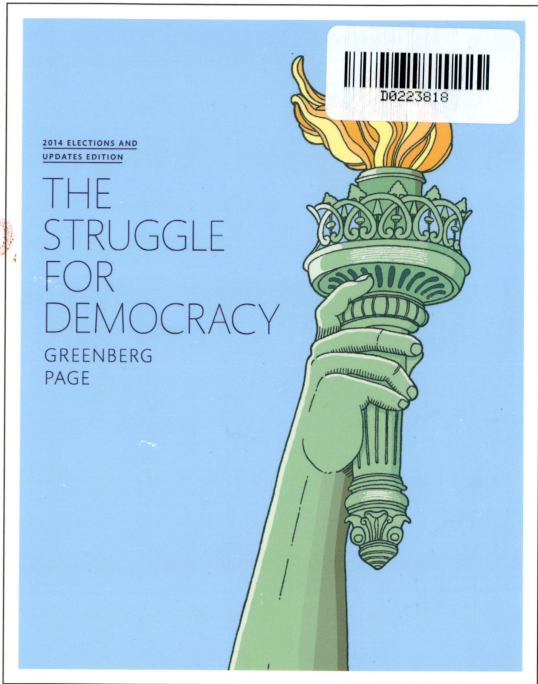

2014 ELECTIONS AND
UPDATES EDITION

# THE STRUGGLE FOR DEMOCRACY

GREENBERG
PAGE

## YOUR TEXTBOOK—IN A BINDER-READY EDITION!

This unbound, three-hole punched version of your textbook
lets you take only what you need to class and incorporate your
own notes—all at an affordable price!

ISBN-13: 978-0-13-391527-3
ISBN-10: 0-13-391527-1

EAN

ALWAYS LEARNING

PEARSON

# THE STRUGGLE FOR DEMOCRACY

# THE STRUGGLE FOR DEMOCRACY

## 2014 ELECTIONS AND UPDATES EDITION

Edward S. GREENBERG

University of Colorado, Boulder

Benjamin I. PAGE

Northwestern University

with assistance by

David Doherty
Loyola University Chicago

Scott L. Minkoff
Barnard College

Josh M. Ryan
Bradley University

**PEARSON**

Boston   Columbus   Indianapolis   New York   San Francisco
Amsterdam   Cape Town   Dubai   London   Madrid   Milan
Munich   Paris   Montréal   Toronto   Delhi   Mexico City   São Paulo   Sydney
Hong Kong   Seoul   Singapore   Taipei   Tokyo

**Editorial Director:** Craig Campanella
**Editor-in-Chief:** Dickson Musslewhite
**Acquisitions Editor:** Jeff Marshall
**Program Team Lead:** Maureen Richardson
**Program Manager:** Beverly Fong
**Editorial Assistant:** Kieran Fleming
**Field Marketing Manager:** Brittany
   Pogue-Mohammed
**Product Marketing Manager:** Tricia Murphy
**Project Management, Team Lead:** Melissa Feimer
**Project Manager:** Carol O'Rourke
**Development:** Ohlinger Publishing
   Services, Judy O'Neill

**Digital Studio Media:** Tina Gagliostro
**Art Director:** Maria Lange
**Cover Design:** Pentagram
**Cover Illustration:** Toby Triumph
**Senior Procurement Supervisor:** Mary Fischer
**Procurement Specialist:** Mary Ann Gloriande
**Composition and Full-Service Project Management:**
   Sneha Pant/Lumina Datamatics, Inc.
Manufactured in the United States by RR Donnelley
**Text Font:** 10.5/13 ACaslonPro Regular

Credits and acknowledgements borrowed from other sources and reproduced with Premission, in this textbook appear on the appropriate page within the text or on page 665.

**Library of Congress Cataloging-in-Publication Data**
Greenberg, Edward S., 1942-
  The struggle for democracy / Edward S.Greenberg, University of Colorado, Boulder Benjamin I.
Page, Northwestern University. — Eleventh ed., 2014 Election Edition
     pages cm
  Includes bibliographical references and index.
  ISBN 978-0-13-391474-0
  ISBN 0-13-391474-7
  1. Democracy—United States.   2. United States—Politics and government—Textbooks.
I. Page, Benjamin I.   II. Title.
  JK274.G692 2016
  320.473—dc23

                                                    2014036620

*To Martha, whose love and support have sustained me while I wrote (with Ben Page)*
*and revised this book through eleven editions spanning more than two decades.*

10 9 8 7 6 5 4
V011

Student Edition:
ISBN 13: 978-0-13391474-0
ISBN 10: 0-13-391474-7
Exam Copy:
ISBN 13: 9-78-0-13391528-0
ISBN 10: 0-13-391528-X
A la Carte Edition
ISBN 13: 978-0-13391527-3
ISBN 10: 0-13-391527-1

# BRIEF CONTENTS

# CONTENTS

# Why study **American government** and

politics and why read this textbook to do it? Here's why: Only by understanding how our complex political system operates and how government works can you play a role in deciding what government does. Only by understanding the obstacles that stand in your way as you enter the political fray, as well as the abundant opportunities you have to advance your ideas and values in the political process, can you play an effective role.

You can learn this best, we believe, by studying what political scientists have discovered about American politics and government. Political science is the systematic study of the role that people and groups play in determining what government does, how government goes about implementing its policy decisions, and what social, economic, and political consequences flow from government actions. The best political science research is testable, evidence-based, and peer-reviewed, as free as possible from ideological and partisan bias as it can be.

*The Struggle for Democracy* not only introduces you to that research, but it also helps you critically analyze the American political system and identify opportunities to make a difference. In *The Struggle for Democracy*, we provide a simple but powerful framework to help you see how government, politics, and the larger society are intertwined and how government policies are a product of the interactions of actors and institutions in these domains. Our hope and expectation is that using *The Struggle for Democracy* will help you to succeed in your introduction to American government and politics.

But we are interested in more than your classroom success. We believe that knowing how politics and government work and how closely they conform to our democratic values gives you a head start in the real world of politics. But we are not naive. We do not believe that making your mark on public policies is or will be an easy matter or that all that you and like-minded individuals need to do is vote. After all, those who have gained the most from government policies have substantial resources to make certain that government treats them well.

But you have resources as well. Change you are interested in may come from, in addition to voting, your involvement in political campaigns, using social media to

## Meet Your Authors

**EDWARD S. GREENBERG**
is Professor Emeritus of Political Science and a Research Professor of Behavioral Science at the University of Colorado, Boulder. Ed's research and teaching interests include American government and politics, domestic and global political economy, and democratic theory and practice, with a special emphasis on workplace issues. His multi-year longitudinal panel study, funded by the NIH, examining the impact of corporate restructuring on employees, has recently been published and is now being revised and updated.

**BENJAMIN I. PAGE**
is the Gordon S. Fulcher Professor of Decision Making at Northwestern University in Evanston, Illinois. Ben's interests include public opinion and policy making, the mass media, empirical democratic theory, political economy, policy formation, the presidency, and American foreign policy. He is currently engaged in a large collaborative project to study Economically Successful Americans and the Common Good and the rise and political consequences of income and wealth inequality in the United States.

persuade others of your views or to organize meetings and demonstrations, participating in social movement organizations, contributing to groups and politicians who share your views, interests, and more. So, much like waging war, making your voice heard requires that you know the "lay of the land," including the weapons you have at your disposal (we would call them political tools), and the weapons of those arrayed against you. But, much like peacemaking, you need to know how and when compromises can be reached that serve the interests of all parties.

Lest all of the above seems too daunting, we also have tried to make this book enjoyable and accessible so that reading it and learning from it will be a great deal of fun for you. We believe we have succeeded in this goal. We only hope you have as much fun reading *The Struggle for Democracy* as we had writing it for you.

# TO THE INSTRUCTOR

## We decided to **write this book** because as **instructors** in large

American government courses, we could not find a book that provided students with usable tools for critically analyzing our political system and making judgments about how well our government works. *The Struggle for Democracy* does not simply present facts about government and politics, but it provides several analytical and normative frameworks for putting the flood of facts we ask our students to absorb into a more comprehensible form. By doing so, we believe we have made it easier and more satisfying for instructors to teach the introductory course.

Our goal, all along, has been to create a textbook that treats students as adults, engages their intellectual and emotional attention, and encourages them to be active learners. Every element in this text is designed to promote the kind of critical thinking skills scholars and instructors believe students need in order to become the engaged, active, and informed citizens that are so vital to any democracy. Over the next several sections, we show the elements we have created to meet these objectives.

## New to This Edition

Key updates to this eleventh edition of *The Struggle for Democracy* include:

- Substantial coverage of the **consequential 2012 national and the 2014 midterm congressional elections**, with special attention to these elections in Chapter 10 on voting, campaigns, and elections and in Chapter 11 on Congress.

- Coverage throughout, but especially in Chapters 3, 10, 14, 15, 16, and 17, on important rulings by the Supreme Court on same-sex marriage, efforts to limit voting rights, immigration, affirmative action, election financing, the commerce clause, and the Affordable Care Act.

- Consideration, especially in Chapter 12, "The Presidency" and Chapter 18, "Foreign Policy and National Defense," on the new challenges posed by the rise of ISIS in Syria and Iraq, nuclear weapons programs in North Korea, Pakistan, and especially Iran, China's emergence as a competing world power, and Russia's attempt to reassert its power in Ukraine and in other countries formerly a part of the Soviet Union.

- Increased attention to the **growing partisan bitterness** in Washington and across much of the nation that affects how government addresses or fails to address virtually every major problem facing the nation whether it be energy, illegal immigration, climate change, or the shrinking middle class (Chapters 9, 10, 11, and 17).

- A focus in several chapters on the question of whether and to what degree income and wealth inequality has increased, and if it has, with what political and public policy consequences. We also look at **globalization and technological change and their impact on Americans.**

- We also look at the ways economic and technological trends shape government action, including new legislation to regulate the financial industry, executive orders increasing gas mileage requirements for cars, and prosecution of government employees who leak confidential government information to social media sites (Chapters 4, 6, 15, 17, and 18).

- **Photos** in this edition were selected not only to capture major events from the last few years but to illustrate politics' relevancy. They show political actors and processes as well as people affected by politics, creating a visual narrative that enhances rather than repeats the text. The data in all of the **figures and tables** have been updated throughout with the intention of helping users think critically not only about political decisions in retrospect but also about pending government action.

# Revel™

**EDUCATIONAL TECHNOLOGY DESIGNED FOR THE WAY TODAY'S STUDENTS READ, THINK, AND LEARN** When students are engaged deeply, they learn more effectively and perform better in their courses. This simple fact inspired the creation of REVEL: an immersive learning experience designed for the way today's students read, think, and learn. Built in collaboration with educators and students nationwide, REVEL is the newest, fully digital way to deliver respected Pearson content.

REVEL enlivens course content with media interactives and assessments—integrated directly within the authors' narrative—that provide opportunities for students to read about and practice course material in tandem. This immersive educational technology boosts student engagement, which leads to better understanding of concepts and improved performance throughout the course.

**Learn more about REVEL** at http://www.pearsonhighered.com/revel/.

# Features

**APPROACH** *The Struggle for Democracy* provides several analytical and normative frameworks for putting the flood of facts we ask our students to absorb into a more comprehensible form. Although all topics that are common and expected in the introductory American government and politics course are covered in this textbook, our three main focal points—the analytical framework for understanding how politics and government work and the questions "How democratic are we?" and "Can government do anything well?"—allow us to take a fresh look at traditional topics.

We pay great attention to *structural factors*—which include the American economy, social change in the United States, technological innovations and change, the American political culture, and changes in the global system—and examine how they affect politics, government, and public policy. These factors are introduced in Chapter 4—a chapter unique among introductory texts—and they are brought to bear on a wide range of issues in subsequent chapters.

We attend very carefully to issues of *democratic political theory*. This follows from our critical thinking objective, which asks students to assess the progress of and prospects for democracy in the United States, and from our desire to present American history as the history of the struggle for democracy. For instance, we examine how the evolution of the party system has improved democracy in some respects in the United States, but hurt it in others.

We also include more *historical perspective* because that is the best way to evaluate the progress of democracy in the United States. We show, for example, how the expansion of civil rights in the United States has been associated with important historical events and trends.

We have integrated substantial *comparative information* because we believe that a full understanding of government and politics and the effect of structural factors on them is possible only through a comparison of developments, practices, and institutions in the United States with those in other nations. We understand better how our system of social welfare works, for example, when we see how other rich democratic countries deal with the problems of poverty, unemployment, and old age.

**COVERAGE**  Part 1 includes an introduction to the textbook, its themes, and the critical thinking tools used throughout the book. Part 2 covers the structural foundations of American government and politics, addressing subjects such as America's economy, political culture, and place in the international system; the constitutional framework of the American political system; and the development of federalism. Part 3 focuses on what we call *political linkage* institutions, such as parties, elections, public opinion, social movements, and interest groups that convey the wants, needs, and demands of individuals and groups to public officials. Part 4 concentrates on the central institutions of the national government, including the presidency, Congress, and the Supreme Court. Part 5 describes the kinds of policies the national government produces and analyzes how effective government is at solving pressing social and economic problems. Our approach also means that the subjects of *civil liberties* and *civil rights* are not treated in conjunction with the Constitution in Part 2, which is the case with many introductory texts, but in Part 5, on public policy. This is because we believe that the real-world status of civil liberties and civil rights, while partly determined by specific provisions of the Constitution, is better understood as the outcome of the interaction of structural, political, and governmental factors. Thus, the status of civil rights for gays and lesbians depends not only on constitutional provisions but also on the state of public opinion, degrees of support from elected political leaders, and the decisions of the Supreme Court.

**PEDAGOGY**  *The Struggle for Democracy* offers unique features that help students better understand, interpret, and critically evaluate American politics and government.

- **Using the Democracy Standard** helps students to think about the American political system as a whole using a normative democracy "yardstick" that measures the degree to which we have become more or less democratic. This yardstick is introduced at the beginning of each chapter and revisited in the final section of each chapter, which asks students what conclusions they have reached regarding "How democratic are we?"

- **Using the Framework** is a unique visual tool that shows the many influences in the American political process and how they shape political decisions and policies. This feature makes clear that government, politics, and society are deeply intertwined in recognizable patterns; that what might be called "deep structures"—the economy, society, political culture, and the constitutional rules—are particularly important for understanding how our system works; and that understanding American politics requires the holistic focus this feature encourages.

- **By the Numbers** encourages students to understand the numbers and statistical information on government, politics, economy, and society and to distinguish between good and bad statistical information in a world increasingly described by numbers. In each box, we describe a particular statistic, telling why it is important, what the story behind the statistic is, why the statistic was first calculated, and what assumptions are embedded in it. We then show how the statistic is calculated, examine what critics and supporters say about its usefulness and validity, and ask students what they think about issues addressed by the statistic, whether it is an issue like party identification or voting turnout.

- **Mapping American Politics** features cartograms—maps that display information organized on a geographical basis with each unit (e.g., a county, state, or country) sized in proportion to the data being reported. This helps students visualize politically consequential numeric information. A broad range of issues—how the geographic bases of the political parties are changing, where American economic and military assistance dollars go, and more—are illuminated.

- **Can Government Do Anything Well?** asks whether government or the market or some combination of the two is the most appropriate instrument for solving our most important national problems. We highlight some important areas of federal government activity that have functioned well over the years and examine claims that the private sector can do a better job. In providing this feature, we hope we help bridge the deep divide that separates those who believe that "government is always the solution" and those who believe that "government is always the problem."

- **Timelines** appear throughout this book to help students develop a sense of historical context. Topics include federalism milestones, development of the U.S. census, a history of the Internet, and the rise and fall of labor unions.

- Every chapter includes a **marginal glossary** to support students' understanding of new and important concepts at first encounter. For easy reference, key terms from the marginal glossary are repeated at the end of each chapter and in the end-of-book glossary.

# Supplements

Make more time for your students with instructor resources that offer effective learning assessments and classroom engagement. Pearson's partnership with educators does not end with the delivery of course materials; Pearson is there with you on the first day of class and beyond. A dedicated team of local Pearson representatives will work with you to not only choose course materials but also integrate them into your class and assess their effectiveness. Our goal is your goal—to improve instruction with each semester.

Pearson is pleased to offer the following resources to qualified adopters of *Government in America*. Several of these supplements are available to instantly download on the Instructor Resource Center (IRC); please visit the IRC **www.pearsonhighered.com/irc** to register for access.

**TEST BANK** Evaluate learning at every level. Reviewed for clarity and accuracy, the Test Bank measures this book's learning objectives with multiple choice, true/false, fill-in-the-blank, short answer, and essay questions. You can easily customize the assessment to work in any major learning management system and to match what is covered in your course. Word, BlackBoard, and WebCT versions available on the IRC and Respondus versions available upon request from **www.respondus.com**.

**PEARSON MYTEST** This powerful assessment generation program includes all of the questions in the Test Bank. Quizzes and exams can be easily authored and saved online and then printed for classroom use, giving you ultimate flexibility to manage assessments anytime and anywhere. To learn more, visit, **www.pearsonhighered.com/mytest.**

**INSTRUCTOR'S MANUAL** Create a comprehensive roadmap for teaching classroom, online, or hybrid courses. Designed for new and experienced instructors, the Instructor's Manual includes a sample syllabus, lecture and discussion suggestions, activities for in or out of class, and essays on teaching American Government. Available on the IRC.

**POWERPOINT PRESENTATION WITH CLASSROOM RESPONSE SYSTEM (CRS)** Make lectures more enriching for students. The PowerPoint Presentation includes a full lecture script, discussion questions, photos and figures from the book, and links to MyPoliSciLab multimedia. With integrated clicker questions, get immediate feedback on what your students are learning during a lecture. Available on the IRC.

# Acknowledgments

We want to thank the many students and Graduate Teaching Assistants who have used this book as a learning and teaching tool and let us know what worked and what didn't work in previous editions. We appreciate their insight and candor. Our thanks go as well to our editors at Pearson, Jeff Marshall and Vikram Mukhija, who have been strong believers in our book and our principal guides into the brave new world of digital learning. Laura Town and Judy O'Neill were magnificent development editors, keeping us on track, offering compelling suggestions for content updates and helping with everything from photo selection to the design of rendered exhibits. Nancy Thorwardson and Scott Minkoff created the cartograms—most originally designed for the fifth edition by Mike Ward of Duke University—for updated and new material in the Mapping feature. Ed Greenberg would like to especially thank the following advanced undergraduate and graduate students who helped with research: Hunter Coohill, Zach Seigel, Corey Barwick, and Bill Jaeger.

This edition of *The Struggle for Democracy* benefited greatly from the wisdom and generosity of David Doherty of Loyola University, Scott Minkoff of Barnard College, and Josh Ryan of Bradley University, who revised eight of the eighteen chapters. Each of these, former head teaching assistants at the University of Colorado and recognized scholars and admired teachers at their respective institutions, have become key collaborators and major contributors to this project. It can be said without exaggeration that this revision could not have been done without them.

# 1

# Democracy and American Politics

## ROBERT MOSES AND THE STRUGGLE FOR AFRICAN AMERICAN VOTING RIGHTS

**T**he right to vote in elections is fundamental to democracy. But many Americans won the right to vote only after long struggles. It took more than 30 years from the adoption of the Constitution, for instance, for most states to allow people without property to vote. Women gained the right to vote in all U.S. elections only in 1920, and young people ages 18 to 20 did so only beginning in 1971. African Americans in the South were not able to vote in any numbers until after 1965, despite the existence of the Fifteenth Amendment—which says the vote cannot be denied to American citizens on the basis of race, color, or previous condition of servitude—adopted in 1870 after the Civil War.

In Mississippi in the early 1960s, only 5 percent of African Americans were registered to vote, and none held elective office, though they accounted for 43 percent of the population. In Walthall County, Mississippi, not a single black was registered, although roughly 3,000 were eligible to vote.[1] What kept them away from the polls was a combination of exclusionary voting registration rules, economic pressures, and violence against those brave enough to defy the prevailing political and social order. In Ruleville, Mississippi, civil rights activist Fannie Lou Hamer was forced out of the house she was renting on a large plantation; fired from her job; and arrested, jailed, and beaten by police after she tried to register to vote.[2]

The Student Non-Violent Coordinating Committee (SNCC) launched its Voter Education Project in 1961 with the aim of ending black political powerlessness in the Deep South. Composed

| 1.1 | 1.2 | 1.3 |
|-----|-----|-----|
| Explain the meaning of democracy and its use as a standard to evaluate American government and politics, p. 4 | Outline a systematic framework for thinking about how government and politics work, p. 15 | Think about ways to analyze the question: "Does government work?" p. 19 |

**WORTH THE WAIT** African American voters wait outside the Haywood County court house in Tennessee to cast their ballots after passage of the 1965 Voting Rights Act.

primarily of African American college students, SNCC worked to increase black voter registration, to challenge exclusionary rules like the poll tax and the literacy test, and to enter African American candidates in local elections. Its first step was to create "freedom schools" in some of the most segregated counties in Mississippi, Alabama, and Georgia to teach black citizens about their rights under the law. Needless to say, SNCC volunteers attracted the malevolent attention of police, local officials, and vigilantes.

The first of the freedom schools was founded in McComb, Mississippi, by a remarkable young man named Robert Parris Moses. Despite repeated threats to his life and more than a few physical attacks, Moses traveled the back roads of Amite and Walthall Counties, meeting with small groups of black farmers and encouraging them to attend the freedom school. At the school, he showed them not only how to fill out the registration forms, but also how to read and interpret the constitution of Mississippi for the "literacy test" required to register to vote. Once people in the school gathered the courage to journey to the county seat to try to register, Moses accompanied them to lend support and encouragement.

Moses paid a price. Over a period of a few months in 1963, he was arrested several times for purported traffic violations; attacked on the main street of Liberty, Mississippi, by the county sheriff's cousin and beaten with the butt end of a knife; assaulted by a mob behind the McComb County courthouse; hit by police while standing in line at the voting registrar's office with one of his students; and jailed for not paying fines connected with his participation in civil rights demonstrations.

Despite the efforts of Moses and other SNCC volunteers, African American registration barely increased in Mississippi in the early 1960s. Black Americans there and in other states of the Deep South would have to await the passage of the 1965 Voting Rights Act, which provided powerful federal government protections for all American citizens wishing to exercise their right to vote.[3] The Voter Education Project was a key building block of a powerful civil rights movement (see Chapters 8 and 16) that would eventually force federal action in the 1960s to support the citizenship rights of African Americans in the South. Robert Moses and many other African Americans were willing to risk all they had, including their lives, to gain full and equal citizenship in the United States. They surely would have been gratified by the election of African American Barack Obama in 2008 as the nation's 44th president.

The struggle for democracy is happening in many countries today, where people fight against all odds for the right to govern themselves and control their own destinies, whether in Afghanistan, Ukraine, Burma, Tunisia, or Sierra Leone. Americans are participants in this drama, not only because American political ideas and institutions have often provided inspiration for democratic movements in other countries, but also because the struggle for democracy continues in our own society. Although honored and celebrated, democracy remains an unfinished project in the United States. The continuing struggle to expand and perfect democracy is a major feature of American history and a defining characteristic of our politics today. It is a central theme of this book.

# Democracy

**1.1** Explain the meaning of democracy and its use as a standard to evaluate American government and politics

*Why should there not be a patient confidence in the ultimate justice of the people? Is there any better, or equal, hope in the world?*

—Abraham Lincoln, First Inaugural Address

**W**ith the exception of anarchists who believe that people can live in harmony without any form of authority, it is generally recognized that when people live together in groups and communities, an entity of some sort is needed to provide law and order; to protect against external aggressors; and to provide essential public goods such as roads, waste disposal, education, and clean water. It is safe to say that most people do not want to live in places where there is no government to speak of at all, as in Somalia, or where there is a failed state, as in Haiti. If government is both necessary and inevitable, certain questions become unavoidable: Who is to govern? How are those who govern to be encouraged to serve the best interests of society? How can governments be induced to make policies and laws that citizens consider legitimate and worth obeying? How can citizens ensure that those who govern both carry out laws and policies the people want and do so effectively? In short, what is the best form of government? For most Americans the answer is clear: democracy.

Democracy's central idea is that ordinary people want to rule themselves and are capable of doing so.[4] This idea has proved enormously popular, not only with Americans, but with people all over the world.[5] To be sure, some people would give top priority to other things besides self-government as a requirement for the good society, including such things as safety and security or the need to have religious law and values determine what government does. Nevertheless, the appealing notion that ordinary people can and should rule themselves has spread to all corners of the globe, and the number of people living in democratic societies has increased significantly over the past two decades.[6]

It is no wonder that a form of government based on the notion that people are capable of ruling themselves enjoys widespread popularity, especially compared with government by the few (e.g., the Communist Party rule in China and Cuba) or by a single person (e.g., the dictatorship of Kim Jong-un in North Korea). There are reasons for its appeal. Some political thinkers think that democracy is the form of government that best protects human rights because it is the only one based on a recognition of the intrinsic worth and equality of human beings. Others believe that democracy is the form of government most likely to produce rational policies because it can count on the pooled knowledge and expertise of a society's entire population: a political version, if you will, of the wisdom of crowds, something like the Wiki phenomenon.[7] Still others claim that democracies are more stable and long-lasting because their leaders, elected by and answerable to voters, enjoy a strong sense of legitimacy among citizens. Many others suggest that democracy is the form of government most conducive to economic growth and material well-being, a claim with some scholarly support. (The relative economic growth in the years ahead of India, a democracy, and China, a party-state, will be a good, real-world test of this proposition.) Others, finally, believe that democracy is the form of government under which human beings, because they are free, are best able to develop their natural capacities and talents.[8] There are many compelling reasons, then, why democracy has been preferred by so many people.

Americans have supported the idea of self-government and have helped make the nation more democratic over the course of our history.[9] Nevertheless, democracy remains an aspiration rather than a finished product. Our goal in this book is to help you think carefully about the quality and progress of democracy in the United States. We want to help you reach your own independent judgments about the degree to which politics and government in the United States make our country more or less democratic. We want to help you draw your own conclusions about which political practices and institutions in the United States encourage and sustain popular self-rule and which ones discourage and undermine it. To do this, we must be clear about the meaning of democracy.

## ☐ Democratic Origins

Many of our ideas about democracy originated with the ancient Greeks. The Greek roots of the word *democracy* are *demos*, meaning "the people," and *kratein*, meaning "to rule." Philosophers and rulers were not friendly to the idea that the *many* can and should rule themselves. Most believed that governing was a difficult art, requiring the greatest sophistication, intelligence, character, and training—certainly not the province of ordinary people. Aristotle expressed this view in his classic work *Politics*, where he observed that democracy "is a government in the hands of men of low birth, no property, and vulgar employments."

Instead, they preferred rule by a select *few* (such as an aristocracy, in which a hereditary nobility rules, or a clerical establishment as in Iran today, where religious leaders rule) or by an enlightened *one*, somewhat akin to the philosopher king

**democracy**

A system of government in which the people rule; rule by the many.

**oligarchy**

Rule by the few, where a minority holds power over a majority, as in an aristocracy or a clerical establishment.

**monarchy**

Rule by the one, such as where power rests in the hands of a king or queen.

**direct democracy**

A form of political decision making in which policies are decided by the people themselves, rather than by their representatives, acting either in small face-to-face assemblies or through the electoral process as in initiatives and referenda in the American states.

described by Plato in his *Republic*, or a hereditary monarch as in England in the time of Elizabeth I. **Democracy**, then, is "rule by the people" or, to put it as the Greeks did, self-government by the many, as opposed to **oligarchy** (rule by the *few*) or **monarchy** (rule by the *one*). The idea that ordinary people might rule themselves represents an important departure from most historical beliefs.[10] In practice, throughout human history, most governments have been quite undemocratic.

Inherent in the idea of self-rule by ordinary people is an understanding that government must serve *all* its people and that ultimately none but the people themselves can be relied on to know, and hence to act in accordance with, their own values and interests.[11]

Interestingly, democracy in the sense described here is more a set of utopian ideas than a description of real societies. Athens of the fifth century BCE is usually cited as the purest form of democracy that ever existed. There, all public policies were decided upon in periodic assemblies of Athenian citizens, though women, slaves, and immigrants were excluded from participation.[12] Nevertheless, the existence of a society in Athens where "a substantial number of free, adult males were entitled as citizens to participate freely in governing"[13] proved to be a powerful example of what was possible for those who believed that rule by the people was the best form of government. A handful of other cases of popular rule kept the democratic idea alive across the centuries. Beginning in the fifth century BCE, for example, India enjoyed long periods marked by spirited and broadly inclusive public debate and discourse on public issues. In the Roman Republic, male citizens elected the consuls, the chief magistrates of the powerful city-state. Also, during the Middle Ages in Europe, some cities were governed directly by the people (at least by men who owned property) rather than by nobles, church, or crown. During the Renaissance, periods of popular control of government (again, limited to male property holders) occurred in the city-states of Venice, Florence, and Milan.

## ☐ Direct Versus Representative Democracy

To the ancient Greeks, democracy meant rule by the common people exercised *directly* in open assemblies. They believed that democracy implied face-to-face deliberation and decision making about the public business. **Direct democracy** requires, however,

**RULE BY THE FEW**

Although the elected president of Iran is influential in determining what the Iranian government does, real power in the country is exercised by an unelected clergy and the Revolutionary Guards, the country's leading security force with considerable influence in the political sphere. The mullahs (or clerics), the ideological custodians of all Iranian institutions and debates, listen to presidential addresses for any slackening in ideological commitment. Is a system that is responsive, in theory, to the many but run, in reality, by the few likely to retain legitimacy over the long term? How might the people of Iran move their system to one where the majority rules rather than the few?

**representative democracy**
Indirect democracy, in which the people rule through elected representatives.

1.1

1.2

1.3

**RULE BY THE MANY**

In small towns throughout New England, local policies and budgets are decided upon at regular town meetings, in which the entire town population is invited to participate. What are some advantages to such a system? What might be the drawbacks? What other kinds of forums might there be where direct democracy is possible?

that all citizens be able to meet together regularly to debate and decide the issues of the day. Such a thing was possible in fifth century BCE Athens, which was small enough to allow all male citizens to gather in one place. In Athens, moreover, male citizens had time to meet and to deliberate because women provided household labor and slaves accounted for most production.

Because direct, participatory democracy is possible only in small communities where citizens with abundant leisure time can meet on a face-to-face basis, it is an unworkable arrangement for a large and widely dispersed society such as the United States.[14] Democracy in large societies must take the representative form, since millions of citizens cannot meet in open assembly. By **representative democracy** we mean a system in which the people select others, called *representatives*, to act on their behalf.

Although representative (or indirect) democracy seems to be the only form of democracy possible in large-scale societies, some political commentators argue that the participatory aspects of direct democracy are worth preserving as an ideal and that certain domains of everyday life—workplaces and schools, for instance—could be enriched by more direct democratic practices.[15] It is worth pointing out, moreover, that direct democracy can and does flourish in some local communities today. In many New England towns, for example, citizens make decisions directly at town meetings. At the state level, the initiative process allows voters in many states to bypass the legislature to make policies or amend state constitutions. Some observers believe that the Internet is empowering people to become more directly engaged and influential in the political process and that this process will accelerate in the future.[16] Increasingly, the Internet, mobile devices, and social media sites enable people to more easily gather information, deliberate with other citizens about important issues, organize political meetings and demonstrations, and directly communicate their interests and demands to political leaders at all levels of government.[17] These new forms of communication and mobilization were especially evident in the so-called Arab Spring in 2011 when popular uprisings drove autocratic leaders from power in several countries and forced leaders in others to pay attention to popular demands.

**popular sovereignty**
The basic principle of democracy that the people are the ultimate source of government authority and of the policies that government leaders make.

**autocracy**
General term that describes all forms of government characterized by rule by a single person or by a group with total power, whether a monarchy, a military tyranny, or a theocracy.

## ☐ Benchmarks of Representative Democracy

In large societies such as our own, then, democracy means rule by the people, exercised indirectly through representatives elected by the people. Still, this definition is not sufficiently precise to use as a standard by which to evaluate the American political system. It does not tell us what features indirect representative systems must have to ensure that those who govern do so on behalf of and in the interest of the people. You will see that this involves more than the existence of elections.[18] To help further clarify the definition of democracy, we add three additional benchmarks drawn from both the scholarly literature and popular understandings of democracy. These benchmarks are *popular sovereignty*, *political equality*, and *political liberty*, with the latter two being necessary for the first (that is to say, for popular sovereignty to work political equality and political liberty must exist). A society in which all three flourish, we argue, is a healthy representative democracy. A society in which any of the three is absent or impaired falls short of the representative democratic ideal. Let us see what each of them means.

**POPULAR SOVEREIGNTY** **Popular sovereignty** means that people are the ultimate source of government authority and that what the government does is determined by what the people want. If ultimate authority resides not in the hands of the *many* but in the hands of the *few* (as in an aristocratic order), or of the *one* (whether a benevolent sovereign or a ruthless dictator), democracy does not exist. Nor does it exist if government consistently fails to follow the preferences and serve the interests of the people.

How can we recognize popular sovereignty when we see it? The following seven conditions are especially important.

***Government Leaders are Selected in Competitive Elections***   The existence of a close match between what the people want and what government does, however, does not necessarily prove that the people are sovereign. In an **autocracy**, for example, the will of the people can be consciously shaped to correspond to the wishes of the leadership. For the direction of influence to flow from the people to the leadership, some mechanism must exist for forcing leaders to be responsive to the people's wishes and to be responsible to them for their actions. The best mechanism ever invented to achieve these goals is the contested election in which both existing and aspiring government leaders must periodically face the people for judgment. (See the "Mapping American Politics" feature on competition in U.S. presidential elections.)

***Elections are Free and Fair***   If elections are to be useful as a way to keep government leaders responsive and responsible, they must be conducted in a fashion that is free and fair. By free, we mean that there is no coercion of voters or election officials and that virtually all citizens are able to run for office and vote in elections. By fair, we mean, among other things, that election rules do not favor some over others and that ballots are accurately counted.

***People Participate in the Political Process***   Although government leaders may be elected in a balloting process that is free and fair, such a process is useful in conveying the will of the people and keeping leaders responsive and responsible only if the people participate. If elections and other forms of political participation only attract a minority of the eligible population, they cannot serve as a way to understand what the broad public wants or as an instrument forcing leaders to pay attention to it. Widespread participation in politics—including voting in elections, contacting public officials, working with others to bring matters to public attention, joining associations that work to shape government actions, and more—is necessary to ensure not only that responsive representatives will be chosen, but that they will also have continuous incentives to pay attention to the people. Because widespread participation is so central to popular sovereignty, we can say that the less political participation there is in a society, the weaker the democracy.

**majority rule**
The form of political decision making in which policies are decided on the basis of what a majority of the people want.

1.1

1.2

1.3

**VOTING AT LONG LAST**

The South Sudanese woman in this photograph is believed to be the oldest voter to cast a vote for independence in a referendum that secured South Sudan's future as a state independent of the much-larger predominately Muslim nation of Sudan. Following a January referendum, South Sudan became an independent nation in July 2011. Is voting a sufficient condition for the existence of democracy or must other conditions exist to ensure that political leaders act as representatives of the people?

***High-Quality Information is Available*** If people are to form authentic and rational attitudes about public policies and political leaders, they must have access to accurate political information, insightful interpretations, and vigorous debate. These are the responsibility of government officials, opposition parties, opinion leaders, and the news media. If false or biased information is provided, if policies are not challenged and debated, or if misleading interpretations of the political world (or none at all) are offered, the people cannot form opinions in accordance with their values and interests, and popular sovereignty cannot be said to exist.

***The Majority Rules*** How can the opinions and preferences of many individual citizens be combined into a single binding decision? Because unanimity is unlikely—so the insistence that new policies should require unanimous agreement for them to be adopted would simply enshrine the status quo—reaching a decision requires a decision rule of some sort. If the actions of government are to respond to all citizens, each citizen being counted equally, the only decision rule that makes sense is **majority rule**, which means that the government adopts the policy that the *most* people want.[19] The only alternative to majority rule is minority rule, which would unacceptably elevate the preferences and the interests of the *few* over the *many*.

# Mapping American Politics

## All the States Are Purple

### Introduction

Voting in elections in which people can choose among competing candidates and political parties is one of the hallmarks of democratic political systems. As we suggest in this chapter, democracy requires other things, such as political equality, civil liberties, and a free press, but competitive elections are essential. For the most part, at all levels of government in the United States, the most important public offices are filled by election, including that of the president. Both the map and the cartogram show the results from the 2012 presidential election won by Democrat Barack Obama over Republican Mitt Romney, focusing on turnout and competition between the candidates.

### Different Maps; Different Stories

The standard geographic map of the United States on this page shows states won by Mitt Romney (in red) and Barack Obama (in blue). Election maps like this are widely distributed in newspapers, magazines, and on television. However, they are misleading in a very fundamental way because they emphasize geographical space over people and overplay the partisan divisions in the country. They take no account of the relative populations of the states and exaggerate the political importance of large, underpopulated spaces. This map suggests a country that is mostly red, or Republican, yet we know that the Democratic candidate won a relatively decisive victory. So, is there a better way to visualize who voted and for whom in 2012?

The second map on this page is called a cartogram. We will be using cartograms throughout this book to learn more about American politics. A cartogram is a way to visually present information that is organized on a geographical basis, with each unit (in this case, state) sized in proportion to the data being reported (in this case, number of voters). So rather than thinking of the cartogram as a "map," think of it as a figure displaying some aspect of American politics in a geographical fashion. Sometimes a cartogram shows geographical units in relation to one another in direct proportion to some simple measure, such as population size. Sometimes a cartogram shows geographical units drawn to reflect some measure on a per capita basis (such as the distribution of homeland security defense dollars to states divided by population size, which we use in Chapter 13). Sometimes a cartogram shows geographical units expanded or diminished from their "normal" geographical scale using mathematical transformations that enable the viewer to easily compare units (such as states and countries) while preserving the rough outlines of the normal shapes of these units. In each "Mapping American Politics" feature in this book, we will specify clearly what sort of cartogram we are using.

The cartogram here uses a simple and direct proportion; each state is sized according to the number of votes cast in the 2012 presidential election. By adjusting the size of the states to reflect the number of citizens who voted for president in 2012, this cartogram shows clearly that California, Florida, New York, Texas, and Ohio have

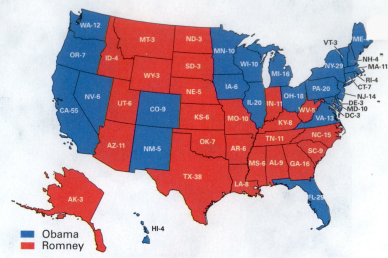

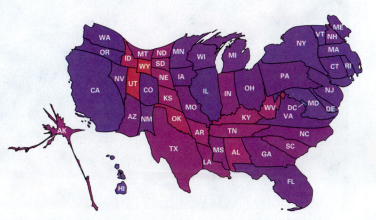

Standard U.S. Map, Blue for Obama States, Red for Romney States

Size of States Adjusted to Reflect Voter Turnout; Each State Is a Mixture of Red and Blue, Reflecting the Percentage of Obama and Romney Voters

Standard U.S. Map

lots of voters and Idaho, Wyoming, Montana, Nebraska, and Maine have relatively few.

Color is often used to convey additional information in cartograms, as we do here. The proportions of blue (for Democratic voters) and red (for Republican voters) in each state reflect the proportions of Democratic and Republican voters in that state. The result is a map with various shades of purple, because all states contain a mix of Democratic and Republican voters. The closer a state comes to the blue end of the spectrum, the more Democratic voters it has relative to Republicans; the closer a state comes to the red end of the spectrum, the more Republicans it has relative to Democrats. There are no pure red or blue states, no pure Republican or Democratic states. Even states that are deep purple (more blue), such as California, have many Republican voters, while states that are more red, such as Utah and Wyoming, have many Democratic voters.

## What Do You Think?

- How does the cartogram convey more information than the conventional map about competition in the 2012 election and where the most voters are located? Do you see anything interesting in either the map or the cartogram that we have not mentioned here? How about your own state? What, if anything, about its portrayal in the cartogram surprises you?

**SOURCE:** U.S. House of Representatives, Office of the Clerk, http://clerk.house.gov/members/electionInfo/2012/Table.htm. Cartogram produced in ArcMap using Tom Gross's Cartogram Geoprocessing Tool (v2). ArcMap uses the Newman-Gastner method [see details in Michael T. Gastner and Mark E. J. Newman, "Diffusion-Based Method for Producing Density-Equalizing Maps," *Proceedings of the National Academy of Sciences* 101 (2004): 7499–7504.]

***Government Policies Reflect the Wishes of the People*** The most obvious sign of popular sovereignty is the existence of a close correspondence between what government does and what the people want it to do. It is hard to imagine a situation in which the people rule but government officials continuously make policies contrary to the expressed wishes of the majority of the people; sovereign people would most likely react by removing such officials from power.

But does the democratic ideal require that government officials always do exactly what the people want, right away, responding to every whim and passing fancy of the public? This question has troubled many democratic theorists, and most have answered that democracy is best served when representatives and other public officials respond to the people after the people have had the opportunity to deliberate among themselves about the issues.[20] We might, then, want to speak of democracy as a system in which government policies conform to what the people want over some period of time.

***Government Policies are Effective*** Finally, for the people to rule, it is not sufficient that government policies are put into place that reflect what the people want it to do. Additionally, these policies must be carried out as intended and must effectively address the problems or concerns that led to the formation of these policies in the first place. Without this seventh and last condition for popular sovereignty, the people might end up with policies in place that reflect their wishes in name only. Government policies must be turned into government actions that work. Thus for example, if the government, in response to popular pressures, institutes a program to provide student loans for higher education, that program must be designed and carried out in such a way that funds for the program get to the intended beneficiaries—they are not wasted or diverted to financial institutions—and access to higher education is expanded. Anything less, and the people cannot be said to fully rule.

**POLITICAL EQUALITY** The second benchmark of representative democracy and a necessary condition for popular sovereignty to exist is **political equality**, the idea that each person, being of equal intrinsic value as other human beings, carries the same weight in voting and other political decision making.[21] Imagine, if you will, a society in which one person could cast 100 votes in an election, another person 50 votes, and still another 25 votes, while many unlucky folks had only 1 vote each—or none at all. Democracy is a way of making decisions in which each person has one, and only one, voice.

Most people know this intuitively. Our sense of what is proper is offended, for instance, when some class of people is denied the right to vote in a society that boasts the outer trappings of democracy. The denial of citizenship rights to African Americans in the South before the passage of the 1965 Voting Rights Act is such an example. We count it as a victory for democracy when previously excluded groups win the right to vote.

Political equality also involves what the Fourteenth Amendment to the Constitution calls "equal protection," meaning that everyone in a democracy is treated the same

**political equality**
The principle that each person carries equal weight in the conduct of the public business.

**1.1**

**1.2**

**1.3**

**civil rights**
Guarantees by government of equal citizenship to all social groups.

**political liberty**
The principle that citizens in a democracy are protected from government interference in the exercise of a range of basic freedoms, such as the freedoms of speech, association, and conscience.

**social contract**
The idea that government is the result of an agreement among people to form one, and that people have the right to create an entirely new government if the terms of the contract have been violated by the existing one.

by government. Government programs, for example, cannot favor one group over another or deny benefits or protections to identifiable groups in the population, such as racial and religious minorities. Nor should people be treated better or worse than others by law enforcement agencies and the courts. Taken together, political equality and equal treatment are sometimes called **civil rights**, a subject we will address in more detail in Chapter 16.

But does political equality require that people be equal in ways that go beyond having a voice in decision making and treatment by government? In particular, does democracy require that inequalities in the distribution of income and wealth not be too extreme? While many do not think this to be the case, thinkers as diverse as Aristotle, Rousseau, and Jefferson thought so, believing that great inequalities in economic circumstances are almost always translated into political inequality.[22] Political scientist Robert Dahl describes the problem in the following way:

> If citizens are unequal in economic resources, so are they likely to be unequal in political resources; and political equality will be impossible to achieve. In the extreme case, a minority of rich will possess so much greater political resources than other citizens that they will control the state, dominate the majority of citizens, and empty the democratic process of all content.[23]

In later chapters, we will see that income and wealth are distributed in a highly unequal way in the United States, that the scale of this inequality has become dramatically more pronounced over the past two decades,[24] and that this inequality is sometimes translated into great inequalities among people and groups in the political arena. We will see for example, how powerful groups representing the most privileged sectors of American society shape not only elections and legislation more than other Americans. We will see how government agencies and leaders administer laws and regulations. In such circumstances, the political equality benchmark is in danger of being violated.

**POLITICAL LIBERTY** A third benchmark of democracy in representative systems, and a necessary condition for popular sovereignty to exist, is **political liberty**. Political liberty refers to basic freedoms essential to the formation and expression of majority opinion and its translation into public policies. These essential liberties include the freedoms of speech, of conscience and religion, of the press, and of assembly and association embodied in the First Amendment to the U.S. Constitution. Philosopher John Locke thought that individual rights and liberties were so fundamental to the good society that their preservation was the central responsibility of any legitimate government and that their protection was the very reason people agreed to enter into a **social contract** to form government in the first place.

Without these First Amendment freedoms, as well as those freedoms involving protections against arbitrary arrest and imprisonment, the other fundamental principles of democracy could not exist. Popular sovereignty cannot be guaranteed if people are prevented from participating in politics or if opposition to the government is crushed by the authorities. Popular sovereignty cannot prevail if the voice of the people is silenced and if citizens are not free to argue and debate, based on their own ideas, values, and personal beliefs, and to form and express their political opinions.[25] Political equality is violated if some people can speak out but others cannot. Voting without liberty can lead to elected autocrats such as Vladmir Putin in Russia and Abdel Fattah al-Sisi in Egypt, an outcome that is clearly undemocratic because opposition voices have been silenced.

For most people today, democracy and liberty are inseparable. The concept of *self-government* implies not only the right to vote and to run for public office, but also the right to speak one's mind; to petition the government; and to join with others in political parties, interest groups, or social movements. Over the years, a number of political philosophers and practitioners have viewed liberty as *threatened* by democracy rather than as essential to it. It is our position that self-government and political liberty are inseparable, in the sense that the former is impossible without the latter.[26] It follows that a majority cannot deprive an individual or a minority group of its political liberty without violating democracy itself.

## Objections to Liberal Democracy

What we have been describing—a system of representative government characterized by popular sovereignty, political equality, and liberty—commonly is called **liberal democracy**. Not everyone is convinced that liberal democracy is the best form of government. Following are the main criticisms that have been leveled against liberal democracy as we have defined it.

**"MAJORITY TYRANNY" THREATENS LIBERTY** James Madison and the other Founders of the American republic feared that majority rule was bound to undermine freedom and threaten the rights of the individual. They created a constitutional system (as you will see in Chapter 2) that was designed to protect certain liberties against the unwelcome intrusions of the majority. The fears of the Founders were not without basis. What they called the "popular passions" have sometimes stifled the freedoms of groups and individuals who have dared to be different. In the 1950s, for example, many people in the movie industry, publishing, and education lost their jobs because of the anticommunist hysteria whipped up by Senator Joseph McCarthy and others.[27] For a time after the 9/11 attacks on the United States, Muslims in the United States became targets of popular hostility (see Chapter 15). As well, Mexican American immigrants have become the object of popular disapproval in many places in the United States recently, blamed for taking jobs from others in the midst of a period of high unemployment.

Although there have been instances during our history of **majority tyranny**, in which the majority violated the citizenship rights of a minority—the chapter-opening story is a good example—there is no evidence that the *many* consistently threaten liberty more than the *few* or the *one*. To put it another way, the majority does not seem

**liberal democracy**
Representative democracy characterized by popular sovereignty, liberty, and political equality.

**majority tyranny**
Suppression of the rights and liberties of a minority by the majority.

1.1

1.2

1.3

**FEAR CAN UNDERMINE DEMOCRACY**

Political hysteria has periodically blemished the record of American democracy. Fear of domestic communism and anarchism, captured in this editorial cartoon, was particularly potent in the twentieth century and led to the suppression of political groups by federal and state authorities acting, in their view, in the name of a majority of Americans. Why was such hysteria able to take hold in the United States? How likely is it that political hysteria will emerge today in the United States given the current economic troubles?

13

to be a special or unique threat to liberty. Violations of freedom seem as likely to come from powerful individuals and groups or from government officials responding to vocal and narrow interests as from the majority of the people.

Liberty is essential to self-government, and threats to liberty, whatever their origin, must be guarded against by all who value democracy. But we must firmly reject the view that majority rule inevitably or uniquely threatens liberty. Majority rule is unthinkable, in fact, without the existence of basic political liberties.[28]

**THE PEOPLE ARE IRRATIONAL AND INCOMPETENT** Political scientists have spent decades studying the attitudes and behaviors of citizens in the United States, and some of the findings are not encouraging. For the most part, the evidence shows that individual Americans do not care a great deal about politics and are rather poorly informed, unstable in their views, and not much interested in participating in the political process.[29] These findings have led some observers to assert that citizens are ill-equipped for the responsibility of self-governance and that public opinion (the will of the majority) should not be the ultimate determinant of what government does.

This is a serious charge and bears a great deal of attention, something we shall address in various places in this book. In Chapter 5, for example, we will see that much of the evidence about individual opinions often has been misinterpreted and that the American public is more informed, sophisticated, and stable in its views than it is generally given credit for, though there remains considerable room for improvement on this front.

**MAJORITARIAN DEMOCRACY THREATENS MINORITIES** We have suggested that when rendering a decision in a democracy, the majority must prevail. In most cases, the minority on the losing side of an issue need not worry unduly about its well-being, because many of its members are likely to be on the winning side in future decisions about other matters. Thus, people on the losing side of one issue, such as welfare reform, may be part of the majority and winning side on another issue, such as how much to spend on education. What prevents majority tyranny over a minority in most policy decisions in a democracy is that the composition of the majority and the minority is always shifting, depending on the issue.

However, what happens in cases that involve race, ethnicity, religion, or sexual orientation, for example, where minority status is fixed? Does the majority pose a threat to such minorities? Many people worry about that possibility.[30] The worry is that unbridled majority rule leaves no room for the claims of minorities. This worry has some historical foundations, because majorities have trampled on minority rights with alarming frequency. Majorities long held, for example, that Native Americans and African Americans were inferior to whites and undeserving of full citizenship. Irish, Eastern European, Asian, and Latin American immigrants to our shores, among others, have been subjected to periods of intolerance on the part of the majority, as have Catholics and Jews. Gays and lesbians have been discriminated against in housing and jobs and have sometimes been violently victimized.

As Robert Dahl points out, however, there is no evidence to support the belief that the rights of minorities are better protected under alternative forms of political government, whether rule by the *few* (note the persecution of the Christian minority in China by the Communist ruling party) or by the *one* (note the persecution of Shia Muslims under the rule of Saddem Hussein in Iraq), and that given the other benefits of majority rule democracy, it is to be preferred.[31]

In any case, democracy, as we have defined it, requires the protection of crucial minority rights. Recall that majority rule is only one of the defining conditions of popular sovereignty and that popular sovereignty is only one of the three basic benchmarks of democracy, the others being political equality and political liberty. The position of minorities is protected in a fully developed liberal democracy, in our view, by the requirements of equal citizenship (the right to vote, to hold public office, to be protected against violence, and to enjoy the equal protection of the law) and access to the full range of civil liberties (speech, press, conscience, and association). To the

## How Democratic Are We?

After this discussion, it should be easy to see how and why the democratic ideal can be used as a measuring rod with which to evaluate American politics. We have learned that the fundamental attributes of a liberal representative democracy are popular sovereignty, political equality, and political liberty. Each suggests a set of questions that will be raised throughout this book to encourage critical thinking about American political life.

■ *Questions about popular sovereignty.* Do citizens participate in politics? Can citizens be involved when they choose to be, and are political leaders responsive? Do political linkage institutions, such as political parties, elections, interest groups, and social movements, effectively transmit what citizens want to political leaders? What is the quality of the public deliberation on the major public policy issues of the day? Do the news media and political leaders provide accurate and complete information? Does government do what citizens want it to do? Does government effectively carry out the policies they have instituted in response to what the people want?

■ *Questions about political equality.* Do some individuals and groups have persistent and substantial advantages over other individuals and groups in the political process? Or is the political game open to all equally? Do government decisions and policies benefit some individuals and groups more than others?

■ *Questions about political liberty.* Are citizens' rights and liberties universally available, protected, and used? Are people free to vote? Can they speak openly and form groups freely to petition their government? Do public authorities, private groups, or the majority threaten liberty or the rights of minorities?

These questions will help us assess where we are and where we are going as a democracy. They will help us go past superficial evaluations based on the existence or nonexistence of this institution or that institution—for example, an elected legislature—and allow us to raise questions about the quality of democracy in the United States and its prospects. Popular sovereignty, political equality, and political liberty are benchmarks to help us in this evaluation. None are attainable, of course, in perfect form. They are, rather, ideals to which our nation can aspire and standards against which we can measure everyday reality.

extent that a majority violates the citizenship rights and liberties of minorities, society falls short of the democratic ideal.

# A Framework for Understanding How American Politics Works

**1.2**  Outline a systematic framework for thinking about how government and politics work

In addition to helping you answer questions about the quality of democracy in the United States, our goal in this textbook is to help you understand how American government and politics work. To help you, we describe in this section a simple way to organize information and to think about how our political system works.

## ☐ Organizing the Main Factors of Political Life

If we are to understand why things happen in government and politics—for example, the passage of the 1965 Voting Rights Act that Robert Moses and his SNCC colleagues did so much to bring about—we must begin with what biologists call *taxonomy*: placing things in their proper categories. We believe that each and every actor, institution, and process that influences what our politics are like and what our national government does can be placed into four main categories: structure, political linkage, government, and government action.

**Jim Crow**
Popular term for the system of legally sanctioned racial segregation that existed in the American South until the middle of the twentieth century.

- *Structure.* Structural factors are enduring features of American life that play key roles in determining what issues become important in politics and government, how political power is distributed in the population, and what attitudes and beliefs guide the behavior of citizens and public officials. This category includes the economy and society, the constitutional rules, the political culture, and the international system: the most fundamental and enduring factors that influence government and politics. They form the foundation upon which all else is built. They are the most enduring parts of the American system, the slowest to change.[32]

- *Political linkage.* Political linkage factors are all of those political actors, institutions, and processes that transmit the wants and demands of people and groups in our society to government officials and that together help shape what government officials do and what policies they adopt. These include public opinion, political parties, interest groups, the news media, and elections. While not a formal part of government, they directly influence what sorts of people are chosen to be government officials and what these officials do once they are in office.

- *Government.* Government factors include all public officials and institutions that have formal, legal responsibilities for making public policy for the United States. These include Congress, the president and the executive branch, the federal bureaucracy, and the federal courts, including the Supreme Court.

- *Government action.* This is about what government does. This category includes the wide range of actions carried out by government: making laws, issuing rules and regulations, waging war and providing national defense, settling civil disputes, providing order, and more.

## ◻ Connecting the Main Factors of Political Life

To understand passage of the landmark legislation, we might begin with *government*, focusing our attention on Congress and its members; President Lyndon Johnson (who was the most vigorous proponent of the voting rights legislation) and his advisers; and the Supreme Court, which was becoming increasingly supportive of civil rights claims in the mid-1960s.

Knowing these things, however, would not tell us all that we needed to know. To understand why Congress, the president, and the Court behaved as they did in 1965, we would want to pay attention to the pressures brought to bear on them by *political linkage* actors and institutions: public opinion (increasingly supportive of civil rights), the growing electoral power of African Americans in the states outside the South, and most important, the moral power of the civil rights movement inspired by people like Robert Moses and Martin Luther King.

Even knowing these things, however, would not tell us all that we needed to know about why the 1965 Voting Rights Act happened. Our inquiry would have to go deeper to include *structural* factors: economic, cultural, and social change; constitutional rules; and the international position of the United States. For example, economic changes in the nation over the course of many decades triggered a "great migration" of African Americans from the rural South to the urban North. Over the long run, this population shift to states with large blocs of Electoral College votes, critical to the election of presidents, increased the political power of African Americans. Cultural change increased the number of Americans bothered by the second-class citizenship of African Americans, even as combat service in World War II and the Korean War led many black Americans to insist on full citizenship rights. Finally, the Cold War struggle of the United States against the Soviet Union played an important role. Many American leaders, recognizing the contradiction between asking for the support of people of color in Third World countries in the struggle against communism while treating African Americans in the United States as second-class citizens, sought an end to the system of official segregation in the South (known as **Jim Crow**).[33]

We see, then, that a full explanation of why the 1965 Voting Rights Act happened (government action) requires that we take into account how governmental, political linkage, and structural factors interact with one another to bring about significant change in American politics.

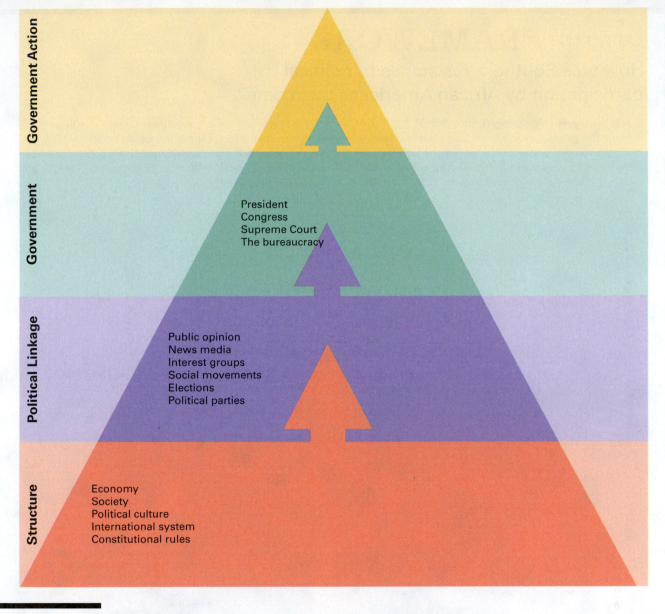

**FIGURE 1.1** THE ANALYTICAL FRAMEWORK

Various actors, institutions, and processes interact to influence what government does in the United States. Structural factors such as the economy, the political culture, the international system, and constitutional rules play a strong role in political events. They may influence the government directly, or, as is more often the case, through political linkages such as elections, parties, and interest groups. In a democratic society, the policies created by the government should reflect these influences.

## ☐ Understanding American Politics Holistically

This way of looking at things—that what government does can only be understood by considering structural, political linkage, and governmental factors—will be used throughout this book and will help bring order to the information presented. We will suggest throughout this book that action by public officials is the product not simply of their personal dessires (although these are important), but also of the influences and pressures brought to bear by other governmental institutions and by individuals, groups, and classes at work in the political linkage sphere. Political linkage institutions and processes, in turn, can often be understood only when we see how they are shaped by the larger structural context, including such things as the national and global economies and the political culture. This way of understanding how American government and politics work is illustrated in the "Using the Framework" feature on page 18. This feature appears in each chapter to explore why particular government actions happen.

You should also keep in mind that, as in all complex systems, feedback also occurs. That is to say, influences sometimes flow in the opposite direction, from government to political linkage actors and institutions to structural factors. For example, federal tax laws

# Using the FRAMEWORK

## How was Southern resistance to political participation by African Americans overcome?

**Background:** The Voting Rights Act of 1965 transformed the politics of the American South. Under federal government protection, the Act permitted African Americans to vote and run for elected office in states where a combination of violence, economic pressure, and state and local government rules made political participation difficult if not impossible prior to 1965. We can understand how such a momentous transformation happened by examining structural, political linkage, and governmental factors.

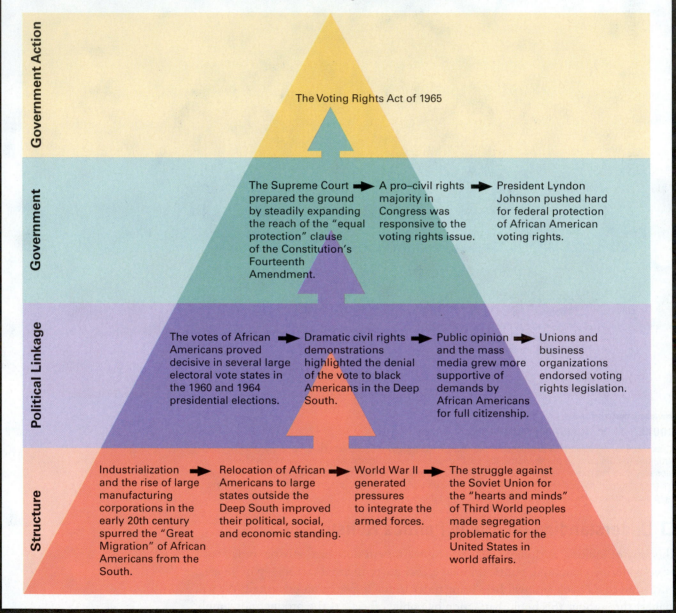

**Government Action**

The Voting Rights Act of 1965

**Government**

The Supreme Court prepared the ground by steadily expanding the reach of the "equal protection" clause of the Constitution's Fourteenth Amendment. → A pro–civil rights majority in Congress was responsive to the voting rights issue. → President Lyndon Johnson pushed hard for federal protection of African American voting rights.

**Political Linkage**

The votes of African Americans proved decisive in several large electoral vote states in the 1960 and 1964 presidential elections. → Dramatic civil rights demonstrations highlighted the denial of the vote to black Americans in the Deep South. → Public opinion and the mass media grew more supportive of demands by African Americans for full citizenship. → Unions and business organizations endorsed voting rights legislation.

**Structure**

Industrialization and the rise of large manufacturing corporations in the early 20th century spurred the "Great Migration" of African Americans from the South. → Relocation of African Americans to large states outside the Deep South improved their political, social, and economic standing. → World War II generated pressures to integrate the armed forces. → The struggle against the Soviet Union for the "hearts and minds" of Third World peoples made segregation problematic for the United States in world affairs.

influence the distribution of income and wealth in society, government regulations affect the operations of corporations, and decisions by the courts may determine what interest groups and political parties are able to do. We will want to pay attention, then, to these sorts of influences in our effort to understand how the American political system works.

You need not worry about remembering exactly which actors and influences belong to which of the four categories. That will become obvious because the chapters of the book are organized into sections corresponding to them. Nor do you need to worry about exactly how the people and institutions in the different levels interact with one another. This will become clear as materials are presented and learned and as you become more familiar with the American political process.

# Does Government Work?

**1.3** Think about ways to analyze the question: "Does government work?"

We bring the democracy standard and the analytical framework together by asking throughout this book about the extent to which government policies reflect the wishes of the people and the degree to which government programs reflecting these wishes are carried out efficiently and effectively. We will want to know, for example, what conditions and developments at the structural level in the analytical model give rise to problems and issues that the American people want addressed. We will want to know the degree to which people can transmit their concerns and wishes to government leaders, and how responsive these leaders are to popular pressures as compared to pressures brought by powerful private interests. As well, we will want to examine how the various branches and levels of government work together in fashioning and carrying out policies the people say they want. Do they cooperate most of the time, for example, or are they at loggerheads and unable to fashion appropriate policies? When government settles on a policy and government officials try to put a policy into practice, is government always handicapped in its efforts either because of obstacles created by political opponents and special interests, or because, as some believe, government is inherently inefficient and ineffective compared to the private sector?

We will address these complex issues at various places in this book, particularly in the feature "Can Government Do Anything Well?" In this feature, we will highlight some important areas of federal government activity that seem to have functioned well over the years, and we will examine claims that the private sector would have done and can do a better job, providing supporting evidence for both positions. We then ask you to weigh the claims and propose what you believe might be the optimal division of labor between the public and private sectors in fulfilling the wishes and needs of the American people regarding a particular area of activity, whether it be interstate highways or overseeing the safety of the food supply. In providing this feature, we hope we can help bridge the deep divide that separates those who believe that "government is always the solution" and those who believe that "government is always the problem."

The debate between pro–free market/anti–big government advocates and regulated markets/pro–big government advocates is an old one in American politics. At various times, one side has controlled the debate and held sway over government policymaking. During the Great Depression, for example, Franklin Roosevelt's New Deal mostly prevailed, with government doing more than most Americans had ever imagined, mostly at the urging of the American people and many business and cultural leaders. Beginning with Ronald Reagan's administration in the early 1980s, however, anti–big government proponents and political actors have steadily gained ground.

We are now deeply into a mostly anti-government moment in American history. The conservative and Tea Party-dominated Republican Party national and state-level landslide election victories in 2010 were an indicator of this trend. So too was the focus of Congress and President Obama in 2011 and 2012 on the problem of budget deficits (which involves deep cuts in government programs) rather than on the problem of stimulating job growth (which often requires new government spending) during the most serious economic crisis since the Great Depression in the 1930s. (The budget deficit debate tends to focus on cutting back government; the stimulating jobs debate tends to center on new or expanded government programs.) To be sure, many liberals also have been unhappy with government as shown by the rapid spread across the nation of the "Occupy Wall Street" movement, whose participants wanted government to do more to rein in the financial industry, create jobs, and make incomes more equal. It is of enduring interest and importance whether anti-government or pro-government advocates and political leaders in the coming years gain the upper hand in response to our present economic difficulties or whether some mixed system of public sector and private sector partnership gains traction. This enduring debate on the role of government will be highlighted throughout this textbook.

# Review the Chapter

## Democracy

**1.1** Explain the meaning of democracy and its use as a standard to evaluate American government and politics, p. 4

Democracy is a system of rule by the people, rooted in three fundamental principles: popular sovereinty (meaning that the people ultimately rule), political equality (meaning that each person has an equal say in determining what government does), and political liberty (meaning that the people are protected from government interference in exercising their rights).

Ensuring that all three aspects of democracy are available and practiced has played an important role in American history, and remains an important theme in our country—as well as many other parts of the world—today.

The United States is a liberal representative democracy—meaning that the people do not rule directly but through elected representatives, and have broad civil and political rights, but the majority does not always get its way.

Because democracy holds a very special place in Americans' constellation of values and is particularly relevant to judging political processes, it is the standard used throughout this text to evaluate the quality of our politics and government.

## A Framework for Understanding How American Politics Works

**1.2** Outline a systematic framework for thinking about how government and politics work, p. 15

The organizing framework presented in this chapter visualizes the world of American politics as a set of interrelated *actors* and *influences*—institutions, groups, and individuals—that operate in three interconnected realms: the *structural*, *political linkage*, and *governmental* sectors. This way of looking at American political life as an ordered, interconnected whole will be used throughout the remainder of the book.

## Does Government Work?

**1.3** Think about ways to analyze the question: "Does government work?" p. 19

People often forget how effective many government programs have been.

We are now in a period of deep distrust of government and what it does.

# Learn the Terms

democracy, p. 6
oligarchy, p. 6
monarchy, p. 6
direct democracy, p. 6
representative democracy, p. 7

popular sovereignty, p. 8
autocracy, p. 8
majority rule, p. 9
political equality, p. 11
civil rights, p. 12

political liberty, p. 12
social contract, p. 12
liberal democracy, p. 13
majority tyranny, p. 13
Jim Crow, p. 16

# Test Yourself

Answer key begins on page T-1.

**1.1** Explain the meaning of democracy and its use as a standard to evaluate American government and politics.

1. Which of the following is the essence of democracy?

   a. Economic well-being
   b. Self-government
   c. Promotion of moral values
   d. Protection of human rights
   e. Creation of rational public policies

**1.2** Outline a systematic framework for thinking about how government and politics work.

2. These factors involve all of the political actors, institutions, and processes that transmit the wants and demands of people and groups in our society to government officials.

   a. Political linkage factors
   b. Public opinion factors
   c. Structural factors
   d. Fundamental factors
   e. Government action factors

**1.3** Think about ways to analyze the question: "Does government work?"

3. Beginning with this president's administration, anti–big government proponents and political actors have steadily gained ground.
   a. George Washington
   b. Ronald Reagan
   c. Richard Nixon
   d. Franklin Roosevelt
   e. Bill Clinton

# Explore Further

## INTERNET SOURCES

Think Progress Blog **thinkprogress.org/** A blog written by liberals.

The Daily Signal **blog.heritage.org/** A blog written by conservatives.

CNN Politics (Political Blog) **politicalticker.blogs.cnn.com/** Political blog by CNN analysts.

*New York Times,* Politics Navigator **www.nytimes.com/pages/ politics/index.html** Internet portal that contains information on a variety of political topics.

International Political Science Association, Top 300 Political Science Websites **ipsaportal.unina.it** A portal to a broad array of web sites on political systems around the world and scholarly research about them.

## SUGGESTIONS FOR FURTHER READING

Bartels, Larry M. *Unequal Democracy: The Political Economy of the New Gilded Age. New York and Princeton*, NJ: The Russell Sage Foundation and Princeton University Press, 2008.

An examination of rising income inequality and how it undermines several of the basic foundational requirements of political democracy.

Dahl, Robert A. *Democracy and Its Critics.* New Haven, CT: Yale University Press, 1989.

A sweeping defense of democracy against its critics by one of the most brilliant political theorists of our time.

Dahl, Robert A. *On Democracy.* New Haven, CT: Yale University Press, 1998.

A brief yet surprisingly thorough examination of classical and contemporary democracy, real and theoretical.

Putnam, Robert D. *Making Democracy Work: Civic Traditions in Modern Italy.* Princeton, NJ: Princeton University Press, 1993.

A brilliant and controversial argument that the success of democratic government depends on the vitality of a participatory and tolerant civic culture.

Taylor, Steven. L., Mathew Sobert Shugart, Arend Liphart, and Bernard Grofman. *A Different Democracy: American Government in a 31-Country Perspective.* New Haven, CT.: Yale University Press, 2014.

An examination of the U.S. brand of democracy in light of the experience of other rich democracies with an eye toward specifying what is unique and what is similar about democratic countries.

Wolfe, Alan. *Does American Democracy Still Work?* New Haven, CT: Yale University Press, 2006.

A pessimistic reading of trends in American politics, society, and economy that are diminishing the quality of American democracy.

Zakaria, Fareed. *The Future of Freedom: Illiberal Democracy at Home and Abroad.* New York: Norton, 2004.

The author suggests that majority rule democracy can only happen and be sustained in societies where individual freedom and the rule of law already exist, suggesting that democracy is unlikely to take hold in places such as Russia and Iraq.

# 2

# The Constitution

## PRESIDENTIAL WAR POWERS GO AIRBORNE

T he constitutional powers of the presidency are always changing; they are not fixed in stone. We can see this in the development of the drone program run by the Central Intelligence Agency (CIA). Though the program began under his predecessor George W. Bush, Barack Obama greatly expanded the use of pilotless drones to kill persons that he and his intelligence team believed to be involved in terrorist plots against the United States. It is estimated that between January 2009, when President Obama took office, and the end of 2013, drones killed around three thousand people, mainly in Pakistan, Yemen, and Somalia. Though it has been reported that the vast majority of those killed were Al Qaeda leaders and operatives, inevitably civilians were killed as well, either family relations of the target or people simply unlucky enough to be nearby. Among those targeted for extermination were four American citizens, including the top leader of Al Qaeda in Yemen, Anwar el-Awlaki, who was born in New Mexico and lived there for the first seven years of his life.

According to supporters, the drone program has many things to commend it. Most important, perhaps, it allows the United States to wage war against Al Qaeda, ISIS, and other terrorist organizations without putting American boots on the ground or risking American casualties. Supporters in the Bush and Obama administrations also argued that, while civilians were often innocent victims of the program, drones killed and wounded fewer civilians than would have been the case if American forces were engaged in ground combat. The drone program appeals to presidents, moreover, because it is popular with Congress, especially at times of seemingly continuous budget crises, and because the American public favors it over direct military action by a two-to-one margin.[1]

All of this said, it is difficult to identify constitutional foundations for the program. The Constitution does specify that the president is commander-in-chief of the American armed forces, but the framers seem to have believed that the decision to wage offensive war—to attack forces

**DRONING ON** Their small size, quiet engines, and surveillance and munitions capabilities makes the use of unmanned aerial vehicles, or drones, an expedient alternative to direct military action and another weapon in the president's expanding war powers arsenal.

23

2.1

2.2

2.3

2.4

2.5

2.6

in another country without being attacked first—should be a matter for Congress, not the president. As George Washington put it in 1792, "The Constitution vests the power of declaring war with Congress; therefore no offensive expedition of importance can be undertaken until after they shall have deliberated upon the subject, and authorized such a measure."[2]

It has been a long time since Congress last declared war (1942), yet American forces have been in action almost every year since World War II ended (1945). This is possible because presidents have greatly expanded their notion of "defensive" war to cover situations and developments that seem to threaten national security, justifying use of American armed forces against real and imagined threats. Examples of presidents using American forces abroad without benefit of a congressional declaration of war are legion: the Korean and Vietnam wars, the invasions of Grenada and Panama, the Gulf War, the Iraq War, and the long post-9/11 war in Afghanistan, among the most notable. With respect to several of these military campaigns, Congress tried to enhance its role in making decisions about the initial use of military forces and the course of combat, but its many resolutions, passage of the War Powers Act, and its control of the budget rarely proved decisive once combat was under way. The upshot: since the end of World War II, the powers of the president as commander-in-chief have grown exponentially even though the wording of presidential powers in the Constitution has not changed one whit. Rather, the expansive reading of presidential war powers has become solidly established because Congress, the courts, and the public have come to accept the president's new role. Presidents now believe these powers to be essential to their office, as do most other actors in the American political system. This is one of the important ways that the Constitution changes without benefit of formal amendment. It is one of the reasons many scholars use the term "living Constitution" when referring to our founding document.

The use of drones represents an additional step in the story of the expansion of presidential war powers. The secret program (albeit not much of a secret), which targets for death the defined enemies of the United States in countries with whom we are not at war, is entirely under the control of the president and run by the CIA, shrouded by national security restrictions on the release of information. Few members of Congress and the public are involved in influencing program policies, nor do they know what the program costs. It is an executive branch operation without much congressional or public oversight. Nevertheless, it has become widely accepted, and future presidents are unlikely to renounce its use, so long as it proves effective and remains popular with Congress and the people. The scope of the president's war powers will continue to expand and change, then, without benefit or need of formal amendment.[3]

## Thinking Critically About This Chapter

This chapter is about the founding of the United States (see Figure 2.1) and the formulation of the constitutional rules that structure American politics to this day.

## Using the Framework

You will see in this chapter how structural factors such as the American political culture, economic developments, and the composition of the Constitutional Convention shaped the substance of our Constitution. You will also see how the Constitution itself is an important structural factor that helps us understand how American government and politics work today.

## Using the Democracy Standard

Using the conception of democracy you learned about in Chapter 1, you will be able to see how and why the framers were uneasy about democracy and created a republican form of government that, although based on popular consent, placed a number of roadblocks in the path of popular rule.

# The American Revolution and the Declaration of Independence

2.1

2.2

2.3

2.4

2.5

2.6

**2.1**  Assess the enduring legacies of the American Revolution and the Declaration of Independence

Initially, the American Revolution (1775–1783) was waged more to preserve an existing way of life than to create something new. By and large, American colonists in the 1760s and 1770s were proud to be affiliated with Great Britain and satisfied with the general prosperity that came with participation in the British commercial empire.[4] When the revolution broke out, the colonists at first wanted only to preserve their traditional rights as British subjects. These traditional rights of life, liberty, and property seemed to be threatened by British policies on trade and taxation. Rather than allowing the American colonists to trade freely with whomever they pleased and to produce whatever goods they wanted, for instance, England was restricting the colonists' freedom to do either in order to protect its own manufacturers. To pay for the military protection of the colonies against raids by Native Americans and their French allies, England imposed taxes on a number of items, including sugar, tea, and stamps (required for legal documents, pamphlets, and newspapers). The imposition of these taxes without the consent of the colonists seemed an act of tyranny to many English subjects in America.

Although the initial aims of the Revolution were quite modest, the American Revolution, like most revolutions, did not stay on the track planned by its leaders. Although it was sparked by a concern for liberty—understood as the preservation of traditional rights against the intrusions of a distant government—it also stimulated the development of sentiments for popular sovereignty and political equality. As these sentiments grew, so did the likelihood that the American colonies would split from their British parent and form a system of government more to the liking of the colonists.

When the Second Continental Congress began its session on May 10, 1775—the First had met only briefly in 1774 to formulate a list of grievances to submit to the British Parliament—the delegates did not have independence in mind, even though armed conflict with Britain had already begun with the battles of Lexington and Concord. Pushed by the logic of armed conflict, an unyielding British government, and Thomas Paine's incendiary call for American independence in his wildly popular pamphlet *Common Sense*, however, the delegates concluded by the spring of 1776 that separation and independence were inescapable.[5] In early June, the Continental Congress appointed a special committee, composed of Thomas Jefferson, John Adams, and Benjamin Franklin, to draft a declaration of independence. The document, mostly Jefferson's handiwork, was adopted unanimously by the Second Continental Congress on July 4, 1776.

## ☐ Key Ideas in the Declaration of Independence

The ideas in the Declaration of Independence are so familiar that we may easily miss their revolutionary importance. In the late eighteenth century, most societies in the world were ruled by kings with authority purportedly derived from God, subject to little or no control by their subjects. Closely following John Locke's ideas in *The Second Treatise on Government*, Jefferson's argument that legitimate government can be established only by the people, is created to protect inalienable rights, and can govern only with their consent, seemed outrageous at the time. However, these ideas sparked a responsive chord in people everywhere when they were first presented, and they remain extremely popular all over the world today. The argument as presented in the Declaration of Independence goes as follows:

- Human beings possess rights that cannot be legitimately given away or taken from them. *"We hold these truths to be self-evident, that all men are created equal, that*

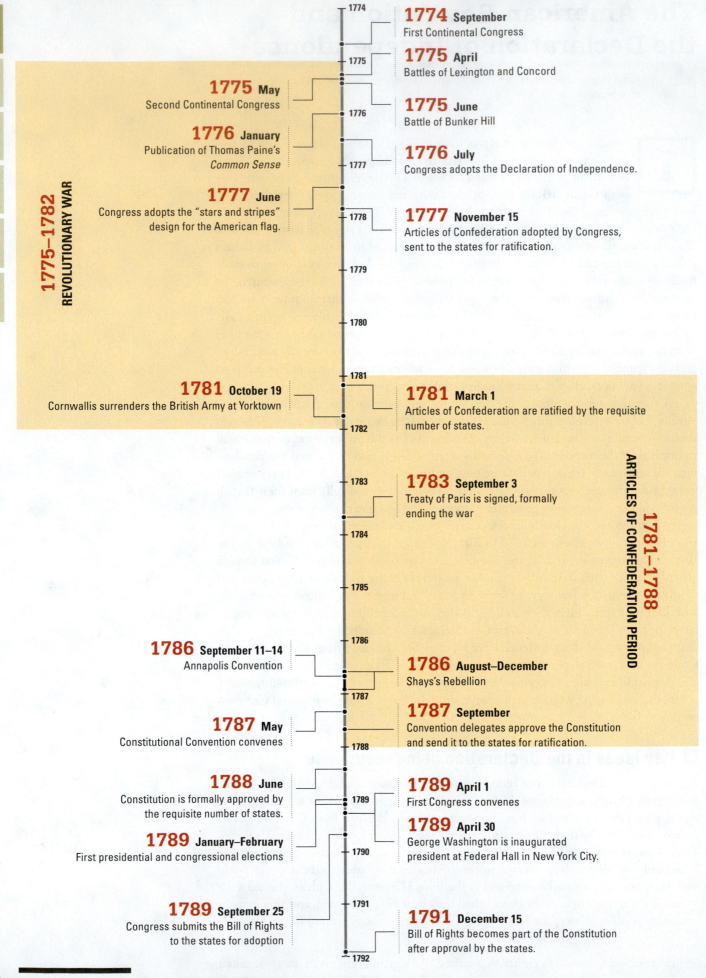

2.1

2.2

2.3

2.4

2.5

2.6

**1775–1782 REVOLUTIONARY WAR**

**1781–1788 ARTICLES OF CONFEDERATION PERIOD**

**1774** September
First Continental Congress

**1775** April
Battles of Lexington and Concord

**1775** May
Second Continental Congress

**1775** June
Battle of Bunker Hill

**1776** January
Publication of Thomas Paine's
*Common Sense*

**1776** July
Congress adopts the Declaration of Independence.

**1777** June
Congress adopts the "stars and stripes"
design for the American flag.

**1777** November 15
Articles of Confederation adopted by Congress,
sent to the states for ratification.

**1781** October 19
Cornwallis surrenders the British Army at Yorktown

**1781** March 1
Articles of Confederation are ratified by the requisite
number of states.

**1783** September 3
Treaty of Paris is signed, formally
ending the war

**1786** September 11–14
Annapolis Convention

**1786** August–December
Shays's Rebellion

**1787** May
Constitutional Convention convenes

**1787** September
Convention delegates approve the Constitution
and send it to the states for ratification.

**1788** June
Constitution is formally approved by
the requisite number of states.

**1789** April 1
First Congress convenes

**1789** January–February
First presidential and congressional elections

**1789** April 30
George Washington is inaugurated
president at Federal Hall in New York City.

**1789** September 25
Congress submits the Bill of Rights
to the states for adoption

**1791** December 15
Bill of Rights becomes part of the Constitution
after approval by the states.

**FIGURE 2.1** TIMELINE OF THE FOUNDING OF THE UNITED STATES, 1774–1791

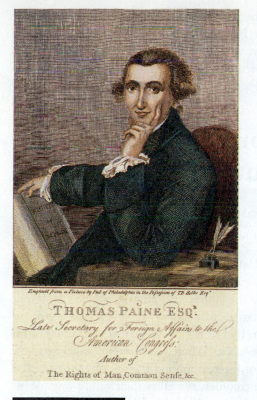

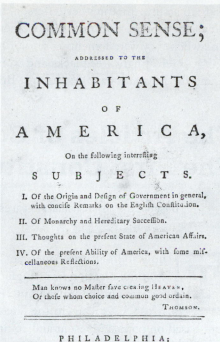

2.1

2.2

2.3

2.4

2.5

2.6

**social contract**
A philosophical device, used by Enlightenment thinkers such as Locke, Rousseau, and Harrington, to suggest that governments are only legitimate if they are created by a voluntary compact among the people.

**CLARION CALL FOR INDEPENDENCE**

American leaders were reluctant at first to declare independence from Great Britain. One of the things that helped change their minds was Thomas Paine's wildly popular—it is said that a higher proportion of Americans read it than any other political tract in U.S. history—and incendiary pamphlet *Common Sense,* which mercilessly mocked the institution of monarchy and helped undermine the legitimacy of British rule. What are some modern-day examples of Paine's pamphlet? Are influential bloggers or tweeters good examples?

*they are endowed by their Creator with certain unalienable Rights, that among these are Life, Liberty, and the Pursuit of Happiness."*

- People create government to protect these rights. *"That to secure these rights, Governments are instituted among Men, deriving their just powers from the consent of the governed."*

- If government fails to protect people's rights or itself becomes a threat to them, people can withdraw their consent from that government and form a new one, that is, void the existing **social contract** and agree to a new one. *"That whenever any Form of Government becomes destructive of these ends, it is the Right of the People to alter or to abolish it, and to institute new Government, laying its foundation on such principles, and organizing its powers in such form, as to them shall seem most likely to effect their Safety and Happiness."*

## ☐ Important Omissions in the Declaration

The Declaration of Independence carefully avoided several controversial subjects, including what to do about slavery. Jefferson's initial draft denounced the Crown for violating human rights by "captivating and carrying Africans into slavery," but this was considered too controversial and was dropped from subsequent versions. The contradiction between the institution of slavery and the Declaration's sweeping claims for self-government, "unalienable" individual rights, and equality ("all men are created equal") was obvious to many observers at the time and is glaringly apparent to us today. The Declaration was also silent about the political status of women and the inalienable rights of Native Americans (referred to in the Declaration as "merciless Indian savages") and African Americans, even those who were not slaves. Indeed, it

**2.1**

**2.2**

**2.3**

**2.4**

**2.5**

**2.6**

**confederation**
A loose association of states or territorial units without any or much power in a central authority.

**constitution**
The basic framework of law for a nation that prescribes how government is to be organized, how decisions are to be made, and what powers and responsibilities government shall have.

**Articles of Confederation**
The first constitution of the United States, adopted during the last stages of the Revolutionary War, created a system of government with most power lodged in the states and little in the central government.

is safe to assume that neither Jefferson, the main author of the Declaration, nor the other signers of the document had women, Native Americans, free blacks, or slaves in mind when they were fomenting revolution and calling for a different kind of political society. Interestingly, free blacks and women would go on to play important roles in waging the Revolutionary War against Britain.[6]

# The Articles of Confederation: The First Constitution

**2.2** Describe the governmental system established by our first constitution

The leaders of the American Revolution almost certainly did not envision the creation of a single, unified nation. At most, they had in mind a loose **confederation** among the states. This should not be surprising. Most Americans in the late eighteenth century believed that a government based on popular consent and committed to the protection of individual rights was possible only in small, homogeneous republics, where government was close to the people and where fundamental conflicts of interest among the people did not exist. Given the great geographic expanse of the colonies, as well as their varied ways of life and economic interests, the formation of a single unified republic seemed unworkable.

## ☐ Provisions of the Articles

Our first written **constitution**—a document specifying the basic organization, powers, and limits of government—passed by the Second Continental Congress in the midst of the Revolutionary War in 1777 (although it was not ratified by the requisite number of states until 1781), created a nation that was hardly a nation at all. The **Articles of Confederation** created in law what had existed in practice from the time of the Declaration of Independence: a loose confederation of independent states with little power in the central government, much like the United Nations today. Under the Articles, most important decisions were made in state legislatures.

The Articles provided for a central government of sorts, but it had few responsibilities and virtually no power. It could make war or peace, but it had no power to levy taxes (even customs duties) to pursue either goal. It could not regulate commerce among the states, nor could it deny the states the right to collect customs duties. It had no independent chief executive to ensure that the laws passed by Congress would be enforced, nor had it a national court system to settle disputes between the states. There were no means to provide a sound national money system. The rule requiring that all national laws be approved by 9 of the 13 states, with each state having one vote in Congress, made lawmaking almost impossible. And, defects in the new constitution were difficult to remedy because amending the Articles required the unanimous approval of the states.

## ☐ Shortcomings of the Articles

The Articles of Confederation did what most of its authors intended: to preserve the power, independence, and sovereignty of the states and ensure that the central government would not encroach on the liberty of the people. Unfortunately, there were also many problems that the confederation was ill-equipped to handle.

Most important, the new central government could not finance its activities. The government was forced to rely on each state's willingness to pay its annual tax assessment. Few states were eager to cooperate. As a result, the bonds and notes of the confederate government became almost worthless, dramatically undermining the creditworthiness of the new country.

2.1

2.2

2.3

2.4

2.5

2.6

**CLASHES ON THE FRONTIER**

As settlers moved west, they inevitably came into conflict with Native Americans already living there. Many of the settlers were angry and distressed when the national government under the Articles of Confederation proved unable to protect them against the people being displaced. This painting shows a battle waged between settlers and Native Americans on the Kentucky frontier in 1785. What weakness of the Articles led to such problems?

The central government was also unable to defend American interests in foreign affairs. Without a chief executive or a standing army, and with the states holding a veto power over actions of the central government, the confederation lacked the capacity to reach binding agreements with other nations or to deal with a wide range of foreign policy problems. These included the continuing presence of British troops in western lands ceded to the new nation by Britain at the end of the Revolutionary War, violent clashes with Native Americans on the western frontier, and piracy on the high seas.

The government was also unable to prevent the outbreak of commercial warfare between the states. As virtually independent nations with the power to levy customs duties, many states became intense commercial rivals of their neighbors and sought to gain every possible advantage against the products of other states. New York and New Jersey, for instance, imposed high tariffs on goods that crossed their borders from other states. This situation was an obstacle to the expansion of commercial activities and economic growth.

# Factors Leading to the Constitutional Convention

**2.3** Analyze the developments that led to the Constitutional Convention

Historians now generally agree that the failings of the Articles of Confederation led most of the leading citizens of the confederation to believe that a new constitution was desperately needed for the fledgling nation. What is left out of many accounts of the convening of the Constitutional Convention in Philadelphia, however, is the story of the growing concern among many of the most influential men in the confederation that the passions for democracy and equality among the common people set loose by the American Revolution were getting out of hand. During the American Revolution, appeals to the people for the defense of freedom and for the spread of the blessings of liberty were often translated by the people to mean their right to better access to the means of government and to the means of livelihood.[7] The common people were convinced that success would bring substantial improvements in their lives.[8]

2.1

2.2

2.3

2.4

2.5

2.6

**republicanism**
A political doctrine advocating limited government based on popular consent, protected against majority tyranny.

**tyranny**
The abuse of the inalienable rights of citizens by government.

# The Eighteenth-Century Republican Beliefs of the Founders

This fever for popular participation and greater equality is not what most of the leaders of the American Revolution had in mind.[9] The Founders were believers in a theory of government known as **republicanism** (please note that we are not referring here to the Republican Party or its members and supporters).[10] Like all republicans of the eighteenth century, the framers were seeking a form of government that would not only be based on the consent of the governed but would prevent **tyranny**, whether tyranny came from the misrule of a single person (a king or military dictator, let us say), a small group of elites (an aristocracy, a clerical theocracy, or moneyed merchant class), or even the majority of the population. The solution to the problem of tyranny for eighteenth-century republican thinkers was threefold: to elect government leaders, limit the power of government, and place roadblocks in the path of the majority. The election of representatives to lead the government, in their view, would keep potentially tyrannical kings and aristocratic factions from power while ensuring popular consent. Limiting the power of government, both by stating what government could and could not do in a written constitution and by fragmenting governmental power, would prevent tyranny no matter who eventually won control, including the majority of the people. The influence of the majority could be limited by making only a portion of government subject to election by the people.

Although eighteenth-century republicans believed in representative government—a government whose political leaders are elected by the people—they were not sympathetic to what we might today call popular democracy. For the most part, they thought that public affairs ought to be left to men from the "better" parts of society. The conduct of the public business was, in their view, the province of individuals with wisdom and experience, capacities associated mainly with people of social standing, substantial financial resources, and high levels of education. They expected that voters would be interested in having such people in office and would cast their ballots consistent with this view. Eighteenth-century republicans believed that once in office, elected representatives should not be overly responsive to public opinion; representatives were to exercise independent judgment about how best to serve the public interest, taking into account the needs and interests of society rather than the moods and opinions of the people. They believed that such a deliberative approach would not only protect liberty but result in better government decisions and policies.[11]

## Why the Founders Were Worried

Eighteenth-century republicans, then, did not believe that the people could or should rule directly. While they favored a system that allowed the common people to play a larger role in public life than existed in other political systems of the day, the role of the people was to be a far more limited one than we find acceptable today. They worried that too much participation by the people could only have a bad outcome. As James Madison put it in *The Federalist Papers*, "[Democracies] have ever been spectacles of turbulence and contention; have ever been found incompatible with personal security or the rights of property; and have in general been as short in their lives as they have been violent in their deaths."[12] (See Table 2.1 on the differences between democracy and eighteenth-century republicanism.)

**AN EXCESS OF DEMOCRACY IN THE STATES** Worries that untamed democracy was on the rise were not unfounded.[13] In the mid-1780s, popular assemblies (called conventions) were created in several states to keep tabs on state legislatures and to issue instructions to legislatures concerning what bills to pass. Both conventions and instructions struck directly at the heart of the republican conception of the legislature as a deliberative body made up of representatives shielded from popular opinion.[14]

**TABLE 2.1** COMPARING EIGHTEENTH-CENTURY REPUBLICANISM AND THE DEMOCRATIC IDEAL

| 18th-Century Republicanism | The Democratic Ideal |
|---|---|
| Government is based on popular consent. | Government is based on popular consent. |
| Rule by the people is indirect, through multiple layers of representatives. | Rule by the people may be direct or indirect through representatives. |
| The term *people* is narrowly defined (by education, property holding, and social standing). | The term *people* is broadly defined. |
| Office holding is confined to a narrow and privileged stratum of the population. | Broad eligibility for office holding. |
| Elected representatives act as "trustees" (act on their own to discover the public good). | Elected representatives act as "delegates" (act as instructed by the people; accurately reflect their wishes). |
| Barriers to majority rule exist. | Majority rule prevails. |
| Government is strictly limited in what it can do. | Government does what a majority of the people want it to do. |
| Government safeguards rights and liberties, with a special emphasis on property rights. | Government safeguards rights and liberties, with no special emphasis on property rights. |

**unicameral**
A legislative body with a single chamber.

**stay acts**
Laws forbidding farm foreclosures for nonpayment of debts.

2.1

2.2

2.3

2.4

2.5

2.6

The constitution of the state of Pennsylvania was also an affront to republican principles. Benjamin Rush, a signatory to the Declaration of Independence, described it as "too much upon the democratic order."[15] This constitution replaced the property qualification to vote with a very small tax (thus allowing many more people to vote), created a **unicameral** (single-house) legislative body whose members were to be elected in annual elections, mandated that legislative deliberations be open to the public, and required that proposed legislation be widely publicized and voted on only after a general election had been held (making the canvassing of public opinion easier).

To many advocates of popular democracy, including Tom Paine, the Pennsylvania constitution was the most perfect instrument of popular sovereignty. To others, like James Madison, the Pennsylvania case was a perfect example of popular tyranny exercised through the legislative branch of government.[16]

**THE THREAT TO PROPERTY RIGHTS IN THE STATES** One of the freedoms that eighteenth-century republicans wanted to protect against the intrusions of a tyrannical government was the right of the people to acquire and enjoy private property. Developments toward the end of the 1770s and the beginning of the 1780s seemed to put this freedom in jeopardy. For one thing, the popular culture was growing increasingly hostile to privilege of any kind, whether of social standing, education, or wealth. Writers derided aristocratic airs; expressed their preference for unlettered, plain-speaking leaders; and pointed out how wealth undermined equal rights.[17] Legislatures were increasingly inclined, moreover, to pass laws protecting debtors. For example, Rhode Island and North Carolina issued cheap paper money, which note holders were forced to accept in payment of debts. Other states passed **stay acts**, which forbade farm foreclosures for nonpayment of debts. Popular opinion, while strongly in favor of property rights (after all, most of the debtors in question were owners of small farms), also sympathized with farmers, who were hard-pressed to pay their debts with increasingly tight money, and believed—with some reason—that many creditors had accumulated notes speculatively or unfairly and were not entitled to full repayment.

What pushed American notables over the edge was the threat of insurrection represented by what came to be called Shays' Rebellion. Named after its leader Daniel Shays, the rebellion occurred in western Massachusetts in 1786 when armed men took over court houses in order to prevent judges from ordering the seizure of farms for nonpayment of state taxes and the incarceration of their owners in debtors prison. The crisis in western Massachusetts was the result of a near "perfect storm" of developments: plummeting prices for crops, a dramatic increase in state taxes to pay off

2.1

2.2

2.3

2.4

2.5

2.6

**SHAYS' REBELLION**

Shays' Rebellion aimed at easing financial pressures on debt-ridden small farmers by closing state courts to prevent foreclosure hearings from taking place. Here, Daniel Shays encourages his fellow citizens to close the courts. Why did the rebellion push American leaders to propose a constitutional convention? Are big changes in forms of government always triggered by some form of social protest?

Revolutionary War debts, and Governor James Bowdoin's insistence that note-holders be paid in full by the state (mostly financial speculators who had bought up the state debt for pennies on the dollar). Unlike most other states in similar circumstances, Massachusetts did not take action to help its debt-ridden farmers. While other states, for example, passed legislation postponing tax and mortgage payments, it instead raised taxes and insisted upon full and timely payment with forfeiture of farms and jail the penalties for noncompliance. Although the state succeeded in putting down the rebellion and reopening the courts, it required the dispatch of the state militia, two pitched battles, and arrests of most of the leaders of the insurrection.

Most of the new nation's leading citizens were alarmed by the apparent inability of state governments to maintain public order under the Articles of Confederation.[18] Shays's Rebellion realized the worst fears of national leaders about the dangers of ineffective state governments and popular democracy spinning out of control, unchecked by a strong national government. As George Washington said, "If government cannot check these disorders, what security has a man?"[19] It was in this climate of crisis in 1786 that 12 delegates from five states meeting in Annapolis issued a call to the other states and Congress to convene a constitutional convention of all the states to correct the flaws in our first constitution. Rather than amend the Articles of Confederation, however, the delegates who gathered at the subsequent convention in Philadelphia in the summer of 1787 did a very surprising thing; they wrote an entirely new constitution.

# The Constitutional Convention

2.1

2.2

2.3

2.4

2.5

2.6

**2.4** Evaluate the framework for government that emerged from the Constitutional Convention

**M**ost of America's economic, social, and political leaders were convinced by 1787 that the new nation and the experiment in self-government were in great peril. These concerns helped convince leaders in the states to select 73 delegates to attend the Constitutional Convention in Philadelphia (only 55 actually showed up for its deliberations). The goal was to create a new government capable of providing both energy and stability.

The convention officially convened in Philadelphia on May 25, 1787, with George Washington presiding. It met in secret for a period of almost four months. By the end of their deliberations, the delegates had hammered out a constitutional framework that has served as one of the structural foundations of American government and politics to the present day.

## ◻ Who Were the Framers?

The delegates were not common folk. There were no common laborers, skilled craftspeople, small farmers, women, or racial minorities in attendance. Most delegates were wealthy men: holders of government bonds, real estate investors, successful merchants, bankers, lawyers, and owners of large plantations worked by slaves. They were, for the most part, far better educated than the average American and solidly steeped in the classics. The journal of the convention debates kept by James Madison of Virginia shows that the delegates were conversant with the great works of Western philosophy and political science; with great facility and frequency, they quoted Aristotle, Plato, Locke, Montesquieu, and scores of other thinkers. Finally, they were a group with broad experience in American politics—most had served in their state legislatures—and many were veterans of the Revolutionary War.[20]

Judgments about the framers, their intentions, and what they produced vary widely. Historian Melvin Urofsky wrote that "few gatherings in the history of this or any other country could boast such a concentration of talent."[21] Supreme Court Justice Thurgood Marshall, the first African American member of the Court, on the other hand, once claimed that the Constitution was "defective from the start" because the convention at which it was written did not include women or blacks.[22]

The most influential criticism of the framers and what they created was mounted in 1913 by the Progressive historian Charles Beard in his book *An Economic Interpretation of the Constitution*.[23] Beard boldly claimed that the framers were engaged in a conspiracy to protect their immediate and personal economic interests. Those who controlled the convention and the ratification process after the convention, he suggested, were owners of government bonds and notes who were interested in a government that could pay its debts, merchants interested in protections of commerce, and land speculators interested in the protection of property rights.

Beard has had legions of defenders and detractors.[24] Historians today generally agree that Beard overemphasized the degree to which the framers were driven by the immediate need to "line their own pockets," failed to give credit to their more noble motivations, and even got many of his facts wrong. So a simple self-interest analysis is not supportable. But Beard was probably on the mark when he suggested that broad economic and social-class motives were at work in shaping the actions of the framers. This is not to suggest that they were not concerned about the national interest, economic stability, or the preservation of liberty. It does suggest, however, that the ways in which they understood these concepts were fully compatible with their own positions of economic and social eminence. It is fair to say that the Constitutional Convention was the work of American notables who were authentically worried about the instability and economic chaos of the confederation as well as the rise of a democratic and equalitarian culture among the common people.[25]

That being said, we must also acknowledge that the framers were launched on a novel and exciting adventure, trying to create a form of government that existed nowhere else during the late eighteenth century. The success of their efforts was not

**2.1**

**2.2**

**2.3**

**2.4**

**2.5**

**2.6**

**Virginia Plan**
Proposal by the large states at the Constitutional Convention to create a strong central government with power in the government apportioned to the states on the basis of population.

**New Jersey Plan**
Proposal of the smaller states at the Constitutional Convention to create a government with slightly more power in a central government than under the Articles, with the states equally represented in a unicameral national legislature.

**Connecticut Compromise**
Also called the *Great Compromise*; the compromise between the New Jersey and Virginia plans formulated by the Connecticut delegates at the Constitutional Convention; called for a lower legislative house based on population size and an upper house based on equal representation of the states.

guaranteed. They were, in effect, sailing in uncharted waters, guided by their reading of history and of the republican philosophers, their understanding of the nature of the unwritten English constitution, and their experience with colonial governments before the Revolution and state governments after the Revolution.

## ☐ Consensus and Conflict at the Convention

The delegates to the convention were of one mind on many fundamental points. Most importantly, they agreed that the Articles of Confederation had to be scrapped and replaced with a new constitution.

Most of the delegates also agreed about the need for a substantially strengthened national government to protect American interests in the world, provide for social order, and regulate interstate commerce. Such a government would diminish the power and sovereignty of the states. Supporters of the idea of a strong, centralized national government, such as Alexander Hamilton, had long argued this position. By the time of the convention, even such traditional opponents of centralized governmental power as James Madison had changed their minds. As Madison put it, some way must be found "which will at once support a due supremacy of the national authority, and leave in force the local authorities so far as they can be subordinately useful."[26]

But the delegates also believed that a strong national government was potentially tyrannical and should not be allowed to fall into the hands of any particular interest or set of interests, particularly the majority of the people, referred to by Madison as the "majority faction." The delegates' most important task became that of finding a formula for creating a republican government based on popular consent but a government not unduly swayed by public opinion and popular democracy. As Benjamin Franklin put it, "We have been guarding against an evil that old states are most liable to, excess of power in the rulers, but our present danger seems to be a defect of obedience in the subjects."[27]

**THE GREAT COMPROMISE** By far the most intense disagreements at the convention concerned the issue of representation in Congress, especially whether large or small states would wield the most power in the legislative branch. The **Virginia Plan**, drafted by James Madison, proposed the creation of a strong central government dominated by a powerful bicameral Congress controlled by the most populous states: Virginia, Massachusetts, and Pennsylvania. The Virginians proposed that seats in the national legislature be apportioned to the states on the basis of population size and that the legislature be vested with the power to appoint executive and judiciary branches and to veto state laws. The smaller states countered with a set of proposals drafted by William Paterson of New Jersey (thereafter known as the **New Jersey Plan**), whose central feature was a unicameral national legislature whose seats were apportioned equally among the states with representatives selected by state legislatures. The New Jersey Plan envisioned a slightly more powerful national government than the one that existed under the Articles of Confederation, but one that was to be organized on representational lines not unlike those in the Articles, in which each of the states remained sovereign and equal. The Virginia Plan, by contrast, with its strong national government run by a popularly elected legislature, represented a fundamentally different kind of national union, one in which national sovereignty was superior to state sovereignty.[28]

Debate over this issue was so intense that no decision could be reached on the floor of the convention. As a way out of this impasse, the convention appointed a committee to hammer out a compromise. The so-called Committee of Eleven met over the Fourth of July holiday while the convention was adjourned. It presented its report, sometimes called the Great Compromise and sometimes the **Connecticut Compromise** (because it was drafted by Roger Sherman of that state), on July 5, 1787. Its key feature was a bicameral (two-house) national legislature in which each state's representation in the House of Representatives was to be based on population (thus favoring the large states), while representation in the Senate was to be equal for each of the states (thus favoring the small states). The compromise, adopted on July 16, broke the deadlock at the convention and allowed the delegates to turn their attention to other matters.[29] (See the "Mapping American Politics" feature for more on the enduring effects of the compromise.)

# Mapping American Politics

## Equal and Unequal Representation in the House and Senate

2.1

2.2

2.3

2.4

2.5

2.6

### Introduction

One of the fundamental decisions made by the framers at the Constitutional Convention in Philadelphia in 1787 was to create a two-chamber legislative branch with each branch based on a different principle of representation. Each state's representation in the House of Representatives is based on its relative population size, with the proviso that no state shall have fewer than one representative. Representation in the House, because it very nearly mirrors the distribution of the American population among the states, then, can fairly be called democratic, based on the principle of one person, one vote. The Senate, on the other hand, is based on equal representation of the states—each state has two senators regardless of its population size—giving disproportionate political power to low-population states. We can see this by comparing the two cartograms.

in the Senate, combined with vast population differences among the states, however, leads to serious representational distortions from a democratic theory point of view. According to 2010 census data, over 37 million people lived in California while about 560,000 people lived in Wyoming—yet each state had two senators. Thus, each California senator represented over 18.5 million people, while each Wyoming senator represented about 280,000. In terms of representation, each person in Wyoming, then, had 66 times the power in the Senate in 2010 as each person in California. The cartogram on the right reflects the representational power of the people in each state in the Senate, measured as the number of senators—always two—divided by state population size. The most populous states, such as California, New York, Texas, and Florida, almost disappear, while less populous states, such as Wyoming, Montana, Delaware, and the two Dakotas, loom large.

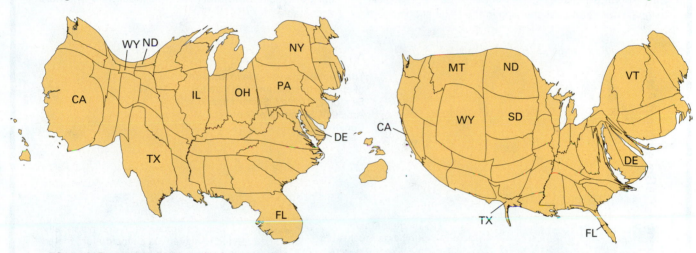

States in Proportion to Number of U.S. Representatives          States in Proportion to Number of Residents per Senator

### Different Maps; Different Stories

The cartogram on the left shows states drawn in proportion to the number of representatives each has in the House of Representatives. Because representation in the House is based roughly on population size, the largest numbers of representatives come from more populous states, such as California, Texas, Florida, Ohio, Illinois, New York, and Pennsylvania, as one would expect in a democratic system. Equal representation of each state

Standard US Map

### What Do You Think?

- For the most part, the framers of the Constitution were eighteenth-century republicans, distrustful of popular democracy. They created the Senate not only as a tactical maneuver to gain ratification of the Constitution by nine states, but to make the legislative branch more deliberative and less prone to follow the ebbs and flows of public opinion. Was it a wise decision by the framers to give equal representation to the states in the Senate? How might Congress make different kinds of policies if the Senate were organized to more closely reflect the size of state populations?

*Note:* Alaska is not shown for reasons of space.

**SOURCES:** United States House of Representatives, http://www.house.gov; U.S. Census Bureau, "Congressional Apportionment," http://www.census.gov/population/www/censusdata/apportionment.html; and www.senate. gov.United States Senate, http://www.senate.gov. Cartogram produced in ArcMap using Tom Gross's Cartogram Geoprocessing Tool (v2). ArcMap uses the Newman-Gastner method [see details in Michael T. Gastner and Mark E. J. Newman, "Diffusion-Based Method for Producing Density-Equalizing Maps," *Proceedings of the National Academy of Sciences* 101 (2004): 7499 -7504.]

2.1

2.2

2.3

2.4

2.5

2.6

**SLAVERY**  Despite great distaste for the institution of slavery among many delegates—it is said that Benjamin Franklin wanted to insert a provision in the Constitution condemning slavery and the slave trade but was talked out of it for fear of splintering the convention[30]—slavery was ultimately condoned in the Constitution, although only indirectly; the word *slavery*, in fact, does not appear in the Constitution at all. But even without using the term, the legal standing of slaves is affirmed in three places. First, the delegates agreed, after much heated debate, to count three-fifths of a state's slave population (referred to as "three-fifths of all other Persons") in the calculation of how many representatives a state was entitled to in the House

## Using the FRAMEWORK

### Why was slavery allowed in the Constitution of 1787?

**Background:** Slavery was allowed in the Constitution until passage, after the Civil War, of the Thirteenth Amendment, which ended involuntary servitude in the United States. Although the words "slave" or "involuntary servitude" never appear in the document, slavery is given constitutional standing in the original document in Article I, Section 2, paragraph 3; Article I, Section 9; and Article IV, Section 2, paragraph 3. For Americans today, it seems almost inconceivable that such a thing could have happened. Taking a broader and more historical view makes the story clearer, though hardly more acceptable.

**Government Action**

The framers allowed the institution of slavery to continue in Article I, Section 2; Article I, Section 9; and Article IV, Section 2 of the Constitution.

**Government**

Slaveholders and merchants involved in the slave trade were well represented among the convention delegates.

Many other delegates, although personally opposed to slavery as an institution, feared that the introduction of a provision to end slavery would cause those states with high numbers of slaves to leave the convention and doom the effort to create a United States of America.

**Political Linkage**

Slaves and free blacks played no significant political role in America during the Articles of Confederation period. Their concerns about slavery had no political weight.

Few private organizations—interest groups, churches, or newspapers—were actively pressing for an end to slavery at the time of the Constitutional Convention.

**Structure**

For the most part, individuals of European descent in America during the time of the constitutional convention did not believe that people of African descent were equal to whites in any respect, nor did they believe they were beings who possessed basic human rights.

The slave trade was a profitable business.

of Representatives (Article I, Section 2, paragraph 3). Much harm was done by this; counting noncitizen slaves for purposes of representation in the House increased the power of the slave states in Congress as well as the number of their electoral votes in presidential elections. This imbalance would continue until 1865, when the Civil War and the Thirteenth Amendment, ratified after the war, ended slavery in the United States. Second, it forbade enactments against the slave trade until the year 1808 (Article I, Section 9). Third, it required nonslave states to return runaway slaves to their owners in slave states (Article IV, Section 2, paragraph 3).

Many Americans today are bothered by the fact that a significant number of the delegates to a convention whose goal was to build a nontyrannical republic were themselves slaveholders (although a few, including George Washington, had provisions in their wills freeing their slaves upon their death). To understand more fully why the delegates did not abolish slavery, see the "Using the Framework" feature.

It would take a terrible civil war to abolish slavery in the United States. At the convention, Virginia delegate George Mason had a foreboding of such an outcome when he observed about slavery that "providence punishes national sins by national calamities."[31]

**THE PRESIDENCY** The Virginia Plan called for a single executive, while the New Jersey Plan called for a multiperson executive. In the spirit of cooperation that pervaded the convention after the Great Compromise, the delegates quickly settled on the idea of a single executive. They could not agree, however, on how this executive should be selected. Both sides rejected direct election of the chief executive by the people, of course, because this would be "too much upon the democratic order," but they locked horns over the Virginia Plan's method of selection: by the vote of state legislatures. The compromise that was eventually struck involved a provision for an **Electoral College** that would select the president. In the Electoral College, each state would have a total of votes equal to its total number of representatives and senators in

**Electoral College**
Elected representatives of the states chosen during the November presidential election, a majority of whose votes cast at a later date formally elect the president of the United States. The number of electors in each state is equal to the total number of its senators and representatives. In all but two states, the candidate who wins a plurality of the popular vote wins all of a state's electoral votes.

**THE FRAMERS RETAIN SLAVERY**
One of the great shortcomings of the framers was their inability or unwillingness to abolish slavery in the Constitution. Here, slaves pick cotton under the watchful eye of an overseer. What were some of the consequences for the nation of the framers allowing slavery in our new nation?

2.1

2.2

2.3

2.4

2.5

2.6

Congress. Selection of electors was left to state legislatures. (Electoral College votes are determined today by popular vote in each state.) Elected members of the Electoral College would then cast their votes for president. Should the Electoral College fail to give a majority to any person, which most framers assumed would usually happen, the House of Representatives would choose the president, with each state having one vote (Article II, Section 1, paragraphs 2 and 3). See the "By the Numbers" feature below in this chapter to better understand how the Electoral College and majoritarian democracy are sometimes at odds.

# By the Numbers

## Did George W. Bush really win the 2000 presidential vote in Florida?

George W. Bush was officially certified the winner of the presidential contest in Florida on December 12, 2000—35 days after the November election—thereby winning all of Florida's 25 electoral votes. This pushed Bush's national electoral vote total to 271, a bare majority but enough to win the White House.

Interestingly, however, a comprehensive review of Florida ballots has come up with several other possible outcomes to the Florida popular vote, depending on different ways the ballots might have been counted. In one of these scenarios, Gore would have won the Florida popular vote, added its electoral votes to his total in the nation, and been declared the winner of the presidential election.

### Why It Matters

Elections must be fair if they are to play the role assigned to them in democratic theory. Part of a fair election is an accurate count of votes cast. Without an accurate count, voter wishes will not be conveyed to public officials, and the legitimacy of elected officials is at risk, making governance more difficult.

### Behind the Vote Count Numbers

A consortium of eight leading news organizations—including *The Wall Street Journal*, *The New York Times*, *The Washington Post*, the Associated Press, and CNN—sponsored a 10-month study by the widely respected National Opinion Research Center at the University of Chicago. Center researchers examined every uncounted "under-vote" ballot (where no vote for president was recorded by the voting machine), with an eye toward determining each voter's intent. Only ballots that showed evidence of clear voter intention were included in the consortium's recount. These included punch card ballots with "hanging" and "pregnant" chads which the machines failed to record and optical scan ballots where voters indicated their vote with a check mark or an "X" rather than filling in the bubble as instructed.

### Calculating the Winner's Margin of Victory

The official tally concluded that Bush won by 537 votes. However, Center investigators found that different counting methods would have yielded the results shown on page 39. There are some incredible ironies in these numbers.

■ **Scenario 1** Had the Gore team gotten everything it asked for from election officials and the courts, Al Gore still would have lost to George W. Bush.

■ **Scenario 2** The U.S. Supreme Court did not steal the election, as many Gore supporters claimed, for had it allowed the Florida Supreme Court's solution to stand, Bush would have won anyway.

■ **Scenario 3** A majority of Florida voters went to the polls on November 8 to cast a vote for Al Gore for president. The method proposed by the U.S. Supreme Court shows this; recounting all "under-count" disputed ballots on a statewide basis using consistent standards yields a Gore victory. The upshot: Gore was badly advised by his team of lawyers, who insisted on recounts in only certain counties that were deemed favorable to him.

Because of the enormous boost in George W. Bush's popularity following the terrorist attack on the United States and the widely supported attack on the Taliban regime in Afghanistan that followed, most Americans ignored the consortium's findings when they were published after 9/11. Most seemed perfectly content to have Bush as president, no matter what had happened in Florida.

### Criticisms of the Florida "Recount"

Some have argued that the consortium's recount was flawed in two major ways:

■ First, it did not include "over-votes" in its estimates—those ballots where the same name was entered more than once—which were also ruled invalid by election officials in Florida. For the most part, these involved ballots where voters wrote in the same name as the candidate they had punched or marked, presumably to make clear to election officials who they had voted for. A substantial majority of over-vote ballots had selected Gore.

■ Second, there is the issue of absentee ballots from overseas armed forces personnel. Had they been counted in the same way other ballots were counted—that is, not counting ballots kicked out because of "under-vote" or "over-vote"

(Continued)

2.1
2.2
2.3
2.4
2.5
2.6

**Bush +493**

**Bush +225**

**Gore +200**

| Scenario 1 | Scenario 2 | Scenario 3 |

**Scenario 1**
If, as the Gore team insisted, "under-votes" from Palm Beach, Miami-Dade, Broward, and Volusia counties were included.

**Scenario 2**
If, as the Florida Supreme Court ruled, "under-votes" were recounted statewide, using standards set by election officials in each county (this solution was rejected by the U.S. Supreme Court as a violation of "equal protection").

**Scenario 3**
If all rejected "under-vote" ballots were tallied on a state-wide basis using uniform standards across the state, as suggested by the U.S. Supreme Court in *Bush v. Gore* (but the Supreme Court also ruled that there was no time left to make such a recount).

problems—Bush would have lost hundreds of votes to Gore and probably lost Florida and the White House.

### What to Watch For

When counting votes, as in all other counts, the rules matter. This is why the lawyers from the Gore and Bush teams fought so ferociously following the Florida election about how to do the recount. Whenever you run across a statistic that involves counting, in one form or another, you might want to look further into what counting rules were used.

### What Do You Think?

Can you think of any other way to decide the winner of an election when the race ends up in a dead heat? Some countries use a "runoff" system in which the two top people run against each other to determine who has won a majority of popular votes before a winner is declared. In the 2000 presidential elections, this would have meant a runoff election between Gore and Bush, without Ralph Nader on the ballot, most of whose votes would probably have gone to Gore in the second round. How might a runoff have changed the face of the election?

## ☐ What the Framers Created

The Constitution of the United States (which is reprinted in its entirety in the Appendix) deserves a careful reading. Each word or phrase tells something important about how American government works. If you keep in mind how the document is organized, it will help you understand the structure of the Constitution, locate specific provisions, and understand what kind of government the framers created. (A brief outline of provisions is provided in Table 2.2.) Let us examine the fundamental design for government laid out in the Constitution.

**A REPUBLICAN FORM OF GOVERNMENT** Recall that eighteenth-century republican doctrine advocated a form of government that, while based on popular consent and some popular participation, places obstacles in the path of majoritarian democracy and limits the purposes and powers of the government in order to prevent tyranny.

*Elections and Representation* Republican government is based on the principle of representation, meaning that public policies are made not by the people directly but by the people's elected representatives acting in their stead. Under the rules created by

2.1

2.2

2.3

2.4

2.5

2.6

**TABLE 2.2** READING THE CONSTITUTION

| Article | What It's About | What It Does |
|---|---|---|
| Preamble | States the purpose of the Constitution | Declares that "we the people" (not just the separate states) establish the Constitution. |
| Article I | The Legislative Branch | Provides for a House of Representatives, elected by the people and apportioned according to population.<br>Provides for a Senate, with equal representation for each state.<br>Discusses various rules and procedures, including the presidential veto.<br>Enumerates specific powers of the Congress, concluding with the necessary and proper clause.<br>Limits Congress's powers.<br>Limits the powers of the states. |
| Article II | The Executive Branch | Vests executive power in a single president of the United States.<br>Describes the Electoral College scheme for electing presidents indirectly (changed, in effect, by the development of a party system).<br>Describes the qualification, removal, compensation, and oath of office for the presidency.<br>Describes presidential powers and duties.<br>Provides for impeachment. |
| Article III | The Judicial Branch | Vests judicial power in a Supreme Court, letting Congress establish other courts if desired.<br>Provides for a limited original jurisdiction and (subject to congressional regulation) for broader appellate jurisdiction (i.e., jurisdiction to review lower court decisions).<br>Specifies a right to jury trials.<br>Defines treason, ruling out certain punishments for it. |
| Article IV | Interstate and Federal Relations | Requires that full faith and credit be given other states.<br>Requires that fugitives (slaves) be delivered up to the authorities.<br>Provides for the admission of new states and the regulation of new territories.<br>Guarantees a republican form of government to the states. |
| Article V | Amending the Constitution | Provides two ways of proposing amendments to the Constitution and two ways of ratifying them.<br>Forbids amendments changing equal state suffrage in the Senate or (before 1808) prohibiting the slave trade or changing the apportionment of taxes. |
| Article VI | Miscellaneous | Assumes the debts of the Confederation.<br>Makes the Constitution, laws, and treaties of the United States the supreme law of the land.<br>Requires an oath by U.S. and state officials. |
| Article VII | Ratification of the Constitution | Provides that the Constitution will be established when ratified by nine state conventions. |

**federal**
Describing a system in which significant governmental powers are divided between a central government and smaller territorial units, such as states.

**supremacy clause**
The provision in Article VI of the Constitution which states that the Constitution and the laws and treaties of the United States are the supreme law of the land, taking precedence over state laws and constitutions.

the Constitution, the president and members of Congress are elected by the people, although in the case of the presidency and the Senate, to be sure, they are elected only indirectly (through the Electoral College and the state legislatures, respectively). The upshot, then, is that government policies at the national level are mostly made by either directly or indirectly elected officials. (The Seventeenth Amendment, ratified in 1913, transferred election of senators from legislatures to the people.) This filters the voices of the people by encouraging the election to office of those "whose enlightened views and virtuous sentiments render them superior to local prejudices and to schemes of injustice."[32] This guarantees a degree of popular consent and some protection against the possibilities of tyrannical government arising from misrule by the *one* or by the *few*, given the electoral power of the *many*, but the many are still several steps removed from direct influence over officials.

*Federalism* The Articles of Confederation envisioned a nation structured as a loose union of politically independent states with little power in the hands of the central government. The Constitution fashioned a **federal** system in which some powers are left to the states, some powers are shared by the states and the central government, and some powers are granted to the central government alone.

The powers in the Constitution tilt toward the center, however.[33] This recasting of the union from a loose confederation to a more centralized federal system is boldly stated in Article VI, Section 2, commonly called the **supremacy clause**:

> This Constitution and the Laws of the United States which shall be made in Pursuance thereof; and all Treaties made, or which shall be made, under the Authority of the United States, shall be the supreme Law of the Land; and the Judges in every State shall be bound thereby, any Thing in the Constitution or Laws of any State to the Contrary notwithstanding.

The tilt toward national power is also enhanced by assigning important powers and responsibilities to the national government: to regulate commerce, to provide a uniform currency, to provide uniform laws on bankruptcy, to raise and support an army and a navy, to declare war, to collect taxes and customs duties, to provide for the common defense of the United States, and more. (See Article I, Section 8.) Especially important for later constitutional history is the last of the clauses in Section 8, which states that Congress has the power to "make all laws which shall be necessary and proper" to carry out its specific powers and responsibilities. We shall see later how this **elastic clause** became one of the foundations for the growth of the federal government in the twentieth century.

The Constitution left it up to each of the states, however, to determine qualifications for voting within their borders. This left rules in place in all the states that denied the right to vote to women, slaves, and Native Americans; it left rules untouched in many states that denied the vote to free blacks and to white males without property. Most states removed property qualifications by the 1830s, establishing universal white male suffrage in the United States. It would take many years and constitutional amendments to remove state restrictions on the voting rights of women and racial minorities, however.

***Limited Government*** The basic purpose of the U.S. Constitution, like any written constitution, is to define the purposes and powers of the government. Such a definition of purposes and powers automatically places a boundary between what is permissible and what is impermissible. By listing the specific powers (as in Article I, Section 8) of the national government and specifically denying others to the national government (as in Article I, Section 9, and in the first 10 amendments to the Constitution, known as the **Bill of Rights**), the Constitution limited what government may legitimately do.

***Checks on Majority Rule*** Afraid of unbridled democracy, the framers created a constitution by which the people rule only indirectly, barriers are placed in the path of majorities, and deliberation is prized over conformity to majority opinion. As political philosopher Robert Dahl puts it, "To achieve their goal of preserving a set of inalienable rights superior to the majority principle . . . the framers deliberately created a framework of government that was carefully designed to impede and even prevent the operation of majority rule."[34] Let us see what the framers did to try to dilute the power of the majority in the national government.

Of the three branches of government, they made only a part of one of them subject to election by the direct vote of the people: the House of Representatives (Article I, Section 2, paragraph 1). They left the election of the president to an electoral college whose members were selected by state legislatures and not by the direct vote of the people. They gave the responsibility of electing senators to state legislatures (since changed by the Seventeenth Amendment). They placed selection of federal judges in the hands of the president and the Senate. They arranged, as well, that representatives, senators, and presidents would serve for different terms (two years for representatives, four years for presidents, and six years for senators), and be beholden to different constituencies. These non-congruencies in terms of office, constituencies, and methods for selecting members of each of the branches were intended to ensure that popular majorities, at least in the short run, would be unlikely to overwhelm those who govern. Finally, the framers rejected the advice of radical democrats, such as Thomas Paine, Samuel Adams, and Thomas Jefferson, to allow the Constitution to be easily amended. Instead, they created an amending process that is exceedingly cumbersome and difficult (see Figure 2.2).

Thus, the framers designed a system in which majority opinion, although given some play (more than anywhere in the world at the time),[35] was largely deflected and slowed, allowing somewhat insulated political leaders to deliberate at their pleasure.

**elastic clause**
Article I, Section 8 of the Constitution, also called the *necessary and proper clause*; gives Congress the authority to make whatever laws are necessary and proper to carry out its enumerated responsibilities.

**Bill of Rights**
The first 10 amendments to the U.S. Constitution, concerned with the protection of basic liberties.

2.1
2.2
2.3
2.4
2.5
2.6

**VENERATING THE CONSTITUTION**

Americans generally believe that the Constitution fashioned by the framers in Philadelphia in 1788 is one of the main reasons the American system of government has proved to be so enduring. Here, young people look at the original document at the National Archives. What reasons might there be for our system enduring, other than the Constitution?

2.1

2.2

2.3

2.4

2.5

2.6

**separation of powers**
The distribution of government legislative, executive, and judicial powers to separate branches of government.

**checks and balances**
The constitutional principle that each of the separate branches of government has the power to hinder the unilateral actions of the other branches as a way to restrain an overreaching government and prevent tyranny.

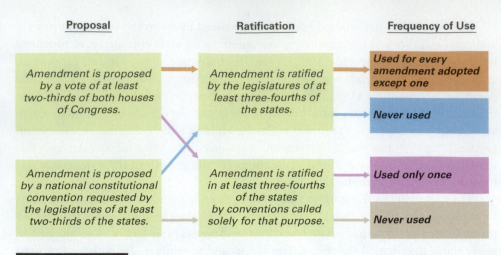

| Proposal | Ratification | Frequency of Use |
|---|---|---|
| Amendment is proposed by a vote of at least two-thirds of both houses of Congress. | Amendment is ratified by the legislatures of at least three-fourths of the states. | Used for every amendment adopted except one |
|  |  | Never used |
| Amendment is proposed by a national constitutional convention requested by the legislatures of at least two-thirds of the states. | Amendment is ratified in at least three-fourths of the states by conventions called solely for that purpose. | Used only once |
|  |  | Never used |

**FIGURE 2.2** AMENDING THE CONSTITUTION

With two ways of proposing a constitutional amendment and two ways of ratifying one, there are four routes to changing the Constitution. In all but one case (the Twenty-First Amendment, which repealed Prohibition), constitutional amendments have been proposed by Congress and then ratified by the state legislatures.

***Separation of Powers; Checks and Balances*** During the American Revolution, American leaders worried mainly about the misrule of executives (kings and governors) and judges. As an antidote, they substituted legislative supremacy in state constitutions and in the Articles of Confederation, thinking that placing power in an elected representative body would make government effective and nontyrannical. The men who drafted the Constitution, however, though still leery of executive and judicial power, were more concerned by 1787 about the danger of legislative tyranny. To deal with this problem, the framers turned to the ancient notion of balanced government, popularized by the French philosopher Montesquieu. The central idea of balanced government is that concentrated power of any kind is dangerous and that the way to prevent tyranny is first to fragment governmental power into its constituent parts—executive, legislative, and judicial—then place each into a separate and independent branch. In the U.S. Constitution, Article I (on the legislative power), Article II (on the executive power), and Article III (on the judicial power) designate separate spheres of responsibility and enumerate specific powers for each branch. We call this the **separation of powers**.

To further ensure that power would not be exercised tyrannically, the framers arranged for the legislative, executive, and judicial powers to check one another in such a way that "ambition . . . be made to counteract ambition."[36] They did this by ensuring that no branch of the national government would be able to act entirely on its own without the cooperation of the others. To put it another way, each branch has ways of blocking the actions of the others. For example, Congress is given the chief lawmaking power under the Constitution, but a bill cannot become law if a president exercises his veto, unless Congress manages to override it with a two-thirds majority in both the House and Senate. The Supreme Court, moreover, has the power (although it is not specifically mentioned) to reject a law formulated by Congress and signed by the president if it is contrary to the Constitution. What is at work here was described nicely by Thomas Jefferson: "The powers of government should be so divided and balanced among several bodies of magistracy, as that no one could transcend their legal limits, without being effectually checked and constrained by the others."[37] We call the provisions that accomplish this objective **checks and balances**. Figure 2.3 shows in detail how each separate branch of the federal government can be checked by the other two. In this constitutional scheme, each branch has power, but none is able to exercise all of its powers on its own, without some concurrence and cooperation from the other branches.

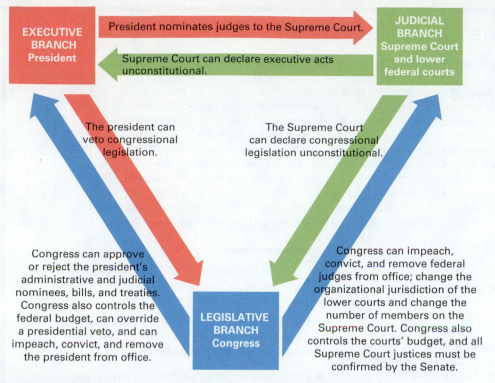

2.1

2.2

2.3

2.4

2.5

2.6

**free enterprise**
An economic system characterized by competitive markets and private ownership of a society's productive assets; a form of capitalism.

**FIGURE 2.3** SEPARATION OF POWERS AND CHECKS AND BALANCES

The framers of the Constitution believed that tyranny might be avoided if the powers of government were fragmented into its executive, legislative, and judicial components and if each component were made the responsibility of a separate branch of government. To further protect against tyranny, they created mechanisms by which the actions of any single branch could be blocked by either or both of the other branches.

**THE FOUNDATIONS FOR A NATIONAL FREE ENTERPRISE ECONOMY** The framers believed that the right to accumulate, use, and transfer private property was one of the fundamental and inalienable rights that governments were instituted to defend, so they looked for ways to protect it. They also believed that the obstacles to trade allowed under the Articles of Confederation were threatening to block the emergence of a vibrant national economy in which most of them were involved.

Property rights are protected in several places in the Constitution. Article I, Section 10, forbids the states to impair the obligation of contracts, to coin money, or to make anything but gold and silver coin a tender in payment of debts. In other words, the states could no longer help debtors by printing inflated money, forgiving debts, or otherwise infringing on the property of creditors, as had happened in such places as Rhode Island and North Carolina under the Articles of Confederation. Article IV, Section 1, further guarantees contracts by establishing that the states must give "full faith and credit" to the public acts, records, and judicial proceedings of every other state, which means that one could no longer escape legal and financial obligations in one state by moving to another. In addition, the Constitution guaranteed that the U.S. government would pay all debts contracted under the Articles of Confederation (Article VI, Section 1). Article IV, Section 2, paragraph 3, even protected private property in slaves by requiring states to deliver escaped slaves back to their owners.

Besides protecting private property, the framers took additional steps to encourage the emergence of a national **free enterprise** economy. Article I, Section 8, grants Congress the power to regulate interstate commerce (thus ending the chaos of individual states' regulations), to coin money and regulate its value (thus establishing a uniform national currency), to establish uniform laws of bankruptcy, and to protect the financial fruits of invention by establishing patent and copyright

2.1

2.2

2.3

2.4

2.5

2.6

# Can Government Do Anything Well?

## Encouraging American Economic Development

The American economy, measured by GDP, is the largest in the world in total size and among the largest in terms of GDP per person. This remains the case even after the financial collapse of 2008 and the deep recession associated with it (the worst since the Great Depression in the 1930s). Over the long haul, and despite many recessions and a few depressions along the way, the American economy has grown at a consistently steady pace over the course of its history. For example, economic historians reckon that between 1820 and 1952, the average American grew eight times richer. Between 1945 and 2007, during the post–World War II boom, the average American became three times richer. Is this story of historic economic growth one that can be explained entirely by the efforts of private individuals—investors, entrepreneurs, and consumers—and private business firms seeking profits in a free market? Or, did government play a significant role as well?

*Support for the claim that government has been a key player in the story of American economic growth:*

**Providing the foundations of a market economy:**

■ Anarchy is not conducive to a thriving, growing economy over the long run. Government provides "law and order," protecting property against both local thieves and foreign invaders.

■ Government provides legal and statutory protections and helpful tools that allow business to operate in a safe and reasonably predictable environment. Contracts are enforced in courts, for example, and invention and innovation are encouraged by a system of copyright and patent law.

■ The federal government also has been and remains responsible for providing a common currency for the nation, easing market transactions for consumers, investors, and firms.

**Instituting policies to stimulate growth:**

■ High tariff barriers in the nineteenth century protected infant American industries from foreign competition.

■ The federal government helped open the West to development when it passed the Homestead Act granting tracts of public land to those who would farm them.

■ The government stimulated the growth of railroads by giving vast tracts of land to railroad companies for rights-of-way and town sites along railroad lines.

■ Major procurements of goods and weaponry during our several wars poured substantial monies into private firms, fueling their expansion and encouraging technological innovation.

■ In the post–World War II period, the federal government invested heavily in higher education and basic scientific research. This better-educated workforce and an array of new technologies flowing from publicly funded research and development, according to most economists, helped fuel the great economic boom of the second half of the twentieth century.

*Rejection of the claim that government has been a key player in the story of American economic growth:*

**A too active government hurts the economy, invites tyranny, and has unintended consequences (the view from the Right):**

■ Beyond providing law and order, a rule-of-law regime, a common currency, and protection against invasion, government action can only interfere in the processes by which the free market makes society richer and intrude upon the freedoms of the people.

■ Heavy taxes to support an active government take away the hard-earned gains of the most successful members of society, taking their private property, as it were, and discouraging others who might create and grow businesses.

■ Real economic growth comes not from distant lawmakers and bureaucrats in Washington but from the private sector, where innovation and investment happen.

■ When government tries to help, it often makes things worse. Lawmakers' and regulators' interest in getting disadvantaged people into their own homes, it has been argued, forced lenders to give loans to people who couldn't afford them.

**Government policies to enhance economic growth have usually served the interests of the wealthy and large business firms (the view from the Left):**

■ Tax breaks, subsidies, and loan guarantees have increased income and wealth inequality in the United States.

■ The deregulation of the financial industry since the 1980s favored large investment banks and hedge funds to the disadvantage of middle class Americans.

## WHAT DO YOU THINK?

What do you think about the past, present, and future role of government in encouraging U.S. economic growth?

- On balance, the federal government has played an important and largely positive role in enhancing American economic growth and should continue to do so in the future.
- The government's record in encouraging economic growth is fairly successful, but it needs to pay more attention in the future to making sure that the benefits of growth are more fairly distributed.
- The government has a legitimate role to play in encouraging economic growth, but it should limit its role as much as possible and defer to the private sector, which is the main engine of economic advancement.
- While government policies can sometimes help economic growth, mostly they are ineffective, inefficient, and wasteful.
- Government's only role should be to protect property rights, enforce contracts, provide law and order, and defend the nation against external attacks. Anything beyond that violates our freedoms.

How would you defend your position to a fellow student? What would be your main line of argument? What evidence do you believe best supports your position? For help in developing your argument, please refer to the source list below.

For sources for this box and for all remaining boxes on the role of government and markets, see: the American Enterprise Institute (www.aei.org); Douglas J. Amy's "Government is Good" website (governmentisgood.com); Brookings (www.brookings.edu); the Cato Institute (www.cato.org); Milton Friedman, *Capitalism and Freedom* (Chicago: University of Chicago Press, 1962); Greg Ip, *The Little Book of Economics: How the Economy Works in the Real World* (New York: John Wiley and Sons, 2010); the Pew Research Center (www.people-press.org); the Heritage Foundation (www.heritage.org); and the Progressive Policy Institute (www.progressivepolicy.org).

laws. At the same time, Article I, Sections 9 and 10, broke down barriers to trade by forbidding the states from imposing taxes or duties on other states' exports, entering into foreign treaties, coining money, or laying any imposts or duties on imports or exports.

It took a little while for a national free enterprise system to emerge and flower in the United States because of the existence of an entirely different sort of economy in the slave South. Although free enterprise was thriving in the northern and western states by the 1820s, it took the destruction of slavery during and after the Civil War to create a free enterprise economy for the country as a whole. (See "Can Government Do Anything Well?" for a discussion of government's role in economic growth and development.)

# The Struggle to Ratify the Constitution

**2.5**  Explain the difficulties of ratifying the Constitution

Congress had instructed the delegates to the convention to propose changes to the Articles of Confederation. Under the provisions of the Articles of Confederation, such alterations would have required the unanimous consent of the 13 states. To follow such a course would have meant instant rejection of the new constitution, because Rhode Island, never friendly to the deliberations in Philadelphia, surely would have voted against it, and one or two additional states may well have joined Rhode Island. Acting boldly, the framers decided that ratification would be based on guidelines specified in Article VII of the unratified

2.1
2.2
2.3
2.4
2.5
2.6

2.1

2.2

2.3

2.4

2.5

2.6

**Federalists**
Proponents of the Constitution during the ratification fight; also the political party of Hamilton, Washington, and Adams.

**Anti-Federalists**
Opponents of the Constitution during the fight over ratification.

document they had just written, namely, approval by nine states meeting in special constitutional conventions. Congress agreed to this procedure, voting on September 28, 1787, to transmit the Constitution to the states for their consideration.

The battle over ratification was heated, and the outcome was far from certain. That the Constitution eventually carried the day may be partly attributed to the fact that the **Federalists** (those who supported the Constitution) did a better job of making their case than the **Anti-Federalists** (those who opposed the Constitution). Their intellectual advantages were nowhere more obvious than in the 85 articles written in defense of the Constitution for New York newspapers, under the name "Publius," by Alexander Hamilton (who wrote the most), James Madison, and John Jay (who wrote only three). Collected later and published as *The Federalist Papers* (which Thomas Jefferson judged to be "the best commentary on the principles of government which ever was written"[38]), these articles strongly influenced the debate over ratification and remain the most impressive commentaries ever written about the U.S. Constitution.

Anti-Federalist opposition to the Constitution was based on fear of centralized power and concern about the absence of a bill of rights.[39] Although the Federalists firmly believed that a bill of rights was unnecessary because of the protection of rights in the state constitutions and the many safeguards against tyranny in the federal Constitution, they promised to add one during the first session of Congress. Without this promise, ratification would probably not have happened. The Federalists kept their word. The 1st Congress passed a bill of rights in the form of 10 amendments to the Constitution (see Table 2.3), and the amendments were eventually ratified by the required number of states by 1791.

Ratification of the Constitution was a close call. Most of the small states quickly approved, attracted by the formula of equal representation in the Senate. Federalists organized a victory in Pennsylvania before the Anti–Federalists realized what had happened. After that, ratification became a struggle. Rhode Island voted no. North Carolina abstained because of the absence of a bill of rights and did not vote its approval until 1790. In the largest and most important states, the vote was exceedingly close. Massachusetts approved by a vote of 187–168; Virginia, by 89–79; and New York, by 30–27. The struggle was especially intense in Virginia, where prominent, articulate, and influential men were involved on both sides. The Federalists could call on George Washington, James Madison, John Marshall, and Edmund Randolph. The Anti-Federalists countered with George Mason, Richard Henry Lee, and Patrick Henry. Patrick Henry was particularly passionate, saying that the Constitution "squints towards monarchy." Although New Hampshire technically put the Constitution over the top, being the ninth state to vote approval, the proponents did not rest easily until Virginia and New York approved it.

**TABLE 2.3** THE BILL OF RIGHTS

| | |
|---|---|
| Amendment I | Freedom of religion, speech, press, and assembly |
| Amendment II | The right to bear arms |
| Amendment III | Prohibition against quartering of troops in private homes |
| Amendment IV | Prohibition against unreasonable searches and seizures |
| Amendment V | Rights guaranteed to the accused: requirement for grand jury indictment; protections against double jeopardy and self-incrimination; guarantee of due process |
| Amendment VI | Right to a speedy and public trial before an impartial jury, to cross-examine witnesses, and to have counsel |
| Amendment VII | Right to a trial by jury in civil suits |
| Amendment VIII | Prohibition against excessive bail and fines and against cruel and unusual punishment |
| Amendment IX | Traditional rights not listed in the Constitution are retained by the people |
| Amendment X | Powers not denied to them by the Constitution or given solely to the national government are retained by the states or the people |

*Note:* See the Appendix for the full text.

# The Changing Constitution, Democracy, and American Politics

**2.6** Identify three processes by which the Constitution changes

**judicial review**
The power of the Supreme Court to declare actions of the other branches and levels of government unconstitutional.

2.1

2.2

2.3

2.4

2.5

2.6

The Constitution is the basic rule book for the game of American politics. Constitutional rules apportion power and responsibility among governmental branches, define the fundamental nature of the relationships among governmental institutions, specify how individuals are to be selected for office, and tell how the rules themselves may be changed. Every aspiring politician who wants to attain office, every citizen who wants to influence what government does, and every group that wants to advance its interests in the political arena must know the rules and how to use them to their best advantage. Because the Constitution has this character, we understand it to be a fundamental *structural* factor influencing all of American political life.

Like all rules, however, constitutional rules can and do change over time, which is why we sometimes speak of the "living Constitution." Constitutional changes come about in three specific ways: formal amendment, judicial interpretation, and political practices.

The Constitution may be formally amended by use of the procedures outlined in Article V of the Constitution (again, refer to Figure 2.2). This method has resulted in the addition of 27 amendments since the founding, the first 10 of which (the Bill of Rights) were added within three years of ratification. That only 17 have been added in the roughly 220 years since suggests that this method of changing the Constitution is extremely difficult. Over the years, proponents of constitutional amendments that would guarantee equal rights for women, ban same-sex marriages, and ban the burning of the American flag have learned how difficult it is to formally amend the Constitution; none of these amendments were added, despite public opinion polls reporting majorities in favor of them. Nevertheless, several formal amendments have played an important role in expanding democracy in the United States by ending slavery; extending voting rights to African Americans, women, and young people ages 18–20; and making the selection of senators the business of voters, not state legislatures.

The Constitution is also changed by decisions and interpretations of the U.S. Supreme Court found in the written opinions of the justices. In *Marbury v. Madison* (1803), the Court claimed the power of **judicial review**—the right to declare the actions of the other branches of government null and void if they are contrary to the Constitution—even though such a power is not specifically mentioned in the Constitution (see Chapter 14 for a full discussion of judicial review). In *Griswold v. Connecticut* (1965), and later in *Roe v. Wade* (1973), actually, to take two more examples, the Court supported a claim for the existence of a fundamental right to privacy even though such a right is not explicitly mentioned in the Constitution. Many conservatives believe that such actions by the Supreme Court are illegitimate because they go beyond the original intentions of the framers, or cannot be justified in the written provisions of the Constitution. Many others disagree, believing that the Court has and must interpret the Constitution in light of changing circumstances that the framers could not have envisioned.

The meaning of the Constitution also changes through changing political practices, which end up serving as precedents for political actors. Political parties, party primaries, and presidential nominating conventions are not mentioned in the Constitution, for example, but it would be hard to think about American politics today without them. It is also fair to say that the framers would not recognize the modern presidency, which is now a far more important office than they envisioned, a change that has been brought about largely by the political and military involvement of the United States in world affairs, tied to vigorous assertion of the office's diplomatic and

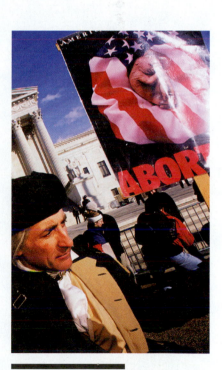

**VOICING CONCERNS AT THE COURT**
The Constitution has evolved over the years in three ways: through the amendment process, through evolving political practices, and through the Supreme Court's changing interpretation of the Constitution's meaning. Here antiabortion protesters demonstrate in front of the Supreme Court building on the anniversary of the Court's *Roe v. Wade* decision to demand a reversal of that landmark decision. How does the Constitution protect both the Supreme Court's decision and these people's public protest of it? How likely is it that the present Supreme Court will listen to these and other voices and overturn *Roe*?

2.1

2.2

2.3

2.4

2.5

2.6

**signing statement**
A document sometimes issued by the president in connection with the signing of a bill from Congress that sets out the president's understanding of the new law and how executive branch officials should carry it out.

commander-in-chief powers by many presidents, and the widespread demand that the president do something during economic crises. The Constitution does not specify, for example, that the Treasury secretary, acting for the president, can force the merger of failing financial firms as was done in the last months of the George W. Bush presidency in the depths of the recession. Nor would they have predicted the increasing use of **signing statements**, by which a president can alter the meaning of a bill even while signing it into law, or the expansion of presidential war powers.

Throughout this book you will see many examples of these three forms of constitutional change that have shaped our current understanding of the meaning of the Constitution and its many provisions. You also will learn that the third factor, changing political practices—itself a product of social and cultural change and pressure from the American people—is at least as important as amendments and judicial rulings in adjusting the Constitution to its times.[40]

# Using the DEMOCRACY STANDARD

## How democratic is the Constitution?

Scarred by the failings of the Articles of Confederation, the framers endeavored to create a republic that would offer representative democracy without the threat of majority tyranny. Consequently, they wrote a number of provisions into the Constitution to control the purported excesses of democracy. These include the separation of powers into executive, legislative, and judicial branches; checks and balances to prevent any of the branches from governing on its own; federalism to fragment government powers between a national government and the states; an appointed federal judiciary with life tenure charged with, among other things, protecting private property; selection of the president by the Electoral College; election of members of the Senate by state legislatures; and a process for changing the Constitution that makes it exceedingly easy for small numbers of people in Congress and a very few states to block amendments favored by a majority of Americans.

Although the framers had every intention of creating a republic and holding democracy in check, the tide of democracy has gradually transformed the original constitutional design. For example, the Seventeenth Amendment created a Senate whose members are directly elected by the people. The Supreme Court, moreover, has extended civil rights protections to racial and ethnic minorities. And, the presidency has become both more powerful and more attentive to majority opinion. By formal amendment, through judicial interpretations, and through changing political practices, government has been fashioned into a more responsive set of institutions that, eventually, must heed the voice of the people.

Yet it can be argued that, despite these changes, the American system of government remains essentially "republican" in nature, with the majority finding it very difficult to prevail. Provisions of the Constitution, designed to keep the majority in check, effectively provide minorities with disproportionate power in government. For example, four times in our history, presidents have taken office after an election without having won a majority of the popular vote (John Quincy Adams, 1825; Rutherford B. Hayes, 1877; Benjamin Harrison, 1889; George W. Bush, 2001). And while the Seventeenth Amendment did make the election of senators more democratic, the Senate itself—which provides equal representation to all states regardless of population—remains skewed toward smaller states, thus serving as a major barrier in the translation of what the American people want into what government does.[41] Moreover, as we will see in later chapters, the ability of private and privileged groups to use the many blocking points provided by the Constitution has grown, often frustrating majority interests and demands.

# Review the Chapter

## The American Revolution and the Declaration of Independence

**2.1** Assess the enduring legacies of the American Revolution and the Declaration of Independence, p. 25

The Revolutionary War and the Declaration of Independence helped establish the ideas of self-government and inalienable individual rights as the core of the American political ideology.

## The Articles of Confederation: The First Constitution

**2.2** Describe the governmental system established by our first constitution, p. 28

The first constitution joining the American states was the Articles of Confederation. Under its terms, the states were organized into a loose confederation in which the states retained full sovereignty and the central government had little power.

## Factors Leading to the Constitutional Convention

**2.3** Analyze the developments that led to the Constitutional Convention, p. 29

Defects in the Articles of Confederation, along with fears that democratic and egalitarian tendencies were beginning to spin out of control, prompted American leaders to gather in Philadelphia to amend the Articles. The delegates chose instead to formulate an entirely new constitution.

## The Constitutional Convention

**2.4** Evaluate the framework for government that emerged from the Constitutional Convention, p. 33

The framers created a constitutional framework for republican government including representative elections, separation of powers, checks and balances, and federalism.

The Connecticut Compromise settled the tensions between large and small states by giving states equal representation in the Senate and representation based on population in the House of Representatives.

The framers legitimated slavery.

The framers created the legal foundations for a thriving commercial republic.

## The Struggle to Ratify the Constitution

**2.5** Explain the difficulties of ratifying the Constitution, p. 45

The Constitution was ratified in an extremely close vote of the states after a hard-fought struggle between the Federalists, who wanted a more centralized republicanism, and the Anti-Federalists, who wanted small-scale republicanism.

The promise by the Federalists to introduce amendments specifying the rights of Americans in the 1st Congress helped swing the vote in favor of ratification in a number of key states.

Despite its "close shave," the Constitution became very popular among the American people within only a few years of the ratification fight.

## The Changing Constitution, Democracy, and American Politics

**2.6** Identify three processes by which the Constitution changes, p. 47

The Constitution changes by three processes: amendments to the document, judicial interpretations of the meaning of constitutional provisions, and the everyday political practices of Americans and their elected leaders.

Because the American people continue to struggle for democracy, the Constitution has become far more democratic over the years than was originally intended by the framers.

# Learn the Terms

# Test Yourself

Answer key begins on page T-1.

## 2.1 Assess the enduring legacies of the American Revolution and the Declaration of Independence

1. At the time of the American Revolution, this concept was understood as the preservation of traditional rights against the intrusion of a distant government.

   a. Democracy
   b. Popular sovereignty
   c. Political equality
   d. Liberty
   e. Justice

## 2.2 Describe the governmental system established by our first constitution

2. According to the Articles of Confederation, all national laws had to be approved by:

   a. 6 of the 13 states
   b. 7 of the 13 states
   c. 8 of the 13 states
   d. 9 of the 13 states
   e. 10 of the 13 states

## 2.3 Analyze the developments that led to the Constitutional Convention

3. Some states passed these types of acts, which forbade farm foreclosures for nonpayment of debts.

   a. Farm acts
   b. Agriculture acts
   c. Revolutionary acts
   d. Stay acts
   e. Debt acts

4. Shays's Rebellion took place in reaction to:

   a. Increased taxes to pay off war debts
   b. Increased taxes and the imprisonment of debtors
   c. Dropping prices for crops, increase in taxes, and an insistence that note holders be paid in full by the state
   d. An increase in taxes, and an insistence that note holders be paid in full by the state
   e. Dropping prices for crops and increased taxes

## 2.4 Evaluate the framework for government that emerged from the Constitutional Convention

5. This plan proposed the creation of a strong central government dominated by a powerful bicameral congress that would be controlled by the most populous states.

   a. New Jersey Plan
   b. Massachusetts Plan
   c. Virginia Plan
   d. Pennsylvania Plan
   e. Maryland Plan

## 2.5 Explain the difficulties of ratifying the Constitution

6. Those who supported the Constitution were known as:

   a. Federalists
   b. Anti-Federalists
   c. Supremacists
   d. Compromisers
   e. Revolutionists

## 2.6 Identify three processes by which the Constitution changes

7. How many amendments are in the Bill of Rights?

   a. 5
   b. 10
   c. 12
   d. 15
   e. 20

# Explore Further

## INTERNET SOURCES

The Library of Congress and The Articles of Confederation **www.loc.gov/rr/program/bib/ourdocs/articles.html**. An overview of the Articles of Confederation with numerous links to other sources involving the writing and development of the articles.

The Avalon Project: Notes on the Debates at the Federal Convention **avalon.law.yale.edu.** As complete a compilation as exists on Madison's notes and the less complete but important notes of other participants.

Best of History Websites **besthistorysites.net/index.php/ american-history/1700/constitution**. A comprehensive collection of links to websites about early American history.

Biographical Sketches of the Delegates to the Constitutional Convention **www.archives.gov/exhibits/charters/constitution_ founding_fathers.html.** Profiles of the delegates to the Constitutional Convention.

Political Science Resources: Political Thought **www. politicalresources.net.** A vast collection of documents on democracy, liberty, and constitutionalism around the world.

## SUGGESTIONS FOR FURTHER READING

Amar, Akhil Reed. *America's Unwritten Constitution: The Precedents and Principles We Live By.* New York: Basic Books, 2012.

A comprehensive guide for understanding why and how the meaning of the Constitution has changed over the course of the nation's history.

Ellis, Joseph J. *Founding Brothers: The Revolutionary Generation.* New York: Alfred Knopf, 2001.

An entertaining and accessible look at the intertwined lives of the men who wrote the Declaration of Independence, fought the Revolutionary War, fashioned the Constitution, and launched the new American government.

Levinson, Sanford. *Our Undemocratic Constitution: Where the Constitution Goes Wrong.* New York: Oxford University Press, 2006.

An argument by a leading constitutional scholar that the framers did their job of protecting against majority rule so well that it severely cripples American democracy today.

Rossiter, Clinton, ed. *The Federalist Papers.* New York: New American Library, 1961.

Classic commentaries on the Constitution and its key provisions, written by Alexander Hamilton, John Jay, and James Madison.

Storing, Herbert J. *What the Anti-Federalists Were For.* Chicago: University of Chicago Press, 1981.

The most complete collection available on the published views of the Anti-Federalists. Includes convincing commentary by Storing.

Sunstein, Cass R. *A Constitution of Many Minds: Why the Founding Document Doesn't Mean What It Meant Before.* Princeton, NJ: Princeton University Press, 2009.

An analysis of why the meaning of the Constitution has changed over the course of American history and will do so in the future.

Wood, Gordon S. *The Creation of the American Republic.* New York: W. W. Norton, 1972.

The most exhaustive and respected source on America's changing ideas during the period 1776–1787, or from the start of the American Revolution to the writing of the Constitution.

Wood, Gordon S. *The Radicalism of the American Revolution.* New York: Alfred Knopf, 1992.

Examines and rejects the argument that the American Revolution was merely a political and not a social and economic revolution.

# 3

# Federalism: States and Nation

## THE AFFORDABLE CARE ACT: WINNING THE BATTLE BUT LOSING THE WAR?

**W**hen the Affordable Care Act (ACA), popularly known as Obamacare, was signed into law on March 23, 2010, few anticipated that the defining legislative achievement of President Barack Obama's first term would be the subject of such a constitutional close call and have such important consequences for American federalism. To help make health care more affordable for all, the ACA instituted a federal requirement that all Americans must have health insurance (either provided to them by their employer or the government or purchased on their own) or pay a penalty. Advocates of the ACA argued that this mandate was necessary to expand the pool of people with health insurance so as to bring down overall costs. Conservative legal scholars, Republican leaders, and some business owners objected to the ACA on the grounds that this mandate was an unconstitutional expansion of federal authority and, as a result, many filed lawsuits aimed at getting the law overturned. For over two years, twenty-six Republican state attorneys general waged a dramatic judicial battle against the ACA. On June 28, 2012, the Supreme Court finally handed down its eagerly awaited decision.

In *National Federation of Independent Business v. Sebelius (NFIB)*, Chief Justice John Roberts Jr. wrote for the 5–4 majority, upholding the constitutionality of the health insurance mandate. For the most part, liberals and Democrats rejoiced on hearing news of the ruling, while conservatives and Republicans were both surprised and angry at Roberts for seemingly

| 3.1 | 3.2 | 3.3 | 3.4 | 3.5 |
|-----|-----|-----|-----|-----|
| Define federalism and explain why we have it, p. 55 | Establish the basis for federalism in the Constitution, p. 57 | Trace the evolution of American federalism, p. 61 | Analyze how federal grants structure national and state government relations, p. 73 | Evaluate the arguments for and against federalism, p. 77 |

**NO TO OBAMACARE** Representative Michele Bachmann (R-MN) spoke at a Tea Party rally in front of the Supreme Court demanding that the justices throw out the requirement in the Affordable Care Act that everyone buy health insurance or face a penalty. The Court supported the mandate, deeply disappointing conservative critics of the law.

abandoning the conservative cause. At first glance, it is easy to view the Court's decision both as a victory for the Obama administration and as an endorsement of the national government's powerful role in the American federal system. However, closer examination reveals that the ruling was neither a true victory for Obama nor a new validation of federal authority.

Here's why. President Obama and Democratic leaders in the U.S. Congress based their health care reform legislation on the commerce clause of the U.S. Constitution. The commerce clause, which gives Congress the power to regulate interstate commerce, has been a reliable constitutional foundation for major expansions of federal power since Franklin Roosevelt's New Deal in 1930s. It has been used to justify reams of legislation that most Americans now take for granted, such as the protection of wetlands from destructive development, the regulation of the safety of the food supply, and the protection of women, the disabled, and ethnic and racial minorities from discrimination. In *NFIB*, however, the Court rejected this justification for the ACA's health insurance mandate, reasoning that, while Congress may *regulate* commerce, it cannot force people *into* commerce by requiring them to buy health insurance. "The commerce clause is not a general license to regulate an individual from cradle to grave," wrote Roberts in his opinion. Instead, he defended the ACA's insurance mandate under Congress's power to tax. According to the Court majority, the penalty for the nonpurchase of health insurance was merely a tax, and a modest one at that. In choosing to uphold the mandate under Congress's taxing power rather than the commerce clause, Roberts struck a blow to a cornerstone of federal power by applying limits to one of the primary tools that the federal government uses to control the states.

Liberal Harvard University professor Laurence Tribe said of the Court's decision, "The narrowing [of the federal commerce power] might be the longest-lasting doctrinal legacy of the ruling." Libertarian attorney David Rivkin, who celebrated the decision despite his disapproval of the mandate, agreed. "It reaffirms with enormous vigor the fundamental limits to the government's power. The administration sailed under the flag of the commerce clause and it was decisively rebuked. No one will try to do this type of mandate again."[1]

Even though the Court upheld the insurance mandate, it rejected as unconstitutional a provision of the ACA that effectively compelled states to expand Medicaid programs to cover a greater number of low-income people. Medicaid is a program administered by the states that pays for health care services for the poor. To help more Americans meet the new health insurance requirement, states were to expand the pool of people eligible for the benefit. Though the ACA provided that the federal government would pay 100 percent of the cost of the expansion of Medicaid for the first two years and 90 percent thereafter, it also imposed a cutoff of all federal Medicaid funds (not just those for the expansion) to states that refused to expand their programs. This inducement would have made it almost impossible for states to turn down the expansion. The Roberts Court therefore ruled that this take-it-or-leave-it proposition represented a coercive use of Congress's spending power. Like the commerce clause, the congressional power to spend has been used for decades as a way to get states to comply with national objectives. By placing conditions on grants, the national government has been able to influence environmental protection, equal opportunity, and highway safety on a nationwide scale. The decision in *NFIB* signified the first time that the Supreme Court had ever found Congress's spending power unconstitutionally coercive. As a result of the *NFIB* decision to strike down the Medicaid expansion provision of the ACA, twenty-five states have decided not to use Medicaid to subsidize those of modest means to affordably remain in compliance with the law.

While the ACA and its health insurance mandate are now firmly the law of the land, the decision in *NFIB* is going to have important long-term consequences for federal authority. With the Roberts Court committed to a more restrictive view of Congress's powers under the commerce clause and Congress's spending power, it is likely that many cases will be brought to the courts by Republicans, conservatives, and business groups questioning the constitutionality of a broad range of federal programs. In *NFIB*, advocates of an activist national government may have won the battle but may yet lose the war.[2]

**federalism**
A system in which governmental powers are divided between a central government and smaller units, such as states.

3.1

**confederation**
A loose association of states or territorial divisions in which very little power or no power at all is lodged in a central government.

3.2

3.3

**unitary system**
A system in which a central government has complete power over its constituent units or states.

3.4

3.5

## Thinking Critically About This Chapter

This complex mixture of state and national government authority and responsibilities highlighted in the chapter-opening story is an important characteristic of American federalism today and in the past.

## Using the Framework

In this chapter, you will learn how and why federalism is one of the most important structural factors that affect American politics and government and shape public policy. You will learn how federalism influences our entire system, from the kinds of political parties we have and the workings of Congress to how domestic programs are affected. You will also learn how federalism itself has changed over time.

## Using the Democracy Standard

Using the evaluative tools you learned in Chapter 1, you will be able to judge for yourself whether federalism enriches or diminishes democracy in the United States.

# Federalism as a System of Government

**3.1**    Define federalism and explain why we have it

T he United States is full of governments. We have not only a federal government in Washington, D.C., but also governments in each of the 50 states and in each of thousands of smaller governmental units, such as counties (about 3,000 of them), cities, towns and townships, school districts, and special districts that deal with such matters as parks and sanitation.

All these governments are organized and related to one another in a particular way. The small governments—those of counties, cities, towns, and special districts—are legal creations of state governments. They can be created, changed, or abolished by state legislatures or by state constitutional revisions, at the convenience of the states or its voters. But state governments themselves have much more weight and permanence because of their prominent place in the Constitution. Together with the central government in Washington, D.C., they form what is known as a federal system. The federal system is part of the basic structure of U.S. government, deeply rooted in our Constitution and history. It is one of the most important features of American politics, since it affects practically everything.

## ☐ The Nature of Federalism

**Federalism** is a system under which significant government powers are divided between the central government and smaller units, such as states or provinces. Neither one completely controls the other; each has some room for independent action. A federal system can be contrasted with two other types of government: a confederation and a unitary government. In a **confederation**, the constituent states get together for certain common purposes but retain ultimate individual authority and can veto major central governmental actions. The United Nations and the American government under the Articles of Confederation are examples. In a **unitary system**, the central government has all the power and can change its constituent units or tell them what to do. China, Japan, Turkey, Iran, and France have this kind of government, as do a substantial majority of nations around the world. These three different types of governmental systems are contrasted in Figure 3.1.

**SECTARIAN VIOLENCE IN AFGHANISTAN**
Deep divisions among Pashtuns, Tajiks, Uzbeks, Hazaris, and Turkmen, as well as religious differences between Shi'ite and Sunni Muslims, mean that the new government in Afghanistan will probably take the form of a federation after the dust settles. This women mourns in the aftermath of the bombing of a Shi-ite mosque by a Pashtun Sunni group. Were there deep ethnic and religious divisions among America's framers? If so, how did it affect their design of federalism?

## ☐ Comparing American Federalism

Some of the elements of federalism go back in history at least as far as the Union of Utrecht in the Netherlands in 1579, but federalism as it exists today is largely an American invention[3], although it has come to take on a variety of forms internationally. Including the United States, only 18 nations, accounting for more than one-third of the world's population and 40 percent of its land area, are however, federal in nature.[4]

**HISTORICAL ORIGINS OF AMERICAN FEDERALISM** American federalism emerged from the way in which the states declared independence from Britain—becoming, in

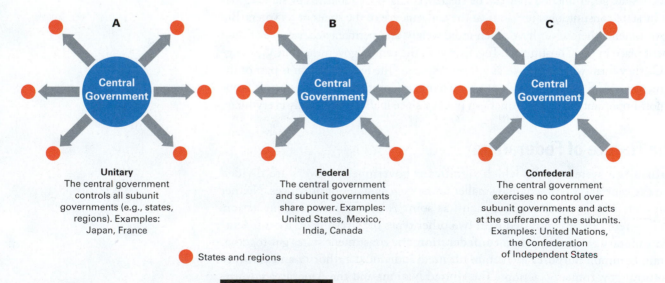

**Unitary**
The central government controls all subunit governments (e.g., states, regions). Examples: Japan, France

**Federal**
The central government and subunit governments share power. Examples: United States, Mexico, India, Canada

**Confederal**
The central government exercises no control over subunit governments and acts at the sufferance of the subunits. Examples: United Nations, the Confederation of Independent States

● States and regions

**FIGURE 3.1** TYPES OF POLITICAL SYSTEMS
A majority of countries have unitary systems (A), in which the central government controls the state and local governments, which in turn exert power over citizens. The United States, however, has a federal system (B), in which the central government has power on some issues, the states have power on other issues, and the central and state governments share power on yet others. In a confederation (C), the central institutions have only a loose coordinating role, with real governing power residing in the constituent states or units.

effect, separate countries—and then joined to form a confederation, and then a single nation, as discussed in Chapter 2. Recall that the framers of the Constitution turned to federalism as a middle-ground solution between a confederation form of government—which was deemed a failed model based on the experience under the Articles of Confederation—and a unitary form of government—which a majority of states, jealous of their independence and prerogatives, found unacceptable. Conveniently, federalism also was a form of government that was consistent with the eighteenth-century republicanism of the framers to the extent that it further fragments government power. But we can gain further insight into *why* the United States adopted and has continued as a federal system if we look at what other countries with similar systems have in common.

**ROLE OF SIZE AND DIVERSITY** Federalism tends to be found in nations that are large in a territorial sense and in which the various geographical regions are fairly distinctive from one another in terms of religion, ethnicity, language, and forms of economic activity. In Canada, for example, the farmers of the central plains are not much like the fishers of Nova Scotia, and the French-speaking (and primarily Catholic) residents of Quebec differ markedly from the mostly English-speaking Protestants of the rest of the country. In Spain there are deep divisions along ethnic and language lines (as in the distinctive Basque and Catalán regions).[5] Other important federal systems include such large and richly diverse countries as India, Pakistan, Russia, and Brazil. In all these countries, federalism gives diverse and geographically concentrated groups the degree of local autonomy they seem to want, with no need to submit in all matters to a unified central government.

The United States, too, is large and diverse. From the early days of the republic, the slave-holding and agriculture-oriented South was quite distinct from the mercantile Northeast, and some important differences persist today. Illinois is not Louisiana; the farmers of Iowa differ from defense and electronics workers in California. States today also vary in their approaches to public policy, their racial and ethnic composition, and their political cultures.[6] In *The Federalist Papers*, the Founders argued that this size and diversity made federalism especially appropriate for the new United States.

While the American system of federalism was truly exceptional at the founding, other large and important countries have adopted federalism in the years since, especially since the end of World War II. To this extent, the United States is no longer the single exception or one among a handful of exceptions to the unitary nature of the majority of the world's governments.

# Federalism in the Constitution

3.2 Establish the basis for federalism in the Constitution

 ederalism is embodied in the U.S. Constitution in two main ways: (1) power is expressly given to the states, as well as to the national government, and (2) the states have important roles in shaping and choosing officials for the national government itself, and in amending the Constitution.

## ☐ Independent State Powers

Although the Constitution makes the central government supreme in certain matters, it also makes clear that state governments have independent powers. The **supremacy clause** in Article VI states that the Constitution, laws, and treaties of the United States shall be the "supreme law of the land," but Article I, Section 8, enumerates what kinds of laws Congress has the power to pass, and the **Tenth Amendment** declares that the powers not delegated to the central government by the Constitution or prohibited by the Constitution to the states are "*reserved to the states* [emphasis added] respectively, or to the people." This provision is known as the **reservation clause**.

**supremacy clause**
The provision in Article VI of the Constitution that the Constitution itself and the laws and treaties of the United States are the supreme law of the land, taking precedence over state laws and constitutions when they are in conflict.

**Tenth Amendment**
Part of the Bill of Rights, the Amendment says that those powers not given to the federal government and not prohibited to the states by the Constitution are reserved for the states and the people.

**reservation clause**
Part of the Tenth Amendment to the Constitution that says powers not given to Congress are reserved to the states or to the people.

**concurrent powers**
Powers under the Constitution that are shared by the federal government and the states.

In other words, the U.S. Constitution specifically lists what the national government can do. Its powers include authority to levy taxes, regulate interstate commerce, establish post offices, and declare war, plus make laws "necessary and proper" for carrying out those powers. The Constitution then provides that all other legitimate government functions may be performed by the states, except for a few things, such as coining money or conducting foreign policy, that are forbidden by Article I, Section 10. This leaves a great deal in the hands of state governments, including licensing lawyers, doctors, and dentists; regulating businesses within their boundaries; chartering banks and corporations; providing a system of family law; providing a system of public education; and assuming the responsibility for building roads and highways, licensing drivers, and registering cars. Under terms of the reservation clause, states exercise what are called their police powers to protect the health, safety, and general well-being of people living in their states. The police powers have allowed states to make decisions independent of the federal government and other states on matters such as stem-cell research, minimum gas mileage standards for cars, the death penalty, emissions of greenhouse gases, and the regulation of abortion services.[7] The reservation clause is unique to the United States and shows how important states are in American federalism. Other federal systems, such as Canada's and Germany's, reserve to the national government all functions not explicitly given to the states.

Lest this sound too clear-cut, there also are broad areas of overlapping or shared powers—called **concurrent powers**; both levels of government, for example, can and do levy taxes, borrow money for public purposes, and spend money for the protection and well-being of their populations (e.g., public health programs and product safety regulation). With both independent national and state powers and responsibilities, as well as concurrent or overlapping powers and responsibilities, the Constitution is not crystal clear about the exact shape of federalism, leaving ample room for the meaning of federalism to change with the times, the preferences of the American people, and the calculations of political leaders. Figure 3.2 shows how powers and responsibilities are distributed.

## ▢ The States' Roles in the National Government

Moreover, the Constitution's provisions about the formation of the national government recognize a special position for the states. The Constitution declares in Article VII that it was "done in Convention by the unanimous consent of the *states* present"

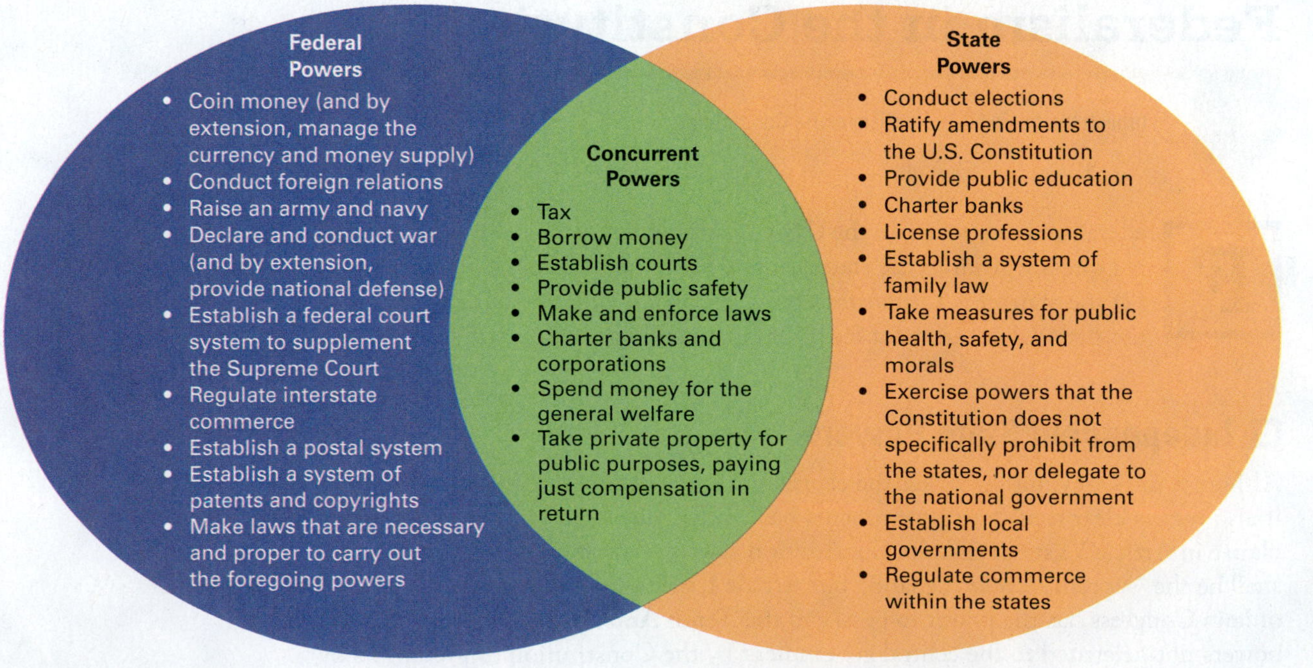

**Federal Powers**
- Coin money (and by extension, manage the currency and money supply)
- Conduct foreign relations
- Raise an army and navy
- Declare and conduct war (and by extension, provide national defense)
- Establish a federal court system to supplement the Supreme Court
- Regulate interstate commerce
- Establish a postal system
- Establish a system of patents and copyrights
- Make laws that are necessary and proper to carry out the foregoing powers

**Concurrent Powers**
- Tax
- Borrow money
- Establish courts
- Provide public safety
- Make and enforce laws
- Charter banks and corporations
- Spend money for the general welfare
- Take private property for public purposes, paying just compensation in return

**State Powers**
- Conduct elections
- Ratify amendments to the U.S. Constitution
- Provide public education
- Charter banks
- License professions
- Establish a system of family law
- Take measures for public health, safety, and morals
- Exercise powers that the Constitution does not specifically prohibit from the states, nor delegate to the national government
- Establish local governments
- Regulate commerce within the states

**FIGURE 3.2** HOW RESPONSIBILITIES ARE DISTRIBUTED IN THE FEDERAL SYSTEM

**horizontal federalism**
Term used to refer to relationships among the states.

BUT LET ME TELL YOU, MR PRESIDENT

State governors and presidents have not always seen eye-to-eye on the issues but the level of conflict among Republican state leaders and Democratic president Barack Obama reached fever pitch during the national debate over health care reform and immigration reform. Arizona governor Jan Brewer, whose state passed harsh anti-immigration measures in 2010 designed to purge undocumented immigrants from the state, defended the legislation as a state-level response to a problem that the federal government was, in Brewer's estimation, neglecting. The Supreme Court later overturned most of the measures as an unconstitutional state intrusion on federal authority in *U.S. v. Arizona* (2012).

(emphasis added) and provides that the Constitution would go into effect, not when a majority of all Americans voted for it, but when the conventions of nine *states* ratified it. Article V provides that the Constitution can be amended only when conventions in or the legislatures of three-quarters of the states ratify an amendment. Article IV, Section 3, makes clear that no states can be combined or divided into new states without the consent of the state legislatures concerned. Thus, the state governments have charge of ratifying and amending the Constitution, and the states control their own boundaries.

The Constitution also provides special roles for the states in the selection of national government officials. The states decide who can vote for members of the U.S. House of Representatives (Article I, Section 2) and draw the boundaries of House districts. Each state is given two senators (Article V) who were, until 1913, to be chosen by the state legislatures rather than by the voters (Article I, Section 3; altered by the Seventeenth Amendment). And the states play a key part in the complicated Electoral College system of choosing a president in which each state has votes equal to the number of its senators and representatives combined, with the president elected by a majority of electoral votes, not a majority of popular votes (Article II, Section 1).

## ❑ Relations Among the States

The Constitution also regulates relations among the states (these state-to-state relations are sometimes called **horizontal federalism**). Article IV of the Constitution is particularly important in this regard (see Table 3.1). For example, each state is required to give "full faith and credit" to the public acts, records, and judicial proceedings of every other state. This means that private contractual or financial agreements among people or companies

**TABLE 3.1** CONSTITUTIONAL UNDERPINNINGS OF FEDERALISM

| Provisions | Where to Find Them in the Constitution | What It Means |
| --- | --- | --- |
| Supremacy of the national government in its own sphere | Supremacy clause: Article VI | The supremacy clause establishes that federal laws and the Constitution take precedence over state laws and constitutions. |
| Limitations on national government powers and reservation of powers to the states | Enumerated national powers: Article I, Section 8<br><br>Limits on national powers: Article I, Section 9; Article IV, Section 3; Eleventh Amendment<br><br>Bill of Rights: First through Tenth Amendments<br><br>Reservation clause: Tenth Amendment | The powers of the federal government are laid out specifically in the Constitution, as are strict limitations on the power of the federal government. Powers not specifically spelled out are reserved to the states or to the people. |
| Limitations on state powers | Original restrictions: Article I, Section 10<br><br>Civil War Amendments: Thirteenth through Fifteenth Amendments | The Constitution places strict limitations on the power of the states in particular areas of activity.<br><br>Compels the states to uphold the civil liberties and civil rights of people living within their borders. |
| State role in national government | Ratification of Constitution: Article VII<br><br>Amendment of Constitution: Article V<br><br>Election of representatives: Article I, Section 2 and Section 4<br><br>Two senators from each state: Article I, Section 3<br><br>No deprivation of state suffrage in Senate: Article V<br><br>Choice of senators: Article I, Section 3 (however, see Seventeenth Amendment)<br><br>Election of president: Article II, Section 1 (however, see Twelfth Amendment) | The states' role in national affairs is clearly laid out. Rules for voting and electing representatives, senators, and the president are defined so that state governments play a part. |
| Regulation of relations among states | Full faith and credit: Article IV, Section 1<br><br>Privileges and immunities: Article IV, Section 2 | Constitutional rules ensure that the states must respect each other's legal actions and judgments.<br><br>Citizens from other states have same rights and privileges as a state's own citizens. |

in one state are valid in all the other states and that civil judgments by the courts of one state must be recognized by the others. Because of this constitutional provision, people in one state cannot evade financial obligations—for example, credit card or department store debts and alimony or child-support payments—by moving to another state.

Same-sex marriage, now legal in more than half the states, is an example of a policy that varies by state with significant consequences. Some states have enacted laws legalizing it; others have been forced into accepting it by way of court rulings; still others ban it. In electing not to hear cases on same-sex marriage in October 2014, the Supreme Court effectively let stand rulings, by four federal circuit judges, that declared bans on same-sex marriage unconstitutional.[8] In November 2014, the Sixth Circuit became the first to uphold a ban on same-sex marriage as constitutional, making it more likely that the Supreme Court will rule explicitly on its constitutionality soon in order to reconcile differences between circuits. When people of the same sex marry in states where their marriages are legally recognized, do they remain legally married when they move elsewhere? Are they eligible for federal benefits? Worried about the contestability of these questions, Congress passed the Defense of Marriage Act (DOMA) in 1996 denying federal benefits (e.g., Medicare) to spouses in same-sex marriages and allowing states to decide whether to recognize their marriages. Later, in *U.S. v. Windsor* (2013), the Supreme Court struck down the portion of DOMA that denied federal benefits to those in same-sex marriages but has yet to rule on whether states must accept other states' same-sex marriages based on "full faith and credit" and is unlikely to do so given its conservative leanings and its propensity to allow Congress broad latitude in regulating interstate relations.[9]

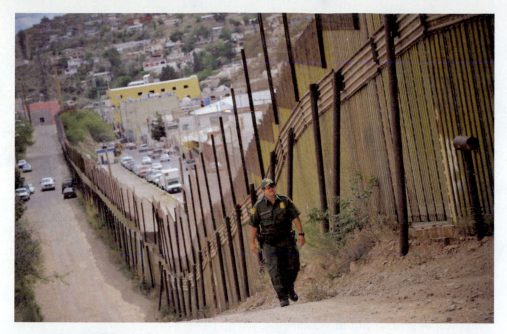

**interstate compacts**
Agreements among states to cooperate on solving mutual problems; requires approval by Congress.

3.1

3.2

**3.3**

3.4

3.5

**BORDER FENCE**

How to control illegal immigration across the U.S.–Mexican border, and what to do about those who make it across, have become contentious issues between several border states and the federal government. Why might this be an issue where some state majorities conflict with the wishes of the national majority?

Article IV also specifies that the citizens of each state are entitled to all the "privileges and immunities" of the citizens in the several states. That means that whatever citizenship rights a person has in one state apply in the other states as well. For example, because of this provision, out-of-state residents have the same access to state courts as in-state residents, as well as an equal right to own property and to be protected by the police. However, the Supreme Court has never clearly defined the meaning of "privileges and immunities," nor have they been entirely consistent in applying them in practice. The Court has allowed states to charge students different tuition rates in their public universities, for example, depending on their in-state or out-of-state status (see the "Using the Framework" feature later in this chapter).

Agreements among a group of states to solve mutual problems, called **interstate compacts**, require the consent of Congress. The framers inserted this provision (Article I, Section 10) into the Constitution as a way to prevent the emergence of coalitions of states that might threaten federal authority or the union itself. Interstate compacts in force today cover a wide range of cooperative state activities. For example, New York and New Jersey created and Congress approved a compact to create the Port Authority of New York & New Jersey. Other compacts among states include agreements to cooperate on matters such as pollution control, crime prevention, transportation, and disaster planning.

# The Evolution of American Federalism

**3.3** Trace the evolution of American federalism

I took a long time after the adoption of the Constitution for the present federal system to emerge. There were (and continue to be) ebbs and flows in the nature of the relationship between the states and national government and in the relative power of the states and the federal government

**nationalist position**
The view of American federalism that holds that the Constitution created a system in which the national government is supreme, relative to the states, and that it granted that government a broad range of powers and responsibilities.

**necessary and proper clause**
Article I, Section 8, of the Constitution, also known as the *elastic clause*; gives Congress the authority to make whatever laws are necessary and proper to carry out its enumerated powers and the responsibilities mentioned in the Constitution's preamble.

as they interacted with one another.[10] Eventually, however, the national government gained ground.[11] There are many reasons for this:

- Economic crises and problems generated pressures on the government in Washington to do something to help fix the national economy. The Great Depression in the 1930s is the primary example, but even today, we expect the president, Congress, and the Federal Reserve to competently manage national economic affairs, something the states cannot do for themselves. Most Americans wanted the government in Washington to do something to get us out of the Great Recession and jobless recovery of 2008–2012, though many did not like what was done in the end (bailing out banks without limiting executive pay and bonuses, for example, or the big deficits that resulted from new government programs and declining tax revenues).

- War and the preparation for war are also important spurs to national-level actions, rather than state-level ones, because only the government in Washington can raise an army and a navy, generate sufficient revenues to pay for military campaigns, and coordinate the productive resources of the nation to make sustained war possible. It is no accident, then, that each of our major wars has served to enhance the power of government in Washington.

- Finally, a number of problems emerged over the course of our history that most political leaders and the public believed could be solved most effectively by the national government rather than by 50 separate state governments: air and water pollution; unsafe food, drugs, and consumer products; the denial of civil rights for racial minorities; anticompetitive practices by some large corporations; poverty; and more.

## The Perpetual Debate About the Nature of American Federalism

From the very beginnings of our nation, two political philosophies have contended with one another over the nature of American federalism and the role to be played by the central government. These are generally referred to as the **nationalist position** and the states' rights position.

**THE NATIONALIST POSITION**  Nationalists believe that the Constitution was formed by a compact among the people to create a single national community, pointing to the powerful phrase that opens the preamble: "We the People of the United States" (not "We the States"). Nationalists also point to the clear expression in the preamble of the purposes for which "we the people" formed a new government, namely to "create a more perfect union . . . and to promote the General Welfare." Also important in the nationalist brief are provisions in the Constitution that point toward a strong central government with expansive responsibilities, including the "commerce clause," the "supremacy clause," and the "elastic" or **"necessary and proper" clause**. Not surprisingly, proponents of the nationalist position such as Alexander Hamilton, Chief Justice John Marshall, Abraham Lincoln, Woodrow Wilson, and the two Roosevelts (Theodore and Franklin) advocated an active national government with the capacity and the will to tackle whatever problems might emerge to threaten the peace and prosperity of the United States or the general welfare of its people. Liberal Democrats, including Barack Obama, are the main proponents of this position today, believing that civil rights and environmental protection, for example, are safer in the hands of the federal government than the state governments.

**THE STATES' RIGHTS POSITION**  Proponents of the states' rights position argue that the Constitution was created as a compact among the states and that the framers meant for the states to be coequal with the national government. They base their argument on a number of things. They note, for instance, that the Constitution was written by representatives of the states; that it was ratified by the states and not by a vote of the public; and that the process for amending the Constitution requires the affirmative votes of three-fourths of the states, not three-fourths of the people. They also point to the Tenth Amendment's "reservation" clause, which says, as we pointed out earlier, that powers not given to the national government nor denied to the states reside in the states and the people.

Not surprisingly, proponents of the **states' rights position** have argued that the Constitution created a form of government in which the national government is strictly limited in size and responsibility and in which states retain broad autonomy in the conduct of their own affairs. Popular among states' rights proponents is the concept of **dual federalism**, which suggests that, much like in a layer cake, there are distinct, nonoverlapping areas of responsibility for the national government and the state governments and that each level of government is sovereign in its own sphere. Thomas Jefferson, John C. Calhoun, the New England and Southern secessionists, the Southern resistors to the civil rights revolution, and many contemporary conservative Republican Tea Party activists are associated with this view of federalism.

We shall see in the pages ahead that the nationalist view has prevailed over the long haul of American history. (See Figure 3.3 for an overview of this history.) However, the states' rights view has always been and remains today a vital position from which to oppose too much power and responsibility in the government in Washington. After the Affordable Care Act was passed in 2010, for example, several states passed laws proclaiming that the mandatory health insurance provisions of the national law did not hold within their boundaries, and 26 state attorneys general took the issue to the federal courts. As we saw in the chapter-opening story, the Supreme Court ruled against the states regarding the mandate.

## ☐ Federalism Before the Civil War

In the late 1790s, during the administration of John Adams, Thomas Jefferson's Democratic Republicans deeply resented the Alien and Sedition Acts, which the Federalists used to punish political dissent by followers of Jefferson. In response, Jefferson and Madison secretly authored the Virginia and Kentucky Resolutions, which declared that the states did not have to obey unconstitutional national laws and left it to the states to decide what was unconstitutional. In this case, the Democratic Republicans, representing the more agricultural South, were advocating states' rights and the principle of dual federalism against a national government run by the more merchant-oriented Federalists of the Northeast. About a decade later, however, the merchants of New England used the Southerners' own arguments to oppose President Madison's War of 1812 against Britain, which they felt interfered with their trade. Neither of these efforts at **nullification** prevailed.

One crucial question about federalism in the early years of the United States concerned who, if anyone, would enforce the supremacy clause. Who would make sure that the U.S. laws and Constitution were actually the "supreme law of the land," controlling state laws? The answer turned out to be the U.S. Supreme Court, but this answer emerged only gradually and haltingly as the Court established its power within the federal system. Only after the strong-willed and subtle John Marshall became chief justice and, in 1803, established the Supreme Court's authority to declare national laws unconstitutional (called judicial review; discussed in detail in Chapter 14) did the Supreme Court turn to the question of national power relative to the states. In *Fletcher v. Peck* (1810), it established the power of judicial review over the states, holding a state law unconstitutional under the U.S. Constitution.[12] Chief Justice Marshall cleverly avoided explicit discussion of the Court's power of judicial review over state laws. He simply took it for granted and used it.

The Supreme Court also provided crucial legal justification for the expansion of federal government power in the historic case of *McCulloch v. Maryland* (1819), which affirmed the supremacy clause and declared that Congress had broad powers under the "necessary and proper" clause. The case involved action by the state of Maryland to impose a tax on the Bank of the United States. The state of Maryland argued

**states' rights position**
The view of American federalism that holds that the Constitution created a system of dual sovereignty in which the national government and the state governments are sovereign in their own spheres.

**dual federalism**
An interpretation of federalism in which the states and the national government have separate jurisdictions and responsibilities.

**nullification**
An attempt by states to declare national laws or actions null and void.

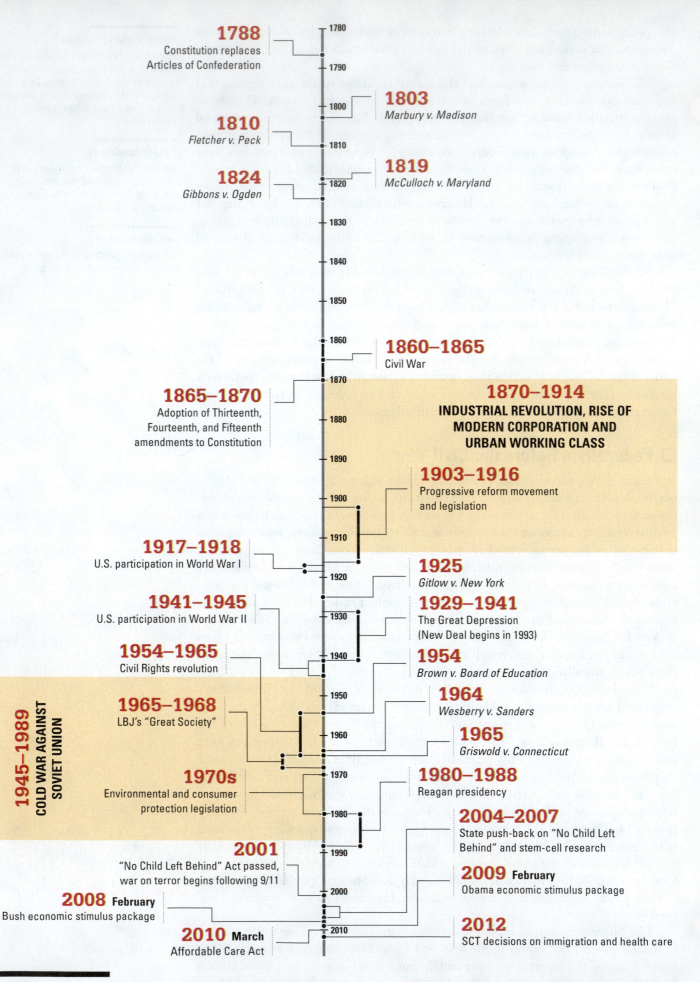

**1788**
Constitution replaces
Articles of Confederation

1780

1790

**1803**
*Marbury v. Madison*

1800

**1810**
*Fletcher v. Peck*

1810

**1819**
*McCulloch v. Maryland*

1820

**1824**
*Gibbons v. Ogden*

1830

1840

1850

**1860–1865**
Civil War

1860

**1865–1870**
Adoption of Thirteenth,
Fourteenth, and Fifteenth
amendments to Constitution

1870

**1870–1914**
**INDUSTRIAL REVOLUTION, RISE OF
MODERN CORPORATION AND
URBAN WORKING CLASS**

1880

1890

**1903–1916**
Progressive reform movement
and legislation

1900

1910

**1917–1918**
U.S. participation in World War I

1920

**1925**
*Gitlow v. New York*

**1941–1945**
U.S. participation in World War II

1930

**1929–1941**
The Great Depression
(New Deal begins in 1993)

**1954–1965**
Civil Rights revolution

1940

**1954**
*Brown v. Board of Education*

1950

**1964**
*Wesberry v. Sanders*

**1965–1968**
LBJ's "Great Society"

1960

**1945–1989
COLD WAR AGAINST
SOVIET UNION**

**1965**
*Griswold v. Connecticut*

**1970s**
Environmental and consumer
protection legislation

1970

**1980–1988**
Reagan presidency

1980

**2004–2007**
State push-back on "No Child Left
Behind" and stem-cell research

**2001**
"No Child Left Behind" Act passed,
war on terror begins following 9/11

1990

**2009** February
Obama economic stimulus package

**2008** February
Bush economic stimulus package

2000

**2010** March
Affordable Care Act

2010

**2012**
SCT decisions on immigration and health care

**FIGURE 3.3** TIMELINE: LANDMARKS IN THE HISTORY OF U.S. FEDERALISM

that the creation of the bank had been unconstitutional, exceeding the powers of Congress, and that, in any case, states could tax whatever they wanted within their own borders.

But Chief Justice Marshall upheld the constitutionality of the bank's creation and its immunity from taxation and, in the process, made a major statement justifying extensive national authority.[13] In his opinion for the Court, Marshall declared that the Constitution emanated from the sovereign people who had made their national government supreme to all rivals within the sphere of its powers, and those powers must be construed generously if they were to be sufficient for the "various crises" of the age to come. Congress, declared Marshall, had the power to incorporate the bank under the clause of Article I, Section 8, authorizing Congress to make all laws "necessary and proper" for carrying into execution its named powers. Moreover, Maryland's tax was invalid because "the power to tax involves the power to destroy," which would defeat the national government's supremacy. Justice Marshall's broad reading of the *necessary and proper* clause laid the foundation for an expansion of what the national government could do in the years ahead. He made it clear that states would not be allowed to interfere.

In several later cases, the Supreme Court also ruled that provisions of the U.S. Constitution excluded the states from acting in certain areas where they might interfere with federal statutes or authority. According to this doctrine known as **preemption**, which remains in place today,[14] states cannot act in certain matters when the national government has authority. The Supreme Court's rejection in 2012 of much of Arizona's immigration law was based on this doctrine.

3.1

3.2

3.3

3.4

3.5

**preemption**
Exclusion of the states from actions that might interfere with federal authority or statutes.

## ☐ The Civil War and the Expansion of National Power

The Civil War profoundly affected the relationship between the states and the national government. First, the unconditional Southern surrender decisively established that

**OUR BLOODY CIVIL WAR**
One important principle of American federalism was settled by the Civil War: the nation is indissoluble; no state or group of states can decide on its own to withdraw from it. Establishing that principle required a bloody contest of arms. Here, Union soldiers rest in camp after an engagement with Confederate troops. Why was this outcome so crucial to the survival of the country?

**Civil War Amendments**
The Thirteenth, Fourteenth, and Fifteenth Amendments to the Constitution, adopted immediately after the Civil War, each of which represented the imposition of a national claim over that of the states.

**due process clause**
The section of the Fourteenth Amendment that prohibits states from depriving anyone of life, liberty, or property "without due process of law," a guarantee against arbitrary government action.

**equal protection clause**
The section of the Fourteenth Amendment that provides for equal treatment by government of people residing within the United States and each of its states.

the Union was indissoluble; states could not withdraw or secede. Hardly any American now questions the permanence of the Union.

Second, passage of what has become known as the **Civil War Amendments** resulted in constitutional changes that subordinated the states to certain new national standards, enforced by the central government. For example, the Thirteenth Amendment abolished slavery, and the Fifteenth gave former male slaves and their descendants a constitutional right to vote. (This right was enforced by the national government for a short time after the Civil War; it was then widely ignored until passage of the 1965 Voting Rights Act.)

Most importantly, the Fourteenth Amendment (1868) included broad language limiting state power in a number of areas: it declared that no state shall "deprive any person of life, liberty, or property, without due process of law, nor deny to any person within its jurisdiction the equal protection of the laws." The **due process clause** eventually became the vehicle by which the Supreme Court ruled that many civil liberties in the Bill of Rights, which originally protected people only against the national government, also provided protections against the states (see Chapter 15). And the **equal protection clause** eventually became the foundation for protecting the rights of African Americans, women, and other categories of people against discrimination by state or local governments (see Chapter 16).

## ☐ Expanded National Activity Since the Civil War

Since the Civil War, and especially during the twentieth century, the activities of the national government expanded greatly, so that they now touch on almost every aspect of daily life and are thoroughly entangled with state government activities.

**THE LATE NINETEENTH CENTURY TO WORLD WAR I**  During the late nineteenth century, the national government was increasingly active in administering western lands, subsidizing economic development (granting railroads enormous tracts of land along their transcontinental lines, for example), helping farmers, and beginning to regulate business, particularly through the Interstate Commerce Act of 1887 and the Sherman Antitrust Act of 1890. Woodrow Wilson's New Freedom domestic legislation—including the Federal Reserve Act of 1913 and the Federal Trade Commission Act of 1914—spurred even greater national government involvement in social and economic issues, as did the great economic and military effort of World War I. During that war, for example, the War Industries Board engaged in a form of economic planning whose orders and regulations covered a substantial number of the nation's manufacturing firms.

**THE NEW DEAL AND WORLD WAR II**  Still more important, however, was Franklin Roosevelt's New Deal of the 1930s. In response to the Great Depression, the New Deal created many new national regulatory agencies to supervise various aspects of business, including communications (the Federal Communications Commission, or FCC), airlines (the Civil Aeronautics Board, or CAB), financial markets (the Securities and Exchange Commission, or SEC), utilities (the Federal Power Commission, or FPC), and labor–management relations (the National Labor Relations Board, or NLRB). The New Deal also brought national government spending to such areas as welfare and relief, which had previously been reserved almost entirely to the states, and established the Social Security old-age pension system.

World War II involved a total economic and military mobilization to fight Germany and Japan. Not surprisingly, directing that mobilization, as well as collecting taxes to support it, planning for production of war materials, and bringing on board the employees to accomplish all of this, was centered in Washington, D.C., not in the states.

**THE POST-WAR PERIOD TO THE 1990s** Ever since World War II, the federal government has spent nearly twice as much per year as all of the states and localities put together. Much of the money has gone in direct payments to individuals (including, most especially, Social Security benefits) and for national defense, particularly during the height of the Cold War with the Soviet Union, and during the Vietnam War.

Two other trends in the last third of the twentieth century enhanced the role of the national government relative to the states. The first was the civil rights revolution (discussed in Chapters 8 and 16), and the second was the regulatory revolution, especially regulation related to environmental and consumer protection (discussed in Chapter 17). With respect to these, national standards, often fashioned by bureaucrats under broad legislative mandates and watched over by federal courts, were imposed on both states and localities. The civil rights revolution also had a great deal to do with the creation of Lyndon Johnson's Great Society program designed both to alleviate poverty and politically empower the poor and racial minorities. The Great Society not only increased the level of domestic spending but also increased the federal role in the political lives of states and localities.

**THE SUPREME COURT'S LONG-TERM SUPPORT FOR THE NATIONALIST POSITION** For several decades, beginning in the late nineteenth century, the U.S. Supreme Court resisted the growth in the federal government's power to regulate business. In 1895, for example, it said that the Sherman Antitrust Act could not forbid monopolies in manufacturing, since manufacturing affected interstate commerce only "indirectly." In 1918, the Court struck down as unconstitutional a national law regulating child labor. During the 1930s, the Supreme Court declared unconstitutional such important New Deal measures as the National Recovery Act and the Agricultural Adjustment Act.[15]

After 1937, perhaps chastened by President Roosevelt's attempt to enlarge the Supreme Court and appoint more friendly justices, the Court became a centralizing force, immediately upholding essential elements of the New Deal, including the Social Security Act and the National Labor Relations Act. In 1942 in *Wickard v. Filburn*, the Court said that Congress has very broad powers under the commerce clause to regulate economic activities even if such activities are only indirectly related to interstate commerce. Since that time, and until the Rehnquist Court began to rethink federalism questions in the 1990s, the Court upheld virtually every piece of national legislation that came before it, even when this legislation preempted or limited powers of the states.

An important example is the Civil Rights Act of 1964, which rests on a very broad *Wickard*-based reading of the commerce clause. In the 1964 act, the national government asserted a power to forbid discrimination at lunch counters and other public accommodations on the grounds that they are engaged in interstate commerce; restaurants serve food imported from out of state, for instance, while hotels buy bedding, towels, flooring, and bathroom fixtures from companies in a variety of states. State economies are so closely tied to each other that by this standard, practically every economic transaction everywhere affects interstate commerce and is therefore subject to national legislative power. Another example of the powerful impetus towards national supremacy by way of the commerce clause (and federal grants) is the interstate highway system, which we discuss in the "Can Government Do Anything Well?" feature.

**DEVOLUTION** During the 1980s and 1990s, **devolution**—the idea that some of the powers and responsibilities of the national government ought to be distributed back to the states—became popular. President Ronald Reagan made this one of the hallmarks of his administration, as did George H.W. Bush, who followed him in office. President Bill Clinton, a former governor of the state of Arkansas, was also an enthusiastic devotee of devolution, freely granting waivers from federal regulations to the states for

**devolution**
The delegation of power over and responsibilities for federal programs to state and/or local governments.

# Can Government Do Anything Well?

## The Interstate Highway System

The federal interstate highway system is so much a part of our lives and has been for so many years that it is hard to imagine a time in America when long-distance car and truck travel was by two-lane roads, rife with dangerous crossroads, innumerable access points to main highways from businesses, schools, and homes, and numerous traffic lights and stop signs in the more popu-lated areas. Car travel and commercial truck transportation was slow and fairly dangerous compared to what was to come. Legislation for a new system of federal multilane, limited-access highways was proposed by Republican president Dwight Eisenhower and passed by Congress in 1956. The planned construction was completed in the early 1980s, but more highway miles have been added each year since then. Today its total length is almost 48,000 miles and it carries about one-fourth of all traffic in the United States though it comprises less than one percent of our highways. The sys-tem is funded by a tax of 18.4 cents per gallon on gasoline—unchanged since 1993—and most of its outlays today are for maintenance and repair.

*Support for the claim that government should be responsible for providing and maintaining national infrastructure, such as interstate highways:* Conservative commentator George Will likes the interstates, calling them "the most successful public works programs in the history of the world." A little over the top, perhaps, but there is no denying the fact that the system helped push economic growth in the United States and bound us together as a nation.

**The most important argument in favor of the federal government's role is that its actions have provided essential infrastructure that no other entity could plan, fund, and complete.**

■ Most products that are used in the United States today get to their destinations by truck. Products come from factories and busi-nesses here in the United States and from producers abroad, trucked to customers from container ports on the east, south, or west coasts, or across the Canadian and Mexican borders. The backbone of this truck-based distribution system is the interstate highway system. Without it, our economy would be less robust and efficient, and our everyday travel on roads shared with trucks would be less safe.

■ Left to itself, the private market has not and cannot provide this public good. We have seen no cases where private firms have built extensive and safe highways on a broad geographic scale that are not associated with the particular activity of their own businesses, say roads to bring out cut timber from forest plots or ores from mining sites. The reason is fairly obvious: though the economy and society as a whole benefit from the existence of such a road system, no single firm or set of firms has an economic interest in making an investment on this scale that might take decades to complete and to see economic payoffs. Nor could private firms secure the financing for such a project.

*Rejection of the claim that government should be responsible for providing and maintaining national infrastructure, such as interstate highways:*

■ There is, of course, the familiar argument that government cannot do anything well and that matters of economic and social development should best be left to the private sector. As Charles Murray has so directly put it in his book *What It Means to Be a Libertarian* (p. 147): "The reality of daily life is that, by and large, the things the government does tend to be ugly, rude, slovenly—and not to work."

■ Cato and the American Enterprise Institute, market-oriented think tanks, on the other hand, accept that the national government did the country a great service in creating the interstate highway system but that it is now so big and so complex that the system cannot be run effectively and efficiently, nor properly maintained and improved, by the federal government. Thinkers there favor either total private ownership or public–private partnerships, with revenues gener-ated by tolls.

■ Critics from all political persuasions lament the fact that the system is showing signs of wear and tear; construction and maintenance are not keeping up with deteriorating roads and bridges. Conservatives believe it is be-cause highway money has been diverted to non-highway purposes such as bike paths, mass transit, and historic preservation. Liber-als believe the problem is not enough money in the highway trust fund and that the federal tax on gasoline is not high enough, falling orders of magnitude short of those in other rich democracies.

(Continued)

## WHAT DO YOU THINK?

What do you think about the past, present, and future role of the government in the interstate highway system? Which of the following positions is closest to your own?

- The government should never undertake such large infrastructure projects.
- Building the interstate highway system represents one of the most successful government programs in the history of the United States and demonstrates the capacity of the public sector to engage in other large-scale projects in the future.
- The interstate highway system represents a government project that was successful in the past, but current infrastructure challenges cannot be handled by the government alone and will need private attention moving forward.

How would you defend this position to a fellow student? What would be your main line of argument? What evidence do you believe best supports your position? For help in developing your argument, please refer to the sources listed in the "Can Government Do Anything Well" feature in Chapter 2 on p. 44.

Additional sources for this feature: "Interstate Facts," The Federal Highway Administration (www.fhwa.dot.gov).

experimenting with new forms of welfare, boasting of cuts in federal government employment, and touting the benefits of state government. And the Republican majority in the 104th Congress, working with President Clinton (but few from his party), passed legislation restricting "unfunded mandates" (about which we will have more to say later) and transferring welfare responsibility to the states. The public seemed to be on board at the time. Polls showed, for example, that a substantial majority of Americans believed that state governments were more effective and more trustworthy than the government in Washington and more likely to be responsive to the people. And Americans said that they wanted state governments to do more and the federal government to do less.[16]

**GUNS FOR SALE**

A gun dealer in Virginia mocks the attempt of (now former) New York City mayor Michael Bloomberg to ban the importation of guns into his jurisdiction by offering customers "Bloomberg give-away-gun tickets," in honor of a federal lawsuit that Bloomberg endorsed to keep firearms out. Such efforts were undermined in 2008 and 2010 when the Supreme Court ruled that gun ownership is an individual constitutional right and that government, consequently, can do little to restrict their sale. In the wake of the tragic Sandy Hook (CT) mass shooting, Bloomberg and like-minded advocates for stricter controls on guns continue to push for laws that would more tightly regulate their sale.

For a time during the height of devolution's popularity, the Rehnquist Court supported increasing the power of the states and decreasing that of the national government. It overruled a number of federal actions and laws on the grounds that Congress had exceeded its constitutional powers, reversing more than half a century of decisions favoring an increased federal government role. In 1995, for example, the Court overturned federal legislation banning guns from the area around schools and legislation requiring background checks for gun buyers, arguing that both represented too broad a use of the commerce power in the Constitution. The Court used similar language in 2000 when it invalidated part of the Violence Against Women Act and in 2001 when it did the same to the Americans with Disabilities Act.

In the last years of Rehnquist's leadership, however, the Court retreated a bit from this states' rights position, supporting federal law over that of the states on issues ranging from the use of medical marijuana to the juvenile death penalty, affirmative action, and gay rights. In each of these areas, several states wanted to go in more liberal directions than the rest of the country—making medical marijuana available, for example, or using affirmative action to create diversity in government hiring and contracting—but the Court affirmed the more restrictive federal statutes.

**NATIONAL POWER REASSERTED** Talk of devolution ended with the Democratic Clinton presidency. Republican George W. Bush, who followed Clinton in the Oval Office, signaled during the 2000 presidential campaign that he was willing to use the federal government to serve conservative ends. He termed his position "compassionate conservatism," suggesting that he would use the power of his office to try to, among other things, end abortion and protect the family, enhance educational performance, and do more to move people from welfare to jobs. While preserving his traditional Republican conservative credentials on a number of fronts—cutting taxes, for example, and pushing for looser environmental regulations on businesses—on gaining the presidency Bush gave a big boost to the power, cost, and scope of the federal government.[17] Most important was his sponsorship of the No Child Left Behind educational reform, which imposed testing mandates on the states, and a prescription drug benefit under Medicare, which substantially increased the cost of the program. Mandatory Medicaid spending by the states also expanded rapidly during the Bush presidency.

The terrorist attacks of September 11, 2001, the subsequent global "war on terrorism" (the president's phrase), and the wars in Iraq and Afghanistan further focused the nation's attention on national leaders in Washington, D.C. As in all wartime situations during our country's history, war and the mobilization for war require centralized coordination and planning. This tendency toward nationalism during war has been further exaggerated by the perceived need for enhancing homeland security, with the national government in Washington playing a larger role in areas such as law enforcement, intelligence gathering, bank oversight (to track terrorist money), public health (to protect against possible bioterrorism), and more. Many of these activities were continued by President Barack Obama when he assumed office in 2008.

Perhaps inevitably, the flow of power to Washington during the Bush years triggered a reaction among the public and leaders in the states, disturbed by the increasing budget demands, regulatory burdens, and loss of state control tied to programs: the No Child Left Behind Act; the Real ID Act, aimed at standardizing driver's license issuance among the states; and changes in states' ability to write work rules in TANF (welfare program for the poor, discussed in Chapter 18). Combined with a sense among many at the state level that important national problems were being ignored and mishandled and the collapse in public support for President Bush and his policies after 2004, the ground was set for a rather extraordinary revitalization of state innovations.[18] Between 2004 and 2008, several states passed laws allowing, and sometimes subsidizing, stem-cell research. Others passed minimum wage legislation, while others legislated gas mileage requirements for cars and trucks. Many legislated incentives for companies and consumers to use energy more efficiently and find alternative fuel sources. California even passed legislation to reduce overall greenhouse gas emissions.

# Mapping American Politics

## Federal Dollars: Which States Win and Which Ones Lose?

Our system of federalism involves a complex set of relationships between the federal government and the states. These relationships are spelled out in the text of the Constitution; decisions of the Supreme Court, interpreting the meaning of constitutional provisions concerning federalism; and bills passed by Congress and signed by the president, creating federal programs and imposing taxes and regulations. One aspect of federalism that often draws attention is the flow of money between the federal government and the states. The flow goes in two directions. Money flows from people and firms in the states to the federal government in the form of taxes (income, corporate, excise, and payroll). Money flows from the federal government to people and firms in the states in the form of grants-in-aid, block grants, and expenditures for specific programs (such as payments to defense contractors) and projects (such as payments for highways and bridges). Given the nature of the political process and differences in the needs and resources of people and firms in the states, some states will inevitably come out ahead in this process, getting more money from Washington than they pay in taxes, and some will come out behind, paying more than they receive.

Note how New York, Illinois, Texas, and California fare; each is dramatically diminished. They receive back from the federal government only a portion of what they pay in taxes.

**Legend**
- Losers: Giving More Money Than Getting
- About Equal
- Winners: Receiving More Money Than Giving

State Sizes Adjusted to Reflect Ratio of Federal Taxes Paid and Federal Monies Received per Capita

### The Story in the Cartogram

The cartogram shows winners and losers in the federalism money story. The size of each state has been adjusted using a mathematical formula derived by Gastner and Newman that takes into account a simple ratio: federal funds received by each state on a per capita basis divided by taxes paid by each state on a per capita basis. If a state received and paid the same amount, the ratio would be 1, meaning that its size in the cartogram would not change from its normal size. States that receive more from Washington than they pay in taxes have ratios higher than 1 and are expanded proportionally in size in the cartogram. States that receive less than they pay have ratios less than 1 and are reduced.

It is readily apparent that a number of states are winners, namely, those in the southeast and the middle south, with Connecticut thrown in (their ratios are above 1, thus expanding its size in the cartogram), while a handful of large states are the biggest losers.

### What Do You Think?

Why do monies flow between Washington and the states as they currently do? What would be the consequences if all states had similar money flow profiles? Do monies flow to where they are needed? Why do you think some states stand out from others on this issue? Where does your own state fit in the overall picture?

Standard U.S. Map

**SOURCES:** IRS Data Book for FY 2012, Table 5; *Statistical Abstract of the United States, 2010;* usaspending.gov, State Summary Table. Cartogram produced in ArcMap using Tom Gross's Cartogram Geoprocessing Tool (v2). ArcMap uses the Newman-Gastner method [see details in Michael T. Gastner and Mark E. J. Newman, "Diffusion-Based Method for Producing Density-Equalizing Maps," *Proceedings of the National Academy of Sciences* 101 (2004): 7499–7504.]

The economic crisis that began in 2008, sometimes called the Great Recession (much like the Great Depression), generated an expanded role for the national government relative to the states in economic affairs. In the last months of the Bush presidency, Congress passed a $700 billion rescue package for financial institutions that gave the Treasury secretary broad powers to rescue and reorganize banks and investment firms even as the Federal Reserve (the Fed), under the leadership of Ben Bernanke, undertook its own rescue and reorganization efforts. These mandates greatly expanded the role of the federal government in managing the economy. When he became president, Barack Obama not only continued to support the efforts of the Treasury and the Fed to bolster the national economy, but insisted on the sale of Chrysler and the managed bankruptcy of General Motors as conditions of a rescue package. Within 30 days of his inauguration as president, Congress passed his $787 billion stimulus bill, which did a great deal to shore up state budgets, almost all of which were in crisis. The stimulus package was a combination of tax cuts and new expenditures in programs that, among other things, extended unemployment benefits, funded new research and development in alternative energy sources, put monies into school construction and keeping teachers on the job, massively increased spending on infrastructure projects (i.e., roads, bridges, canals, and the like), and helped the states pay for some of their rising Medicaid outlays.

Perhaps most consequentially, in a long-term sense, President Obama and the Democratic Congress passed a health care bill that will transform America's health care system and a financial regulation bill they hope will prevent the type of financial collapse that happened in 2008 and brought on the Great Recession.[19] President Obama also proposed a major effort to make the nation less dependent on fossil fuels, hoping that the tragic Gulf oil spill and the environmental disaster that followed would convince Americans that the time was ripe for such a change. Republicans and coal-state Democrats stopped the climate bill in the Senate, however, in July 2010.

**RECENT PUSHBACK** As suggested earlier in this chapter, there has been a great deal of pushback at this increase in national government power relative to the states, suggesting that the states remain significant actors in the American system. As the opening story of the chapter details, many states (primarily Republican) have passed laws opposing the Affordable Care Act and have challenged its constitutionality in Court. Republican governors Rick Scott of Florida, John Kasich of Ohio, and Scott Walker of Wisconsin have also all turned down federal funding for high-speed rail projects that would have obligated their states to make future outlays to maintain new rail systems.[20] The anti-tax, anti–big government Tea Party movement has become a major force in deciding who GOP nominees are in local, state, and national contests, and has influenced Republicans in Congress to act as a united front against virtually every important proposal offered by President Obama. The Tea Party also helped change the agenda in Washington from stimulus and job creation efforts after Obama was elected in 2008, to doing something about the deficit problem following the dramatic victory of the Republicans in the 2010 national elections. The Supreme Court joined in with decisions in 2011 and 2012 that affirmed state sovereignty in several areas, basing its decisions on the Tenth Amendment, thereby echoing many of the federalism rulings of the Rehnquist Court.[21] In 2012, the Supreme Court, while approving most of the Affordable Care Act, signalled that it wanted to rein-in federal government powers on a broader front, saying that Congress long had been giving too broad a reading of its powers under the commerce and spending clauses.

**CHANGING AMERICAN FEDERALISM** Today's federalism is very different from what it was in the 1790s or early 1800s.[22] One major difference is that the national government is dominant in many policy areas; it calls many shots for the states. Another difference is that state and national government powers and activities have become deeply intertwined and entangled. The old, simple metaphor for federalism was a "layer cake": a system of dual federalism in which state and national powers were neatly divided into separate layers, with each level of government going its own way, unencumbered by the other. If we stay with bakery images, a much more accurate metaphor for today's federalism is a "marble cake," in which elements of national and state influence swirl around each other, without very clear boundaries.[23] The "marble cake" itself has taken on several forms. During the 1960s and 1970s, for example, the federal and state governments seemed to many to be working smoothly together to solve problems, leading scholars and politicians to use the term **cooperative federalism** to characterize the period. Today, no one talks any longer of cooperative federalism, although no single term has replaced it.

Whether cooperative or not, our federal system today is a marble cake in which the federal government and state governments are densely intertwined. Much of this intertwining is a product of the financial links among the national and state governments, which we address in the next section, as well as in the "Mapping American Politics" feature.

# Fiscal Federalism

O ne of the most important elements of modern American federalism is **fiscal federalism**—the transfer of money from the national government to state and local governments. These **grants-in-aid** have been used to increase national government influence over what the states and localities do. The grants have grown from small beginnings to form a substantial part of state government budgets. In the following sections, you will learn how and why this trend began, what kinds of grants have and are being made, and how they affect national–state relationships.

## ☐ Origin and Growth of Grants

National government grants to the states began at least as early as the 1787 Northwest Ordinance. The U.S. government granted land for government buildings, schools, and colleges in the Northwest Territory and imposed various regulations, such as forbidding slavery there. During the early nineteenth century, the federal government provided some land grants to the states for roads, canals, and railroads, as well as a little cash for militias; after 1862, it helped establish agricultural colleges. Some small cash-grant programs were begun around 1900 for agriculture, vocational education, and highways.[24]

However, it was during the 1950s, 1960s, and 1970s, under both Republican and Democratic administrations, that federal grants to the states really took off. Such programs as President Dwight Eisenhower's interstate highway system and President Lyndon Johnson's Great Society poured money into the states.[25] After a pause during the Reagan presidency, grants began to increase again in the 1990s (see Figure 3.4). Federal grants to the states increased because presidents and Congress sought to deal with many nationwide problems—especially transportation, education, HIV/AIDS, poverty, crime, and air and water pollution—by setting policy at the national level and providing money from national tax revenues, while having state and local officials carry out the policies. The big jump in grant totals in 2009 and 2010 were tied to various efforts by the federal government to stimulate the economy during the Great Recession, including assistance to states for Medicaid, unemployment insurance, education, and infrastructure.[26]

## ☐ Types of Grants

Over the years, many of the new programs were established through **categorical grants**, which give the states money but clearly specify the category of activity for which the money has to be spent and often define rather precisely how the program should work. For example, Lyndon Johnson's antipoverty initiatives—in the

**cooperative federalism**
Federalism in which the powers and responsibilities of the states and the national government are intertwined and in which they work together to solve common problems; said to have characterized the 1960s and 1970s.

**fiscal federalism**
That aspect of federalism having to do with federal grants to the states.

**grants-in-aid**
Funds from the national government to state and local governments to help pay for programs created by the national government.

**categorical grants**
Federal aid to states and localities clearly specifying what the money can be used for.

**block grants**
Federal grants to the states to be used for general activities.

**general revenue sharing**
Federal aid to the states without any conditions on how the money is to be spent.

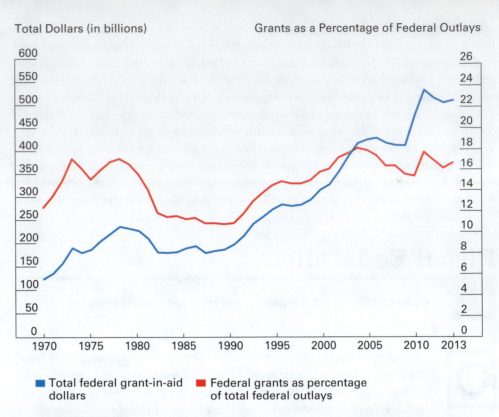

Total Dollars (in billions)                    Grants as a Percentage of Federal Outlays

■ Total federal grant-in-aid dollars    ■ Federal grants as percentage of total federal outlays

**FIGURE 3.4** THE GROWTH IN FEDERAL GRANTS-IN-AID TO STATES AND LOCALITIES (in billions of dollars)

Federal grants-in-aid to state and local governments have grown steadily since 1970, the only exception being during the Reagan presidency in the first half of the 1980s. A big jump occurred in 2010 and 2011 as federal assistance to the states increased to address problems caused by financial collapse and economic recession.

*Note:* All grant spending totals in constant 2005 dollars.
*Source:* Budget of the United States Government, Fiscal Year 2013: Historical Tables, Table 12.1.

areas of housing, job training, medical assistance, and more—funneled substantial federal money to states and localities, but attached strict rules on how the money could be used.

Responding to complaints from the states and seeking to reduce federal government power to better fit their ideas about the proper role of government, Republican presidents Nixon and Ford succeeded in convincing Congress to loosen centralized rules and oversight, first instituting **block grants** (which give money for more general purposes, such as secondary education, and with fewer rules than categorical grant programs), then, for a short time, **general revenue sharing**, which distributed money to the states with no federal controls at all. President Nixon spoke of a "New Federalism" and pushed to increase these kinds of grants with few strings attached. General revenue sharing ended in 1987 when even proponents of a smaller federal government realized that giving money to the states with "no strings attached" meant that elected officials in the federal government were losing influence over policies in which they wanted to have a say.[27]

Categorical and block grants often provide federal money under an automatic formula related to the statistical characteristics of each state or locality (thus the term "formula grant"), such as the number of needy residents, the total size of the population, or the average income level. Disputes frequently arise when these formulas benefit one state or region rather than another. Because statistical counts by the census affect how much money the states and localities get, census counts themselves have become the subject of political conflict.

## ☐ Debates About Federal Money and Control

Most contemporary conflicts about federalism concern not just money but also control.

**CONDITIONS ON AID** As we have seen, categorical grant-in-aid programs require that the states spend federal money only in certain restricted ways. Even block grants—such as grants that support social welfare for the poor—have conditions attached, thus the term **conditional grants**. In theory, these conditions are "voluntary" because the states can refuse to accept the aid. But in practice, there is no clear line between incentives and coercion. Because the states cannot generally afford to give up federal money, they normally must accept the conditions attached to it.

Some of the most important provisions of the 1964 Civil Rights Act, for example, are those that declare that no federal aid of any kind can be used in ways that discriminate against people on grounds of race, gender, religion, or national origin. Thus, the enormous program of national aid for elementary and secondary education, which began in 1965, became a powerful lever for forcing schools to desegregate. To take another example, the federal government in 1984 used federal highway money to encourage states to adopt a minimum drinking age of 21. As we saw in the chapter opening story on the ruling on the Affordable Care Act, the Court now seems inclined to entertain challenges to grant programs to the states that are unduly coercive.

**MANDATES** The national government often imposes a **mandate**, or demand, that the states carry out certain policies even when little or no national government aid is offered. (An "unfunded" mandate involves no aid at all or less aid than compliance will cost.) Mandates have been especially important in the areas of civil rights and the environment. Most civil rights policies flow from the equal protection clause of the Fourteenth Amendment to the U.S. Constitution or from national legislation that imposes uniform national standards. Environmental regulations also come from the national government, since problems of dirty air, polluted water, and acid rain spill across state boundaries. Recently, the Supreme Court even ruled, in *EPA v. EME Homer City Generation* (2013), that the EPA has the authority to set standards that account for how air pollution travels from one state to another.

National legislation and regulations have required state governments to provide costly special facilities for the disabled, to set up environmental protection agencies, and to limit the kinds and amounts of pollutants that can be discharged. The states often complain bitterly about federal mandates that require state spending without providing the money.

**conditional grants**
Federal grants with provisions requiring that state and local governments follow certain policies in order to obtain funds.

**mandate**
A formal order from the national government that the states carry out certain policies.

3.1

3.2

3.3

3.4

3.5

**SPEWING POLLUTION**
Industrial pollution, such as these untreated emissions from this coal-burning power plant in Tennessee, often affects people of more than one state and requires the participation of the national government to clean up the mess and prevent recurrences. What role should the federal government take in environmental issues within states whose effects spill over into other states?

# Using the FRAMEWORK

## I thought that attending a public university would save a lot of money, but it hasn't because I have to pay out-of-state tuition. Why do I have to pay so much money?

**Background:** All over the United States, students who choose to attend out-of-state public universities pay much higher tuition than state residents. For example, at the University of Colorado, Boulder, estimated annual tuition for in-state students is, at present, $10,971; out-of-state students pay on average $33,333. Some educational reformers have suggested that the system be reformed so that students might attend public universities wherever they choose without financial penalty. They have suggested that over the long haul and on average, such a reform would not have much impact on state budgets because students would randomly distribute themselves across state borders. Such proposals have never gotten very far. Taking a broad view of how structural, political linkage, and governmental factors affect this issue will help explain the situation.

**Government Action**

The Supreme Court rules that different tuition rates for in-state and out-of-state residents do not violate the "privileges and immunities" section of Article IV, Section 2, of the Constitution.

State legislatures decline to pass uniform tuition legislation.

**Government**

Elected leaders know that voters want access to low-cost higher education for state residents. → Elected leaders are not subject to political pressures to change tuition policy. → Elected leaders are concerned with short-term budget issues; high out-of-state tuition allows them to raise part of the higher education budget.

**Political Linkage**

Voters in each state insist on access for their children and the children of their neighbors to low-cost public higher education. → There is little political pressure on elected leaders within the states to lower or eliminate out-of-state tuition, whether from
– Public opinion and voters,
– Parties,
– The mass media,
– Interest groups,
– Social movements. → Out-of-state students rarely vote in the states where they go to school; politicians have no incentive to think seriously about their tuition concerns.

The states are mainly responsible for education in our federal system; standardizing national tuition rates would require agreements among all the states, or federal legislation preempting the states.

Cutting back on these "unfunded mandates" was one of the main promises in the Republicans' 1994 Contract with America.[28] The congressional Republicans delivered on their promise early in 1995 with a bill that had bipartisan support in Congress and that President Clinton signed into law. Because it did not apply to past mandates, however, and did not ban unfunded mandates but only regulated them (e.g., requiring cost–benefit analyses), unfunded mandates have continued to proliferate, as has the debate about their use. The main complaints coming from governors today concern the substantial costs imposed on the states by the No Child Left Behind testing program and by the rising costs to the states of required Medicaid support for certain categories of people. Pressures on state budgets became especially pronounced during the Great Recession when revenues from sales and other taxes plummeted because of the national economic downturn. Hard-fought budget agreements between Congress and President Obama in 2013 to address the problem of federal government deficits cut federal spending across a wide range of programs—including money to keep teachers and first-responders from being laid off and help with Medicaid—and plunged most states even further into the red. Many responded by making deep cuts in education, social programs for the poor, and programs for maintaining and improving infrastructure (roads, bridges, and dams, for example). Several governors, such as Governor Walker of Wisconsin, tried to tame public employee unions or rescind the collective bargaining rights of state workers.

**PREEMPTION**  The doctrine of preemption, based on the supremacy clause in the Constitution and supported by a series of Supreme Court decisions, says that federal treaties, statutes, and rules must prevail over state statutes and rules when the two are in conflict. For example, in *U.S. v. Arizona* (2012), the Supreme Court preempted the portions of Arizona's tough immigration law, including one that required immigrants to carry documentation of their legal residency, ruling that immigration enforcement is the responsibility of the federal government. However, even when national laws preempt state laws, the national government may still choose not to interfere. To some extent this has been the case in Colorado and Washington, which have legalized marijuana use despite federal laws prohibiting it. While the federal law remains supreme, the Obama administration has chosen not to block the Colorado and Washington laws so long as certain aspects of marijuana distribution are regulated (such as distribution to minors), arguing that it is not the best use of federal resources.[29]

# U.S. Federalism: Pro and Con

**3.5**    Evaluate the arguments for and against federalism

 ver the years, from the framing of the U.S. Constitution to the present day, people have offered a number of strong arguments for and against federalism, in contrast to a more unitary system. Let us consider some of these arguments.

**PRO: DIVERSITY OF NEEDS**  The oldest and most important argument in favor of decentralized government is that in a large and diverse country, needs and wants and conditions differ from one place to another. Why not let different states enact different policies to meet their own needs? California, New York, and New Jersey, for example, all densely populated, have tougher fuel mileage standards in place than those set by the federal government. (See the "Using the Framework" feature on tuition for out-of-state students.) The border state of Arizona, feeling overwhelmed by illegal immigrants, passed a law in 2010 allowing police to stop and interrogate people they think may be in the country illegally. A federal judge threw out most provisions of the law soon after, a decision that was upheld by the Ninth Circuit Court of Appeals. The Supreme Court ruled in 2012 that the state had gone too far in usurping the powers of the federal government on issues of immigration.

**CON: THE IMPORTANCE OF NATIONAL STANDARDS**  However, the needs or desires that different states pursue may not be worthy ones. Political scientist William Riker has pointed out that, in the past, one of the main effects of federalism was to let white majorities in the Southern states enslave and then discriminate against black people, without interference from the North.[30] Perhaps it is better, in some cases, to insist on national standards that apply everywhere.

**PRO: CLOSENESS TO THE PEOPLE**  It is sometimes claimed that state governments are closer to the ordinary citizens, who have a better chance to know their officials, to be aware of what they are doing, to contact them, and to hold them responsible for what they do.

**CON: LOW VISIBILITY AND LACK OF POPULAR CONTROL**  However, others respond that geographic closeness may not be the real issue. More Americans are better informed about the federal government than they are about state governments, and more people participate in national than in state elections. When more people know what the government is doing and more people vote, they are better able to insist that the government do what they want. For that reason, responsiveness to ordinary citizens may actually be greater in national government.

**PRO: INNOVATION AND EXPERIMENTATION**  When the states have independent power, they can try out new ideas. Individual states can be "laboratories." If the experiments work, other states or the nation as a whole can adopt their ideas, as has happened on such issues as allowing women and 18-year-olds to vote, fighting air pollution, reforming welfare, and dealing with water pollution. Massachusetts passed a law in 2006 mandating health insurance coverage for every person in the state. Also in 2006, California passed a law committing itself to reducing greenhouse gas emissions to 1990 levels by 2020.

Likewise, when the national government is controlled by one political party, federalism allows the states with majorities favoring a different party to compensate by enacting different policies. This aspect of diversity in policymaking is related to the Founders' contention that tyranny is less likely when government's power is dispersed. Multiple governments reduce the risks of bad policy or the blockage of the popular will; if things go wrong at one governmental level, they may go right at another.

**CON: SPILLOVER EFFECTS AND COMPETITION**  Diversity and experimentation in policies, however, may not always be good. Divergent regulations can cause bad effects that spill over from one state to another. When factories in the Midwest spew out oxides of nitrogen and sulfur that fall as acid rain in the Northeast, the northeastern states acting on their own can do nothing about it. Only nationwide rules can solve such problems. Similarly, it is very difficult for cities or local communities in the states to do much about poverty or other social problems. If a city raises taxes to pay for social programs, businesses and the wealthy may move out of town, and the poor may move in, impoverishing the city.[31]

**WHAT SORT OF FEDERALISM?**  As the pros and cons indicate, a lot is at stake in determining the nature of federalism. It is not likely, however, that Americans will ever have a chance to vote yes or no on the federal system as a whole or to choose a unitary government instead. What we can decide is exactly *what sort* of federalism we will have—how much power will go to the states and how much will remain with the federal government. Indeed, we may want a fluid system in which the balance of power varies from one kind of policy to another. Over the long term of American history, of course, the nationalist position on federalism has generally prevailed over the states' rights position, but the states remain important, and there are many reasons to expect that the American people will continue to want the states to play an important role in fashioning policies that affect them.

It is important to keep in mind that arguments about federalism do not concern just abstract theories; they affect who wins and who loses valuable benefits. People's opinions about federalism often depend on their interests, their ideologies, and the kinds of things they want government to do.

# Using the DEMOCRACY STANDARD

## American Federalism: How Democratic?

Federalism is one of the foundation stones of the Constitution of the United States. Along with the separation of powers and checks and balances, its purpose, from the framers' point of view, was to make it impossible for any person or group (and, most especially, the majority faction) to monopolize the power of government and use it for tyrannical purposes. By fragmenting government power among a national government and 50 state governments and by giving each of the states some say on what the national government does, federalism makes it difficult for any faction, minority or majority, to dominate government. On balance, federalism has served the intentions of the framers by toning down the influence of majoritarian democracy in determining what the national government does, even while maintaining the principle of popular consent.

Federalism successfully constrains democracy in at least five ways:

1. It adds complexity to policymaking and makes it difficult for citizens to know which elected leaders to hold responsible for government actions.
2. Many policy areas, including education and voting eligibility, are mainly the responsibility of the states, where policymakers are insulated from national majorities, although not from majorities in their own states.
3. Small-population states play a decisive role in the constitutional amending process, where each state counts equally, regardless of the size of its population.
4. Small and large states have equal representation in the Senate, meaning that senators representing a minority of the population can block actions favored by senators representing the majority.
5. State politics are much less visible to the public; citizens are much less informed about what goes on in state governments where many important policies are made, and thus, popular participation tends to be lower.

All of this makes state-level politics especially vulnerable to the influence of special interests and those with substantial political resources. Because the well-organized and the affluent have extra influence, political equality and popular sovereignty have pretty tough challenges in many of the states.

In the end, the story of federalism is not entirely about the persistence of the framer's initial eighteenth-century republican constitutional design. The democratic aspirations of the American people have also shaped federalism and turned it into something that might not be entirely familiar to the framers. We noted in this chapter how the nature of federalism has changed over the course of American history, with the national government assuming an ever-larger role relative to the states. Much of this, we have suggested, has been brought about by the wishes of the American people as expressed in elections, public opinion polls, and social movements. Repeatedly, Americans have said they want a national government capable of addressing a broad range of problems, including economic difficulties (such as depressions, recessions, and inflation); persistent poverty; environmental degradation; unsafe food, drugs, and other consumer products; racial and ethnic discrimination; and foreign threats to the United States. Over the years, public officials and candidates have responded to these popular aspirations, altering federalism in the process.

# Review the Chapter

## Federalism as a System of Government

**3.1** Define federalism and explain why we have it, p. 55

Federalism is a system under which political powers are divided and shared between the state and federal governments, and is a key structural aspect of American politics.

Federalism in the United States was the product of both important compromises made at the Constitutional Convention and eighteenth-century republican doctrines about the nature of good government.

## Federalism in the Constitution

**3.2** Establish the basis for federalism in the Constitution, p. 57

There is no section of the Constitution where federalism is described in its entirety. Rather, federalism is construction from scattered clauses throughout the document that describe what the federal government may do and not do, how relations among the states are structured, the role of the states in amending the Constitution and electing the president, and how the states are represented in the national government.

The U.S. Constitution specifies the powers of the national government and reserves all others (except a few that are specifically forbidden) to the states. Overlapping, or concurrent, powers fall within the powers of both the national government and the states.

## The Evolution of American Federalism

**3.3** Trace the evolution of American federalism, p. 61

The story of American federalism is the story of the increasing power of the federal government relative to the states.

The trend toward national power is lodged in the "supremacy" and "elastic" clauses in the Constitution and propelled by war and national security demands, economic troubles and crises, and a range of problems that no state could handle alone.

## Fiscal Federalism

**3.4** Analyze how federal grants structure national and state government relations, p. 73

Contemporary federalism involves complex "marble cake" relations among the national and state governments, in which federal grants-in-aid play an important part. Except for the Reagan years, grant totals have grown steadily; they took a big jump upward as the country battled the Great Recession and jobless recovery in the 2008–2012 period, then leveled out after the anti-tax, anti-government, deficit-reducing agenda came to dominate Washington politics.

The national government also influences or controls many state policies through mandates and through conditions placed on aid.

## U.S. Federalism: Pro and Con

**3.5** Evaluate the arguments for and against federalism, p. 77

Arguments in favor of federalism have to do with diversity of needs, closeness to the people, experimentation, and innovation.

Arguments against federalism involve national standards, popular control, and needs for uniformity.

# Learn the Terms

# Test Yourself

Answer key begins on page T-1.

## 3.1 Define federalism and explain why we have it

1. What is federalism?

   a. A system of government where the states are sovereign and have authority over the central government.
   b. A system of government where the central government has complete power and can tell lower levels of government what to do.
   c. A system of government where local representatives are elected directly by the voters. These representatives then select the members of the central government.
   d. A system of government where the representatives of the central government are elected directly by the voters. These representatives then select the members of the local government.
   e. A system of government where power is divided between the central government and smaller units, such as states.

2. Why did the authors of the U.S. Constitution create a federal system of government?

   a. Federalism is best suited for small, homogenous countries such as the United States was at its founding.
   b. The U.S. Constitution was modeled after European countries, most of which used a federal system.
   c. Federalism had worked well under the Articles of Confederation, and the framers wanted to build on this success.
   d. Federalism was a reasonable compromise between a confederation and a unitary system.
   e. The system would help ensure a concentration of powers between the federal government and the state governments.

## 3.2 Establish the basis for federalism in the Constitution

3. The reservation clause in Article IV states that the constitution, laws, and treaties of the United States shall be the "supreme law of the land."
   True/False

4. This amendment says that those powers not given to the federal government and not prohibited are reserved for the states and the people.

   a. Sixth Amendment
   b. Tenth Amendment
   c. Second Amendment
   d. Eighth Amendment
   e. Fourth Amendment

## 3.3 Trace the evolution of American federalism

5. Who enforced the supremacy clause?

   a. Thomas Jefferson
   b. John Adams
   c. The Supreme Court
   d. James Madison
   e. Congress

6. This eventually became the vehicle by which the Supreme Court ruled that many civil liberties in the Bill of Rights also provided protections against the states.

   a. Due process
   b. Equal protection
   c. Civil War Amendments
   d. Preemption
   e. Nullification

## 3.4 Analyze how federal grants structure national and state government relations

7. One of the most important elements of modern American federalism is fiscal federalism.
   True/False

8. These types of grants give money for more general purposes such as secondary education.

   a. General grants
   b. Sharing grants
   c. Categorical grants
   d. Block grants
   e. Growth grants

## 3.5 Evaluate the arguments for and against federalism

9. One of the main effects of federalism allowed slavery in the South.
   True/False

10. The purpose of federalism, from the framers' point of view, was to make it impossible for:

    a. One group or person to monopolize power and use it for tyrannical purposes
    b. The government to fall
    c. One party to be in complete control of the United States
    d. Democracy to turn into communism
    e. States to be in control of the government

# Explore Further

## INTERNET SOURCES

History of Federalism **plato.stanford.edu/entries/federalism/**
A comprehensive study of the history of federalism in the west.

Federalism: National vs. State Government **usgovinfo.about.com/od/rightsandfreedoms/a/federalism.htm**
A site explaining the powers of national and state governments with links to articles on the federalist papers.

Block Grants **www.urban.org/publications/310991.html**
A historical overview of block grants.

National Conference of State Legislatures **www.ncsl.org**
Information about state governments and federal relations, including the distribution of federal revenues and expenditures in the states. Links to the "Mandate Monitor" and the "Preemption Monitor."

State Constitutions **www.findlaw.com/**
A site where the constitutions of all the states may be found.

Stateline **www.stateline.org**
A comprehensive, nonpartisan look at politics and policies in the American states.

## SUGGESTIONS FOR FURTHER READING

Beer, Samuel H. *To Make a Nation: The Rediscovery of American Federalism.* Cambridge, MA: Belknap Press, 1998.
A historical argument that the Constitution was written with national supremacy over the states in mind.

Brinkley, Douglas G. *The Great Deluge: Hurricane Katrina, New Orleans, and the Mississippi Gulf Coast.* New York: Harper Collins, 2006.

Much more than a blow-by-blow telling of the Hurricane Katrina story, this text provides a detailed description of how the complex interactions of local, state, and federal politics and policies over the years contributed to the disaster.

Derthick, Martha. *Keeping the Compound Republic: Essays in American Federalism.* Washington, D.C.: Brookings, 2001.
An examination of the enduring features of federalism, as well as its most important changes, in light of the framers' original design, in Madison's words, of a compound republic.

Hero, Rodney E. *Faces of Inequality: Social Diversity in American Politics.* New York: Oxford University Press, 1998.
An impressive argument with strong empirical evidence that the racial and ethnic composition of states matters for patterns of state politics.

Nagel, Robert. *The Implosion of American Federalism.* New York: Oxford University Press, 2002.
Argues that American federalism has largely disappeared as power in the United States has flowed steadily to Washington, D.C.

Peterson, Paul E. *The Price of Federalism.* Washington, D.C.: Brookings Institution, 1995.
Describes modern federalism and argues that the national government is best at redistributive programs, while the states and localities are best at economic development.

Riker, William H. *The Development of American Federalism.* Boston: Kluwer Academic, 1987.
An influential discussion of what American federalism is and how it came about.

# 4

# The Structural Foundations of American Government and Politics

## THE WALMARTIZATION OF AEROSPACE?

**F**ifty-six thousand jobs is a lot of leverage, and Boeing executives were anxious to use it. Another lever? The manufacturing contract to build the new Boeing 777X, a stretched and more-fuel efficient version of the Boeing 777, the most popular and all-time best-selling twin-aisle big jet ever produced. No doubt attracted by a super-efficient aircraft capable of carrying four hundred passengers and, unlike the Airbus 380, able to use existing Jetways and gates at major airports because of its revolutionary folding wings, airline carriers placed more than three hundred orders for the 777X at the 2013 Dubai air show before Boeing had built a single plane. With this fast start, the 777X looks like a long-term winner for Boeing.

But where will Boeing choose to make the new plane? Where will the jobs land, so to speak? According to most observers, the logical place is Boeing's Everett, Washington, plant, where the current 777 and the 787 Dreamliner are assembled. Everett has a highly educated and trained

| **4.1** | **4.2** | **4.3** | **4.4** |
|---|---|---|---|
| Determine how the changing demography of the U.S. population has effected American politics, p. 87 | Assess how the American economy shapes government and politics, p. 98 | Evaluate how America's power in the world has changed and why it matters, p. 103 | Analyze Americans' political culture and its implications for government and politics, p. 104 |

**GLOBAL BOEING** Two new Boeing 787 Dreamliners wait for delivery to Air India and All Nippon Airways. Indian and Japanese companies were not only customers for the new aircraft but suppliers and partners in its design and production as well. Do such global arrangements cause jobs to depart the United States or help to create new ones? What should government do to encourage further job growth in the United States.

workforce, with extensive experience in design, engineering, building, final assembly, and testing. Everett also has the advantage of being near the Port of Seattle, where parts and sections from Boeing's main Japanese supplier enter the country. But before agreeing to manufacture the 777X in Everett, Boeing wanted special subsidies from the state of Washington and major concessions from the International Association of Machinists (IAM), Local 751, which represents Everett labor. Unless satisfied on both counts, Boeing would look elsewhere.

Washington complied. In a one-day special session of the legislature, the state agreed to grant Boeing, among other things, almost $9 billion in tax breaks over sixteen years, the most generous series of tax subsidies ever granted to an American corporation by a state. Washington agreed to these subsidies despite the fact that Boeing was thriving and not in apparent need of assistance. In 2013, Boeing enjoyed record profits—more than $4 billion—with its stock price hitting an all-time high.

Though the IAM had a contract in effect until 2016, Boeing insisted that the union revise it on a "take it or leave it" basis. Boeing's proposal, sweetened by a one-time $10,000 payment to each employee, would stretch to 2024, increase employee health insurance premiums, freeze pensions, and limit pay increases to 1 percent every other year, regardless of company profitability or the inflation rate.

Boeing said these changes were required if the company was to keep its long-term costs down and remain a player in the increasingly competitive commercial aircraft market. Several times in the recent past Boeing had tried to deal decisively with its labor costs. First, it turned to massive partnering and outsourcing, with much of the design, engineering, and manufacturing of the carbon-fiber 787 Dreamliner—along with the attendant jobs—outsourced to 135 locations around the world. Disastrous production snags and difficulty in coordinating a global supply chain delayed delivery of the 787 by three years. Battery fires on the 787 after it went into service were equally damning. To save the 787 project, Boeing brought much of the work back to Everett and created an additional 787 production line in non-union South Carolina. With less well-trained and less experienced aerospace workers, the South Carolina operation never reached production targets, and many of the planes assembled there needed to go to Everett for repair before going into service. Thus, the surprise demand in 2013 to reopen the IAM contract on pain of losing 777X jobs to another location represented Boeing's third try to lower its costs.

After IAM District 751 members voted down the proposal by a two-to-one margin, Boeing made good on its threat, inviting other states and communities to bid for the 777X assembly operation. Many did. Scared by the prospect of permanently losing jobs in the Puget Sound area, local Democratic leaders and state officials pressed local 751 to reconsider its contract vote. It refused to do so until a second vote on the contract was ordered by officials from the national office of the machinists union. The contract was approved by a very narrow margin on the second vote.

Machinists at Boeing are worse off than before Boeing made its bold threat to leave Everett. Boeing was able to take on one of the most powerful remaining unions in the United States and win. The machinists who assemble airplanes are among the last production workers in the United States who, because of their unions and the generous wages and benefits that come with union protection, have been able to live middle-class lifestyles. This may now be at risk as Boeing has every incentive to employ the same bargaining tactics in the future when it comes to decisions about where to assemble new or upgraded airplane models. Whatever one thinks of unions, whether one is for them or against them in terms of economic efficiency, it is undeniable that the decline of labor unions in the private sector—now only about 6 percent of private-sector workers, down from 33 percent in the mid-1950s—is one of the main reasons why the middle class is being steadily hollowed out.[1]

Many Americans are worried about whether the nation's high standard of living can be maintained and whether they can continue to provide for themselves and their families. When they are worried about such matters, Americans tend to turn to their elected officials for solutions. Some want outsourcing to be stopped or regulated. Others want government to provide health insurance so that they will not be left in the lurch when companies downsize their workforces. Still others want more retraining and education assistance. And others want lower taxes and fewer regulations to help the competitiveness of American companies. Whatever the particulars might be, it is inevitably the case that big economic and technological changes, and the choices corporations make in the face of such changes, find expression in the political arena and shape what government does. What to do about such things is part of the continuing debate between Democrats and Republicans and liberals and conservatives.

**demographic**
Pertaining to the statistical study and description of a population.

4.1

4.2

4.3

4.4

### Thinking Critically About This Chapter

This chapter is about the founding of the United States (see Figure 4.1) and the formulation of the constitutional rules that structure American politics to this day.

### Using the Framework

You will see in this chapter how structural factors such as the American political culture, economic developments, and the composition of the Constitutional Convention shaped the substance of our Constitution. You will also see how the Constitution is itself an important structural factor that helps us understand how American government and politics work today.

### Using the Democracy Standard

Using the conception of democracy you learned about in Chapter 1, you will be able to see how and why the framers were uneasy about democracy and created a republican form of government that, although based on popular consent, placed a number of roadblocks in the path of popular rule.

# America's Population

4.1  Determine how the changing demography of the U.S. population has affected American politics

**W** here we live, how we work, our racial and ethnic composition, and our average age and standard of living have all changed substantially over the course of our history. Each change has influenced and continues to influence our political life. In this section we highlight several of the most important of these **demographic** characteristics.

## ☐ Growing

Unlike most other rich democracies, the United States continues to experience significant population growth. According to the Bureau of the Census, the population grew almost 10 percent between 2000 and 2010 to a total of almost 309 million people and had passed 318 million by the end of 2014. This leaves the United States as the third most populous country in the world, trailing only China at 1.36 billion and India at

1.24 billion. During the same period, other countries experienced stagnant growth or their population actually declined, as it did in Japan and Russia. Population growth has been the product of both a higher-than-replacement birth rate (more people are being born than dying[2]) and immigration. While the U.S. birth rate and immigration fell after the 2007 recession hit, both rebounded a bit in 2013. Both births and immigration are important for economic growth and fiscal health. When a country's population grows, more people become part of the working, tax-paying population, helping to cushion the burden on national budgets of those who have retired, and more businesses are formed to service the needs of new and growing households. There is a growing market in countries with increasing populations for houses and apartments, furniture, appliances, electronics, cars, and all the multitude of services and products associated with them.

Some worry, however, that population growth in a rich country like the United States must at some point run up against the limits of available resources, such as oil, and that the natural environment will be hurt as more people invariably produce more pollutants. Of course, an increase in population need not lead to such outcomes if business firms and consumers use more efficient and less polluting forms of energy, let us say, and use and dispose of other resources in more environmentally friendly ways. How to do this and what the relative roles government and the private sector should play in accomplishing these outcomes is a recurring element of political debate in the United States today.

## ◻ Becoming More Diverse

Based on a long history of immigration, ours is an ethnically, religiously, and racially diverse society.[3] The white European Protestants, black slaves, and Native Americans who made up the bulk of the U.S. population when the first census was taken in 1790 were joined by Catholic immigrants from Ireland and Germany in the 1840s and 1850s (see Figure 4.1). In the 1870s, Chinese migrated to America,

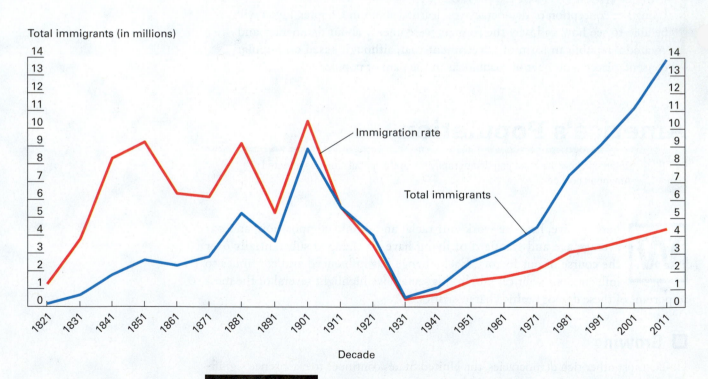

**FIGURE 4.1** IMMIGRATION TO THE UNITED STATES, BY DECADE

Measuring immigration to the United States in different ways gives rise to quite different interpretations of its scale. Measured in total numbers, the largest numbers of immigrants in U.S. history came to the United States in the decade between 2000 and 2010. However, the immigration rate (total number of immigrant/U.S. population × 1000) is a much more important comparative statistic. As the figure demonstrates, the rate of U.S. immigration was highest in the middle and late nineteenth century and in the early part of the twentieth century but fell after that as stringent immigration laws came into force. The rate of recent immigration, relative to the total U.S. population—even with the high numbers of immigrants who have come to the country over the past two decades—remains historically low, although it has been increasing steadily since its low point in the 1930s. In what ways do we still see the effects of this immigration history?

*Source:* U.S. Census Bureau.

drawn by jobs in railroad construction. Around the turn of the twentieth century, most emigration was from eastern, central, and southern Europe, with its many ethnic, linguistic, and religious groups. Today most emigration is from Asia and Latin America, with people from Mexico representing the largest single component. Starting in the 1990s and continuing today, the number of immigrants from the Middle East and other locations with Muslim populations has been significant. More than 1 million people from predominantly Muslim countries in the Middle East, Africa, and Asia immigrated to the United States between 2000 and 2013, bringing their total to about 3.5 million.[4]

Until the Great Recession and tougher border enforcement slowed it down in the years 2008 through 2011, immigration to the United States was substantial. During the 1990s, for example, more immigrants arrived on U.S. soil than in any previous decade in American history; that record was topped during the next decade with the arrival of 13.9 million immigrants in the 2000s.[5] Of the 1990s and 2000s total, just over three-fourths were legal and just under one-fourth were illegal. As a result of this and other immigration streams, the percentage of foreign-born people resident in the United States has more than tripled since 1970, reaching almost 12.7 percent of the population in 2010, about 40 million people.[6] Although the foreign-born population is concentrated in a handful of states—mainly California, New York, New Jersey, Florida, Illinois, New Mexico, Arizona, and Texas—and a handful of cities and localities—mainly Miami, New York, Los Angeles–Long Beach, Orange County, Oakland, and Houston—the presence of new immigrants is being felt almost everywhere in America, including the Midwest (Ohio, Michigan, and Wisconsin) and the Deep South (North Carolina and Georgia, especially). In California, more than 27 percent of the population is foreign-born.[7]

The natural outcome of this history of immigration is substantial racial and ethnic diversity in the American population. Although the largest segment of the population in the United States is still overwhelmingly non-Hispanic white (61.8 percent by 2015, as shown in Table 4.1), diversity is growing with every passing year because of continuing immigration and differential birth rates among population groups. Fully 92 percent of U.S. population growth between 2000 and 2010 was accounted for by minorities, with almost half of that accounted for by Hispanics, who increased their numbers by 43 percent. The non-Hispanic white population grew quite slowly by contrast, at only 1.9 percent during the decade, and, in 2012, for the first time, births among non-Hispanic whites fell below 50 percent of total births in the United States.[8] Hispanics are now the nation's

**TABLE 4.1** RACE AND ETHNICITY IN THE UNITED STATES

| | 2000 | 2015 (estimate) |
|---|---|---|
| Non-Hispanic White | 69.1% | 61.8% |
| Latin or Hispanic (of any race) | 12.5% | 17.8% |
| African American | 12.1% | 12.4% |
| American Indian and Alaskan Native | 0.7% | 0.8% |
| Asian | 3.6% | 5.1% |
| Native Hawaiian and other Pacific Islander | 0.1% | 0.2% |
| Two or more races | 1.6% | 2.1% |

*Note:* Because Latino-Hispanic is defined as an ethnic group rather than a race, the columns in this table do not add up to 100 percent.

*Sources:* U.S. Census Bureau, Census 2000, Population by Race and Hispanic or Latino Origin for the United States: 1990 and 2000, Table 1, https://www.census.gov/population/www/cen2000/briefs/phc-t1/index.html; U.S. Census Bureau, 2012 National Population Projections, Table 6, Percent Distribution of the Projected Population by Race, and Hispanic Origin for the United States: 2015 to 2060, http://www.census.gov/population/projections/data/national/2012/summarytables.html.

**nativist**

Antiforeign; applied to political movements active in the nineteenth century in the United States.

largest minority group and will account for 17.8 percent of the U.S. population by 2015.[9] The African American population is the second largest minority group at 12.4 percent of people in the United States. Asian Americans were the fastest-growing group in percentage terms between 2010 and 2013, primarily because of the slowdown of the inflow of immigrants from Mexico, but they still will account only for about 5 percent of the population by 2015. Demographers predict that these trends will continue and that current minority groups, taken together, will become the majority of the U.S. population by 2050, though non-Hispanic whites will remain the largest single group for a long time after that.[10]

The most recent wave of immigration, like all previous ones, has added to our rich linguistic, cultural, and religious traditions; it has also helped revitalize formerly poverty-stricken neighborhoods in cities such as Los Angeles, New York, and Chicago. Immigrants from Asia and Europe especially have also made a mark in science and technology, earning a disproportionate share of PhDs in the sciences as well as technology patents, and are responsible for creating some of the hottest high-technology companies (e.g., Comcast, Google, SpaceX, WhatsApp, Yahoo!, and YouTube). Because immigrants tend to be younger and have more children than non-immigrants, they have slowed the rate at which the American population is aging, particularly when compared with the rapidly aging populations of Japan, Russia, China, and most of Europe.

But immigration also has generated political and social tensions at various times in our history. The arrival of immigrants who are different from the majority population in significant ways has often sparked anti-immigration agitation and demands that public officials stem the tide. **Nativist** (antiforeign) reactions to Irish Catholic migrants were common throughout the nineteenth century. Anti-Chinese agitation swept the western states in the 1870s and 1880s. Alarm at the arrival of waves of immigrants from eastern, southern, and central Europe in the early part of the last century led Congress virtually to close the doors of the United States in 1921 and keep them closed until the 1950s.

The current wave of Hispanic immigration, much of it illegal, has caused unease among some Americans. In 2013, 41 percent of Americans said that immigrants today are a burden "primarily because they take jobs and housing and receive public benefits." (It should be noted that this sentiment has decreased dramatically from 63 percent in 1994.)[11] Concerns about illegal immigration are among the most often expressed discontents of people who are active in the Tea Party movement, for example, and have led to stringent state-level efforts in Georgia and Arizona to reduce the numbers of such immigrants. Showing how complex this issue remains, surveys in 2013[12] show that almost three-quarters of Americans approve of tougher measures at the border to stem the flow of illegal immigrants (a Tea Party objective); another 71 percent, countering Tea Party goals, wanted to find a way for them to stay in the country legally (though only 44 percent favored a pathway to citizenship for undocumented immigrants already living here). Finally, Russell Pearce, the powerful Republican state legislator who wrote, sponsored, and pushed through the tough Arizona law, was defeated by another, more moderate Republican in a special recall election in 2011.

President Obama acted inconsistently on how or whether to address the problem of illegal immigration. He started slowly. In 2009, he made sweeping changes in the immigration detention system by executive order, thus reducing the number of people in prison awaiting determination of their cases. However, he found it prudent to avoid introducing a major new immigration bill in 2010 as he had promised to do during his campaign because Democrats in Congress were reluctant to take up such a controversial piece of legislation with elections on the horizon; nor did he support major legislation over the next two years. Following the uproar over passage of the law in Arizona allowing police to interrogate people suspected of being in the country illegally, Obama dispatched troops to help guard Arizona's border as a way to tamp down some of the discontent that led to the new law (the Supreme Court rendered most of the law unconstitutional). In 2012, however, he issued an executive order allowing undocumented people brought here as children to stay without fear of deportation for a period of three years so long as they had not been in trouble with the law.

Where immigrants settle is very important for American politics. As is clear from the many news stories about the issue, states and localities with high concentrations of immigrants must find additional monies for social services, health care, and education in order to service a growing and changing population, though the taxes paid by immigrants, whether legal or illegal, help pay for these things. A less well-known impact of immigrant populations is the increase that destination states gain in Congress, where apportionment of seats in the House of Representatives is calculated on the basis of a state's entire adult population regardless of legal status. And, because each state's Electoral College vote is the sum of the number of its representatives in the House and its two senators, high-immigration states play a larger role in presidential elections than they might if only adult citizens and legal aliens were counted in population surveys.

Even while waves of immigration often trigger an initial negative response from the native population (among all races and ethnic groups, it is important to add) and opportunistic politicians, elected officials invariably begin to pay attention to immigrant groups as more become citizens and voters. Indeed, immigrants now represent the fastest-growing voting bloc in the American electorate.[13] The upshot of this change is that elected officials at all levels of government are likely to become more responsive to the needs and interests of recent immigrant groups, even as they try to balance demands from anti-immigration groups who want the border with Mexico sealed. The growing political importance of immigrants in the United States, especially Hispanics, reflects both sheer numbers and the geographic concentration of immigrants in states with very large or closely contested blocs of electoral votes in presidential elections. In 2012, Hispanic voters accounted for 10 percent of all voters in the United States and cast 71 percent of their ballots for President Barack Obama, a Democrat.[14] Their votes were especially important in several battleground states won by Obama, including Florida, New Mexico, Nevada, and Colorado. The GOP is paying attention. Leading contenders for the 2016 Republican presidential nomination include Latinos Ted Cruz of Texas and Marco Rubio of Florida.

## ☐ Moving West and South, and to the Suburbs

During the first decade of the twenty-first century, Americans continued a decades-long trend of moving to the South and West, and to metropolitan areas from rural areas. The Great Recession slowed both processes down a bit—Americans had trouble selling their homes and moving elsewhere because of the housing market collapse—but did not stop them. While the Northeast and Midwest still grew from 2000 to 2010—3 percent and 4 percent respectively—these regions were outpaced by the South and the West, each of which expanded by 14 percent. Almost everywhere, rural areas are losing population—the exception being energy boom states such as North Dakota and Wyoming—as people move to metropolitan areas, locating mostly in the suburbs. The 2010 census reported that 93.7 percent of Americans live in urban areas, with almost all of the growth occurring in suburbs. Although we began as a country of rural farms and small towns, we rapidly became an urban people. By 1910, some 50 cities had populations of more than 100,000, and 3 (New York, Philadelphia, and Chicago) had more than 1 million. **Urbanization**, caused mainly by **industrialization**—the rise of large manufacturing firms required many industrial workers, while the mechanization of farming meant that fewer agricultural workers were needed—continued unabated until the mid-1940s. After World War II, a massive federal and state road-building program and government-guaranteed home loans for veterans started the process by which the United States became an overwhelmingly suburban nation (see Figure 4.2). In recent years, "exurbia"—the areas beyond the older, first-ring of suburbia—has become the fastest-growing part of America's metropolitan areas, though high gas prices and the real estate collapse (and many foreclosures in the exurbs) during the Great Recession and jobless recovery of 2008–2012 slowed the process down and even reversed it in

**urbanization**
The movement of people from rural areas to cities.

**industrialization**
The transformation of a society's economy from one dominated by agricultural pursuits to one dominated by manufacturing.

4.1

4.2

4.3

4.4

**Sun Belt**
States of the Lower South, Southwest, and West, where sunny weather and conservative politics have often prevailed.

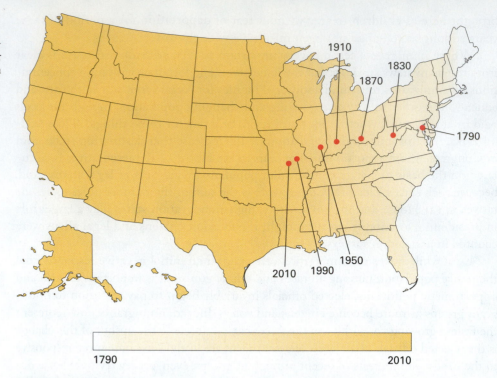

**FIGURE 4.2** CENTER OF AMERICAN POPULATION

The mean center of the American population has gradually moved west and south over the course of our history from near the Chesapeake Bay in Maryland in 1790 to near Plato, Missouri in the most recent census. This change in the center of population has given western and southern states more power in the Senate and in the Electoral College.

*Source:* Bureau of the Census, http://2010.census.gov/2010census/data/center-of-population.php

some areas. Meanwhile, rural communities across the country, but especially in the northern Rockies and western Great Plains states, are losing population.[15]

These changes have important political consequences. The continued drain of population from rural areas, for instance, has diminished the power of the rural voice in state politics, though more rural, low-population states continue to exercise disproportionate power in national politics because of the constitutional provision granting equal power to the states in the Senate. Thus, states like Wyoming and Idaho have the same number of seats in that body as large-population, highly urbanized states such as California and Florida. For their part, suburban voters have become more visible, persuading politicians to talk more about issues such as traffic congestion, urban sprawl, and the price of gasoline and less about inner-city problems like poverty. However, when the economy enters a free-fall, as it did during the Great Recession, the concern about jobs and economic growth, as well as about the fiscal health of the country, trumped most other issues.

The population shift to the South and West has led to changes in the relative political power of the states. Following each census from 1950 to 2000, states in the East and the upper Midwest lost congressional seats and presidential electoral votes. States in the West and the South—often referred to as the **Sun Belt** because of their generally pleasant weather—gained at their expense. After the 2010 census, Missouri, Ohio, Pennsylvania, New York, Massachusetts, Louisiana, New Jersey, Illinois, and Michigan lost House seats and electoral votes; Florida, Georgia, Texas, South Carolina, Arizona, Utah, Washington, and Nevada picked up seats and electoral votes, with Texas the big winner with four.

## ☐ Growing Older

One of the most significant demographic trends in the United States and in other industrialized countries is the aging of the population. In 1800, the median age of the United States was just under 16; today it is a bit more than 35. By 2030, it will be about 38. The proportion of the population over age 65 has been growing, while the proportion between the ages of 18 and 64 has been shrinking. Today 13 percent of Americans are elderly. Moreover, the number of the very old—over age 85—is the fastest-growing age segment of all. By 2030, this figure is likely to rise to about 20 percent.[16] Meanwhile, the proportion of the population in the prime working years is likely to fall from 61.4 percent today to about 56.5 percent in 2030. Thus, an increasing proportion of Americans is likely to be dependent and in need of services, and a shrinking proportion is likely to be taxpaying wage or salary earners, though, to be sure, more Americans over 65 are staying employed, both for financial reasons and for reasons of staying active and engaged.[17] The United States is aging much less rapidly, however, than other countries and regions, primarily because so many young immigrants of childbearing age are coming here. Aging is happening much more rapidly in Japan, South Korea, Italy, Russia, and China, for example.[18]

Because the population is aging, how to finance Social Security and Medicare is likely to remain an important political question for the foreseeable future. The voting power of the elderly is likely to make it difficult for elected officials to substantially reduce social insurance programs for Americans over the age of 65. Meanwhile, the tax load on those still in the workforce may feel increasingly burdensome. Also, more and more middle-aged people are trying to figure out how to finance assisted-living and nursing home care for their elderly parents. How these issues will play out in the political arena in the near future will be interesting to follow.

## ☐ Becoming More Unequal

The United States enjoys one of the highest standards of living in the world, consistently ranking among the top countries in **gross domestic product (GDP)** per capita[19]— Luxembourg, Denmark, Switzerland, Singapore, Qatar, and Norway are the other countries always in the running for the top spot—and is ranked third on the U.N.'s Human Development Index, which takes into account education and life expectancy as well as per capita GDP—others in the top group include Australia, Belgium, Canada, France, Ireland, Germany, Norway, Iceland, the Netherlands, Japan, New Zealand, and Sweden.[20] However, the high standard of living represented by these numbers is not shared by all Americans.

**INCOME** Overall, **median household income** in the United States (in constant dollars, taking account of inflation) has grown only modestly over the past four decades, has lagged significantly behind the overall rate of growth in the economy, and fell significantly after the economic crisis hit in late 2007 (see Figure 4.3).[21] Median household income in 2007 was up about 30 percent from 1967 in constant dollars, but the overall economy, measured as GDP, grew by more than 1,000 percent over the same period. This suggests that households in the middle were not reaping the rewards of America's economic growth even before the recent recession hit. The recession, which officially began in the first quarter of 2008, was especially harsh on median family income. Between 2007, the last year before the recession, and 2012, it fell by 8.3 percent. It is worth noting that median household income in constant dollars was lower in 2012 than it was in 2000, meaning that the household in the exact middle of income distribution in the United States was making less in 2012 than it was making at the beginning of the new century.[22] Given the "jobless recovery" from the Great Recession, the unemployment rate hovering around 8 percent in 2011 and 2012, and continuing wage stagnation,[23] it is unlikely that the median household income of Americans is likely to improve much in the next few years.

It is important to point out that median household income varies across demographic groups. African American and Hispanic households have the lowest household incomes—and took the hardest hits in the economic collapse—while Asian Americans and non-Hispanic whites have the highest. In the recent recession, white non-college-educated men also were hit hard because they were the most directly affected by the decline in manufacturing. Men working full time in 2010 made on average in constant dollars less than they made in the mid-1970s.[24] And the wages share of total GDP fell to a record low of 43.5 percent in 2012, down from 49 percent in 2001.[25]

**gross domestic product (GDP)**
Monetary value of all goods and services produced in a nation each year, excluding income residents earn abroad.

**median household income**
The midpoint of all households ranked by income.

**poverty line**
The federal government's calculation of the amount of income families of various sizes need to stay out of poverty. In 2013 it was $23,550 for a family of four.

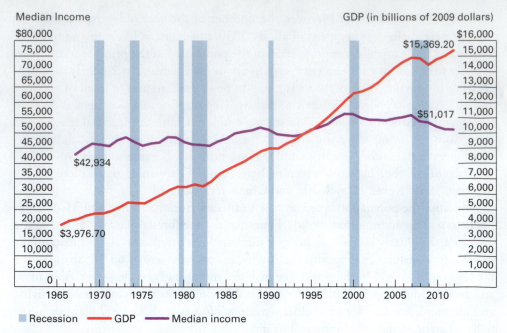

Median Income                                         GDP (in billions of 2009 dollars)

**FIGURE 4.3** MEDIAN HOUSEHOLD INCOME (in 2012 dollars) AND GDP (in constant 2009 dollars)
While the size of the economy grew by more than 1,000 percent between 1967 and the fourth quarter of 2007, median household income increased by only 30 percent. It is worth noting that income distribution became more unequal over time, with more going to the top income earners, suggesting that household incomes for many Americans did not increase at all over this time period. How might the slow gains in household income for most Americans affect what people want from government?

*Sources:* Carmen DeNavas-Walt, Bernadette D. Proctor, and Jessica C. Smith, *Income, Poverty, and Health Insurance Coverage in the United States: 2012* (Washington, DC: U.S. Census Bureau, September 2013), https://www.census.gov/prod/2013pubs/p60-245.pdf. For GPD data see Bureau of Economic Analysis, https://www.bea.gov/national/index.htm (Current-dollar and "real" GDP).

Changes in household income can have important political effects. Not surprisingly, when household income is rising, Americans tend to express satisfaction with their situation and confidence in elected leaders. During periods of stagnation and decline, the opposite is evident. During the long 1973–1983 period of stagnation, for example, political observers talked about the rise of an angry middle class as the main new factor in American politics leading to the decline of the Democrats, capped in 1980 by the election of Ronald Reagan and a Republican Senate.[26] In 2008, with the United States mired in an economic recession, 81 percent of Americans said that "things have pretty seriously gotten off on the wrong track" in the country—the highest percentage ever recorded on this standard survey question—while President Bush's approval dropped to only 28 percent.[27] What to do about the deeply troubled American economy became an important issue during the 2008 presidential election contest and had a great deal to do with Barack Obama's win over John McCain. Not surprisingly, Obama and the Democrats ran into trouble in the 2010 congressional elections when income and wages failed to rebound in the jobless recovery from the Great Recession; Tea Party Republicans were the big winners.

**POVERTY** In 1955, almost 25 percent of Americans fell below the federal government's official **poverty line** (how it is calculated is addressed in detail in the "By the Numbers" feature in Chapter 17). Things improved a great deal after that, dropping to 11.1 percent in 1973. It then rose again to about 15 percent during and after the recessions of the early 1980s and early 1990s, then fell (i.e., poverty decreased) through the 1990s economic boom, dropping to 11 percent in 1999. During the first decade of the twenty-first century, things took a dramatic turn for the worse. By 2012, 15 percent of Americans were officially below the government's poverty line, the most since 1993.[28] Using what scholars and statisticians consider to be a better measure, the "Supplemental Poverty Measure" (see Chapter 17), fully 16 percent of Americans are poor.

Is poverty a problem? Here is why many people think so:

- A distressingly large number of Americans live in poverty: using the standard poverty line measure, almost 46.5 million in 2012, a record number.

- The poverty rate is unlikely to fall much unless there is sustained job growth, especially in jobs that will be available to low-skill workers who make up the bulk of the poor. This seems unlikely in light of slow job growth in the private economy and deep cuts in the budgets of local, state, and federal governments as politicians vie with one another to slash the size of government. This means fewer government workers and fewer workers in programs funded by government that traditionally have helped the poor and less skilled.

- The poverty rate in the United States remains substantially higher than in the other rich democracies, even though they have had troubles of their own, particularly in parts of the European Union.

The distribution of poverty is not random. It is concentrated among racial minorities and single-parent, female-headed households and their children.[29] In 2012, over 27 percent of African Americans and almost 26 percent of Hispanic Americans lived in poverty, for example (although a sizable middle class has emerged in both communities), compared with 9.7 percent among non-Hispanic whites and 11.7 percent among Asians. And 21.8 percent of children under the age of 18 lived in poverty, as did 30.9 percent of people in single-parent, female-headed households.[30]

Obviously, the extent of poverty is politically consequential. While the poor have little voice in the American political system—a point that will be elaborated in several later chapters—poverty tends to be linked to a range of socially undesirable outcomes, including crime, drug use, and family disintegration,[31] which draws the attention of other citizens who want government to do something about these problems. The cause of poverty reduction has also drawn the attention of many Americans who are offended on moral and other grounds by the extent of the poverty that exists in what is still the world's largest economy. (See "Using the Framework" for insight into why it has been so difficult to further diminish poverty in the United States.)

**INEQUALITY** The degree of income and wealth inequality has always been higher in the United States than in the other rich democracies.[32] Over the past three decades, income and wealth inequality has become even more pronounced; income and wealth inequality actually grew during the economic booms of the 1980s and 1990s. By 2012, the top quintile (the top 20 percent) of households took home more than 51 percent of national income (see Figure 4.4 on p. 97), the highest ever recorded (the second highest was in 2006 at 50.6 percent).[33] By way of comparison, in the early 1970s the top 1 percent captured only about 8 percent of national income. During the first three years of the economic recovery after the Great Recession of 2008, the top 1 percent enjoyed 95 percent of the gain in national income, so inequality has been getting worse in recent years.

More gains at the top have come from annual bonuses. In 2006, for example, three hedge fund managers each earned more than $1 billion in salary and bonuses. Big bonuses were handed out to top executives in 2008 and 2009 at several large commercial and investment banks receiving government bailout money, including Bank of America, JPMorgan Chase, and Goldman Sachs, prompting public outcry and congressional hearings. Despite these well-documented bonuses, the Great Recession ultimately took a small toll on the top people in the biggest companies. *The Wall Street Journal* reported in its annual compensation survey of the top 200 American companies that CEO total compensation declined 2 percent between 2007 and 2008, from $11.2 million to $10.9 million.[34] It had rebounded to $11.4 by 2013.[35] In 2011, after the death of Steve Jobs, Apple rewarded its new leader Tim Cook with a one-time payment of company stock worth $376 million; it was worth over $600 million by mid-2012.[36]

# Using the FRAMEWORK

## It's easy to understand why the number of poor people increases during recessions, but why did poverty only barely decline during recent periods of strong economic growth?

**Background:** Despite strong economic growth in the United States from 1993 to 2000, and from 2003 to 2006, the rate of poverty during these years never dropped below 12 percent. (The poverty line for a family of four in 2013 was $23,550. See more on the poverty line in the By the Numbers feature in Chapter 17.) Surveys show that Americans would like government to do something to help the poor, although there is not much consensus on precisely what should be done to solve the problem of persistent poverty, except for a general unwillingness to go back to the traditional system of welfare that ended in 1996 (again, see Chapter 17). So, why doesn't the federal government do more to try to end poverty? Taking a look at how structural, political linkage, and governmental factors interact on this issue will help explain this situation.

### Government Action

While the national government provides small safety nets for the poor, it has not created major programs to eliminate poverty.

### Government

Proposals to eliminate poverty do not improve the electoral prospects of public officials. → Elected leaders in both parties have voiced support for balanced budgets, deregulation, and a friendly environment for investors rather than poverty reduction.

### Political Linkage

The poor are politically invisible; they represent a small minority of the electorate and have had few organized groups to push their interests. → Wealthier Americans and large corporations make large contributions to candidates who promise to keep taxes low and government small. → Public opinion opposes big federal government programs to redistribute income.

The decline of organized labor has lowered the voice of an important advocate for poverty reduction. → Democrats have been reluctant to propose programs that might tag them with the "tax and spend" label.

### Structure

American core beliefs about individualism, initiative, and opportunity make it difficult for proposals to assist the poor to gain recognition. → The economic booms of the 1990s and mid-2000s reinforced the belief that anyone who wanted to work could find a job. → The decrease in the number of high-wage, high-benefit jobs in manufacturing has diminished the economic prospects for unskilled, less-educated people.

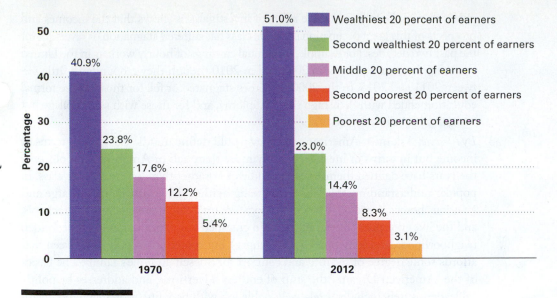

**FIGURE 4.4** U.S. HOUSEHOLD INCOME DISTRIBUTION BY QUINTILES, 1970 VERSUS 2012

Income inequality has been increasing in the United States, reaching levels not seen since the 1920s. A standard way to measure income inequality is to compare the proportion of national income going to each 20 percent (*quintile*) of households in the population. Especially striking is the shrinking share of the bottom 60 percent, the lack of improvement among the second highest quintile over four decades, and the increasing share of the top 20 percent.

*Source:* Carmen DeNavas-Walt, Bernadette D. Proctor, and Jessica C. Smith, *Income, Poverty, and Health Insurance Coverage in the United States: 2012* (Washington, DC: U.S. Census Bureau, September 2013), https://www.census.gov/prod/2013pubs/p60-245.pdf.

In the United States, wealth (assets such as real estate, stocks and bonds, art, bank accounts, cash-value insurance policies, and so on) is even more unequally distributed than income. Wealth distribution became slightly more equal during the Great Recession, when stocks, mostly owned by upper-income groups, took a beating. But since the recovery, the wealthy have regained their pre-recession share of national economic and financial assets. According to Edward Wolff, the nation's leading authority on the subject, in 2010 the top 1 percent of households accounted for slightly more than 42 percent of the America's total net worth.[37]

For more on how to conceptualize and measure inequality and on what inequality might mean for American politics, especially as it affects the distribution of power in political affairs, see the "By the Numbers" feature.

**A TROUBLED MIDDLE CLASS** By every indication, the American middle class is in trouble. This is true no matter how we define the middle class.

1. *By income*: One way to define classes is in terms of how much money people make. If we divide American households into income quintiles, as we did in Figure 4.4, we could simply define the middle class as those households in the middle three quintiles. These middle quintiles, making up 60 percent of the population, had average household incomes of between $29,696 and $82,098 in 2012.[38] As you saw above, the three middle quintiles have made very little progress since the mid-1970s and actually fell back during the 2000s. This happened even as Americans worked longer hours and more people in each household, notably women, entered the paid labor force.[39]

2. *By occupation*: Sociologists usually talk of social stratification rather than social classes, per se, focusing mainly on occupations.[40] At the top are independent professionals with advanced degrees (lawyers, doctors, and accountants, for example), top managers and executives in large corporations, and so-called "rentiers" who derive their income from the ownership of property, including real estate, stocks, bonds, and precious commodities. At the bottom of the stratification structure are people without regular and strong ties to the workforce. Income for people in this stratum comes from the underground economy, occasional minimum wage jobs, and/or assistance from government and private charities. The middle class would include everyone else, including blue-collar manufacturing workers, and white-collar and service workers in either the private or

public sectors. Data from a wide range of investigations shows that the incomes and prospects of this great occupational middle class has suffered stagnation or reverses over the past two decades. For example, the annual earnings of hourly workers in the United States fell by over 2 percent in 2009 and in 2010 though they rebounded a little between 2011 and 2013. In the 2000s, incomes stagnated or fell for those whose formal education ended with their high school diploma, and for those with some college but without a bachelor's degree.[41]

3. *By lifestyle*: Ask most Americans and they would define middle class not in terms of income but in terms of lifestyle. Slightly more than half of Americans in polls over the years have defined themselves as middle class rather than lower or upper class. In popular understanding, this has meant being neither rich (with, let us say, large and luxurious homes in exclusive neighborhoods, country club memberships, prep schools, and the like) nor poor (living, let us say, in cramped rental properties in crime-ridden neighborhoods, and sometimes going hungry), but something solidly in between that affords some degree of security and comfort for oneself and one's family. The basics of the "American Dream," the stuff of endless advertising and addresses by political leaders, surely includes a relatively stable job with benefits (retirement and health care), making enough money in that job to own a home in a safe neighborhood with enough left over to have a new or late model used car and to be able to take one's family on an annual vacation. In popular accounts, the Dream also includes access for one's children to good public schools and affordable post-secondary education. Leaving aside the question of whether this version of the "American Dream" is sustainable from a resource availability or an environmental point of view—we are agnostic on the issues—it is certainly true that Americans in the middle have been having more difficulty in attaining or holding on to the Dream over the past several decades. Health care is more expensive, and fewer companies provide health insurance for their employees today, for example, than they did in the 1970s and 1980s. Jobs are less secure because of technological change and outsourcing, moreover, and college tuitions have risen far faster than the overall cost of living or wages and salaries.[42] And many Americans lost their homes when the real estate bubble burst and the financial system collapsed in 2008.

However one defines middle class, a troubled middle class tends to be an angry and fearful middle class, and this has important consequences for American politics, as we pointed out above in the section on income. A *Wall Street Journal*/NBC News poll reported widespread support for both the Tea Party and Occupy Wall Street anti–Wall Street/antigovernment agendas in late 2011, with the strongest support for both coming from solidly middle class and middle-aged people, especially men, who once felt secure in their situations but are now most fearful of the changes they are seeing.[43] These developments may explain part of the volatility of recent elections in which one party then the other is swept into power to "clean up the mess" in Washington or a state capital. It may partially explain why voters are increasingly prone to elect hard partisans to office who offer easily digestible explanations of who is to blame for stagnant or declining living standards. It may partially explain the rising incivility in our civic life where angry confrontations have become more common, whether in school board meetings or town hall-type meetings in congressional districts.[44]

# America's Economy

**4.2**  Assess how the American economy shapes government and politics

 irtually everything we have discussed so far in this chapter is shaped by the American economy. The growth, diversification, and geographic dispersion of the American population, for example, can be traced directly to changes in the economy. The way we earn our livings, our standard of living, and the distribution of income and wealth in the nation are closely connected to the operations of our economic institutions. Even important elements of the American political culture, as we shall soon see, are associated with our economy and how it works.

America's economy is a capitalist one, meaning that it is an economy where the productive assets of society (e.g., land, machinery, factories and offices, financial capital) are privately owned and where most decisions about how to use them are made not by the government but by individuals and firms. Buying and selling products and services in the pursuit of profits is the driving engine of such an economy. For the most part, prices for products and services are set by buyers and sellers in the market, as are incomes and profits to individuals and firms. Although the role of government today varies quite considerably among countries with capitalist economies, they all see protecting property rights, creating the legal framework for allowing markets to operate, providing currencies for market transactions, and providing law and order as a minimum set of government responsibilities.[45]

# By the Numbers

## Is America becoming more unequal?

Scholars and journalists have been claiming for some time now that economic inequality in the United States is not only the highest among all rich democracies, but is becoming steadily more pronounced. As the highly respected *Economist* put it, "Income inequality [in the United States] is growing to levels not seen since the Gilded Age, around the 1880s."[a]

### Why It Matters

Rising income inequality has troubling implications for the practice of democracy in the United States. It is undeniably the case that such inequalities all too often spill over into inequalities in politics. Those with substantially more income and wealth tend to have a stronger voice in politics and better access to political decision makers than people with lower incomes. Those at the top are more likely to vote; can and do make more contributions to candidates, parties, and advocacy groups; and have more information available to them than those on the bottom. They are more influential than the average citizen, with agencies writing rules that affect their well-being. The fundamental democratic principle of political equality is at risk when economic inequality is substantial.[b]

### Calculating the Numbers

We show three ways that income inequality generally is measured. Each provides a slightly different angle for viewing the issue. We have already, in Figure 4.4 and discussion in the text, discussed the first, which examines the shares of national income going to different percentiles of the population, say the top fifth or the top 1 percent of income earners. Here we examine two other measures of income inequality collected by an international organization that allows us to compare how the United States is doing on the distribution of earnings—money earned by working—with other rich countries. The graph on the left from the Organization of Economic Cooperation and Development (OECD) reports ratios created by dividing the earnings among full-time employed individuals

in the 90th percentile of the population by the earnings of working individuals in the 10th percentile. (These data, called P90/P10 ratios, were collected at two points in time, in 1979 and 2011.) Higher ratios mean higher levels of inequality. Thus, a ratio score of 2 means that individuals in the 90th percentile earn twice as much as individuals in the 10th percentile. A ratio score of 8 means that those in the 90th percentile earn eight times as much. From the graph, several things are apparent. First, the more recent P90/P10 ratio is higher in the United States than in the other comparison countries, with the average individual in the 90th percentile earning more than six times the average individual in the 10th percentile. Second, earnings inequality has increased in all the rich countries. Third, the rise in earnings inequality over this time period was more pronounced in the United States than in any measured country except the United Kingdom, Japan, and New Zealand.

The second graph from the Organization for Economic Cooperation and Development shows Gini coefficients of inequality. The Gini coefficient is a number between "0" and "1," where "0" is perfect equality (everyone has the same earnings) and "1" is perfect inequality (where one person or household takes all earnings, leaving nothing for anyone else). The higher the Gini coefficient, the higher the measured inequality. The most obvious conclusion that can be drawn from the graph is that the United States has by far the highest level of inequality among the rich countries, with only Japan, the United Kingdom, and Australia coming anywhere close.

### What Do the Numbers Mean, Really?

Calculations using alternative data sources yield roughly the same result: the United States ranks very high on measures of economic inequality—and has been growing more unequal. But, does high and rising inequality mean that those at the bottom of the distribution are worse off? Not necessarily. During the 1990s, for example, even as earnings inequality was increasing in the United States, poverty rates were falling (poverty has

*(Continued)*

(Continued)

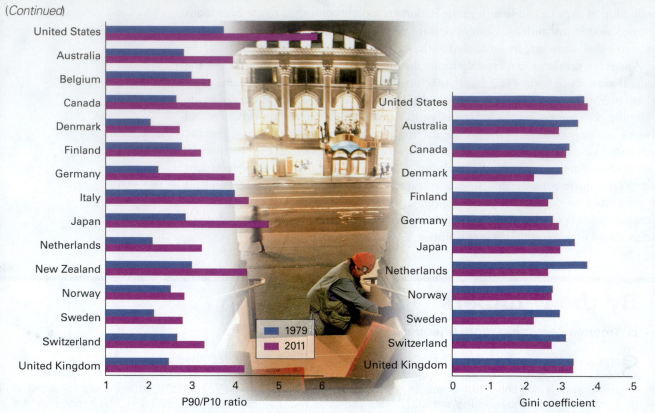

| | 1979 |
|---|---|
| | 2011 |

P90/P10 ratio

Gini coefficient

*Source:* The 90/10 ratio graph is based on data from "Income Distribution and Poverty, P90/P10 Table," OECD StatExtracts, at stats.oecd.org, accessed on June 20, 2014.

*Source:* The Gini coefficient graph is based on data from "Income Distribution and Poverty, GINI ratio Table," OECD StatExtracts, at stats.oecd.org, accessed on June 20, 2014.

P90/P10 RATIOS FOR EARNINGS AMONG FULL-TIME EMPLOYED INDIVIDUALS, 1979–2011
GINI COEFFICIENTS FOR MARKET INCOME AMONG WORKING-AGE HOUSEHOLDS, 1979–2011

increased dramatically, however, since 2000, as you have seen). How can this be? The answer is that rising inequality can be the outcome of a number of income distribution processes, only one of which involves the worst off becoming even worse off. These processes include the following: (1) the people on top become better off while those on the bottom become worse off; (2) the people on both the top and the bottom become worse off, but those on the bottom decline faster; (3) everyone is better off, but incomes rise faster for those on the top than those on the bottom. Situation 1 is what many critics say has been going on and what many people tend to think is going on when they see inequality statistics. Situation 3 is what many defenders of the American economy say was going on during the 1990s and 2000s, although many acknowledge that improvements at the bottom of the income scale have been modest.[c] Oddly, inequality tends to decrease a little during deep recessions as the assets of the wealthy become less valuable; this is what happened in the United States during the Great Recession that began in 2008.

### What Do You Think?

Some people think that inequality is inherently unjust and that rising inequality, even in cases where people on the bottom are better off in an absolute sense, is something that society must rectify.

- How do you feel about this? Why might one argue that inequality is acceptable if people in all parts of the income structure are better off even if those on the bottom only improve a little? What do you think about the issue of inequality and democracy? If those on the top have relatively more income every year, what might be the effect of their continually increased political influence?

[a]"Ever Higher Society, Ever Harder to Ascend," *The Economist* (January 1, 2005), p. 22.
[b]"American Democracy in an Age of Rising Inequality," Report of the American Political Science Association's Taskforce on Inequality and American Democracy, *Perspectives on Politics* 2 (2004), pp. 651–666; Larry M. Bartells, "Is the Water Rising? Reflections on Inequality and American Democracy," *PS* (January 2006), pp. 39–42.
[c]Gregg Easterbrook, *The Progress Paradox: How Life Gets Better While People Feel Worse* (New York: Random House, 2003).

**capitalism**

An economic system characterized by private ownership of productive assets where most decisions about how to use these assets are made by individuals and firms operating in a market rather than by government.

## ☐ Main Tendencies

**Capitalism** has some important tendencies that have political consequences.

1. Capitalist economies are tremendously productive. It is no mystery that societies with the highest standards of living for their populations and the most wealth— usually measured by gross domestic product—are capitalist in one form or

another. Capitalism, unlike, let us say, the Soviet-style command economies of the Soviet Union and its Eastern European satellite nations for most of the post-WWII era, and China and India until quite recently, rewards entrepreneurial risk-taking, innovation, and responsiveness to consumer preferences. Productivity gains and economic growth tend to follow, at least over the long run. The tremendous performance of China, Brazil, and India in the current period is related to their loosening of many state controls on individuals and firms, opening up to world markets, and doing more to protect property rights. They have become more capitalist, that is to say—though the Chinese state continues to exercise much more control over individuals and firms than is the norm in the United States and Western Europe.

2. Capitalist economies tend to produce substantial income, rewarding individuals with high skills and entrepreneurs and firms that successfully innovate and satisfy consumers. Moreover, earners of high incomes inevitably convert their income into property assets such as real estate, jewelry, art, and stocks. Because the value of such property tends to grow faster than the overall economy over time, as economist Thomas Pikkety has demonstrated, wealth inequality increases even faster than income inequality.[46] The wealthy not only generate additional income for themselves and their families from their property holdings but pass on their estates to their heirs so that wealth inequality comes to expand across generations. These dynamics are happening as well in fast-growing Brazil, China, and India, where income and wealth inequality are on the rise. Where capitalist countries differ considerably is the degree to which government acts to alter this situation by redistributing income and wealth, by imposing higher tax rates on high-income earners, and by delivering generous educational, unemployment, retirement, and medical benefits for all. The United States does less redistributing than virtually any other rich capitalist country.[47]

3. Capitalist economies are unstable. They invariably have business cycles, alternating periods of high and low (or even negative) economic growth. In the former, firms, investors, and those who have jobs all tend to gain, to one degree or another; in the latter down period, rewards to firms, investors, and workers grow only slowly, stagnate, or even decline. Historically, capitalism has experienced these fluctuations around a general upward trend of economic growth. One reason for this overall growth, despite periods of negative growth, seems to be that in bad times, inefficient and ineffective firms fall by the wayside and innovative and nimble firms emerge better positioned for the next phase of growth. During the Great Depression, for example, big technical advances were made in radio, television, and automobiles.

At times, the up and down cycles can become quite extreme, a so-called boom-and-bust pattern. The biggest bust of the twentieth century in American capitalism was the Great Depression of the 1930s, when industrial production fell by half and unemployment at one point reached 31 percent. Our current economic troubles—a long and deep recession and a very slow and "jobless" recovery—followed the bursting of a gigantic real estate bubble (fueled by a flood of easy credit) and the collapse of the financial industry, and has been the deepest downturn since the Great Depression.

## ☐ Globalization and Hyper-Competition

For roughly three decades following the end of the Second World War in 1945, the American version of capitalism enjoyed unparalleled success. By 1975, for example, 11 of the largest 15 corporations in the world were American; by 1981, 40 percent of the world's total foreign direct investment was accounted for by the United States.[48]

American corporations were in the saddle in the years stretching from the end of World War II to the mid-1970s. Most major industries in the United States were dominated by three or four firms—such as GM, Ford, and Chrysler, or the "Big Three," in autos—that mass-produced commodities such as steel, cars, and refrigerators. Facing little domestic or foreign competition in the U.S. market and protected in their market dominance by federal regulators, major companies enjoyed substantial and stable profits over many years. Because they could easily pass on their costs in the

**globalization**
The increasing tendency of information, products, and financial capital to flow across national borders, with the effect of more tightly integrating the global economy.

prices they charged consumers, corporations were happy to enter into contracts with labor unions that provided good wages and benefits for their employees as well as employment stability, and predictability for themselves. One result was an impressive expansion of the middle class and a general rise in the American standard of living.

The relatively protected and stable world of the post–World War II corporation is gone, replaced by a form of capitalism in the United States where major companies face intense and unrelenting competition at home and abroad. Their changed situation was brought about by a set of near-simultaneous transformations across a broad front that accelerated the introduction of labor-saving technologies and the pace of **globalization**. There was, for example, the digital revolution that brought advances in computer hardware and software and the explosive growth in the Internet. There were dramatic improvements in the speed and costs of moving raw materials and commodities here and abroad: containerized trucking and shipping, bigger and faster jet planes, high-speed trains, and improved highways. There was also a strong move in the United States, beginning in the 1970s and picking up steam after that, to deregulate a broad range of industries (including shipping, banking, securities, and telecommunications, among others) in hopes of fighting inflation and improving American competitiveness in the face of the galloping economies of Japan, the so-called Asian Tigers, and the European Union. And, finally, a number of international agreements came into force that diminished barriers to trade and investment across national borders.

*Globalization*[49] is the term that is often used to describe this new world where goods, services, and money flow easily across national borders. In this new world, companies can and must produce and sell almost anywhere and seek hard-working and talented employees where they can find them. They can also find subcontractors and partner companies in diverse geographical locations to supply them with parts, as Boeing does for the airplanes it assembles, or with finished products, as Walmart does to supply its many stores. With the infrastructure provided by global financial markets and services, investors can move money to those places and into those companies wherein they believe they can get the highest rate of return. Customers, having a wider range of choices, increasingly insist on the best possible products at the lowest possible prices, and will switch where they shop with breathtaking speed to make sure this happens.[50]

**GLOBALIZATION**

Production and distribution of most manufactured products is now global, a trend that has been accelerated by a wide range of technological changes including containerization shown in this massive container shipping complex in Hamburg, Germany. How does globalization shape the issues that concern the American public and how does it affect what government does?

With many emerging markets, new industry-spawning technologies, fickle investors and customers, and ample investment capital for new companies—though lending fell sharply during the Great Recession—large companies everywhere face fierce competition. Growth and profitability, even survival, for many of them, are no longer routine as they were for much of the postwar period. Some formerly powerful companies, for example, simply disappeared (including TWA, Eastern, and Pan Am among American airlines), giving way to more innovative and nimble challengers (e.g., JetBlue and Southwest), while others were forced to dramatically change their business model (e.g., Kodak shifting from film to digital photography and IBM focusing on IT services after offloading its computer manufacturing division to the Chinese company Lenovo). With the possible exception of large oil companies, even the most powerful companies today dare not stand pat for fear of losing out to new competitors. Microsoft, for example, must figure out how to compete with Apple in the smart phone and tablet markets, and with Google and its cloud-based software model for enterprise computing. Apple cannot afford to rest on its considerable laurels when Amazon is pushing hard to become the main supplier of cloud computing capacity and using its own access to books, movies, and media content for the Kindle line of devices to challenge Apple's dominance of the tablet market.

To a great extent, globalization and rapid technological innovation have been good for Americans. They have helped drop prices for a wide range of consumer goods and brought new, exciting, and useful products to market. But globalization and hypercompetition, in association with the introduction of labor-saving technologies, also have had negative impacts. In a global economy where companies fight for advantage, many choose to become "lean and mean," trimming or eliminating health care and retirement plans and shedding employees. For example, Google announced in late 2013 that it was investing heavily in robotics to make supply-chain distribution channels faster and more efficient, with need for fewer and fewer workers. As the engineer in charge of the project noted with some amazement, "There are still people who walk around in factories and pick things up in distribution centers and work in the back rooms of grocery stores."[51] Some companies, moreover, believe they must outsource to lower-cost suppliers and shift some operations to other locations to be closer to overseas customers. This happened first with basic manufacturing (think cars and steel), then with back-office low-skilled service activities (think call centers and mortgage processing services), and increasingly today with highly skilled work in design engineering, research and development, advanced manufacturing,[52] and some medical services (medical records, radiology, and the like). Faced with this combination of labor-saving technologies and globalization, employees here have lost much of their bargaining power with employers.[53]

All of this affects the well-being and mood of the American people and gets reflected, sooner or later, in our politics. For example, polls show that Americans are deeply concerned about rising inequality, wage and salary stagnation, and the economic futures of the country and their children. And they want elected officials to do something about it.

# America in the World

**4.3**    Evaluate how America's power in the world has changed and why it matters

In addition to its prominent, though reduced, role in the global economy, America's powerful diplomatic, cultural, and military standing in the world is another important structural fact that has shaped our politics and government. While the United States has economic, diplomatic, cultural, and military rivals in the world, no other country can lay claim to leadership in all four areas as America can. While the United States has been so positioned since the end of World War II, matters crystallized in the 1990s, when startling changes happened in the world's military, political, and economic systems that heightened, for a time, U.S. power in the world. Communism collapsed in Eastern Europe. The Soviet Union ceased to exist. Communist China switched to a market economy. Most developing countries rejected the socialist development model, embraced "privatization," and welcomed foreign investment. Moreover, the United States took the lead in organizing the global economy. Many observers began to refer to the United States as the world's only superpower.

Wars in Iraq and Afghanistan, the Great Recession, and the collapse of the U.S. financial system have lessened the appeal of the U.S. economic model. Endless gridlock, repeated budget crises, and intense partisanship have also made suspect the U.S. model of government. One hears much less talk of the U.S.A. as a superpower that others should emulate. China presents an alternative state-led economic model , and its rapid military modernization worries some about the balance of power over the long term.

Even if it is reasonable to argue that the United States remains the most powerful nation in the world in terms of military strength and even if President Obama is the most popular leader in the world,[54] the United States has not been having its way on many important matters on the international front, either with allies or adversaries, nor is it likely to do so in the future. With the threat of the Soviet Union no longer holding them together, U.S. allies feel freer to act unilaterally. In 2011, Germany refused to be part of the NATO mission that helped Libyans depose longtime dictator Muammar Gaddafi, and members of NATO remain deeply divided about the lengthy civil war in Syria. Disagreements about NATO expansion, human rights, and intervention in Ukraine have strained U.S. relations with Russia, while security issues, cyber warfare, trade imbalances, and intellectual property irritate our relations with China. In spite of all of its power, America seems unable to bring the Palestinians and Israelis together. Finally, the threat of a terrorist attack is not over.

America's expansive role in the post-World War II world has had many implications for U.S. politics and policies. (1) U.S. leaders and the public have judged that we require a large military establishment and, consequently, have tilted spending toward national security. (2) Expanded U.S. involvement overseas has enhanced the role of the president in policy making and diminished that of Congress. (3) Being the dominant military power has been very costly, not simply in a budgetary sense. Fighting in Iraq and Afghanistan stretched the manpower resources of the military, leading to a greater-than-normal reliance on reserve and National Guard units as well as on multiple deployments.

It is not entirely clear if the people are prepared for the United States to continue to play a leading role on the world stage, though there is no reason to believe that the United States will turn isolationist. The U.S. economy is too big and too globally interconnected. The U.S. dollar remains the global currency of choice, despite rumblings from China, and the United States remains the world's foremost military power. Even so, public opinion[55] and elected officials across the political spectrum signal support for doing less in the world. The so-called sequester, brought on by the deep partisan divide in Washington, resulted in across-the-board budget cuts in 2013 and 2014 for all federal departments and agencies, including the Pentagon, the Central Intelligence Agency, and the Department of State.

# America's Political Culture

**4.4**    Analyze Americans' political culture and its implications for government and politics

**E**vidence strongly suggests that Americans share a core set of beliefs about human nature, society, and government that is very different from the core beliefs of people in other societies.[56] To be sure, we are a vast, polyglot mixture of races, religions, ethnicities, occupations, and lifestyles. Nevertheless, one of the things that has always struck foreign observers of the American scene, ranging from Alexis de Tocqueville (*Democracy in America*, 1835 and 1840) to James Bryce (*The American Commonwealth*, 1888) and John Micklethwait and Adrian

Wooldridge (*The Right Nation*, 2004), is the degree to which a broad consensus seems to exist on many of the **core beliefs** that shape our attitudes and opinions, our ways of engaging in politics, and what we expect of our government, and how different the elements of this consensus are from political cultural elements elsewhere. To be sure, consensus on core beliefs does not mean that people always agree on what government should do in particular situations. Thus, people who agree that government's role should be limited might disagree on what specific things government should do (say, national defense or school lunch programs). Though people in other societies share some of the core beliefs of Americans, the package of core beliefs is truly exceptional.

Understanding our **political culture**—the set of core beliefs about human nature, society, and government—is important for understanding American politics and government. Why? Because the kinds of choices Americans make in meeting the challenges posed by a changing economy, society, and post–Cold War world depend a great deal on the core beliefs Americans hold about human nature, society, economic relations, and the role of government. In Chapter 5 we examine in some detail how Americans pass on these core beliefs to each new generation—a process called **political socialization**. In the remainder of this chapter, we look at the content of these core beliefs.

**core beliefs**
The most fundamental beliefs in a national population about human nature, the country, government, and the economy.

**political culture**
The set of core beliefs in a country that help shape how people behave politically and what they believe government should do.

**political socialization**
The process by which individuals come to have certain core beliefs and political attitudes.

4.1

4.2

4.3

4.4

## ☐ Individualism

Americans believe that individuals have, as the Declaration of Independence puts it, inalienable rights, meaning that individual rights take priority over rights that might be attributed to society or government. Indeed, the very purpose of government, following John Locke's ideas in *The Second Treatise on Government* (1690) and Jefferson's in the Declaration (1776), is to protect these rights. In formal, legal terms, this has meant that Americans have worked hard to protect the constitutional rights of speech, belief, and association (among others). In a more informal sense, this has meant an abiding belief among Americans in the importance of personal ambition and choosing one's own life goals and way of life.

American individualism is also expressed as a belief that one's fate is (and ought to be) in one's own hands, rather than the product of impersonal social and economic forces beyond one's own control. In particular, one's fortunes are tied to one's own efforts. Those with talent, grit, and the willingness to work hard, Americans believe, are more likely than not to end up on top; those without at least some of these qualities are more likely to wind up at the bottom of the heap. Americans tend to assume that people generally get what they deserve in the long run.

Americans are also more likely to believe that people are naturally competitive, always striving to better themselves in relation to others. Popular literature in America has always conveyed this theme, ranging from the Horatio Alger books of the late nineteenth century to the many contemporary self-help books with keys to "getting ahead," "making it," and "getting rich." The French have been known to refer to this celebration of the competitive individual over the community as the "Anglo-Saxon disease" (thus including the English) and profess to want no part of it in continental Europe.

This core belief about individualism affects American attitudes toward many issues, including inequality and what should be done about it.[57] Americans overwhelmingly endorse the idea of "equality of opportunity" (the idea that people ought to have an equal shot in the competitive game of life), for instance, yet they also overwhelmingly reject the idea that people should be guaranteed equal rewards, especially if this outcome comes from actions by government.[58]

Not surprisingly, Americans tend to look favorably on government programs that try to equalize opportunity—Head Start, education programs of various kinds, school lunch programs, and the like—but are less favorable to welfare-style programs that seem to redistribute income from the hard-working middle class to individuals who are considered "undeserving."[59] Not surprisingly, given this core belief, Americans are less likely to support government efforts to equalize matters than are people in other rich democracies, especially if efforts to equalize outcomes in society involve imposing limits on individual striving and achievement[60] (see Figure 4.5).

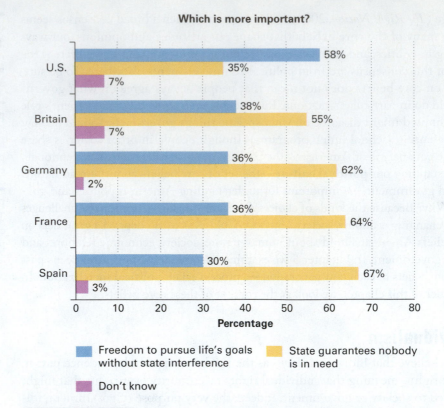

**Which is more important?**

**FIGURE 4.5** INDIVIDUALISM

More than any other people among the richest democracies in the world, Americans are the least likely to want government to play a major role in determining life's economic outcomes. How does this aspect of our political culture affect what we want government to do?

*Source:* Pew Research Global Attitudes Project, "The American-Western European Values Gap," Pew Research Center, November 17, 2011, updated February 29, 2012, http://www.pewglobal.org/2011/11/17/the-american-western-european-values-gap/.

## ☐ Distrust of Government

From the beginning, Americans have distrusted government. The framers created a republican constitutional system precisely because they distrusted government and were trying to create a set of constitutional rules that would deny government the means to act in mischievous or evil ways. Americans have long believed that when governments are imbued with too much power, they are tempted to interfere with private property, individual rights, and economic efficiency. Distrust of government still remains attractive to most Americans today, even though most Americans expect government to do far more than the framers ever imagined, such as providing Social Security, Medicare, and environmental protection, and trying a variety of measures to get the country out of its recent deep recession. In this respect—distrusting government yet supporting a range of programs that seem essential to the public's well-being—Americans are conflicted, to some extent, being what some have called ideological conservatives and operational liberals. As Ben Page and Lawrence Jacobs put it: ". . . most Americans are philosophical conservatives but also pragmatic egalitarians. They look to government for help in ensuring that everyone has genuine equal opportunity plus a measure of economic security with which to exercise that opportunity."[61] But their distrust of government increases further when the help provided by government does not, in reality, seem to help or seems to help those who are already powerful and privileged, as in the bank and auto company bailouts in the midst of the Great Recession.[62] (See the "Can Government Do Anything Well?" feature for the big role the federal government has played in economic development over the course of American history.)

Distrust of government remains the "default" position of a majority of Americans. Even when they support particular government programs, they worry that government is getting too big, too expensive, and too involved in running things. During the health care debate in 2009, for example, the respected Pew survey discovered that a majority supported each major element of the Democrats' health care package, but only 34 percent

**ALL FOR ONE, ONE FOR ALL**

In Japan, commitment to the work team and the company are more important cultural values than they are in the United States. These Japanese supermarket workers start their day as a team. What might be some advantages and disadvantages to the Japanese viewpoint?

favored the package as a whole, with widespread concern that the bill created too much government control.[63] As one commentator put it, "... Americans are looking to the government for help, but they still don't like the government."[64] This core belief is not universally shared. In Germany, Sweden, and France, for example, where governments have always played an important role in directing society and the economy, people are much more likely to trust the intentions and trustworthiness of their national governments even when they disagree with political leaders on particular government policies.

## ☐ Belief in Democracy and Freedom

Certain beliefs about what kind of political order is most appropriate and what role citizens should play shape the actual daily behavior of citizens and political decision makers alike.

**DEMOCRACY** At the time of the nation's founding, democracy was not highly regarded in the United States. During our history, however, the practice of democracy has been enriched and expanded, and the term *democracy* has become an honored one.[65] While regard for democracy is one of the bedrocks of the American belief system today, Americans have not necessarily always behaved democratically. After all, African Americans were denied the vote and other citizenship rights in many parts of the nation until the 1960s. It is fair to say, nevertheless, that most Americans believe in democracy as a general principle and take seriously any claim that their behavior is not consistent with it. For example, public opinion surveys done during the past 25 years consistently show that about 60 to 70 percent of Americans want to abolish the Electoral College in favor of a direct, popular vote for the president.

**FREEDOM** Foreign visitors have always been fascinated by the American obsession with individual "rights," the belief that in the good society, government leaves people alone in their private pursuits. Studies show that freedom (also called *liberty*) is at the very top of the list of American beliefs and that it is more strongly honored here than elsewhere.[66] From the very beginning, what attracted most people to the United States was the promise of freedom in the New World. Many came for other reasons, to be sure: a great many came for strictly economic reasons, some came as convict labor, and some came in chains as slaves. But many who came to these shores seem to have done so to taste the

# Can Government Do Anything Well?

## Backing Research and Development

One of the most important functions of the federal government in the post–World War II era has been to support basic research and development in every area of science and technology. Most of the monies have gone to major research universities, though some have been directed to private firms. Four entities account for the virtually all of this funded research: the National Science Foundation (NSF) for basic science, the National Institutes of Health (NIH) for biomedical research, the Defense Advanced Research Projects Agency (DARPA) for new military-related technologies, and the National Aeronautics and Space Administration (NASA) for space-related sciences.

*Support for the claim that government should play a significant role in encouraging research and development*

It is generally recognized that while private companies and investors will spend for research and development on projects related to their existing or planned product lines—for example, pharmaceutical companies designing and testing a new drug—it is not in their interest to fund fundamental science that doesn't have an understood payoff for shareholders. Though basic scientific research benefits society and the economy in the long run, it is hard to convince shareholders that the firm should finance expensive activities whose benefits may go to other companies and not to one's own. The last private corporation to fund basic research unrelated to its own product line or industry was Bell Labs (whose scientists won several Nobel Prizes). It stopped doing research unrelated to its own product lines after AT&T lost its monopoly position in the telephone industry in the wake of deregulation.

NSF, NIH, DARPA, and NASA funding helped make the United States the world leader in science and technology development and its universities the envy of the world. Basic scientific discoveries in mathematics, physics, astrophysics, cell biology, chemistry, neuroscience, computers (including the Internet), human systems, nanotechnology, telecommunications, and more have formed the basis of entire new industries and enhanced the competitiveness of the American economy. In the medical field, NIH-funded research led to breakthroughs that have rid the United States of polio, cholera, and smallpox and radically reduced the risk of hepatitis B, measles, mumps, tetanus, rubella, and diphtheria.

- The main criticism of the federal government's role in basic research and development is that it is no longer doing enough and that American competitiveness is at risk. NSF, for example, today awards no more fellowships for training PhD scientists and engineers than it did in the 1960s. Even some Republicans, hostile to a big role for the federal government as a matter of principle, have recognized that more needs to be done. In his 2006 State of the Union Address President Bush, in asking for more money for basic science agencies, said the following: "For the U.S. to maintain its global economic leadership, we must ensure a continuous supply of highly trained mathematicians, scientists, engineers, technicians, and scientific support staff."

*Rejection of the claim that government should play a significant role in encouraging research and development*

Opposition to the federal government's role in funding basic scientific research takes a number of forms:

- Critics point out that funding agencies often support projects that seem, on their face, to be wasteful or frivolous.

- In the biological sciences, funded researchers often focus on areas that offend the religious beliefs of some Americans, especially in the areas of embryonic stem cells and contraception.

- Climate science research is troubling to some Americans and industry interest groups, either because they believe climate change is not a real phenomenon, is unrelated to human activities, or because the findings of research in this area may lead to policies that demand economic sacrifices.

- Free-market–oriented think tanks such as Cato take the position that basic research would be done by private firms if a patent system was in place that would allow private inventors or firms supporting research to enjoy a monopoly over their findings, allowing them to realize a profit.

*(Continued)*

**WHAT DO YOU THINK?**

What do you think about the past, present, and future role of the government in encouraging research and development in agencies such as NIH, NSF, and DARPA? Which of the following positions is closest to your own?

- Government support in encouraging research and development plays an integral role in ensuring the success of R&D and maintaining the U.S. global position and should be enhanced.
- Government-spurred R&D projects have been mostly successful, but current challenges cannot be handled by government-funded, university-based research alone and will need private sector attention.
- The government has no place in funding research and development, as these programs can always be completed more efficiently and effectively by the private sector.

How would you defend this position to a fellow student? What would be your main line of argument? What evidence do you believe best supports your position?

freedom to speak and think as they chose, to worship as they pleased, to read what they might, and to assemble and petition the government if they had a mind to do so.

As in many cases, however, to believe in something is not necessarily to act consistently with that belief. There have been many intrusions on basic rights during our history. Later chapters address this issue in more detail.

**populism**
The belief that the common person is every bit as good as those with wealth and power.

## ☐ Populist

The term **populism** refers to the hostility of the common person to concentrated power and the powerful. While public policy is not often driven by populist sentiments (for the powerful, by definition, exercise considerable political influence), populism has always been part of the American core belief system and has sometimes been expressed in visible ways in American politics.

One of the most common targets of populist sentiment has been concentrated economic power and the people who exercise it. The Populist movement of the 1890s aimed at taming the new corporations of the day, especially the banks and the railroads. Corporations were the target of popular hostility during the dark days of the Great Depression and also in the 1970s, when agitation by consumer and environmental groups made the lives of some corporate executives extremely uncomfortable. Populism is a staple of contemporary conservatism in the United States with its attacks on Hollywood, the media, and academic elitists.[67] Members of the modern Tea Party movement have directed their anger at bankers and bank bailouts, big government and taxes, and bicoastal elites who fail, they believe, to appreciate the values of ordinary Americans. Occupy Wall Street supporters, we have seen, also denigrate Wall Street and a government that seems to consistently come to its aid.

Populism celebrates the ordinary person. Given this widespread belief, it behooves political candidates in America to portray themselves as ordinary folks, with tastes and lifestyles very much like everyone else's. How else might one explain private school-educated and aristocratically born-and-bred George H.W. Bush expressing his fondness for pork rinds and country and western music during the 1988 presidential campaign? His son George W. Bush—a student at a prestigious prep school, an undergraduate at Yale, and an MBA student at Harvard—wanted to be seen (and perhaps saw himself) as a hard-working rancher on his Texas spread.

## ☐ Religious

The United States is, by any measure, a strikingly religious society.[68] Polls conducted over the past three or four decades show that more Americans believe in God, regularly attend church, and say that religion is important in their lives, than people in any of the other rich democracies (see Figure 4.6). Levels of religiosity in the United States, in fact, approach those found in Muslim countries of the developing world.[69] This commitment to religion has existed from the beginning of the republic and is integrally related to the practice of politics in the United States—something that often

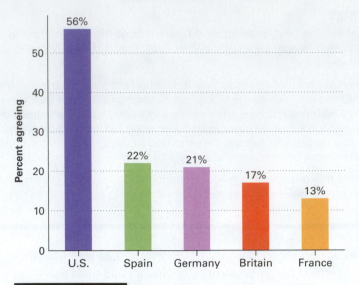

**Religion is important in my life**

Percent agreeing

- U.S.: 56%
- Spain: 22%
- Germany: 21%
- Britain: 17%
- France: 13%

**FIGURE 4.6** RELIGIOUS COMMITTMENT

Americans are the most religious among people in the rich democracies of the world as this survey question and many others show. How does this aspect of our political culture affect the nature of our public policies?

*Source:* Pew Research Global Attitudes Project, "The American-Western European Values Gap," Pew Research Center, November 17, 2011, updated February 29, 2012, http://www.pewglobal.org/2011/11/17/the-american-western-european-values-gap/.

baffles foreign observers.[70] Religious sentiments have been invoked by most important political leaders in the United States in their public pronouncements, and Americans have come to expect religious references when leaders talk about public matters. During the intense Democratic presidential nomination campaign in 2008, for example, Hillary Clinton and Barack Obama spoke often of their religious faith, something one is unlikely to hear in political campaigns in other rich democracies.

Religious faith affects politics in important ways. For one thing, it affects which issues become part of political debate and election campaigns. School prayer and the teaching

**PRAYING BEFORE DOING BATTLE**

Public displays of piety by political leaders are common and expected in the United States, something that is quite rare in other rich democracies. Here President Obama and Republican House Speaker John Boehner say a prayer together before holding a contentious meeting on issues dividing the president and congressional Republicans. How does the strong religious culture of the United States affect the kinds of public policies we have here compared to other countries?

of evolution have not been part of the political debate in many other democracies, for example, as they have here. For another thing, religious belief has been important in drawing ideological lines. While churches and religious believers have often been on the liberal side of the political divide, to be sure—note the substantial involvement of religious leaders, organizations, and believers in the civil rights and anti–Vietnam War movements—strong religious beliefs are most associated with conservative tendencies in American politics. Public opinion polls show that the most religiously committed Americans (of all denominations) are also the most conservative Americans on issues ranging from abortion to prayer in the schools, social welfare, and military spending; church attendance, in the end, is a better predictor of party affiliation than income.

# Using the DEMOCRACY STANDARD

## Do structural factors in the United States support democracy?

Throughout this book, we have examined a number of structural factors that influence American politics. This chapter considered the main features of American society, economy, political culture, and America's place in the world, and how each influences important aspects of politics and government in the United States. All of these structural factors are interrelated. The constitutional rules are substantially shaped by our beliefs about the nature of the individual, society, and government that make up our political culture. The political culture, in turn—with its celebration of the market, competitive individualism, and private property—is perfectly attuned to a capitalist economy. How the economy operates and develops has a lot to do with the American people (where people live, what kind of work they do, and so on), as does the nation's place in the world. The demographic characteristics of the American population trigger their own effects; the populace's level of education and skill has a lot to do with American economic performance, for instance.

The interplay of these factors—and the ways in which they are interpreted and played out through government policy and action—affects the quality and nature of democracy in the United States. But there is some disagreement on whether or not the American political structure, created by economics, culture, and social realities, fosters democracy.

On the one side, some argue that American society is open, diverse, and filled with opportunity for those who are ambitious and hard working. Economic growth is raising the living standards of the population (if modestly for most), which bodes well for democracy; note the evidence that high living standards and democracy seem to go together. Also, economic, technological, and social changes—including the Internet, ease of travel, medical advances, and more—are allowing more and more people to develop their unique abilities and capacities, to become informed, to link together with others who share their public concerns, to get involved in community and political affairs, and to have their voices heard by public officials. Most importantly, perhaps, these developments make it possible for Americans to shape their own lives, improving their situations and those of their families, without the help of government. In short, equality of opportunity and technological and social changes are making American society more hospitable to democracy.

Yet others counter that the American society fails to live up to the promise of equal opportunity and access to government, making it, in fact, far less democratic than other wealthy democracies. The economic system of the United States, while incredibly productive, distributes wealth and income in a highly unequal way, leaving the very few at the top with the lion's share. This leads to substantial inequalities in political power and influence among different income and wealth groups, as well as dividing Americans along ethnic, racial, religious, and regional lines. Such divisions undermine democracy because economic inequality always spills over into political inequality. To make matters worse, the American political culture celebrates an extreme form of individualism and antigovernment sentiment that makes it hard for Americans to agree on a way to use government to best serve public purposes.

# Review the Chapter

## America's Population

**4.1** Determine how the changing demography of the U.S. population has affected American politics, p. 87

The most important changes in the American population are its diversification along ethnic, religious, and racial lines and its relocation from rural to urban and suburban areas and to the Sun Belt.

These changes have enhanced the political influence of the southern and western states in Congress and in presidential elections, and of voters in suburban areas around the country. The influence of rural voters has diminished.

Minority racial and ethnic groups have gained political influence as their numbers have grown.

Income and wealth in the United States are more unequally distributed than in any other rich democracy and are becoming more so.

Poverty increased dramatically during the 2000s, and median household income declined.

## America's Economy

**4.2** Assess how the American economy shapes government and politics, p. 98

The American economy is a capitalist economy that has evolved from a highly competitive, small-enterprise form to one that is corporate dominated and with a global reach.

The American economy has shown itself to be highly efficient and wealth producing, resulting in a high standard of living, yet it has also produced high levels of income and wealth inequality and periods of economic instability and financial difficulties.

The political responses to difficult economic times like the Great Depression of the 1930s, and the Great Recession and jobless recovery of 2008–2012, have increased the role of government in society and the economy.

## America in the World

**4.3** Evaluate how America's power in the world has changed and why it matters, p. 103

America's diplomatic, political, and military standing in the world has been largely unrivaled since the downfall of the Soviet Union. But the power of the United States in world affairs is limited in important ways and becoming ever more limited, making it harder for the country to get its way in foreign affairs. The rise of China as an economic power is particularly challenging to American preeminence.

The status of the United States as a military superpower has changed the content of foreign policy, the balance of power between the president and Congress, the size of the federal government, and the priorities of the government's budget.

## America's Political Culture

**4.4** Analyze Americans' political culture and its implications for government and politics, p. 104

Americans believe strongly in individualism, limited government, and free enterprise. Beliefs about democracy, liberty, the primacy of the common people, and a strong religious orientation also help define the political culture.

The political culture shapes American ideas about what the good society should look like, the appropriate role for government, and the possibilities for self-government.

# Learn the Terms

demographic, p. 87
nativist, p. 90
urbanization, p. 91
industrialization, p. 91
Sun Belt, p. 92

gross domestic product (GDP), p. 93
median household income, p. 93
poverty line, p. 94
capitalism, p. 100
globalization, p. 102

core beliefs, p. 105
political culture, p. 105
political socialization, p. 105
populism, p. 109

# Test Yourself

Answer key begins on page T-1.

**4.1** Determine how the changing demography of the U.S. population has affected American politics

1. _____ percent of U.S. population growth between 2000 and 2010 was accounted for by minorities.

   a. 10
   b. 22
   c. 30
   d. 85
   e. 92

**4.2** Assess how the American economy shapes government and politics

2. For about three decades following this war, the American version of capitalism enjoyed unparalleled success.

   a. World War I
   b. World War II
   c. The Vietnam War
   d. The Cold War
   e. The Gulf War

**4.3** Evaluate how America's power in the world has changed and why it matters

3. In 2011, this country refused to be part of NATO military activities that helped Libyans depose their dictator, Muammar Gaddafi.

   a. France
   b. Russia
   c. Poland
   d. Germany
   e. Turkey

**4.4** Analyze Americans' political culture and its implications for government and politics

4. The French have been known to refer to the celebration of the competitive individual over the community as:

   a. Advanced capitalism
   b. Anglo-Saxon disease
   c. Western capitalism
   d. Anglo-Saxon capitalism
   e. Western disease

# Explore Further

## INTERNET SOURCES

Fedstats **www.fedstats.gov/**
Statistical information on the U.S. economy and society from more than 70 government agencies.

Immigration in the United States **http://ocp.hul.harvard.edu/immigration/timeline.html**
A timeline of important dates and landmarks in immigration to the United States from 1789–1940.

Pew Hispanic Center **http://pewhispanic.org**
A rich site for data on Hispanic immigration to the United States and polling information on public opinion on immigration topics.

Religious Freedom in the United States and Abroad **http://www.state.gov/g/drl/irf/**
The State Department's site documenting reports on international religious freedom.

Statistical Abstract of the United States **www.census.gov/compendia/statab/**
A vast compendium of statistical information on the government, the economy, and society.

## SUGGESTIONS FOR FURTHER READING

Bartels, Larry M. *Unequal Democracy: The Political Economy of the New Gilded Age.* New York and Princeton, NJ: Russell Sage Foundation and Princeton University Press, 2008.
An examination of growing income and wealth inequality in America and how it is shaped by and shapes our politics.

Gosselin, Peter. *High Wire: The Precarious Financial Lives of American Families.* New York: Basic Books, 2008.
Suggests that more and more Americans are close to financial disaster because of cutbacks in public and private safety nets.

Hochschild, Jennifer L. *Facing Up to the American Dream.* Princeton, NJ: Princeton University Press, 1995.
A brilliant examination of the ideology of the American dream and how race and social class affect its interpretation and possibilities.

Page, Benjamin I., and Lawrence R. Jacobs. *Class War: What Americans Really Think About Economic Inequality.* Chicago: University of Chicago Press, 2009.
Based on their own national opinion survey, the authors suggest that Americans across the board recognize and are worried about rising inequality and support many specific government programs to improve the lot of those less well off.

Piketty, Thomas. *Capitalism in the Twenty-First Century.* Cambridge, MA: Harvard University Press, 2014.
A compelling and controversial empirical and theoretical work that shows how and why ever-rising wealth inequality remains an integral part of capitalism except in times of war, economic depression, and government intervention on behalf of the non-wealthy.

Reich, Robert B. *Supercapitalism: The Transformation of Business, Democracy, and Everyday Life.* New York: Alfred A. Knopf, 2007.
A description of how the arrival of hyper-competitive capitalism has increased our power as consumers and investors but decreased our power as citizens.

Zolberg, Aristide R. *A Nation by Design: Immigration Policy in the Fashioning of America.* New York and Cambridge, MA: Russell Sage Foundation and Harvard University Press, 2006.
The definitive work on the U.S. immigrant mix.

# 5

# Public Opinion

## THE VIETNAM WAR AND THE PUBLIC

O n August 2, 1964, the Pentagon announced that the U.S. destroyer *Maddox*, while on "routine patrol" in international waters in the Gulf of Tonkin near Vietnam, had undergone an "unprovoked attack" by three communist North Vietnamese PT boats. Two days later, the Pentagon reported a "second deliberate attack." In a nationwide television broadcast, President Lyndon Johnson referred to "open aggression on the high seas" and declared that these hostile actions required that he retaliate with military force. Air attacks were launched against four North Vietnamese PT boat bases and an oil storage depot.[1]

Years later, the *Pentagon Papers*, a secret Defense Department study leaked to the news media by defense analyst Daniel Ellsberg, revealed that the American people had been deceived. The *Maddox* had not been on an innocent cruise; it had, in fact, been helping South Vietnamese gunboats make raids on the North Vietnamese coast. The second "attack" apparently never occurred. At the time, however, few skeptics raised questions. On August 7, 1964, by a vote of 98–2, the Senate passed the Tonkin Gulf Resolution, which approved the president's taking "all necessary measures," including the use of armed force, to repel any armed attack and to assist any ally in the region. A legal basis for full U.S. involvement in the Vietnam War had been established.

For more than a decade, the United States had been giving large-scale military aid to the French colonialists, and then to the American-installed but authoritarian South Vietnamese government, to fight nationalists and communists in Vietnam. More than 23,000 U.S. military advisers were there by the end of 1964, occasionally engaging in combat. On the other side of the world, the American public knew and cared little about the guerrilla war. In fact, few knew exactly

| 5.1 | 5.2 | 5.3 | 5.4 | 5.5 |
|---|---|---|---|---|
| Characterize the ideal role of public opinion in a democracy, p. 117 | Describe methods used to measure public opinion, p. 118 | Analyze the process of political socialization, p. 121 | Relate political attitudes to race, gender, age, income, and other factors, p. 123 | Assess the American public's ability to rule, p. 134 |

**AWAITING EVACUATION** This marine is waiting for a medical evacuation helicopter during the bloody battle for Hill 937 in Vietnam near the Laos border. Rising casualties and limited success in Vietnam undermined public support for the war over the course of the conflict and led to an American withdrawal.

where Vietnam was. Nevertheless, people were willing to go along when their leaders told them that action was essential to resist communist aggression.

After the Tonkin incident, people paid more attention. Public support for the war increased. When asked in August what should be done next in Vietnam, 48 percent said to keep troops there, get tougher, or take definite military action while only 14 percent said to negotiate or get out.[2] Through the fall of 1964, more people wanted to step up the war than wanted to pull out, and many endorsed the current policy.

But the number of U.S. troops in Vietnam rose rapidly, reaching 536,100 at the end of 1968, and casualties increased correspondingly. Just over 30,000 Americans were killed by the end of 1968.[3] Television news began to display weekly casualty counts in the hundreds, with pictures of dead American soldiers going home in body bags. The war became expensive, as politicians put it, in "American blood and treasure." Senate hearings aired antiwar testimony. Although in 1965 only 24 percent of Americans said sending troops to Vietnam had been a mistake, by December 1967, pressure to end the war was mounting. About as many people (45 percent) agreed as disagreed with the proposition that it had been a "mistake" to send troops to fight in Vietnam.

Then catastrophe struck. In January 1968, during Vietnam's Tet holidays, the North Vietnamese army launched what became known as the *Tet Offensive*: massive attacks throughout South Vietnam, including an assault on the U.S. embassy in Saigon. The American public was shocked by televised scenes of urban destruction and bloody corpses, of U.S. soldiers destroying Ben Tre village "in order to save it," of marines bogged down in the rubble of the ancient city of Hue, and of a 77-day siege of the American firebase at Khe Sanh. The chief lesson seemed to be that a U.S. victory in Vietnam, if feasible at all, was going to be very costly in terms of lives and dollars.

After Tet, criticism of the war—by politicians, newspaper editorials, and television commentators such as Walter Cronkite and others—mushroomed, and public support for the war diminished. President Johnson, staggered by a surprisingly strong vote for antiwar candidate Eugene McCarthy in the New Hampshire primary, announced that he would limit the bombing of North Vietnam, seek a negotiated settlement, and withdraw as a candidate for reelection. In March 1968, only 41 percent of Americans described themselves as hawks (supporters of the war), a sharp drop from the 61 percent of early February. Anger over Vietnam contributed to the election defeat of the Democrats the following November.

After taking office in January 1969, President Richard Nixon announced a plan to begin a slow withdrawal of troops from Vietnam, with the aim of turning the fighting over to South Vietnamese forces. A majority of the public supported the plan but soon supported calls for a more rapid withdrawal, telling pollsters they wanted to move in this direction even if it might lead to the collapse of the South Vietnamese government. The shift in mood was propelled, no doubt, by rising American casualties, numerous congressional hearings on the war, and massive antiwar demonstrations. After a slow start on withdrawals in 1969 (about 100,000), the pace picked up, and most American troops were gone by mid-1973. There can be little doubt that public opinion influenced U.S. disengagement from the war.

The Vietnam story shows how government officials can sometimes lead or manipulate opinion, especially when it concerns obscure matters in faraway lands, and how opinion is affected by events and their presentation in the news media. The story also shows that public opinion, even on foreign policy matters, can sometimes have a strong effect on policymaking. This complex interaction among public opinion, the news media, elected officials, and foreign policy in Vietnam is not very different from what happened with the war in Iraq, where a substantial majority of the public, believing Bush administration claims about the existence of weapons of mass destruction in Iraq (since proved untrue), supported the invasion of that country in 2003 to topple Saddam Hussein. By 2006, however, a majority of Americans were telling pollsters that the war was a mistake, a shift in mood propelled by mounting American casualties, a lack of progress in achieving either democracy or stability in Iraq, and news about the mistreatment of prisoners at the Abu Ghraib prison. The shift in public attitudes was a major factor in the Democratic Party's victory in the 2006 congressional elections and Barack Obama's win in 2008.

## Thinking Critically About This Chapter

This chapter is about public opinion, how it is formed, and what effect it has on American politics and government.

## Using the Framework

You will learn in this chapter how structural-level factors—including historical events, the political culture, and economic and social change—as well as family and community socialization, shape public opinion. You will also learn how public opinion influences the behavior of political leaders and shapes many of the policies of the federal government.

## Using the Democracy Standard

Based on the standard of democracy, public opinion should be one of the decisive factors in determining what government does. You will see in this chapter, however, that while the influence of public opinion is important, public officials must pay attention to other political forces as well. They sometimes pay close attention to public opinion; at other times, they pay only slight attention to it.

**core beliefs (political)**
Individuals' views about the fundamental nature of human beings, society, the economy, and the role of government; taken together, they comprise the political culture.

**political attitudes**
Individuals' views and preferences about public policies, political parties, candidates, government institutions, and public officials.

**public opinion**
The aggregated political attitudes of ordinary people as revealed by surveys.

5.1
5.2
5.3
5.4
5.5

# Democracy and Public Opinion

**5.1** Characterize the ideal role of public opinion in a democracy

Most Americans share certain **core beliefs** about the nature of human beings, society, and the political order. These core beliefs—including beliefs in individualism, limited government, and a market economy, among others—make up the American political culture. In addition to their overarching core beliefs, most Americans also have **political attitudes** about the specific political issues of the day, including attitudes about government policies, public officials, political parties, and candidates. **Public opinion** refers to these political attitudes expressed by ordinary people and considered as a whole—particularly as they are revealed by polling surveys.

Public opinion is particularly important in a democracy if we understand democracy to be fundamentally about the rule of the people. For the people to rule, they must have their voice heard by those in government. To know whether or not the people rule, we require evidence that those in government are responsive to the voice of the people. The best evidence that those in power are responsive to the voice of the people is that what the people want and what government does are congruent. The wishes of the people can be discerned in elections, to be sure, but a particularly powerful way to know what the people want is to ask them directly in a polling survey. In a real democracy, there must be a close match between public opinion and government policies and actions, at least in the long run.

Curiously, however, many leading political theorists, including some who say they believe in democracy, have expressed grave doubts about the wisdom of the public. James Madison, Alexander Hamilton, and other Founders of our national government worried that the public's "passions" would infringe on liberty and that public opinion would be susceptible to radical and frequent shifts.[4] Journalist and statesman Walter Lippmann declared that most people do not know what goes on in the world; they have only vague, media-provided pictures in their heads. Lippmann approvingly quoted Sir Robert Peel's reference to "that great compound of folly, weakness, prejudice, wrong feeling, right feeling, obstinacy and newspaper paragraphs which is called public opinion."[5]

Modern survey researchers have not been much kinder. The first voting studies, carried out during the 1940s and 1950s, turned up what scholars considered appalling evidence of public ignorance, lack of interest in politics, and reliance on group or party loyalties rather than judgments about the issues of the day. Repeated surveys of the same individuals found that their responses seemed to change randomly from one

**WHAT DO THE PEOPLE KNOW?**
Polls conducted at the time the Supreme Court upheld the constitutionality of the Affordable Care Act in 2012 showed that a substantial majority of Americans did not know very much about what was in the new law. Does this call into question the role that public opinion should play in our system of democracy or is specific knowledge about issues and policies not all that important?

interview to another. Philip Converse, a leading student of political behavior, coined the term *nonattitudes*: on many issues of public policy, many or most Americans seemed to have no real views at all but simply offered "doorstep opinions" to satisfy interviewers.[6] Political scientist Larry Bartels recently demonstrated in a rigorous analysis of a multitude of surveys that middle-class and lower-income Americans know surprisingly little about the economy and tend to support government policies that make their economic positions worse.[7] Economist Bryan Caplan argues that public opinion is more influential than it should be, having shown that widespread public ignorance about how the economy works leads people to support harmful public policies.[8]

What should we make of this? If ordinary citizens are poorly informed and their views are based on whim, or if they have no real opinions at all, or if these opinions are wrong-headed in a serious way, it hardly seems desirable—or even possible—that public opinion should determine what governments do. Both the feasibility and the attractiveness of democracy seem to be thrown into doubt. When we examine exactly what sorts of opinions ordinary Americans have, however, and how those opinions are formed and changed, we will see that such fears about public opinion are somewhat exaggerated.

# Measuring Public Opinion

**5.2**  Describe methods used to measure public opinion

ecades ago, people who wanted to find out anything about public opinion had to guess, based on what their barbers or taxi drivers said, on what appeared in letters to newspaper editors, or on what sorts of one-liners won cheers at political rallies. But the views of personal acquaintances, letter writers, or rally audiences are often quite different from those of the public as a whole. Similarly, the angry people who call in to radio talk shows may not hold views that are typical of most Americans. To figure out what the average American thinks, we cannot rely on unrepresentative groups or noisy minorities. Fortunately, social scientists have developed some fairly reliable tools for culling and studying the opinions of large groups of people.

## ☐ Public Opinion Polls

A clever invention, the public opinion poll, or **sample survey**, now eliminates most of the guesswork in measuring public opinion. A survey consists of systematic interviews conducted by trained professional interviewers who ask a standardized set of questions of a rather small number of randomly chosen Americans—usually between 1,000 and 1,500 of them for a national survey. Such a survey, if done properly, can reveal with remarkable accuracy what the rest of us are thinking.

The secret of success is to make sure that the sample of people interviewed is representative of the whole population; that is, that the proportions of people in the sample who are young, old, female, college-educated, black, rural, Catholic, southern, western, religious, secular, liberal, conservative, Democratic, Republican, and so forth are all about the same as in the U.S. population as a whole. This representativeness is achieved best when the people being interviewed are chosen through **random sampling**, which ensures that each member of the population has an equal chance of being selected. Then survey researchers can add up all the responses to a given question and compute the percentages of people answering one way or another. If for some reason some element of the population is underrepresented or overrepresented in the sample—say, young people or people living in rural areas—researchers can "weight" the relevant population group, giving it more or less importance in the total sample, so that the mix of elements in the final sample closely matches the general population. Statisticians can use probability theory to tell how close the survey's results are likely to be to what the whole population would say if asked the same questions. Findings from a random sample of 1,500 people have a 95 percent chance of accurately reflecting the views of the whole population within about 2 or 3 percentage points. This **sampling error** is typically labeled the margin of error.[9]

For a number of reasons, perfectly random sampling of a national population is not feasible. Personal interviews have to be clustered geographically, for example, so that interviewers can easily get from one respondent to another. Telephone interviews—the cheapest and most common kind—are clustered within particular telephone exchanges. Still, the samples that survey organizations use are sufficiently representative so that survey results closely reflect how the whole population would have responded if everyone in the United States had been asked the same questions at the moment the survey was carried out.

## ☐ Challenges of Political Polling

Those who use poll results—including citizens encountering political polls in newspapers and on television—should be aware of the following problems with polls and what competent pollsters try to do about them.

**ISSUES OF WORDING**  The wording of questions is important; the way in which a question is worded often makes a big difference in the way it is answered.

- A question that asks, "Do you favor the death penalty?" is likely to get a higher proportion of people saying they are in favor than a question that asks, "Do you favor or oppose the death penalty?" because the former gives only one option.[10] Attaching the name of a popular president or an unpopular one to a survey question—as in "Do you support President X's proposal for Medicare reform?"—affects how people respond. Good survey questions try to avoid such "leading" wording.

• "Closed-ended" or "forced-choice" questions, which ask the respondents to choose among preformulated answers, do not always reveal what people are thinking on their own or what they would come up with after a few minutes of thought or discussion. So, in this sense, a survey may not always be capturing what people think is important or what choices they would make. Some scholars believe that such questions force people to express opinions about matters on which they really don't have an opinion or when they don't even know what the question means.[11] For these reasons, "open-ended" questions are sometimes asked in order to yield more spontaneous answers, and small discussion groups or "focus groups" are brought together to show what emerges when people talk among themselves about the topics a moderator introduces.

**ISSUES OF INTENSITY AND TIMING** Often, while the wording of a question may be perfectly acceptable, the question may not capture the relative intensity of respondents' feelings about some policy or political issue. Pollsters attempt to address this shortcoming by building intensity measures into responses offered to survey participants. Most commonly, pollsters provide more than simple "agree or disagree" answer options, including instead a set of five to seven options ranging from "strongly agree" to "strongly disagree." At other times, surveys ask respondents to rank the importance of certain problems or policies.

The timing of a survey can be important. For elections, in particular, polling needs to happen as close to Election Day as possible in order not to miss last-minute switches and surges. Most famously, survey organizations in 1948 predicted a comfortable victory for Republican Thomas Dewey over Democratic president Harry Truman, feeling so confident of the outcome that they stopped polling several weeks before Election Day, missing changes in public sentiments late in the campaign.

**ISSUES OF SAMPLING** Scholars and survey professionals worry about a number of things that can undermine the validity of survey research by making it difficult to draw a sample that is random, meaning representative of the entire population. In some cases, the problems seem to be getting worse. Some of the issues survey researchers have to deal with include:

**THE POLLSTERS GET IT WRONG**

Harry Truman ridicules an edition of the *Chicago Daily Tribune* proclaiming his Republican challenger, Thomas Dewey, president. Opinion polls stopped asking questions too early in the 1948 election campaign, missing Truman's last-minute surge. Top pollsters today survey likely voters right to the end of the campaign. Is it ever safe to rely heavily on polls?

• If pollsters wish to interview people face-to-face, they must interview clusters of respondents who live close together as it is far too costly for pollsters to travel to interview one person in each of hundreds of locations. In addition, conducting face-to-face interviews takes a great deal of time, making it virtually impossible to use this approach in the context of what may be a fast-paced election.

• Telephone surveys are a cheaper, more efficient alternative to face-to-face interviews, but because Americans are inundated with calls from advertisers who may pose as researchers, they have become less willing to answer surveys. In addition, many Americans screen calls and refuse to pick up when a caller's number is not known.

• More and more Americans are turning to cell phones and cutting their reliance on landlines. Because mobile phones are often turned off, survey researchers cannot always get through to people who are part of the prospective random sample. Also, because people don't want to use up their minutes when they are reached, many are unwilling to take part in lengthy surveys. And, pollsters cannot use autodialing technology to randomly call hundreds or thousands of potential respondents because federal law requires that pollsters dial cell numbers directly. So, calling cell phones is more expensive because people must be hired to punch in phone numbers.

- The Internet offers a promising new way to conduct public opinion surveys. However, most online surveys fall prey to the problem of nonrandom sampling. Not all Americans own computers with Internet access and, even if they did, it would be difficult to identify a random sample of people to interview by collecting responses from individuals choosing to visit a particular website. Some firms are working on ways to overcome these obstacles through statistical techniques and innovative sampling procedures.

The top academic and commercial polling firms claim they are taking steps to overcome these problems by using repeated callbacks and statistical methods to fill in for missing people, for example, but the problems are likely to get worse before they get better. For now, we will have to make do with polling results from quality researchers and firms that can be relied on to use best practices, even if this is more expensive for them. A good rule of thumb is to see which polls are most relied upon by public opinion scholars and other specialists in American politics.

# Political Socialization: Learning Political Beliefs and Attitudes

T he opinions and attitudes revealed by public opinion polls do not form in a vacuum. A number of important factors—among them families, schools, churches, the news media, and social groups with which individuals are most closely associated—significantly influence both our core beliefs and our political attitudes. Political scientists refer to the process by which individuals acquire these beliefs and attitudes as **political socialization**. The instruments by which beliefs and attitudes are conveyed to individuals in society (such as our families, schools, and so on) are called **agents of socialization**.

Political socialization is a lifetime process in the sense that people engage in political learning throughout the life-course.[12] However, childhood and adolescence seem to be particularly important times for people's incorporation of core beliefs and general outlooks about the political world, especially party identification, ideological leanings, and racial and ethnic identity, though scholars are beginning to believe that early adulthood is almost as important.[13]

The *family* plays a particularly important role in shaping the outlooks of children. It is in the family—whether in a traditional or nontraditional family—that children pick up their basic outlook on life and the world around them. It is mainly from their family, for example, that children learn to trust or distrust others, something that affects a wide range of political attitudes later in life. It is from the family, and the neighborhood where the family lives, that children learn about which ethnic or racial group, social class or income group, and religion they belong to and begin to pick up attitudes that are typical of these groups. In dinner table conversations and other encounters with parents, children start to acquire ideas about the country—ideas about patriotism, for example—and their first vague ideological ideas: whether government is a good or bad thing, whether taxes are a good or bad thing, and whether certain people and groups in society are to be admired or not (welfare recipients, rich people, corporations, and the like). Most importantly, because it represents the filter through which a great deal of future political learning takes place, many children adopt the political party identifications of their parents, especially if the parents share the same party identification. Although the relationship between parent and child party identification is weaker now than it was in the 1940s and 1950s, a majority of adult Americans still identify with the same party as their parents.

**political socialization**
The process by which individuals come to have certain core beliefs and political attitudes.

**agents of socialization**
Those institutions and individuals that shape the core beliefs and attitudes of people.

*Schools* are also important as agents of political socialization. In the early grades, through explicit lessons and the celebration of national symbols—such as the flag in the classroom, recitation of the Pledge of Allegiance, pictures on the walls of famous presidents, patriotic pageants, and the like—schools convey lessons about American identity and patriotism. In the middle grades, schools teach children about the political process by sponsoring mock presidential elections and elections to student government. In the upper grades, most students in most school districts take courses in American history and American government and continue learning about participation through student government.

*Popular culture*—movies, music, and advertising—also shapes the budding political outlooks of young people.[14] To be sure, most of the messages coming from the popular culture have more to do with style, fashion, and attitude. But much in popular culture conveys political messages. Many performers, such as U2, Bruce Springsteen, and Lady Gaga, for example, embed political messages in their songs. Many Hollywood movies come with a political message; themes of sleazy politicians and untrustworthy or corrupt elected officials are quite common.

Political socialization does not stop when children become adults. Substantial evidence shows that a *college education* affects people's outlooks about public policies and the role of government. People with a college education, for example, are more likely to support government programs to protect the environment. We know, moreover, that people's political outlooks are shaped by *major events* or developments that affect the country during their young adult years. In the past, such events have included the Great Depression, World War II, the civil rights movement and the countercultural revolution of the 1960s, the Reagan Revolution of the 1980s, and the 9/11 terrorist attacks on the United States. The recent Great Recession may similarly shape long-term outlooks as sustained economic troubles have derailed people's hopes of attaining the American Dream.[15] The effect of these events and developments seems most pronounced for young people who are just coming to have a sense of political awareness. Political scientists identify this phenomenon as a *generational effect*. Thus, young people coming of age politically during the 1960s turned out to be much more liberal

**LEARNING ABOUT DEMOCRACY**

Children gain many of their initial ideas about how the American political system works in their school classrooms. In the early grades, children gain impressions about the nation, its most important symbols (such as the flag), and its most visible and well-known presidents. They also learn the rudiments of democracy. Here, elementary school students take part in a mock election. How might developing an entire generation of active participants change the face of American politics?

throughout their lives than young people coming of age during the 1950s or during the Reagan years.

Finally, a number of socializing agents affect people's attitudes and expressed political opinions throughout adulthood. *Jobs* and experiences at work can affect the confidence that people express about the future for themselves and their families. The *news media* affects people's attitudes by how they select and frame the issues they cover. Getting *married* and buying a home—because they bring new concerns with things such as the quality of local schools and neighborhoods, interest rates on home mortgages, and more—cause many people to alter their positions on political parties, candidates, and issues. So too does *retirement*, which often brings a new sense of urgency about government support for retirement and health care benefits.

# How and Why People's Political Attitudes Differ

**5.4** Relate political attitudes to race, gender, age, income, and other factors

A mericans share a range of core beliefs. And, as we learned in the previous section, a broad range of socialization agents—from the news media and popular entertainment to government leaders and the schools—reinforce one another to shape our ideas about what it means to be an American and to live in the United States. However, Americans also grow up and live in a variety of distinctive environments that shape general political outlooks and specific attitudes in distinctive ways. In this section, we explore some of the most significant circumstances that define and often divide us in our political views.[16]

## ☐ Race and Ethnicity

Polling reveals differences in political attitudes that divide significantly along racial and ethnic lines. Among the biggest differences are those between white and black Americans. Hispanics and Asian Americans also have some distinctive political opinions. Many white ethnic groups, however, are no longer much different from other members of the population.

**AFRICAN AMERICANS** On most core beliefs about the American system, few differences are discernible between black Americans and other Americans.[17] Similar percentages of each group believe, for example, that people can get ahead by working hard, that providing for equal opportunity is more important than ensuring equal outcomes, and that the federal government should balance its budget. Equal numbers say they are proud to be Americans and believe democracy to be the best form of government. On a range of other political issues, however, the racial divide looms large,[18] particularly with respect to what role government should play in helping people and making America more equal. But Barack Obama's election to the presidency made African Americans more confident in the country and their place in it. Indeed, African Americans now believe more than white Americans that voting is a duty and that casting a ballot makes a difference.[19]

Partisanship is one important area where African Americans differ from whites. Blacks, who stayed loyal to the Republican party (the party of Lincoln and of Reconstruction) long after the Civil War, became Democrats in large proportions in the 1930s during the presidency of Franklin D. Roosevelt, whose New Deal greatly expanded the federal government's role in providing safety nets for the poor and unemployed. During the civil rights struggles of the 1960s, African Americans began to identify overwhelmingly as Democrats and continue to do so today. In 2012, African Americans were the most solidly Democratic of any group in the population: 87 percent said they were Democrats or independents who leaned toward the Democrats, while less than 5 percent called themselves Republicans or Republican leaners (see Figure 5.1). In 2012, 95 percent of African Americans voted for African American Democrat Barack Obama; only 3 percent supported Republican Mitt Romney.[20]

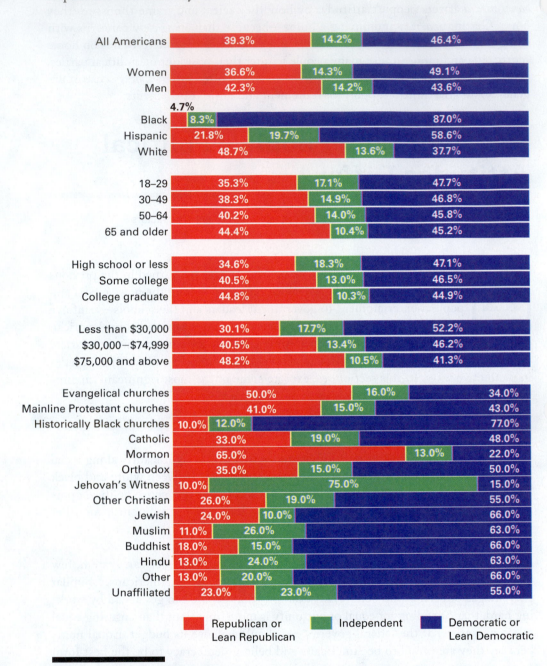

**FIGURE 5.1** PARTY IDENTIFICATION AMONG VARIOUS DEMOGRAPHIC GROUPS

*Source:* Pew Research Center; American National Election Study (2012).

African Americans also tend to be much more liberal than whites on a range of issues that require an activist government to solve pressing problems. This liberalism reflects African Americans' economically disadvantaged position in American society and the still-real effects of slavery and discrimination. However, blacks tend to hold strong religious values and to be rather conservative on some social issues.[21] More are opposed to abortion, for example, than are whites. In general, however, African Americans are very liberal (i.e., favor an activist government to help solve social ills; see Figure 5.2). More blacks identify themselves as liberals than as conservatives or moderates, a pattern that is almost exactly reversed among whites.[22] African Americans also are more likely than Americans in general to favor government regulation of corporations to protect the environment and to favor labor unions.[23] Black and white divisions are most apparent on issues related to affirmative action. For example, 54 percent of African Americans but only 22 percent of whites think the government should play a major role in trying to improve the social and economic position of blacks and other minority groups in this country.[24]

**HISPANICS** Hispanics—people of Spanish-speaking background—are the fastest-growing ethnic group in America and the largest minority group in the nation. As a whole, the Hispanic population identifies much more with the Democrats than with the Republicans; among this group, Democrats enjoy a 59 percent to 22 percent advantage over Republicans (see Figure 5.1). However, the Hispanic population itself is quite diverse. Cuban Americans, many of them refugees from the Castro regime, tend to be conservative, Republican, strongly anticommunist, and skeptical of government

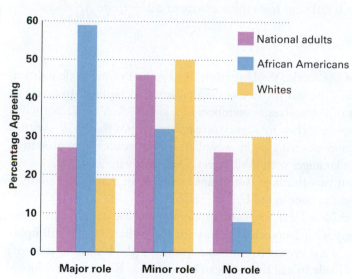

How much of a role, if any, do you think the government should have in trying to improve the social and economic position of blacks and other minority groups in this country—a major role, a minor role, or no role at all?

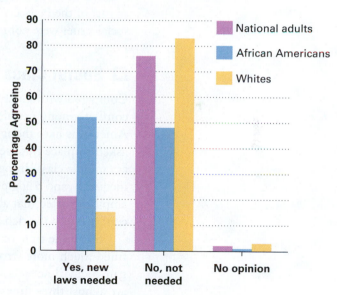

Do you think new civil rights laws are needed to reduce discrimination against blacks, or not?

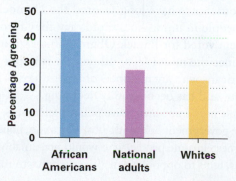

Government must plan an active role in regulating the marketplace and ensuring that the economy benifits people like me.

**FIGURE 5.2** THE RACIAL AND ETHNIC DIVIDE

*Source:* USA Today/Gallup, August 4–7, 2011; and Allstate/National Journal/Heartland Monitor Poll, June 2011.

programs. The much more numerous Americans of Mexican, Central American, or Puerto Rican ancestry, by contrast, are mostly Democrats and quite liberal on economic matters. In 2012, 71 percent of the Hispanic vote went to Democrat Barack Obama. Republican sponsorship and support for laws to crack down on illegal immigrants and on people who help them may make this group view Democrats even more favorably in the future. On the other hand, because Hispanics are predominantly Roman Catholic, one may expect them to be more conservative—and hence more attracted to Republicans—on social issues. On some issues this is true. Hispanics tend to be more conservative than Americans in general on abortion. On other issues—like those pertaining to homosexuality—their preferences are similar to those of the rest of the population.[25]

**ASIAN AMERICANS** Asian Americans, a small but growing part of the U.S. population—a little under 5 percent of the population in 2010—come from quite diverse backgrounds in the Philippines, India, Vietnam, Korea, Thailand, Japan, China, and elsewhere. As a group, Asian Americans are more educated and economically successful than the general population but are less likely to vote and express an interest in politics than people of equal educational and financial status. Though there is only sparse systematic research on the politically relevant attitudes of Asian Americans, we do know the following.[26] On social issues, Asian Americans are somewhat more conservative than other Americans; a majority supports the death penalty and opposes same-sex marriage, for example. On the role of government, they are more liberal, however. For example, a small majority supports efforts to provide universal health care. Importantly, though once split fairly evenly between Republican and Democratic identifiers, they have been trending more Democratic in recent elections; in 2012, 71 percent voted for Obama.

**WHITE ETHNICS** Other ethnic groups are not so distinctive in their political opinions. Americans of Italian, Polish, and Irish ancestry, for example, became strong Democrats as part of the New Deal coalition, but by the 1980s, their attitudes about political and social issues were not much different from the majority of other white Americans.

## □ Social Class

Compared with much of the world, the United States has had rather little political conflict among people of different income or occupational groupings. In fact, few Americans have thought of themselves as members of a social "class" at all, but when asked to place themselves in a class by survey researchers, more than half say they are middle class. Things may be changing, however, after the decades-long growth in inequality, and rising popular anger with Wall Street. One survey in early 2012, for example, reported that about two-thirds of Americans now believe that strong conflicts exist between the rich and the poor in the United States.[27]

Since the time of the New Deal, low- and moderate-income people have identified much more strongly with Democrats than with Republicans. This still holds true today;[28] households in the lowest two income quintiles (the lowest 40 percent) are almost three times as likely to call themselves Democrats as Republicans. Upper-income people—whether high-salaried business executives, doctors, accountants, and lawyers or asset-rich people with no need to hold a job—have identified more strongly with the Republican Party for a long time.[29]

People in union households have long favored the Democrats and continue to do so. About 6 in 10 people in union households say they favor the Democrats. In 2012, 58 percent of them voted for Barack Obama. This Democratic advantage has changed hardly at all since the mid-1970s, although it is important to be aware that the proportion of Americans who are members of labor unions is quite low compared with other rich countries and has been steadily declining.

Lower-income people have some distinctive policy preferences. Not surprisingly, they tend to favor much more government help with jobs, education, housing, medical care, and the like, whereas the highest-income people, who would presumably pay more and benefit less from such programs, tend to oppose them.[30] To complicate matters, however, many

**THE UAW ON BOARD**
Barack Obama and other Democratic candidates can generally count on the support of union members, like these members of United Auto Workers Local 550 in Indianapolis. How might Republicans enhance their appeal to labor?

lower- and moderate-income people, primarily for religious and cultural reasons, favor Republican conservative positions on social issues such as abortion, law and order, religion, civil rights, education, and gay rights. Non–college-educated, moderate-income white men, to take another example, are less likely than in the past to identify with Democrats, with race issues such as welfare and affirmative action playing a key role in this change. Furthermore, some high-income people—especially those with postgraduate degrees—tend to be very liberal on lifestyle and social issues involving sexual behavior, abortion rights, free speech, and civil rights. They also tend to be especially eager for government action to protect the environment. But on the whole, the relationship of income to party choice and economic policy matters still holds; upper-income people are more likely than others to favor Republicans and conservative economic policies, while moderate- and lower-income Americans are more likely to favor Democrats and liberal economic policies.[31]

## ☐ Region

Region is an important factor in shaping public opinion in the United States. Each region is distinctive, with the South especially so. Although southern distinctiveness has been reduced somewhat because of years of migration by southern blacks to northern cities, the movement of industrial plants and northern whites to the Sun Belt, and economic growth catching up with that of the North, the legacy of slavery and segregation, a large black population, and late industrialization have made the South a unique region in American politics.[32]

Even now, white southerners tend to be somewhat less enthusiastic about civil rights than northerners; only people from the Mountain West (excluding Colorado and New Mexico) are as conservative on race. Southern whites also tend to be more conservative than people in other regions on social issues, such as school prayer, crime, and abortion, and supportive of military spending and a strong foreign policy (although they remain fairly liberal on economic issues, such as government health insurance, perhaps because incomes are lower in the South than elsewhere).[33]

These distinctive policy preferences have undercut southern whites' traditional identification with the Democrats, especially since the 1960s and 1970s, when Democrats became identified with liberal social policies. The white South's switch to the Republican Party in the 1994 elections, in fact, is one of the major reasons Republicans were able to maintain control of Congress for a dozen years until the Democrats won back both houses in 2006. Though a plurality of southerners say they favor Republicans, more of them than in the past say they identify as independents.[34] This may help explain why moderate Democrats who appeal to independents have made some inroads in the region; Jim Webb won a Senate seat in Virginia in 2006, as did Kay Hagen in North Carolina in 2008. However, a Republican tide swept the South in 2010.[35] In 2012, the trend towards a strongly Republican South continued, as the GOP won five formerly Democratic House seats in North Carolina, Arkansas and Kentucky. Democrats Timothy Kaine and Bill Nelson, however, won Senate races in Virginia and Florida. In the 2014 midterms, Kay Hagan lost her Senate seat to Republican Thom Tillis and Democratic Arkansas Senator Mark Pryor lost by a wide margin to Republican challenger Tom Cotton.

On many issues, northeasterners tend to be the most different from southerners, being the most liberal of any region on social and economic issues, and most likely to be Democratic identifiers. On most issues and party identification, Midwesterners, appropriately, are about in the middle between the South and the northeast. Pacific Coast residents resemble northeasterners in many respects, but the Rocky Mountain States, with the exception of Colorado and New Mexico, tend to be quite conservative, with majorities opposed to a big government role in health insurance, for example.[36]

These regional differences should not be exaggerated, however. Long-term trends show a narrowing in regional differences on many core beliefs and political attitudes.[37] This is the outcome of years of migration of Americans from one region to another and the rise of a media and entertainment industry that is national in scale, beaming messages and information across regional lines.

## ☐ Education

The level of formal education that people reach is closely related to their income level because education helps people earn more and also because the wealthy can pay for more and better schooling for their children. But education has some distinct political effects of its own.

Education is generally considered the strongest single predictor of participation in politics. College-educated people are much more likely to say that they vote, talk about politics, go to meetings, sign petitions, and write letters to officials than people who have attained only an elementary or a high school education. The highly educated know more about politics. They know what they want and how to go about getting it—joining groups and writing letters, faxes, and e-mail messages to public officials. Within every income stratum of the population, moreover, college-educated people are somewhat more liberal than others on non-economic issues such as race, gay rights, and the environment.[38] They also are more likely than other people in their same income stratum to favor multilateralism in international affairs, favoring the use of diplomacy, multination treaties, and the United Nations to solve global problems.[39]

People who have earned postgraduate degrees also have some distinctive policy preferences. They are especially protective of the civil rights, civil liberties, and individual freedom of atheists, homosexuals, protesters, and dissenters. Education may contribute to tolerance by exposing people to diverse ideas or by training them in elite-backed norms of tolerance.

## ☐ Gender

A partisan "gender gap" first appeared in the 1980s and persists today, with the percentage of women who identify themselves as Democrats about 6 percentage points higher than men (see Figure 5.1). What seems to have been happening is a decline in the proportion of men who identify as Democrats, and a sharp rise in identification as Democrats among unmarried women.[40] The differences show up in elections; in 2012, only 44 percent of women voted for Republican Mitt Romney, compared with 54 percent of men. However, although the partisan gender gap is real and

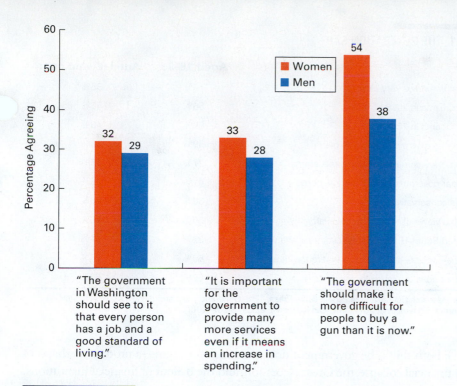

FIGURE 5.3  THE GENDER GAP

*Source:* American National Election Study, (2012).

persistent—women identify more with the Democrats and are more likely to vote for Democratic candidates—the scale of the gap is not enormous, leading some scholars to suggest that the gender gap issue has been exaggerated.[41]

Women also differ somewhat from men in certain policy preferences (see Figure 5.3). Women tend to be somewhat more supportive of protective policies for the poor, the elderly, and the disabled. Women tend to be more opposed to violence, whether by criminals or by the state. More women over the years have opposed capital punishment and the use of military force abroad and favored arms control and peace agreements.[42] Perhaps surprisingly, there is no gender gap on the issue of abortion.[43]

## ☐ Age

Younger citizens are less likely to identify with a political party than older cohorts, although those who do are increasingly leaning toward the Democrats.[44] The young and the old also differ on certain matters that touch their particular interests: the draft in wartime, the drinking age, and, to some extent, Social Security and Medicare. But the chief difference between old and young has to do with the particular era in which they were raised. Those who were young during the 1960s were especially quick to favor civil rights for blacks, for example. In recent years, young people have been especially concerned about environmental issues, and they are much less supportive than other Americans of traditional or conservative social values on homosexuality and the role of women in society. More than any other age cohort, those between the ages of 18 and 34 support the idea of government-sponsored universal health insurance and legalization of same-sex marriage.[45] They were particularly attracted to youthful presidential candidate Barack Obama in 2008 and 2012, with 66 and 60 percent voting for him, respectively ( Table 5.1).

Often social change occurs by generational replacement in which old ideas, like the Depression-era notion that women should stay at home and "not take jobs away from men," die off with old people. But it is worth noting that older Americans are not necessarily entirely fixed in their views; like other Americans, those over the age of 60 have become, over the past decade or so, more tolerant of homosexuality and more supportive of the idea of women pursuing careers.[46] There is no difference between the generations, moreover, on the privileged position of the wealthy in the American political system (see

**TABLE 5.1** THE GENERATION GAP

|  | Aged 18–29 | Aged 65 and over |
|---|---|---|
| Follow election news very closely | 17% | 36% |
| Voted for Obama in 2008 | 66% | 45% |
| Voted for Obama in 2012 | 60% | 46% |
| Favor allowing gays and lesbians to marry | 59% | 33% |
| Agree that "Newcomers threaten our customs." | 27% | 45% |
| Want bigger government, with more services | 41% | 25% |
| Identify as conservatives | 30% | 46% |
| Unfavorable views of the Democratic Party | 36% | 56% |
| "The United States is the greatest country in the world." | 32% | 64% |
| Keep Social Security and Medicare where they are | 53% | 64% |
| Government does too much for the wealthy | 62% | 63% |

*Source:* Pew Research Center for the People & the Press, "The Generation Gap and the 2012 Election," Pew Research Center, November 3, 2011; American National Election Study (2012).

Table 5.1); both think the government does too much for them—a product, perhaps, of the 2008 financial collapse, the Great Recession, and the bailout of financial institutions.

## ☐ Religion

Although religious differences along denominational lines are and have always been important in the United States,[47] the differences between the religiously observant of all denominations and more secular Americans is becoming wider and more central to an understanding of contemporary American politics. We look first at denominational differences, then at what has come to be called the "culture wars."

**RELIGIOUS DENOMINATIONS** Roman Catholics, who constitute about 24 percent of the U.S. population, were heavily Democratic after the New Deal and now identify with Democrats over Republicans by a margin of 48 to 33 percent, a sign, perhaps, of the growing numbers of practicing Catholics of Hispanic dissent in America. (see Figure 5.1).[48] Catholics' economic liberalism has faded somewhat with rises in their income, although this liberalism remains substantial. Catholics have tended to be especially concerned with family issues and to support measures to promote morality (e.g., antipornography laws) and law and order. But American Catholics disagree with many church teachings; they support birth control and the right to have abortions in about the same proportions as other Americans, for example.

A majority of Americans are Protestant. Protestants come in many varieties, however. There are the relatively high-income (socially liberal, economically conservative) Episcopalians and Presbyterians; the generally liberal Unitarian-Universalists and middle-class Northern Baptists; and the lower-income and quite conservative Southern Baptists and evangelicals of various denominations. The sharpest dividing line seems to be that between evangelical Protestants and mainstream Protestants. Evangelicals are much more likely to identify themselves as Republicans than as Democrats, 50 percent compared to 34 percent, whereas members of mainline Protestant churches are pretty evenly split between Republicans and Democrat (see Figure 5.1). Evangelicals and mainstream Protestants also are sharply divided on issues, with evangelicals taking decidedly more conservative positions on homosexuality and abortion.[49] In 2012, evangelicals cast an astounding 79 percent of their votes for Mitt Romney.

A little under 2 percent of Americans are Mormons, members of the fast-growing Church of Jesus Christ of Latter-Day Saints. They are the most staunchly conservative and most solidly Republican of any major religious denomination in the country. Sixty percent claim to be conservative in their political orientation, with only 10 percent choosing liberal. They also favor Republicans over Democrats by a margin of 65 percent to 22 percent. Not surprisingly, two candidates for the 2012 GOP presidential nomination were Mormons, Jon Huntsman and Mitt Romney.

**SHOULDER TO SHOULDER**

Americans who came of age during the civil rights struggles of the 1960s are more likely than others to favor civil rights protections for African Americans. Here, demonstrators march together in Selma, Alabama, in 1965 in support of voting rights for African Americans. Why do relatively short time periods, such as the Great Depression or the civil rights movement, have such a lasting influence on one's political outlook?

American Jews (like Mormons, just under 2 percent of the U.S. population and very much their mirror image politically) began to join the Democratic Party in the 1920s and did so overwhelmingly in the 1930s, in response to Franklin D. Roosevelt's New Deal social policies and his foreign policy of resisting Hitler. Most Jews have stayed with the party. Next to African Americans, they remain the most Democratic group in the United States: about 66 percent identify themselves as Democrats and only 24 percent as Republicans. Jews are exceptionally liberal on social issues, such as civil liberties and abortion. They also tend to be staunch supporters of civil rights. Although rising incomes have somewhat undercut Jews' economic liberalism, they remain substantially more supportive of social welfare policies than other groups. In the 2012 presidential election, Jews cast 69 percent of their votes for Obama and only 30 percent for Romney.

The best estimates are that about 2 percent of people in the United States are Muslim and that most Muslims identify as Democrats. We do know that a high proportion of American Muslims feel discriminated against, are less supportive of state and federal law enforcement agencies, and vote in small numbers in national elections.[50]

People who say they are not affiliated with any religious institution or belief system at all are strongly Democratic in their party identification and relatively liberal on most social issues; 55 percent are Democrats and 23 percent are Republicans. Seventy percent of the unaffiliated say that abortion should always be legal or legal most of the time. Seventy-one percent of them agree with the statement that "homosexuality should be accepted by society."

## RELIGIOUSLY COMMITTED VERSUS THE LESS COMMITTED AND SECULAR

Among the factors that most differentiate Americans on political attitudes and partisanship is their degree of religious belief and practice.[51] The religiously

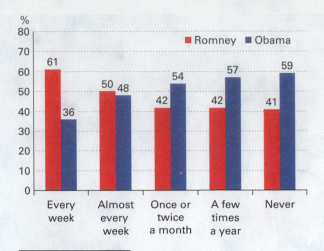

**FIGURE 5.4** CHURCH ATTENDANCE AND THE VOTE IN THE 2012 PRESIDENTIAL ELECTION (PERCENTAGE VOTING FOR EACH CANDIDATE)

*Source:* American National Election Study (2012).

committed, no matter the religious denomination, are the most likely Americans to vote Republican and to hold conservative views, particularly on social issues such as abortion, the death penalty, same-sex marriage, and stem cell research. Committed and observant Catholics, Jews, and Protestants are not only much more Republican and socially conservative than people who practice no religion and/or claim to be totally secular, but they are also more Republican and socially conservative than their less committed and observant co-religionists. Taking all denominations together, to look at another example of how relative religious commitment matters, the "churched" are far more likely to vote Republican than those who are less "churched" or who don't go to church (or synagogue or mosque) at all (see Figure 5.4). In 2012, about 60 percent of people who reported attending religious services every week voted for Romney. Among those who reported attending services only a few times a year or never, Obama won about 60 percent of the vote.

The gap between the religiously committed and other Americans—particularly those who say they never or almost never go to church—on matters of party identification, votes in elections, and attitudes about social issues has become so wide and the debates so fierce that many have come to talk about America's culture wars. On a range of issues—including Supreme Court appointments, abortion, the rights of gays and lesbians, prayer in the public schools, and the teaching of evolution—passions on both sides of the divide have reached what can only be called white-hot fever pitch. To be sure, much of the noise in the culture wars is being generated by leaders of and activists in religiously affiliated organizations and advocacy groups, exaggerating, perhaps, the degree to which most Americans disagree on most core beliefs and political attitudes.[52] But, the battle between the most and least religiously observant and committed has helped heat up the passions in American politics because each group has gravitated to one or the other political party—the former to the Republicans and the latter to the Democrats—and become among the strongest campaign activists and financial contributors within them.[53]

# ☐ Party

People who say they are Democrats differ considerably in their political attitudes from those who say they are Republicans. More than any other factor, one's political party identification structures how one sees the world, helps interpret what is going on in political life in the country, and determines which government polices one will support.[54] Much more than in the past, Republicans are more likely than Democrats to vote for Republican candidates and approve of Republican presidents; they tend

**LIBERAL BELIEVERS**

Although they are a distinct minority among believers, there is an increasing number of religiously committed people in all denominations who take liberal positions on matters such as global warming, economic inequality, poverty and its alleviation, and gay rights. Here, believers demonstrate in support of same-sex marriage in front of the state capitol in Olympia, Washington. How does this affect your view of religion as it relates to important public policies?

to belong to different social and economic groups; and they are more likely to favor policies associated with the Republican Party. Republicans are much more likely than Democrats to support big business and an assertive national security policy, and to be against stem-cell research, same-sex marriage, and abortions, for example; Democrats are much more likely than Republicans to support government programs to help the poor and to help racial minorities get ahead, to regulate business for consumer protection and greenhouse gas emissions, and to support gay rights and abortion on demand. Table 5.2 shows big differences on some of the major issues of the day between Republicans and Democrats. Figure 5.5 shows that the differences between them are growing ever wider. Republicans and Democrats face each other today across a wide chasm, particularly among the most committed and active among them.

**TABLE 5.2** PARTISANSHIP AND ISSUE POSITIONS

| Survey Statement | Percent Agreeing with Survey Statement | |
|---|---|---|
| | Democrats | Republicans |
| Favor reducing the federal deficit | 69% | 81% |
| Think that the federal government should spend more on Social Security | 58% | 39% |
| Think that gay and lesbian couples should be allowed to legally marry | 56% | 19% |
| Feel that it is extremely important being an American | 50% | 69% |
| Think that immigration levels should be decreased | 36% | 52% |
| Think that abortion should never be permitted or only be permitted in cases of rape, incest, or when the women's life is in danger | 27% | 57% |
| Favor allowing universities to increase enrollment of African Americans at their schools by considering race along with other factors on admission | 24% | 6% |

*Source:* American National Election Study (2012).

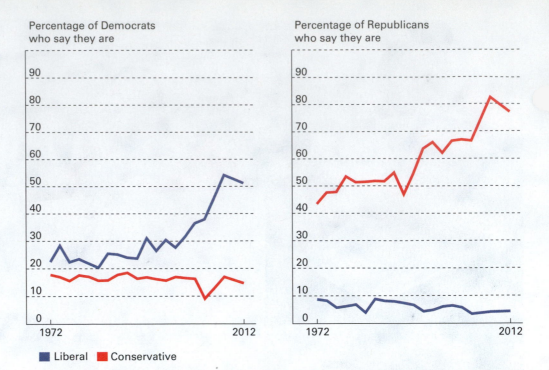

Percentage of Democrats who say they are

Percentage of Republicans who say they are

■ Liberal  ■ Conservative

**FIGURE 5.5**  TRENDS IN THE RELATIONSHIP BETWEEN PARTY IDENTIFICATION AND POLITICAL IDEOLOGY

Party identification and political ideology are becoming more closely related. Republican identifiers, more conservative than Democratic Party identifiers anyway, are becoming dramatically more conservative. At the same time, Democratic Party identifiers are becoming more liberal. The deep divide that reflects the confluence of parties and ideologies has become a key feature of modern American politics and contributes to much of the incivility and intensity of public affairs in recent years.

*Source:* American National Election Studies (1972–2012).

# The Contours of American Public Opinion: Are the People Fit to Rule?

**5.5**  Assess the American public's ability to rule

 ow that we know more about how public opinion is measured and why people hold certain core beliefs and political attitudes, we can return to the issue raised in the opening pages of this chapter concerning the place of public opinion in a society that aspires to be a democracy. Recall from the earlier discussion that many observers of American politics in the past and today have had little confidence in the abilities of the average person to understand vital public issues or to rationally engage in public affairs. If, as they have feared, ordinary citizens are uninformed, prone to rapid and irrational changes in their political attitudes, and easily led astray, there is not much reason to assume that public opinion can or ought to play a central role in deciding what government should do. However, as we will see in this section, further examination of the opinions of ordinary Americans and how they change in response to events and new information will demonstrate that such fears about an uninformed and irrational public may have been exaggerated.

## ☐ What People Know About Politics

Several decades of polling have shown that most ordinary Americans do not know or care a lot about politics.[55] Nearly everyone knows some basic facts, such as the name of the capital of the United States and the length of the president's term of office. But only about two-thirds of adults know which party has the most members in the House of Representatives. Only about 30 percent know that the term of a U.S. House member is two years; only about one-half know that there are two U.S. senators from their state.[56] And barely one in four Americans can explain what is in the First Amendment. Furthermore, people have particular trouble with technical terms, geography, abbreviations, and acronyms like NATO (the North Atlantic Treaty Organization) and NAFTA (the North American Free Trade Agreement). Americans don't have detailed knowledge, moreover, about important public policies and the way our economic system works. For example, in 2014, only 20 percent of Americans knew that the federal government spends more on Social Security than on foreign aid, transportation, or interest on the national debt.[57] People also consistently and dramatically underestimate the degree of income and wealth inequality that exists in the United States and fail to understand how things like tax policies affect who gets what in American society.[58] Many Americans do not even know they are involved in a government program and receive benefits from it, including many young people who participate in one of the several student loan programs.[59] Forty-four percent of Social Security beneficiaries and 40 percent of those covered by Medicare do not realize they are using a government program.[60] And, despite the explosion of information sources—including the Internet and 24-hour cable news—there has been no improvement in Americans' political knowledge over the past two decades.[61]

Some have argued that things that most Americans don't know may not be vital to their role as citizens, however. If citizens are aware that trade restrictions with Canada and Mexico have been eased, does it matter that they recognize the acronym NAFTA? How important is it for people to know about the two-year term of office for the U.S. House of Representatives, as long as they are aware of the opportunity to vote each time it comes along? Perhaps most people know as much as they need to know in order to be good citizens, particularly if they can form opinions with the help of better-informed cue givers (experts, political leaders, media sources, informed friends, interest groups, and so on) whom they trust or by means of simple rules of thumb that simplify and make the political world more coherent and understandable.[62]

To be sure, there are consequences that flow from people's lack of political knowledge and attention. When policy decisions are made in the dark, out of public view, interest groups often influence policies that an informed public might oppose. Nor do we mean to encourage complacency, fatalism, or ignorance. Individuals should take the personal responsibility to be good citizens, and organized efforts to alert and to educate the public are valuable. But low levels of information and attention are a reality that must be taken into account. Perhaps it is unrealistic to expect everyone to have a detailed knowledge of a wide range of political matters.

By the same token, we perhaps should not expect the average American to have an elaborately worked-out **political ideology**, a coherent system of interlocking attitudes and beliefs about politics, the economy, and the role of government. You yourself may be a consistent liberal or conservative (or populist, socialist, libertarian, or something else), with many opinions that hang together in a coherent pattern. But surveys show that most people's attitudes are only loosely connected to each other. Most people have opinions that vary from one issue to another: conservative on some issues, liberal on others. Surveys and in-depth interviews indicate that these are often linked by underlying themes and values, but not necessarily in the neat ways that the ideologies of leading political thinkers would dictate.[63] Often, issues are not thought through very well. One recent *New York Times* poll discovered that many critics of government benefit programs, such as Social Security, Medicare, food stamps, and unemployment insurance, receive benefits from these very same programs but are unable to recognize or explain the evident contradiction.[64]

For the same reasons, we should not be surprised that most individuals' expressed opinions on issues tend to be unstable. Many people give different answers when the

**political ideology**
A system of interrelated and coherently organized political beliefs and attitudes.

**5.1**

**5.2**

**5.3**

**5.4**

**5.5**

**collective public opinion**
The political attitudes of the public as a whole, expressed as averages, percentages, or other summaries of many individuals' opinions.

**rational public**
The notion that collective public opinion is rational in the sense that it is generally stable and consistent and that when it changes it does so as an understandable response to events, to changing circumstances, and to new information.

same survey question is repeated four years or two years or even a few weeks after their first response. Scholars have disagreed about what these unstable responses mean, but uncertainty and lack of information very likely play a part.

Even if the evidence leads you to the conclusion that individual Americans are politically uninformed and disengaged, it does not necessarily follow that you must take the position that the opinions of the public, taken as a whole, are unreal, unstable, or irrelevant. We would suggest that the *collective whole* is greater than its individual parts in this case. Here is why: even if there is some randomness in the average individual's expressions of political opinions—even if people often say things off the top of their heads to survey interviewers—the responses of thousands or millions of people tend to average out this randomness and reveal a stable **collective public opinion**. Americans' collective policy preferences are actually very stable over time. That is, the percentage of Americans who favor a particular policy usually stays about the same, unless circumstances change in important ways, such as a major war or economic depression. Moreover, even if most people form many of their specific opinions by deferring to others whom they trust (party leaders, television commentators, and the like) rather than by compiling their own mass of political information, the resulting public opinion need not be ignorant or unwise because the trusted leaders may themselves take account of the best available information. Finally, there is mounting evidence that indicates that Americans' collective policy preferences react rather sensibly to events, to changing circumstances, and to the quality of the information that is available to them, so that we can speak of a **rational public**.[65] So, at the individual level, we may not be impressed with the capacities or rationality of the public. But when we aggregate individual attitudes and understandings, that is, put them together and look at the average of public opinion over time, we are on somewhat firmer ground in suggesting a sort of public rationality.[66]

## ☐ Attitudes About the System in General

At the most general level, Americans are proud of their country and its political institutions. In 2013, for example, 85 percent of Americans said they were either very or extremely proud to be an American.[67] In a survey a few years earlier, only 43 percent of British, 33 percent of French, and 23 percent of Germans said the same about their own countries.[68] In 2011, about one-half of Americans said they believed "our culture is superior to others," compared to only a little more than one-fourth of the French.[69] Additionally, about 7 in 10 Americans say they feel it is important to vote.[70]

However, there are indications that Americans have become more pessimistic about the ability of the country to solve its problems. There are any number of ways to see evidence of rising pessimism. There is, first, the steady decline in what pollsters and public opinion scholars call "trust in government." The Pew Research Center, for example, reporting results from its own polls and other leading surveys, put the level of "trust in government"—those who say they trust government to do the right thing "always" or "most of the time"—at around 19 percent in 2013, down from the 40 percent average for most of the 1980s, and the 70 percent trust in government levels during the 1960s (see Figure 5.6).[71] This is perhaps no surprise given the wars in Iraq and Afghanistan, the decades-long stagnation in income for most Americans and rise in income and wealth inequality, the Great Recession and slow job recovery, mounting evidence of partisan gridlock in our political system, and difficulties with the rollout of Obamacare.

Another standard way that both pollsters and scholars assess the general mood of the country is questions that ask about whether we are moving in the right or wrong direction. In early 2014, Gallup reported that fully 73 percent of Americans were "dissatisfied with the way things are going in the United States at this time," a finding consistent with the results from other polling organizations.[72] Again, this is hardly surprising given that the country then was still mired in a deep economic slump and the political establishment in Washington

**FIGURE 5.6** PUBLIC TRUST IN GOVERNMENT

*Source:* Pew Research Center for the People & the Press, "Trust in Government, 1958–2013," Pew Research Center, October 18, 2013, based on polling by Gallup, the Pew Research Center, National Election Studies, ABC/Washington Post, CBS/New York Times, and CNN.

remained deadlocked on what to do about the budget and to create jobs. (See the "Can Government Do Anything Well?" feature so you can judge whether Americans' lack of confidence is justified in light of what government has done in the area of financial regulation.)

One important aspect of happiness or unhappiness with government is a judgment about how well Congress is doing. For much of the past four decades or so, the proportion of Americans disapproving of the job Congress is doing has been twice as high as the proportion approving. Things became especially bad for Congress in the last year of the Bush administration when unpopular bailouts of financial institutions were approved. By the end of 2013, Congress's approval had dropped to 12 percent.[73] In fact, one poll conducted in 2013 found that Americans reported having a higher opinion of cockroaches, root canals, lice, and traffic jams than of Congress.[74]

Another indicator of government performance is how well Americans judge the president has been doing his job. The public's evaluations of presidents' handling of their jobs depend on how well things are actually going. The state of the economy is especially important: when the country is prosperous and ordinary Americans are doing well and feeling confident about the future, the president tends to be popular; when there is high inflation or unemployment or when general living standards remain stagnant, the president's popularity falls. Pollsters have been asking Americans for many decades whether they approve or disapprove of the way the president is doing his job. The percentage of people saying they approve—the **presidential job approval rating**—is taken as a crucial indicator of a president's popularity. Job approval fluctuates up and down with particular events and trends—Lyndon Johnson's approval fluctuated with events in Vietnam, and he decided not to run for reelection when his ratings fell to historic lows after the Tet Offensive—but in the current era, most presidents have come on hard times. Richard Nixon, Gerald Ford, and Jimmy Carter all had low approval ratings by the end of their terms. George H. W. Bush reached a then-record 89 percent approval in March 1991 in the aftermath of the Gulf War but fell below 30 percent by the summer, an unprecedented collapse. Oddly, Bill Clinton enjoyed the highest job approval ratings of any recent president for the final two years of the presidential term, in spite of the fact that he was impeached by the

**presidential job approval rating**
A president's standing with the public, indicated by the percentage of Americans who tell survey interviewers that they approve a president's "handling of his job."

# Can Government Do Anything Well?

## Regulating the Financial System

Following the Great Depression, the U.S. government increased its regulatory capacity in the financial system, most importantly separating banking and investment functions in financial institutions so that such institutions could not gamble with other people's savings. Government regulation is generally credited with successfully preventing large-scale financial collapses until the spectacular failure in 2008. Most economists believe that the deregulation of the financial industry in the 1990s, engineered by lobbyists for the financial industry and Republican and Democratic elected officials who believed that regulation was stifling financial innovations like derivatives and mortgage-backed securities, was decisive in the collapse, allowing reckless behavior by financial institutions that fueled the crisis. Repeal of the Depression-era Glass-Steagall Act in 1999 was the final step in a series of deregulatory steps.

Interestingly, the deregulation of the financial industry in the 1990s was done largely out of public view. Public opinion did not drive the change nor did polling show much public interest in the matter at the time. Furthermore, while the public remained angry with Wall Street after the 2008 financial collapse and the Great Recession associated with it, much of the public reserved its anger for the government. The narrative, that is to say, switched from the bad behavior of Wall Street to the incompetence or indifference of government, with the Obama administration getting much of the blame. Gallup reported in 2011, for example, that 70 percent of Americans believed that "government creates more problems than it solves." This probably was the result of the quick recovery of financial firms (and the big bonuses they paid their top people) coupled with the agonizingly slow and jobless economic recovery in the country, even after the large stimulus bill passed in early 2009. In this atmosphere of antigovernment sentiment and in the absence of public attention to the fine details of governing, Republicans in Congress were able to extract cuts to the budgets of financial industry regulatory watchdogs such as the Securities and Exchange Commission and the Commodities Futures Trading Commission as part of the deal to end the budget ceiling crisis in 2011.

*Support for the claim that government should play a significantly larger role today in regulating the financial system:*

- Financial instruments have become so complex that regulations are needed to increase transparency so that Wall Street firms, investors, consumers, and regulators can more accurately determine the real value and assess the risk of securities, including derivatives, mortgage-backed securities, collateralized debt obligations, credit default swaps, and the like.

- Financial institutions should keep higher capital reserves on hand so they can pay off their creditors when crises hit—thus avoiding "too big to fail" bailouts—and be required to invest more of their own money in potentially risky investments so they will not be tempted to play only with other people's and firms' money. This will make them more prudent.

*Rejection of the claim that government should play a significantly larger role in regulating the financial system:*

- There are already enough regulations and regulators. Regulators simply didn't do their jobs in the years leading up to the financial collapse. In fact, in the view of Cato-associated commentators, the failure of regulators to do their jobs was a prime cause of the collapse.

- More regulations and regulators will not only fail to enhance the safety and transparency of the financial system but will stifle innovation in the industry and encourage financial firms and the most talented individuals to go elsewhere.

- Markets are self-correcting. Government should stay out of the industry.

## WHAT DO YOU THINK?

What do you think about the past, present, and future role of the government in regulating the financial sector? Which of the following positions is closest to your own?

- Government deregulation was the principle cause of the financial collapse of 2008 and it is only with new regulations that the financial system can be stabilized and economic growth can take off.
- Government deregulation was one of the causes of the financial collapse, and some regulation, better executed, must be part of the solution.
- Government deregulation of the financial industry will hurt innovation and slow economic recovery.

How would you defend your position to a fellow student in this class? What would be your main line of argument? What evidence do you believe best supports your position?

**SOURCE:** Crotty, J. (2009, April 30). Structural causes of the global financial crisis: a critical assessment of the "new financial architecture." *Cambridge Journal of Economics 33*(4), 563–580. Retrieved from cje.oxfordjournals.org////.short.

**SOURCE:** Strahan, P. E. (2002, September). The Real Effects of U.S. Banking Deregulation. *Financial Institutions Center–Wharton School of Business*, 2–39. Retrieved from fic.wharton.upenn.edu////.pdf.

**POPULAR TO THE END**

Despite his tumultuous presidency and efforts by Republicans in Congress to remove him from office, Bill Clinton's approval rating among the American public at the end of his presidency was higher than that of any president since the end of World War II, with the exception of Eisenhower. Ronald Reagan came close, but still trailed Clinton. How can a president retain such popularity in the face of such conflict?

Republican-controlled House of Representatives. George W. Bush's 90 percent job approval in late 2001 broke his father's record. By fall 2008, however, Bush's approval hovered in the mid-20s, the lowest presidential approval ratings in 50 years. President Barack Obama began his term in early 2009 with a job approval rating in the mid-60s; by fall 2014 his approval had fallen to the low 40s—a lack of popularity that likely contributed to Democratic losses in the mid-term elections.[75]

These trends in trust in government, the direction of the country, and evaluations of the job performance of Congress and the president by the public seem perfectly sensible and rational. They reflect the difficulties many Americans have been living through, news media attention to the country's economic downturn and Washington's governing problems, and the ferocious manner in which the parties have waged political combat over the causes and solutions to the nation's problems.

With the rise of the Tea Party, pessimism about government and the economy and discomfiture with the direction of the country turned into outright anger. Adherents have said they are angry about illegal immigrants, government deficits, bailouts and loan guarantees to financial institutions, and a growing national government involved in everything from owning financial institutions and auto companies to mandating health insurance coverage. Much like earlier manifestations of populist-style anger, cultural, media, and academic elites are handy targets for seemingly supporting many of the disruptive changes in the country. And they were particularly exercised about programs that, in their view, direct government benefits to the "undeserving," those unwilling to work or who have just come into the country.[76] Though the Tea Party movement was encouraged and partially organized by conservative talk radio and cable television personalities such as Glenn Beck on Fox News, its rise reflects real concerns about the state of matters in the country for many people. Their enthusiastic support of the Republican Party in 2010—and a lack of similar enthusiasm among groups in the Democratic Party base—helped the GOP make historic gains in that year's national, state, and local elections.

**5.1**

**5.2**

**5.3**

**5.4**

**5.5**

**economic conservatives**
People who favor private enterprise and oppose government regulation of business.

**economic liberals**
People who favor government regulation of business to protect the public from harm, and government spending for social programs.

**social (lifestyle) liberals**
People who favor civil liberties, abortion rights, and alternative lifestyles.

**social (lifestyle) conservatives**
People who favor traditional social values; they tend to support strong law-and-order measures and oppose abortion and gay rights.

In 2011, populist anger took shape on the left of the political spectrum with the rise and rapid spread of the Occupy Wall Street movement. Though their overall message was less than crystal clear given the spontaneity of the movement and the many groups involved in it, in the end it was mostly a protest about rising income and wealth inequality in the country, high unemployment, and sluggish job growth, particularly for young people. Unlike the Tea Party, this movement wants government to do more.

## ☐ Liberals and Conservatives

Although most Americans do not adhere to a rigid political ideology of the sort beloved by political philosophers or adhered to by many people around the world—for example, Marxism, communism, socialism, fascism, anarchism, radical political Islam, and the like—they do divide on the role they believe government should play. To complicate matters, Americans generally divide along two dimensions when it comes to government: one related to government's role in the economy, the other related to government's role in society. Some Americans—those we usually label **economic conservatives**—tend to put more emphasis on economic liberty and freedom from government interference; they believe that a free market offers the best road to economic efficiency and a decent society. Others—whom we usually label **economic liberals**—stress the necessary role of government in ensuring equality of opportunity, regulating potentially damaging business practices, and providing safety nets for individuals unable to compete in the job market. Government regulation of the economy and spending to help the disadvantaged are two of the main sources of political disputes in America; they make up a big part of the difference between the ideologies of liberalism and of conservatism. However, this accounts for only one of the two dimensions. It is also useful to distinguish between **social (or lifestyle) liberals** and **social (or lifestyle) conservatives**, who differ on such issues as abortion, prayer in the schools, homosexuality, pornography, crime, and political dissent. Those who favor free choices and the rights of the accused are often said to be liberals, while those preferring government enforcement of order and traditional values are called conservatives (see Table 5.3).

It should be apparent that opinions on economic and social issues do not necessarily go together. Many people are liberal in some ways but conservative in others. A gay activist, for example, would likely be a social liberal, but might also be a small business owner who is an economic conservative when it comes to taxes and regulation of business. An evangelical minister preaching in a poor community might be a social conservative on issues such as homosexuality and

**TABLE 5.3** POSITIONING PROMINENT AMERICANS

| | Economic Liberal | Economic Conservative |
|---|---|---|
| | (favors more government regulation of business to protect the environment and consumers, more progressive taxes, and more programs to help low-income Americans) | (favors less government involvement in economy and society, leaving more to the private sector) |
| **Social Liberal** | | |
| (favors the right to abortion, more rights for gays and lesbians, more civil rights protections for minorities, and separation of church and state) | Barack Obama Nancy Pelosi | Gary Johnson Ron Paul |
| **Social Conservative** | | |
| (against abortion, supports traditional families and gender roles, favors more religious practices in public life) | Rev. Rick Warren Bart Stupak | Ronald Reagan Rick Santorum |

pornography but an economic liberal when it comes to government programs to help the disadvantaged.

**policy preferences**
Citizens' ideas about what policies they want government to pursue.

5.1

5.2

5.3

5.4

5.5

## ☐ Policy Preferences

According to democratic theory, one of the chief determinants of what governments do should be what the citizens *want* them to do, that is, citizens' **policy preferences**. We see in Figures 5.7 and 5.8 that public opinion on what government should do is either relatively unchanging or has changed because of fairly well, understood developments in American society.

**SPENDING PROGRAMS**  By and large, while more Americans say they are conservative or moderate than say they are liberal, many want government to do a great deal to address societal needs. One might say that a majority of Americans are philosophical conservatives and moderates but operational liberals. Figure 5.7 shows Americans have been consistent over the years in their positions on a range of things they want from government. We can see that large and rather stable numbers of Americans think we are spending "too little" on fighting crime, providing health insurance, and other government services. Many polls show that the public also gives consistent supermajority support to Social Security, Medicare, and environmental protection programs. Substantial majorities, moreover, have said for many years that they want the government to pay for more research on diseases such as cancer and AIDS and to "see to it" that everyone who wants to work can find a job.

By contrast, few people think too little is being spent on foreign aid; many more think too much is being spent. Except for disaster relief, such as for the 2010 Haitian earthquake disaster, foreign aid is generally unpopular. (The reason may be, in part, that few realize how little is spent on foreign aid—only about 1 percent of the annual federal budget is devoted to economic and humanitarian assistance; when this is made clear, support for economic aid rises sharply.[77]) Large majorities of the public oppose military aid or arms sales abroad.

When public opinion changes, it usually does so for perfectly understandable reasons. After the financial collapse in September 2008, more Americans than before said

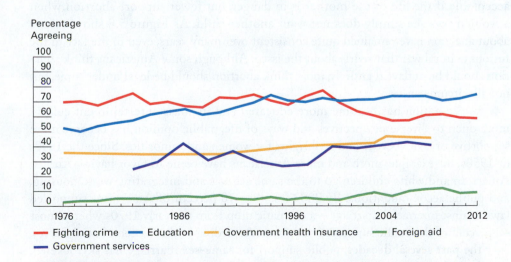

Percentage Agreeing

1976  1986  1996  2004  2012

— Fighting crime  — Education  — Government health insurance  — Foreign aid
— Government services

**FIGURE 5.7** PUBLIC SUPPORT FOR INCREASED GOVERNMENT SPENDING PROGRAMS

Large, fairly stable majorities of Americans have favored increased spending for fighting crime, aiding education, and government health insurance, but very few have favored increased foreign aid over the years (though support increased after 2000).

*Source:* The American National Election Studies, Aug. 23, 2010; General Social Survey, Cumulative Data File (1972–2012).

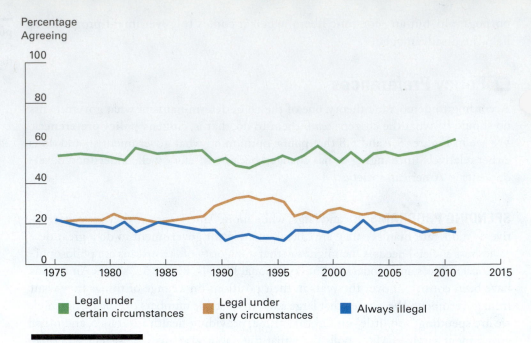

Percentage
Agreeing

**Legal under certain circumstances**

**Legal under any circumstances**

**Always illegal**

**FIGURE 5.8** VIEWS ABOUT ABORTION

Only a minority of Americans supports or rejects abortion under any and all circumstances. For a long time now, a majority of Americans have said they believe abortion should be legal, but only under certain circumstances.

*Sources:* General Social Survey and the Pew Research Center.

they wanted the government to increase regulation of the industry whose unregulated bets and speculation helped bring on the Great Recession. In 2010, 61 percent said they wanted to see the industry more closely regulated.[78]

**SOCIAL ISSUES**  As Figure 5.8 shows, Americans make distinctions among different circumstances when deciding whether they favor permitting abortions. For much of the past three decades, a majority of Americans have reported that they support the legality of abortion under certain circumstances. Thus, more are likely to find abortion acceptable if the life of the mother is in danger, but fewer support abortion when a woman says she simply does not want another child. As Figure 5.8 shows, views about abortion have remained quite consistent over many years, even in the face of the furious cultural war that swirls about the issue. Although some Americans think abortion should be outlawed entirely, most think abortion should be legal under some, but not all, circumstances.

As the nation has become more educated and its mass entertainment culture more open to diverse perspectives and ways of life, public opinion has become more supportive of civil liberties and civil rights for women and minorities. Since the 1940s or 1950s, for example, more and more Americans have come to favor having African American and white children go to the same schools and integrating work, housing, and public accommodations. By 2002 less than 10 percent of Americans supported laws against interracial marriage—a dramatic drop from the early 1970s when almost 40 percent of the public supported such bans. According to the General Social Survey, over the past several decades, public support for same-sex marriage has skyrocketed, from only 12 percent supporting it in 1988 to 49 percent supporting it in 2012. By early 2014 surveys indicated that a majority of the public—as much as 55 percent—supported same-sex marriage.[79]

On a number of issues, Americans support positions favored by social conservatives. Large majorities, for example, have consistently favored allowing organized prayer in the public schools, banning pornography, preventing flag burning, penalizing drug use, punishing crimes severely, and imposing capital punishment for murder. Moreover, 62 percent of Americans said in 2010 that they approved police questioning of anyone they suspected of being in the country illegally, the heart of the controversial law passed in Arizona; this section was upheld by the Supreme Court in 2012.[80]

**FOREIGN POLICY AND NATIONAL SECURITY** In the realm of foreign policy and national security, public opinion sometimes changes rapidly in response to crises and other dramatic events. Major international events affect opinions, as we saw in the chapter-opening story on public reactions to the Tet Offensive during the Vietnam War. The percentage of Americans saying we were wrong to invade Iraq steadily increased as the news from there got worse. Confidence in the effectiveness of American foreign and military policies declined sharply between 2005 and 2007.[81] This seems understandable given events on the ground. But often foreign policy opinions are quite stable. Since World War II, for example, two-thirds or more of those giving an opinion have usually said that the United States should take an "active part" in world affairs. The percentage supporting a U.S. role has remained relatively high, but declined somewhat by 2011.[82]

The public has been quite hesitant to use troops abroad, however, unless the threat to the United States is tangible. Just before U.S. troops were sent as peacekeepers to Bosnia in 1994, for example, 56 percent of the public opposed the idea and only 39 percent were in favor.[83] Opposition faded as the operation began to look less risky. The public strongly supported the use of the military to destroy Al Qaeda and the Taliban regime in Afghanistan[84] and initially supported President Bush's decision to invade Iraq in 2003, when only 23 percent of those surveyed said the United States "made a mistake sending troops to Iraq." By summer 2010, the proportion of the public who thought it was a mistake had soared to 55 percent.[85] Support for the armed conflict in Afghanistan was low by mid-2014, about thirteen years after it began; only 27 percent of Americans said it was "worth fighting."[86]

Although not many Americans embrace pure **isolationism**—the view that the United States should not be involved abroad and should only pay attention to its own affairs—the public (and political and economic leaders, as well) is divided over whether its involvement in the world should take a **unilateralist** or a **multilateralist** form. Unilateralists want to go it alone, taking action when it suits our purposes, and not necessarily seeking the approval or help of international organizations such as the United Nations or regional organizations such as NATO. Unilateralists are also uncomfortable with entering into too many international treaties. Multilateralists believe that the protection of American interests requires continuous engagement in the world, but do not think that the United States has the resources or ability to accomplish its ends without the cooperation of other nations and with international and regional organizations. According to most surveys, roughly two out of three Americans are in the multilateralist camp, telling pollsters they oppose unilateral U.S. military intervention in most cases and support cooperation with the United Nations and NATO and international treaties on human rights, the environment, and arms control. In this regard, they are considerably more multilateralist than American legislative and executive branch officials.[87]

## ☐ The People's "Fitness to Rule" Revisited

This examination of collective public opinion, its evident stability on a wide range of issues over time, and why it sometimes changes on some issues leads us to conclude that confidence in the role of the public in the American political system is warranted.

**isolationism**
The policy of avoiding undue involvement in the affairs of other countries and multilateral institutions.

**unilateralist**
The stance toward foreign policy that suggests that the United States should "go it alone," pursuing its national interests without seeking the cooperation of other nations or multilateral institutions.

**multilateralist**
The stance toward foreign policy which suggests that the United States should seek the cooperation of other nations and multilateral institutions in pursuing its goals.

5.1

5.2

5.3

5.4

5.5

The evidence demonstrates that collective public opinion is quite stable and sensible when it comes to core beliefs and attitudes about government, the parties, and policy preferences.[88] The evidence further shows that when collective public opinion does change, it does so for perfectly understandable reasons: dramatic events, new information, or changes in perspective among American leaders. The conclusion we draw is a simple yet powerful one: the American people are fit to rule. The next question to address is whether the people, in fact, do rule.

# Using the DEMOCRACY STANDARD

## Do the public's opinions determine what government does?

We have argued that a crucial test of how well democracy is working is how closely a government's policies match the expressed wishes of its citizens over time. Do the actions of the U.S. government match what collective public opinion says it wants government to do? Some scholars claim that yes, the government generally acts in ways that reflect public opinion. But others argue that public officials sometimes ignore public opinion; that public opinion is often heavily manipulated by government leaders so that it tends to reflect rather than influence government action; and that the public is inattentive and has no opinions on many important policy issues, leaving political leaders free to act on their own. In the remainder of this chapter, we'll take a look at just how much of an impact public opinion has on government action, and consider whether public opinion works in the United States to make our system more democratic.

## The case for saying that public opinion substantially determines what government does

As our opening story about the Vietnam War suggests, at least under some circumstances, public opinion significantly affects policymaking by government leaders (see Figure 5.9). We have encountered other examples that tell the same "government responsiveness" story in this book. President Bush's attempt to alter Social Security in 2005, for example, was blocked by congressional opponents backstopped by strong public support for the current system.

These stories about government responsiveness to public opinion have been buttressed by important scholarly assessments that indicate a strong statistical correlation between public opinion and government action.[89] Looking at many different policy issues—foreign and domestic—one scholar found, for example, that about two-thirds of the time, U.S. government policy coincides with what opinion surveys say the public wants. The same two-thirds correspondence has appeared when other scholars investigated how *changes* in public opinion relate to changes in federal, state, and local policies. Moreover, when public opinion changes by a substantial and enduring amount and the issue is prominent, government policy has moved in the same direction as the public 87 percent of the time within a year or so afterward.[90] Yet another influential study shows that substantial swings in the national political mood have occurred over the past half century or so and that public policy has followed accordingly. As the American people have moved first in a liberal direction, then a conservative direction, and back again over the years, elected leaders in Washington have shaped their policies to fit the public mood, being more activist in liberal periods and less activist in conservative periods.[91] Finally, after carefully reviewing the results of 30 studies, one scholar concludes that public opinion almost always has some effect on what government does, and when an issue is visible and important to the people, public opinion is the decisive factor in determining the substance of government policy.[92]

## Not so fast; when public opinion only *seems* to shape what government does

Although these studies seem to lend substantial support for the idea that public opinion is a powerful determinant of what government does in the United States, showing a strong statistical correlation between public opinion and government policy does not prove that public opinion *causes* government policies. There are any number of plausible reasons why a "causal relationship" may not really exist. Here is what the critics say:[93]

- It may be the case that public opinion and government policies move in the same direction because some third factor, usually interest groups or the news media, causes both of them to change in similar directions. (See Figure 5.9.) In this example, the true cause of government action is this third factor, not public opinion. There are many real-world instances in which this has happened. For example, the news media often play up a particular incident or situation and persuade both public opinion and government policymakers that action is needed. Thus the public and various government officials became interested in the near-genocidal situation in the Darfur region of Sudan in the mid-2000s after news networks and major newspapers highlighted the story.[94] Or interest groups may simultaneously sway public opinion and government officials in the same direction, as medical, insurance, and hospital associations did when they launched a successful campaign to sink Bill Clinton's health care initiative in 1994. Or to take another example, financial industry groups persuaded both the public and government leaders that deregulating the industry would be a good thing, which happened throughout the 1990s, with well-known disastrous results in 2008 when financial institutions collapsed.

- Even if public opinion and government actions are highly correlated, it may be the case that political leaders shape public opinion, not the other way around. (See Figure 5.9.) In statistical language, we might say that the causal arrow is reversed, going not from the public to government, but the reverse: that officials act to gain popular support for policies and actions these officials want.[95] Such efforts can range from outright manipulation of the public—the Tonkin Gulf incident described in the opening story in this chapter is such a case; some would claim that the use of the "weapons of mass destruction" rhetoric to raise support for the invasion of Iraq in 2003 is another compelling case[96]—to the conventional public relations efforts carried out every day by government officials and

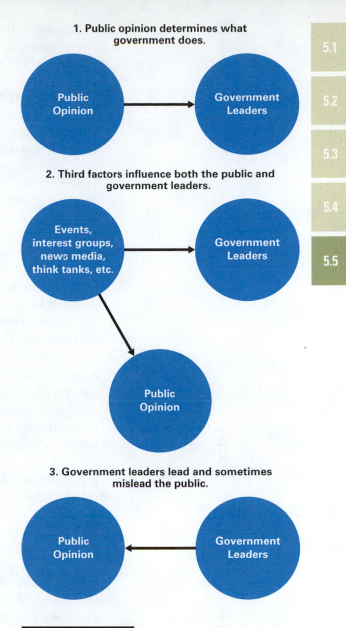

1. **Public opinion determines what government does.**

Public Opinion → Government Leaders

2. **Third factors influence both the public and government leaders.**

Events, interest groups, news media, think tanks, etc. → Government Leaders

Events, interest groups, news media, think tanks, etc. → Public Opinion

3. **Government leaders lead and sometimes mislead the public.**

Government Leaders → Public Opinion

**FIGURE 5.9** PUBLIC OPINION'S ROLE IN DECIDING WHAT GOVERNMENT DOES, ALTERNATIVE SCENARIOS

agencies. This is why both the legislative and executive branches of the federal government are so well equipped with communications offices, press secretaries, and public liaison personnel.

**THE MIXED REALITY** So where does all of this leave us on the question of public opinion's influence on government? It is probably reasonable to say that public opinion often plays an important role in shaping what government does: political leaders seem to pay attention to public opinion when they are in the midst of deciding on alternative courses of action. Some would argue that they do entirely too much of this, in fact, pandering to the whims of the public rather than exercising leadership. This desire to find out what the public thinks and what it wants is why congressional incumbents, candidates for office, presidents, and government agencies spend so much time and money polling their relevant constituencies. And it is no mystery why elected officials do this, as do their challengers: public opinion is eventually translated into votes at election time. So, staying on the right side of public opinion—giving people what they want in terms of policies—is how people gain and keep elected offices.

But the public does not always pay attention or have an opinion about important matters. This has led scholars to suggest that while public opinion plays an important role in shaping government policy under certain conditions, it plays a lesser role in others. In particular, public opinion seems to matter most when issues are highly visible to the public (usually because there has been lots of political conflict surrounding the issue), are about matters that affect the lives of Americans most directly, and concern issues for which people have access to reliable and understandable information. When economic times are tough—during a recession, for example—no amount of rhetoric from political leaders, the news media, or interest groups is likely to convince people "that they never had it so good." People have a reality check in such circumstances.

By the same token, many foreign policy questions are distant from people's lives and involve issues about which information is scarce or incomplete. In this circumstance, government officials act with wide latitude and play an important role in shaping what the public believes. After studying decades' worth of surveys of public and elite opinion on foreign policy issues collected by the Chicago Council on Foreign Relations, for example, researchers concluded that a deep disconnect exists between the public and elites, with the public much less eager than elites to use force in foreign affairs and more supportive of international cooperation—in the form of international treaties and the United Nations—to tackle global problems.[97]

Additionally, some issues, such as the details of tax legislation or the deregulation of the telecommunications industry, are so obscure and complex that they become the province of interest groups and experts, with the public holding ill-formed and not very intense opinions.[98] Moreover, public opinion is only one factor in shaping what government does, something we will address in later chapters. A range of other political actors and institutions including political parties, interest groups, the news media, and social movements also influence government, and many scholars argue that their combined influence has far more of an effect than public opinion on what government does.

It is probably reasonable to say, moreover, that the influence of public opinion on government is significantly less than the statistical studies suggest (e.g., the "two-thirds" rule) for the reasons given: the impact of third factors on both opinion and government and the significant amount of influence government officials have over popular opinion.[99] And it is hard to avoid noticing the many times government acts

# Using the FRAMEWORK

## If a majority of Americans say they want gun control, why hasn't the federal government done much about it?

**Background:** Polls have consistently indicated high public support for stricter federal gun control laws. At a general level, around two-thirds of Americans say they want stricter laws. Several specific proposals receive even higher levels of support. For example, about 80 percent of Americans say they want a nationwide ban on assault weapons, while 70 percent want the government to ban gun sales by mail order and over the Internet. Although some laws, such as the Brady Bill—which requires background checks of gun buyers and a waiting period—have passed Congress, proposals for stricter control over the sale and distribution of weapons almost never get very far. Taking a broad look at how structural, political linkage, and governmental factors affect gun control legislation will help explain the situation.

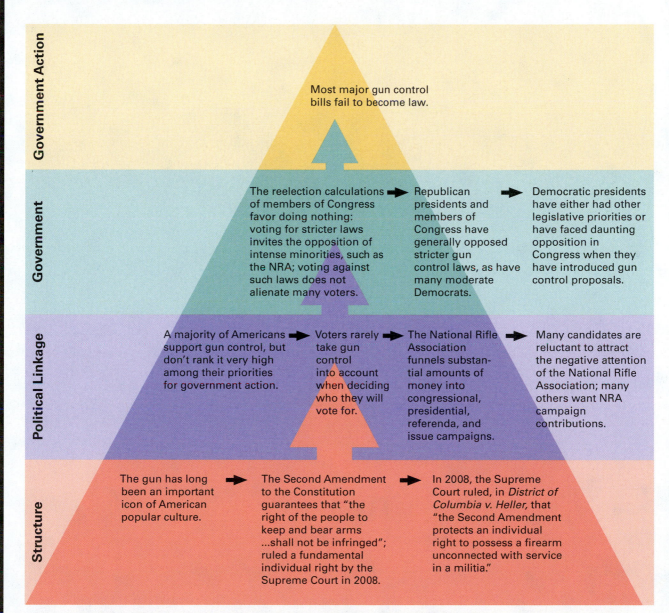

**Government Action**

Most major gun control bills fail to become law.

**Government**

The reelection calculations of members of Congress favor doing nothing: voting for stricter laws invites the opposition of intense minorities, such as the NRA; voting against such laws does not alienate many voters. → Republican presidents and members of Congress have generally opposed stricter gun control laws, as have many moderate Democrats. → Democratic presidents have either had other legislative priorities or have faced daunting opposition in Congress when they have introduced gun control proposals.

**Political Linkage**

A majority of Americans support gun control, but don't rank it very high among their priorities for government action. → Voters rarely take gun control into account when deciding who they will vote for. → The National Rifle Association funnels substantial amounts of money into congressional, presidential, referenda, and issue campaigns. → Many candidates are reluctant to attract the negative attention of the National Rifle Association; many others want NRA campaign contributions.

**Structure**

The gun has long been an important icon of American popular culture. → The Second Amendment to the Constitution guarantees that "the right of the people to keep and bear arms ...shall not be infringed"; ruled a fundamental individual right by the Supreme Court in 2008. → In 2008, the Supreme Court ruled, in *District of Columbia v. Heller,* that "the Second Amendment protects an individual right to possess a firearm unconnected with service in a militia."

almost exactly contrary to public opinion—Congress's decision to go ahead with the impeachment and trial of Bill Clinton in late 1998 and early 1999 in the face of strong public opposition comes to mind, as does inaction on gun control (see the "Using the Framework" feature). Most recently, the turn of the president and Congress to matters of controlling the deficit was not the product of public opinion. Polls showed throughout 2010 and 2011 that the public wanted government leaders to focus on job creation as the first order of business; deficit control was way down the list of public concerns.

# Review the Chapter

## Democracy and Public Opinion

**5.1** Characterize the ideal role of public opinion in a democracy, p. 117

Public opinion consists of the core political beliefs and political attitudes expressed by ordinary citizens; it can be measured rather accurately through polls and surveys.

The democratic ideals of popular sovereignty and majority rule imply that government policy should respond to the wishes of the citizens, at least in the long run. An important test of how well democracy is working, then, is how closely government policy corresponds to public opinion.

## Measuring Public Opinion

**5.2** Describe methods used to measure public opinion, p. 118

Today most polling is done by telephone.

The foundation of a legitimate survey is that respondents in a sample are randomly selected.

The increased use of answering machines on landlines and of mobile phones makes it more difficult to develop a random sample.

## Political Socialization: Learning Political Beliefs and Attitudes

**5.3** Analyze the process of political socialization, p. 121

People learn their political attitudes and beliefs from their families, peers, schools, and workplaces, as well as through their experiences with political events and the mass media. This process is known as political socialization.

Changes in society, the economy, and America's situation in the world affect political attitudes and public opinion.

## How and Why People's Political Attitudes Differ

**5.4** Relate political attitudes to race, gender, age, income, and other factors, p. 123

Opinions and party loyalties differ according to race, religion, region, urban or rural residence, social class, education level, gender, and age. Blacks, Jews, city dwellers, women, and low-income people tend to be particularly liberal and Democratic; white Protestants, suburbanites, males, and the wealthy tend to be more conservative and Republican.

## The Contours of American Public Opinion: Are the People Fit to Rule?

**5.5** Assess the American public's ability to rule, p. 134

Political knowledge among the public is low, but cue-givers allow people to make fairly rational decisions about their policy preferences.

Public opinion, considered in the aggregate as a collection of randomly selected respondents, tends to be stable, measured, and rational over the years. Some political scientists call this the "rational public."

# Learn the Terms

# Test Yourself

Answer key begins on page T-1.

**5.1**  Characterize the ideal role of public opinion in a democracy

1. In a real democracy, there must be a close match between government policies and actions and:

   a. Public opinion
   b. Political attitudes
   c. Political beliefs
   d. Laws
   e. Government power

**5.2**  Describe methods used to measure public opinion

2. The three main problems that arise with political polls are:

   a. Issues of wording, issues of intensity and timing, and issues of understanding
   b. Issues of information, issues of understanding, and issues of sampling
   c. Issues of wording, issues of timing, and issues of information
   d. Issues of intensity and timing, issues of sampling, and issues of understanding
   e. Issues of wording, issues of intensity and timing, and issues of sampling

**5.3**  Analyze the process of political socialization

3. Three important agents of political socialization are:

   a. Family, popular culture, and schools
   b. Books, children, and family
   c. Political rallies, schools, and college education
   d. Political rallies, wars, and schools
   e. Family, political parties, and popular culture

**5.4**  Relate political attitudes to race, gender, age, income, and other factors

4. People in union households have long favored:

   a. Liberals
   b. Conservatives
   c. Independents
   d. Democrats
   e. Republicans

**5.5**  Assess the American public's ability to rule

5. Polling data from the Pew Research Center (2013) places Americans' "trust in government" closest to which percentage?

   a. 10 percent
   b. 20 percent
   c. 30 percent
   d. 40 percent
   e. 50 percent

# Explore Further

## INTERNET SOURCES

American Association for Public Opinion Research **www.aapor .org/Poll_andamp_Survey_FAQs.htm**
An online guide for understanding and interpreting polls.
Rock the Vote Polls **www.rockthevote.com/about/ about-young-voters/polling/**
Polls of 18- to 29-year-olds on voting and politics.
Measuring Public Opinion **www.ushistory.org/gov/4c.asp**
The history of polling, as well as links to many public opinion organizations.
Gallup Organization **www.gallup.com**
Access to recent Gallup polls as well as to the Gallup archives. Some content requires a paid subscription.
American National Election Studies **www.electionstudies.org**
Biennial survey of voters, focusing on electoral issues; the gold standard for political scientists.
Pew Research Center for the People and the Press **pewresearch.org**
Complex, in-depth polls on domestic and foreign issues.
Political Compass **www.politicalcompass.org**
Determine where you stand in ideological terms by completing the online survey.

Polling Report **www.pollingreport.com**
A compilation of surveys from a wide variety of organizations on politics and public affairs.
Public Agenda Beyond the Polls **www.publicagenda.org/pages/ our-blog**
A comprehensive collection of opinion polls and background reports on public issues.

## SUGGESTIONS FOR FURTHER READING

Asher, Herbert. *Polling and the Public: What Every Citizen Should Know.* Washington, D.C.: CQ Press, 2011.
How public opinion surveys are done and what they mean.
Caplan, Bryan. *The Myth of the Rational Voter: Why Democracies Choose Bad Policies.* Princeton, NJ: Princeton University Press, 2007.
Argues that the public is systematically—rather than randomly—misinformed about economic matters and that this leads to irrational government policies to the extent that government leaders follow public opinion.
Erikson, Robert S., and Kent L. Tedin. *American Public Opinion,* 8th ed. New York: Longman Publishers, 2011.
A comprehensive survey of what we know about American public opinion and how we know it.

Page, Benjamin I., with Marshall Bouton. *The Foreign Policy Disconnect: What Americans Want from Our Leaders but Don't Get.* Chicago: University of Chicago Press, 2006.

Based on surveys of the public and elites sponsored by the Chicago Council on Foreign Relations, the authors demonstrate the existence of a deep disconnect between the public and elites on what kind of foreign policy the United States should have.

Shapiro, Robert Y., and Lawrence R. Jacobs, eds. *The Oxford Handbook of American Public Opinion and the Media.* Oxford: Oxford University Press, 2011.

A state-of-the-art compendium of what we know about public opinion and how we know it, by leading scholars in the field.

Weissberg, Robert. *Polling, Policy, and Public Opinion: The Case Against Heeding the "Voice of the People."* New York: Palgrave, 2002.

A passionate argument on why government officials should not be too responsive to public opinion.

Wolfe, Alan. *Does American Democracy Still Work?* New Haven, CT: Yale University Press, 2006.

Suggests that Americans are neither interested in nor informed about public affairs and that the effects of these twin conditions undermine democracy in the nation.

# 6

# The News Media

## BIG STORIES WITHOUT LEGS

**I**t had all the makings of a major news story that would rock Washington and trigger a major rethinking of war policies in Iraq.[1] All the pieces appeared to be in place. In an article published on April 30, 2005, the prestigious British newspaper, *The Times* of London, reported the minutes of a secret meeting between Prime Minister Tony Blair and his top military and intelligence officials that featured a report by a British intelligence operative that Washington officials had "cooked the books" to justify the invasion of Iraq in spring 2003. The operative had been at several prewar meetings with White House and Pentagon officials where it was evident, he claimed, that the decision for war already had been made and that intelligence information about Saddam Hussein's purported "weapons of mass destruction" program and ties to the 9/11 terrorists was being organized and interpreted to build a case for going to war. In his words, the "facts were being fixed around the policy."[2]

As news stories go, the seeming blockbuster turned out to be a dud. The story failed to merit a lead on any of the network newscasts. While the story of the so-called Downing Street memo appeared on the front page of the *Washington Post,* it was there for only a single day. Other newspapers relegated it to the inside pages. For the most part, the story was ". . . treated as old news or a British politics story" rather than a story about Americans being misled into war by the Bush administration, something that might call into question the entire enterprise.[3] The liberal blogosphere jumped on the issue, but the story failed to stir more mainstream media attention or action from congressional Democrats, who were in the minority in both the House and Senate and unsure about what position to take on the war in the upcoming 2006 elections. When Representative John Conyers (D–MI) sought to bring attention to the misuse of intelligence information to encourage the Iraq war by holding an "informational hearing" (being

**6.1**

Evaluate the various roles of the news media in a democracy, p. 155

**6.2**

Assess the respective roles of traditional and other news media today, p. 156

**6.3**

Analyze how the news is gathered and disseminated and evaluate the outcomes of this process, p. 163

**6.4**

Identify the ways in which the news media affect public opinion and policymaking, p. 176

**WEAPONS OF MASS DESTRUCTION** The Bush administration sold the American people on the invasion of Iraq in 2003 on the grounds that Saddam Hussein had developed nuclear and biological weapons that threatened the region and the world. We learned later from British government sources that the intelligence was "cooked" to support the invasion—there were no such military capabilities—but the new information failed to become important news in America's media. Was this an unusual occurrence or all too common regarding important public affairs? If the latter, what does this mean for creating an informed public in a democracy?

in the minority, the Democrat Conyers could not schedule an official set of hearings), the *Washington Post* treated it as a joke; the headline read "Democrats Play House to Rally Against the War" and opened with the line, "In the Capitol basement yesterday, long suffering House Democrats took a trip to the land of make-believe."[4]

Similarly, in an article published in early 2006—roughly three years after the invasion of Iraq—the *New York Times* reported a British press story, based on a memo written by a Blair aide who had attended a prewar January 2003 meeting of Prime Minister Tony Blair and President George W. Bush at the White House, where the president had made it clear to the British leader that he was determined to go to war even without evidence that Iraq was building weapons of mass destruction or had links to Al Qaeda. (At the same time, the president was making numerous statements that he had not made up his mind about an invasion and was making every effort to solve the issue diplomatically in cooperation with the United Nations and close allies.) While the revelation elicited a few comments from Democratic leaders and some blog activity, it didn't get a mention on CBS, NBC, or Fox News, and no follow-up stories appeared in the *Los Angeles Times*, the *Wall Street Journal*, the *Washington Post*, or *USA Today*. At around the same time this story about the Bush–Blair meeting came and went with hardly a murmur, a feeding frenzy was swirling around an unfortunate incident in which Vice President Richard Cheney accidentally shot a long-time friend in the face while hunting. For four or five days after the accidental shooting, every type of news media outlet—including the network and cable news networks, news magazines, local and national newspapers, news websites, and blogs—ran full coverage on the story, examining every nuance and speculating about why it happened, why an official press release about it was delayed for a few hours, and what it might all mean. Late-night comedy hosts had a field day with the story for months.

Many critics claim the news media are biased and cannot be relied upon to tell an objective story. Other critics claim that the mainstream news media in particular are becoming irrelevant in the face of the Internet, with its multiple information and opinion sources. We suggest that the principal problems of the news media concern their underreporting of stories that might help American citizens better understand events and trends that are affecting their lives, including those involving government and political leaders, and overattention to stories that involve sensation, entertainment, or scandals. This chapter is about the news media and why certain things become news we pay attention to while other things, many of them very important to public conversations about government policies and the direction of the country, do not.

## Thinking Critically About This Chapter

In this chapter, we turn our attention to the diverse news media in the United States to learn how they are organized, how they work, and what effects they have on the quality of our political life.

## Using the Framework

In this chapter, you will learn about the role the news media play in influencing significant actors in the political system, including citizens and elected leaders. You also will learn how the news media can shape what government does. And you will learn how the news media are influenced by changes in technology and business organization.

## Using the Democracy Standard

Using the tools already presented, you will be able to evaluate the degree to which the news media advance democracy in the United States or retard it. You will be able to judge whether the media promote popular sovereignty, political equality, and liberty. Finally, you will see how certain changes in the media may be cause for concern in terms of the health of democracy.

# Roles of the News Media in Democracy

**watchdog**
The role of the media in scrutinizing the actions of government officials.

6.1

6.2

6.3

6.4

**T**he central idea of democracy is that ordinary citizens should control what their government does. However, citizens cannot hope to control officials, choose candidates wisely, speak intelligently with others about public affairs, or even make up their minds about which policies they favor unless they have good information about politics and policies. Most of that information must come through the news media, whether newspapers, radio, television, or, increasingly, the Internet. How well democracy works, then, depends partly on how good a job the news media are doing. The news media, ideally, should fulfill several roles in this democracy.

## ☐ Watchdog Over Government

One role of the news media in a democracy is that of **watchdog** over government. The Founders, although not entirely enamored of democracy, as we have seen, nevertheless fully subscribed to the idea that a free press was essential for keeping an eye on government and checking its excesses. This is why protection of press freedom figured so prominently in the First Amendment. This role for the press is essential to the practice of democracy as well. The idea is that the press should dig up facts and warn the public when officials are doing something wrong. Citizens can hold officials accountable for setting things right only if they know about errors and wrongdoing.

The First Amendment to the Constitution ("Congress shall make no law . . . abridging the freedom . . . of the press") helps ensure that the news media will be able to expose officials' misbehavior without fear of censorship or prosecution. This is a treasured American right that is not available in many other countries. Under dictatorships and other authoritarian regimes, the news media are usually tightly controlled, with government censorship of the press and intimidation of journalists all too common.[5] Even in a democratic country such as Great Britain, strict secrecy laws limit what the press can say about certain government activities. In many countries, including France, Israel, and Sweden, the government owns and operates major television channels and sometimes pressures news executives to tone down their criticism of political leaders, though citizens in these countries have access to alternative channels by satellite and on the Internet.

As you will see, even without formal censorship or government ownership of the media, various factors, including the way in which the news media are organized as privately owned, profit-seeking enterprises, and their routines of news gathering, may limit how willing or able the news media are to be critical of government policies. In addition, the media may be too quick to blow scandals out of proportion and to destroy political leaders' careers.[6]

## ☐ Clarifying Electoral Choices

A second role of the news media in a democracy is to make clear what electoral choices the public has: what the political parties stand for and how the candidates shape up in terms of personal character, knowledge, experience, and positions on the issues. Without such information, it is difficult for voters to make intelligent choices. Unfortunately, the news media tend to pay attention more to the "horse race" (who is ahead? who is behind?) aspect of campaigns, or go overboard digging up dirt and reporting negative material, rather than covering the policy positions of the candidates.

## ☐ Providing Policy Information

A third role of the news media is to present a diverse, full, and enlightening set of facts and ideas about public policy. Citizens need to know about emerging problems that will need attention and how well current policies are working, as well as the pros and

**DARNED REPORTERS**

Richard Nixon resigned his presidency in August, 1974 rather than face a trial in the Senate following his impeachment in the House after investigative reporters Bob Woodward and Carl Bernstein of The Washington Post uncovered evidence of the president's close involvement in illegal spying on political opponents and in efforts to cover-up these activities from law enforcement authorities in what has come to be called the Watergate Affair. Here he leaves Washington after his resignation. Do you believe the news media played an important role in enhancing American democracy in this case or did reporters like Woodward and Bernstein go too far?

cons of alternative policies that might be tried. In a democracy, government should respond to public opinion, but that opinion should be reasonably well informed. You will see later in this chapter why many observers worry that the news media do not provide quality information and analyses on a consistent basis.

# Mainstream and Alternative News Media

**6.2**  Assess the respective roles of traditional and other news media today

The Pew Research Center's Project for Excellence in Journalism (www .journalism.org) claims that the coming of the digital age in the news media represents "an epochal transformation, as momentous probably as the invention of the telegraph or television."[7] This new digital age in news is described as one in which there is virtually unlimited access to information, news, and analysis, untold opportunities for ordinary people to express their views on public issues, and a decline in the presence and importance of the mainstream or traditional media.[8] Despite the unmistakable and dramatic growth of alternative news and information sources and outlets for people to express themselves and to report what is going on around them (at a political demonstration such as Occupy Wall Street, for example), however, we suggest that the mainstream media and traditional forms of reporting remain at the center of the news operations that most affect American politics and government.

## ☐ Alternatives to the Mainstream

The most important development in the collection, organization, and distribution of information of all kinds is, of course, the Internet, allowing instant access to a vast

**BLOGGING THE REPUBLICAN NATIONAL CONVENTION**

Alternative media are becoming increasingly mainstream. Both the Republican and Democratic conventions allocate space not only to the mainstream media but to bloggers as well. To what extent does live blogging and tweeting enhance the quality of political information that is available to the public?

treasure trove of digitalized information in every field of human knowledge. (See Figure 6.1 for a timeline on the development of the Internet.) The way people access political information is no exception to this trend. In recent years we have seen substantial growth in the number of online sources of political information. Findings from a recent report published by the Pew Research Center Journalism Project indicate that thousands of people now work full time at one of hundreds of digital news outlets producing content for the 50 percent of adults who consume news online on any given day.[9] This dynamic has transformed the news media landscape and provides interested citizens with virtually unlimited access to information, news, and analysis as well as with opportunities to express their own viewpoints on political and governmental issues by commenting on and sharing stories, links, videos, and photos on platforms like Facebook, Google+, Twitter, and YouTube.[10]

To be sure, most people use the Internet for such nonpolitical activities as sending and receiving e-mail, sharing photos and videos, sending tweets about their lives, arranging travel and vacations, participating in online auctions, shopping for products, playing interactive games, following their friends and relations on Facebook, and more. But many millions use it for explicitly political purposes, to both inform and express themselves. Here are a few examples:

- People visit political party and candidate websites, as well as interest and advocacy group websites, to get information, make contributions, learn how to organize, and leave comments. They also visit fact-check sites to test the claims of government officials, candidates, and parties.

- People visit government websites to access a vast trove of information ranging from statistics on demographic change and performance of the economy to the details of the U.S. budget and bills being considered by Congress. Over 100 million people have done so.[11]

- People read commentaries on thousands of political blogs, or follow politically oriented people via Twitter and Facebook, and respond with their own commentary. Or they can easily set up their own blogs, Twitter accounts, or Facebook pages to convey their political commentaries.

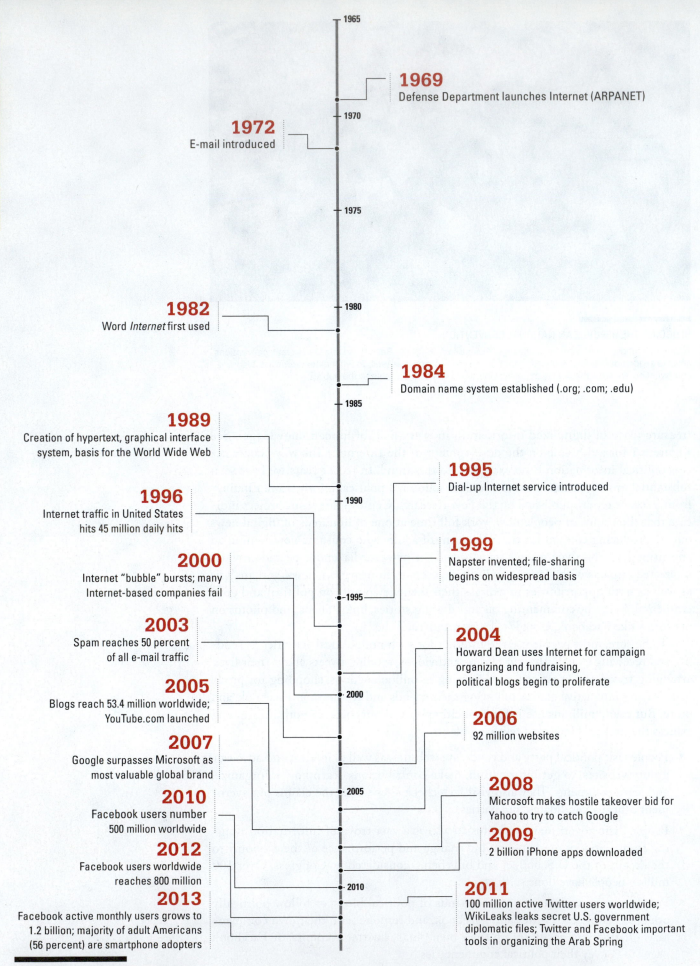

**1965**

**1969**
Defense Department launches Internet (ARPANET)

**1972**
E-mail introduced

1970

1975

**1982**
Word *Internet* first used

1980

**1984**
Domain name system established (.org; .com; .edu)

1985

**1989**
Creation of hypertext, graphical interface
system, basis for the World Wide Web

**1995**
Dial-up Internet service introduced

**1996**
Internet traffic in United States
hits 45 million daily hits

1990

**1999**
Napster invented; file-sharing
begins on widespread basis

**2000**
Internet "bubble" bursts; many
Internet-based companies fail

1995

**2003**
Spam reaches 50 percent
of all e-mail traffic

**2004**
Howard Dean uses Internet for campaign
organizing and fundraising,
political blogs begin to proliferate

**2005**
Blogs reach 53.4 million worldwide;
YouTube.com launched

2000

**2006**
92 million websites

**2007**
Google surpasses Microsoft as
most valuable global brand

2005

**2008**
Microsoft makes hostile takeover bid for
Yahoo to try to catch Google

**2010**
Facebook users number
500 million worldwide

**2009**
2 billion iPhone apps downloaded

**2012**
Facebook users worldwide
reaches 800 million

2010

**2011**
100 million active Twitter users worldwide;
WikiLeaks leaks secret U.S. government
diplomatic files; Twitter and Facebook important
tools in organizing the Arab Spring

**2013**
Facebook active monthly users grows to
1.2 billion; majority of adult Americans
(56 percent) are smartphone adopters

**FIGURE 6.1** TIMELINE: THE INTERNET

*Sources:* Infoplease, www.infoplease.com; "The New News Landscape: Rise of the Internet" (Washington, D.C.: Pew Research Center, March 1, 2010); "Overseas Users Power Facebook's Growth; More Going Mobile-Only," Fact Tank, Pew Research Center, February 4, 2014; Aaron Smith, "Smartphone Ownership 2013," Pew Research Center, June 5, 2013.

6.1

6.2

6.3

6.4

- People visit specialized political news websites, some with their own reporters like Politico.com or the Huffington Post, for breaking news and background information on what is going on in Washington or state capitals.

- Millions of people go to the websites of traditional news organizations such as CNN, the *New York Times,* and the *Wall Street Journal* for their news. They also go to news aggregator sites such as Instapaper, Yahoo! News, and Google News.

- People use the Internet to access public affairs information from online university and public libraries, as well as from online encyclopedia-type sites such as Wikipedia.

- People watch newscasts, political commentators, and breaking or audience-generated news on video sites like YouTube.

- People increasingly use social-networking sites like Twitter and Facebook to inform others about breaking stories—demonstrations in Cairo, for example, or a sighting of financial swindler Bernie Madoff walking near his condo in Manhattan—to pass on bits and pieces of news stories from other sources. They also sometimes use social-networking sites to organize demonstrations, as Tea Party activists did several times in their effort to stop health care reform and the Occupy movement did to protest economic inequality and the lack of jobs.

At the same time that Internet use has expanded at an exponential rate, there has been a decline in the audience for the most traditional news outlet: newspapers (see

**SIGHTING POPE FRANCIS**

Phones with cameras together with social media sites like Instagram and Twitter make it easy for anyone to play the role of a reporter. These technologies and services allow individual citizens to share photos and other first-hand information about politicians and public figures with their friends, followers, and acquaintances, as well as with traditional news outlets. In what ways have such new technologies refashioned how Americans engage in political life?

**wire services**

Organizations such as the Associated Press and Reuters that gather and disseminate news to other news organizations.

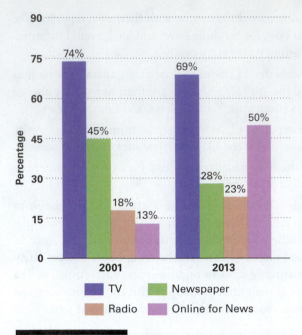

**FIGURE 6.2** WHERE PEOPLE GET THEIR NEWS

Surveys that ask respondents how they get most of their national and international news show, in recent years, that people have turned increasingly to the Internet as a source of news, while decreasing somewhat their reliance on television and newspapers. Although the Internet still trails television as people's main source of news, it is closing the gap.

**Note:** Respondents could cite up to two sources.

*Source:* Pew Research Center.

Figure 6.2). People consistently report that television is their main source of news over newspapers and news magazines, with the Internet closing fast. The collapse in circulation for metropolitan newspapers has been stunning. By 2013 total print advertising revenue for newspapers had plummeted from a high of over $65 billion to less than $20 billion–the lowest since 1950.[12] Young people have almost entirely given up on newspaper reading; one survey reports that only 16 percent of 18- to 30-year-olds said they read a newspaper every day.[13] By early 2012, only 11 percent of this group said that newspapers were an important source of news for them. Although television remains the favorite source of political news for Americans, network news programs on ABC, CBS, and NBC have now fallen behind cable TV as important sources of campaign and political news, headed by Fox News, CNN, and MSNBC. Though network and cable news networks have changed positions, television remains the favorite source of political news for Americans (refer again to Figure 6.2).[14] A substantial fraction of younger news consumers report that they also rely on satirical television shows like *The Daily Show* or *The Colbert Report* on Comedy Central for their news.

## ☐ The Continuing Importance of the Mainstream

Despite the rapid rise and development of alternatives to the mainstream media, the mainstream media retain their central role in the gathering and reporting of serious political and governmental news. The mainstream or traditional news media are the collection of nationally prominent newspapers (such as the *Wall Street Journal,* the *New York Times,* and the *Washington Post*), national news magazines (such as *Time* and the *National Review*), TV network news organizations, local newspapers, and local TV news operations that gather, analyze, and report politically important events, developments, and trends, usually with the help of **wire services** such as the Associated Press (AP) and Reuters, the resources of newspaper chains, and syndication services, but sometimes on their own.[15] Research by media scholars shows that the mainstream news organizations, taken as a whole, remain the most important set of institutions for setting the agenda of American politics and shaping how we interpret what is going on in politics and government.

**NEWS WITH LAUGHS**

Increasingly, young people report that their most trusted news sources are to be found on Comedy Central on shows like *The Daily Show* and *The Colbert Report*, rather than from the major network or cable news offerings. Stephen Colbert's success at integrating humor and current events, along with his comic interviews with public figures, led to his selection as David Letterman's replacement as the host of CBS's *The Late Show* after Letterman retires in 2015.

There are a number of reasons the mainstream or traditional news organizations remain central to political news. For one thing, much of the rich and diverse information on the Internet, whether in the form of advocacy organization websites, political blogs, citizen journalism, or academic and government reports, only reach small and fragmented audiences and usually have an impact only when and to the extent they can attract the attention of the mainstream news media. Bloggers' unearthing of news anchor Dan Rather's sloppy reporting on President George W. Bush's National Guard service during the Vietnam War, for example, only mattered once the story began to run in the nation's leading newspapers and on network and cable news networks. Tens of thousands of bloggers voice their views every day, to take another example, but few gain an audience. One scholar, using a vast database to chronicle the number of daily hits on blogger sites, has determined that only 10 to 20 of them have a readership of any size. Of the 5,000 most-visited political blog sites, for example, the top 5 of them accounted for 28 percent of all blog visits, while the top 10 accounted for almost half. Also, fully half of the top 10 bloggers are or were at one time professional journalists.[16]

An additional piece of evidence that traditional news outlets continue to play a central role in the contemporary news media landscape is that, with the exception of the Huffington Post, the most visited hard-news sites are those that are run by traditional media organizations. Among the most popular are those of CBS News, ABC News, the *New York Times*, the *Washington Post*, CNN, Fox News, and MSNBC.

Much more telling, most political and public policy-related news on the Internet at news aggregator sites such as Yahoo! News and Google News is simply content collected from the mainstream wire services and major newspaper and network news organizations. The same is true for the matters that most political bloggers talk about, and the bits of news that get passed around on social-networking sites: they come mainly from material that has been collected by reporters in the traditional news sector. The grist for commentary at the most popular political sites, including the liberal *Huffington Post* and the conservative *Free Republic* and Townhall.com, comes mainly from traditional news organizations. Much of the airtime on cable news networks such as Fox News, moreover, is devoted to reporting or commenting on material gathered from the major wire services such as the AP or Reuters or prestigious newspapers. And it is to the mainstream media that eager politicians and government officials generally look for clues about what the public and other leaders want and where they try to gain attention for their own views and achievements.

What seems on the surface, then, to be a fantastic expansion in the amount of political news in reality is an expansion in the number of ways in which the news is distributed. It is the same news being passed around and around on the Internet. An exponential growth in commentary on that news is not the same thing as an expansion in the size or quality of the core of political news.[17] As far as scholars have been able to tell, the new digital age news operations have done very little by way of original, in-depth stories.[18] To be sure, this may change before too long. Some mainstream media organizations have been quite aggressive in using citizen reporters to gather and submit news stories—see CNN's iReport website—while new types of social media sites have found ways for people to arrange Facebook posts and tweets, often of a political nature, into chronological narratives to be reposted to social media sites. Mainstream media also use the new media as sources for constructing their own news stories, as when in 2010 the *New York Times* reported about and released much of the raw diplomatic cables gathered by WikiLeaks under the leadership of its founder, Julian Assange.

So, while the news media have changed greatly over our history and continue to change ever more rapidly, and while people can get their news and commentary from many different places ranging from the Internet to cable television, talk radio, and television satire and comedy programs, mainstream news organizations remain the most important set of institutions in the American political news system, even if they are fighting for their lives in an economic sense. It is the reason we mostly focus on the mainstream news media in this chapter, asking how well they play the role assigned to them by democratic theorists.

**WIKILEAKS FOUNDER IN TROUBLE**

WikiLeaks a web-based virtual organization, says it is committed to ending secrecy in government. To that end, it released a massive library of raw American diplomatic cables that came into its possession, causing great embarrassment to American officials and officials in many other countries. Here WikiLeaks founder Julian Assange leaves a hearing before the High Court in Great Britain in 2011. He was fighting his extradition to Sweden, where he faced sexual assault charges. His followers claim these charges were fabricated by government leaders concerned about the spread of the WikiLeaks phenomenon. To what extent should there be secrecy in government? Does a democracy require complete openness?

# How the Mainstream News Media Work

**6.3** Analyze how the news is gathered and disseminated and evaluate the outcome of this process

Whether citizens get from the news media the kinds of information they need for democracy to work properly depends on how the media are organized and function. In the remainder of this chapter, we focus on news media organizations and journalists with an eye toward better understanding the influences that affect the content of their news product and how the news shapes politics and government in the United States.

## Organization of the News Media

News media in the United States are almost entirely privately owned businesses. Most are either very large businesses in their own right or, more typically, part of very large corporate empires.

**CORPORATE OWNERSHIP** Some television stations and newspapers—especially the smaller ones—are still owned locally by families or by groups of investors, although they account for a rapidly declining share of the total. Most of the biggest stations and newspapers, however, as well as the television and cable networks, are owned by large media corporations, some of which, in turn, are subsidiaries of enormous conglomerates.

Each media sector is dominated by a few firms.[19] Gannett dominates the newspaper business, a media sector that has fallen on hard times because of declining readership, especially among young adults, and shrinking ad revenues as classified advertising migrates to online sites such as Craigslist. Time Warner dominates magazine

**I WANT MORE**

Rupert Murdoch has created a global entertainment and news operation that gives him influence with the public, opinion leaders, and government officials in a wide range of countries. Though revelations about reporters from several of his publications in Britain illegally tapping into cell phones damaged his reputation, his company, News Corp., continues to be among the biggest players in the world and in the United States. Does this development of giant media empires diminish the number of viewpoints citizens get to consider, or is there sufficient alternative information from other outlets such as the Internet?

**media monopoly**

Term used to suggest that media corporations are so large, powerful, and interconnected that the less economically and politically powerful cannot have their views aired.

publishing. Comcast, Disney, CBS, News Corp., and Time Warner dominate network and cable television. Clear Channel owns over 800 stations across the country and dominates radio, reaching 110 million listeners every week. And six firms (Paramount, Warner Brothers, Columbia, Disney, Universal, and 20th Century Fox) receive most of the gross box office revenues from movies.[20]

Mergers across media lines have accelerated in recent years, leaving a handful of giant conglomerates. Disney, for example, owns not only its theme parks, movie production and distribution operations, and sports teams, but the ABC television network, local TV and radio stations in the nation's largest cities, cable television operations, and book publishers. Rupert Murdoch's News Corp. owns local TV stations in many of the nation's largest cities, cable and satellite operations (including Fox News and DirecTV), the 20th Century Fox film company, the *New York Post* and major newspapers in Great Britain and Australia, a stable of magazines and journals, HarperCollins and Harper-Morrow book companies, and radio and TV operations in Europe and Asia. In 2007, he acquired one of the most influential news organizations in the world, the *Wall Street Journal*. (Journalists at the paper were dismayed, perhaps because Murdoch says he "finds long stories about complicated subjects to be rather trying").[21]

So, behind the apparent proliferation of news sources—new magazines, online news and opinion operations, cable television news and commentary, handheld devices with links to the Web, and the like—is substantial concentration of ownership and dense interconnections among the vast cornucopia of news and entertainment outlets. Some have used the term **media monopoly** to suggest how serious the situation is, though most scholars are loath to go that far, believing that much competition remains among the giant firms.[22]

Scholars disagree about the effects of corporate ownership and increased media concentration. A few see efficiency gains and an increase in the output and availability of information. But some critics maintain that the concentrated corporate control of our media adds dangerously to the already strong business presence in American politics. Those who use the term *media monopoly* worry that media corporations are so large, powerful, and interconnected that alternative voices to the economically and politically powerful are unlikely to be aired. Still others are concerned that concentration of ownership may lead to less diversity of news and opinion or failure to provide citizens with substantive information about politicians and public policies, preferring instead to focus on entertaining audiences due to an excessive focus on the bottom line. Still others worry that news organizations may pull their punches when reporting about the activities of their corporate parents or partners. Will ABC News go easy on problems at Disney, which owns ABC?

**UNIFORMITY AND DIVERSITY**  Whoever owns them, most newspapers and television stations depend largely on the same sources for news. Political scientist Lance Bennett points out that while there is a growing diversity of news outlets in the United States—more specialized magazines, television channels, and newspaper home pages on the Web—news sources are contracting. That is to say, much of what comes to us over a multitude of media avenues originates in fewer and fewer centralized sources.[23] Local radio stations increasingly buy headlines for their brief on-the-hour updates from a handful of headline service providers. Television news increasingly buys raw video footage, for in-house editing and scripting, from a handful of providers, including Independent Television News (ITN), rather than having their own reporters and film crews on the ground. The AP supplies most of the main national and international news stories for newspapers and local news (although Reuters is increasingly important)—even those that are rewritten to carry a local reporter's byline. Most of what appears on network and cable television news, too, is inspired by the AP wire, although they often take their lead on the major stories of the day from the major national newspapers such as the *New York Times,* the *Wall Street Journal,* and the *Washington Post.*[24] National and local television news organizations depend on centralized news and video suppliers, with fewer of them using their own reporters. This is why viewers are likely to see the same news (and sports) footage on different stations as they switch channels, although each station adds its own "voiceover" from a reporter or news anchor. In most cases, the person doing the voiceover has no direct relationship to the story. (For more on the state of local news, see the "By the Numbers" feature.)

# By the Numbers

## How much serious crime is there in the United States?

"If it bleeds, it leads" seems to be the mantra of television news. Indeed, we are in danger in this country of being overwhelmed by news stories about crime, and the problem seems to be getting worse. While coverage of public affairs and foreign affairs has been falling, news coverage of crime has flourished, especially on local news telecasts.

### Why It Matters

If television news broadcasts are accurately portraying real trends in crime, then they are doing a public service. If portrayals are inaccurate, then the public is being misled. This is problematic because public and official perceptions about the scale of particular social problems affect politics and government deeply. For example,

- When pressed by the public to address a perceived problem, government officials respond by redirecting resources at the problem and make budget and personnel decisions in light of it. If the problem is a false one, then government attention and resources get used ineffectively.

- Candidates campaign on issues that are most salient to the public. When the public misperceives the scale of a problem, it makes electoral choices based on irrelevant grounds.

- The more threatening the public finds a particular problem, the more it pushes aside other public priorities, such as education and health care.

### The Story Behind the Crime Numbers

How accurately are the news media portraying the true state of affairs? To put it bluntly, not very well. Crime in general, and violent crime in particular, declined substantially during the 1990s, at precisely the same time that concerns about crime were at the forefront of media, popular attention, and political saliency. How do we know this to be the case?

The two most widely used measures of the incidence of crime in the United States are the Uniform Crime Report (UCR) of the FBI and the National Crime Victimization Survey (NCVS) of the Department of Justice. Each counts the incidence of crime in a different way. The UCR is based on reports from law enforcement agencies and is meant to help state and local police departments track their own performance and plan their budgets. The NCVS is based on a survey of victims of crime and is used to assess how crime is experienced by Americans and how it affects them and their families.

### Calculating the Crime Rate

The FBI's UCR, based on reports submitted voluntarily by state and local law enforcement agencies, counts the annual incidence of "violent crimes" (murder, forcible rape, robbery, and aggravated assault), "property crimes" (burglary, larceny-theft, motor vehicle theft, and arson), and "serious crimes" (all of the above). However, here is what is most important about the FBI's methodology: *it only counts crimes that come to the attention of police.*

The Justice Department's NCVS is based on an annual survey of roughly 50,000 randomly selected U.S. households. One person over the age of 18 in each household is interviewed about any crimes that may have been committed against any member of the household during the previous year. The result is annual crime *victimization* information for more than 100,000 people, a very large number for a national survey. Because the NCVS includes crimes experienced by people that are never reported to the authorities, it tends to show higher rates of serious crime than the UCR.

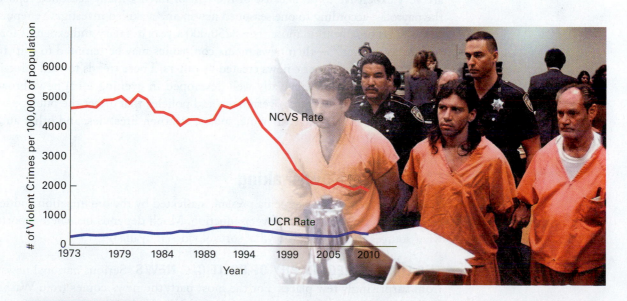

**SERIOUS VIOLENT CRIMES**

*Source: Crime Victimization 2011 and Uniform Crime Reports,* Bureau of Justice Statistics, 2011.

*(Continued)*

### Criticisms of Crime Rate Calculations

The experts generally prefer the NCVS numbers to those of the UCR for understanding the dimensions of the crime problem. The principal problems with the UCR concern the accuracy of recording and reporting crime. For example,

- Many serious crimes, especially rape, go unreported to police. The fact that the UCR came closer to the NCVS numbers starting in the 1990s may mean that more crimes are being reported than in the past.

- Ideas about what constitutes a serious crime may change as social mores change. Domestic violence was treated in the past by police as a family matter; now it tends to get recorded and reported by police.

- A small number of law enforcement agencies do not participate in the UCR reporting system or do not treat it with the seriousness that the FBI hopes for.

### What to Watch for

Each way of measuring crime is valid and has its purposes. Although the UCR measure has some problems, it does a fairly good job of telling us what is going on year to year with respect to police encounters with crime. This, in turn, is useful to national, state, and local governments in deciding on budget and staffing issues for law enforcement. The NCVS does a very good job of telling us what is going on year to year with respect to overall victimization trends, and gives us a handle on the size of the underlying crime problem. The lesson here is to use the statistic that conforms most closely to the purposes of your inquiry.

### What Do You Think?

How do television news programs underplay or overplay the incidence of violent crime? Monitor local and national news for the next week or so and try to keep a running count of stories about crime. How does your count match what the UCR and NCVS numbers are telling us about crime?

---

**infotainment**

The merging of hard news and entertainment in news presentations.

**PROFIT MOTIVES** Media companies, like other companies, are in business to make a profit. This is entirely appropriate in general terms but has some important and unfortunate consequences for how media companies create and disseminate the news. For many newspapers and television news organizations, this often means closing down foreign bureaus and cutting the number of reporters focused on government affairs in Washington or the economy and financial system. For many traditional news organizations, there are market pressures to alter their news coverage to appeal to audiences who are more interested in entertainment than public affairs and want their news short, snappy, and sensational. This sort of **infotainment** is increasingly offered on network and cable television news and in *USA Today*. If consumers of the news do not want long and detailed investigative reports, and given that such stories are very expensive to do because of the cost of having many seasoned reporters on the payroll—according to one seasoned newsman, "a skilled investigative reporter can cost a news organization more than $250,000 a year in salary and expenses for only a handful of stories"[25]—then news media companies may be tempted to shift to infotainment or to use generic news created by others. These trends toward infotainment and generic news are especially well developed in evening local news broadcasts, where coverage of politics, government, and policies that affect the public have been "crowded out by coverage of crime, sports, weather, lifestyles, and other audience-grabbing topics."[26]

## ☐ Political Newsmaking

The kind of news that the media present is affected by the organization and technology of news gathering and news production. Much depends on where reporters are, what sources they talk to, and what sorts of video is available.

**THE LIMITED GEOGRAPHY OF POLITICAL NEWS** Serious national news comes from surprisingly few places. For the most part, the news comes from Washington, D.C., the seat of the federal government, and New York City, the center of publishing and finance in the United States. This is where most news media companies locate their reporters, though a few other areas get coverage as well. We show how the news is geographically concentrated in the "Mapping American Politics" feature.

# Mapping American Politics

## The Limited Geography of National News

### Introduction

Most national political reporters are located in and file their stories from two main locations: Washington, D.C., site of the federal government and most of the nation's most influential think tanks and interest group organizations, and New York City, the center of most media operations and key national and global financial institutions. For national news involving more than politics and governmental affairs or closely related economic issues, reporters tend to file stories from a broader range of geographical locations, although not equally from all areas around the United States. This is hardly surprising: maintaining reporters is expensive, so news organizations concentrate their news gathering where they will get the most bang for the buck—where the most important news occurs.

### Mapping the News

The cartogram depicts the states and the District of Columbia resized from normal in proportion to the number of headlines in wire service stories originating from these locations in recent years. If news stories had originated in various states in proportion to their populations, the states' size would correspond to the relative sizes of their populations. In this cartogram, however, New York City, New York State, New Jersey, and California stand out as sites that generate a disproportionate share of news stories, as do Georgia, Florida, and, given its tiny geographic area (less than 10 miles square), Washington, D.C. New York City, its metropolitan area (which includes parts of New York State, New Jersey, and Connecticut),

and Washington, D.C. generate so much news for the reasons cited earlier. Georgia's relatively large size may be due to the fact that both CNN and the federal government's Centers for Disease Control and Prevention are based there. Florida is in the news often because of tight and controversial political contests as well as more than its share of hurricanes. California generates many stories from the entertainment industry, much of which is centered there, as well as from Silicon Valley, the heart of the nation's high-tech industry. Some states virtually disappear, with very few news stories originating in the Mountain West, Southwest, Great Plains, and Midwest (other than Illinois), or the New England states of New Hampshire, Vermont, and Maine. News stories from Texas are less than one might expect, given the importance of the state in American politics, energy production, music, and the high-tech industry in Austin.

### What Do You Think?

Why might one argue that it is reasonable that news stories are concentrated in America's centers of governance, communications, finance, and entertainment? Can you think of some way that news might be gathered to avoid such concentrations? Some people say that the news media are out of touch with the American people. What is the basis of this argument? Does the pattern in the cartogram showing the origins of news stories help explain the situation?

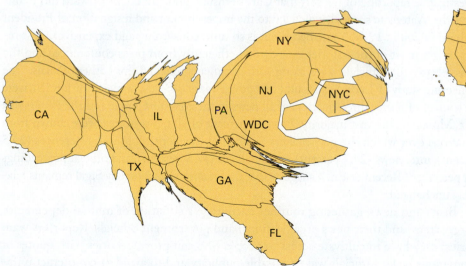

**Headline News: Size of States in Proportion to Number of Headlines**

**MAP NOTE:** Alaska is not shown (although information about Alaska is included in calculations where relevant), and Hawaii is moved closer to the mainland.

**SOURCE:** Data from Michael Gastner and described in M. T. Gastner and M. E. J. Newman, "Diffusion-Based Method for Producing Density-Equalizing Maps," *Proceedings of the National Academy of Sciences* 101 (May 18, 2004), pp. 7499–7504. Wire service news headlines from 1994 to 1998.

**beat**
The assigned location where a reporter regularly gathers news stories.

The major television networks and most newspapers cannot afford to station many reporters outside Washington, D.C. or New York.[27] The networks usually add just Chicago, Los Angeles, Miami, and Houston or Dallas. When stories break in San Francisco or Seattle, news organizations can rush reporters to the area or turn to part-time "stringers" (local journalists who file occasional reports) to do the reporting. Some significant stories from outside the main media centers simply do not make it into the national news.

While some newspapers have strong regional bureaus, the majority print mostly wire service reports of news from elsewhere around the country. The television networks' assignment editors also rely on the wire services to decide what stories to cover.

Because so much expensive, high-tech equipment is involved, and because a considerable amount of editing is required to turn raw video into coherent stories, most television news coverage is assigned to predictable events—news conferences and the like—long before they happen, usually in one of the cities with a permanent television crew. For such spontaneous news as riots, accidents, and natural disasters, special video camera crews can be rushed to the location, but they usually arrive after the main events occur and have to rely on "reaction" interviews or aftermath stories. This is not always true; occasionally television news organizations find themselves in the middle of an unfolding series of events and can convey its texture, explore its human meaning, and speculate about its political implications in particularly meaningful ways. This was certainly true of television coverage of the Hurricane Katrina disaster and its immediate aftermath.

**DEPENDENCE ON OFFICIAL SOURCES**  Most political news is based on what public officials say. This fact has important consequences for how well the media serve democracy.

*Beats and Routines*  A newspaper or television reporter's work is usually organized around a particular **beat**, which he or she checks every day for news stories. Most political beats center on some official government institution that regularly produces news, such as a local police station or city council, the White House, Congress, the Pentagon, an American embassy abroad, or a country's foreign ministry.

In fact, many news reports are created or originated by officials, not by reporters. Investigative reporting of the sort that Carl Bernstein and Robert Woodward did to uncover the Watergate scandal, which led to the impeachment and resignation of President Richard Nixon in 1974, is rare because it is so time-consuming and expensive. Most reporters get most of their stories quickly and efficiently from press conferences and the press releases that officials write, along with comments solicited from other officials. One pioneering study by Leon Sigal found that government officials, domestic or foreign, were the sources of nearly three-quarters of all news in the *New York Times* and the *Washington Post*. Moreover, the vast majority, 70 to 90 percent of all news stories, were drawn from situations over which the newsmakers had substantial control: press conferences (24.5 percent), interviews (24.7 percent), press releases (17.5 percent), and official proceedings (13 percent).[28] Recent research suggests that the situation described by Sigal remains relatively unchanged.[29]

Beats and news-gathering routines encourage a situation of mutual dependence by reporters (and their news organizations) and government officials. Reporters want stories; they have to cultivate access to people who can provide stories with quotes or anonymous leaks. Officials want favorable publicity and to avoid or counteract unfavorable publicity. Thus, a comfortable relationship tends to develop. Even when reporters put on a show of aggressive questioning at White House press conferences, they usually work hard to stay on good terms with officials and to avoid fundamental challenges of the officials' positions. Cozy relationships between the Washington press corps and top government officials are further encouraged by the fact that the participants know each other so well, often living in the same neighborhoods, attending the same social gatherings, and sending their children to the same private schools.[30]

While often decried by officials hurt by a damaging revelation, the **leak** is an important part of news gathering that is useful both to journalists and officials, and so is a part of the normal currency of journalist–official working relationships. Indeed, Woodward and Bernstein's Watergate story got its start with leaks from the anonymous "Deep Throat," revealed in 2005 to be Mark Felt, deputy director of the FBI during the Nixon administration. Most commonly, leaking is a way for officials to float policy ideas, get themselves noticed and credited with good deeds, undercut rivals in other government agencies, or report real or imagined wrongdoing. Because the practice is so common and useful, it is likely to remain central to how news is made.

***Government News Management*** The news media's heavy reliance on official sources means that government officials are sometimes able to control what journalists report and how they report it.[31] This is commonly referred to as **spin**. Every president and high-ranking official wants to help reporters spin a story in a way that is most useful or favorable to the office holder. The Reagan administration was particularly successful at picking a "story of the day" and having many officials feed that story to reporters, with a unified interpretation.[32] The Clinton administration tried to do the same but was not disciplined enough to make it work. President George W. Bush's administration pushed the news management envelope the farthest, eventually acknowledging that it had paid three journalists to write favorable stories, encouraged executive agencies to create news videos for media outlets without revealing the source of the videos, and allowed a political operative to be planted among the accredited White House press corps to ask questions at presidential news conferences.[33] President Obama's team ran an impressive news management operation using many of the same Internet-based tools honed during his nomination and election campaigns to get his administration's story out, partially bypassing the traditional news media. But he also generated a great deal of criticism when his press aides announced that the president and his administration would have nothing more to do with Fox News because the network, in their view, failed to separate its news reporting and editorial (strongly conservative) functions. Obama did this after Fox News allowed on-screen personalities like Glenn Beck and Sean Hannity to help mobilize the Tea Party movement to hold rallies across the country to protest the health reform bill, then sent its news cameras and correspondents to give the gatherings extensive coverage.

**NEWS FROM THE FIELD**

Increasingly, news from the battlefield is reaching the public from soldiers blogging about their experiences and observations. Tight control of the news by officials has become more difficult because of this. To what extent does this help or hinder the public's understanding of our engagement in armed conflict abroad?

---

**leak**
Inside or secret information given to a journalist or media outlet by a government official.

**spin**
The attempt by public officials to have a story reported in terms that favor them and their policies; see news management.

**newsworthy**
Worth printing or broadcasting as news, according to editors' judgments.

Managing images in press reports is also important. Every administration in the modern era has tried to manage public perceptions by staging events that convey strong symbolic messages. For example, George W. Bush announced that the invasion of Iraq had been successfully concluded not in a press release but from the deck of the aircraft carrier *USS Lincoln* on May 2, 2003, in front of a massive sign "Mission Accomplished," after landing in a jet on its runway. Barack Obama told Americans about his new strategy in Afghanistan not from his desk in the Oval Office but in a televised address in front of the cadets at West Point.

Of course, news management doesn't always work as planned. When the war in Iraq took a bad turn, Bush's "Mission Accomplished" came to seem false and hollow to many Americans, and the president's popularity took a dramatic plunge. With fewer American casualties in Afghanistan—by 2012, most of the fighting there was being done by Special Forces units and drone aircraft—President Obama was more insulated from the effects of bad war news.

***Military Actions*** Dependence on official sources is especially evident in military actions abroad. Because it is wary of the release of information that might help an adversary or undermine public support for U.S. actions—as happened during the Vietnam conflict—the Defense Department tries to restrict access of reporters to military personnel and the battlefield and provide carefully screened information for use by the news media. Information management was especially evident during the 1991 Gulf War to expel Saddam Hussein from Kuwait, with its carefully stage-managed news briefings at U.S. military headquarters in Saudi Arabia featuring video of "smart" weapons, Defense Department organization of press pools to cover parts of the war, and tight restrictions on reporters' access to the battlefields in Kuwait and Iraq.

During the rapid advance to Baghdad to topple Hussein's regime in 2003, the Defense Department encouraged coverage of combat by journalists embedded in combat units, although administration officials continued to exercise control over information about the big picture during the initial stages of the war. In the end, however, the administration was unable to control news about military and civilian casualties during the long occupation, the difficulties of helping to create a new constitution and government for that country, and the abuse of Iraqi prisoners at Abu Ghraib and other prisons. There were simply too many journalists and news organizations from around the world reporting on events there—and too many American soldiers and Iraqi civilians posting what they were seeing and experiencing to blogs—for the administration and military officials to be able to control the news.

**NEWSWORTHINESS** Decisions about what kinds of news to print or televise depend largely on professional judgments about what is **newsworthy**. Exactly what makes a story newsworthy is difficult to spell out, but experienced editors make quick and confident judgments of what their audiences (and their employers) want. If they were consistently wrong, they would probably not remain in their jobs for very long.

In practice, newsworthiness seems to depend on such factors as novelty (man bites dog, not dog bites man), drama and human interest, relevance to the lives of Americans, high stakes (physical violence or conflict), and celebrity. Some trivial topics are judged newsworthy, such as the recurring troubles of movie actress Lindsay Lohan. As the term *news story* implies, news works best when it can be framed as a familiar kind of narrative: an exposé of greed, sex, or corruption; conflict between politicians; or a foreign affairs crisis. On television, of course, dramatic or startling film footage helps make a story gripping. Important stories without visuals are often pushed aside for less important stories for which visuals exist.

This can often lead to missing very big stories in the making. For example, though experts had been worried for many years about the safety of New Orleans, and had been publishing their research results in specialized journals for some time, the news media did not pay much attention until the levees broke when Hurricane Katrina struck in 2005. To take another example, no reporters were at an important 2004 meeting of the Securities and Exchange Commission when the SEC decided to relax capital requirements—how much money firms had to have on hand to deal with crises—for big financial firms.[34] This decision played an important role in the collapse of the financial system in the late summer and early fall of 2008.

**TEMPLATES** On many important stories, a subtle "governing template" may prevail—a sense among both reporters and editors that news stories must take a generally agreed-upon slant to be taken seriously and to make it into the news broadcast or the newspaper. This is not because of censorship but because of the development of a general agreement among news reporters and editors that the public already knows what the big story looks like on a range of issues—filling in the details is what is important. Take reporting from China as an example. For many years, editors only wanted to hear about economic prosperity, emerging democratic freedoms, and happy peasants liberated from the economic and personal straightjacket of the Maoist collective farm system. After the pro-democracy demonstrations in Tiananmen Square were brutally repressed by the People's Liberation Army, however, reporters say that it became almost impossible to write anything positive about China, because the prevailing template about China had changed.[35] Now that China has become a very important trading partner, stories about the Chinese economic miracle have proliferated (as well as some worrying about China as a potential economic, diplomatic, and military rival and as a source of tainted goods). Coverage of the Beijing Olympics became almost euphoric, despite ill-treatment of dissidents during the Games.

**EPISODIC FOREIGN COVERAGE** Very few newspapers other than the *New York Times* can afford to station reporters abroad. Even the *Times* and the networks and wire services cannot regularly cover most nations of the world. They keep reporters in the countries of greatest interest to Americans—those that have big effects on American interests or enjoy close economic or cultural ties with the United States, such as Great Britain, Germany, Japan, Israel, Russia, and China—and they have regional bureaus in Africa and Latin America. In many countries, however, they depend on "stringers." During major crises or big events, the media send in temporary news teams, such as the armies of reporters that swarmed to Bosnia and Kosovo during the conflicts with the Serbs. The result is that most media devote the majority of their attention to limited areas of the world, dropping in only occasionally on others.

Foreign news, therefore, tends to be episodic—viewers are presented with a brief window into a foreign affairs issue but given little in the way of contextual information to help them make sense of what is going on. An unfamiliar part of the world, such as the Borno state in Nigeria, suddenly jumps into the headlines in a spectacular story of a kidnapping or an invasion and comes as a surprise to most Americans because they have not been prepared by background reports. (Journalism.org, the website of the Columbia Journalism Review, reports that only 0.2 percent of news coverage in the United States in 2011 was about Sub-Sahara Africa.)[36] For a few days or weeks, the story dominates the news, with intensive coverage through pictures, interviews, and commentaries. Then, if nothing new and exciting happens, the story grows stale and disappears from the media. Most viewers are left with little more understanding of the country than they began with. Thus, they find it difficult to form judgments about U.S. foreign policy.[37]

**INTERPRETING** Political news may not make much sense without an interpretation of what it means. Under the informal rules of **objective journalism**, taught in university journalism schools and practiced by the nation's leading newspapers and network news programs, however, explicit interpretations by journalists are avoided, except for commentary or editorials that are labeled as such (some cable news operations, however, and without apology, freely mix commentary and news). Thus, even if a reporter knows that an official is lying, he or she cannot say so directly but must find someone else who will say so for the record.[38] Staged events—such as a president holding a "town meeting" using carefully selected and screened audience members—are rarely identified by reporters as staged events. In news stories, most interpretations are left implicit (so that they are hard to detect and argue with) or are given by so-called

**objective journalism**
News reported with no evaluative language and with opinions quoted or attributed to a specific source.

**pundits**
Somewhat derisive term for print, broadcast, and radio commentators on the political news.

**WAITING FOR HELP**

Refugees from genocidal conflicts wait endlessly for daily food rations, along with thousands of other displaced persons, in camps lacking even basic necessities. News coverage of their plight is spotty, however, gaining attention for a time only when a celebrity or prominent politician visits or when a demonstration takes place in a major city in Europe or the United States. Why isn't media coverage of these kinds of international issues more consistent?

experts who are interviewed for comments. Often, particular experts are selected by print, broadcast, and telecast journalists because the position the experts will take is entirely predictable.

Experts are selected partly for reasons of convenience and audience appeal: scholars and commentators who live close to New York City or Washington, D.C., who like to speak in public, who look good on camera, and who are skillful in coming up with colorful quotations on a variety of subjects, are contacted again and again. They often show up on television to comment on the news of the day, even on issues that are far from the area of their special expertise. In many cases, these **pundits** are simply well-known for being on television often and are not experts on any subject at all. The experts and commentators featured in the media are often ex-officials. Their views are usually in harmony with the political currents of the day; that is, they tend to reflect a fairly narrow spectrum of opinion close to that of the party in power in Washington, D.C., or to the prevailing "conventional wisdom" inside the Beltway.

# Ideological Bias

Few topics arouse more disagreement than the question of whether the mass media in the United States have a liberal or conservative **bias**—or any bias at all. It is perhaps impossible to pinpoint what an "unbiased" story would look like. This is particularly true given that media reports are typically quite brief. Should a story about a proposal to raise the minimum wage cite statistics on income inequality or would that introduce a "liberal bias"? Should research suggesting that raising the minimum wage may increase unemployment be cited or would that introduce a "conservative bias"? What if studies reach competing conclusions, suggesting that raising the minimum wage increases or reduces unemployment? Journalists must make choices about what facts and perspectives to present. A decision to include a particular fact may be seen as biased by some but as indicative of bias by others if excluded.

Though it is difficult to agree on what it means for a particular news report to be unbiased, innovative research provides some interesting insights. In one fascinating study, Gentzkow and Shapiro analyzed the words and phrases commonly used by Democrats and Republicans in Congress.[39] They found, for example, that Democrats and Republicans typically used different language to refer to the federal tax paid on multimillion dollar estates after an owner dies. Democrats overwhelmingly referred to this tax as an "estate tax," presumably to highlight the fact that it applies only to wealthy individuals. In contrast, Republicans described the tax as a "death tax," perhaps to suggest that it affects everyone. The researchers then assessed how often various newspapers used these terms to construct a measure of media slant. Newspapers that used language similar to that of Republican elected officials were considered more conservative; those that used the language of Democrats, more liberal. Although studies like this can identify variation in newspapers' slants, it is important to note that they cannot prove or disprove bias. However, the fact that news outlets appear to vary in their ideological leanings raises the question why. What factors might affect the ideological leanings of news outlets? We consider three explanations.

**LIBERAL REPORTERS** Surveys of reporters' and journalists' opinions suggest that these individuals tend to be somewhat more liberal than the average American on certain matters, including the environment and such social issues as civil rights and liberties, affirmative action, abortion, and women's rights.[40] This is especially true of those employed by certain elite media organizations, including the *New York Times,* the *Washington Post,* and PBS. It is likely that reporters' liberalism has been reflected in the treatment of issues such as global warming, same-sex marriage, and abortion. In recent years, to be sure, more conservative reporters and newscasters have gained prominence, especially on cable news telecasts.

There is, however, little or no systematic evidence that reporters' personal values regularly affect what appears in the mainstream news media.[41] Journalists' commitment to the idea of objectivity helps them resist temptation, as do critical scrutiny and

**bias**
Deviation from ideal standards such as representativeness or objectivity.

**STUNNED BY KATRINA**
Many conservative commentators charged that the news media focused on poor African Americans in New Orleans as the main victims of Hurricane Katrina when, in fact, the range of victims was much more diverse and living across a broader swath of Gulf Coast states. Is this a fair assessment of the media coverage?

rewriting by editors. In any case, the liberalism of journalists may be offset by their need to rely on official sources, their reliance on experts who are either former officials or associated with centrist or conservative think tanks, and the need to get their stories past editors who are accountable to mostly conservative owners and publishers.

**NOT-SO-LIBERAL OWNERS AND CORPORATIONS** The owners and top managers of most news media organizations tend to be conservative and Republican. This is hardly surprising. The shareholders and executives of multi-billion-dollar corporations are not very interested in undermining the free enterprise system, for example, or, for that matter, increasing their own taxes, raising labor costs, or losing income from offended advertisers. These owners and managers ultimately decide which reporters, newscasters, and editors to hire or fire, promote or discourage. Journalists who want to get ahead, therefore, may have to come to terms with the policies of the people who own and run media businesses.[42]

**REPUTATION FOR QUALITY** A final factor that may affect the ideological slant of a news outlet is closely connected to the profit motive. News organizations that do not attract and maintain an audience ultimately, fail. Thus, when reporting on politics, they may strive to present stories in a way that their audience will interpret as high quality. One way to convey quality to may be to avoid telling stories in ways that challenge audience beliefs.[43] For example, among people who cited Fox News as their primary source of news, a recent survey found that 94 percent identified themselves as Republicans or Republican leaners and 97 percent disapproved of President Obama's job performance.[44] If Fox News airs stories that cast Obama in a favorable light, its viewers may tune out, reasoning that liberal bias has infiltrated what had previously been a "high-quality" outlet. Put simply, a desire to gain and retain audience, not the ideological preferences of reporters or owners, may be a key driver of ideological media bias.

## ◻ Nonideological Biases

Nonideological biases in reporting may also push news organizations to engage in practices that are harmful to their roles in a democratic society and that undermine their effectiveness as watchdogs and as providers of relevant information. These biases include reporters' dependence on official sources of information, the eagerness with which they pursue sensational stories, and profit seeking—all matters examined earlier—but there are others.

**NATIONALISM** Although perhaps not terribly surprising, most news about foreign affairs takes a definitely pro-American, patriotic point of view, usually putting the United States in a favorable light and its opponents in an unfavorable light. This tendency is especially pronounced in news about military conflicts involving U.S. troops, as in Iraq and Afghanistan, but it can be found as well in a wide range of foreign affairs news reports, including those concerning conflicts with other governments on trade, arms control, immigration, and intellectual property rights.

News organizations also focus on subjects that interest and concern ordinary Americans, regardless of their importance in the larger picture. For example, in the early 1990s, they exhaustively covered a U.S. pilot, Scott O'Grady, who had been shot down over Bosnia. But much less attention was paid to the slaughter of millions of people during the same time in Indonesia, Nigeria, East Timor, Cambodia, and Rwanda.

This nationalistic perspective, together with heavy reliance on U.S. government news sources, means that coverage of foreign news generally harmonizes well with official U.S. foreign policy. Thus, the media tend to go along with the U.S. government in assuming the best about our close allies and the worst about official "enemies." When the United States was assisting Iraq in its war against Iran during the 1980s, for example, Saddam Hussein was depicted in a positive light; during the later Gulf War and the Iraq War, media characterizations of him turned dramatically negative.

In foreign policy crisis situations, the reliance on official news sources means that the media sometimes propagate government statements that are false or misleading, as in the announcement of unprovoked attacks on U.S. destroyers in the Gulf of Tonkin at the beginning of the Vietnam War. Secret information can also be controlled by the government. And political leaders know that the news media will be cautious in its criticism when troops are deployed and put in harm's way.

It is important to point out that when the use of American armed forces abroad drags on beyond expectations and goals are not met (as in the conflicts in Vietnam, Iraq, and Afghanistan), the news media can and do become negative in their coverage. This may simply reflect the mood change among nonadministration leaders and the public, or it might be a reaction among journalists and news organizations to their initial uncritical coverage of administration policies.

**APPROVAL OF THE AMERICAN ECONOMIC SYSTEM** Another tendency of the news media is to run stories generally approving of the basics of the American free enterprise system—free markets, strong property rights, and minimal government—and critical of systems that take a different approach. European social democracies with comprehensive social welfare programs, for example, rarely win praise and are often chided for their economic inefficiencies. Countries such as France, Italy, and Germany are commonly criticized for labor policies that make it difficult to fire employees and downsize companies, again on economic efficiency grounds. Meanwhile, countries whose economic policies mirror those of the U.S. economy, such as Poland and Chile, win praise. To be sure, individual U.S. companies (e.g., Lehman Brothers, AIG, and Goldman Sachs) and particular industries (e.g., the sub-prime mortgage sector) are criticized for errors and misdeeds, but the basics of the economic system itself are rarely challenged. When an economic disaster like the Great Recession happens, news consumers and news organizations are eager to focus on "who is to blame" rather than on issues like the instability that may be inherent in market-driven financial systems.[45]

**NEGATIVITY AND SCANDAL** Journalists are also eager to cover and magnify scandals involving political leaders and candidates of all stripes. Although the catalyst for these stories may be leaks from inside the government; negative ads aired by rival candidates, political parties, or advocacy groups; or postings to partisan and ideological blogs, they often are picked up by major news media outlets and developed further, occasionally with great gusto.[46] These stories are especially compelling to the news media when even the appearance of wrongdoing in the personal lives of prominent people creates dramatic human interest stories. Sex scandals dogged Bill Clinton for most of his presidency and contributed to his eventual impeachment. In 2011 Anthony Weiner (D-NY) resigned from Congress after being caught in a sexting scandal. Weiner—a married man—admitted to sending sexually explicit images to women he had met online. In 2013 he attempted to revive his political career, vying to be the Democratic nominee in the New York City mayoral race. After he was caught in a second scandal, admitting to more sexting in 2012 and 2013, he stayed in the race nonetheless and came in fifth place, winning fewer than 35,000 votes.

**INFOTAINMENT** The prominent place of scandal in the news media is but one example of a larger and troubling trend. Together with the multiplication of news outlets and increasing competition for audience share, the desire to attract viewers, readers, or listeners has led to the massive invasion of entertainment values into political reporting and news presentation. The best way to gain and retain an audience, media executives have discovered, is to make the news more entertaining, for the worst sin of this brave new media world is to be boring.[47] All too often, "more entertaining" means that sensation and scandal replace consideration of domestic politics, public policies, and international affairs. In 2009, Michael Jackson accounted for 60 percent of television news shows during the two days following his death, far more coverage than the mass antigovernment demonstrations in Iran.[48] More entertaining also means short and snappy coverage rather than longer, more analytical coverage; dramatic visuals push aside stories that cannot be easily visualized; and stories that feature angry conflict displace stories in which political leaders are trying to make workable compromises.[49]

When news organizations do cover political topics they tend to prioritize stories that feature conflict. The current culture wars between liberals and conservatives over the various legacies of the 1960s involving issues such as abortion, affirmative action, religious values, teaching evolution in schools, same-sex marriage, and more are perfect grist for the infotainment

**agenda setting**
Influencing people's opinions about what is important.

mill.[50] Thus, a current staple of cable and broadcast television public affairs programming is the gathering of pundits from both sides of the cultural and political divide angrily shouting at one another for 30 or 60 minutes. And, because bringing together shouting pundits is far cheaper than sending reporters into the field to gather hard news, this form of news coverage is becoming more and more common, especially in the world of cable TV. It is highly unlikely that this emergent journalism of assertion and attack improves public understanding of the candidates, political leaders, or public policies.

Conflict and contest are also evident in coverage of campaigns, where the media concentrate on the "horse-race" aspects of election contests, focusing almost exclusively on who is winning and who is losing the race and what strategies candidates are using to gain ground or to maintain their lead. When candidates sometimes make a stab at talking seriously about issues, the media almost always treat such talk as a mere stratagem of the long campaign.[51] The perpetual struggle between Congress and the president, built into our constitutional system, is also perfect for the infotainment news industry, especially if the struggle can be personalized, as it was when President Obama was doing battle with House Speaker John Boehner over raising the debt ceiling.

**LIMITED, FRAGMENTED, AND INCOHERENT POLITICAL INFORMATION** Most communications scholars agree that the media coverage of political news has certain distinctive features that result from characteristics of the mass media themselves, including the prevailing technology and organization of news gathering, corporate ownership, and the profit-making drive to appeal to mass audiences. These characteristics of the media mean that news, especially on television, tends to be episodic and fragmented rather than sustained, analytical, or dispassionate. Information comes in bits and pieces, out of context, and without historical background. Its effect is to entertain more than to inform. This may or may not be what people want—some scholars suggest that the people, in fact, do not want hard news at all; others suggest that they want a strong dose of entertainment and diversion with their news[52]—but it is what they get.

Having said that, it is important to point out that the news media often do deep and thorough investigative reporting that matters. But the pressure to stick to infotainment is relentless, and all news organizations feel it in one way or another—even the best of them.

# Effects of the News Media on Politics

**S**ocial scientists have gone from speculating that the media dramatically and directly influence political views to believing instead that the media have only "minimal effects" on people's attitudes. Both of these possibilities has been discredited in favor of a more nuanced understanding of the effect of the media on public opinion and policymaking, including the media's effect on setting the agenda for public debate and on framing how issues are understood.[53] News reports may also affect people's broader orientation toward the political world by fostering cynicism and fragmented knowledge of the political world.

## ☐ Agenda Setting

Several studies have demonstrated the effect known as **agenda setting**. The topics that get the most coverage in the news media at any point in time are the same ones that most people tell pollsters are the most important problems facing the country. This correlation does not result just from the news media's reporting what people are most interested in; it is a real effect of what appears in the news. In controlled experiments, people who are shown doctored television news broadcasts emphasizing a particular problem (e.g., national defense) mention that problem as being important more often than people who have seen broadcasts that have not been tampered with.[54] Another line of research has shown that news media polling often is used as the basis for reporting about what the American people want regarding a certain policy (say, intervening in the civil war in Syria) when few Americans know or care about the subject matter of the opinion survey. The polling story, if it is picked up by other news media outlets, bloggers, and pundits, however, then becomes part of the general news landscape and sparks interest among much of the public about that subject. It becomes part of the public agenda.[55]

Of course, media managers do not arbitrarily decide what news to emphasize; their decisions reflect what is happening in the world and what American audiences care about. If there is a war or an economic depression, the media report it. But some research has indicated that what the media cover sometimes diverges from actual trends in problems. Publicity about crime, for example, may reflect editors' fears or a few dramatic incidents rather than a rising crime rate. When the two diverge, it seems to be the media's emphasis rather than real trends that affects public opinion.[56]

When the media decide to highlight a human rights tragedy in "real time," such as Boko Haram's kidnapping of more than 200 Nigerian schoolgirls, public officials often feel compelled to act. (This is sometimes called the CNN effect.) When the media ignore equally troubling human tragedies, such as the genocide in Darfur, public officials can attend to other matters. One scholarly study shows that in the foreign policy area, media choices about coverage shape what presidents pay attention to.[57] But influences go in both directions. News media scholar Lance Bennett suggests that journalists and the news organizations they work for are very attuned to the relative power balance in Washington between Democrats and Republicans, and between liberals and conservatives, and focus on matters that are of most concern to those in power at any particular time. Thus, Social Security reform becomes an important issue in the press when important political actors want to talk about it. The same is true for other issues, whether it's taxes or nuclear threats from countries such as Iran and North Korea.[58]

## ☐ Framing and Effects on Policy Preferences

Experiments also indicate that the media's **framing**, or interpretation of stories, affects how people think about political problems and how they assign blame.[59] Several commentators noticed during the Katrina disaster in New Orleans, for example, that TV news stories featuring whites talked of "foraging for food and supplies," while those featuring blacks talked of looting. There are reasons to believe that public impressions of what was going on in the city were affected by this coverage. To take another example, whether citizens ascribe poverty to the laziness of the poor or to the nature of the economy, for example, depends partly on whether the news media run stories about poor individuals (implying that they are responsible for their own plight) or stories about overall economic trends such as economic recessions and unemployment.[60] (See the "Using the Framework" feature for another example.)

What appears in the news media affects people's policy preferences as well. One study found, for example, that the public is more likely to favor government programs to help African Americans when the news media frame racial problems in terms of failures of society to live up to the tradition of equality in the United States. The public is less supportive of these programs when the news media frame the origins of racial problems in terms of individual failures to be self-reliant and responsible.[61] Another study found that changes in the percentages of the public that favored various policies could be predicted rather accurately by what sorts of

**framing**
Providing a context for interpretation.

6.1

6.2

6.3

6.4

**THE TELEVISED WAR**

The Vietnam War was the first American war fully covered by television. Footage of American deaths and casualties, as well as visual reminders of the terrible consequences of the conflict on the Vietnamese civilian population, helped turn public opinion in the United States against the war. This still from television footage of children napalmed by an accidental American attack on a village of Trang Bang in 1972 is a particularly powerful example of the war coming home to American living rooms. How do the media continue to influence American public opinion about our role in foreign conflicts?

stories appeared on network television news shows between one opinion survey and the next. News from experts, commentators, and popular presidents had especially strong effects.[62]

## ☐ Fueling Cynicism

Americans are quite cynical about the political parties, politicians, and most incumbent political leaders. To some extent, this has been true since the founding of the nation. Nevertheless, scholars and political commentators have noted a considerable increase in negative feelings about the political system over the past two decades or so. Many students of the media believe that news media coverage of American politics has a great deal to do with this attitude change.[63] As the adversarial-attack journalism style and infotainment have taken over political reporting, serious consideration of the issues, careful examination of policy alternatives, and dispassionate examination of the actions of government institutions have taken a back seat to a steady diet of charges about personal misbehavior and political conflict. When President George H. W. Bush joined a world leader at a press conference in 1992 to describe the nature of the agreement they had reached, reporters asked him instead about rumors of an extramarital affair a few years earlier. With the message being delivered by the mass media that political issues are really about special-interest maneuvering, that political leaders and aspiring political leaders never say what they mean or mean what they say, that all of them have something in their personal lives they want to hide, and that even the most admired of the lot have feet of clay, is it any wonder that the American people are becoming increasingly disenchanted with the whole business?

News reports feed a constant stream of messages about the failure of government: programs that don't work, wasteful spending, lazy and incompetent public employees, looming government deficits, and people receiving benefits they don't deserve. Though not entirely absent, stories about government working in a way that enhances the well-being of Americans are less common, probably because such stories are not terribly dramatic. Mail gets delivered every day into the remotest regions of the country,

# Using the FRAMEWORK

## Why talk of deficits filled the air rather than talk of jobs

**Background:** The battle between Democrats and Republicans, and President Barack Obama and the Republican-controlled House of Representatives over increasing the national government's debt ceiling—how much the government could borrow—was dominated by talk of decreasing the size of the annual federal deficit, with the threat of a government shutdown and default on U.S. debts looming. While this was going on in the summer of 2011, the United States was in the midst of its longest period of economic stagnation since the Great Depression, characterized by tepid GDP growth, an unemployment rate of over 9 percent (the underemployment rate was near 17 percent), and long-term unemployment at its highest level since the end of World War II. When asked what their most important concerns were, every major poll showed that Americans listed jobs first, with deficit reduction down the list at eighth or ninth position. This disconnect between what was happening in Washington and what the American people wanted had many causes, but one was surely the news media's tendency to emphasize issues of greatest concern to our leading political actors. We see here how structural, political, and governmental factors combine to create this outcome.

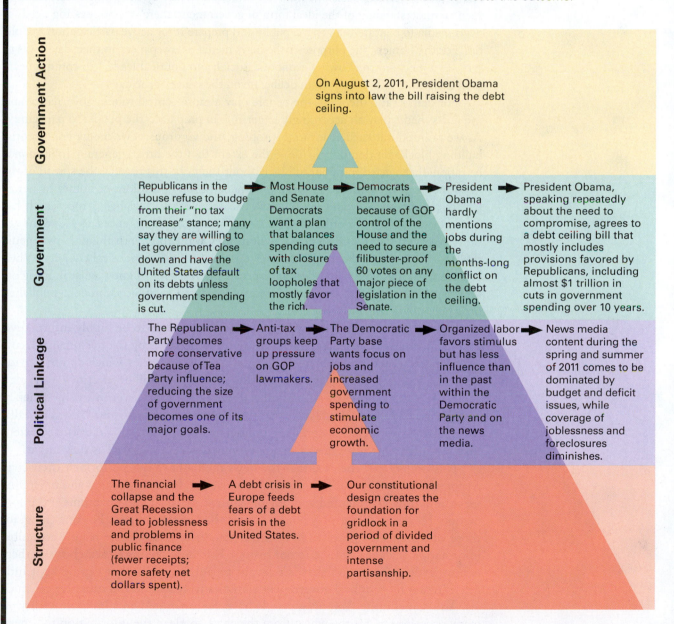

**Government Action**

On August 2, 2011, President Obama signs into law the bill raising the debt ceiling.

**Government**

Republicans in the House refuse to budge from their "no tax increase" stance; many say they are willing to let government close down and have the United States default on its debts unless government spending is cut. → Most House and Senate Democrats want a plan that balances spending cuts with closure of tax loopholes that mostly favor the rich. → Democrats cannot win because of GOP control of the House and the need to secure a filibuster-proof 60 votes on any major piece of legislation in the Senate. → President Obama hardly mentions jobs during the months-long conflict on the debt ceiling. → President Obama, speaking repeatedly about the need to compromise, agrees to a debt ceiling bill that mostly includes provisions favored by Republicans, including almost $1 trillion in cuts in government spending over 10 years.

**Political Linkage**

The Republican Party becomes more conservative because of Tea Party influence; reducing the size of government becomes one of its major goals. → Anti-tax groups keep up pressure on GOP lawmakers. → The Democratic Party base wants focus on jobs and increased government spending to stimulate economic growth. → Organized labor favors stimulus but has less influence than in the past within the Democratic Party and on the news media. → News media content during the spring and summer of 2011 comes to be dominated by budget and deficit issues, while coverage of joblessness and foreclosures diminishes.

**Structure**

The financial collapse and the Great Recession lead to joblessness and problems in public finance (fewer receipts; more safety net dollars spent). → A debt crisis in Europe feeds fears of a debt crisis in the United States. → Our constitutional design creates the foundation for gridlock in a period of divided government and intense partisanship.

for example, while cars and trucks make heavy use of the interstate highway system. The Center for Disease Control keeps on constant alert for dangerous pathogens, even as park rangers keep watch on our national parks.

## Using the DEMOCRACY STANDARD

### Do the news media help or hinder democracy?

The framers favored a form of government based on the consent of the governed, but one in which most of the governed played only a limited and indirect role in political life. They believed that government was best run by talented, educated, and broad-minded individuals who attained office through indirect elections based on a limited franchise, and whose governing decisions were not directly dictated by the people. According to such an understanding of the ideal form of government, there was no pressing need for news media to educate the general public and prepare it for active participation in politics. For the framers, the purpose of the news media—newspapers, in their day—was to serve as a mechanism allowing economic, social, and political leaders to communicate with each other and to help them deliberate on the issues of the day.

For democratic theorists, the people play a more central role in governance and the news media play an accordingly larger role in preparing the people to participate. As we pointed out earlier, accurate, probing, and vigorous news media are essential building blocks for democratic life to the extent that the broad general public cannot be rationally engaged in public affairs without them. In this respect, the spread of the news media in the United States, and the penetration of millions of homes by newspapers, radio, television, and the Internet, has undoubtedly enriched democracy. It has made it much easier for ordinary citizens to form policy preferences, to judge the actions of government, and to decide whom they want to govern them. News media thus tend to broaden the scope of conflict and contribute to political equality. When citizens as well as political leaders and special-interest groups know what is going on, they can have a voice in politics. Moreover, interactive media and media-published polls help politicians hear that voice.

Scholars and media critics who want the news media to be highly informative, analytical, and issue oriented, however, are often appalled by the personalized, episodic, dramatic, and fragmented character of most news stories, which do not provide sustained and coherent explanations of what is going on. Still other critics worry that constant media exposés of alleged official wrongdoing or government inefficiency, and the mocking tone aimed at virtually all political leaders by journalists and talk-radio hosts, have fueled the growing political cynicism of the public. To the extent that this is true, the news media are not serving democracy as well as they might.

It is undeniably the case that the news media have not performed their civic responsibilities very well. They do tend to trivialize, focus on scandal and entertainment, and offer fragmented and out-of-context political and governmental information. However, things may not be quite as bad as they appear. For one thing, for those who are truly interested in public affairs, there is now more readily accessible information than at any time in our history. For those willing to search for it, there is now little information that is relevant to public affairs that can be kept hidden, ranging from official government statistics to academic and other expert studies. Additionally, the American people have demonstrated an admirable ability on many occasions to sift the wheat from the chaff, to glean the information they need from the background noise, as it were.[64] On balance, then, the news media have probably helped advance the cause of democracy in the United States and helped transform the American republic into the American democratic republic. There is no doubt, however, that the news media could also do a considerably better job than they do at the present time.

# Review the Chapter

## Roles of the News Media in Democracy

**6.1** Evaluate the various roles of the news media in a democracy, p. 155

One role for the news media in a democracy is to serve as a watchdog over government, uncovering government corruption and keeping government officials accountable to the public.

Other important roles are to help citizens evaluate candidates for public office and to think about what kinds of government policies might best serve the public interest.

## Mainstream and Alternative News Media

**6.2** Assess the respective roles of traditional and other news media today, p. 156

Traditional news media such as newspapers and television still gather and report the most news, even as more people get their information from the Internet.

Internet news is rarely based on independent reporting. Most is from the traditional media, either taken directly, rewritten, or commented upon.

Television is still the most trusted source of news.

## How the Mainstream News Media Work

**6.3** Analyze how the news is gathered and disseminated and evaluate the outcome of this process, p. 163

The shape of the news media in the United States has been determined largely by structural factors: technological developments; the growth of the American population and economy; and the development of a privately owned, corporation-dominated media industry.

New Internet-based media have not replaced traditional reporting and news organizations. For the most part, these new media use materials gathered by old media.

News gathering is limited by logistics. Most news gathering is organized around New York City, Washington, D.C., and a handful of major cities in the United States and abroad. Most foreign countries are ignored unless there are crises or other big stories to communicate.

## Effects of the News Media on Politics

**6.4** Identify the ways in which the news media affect public opinion and policymaking, p. 176

News media stories have substantial effects on the public's perceptions of problems, its interpretations of events, its evaluations of political candidates, and its policy preferences.

The news media affects the public not only by providing information but also by agenda setting and framing.

# Learn the Terms

watchdog, p. 155
wire services, p. 160
media monopoly, p. 164
infotainment, p. 166
beat, p. 168

leak, p. 169
spin, p. 169
newsworthy, p. 170
objective journalism, p. 171
pundits, p. 172

bias, p. 173
agenda setting, p. 176
framing, p. 177

# Test Yourself

Answer key begins on page T-1.

**6.1** Evaluate the various roles of the news media in a democracy

1. The three roles of the news media in democracy are:

   **a.** Be a watchdog over the government, present electoral choices, and expose scandals.
   **b.** Present electoral choices, expose scandals, and cover breaking news stories.
   **c.** Be a watchdog over the government, present breaking news stories, and provide information about public policy.
   **d.** Be a watchdog over the government, present electoral choices, and provide information about public policy.
   **e.** Expose scandals, cover breaking news stores, and protect the reputation of high-ranking government officials.

**6.2** Assess the respective roles of traditional and other news media today

2. The preferred source for political news for Americans is:

   **a.** Printed newspapers
   **b.** Online newspapers
   **c.** Campaign websites
   **d.** Facebook
   **e.** Television

**6.3** Analyze how the news is gathered and disseminated and evaluate the outcome of this process

3. This is a common way for officials to float policy ideas, get noticed, undercut rivals, and report real or imagined wrongdoing.

   **a.** Floating information
   **b.** Spinning information
   **c.** Leaking information
   **d.** News management
   **e.** Tipping information

**6.4** Identify the ways in which the news media affect public opinion and policymaking

4. Many students of media believe that news media coverage of American politics has a lot to do with this growing feeling in the American people:

   **a.** Cynicism
   **b.** Happiness
   **c.** Anger
   **d.** Disappointment
   **e.** Security

# Explore Further

## INTERNET SOURCES

The Pew Research Center Journalism Project **www .stateofthenewsmedia.org**
Annual scholarly review of the state of the news media, with attention to new developments.
The Berkman Center for Internet & Society **cyber.law.harvard.edu**
A research and information center at the Harvard Law School that follows the development of the Internet and its impact on law and society.
The Columbia Journalism Review **www.cjr.org/**
The website of the leading scholarly monitor of journalism and journalists; loaded with useful information about all aspects of newsmaking and dissemination.
The Pew Research Center for the People and the Press **www .people-press.org**
The most complete public opinion surveys on citizen evaluations of the quality of media coverage of public affairs.
Wired Magazine Online **www.wired.com**
Attempts to report on what is at the cutting edge in terms of technology, computing, and the Internet with some coverage of their economic, social, and political impacts.
News Bias Explored: The Art of Reading the News **www.umich .edu/~newsbias/links.html**
A comprehensive collection of links to objective sources discussing omission and bias in news reporting.
The New York Times **www.nytimes.com**
The home page for *The New York Times.*
The Huffington Post **www.huffingtonpost.com**
The home page for *The Huffington Post.*

## SUGGESTIONS FOR FURTHER READING

Alterman, Eric. *What Liberal Media? The Truth About Bias and the News.* New York: Basic Books, 2003.
An impassioned yet well-documented answer to the charge that the news media are biased against conservatives.
Bennett, W. Lance. *News: Politics of Illusion,* 9th ed. New York: Longman, 2011.
A critique of the news as trivial and uninformative.
Bennett, W. Lance, Regina G. Lawrence, and Steven Livingston. *When the Press Fails: Political Power and the News from Iraq to Katrina.* Chicago: University of Chicago Press, 2007.
A devastating critique of the news media limited by the pressures of the marketplace and the balance of political power in Washington.
Goldberg, Bernard. *Bias: A CBS Insider Exposes How the Media Distort the News.* New York: Harper Paperbacks, 2003.

A conservative critique of CBS News in particular and the mainstream news media in general.

Hindman, Matthew. *The Myth of Digital Democracy.* Princeton, NJ: Princeton University Press, 2009.

Based on compelling empirical evidence, the author shows that many of the inequalities that characterize American society and politics are recreated on the Internet.

Graber, Doris. *Mass Media and American Politics,* 8th ed. Washington, D.C.: CQ Press, 2010.

A comprehensive examination of the news media's effect on American politics.

Shapiro, Robert Y. and Lawrence R. Jacobs, eds. *The Oxford Handbook of American Public Opinion and the Media.* Oxford: Oxford University Press, 2011.

A comprehensive collection of articles by leading scholars on the organization, operations, and impact of the news media, both old and new.

# 7

# Interest Groups and Business Corporations

## DISASTER IN THE GULF

I n the Gulf of Mexico on April 20, 2010, just before midnight the Deepwater Horizon drilling rig was ripped apart by a series of spectacular explosions that killed 11 oil rig workers and unleashed an oil spill of near-historic proportions.[1] The Deepwater Horizon, owned by the Transocean Corporation and leased to oil giant BP, was finishing the final phases of drilling a well more than a mile beneath the platform when disaster struck. The temporary cement cap that topped off the well failed, releasing a potent and out-of-control flow of a natural gas and crude oil mixture to the platform where a spark set off the explosion. The shattered pipe in the middle of the drill hole poured natural gas and crude oil into the Gulf at the rate of 35,000 to 60,000 barrels a day, defying initial efforts to cut off the flow at the pipe. Efforts to funnel the crude oil to storage and transport vessels on the surface in the months after the blowout, even as relief wells were being drilled, did some good, but massive amounts of natural gas and crude oil continued to escape for months. The spill fouled the beaches and marshlands of Gulf Coast states and formed deep, underwater

| 7.1 | 7.2 | 7.3 | 7.4 | 7.5 | 7.6 |
|-----|-----|-----|-----|-----|-----|
| Compare and contrast theories about the role of interest groups in a democracy, p. 188 | Distinguish the two kinds of interests at work in American politics, p. 190 | Explain why interest groups have proliferated, p. 195 | Distinguish the methods through which interest groups try to shape government policy, p. 198 | Determine the biases in the interest group system, p. 204 | Assess the steps that have been taken to control factions, p. 212 |

**DISASTER IN THE GULF** Risky behavior by drilling companies, pressure from the parent oil company BP, and lax government regulatory oversight, all contributed to the Deepwater Horizon disaster in the Gulf of Mexico in 2010. By all accounts, it represents the most serious environmental disaster in American history, with its effects still being felt in the Gulf region. What can and should be done to prevent similar such disasters in the future?

natural gas and oil plumes, whose long-term environmental effects are unknowable at this time. Needless to say, the Gulf Coast fishing and shrimping industries suffered serious losses, with many customers turning to foreign sources of supply.

How did it happen? We know that BP, putting cost-saving before safety, insisted that the platform operator, Transocean, take a number of operational steps that were quite risky and ill-advised. These included using too few "centralizers" to stabilize the cement that held the drilling pipe in place in the ocean floor, skipping critical inspections and tests of emergency cut-off mechanisms, using one rather than the industry-standard two pipe "pinchers" (called "blind shear rams") to cut off oil flow in the main pipe in the event of a blowout, and using pipes of lower quality than BP's own experts advised. Though Transocean engineers and many workers aboard the Deepwater rig apparently expressed concerns about these decisions, operations never slowed as BP executives pushed everyone to finish on time and under budget so it could temporarily cap the well and move on to other drilling opportunities.

Though BP was at fault in this case, it emerged in congressional testimony during early summer 2010 that other oil company operators doing deep well drilling in the Gulf and other places in the world had no better solutions to a blowout at these depths than BP did. Oil and drilling company executives testified that, at a minimum, more onsite testing of critical blowout preventers should be done in light of the Deepwater Horizon event, but they were somewhat at a loss for words when congressional committee members produced a report from the industry itself pointing out that most companies cut corners in their testing programs given the costs involved: about $700 a minute to suspend operations while testing.

We have a rough idea, then, of why the Deepwater Horizon happened from a technical point of view. But other factors involving the oil industry's political influence are also important in this story. There is, first, the absence of a national energy policy that might encourage the development and use of renewable energy. Without this, for now and the foreseeable future, Americans must depend on fossil fuels, especially coal, natural gas, and oil, to provide the power they need to run a modern, industrial society. Inevitably, as easily recoverable oil reserves are depleted, and as global climate change concerns put a damper on a greater reliance on coal, oil companies are forced to look in less hospitable places for oil, including the deep ocean floor. But the absence of a national energy policy is itself the result of the long-term oil industry influence in American politics; the industry has been among the very largest contributors to the campaigns of presidential, congressional, and state-level candidates and among the industries that spend the most on direct lobbying to keep oil at the center of our energy economy.

The oil industry also has been a central player in the four-decade-long effort to deregulate the American economy, that is, leave more and more decisions to private firms operating in the marketplace, largely freed from federal and state government oversight. Business leaders, the economics profession, conservative think tanks, and Republican and centrist Democrats came to believe that government is generally bad for economic efficiency and growth and ought to exit the game, as it were.[2] The oil industry contribution to the deregulation movement has been multifaceted, including campaign contributions and lobbying, but also the generous funding of anti–big government think tanks that have churned out reports on the evils of regulation for many years. Deregulation has had some good outcomes, to be sure, as in restraining air travel and freight shipping costs, but bad ones in a wide range of areas, including the collapse of the financial system as the most obvious recent case. But the deregulation spirit has infused the oil industry as well, with fewer personnel in agencies that are responsible for oversight and less willingness on the part of mid-level government bureaucrats, given the political environment, to ask too much of industry operators. One of the things congressional testimony revealed in summer 2010 was how few rules the Minerals Management Service (MMS) issued regarding deep ocean drilling and how often they failed to enforce the few rules that were in place.

Finally, there is what political scientists call "agency capture," in which a regulatory agency, designed to regulate an industry in the public interest, comes to act as a partner instead. This happens for a number of reasons, including possible future employment in the regulated industry for the regulator, dependence on the industry for the technical information that the agency needs to issue regulations and monitor performance, and long-term relationships among regulators and firms that encourage commonality in points of view. Sometimes, there is even gift-giving from the wealthy industry to those who work in the regulatory agency.

Each of these elements of "capture" can be seen in the MMS oil and drilling industry relationship. Congressional hearings and an Interior Department inspector general's report in 2010 revealed, for example, that companies paid for meals and hotel stays, elaborate vacations, and tickets to premium athletic events for agency employees and that several inspectors had examined operations at companies where they hoped to work. The hearings and report also uncovered the cozy relationship that developed between oil rig inspectors and drilling companies. For example, many instances were uncovered in which industry officials were allowed to fill out MMS inspection report forms in pencil, with the inspectors going over the pencil traces later in pen. Equally important, the MMS was entirely dependent on the technical information provided by regulated companies, having neither the personnel nor agency resources to develop information or independent testing equipment and instruments "in-house." During the Coast Guard inquiry on the failure of the various safety devices to work at the Deepwater Horizon platform, Captain Hung Nguyen was astonished when he received a simple "yes" answer from the MMS's regional supervisor for field operations to the following question: "So my understanding is that [the shear ram tool] is designed to industry standard, manufactured by industry, installed by industry, with no government witnessing oversight of the construction or the installation. Is that correct?"

Much of what the federal government does in the United States is influenced by what the general public wants it to do. Elected and other public officials, you have seen, pay attention to things such as public opinion polls and news media characterizations of popular preferences. You will see in later chapters in this book, moreover, that, political leaders must be responsive to the electorate if they want to gain and retain their elected offices. But it is also the case that a wide array of private interest and advocacy groups, with business leading the way, also play an enormously important, although less visible, role in determining what government does and influencing who wins and who loses from public policies. Some commentators go so far as to suggest that Washington is now run by a massive and powerful interest group industry that either clogs the governmental machinery—with a multitude of dispersed special interests vetoing government actions they oppose, whether legislation or administrative rule-making and enforcement—or gets their way most of the time on government actions that directly affect them. Conservative *New York Times* commentator David Brooks terms this system "interest group capitalism."[3]

## Thinking Critically About This Chapter

This chapter is about the important role interest groups play in American government and politics, how they go about achieving their ends, and what effects they have in determining government policies in the United States.

## Using the Framework

You will see in this chapter how interest groups, in combination with other political linkage institutions, help convey the wishes and interests of people and groups to government decision makers. You will also learn how the kind of interest group system we have in the United States is, in large part, a product of structural factors, including our constitutional rules, political culture, social organization, and economy.

## Using the Democracy Standard

Interest groups have long held an ambiguous place in American politics. To some, interest groups are "special" interests that act without regard to the public interest and are the instruments of the most privileged parts of American society. To others, interest groups are simply another way by which people and groups in a democratic society get their voices heard by government leaders. Using the democracy standard, you will be able to evaluate these two positions.

7.1

7.2

7.3

7.4

7.5

7.6

**interest groups**
A private organization or voluntary association that seeks to influence public policy as a way to protect or advance its interests.

**factions**
Madison's term for groups or parties that try to advance their own interests at the expense of the public good.

# Interest Groups in a Democratic Society: Contrasting Views

**7.1** Compare and contrast theories about the role of interest groups in a democracy

**I**nterest groups are private organizations and voluntary associations that seek to advance their interests by trying to influence what government does. They are not officially a part of government. Nor are they political parties that try to place candidates carrying the party banner into government offices, though, as shown later in this chapter, interest groups play an important role in U.S. elections. Interest groups are formed by people or firms that share an interest or cause they are trying to protect or advance with the help of government.[4] The interests and causes they press on government range from narrowly targeted material benefits (e.g., passage of a favorable tax break or the issuance of a helpful regulation) to more broadly targeted outcomes for society at large (e.g., new rules on auto emissions or abortion availability). To do this, interest groups try to influence the behavior of public officials, such as presidents, members of Congress, bureaucrats, and judges. The framers knew that interest groups were inevitable and appropriate in a free society but were potentially harmful as well, so they paid special attention to them in the design of the Constitution.

## ☐ The Evils of Faction

The danger to good government and the public interest from interest groups is a familiar theme in American politics. They are usually regarded as narrowly self-interested, out for themselves, and without regard for the public good.

This theme is prominent in *The Federalist* No. 10 (see the Appendix), in which James Madison defined **factions** (his term for interest groups and narrow political parties) in the following manner: "A number of citizens, whether amounting to a majority

**BOSSES OF THE SENATE**

In the late nineteenth century, most Americans thought of the Senate as the captive of large corporate trusts and other special-interest groups, as depicted in this popular cartoon, "Bosses of the Senate." How has the public's view changed, if at all? Is there any basis for believing that the situation today is substantially different from that of the late nineteenth century?

or a minority of the whole, who are united and actuated by some common impulse of passion, or of interest, adverse to the rights of other citizens or to the permanent and aggregate interests of the community."[5] The "evils of faction" theme recurs throughout our history, from the writings of the "muckrakers" at the turn of the twentieth century to news accounts and commentary on the misdeeds of the leaders of the financial industry in the 2008 financial collapse.

**pluralism**
The political science position that American democracy is best understood in terms of the interaction, conflict, and bargaining of groups.

## ☐ Interest Group Democracy: The Pluralist Argument

According to many political scientists, however, interest groups do not hurt democracy and the public interest but are an important instrument in attaining both. This way of looking at American democracy is called **pluralism** and takes the following form (also see Figure 7.1):[6]

- Free elections, while essential to a democracy, do not adequately communicate the specific wants and interests of the people to political leaders on a continuous basis. These are more accurately, consistently, and frequently conveyed to political leaders by the many groups and organizations to which people belong.

- Interest groups are easy to create; people in the United States are free to join or to organize groups that reflect their interests.

- Because of federalism, checks and balances, and the separation of powers, government power in the United States is broadly dispersed, leaving governmental institutions remarkably porous and open to the entreaties of the many and diverse groups that exist in society.

- Because of the ease of group formation and the accessibility of government, all legitimate interests in society can have their views taken into account by some public official. Farmers and business owners can get heard; so too can consumers and workers. Because of this, the system is highly democratic.

Pluralists see interest groups, then, not as a problem but as an additional tool of democratic representation, similar to other democratic instruments such as public opinion and elections. We shall explore the degree to which this position is valid in this and other chapters.

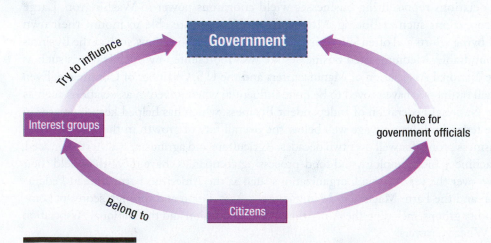

**FIGURE 7.1** THE PLURALIST VIEW OF AMERICAN POLITICS

In the pluralist understanding of the way American democracy works, citizens have more than one way to influence government leaders. In addition to voting, citizens also have the opportunity to participate in organizations that convey member views to public officials. Because of weak political parties, federalism, checks and balances, and the separation of powers, access to public officials is relatively easy.

# The Universe of Interest Groups

hat kinds of interests find a voice in American politics? A useful place to start is with political scientist E.E. Schattschneider's distinction between "private" and "public" interests. Although the boundaries between the two are sometimes fuzzy, the distinction remains important. **Private interests** are organizations and associations that try to gain protections or material advantages from government for their own members rather than for society at large.[7] For the most part, these represent economic interests of one kind or another. **Public interests**—often called **advocacy groups**—are organizations and associations that try to gain protections or benefits for people beyond their own members, often for society at large. Some are motivated by an ideology or by the desire to advance a general cause—animal rights, let us say, or environmental protection—or by the commitment to some public policy—gun control or an end to abortion. Some represent the nonprofit sector, and some even represent government entities, such as state and local governments.

Private and public interest groups come in a wide range of forms. Some, including the AARP, are large membership organizations with sizable Washington and regional offices. Some large membership organizations have passionately committed members active in their affairs—such as the National Rifle Association—while others have relatively passive members who join for the benefits the organization provides—such as the American Automobile Association with its well-known trip assistance and car buying service. Other groups are trade associations whose members are business firms. Still others are rather small organizations without members; are run by professionals and sustained by foundations and wealthy donors; and have sizable mailing, Internet, and telephone lists for soliciting contributions—the Children's Defense Fund and the National Taxpayers Union come to mind. We examine these in more detail below (see also Table 7.1).

## ☐ Private Interest Groups

Many different kinds of private interest groups are active in American politics.

**BUSINESS** Because of the vast resources at the disposal of businesses and because of their strategic role in the health of local, state, and national economies, groups and associations representing businesses wield enormous power in Washington. Large corporations such as Boeing, Microsoft, and Google are able to mount their own **lobbying** efforts and often join with others in influential associations, such as the Business Roundtable. Medium-sized businesses are well represented by organizations such as the National Association of Manufacturers and the U.S. Chamber of Commerce. Even small businesses have proved to be quite influential when joined in associations such as the National Federation of Independent Business, which has helped keep increases in the federal minimum wage well below the overall rate of growth in the economy and business profits for well over two decades. Agriculture and agribusinesses (fertilizer, seed, machinery, biotechnology, and food-processing companies) have more than held their own over the years through organizations such as the American Farm Bureau Federation and the Farm Machinery Manufacturer's Association and through scores of commodity groups, including the American Dairy Association and the National Association of Wheat Growers.

**THE PROFESSIONS** Several associations represent the interests of professionals, such as doctors, lawyers, dentists, and accountants. Because of the prominent social position of professionals in local communities and their ability to make substantial campaign contributions, such associations are very influential in the policymaking process on matters related to their professional expertise and concerns. The American Medical

7.1

7.2

7.3

7.4

7.5

7.6

**TABLE 7.1** THE DIVERSE WORLD OF INTEREST ASSOCIATIONS

| Interest | Interest Subtypes | Association Examples |
|---|---|---|
| *Private Interests (focus on protections and gains for their members)* | | |
| Business | Corporations that lobby on their own behalf | Google Boeing |
| | Trade associations | Chemical Manufacturers Association |
| | | Health Insurance Association of America |
| | Peak business organizations | Business Roundtable |
| | | Federation of Small Businesses |
| Professions | Doctors | American Medical Association |
| | Dentists | American Dental Association |
| | Accountants | National Society of Accountants |
| | Lawyers | American Bar Association |
| Labor | Union | International Association of Machinists |
| | Union federation | AFL-CIO |
| *Public Interests (focus on protections and gains for a broader public or society in general)* | | |
| Ideological and cause | Environment | Environmental Defense (formerly Environmental Defense Fund) |
| | Pro-choice | National Abortion Rights Action League |
| | Pro-life | National Right to Life Committee |
| | Anti-tax | Americans for Tax Reform |
| | Civil rights | National Association for the Advancement of Colored People |
| | | Human Rights Campaign |
| Nonprofit sector | Medical | American Hospital Association |
| | Charitable | American Red Cross |
| Governmental entities | State | National Conference of State Legislatures |
| | Local | National Association of Counties |

Association (AMA) and the American Dental Association (ADA), for instance, lobbied strongly against the Clinton health care proposal and helped kill it in the 103rd Congress. (These associations changed their tune in 2010, however, by backing the Affordable Care Act, perhaps because the new law promised to bring about 32 million more insured people into the existing system.) The Trial Lawyers Association has long been a major financial contributor to the Democratic Party and has been active in blocking legislation to limit the size of personal injury jury awards.

**LABOR** Although labor unions are sometimes involved in what might be called public interest activities (such as supporting civil rights legislation), their main role in the United States has been to protect the jobs of their members and to secure maximum wages and benefits for them. Unlike labor unions in many parts of the world, which are as much political and ideological organizations as economic, American labor unions have traditionally focused on so-called bread-and-butter issues. As an important part of the New Deal coalition that dominated American politics well into the late 1960s, labor unions were influential at the federal level during the years when the Democratic Party controlled Congress and often won the presidency.

Although organized labor is still a force to be reckoned with in electoral politics—they played a big role in fund-raising and mobilizing voters for Barack

7.1

7.2

7.3

7.4

7.5

7.6

**TINA FEY ON THE PICKET LINE AT NBC HEADQUARTERS**

A long strike in 2007 by television and film writers to gain concessions from the networks and film studios on use of writers' materials on the Internet was successful, party because of the strong support it received from leading actors and performers, including Tina Fey (herself a writer and a member of the Writers Guild of America). Despite success such as this one, union membership has been steadily declining in the United States. What accounts for declining union membership?

Obama and the Democrats in the 2008 and 2012 presidential and congressional races—most observers believe that the political power of labor unions has eroded in dramatic ways over the past several decades.[8] Organized labor's main long-range problem in American politics and its declining power relative to business in the workplace is its small membership base; in 2013, only 11.3 percent of American wage and salary workers—and only 6.7 percent of private sector workers—were members of labor unions compared with 35 percent in 1954.[9] The long but steady decline in union membership in the private sector is explained by a number of things. First, there has been a dramatic decline in the proportion of American workers in manufacturing, the economic sector in which unions have traditionally been the strongest. Fewer manufacturing workers are needed now than in the past because of outsourcing, gains in productivity (more can be manufactured with fewer workers), and pressures on companies to cut operating costs in a hyper-competitive global economy.[10] Second, business firms have become much less willing to tolerate unions and have become much more sophisticated at efforts to decertify unions and undermine union organization drives.[11] The long-term decline of private sector labor unions was vividly on display in the successful campaign by business groups and associations to pass so-called right to work laws in 2012 in Indiana and Michigan, historically important manufacturing states with strong labor unions. GOP control of the legislatures and governorships in both states after the 2010 elections made it possible. Right to work laws, which say that workers cannot be forced to join unions or pay union dues as a condition of getting or keeping a job, have long been considered anathema to organized labor, but, despite strenuous efforts, labor was unable to prevent Indiana and Michigan

7.1
7.2
7.3
7.4
7.5
7.6

**RECALL GOVERNOR WALKER**

Teachers and other public sector workers and sympathizers took over the Wisconsin Capital Rotunda in 2011 to protest Governor Scott Walker's plan to end collective bargaining rights for state government employees. Walker was successful in passing the new law and survived a state-wide effort to recall him from office in 2012.

from legislating them (though in 2013 a state judge ruled the Indiana statute unconstitutional).

The overall decline in labor union membership would have been more precipitous had it not been for the substantial levels of unionization among public sector workers such as teachers, firefighters, police, and civil servants in local and state governments, 35 percent of whom belong to unions in 2013. Today there are more public sector workers than private sector workers in labor unions in the United States. Though stable for several decades now, union density in the public sector has been undercut recently, no doubt a product of successful efforts to pass laws weakening public-sector labor unions in Wisconsin and Michigan. Voters in Ohio, where labor unions played a key role in voter mobilization, have also over-turned a similar law taking away collective bargaining rights from government workers as they have vowed to do.[12]

The changing fortunes of private sector organized labor can be seen, first, in the passage of a minimum wage law during the Great Depression as unions flexed their growing organizational muscle; second, in the steady rise in the minimum wage during the height of union political power in the three decades following the end of World War II; and third, in the erosion of the purchasing power of the minimum wage as union membership and political influence began to wane after that, continuing to the present day. We examine the pros and cons of the minimum wage in the "Can Government Do Anything Well?" feature.

7.1
7.2
7.3
7.4
7.5
7.6

# Can Government Do Anything Well?

## The Federal Minimum Wage

The minimum wage and 40-hour workweek were first introduced in 1938 by Congress in the Fair Labor Standards Act. FDR claimed the law was "the most far-sighted program for the benefit of workers ever adopted," arguing that fair wages ensure a "minimum standard of living necessary for health, efficiency and general well-being." The FLSA established minimum wage, overtime pay, recordkeeping, and youth employment standards affecting employees in the private sector and in governments at all levels. Covered workers today are entitled to a minimum wage of not less than $7.25 per hour, and overtime pay of at least 150 percent of the regular rate of pay.

The U.S. Chamber of Commerce, one of the largest and most influential interest groups in the United States with over 3 million business and organizational members, has been a staunch foe of the minimum wage. Their opposition over the years, and their role in campaign finance, is one of the reasons that members of Congress have been reluctant to increase the minimum wage to keep up with the cost of living. When adjusting for inflation, the minimum wage was almost $2/hour higher in the 1960s and 1970s than it is today.

The value of the minimum wage peaked in 1968, a product of Lyndon Johnson's Great Society, the high water mark of postwar Democratic Party liberalism and the political influence within the Democratic Party of organized labor. The decline of organized labor, the main interest group in favor of a generous minimum wage, is another reason why the minimum wage has not kept pace.

*Support for the claim that government should specify a minimum wage:*

- The minimum wage guarantees a basic, if low, income safety net for Americans who are working; it keeps more people from becoming poor when the gap between rich and poor is widening.
- The minimum wage helps the economy by increasing overall purchasing power; it allows low-income working Americans to be able to buy more products and services from private firms than they might otherwise be able to do.
- Major academic studies do not support the claims below that the minimum wage significantly and adversely affects overall employment levels or increases inflation.

*Rejection of the claim that government should specify a minimum wage:*

- Wage determination should always be left to the free market; it is the most efficient and fairest way to determine wages.
- Because employers cannot pay less than the minimum wage, it makes them less able and likely to hire teens and the unskilled with spotty work histories; unemployment among these groups, particularly African Americans, remains higher than it might be.
- Unemployment is increased when the minimum wage goes up because it becomes more expensive for businesses to keep workers.
- Because minimum wage laws mean employers must pay higher wages than given by market forces, prices for consumers must be higher to cover the additional costs.

### WHAT DO YOU THINK?

What do you think about the past, present, and future role of the government in legislating a minimum wage?

- Increases to the minimum wage (specifically over the past decade) have increased the standard of living for the lowest socioeconomic classes and have not increased unemployment in the United States.
- Increases to the minimum wage (specifically over the past decade) have contributed to modest increases in the standard of living for the lowest socioeconomic classes, but have also contributed to increasing unemployment in the United States.
- Increases to the minimum wage (specifically over the past decade) have not increased the standard of living for the lowest socioeconomic classes and have contributed significantly to increased unemployment in the United States.

How would you defend this position to a fellow student? What would be your main line of argument? What evidence do you believe best supports your position?

Additional sources for this feature: The Living Wage Calculator at www.livingwage.geog.psu.edu/states/25, the Chamber of Commerce website at www.uschamber.com, and the Wage and Hour Division of the U.S. Department of Labor at www.dol.gov/whd/flsa.

## Public Interest Groups

Public interest groups or associations try to get government to act in ways that will serve interests that are broader and more encompassing than the direct economic or occupational interests of their own members. Such groups claim to be committed to protecting and advancing the public interest, at least as they see it.[13]

One type of public interest group is the advocacy group. People active in advocacy groups tend to be motivated by ideological concerns or a belief in some cause. Such advocacy groups have always been around, but a great upsurge in their number and influence has taken place since the late 1960s.[14] Many were spawned by social movements. In the wake of the civil rights and women's movements, it is hardly surprising that a number of associations have been formed to advance the interests of particular racial, ethnic, and gender groups in American society. The National Organization for Women advocates policies in Washington that advance the position of women in American society. For example, the League of Latin American Citizens has been concerned, among other things, with national and state policies that affect migrants from Mexico and other Latin American countries. Similarly, the NAACP and the Urban League are advocates for the interests of African Americans. The environmental movement created organizations such as the Environmental Defense Fund, the Nature Conservancy, Clean Water Action, and the Natural Resources Defense Council, to take another example. The evangelical Christian upsurge led to the creation of such organizations as the Moral Majority, the Christian Coalition, the National Right to Life Committee, Focus on the Family, and the Family Research Council. The gay and lesbian movement eventually led to the creation of organizations such as the Gay and Lesbian Alliance Against Defamation (GLAAD). Some have been around for many years, such as the American Civil Liberties Union, committed to the protection of First Amendment freedoms, and the Children's Defense Fund, an advocate for poor children.

Most advocacy groups retain a professional, paid administrative staff and are supported by generous large donors (often foundations), membership dues, and/or donations generated by direct mail campaigns. While some depend on and encourage grassroots volunteers and some hold annual membership meetings through which members play some role in making association policies, most advocacy associations are organizations without active membership involvement (other than check writing) and are run by lobbying and public education professionals.[15]

Two other types of public interest groups play a role in American politics, although usually a quieter one. First, associations representing government entities at the state and local levels of our federal system attempt to influence policies made by lawmakers and bureaucrats in Washington. The National Association of Counties is one example, as is the National Governors Association. Second, nonprofit organizations and associations try to influence policies that advance their missions to serve the public interests. Examples include the American Red Cross and the National Council of Nonprofit Associations.

**lobbyists**
A person who attempts to influence the behavior of public officials on behalf of an interest group.

7.1

7.2

7.3

7.4

7.5

7.6

# Why There Are So Many Interest Groups

| 7.3 | Explain why interest groups have proliferated |

Nobody knows exactly how many interest groups exist in the United States, but there is wide agreement that the number began to mushroom in the late 1960s and grew steadily thereafter. We can see this increase along several dimensions. The number of groups listed in the *Encyclopedia of Associations*, for example, has increased from about 10,000 in 1968 to about 22,000 today. Moreover, the number of paid **lobbyists**, that is, people who work for

7.1

7.2

7.3

7.4

7.5

7.6

interest groups in Washington and try to affect government policies on their behalf, today totals about 35,000, double what it was then, and that number does not include thousands of others who work for law firms whose main business is lobbying. One estimate is that about 260,000 people in Washington and its surrounding areas work in the lobbying sector.[16] (Even more work in public relations, accounting, and technology firms linked to the lobbying sector.) Although lobbying Congress is only a part of what interest groups do, these associations and other lobbyists spent around $3.5 billion on lobbying efforts in Washington in 2010. That amount was double what was spent in 2000, though expenditures declined a bit after 2010 because of a mostly deadlocked Congress that did little legislatively.[17] There are a number of reasons so many interest groups exist in the United States.

## ☐ The Constitution

The constitutional rules of the political game in the United States encourage the formation of interest groups. The First Amendment to the Constitution, for instance, guarantees citizens the right to speak freely, to assemble, and to petition the government, all of which are essential to citizens' ability to form organizations to advance their interests before government. Moreover, the government is organized in such a way that officials are relatively accessible to interest groups. Because of federalism, checks and balances, and the separation of powers, there is no dominant center of decision making, as there is in unitary states such as Great Britain and France. In unitary states, most important policy decisions are made in parliamentary bodies. In the United States, important decisions are made by many officials, on many matters, in many jurisdictions. Consequently, there are many more places where interest group pressure can be effective; there are more access points to public officials.

## ☐ Diverse Interests

Being a very diverse society, there are simply myriad interests in the United States. Racial, religious, ethnic, and occupational diversity is pronounced. Also varied are the views about abortion, property rights, prayer in the schools, and environmental protection. Our economy is also strikingly complex and multifaceted, and becoming more so. In a free society, these diverse interests usually take organizational forms. Thus, the computer revolution spawned computer chip manufacturers, software companies, software engineers, computer magazines and blogs, Internet services, technical information providers, computer component jobbers, Web designers, social media sites, and countless others. Each has particular interests to defend or advance before government, and each has formed an association to try to do so.[18] Thus, software engineers have an association to look after their interests, as do software and hardware companies, Internet access providers, digital content providers, industry writers, and so on. After it went public in 2004, Google opened its own Washington office to ensure that its interests were protected before Congress and important regulatory agencies against competing interests such as Microsoft and wireless phone carriers.[19] Facebook opened a Washington D.C. office in 2010, another indication that many of Silicon Valley's technology firms are actively cultivating influence in the capital.

## ☐ A More Active Government

Government does far more today than it did during the early years of the Republic. As government takes on more responsibilities, it quite naturally comes to have a greater effect on virtually all aspects of economic, social, and personal life. People, groups, and organizations are increasingly affected by the actions of government, so the decisions made by presidents, members of Congress, bureaucrats who write regulations, and judges are increasingly important. It would be surprising indeed if in response, people, groups, and organizations did not try harder to influence the public officials' decisions that affect them.[20] During the long, drawn-out deliberations in Congress in 2009 and 2010 that resulted in new rules for banks and the financial industry, bank and financial industry lobbyists flooded Capitol Hill to make sure that the most onerous provisions—for example, a limit on the size of banks so they would not be "too big to fail"—did not make it into the final bill.

Some part of the growth in lobbying by business firms and industry and trade groups may be tied to the emergence of hyper-competition in the global economy, where even giant enterprises like Microsoft must fight to protect their positions not only against competitors but against threatening actions by one or more government agencies. The Seattle-based company has been fighting antitrust actions initiated by the U.S. Justice Department and the European Union Commission for many years and has dramatically enhanced its lobbying presence in Washington (and Brussels) and increased its campaign contributions.[21]

Some groups form around government programs in order to take advantage of existing government programs and initiatives. The creation of the Department of Homeland Security (DHS), with its large budget for new homeland defense technologies, stimulated the formation of new companies to serve this market, as well as new trade associations—including the Homeland Security Industries Association—to represent them. For-profit higher education institutions such as the University of Phoenix receive about 90 percent of their funding from the federal student loan program and other forms of federal aid. Is it any wonder that the industry lobbies heavily against proposals to tie federal dollars to measures of performance like graduation rates and job placement?[22]

## ☐ Disturbances

The existence of diverse interests, the rules of the game, and the importance of government decisions and policies enable and encourage the formation of interest groups, but formation seems to happen only when interests are threatened,

**LOBBYING FOR ETHANOL**

Corn farmers and organizations that represent them have been very successful in convincing Americans and their elected officials to pass laws requiring that ethanol from corn be added to gasoline and to keep out—mainly by the imposition of high tariffs—more efficiently produced ethanol from other countries, especially Brazil, which uses sugar cane and switchgrass. Billboards along major highways such as this one near Boone, Missouri, have been very effective tools of public persuasion in this campaign by corn and domestic ethanol producers, but they deploy many other tools as well. What are some other powerful lobbying tools?

7.1
7.2
7.3
7.4
7.5
7.6

7.1

7.2

7.3

7.4

7.5

7.6

**disturbance theory**
A theory positing that interest groups originate with changes in the economic, social, or political environment that threaten the well-being of some segment of the population.

**earmarks**
Provisions written into congressional legislation that appropriate money for specific pet projects of members of Congress, usually done at the behest of lobbyists, and added to bills at the last minute with little opportunity for deliberation.

usually by some change in the social and economic environment or in government policy. This is known as the **disturbance theory** of interest group formation.[23] To take one example, Focus on the Family, a conservative religious advocacy group, was formed when many evangelical Christians began to feel threatened by what they considered to be a rise in family breakdown, an increase in the number of abortions, the sexual revolution, and the growing visibility of gays and lesbians in American life.

# What Interest Groups Do

**7.4**    Distinguish the methods through which interest groups try to shape government policy

I nterest groups, whether public or private in nature, are in the business of conveying the policy views of individuals and groups to public officials. There are two basic types of interest group activity: the inside game and the outside game.[24] The inside game—the older and more familiar of the two—involves direct, personal contact between interest group representatives and government officials. Some political scientists believe this inside game of influencing the actions of those who make and carry out government policy in Washington—representatives and senators, judges, and regulators—is the thing that big interest groups and business corporations care about the most in politics and where they put most of their political resources. As they put it, "For powerful groups the center of action is in Washington, not the swing states."[25] The outside game involves interest group mobilization of public opinion, voters, and important contributors in order to bring indirect pressure to bear on elected officials. Increasingly today, the most powerful interest groups use both inside and outside methods to influence what policies government makes and carries out.

## ☐ The Inside Game

When lobbying and lobbyists are in the news, the news generally is not good. In early 2006, "super-lobbyist" Jack Abramoff pled guilty to three felony counts for fraud, tax evasion, and conspiracy to bribe public officials; he was then convicted and sentenced to 10 years in prison. Prosecutors had amassed evidence that he had funneled millions on behalf of his clients to a long list of representatives and senators, mostly on the Republican side of the aisle, for campaign war chests and elaborate gifts, including vacations. **Earmarks**—setting aside money in appropriations bills for pet projects for constituents and private interests, usually at the behest of lobbyists—were banned by Congress in 2011. Action finally happened after (1) John McCain made earmarks an issue during his 2008 run for the presidency[26] and (2) public anger against Congress over deficits and corporate welfare reached the boiling point, pushed by both liberal and conservative activists (the Occupy movement and the Tea Party, respectively).

The inside game of lobbying—so named because of the practice of interest group representatives talking to legislators in the lobbies outside House and Senate committee rooms—does not customarily involve bribing legislators, however. Rather, it is more the politics of insiders and the "good ole' boy" network (although, increasingly, women are also part of the network). It is the politics of one-on-one persuasion, in which the skilled lobbyist tries to get a decision-maker to understand and sympathize with the interest group's point of view or to see that what the interest group wants is good for the politician's constituents. Access is critical if one is to be successful at this game.

Many of the most successful lobbyists are recruited from the ranks of retired members of the House and Senate, congressional staff, and high levels of the bureaucracy. Almost 30 percent of outgoing lawmakers, for example, are hired by lobbying firms or hang out their own lobbying shingle.[27] Former Democratic Senate leader Tom Daschle consults for the United Health Group, an association of health insurance giants deeply involved in the formulation of the health care reform bill.[28] Between 1998 and 2009, 29 people associated with Mitch McConnell (R–KY) became high-profile lobbyists, as did 21 with Nancy Pelosi (D–CA). The promise of lucrative employment based on their skills—and especially on their many contacts—is what keeps so many of them around Washington after they leave office or quit federal employment.

The inside game seems to work best when the issues are narrow and technical, do not command much media attention or public passion, and do not stir up counteractivity by other interest groups.[29] This is not to say that interest groups play a role only on unimportant matters. Great benefit can come to an interest group or a large corporation from a small change in a single provision of the Tax Code or in a slight change in the wording of a regulation on carbon emissions or what percentage of deposits banks must keep in reserve. Enron was very successful at getting Congress to remove federal oversight on many of its energy-trading and acquisitions activities. These stayed well out of public view until they came to light after Enron's spectacular collapse in 2001.

Lobbyists from citizens groups also play the inside game, often with great skill and effect. Many environmental regulations have been strengthened because of the efforts of skilled lobbyists from the Sierra Club, for example, and the National Rifle Association (NRA) is virtually unbeatable on issues of gun control. But it is inescapably the case that lobbyists representing business and the wealthy are far more numerous and deployed on a wider range of issues than those of any other interest, as we will show later in the chapter.

Political scientist E.E. Schattschneider has pointed out that the inside game—traditional lobbying—is pretty much outside the view of the public.[30] That is to say, the day-to-day details of this form of lobbying takes place behind closed doors.

**LOBBYING CONGRESS** In Congress, lobbyists try to accomplish two essential tasks: (1) have bills and provisions in bills they favor pass; (2) stop bills and provisions of bills they do not like from seeing the light of day. The essence of the inside game in Congress is twofold. First, lobbyists remind key actors of the electoral consequences of opposing group interests. The NRA, which plays the inside game very well, has been deeply involved not only in blocking bills it opposes but in helping to write NRA-friendly provisions into the few gun control bills that Congress has passed over the last two decades. After the Newtown school shootings prompted widespread calls for gun control, NRA lobbyists worked with Senator Joe Manchin (D–WV) on a bill to extend background checks on gun purchasers. Bans on assault rifles never made it into the bill, thanks to NRA lobbyists, who also pressed for watered-down background restraints. Though it was successful in shaping the post-Newton bill, the NRA eventually withdrew its support and the bill failed. Senators facing elections in closely contested states were reluctant to provoke NRA opposition.[31] Second, lobbyists cultivate personal relationships with people who matter, both influential and well-placed legislators and their staffs.[32] Because a lot of action in Congress takes place in committees, relationships with legislative and committee staff people is imperative.

Lobbyists are also expected to make substantial contributions to congressional campaigns and to persuade their clients to do the same.[33] "About one-third of my day is spent raising money from my clients to give to people I lobby," according to one well-placed lobbyist.[34]

**LOBBYING THE EXECUTIVE BRANCH** After bills become law, they must be carried out or implemented. This is done by the executive branch. In this process of implementation, career civil servants, political appointees in top executive branch bureaus and departments, and regulators have a great deal of discretionary authority in deciding how to transform the wishes of the president and Congress into action on the ground. This happens because Congress and the president usually legislate broad policies, leaving it to executive branch bureaus and agencies to promulgate procedures,

7.1

7.2

7.3

7.4

7.5

7.6

7.1

7.2

7.3

7.4

7.5

7.6

rules, and regulations to fill in the details of how laws will actually work in practice and how the mandates of regulatory agencies will be accomplished. So, for example, while Congress appropriates monies for the Army Corps of Engineers, it is, for the most part, decision-makers in the Corps who decide which specific levee and river dredging projects will be funded. Lobbyists for big contractors and for state and local governments try to make sure they have a regular presence with the Corps' top officials and staffers.

Because of the technical complexity of many of the issues that come before them, regulatory agencies such as the SEC (Securities and Exchange Commission), the EPA (the Environmental Protection Agency), and the FCC (the Federal Communications Commission) have been granted broad leeway in promulgating rules designed to meet the goals the president and Congress have set for them. The rules they issue have the force of law, moreover, unless these rules are subsequently overturned by Congress (which is very hard for Congress to do) or the courts. Congress rarely passes legislation involving details of television and radio broadcasting, for example, leaving regulatory decisions to the Federal Communications Commission. Because of this, the National Association of Broadcasters focuses its time and energies on the FCC, trying to establish stable and friendly relationships with them. The payoffs can be quite high for lobbying executive branch agencies like the FCC. In 2003, for example, large media company and news organization leaders and lobbyists met with the top staff of the FCC in a successful effort to get the agency to loosen rules on ownership so that big companies could grow even bigger.

The key to success in lobbying the executive branch is similar to that in lobbying Congress: personal contact and cooperative long-term relationships that a civil servant, a department or bureau leader, or a regulator finds useful.[35] Interest group representatives can convey technical information, for example, provide the results of their research, help a public official deflect criticism, and show that what the group wants is compatible with good public policy and the political needs of the official.

### CELEBRATING A HISTORIC COURT DECISION

Dick Heller—here signing his autograph on the placards of gun rights advocates in front of the Supreme Court in June 2008—won his suit against the city government of Washington, D.C., in a case that established a constitutional right to own a firearm. The legal and financial resources that made his suit possible were provided by the NRA and other organizations against gun control. Why are gun lobbies such a powerful force in American politics?

**LOBBYING THE COURTS** Interest groups sometimes lobby the courts, although not in the same way as they lobby the other two branches. A group may find that neither Congress nor the White House is favorably disposed to its interests and will bring a test case to the courts. Realizing that the improvement of the lot of African Americans was very low on the agenda of presidents and members of Congress during the 1940s and 1950s, for example, the NAACP turned to the courts for satisfaction. The effort eventually paid off in 1954 in the landmark *Brown v. Board of Education* decision.

Interest groups sometimes lobby the courts by filing *amicus curiae* ("friends of the court") briefs in cases involving other parties. In this kind of brief, a person or an organization that is not a party in the suit may file an argument in support of one side or the other in the hope of swaying the views of the judge or judges. Major controversies before the Supreme Court on such issues as abortion, free speech, or civil rights attract scores of *amicus curiae* briefs. Nineteen *amicus* briefs were filed by supporters and opponents of gun control, for example, in the recently decided case, *District of Columbia v. Heller* (2008), in which the Court ruled that Americans have an individual right under the Constitution to own a gun.

Interest groups also get involved in the appointment of federal judges. Particularly controversial appointments, such as the Supreme Court nominations of Robert Bork (whom many women's and civil rights interests considered too conservative) in 1987, Clarence Thomas (who was opposed by liberal and women's groups) in 1992, and Samuel Alito in 2005 (Democrats and liberals considered him much too conservative on a wide range of issues), drew interest group attention and strenuous efforts for and against the nominees. Though they ultimately failed, conservative groups mobilized in 2009 to block the appointment of Sonia Sotomayor to the Court.

## ☐ The Outside Game

The outside game is being played when an interest group tries to mobilize local constituencies and shape public opinion to support the group's goals and to bring that pressure to bear on elected officials. Defenders of the status quo can mostly depend on the inside game; those who are trying to change existing policies or create new legislation are more likely to use the outside game.[36] By all indications, the outside game—sometimes called **grassroots lobbying**—has been growing steadily in importance in recent years.[37] This may be a good development for democracy, and here is why. Although groups involved in the outside game often try to hide their true identities—Americans for Fair Drug Prices, for example, may well be funded by the pharmaceutical industry—and while some groups involved in the outside game have more resources than others, it is still the case that this form of politics has the effect of expanding and heightening political conflict. This brings issues out into the open and subjects them to public scrutiny—what Schattschneider has called the "socialization of conflict."[38]

**MOBILIZING MEMBERSHIP** Those interest groups with a large membership base try to persuade their members to send letters and to make telephone calls to senators and representatives when an important issue is before Congress. They sound the alarm, using direct mail and, increasingly, e-mail. They define the threat to members; suggest a way to respond to the threat; and supply the addresses, phone numbers, and e-mail addresses of the people to contact in Washington. Members are grouped by congressional district and state and are given the addresses of their own representatives or senators. The National Rifle Association (NRA) is particularly effective in mobilizing its considerable membership whenever the threat of federal gun control rears its head. Environmental organizations such as Friends of the Earth sound the alarm to people on their mailing list whenever Congress threatens to loosen environmental protections.

*amicus curiae*
Latin for "friend of the court"; a legal brief in which individuals not party to a suit may have their views heard in court.

**grassroots lobbying**
The effort by interest groups to mobilize local constituencies, shape public opinion to support the group's goals, and bring that pressure to bear on elected officials.

7.1

7.2

7.3

7.4

7.5

7.6

7.1

7.2

7.3

7.4

7.5

7.6

**ORGANIZING THE DISTRICT** Members of Congress are especially attuned to those in their states or districts who can affect their reelection prospects. Smart interest groups, therefore, not only convince their members in the state and district to put pressure on a senator or congressional representative but also make every effort to be in touch with important campaign contributors and opinion leaders there. Republicans in office are especially wary of groups like the Club for Growth and American Crossroads, which target any in the party who supports tax increases and more spending and which threaten to finance the campaigns of their primary election opponents. Democrats are wary of bucking labor unions and pro-choice groups for the same reasons.

**SHAPING PUBLIC OPINION** "Educating" the public on issues that are important to the interest group is one of the central features of new-style lobbying. The idea is to shape opinion in such a way that government officials will be favorably disposed to the views of the interest group. These attempts to shape public and elite opinion come in many forms. One strategy is to produce and distribute research reports that bolster the group's position. Citizen groups such as the Food Research and Action Center have been very adept and effective in this area.[39]

Another strategy is media advertising. Sometimes this takes the form of pressing a position on a particular issue, such as the Teamsters Union raising the alarm about open borders with Mexico, focusing on the purported unsafe nature of Mexican trucks roaming American highways. Sometimes it is "image" advertising, in which some company or industry portrays its positive contribution to American life.[40] Thus, large oil companies often feature their regard for the environment in their advertising, showing pristine forests or beaches, with nary a pipeline, a tanker, or a refinery in sight.

In the effort to shape public opinion, the well-heeled interest group will also prepare materials that will be of use to radio and television broadcasters and to newspaper and magazine editors. Many produce opinion pieces, magazine articles, television spots and radio "sound bites," and even television documentaries. Others stage events to be covered as news. The environmentalist group Greenpeace puts the news media on full alert, for example, when it tries to disrupt a whaling operation.

Finally, interest groups, using the latest computer technology, identify target groups to receive information on particular issues. Groups pushing for cuts in the capital gains tax rate, for instance, direct their mail and telephone banks to holders of the American Express card or to addresses in ZIP code areas identified as upper-income neighborhoods. They are increasingly using the Internet, as well, in the effort to mobilize the public on issues of concern to them. For example, most have their own websites and publish position papers and other materials there. Many arrange postings to friendly blogs in hopes of further disseminating their message. Some will use their websites and e-mail to organize e-mails to lawmakers from their constituents.[41] Many interest and advocacy groups have made big commitments recently to the use of social media such as Facebook and Twitter to spread their message.

**GETTING INVOLVED IN CAMPAIGNS AND ELECTIONS** Interest groups try to increase their influence by getting involved in political campaigns.[42] Many interest groups, for example, issue a report card indicating the degree to which members of the House and Senate supported the interest group's position on a selection of key votes. The report card ratings are distributed to the members of the interest group and other interested parties in the hope that the ratings will influence their voting behavior. We show how groups do this in the "By the Numbers" feature. Interest groups also encourage their members to get involved in the electoral campaigns of candidates who are favorable to their interests. Groups often assist campaigns in more tangible ways—allowing the use of their telephone banks; mail, telephone, and e-mail lists; fax and photocopy machines; computers; and the like. Some interest groups help with fund-raising events or ask members to make financial contributions to candidates.

Interest groups also endorse particular candidates for public office. The strategy may backfire and is somewhat risky, for to endorse a losing candidate is to risk losing access to the winner. Nevertheless, it is fairly common now for labor unions,

7.1
7.2
7.3
7.4
7.5
7.6

# By the Numbers

## Is there a reliable way to evaluate the performance of your representative in Congress?

Imagine you are at the end of the semester and four different teachers give you a grade in your introductory political science course. One looks at your performance and gives you a grade of 100 percent. Your day is made! Teacher number 2 gives you an 83. OK, you might say, "I can live with that." Teachers 3 and 4 slam you with a 20 and a 10. Ouch! How to make sense of all of this? Why is it that two teachers love you and two hate you? Surely they must be biased in some way.

This is exactly what happens to members of Congress when they are graded on their performance by interest groups. Unlike you, the confused student in the preceding example, congressional representatives expect the wide disparity in the grades they receive, understand what is going on, and are even proud of most of their grades, whether high or low. Note the wildly contrasting grades for Republican Senator Jeff Flake of Arizona and Democratic Senator Ben Cardin of Maryland given by four organizations: the Americans for Democratic Action (ADA), the American Conservative Union (ACU), the League of Conservation Voters (LCV), and the National Taxpayers Union (NTU).

### Why It Matters

Having a consistent and reliable way to grade each member of Congress can help voters make more rational electoral choices. Without such grades, each citizen would have to investigate the record of his or her member of Congress, rely on news reports, or depend on information provided by the member.

### Behind the Numbers

How are members of Congress graded? The answer is pretty straightforward. Each interest group in this example is strongly ideological or committed to a certain set of concerns, and each grades members of Congress in terms of these standards. The ADA is very strongly liberal—interested in civil liberties, civil rights, and economic and social justice; while the ACU is strongly conservative—in favor of capitalism, traditional moral values, and a strong national defense. The LCV supports legislation to protect the environment, while the NTU wants lower taxes, less wasteful government spending, and a balanced budget. So, members of Congress who vote to increase spending on child welfare programs, let us say, are likely to get high grades from the ADA, but low grades from the ACU and the NTU. Members who vote to open the Alaska National Wildlife Reserve for oil exploration would surely receive a low grade from the folks at LCV.

### Calculating Interest Group Scores

Although each group uses a slightly different method to do its grading, at base, each approaches grading in pretty much the same way. For each interest group, its professional staff, sometimes in conjunction with outside experts, selects a set of key votes on which to assess members of Congress. The particular votes selected by each group will differ—a group interested solely in civil rights issues will not, for example, use a vote on the defense budget for its scorecard—but each identifies a set of votes it considers to be a good indicator of ideological or policy loyalty. On each vote, members of Congress are scored "with the group" or "against the group." The numbers are added up, then transformed to percentage terms, with 100 being the highest score and 0 the lowest.

### What to Watch for

Oddly enough, although not terribly sophisticated in either conceptual or computational terms, these are numbers you can trust. You can, as they say, "Take them to

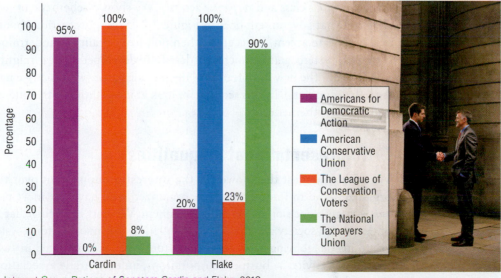

Interest Group Ratings of Senators Cardin and Flake, 2013
*Source:* Project Vote Smart

7.1

7.2

7.3

7.4

7.5

7.6

*(Continued)*

the bank." Why? Because each interest group is clear about what it stands for, and each makes it clear that it is judging members of Congress from a particular perspective. When you are considering whether to vote for or against an incumbent member of Congress, a good method would be to check member scores from organizations whose ideology and/or policy views you support.

**What Do You Think?**

How does your representative in Congress score with those groups whose values and policy positions come closest to your own? You can investigate this at the Project Vote Smart website at www.votesmart.org, where you can find how your representative is evaluated by different interest groups.

environmental organizations, religious groups, and liberal and conservative ideological groups to make such endorsements.

Interest groups are also an increasingly important part of campaign fund-raising. The rise of super PACs and 501cs is especially noteworthy, injecting super-rich individuals and companies directly into the middle of electoral campaigns. This topic will be explored briefly in the next section and more extensively later in the book.

# Interest Groups, Corporations, and Inequality in American Politics

**7.5** Determine the biases in the interest group system

Overall, between the inside game and the outside game, interest groups have a diverse set of tools for influencing elected officials, bureaucrats in the executive branch, judges, and the public. And the number of groups capable of deploying these tools is large and growing every year. On the surface, it might look like the proliferation of interest groups has enhanced the democratic flavor of our country, allowing more and more Americans to have their interests represented. But not all scholars and students of politics agree that this is so.

Political scientist E.E. Schattschneider once observed that the flaw in the pluralist (or interest group) heaven is "that the heavenly chorus sings with a strong upper class accent."[43] We would amend this, based on our reading of the evidence, in the following way: the flaw in the pluralist heaven is "that the heavenly chorus sings with a strong upper class and *corporate* accent." We show a schematic of how this works in shaping what government does in Figure 7.2. If this observation about an "upper class and corporate accent" is accurate, then political equality is undermined by the interest group system, and democracy is less fully developed than it might be, even taking into account the new importance of the outside game (which, as we have said, tends to "socialize conflict"). In this section, we look at inequalities in the interest group system and evaluate their effects.

## ☐ Representational Inequalities

We would suggest that power in the interest group system over time goes to the organized and to those among the organized who have the most resources and the best access to decision makers in government. We start by noting that not all segments of American society are equally represented in the interest group system. The interest group inside lobbying game in Washington, D.C., is dominated in sheer numbers and weight of activity, by business corporations, industry trade associations, and associations of the professions, although liberal and conservative advocacy groups lobby as well.[44] Organized labor, we have seen, although still a powerful player in Washington,

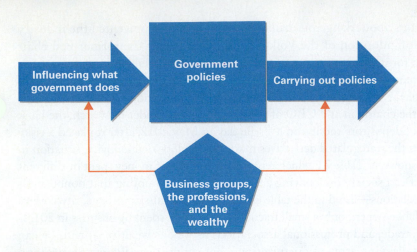

**FIGURE 7.2** THESE INTERESTS EXERCISE THE MOST INFLUENCE AT EACH STAGE OF THE POLICY-MAKING PROCESS?

7.1

7.2

7.3

7.4

7.5

7.6

has lost much of its lobbying clout in recent years, mainly because of declining membership. Passage in 2005 of several pro-business bills that it strongly opposed—namely, bills making it more difficult to declare bankruptcy and to bring class-action lawsuits in state courts—showcases labor's declining fortunes. For their part, the vast majority of advocacy groups, even those that perceive themselves as liberal and lean toward the Democrats, attract members and contributors who have much higher incomes, more elite occupations, and more education than the general public. Not surprisingly, given those whom these advocacy groups represent, they tend to focus less on issues of poverty, jobs, and income inequality, the traditional purview of labor unions, let us say, and more on "quality of life" issues such as environmental protection, consumer protection, globalization, women's rights, racial and ethnic civil rights, gay and lesbian rights, and civil liberties.[45]

## ☐ Resource Inequalities

Business corporations and financial institutions, corporate and financial institution executives and top managers, heads of private equity and hedge funds, and professionals are the most economically well-off parts of American society. As firms, they are the most important actors; as individuals, they account for a disproportionately large share of income and wealth in the United States. It is hardly surprising that interest groups representing them can afford to spend far more than other groups to hire professional lobbying firms, form their own Washington liaison office, place advertising in the media, conduct targeted mailings on issues, mobilize their members to contact government officials, and pursue all of the other activities of old- and new-style lobbying. Lobbying in Washington is heavily dominated by lobbyists and lobbying firms that represent business.[46] Registered lobbyists for the various drug companies, for example, typically total more than the combined membership of the House and Senate;[47] in 2013 there were 1,359 registered lobbyists for the pharmaceutical industry, according to the Center for Responsive Politics. (You can learn more about the influence of business in Washington in the "Using the Framework," which examines the business-friendly outcomes of Supreme Court decisions under Justice Roberts.)

The story is the same elsewhere. More than 3,000 lobbyists worked to kill provisions of the Dodd-Frank bill—passed in 2010 to forestall a recurrence of the 2008 financial collapse—aimed at keeping banks from becoming "too big to fail," such as higher capital requirements. After passage, financial industry lobbyists managed to slow down the work of the rule-making executive branch agencies charged with administering Dodd-Frank.[48] Anger at the financial community and fear among

7.1

7.2

7.3

7.4

7.5

7.6

**political action committees (PACs)**
An entity created by an interest group whose purpose is to collect money and make contributions to candidates in federal elections.

enough regulators about dangerous bank practices, however, prevented the industry from heading off adoption of the Volker rule (named after the former Fed chair who advocated for it), which separated trading and commercial banking operations, disallowing financial institutions thereby from speculating with their customers' money. (One of the leading advocates of letting the banking industry regulate itself is Jamie Dimon, the chairman and CEO of JPMorgan Chase. Under his watch, the bank lost $2 billion of depositors' money on a single day in May 2012, after it placed a risky and failed bet in the unregulated derivatives market.) The lopsided lobbying situation in Washington is shown in Table 7.2 which reports the amount of money spent by different sectors of American society on lobbying activities. It is worth noting that nonbusiness groups and associations—listed in the table as other, ideological/single-issue, city/county, and organized labor—spent only a small fraction of what was spent by business in 2013.

Corporate, trade, and professional associations as well as wealthy individuals can contribute to a dizzying array of organizations that support candidates, parties, and issues during political campaigns. Among the most important targets for politically oriented contributions are **political action committees (PACs)**, 527 and 501c social welfare organizations, and Super PACS. PACs are regulated, donations are on the public record, and caps exist on how much can be given to candidates in federal elections and to party committees. 527, 501c, and Super PAC organizations, often labeled "outside money," are largely unregulated and have no limits on how much money can be raised from individuals, corporations, and labor unions or spent to influence the outcome of elections. These relatively new forms of campaign organizations were made possible by the hollowing out of campaign finance laws by two Supreme Court cases, *Citizens United v. FEC* (2010) and *Speechnow.org v. FEC* (2010), in which the Supreme Court ruled that many of these laws and rules written under them violated the free speech rights of corporations, unions, and individuals.[49] These organizations have come to play an ever-larger role in funding presidential and congressional elections and in shaping public opinion about public issues.

The *Citizens United* decision turned heavily on the doctrine that corporations are "persons" with the same rights and privileges as any natural person residing in the United States, including free speech. Several scholars have pointed out that this doctrine has been pushed for a very long time in the courts by legal firms representing corporations in a broad set of cases. It need hardly be pointed out that the decades-long effort required a staying power based on access to substantial financial resources not available to most individuals, advocacy groups, or labor unions. Interestingly, corporations have managed to avoid criminal prosecution even when they have broken the law because criminal punishment is relevant only to "natural" persons. This is why most of the key players that brought about the financial collapse in 2008 have not gone to jail.[50]

**TABLE 7.2** MAJOR SPENDING ON FEDERAL LOBBYING, BY INDUSTRY SECTOR

| Sector | Total |
| --- | --- |
| Finance, insurance, and real estate | $484,701,853 |
| Health | $480,463,898 |
| Miscellaneous business | $479,619,408 |
| Energy and natural resources | $356,545,408 |
| Communications/electronics | $391,131,203 |
| Transportation | $221,534,856 |
| Ideological/single-issue | $143,053,727 |
| Agribusiness | $149,818,306 |
| Defense | $133,835,857 |
| Construction | $49,151,726 |
| Organized labor | $46,367,803 |
| Lawyers and lobbyists | $22,127,084 |

*Source:* Center for Responsive Politics, Influence and Lobbying, Top Industries (by sector), 2013.

Corporate, trade, and professional donors have dominated all forms of campaign finance organizations during recent election cycles, though labor unions have had a big presence as well.[51] For example, PACs representing the least-privileged sectors of American society are notable for their absence. As former Senator (R-KS) and presidential candidate Bob Dole once put it, "There aren't any poor PACs or food stamp PACs or nutrition PACs or Medicaid PACs."[52] Notably, very wealthy individuals, not interest groups, have written the biggest checks for Super PACs. During the 2011–2012 election cycle, the Super PAC "Winning Our Future," funded entirely by gambling magnate Sheldon Adelman, contributed more than $17 million to help Newt Gingrich win the Republican nomination (it did not work). In all, Super PACs spent roughly $610 million in that cycle, two-thirds on Republican and conservative candidates and causes.[53]

## ☐ Access Inequality

Inequalities of representation and resources are further exaggerated by vast inequalities in access to government decision makers. Powerful interest organizations and lobbying firms that primarily represent business, professionals, and the wealthy have the resources to employ many former regulators and staff from independent regulatory agencies, former members of Congress and congressional staff, and top employees of other federal executive departments, including many from the Department of Defense and the Internal Revenue Service. They are hired partly for their technical expertise but also for the access they can provide to those with whom they formerly worked. *Bloomberg/Businessweek* reported, for example, that firms hired 60 former staffers from Congress in 2011 to work solely on convincing Congress to repeat a tax holiday on "repatriated earnings" (earnings brought back to the United States by global firms, normally taxed at the rate of 35 percent) that dropped the tax rate to 5.25 percent in 2004, saving firms $312 billion.[54]

Access inequality may also be seen in the ability of some groups to play a central role in the formation and implementation of government policies based on the membership of these groups in informal networks within the government itself. These networks are of two kinds. The first, **iron triangles** or **sub-governments**, customarily include a private interest group (usually a corporation or business trade association), an agency in the executive branch, and a committee or subcommittees in Congress, which act together to advance and protect certain government programs that work to the mutual benefit of their members. Most scholars believe that iron triangles have become less important in American government.[55] The second, called **issue networks**, are understood to be more open and inclusive than iron triangles. They are said to be coalitions that form around different policy areas that include a range of public and private interest groups and policy experts as well as business representatives, bureaucrats, and legislators. Iron triangles suggest a closed system in which a small group of actors controls a policy area. Issue networks suggest a more fluid situation with more actors and visibility, where control of policymaking is less predictable.

Be that as it may, corporations, trade associations, and associations of professionals not only play a prominent role in issue networks, but also participate in those iron triangles that are still around.[56] These are especially prominent in shaping and carrying out public policies in the areas of agriculture, defense procurement, public lands, highway construction, and water. Large-scale water projects—dams, irrigation, and levees, for example—are supported by farm, real estate developer, construction, and barge-shipping interest groups; members of key Senate and House committees responsible for these projects, who can claim credit for bringing jobs and federal money to their constituencies; and the Army Corps of Engineers, whose budget and responsibilities grow apace as it builds the projects. Another iron triangle is shown in Figure 7.3.

## ☐ The Privileged Position of Business Corporations

Economist and political scientist Charles Lindblom has argued that corporations wield such disproportionate power in American politics that they undermine democracy. He closes his classic 1977 book *Politics and Markets* with this observation:

**iron triangles**
An enduring alliance of common interest among an interest group, a congressional committee, and a bureaucratic agency.

**sub-governments**
Another name for an iron triangle.

**issue networks**
Broad coalitions of public and private interest groups, policy experts, and public officials that form around particular policy issues; said to be more visible to the public and more inclusive.

7.1

7.2

7.3

7.4

7.5

7.6

7.1

7.2

7.3

7.4

7.5

7.6

**FIGURE 7.3** IRON TRIANGLE

In an iron triangle, an alliance based on common interests is formed among a powerful corporation or interest group, an agency of the executive branch, and congressional committees or subcommittees. In this example from the defense industry, an alliance is formed among parties that share an interest in the existence and expansion of defense industry contracts. Most scholars think iron triangles are less common today than in the past, though they are alive and well in a number of policy areas, including the one illustrated here.

"The large private corporation fits oddly into democratic theory. Indeed, it does not fit."[57] Twenty years later, political scientist Neil Mitchell concluded his book *The Conspicuous Corporation*, which reported the results of careful empirical testing of Lindblom's ideas, with the conclusion that "business interests (in the United States) are not routinely countervailed in the policy process. Their political resources and incentives to participate are usually greater than other interests."[58] Let's see why these scholars reached their somber conclusion about business corporations in American politics.

We have already learned about many of the advantages that corporations and business trade associations representing groups of corporations enjoy over others in the political process. The largest corporations are far ahead of their competitors in the number of lobbyists they employ, the level of resources they can and do use for political purposes, their ability to shape public perceptions and opinions through such instruments as issue advertising and subsidization of business-oriented think tanks like the American Enterprise Institute, and the ease of access they often have to government officials.

An additional source of big business power is the high regard in which business is held in American society and the central and honored place of business values in our culture. Faith in free enterprise gives special advantages to the central institution of free enterprise, the corporation. Any political leader contemplating hostile action against corporations must contend with business's special place of honor in the United States. To be sure, scandals involving large business enterprises such as Enron, Goldman Sachs, and BP can tarnish big business now and then, but in the long run, as President Coolidge is known to have once famously said, the business of America is business.

Business corporations are also unusually influential because the health of the American economy—and thus the standard of living of the people—is tied closely to the economic well-being of large corporations. It is widely and not entirely unreasonably believed that what is good for business is good for America. Because of their vital role in the economy, government officials tend to interpret business corporations

7.1
7.2
7.3
7.4
7.5
7.6

# Using the FRAMEWORK

## How does business fare on the Roberts Court?

**Background:** Recent research has shown that the Supreme Court has become steadily more pro-business since 1946 and that the Roberts Court is the most pro-business since the end of World War II. Five of the ten most pro-business justices since 1946 sit on the current Court. Even two liberal judges—Stephen Beyer and Ruth Bader Ginsburg—side with business about 40 percent of the time in cases involving issues ranging from anti-trust and copyrights to union and employee relations. We can better understand these developments by examining how structural, political linkage, and governmental factors interact to produce pro-business decisions on the Roberts Court.

*Source:* Lee Epstein, William M. Landes, and Richard A. Posner, "How Business Fares in the Supreme Court," *Minnesota Law Review* 97, no. 1 (2012).

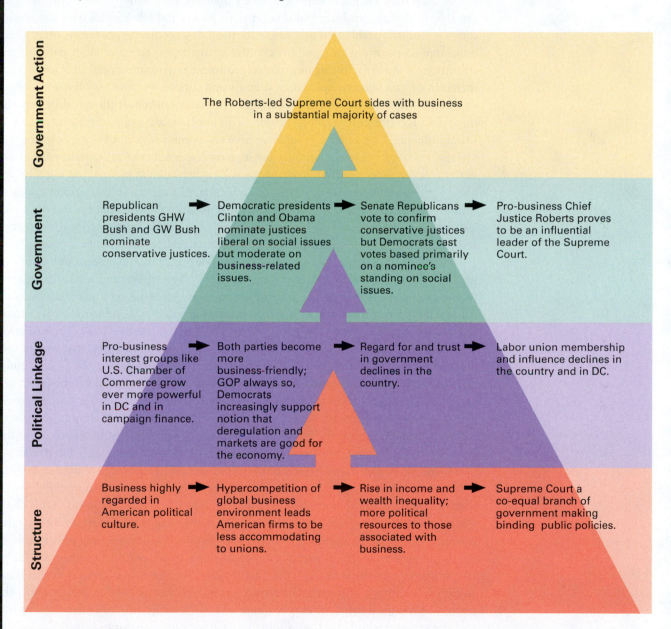

**Government Action**

The Roberts-led Supreme Court sides with business in a substantial majority of cases

**Government**

Republican presidents GHW Bush and GW Bush nominate conservative justices. → Democratic presidents Clinton and Obama nominate justices liberal on social issues but moderate on business-related issues. → Senate Republicans vote to confirm conservative justices but Democrats cast votes based primarily on a nominee's standing on social issues. → Pro-business Chief Justice Roberts proves to be an influential leader of the Supreme Court.

**Political Linkage**

Pro-business interest groups like U.S. Chamber of Commerce grow ever more powerful in DC and in campaign finance. → Both parties become more business-friendly; GOP always so, Democrats increasingly support notion that deregulation and markets are good for the economy. → Regard for and trust in government declines in the country. → Labor union membership and influence declines in the country and in DC.

**Structure**

Business highly regarded in American political culture. → Hypercompetition of global business environment leads American firms to be less accommodating to unions. → Rise in income and wealth inequality; more political resources to those associated with business. → Supreme Court a co-equal branch of government making binding public policies.

7.1

7.2

7.3

7.4

7.5

7.6

not as "special interests" but as the voice of the national interest and to listen more attentively to their demands than they do to those of other sectors of American society. Some companies are so important for the overall operation of the American and global economies that they are considered "too big to fail"—think AIG, Citigroup, Bank of America, and General Motors, among others in 2008 and 2009—and were bailed out even when their downfall was from self-inflicted wounds. In this sense, corporations enjoy an especially privileged position in American politics. (See the "Mapping American Politics" feature for an example of how the power of large auto and oil companies has had important negative impacts on the environment.)

Corporations are also powerful because their mobility is an important counterweight to any government effort (local, state, or national) to raise taxes or impose regulations that business deems especially onerous. Increasingly, large corporations are able to design, produce, and market their goods and services all over the world; they are not irrevocably tied to a single location. If government threatens their interests, large corporations can credibly counter with a threat to move all or part of their operations elsewhere. In this new global economic environment, political leaders are increasingly of a mind to maintain a friendly and supportive business climate.

Large corporations do not, of course, run the show entirely. Although they have the most resources, for instance, these resources do not translate automatically into real political influence. One interest group may have enormous resource advantages over other interest groups, for instance, but may use its resources ineffectively. Or an interest group with great resources may find itself opposed by other interest groups that together are able to mobilize impressive resources of their own. A powerful interest group may also find that an elected politician is not cooperative because the voters in the district are of a different mind from the interest group. So even with this immense set of resources, business power is not automatically and inevitably translated into political power.[59]

Nor does business always get its way in Washington. There are many issues of great importance on which business in general, or one corporation in particular, loses in the give-and-take of politics. There are times when business finds itself squared off against powerful coalitions of other interest groups (labor, consumer, and environmentalist groups, let us say). Corporations have not gotten their way on loosening immigration controls or expanding the pool of H1-B visas, something that would have allowed them access to a larger pool of cheap labor had they won on the former, and a pool of highly skilled scientific and technical workers, had they won on the latter. On many occasions, corporations also find themselves at odds with one another on public policy issues. Thus, Internet service providers, computer and handheld device makers, software developers, and the music and film industries are locked in a battle over the ease of file-sharing and royalty compensation for distributed copyrighted material.

Corporations are most powerful when they can build alliances among themselves. Most of the time, corporations are in competition with one another; they do not form a unified political bloc capable of moving government to action on their behalf. On those occasions when corporations feel that their collective interests are at stake, however—as on taxes, for example, or executive compensation—they are capable of coming together to form powerful and virtually unbeatable political coalitions.[60] Large corporations and the wealthy—the vast majority of the top 1 percent derive their wealth from their positions as corporate executives, hedge fund managers, and the leaders of financial firms, so corporations and the wealthy can be understood as one and the same—recently have won some notable long-term victories.[61]

1. The long-term tax rates of the super-wealthy have declined (see Figure 7.4).

2. The minimum wage has hardly increased at all over the past three decades.

3. The financial services industry was deregulated (with disastrous results in 2008).

4. Laws were passed shielding corporate executives from lawsuits by stockholders, thereby allowing executive compensation to skyrocket in the 1990s and 2000s.

5. IRS audits of top income earners decreased during the past three decades even as audits of the working poor recently increased (those who use the Earned Income Tax Credit).

7.1

7.2

7.3

7.4

7.5

7.6

# Mapping American Politics

## Greenhouse Emissions from the Use of Fossil Fuels

### Introduction

The United States is a major emitter of greenhouse gases. For the most part, U.S. emissions reflect the enormous amount of fossil fuel required to power the U.S. economy, with a great deal of these fuels taking the form of gasoline to power cars and trucks. All wealthy countries use enormous amounts of fossil fuel, fossil fuel being essential for powering industrialization, people's homes and apartments, and modern transportation and shipping systems, including cars, trucks, trains, and planes. Recently, rapidly industrializing and modernizing countries such as India and China have joined the ranks of high–fuel-consuming nations. With the many benefits that come with high fuel consumption, however, come some problems, not the least of which is the release of massive amounts of carbon into the atmosphere when fossil fuels are burned. Such emissions contribute to the problem of global climate change. Whether or not one chooses to accept this conclusion—and, according to public opinion polls, many in the United States do not—it is indisputable that the accumulation of fossil fuel emissions in the atmosphere contributes to pollution that adversely affects human health.

### Mapping Fuel Useage

The cartogram below graphically represents the relative contribution to total global carbon emissions of every country in the world in 2011 (the latest year for which data are available). In the cartogram, the normal geographical size of each country is proportionally increased or decreased by its proportional share of global emissions. Examining the cartogram, it is evident that the United States, as well as China (now the world's largest emitter), Western Europe, Japan, and India, are the main contributors, in a relative sense, to greenhouse gas emissions. Given the level of economic development and the high standard of living in the United States, Europe, and Japan and the rapid economic development of China and India, none of this is surprising. (Somewhat surprising is Russia's low greenhouse emissions profile as well as the relatively high profile of Saudi Arabia and Iran.)

There are many reasons why Americans are such high greenhouse gas emitters. Consider the amount of emissions in America attributable to the use of vehicle-related gasoline. The vast size of the country, the expansion of cities into suburban-dominated metropolitan areas, excellent U.S. road systems, and low investment in mass transportation factor into American rates of emission. Also important is the low-gas-mileage efficiency of U.S. cars and trucks, a consequence of the lobbying activities of oil companies and automobile manufacturers that block higher CAFE (corporate average fuel economy) requirements. Although rising gasoline prices and troubles in oil-producing nations and regions, such as Nigeria, Venezuela, and the Persian Gulf, finally compelled U.S. lawmakers to increase CAFE requirements for cars and trucks in 2007, the tougher standards were a long time coming because of the resistance of American industries. The EPA increased CAFE requirements even more in 2009 and 2011, under directives from President Obama, but will take some time to go into effect. Under the new standards, automakers must boost the average fuel efficiency for cars and small trucks (including SUVs) to 54.5 mpg by 2025.

### What Do You Think?

How concerned are you about global climate change and what do you believe might be its relationship to carbon emissions from fossil fuels? How concerned are you about the adverse health effects from air pollution caused by such emissions? Are there ways to cut greenhouse gas emissions without undermining the American standard of living and the economic well-being of its people? Does solving the emissions problem require curtailing the lobbying power of energy and automobile industries, or would curtailment be an unacceptable limitation of free speech and the right to petition the government? Or might the rapid transition of electricity generation from coal to natural gas and the increased fuel efficiency of automobile and trucks in the United States help us solve the problem without too much pain? Finally, does the rapid economic rise of China and India make our efforts at improvement beside the point given their increasing role in greenhouse gas emissions?

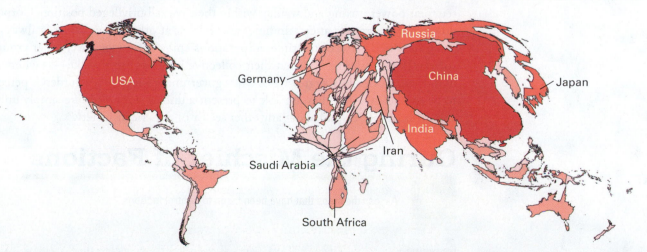

*Source:* Total Carbon Dioxide Emissions from the Consumption of Energy, International Energy Statistics, U.S. Energy Information Administration. Cartogram produced in ArcMap using Tom Gross's Cartogram Geoprocessing Tool (v2). The tool uses the Newman-Gastner method [see details in Michael T. Gastner and Mark E. J. Newman, "Diffusion-Based Method for Producing Density-Equalizing Maps," *Proceedings of the National Academy of Sciences* 101 (2004): 7499–7504].

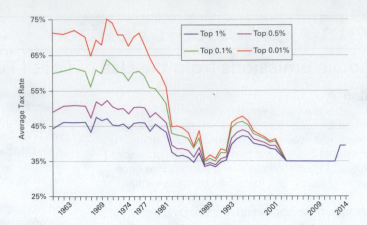

**FIGURE 7.4** TAX RATES FOR THE WEALTHIEST AMERICANS

Tax rates for the wealthiest Americans, particularly the super-wealthy, have dropped dramatically since the 1960s. The drops occurred not only when Republicans were in control in Washington, but during the Democratic Carter administration, and during periods when Democrats controlled Congress and Republicans held the presidency. This suggests that the political influence of these Americans has been fairly constant no matter which party was heading the government.

*Source:* 1960–2001 data from Thomas Piketty and Emmanuel Saez, "How Progressive Is the U.S. Federal Tax System?" Working Paper 12404, National Bureau of Economic Research (July 2006), Table A3. All other data are authors' calculations.

6. The National Labor Relations Board became less willing during the 1980s, 1990s, and 2000s to penalize corporations for illegal anti-union activities.

7. Until Democrats eliminated the use of the filibuster for executive branch nominations in 2013, Congress refused to confirm appointments of top officials to new financial industry regulatory agencies that business did not approve of.

8. Though the published corporate tax rate is 35 percent, the effective rate—what large, profitable corporations actually pay as a percentage of their earnings—is only 12.6 because of credits, exclusions, and shelters.[62]

These "wins" on important government policies that advance their interests are the best evidence available confirming political scientist David Vogel's observation that "when business is both mobilized and unified, its political power can be formidable."[63] Until recently interest group specialists in political science had not been able to empirically demonstrate links between things like money spent in lobbying or campaign contributions and specific votes in Congress or major federal policy developments.[64] But a growing body of ground-breaking empirical research shows that what the government in Washington does is overwhelmingly tied to the wishes of the wealthiest Americans and interest groups that represent our largest corporations and not to the wishes of average citizens.[65]

In our view, the best way to think about corporations in American politics is to see their power waxing and waning within their overall privileged position. Corporate power may be greater at certain times and weaker at other times, but it is always in a game in which, most of the time, corporations enjoy advantages over other groups in society. If corporations feel that their collective interests are at stake—as when labor unions are particularly aggressive or when government's regulatory burden is perceived to be too heavy—and they are able to present a united front, they are simply unbeatable. This cannot be said about any other sector of American society.[66]

# Curing the Mischief of Factions

**7.6** Assess the steps that have been taken to control factions

Americans have worried about the "mischief of factions" ever since James Madison wrote about them in *The Federalist* No. 10 (see the Appendix). Over the years, various things have been tried to control the purported negative effects of these special interests.[67] Disclosure has been the principal tool of regulation. In 1946, Congress imposed a requirement (in the Federal Regulation of Lobbying Act) that all lobbyists working in Congress be registered. The Lobby Disclosure Act of 1995 requires a wider range of political actors to register as lobbyists and makes them report every six months on which policies they are trying to influence and how much they are spending to do it.

Reformers have also tried to regulate some of the most troublesome abuses of the politics of factions. Sections of the Ethics in Government Act (1978) aim at the so-called **revolving door** in which former government officials become lobbyists for interests with whom they formerly dealt in their official capacity. A 1995 measure specifies that former U.S. trade representatives and their deputies are banned for life from lobbying for foreign interests. The 2007 measure increases the one-year waiting period in the 1995 measure to two years and adds representatives and senators to those who must wait.

Reformers have also tried to control the effects of interest group money in politics. The McCain–Feingold bill, passed in 2002, was designed to limit the use of soft money, but it left a huge loophole for nonprofit, advocacy 527 organizations—so named because of their location in the Tax Code—to use unlimited amounts of money to support or oppose candidates and issues, the only restrictions being a ban on radio and television advertising for a period before elections. It also increased the amount people could give to PACs. As described above, however, the Supreme Court has invalidated many key provisions of campaign finance laws, and political deadlock between Democrats and Republicans on the Federal Election Commission has crippled the commission's ability to examine and issue regulations regarding newly prominent entities such as 501s and Super PACs. The upshot is that that interest and advocacy groups have virtual free rein in financing candidates and advocating policies in federal election campaigns. Another measure passed in 2007 requires congressional leaders to identify all earmarks in appropriations bills and post them to the Internet at least 48 hours before their consideration by the full House and Senate, along with information about their sponsors and intended purposes. The same measures require lobbyists to certify that no one in their firm or organization has provided gifts to members of Congress or their staffs and post this to a site on the Internet. Moreover, the measures require lobbyists to file and also post to the Internet quarterly reports on their lobbying activities in Congress.

The 2007 lobbying reform measure was passed in the wake of the corruption conviction of super-lobbyist Jack Abramoff, revelations of widespread influence peddling by lobbyists who formerly worked in Congress or the executive branch agencies, and the explosion of special interest earmarks in appropriations bills. Most keen Washington observers remain unconvinced that the new rules will diminish in a major way the influence of privileged interest groups in shaping what government does. Like water seeking its own level, it may be that powerful and wealthy interests will find a way to have their needs and wishes attended to in one way or another.

7.1

7.2

7.3

7.4

7.5

7.6

## Using the DEMOCRACY STANDARD

### Do interest groups help or hinder American democracy?

There is no doubt that the interest group system plays an important role in shaping what government does in the United States; elected officials pay lots of attention to them, for all the reasons explored in this chapter. Whether the interest group system advances or retards democracy, however, can only be determined by knowing which sectors of the American population are represented by interest groups, and how well interest groups represent the people they claim to be representing. There is considerable disagreement regarding the role that interest groups play in American politics and governance.

There are many who believe that the interest group system enhances democracy because it gives individuals and groups in American society another tool to keep

7.1

7.2

7.3

7.4

7.5

7.6

elected and appointed officials responsive and responsible to their needs, wants, and interests. Political parties are important for making popular sovereignty work, to be sure, but being broad and inclusive umbrella organizations, they often ignore the interests of particular groups. And, although elections are essential for keeping public officials on their toes, they happen only every two to four years. Proponents of this pluralist view argue that the day-to-day work of popular sovereignty is done by interest groups. Additionally, pluralists point to the rise of advocacy groups—supported by thousands of ordinary people with ordinary incomes—as an indication that the interest group system is being leveled, with a wider range of groups representing a broad swath of the population now playing a key role in the political game.

Having said that, there is more than ample evidence that narrow, special, and privileged interests dominate the interest group world and play the biggest role in determining what government does in the United States. The powerful interest groups that play the largest role in shaping public policies in the United States represent, by and large, wealthier and better-educated Americans, corporations, and other business interests and professionals, such as doctors and lawyers. In this view, the proliferation of interest groups, mostly in the form of associations and firms that represent business, has made American politics less and less democratic. This inequality of access and influence violates the democratic principle of political equality, with less influence in the hands of ordinary Americans. Thus, some argue, the present interest group system poses a real threat to democratic ideals.

# Review the Chapter

## Interest Groups in a Democratic Society: Contrasting Views

> **7.1** Compare and contrast theories about the role of interest groups in a democracy, p. 188

Americans have long denigrated special interests as contrary to the public good. Many political scientists, however, see interest groups as an important addition to the representation process in a democracy, enhancing the contact of citizens with government officials in the periods between elections.

## The Universe of Interest Groups

> **7.2** Distinguish the two kinds of interests at work in American politics, p. 190

Private interests are organizations and associations that try to gain protections or material advantages from government for their own members rather than for society at large. For the most part, these represent economic interests of one kind or another.

Public interests are organizations and associations that try to gain protections or benefits for people beyond their own members, often for society at large. Public interests are motivated by ideological or issue concerns.

## Why There Are So Many Interest Groups

> **7.3** Explain why interest groups have proliferated, p. 195

There has been a significant expansion in the number of public interest or citizen groups since 1968.

The United States provides a rich environment for interest groups because of our constitutional system, our political culture, and the broad responsibilities of our government.

Interests tend to proliferate in a complex and changing society, which creates a diversity of interests.

Government does more than it did in the past and affects the interests of various people, groups, and firms who organize to exert influence over laws and regulations.

## What Interest Groups Do

> **7.4** Distinguish the methods through which interest groups try to shape government policy, p. 198

One way that interest groups attempt to influence the shape of public policy is the inside game: interest group representatives are in direct contact with government officials and try to build influence on the basis of personal relationships.

The outside game is being played when an interest group tries to mobilize local constituencies and shape public opinion to support the group's goals and to bring that pressure to bear on elected officials.

## Interest Groups, Corporations, and Inequality in American Politics

> **7.5** Determine the biases in the interest group system, p. 204

Some groups, especially corporations, trade associations, high-income professionals, and the wealthy, have more resources to put into lobbying officials and better access to them than other groups.

The business corporation enjoys what has been called a "privileged position" in American society that substantially enhances its influence on government policies.

Business corporations and the wealthy made big gains in a number of important areas of government policy during the past two decades, particularly on policies related to taxes, financial deregulation, and executive compensation.

## Curing the Mischief of Factions

> **7.6** Assess the steps that have been taken to control factions, p. 212

Lobbying reform has focused on requiring interest and advocacy groups to report on their lobbying activities, trying to control the revolving door, and limiting what private and public interest groups are allowed to spend in elections.

# Learn the Terms

# Test Yourself

Answer key begins on page T-1.

**7.1** Compare and contrast theories about the role of interest groups in a democracy

1. Government power in the United States is broadly dispersed, leaving governmental institutions porous and open to the entreaties of diverse groups that exist in society. This can be attributed to

   a. Federalism and checks and balances
   b. The separation of powers
   c. Federalism, checks and balances, and the separation of powers
   d. Interest groups
   e. Factions

**7.2** Distinguish the two kinds of interests at work in American politics

2. The main role of labor unions in the United States has been to

   a. Support public interest groups
   b. Support political parties and protect the jobs of their members
   c. Protect the jobs of their members
   d. Secure maximum wages for their members
   e. Protect the jobs and secure maximum wages and benefits for their members

**7.3** Explain why interest groups have proliferated

3. According to the disturbance theory, interest group formation often seems to happen when:

   a. Interests are threatened
   b. Congress passes a law
   c. The government acquires too much power
   d. New interest groups are formed
   e. There is an increase in lobbying

**7.4** Distinguish the methods through which interest groups try to shape government policy

4. This describes a legal brief in which individuals not involved in a suit may have their views heard in court:

   a. Grassroots lobbying
   b. *Amicus curiae*
   c. Lobbying Congress
   d. Earmarking
   e. Disturbance theory

**7.5** Determine the biases in the interest group system

5. Coalitions that which form around different policy areas that include public and private interest groups and policy experts are called

   a. Iron triangles
   b. Sub-triangles
   c. Informal networks
   d. Issue networks
   e. Sub-governments

**7.6** Assess the steps that have been taken to control factions

6. This bill, passed in 2002, was designed to limit the effect of interest group money in politics.

   a. Revolving door
   b. McCain–Feingold
   c. Ethics in government
   d. Federal regulation of lobbying
   e. Lobby disclosure

# Explore Further

## INTERNET SOURCES

Center for Responsive Politics **www.opensecrets.org/**
Follow the money trail—who gets it? who contributes?—in American politics.

National Taxpayers Union **www.ntu.org**
Conservative group that advocates for lower taxes.

National Organization for Women **www.now.org**
The women's organization that has long been a "player" in Washington politics.

National Rifle Association **www.nra.org**
Home page of one of America's most politically successful interest groups.

Project VoteSmart **www.votesmart.org**
Information on interest group campaign contributions to and ratings for all members of Congress.

U.S. Chamber of Commerce **www.uschamber.org**
The leading peak association lobbying for business.

Student Environmental Action Coalition **www.seac.org**
A grassroots coalition of student environmental groups.

Townhall **www.townhall.com**
A portal to scores of conservative organizations and citizen groups.

Yahoo/Organizations and Interest Groups **www.yahoo.com/ Government/Politics/**
Direct links to the home pages of scores of public and private interest groups as well as to Washington lobbying firms.

U.S. Public Interest Research Group **www.uspirg.org**
A site dedicated to information on public interest research groups.

Association of Government Relations Professionals **www.alldc.org**
The Association of Government Relations Professionals is a site dedicated to educating others about the profession of lobbying.

Lobbyists.info **www.lobbyists.info**
A database of lobbyists, lobbying firms, and organizations.

## SUGGESTIONS FOR FURTHER READING

Ainsworth, Scott H. *Analyzing Interest Groups: Group Influence on People and Policies.* New York: W. W. Norton, 2002.
Shows how economic forms of reasoning can be used to better understand how interest groups work and what effect they have on politics and government.

Andres, Gary J. *Lobbying Reconsidered: Under the Influence.* New York: Pearson Longman, 2009.
A fascinating tour of the world of lobbying by an author who not only knows the scholarly literature on the subject, but also has years of experience as a lobbyist.

Berry, Jeffrey M., and Clyde Wilcox. *The Interest Group Society*, 5th ed. New York: Pearson Longman, 2009.
A leading textbook on interest groups, filled with up-to-date insights from scholars and political journalists.

Dahl, Robert A. *A Preface to Democratic Theory.* Chicago: University of Chicago Press, 1956.
The leading theoretical statement of the pluralist position and the democratic role of interest groups.

Davidson, Roger H., Walter J. Oleszek, and Frances E. Lee. *Congress and Its Members*, 14th ed. Washington, D.C.: CQ Press, 2014.
A comprehensive book on Congress that carefully examines the role of organized interests in the legislative process.

Gilens, Martin. *Affluence and Influence: Economic Inequality and Political Power in America.* New York and Princeton, NJ: Russell Sage Foundation and Princeton University Press, 2012.
Ground-breaking work that empirically demonstrates the close linkage between government policies and the positions on public affairs of corporations, powerful interest groups, and the wealthy.

Hacker, Jacob S., and Paul Pierson. *Winner-Take-All Politics: How Washington Made the Rich Richer—and Turned Its Back on the Middle Class.* New York: Simon and Schuster, 2010.
Shows how interest groups representing business and the wealthy have dominated public policymaking in Washington and made the distribution of income and wealth much more unequal.

Skocpol, Theda. *Diminished Democracy: From Membership to Management in American Civil Life.* Norman, OK: University of Oklahoma Press, 2003.
An analysis of the decline of mass membership associations and how it hurts American civic life and the middle class.

Smith, Mark A. *American Business and Political Power: Public Opinion, Elections, and Democracy.* Chicago: University of Chicago Press, 2000.
An argument, counter to that of Lindblom, that business corporations are not as powerful in American politics as often perceived.

# 8

# Social Movements

## WOMEN WIN THE RIGHT TO VOTE

**T**he struggle for women's suffrage (i.e., the right to vote) was long and difficult. The main instrument for winning the struggle to amend the Constitution to admit women to full citizenship was a powerful social movement that dared to challenge the status quo, used unconventional tactics to gain attention and sympathy, and demanded bravery and commitment from many women.[1] One of these women was Angelina Grimké.

Abolitionist Angelina Grimké addressed the Massachusetts legislature in February 1838, presenting a petition against slavery from an estimated 20,000 women of the state. In doing so, she became the first woman to speak before an American legislative body. Because women at this time were legally subordinate to men and shut out of civic life—the life of home and church were considered their proper domains—Grimké felt it necessary to defend women's involvement in the abolitionist movement to end slavery. She said the following to the legislators:

> Are we aliens because we are women? Are we bereft of citizenship because we are mothers, wives and daughters of a mighty people? Have women no country—no interests staked in public weal—no partnership in a nation's guilt and shame? . . . I hold, Mr. Chairman, that American women have to do this subject [the abolition of slavery], not only because it is moral and religious, but because it is political, inasmuch as we are citizens of the Republic and as such our honor, happiness and well-being are bound up in its politics, government and laws.

Although this bold claim of citizenship for women did not fall on receptive ears—Grimké was derided as ridiculous and blasphemous by press and pulpit—it helped inspire other women who had entered political life by way of the abolitionist movement to press for women's rights as well. Meeting at Seneca Falls, New York, in 1848, a group of women issued a declaration written by

**DEMANDING THE RIGHT TO VOTE** Here a member of a women's suffrage organization speaks on a street corner in New York demanding that women be granted the right to vote in the United States. Women's struggle to gain the vote blew hot and cold for over 130 years, but persistence paid off at last in 1920 when the Nineteenth Amendment was adopted. How might one explain why such a basic democratic right was so long in coming?

Elizabeth Cady Stanton stating that "all men and women are created equal, endowed with the same inalienable rights." The declaration, much like the Declaration of Independence on which it was modeled, then presented a long list of violations of rights.

The Seneca Falls Declaration remains one of the most eloquent statements of women's equality ever written, but it failed to have an immediate effect because most politically active women (and men) in the abolitionist movement believed that their first order of business was to end slavery. Women's rights would have to wait.

After the Civil War destroyed the slave system, women's rights leaders such as Stanton, Susan B. Anthony, and Lucy Stone pressed for equal citizenship rights for all, white or black, male or female. They were bitterly disappointed when the Fourteenth Amendment, ratified after the war, declared full citizenship rights for all males born or naturalized in the United States, including those who had been slaves, but failed to include women. Women's rights activists realized that they would have to fight for rights on their own, with their own organizations.

Women's rights organizations were formed soon after the Civil War. For more than two decades, though, the National Woman Suffrage Association (NWSA) and the American Woman Suffrage Association (AWSA) feuded over how to pressure male politicians. Susan B. Anthony (with the NWSA) and Lucy Stone (with the AWSA) were divided by temperament and ideology. Anthony favored pressing for a broad range of rights and organized dramatic actions to expose men's hypocrisy. At an 1876 centennial celebration of the United States in Philadelphia, Anthony and several other women marched onto the platform, where the emperor of Brazil and other dignitaries sat, and read the declaration aloud. Stone favored gaining the vote as the primary objective of the rights movement and used quieter methods of persuasion, such as petitions.

In 1890, the two main organizations joined to form the National American Woman Suffrage Association (NAWSA). They dropped such controversial NWSA demands as divorce reform and legalized prostitution in favor of one order of business: women's suffrage. The movement was now focused, united, and growing more powerful every year.

In 1912, the NAWSA organized a march to support a constitutional amendment for suffrage. More than 5,000 women paraded through the streets of Washington before Woodrow Wilson's inauguration. The police offered the marchers no protection from antagonistic spectators who pelted the marchers with rotten fruit and vegetables and an occasional rock, despite the legal parade permit they had obtained. This lack of protection outraged the public and attracted media attention to the suffrage movement.

Almost immediately after the United States entered World War I in April 1917, with the express purpose of "making the world safe for democracy," women began to picket the White House, demanding that full democracy be instituted in America. One demonstrator's sign quoted directly from President Wilson's war message, "We shall fight for the right of those who submit to authority to have a voice in their own government,"[2] and asked why women were excluded from American democracy. As the picketing at the White House picked up in numbers and in intensity, the police began arresting large groups of women. Other women took their place. The cycle continued until local jails were filled to capacity. When suffragists began a hunger strike in jail, authorities responded with forced feedings and isolation cells. By November, public outrage forced local authorities to relent and free the women. By this time, public opinion had shifted in favor of women's right to vote.

In the years surrounding U.S. entry into the war, other women's groups worked state by state, senator by senator, pressuring male politicians to support women's suffrage. After two prominent senators from New England were defeated in 1918 primarily because of the efforts of suffragists and prohibitionists, the political clout of the women's groups became apparent to most elected officials. In June 1919, Congress passed the Nineteenth Amendment, and the necessary 36 states ratified it the following year. By uniting around a common cause, women's organizations gained the right to vote for all women.

Although few social movements have been as effective as the women's suffrage movement in reaching their primary goal, other social movements have also played an important role in American political life. This chapter is about what social movements are, how and why they form, what tactics they use, and how they affect American political life and what government does.

## Thinking Critically About This Chapter

This chapter is about the important role of social movements in American government and politics.

## Using the Framework

You will see in this chapter how social movements are a response to structural changes in the economy, culture, and society and how they affect other political linkage actors and institutions—parties, interest groups, and public opinion, for example—and government. You will learn, most importantly, under what conditions social movements most effectively shape the behavior of elected leaders and the content of government policies.

## Using the Democracy Standard

At first glance, because social movements are most often the political instrument of numerical minorities, it may seem that they have little to do with democracy, which is rooted in majority rule. You will see in this chapter, however, that social movements play an especially important role in our democracy, principally by broadening public debate on important issues and bringing outsiders and nonparticipants into the political arena.

**social movement**
A loosely organized group that uses unconventional and often disruptive tactics to have their grievances heard by the public, the news media, and government leaders.

8.1

8.2

8.3

8.4

8.5

8.6

# What Are Social Movements?

**8.1**  Define social movements and who they represent

**S**ocial movements are loosely organized collections of ordinary people, working outside normal political channels, to get their voices heard by the public at large, the news media and leaders of major institutions, and government officials, in order to promote, resist, or undo some social change. They are different than interest groups, which are longer lasting and more organized, with permanent employees and budgets, for example, and more committed to conventional and nondisruptive methods such as lobbying and issue advertising. They are different than political parties, whose main purpose is to win elective offices for candidates who campaign under the party banner and to control government and what it does across a broad range of policies. Social movements are more ephemeral in nature, coming and going as people feel they are needed, sometimes leaving their mark on public policies, sometimes not. What sets social movements apart from parties and interest groups is their focus on broad, society-wide issues and their tendency to act outside the normal channels of government and politics, using unconventional and often disruptive tactics.[3] Some scholars call social movement politics "contentious politics."[4] When suffragists disrupted meetings, went on hunger strikes, and marched to demand the right to vote, they were engaged in contentious politics. The most important such social movement in recent times is the civil rights movement, which pressed demands for equal treatment for African Americans on the American public and elected officials, primarily during the 1960s.

This general definition of social movements requires further elaboration if we are to understand their role in American politics.[5] Here we highlight some important things to know about them:

- *Social movements are the political instrument of political outsiders.* Social movements often help people who are outside the political mainstream gain a

8.1

8.2

8.3

8.4

8.5

8.6

**secularization**
The spread of nonreligious values and outlooks.

hearing from the public and from political decision makers. The women's suffrage movement forced the issue of votes for women onto the public agenda. The civil rights movement did the same for the issue of equal citizenship for African Americans. Gays and lesbians forced the country to pay attention to issues that had long been left "in the closet." Insiders don't need social movements; they can rely instead on interest groups, political action committees (PACs), lobbyists, campaign contributions, and the like to make their voices heard.

Christian conservatives, now a political force to reckon with, with many well-established interest groups, such as the Family Research Council and the remarkable influence within the Republican Party, were at one time largely ignored by the cultural and political establishment. Their grassroots movement to resist the general **secularization** of American life and to promote their vision of religious values in American life was built at first around local churches and Bible reading groups and often took the form of protests, whether at abortion clinics or at government locations where some religious symbol (like a manger scene at Christmas-time) was ordered removed by the courts because it violated the principle of separation of church and state.

- *Social movements are generally mass grassroots phenomena.* Because outsiders and excluded groups often lack the financial and political resources of insiders, they must take advantage of what they have: numbers, energy, and commitment. They depend on the participation of large numbers of ordinary people to act in ways that will move the general public and persuade public officials to address issues of concern to those in the movement.

- *Social movements are populated by individuals with a shared sense of grievance.* People would not take on the considerable risks involved in joining others in a social movement unless they felt a strong, shared sense of grievance against the status quo and a desire to bring about social change. Social movements tend to form when a significant number of people come to define their own troubles and problems, not in personal terms, but in more general social terms (the belief that there is a common cause for all of their troubles) and when they believe that the government can be moved to take action on their behalf. Because this is a rare combination, social movements are very difficult to organize and sustain.

- *Social movements often use unconventional and disruptive tactics.* Officials and citizens almost always complain that social movements are ill-mannered and disruptive. For social movements, that is precisely the point. Unconventional and disruptive tactics help gain attention for movement grievances. While successful movements are ones that eventually bring many other Americans and public officials over to their side, it is usually the case that other Americans and public officials are not paying attention to the issues that are of greatest concern to movement participants, so something dramatic needs to be done to change the situation.

- *Social movements often turn into interest groups.* Although particular social movements eventually fade from the political scene, for reasons we explore later, the more successful ones create organizations that carry on their work over a longer period of time. Thus, the women's movement spawned the National Organization for Women, while the environmental movement created organizations such as Environmental Defense Fund and the Nature Conservancy. The movement of Christian evangelicals spurred the creation of groups such as the Family Research Council and the National Right to Life Committee.

**TEA'D OFF**

The Tea Party movement, deeply opposed to President Obama and his agenda for an energetic government to solve the economic crisis and longer-term problems like health care, became a force to be reckoned within American politics only months after the president's inauguration. These people gathered in Freedom Plaza in Washington, D.C., to express their anger at passage of the economic "stimulus package."

# Major Social Movements in the United States

8.1

8.2

8.3

8.4

8.5

8.6

**8.2** Illustrate how important social movements have shaped American society

**M**any social movements have left their mark on American political life and have shaped what government does in the United States. Here we describe some of the most important.

## ☐ The Abolitionists

This movement's objective was to end slavery in the United States. The movement was most active in the northern states in the three decades before the outbreak of the Civil War. Their harsh condemnation of the slave system helped heighten the tensions between the North and the South, eventually bringing on the war that ended slavery. Their tactics included antislavery demonstrations and resistance (sometimes violent) to enforcement of the Fugitive Slave Act, which required all states to identify, capture, and return runaway slaves to their owners.

8.1

8.2

8.3

8.4

8.5

8.6

## ☐ The Populists

The Populist movement was made up of disaffected farmers of the American South and West in the 1880s and 1890s who were angry with business practices and developments in the American economy that were adversely affecting them. Their main grievance was the concentration of economic power in the banking and railroad industries, both of which favored (with loans on better terms, cheaper shipping rates, and the like) their larger customers. The aim of the movement was to force public ownership or regulation of banks, grain storage companies, and the railroads. Small demonstrations at banks and at foreclosed farms were part of their repertoire, but they used the vote as well. For a short time, they were quite successful, winning control of several state legislatures, sending members to Congress, helping to nominate William Jennings Bryan as the Democratic candidate for president in 1896, and forcing the federal regulation of corporations (e.g., in the Interstate Commerce Act of 1887).

## ☐ Women's Suffrage

This movement, active in the late nineteenth and early twentieth centuries, aimed to win women the right to vote. As we saw in the chapter-opening story, the movement won its objective when the Nineteenth Amendment to the Constitution was ratified in 1920. We also saw that the tactics of the movement were deliberately disruptive and unsettling to many.

## ☐ The Labor Movement

The labor movement represented efforts by working people over the years to protect jobs, ensure decent wages and benefits, and guarantee safe workplaces. The periods of greatest militancy—when working people took to the streets and the factory floors to demand recognition of their unions—were in the 1880s, the 1890s, and the 1930s. (Their militancy during the Great Depression, joined with that of other groups pressing for a more activist government committed to social justice, led to the passage of the Social Security Act, which we examine in the "Can Government Do Anything Well?" feature.) The labor movement eventually forced the federal government to recognize the right of working people to form labor unions to represent them in negotiations with management. However, labor unions, the fruit of this successful movement, have been steadily losing members, especially in the private sector.

## ☐ The Civil Rights Movement

The civil rights movement began in the mid-1950s, reached the peak of its activity in the mid-1960s, and gradually lost steam after that (see Figure 8.1). The movement, which was committed to nonviolent civil disobedience as one of its main tactics, remains one of the most influential on record, having pressed successfully for the end of formal segregation in the South and discriminatory practices across the nation. The main weapons of the movement were nonviolent civil disobedience and mass demonstrations. The outbreak of violence in urban centers after the assassination of Martin Luther King, Jr. in 1968 and the rise in prominence at the same time of black power advocates like Stokely Carmichael and Malcolm X,[6] who rejected nonviolence as a basic principle, marked for many people the end of the movement.

## ☐ Contemporary Antiwar Movements

Antiwar movements have accompanied virtually every war the United States has waged. The most important ones that have affected American politics in contemporary times were associated with military conflicts in Southeast Asia and the Middle East. The *anti–Vietnam War* movement was active in the United States in the late 1960s and early 1970s. Its aim was to end the war in Vietnam. It used a wide variety of tactics in this effort, from mass demonstrations to voting registration and nonviolent civil disobedience. Fringe elements even turned to violence, exemplified by the Days

8.1
8.2
8.3
8.4
8.5
8.6

# Can Government Do Anything Well?

## Old-age pensions in Social Security

Social Security was passed in 1936 as part of Franklin Roosevelt's New Deal program to fight the Great Depression. In the beginning it provided very modest provisions for a limited number of working Americans once they reached the age of 65. It was the product not only of the liberal political thinking of the day, but of mass movements rocking the country demanding greater economic justice and security across the board in the United States. The Communist and Socialist parties had made significant gains in American politics since the beginning of the Depression, while radical populist politicians demanding "soak the rich" and poor relief programs such as the radio priest Father Coughlin and Louisiana governor Huey Long had gained enormous followings. Labor unions were on the rise, demanding not only better wages and working conditions but a better deal for other ordinary Americans. Most importantly, the Townsend Movement, which advocated that everyone over 65 be given a $200 per month benefit (so long as all the money was spent by the recipient), was gaining adherents by the millions as established by signed petitions that poured into the White House and Congress. Franklin Roosevelt, his labor secretary Francis Perkins, and members of Congress felt that something had to be done. Some have suggested, to be sure, that Roosevelt and other Social Security advocates used the popular pressures created by these movements to achieve something they had wanted to do all along.

Since its original passage, the average Social Security monthly payment gradually has grown larger and a higher proportion of Americans are now covered. This has happened because the program has become incredibly popular, and elected leaders, recognizing the voting power of those near or over 65, lean much more strongly toward increasing the size and reach of benefits and try to avoid any cutbacks in benefits. It is telling that there have been signs at antigovernment Tea Party rallies saying, "Keep government out of my Social Security." Today, the average benefit is $1,294 a month, and 90 percent of those over 65 years of age receive Social Security benefits. Two-thirds of all recipients receive 50 percent or more of their total income from their Social Security checks.

*Support for the claim that government should provide at least the current levels of income support for the elderly:*

- Social Security is the nation's most important antipoverty program; poverty among the elderly, once the highest among population age groups, is now the lowest.
- Social Security pensions, though not overly generous, allow most of our elderly to live with dignity, especially when paired with Medicare.
- The purported Social Security financing crisis is easily fixed by raising the retirement age or raising the payroll tax or raising the ceiling on income subject to payroll taxes (benefit payments could be cut theoretically, but this is politically unpalatable).
- Privatizing Social Security would subject all retirees to the vagaries of the market, leaving many in dire straits, if things go badly on Wall Street, just when they need it most.

*Rejection of the claim that government should provide at least the current levels of income support for the elderly:*

- The current system is expensive and inefficient. Part of the problem could be solved by partially privatizing the system, allowing working Americans to put all or part of the payroll tax into 401(k)-style private accounts.
- The long-term budget crisis of the country cannot be seriously addressed without making substantial cuts in entitlement programs, among which Social Security and Medicare are the largest.
- As the American population ages there will be more older Americans receiving Social Security benefits every year and fewer younger working Americans paying payroll taxes, so the fiscal crisis of the system is bound to get worse unless major steps are taken to cut the program or raise the retirement age. Increasing taxes is off the table because of the depressing impacts such taxes would have on the overall economy.

### WHAT DO YOU THINK?

What do you think about the past, present, and future role of the government in providing old-age pensions under Social Security?

- Government was right to establish Social Security and now needs to make it more generous.
- Government was right to establish Social Security and, because it is working well, should leave it unchanged.
- Government was right to establish Social Security but now needs to cut it back.
- Government should not have created Social Security in the first place. At most, it should have used tax incentives to encourage people to establish private accounts.

How would you defend this position to a fellow student? What would be your main line of argument? What evidence do you believe best supports your position?

Additional sources for this feature: David Kennedy, *Freedom from Fear: The American People in Depression and War* (Oxford, UK: Oxford University Press, 1999); and the Social Security Administration at www.ssa.gov.

8.1
8.2
8.3
8.4
8.5
8.6

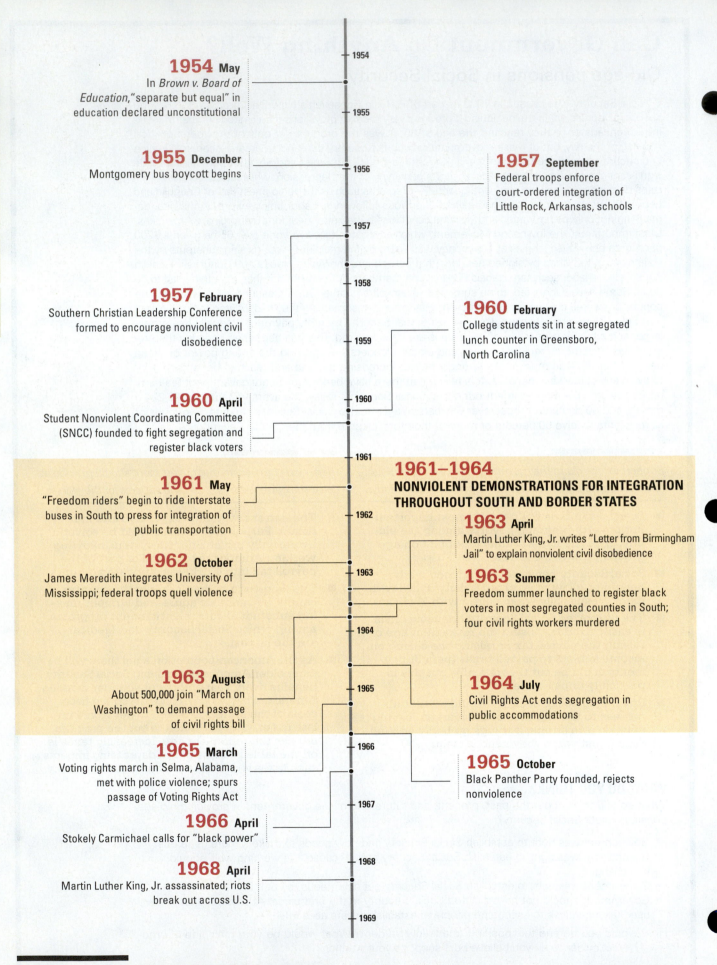

**1954** May
In *Brown v. Board of Education*, "separate but equal" in education declared unconstitutional

**1955** December
Montgomery bus boycott begins

**1957** September
Federal troops enforce court-ordered integration of Little Rock, Arkansas, schools

**1957** February
Southern Christian Leadership Conference formed to encourage nonviolent civil disobedience

**1960** February
College students sit in at segregated lunch counter in Greensboro, North Carolina

**1960** April
Student Nonviolent Coordinating Committee (SNCC) founded to fight segregation and register black voters

**1961–1964**
**NONVIOLENT DEMONSTRATIONS FOR INTEGRATION THROUGHOUT SOUTH AND BORDER STATES**

**1961** May
"Freedom riders" begin to ride interstate buses in South to press for integration of public transportation

**1963** April
Martin Luther King, Jr. writes "Letter from Birmingham Jail" to explain nonviolent civil disobedience

**1962** October
James Meredith integrates University of Mississippi; federal troops quell violence

**1963** Summer
Freedom summer launched to register black voters in most segregated counties in South; four civil rights workers murdered

**1963** August
About 500,000 join "March on Washington" to demand passage of civil rights bill

**1964** July
Civil Rights Act ends segregation in public accommodations

**1965** March
Voting rights march in Selma, Alabama, met with police violence; spurs passage of Voting Rights Act

**1965** October
Black Panther Party founded, rejects nonviolence

**1966** April
Stokely Carmichael calls for "black power"

**1968** April
Martin Luther King, Jr. assassinated; riots break out across U.S.

**FIGURE 8.1** TIMELINE: THE NONVIOLENT CIVIL RIGHTS MOVEMENT

8.1
8.2
8.3
8.4
8.5
8.6

**NON-VIOLENT PROTEST SPARKS A MOVEMENT**

When African American college students sat at the whites-only lunch counter of a Woolworth's department store in Greensboro, North Carolina in 1957 to protest the company's segregationist policies, often braving assaults by angry counter-demonstrators like this one spraying insect repellant, it inspired college students across the nation to conduct sit-ins in their own communities.

of Rage vandalism along Chicago's Gold Coast mounted by a wing of Students for a Democratic Society and the bombing of a research lab at the University of Wisconsin in which a graduate student was killed.

An *anti–Iraq War* movement quickly formed in the months leading up to the U.S. invasion of Iraq in 2003. The movement's most dramatic political act was the organization of massive demonstrations across the world on February 15, 2003. In the United States, demonstrations took place in 150 cities; in New York, the crowd converging on the U.N. headquarters building filled a space 20 blocks long, along First and Second Avenues (huge demonstrations occurred around the world as the "Mapping American Politics" feature shows).[7] The massive demonstrations did not convince President Bush to put off the Iraq invasion, however. The movement lost support after the invasion of Iraq in April 2003, as patriotic feelings rose as troops went into battle, but the subsequent insurgency, and the high cost to the United States of the insurgency in lives and money, rekindled the movement in late 2005. Changing public opinion on the war, some of it attributable to the antiwar demonstrations, perhaps, helped set the stage for the Republicans' big losses in the 2006 congressional elections.

## ☐ The Women's Movement

This movement has been important in American life since the late 1960s. Its aim has been to win civil rights protections for women and to broaden the participation of women in all aspects of American society, economy, and politics. Although it did not win one of its main objectives—passage of the **Equal Rights Amendment (ERA)** to the U.S. Constitution that guaranteed equal treatment for men and women by all levels of government—the broad advance of women on virtually all fronts in the United States attests to its overall effectiveness. The movement has been sufficiently successful, in fact, that it helped trigger a counter-movement among religious conservatives of all denominations worried about purported threats to traditional family values.

**Equal Rights Amendment (ERA)**

Proposed amendment to the U.S. Constitution stating that equality of rights shall not be abridged or denied on account of a person's gender; it failed to win the approval of the necessary number of states.

8.1
8.2
8.3
8.4
8.5
8.6

# Mapping American Politics

## Worldwide Demonstrations Against the Invasion of Iraq

### Introduction

The buildup to the invasion of Iraq was a long time coming. President Bush named Iraq one of the three members of his "axis-of-evil" countries in his State of the Union address in January 2002 because of their purported weapons of mass destruction (WMD) programs. U.S. diplomats urged the U.N. Security Council to pass a resolution pushing for renewed inspections of possible violations of international restrictions on chemical, biological, and nuclear weapons programs in Iraq. U.N. inspectors found very little and reported skepticism that such programs still existed. The administration kept up the pressure, gaining congressional approval in October 2002 for the use of force against Iraq if there was evidence of WMD programs and the United Nations failed to act. Other Security Council members were not convinced by Secretary of State Colin Powell's presentation of evidence for WMDs in early 2003, causing the United States to withdraw its resolution for the use of force in early March 2003. The United States then pulled together a group of 18 countries that President Bush called the "coalition of the willing" that agreed to use force if necessary and warned U.N. weapons inspectors to leave Iraq. The invasion of Iraq began on March 20, 2003.

### Mapping World Demonstrations

Rough estimates are that about 16 million people worldwide gathered over the weekend of February 13–15, 2003, to protest against the coming invasion of Iraq. Researchers at Worldmapper found evidence of protest demonstrations in 96 of the world's mapped countries and territories. The cartogram map, showing the proportion of the world total accounted for by each country, reveals that the largest demonstrations took place in Europe, especially in Italy, Spain, and the United Kingdom, and also in the United States. The demonstrations in Rome drew 3 million; the ones in London, about 1.4 million. New York saw about 125,000 protestors, while the march in San Francisco drew about 65,000. It is worth noting, however, as you look at this map, that estimates of the size of demonstrations are just that—estimates—though whenever possible, the researchers depended on more than a single source, leaning toward academic, press, and official estimates rather than those of the demonstration organizers. (See the "By the Numbers" feature in this chapter on how to count crowds.)

### What Do You Think?

Why might the president and his advisers make decisions or policies with which large portions of the domestic and foreign publics disagree? Given what occurred in Iraq after the invasion in March 2003, how could American officials have better taken into account what protesters around the world and in the United States were saying? Even if you believe that presidents must be free to act as they choose, within the constitutional boundaries of their office, how should global and American public opinion factor into their policymaking, if at all?

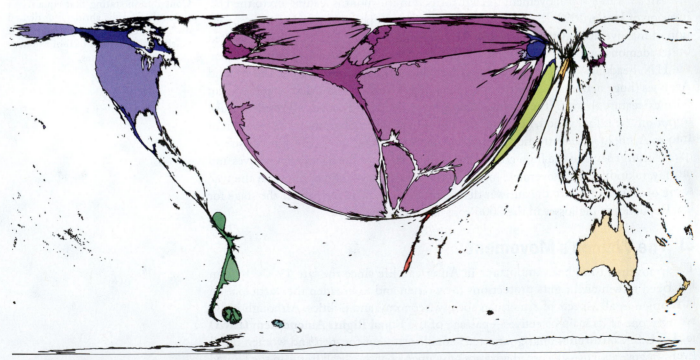

Worldwide Demonstrations Against the Invasion of Iraq
*Source:* © 2006 SASI Group (University of Sheffield) and Mark Newman (University of Michigan).

## The Environmental Movement

The environmental movement has been active in the United States since the early 1970s. Its aim has been to encourage government regulation of damaging environmental practices and to raise the environmental sympathies of the public. While the vitality of the movement has waxed and waned over the years, the public's strong support for environmental regulation suggests that it has been unusually successful. Although disruptive and even violent tactics have sometimes been used, the movement has depended more on legal challenges to business practices and the creation of organizations to lobby in Washington. Rising concerns among many Americans about fuel shortages, high gasoline prices, and global climate change have revitalized the movement and enhanced its influence.

## The Gay and Lesbian Movements

These movements began in earnest in the late 1960s. Their aim was to gain the same civil rights protections under the law enjoyed by African Americans and other minority groups and to gain respect from the public. Ranging from patient lobbying and voting to mass demonstrations and deliberately shocking actions by groups such as ACT-UP, the movement's efforts have been only partially successful. They also have sparked strong counterattacks by groups such as the Christian Coalition and Focus on the Family that are opposed to their objectives.

## Religious Conservatives

Religious conservative movements have occurred at several different moments in American history and have been very influential. These movements have brought together strongly religious people trying to infuse American society and public policies with their values. The contemporary movement of religious conservatives falls within this tradition and has become very important in American politics, especially on the issues of abortion, school prayer, educational curriculum, and same-sex marriage. The *pro-life (anti-abortion)* movement is part of this larger religious conservative movement. Its main objective is to end the legal availability of abortion in the United States.

## The Antiglobalization Movement

An emergent antiglobalization movement announced itself to the public with demonstrations in Seattle in late 1999 targeted at the World Trade Organization (WTO), whose trade ministers were meeting in the city to fashion an agreement to further open national borders to trade and foreign investment.[8] The demonstrations were mostly peaceful, but some demonstrators turned violent. This movement is extremely diverse and includes people who are worried about the effects of globalization on the environment, income inequality in the United States and Third World countries, food safety, labor rights, sweat shops, unfair trade, and national sovereignty. The movement remains intermittently active, with protesters showing up at large WTO gatherings, as well as those put on by the World Bank, the International Monetary Fund, the World Economic Forum (which meets annually in Davos, Switzerland), and meetings of the leaders of the major industrial democracies, such as the G8.

## Undocumented Immigrants Movement

A series of massive demonstrations in the spring of 2006 in cities across the nation signaled the rise in the United States of a movement of and for illegal immigrants. Although the goals of movement leaders, activists, and joiners were quite diverse, they were joined by a wish to give legal status to those presently living and working in the United States illegally, to allow more legal immigration from Mexico, and to increase Americans' understanding of the positive role played by immigrants—legal and illegal—in the American economy. Demonstration participants included not only legal immigrants, American citizens of Mexican descent, and sympathizers from many

8.1

8.2

8.3

8.4

8.5

8.6

8.1

8.2

8.3

8.4

8.5

8.6

other ethnic and racial groups but, remarkably, tens of thousands of undocumented people subject to deportation if they came to the attention of the authorities.[9] This and subsequent demonstrations failed to convince Republicans in Congress in 2007 to support an immigration bill favored by President Bush that included a path toward citizenship for people living in the United States illegally. It also helped galvanize groups of Americans opposed to illegal immigration and later made it impossible for President Obama to convince Congress to pass his own comprehensive immigration reform ideas that included a pathway to citizenship.

## □ Tea Party Movement

This movement exploded onto the American political scene on tax deadline day (April 15) 2009, with demonstrations in scores of locations around the country denouncing bank bailouts, the Democrats' health care reform effort, rising government deficits, taxes and regulations, illegal immigration, and, for many among the participants, the legality of the Obama presidency. Urged on by conservative talk radio hosts and the intense coverage of their activities by Fox News, and funded by the Koch brothers' oil fortune, the Tea Party staged a series of demonstrations across the country and mobilized in August 2009 to flood and take over health care town hall meetings held by Democratic members of Congress. By 2010, it had become a major force within the Republican Party, defeating many establishment candidates with Tea Party adherents and helping Republicans win control of legislatures and governorships in many states and in the U.S. House of Representatives. The movement seems to represent a modern-day angry populism directed against an activist federal government that, in the view of movement activists and followers, has been taking too many taxes from hard-working people and saddling the country with huge debts, all for programs that support the undeserving poor (people unwilling to work), and those who are in the country illegally. (See Figure 8.2 for how Tea Party sympathizers differ from other Americans and other Republicans.)

**FIGURE 8.2** TEA PARTY PROPONENTS ON THE ISSUES

Polls show that while Tea Party identifiers are overwhelmingly Republican, they are from the most conservative wing of the party, with stronger antigovernment and anti-immigration views than mainstream Republicans. Their views diverge even farther from those of all registered voters. This poll was conducted right after the Tea Party's rise to prominence in the 2010 national elections, when many Tea Party candidates won nomination fights against Republican establishment candidates and the GOP won control of the House of Representatives. It demonstrates that a determined minority can be successful in very low turnout elections such as party primaries and caucuses where House candidates are nominated and off-year congressional elections when there is no presidential contest.

*Source:* Scott Clement and John Green, "The Tea Party, Religion, and Social Issues," (Washington, D.C.: Pew Forum on Religion and Public Life, February 23, 2011).

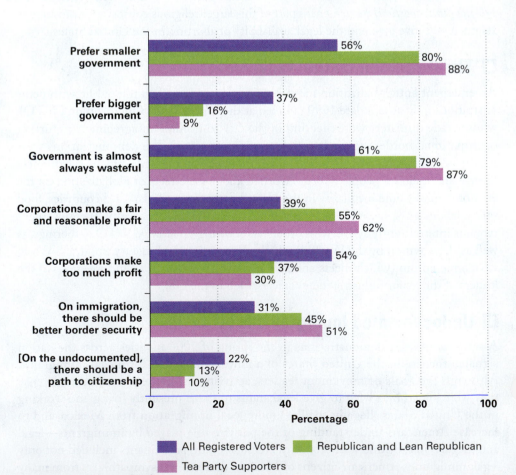

## The Occupy Wall Street Movement

This movement, organized almost wholly through the new social media, came dramatically to public attention in September 2011 when protestors took over Zuccotti Park in the Wall Street section of New York. The number of occupiers quickly increased in New York, then Occupy sites rapidly spread to many cities and communities across the country. Though the message of the movement was somewhat garbled because of the many diverse groups it attracted, its most common underlying theme alleged economic unfairness, asserting the failure of government to do anything about diminished job prospects, stagnant wages, crippling student loan debt, declining living standards, or rising income and wealth inequality while bailing out banks whose top executives raked in bonus upon bonus. The movement coined the phrase, "We are the 99 percent," as a way of calling attention to their contention that most of the gains of economic growth over the past two decades had gone to the top 1 percent. Some labor unions joined the protests in New York and Oakland, among other places, and many celebrities voiced support and made contributions. Because the movement believed in actual "occupation," setting up tents, feeding stations, first-aid centers, and the like in the places they took over, police eventually moved in to clear away the demonstrators, with officials citing safety concerns as their motivations. In New York, closing down the Occupy site was relatively peaceful; in Oakland and Berkeley it proved to be more violent. Though the movement has receded from view recently, its issues are sufficiently consistent with the views of a substantial number of Americans to suggest that it will reappear from time to time. As the Zuccotti Park occupation moved into its second month, a Pew poll showed that 39 percent of Americans said they agreed with the movement's goals, more than said they supported the Tea Party's (32 percent).[10]

# Social Movements in a Majoritarian Democracy

**8.3** Evaluate how social movements make U.S. politics more democratic

**A**t first glance, social movements do not seem to fit very well in a democracy. First, social movements usually start out with only a small minority of people, whereas democracy requires majority rule. Second, social movements often use disruptive tactics—though rarely overtly violent ones—when it seems that many channels already exist (e.g., voting, petitioning and writing to policymakers, and writing letters to newspapers) for people to express their grievances. In this section, we talk about how social movements can (and often do) help make American politics more democratic.

## Encouraging Participation

Social movements may increase the level of popular involvement and interest in politics. In one sense, this is true simply by definition: social movements are the instruments of outsiders. Thus, the women's suffrage movement showed many middle-class women that their activities need not be confined exclusively to home, family, church, and charity work and encouraged them to venture into political life by gathering petitions or joining demonstrations demanding the vote for women. The civil rights movement in the 1960s encouraged southern African Americans, who had long been barred from the political life of their communities, to become active in their own emancipation. The religious fundamentalist movement spurred the involvement of previously politically apathetic evangelicals. The pro-immigration movement may yet spur increased political participation by Hispanic citizens.

8.1

8.2

8.3

8.4

8.5

8.6

8.1
8.2
8.3
8.4
8.5
8.6

**scope of conflict**
Refers to the number of groups involved in a political conflict; a narrow scope of conflict involves a small number of groups, and a wide scope of conflict involves many.

**mass mobilization**
The process of involving large numbers of people in a social movement.

**Great Depression**
The period of economic crisis in the United States that lasted from the stock market crash of 1929 to America's entry into World War II.

Social movements also encourage popular participation by dramatizing and bringing to public attention a range of issues that have been ignored or have been dealt with behind closed doors. The reason is that their contentious actions make these movements' members highly visible. They offer irresistible fare for the television camera. This ability to make politics more visible—called broadening the **scope of conflict** by political scientist E.E. Schattschneider[11]—makes politics the province of the many rather than the few.

## ☐ Overcoming Political Inequality

Social movements also sometimes allow individuals and groups without substantial resources to enter the game of politics. Many social movements are made up of people who do not have access to the money, time, contacts, or organizational resources that fuel normal politics.[12] The ability of those without resources to disrupt the status quo by mobilizing thousands to take to the streets to voice their demands—what sociologists call **mass mobilization**—is a powerful political tool for people on the outside looking in. In the right circumstances, the disruptive politics of social groups can become as politically useful as other resources such as money and votes. Seemingly politically powerless women were able to mobilize to win the vote in the early part of the twentieth century; seemingly politically powerless African Americans in the Deep South were able to secure full citizenship rights in the 1960s.

## ☐ Creating New Majorities

Over time, social movements may also help create new majorities in society. Social movements are the province of numerical minorities in most cases, and in a majoritarian democracy, minorities should have their way only if they can convince enough of their fellow citizens that what they want is reasonable. Before the 1930s, for instance, only a minority of Americans may have been convinced that labor unions were a good idea. The **Great Depression** and a vigorous, militant labor movement changed the opinion climate in the nation and created the basis for federal laws protecting the right of working people to form labor unions. Such issues as gender-based job discrimination and pay inequity, to take another example, were not important to the general public until they were brought center stage by the women's movement.

## ☐ Overcoming Constitutional Limitations on Change

Sometimes it takes the energy and disruption of a social movement to overcome the antimajoritarian aspects of our constitutional system and get anything done at all.[13] As political scientist Theodore Lowi describes the issue:

> Our political system is almost perfectly designed to maintain an existing state of affairs. Our system is so designed that only a determined and undoubted majority could make it move. This is why our history is replete with social movements. It takes that kind of energy to get anything like a majority . . . Change comes neither from the genius of the system nor from the liberality or wisdom of its supporters and of the organized groups. It comes from new groups or nascent groups—social movements—when the situation is most dramatic.[14]

It is important to note that many of the social reforms of which most Americans are most proud—women's right to vote, equal citizenship rights for African Americans, Social Security, collective bargaining, and environmental protection—have been less the result of "normal" politics than of social movements started by determined and often disruptive minorities.[15]

8.1

8.2

8.3

8.4

8.5

8.6

# Factors That Encourage the Creation of Social Movements

**8.4**    Identify factors that give rise to social movements

 certain combination of factors seems necessary for a social movement to develop.[16] We review the most important ones here.

## ☐ Real or Perceived Distress

People who are safe, prosperous, respected, and contented generally have no need of social movements. By contrast, those whose lives are difficult and unsafe, whose way of life or values are threatened, or whose way of life is disrespected often find social movements an attractive means of calling attention to their plight and of pressing for changes in the status quo.[17]

Social distress caused by economic, social, and technological change helped create the conditions for the rise of most of the major social movements in American history. For example, the Populist movement occurred after western and southern farmers suffered great economic reverses during the latter part of the nineteenth century. The labor movement during the 1930s was spurred by the Great Depression—the virtual collapse of the industrial sector of the American economy, historically unprecedented levels of unemployment, and widespread destitution. The rise of the Christian conservative movement seems to be associated with the perception among conservatives that religious and family values had been declining in American life. For many women, distress caused by discriminatory hiring, blocked career advancement—in the form of the "glass ceiling" and the "mommy track"—and unequal pay at a time when they were entering the job market in increasing numbers during the 1960s and 1970s made participation in the women's movement attractive.[18] Discrimination, police harassment, and violence directed against them spurred gays and lesbians to turn to "contentious politics."[19] The AIDS epidemic added to their sense of distress and stimulated further political participation.[20] The rise of the Minute Men volunteers to help control the border with Mexico and legislation in several border states to deny certain benefits to illegal immigrants helped spur the mass demonstrations in 2006 and 2007 in favor of both legal and illegal immigrants. The Great Recession, rising student loan debt, and the slow job recovery that followed sowed the seeds for the Occupy Wall Street movement.

Ironically, perhaps, as is evident from the previous paragraph, the rise of one social movement demanding a change in how its people are regarded and treated often triggers the rise of a counter–movement among people who come to feel distressed in turn. Thus, the women's and gay and lesbian movements were powerful stimulants for the rise of the Christian conservative movement, whose people worried that traditional family values were under assault.

## ☐ Availability of Resources for Mobilization

Social strain and distress are almost always present in society. But social movements occur, it seems, only when aggrieved people have the resources sufficient to organize those who are suffering strain and distress. A pool of potential leaders and a set of institutions that can provide infrastructure and money are particularly helpful. The grievances expressed by the labor movement had existed for a long time in the United States, but it was not until a few unions developed—generating talented leaders like John L. Lewis and Walter Reuther, a very active labor press, and widespread media attention—that the movement began to take off. Martin Luther King, Jr. and the nonviolent civil rights movement found traction in the 1960s partly because network news telecasts had just

**consciousness-raising groups**
Meetings of small groups of women designed to raise awareness of discrimination against women and to encourage involvement in movement activities.

**political efficacy**
The sense that an individual can affect what government does.

increased from 15 minutes to half an hour and civil rights demonstrations and marches, and the sometimes violent response to them, provided dramatic footage to fill out the news programs. The women's movement's assets included a sizable population of educated and skilled women, a lively women's press, and a broad network of meetings to talk about common problems[21] (generally called **consciousness-raising groups**). The Christian conservative movement could build on a base of skilled clergy (for instance, Jerry Falwell and Pat Robertson), an expanding evangelical church membership, religious television and radio networks, and highly developed fund-raising technologies. The antiglobalization and anti–Iraq War movements, highly decentralized and organizationally amorphous, skillfully used networking and mobile communications to spread information, raise money, and organize demonstrations here and abroad.[22] Spanish-language radio stations played a big role in mobilizing people to join pro-immigrant marches and rallies in spring 2006.

## ☐ A Supportive Environment

The rise of social movements requires more than the existence of resources for mobilization among aggrieved groups. The times must also be right, in the sense that a degree of support and tolerance must exist for the movement among the public and society's leaders.[23] The civil rights movement took place when overt racism among the public was declining (even in the then-segregated South) and national leaders were worried about the bad effects of segregation in the South on American foreign policy. Christian conservatives mobilized in an environment in which many other Americans were also worried about changes in social values and practices and when the Republican Party was looking for a way to detach traditional Democratic voters from their party. The labor movement's upsurge during the 1930s coincided with the electoral needs of the Democratic Party.[24] The women's movement surged at a time when public opinion was becoming much more favorable toward women's equality.[25] In 1972, for example, two out of three Americans reported to pollsters that they supported the proposal for an Equal Rights Amendment; the same proportion said they believed that the issues raised by the women's movement were important.[26] Toleration toward alternative lifestyles, including homosexuality, that have developed in the United States since the late 1960s have benefited gays and lesbians. The Pew Research Center reported that, as of 2013, 60 percent of Americans thought "homosexuality should be accepted by society," while 50 percent said they supported the right of same-sex couples to marry (the percentage jumped to 65 percent for Americans under the age of 30).[27] The Occupy movement almost surely reflected a widespread sentiment that there is too much inequality in the country and that government mostly helps the wealthy (54 percent of Americans agreed).[28]

Especially important for a social movement is acceptance among elites that the concerns and demands of a social movement are worth supporting. A group of corporate leaders in the 1930s, for example, believed that labor peace was crucial for ending the Great Depression and making long-term economic stability possible, and openly supported labor union efforts to organize industries and enter into labor-management contracts.[29] As noted earlier, in the 1950s and 1960s, American political leaders—concerned that widespread reports of violence and discrimination against African Americans were undermining U.S. credibility in the struggle against the Soviet Union for the loyalties of people of color in Asia, Africa, and Latin America—were ready for fundamental changes in race relations in the South and supported the civil rights movement. Leaders of the film, music, and television industries, whether for reasons of belief or economic gain, have increased the visibility of gay and lesbian performers and themes in their offerings.

## ☐ A Sense of Efficacy Among Participants

Some scholars believe that to develop an effective social movement, people who are on the outside looking in must come to believe that their actions can make a difference, that other citizens and political leaders will listen and respond to their grievances.[30] Political scientists call this "I can make a difference" attitude a sense of **political efficacy**.

Without a sense of efficacy, grievances might explode into brief demonstrations or riots, but they would not support a long-term effort requiring time, commitment, and risk.

It may well be that the highly decentralized and fragmented nature of our political system helps sustain a sense of efficacy, because movements often find places in the system where they will be heard by officials. Christian conservatives have had little effect on school curricula in unitary political systems like that of Great Britain, for instance, where educational policy is made centrally, so few try to do anything about it. In the United States, however, they know they can gain the ear of local school boards and state officials in parts of the country in which conservative religious belief is strong. For their part, gays and lesbians have been able to convince public officials and local voters to pass antidiscrimination ordinances in accepting communities—such as San Francisco, California, and Boulder, Colorado—and to win cases in several state courts.

Some scholars have suggested that a strong sense of common identity among protest groups contributes to efficacy. Knowing that one is not alone, that others see the world in common ways and have common concerns, is often the basis for people's willingness to commit the time and energy and to take the risks that social movements require. (Large demonstrations often help in this development; how the size of demonstrations is calculated is shown in the "By the Numbers" feature.) Growing gay and lesbian identity seems to be an important component of the rising political self-confidence of this movement.[31] The same can be said for Christian conservatives and Tea Party activists.

8.1

8.2

8.3

8.4

8.5

8.6

# By the Numbers

## Just how many people were at that demonstration?

Calculating the size of demonstrations has always depended on estimates, although, as we will see, some estimates are more reliable than others. It was once standard practice for people to make educated guesses, with demonstration organizers always guessing on the very high side and officials in charge of controlling the crowd or sometimes unfriendly to the message of the demonstrators guessing on the very low side. For example, the organizers of the March 2003 antiwar rally in Washington, D.C., variously claimed, depending on which one was being quoted, a crowd of between 200,000 and 600,000, while D.C. police said it was more like 60,000. The same mismatch happened in 1996 when Louis Farrakhan claimed a crowd between 1.5 and 2 million at his Million Man March, a bit higher, to say the least, than the National Park Service's estimate of 400,000. Farrakhan threatened to sue over the disparity, arguing that the Park Service was out to discredit him and his movement.

### Why It Matters

Whether it makes sense or not, demonstration organizers, sympathetic supporters, and critics of any particular protest demonstration often use the size of the crowd to convey the reach and strength of a movement and make it the foundation for why the public and elected officials should pay attention to it or not. Organizers want a big number; critics want a small number. Journalists often simply average the high and low estimates and report that as the actual number. The rest of us would probably like a reliable number. But how to do that without lining everyone up and counting them or having them go through a turnstile on their way to a demonstration?

### Calculating Crowd Sizes

A fairly reliable method has emerged based on advances in aerial photography and digitalized remote sensing. What is now done regularly by news organizations and many governments is to take an aerial photograph, divide the area the crowd occupies into grids, then determine the density of each area, namely, how many people are in the bounded area of the grid. Researchers do not take the time, of course, to count each person in each grid, but divide the grids into a range of density types—from very tightly packed to very thinly packed—count the actual number in a sample grid of each type, then multiply by the number of grids of each. As an example, say that one type of $10' \times 10'$ grid packs in 25 people, another $10' \times 10'$ type packs in 20 people, and yet another has only 10 people wandering around the space. If there are 100 grids of the first type (let's call it "very dense"), 100 grids of the second type (let's call it "dense"), and 100 grids of the third type (let's call it "not very dense"), then the total crowd is 5,500 based on the formula: $(25 \times 100) + (20 \times 100) + (10 \times 100)$. This is not a very big crowd, of course, not likely to make an impression, but you get the idea.

### What to Watch for

What to mainly watch out for and avoid are crowd estimates based on guesswork methods from "interested" parties, that is, from those who have an "axe to grind." Numbers from demonstration organizers should simply not be believed because they have an interest in reporting as high a number as they can. Numbers from critics of a demonstration—say, spokespersons from

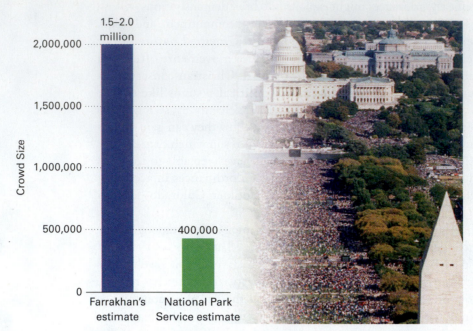

Variations in Crowd Size Estimates at the Million Man March

pro-life organizations estimating the size of a pro-choice rally—should be dismissed out of hand. Rely instead on reports from disinterested parties such as mainstream news organizations or academics, if possible, who use one form or another of counting using aerial photography. But note as well, even here, that the photograph/grid method is an estimate (just how dense is that grid, one might ask?), though it comes closer than any other method available for producing a hard and accurate number.

**What Do You Think?**

Do you think that the size of a demonstration or a series of demonstrations is a good indicator of the strength of a movement? If not, why not? Should movements that are able to mount large demonstrations, like the Tea Party did on April 15, 2009 (tax deadline day), in Washington and in many other cities across the nation, have more attention paid to them by the public and elected officials than movements that can't do so? Why? Can you think of mass demonstrations that have had a big impact on what government does? Or, on the other hand, can you think of mass demonstrations that have had no impact at all?

*Sources:* Farouk El-baz, "Remote Sensing, Controversy, and the Million Man March," Earth *Observation Magazine* (February 1996), accessed at www.eomonline.com/Common/Archives/1996feb; J. Patrick Coolican, "Crowd Count Adds Up to Infinite Interpretation," *Seattle Times* (February 17, 2003), p. 1; "Using Aerial Photography to Estimate the Size of Sunday's Peace March in San Francisco," *The San Francisco Chronicle* (February 21, 2003).

## ☐ A Spark to Set Off the Flames

Social movements require, as we have seen, a set of grievances among a group of people, the resources to form and sustain organization, a supportive environment, and a sense of political efficacy among the potential participants in the movement. But they also seem to require something to set off the mix, some dramatic precipitating event (or series of events), sometimes called a *catalyst*, to set them in motion. Passage of the Fourteenth Amendment, protecting the citizenship rights of males, galvanized the early women's suffrage movement, as we saw in the chapter-opening story. The gay and lesbian movement seems to have been sparked by the 1969 "Stonewall rebellion"—three days of rioting set off by police harassment of the patrons of a popular gay bar in New York City's Greenwich Village. An important catalyst for the civil rights movement was Rosa Parks's simple refusal to give up her seat on a Montgomery, Alabama, bus in 1957. Sending her to jail spurred the Montgomery bus boycott and associated demonstrations, led by a young minister named Martin Luther King, Jr. In 2006, Latinos were moved to action when the House passed a bill sponsored by James Sensenbrenner (R–WI) making illegal immigrants felons, subjecting long-time undocumented immigrants to deportation, and beefing up control of the U.S.–Mexican border.

# Tactics of Social Movements

**8.5** Evaluate tactics used by social movements to influence what government does

8.1

8.2

8.3

8.4

8.5

8.6

**sit-down strike**
A form of labor action in which workers stop production but do not leave their job site.

**civil disobedience**
Intentionally breaking a law and accepting the consequences as a way to publicize the unjustness of the law.

**B**ecause they often represent people and groups that lack political power, social movements tend to use unconventional tactics to make themselves heard. Such tactics depend on the dramatic gesture and are often disruptive.[32] As you saw in the chapter-opening story, the women's suffrage movement used mass demonstrations and hunger strikes to great effect. The labor movement invented **sit-down strikes** and plant takeovers as its most effective weapons in the 1930s. Pro-life activists added to the protest repertoire clinic blockades and the harassment of clinic patients, doctors, and employees. The Occupy Wall Street movement learned to take over and prevent any other activities from happening in publicly prominent urban spaces such as parks, squares, and in front of government buildings and banks.

The most effective tool of the civil rights movement was nonviolent **civil disobedience**, a conscious refusal to obey a law that a group considers unfair, unjust, or unconstitutional, courting arrest by the authorities and assault from others, without offering resistance, as a way to highlight injustice and gain broader public sympathy. Dr. Martin Luther King, Jr. was the strongest advocate for and popularizer of this strategy, having borrowed it from Mahatma Gandhi, who used it as part of the campaign that ended British colonial rule in India after the Second World War.[33] A particularly dramatic and effective use of this tactic took place in Greensboro, North Carolina. Four black students from North Carolina Agricultural and Technical State University sat down at a "whites only" lunch counter in a Woolworth's store on February 1, 1960, and politely asked to be served. When requested to leave, they refused. They stayed put and remained calm even as a mob of young white men screamed at them, squirted them with ketchup and mustard, and threatened to lynch them. Each day, more students from the college joined them. By the end of the week, more than 1,000 black students had joined the sit-in to demand an end to segregation. These actions ignited the South. Within two months, similar sit-ins had taken place in nearly 60 cities

**PROTEST COMMUNITY**
The Occupy Wall Street movement was formed not only to protest rising income inequality and the dim job prospects for young people but to highlight the possibilities for forming a sense of community amidst a competitive, individualistic-oriented society. Here protesters work together to clean up their camp site in New York's Zuccotti Park in 2011.

## 8.1
## 8.2
## 8.3
## 8.4
## 8.5
## 8.6

**integration**
Policies encouraging the interaction between different races in schools or public facilities.

across nine states; almost 4,000 young people, including a number of white college students from outside the South, had tasted a night in jail for their actions. Their bravery galvanized blacks across the nation and generated sympathy among many whites. The student sit-in movement also spawned a new and more impatient civil rights organization, the Student Non-Violent Coordinating Committee (SNCC).

For his part, Dr. King led a massive nonviolent civil disobedience campaign in Birmingham, Alabama, in 1963, demanding that the city abide by the Supreme Court's decision in *Brown v. Board of Education* (1954) to end the segregation of schools in addition to the more broadly based **integration** of public services, especially public transportation. Nonviolent demonstrators, many of them schoolchildren, were assaulted by snarling police dogs, electric cattle prods, and high-pressure fire hoses that sent demonstrators sprawling. Police Commissioner Eugene "Bull" Connor filled his jails to overflowing with hundreds of young marchers, who resisted only passively, alternately praying and singing civil rights songs, including "We Shall Overcome." The quiet bravery of the demonstrators and the palpable sense among public officials and private sector leaders in the nation that matters were quickly spinning out of control convinced President John Kennedy on June 11, 1963, to introduce his historic civil rights bill for congressional consideration.

This is not to say that unconventional and disruptive tactics always work, something addressed in more detail in the next section. No matter how peaceful, some fail to strike a chord with the public or elites. And, there are times when fringe elements within movements do things that are so disruptive or violent that the movement itself is discredited. In the late 1960s, urban riots and the rise of African American leaders and groups committed to black power undermined the broad popularity of the civil rights movement. The antiglobalization movement has been similarly undermined by its anarchist wing, which, committed to violence against property and confrontations with police, usually draws the most attention from the television cameras at antiglobalization gatherings, whether in Seattle or Davos.

**COURAGE UNDER FIRE**
Under the leadership of Chief of Public Safety "Bull" Connor, peaceful civil rights demonstrators protesting segregation in Birmingham, Alabama were met with fire hoses, police billy clubs, snarling police dogs, and jail in 1963. The national and international outcry over the treatment of peaceful protestors contributed to passage of the 1964 Civil Rights Act ending most forms *de jure* segregation in the United States.

# Why Some Social Movements Succeed and Others Do Not

8.1

8.2

8.3

8.4

8.5

8.6

**8.6**  Determine what makes a social movement successful

ocial movements have had a significant effect on American politics and on what government does. Not all social movements are equally successful; here is why:[34]

- *The proximity of the movement's goals to American values.* Movements that ask for fuller participation in things that other Americans consider right and proper—such as voting and holding office or opportunities for economic advancement—are more likely to strike a responsive chord than movements that, let us say, demand a redistribution of income from the rich to the poor.

- *The movement's capacity to win public attention and support.* Potential movements that fail to gain public attention, either because the news media do not pay much attention, or because there is little sympathy for the cause the movement espouses, never get very far. Things become even more problematic when a social movement stimulates the formation of a counter–social movement.

- *The movement's ability to affect the political fortunes of elected leaders.* Politicians tend to pay attention to movements that can affect their electoral fortunes one way or another. If support for the aims of a movement will add to their vote totals among movement members and a broader sympathetic public, politicians likely will be more inclined to help. If opposition to the movement is a better electoral strategy for politicians, they are likely to act as roadblocks to the movement.

We can see how these factors play out in the life-histories of the social movements that have made their mark or tried with varying degrees of success to make their mark in American political life.

## ☐ Low-Impact Social Movements

The poor people's movement, which tried to convince Americans to enact policies that would end poverty in the United States, failed to make much of a mark in the late 1960s. This social movement was never able to mobilize a large group of activists, had little support among the general public because of its fairly radical proposals for income redistribution, and was unable to disrupt everyday life significantly or to affect the electoral prospects of politicians.

The women's movement, while successful in a number of areas, was unable to win passage of a proposed Equal Rights Amendment to the Constitution banning discrimination on the grounds of gender. The ERA failed to receive the approval of the necessary three-fourths of the states by the amendment's 1979 deadline, mainly because the effort to ratify this new amendment stirred up a counter-movement among religious conservatives in every religious denomination.[35]

## ☐ Repressed Social Movements

Social movements committed to a radical change in the society and the economy tend to threaten widely shared values and the interests of powerful individuals, groups, and institutions.[36] As a result, they rarely gain widespread popular support and almost always arouse the hostility of political leaders. Such movements very often face repression of one kind or another.[37] In the late nineteenth and early twentieth centuries, for instance, the labor movement was hindered by court injunctions forbidding strikes and boycotts, laws against the formation of labor unions, violence by employer-hired armed gangs, and strikebreaking by the National Guard and the U.S. armed forces. In 1877, 60,000 National Guardsmen were mobilized in 10 states to break the first national railroad strike. The strike against Carnegie Steel in 1892 in Homestead, Pennsylvania, brought the

8.1

8.2

8.3

8.4

8.5

8.6

mobilization of 10,000 militiamen, the arrest of 16 strike leaders on conspiracy charges, and the indictment of 27 labor leaders for treason.

## ☐ Partially Successful Social Movements

Some social movements have enough power and public support to generate a favorable response from public officials but not enough to force them to go very far. In these situations, government may respond in a partial or halfhearted way. President Franklin D. Roosevelt responded to the social movements pressing for strong antipoverty measures during the Great Depression by proposing the passage of the Social Security Act, which fell far short of movement expectations.[38] The pro-life movement discovered that President Reagan was willing to use movement rhetoric to appoint sympathetic judges but was unwilling to submit anti-abortion legislation to Congress. Christian conservatives enjoyed some legislative successes during the height of their power in the 1990s and were important voices in the nominations of John Roberts and Samuel Alito to the Supreme Court by President Bush in 2005, but they failed to achieve some of their primary objectives: enact a law to ban late-term (in their words, "partial birth") abortions, pass a constitutional amendment banning same-sex marriages, and remove Bill Clinton from the presidency by impeachment and trial. Although public opinion has become increasingly supportive of the rights of gays and lesbians, same-sex marriages and civil unions continue to be illegal in many states and the Defense of Marriage Act (DOMA), which became law in 1996, continued to deny federal benefits and recognition to same-sex couples until the Supreme Court overturned that key DOMA provision in 2013. To understand how this important change in public policy happened, we need to examine the interaction of structural, political linkage, and governmental factors by applying the analytical framework (see p. 241).

## ☐ Successful Social Movements

Social movements that have many supporters, win wide public sympathy, do not challenge the basics of the economic and social orders, and wield some clout in the electoral arena are likely to achieve a substantial number of their goals. The women's suffrage movement, described in the chapter-opening story, is one of the best examples. The civil rights movement is another, yielding, after years of struggle, the Civil Rights Act of 1964, which banned segregation in places of public accommodations such as hotels and restaurants, and the Voting Rights Act of 1965, which put the might of the federal government behind efforts to allow African Americans to vote and hold elected office. These enactments helped sound the death knell of the "separate but equal" doctrine enunciated in the infamous *Plessy* decision (1896), and engineered the collapse of legal segregation in the South.

The Voting Rights Act was particularly important in transforming the politics of the South. Black registration and voting turnout increased dramatically all over the region during the late 1960s and the 1970s. Elected black officials filled legislative seats, city council seats, the mayors' offices in large and small cities, and sheriffs' offices. Between 1960 and 2011—the last year for which this statistic is available—the number of elected black officials in the United States increased from a mere 40 to more than 10,500.[39] Also, white politicians, tacking with the new winds of change, began to court the black vote in the years after passage of the Voting Rights Act. George Wallace, who first became famous by "standing in the schoolhouse door" to prevent the integration of the University of Alabama and who once kicked off a political campaign with the slogan, "Segregation Now, Segregation Tomorrow, Segregation Forever," actively pursued the black vote in his last run for public office.

To be sure, being successful in achieving specific policy goals may not in the end make matters better for a group across the board. Though the civil rights movement achieved its legislative goals—passage of the Civil Rights Act in 1964 guaranteeing equal treatment in public accommodations and the 1965 Voting Rights Act protecting African Americans' right to vote—the social and economic condition of African Americans today lags behind that of other Americans. This is true with respect to educational attainment, income and wealth, and life expectancy, for example.[40]

Movements can be successful even if no new laws are passed. Other measures of success include increased respect for members of the movement, changes in

8.1
8.2
8.3
8.4
8.5
8.6

# Using the FRAMEWORK

## How did DOMA get overturned?

**Background:** Acting in response to a ruling by the Hawaii Supreme Court in 1993 that same-sex couples had the right to marry in the state, Congress passed and President Clinton signed the Defense of Marriage Act (DOMA) in 1996. The new law said (1) that no state could be forced to recognize the legality of same-sex marriages performed in other states and (2) that people in same-sex marriages would not be considered spouses under federal law. Under section 3 of DOMA, federal programs and benefits, including Social Security, Medicare, tax deductions and exclusions, inheritance rights, veterans benefits, and more, did not apply to same-sex spouses. By 2014, however, some seventeen states and the District of Columbia had legalized same-sex marriage and DOMA had been challenged in the courts. In 2013, in *United States v. Windsor*, the Supreme Court ruled that section 3 of DOMA was unconstitutional. Writing for the majority, Justice Kennedy called section 3 "a deprivation of the liberty of the person protected by the Fifth Amendment," but states remained free after this decision to allow or disallow same-sex marriages and unions. After *Windsor*, a cascade of state laws and constitutional provisions banning same-sex marriage were overturned by state and federal judges.

**Government Action**

The Supreme Court rules in *United States v. Windsor* (2013) that section 3 of the Defense of Marriage Act (DOMA) is unconstitutional.

**Government**

After leaving office in 2001, President Clinton calls for the repeal of DOMA. → Presidential candidate Obama calls for the end of DOMA during his campaign for the presidency. → By 2010, courts or legislatures had approved same-sex marriage in nine states and the District of Columbia. → President Obama announces that Justice Department will not defend DOMA in federal court cases. → Justice Kennedy, a conservative on most matters, joins the four liberal justices on the Supreme Court to form the majority in the case challenging the constitutionality of DOMA.

**Political Linkage**

Triggered by the Stonewall riots in NYC in 1969, gays and lesbians create a social movement demanding equal treatment. The social movement creates a multitude of LGBT advocacy groups to lobby, to bring suits in state and federal courts, and to get involved in election campaigns. → Public opinion shifts dramatically after 2000 in favor of gay and lesbian rights and in support of same-sex marriage. → The GOP continues to court religious conservatives and supports DOMA in its party platforms. Democrats welcome gay and lesbian voters and candidates and call for overturning of DOMA in 2008 platform. → In 2012 voters in Maine, Maryland, and Washington vote in favor of referenda allowing same-sex marriage.

**Structure**

Our federal constitutional system allows states to fashion their own laws regarding marriage. → The federal government retains the power to make rules regarding federal programs. → The political culture is religious, generating opposition to same sex unions—but also supportive of individual freedom —generating support for people making their own life-style choices. → Educational levels have increased in the United States. More highly educated people are more tolerant of alternative life-styles, including homosexuality. → American popular culture is more accepting of homosexuality; movies, television shows, and music performances increasingly show LGBT characters in a favorable light.

8.1

8.2

8.3

8.4

8.5

8.6

fundamental underlying values in society, and increased representation of the group in decision-making bodies. The women's movement has had this kind of success. Although the Equal Rights Amendment (the movement's main goal) failed, women's issues came to the forefront during these years, and, to a very substantial degree, the demands of the movement for equal treatment and respect made great headway in many areas of American life.[41] Issues such as pay equity, family leave, sexual harassment, and attention to women's health problems in medical research are now a part of the American political agenda. Women have made important gains economically and are becoming more numerous in the professions, corporate managerial offices (although only 17 percent of corporate board members and 4 percent of CEOs of Fortune 500 companies in the United States were female in 2013),[42] and political office. In 2008, Hillary Clinton came close to winning the Democratic presidential nomination, and Sarah Palin gained the GOP's vice presidential nomination.

## Using the DEMOCRACY STANDARD

### Do social movements make us more or less democratic?

The story of American democracy has been shaped by social movements—from the first stirrings of rebellion in the British colonies to the emancipation of African American slaves to the granting of the right to vote to women. But in a nation that is supposed to be governed by majority rule, expressed primarily through elections, are social movements that empower minorities truly democratic? Just what role do social movements play in a democracy?

In a perfect democratic society, of course, social movements would be unnecessary: change would happen through political linkages like elections and public opinion and through party and interest group activity. Indeed, a democracy that depended entirely on social movements to bring needed change would not be working very effectively at all. But in an imperfect and incomplete democracy like ours, social movements play a valuable and important role, creating an additional linkage between portions of the American public and their government.

Social movements affect our democracy in several ways. First of all, social movements represent a way—a difficult way, to be sure—by which political outsiders and the politically powerless can become players in the political game. Our constitutional system favors the status quo—federalism, separation of powers, and checks and balances make it extremely difficult to institute fundamentally new policies or to change existing social and economic conditions. The primacy of the status quo is further enhanced by the political power of economically and socially privileged groups and individuals who generally resist changes that might undermine their positions. Movements present a way for outsider groups and individuals to gain a hearing for their grievances, work to win over a majority of their fellow citizens, and persuade elected leaders to take action. Equal citizenship for women and for African Americans, for example, would not have happened at all, or would have been much longer in coming, if not for the existence of social movements demanding change. Thus, social movements are valuable tools for ensuring that popular sovereignty, political equality, and political liberty—the key ingredients in a democracy as we have defined it—are more fully realized.

To be sure, in some cases, at least theoretically, social movements can pose a threat to democracy. Small minorities who force elected officials to respond to their demands because of the tangible threat of social disruption might occasionally get their way, even though the majority does not favor such action. Some social movements, moreover, might push policies that run counter to democratic ideals of popular sovereignty, political equality, and political liberty, making them dangerous for democracy if they take hold. Anti-immigrant movements during several periods in the nineteenth century, for example, tried to deny citizenship rights to various groups, including people from China and Southern and Eastern Europe. But these threats to the fundamentals of democracy emanating from social movements seem minor compared to the persistent citizen inequalities that arise from other quarters, including the interest group system described in the previous chapter.

# Review the Chapter

## What Are Social Movements?

**8.1** Define social movements and who they represent, p. 221

Social movements emphasize rather dramatically the point that the struggle for democracy is a recurring feature of our political life.

Social movements are mainly the instruments of political outsiders with grievances who want to gain a hearing in American politics.

## Major Social Movements in the United States

**8.2** Illustrate how important social movements have shaped American society, p. 223

Social movements, by using disruptive tactics and broadening the scope of conflict, can contribute to democracy by increasing the visibility of important issues, encouraging wider participation in public affairs, often creating new majorities, and sometimes providing the energy to overcome the many antimajoritarian features of our constitutional system.

## Social Movements in a Majoritarian Democracy

**8.3** Evaluate how social movements make U.S. politics more democratic, p. 231

Social movements often produce changes in government policies.

Social movements try to bring about social change through collective action.

Movements can also serve as a tension-release mechanism for aggrieved groups even when major policy shifts do not happen.

Social movements have had an important effect on our political life and in determining what our government does. Some of our most important legislative landmarks can be attributed to them.

Social movements do not always get what they want. They seem to be most successful when their goals are consistent with the central values of the society, have wide popular support, and fit the needs of political leaders.

## Factors that Encourage the Creation of Social Movements

**8.4** Identify factors that give rise to social movements, p. 233

Social distress caused by economic, social, and technological change often creates the conditions for the rise of social movements in the United States.

Social distress that encourages the formation of social movements comes from change that proves difficult and unsafe for people, threatens their way of life or basic values, and lessens the respect they feel from others.

Social movements can be a means for calling attention to their plight and pressing for changes in the status quo.

## Tactics of Social Movements

**8.5** Evaluate tactics used by social movements to influence what government does, p. 237

Social movements use unconventional and often disruptive tactics to attract attention to their cause.

Social movements tend to be most successful when the political environment is supportive, in the sense that at least portions of the general population and some public officials are sympathetic to the movements' goals.

Movement ideas often are taken up by one of the major political parties as it seeks to add voters.

To the degree that parties attract new voters and change the views of some of their traditional voters because of social movement activities, elected officials are more likely to be receptive to responding to grievances.

Social movements sometimes spark counter–social movements, which, if strong enough, can make government leaders reluctant to address grievances.

## Why Some Social Movements Succeed and Others Do Not

**8.6** Determine what makes a social movement successful, p. 239

Social movements that have many supporters, win wide public sympathy, do not challenge the basics of the economic and social orders, and wield some clout in the electoral arena are most likely to achieve their goals.

# Learn the Terms

# Test Yourself

Answer key begins on page T-1.

**8.1** Define social movements and who they represent

1. Which statement about social movements is NOT true:

    a. Social movements are the political instrument of political outsiders.
    b. Social movements are generally mass grassroots phenomena.
    c. Social movements use unconventional and disruptive tactics.
    d. Social movements are often easily organized and sustained.
    e. Social movements often turn into interest groups.

**8.2** Illustrate how important social movements have shaped American society

2. One antiwar movement that most affected American politics had to do with this war:

    a. World War I
    b. World War II
    c. Vietnam War
    d. Persian Gulf War
    e. Afghanistan War

**8.3** Evaluate how social movements make U.S. politics more democratic

3. Over time, social movements may also help create
    a. More social reforms
    b. Social equality in society
    c. New majorities in society
    d. More labor unions
    e. New minorities in society

**8.4** Identify factors that give rise to social movements

4. In addition to the existence of resources for mobilization, the rise of social movements requires two things:

    a. Acceptance of the movement among elites, and financial resources
    b. The right timing, and acceptance of the movement among elites
    c. Financial resources, and the right timing
    d. More than 1,000 people, and the right timing
    e. More than 1,000 people, and a strong leader

**8.5** Evaluate tactics used by social movements to influence what government does

5. The antiglobalization movement has been undermined by

    a. Media coverage
    b. Peaceful sit-ins
    c. Civil disobedience
    d. Nonviolent protests
    e. Violent protests

**8.6** Determine what makes a social movement successful

6. Between 1960 and 2011, the number of elected black officials in the United States increased from.

    a. 5 to 50,000
    b. 20 to 100
    c. 40 to 10,500
    d. 50 to 65
    e. 100 to 400

# Explore Further

## INTERNET SOURCES

Center for the Study of Social Movements, Notre Dame University **nd.edu/~cssm/**
A leading academic research center that disseminates the research of its own distinguished faculty and provides information about current social movements.

Family Research Council **www.frc.org**
Information, news, and links from one of the nation's most influential Christian conservative organizations.

The Gay and Lesbian Alliance Against Defamation **www.glaad.org**
News, issues, and links related to the gay and lesbian movement.

Pew Research Center's Hispanic Trends Project **pewhispanic.org**
A rich site for data on Hispanic immigration to the United States and public opinion polling information on immigration topics.

The Smithsonian Exhibits: Disability Rights **americanhistory .si.edu/disabilityrights/welcome.html**
A Smithsonian online exhibit featuring the history of the disability rights movement.

Tea Party Patriots **www.teapartypatriots.org**
The official website of the Tea Party movement.

## SUGGESTIONS FOR FURTHER READING

Alquist, John S. and Margaret Levi. *In the Interest of Others: Organizations and Social Activism.* Princeton, NJ: Princeton University Press, 2013.
An analysis that shows how and why some trade unions foster among its members a concern for the interests of others and how and why some remain narrowly self-interested.

Branch, Taylor. *Parting the Waters: America in the King Years, 1954–1963.* New York: Simon & Schuster, 1988.
A detailed and compelling description of the civil rights movement, with a particular focus on Martin Luther King, Jr.; winner of the National Book Award and the Pulitzer Prize.

Chafe, William H. *The Unfinished Journey: America Since World War II.* New York: Oxford University Press, 2006.
A justly celebrated history of America since 1945, with a particular focus on the civil rights and women's movements.

Dudziak, Mary L. *Cold War Civil Rights.* Princeton, NJ: Princeton University Press, 2002.
A compelling history of how the Cold War struggle with the Soviet Union provided a supportive environment for the civil rights movement.

Horton, Carol A. *Race and the Making of American Liberalism.* New York: Oxford University Press, 2005.
Suggests that American liberalism has been useful in ending discrimination and expanding diversity, but much less useful in diminishing dramatic racial inequalities in status, power, and wealth.

McAdam, Doug, Sidney Tarrow, and Charles Tilly. *Dynamics of Contention.* Cambridge, UK: Cambridge University Press, 2001.
A book that attempts to bridge the gap between the leading but competing theories of social movements by the field's three leading scholars.

Opp, Karl-Dieter. *Theories of Political Protest and Social Movements.* New York: Routledge, 2009.
A comprehensive examination of the scholarly debates surrounding our understanding of social movements and the role they play not only in the United States but in other countries as well.

Rosen, Ruth. *The World Split Open: How the Modern Women's Movement Changed America.* New York: Penguin, 2006.
A history of the modern women's movement, filled with detailed accounts of its origins, operations, and impacts.

# 9

# Political Parties

## BROKEN POLITICS, BUSTED BUDGETS

very year Congress must pass and the president must sign the appropriations bills necessary to fund the government. Since the beginning of the twentieth century, the government has chosen, more often than not, to spend more than it has taken in. These annual deficits result in an increasing national debt and an increasing need for the government to borrow from individuals, financial institutions, and other nations. Increasing debts can push the United States above its debt ceiling—the amount of debt above which the government must stop all its borrowing and default on some of its existing obligations—unless a law is passed to raise it. A debt ceiling has served as a tool of fiscal accountability since 1917. Surpassing it, however, can have such grave financial consequences that some question its usefulness, and legislation to raise the debt ceiling has historically been routine.[1]

The routine response to the national debt changed in 2011, when recently elected Tea Party-supported members of Congress convinced the Republican leadership to reject calls to raise the debt ceiling unless the Democrats agreed to slash federal spending and decrease taxes. Tea Party Republicans vowed to win on this issue even if it meant exceeding the debt limit and defaulting on the country's financial obligations. In the view of most economists and financial experts, default would bring on steep declines in stocks and in the value of the dollar along with a substantial increase in the cost of borrowing. Business loans, mortgages, car loans, and student loans would all cost Americans more. A new recession and a downgrade in America's AAA bond rating were likely looming.

On July 21, 2011, with the economy on the brink of another serious downturn, Republican House Speaker John Boehner was forced to withdraw a compromise debt-ceiling bill that he

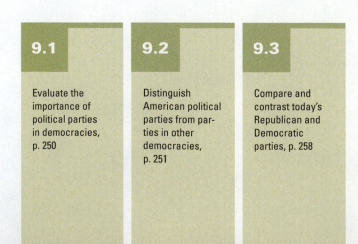

| 9.1 | 9.2 | 9.3 |
|---|---|---|
| Evaluate the importance of political parties in democracies, p. 250 | Distinguish American political parties from parties in other democracies, p. 251 | Compare and contrast today's Republican and Democratic parties, p. 258 |

**TO THE BRINK** In 2011 the bitter partisan deadlock over a bill to raise the debt ceiling almost caused the country to default on its national debt. The high drama surrounding this and other budget issues kept Congress and the White House from addressing important problems like high unemployment, leading everywhere to lengthier lines at job fairs and unemployment bureaus. Despite the earnest negotiations of President Barack Obama and Speaker John Boehner, the deal that they were ready to strike fell through. Why has it been so difficult to put the federal government on a sustainable fiscal footing? And why, time after time, do the parties fail to make any compromises on major issues?

had painstakingly put together with President Obama over the preceding months. Boehner lacked the Republican votes to pass it. Over in the Senate, Democrats were also balking at the bill. The size of the cuts in government spending, without any contribution to deficit reduction by raising taxes on the wealthy, was too much for them to stomach.

Pushed by the business community, foreign governments, and growing unease among the public, just two days before the default deadline the president and congressional leaders finally made a deal to raise the debt ceiling and structure the process for determining funding levels over the coming months.[2] But even with the deal, the damage had already been done. Credit rating agencies, worried about the ability of the United States to address its long-term budget problems, downgraded America's credit rating. The *Economist* blamed these downgrades on the growing partisan dysfunction of American politics, arguing that "the gulf between the political parties was becoming unbridgeable, and that policymaking was becoming unpredictable."[3]

Although the deal raised the debt ceiling, much of the hard work of actually determining tax and spending levels was deferred to a House–Senate Super Committee created by the deal. To spur the Super Committee to action, the debt-ceiling legislation contained a deadly trigger: if a budget agreement was not reached, there would be automatic deep cuts in programs favored by both parties at the start of 2013. One week before the January 2013 deadline, Super Committee negotiations broke down in partisan acrimony, and the automatic cuts went into effect.[4]

Unfortunately, the story does not end there. At this point the government was facing the prospect of a shutdown because of the failure to pass the appropriations bills and *yet another* pending breach of the debt ceiling. This time, President Obama publicly stated he would not negotiate over the debt ceiling while Republicans were demanding drastic changes to Obama's signature legislative achievement, The Affordable Care Act (ACA), before agreeing to fund the government or raise the debt ceiling. Sure enough, the government shut down on October 1, 2013, furloughing all nonessential government employees and closing important agencies. The shutdown ended fifteen days later after Republicans (who were taking the brunt of the criticism for dysfunction in Washington) agreed to a deal that was favorable to Democrats, a deal that funded the government, increased the debt limit, and made no major changes to the ACA.[5]

This story illustrates recent big changes in the American party system. American political parties often are described as "big tent" parties comprising broad and diverse coalitions of groups and viewpoints. This has been generally true for most of our history. Since the 1980s, however, the Democratic Party has become slightly more economically and socially liberal while the Republican Party has become much more economically and socially conservative. The number of moderates (especially moderate Republicans) in Congress has declined, and, increasingly, Republicans in the House and Senate vote on important bills as relatively homogeneous blocs rather than as bipartisan coalitions. For example, in 2009 the Obama economic stimulus bill drew no Republican votes in the House and only three in the Senate and the health care reform bill drew only a single Republican vote in the House of Representatives and not one in the Senate.

American politics is no stranger to partisanship; Democratic and Republican leaders have always been in the business of making the other party look bad. It's good politics. However, most veteran observers of American politics agree that things are getting worse.[6] Democrats and Republicans in Washington and across the country have become engaged in increasingly bitter disputes over many issues, including abortion, same-sex marriage, global warming, spending and taxes, and judicial appointments, to name just a few. Incivility has become the order of any day on which party leaders and elected officials deal with one another. Opponents in Congress accuse each other of being liars and cowards instead of colleagues, and, more often than not, those who try to work together are vilified by their co-partisans.

What accounts for the intense partisanship of American politics today? Scholars and journalists have lots of ideas on this. Many point to the explosion in the number and influence of liberal and conservative advocacy groups who demand unity on bedrock issues like tax increases.

Others point to the increased number of "safe" congressional districts that allow most representatives to win elections without considering the opinions of voters from the other party. Others suggest that our presidential primary system and close elections force candidates to play too much to their party bases. What better way to do this than to get partisans angry with the other party and fearful of a world where the other party controls government?[7]

Despite these changes, this chapter will show that political parties are an important part of democratic political systems. How well they function and fulfill their responsibilities has a lot to do with the health and vitality of democratic polities. As you will see, partisanship can play an important role in enhancing democracy, but it also often leads to gridlock in our constitutional system of separated powers.

## Thinking Critically About This Chapter

This chapter is about American political parties, how they evolved, what they do, and how their actions affect the quality of democracy in the United States.

## Using the Framework

You will see in this chapter how parties work as political linkage institutions connecting the public with government leaders and institutions. You will see, as well, how structural changes in the American economy and society have affected how our political parties function.

## Using the Democracy Standard

You will see in this chapter that political parties, at least in theory, are one of the most important instruments for making popular sovereignty and majority rule a reality in a representative democracy, particularly in a system of checks and balances and separated powers such as our own. Evaluating how well our parties carry out these democratic responsibilities is one of the main themes of this chapter.

**political party**
An organization that tries to win control of government by electing people to office who carry the party label.

**party platform**
A party's statement of its positions on the issues of the day passed at the quadrennial national convention.

# The Role of Political Parties in a Democracy

**9.1**    Evaluate the importance of political parties in democracies

 lthough the framers worried about the possible pernicious effects of factions, a category that included interest groups and political parties in today's terminology, and designed a constitution to address these effects, most political thinkers today believe that political parties are essential to democracy. They agree with E.E. Schattschneider that "political parties created democracy and . . . modern democracy is unthinkable save in terms of the parties."[8] So, what are political parties and why are they essential to the practice of democracy?

A "**political party** is a group organized to nominate candidates, to try to win political power through elections, and to promote ideas about public policies."[9] In representative democracies, parties are the principal organizations that recruit candidates for public office, run their candidates against the candidates of other political parties in competitive elections, and try to organize and coordinate the activities of government officials under party banners and programs. In going about the business of electing people to office and running government, political parties make it possible for the people to rule,[10] for parties can only gain power and govern with the approval of the majority. Majority rule is one of the things that makes popular sovereignty possible. As Schattschneider once put it: "The parties are the special form of political organization adapted to the mobilization of majorities. How else can the majority get organized? If democracy means anything at all it means that the majority has the right to organize for the purpose of taking over the government."[11]

In theory, political parties can do a number of things to make popular sovereignty and political equality possible:[12]

- *Keep elected officials responsive.* Competitive party elections help voters choose between alternative policy directions for the future. They also allow voters to make a judgment about the past performance of a governing party and decide whether to allow that party to continue in office. And, a party can adjust its **party platform**— the party's statement of its position on the issues—to reflect the preferences of the public as a way to win elections.

- *Stimulate political interest.* When they are working properly, moreover, political parties stimulate interest in politics and public affairs and increase participation. They do this as a natural by-product of their effort to win or retain power in government; they mobilize voters, bring issues to public attention, and educate on the issues that are of interest to the party.[13] Party competition, by "expanding the scope of conflict," attracts attention and gets people involved.[14]

- *Ensure accountability.* Parties can help make office holders more accountable. When things go wrong or promises are not kept, it is important in a democracy for citizens to know who is responsible. Where there are many offices and branches of government, however, it is hard to pinpoint responsibility. Political parties can simplify this difficult task by allowing for collective responsibility. Citizens can pass judgment on the governing ability of a party as a whole and decide whether to retain the incumbent party or to throw it out of office in favor of the other party.

- *Help people make sense of complexity in politics.* Party labels and party positions on the issues help many people make sense of the political world. Few people have the time or resources to learn about and reach decisions on every candidate on the ballot or the issues before the public at any period in time. Party labels and policy positions can act as useful shortcuts or cues enabling people to cut through the complexities and reach decisions that are consistent with their own values and interests.[15]

- *Make government work.* In a system like ours of separation of powers and checks and balances, designed to make it difficult for government to act decisively, political parties can encourage cooperation across the branches of government among public officials who are members of the same party. Thus, some of the constitutionally induced tension between a president and Congress may diminish when they are members of the same political party.

Political parties, then, can be tools of popular sovereignty. Whether our own political parties fulfill these responsibilities to democracy is the question we explore in the remainder of this chapter. We will see that our political parties fulfill many of the democracy-supporting roles listed above. But we also will see that rising cohesion within our political parties and intensified and increasingly bitter competition between them is making it more difficult when there is divided government to achieve the kinds of cooperation needed to allow our political system to address the most important problems facing the nation today. We saw some of this in our opening story.

# The American Two-Party System

| 9.2 | Distinguish American political parties from parties in other democracies |

The United States comes closer to having a "pure" **two-party system** than any other nation in the world. Most Western democracies have **multiparty systems.** In the United States, however, two parties have dominated the political scene since the mid-nineteenth century. As eminent political party scholar Marjorie Randon Hershey shows in Table 9.1, there have only been five major parties in the history of the United States, that is, parties that have led at least one of the branches of the national government at one time or another. Minor or third parties have rarely polled a significant percentage of the popular vote in either presidential or congressional

**TABLE 9.1** MAJOR POLITICAL PARTIES IN AMERICAN HISTORY

1. **The Federalist Party, 1788–1816.** The champion of the new Constitution and strong national government, it was the first American political institution to resemble a political party, although it was not a full-fledged party. Its strength was rooted in the Northeast and the Atlantic Seaboard, where it attracted the support of shopkeepers, manufacturers, financiers, landowners, and other established families of wealth and status. Limited by its narrow electoral base, it soon fell before the success of the Democratic-Republicans.

2. **The Democratic-Republican Party, 1800–1832.** Many of its leaders had been strong proponents of the Constitution but opposed the extreme nationalism of the Federalists. This was a party of the small farmers, workers, and less privileged citizens, plus southern planters, who preferred the authority of the state governments and opposed centralizing power in the national government. Like its leader, Thomas Jefferson, it shared many of the ideals of the French Revolution, especially the extension of the right to vote and the notion of direct popular self-government.

3. **The Democratic Party, 1832–Present.** Growing out of the Jacksonian wing of the Democratic-Republicans, it was the first really broad-based, popular party in the United States. On behalf of a coalition of less-privileged voters it opposed such business-friendly policies as national banking and high tariffs. It also welcomed the new immigrants (and sought their votes) and opposed nativist (anti-immigrant) sentiment.

4. **The Whig Party, 1834–1856.** This party, too, had roots in the old Democratic-Republican Party, but in the Clay–Adams faction and in opposition to the Jacksonians. Its greatest leaders, Henry Clay and Daniel Webster, stood for legislative supremacy and protested the strong presidency of Andrew Jackson. For its short life, the Whig Party was an unstable coalition of many interests, among them nativism, property, and business and commerce.

5. **The Republican Party, 1854–Present.** Born as the Civil War approached, this was the party of northern opposition to slavery and its spread to the new territories. Therefore it was also the party of the Union, the North, Lincoln, the freeing of slaves, victory in the Civil War, and the imposition of Reconstruction on the South. From the Whigs it also inherited a concern for business and industrial expansion.

*Source:* Hershey, Marjorie R. PARTY POLITICS IN AMERICA, 14th Ed., c 2011, p. 15. Reprinted and Electronically reproduced by permission of Pearson Education, Inc., Upper Saddle River, New Jersey.

9.1

9.2

9.3

**two-party system**
A political system in which two parties vie on relatively equal terms to win national elections and in which each party governs at one time or another.

**multiparty system**
A political system in which three or more viable parties compete to lead the government; because a majority winner is not always possible, multiparty systems often have coalition governments where governing power is shared among two or more parties.

**proportional representation**
The awarding of legislative seats to political parties to reflect the proportion of the popular vote each party receives.

elections (more will be said later about third parties), although they are sometimes successful at the state and local levels. Jesse Ventura, for example, a former professional wrestler, was elected governor of Minnesota in 1998 as the nominee of the Reform Party.

## ❑ Why a Two-Party System?

Why are we so different from other countries? Why do we have only two major parties? There are several reasons.

**ELECTORAL RULES** The kinds of rules that organize elections help determine what kind of party system exists.[16] Which rules are chosen, then, have important consequences for a nation's politics.

*Proportional Representation* Most other democratic nations use some form of **proportional representation** (PR) to elect their representatives. In PR systems, each party is represented in the legislature in rough proportion to the percentage of the popular vote it receives in an election. In a perfect PR system, a party winning 40 percent of the vote would get 40 seats in a 100-seat legislative body, a party winning 22 percent of the vote would get 22 seats, and so on. In such a system, even very small parties would have a reason to maintain their separate identities because no matter how narrow their appeal, they would win seats as long as they could win a proportion of the popular vote. Voters with strong views on an issue or with strong ideological outlooks could vote for a party that closely represented their views. A vote for a small party would not be wasted, because it would ultimately be translated into legislative seats and, perhaps, a place in the governing coalition.

Israel and the Netherlands come closest to having pure PR systems, organized on a national basis; most Western European nations depart in various ways from the pure form. Most, for instance, vote for slates of party candidates within multimember electoral districts, apportioning seats in each district according to each party's percentage of the vote. In Germany, seats in the Bundestag (the lower house of the national parliament) are filled by a combination of elections from single-member districts and a party's share of the nationwide vote. Most democracies that use proportional representation also have a minimum threshold (often 5 percent) below which no seats are awarded to a party. For example, 21 parties ran in the 2013 Norwegian elections with eight of them garnering enough support to win parliamentary seats.

*Winner-Take-All, Plurality Election, Single-Member Districts* Elections in the United States are organized on a winner-take-all, single-member-district basis. Each electoral district in the United States—whether it is an urban ward, a county, a congressional district, or a state—elects only one person to a given office and does so on the basis of whoever wins the *most* votes (not necessarily a majority). This is why our way of electing leaders is sometimes called a "first past the post" system, analogous to a horse race. This arrangement creates a powerful incentive for parties to coalesce and for voters to concentrate their attention on two big parties. The two-party outcome of plurality elections in single-member-district voting systems is often called Duverger's Law after the French political scientist who first discovered and systematically examined the relationship.[17] Here is how it works.

From the vantage point of party organizations, this type of election discourages minor-party efforts because failure to come in first in the voting leaves a party with no representation at all. Leaders of such parties are tempted to merge with a major party. Also, a disaffected faction within a party is unlikely to strike out on its own because the probability of gaining political office is very low. Tea Party candidates in the 2010, 2012, and 2014 elections are a case in point. Knowing they had little chance on their own, they ran as Republicans and pushed the already strongly conservative Republican Party establishment in an even more conservative direction. From the voter's point of view, a single-member, winner-take-all election means that a vote for a minor party is wasted. People who vote for a minor party may feel good, but most voters have few illusions that such votes will translate into representation and so are not inclined to cast them.

IT'S ALL ABOUT THE ELECTORAL COLLEGE

The winner of the presidential election is the candidate who receives a majority of Electoral College votes, not the candidate who wins the most popular votes. Here two workers fill in the winner of each state on a U.S. map drawn on the ice rink at Rockefeller Center in New York as election night results are tallied. Why is the Electoral College method preferable to a majority popular vote? Or is it?

Note that the most important office in American government, the presidency, is elected in what is, in effect, a single-district (the nation), winner-take-all election. The candidate who wins a majority of the nation's votes in the Electoral College wins the presidency. A party cannot win a share of the presidency; it is all or nothing. In parliamentary systems, the executive power is lodged in a cabinet, however, where several parties may be represented.

**RESTRICTIONS ON MINOR PARTIES** Once a party system is in place, the dominant parties often establish rules that make it difficult for other parties to get on the ballot.[18] A number of formidable legal obstacles stand in the way of third parties and independent candidates in the United States. While many of these restrictions have been eased because of successful court challenges by recent minor-party and independent presidential candidates such as Ross Perot, the path to the ballot remains tortuous in many states, where a considerable number of signatures are required to get on the ballot. Moreover, the requirements for ballot access are different in every state. While the two main parties, with party organizations in place in each of the states and well-heeled national party committees, are able to navigate this legal patchwork, new and small parties find it quite difficult.

The federal government's partial funding of presidential campaigns has made the situation of third parties even more difficult. Major-party candidates automatically qualify for federal funding once they are nominated. Minor-party candidates must attract a minimum of 5 percent of the votes cast in the general election to be eligible for public funding, and they are not reimbursed until after the election. In recent decades, only the Reform Party among the legion of minor parties has managed to cross the threshold to qualify for federal funding. Because the Green Party's candidate, Ralph Nader, won only 2.7 percent of the national vote in the 2000 election, it was not eligible for federal funding for the 2004 election, something that hobbled its candidate.

**realignment**
The process by which one party supplants another as the dominant party in a two-party political system.

David Cobb, the Green Party's presidential candidate in 2004, hardly registered at the polls, winning about 0.1 percent of the vote.

## The Role of Minor Parties in the Two-Party System

Minor parties have played a less important role in the United States than in virtually any other democratic nation, and have become even less important over time.[19] In our entire history, only a single minor party (the Republicans) has managed to replace one of the major parties. Only six (not including the Republicans) have been able to win even 10 percent of the popular vote in a presidential election, and only seven have managed to win a single state in a presidential election. In countries with PR systems, minor parties play a much more important role because they are likely to have at least some representation in the legislature and can work with the bigger parties to make policy.

Minor parties have come in a number of forms:

- *Protest parties* sometimes arise as part of a social movement. The Populist Party, for instance, grew out of the western and southern farm protest movements in the late nineteenth century. The Green Party is an offshoot of the environmental and antiglobalization movements.

- *Ideological parties* are organized around coherent sets of ideas. The several Socialist parties have been of this sort, as has the Libertarian Party. The Green Party ran in the 2000 elections on an anticorporate, antiglobalization platform.

- *Single-issue parties* are barely distinguishable from advocacy groups. What makes them different is their decision to run candidates for office. The Prohibition Party and the Free-Soil Party fall into this category, as did Perot's "balanced budget" Reform Party in 1996.

- *Splinter parties* form when a faction in one of the two major parties bolts to run its own candidate or candidates. An example is the Bull Moose Progressive Party of Teddy Roosevelt, formed after Roosevelt split with Republican Party regulars in 1912.

Minor parties do a number of things in American politics. Sometimes they articulate new ideas that are eventually taken over by one or both major parties. Ross Perot's popular crusade for a balanced budget during his 1992 campaign helped nudge the major parties toward a budget agreement that, for a while, eliminated annual deficits in the federal budget. It is also the case that third parties can sometimes change the outcome of presidential contests by affecting the outcome of the electoral vote contest in the various states. In 1992, a substantial portion of the Perot votes were cast by people who otherwise would have voted Republican, allowing Bill Clinton to win enough states to beat George H. W. Bush (and Perot's success in 1992 resulted in the formation of the short-lived Reform Party under which he ran in 1996). In 2000, a substantial portion of the Ralph Nader votes in Florida were cast by people who otherwise would have voted Democratic, allowing George W. Bush to win Florida's electoral votes and the presidency over Al Gore.[20]

## Shifts in the American Two-Party System

Scholars have identified a number of party eras in the United States so that we can better understand why parties are powerful at particular moments in history. Each era is different in one or more important ways from the others. The transition from one era to the next is generally referred to as a **realignment**.[21] There is some disagreement amongst scholars of the American party system about exactly when party eras begin and end; however, realignments are always reflective of shifting voting coalitions in the country. Though scholars have identified several party eras before the onset of the Great Depression in the 1930s, in this section we examine only the three most recent party eras: The New Deal Party Era, the Dealignment Era, and the Parties at War Era. Taken together, these three eras tell the story of contemporary American political parties as they developed around the New Deal, reshuffled around civil rights and international conflicts, and settled into the combative ideological camps we see today.

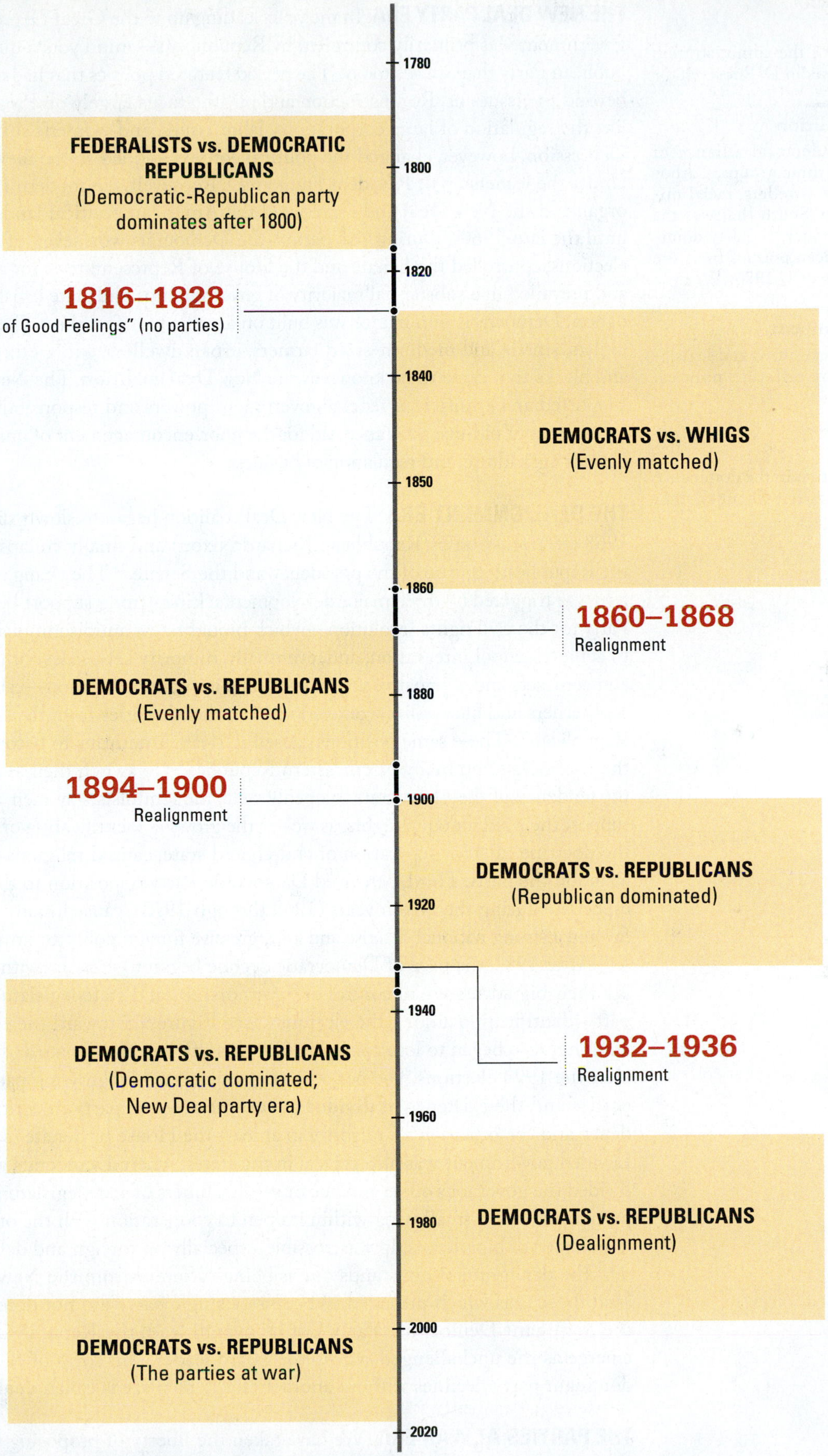

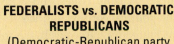

FEDERALISTS vs. DEMOCRATIC
REPUBLICANS
(Democratic-Republican party
dominates after 1800)

1780

1800

1820

**1816–1828**
"Era of Good Feelings" (no parties)

1840

DEMOCRATS vs. WHIGS
(Evenly matched)

1850

1860

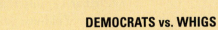

**1860–1868**
Realignment

DEMOCRATS vs. REPUBLICANS
(Evenly matched)

1880

**1894–1900**
Realignment

1900

DEMOCRATS vs. REPUBLICANS
(Republican dominated)

1920

1940

**1932–1936**
Realignment

DEMOCRATS vs. REPUBLICANS
(Democratic dominated;
New Deal party era)

1960

1980

DEMOCRATS vs. REPUBLICANS
(Dealignment)

2000

DEMOCRATS vs. REPUBLICANS
(The parties at war)

2020

**FIGURE 9.1** TIMELINE: PARTY ERAS IN THE UNITED STATES
American politics has been characterized by a series of relatively stable political party eras punctuated by
periods of transition—some sudden, others much more drawn out—from one party era to another.

**THE NEW DEAL PARTY ERA** In the years leading up to the Great Depression, American government was primarily controlled by Republicans—mind you, a quite different Republican Party than we see today. The period featured politics that had moved somewhat beyond the issues of Reconstruction and put the focus largely on Progressive concerns like the regulation of large corporations, labor issues, and women's suffrage. The Great Depression, however, changed the political context and led to the New Deal party era. Under the leadership of President Franklin D. Roosevelt, the modern Democratic Party organized the **New Deal** and dominated the American political landscape from 1933 until the late-1960s. During this period, the Democrats won seven of nine presidential elections, controlled the Senate and the House of Representatives for all but four years, and prevailed in a substantial majority of governorships and state legislatures across the nation. Democratic dominance was built on an alliance of workers, Catholics, Jews, unionists, small- and medium-sized farmers, urban dwellers, white ethnics, southerners, and blacks that came to be known as the **New Deal coalition**. The New Deal coalition supported an expansion of federal government powers and responsibilities, particularly in the areas of old-age assistance, aid for the poor, encouragement of unionization, subsidies for agriculture, and regulation of business.

**THE DEALIGNMENT ERA** The New Deal coalition began to slowly disintegrate in the 1968 election (won by Republican Richard Nixon) and finally collapsed in 1980 with the Republican capture of the presidency and the Senate.[22] The change in the party system was triggered by three major developments. First, strong support by the Democratic Party for the civil rights revolution—which brought new antidiscrimination laws, busing to achieve school integration, and, eventually, minority set-asides for government jobs and contracts and affirmative action programs in higher education—caused many white southerners and blue-collar workers to switch their loyalties from the Democrats to the Republicans. These same positions caused African Americans to become more loyal to the Democrats and many Northeastern Republicans to switch their alliances.[23] Second, the tendency of the Democrats to openly welcome feminists, gay men, and lesbians and support their bid for equal rights, as well as the growing identification of Democrats with the doctrine of strict separation of church and state, caused religious conservatives to abandon the party. Third, perceived Democratic Party opposition to the Vietnam War, especially during the Nixon years (1969 through 1973), caused many Americans who favored a strong national defense and an aggressive foreign policy to drift away as well.

After 1980, the pace of Democratic decline began to pick up, with Democrats losing their big advantage in control of governorships and state legislatures, as well as in party identification among the electorate (see Figure 9.5 toward the end of this chapter). They also began to lose control in Congress, first in the Senate and then the House after the 1994 elections. The period was characterized by growing parity between the parties and the existence of **divided government**—one party in control of the presidency and the other with a majority in at least the House or Senate (sometimes both). Divided government was also typical in the states, where Democrats and Republicans divided the governor's office and one or two chambers of state legislatures. Because each party contained a small wing within it open to cooperation with the other party, a certain degree of bipartisanship was possible, especially on foreign and defense policies.[24]

The dealignment era stands out as being different from the New Deal party era (and those eras which preceded it) because a single party did not dominate it. While the dominant Democratic Party lost its overall lead, the Republican Party did not emerge as the unchallenged, across-the-board leader. This form of change in which a dominant party declines without another taking its place is called **dealignment**.[25]

**THE PARTIES AT WAR ERA** We have taken the liberty of proposing in this book the emergence of another party era in the mid-1990s that we call the "parties at war" era. The exact date it started is hard to pin down. But two developments are particularly important. First, there was the historic victory for Republicans in the congressional elections of 1994 in which they gained control of both houses of Congress for the first time since 1946, with much of the credit going to a unified conservative surge led

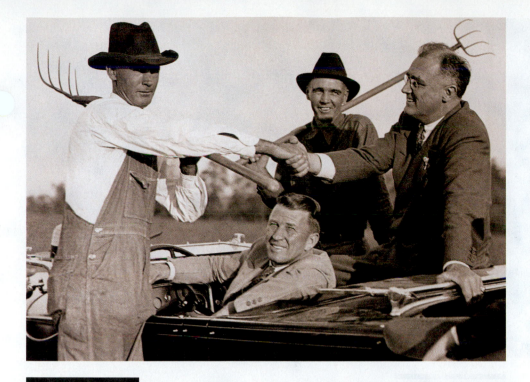

**FDR ADDS TO HIS COALITION**

The wealthy and patrician Franklin D. Roosevelt attracted a wide range of common people to his Democratic Party, including industrial workers, poor farmers, and farm laborers. Here he talks with Georgia farmers during his campaign for the presidency in 1932. How did a man of wealth and privilege become so popular among America's working class?

by Republican House leader Newt Gingrich (R–GA) and supported by an array of conservative think tanks, media, and advocacy groups. Second, there was the successful effort by House Republicans to impeach Democratic president Bill Clinton in 1998 and a close vote along party lines in the Senate in early 1999 that fell just short of removing him from office—despite Democratic gains in the 1998 congressional elections and large majorities among the public saying they opposed these actions.

By the time of the historic and disputed 2000 Bush–Gore presidential election, the new era was solidly in place. National elections from then on would be fought by two well-funded and ideologically unified parties. The central electoral strategy of the parties increasingly focused on using emotional appeals to turn out one's own party base voters on Election Day as the first priority, gaining just enough independents to tip the balance. Adding to the partisan warfare was the fact that election outcomes (with the exception of 2006) in state and national races became extremely close, with Democratic and Republican votes on a national basis closely divided, and control of the House, the Senate, and the presidency seemingly hanging in the balance at every election.[26] In the governing process, bipartisanship largely absented the scene, as we showed in the chapter-opening story; consultations across the aisles in Congress and between the president and Congress during periods of divided government became rare. Compromise with the other party came to be seen as traitorous, so wedded were the parties to core policy positions. Underlying it all has been a fundamental settling in of a new electoral geography defined by the shift of the South to the Republicans and the Northeast and coastal West to the Democrats (see the "Mapping American Politics" feature on this shift).

Debate is common about whether party polarization is just an elite affair or a true reflection of views in the mass electorate. One leading scholar argues that the public at large remains fairly moderate on most issues that deeply divide the parties, while party office holders, activists, and advocacy groups associated with each party have become more internally unified and partisan.[27] Other leading scholars counter that voters—particularly informed and active ones—have become more ideologically polarized in recent years.[28] One thing is clear: elections and governing are now characterized by partisan warfare at nearly every turn.

**PARTISANSHIP AT THE BOILING POINT**

Republican members of Congress show their displeasure with President Barack Obama during an address to Congress in which he outlined his health care reform proposal. Representative Joe Wilson of South Carolina, at center, shocked much of the country when he shouted out "you lie" in response to the president's statement that his plan would not insure immigrants illegally in the country. While the incident was roundly criticized and Wilson later apologized, it demonstrates the poisonous level of party division that has prevailed in Washington. Does this heightened partisanship serve some useful purpose in our system of government or does it make successful self-government less likely?

# The Democratic and Republican Parties Today

**9.3**　Compare and contrast today's Republican and Democratic parties

T hough our two major parties, the Republican Party and the Democratic Party, remain more decentralized and free-wheeling than parties in other rich democracies, each has become much more organized and ideologically cohesive than has traditionally been the case in American politics.

## ☐ The Parties as Organizations

The Republican and Democratic parties are not organizations in the usual sense of the term, but rather loose collections of local and state parties, campaign committees, candidates and office holders, and associated interest and advocacy groups that get together every four years to nominate a presidential candidate. Unlike a corporation, a bureaucratic agency, a military organization, or even a political party in most other countries, the official leaders of the major American parties cannot issue orders that get passed down a chain of command. Even popular, charismatic, and skillful presidents, including George Washington, Abraham Lincoln, Woodrow Wilson, Franklin Roosevelt, Harry Truman, John Kennedy, and Ronald Reagan, have had nearly as much trouble controlling the many diverse and independent groups and individuals within their own parties as they have had dealing with the opposition. George W. Bush discovered this in his second term when a significant number of Republican members of the House and Senate, loyal followers throughout his first term, abandoned him on his plans for a pathway to citizenship for many undocumented immigrants.

**PARTY MEMBERSHIP** The ill-defined nature of Republican and Democratic party membership is another indicator of how different American political parties are from political parties in other countries, as well as from private organizations. What does it mean, in fact, to be a Republican or a Democrat in the United States? Americans do not join parties in the sense of paying dues and receiving a membership card. To Americans, being a member of a party may mean voting most of the time for the candidate of a party or choosing to become a candidate of one of them. Or it may mean voting in a party primary. Or it may mean contributing money to, or otherwise helping in, a local, state, or national campaign of one of the party candidates. Or it may just mean generally preferring one party over another most of the time. These are loose criteria for membership, to say the least—looser than for virtually any other organization that might be imagined.

However, membership in the sense of feeling closer to and identifying with one party or another—what political scientists call **party identification**—has proved to be a very powerful thing indeed. A majority of Americans say they identify with or lean towards one of the two major parties. Party identification is important on a number of accounts. Most importantly, what party one identifies with and how strongly one holds that identification shapes how a person feels about a wide range of public issues, how likely that person is to vote, and which candidates the person votes for. (Party identification is addressed in greater depth later in this chapter.)

Among party identifiers one can identify groups of people who are especially strong supporters of the party and its candidates at all levels. Each party has a set of core supporters—often called the party base[29]—upon which it can count for votes, campaign contributions, and activists to advance the fortunes of the parties and their candidates for elected office.[30] The strongest Republican supporters may be found among whites (particularly in the South and Rocky Mountain West), conservative Christians and the most religiously committed (those who express a belief in God and say they regularly attend religious services) among all denominations, businesspeople (whether small business owners or top executives in large corporations), economic

**party identification**
The sense of belonging to one or another political party.

9.1

9.2

9.3

**YET ANOTHER CONSERVATIVE ALTERNATIVE**
Many conservatives were disappointed during the Republican presidential nomination contest that Mitt Romney remained the front-runner from the first. They supported a series of conservative alternatives, including Michelle Bachmann, Herman Cain, Newt Gingrich, and, finally Rick Santorum (shown here), before rallying behind Romney when none proved successful.

# Mapping American Politics

## The Shifting Geography of the Parties

### Introduction

The centers of strength of each of the major political parties changed during the last half century. In 1960 the Democrats tended to dominate in the southern states and in the industrial states of the Middle Atlantic and upper Midwest, while Republicans were particularly strong in parts of New England, the Great Plains, the Mountain West, and the Pacific Coast. Until 2004, the Plains and Mountain West states (other than Colorado) had become more reliably Republican, and the South moved solidly into the Republican column. At the same time, the Pacific Coast and New England became more reliably Democratic. In the 2008 election, Barack Obama's big victory can be attributed to his success in former Republican or battleground states, including Colorado, New Mexico, Iowa, Indiana, Ohio, Virginia, North Carolina, and Florida.

Because of population shifts, moreover, the distribution of electoral votes has shifted among the states over time, changing the calculations of those who plan and wage presidential campaigns.

### Mapping Party Electoral Votes

The states in the three cartograms are sized in proportion to their electoral votes in presidential elections and colored by whether they cast their electoral votes for Democrats (blue) or Republicans (red) in 1960, 2004, and 2008. Because each state's electoral votes are the total of their representatives and senators in Congress, they are roughly proportional to the size of their populations. We can see at least three important things in the cartograms. First, between 1960 and 2008, electoral votes of the Middle Atlantic states, New England, and the upper

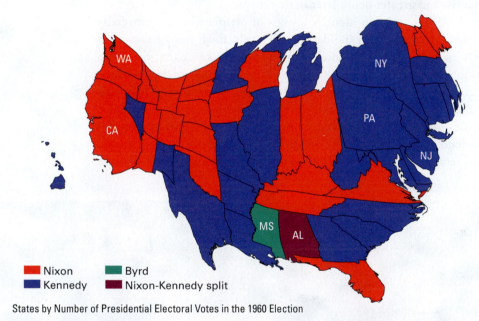

States by Number of Presidential Electoral Votes in the 1960 Election

*Source:* Election data are from historical tables, U.S. Bureau of the Census, Statistical Abstract of the United States, 2010.

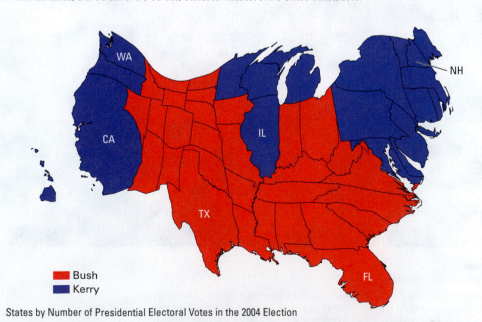

States by Number of Presidential Electoral Votes in the 2004 Election

*Source:* Election data are from historical tables, U.S. Bureau of the Census, Statistical Abstract of the United States, 2010.

(Continued)

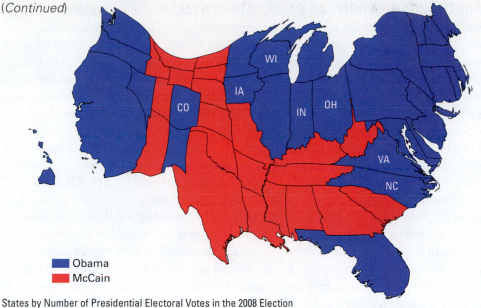

Obama
McCain

States by Number of Presidential Electoral Votes in the 2008 Election

*Source:* Election data are from historical tables, U.S. Bureau of the Census, *Statistical Abstract of the United States*, 2010.

Standard US Map

Midwest decreased while they increased in California, the Southwest, and the South, reflecting the shift in the populations of the states over this time period. Second, the states that came together to elect Democrats John F. Kennedy in 1960 and Barack Obama in 2008 were quite different. These changes have altered the strategies of the parties. The Democrats today can pretty much count on winning California, Washington, Illinois, the New England states, New York, and New Jersey; Republicans can count on the South, outside of Florida, and the Southwest, Mountain West, and Plains states. The remaining states—often called battleground states—are where presidential campaigns are now waged and where presidential elections are won and lost. These realities defined presidential campaign strategies in 2012 and will do so again in 2016.

**What Do You Think?**

Why does it make sense to elect presidents by electoral votes rather than direct popular vote when so many states are safe for one party or the other? Some critics argue that having so many noncompetitive states in the Electoral College, with the bulk of the electioneering going on in the handful of states where the outcome is in doubt, deprives the majority of Americans of being fully engaged in the process of electing the president. How would you support this argument? How would you dispute it?

**MAP NOTE:** In 1960, Mississippi electoral votes were cast for Harry Byrd, an independent candidate. Alabama split its 11 electoral votes: 6 for Kennedy and 5 for Nixon.

**SOURCE:** Election data are from historical tables, U.S. Bureau of the Census, *Statistical Abstract of the United States*, 2010.

and social conservatives, people in rural areas, and those with the highest incomes. The strongest Democratic supporters may be found among African Americans, Jews, non-Cuban Hispanics, people who are secular in belief, people with postgraduate degrees, union households, economic and social liberals, people living on the West Coast and the Northeast, and lower-income people. Democrats find strong support, as well, among teachers and other government employees at the local, state, and national levels, and people living in university towns and science and technology research centers such as the Silicon Valley (stretching from San Jose to San Francisco), Austin, Seattle, Boulder, the Research Triangle area in North Carolina, and the Route 128 economic corridor around Boston and Cambridge.[31]

Increasingly in recent years, Republicans and Democrats have tried to win elections by first mobilizing these core supporters—in a process often called "rallying the base"—by focusing on issues and symbolic gestures that will bring them to the polls, then trying to win a majority among those voters not automatically predisposed to one party or the other (Catholics are a good example of such a swing vote, as are self-identified independents). In a situation where Republican and Democratic core supporters are about equal in strength, winning even a small majority among these less partisan groups while mobilizing one's own partisans is the key to winning elections. Issue and ideological appeals are important in these efforts.

**PARTY ORGANIZATIONS AS CANDIDATE-CENTERED** Unlike a traditional organization and unlike political parties in other democracies, the various elements of the Democratic and Republican parties are relatively independent from one another and act in concert not on the basis of orders, but on the basis of shared interests, sentiment, ideology, fund-raising, and the desire to win elections.[32] (See Figure 9.2.) Most important, perhaps, the official party organizations do not control the nomination of candidates running under the party label—their most vital political role—or the flow of money that funds electoral campaigns or the behavior of their office holders once elected. Party organizations have become, in effect, campaign machines in the service of candidates running for elected office.[33] As such, many commentators have come to describe American political parties as "candidate-centered" (as opposed to "party-centered").[34] The 2010 and 2012 elections exemplify the extent to which American elections are candidate-centered. In these elections, Tea Party insurgents enjoyed success in wresting the Republican nominations for congressional and gubernatorial seats away from candidates favored by party leaders. In the past, party candidates were usually nominated in district, state, and national conventions, where party regulars played a major role. They are now almost exclusively nominated in primaries or grassroots caucuses in the states, where the party organizations help but do not run the show. Nomination comes to those who are best able to raise money, gain access to the media, form their own campaign organizations, and win the support of powerful interest and advocacy groups (such as the National Rifle Association in the GOP and the National Education Association in the Democratic Party). To a very large extent, Democratic and Republican party organizations are there to help candidates in these efforts, not order them about.[35] Party presidential nominees who go on to win the office in the November elections often reward supporters and contributors by appointing them to positions in the executive branch. (Sometimes these appointees are not up to the task; see the "Can Government Do Anything Well?" feature.)

**THE PARTY CONVENTIONS** The national party conventions are the governing bodies of the parties. Convention delegates meet every four years not only to nominate presidential and vice presidential candidates but also to write a party platform and revise party rules.

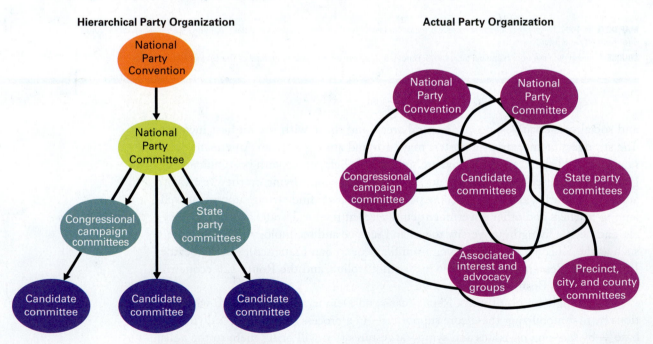

**Hierarchical Party Organization**

**Actual Party Organization**

**FIGURE 9.2** POLITICAL PARTY ORGANIZATION IN THE UNITED STATES

The graphic on the left shows a hypothetical organizational chart of the Republican and Democratic parties as if they were structured hierarchically like many other organizations you are familiar with. It would be a mistake, however, to think of our national parties this way. The drawing on the right, which depicts our national parties as network or web-like organizations, where there is neither central authority nor a chain of command, is closer to reality. The ties between elements of the parties include money, ideology, sentiment, and common interests.

# Can Government Do Anything Well?

## FEMA and disaster relief

Democrats and Republicans each have their favored agencies in the executive branch in which to hide party activists and financial contributors who want a position in the administration but bring with them few qualifications. They tend to be agencies for which the party in power has little respect or regard. For the Democrats, the Commerce Department has traditionally been that place. For Republican president George W. Bush, the Federal Emergency Management Agency, which merged into the Department of Homeland Security in 2003, was one of the favored destinations. To head that agency, he placed Michael Brown, a lawyer from Enid, Oklahoma, and the commissioner of the International Arabian Horse Association, who had had no emergency management or relief experience other than a stint in the White House on a committee planning assistance to New York City following the 9/11 attacks. This ill prepared him for handling coordination of the relief and recovery effort following Hurricane Katrina that devastated New Orleans and a long stretch of the Gulf Coast in Louisiana and Mississippi.

FEMA was created in 1979 and is responsible for coordinating relief efforts with state and local first responders and authorities and for mobilizing and delivering resources that are beyond what is available on the ground in the immediate aftermath of a disaster. FEMA has had a checkered history. It failed miserably, by all accounts, in responding to the Loma Prieta, California, earthquake in 1989 (one California member of Congress concluded that FEMA "could screw up a two-car parade"), Hurricane Hugo in Puerto Rico that same year, and Hurricane Andrew in Florida in 1992 (failed to appear for three days, late with supplies and field hospitals, botched coordination of relief efforts, and more). With 10 times the number of political appointees as the average federal agency, FEMA was headed by political contributors and activists, not emergency relief specialists. After Congress threatened to eliminate FEMA and gave it a clearer mission and set of guidelines, the newly elected president Bill Clinton, a believer in an activist government run by highly qualified people, cleaned house and filled top positions with experienced disaster relief people from other federal agencies and from several states. The transformation was almost immediate, with the agency receiving high marks for its responses in 1993 to a series of floods in the Midwest and the Oklahoma City bombing. The agency performed well for the remainder of the 1990s. After the 2000 election, however, FEMA again became a place to put people who had supported a party that believed a strong federal government was not such a good thing.

*Support for the claim that government can and should play a significant role in disaster relief through FEMA:*

- FEMA performance during the presidency of Bill Clinton and its highly praised response to 2012's superstorm Sandy and 2013's Colorado floods suggest that committed and talented leadership of the agency can make it a valuable participant in the emergency response to human-made and natural disasters.
- FEMA can only do its job, however, if properly funded and its mission redirected to immediate relief only, leaving long-term recovery to other federal agencies and state and local authorities.
- The agency needs to be led by people who are professionally trained in and have experience in emergency relief; President Obama put the agency's leadership back into the hands of professionals beginning in 2009.
- Proper leadership of the agency, adequate resources, and clarity of mission are only possible if the president, Congress, and the people pay attention to it on a continuous basis rather than treat it as an afterthought until disaster strikes.

*Rejection of the claim that government can and should play a significant role in disaster relief through FEMA:*

- FEMA's long history of botched emergency responses shows that the federal government cannot do this job properly.
- Presidents are increasingly prone to issue FEMA emergency declarations, with President Obama on a near-record pace; this is done more for political reasons than for addressing real emergencies and strains FEMA capacities.
- Because disasters vary so much from community to community and because local authorities and citizens best know what needs to be done in particular places, emergency relief should be decentralized to states and localities; there is no need for federal government involvement except for topping up money and supplies as needed.
- Dependence on FEMA allows states and localities to skimp on their own emergency relief preparations; elimination of FEMA would force states and localities to build emergency preparation capabilities.

## WHAT DO YOU THINK?

What do you think about the past, present, and future role of the federal government in disaster relief through agencies such as FEMA?

- The government should play a *big* role in the immediate response to disasters through agencies such as FEMA, but to function properly, these agencies need increased funding and adequate leadership.
- The government should play *some* role in the immediate response to disasters through agencies such as FEMA, mostly offering logistical support for state and local efforts and other aid as requested.
- There is no need for the federal government to play a role in disaster relief and recovery. This should be a state and local responsibility, possibly in partnership with the private sector.

How would you defend your position to a fellow student? What would be your main line of argument? What evidence do you believe best supports your position?

Additional sources for this feature: Daniel Franklin, "The FEMA Phoenix: Reform of the Federal Emergency Management Agency," *The Washington Monthly* (July/August, 1995), pp. 14–17; "Report on FEMA Performance During the Hurricane Katrina Disaster," (Washington, D.C.: Government Accounting Office, 2006).

Although the national convention is the formal governing body of each of the parties, it cannot dictate to party candidates or party organizations at other levels of jurisdiction. The presidential nominee need not adhere to either the letter or the spirit of the party platform, for instance, although most nominees stay fairly close to the platform most of the time (usually because the winning candidate's supporters control the platform-writing committee). State and local party organizations may nominate whomever they choose to run for public office and may or may not support key planks in the national party's platform.

**NATIONAL PARTY COMMITTEES** The Democratic and Republican national committees conduct the business of the parties during the four years between national conventions. The national committees are made up of elected committeemen and committee women from each of the states, a sizable staff, and a chairperson, but they rarely meet. The real business of the committee is run by the party chair, assisted by the committee staff. The chair exercises little power when a president from the party is in office, because the party chair is compelled to take direction from the White House. When the opposition controls the presidency, the party chair exercises more influence in party affairs, although the extent of that power is still not very great.

Although the national committees have little direct power, they have become increasingly important as campaign service organizations for party candidates running for national and state offices.[36] In addition to substantial financial contributions to candidate campaign organizations, they do a wide variety of things to help. Out of their Washington, D.C., in-house TV and radio studios come attack ads aimed at the other party and its candidates, tailored to the particular district or state in which the ads will be used. Other ads extol the sponsoring party and its achievements. Direct mail campaigns are mounted to disseminate information and party positions on the issues and to make appeals for campaign contributions, increasingly using sophisticated data-mining techniques to allow very narrow targeting of messages to different groups of people.[37] News releases are prepared for the media, as are campaign-oriented sound and video bites to be used as news clips on local radio and television. Each party also produces training courses for potential candidates, complete with "how-to" manuals and videos. Each has a website where people can access information about the party, get news about the nefarious behavior of the opposition, and make monetary contributions to the party and party candidates. And, they funnel campaign money to state and local party organizations, with the bulk going to states where competition between the parties is closest.[38]

To carry out these activities, both the Republican and Democratic national committees have steadily increased the number of employees in their national offices, especially in the areas of finance, advertising, information technology, campaign planning, and video specialist and support personnel, and they have expanded their budgets to carry out an ever-broader range of campaign activities for party candidates. Each of the national committees has become a highly professional campaign organization, filled with highly skilled people able to provide party candidates with what they need to wage first-rate electoral campaigns.

**CONGRESSIONAL CAMPAIGN COMMITTEES** Almost as old as the national party committees, but entirely independent of them, are the four congressional campaign committees—Republican and Democratic, for the House and for the Senate—that aid members of Congress in their campaigns for reelection. They help raise money, provide media services (e.g., making short videotapes of the members of Congress for local television news shows), conduct research, and do whatever else the party members in Congress deem appropriate. Increasingly, these committees have turned their attention to identifying and encouraging quality party candidates in districts and states where competition between the parties is close. Rahm Emanuel (D–IL), later President Obama's chief of staff, and currently mayor of Chicago, did this particularly well during the 2005–2006 elections cycle when he was head of the Democratic House Campaign Committee; many gave him the main credit for the Democrats' retaking the House in the 2006 elections.[39] These committees are controlled by the party members in Congress, not the party chair, the national committees, or even the president. Much as with the national committees, the congressional campaign committees have become highly professional and well funded.[40]

**STATE PARTY ORGANIZATIONS** As expected in a federal system, separate political party organizations exist in each of the states. Although tied together by bonds of ideology, sentiment, and campaign money and constrained in what they can do according to rules set by the national party committees and conventions—rules on how and when to choose delegates to the national convention, for example—the state party organizations are relatively independent of one another and of the national party.

**ASSOCIATED INTEREST AND ADVOCACY GROUPS** Although not technically part of the formal party organizations, some groups are so closely involved in the affairs of the parties that it is hard to draw a line between them and the political parties.[41] Some have even argued that networks of conservative organizations such as American Crossroads (founded by Karl Rove), the American Action Network, and Americans for Prosperity (backed by the energy billionaire Koch brothers) have taken over much of the role of the Republican National Committee with regard to fund-raising, campaign messaging, and recruiting new party candidates.[42] Organized labor (e.g. AFL-CIO, SEIU) has had a similar relationship with the Democratic Party since the Great Depression and the New Deal.

The main effect of the rise of advocacy groups in recent years has been to push the parties and their candidates into more ideological and partisan directions. MoveOn .org, for example, and liberal blogs such as the Daily Kos and the *Huffington Post*, push Democrats to be more assertive in opposing Republicans, offering a more liberal policy agenda, and pushing the candidacy of people they favor. Republican advocacy groups, talk radio hosts such as Rush Limbaugh, and conservative blogs push the party and its candidates to oppose abortion and more open borders for immigrants and to favor tax cuts and fewer government regulations. We look at the issue of ideology in the parties in more detail in the next section.

# ☐ Party Ideologies

Ideology may be understood as a coherently organized set of beliefs about the fundamental nature of a good society and the role government ought to play in achieving it. Because the Republican and Democratic parties have traditionally organized themselves as fairly broad coalitions, seeking to attract as many voters as possible in order to prevail in winner-take-all, single-member-district elections, there always have been

**liberal**

The political position, combining both economic and social dimensions, that holds that the federal government has a substantial role to play in providing economic justice and opportunity, regulating business in the public interest, overcoming racial discrimination, protecting abortion rights, and ensuring the equal treatment of gays and lesbians.

**conservative**

The political position, combining both economic and social dimensions, that holds that the federal government ought to play a very small role in economic regulation, social welfare, and overcoming racial inequality, that abortion should be illegal, and that family values and law and order should guide public policies.

strong pressures on them to tone down matters of ideology.[43] However, each party also has a core of loyal supporters and party activists, such as delegates to the party convention and caucus attendees, contributors to election campaigns, and closely allied advocacy groups, who are more ideologically oriented than the general public (38 percent of whom call themselves independents).[44] Each party, moreover, has a stable core set of voters from groups concerned about particular issues and problems and committed to particular government policies. The result is a party system composed of parties with significant and growing ideological and policy unity within them and differences between them.[45] One veteran observer even claims that today, "Political leaders on both sides now feel a relentless pressure for party discipline and intellectual conformity more common in parliamentary systems than through most of American history,"[46] (see the "Using the Framework" feature to see how greater ideological cohesion and discipline have affected party behavior in Congress).

While Americans of all political stripes hold a range of core beliefs about free enterprise, individualism, the Constitution, and the Bill of Rights, the differences between Democrats and Republicans are becoming clearer every day. The Republican Party tends to endorse positions held by social and economic conservatives; for example, opposing abortion and same-sex marriage and regulating business, higher taxes, and generous social safety nets. The Democratic Party tends to endorse positions held by social and economic liberals; for example, supporting a strong government role in guiding the economy and protecting the environment and the civil rights of ethnic, racial, and gay and lesbian minorities. Ideological and policy differences between the Democrats and Republicans are becoming so marked, and the tendency of the Republicans to become a more internally cohesive conservative party is so pronounced, that a number of observers now talk about the "Europeanization" of the American party system.[47] Pressure from Tea Party activists on candidates for nominations in the Republican Party in 2010 and 2012 helped make the GOP even more conservative than it had been. For example, Senator Orrin Hatch (R-UT), sensing pressure from the Tea Party, began to vote even more consistently conservative in the Senate. In 2010 and 2011, Hatch averaged a score of 99.5 from the conservative advocacy group Club for Growth, well above his lifetime score of 78 awarded to him previously by that group. For his part, Mitt Romney, a fairly moderate Republican for most of his career, took on a much more conservative ideological hue in the course of gaining the GOP's presidential nomination in 2012, repudiating his previous positions on issues such as immigration, health insurance mandates, and affirmative action.

Let's see how ideological and policies differences manifest themselves in our political parties.

**IDEOLOGY AND PARTY IN PUBLIC PERCEPTIONS** For one thing, the Democratic and Republican parties differ in the electorate's perceptions of them; in 2012, for example, 75 percent of Americans reported that they see important differences between the parties.[48] Most accurately see the Democrats as the more **liberal** party (in the sense of favoring an active federal government; helping citizens with jobs, education, and medical care; supporting a woman's right to choose; and protecting civil rights) and the Republicans as the more **conservative** party (opposing such government activism, supporting business, and opposing abortion and same-sex marriage) (See Figure 9.3).[49] Democrats, moreover, are much more likely to say they are liberals; Republicans are much more likely than others to say they are conservative.[50] Additionally, those Americans who classify themselves as liberals overwhelmingly support Democratic candidates; self-described conservatives overwhelmingly support Republicans. In 2012, for example, 93 percent of self-identified Republicans voted for Mitt Romney for president, while 92 percent of Democrats voted for Barack Obama.[51] This association of liberalism with the Democrats and conservatism with the Republicans is growing stronger all the time, with the gap in outlooks between the two parties growing ever larger.[52]

# Using the FRAMEWORK

## How did Republicans manage to pass so many laws with such small majorities after they came to power in 2001?

**Background:** In the 1990s, official Washington seemed to grind to a screeching halt. Divided government was the rule. Not only was major legislation tough to come by, but partisan warfare between a Republican-dominated Congress and a Democratic president (Clinton) led to a budget crisis that twice closed the federal government (except for essential services) and to the impeachment of Bill Clinton on a straight party-line vote in the House. After the disputed election of George W. Bush in 2000, however, new bills were passed with a fair degree of regularity despite very slim majorities for Republicans in Congress: three different tax cuts, No Child Left Behind, a new prescription drug benefit under Medicare, creation of the Department of Homeland Security, the USA Patriot Act, restrictions on class-action lawsuits, the Energy Policy Act of 2005, the Bankruptcy Act of 2005, and the Sarbanes-Oxley Act regulating corporate accounting practices. Taking a look at how structural, political linkage, and governmental factors affect policymaking in Washington will help explain the changed situation from 2001 through 2005.

**Government Action**

Major bills are passed by Congress and signed into law by President Bush.

**Government**

Because of their extremely high levels of party unity and discipline in both houses of Congress, Republicans were able to control the legislative agenda without much need of help from the Democrats, even though they held very slim majorities in the House and Senate.

The elections of 2000, 2002, and 2004 resulted in unified government, with a tightly disciplined and unified Republican party in control of Congress and the presidency.

**Political Linkage**

The political parties became more ideological, with the virtual disappearance of conservative Democrats in the South and Mountain West and liberal Republicans in New England.

→ Partisan warfare and scandals became standard fare in the mass media, making cooperation and civility in public affairs, in general, and between the parties, in particular, less likely.

Neither party enjoyed a commanding lead in party identification nationally during the 1990s or 2000s.

→ Congressional elections became very close and hotly contested, with control of Congress hanging in the balance every two years, so partisanship increased.

**Structure**

Separation of powers and checks and balances in the Constitution make gridlock the "default" condition in Washington.

→ A sense of patriotism and shared threat arising from the 9/11 attacks in 2001 permeates society and creates a brief period of political cooperation.

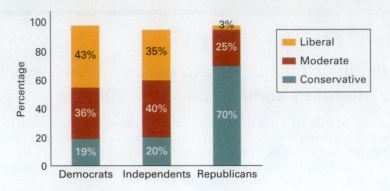

**FIGURE 9.3** PARTY IDENTIFICATION AND IDEOLOGY

Party identification and political ideology go hand in hand, something that has not always been the case in the United States. In 2013, Democrats were overwhelmingly liberal. Among Republicans, only a tiny percentage of their identifiers called themselves liberal. Not surprisingly, perhaps, a majority of independents—the largest group among Americans—defined its ideology as moderate.

*Source:* Jeffrey M. Jones, "Liberal Self-Identification Edges Up to New High in 2013," Gallup Politics, January 10, 2014, http://www.gallup.com/poll/166787/liberal-self-identification-edges-new-high-2013.aspx.

**IDEOLOGY AND POLICIES IN PARTY PLATFORMS**  Our parties also tend to write political platforms at their conventions that differ significantly from one another. Scholars have discovered persistent differences in the platforms of the two parties in terms of rhetoric (Republicans tend to talk more about opportunity and freedom), issues (Democrats worry more about poverty and social welfare), and the public policies advocated.[53]

**THE IDEOLOGIES OF PARTY ACTIVISTS**  The activists of one party are quite different in their views from activists and voters in the other party, as well as the general public. Republican delegates to recent national conventions, for example, have been far more conservative than Republican voters and much more conservative than the average registered voter (see Table 9.2). They were also much more hostile to affirmative action, same-sex marriage, social spending programs, and gun control than Republican voters and registered voters in general. Analogously, delegates to the Democratic National Convention were far more liberal than Democratic voters and registered voters and much more favorable to gun control, affirmative action, gay rights, and a woman's right to an abortion than the other two groups.[54]

**DIVISIONS WITHIN THE PARTIES**  While differences between Democrats and Republicans have become more pronounced, and while ideological and policy cohesion within the parties has been increasing, especially in the GOP, there are still important disagreements within each of the parties.[55] There is not near-perfect unity, as one might have found in the past within communist and socialist parties, let us say, or as exists today in some Islamist parties, such as the Muslim Brotherhood in Egypt. The division in the Democratic Party is between a very liberal wing—found among Democratic activists and advocacy groups and among most office holders in the West Coast and northeastern states—and a more "centrist" wing—typified by moderates elected in traditionally Republican areas such as senators Claire McCaskill (D-MO), Jon Tester (D-MT), and Mark Pryor (D-AR). The liberal wing supports traditional Democratic Party programs in which government plays a central role in societal improvement, leveling the playing field for minorities and women, supporting gay rights, protecting union jobs, providing substantial social safety nets, protecting civil liberties, and trying to avoid the use of military power in foreign affairs. The smaller centrist wing of the party tends to oppose racial preferences and support lower taxes, free trade, deregulation, a crackdown on crime, and a strong military supported by a large defense budget.

Fissures have existed for a long time in the Republican Party, with the fault lines most evident between economic and social conservatives, between, that is to say, those whose main priority is lower government spending, taxes, and regulations pitted against those who most want to emphasize "family values" and religious beliefs.

**TABLE 9.2** COMPARING DELEGATES TO THE 2008 NATIONAL PARTY CONVENTIONS WITH OTHER AMERICANS

| | Delegates to Democratic National Convention | Democratic Voters | All Voters | Republican Voters | Delegates to Republican National Convention |
|---|---|---|---|---|---|
| Is it more important to provide **health care** coverage for all Americans or hold down taxes? (percent saying "health care") | 94 | 90 | 67 | 40 | 7 |
| Looking back, do you think the United States did the right thing in taking military action against **Iraq**, or should the U.S. have stayed out? (percent saying "right thing") | 2 | 14 | 37 | 70 | 80 |
| Should protecting the environment or developing new sources of **energy** be a higher priority for the government? (percent saying "environment") | 25 | 30 | 21 | 9 | 3 |
| Should **abortion** be generally available to those who want it, be available but under stricter limits than it is now, or should it not be permitted? (percent saying "should not be permitted") | 3 | 16 | 24 | 37 | 43 |
| Should **gay couples** be allowed to legally marry, be allowed to form civil unions but not legally marry, or should there be no legal recognition? (percent choosing "same-sex marriage") | 55 | 49 | 34 | 11 | 6 |

*Note:* The last survey of this type was done in 2008.

*Source: New York Times*/CBS News Poll, "What Democratic Convention Delegates Say About . . . ," *New York Times,* August 24, 2008, http://www.nytimes.com/ref/washington/20080825-poll-graphic.html; CBS News/*New York Times* News Poll, "McCain, Bush, the Nomination Process, and the Republican Delegates," CBS News, July 23-August 26, 2008, http://www.cbsnews.com/htdocs/pdf/RNCDelegates_McCain_Bush.pdf.

However, the Republican Party has become even more fractured in recent years with the appearance of the Tea Party. Among economic conservatives there is a split between those who recognize that a long-term budget solution for the country must involve some revenue enhancements as well as cuts in government spending and those in the Tea Party wing who believe that cutting spending is paramount and that every action must be taken to win that goal even if it means default on the public debt and a shutdown of the government.

Divisions are evident as well in the Democratic Party, particularly between the liberal base and the more moderate office holders. The liberal wing of the party, for example, was not happy with many actions and policies of President Obama that seemed to hug the middle of the public policy spectrum: continuing many Bush-era policies on bailouts and financial industry regulation; giving in to Republican congressional demands at almost every turn to cut government spending without much in the way of tax increases on top income groups in exchange; failing to close the detainee facilities at Guantanamo Bay; and continuing for a number of years the wars in Iraq and Afghanistan.[56]

## □ The Parties in Government and in the Electorate

The Republican and Democratic parties exist not only as network-like organizations of candidates, activists, contributors, and interest and advocacy groups, but as a presence in government and in the electorate.

**GOVERNMENT** Fearful of the tyrannical possibilities of a vigorous government, the framers designed a system of government in which power is so fragmented and competitive that effectiveness is unlikely. One of the roles that political parties can play in a democracy such as ours is to overcome this deadlock by persuading officials of the same party in the different branches of government to cooperate with one another on the basis of party loyalty.[57] The constitutionally designed conflict between the

**unified government**
Control of the executive and legislative branches by the same political party.

**gridlock**
A situation in which things cannot get done in Washington, usually because of divided government.

president and Congress can be bridged, it has been argued, when there is **unified government**—when a single party controls both houses of Congress and the presidency—as the Democrats did during much of the 1960s and during Barack Obama's presidency in 2009 and 2010, and the Republicans did between 2001 and 2006 when George W. Bush was in office. When the parties are strong and unified, this bridging can occur even when a party controls the legislative branch with the tiniest of margins. On the other hand, strong parties in periods of divided government often leads to **gridlock**.[58] Very little was done when Bill Clinton was president and the Republicans controlled both houses of Congress (1995-2000) or has been done since 2010, when Republicans gained the House two years into Obama's presidency. With the Republicans winning control of the Senate in the 2014 mid-term elections, an even less productive final two years of the Obama presidency is likely.

It matters a great deal whether Democrats or Republicans control the House, the Senate, and the presidency, because the two parties differ in what they do when they win control of government. Republican members of Congress tend to vote differently from Democrats; for example, the former are considerably more economically and socially conservative on domestic issues. This difference translates into public policy. Republicans and Democrats produce different policies on taxes, corporate regulation, abortion and stem cell research, and social welfare when they are in power.[59] It also matters whether a single party controls Congress and the presidency or whether control is divided between two parties not only for what bills become law but also for the composition of the federal judiciary and for what policies are implemented and what actions are taken by executive branch agencies. Consideration of the many complex issues associated with how political parties act in office and why it matters will be left to chapters later in this book that look in depth at the branches of the federal government.

**THE ELECTORATE** Parties are not only political organizations and sets of office holders in government, but also images in the minds of voters and potential voters—that is, mental cues that affect the behavior of the electorate. This aspect of the parties is called party identification. The distribution of party identification among the American people is important on a number of grounds. First, party identification helps determine people's political attitudes on a wide range of issues; for a majority of Americans, party identity is a stable and powerful shaper of one's overall political identity. People use the party label to help organize their thinking about politics: to guide them in voting, judging new policy proposals, and evaluating the government's performance.[60] Second, how the parties stand relative to one another in the affections of the American people has a lot to do with who wins elections and thereby determining which party controls the presidency, Congress, and, eventually, the federal courts. That distribution has changed over time and has affected what government does. (How party identification is measured by political scientists is shown in the "By the Numbers" feature.)

Beginning at the time of Roosevelt's highly popular New Deal in the 1930s and continuing to the 1980s, the Democratic lead over Republicans among party identifiers was substantial, making them the majority party. At times their advantage was on the order of 35 percentage points. From the 1980s through the early 2000s, the Democrats gradually lost their big lead primarily because of the increasing number of Americans who say they are independent. Since the early 2000s, the Democratic lead over Republican identifiers has become much smaller. Democrats currently maintain an 8-point advantage over Republicans (see Figure 9.4). While the Democrats retain a small lead over Republicans, the parties are closer than they have been in a very long time among those Americans who identify with one or the other. Because they are so close, even very small swings from election to election in Democratic and Republican voting turnout and the parties' ability to attract independent "leaners" have had big effects on who wins and loses in presidential and congressional contests. Barack Obama's strong "get out the vote" effort among Democrats and independents helped him win big in the 2008 presidential election. Similar Republican efforts in 2010 led to huge GOP gains in Congress, governorships, and state legislative chambers across the country.

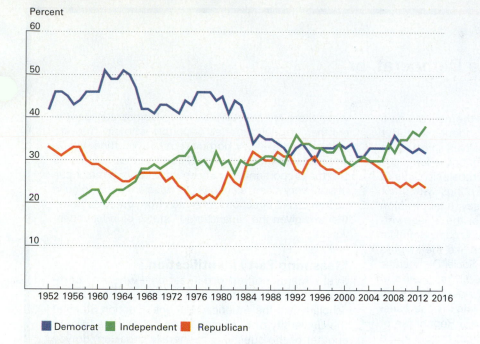

Percent

**FIGURE 9.4** TRENDS IN PARTY IDENTIFICATION

The decades-long gap between the percentages of those who call themselves Democrats and those who call themselves Republicans has been getting smaller. This has happened because fewer Americans than in the 1950s are identifying as Democrats and more are identifying as independents. Interestingly, there has not been much change in the proportion of Americans who identify as Republicans over the years. If these trends continue, how might the landscape of American politics change?

*Source:* American National Election Studies (through 2008); (after 2008) data from Data Trend, Party Identification, Pew Research Center, http://www.pewresearch.org/data-trend/political-attitudes/party-identification/.

While Democratic and Republican identifiers are moving farther apart on which policies they support, the distances are even greater between Democratic and Republican **active partisans**, those Republican and Democratic identifiers who not only vote but are engaged in other party, candidate, and party-support activities, such as making campaign contributions, attending candidate meetings, making phone calls for the parties and candidates, knocking on doors to get out the party vote, putting bumper stickers on their cars, and the like. Democratic active partisans are strongly liberal, with, for example, 78 percent supporting abortion, 70 percent supporting the use of diplomacy over force in international relations, and 70 percent favoring environmental protection over job protection. For their part, Republican active partisans are a near mirror image, reporting only 41 percent, 11 percent, and 24 percent approval, respectively, for these things.[61]

The proportion of people who say they are independents—including **leaners**, or those who say they are independents but lean fairly consistently to one party or another—has steadily increased, from the low 20s in the 1960s to the high 30s today (the remainder are respondents who choose "no preference" or "don't know"). Although some scholars maintain that these figures exaggerate the rise of independents because many leaners behave the same way as people who say they consider themselves Republicans or Democrats[62]—in 2009, 17 percent of independents said they leaned Democratic, while 12 percent leaned Republican[63]—there has clearly been a decline in the proportion of Americans who identify outright with either of the two major parties. Oddly, then, while a growing proportion of the American population is calling itself independent—though a large majority of Americans identify with one or the other of the two parties—views about public policies in the United States are becoming increasingly polarized along party lines, primarily because partisans vote more than independents and participate more in campaigns, electing more liberal Democrats and conservative Republicans and fewer moderates in either party. Independents tell journalists, pollsters, and scholars that they are fed up with the general nastiness in politics and government ineffectiveness that seems to be associated with the intensification of partisanship in the political life of the country.[64]

**active partisans**
People who identify with a party, vote in elections, and participate in additional party and party-candidate activities.

**leaners**
People who claim to be independents but consistently favor one party over another.

271

# By the Numbers

## Are you a Republican, a Democrat, or an independent?

One often hears people refer to themselves as a Republican or a Democrat or an independent. But what does that mean? Do people formally join a party organization? Do they fill out a paper or online form, pay annual membership dues, receive membership cards to slip into their wallets, and attend meetings with other members? Is it like joining, let us say, a labor union like the United Automobile Workers or the Screenwriters Guild? Is it like joining a service organization like the Rotary or a religious organization like the Knights of Columbus? Or is it like joining the Social Democratic Party in Germany, where people do, in fact, join the party organization? And where do independents go in the United States? Who do they join? These questions are, of course, rhetorical. To be a Republican or a Democrat or an independent for most people in the United States—except for people who are, let us say, employed by or do volunteer work for the Democratic or Republican National Committees—is really a matter of sentiment, about which party one identifies with most of the time.

### Why It Matters

As you have learned in this chapter, one's party identification is very important in how one thinks about issues and decides who to vote for. Notice the directionality in this statement. There is growing evidence that people do not take on a party identification after assessing the issues and the candidates for elective office but the other way around: party identification does most of the shaping. Party identification matters not only because it influences the choices people make in politics but also because the distribution of party identifiers in the population is decisive in determining the outcome of elections and who controls the government. This is because party identifiers almost always vote for candidates with their preferred party's label. During times when Democratic identifiers enjoy strong pluralities—that is,

when there are substantially more Democratic identifiers than Republican ones or people who say they are independents—they dominate elective office. When self-declared independents lead the other categories and the proportions identifying with the two major parties are very close, elections are close and likely to go in unpredictable directions or switch from one election to the next given the "unanchored" status of independent voters.

### Measuring Party Identification

Every major polling organization—whether commercial like Gallup, nonprofit like Pew, or academic/scholarly like the American National Election Study at the University of Michigan—asks people one form or another of the question: "Generally speaking, do you usually think of yourself as a Republican, Democrat, independent, or what?" (Pew); or "In politics, as of today, do you consider yourself a Republican, a Democrat, or an independent?" (Gallup). Typically, the polling organizations then ask people who have answered Republican or Democrat whether they consider themselves to be strong or weak Republicans and Democrats. Independents are asked if they generally lean toward one of the two major parties, or whether they tend to vote for candidates of one party or the other. These so-called leaners, according to some researchers, tend to vote for the candidates of a particular party almost as frequently as people who pick a party identification. Other researchers are not convinced.

### What to Watch for

Pay attention in reports of whether Republicans or Democrats are in the lead in the country to how independents and leaners are counted. For example, in a report issued in 2012, Pew reported that Democrats were the biggest group at 48 percent, with Republicans a little ways back at 43 percent. In this report,

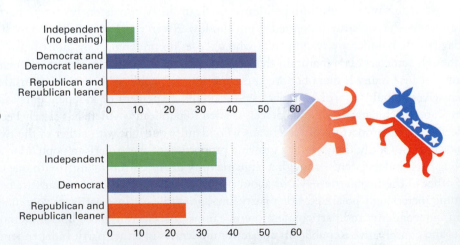

**FIGURE 9.5** PARTY IDENTIFICATION IN THE UNITED STATES, 2012, BY THE PEW RESEARCH CENTER

*Source:* Pew Research Center for the People and the Press, "Party Identification with Leaners among Registered Voters," Table 3, 2012, http://www.people-press.org/files/legacy-detailed_tables/Detailed%20tables%20for%20Party%20ID.pdf.

**FIGURE 9.6** PARTY IDENTIFICATION IN THE UNITED STATES, 2012, BY THE GALLUP POLL

*Source:* Gallup Poll, "Party Affiliation," December 19-22, 2012, http://www.gallup.com/poll/15370/party-affiliation.aspx.

*(Continued)*

Pew put Democratic leaners into the Democratic camp and Republican leaners into the Republican side of the ledger, leaving only 10 percent as independents. The Gallup Poll, by contrast, in its 2012 report, put all independents together, whether pure or party leaners, so they come up with different numbers for Democrats and Republicans. They reported a bigger Democratic advantage over Republicans, with independents sharing the lead.

**What Do You Think?**

Do you identify with one party rather than the other? If so, are you a strong or weak partisan? Or do you consider yourself an independent? How do you think this identification affects how you think about the issues and who you vote for? What is your reaction to the fact that people so often respond to political developments in the context of the party they identify with? Why do people respond in this way?

**SOURCE:** L. Sandy Maisel, *American Political Parties and Elections* (New York: Oxford University Press, 2007).

# Using the DEMOCRACY STANDARD

## How do our major political parties affect democracy?

Democratic theorists, you will recall, believe that vigorous and healthy political parties are essential for democracy. They are essential because, in theory at least, they are among the principal political institutions that can make popular sovereignty and political equality a reality. They are able to do so—again, in theory—because they can help keep elected officials responsive and responsible to the broad public, stimulate interest and participation among ordinary Americans, include a broad range of groups from all economic and social levels of the population, simplify voter choices, and make government work for the people by overcoming the problems of democratic government created by the separation of powers and checks and balances. For all these reasons, of course, the framers looked askance at political parties and worried about their effects on republican government. They were not inclined to include all groups in the population in political life, they were certainly not interested in stimulating widespread interest and participation by ordinary Americans, and they most certainly were not in favor of an institution that might overcome the constraints on the national government they had created.

The framers might have rested a bit easier had they known that our political parties were never quite able to fulfill their democratic promise primarily because the constitutional system they created makes it hard for even unified parties, swept into power by electoral majorities, to get their way. In the Senate, for example, a unified minority party representing a minority of Americans (because each state gets two senators no matter the size of its population) can block important bills favored by the majority party. Still, our parties are the only mechanism we have for allowing voters to decide on a program for the government and to hold elected officials responsible in a collective sense, even if imperfectly. Interest groups and social movements are much too narrow in their outlooks and policy objectives, and voters have no control over what they do. Our parties are becoming better organized and more ideologically distinctive and clearer on the policy alternatives offered to the public, so voters increasingly know what they are getting when they put a party into office. However, the rise in the ideological coherence of the parties, potentially a boon to responsiveness and responsibility in government when a single party controls the presidency and Congress, adds to the possibilities of gridlock in periods of divided government, which are now quite common.

# Review the Chapter

## The Role of Political Parties in a Democracy

**9.1** Evaluate the importance of political parties in democracies, p. 250

Theoretically, the electoral activities of political parties enable citizens to determine what the government does and to hold elected leaders accountable for achieving or failing to achieve what they promise.

Theoretically, some of the gridlock built into our constitutional system can be overcome when the same party controls more than one branch of government.

## The American Two-Party System

**9.2** Distinguish American political parties from parties in other democracies, p. 251

The American party system is unique among the Western democracies in that it is a relatively pure two-party system and has been so since the 1830s.

The American parties are candidate-centered, having very little power in their national party organizations to affect the behavior of individual candidates, office holders, or state and local party organizations.

American parties traditionally have been less unified internally and less ideologically coherent than parties in many other democracies, although partisanship between the parties and ideological coherence within the parties are becoming much more pronounced and politically important.

## The Democratic and Republican Parties Today

**9.3** Compare and contrast today's Republican and Democratic parties, p. 258

The Republican and Democratic parties differ from one another in the demographic groups that make up their electoral coalitions, the interest and advocacy groups that support them, and their stance on a wide range of public policies.

The parties are becoming more ideologically coherent; the GOP is increasingly conservative on social and economic issues while Democrats are increasingly liberal, though the Democrats have many more moderate supporters and elected officials than their Republican counterparts.

It matters a great deal which party is in power for the kinds of public policies that the federal government produces.

# Learn the Terms

political party, p. 250
party platform, p. 250
two-party system, p. 251
multiparty system, p. 251
proportional representation, p. 252
realignment, p. 254

New Deal, p. 256
New Deal coalition, p. 256
divided government, p. 256
dealignment, p. 256
party identification, p. 259
liberal, p. 266

conservative, p. 266
unified government, p. 270
gridlock, p. 270
active partisan, p. 271
leaners, p. 271

# Test Yourself

Answer key begins on page T-1.

**9.1** Evaluate the importance of political parties in democracies

1. Which factor listed below is NOT something political parties can do to make popular sovereignty and political equality possible:

   a. Keep elected officials responsible
   b. Discourage cooperation between parties
   c. Ensure accountability
   d. Stimulate political interest
   e. Help people make sense of politics

**9.2** Distinguish American political parties from parties in other democracies

2. This slowly began to disintegrate in the 1968 election and finally collapsed in 1980 with the Republican capture of the presidency and the Senate.

   a. The New Deal Coalition
   b. The New Deal
   c. The Democratic Party
   d. The Independent Party
   e. The Reform Party

**9.3** Compare and contrast today's Republican and Democratic parties

3. The Republican Party typically attracts supporters who fit into which of the following categories:

   a. People who have secular beliefs, union households, and those with lower incomes
   b. People who have secular beliefs, people with postgraduate degrees, and people in suburban areas
   c. White southerners, people with postgraduate degrees, and those with lower incomes
   d. Conservative Christians, people in rural areas, and those with the highest incomes
   e. Conservative Christians, people in suburban areas, and those with the highest incomes

# Explore Further

## INTERNET SOURCES

A Plain Blog About Politics **plainblogaboutpolitics.blogspot.com**
A blog on politics, but scholarly—active political scientists with links to other first-rate scholarly and journalist blogs of all persuasions.

Democratic National Committee **www.democrats.org**
Information about Democratic Party candidates, party history, convention and national committees, state parties, stands on the issues, affiliated groups, upcoming events, and more.

National Political Index **www.politicalindex.com**
Links to state and local parties and affiliated organizations and interest groups, as well as news and information about the parties.

Real Clear Politics **www.realclearpolitics.com**
News and commentary on American politics from a wide and diverse range of sources.

Project Vote Smart **www.votesmart.org**
A comprehensive collection of information on national and state party candidates and public officials, including biographies, voting records, and campaign finances.

Republican National Committee **www.gop.com**
Information about Republican Party candidates, party history, convention and national committees, state parties, stands on the issues, affiliated groups, upcoming events, and more.

## SUGGESTIONS FOR FURTHER READING

Aldrich, John H. *Why Parties? A Second Look*. Chicago: University of Chicago Press, 2012.
A classic and groundbreaking work on the origins and functions of American political parties brought up to date.

Black, Earl, and Merle Black. *Divided: The Ferocious Power Struggle in American Politics*. New York: Simon and Schuster, 2007.
The authors demonstrate the extent to which the regional bases of the two major parties have changed and why it happened.

Brownstein, Ronald. *The Second Civil War: How Extreme Partisanship Has Paralyzed Washington and Polarized America*. New York: Penguin Press, 2007.
A passionate chronicle of the growth of partisanship, the coarsening of public life, and our consequent inability, in the author's view, to tackle the nation's problems.

Gould, Lewis. *Grand Old Party: A History of the Republicans*. New York: Random House, 2003.
A comprehensive history of the Republican Party in the United States.

Hershey, Marjory. *Party Politics in America*, 14th ed. New York: Pearson Longman Publishers, 2011.
A leading textbook on political parties in the United States; comprehensive, detailed, yet engaging.

Maisel, L. Sandy. *American Political Parties and Elections: A Very Short Introduction*. New York: Oxford University Press, 2007.
The best short guide to American parties and elections.

Mann, Thomas E., and Norman J. Ornstein. *It's Even Worse Than It Looks: How the American Constitutional System Collided with the New Politics of Extremism*. Basic Books, 2013.
How the deadlock in Washington caused by the interaction of hyperpartisanship with our constitutional system has made gridlock a relatively fixed feature of our political system.

Witcover, Jules. *Party of the People: A History of the Democrats*. New York: Random House, 2003.
A comprehensive history of the Democratic Party in the United States.

# 10
# Voting, Campaigns, and Elections

## BARACK OBAMA WINS A SECOND TERM

**A** fter an exhausting and expensive campaign, incumbent president Barack Obama scored a decisive electoral vote victory over Republican challenger Mitt Romney in the 2012 presidential election, winning by a margin of 332 to 206. The Obama-Biden ticket's victory in the national popular vote was narrower, though it prevailed over the Romney-Ryan ticket by almost 3 million votes (out of more than 126 million votes cast), winning by a margin of 50 percent to 48. To forge this victory, Obama maintained the coalition that helped him win in 2008, one made up largely of women and young, urban, and minority voters.

President Obama's reelection victory was not a foregone conclusion. When Romney announced his candidacy in 2011, Obama seemed quite vulnerable. The United States was still mired in wars in Iraq and Afghanistan. The country's economy was in serious trouble—unemployment topped 9 percent, GDP growth was tepid, and the housing market remained in the doldrums. Additionally, the Gallup organization reported that fewer than 50 percent approved of the way President Obama was doing his job, and 74 percent thought the "country was on the wrong track." Romney's assumption was that focusing on the weak economy and the president's failure to improve it, would be sufficient to win the election. Adding to the Romney campaign's confidence was the belief that enthusiasm had waned for Obama among groups that had been central to his 2008 election winning coalition, and that turnout among these groups would be lower in 2012.

Unfortunately for Romney and his running mate, Paul Ryan, they were wrong on almost all counts. First Barack Obama remained personally popular, even among those who did not

<table>
<tr><td>

**10.1**

Evaluate three models of how elections can lead to popular control, p. 279

</td><td>

**10.2**

Distinguish American elections from those in other countries, p. 282

</td><td>

**10.3**

Analyze the importance of political participation in elections, p. 285

</td><td>

**10.4**

Identify demographic factors that increase the likelihood of voting, p. 291

</td><td>

**10.5**

Outline the process of campaigns for the presidency and Congress, p. 295

</td><td>

**10.6**

Assess how presidential elections are decided, p. 308

</td></tr>
</table>

**CONTEMPLATING HIS SECOND TERM** A solemn President Barack Obama waves to his enthusiastic supporters at McCormick Place in Chicago late on the evening of November 7 after his decisive electoral vote win over Republican Mitt Romney in the 2012 presidential election. His mood may have been tempered by the prospect of having to deal at the start of his second term with a Republican-dominated House of Representatives on a wide range of pressing issues.

think he was doing a good job on the economy. Moreover, though the Romney campaign believed that people would blame the president for the country's economic troubles, exit polls showed that Americans overwhelmingly blamed his predecessor George W. Bush. To make matters worse for Romney's prospects, the economy slowly improved in the months before the election, with evidence of private sector job growth, a fall in the unemployment rate below 8 percent, a boom in the auto sector, and a surge in U.S. exports, all of which caused the president's job approval to rise to about 50 percent in the weeks before the election.[1] Finally, while turnout was not as high as it was in 2008, young, urban dwellers, racial and ethnic minorities, and women still voted in relatively high numbers and overwhelmingly cast their ballots for the Obama-Biden ticket. For example, 93 percent of African Americans voted for Obama, as did 55 percent of women, 71 percent of Asian Americans, 71 percent of Hispanics, 69 percent of people in big cities, 60 percent of 18-29 year olds, 55 percent of people with post-graduate degrees, and 92 percent of Democrats.

Romney did best among white men 45 and older who did not have college degrees, still a substantial size of the electorate, but a shrinking population. The decline in Hispanic support was especially troubling for Republicans. After all, only eight years earlier, Republican George W. Bush managed to win 40 percent of Hispanic voters, a group whose share of the electorate will only increase in future elections.

A number of actions by Republican office-holders and candidates seems to have driven Hispanics and women towards the Democrats. Many of these voters were troubled by harsh anti-immigration measures passed in states that often brought legal immigrants and citizens of Hispanic ancestry into unwelcome contact with authorities and by tough rhetoric from the main contenders during the Republican primary. At one point, Romney promised such strict laws that people would "self deport." Many women (not all, to be sure) were troubled by strong anti-abortion rhetoric and were shocked by the remarks of two Republican senate candidates who talked of "legitimate rape" and pregnancy following a rape as part of God's plan. In the many post-mortems after the election, leading conservatives expressed grave concern about trends for the future of the GOP.

Another factor in the election, though it is difficult to measure empirically, was the "ground game," the ability of the campaign organizations to identify supporters and get them to cast their votes. Observers agreed that the Obama team was much better at this than the Romney team. The Obama ground game was especially effective in the battleground states.

## Thinking Critically About This Chapter

The story of the 2012 presidential election focuses our attention on the issue of democratic control of the national government through the electoral process and on the degree to which the public participates in this key activity of the representative democratic process.

## Using the Framework

You will see in this chapter that elections are affected by the different rates of participation of groups in American society and how structural factors such as constitutional rules, unequal access to resources, and cultural ideas help determine why some groups participate more than others. You will also learn how elections affect the behavior of public officials.

## Using the Democracy Standard

We suggest in this chapter that elections are the lynchpin of any discussion about the democratic quality of any system of government because they are, in theory, what makes popular sovereignty possible. You will see in this chapter that while elections in the United States do much to make our system democratic, they fall short of their democratic promise.

# Elections and Democracy

**10.1** Evaluate three models of how elections can lead to popular control

10.1

10.2

10.3

10.4

10.5

10.6

**prospective voting model**
A theory of democratic elections in which voters decide what government will do in the near future by choosing one or another responsible party.

**responsible party**
The notion that a political party will take clear and distinct stands on the issues and enact them as policy once elected to office.

 lections are fundamental to democratic politics, the chief means by which citizens control what their government does. Many important struggles for democracy in the United States have involved conflicts over the right to vote. But can elections actually ensure that governments will do what their people want?

Democratic theorists have suggested several ways that elections in a two-party system like that found in the United States can bring about popular control of government. We will briefly discuss three of these ways, indicating how they might work in theory.[2] The remainder of this chapter is concerned with what actually happens in American national elections and with the question of whether these elections really bring about popular control of government.

## ☐ The Prospective (or Responsible Party) Voting Model

The **prospective voting model** requires that parties stake out different positions on the issues of the day and that voters cast ballots based on these differences. In this way, parties are responsible because they offer a "real choice" on important issues and, once elected, they work to implement their stated policies. Simply put, voters know what a **responsible party** stands for and know what to expect once a party is elected.

**THEORY** For this system to work perfectly, each of the two parties must be cohesive and unified; each must take clear policy positions that differ significantly from the other party's positions; citizens must accurately perceive these positions and vote on the basis of them; and the winning party, when it takes office, must try to implement the policies it advocated. It is in this sense—that parties stand for something and have the wherewithal and willingness to follow through once in power—that the model also is called the responsible party model. If all these conditions are met, then the party with the more popular policy positions will win and enact its program. In such an electoral system, government will do what the majority of the voters want.[3]

**POTENTIAL PROBLEMS** One potential problem of elections fought by responsible parties is that it might increase the frequency and intensity of political conflicts in the country. If each party in such a system stands for ideologies and policies different from the other party, feels duty-bound to put promises into effect on attaining power, and has the means to do so, there would be little reason for the victorious party to reach compromises with the losing party, even if it won by a razor-thin margin. The party in power can make the policies it wants, disregarding the objections of the losing party. The high stakes involved in winning and losing elections in such a system would make campaigns and elections very heated.

Others have pointed out that while responsible parties might make choices at the ballot box easier for voters, in a system of separation of powers and federalism, it is likely to lead to gridlock—a situation in which government cannot function very well because the different branches of government are controlled by different parties that are not prone to compromise with one another. It is quite common, for example, for Congress to be controlled by one party and the presidency by another (something that cannot happen in a parliamentary system) and, if the parties controlling them disagree clearly and fundamentally, then it's hard to get things done.[4] This has been a common theme during Barack Obama's presidential term, as partisan warfare with congressional Republicans has made it difficult to achieve even the most mundane tasks, such as raising the debt ceiling and funding the government. The frequency of these types of events is likely to increase if our parties become more responsible, as seems to be happening.[5]

10.1

10.2

10.3

10.4

10.5

10.6

**electoral competition voting model**
A form of election in which parties seeking votes move toward the median voter or the center of the political spectrum.

**median voter**
The voter who is, ideologically, at the center of the political issue spectrum.

Another potential problem, because the parties focus on their differences, is that polarization among elites and voters tends to occur, exacerbating ideological differences and further encouraging the parties to grow apart. The result is a destructive cycle in which extreme voters and activists encourage the parties and individual candidates to become more extreme, which in turns promotes more gridlock, more heated rhetoric, and less willingness to compromise.

## ☐ The Electoral Competition Voting Model

A very different, and less obvious, sort of democratic control can be found in what political scientists call the **electoral competition voting model** of democratic elections. In this sort of electoral model, unified parties compete for votes by taking the *most popular* positions they can. They do so by trying to take positions that will appeal to the voter in the middle of the political spectrum, the so-called **median voter**. Both parties are therefore likely to end up standing for the *same* policies: those favored by the most voters.

**THEORY** This electoral competition model relies on the assumption that citizens can be arranged along a single dimension from liberal to conservative, as shown in Figure 10.1, and that voters prefer the party or candidate who is closest to their own beliefs. There is substantial evidence, for most of American history, that issues, voters, and elected officials can all be placed in a single economic-social dimension.[6] Parties are thought of as vote-seeking entities without particular ideological preferences. As a result, both parties take positions exactly at the *median* of public opinion, that is, at the point where exactly one-half the voters are more liberal and one-half are more conservative. It can be shown mathematically that the party that captures the median will always win the election, meaning that if either party took a position even a little bit away from the median, the other party would win more votes.[7]

If electoral competition drives parties together in this way, and if they keep their promises, then, in theory, it should not matter which party wins; the winner enacts the policies that the most voters want. Democracy is ensured by the hidden hand of competition, much as efficiency is ensured by competitive markets, according to standard economic theory.

**POTENTIAL PROBLEMS** The most important criticism of the electoral competition voting model is that certain pressures prevent parties from moving to the middle. Parties need the backing of financial contributors for campaign money, and candidates need the backing of party activists during primary elections. Both groups, contributors and activists, tend to be more extreme and will only support the party if it too supports extreme policy positions. Further, individual candidates who are ideological may win a

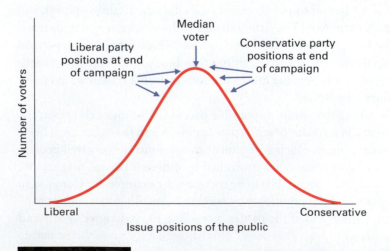

**FIGURE 10.1** ELECTORAL COMPETITION MODEL
The electoral competition voting model suggests that, as campaigns progress, parties move toward the median voter (where most votes are to be found) in pursuit of election wins.

primary election, and may simply refuse to moderate their positions due to their own personal beliefs. Because American political parties have little control over what individual candidates say and do, there is virtually no way a party can force its own candidates toward the center.

Still, the conditions necessary for the electoral competition voting model are close enough to the truth so that the model does work, to a significant extent, in real elections. Extreme candidates win less frequently, especially when the electorate is large and diverse (such as in Senate or presidential campaigns), creating a powerful incentive for parties and their candidates to remain near the median. Indeed, electoral competition is probably one of the main ways that elected officials are influenced by public opinion.

## The Retrospective (or Reward and Punishment) Voting Model

A third model by which elections might bring about popular control of government is the **retrospective voting model**, also known as the **electoral reward and punishment model**, which claims voters judge how well the party in power has governed and then decide if they want the party and its members to continue in office.

**THEORY** Here the idea is that the voters simply make retrospective, backward-looking judgments about how well incumbent officials have done in the past, rewarding success with reelection and punishing failure by throwing the incumbents out. The result, in theory, is that politicians who want to stay in office have strong incentives to bring about peace and prosperity and to address the problems that occur, such as a bad economy, rising inflation, or threats from a foreign country.[8] The reward-and-punishment process of democratic control has the advantage of simplicity. It requires very little of voters: no elaborate policy preferences, no study of campaign platforms, just judgments of how well or how badly things have been going. Voters seem to have punished Republicans in 2006 in such a way, expressing their displeasure with George W. Bush over the wars in Iraq and Afghanistan and again in 2008 over a collapsed economy.[9] Likewise, in 2014, voters seemed to use the retrospective voting model to penalize Democrats for the country's economic failures. Polling taken at the time suggested congressional Republicans were much more unpopular than both the president and congressional Democrats. Yet, as the model suggests, voters punished the presidential "in" party (in this case, the Democrats), expressing their displeasure with the direction of the country by sending Republicans to Congress.

**POTENTIAL PROBLEMS** However, reward and punishment may be a rather blunt instrument. It gets rid of bad political leaders only after (not before) disasters happen, without guaranteeing that the next leaders will be any better. It relies on politicians *anticipating* the effects of future policies, which they cannot always do successfully. Moreover, the reward-and-punishment process focuses only on the most prominent issues and may leave room for unpopular policies on matters that are less visible. It may also encourage politicians to produce deceptively positive but temporary results that arrive just in time for Election Day and then fade away.

## Imperfect Electoral Democracy

We will see that each of the three processes of democratic control we have discussed exists, to some extent, in American elections. On occasion, the models converge and help produce an election that is enormously consequential for the direction of the nation, as in the 1932 election, which elevated Franklin Roosevelt to the presidency during the Great Depression. To understand this important election more fully, see the "Using the Framework" feature.

But none of the three processes works well enough to guarantee perfectly democratic outcomes most of the time. In certain respects, they conflict: responsible parties and electoral competition, for example, tend to push in opposite directions. In other respects, all three processes require similar conditions that are not met in reality.

10.1
10.2
10.3
10.4
10.5
10.6

**retrospective voting model (or electoral reward and punishment model)**
A theory of democratic elections in which voters look back at the performance of a party in power and cast ballots on the basis of how well it did in office.

10.1

10.2

10.3

10.4

10.5

10.6

**provisional ballot**
A vote that is cast but not counted until determination is made that the voter is properly registered.

For example, none of the three can ensure government responsiveness to all citizens unless *all* citizens have the right to vote and exercise that right. Unfortunately, tens of millions of Americans cannot or do not go to the polls. Their voices are not heard; political equality is not achieved.

Another problem with our system of elections was brought to public attention by the chaos and uncertainty of the disputed 2000 presidential election in Florida: not all ballots cast by voters are actually counted. For a variety of reasons, ranging from lack of voter education to confusing ballot layouts and malfunctioning voting machines, a number of ballots in every election in the United States are disqualified and not included in the final vote tally. A study commissioned by Congress on the 2000 election estimated that from 4 to 6 million votes of the roughly 100 million cast nationally were not counted, with the votes of poor people and members of racial minorities three times more likely than those of other Americans to be uncounted in the 2000 election.[10]

# The Unique Nature of American Elections

**10.2** Distinguish American elections from those in other countries

merican elections differ quite dramatically from those of most other democratic countries. The differences are the result of rules—mainly found in the Constitution but also in federal statutes and judicial decisions—that define offices and tell how elections are to be conducted. Here are the distinguishing features of elections in the United States:

**ELECTIONS ARE NUMEROUS AND FREQUENT** In some sense, we are "election happy" in the United States. We not only elect the president and members of Congress (senators and representatives), but also, being a federal system, we elect governors, state legislators, and (in most states) judges. In addition, state constitutions allow autonomy for counties, cities, and towns, and all of their top officials are elected by the people. All in all, we fill about 500,000 offices through elections.[11] We also elect school boards in most places, and the top positions in special districts (e.g., water or conservation districts). And then there are the many state and local ballot initiatives that add to the length and complexity of the ballot at election time. No other country holds so many elections, covering so many offices and public policy issues.

**ELECTIONS ARE SEPARATE AND INDEPENDENT FROM ONE ANOTHER** Not only do we have a multitude of elections, but the election to fill each particular office is separate and independent from the others. In parliamentary systems, one votes for a party, and the party that wins a majority gets to appoint a whole range of other officials. The majority party in the British parliament (the legislative branch), for example, chooses the prime minister and cabinet ministers (the executive branch), who run the government. The government, in turn, appoints officials to many posts that are filled by elections here. In the United States, the president and members of Congress are elected independently from one another, as are governors, state legislators, mayors of cities, city council members, and school boards.

**INCONSISTENT ELECTION PROCEDURES AND VOTE-COUNTING** With very few exceptions—such as the 1965 Voting Rights Act to protect the rights of African American voters and the 2002 law allowing the use of **provisional ballots** when voter registration issues arise on election day—the federal government plays no role in regulating and overseeing elections. This mainly is the role of states that, in most cases, further decentralize the process by lodging the management of elections in the hands of county officials.

10.1

10.2

10.3

10.4

10.5

10.6

# Using the FRAMEWORK

## Do elections matter? Has an election ever fundamentally changed the course of American government?

**Background:** Occasionally in American history, a national election is so consequential that it alters the overall direction of government policy and the role of government in the United States. The election of Franklin Delano Roosevelt and an overwhelmingly Democratic Congress in the 1932 elections was just such a moment. In the first 100 days of his administration, Roosevelt launched his New Deal, convincing Congress to pass bills to regulate the banking and securities industries, to bail out failing banks and protect the deposits of the public, to launch public works and relief efforts, and to provide price supports for farmers. This revolution in the role of the federal government was made possible by the 1932 elections, but to fully understand what happened, structural, political linkage, and governmental factors have to be taken into account.

### Government Action

Major emergency and reform legislation is passed beginning in early 1933, launching the New Deal.

### Government

Franklin Roosevelt interpreted the 1932 election as a mandate for immediate and far-reaching actions by the federal government to meet the crisis of the Great Depression. → Roosevelt mobilized business and labor leaders, as well as the public, behind his emergency program. → The Democratic-controlled Congress, aware of Roosevelt's enormous popularity, and concerned about the national crisis, passed all the president's emergency measures.

### Political Linkage

Public opinion strongly supported a greater role for the federal government in fighting the depression. → Social disorder was widespread, leading to concerns that the country was near the point of collapse. → Social movements that demanded government action were growing and making their presence felt. → Democrats won big majorities in the House and the Senate in 1932. → Roosevelt won an overwhelming victory in the 1932 presidential election, tallying 472 electoral votes to Hoover's 59.

### Structure

The 1932 election was held in the midst of the Great Depression, with unemployment reaching 33 percent, bank failures at an all-time high, and industrial and farm production at 50 percent of their levels in the mid-1920s. → The preamble to the Constitution says that the Constitution was intended to create a government that would "...insure Domestic tranquility...[and]...promote the general Welfare."

283

10.1

10.2

10.3

10.4

10.5

10.6

The result is wide variation across the country in voter registration rules, how absentee and early ballots are handled and counted, what types of election devices are used (paper ballots, either counted by hand or scanned, computerized touch screen systems, and more), when and how recounts are done, and how election disputes are resolved.[12]

**ELECTED POSITIONS HAVE FIXED TERMS OF OFFICE** The office of president of the United States is fixed at four years, representatives serve for two years, and senators for six. At the state level, terms of office for all important elected positions are fixed, whether for governors or legislators. The same holds true for county, city, and town elected offices. In parliamentary systems, the government can call an election at any time within a certain number of years (in Britain, it is five years), timing the election to maximize chances for reelection. One implication of fixed elections in the United States is that presidents cannot call for new elections in hopes of changing the party mix in Congress to their advantage. It also means that an unpopular president stays in office until the next election, because there is no method to remove him other than by impeachment and trial. In parliamentary systems, elections customarily are held when the majority party or majority coalition in parliament loses support among its members, shown in a defeat on a major bill proposed by the government (the prime minister and cabinet) or on a "vote of confidence" called by the opposition. Governments deemed not up to the task of rescuing their countries from impending financial collapse were replaced in both Greece and Italy during the European debt crisis in 2011, for example.

**ELECTIONS ARE HELD ON A FIXED DATE** In 1845, Congress determined that elections for president and members of Congress will occur on the Tuesday after the first Monday in November (the Constitution only requires that national elections be held on the same day throughout the country). States have generally followed suit for election of governors and members of the legislature. One implication, related to the fixed terms of offices just described, is that neither presidents nor governors can time elections to their political advantage as we have seen can happen in parliamentary systems. Another implication

**PARLIAMENTARY ELECTIONS IN INDIA**
Prime ministerial candidate Narendra Modi, of the opposition Bharatiya Janata Party (BJP), won the highest office in the world's largest democracy in parliamentary elections that spanned more than a month to accommodate India's hundreds of millions of eligible voters.

is that Tuesday elections may cut down on participation. In other democracies, elections are held either on the weekend or on days that are declared a national holiday.

**"FIRST-PAST-THE-POST" WINS** Winners in most elections in the United States are those who win the most votes—not necessarily a majority—in a particular electoral district. This type of election is often called "first-past-the-post," as in a horse race where the winner is the first past the finish line. This includes congressional elections and presidential contests for electoral votes in each of the states. We do not have proportional representation in national-level races, nor do we have "run-off" elections between the top two vote-getters in presidential or congressional elections to ensure a majority victor. If no one wins an absolute majority (more than 50 percent of the vote), the winner is the candidate who wins a **plurality**, or the most votes among all candidates. Presidential candidates often fail to win a majority of votes. In 1992, Bill Clinton won only 43 percent of the vote because third-party candidate Ross Perot took 19 percent. Though Bill Clinton won a plurality, 56 percent of ballots were cast either for Perot or the Republican nominee, incumbent president George H. W. Bush! In contrast, in France and Finland, if no candidate wins a majority in the first round of voting for president, a second election is held, ensuring that the person elected enters office with majority support.

# Voting in the United States

Analyze the importance of political participation in elections

I n this section, we turn our attention to political participation. For elections to be democratic—whether in the prospective, electoral competition, or retrospective voting models—participation in elections must not only be at high levels, but also must not vary substantially across social groups in the population (e.g., by race, gender, income, occupation, religion, ethnicity, region, and so on), or else the principle of political equality would be violated.

## ☐ Expansion of the Franchise

Until passage of the Fourteenth and Fifteenth Amendments after the Civil War, it was up to each state to determine who within its borders was eligible to vote. In the early years of the United States, many of the states limited the legal right to vote—called the **franchise**—quite severely. In fact, a majority of people could not vote at all. Slaves, Native Americans, and women were excluded altogether. In most states, white men without property or who had not paid some set level of taxes were not allowed to vote. In some states early on, white men with certain religious beliefs were excluded. One of the most important developments in U.S. political history, an essential part of the struggle for democracy, has been the expansion of the right to vote. The extension of the franchise has been a lengthy and uneven process, spanning 200 years.[13]

**WHITE MALE SUFFRAGE** The first barriers to fall were those concerning property and religion. So strong were the democratic currents during Thomas Jefferson's presidency (1801–1809) and in the years leading up to the election of Andrew Jackson in 1828 that by 1829, property, taxpaying, and religious requirements had been dropped in all states except North Carolina and Virginia. That left universal **suffrage**, or the ability to vote, firmly in place for most adult white males in the United States. Most of Europe, including Britain, did not achieve this degree of democracy until after World War I.

**BLACKS, WOMEN, AND YOUNG PEOPLE** Despite this head start for the United States compared with the rest of the world, the struggle to expand the franchise to include African Americans, women, and young people proved difficult and painful. Ironically, universal white male suffrage was often accompanied by the withdrawal

**plurality**
More votes than any other candidate but less than a majority of all votes cast.

**franchise**
The legal right to vote; see suffrage.

**suffrage**
The legal right to vote; see franchise.

10.1
10.2
10.3
10.4
10.5
10.6

10.1

10.2

10.3

10.4

10.5

10.6

**Electoral College**
Representatives selected in each of the states, their numbers based on each state's total number of its senators and representatives; a majority of Electoral College votes elects the president.

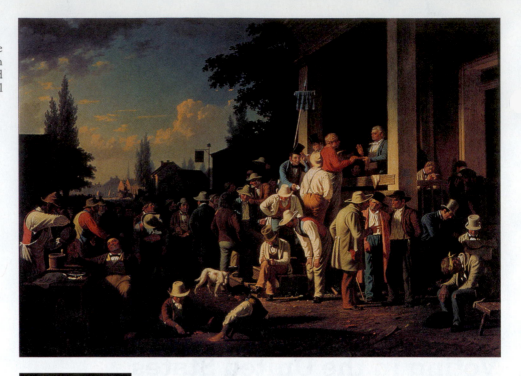

**AT THE POLLS**

Early U.S. elections were poorly organized and hard to get to. In addition, only a small proportion of the population was eligible to vote. Here a group of white men, the only people with the right to vote in most places in the United States at the time, wait to vote in the presidential election of 1824 at a polling station in Saline County, Missouri. How did the voter profile of the time shape government policies?

of voting rights from black freedmen, even in states that did not permit slavery.[14] It took the bloody Civil War to free the slaves and the Fifteenth Amendment to the U.S. Constitution (1870) to extend the right to vote to all black males, both North and South. Even so, most blacks were effectively disfranchised in the South by the end of the nineteenth century and remained so until the 1960s civil rights movement and the Voting Rights Act of 1965.

Women won the right to vote in 1920 in all the states with the Nineteenth Amendment to the Constitution, after a long political battle. Residents of the District of Columbia were allowed to vote in presidential—but not congressional—elections after 1961, and 18- to 20-year-olds gained the franchise in 1971.

The result of these changes at the state and national levels was an enormous increase in the proportion of Americans who were legally eligible to vote: from about 23 percent of the adult population in 1788–1789 to nearly 98 percent by the beginning of the 1970s—practically all citizens above the age of 18, except people who have recently moved to another state, people in mental institutions, and incarcerated felons (and, in many states, former felons).

**DIRECT PARTISAN ELECTIONS**  A related trend has involved more direct elections of government officials, replacing the old indirect methods that insulated officials from the public. At the same time, the development of a two-party system has clarified choices by focusing citizens' attention on just two alternatives for each office.

The election of the president, even with the existence of the **Electoral College**, has become more directly democratic. By the time of the Jefferson–Adams presidential campaign of 1800, which pitted the new Republican and Federalist parties against each other, most state legislatures had stopped picking the presidential electors themselves (as the Constitution permits). Instead, the legislatures allowed a popular vote for electors, most of whom were pledged to support the presidential candidate of one party or the other.

This is the same system we use today: in practically every state, there is a winner-take-all popular vote for a slate of electors—positions usually awarded by each of the political parties to loyal party workers and contributors—who are pledged to a particular presidential candidate. In fact, only the name of the candidate and the party to whom the electors are pledged, not the names of the electors we are actually voting for, appear on the ballot. Thus, when the winning electors meet as the Electoral College in their respective states and cast ballots to elect the president, their actions are generally controlled by the popular vote that chose them. This system, odd and cumbersome as it is, almost always ensures that American citizens choose their president more or less directly. One recent exception is the 2000 election, when Democrat Al Gore won the popular vote by more than 500,000, but Republican George W. Bush captured a majority of the electoral votes after the Supreme Court ruled in Bush's favor on who should receive Florida's 25 electoral votes.

By 1840, the parties had started nominating presidential candidates in national **party conventions** instead of in congressional party caucuses. Later still, the parties began letting voters select many convention delegates directly in state **primary elections** instead of having party activists choose them in political party conventions in each of the states. Today, most delegates to the Republican and Democratic national conventions are selected in primary elections or in state **party caucuses** in which party supporters and activists hold neighborhood and area-wide meetings to select delegates. The important role of primaries and caucuses in nominating party candidates for elected office enhances democratic control of government, although we will see that each of them has antidemocratic features, too.

Until 1913, when the Seventeenth Amendment to the Constitution was ratified, U.S. senators were selected by state legislatures rather than directly by the people. Since then, all members of the Senate have been subject to direct choice by the voters.

Taken together, the expansion of the franchise and the development of direct, two-party elections have represented major successes in the struggle for democracy. But problems remain on the voting participation front.

## ☐ Low Voting Turnout

During the first 100 years or so of the United States's existence, not only did more and more people gain the right to vote, but also higher and higher proportions of voters actually turned out on Election Day and voted. Because of data inaccuracies and voter fraud, it is difficult to determine voter **turnout** accurately in early American elections. But the percentage of American voters appears to have increased rapidly, from roughly 11 percent of eligible voters in 1788–1789, to about 31 percent in 1800 (when Thomas Jefferson was first elected), and to about 57 percent in 1828 (Andrew Jackson's first victory). By 1840, the figure had reached 80 percent, and it stayed at about that level until 1896.[15]

The disturbing fact is that today, despite higher turnout in recent presidential elections, proportionally fewer people vote than during most of the nineteenth century. Since 1912, only about 50 to 65 percent of Americans have voted in presidential elections (see Figure 10.2) and still fewer in other elections: 40 to 50 percent in off-year (non-presidential-year) congressional elections and as few as 10 to 20 percent in primaries and minor local elections, although the exact number depends on how turnout is measured (see the "By the Numbers" feature). In addition, turnout in presidential elections remains well below turnout in other democratic countries; in Western Europe, turnout rates regularly top 75 percent, and in Australia, where voting is required by law, turnout is, unsurprisingly, higher than 90 percent.

Why do so few Americans vote compared to people in other democracies? Scholars have identified several possible factors.[16]

**BARRIERS TO VOTING** In the United States, only citizens who take the initiative to register in advance are permitted to vote in an election. Most commonly, the registration period is ten to thirty days before an election (nine states allow same-day registration)[17]. Many people do not make the extra effort to register, or circumstances make it difficult.

**party convention**
A gathering of delegates who nominate a party's presidential candidate.

**primary election**
Statewide elections in which voters choose delegates to the national party conventions.

**party caucuses**
The process for selecting delegates to the national party conventions characterized by neighborhood and area-wide meetings of party supporters and activists.

**turnout**
The proportion of either eligible or all voting-age Americans who actually vote in a given election; the two ways of counting turnout yield different results.

10.1

10.2

10.3

10.4

10.5

10.6

10.1
10.2
10.3
10.4
10.5
10.6

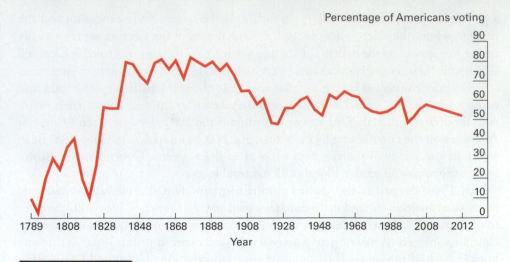

Percentage of Americans voting

**FIGURE 10.2** THE RISE AND FALL OF TURNOUT IN PRESIDENTIAL ELECTIONS, 1789–2012

Turnout in presidential elections rose sharply during the nineteenth century—except during the "era of good feelings" when there was no party competition and little interest in politics among the public—but declined in the twentieth century. In 2004, turnout increased dramatically, but only to a level typical of the 1950s and 1960s.

*Note:* From 1920, the Census Bureau has calculated voting turnout as the percentage of the voting-age population voting, not as a percentage of the total voting-eligible population.

*Source:* U.S. Bureau of the Census, 2009; post-election estimates the authors based on data collected by Michael McDonald, "United States Elections Project," George Washington University, November 7, 2012.

For example, people who move, either within a state or to another state, must find out where and when to register in their new location. Many procrastinate and do not register in time, lowering turnout, according to one study, by 9 percentage points.[18] In most European countries with high turnout rates, the government, rather than individual citizens, is responsible for deciding who is listed as eligible to vote and registers them automatically.

If one's goal is to increase voting turnout, then doing things to make registering easier seems sensible. That is because research has shown a strong relationship between being registered and voting. We know, for example, that voting turnout in the United States among those who have registered to vote has hovered at about 85 percent and that voting participation in the states that allow same-day registration has been significantly higher than in other states.[19] In Minnesota and Wisconsin in 2012, where same-day registration is in effect, turnout was 76 percent and 73 percent, respectively, similar to turnout in other rich democracies. These findings suggest that the registration requirement for voting is probably a significant barrier to participation, because participation rates go up when such barriers are lowered.

A number of reforms have been instituted to make registration and voting more convenient. The National Voter Registration Act came into force in 1996, requiring states to allow people to sign up to vote in a variety of places where they are in contact with state and local government, as in welfare offices and motor vehicle facilities (why it is almost always called the "Motor Voter" law). Interestingly, while registration rates went up after the law came into being, voting turnout did not increase at similar rates, surprising advocates of the law and many scholars.[20]

Other reforms designed to ease the voting act itself have been instituted at the state level. These include allowing an extended voting period—usually called early voting—which many states have instituted in recent elections; and expanding the use of mail balloting over a period of several weeks, which a growing number of states allow.

Several reform ideas have not gotten very far. One is to make Election Day a legal holiday when people could vote without missing work, as many European countries do. Some have even suggested that people be required to vote, as many countries do. Needless to say, we do not require people to vote in this country and it does not seem likely to happen here any time soon.

Though much has been done recently to make registration and voting easier, there is a countermovement tied directly to the "parties at war" narrative that seeks to make registration and voting harder for many. It has been mostly Democrats who have sought an expanded electorate, believing, perhaps, that those least likely to vote under older arrangements—lower-income and less educated people, and racial and ethnic minorities—would more likely vote for them. Claiming they are interested in rooting out voter fraud in our present system, but also wishing perhaps to take away Democratic votes, Republicans have been pushing hard to more tightly regulate the voting process. In virtually every state where they ended up in control of state government in the wake of their 2010 electoral landslide victory, Republicans passed laws requiring government-issued photo IDs for voting, while many of them, including Ohio and Florida, cut back the length of early voting periods. Maine ended same-day registration. Alabama and Kansas now require proof of citizenship. Florida and Iowa no longer allow ex-felons (presumably, "ex" means they have served their sentences and paid their debts to society) to vote. Other states, such as Wisconsin and Tennessee, have sought to make it harder for college students to vote by not allowing the use of college identification cards as a valid form of voter identification, among other limitations. It remains to be seen what the turnout effects of these changes will be, though no one doubts that it will keep many eligible citizens from voting, especially those most likely to cast their ballots for Democrats.[21]

**TOO MUCH COMPLEXITY** As we suggested earlier, when voters go to the polls in the United States, they must make voting choices for a multitude of federal, state, and local offices and often decide on constitutional and policy measures put on the ballot by state legislatures (called **referenda**) or the public (called **initiatives**), especially in states such as California and Colorado where these are common. Research demonstrates that many potential voters are simply overwhelmed by the complexity of the issues and the number of choices they must make; some choose to stay home.[22]

**A DECLINE IN COMPETITIVE ELECTIONS** It may seem exceedingly odd to suggest, given the rise of intense partisanship, an increase in the shrillness and incivility in recent election campaigns, and the frequency of close elections in recent electoral rounds for the presidency and control of Congress, that very few Americans experience competitive elections where they live.[23] In the most recent congressional elections, for example, no more than 51 or so of the 435 seats in the House really have been up for grabs (in 2008, it rose to about 60; in 2010, it jumped to about 100[24]). The remainder have resided safely in the hands of incumbents who won with at least 55 percent of the vote. In presidential elections, most states find themselves solidly in the Democratic or Republican columns, and little campaigning takes place in them. California is safely Democratic in presidential elections, for example, so Republican presidential candidates don't spend much time or money there. Democratic candidates tend to skirt places that are reliably Republican, such as Texas. In the last few elections, battleground states have included North Carolina, Nevada, Colorado, Iowa, Ohio, Virginia, and Florida. In a recent presidential election (see the "Mapping American Politics" feature later in this chapter), 88 percent of media ad buys in the last month of the presidential campaign were concentrated in only 10 states. If competition drives up voter turnout, as political scientists suggest, then an important reason for low turnout in the United States may be that most Americans do not live in an environment where elections are strongly contested.

**WEAK VOTER MOBILIZATION BY LOCAL PARTIES** Low turnout may be tied to the failure of the political parties to rouse people broadly and get them to the polls to vote. The national parties mostly are in the business of getting their own supporters to the polls, to rally the base, as it were, not in the business of increasing the voter turnout in general as a sort of civic duty. The problem is that aiming at your own voters with highly partisan appeals delivered by mail, telephone, television, e-mail, and social media by highly professional but distant party organizations and advocacy groups does not increase turnout among the non-committed public and may even persuade many of them to stay home.[25] Old-style, door-to-door canvassing in neighborhoods, historically the province of local party organizations that now seem increasingly enfeebled, is more effective in raising turnout than modern methods but less commonly used than in the past. Both parties have renewed their efforts in this area,[26] however, with the

**referenda**
Procedures available in some states by which state laws or constitutional amendments proposed by the legislature are submitted to the voters for approval or rejection.

**initiatives**
Procedures available in some states for citizens to put proposed laws and constitutional amendments on the ballot for voter approval or rejection.

10.1
10.2
10.3
10.4
10.5
10.6

10.1

10.2

10.3

10.4

10.5

10.6

# By the Numbers

## Is voting turnout declining in the United States?

Commentators have been decrying the declining rate of voting in the United States for many years now. All sorts of explanations have been advanced to explain the decline; all sorts of remedies for the problem have been proposed. But what if the decline is less severe than generally believed?

### Why It Matters

We have argued in this chapter that widespread participation in voting and other civic activities is one measure of the health of democracy in any society. If the way we measure participation is inaccurate, we cannot do a good job of assessing the quality of democracy in the United States, or identify what problems and shortcomings in our political system need to be addressed to make it more democratic.

### Behind the Traditional Voting Turnout Measure

Voter turnout in American elections *normally* is determined by a very simple calculation: the number of people who vote in a national election divided by the number of people in the United States who are of voting age, that is, 18 years of age and older. The denominator for this equation—voting-age population, or VAP—is provided by the Census Bureau. But there is a problem: the denominator may be misleading, because it includes millions of people who are not eligible to vote at all—residents who are not citizens, felons (some states), people with past felonies (some states), and the mentally incompetent. If we calculated voting turnout as the number of voters divided by the number of people in the United States who *actually* are eligible to vote—the voting-eligible population, or VEP—turnout would always be higher than is now reported because the denominator would be smaller.

### Calculating a VEP-based Measure of Turnout

Two political scientists, Michael McDonald and Samuel Popkin, have done us the great service of transforming the Census Bureau's VAP number to a VEP number for every national election from 1948 to 2012, pulling out noncitizens and ineligible felons and former felons in states where they cannot vote. Using the voting-eligible population rather than the resident population over the age of 18 as the denominator in the voting turnout equation, McDonald and Popkin's figures show the following:

- Voting turnout is actually four or five percentage points higher in recent elections than usually reported.

- Voting turnout declined between 1960 and 1972 regardless of which method was used. However, voting turnout appears to have declined further after 1972 only when using the traditional VAP method; the VEP method shows declines only in 1996 and 2012.

- Voting turnout jumped substantially in 2004 and 2008 for the hotly contested races between John Kerry and George W. Bush, and Barack Obama and John McCain, whether using the VEP numbers or the VAP numbers. Turnout dropped in 2012 for the Obama-Romney contest, however.

The main reason voting turnout has declined in recent elections using the traditional VAP method is that the number of people who are residents of the United States but who are not eligible to vote in American elections has increased at every election, mostly due to the number of noncitizens living here.

### Criticism of the VEP-based Measure of Turnout

Some critics suggest that the old way of calculating voting turnout serves a very useful purpose, namely, pointing out how far short we fall in our claim to being a democratic society. The low turnout number reported by VAP, it is argued, helps focus attention on the

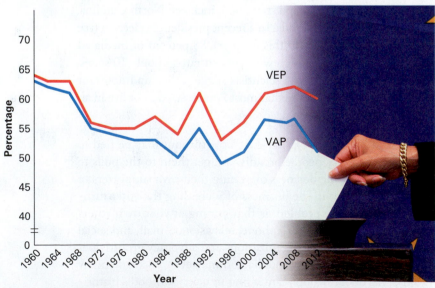

Voting Turnout in Presidential Elections by Year

*Sources:* Michael P. McDonald and Samuel L. Popkin, "The Myth of the Vanishing Voter," The American Political Science Review, 95, no. 4 (December 2001), pp. 963–974; authors' estimates based on data from Michael McDonald, "United States Elections Project," George Washington University, November 7, 2012.

10.1

10.2

10.3

10.4

10.5

10.6

*(Continued)*

issue of nonvoting in the United States and encourages efforts to reform voting rules to increase turnout. Even using the VEP-based measure, American voting turnout remains the lowest among the rich democracies of the world.

### What to Watch for

When you come across voter turnout numbers, pay attention to whether the figure has been calculated based on the voting-age population or on the voting-eligible population. The latter will always be higher than the former. It is important to be aware that both methods of

calculating turnout make sense in their own way; each has a slightly different story to tell.

### What Do You Think?

How could the United States increase the rate of voting turnout, which, regardless of the calculation method, is low in comparison to other democratic countries? Should we have compulsory voting in the United States like several other democratic countries? What are the pros and cons of making noncitizens—who pay taxes and are subject to U.S. laws—eligible to vote? How about former felons who have paid their debt to society?

Obama campaign in 2008 particularly effective in increasing voter turnout by knocking on the doors of potential voters.

**OTHER POSSIBILITIES** Political scientists, journalists, and political practitioners have suggested a number of other possible reasons for low turnout. For example, it may be that the increase in negative advertising, the increasing partisanship, and the growing incivility of American politics overall are adding to peoples' cynicism about the political system and politicians, causing Americans to turn away in disgust or despair. There has been some speculation that the time available to Americans for political participation has declined either because of longer working hours for many or because of the availability of other diversions, most especially television and the Internet. Unfortunately, scholars still are tussling with these issues; there is much disagreement among them about whether and the extent to which these factors affect voting turnout.[27]

# Who Votes?

**10.4**   Identify demographic factors that increase the likelihood of voting

Voting in the United States varies a great deal according to people's income, education, age, and ethnicity. This means that some kinds of people have more representation and influence with elected officials than others, and, other things being equal, they are more likely to have their preferences and interests reflected in what government does.

## ☐ Income and Education

For the most part, politically active people tend to be those with higher-than-average incomes and more formal education.[28] These people also are more likely to vote, even in off-year elections when there is not a presidential contest, when voting turnout for the entire population is about half of that during presidential election years. In the 2010 midterm elections, about 59 percent of those with incomes of $100,000 or above said they had voted, but only 43 percent of those with incomes under $50,000 said they had done so (see Figure 10.3). About 63 percent of those earning postgraduate degrees reported that they had voted, but only 35 percent of high school graduates and 21 percent of those who had not graduated from high school had done so. Some statistical analyses have indicated that the most important factor determining whether people vote is their level of formal education. When other factors are controlled—including race, income, and gender—college-educated people are much more likely to tell interviewers that they have voted than are the less educated. There are several possible reasons: people with more education learn more

10.1

10.2

10.3

10.4

10.5

10.6

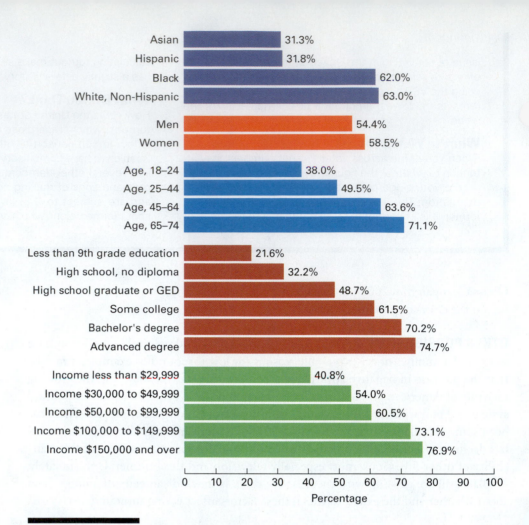

**FIGURE 10.3** CONGRESSIONAL ELECTION TURNOUT BY SOCIAL GROUP, 2012 ELECTIONS

Age, education, race, ethnicity, income, and gender all affect voting behavior. Members of certain social groups are more likely to vote in elections than others. The Census Bureau warns that these numbers may be inflated because of people's tendency to want to report positive citizen behavior to interviewers. What is important here, however, is not necessarily the accuracy of the turnout totals but the comparison between groups of people. The relative turnout comparisons between groups fit the general picture available from other academic research and government sources.

*Source:* U.S. Bureau of the Census, Voting and Registration in the Election of November 2012.

about politics, are less troubled by registration requirements, and are more confident in their ability to affect political life.

Looking at political participation more broadly, citizens with lower incomes are also less likely to work in campaigns, give money, contact officials, and the like. Wealthier Americans, who have more time, more money, and more knowledge of how to get things done, tend to be much more active politically. As a result, they may have more political clout than their fellow citizens.

## ☐ Race and Ethnicity

In the past, turnout among African Americans was lower than among whites, but the percentages have now become nearly equal. In fact, African Americans are at least equally like to vote, and sometimes more likely to vote, than whites of similar educational and income backgrounds. The 2012 presidential election reflects this trend. For the first time ever, among those who were registered to vote, turnout was higher among African Americans than whites, with 66.2 percent of voting-eligible African Americans voting compared with 64.1 percent of voting-eligible whites.[29]

In contrast, Hispanic voters have historically had very low participation rates; many are discouraged from participating by low incomes, language problems, or suspicion of government authorities. Although Hispanics continue to vote at lower rates than other Americans with a similar income and educational profile, their turnout at the polls has been increasing, reaching 31.8 percent in 2012.[30] In both 2008 and 2012, the presidential candidates made special efforts to win over this increasingly influential group, and the role of Hispanics in closely contested battleground states such as Florida, Nevada, Colorado, and New Mexico—all won by Barack Obama—demonstrates their rising importance. It may be that the harsh anti-immigrant legislation passed in the last few years by Alabama, Arizona, Georgia, Indiana, and South Carolina, which have angered Latinos, against whom these laws have been directed, may increase voting turnout among Latinos, as these things generally do. To have a big impact, however, Latinos would need to raise their rates of voter registration, which are well below those of other groups in the population. In 2012, for example, only 42 percent of eligible Latino voters in Nevada were registered, and only 35 percent were registered in Virginia, both important battleground states.[31]

Voting has also been relatively low among Asian Americans; about 31.3 percent reported voting in 2012, very similar to turnout for Latinos. Like Latinos, voting turnout has increased in recent elections, as have Asian American contributions to candidates and parties. Moreover, Asian American individuals and organizations have become more active in local politics.

Two important trends will change the American electorate dramatically over the next fifty years. The first is the decreasing share of the overall population that is white. The second is increasing turnout among other racial groups, especially Hispanics and Asian Americans. These two trends are combining to produce an electorate that is increasingly nonwhite. In the 1996 presidential election, 82.5 percent of all voters were white. That number has decreased in every subsequent presidential election, and by 2012, it was only 73.7 percent. Demographers and political scientists expect it to keep dropping for the foreseeable future, dramatically altering the national political landscape.[32]

## ☐ Age

Age is one of the most important variables when explaining why some people vote and others do not. The youngest groups of eligible voters go to the polls much less often than older voters. This was true even in the exciting 2008 presidential election when young people played such a visible role in the Obama campaign in organizing state and local campaign organizations and get-out-the-vote efforts. Though 2 million more 18- to 24-year-olds voted than in 2004, their voting turnout was still only 48.5 percent (up 2 percent from the previous presidential election, to be sure).[33] In comparison, turnout among older voters age 65 to 74 was 70 percent. In the 2012 election, turnout among 18- to 24-year-olds was only 38 percent, while among those 65 and older, it was about 71 percent. The reasons for low turnout among young people may be that they tend to be less rooted in communities, less familiar with registration and voting procedures, less in the habit of voting, and have less time away from school and work to vote.[34]

## ☐ Gender

Women were prevented from participating in politics for a large part of our history; they got the vote, by constitutional amendment, only in 1920. Not all women immediately took advantage of this new opportunity. For many years, women voted and participated in politics at lower rates than men—about 10 or 15 percent lower in the elections of the 1950s, for example. The gender gap in voting and other forms of political participation disappeared in the United States by the end of the 1980s and today women actually vote at a higher rate than men (by about 4 percent).[35] (Refer again to Figure 10.3.) This marks a dramatic change over the past two or three decades and can probably be traced to the improvement in the educational attainments of women, the entrance

10.1

10.2

10.3

10.4

10.5

10.6

10.1

10.2

10.3

10.4

10.5

10.6

of more women than ever into the paid workforce, and the increased importance of issues such as pay equity and abortion on the American political agenda.

## ☐ Does It Matter Who Votes?

Some observers have argued that it doesn't matter if many people don't vote, because their preferences aren't much different from those who do; the results would be about the same if everyone voted. In some elections, nonvoters have shown support for the same candidate who won, so their votes would apparently have changed nothing,[36] and some surveys have indicated that nonvoters' policy preferences differ little from those of voters.

However, we should not be too quick to accept these arguments, just as few now accept the nineteenth-century view that there was no need for women to vote because their husbands could protect their interests. Even when the expressed preferences of nonvoters or nonparticipators do not look very distinctive, their objective circumstances, and therefore their needs for government services, may differ markedly.[37] Latinos, the young, and those with low incomes might benefit from government programs that are of less interest to other citizens.[38] A political system that included and mobilized these people vigorously might produce quite different government policies. There is a growing body of evidence, in fact, that high- and low-income people in the United States have very different preferences about what government should do and that elected officials are more likely to attend to the views of higher-income groups than others.[39] It is also known that government efforts to compensate people with low incomes in the rich democracies are associated with the degree to which low-income people vote, with the United States, where low-income people participate at far lower rates than others, doing the least in this area of government activity.[40]

**MOBILIZING THE YOUTH VOTE**
College Democrats at Boston University register students to vote in the upcoming national elections, trying to match the high turnout of the youth vote that occurred in 2008 that was so helpful to Democrats.

# Campaigning for Office

T he ideas we discussed about how elections might ensure democratic policymaking all depend in various ways on what sorts of choices are presented to the voters. It makes a difference what kind of people run for office, whether they take clear policy stands, whether those stands differ from each other, and whether they stand for what the average voter wants. In evaluating how democratic our elections are, therefore, we need to examine what kinds of alternatives are put before the voters in campaigns. We consider these issues in this section focusing on presidential elections only.

## ☐ Gaining the Nomination

The first step for someone seeking the presidency is winning the nomination of one's own party. (For sitting presidents seeking a second term, such as George Bush in 2004 and Barack Obama in 2012, this is normally not a serious problem; they are the presumptive nominees of their party.) In a formal sense, the Republican and Democratic presidential nominees are selected at their national conventions the summer before the presidential election. In both parties, the nomination goes to the winner of a majority of delegates to the national party convention mostly chosen in state primaries and caucuses (to be described later). The Democrats' popularly elected primary and caucus delegates are supplemented by **superdelegates**, usually party luminaries and elected officials, including members of Congress, and state and local officials. In 2012, about one-in-five delegates to the Democratic National Convention fell into this category. About the same proportion of delegates to the Republican National Convention were "unpledged," not called superdelegates, but playing the same role as superdelegates in the Democratic nominating process: allowing the party establishment to have a voice at the national convention, serving as a counterweight to delegates selected in primaries and caucuses dominated by the most ideologically committed party voters.

**WHO HAS A CHANCE**  In any given presidential election, only a handful of candidates are serious possibilities. So far in American history, these have virtually always been middle-aged or elderly white men with extensive formal educations, fairly high incomes,[41] and substantial experience as public figures—usually as government officials (especially vice presidents, governors, or senators) or military heroes. The Democrats broke the white male mold in 2008 when Hillary Clinton came close to winning the nomination in a tight race with the eventual winner, Barack Obama, an African American. Movie stars, media commentators, business executives, and others who would be president almost always have to perform important government service before they are seriously considered for the presidency. Ronald Reagan, for example, most of whose career was spent acting in motion pictures and on television, served as governor of California before being elected president. In addition to being a successful businessman at Bain Capital, 2012 Republican presidential nominee Mitt Romney served as governor of Massachusetts. His Republican rivals for the nomination also had extensive government experience. Rick Santorum was a former U.S. senator from Pennsylvania. Newt Gingrich, best known at the beginning of the 2011–2012 election cycle as a conservative media commentator, writer, and lobbyist, served in the 1990s as the Republican Speaker of the House.

The single best stepping-stone to becoming president has been the vice presidency, which is usually filled by former senators or governors. Since 1900, 5 of the 18 presidents have succeeded from the vice presidency after the president's death or resignation, and two others, Nixon and Bush (the elder), were former vice presidents elected in their own right.

It used to be the case that serious candidates for president almost invariably represented mainstream American values and policy preferences. Seldom had an "extreme"

**superdelegates**
Elected officials from all levels of government who are appointed by party committees to be delegates to the national convention of the Democratic Party; not selected in primary elections or caucuses.

10.1

10.2

10.3

10.4

10.5

10.6

10.1

10.2

10.3

10.4

10.5

10.6

**GATHERING VOTES**

In addition to living room coffee klatches and rallies, contenders for the presidential nomination in each of the parties spend considerable time on the phones with potential voters trying to get them to the polls. During New Hampshire's presidential primary, in early 2012, eventual Republican nominee Mitt Romney joined campaign staffers in asking potential voters for their support. Must candidates engage in these forms of retail politics to gain the nomination or would television advertising, use of social media, and rallies be a better use of the time and resources of candidates?

candidate—that is, a candidate who appeals only to active partisans in a party—gotten very far. In the 2011–2012 election cycle, Newt Gingrich, and then Rick Santorum, made a serious run for the Republican nomination, having generated much excitement among the most conservative Republicans and Tea Party activists, but the nomination went to so-called establishment candidate Mitt Romney. Most of the time, serious candidates must be acceptable not only to the party base but to the business community and have enthusiastic support from at least some sectors of industry or finance. They also must be considered "presidential" by the news media and find some support among independent voters. And they must be attractive to those individuals and groups that fund campaigns. With the rise of super PACs, however, more nonmainstream candidates may be able to hang around longer. A big contribution by a rich contributor to a super PAC supporting such a candidate can keep him or her in a nomination contest even if that candidate has not won a string of state contests. That happened in the 2012 GOP nomination race when Newt Gingrich was supported by Winning Our Future, largely funded by Las Vegas gambling and hotel magnate Sheldon Adelson. Though he had only a handful of delegates and no chance of winning the Republican nomination, his rich backers allowed Gingrich to stay in the nomination race until late April.

**GETTING STARTED** A person who wants to run for the presidency usually begins at least two or three years before the election by testing the waters, asking friends and financial backers if they will support a run, and observing how people react to the mythical "Great Mentioner." A friendly journalist may write that Senator Blathers "has been mentioned" as a smart, attractive, strong candidate; Blathers waits to see whether anyone agrees. The would-be candidate may commission a national survey to check for name recognition and a positive image. He or she may put together an exploratory committee to round up private endorsements, commitments, and financial contributions, perhaps setting up private political action committees to gather money.

If all goes well in the early stages, the presidential aspirant becomes more serious, assembling a group of close advisers, formulating strategy, officially announcing his or her candidacy, forming a fund-raising operation, setting up campaign and personal websites, and putting together organizations in key states. Early money is crucial to finance organization and advertising.[42] Raising serious money from donors big and small—the latter, primarily through the Internet—is a clear sign to party bigwigs, associated interest and advocacy groups, and the news media that a candidate ought to be taken seriously. The relationship between money-raising and consideration as a serious candidate is now so important that it is commonly called the "invisible primary" and the "money primary."[43]

It is a vicious cycle of sorts. If a candidate can't raise money, she or he is not taken seriously. If a candidate is not taken seriously, then raising money becomes even more difficult. And with little money in the bank and not much coming in, failure in the first primaries and caucuses is inevitable. Candidates who can't raise money drop out early. In 2008, Bill Richardson, John Edwards, and Christopher Dodd were gone early from the Democratic nomination race, facing the awesome campaign finance machines of Hillary Clinton and Barack Obama, each of whom had raised about $100 million by the end of 2007 and each of whom was spending money almost as fast as it was coming in. In 2012, Mitt Romney easily won the money contest, persuading those without much money (or standing in the polls), such as Michele Bachmann, Jon Huntsman, and Tim Pawlenty to drop out. According to most estimates, the candidates, the parties, and political action committees combined to spend almost $1 billion *per candidate* during the primary and general election campaigns in 2012.

At one time, an important early decision was whether to be a part of the public campaign finance system—in which the federal government matches the first $250 from each individual donor on condition that candidates in the 2007–2008 election cycle limit preconvention campaign spending to around $50 million—or to go it alone, raise hard money contributions from individuals (limited to $2,500 in 2012) and PACs (limited to $5,000), and spend what they wish. But things began to change in 2000 when George W. Bush became the first serious candidate to eschew public financing since it was first established in 1976. Democrats John Kerry and Howard Dean, as well as Republican President Bush, skipped public funding in 2004. In the 2007–2008 election cycle, none of the leading contenders for the presidential nomination in either party, with the exception of John Edwards, chose public funding with its attendant spending limits, nor did any of the major contenders do so in the 2011–2012 cycle.

Public financing of presidential nomination campaigns seems to be going by the wayside for two reasons. First, the costs of running a credible campaign for the party presidential nomination have gone up much faster than the amount that candidates who choose the public funding route are allowed to spend. Most candidates do not want to handcuff themselves in this way. Second, it is easier now to raise money outside the public financing system. The campaign reform act in 2002 substantially increased the amount of money individuals can give to candidates. The Internet—typically e-mail blasts and appeals on social media sites such as Facebook—has proved to be an incredibly efficient and cost-effective device for raising lots of money from individual contributors, something Barack Obama did particularly well in both 2008 and 2012. And, though not officially part of their campaigns, super PACs and 501 advocacy organizations, often run by close associates and friends of the candidates, can raise unlimited amounts of money from corporations, unions, and wealthy individuals, then spend that money on advertising supporting that candidate and attacking his or her opponents.

Another important early decision involves which state primaries and caucus contests to enter. Each entry takes a lot of money, energy, and organization, and any loss is damaging; many candidates drop out after just a few early defeats, as John Edwards, Fred Thompson, and Mitt Romney did in 2008 and Michele Bachmann, Tim Pawlenty, and Rick Perry did in 2012. To win the nomination, it is generally necessary to put together a string of primary and caucus victories, something John McCain was able to do in 2008, starting with New Hampshire. By the end of the day on March 4, after winning the big primaries in Ohio and Texas, he had secured the nomination with a majority of Republican convention delegates pledged to him, an outcome made possible by the

10.1

10.2

10.3

10.4

10.5

10.6

10.1

10.2

10.3

10.4

10.5

10.6

winner-take-all rules then in effect in the Republican Party. With fewer winner-take-all state primaries and caucuses in effect in the Republican Party in 2012, and with many in the base of the party trying out first one, then another conservative alternative to Mitt Romney—Rick Perry, Newt Gingrich, Rick Santorum, and, for a dedicated handful, Ron Paul—it took much longer for Romney to emerge as the presumptive nominee.

**PRESIDENTIAL PRIMARIES AND CAUCUSES** Since 1952, no national party convention has taken more than one ballot to nominate its candidate for the presidency, and the pre-convention front-runner has always been the nominee.[44] Since the 1970s, a majority of the delegates to the conventions in each party have been chosen in state primary or caucus elections, with direct voting by citizens. A small majority of these primaries are closed, meaning they are open only to voters who have registered Republican or Democrat before the date of the primary; the others are open to all voters, who can decide on the day of the election which party's ballot they wish to take into the voting booth. Republicans had 12 open primaries or caucuses during the 2012 nomination season, while Democrats had 18. Parties have been known to encourage their supporters to enter the other party's primary in a bid to damage the opposition's front-runner. There were press reports in 2012, for example, that party officials were encouraging Democrats to vote for Rick Santorum in the Ohio primary as a way to deny a victory to the presumptive front-runner, Mitt Romney (it didn't work; Romney eked out a victory). Whether a primary is closed or open also can affect how candidates run their campaigns. Because closed primaries mean that the bulk of the voters likely will be party loyalists, candidates tend to pitch their appeal to the party base. (Thus the frequent attacks on government regulatory agencies such as the Environmental Protections Agency. See the "Can Government Do Anything Well?" feature.) In open primaries with more diverse voters, candidates tend to make broader appeals. Many states—most famously Iowa, with the first on the calendar—use caucuses, where active party members and officials gather in meetings to select the delegates to the national convention. To confuse matters even further, some states select convention delegates in primaries and caucuses.

It is especially important for a candidate to establish momentum by winning early primaries and caucuses. Early winners get press attention, financial contributions, and better standings in the polls as voters and contributors decide they are viable candidates and must have some merit if people in other states have supported them. All these factors—attention from the media, money, and increased popular support—help the candidates who win early contests go on to win more and more contests.[45]

Because the states and the parties—not Congress or the president—control this nominating process, the system is a disorganized, even chaotic one, and it changes from one election to the next. Some states have primaries for both parties on the same day (including the important New Hampshire primaries); others hold primaries for the parties on separate dates. States are particularly anxious that they are not ignored, so an increasing number of them have moved their primary and caucus dates forward in the calendar. States with late primaries, even very large ones such as California, discovered in recent elections that the winners of early primaries had, for all intents and purposes, sewed up the party nominations, discounting the importance of their own primaries and caucuses. As a result, the primary and caucus season started to get "front-loaded" in 2004, then accelerated in 2008 when it became a stampede, with states leap-frogging over the others to position themselves earlier in the calendar. The result in 2008 was that 20 states—including big ones such as New York, New Jersey, Illinois, Missouri, and California—held their primaries on February 5, only a little more than a month after the first caucus in Iowa on January 3 (always the first caucus by state law) and a little less than a month after the first-in-the-nation primary in New Hampshire (always the first primary by state law) on January 8. The large states of Florida and Michigan held their Democratic primaries in mid and late January, respectively, against the rules of the Democratic National Committee, and were penalized for doing so. Perhaps ironically, the Clinton–Obama race was so close that states with late primaries, such as North Carolina and Indiana, became very important in 2008.

Both parties passed rules after this to slow or reverse the trend toward front-loading and early winner-take-all primaries, but Florida, Michigan, and Arizona Republicans

10.1

10.2

10.3

10.4

10.5

10.6

# Can Government Do Anything Well?

## The Environmental Protection Agency

Candidates for the 2012 GOP presidential nomination couldn't get enough of the EPA. The agency came up in nearly every televised debate. Michele Bachmann said she wanted to "padlock the EPA's doors." Newt Gingrich proposed that the EPA be eliminated, as did Rick Santorum. Rick Perry proposed an immediate moratorium on new EPA regulations. (As Texas governor, Perry led a group of states in a lawsuit to prevent the EPA from issuing rules on greenhouse gas emissions from power plants, refineries, and mining operations.) Ron Paul saw no need for a significant federal role, believing that the proper tax incentives would allow the private sector to address $CO_2$ emissions and other pollutants. Mitt Romney, somewhat favorable at times to the EPA, still said he wanted the EPA to stop issuing regulations on $CO_2$ emissions.

The Environmental Protection Agency was created in 1970 during the presidency of Republican Richard Nixon. Its mission was to conduct or sponsor scientific research on the human impacts of air and water pollution and to issue regulations affecting private firms and government entities that emit pollutants. In issuing regulations, the agency is responsible for maintaining national standards set by federal statutes that limit air pollution, water pollution, and hazardous waste. From the beginning, business has been hostile to the agency, claiming that its rules make doing business more expensive, undercutting profits and destroying jobs. Over the years, the Republican Party has joined business in opposition to the EPA. Democrats, more supportive of an activist government primed to solve social and economic problems, have become champions of the agency.

What has widened the partisan divide even further was the declaration in 2009 by the EPA that greenhouse gas emissions posed a threat to human health because of their role in causing global warming and that it would issue rules regulating such emissions. Acting on a suit brought by a broad coalition of industry groups, the Supreme Court ruled in 2011 that the EPA was acting properly under authority granted to it by Congress. The Supreme Court affirmed, in 2014, the EPA's regulation of emissions from power plants, which will affect mainly plants fueled by coal. Needless to say, Republicans were not pleased, given the widespread belief among party supporters and activists that global warming does not exist and, if it does, is not caused by human activity, including $CO_2$ emissions.

*Support for the claim that government can and should regulate air and water pollution and greenhouse gas emissions:*

- The EPA has a solid record in regulating pollutants that degrade human health: lead in paints and gasoline, DDT and other harmful pesticides and herbicides, for example.

- EPA rules have forced local governments to provide safe drinking water.

- The EPA played in big role in the effort to eliminate ozone layer–depleting fluorocarbons in products.

- Agency rules forced a cutback in dumping sewage in coastal waters.

- Agency rules on emissions from chemical plants in 1997 led to the reduction of air pollutants from that source by 90 percent.

- Solid scientific research supports the move by the EPA, using its authority under the Clean Air Act, to define $CO_2$ emissions as harmful to human health and issue rules starting in 2011 to lower such emissions.

*Rejection of the claim that government can and should regulate air and water pollution and greenhouse gas emissions:*

- EPA regulations hurt business by increasing their operating expenses, and when businesses are hurting they do not hire.

- EPA regulations cost state and local governments a great deal of money to comply; this takes money away from other needs and raises taxes for the people.

- Like most regulatory agencies, the EPA over-regulates; it does more than what is optimal to guard against pollution and its effects.

- Many EPA regulations are based on poor science; this is especially true for the research linking $CO_2$ to global warming and to ill effects on humans.

- EPA regulations adversely affect economic growth, which is a key correlate of a healthy population; by slowing growth, the EPA adversely affects human well-being in the United States.

- EPA regulations are hurting the economic recovery from the Great Recession, the deepest since the Great Depression.

10.1
10.2
10.3
10.4
10.5
10.6

(Continued)

## WHAT DO YOU THINK?

What do you think about the past, present, and future role of the EPA in regulating air and water pollution and greenhouse gas emissions?

- EPA policies and regulations have been beneficial to the United States as a whole, and the EPA should vigorously pursue its mandate in rule-making; funding should continue to be allocated to this important government agency.
- EPA policies and regulations have been net beneficial to the United States as a whole, but at times efforts have been contrary to business interests; it should rescind its most egregious regulations and refrain from issuing new ones that hurt the economy.
- EPA policies are almost always contrary to business interests and hurt the economy; the agency should have its budget drastically reduced or be abolished.

How would you defend your position to a fellow student? What would be your main line of argument? What evidence do you believe best supports your position? For help in developing your argument, please refer to the sources listed in the "Can Government Do Anything Well" feature in Chapter 2 on p. 48.

bucked party rules to hold their binding primaries in January and February during the 2012 nomination season even though doing so cost them one-half of their delegates at the Republican National Convention. Nevertheless, by dissuading a number of states from moving up in the calendar and with a number of states moving from a winner-take-all to proportional selection of delegates, the Republican nomination battle extended far later into the spring than usually is the case for the Republican Party. No candidate, including the early presumptive party nominee Mitt Romney, could deliver an early knockout blow and secure the nomination. Like Obama in 2008, Romney failed to win in the first two months after Iowa and New Hampshire but was able to slowly and steadily accumulate delegates over a longer period leading up to the convention.

**THE PRESIDENTIAL NOMINATING CONVENTIONS** Because the front-runner now comes to the national convention with enough delegates to win on the first ballot, the gathering has become a coronation ceremony in which pre-pledged delegates ratify the selection of the leading candidate, accept that candidate's choice for the vice presidency, and put on a colorful show for the media and the country. Enthusiasm and unity are staged for the national television audience. Barack Obama's acceptance speech before 80,000 wildly cheering supporters at Invesco Field in Denver drew a national television audience of more than 38 million in 2008, though the crowd was much smaller for his acceptance speech in Charlotte, North Carolina, in 2012, reflecting lower enthusiasm among his supporters. John McCain's "town hall–style" acceptance speech at the Republican National Convention in St. Paul, Minnesota, before an equally enthusiastic crowd, drew an even larger national television audience, though only about 30 million Americans, around 1 in 8, watched Romney's acceptance speech in 2012.

It is a disaster for a political party if serious conflicts break out or the timing of the elaborate nomination process goes wrong. The Democrats were in turmoil over the Vietnam War at their 1968 gathering, for example, with the conflict played out on the convention floor and in the streets of Chicago, carried live on television. By all accounts, the conflict and disunity played a role in Hubert Humphrey's loss in the general election to Republican Richard Nixon. In 1972, conflict between the eventual nominee George McGovern and Ted Kennedy, as well as procedural snafus, meant that McGovern didn't deliver his televised acceptance speech until early morning, well after most people on the East Coast and in the Midwest had gone to bed.

**NOMINATING INCUMBENT PRESIDENTS** We have been focusing on how outsiders and political challengers try to win party presidential nominations. Things are very different for incumbent presidents seeking reelection, like Bill Clinton in 1996 or George W. Bush in 2004 or Barack Obama in 2012. These candidates must also enter and win primaries and caucuses, but they have the machinery of government working for them and, if times are reasonably good, a unified party behind them. They also have an easier time getting campaign contributions, especially for the primaries when incumbent presidents only occasionally meet serious competition. They campaign on the job, taking credit for policy successes while discounting or blaming others, such as Congress, for failures. Winning renomination as president is usually easy, except in cases of disaster such as the 1968 Vietnam War debacle for Lyndon Johnson.

**NOMINATION POLITICS AND DEMOCRACY**  What does all this have to do with democratic control of government? Several things. On the one hand, as we have indicated, the presidential nomination process has some success in coming up with candidates who take stands with wide popular appeal, much as electoral competition theories dictate. On the other hand, as the sharp differences between Republican and Democratic convention delegates suggest (see Table 9.2), Republican and Democratic nominees tend to differ in certain systematic ways, in responsible party fashion. Party platforms—the parties' official statements of their stand on issues—tend to include appeals to average voters but also distinctive appeals to each party's base constituencies.

Both these tendencies might be considered good for democracy. However, the crucial role of party activists and money-givers in selecting candidates means that nominees and their policy stands are chosen partly to appeal to party elites, financial contributors, and strong partisans rather than to ordinary voters. Thus, neither party's nominee may stand for what ordinary citizens want, the result being voter dissatisfaction and no ideal democratic outcome.

10.1
10.2
10.3
10.4
10.5
10.6

THE PUBLIC FACE OF PARTY CONVENTIONS

The impression conveyed by political conventions can have an important impact on elections. The apparent unhappiness of many anti–Vietnam War delegates with their party's selection at the 1968 Democratic convention in Chicago severely damaged the campaign of nominee Hubert Humphrey. In contrast, the 1984 Republican convention that selected Ronald Reagan as its nominee more nearly resembled a coronation and gave Reagan and the GOP a fast start in the fall campaign. Are party conventions still necessary? Might there be an easier way to certify each party's nominee? Do they still exist because of their pep-rally appeal?

10.1

10.2

10.3

10.4

10.5

10.6

# ☐ The General Election Campaign

The general election campaign pitting the candidates of the two major parties against one another, with an occasional third party thrown into the mix, is a very different sort of contest than the run for party nomination. It requires different things from the candidates, campaign organizations, and associated interest and advocacy groups, and has an entirely different tone and set of rules, both formal and informal. The general election campaign season, much like the nomination campaign season, has gotten much longer as well. For a discussion of the 2012 presidential campaign and election, please refer again to the chapter-opening story.

**GETTING THE CAMPAIGN UP AND RUNNING**  In the not-too-distant past, the general election campaign generally began on or about Labor Day, some weeks after the Republican and Democratic conventions were done with their business. That's why it was referred to as the "autumn campaign" and the "fall campaign." Today, however, as we have suggested, the presidential nominees for both parties are known months before the conventions even convene and they begin to campaign for the presidency months before their formal nomination. Flush with campaign money and unworried about their no-longer-relevant challengers within their own party, the presumptive nominees of each party begin to reposition their campaigns by mid-spring to take on their general election foe: setting up a campaign organization in each state, sending aides to coordinate backers and local party leaders, and continuing the money-raising effort. Barack Obama swung into general election mode by early June in 2008 once he had bested Hillary Clinton for the nomination. In 2012, major advertising campaigns by the Obama and Romney camps were well underway in important swing states by late May, months before either was confirmed as the official nominee of his respective party.[46]

Once the post-convention autumn campaign begins in September, the candidates' staffs have the nominees making speeches in six or seven media markets each week, with the pace intensifying as the November election draws closer, concentrating on so-called battleground states, where the contest between the presidential candidates is deemed to be very close and could go either way (see the "Mapping American Politics" feature on campaign ad buys). In all of this, hired pollsters and campaign consultants are deeply involved, playing a role in virtually all tactical and strategic decision making.[47]

Besides speeches, campaigns invest heavily in television advertising. Much of the advertising consists of "attack" ads. In 2012, Barack Obama's campaign ran ads targeting Mitt Romney's income and investments, accusing Romney of hiding money in Caribbean banks accounts to avoid paying U.S. taxes. Romney ran ads that pilloried the president for doing nothing about a worsening economy. Political consultants use voter focus groups to identify hot-button emotional appeals. Negative advertising, whether print, on television, or on the Internet, has been heavily criticized as simplistic and misleading, but it has often proved effective and is difficult to control or counteract. (Some scholars even argue that such ads increase voter interest and provide needed information.)[48]

Each campaign uses micro-targeting techniques to identify and communicate with base supporters and persuadable voters who might be convinced to vote for the candidate. Sophisticated software allows campaign organizations to combine surveys, census tract data, and materials from marketing research firms to identify base and persuadable voters and to tailor messages to particular groups and people and deliver the message by mail, door-to-door canvassing, e-mail, and social-network tools. Republican messages are directed, for example, not only to well-off people but more specifically to those who subscribe to *Golf Weekly* and shop at Saks Fifth Avenue. Democratic messages, using the same micro-targeting, might be directed to members of teachers unions and contributors to the American Civil Liberties Union.[49]

In all of these activities, presidential candidates, with lots of help to be sure, run their own campaigns. They and not the political parties decide on campaign themes, schedules, and strategies. The national party organizations are there to help, running parallel advertising campaigns supporting their candidate and attacking the opponent, channelling money to state and local party organizations, and getting potential supporters registered and to the polls. Meanwhile, interest groups and advocacy

10.1

10.2

10.3

10.4

10.5

10.6

**OBAMA ON THE CAMPAIGN TRAIL**

Until the early years of the twentieth century, it was considered unseemly for a sitting president to campaign for his own reelection. Modern presidents are deeply engaged in their campaigns, spending as much time as possible on television and video-friendly events available for broad distribution.

organizations run their own ad campaigns and get-out-the-vote efforts. Liberal advocacy organizations such as MoveOn.org, for example, run ads in support of the Democratic presidential candidate (and House and Senate Democratic candidates), raise money, and work on turning out Democrats, while conservative Christian groups and business-oriented organizations work to help the Republican side. Now, since *Citizens United v. Federal Election Commission* (2010), corporations, unions, and rich individuals can give without limit in support of or in opposition to candidates so long as they don't give money directly to the candidates' official campaign organizations.

**INFORMING VOTERS** What kinds of information do voters get in presidential campaigns? Among other things, voters get information on the candidates' stands on the issues, their past performances, and their personal characteristics.

***Issues*** Some of the information voters get concerns issues. In accord with electoral competition theories, both the Republican and the Democratic candidates typically have tried to appeal to the average voter by taking similar, popular stands on a range of policies, whether it be support for federal student loan programs or proposals to create more jobs. In recent elections, however, intensification of partisanship has moved American presidential and congressional electoral campaigns in a more responsible party direction, with clear stands on the issues, differentiated from the other party. In 2012, Barack Obama and Mitt Romney took decidedly different stands on major issues, especially on the economy and the size of the national debt, abortion, global climate change, and health care reform. On these issues, the Democratic candidate tends to take a more liberal (on both economic and social dimensions) stand than the Republican, just as Democratic Party identifiers, activists, money givers, and convention delegates tend to be more liberal than their Republican counterparts.

***Past Performance*** Often candidates focus on past performance in their campaigns. The "outs" blame the "ins" for wars, recessions, and other calamities. The "ins" brag about how they have brought peace and prosperity and paint a warm picture of a glorious future, without saying exactly how it will come about. When these issues become the overriding theme in a campaign, the result is a "retrospective," "reward–punish" type of election. Democrat Franklin Roosevelt won a landslide victory in 1932, for example,

**303**

10.1

10.2

10.3

10.4

10.5

10.6

because of popular discontent with government performance under Herbert Hoover in the face of the Great Depression; Republican Ronald Reagan capitalized on economic and foreign policy troubles under Jimmy Carter to win in 1980.

***Personal Characteristics*** Most of all, however, voters get a chance during the general election campaign to learn about the real or alleged personal characteristics of the candidates. Even when the candidates are talking about something else, they give an impression of either competence or incompetence and likeability. Mitt Romney, for example, often seemed like he didn't understand the common voter, which may have hurt him in the election.

Candidates also come across as interpersonally warm or cold. Dwight D. Eisenhower's radiant grin appeared everywhere in 1952 and 1956, as Reagan's did in 1984, but Richard Nixon was perceived as cold and aloof in 1968, despite clever efforts at selling his personality.

Still another dimension of candidates' personalities is a candidate's presumed strength or weakness, which is especially important to voters when considering how the candidates will deal with foreign governments and enemies. In 2004, George W. Bush was perceived as being better able to deal with terrorism compared to his opponent John Kerry, whom the Bush campaign sought to portray as weak on terrorism.

The sparse and ambiguous treatment of policy issues in campaigns, as well as the emphasis on past performance and personal competence, fits better with ideas about electoral reward and punishment than with responsible parties or issue-oriented electoral competition models of democratic elections. To be sure, candidate personalities are not irrelevant to the democratic control of government. Obviously, it is useful for voters to pick presidents who possess competence, warmth, and strength. And citizens may be more skillful in judging people than in figuring out complicated policy issues.

Voters can be fooled, however, by dirty tricks or slick advertising that sells presidential candidates' personalities and tears down the opponent. Moreover, the focus on personal imagery may distract attention from policy stands. If candidates who favor unpopular policies are elected on the basis of attractive personal images, democratic control of policymaking is weakened. By the purchase of advertising and the hiring of smart consultants, money may, in effect, overcome the popular will.

## ☐ Money in General Elections

Money plays a crucial role in American general election campaigns and elections. Not surprisingly, parties and candidates spend much of their time and effort raising money for campaigns.

**THE SCALE OF CAMPAIGN MONEY AND WHERE IT COMES FROM** Presidential campaigns cost a great deal of money, although the system is so complex that even seasoned observers can make only educated guesses about the total. We have good data on money coming from certain sources but not from others. For example, we know that federal candidates during the 2007–2008 election cycle spent around $5.3 billion,[50] and more than $6 billion during the 2011–2012 cycle,[51] but we are less sure about a wide range of other expenditures on their behalf by advocacy groups. What we do know is that, considering only monies officially reported (so-called hard money), the total that is raised and spent from one presidential election cycle to the next keeps increasing and shows no signs of slowing down (see Figure 10.4).

**"HARD" AND "SOFT" MONEY** Hard money refers to contributions made directly to candidates and party committees that fall under the jurisdiction of the Federal Election Commission (the FEC). FEC rules are the result of (1) the Federal Election Campaign Act (FECA), and its later amendments passed during the 1970s, and (2) the Bipartisan Campaign Reform Act of 2002, also called the McCain-Feingold bill after its two primary sponsors. The implementation of both laws is governed by Supreme Court rulings and by administrative rules established by the FEC. Hard money is difficult to raise because of regulations on the size of donations, but it can be used for most campaign activities, including advocating for or against candidates. Soft money is not as tightly regulated by the FEC because it is donated to state or local, as opposed to federal, parties or candidates. Soft money was originally intended to be used for "party-building"

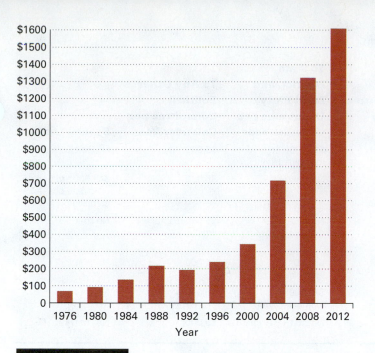

10.1

10.2

10.3

10.4

10.5

10.6

**FIGURE 10.4** THE GROWTH IN HARD MONEY SPENDING IN PRESIDENTIAL ELECTIONS (in millions of dollars)*

*Spending by candidates, party, and independent committees as reported to the Federal Election Commission. All numbers are based on summary reports filed with the FEC. The election data for 2012 are based on preliminary estimates.

*Source:* The Center for Responsive Politics.

activities like voter drives, not for advocating for specific candidates. However, in the past soft money has often been used to run "issue" ads, criticizing candidates for their positions without directly championing their defeat. After the 2002 election cycle, when both parties raised more than $500 million in soft money, Congress aimed to increase regulation of soft money with the passage of the McCain-Feingold law.

***Individuals*** The largest single source of hard money funding for presidential campaigns is from individual contributors, ranging from those who made small contributions to the candidates in response to an e-mail or letter solicitation or a call from a party worker, to wealthier individuals who gave the maximum amount allowed in 2013 of $2,600 to a single candidate (or a total of $46,200 to several candidates) and $32,400 to a national party committee per year. (See Table 10.1 for FEC rules on contributions limits for the 2013–2014 election cycle.) Before passage of the Federal Election Campaign Act (FECA), individuals could make contributions of unlimited size, and candidates and the parties depended on a handful of very rich individuals to fund their operations. After limits were placed on the size of allowable contributions, both parties invented a variety of ways to attract small contributions from hundreds of thousands of people, beginning with targeted mail and telephone solicitations. The rise of Internet fund-raising has made campaigns much more reliant on small donations from individual contributors but has also allowed candidates to raise much more money because of the sheer number of individuals who contribute. Indeed, Barack Obama raised approximately $233 million from small contributors in 2012, while Mitt Romney raised about $80 million.

***Candidates*** Candidates seeking a party's nomination will sometimes contribute or lend money to their campaigns; both John McCain and Hillary Clinton did this during the primaries in 2007 and 2008. Once each party chooses its nominee for the presidency, candidates have no need to use personal resources because money is coming in from other sources.

***Political Action Committees (PACs)*** You will recall that PACs are entities created by interest groups—whether business firms, unions, membership organizations, or liberal and conservative advocacy groups—to collect money and make contributions to candidates in federal elections (i.e., to candidates for the presidency, the House of Representatives, and the Senate). In 2012, PACs raised about $2 billion to contribute to presidential and congressional candidates, party committees, and their own electioneering campaigning (television, radio, and Internet advertising on the issues or candidates).[52]

10.1
10.2
10.3
10.4
10.5
10.6

**TABLE 10.1** HARD MONEY CONTRIBUTION LIMITS, 2013–2014

| | To Each Candidate or Candidate Committee per Election | To National Party Committee per Calendar Year | To State, District, and Local Party Committee per Calendar Year | To Any Other Political Committee per Calendar Year | Special Limits |
| --- | --- | --- | --- | --- | --- |
| Individual | $2,600* | $32,400* | $10,000 (combined limit) | $5,000 | No limit |
| National Party Committee | $5,000 | No limit | No limit | $5,000 | $45,000* to Senate candidate per campaign |
| State, District, and Local Party Committee | $5,000 (combined limit) | No limit | No limit | $5,000 (combined limit) | No limit |
| PAC (multicandidate) | $5,000 | $15,000 | $5,000 (combined limit) | $5,000 | No limit |
| PAC (not multicandidate) | $2,600* | $32,400* | $10,000 (combined limit) | $5,000 | No limit |
| Authorized Campaign Committee | $2,000 | No limit | No limit | $5,000 | No limit |

*Indexed for inflation.
*Source:* Federal Election Commission, "Quick Answers to General Questions: How Much Can I Contribute?" Contribution Limits, 2013–14.

***Political Parties*** The political parties also play an important role in helping out the party presidential nominee. Though campaign finance laws limit the amount of money that parties can give to the candidate's official campaign committee, they also are allowed to spend a regulated amount on candidate services such as polling and advertising for get-out-the-vote efforts. More importantly, as described later, parties can also run very large and mostly unregulated "independent" campaigns on behalf of candidates. For these various campaign activities, the Republican National Committee raised almost $351 million in 2011–2012, while the Democratic National Committee raised a little more than $267 million.[53]

**PUBLIC FUNDING** Since 1971, presidential candidates have had the option of accepting campaign money from the federal treasury, paid for by taxpayers through a $3 donation on tax returns. The government uses these taxpayer contributions to provide matches for money contributors give to candidates during the primary and general election campaigns of those candidates. In 2004, the Kerry and Bush campaigns each received $74.4 million in public funds for the general election in the fall, and in 2008, Republican John McCain accepted public funding of roughly $84 million.

By accepting public funds, the candidates agree not to raise or spend any additional money. Usually, this has still been a good deal for presidential nominees, because the federal matching funds have been about the same amount as they would have raised without requiring the candidate to spend a lot of time and effort to fund-raise.

Dramatically breaking with tradition, Democratic nominee Barack Obama chose in 2008 to reject public funding with its accompanying spending limits, primarily because of his remarkably successful fund-raising operation. He was able to raise so much money from millions of small and medium-sized donations through his online system that he realized he was better off raising his own money and not adhering to the limits the public financing system would have placed on his campaign. In doing so, he went back on a promise to use public funding and limit his spending, saying he needed to do so because of expected attacks from independent conservative advocacy groups and 527 and 501 organizations. In 2012, neither Democrat Barack Obama nor Republican Mitt Romney accepted public funding, effectively killing the system.

A similar system is in place for the primary campaign. Similar to the general election system, the federal government would match individual donations until the candidate had raised about $50 million. Things began to change in 2000 when George

10.1

10.2

10.3

10.4

10.5

10.6

W. Bush became the first serious candidate to eschew public financing since it was first established in 1976. Since then, virtually none of the leading contenders in either party has accepted public funding with its attendant spending limits.

As noted earlier, public financing of presidential nomination campaigns is no longer viable for two reasons. First, the costs of running a credible campaign for the party presidential nomination have gone up much faster than the amount given to the candidates by the government. Second, most candidates do not want to limit their spending as required by the public financing system. It is much easier for campaigns to raise money now because of the growth of the Internet and the importance of individual contributions. Though Barack Obama was particularly good at raising money through e-mail and social media in 2008 and 2012, other campaigns have adopted the same tools and strategies.

**OTHER MONEY** After soft money to political parties was banned, 527, 501, and super PAC organizations gained favor.

***527s*** So named because of where they are defined in the Tax Code, 527s are entities that can use unregulated money to talk about issues, mobilize voters, and praise or criticize candidates and office holders. There are no limits on contributions to them, nor are 527s limited in what they can spend. Many of these groups devoted to liberal or conservative causes and candidates sprouted up after passage of McCain–Feingold and played a very large role in the 2004 presidential election—Swift Boat Veterans for Truth (anti-Kerry) and MoveOn.org (anti-Bush) were the most prominent—and the 2006 congressional elections. Many of these groups depend on very large contributions from a handful of rich individuals; George Soros contributed more than $15 million to anti-Bush 527s in 2004, while Texas oilman T. Boone Pickens gave $4.6 million to anti-Kerry groups.

***501s*** Although 527s are still around, they have lost favor. For one thing, both John McCain and Barack Obama condemned them in 2008 and informed 527 groups that they did not want their help. Perhaps more importantly, a better entity was discovered. 527s are required to report their total receipts and expenditures to the Internal Revenue Service (IRS) and report the identity of their contributors and how much they gave. 501 tax-exempt organizations—entities whose main purpose is to encourage "civic engagement"—must also report receipts and expenditures to the IRS, but less frequently than 527s, and they are not obligated to report the identities of their contributors. And,

**GETTING "SWIFT BOATED"**

In the 2004 presidential campaign, 527 advocacy organizations became very important, mostly by running attack ads. One of the most effective was the Swift Boat group, which attacked Democratic candidate John Kerry's war record, calling his wartime awards and citations "dishonest and dishonorable." By law, such 527 groups are not allowed specifically to ask voters to vote for a particular candidate or to not vote for a particular candidate, though they can praise or criticize them. Is it truly possible or even reasonable for an organization to promote certain issues while not endorsing a candidate, or to praise or criticize a candidate without the same effect?

10.1

10.2

10.3

10.4

10.5

10.6

like 527s, there are no limits on how much money they can collect or spend. Not surprisingly, 501s have come to play a bigger role in the campaign finance system.

**Super PACs** These are nonprofit entities—usually organized as 527 organizations—that can accept unlimited amounts in donations from corporations, unions, groups, and individuals. They can use these monies to advocate issues and for and against candidates for public office, though (unlike PACs) they cannot give money directly to candidates. They must issue periodic reports to the Federal Election Commission and identify their donors, though donors may be 501 organizations that need not report who their donors are. Super PACs played a major role in the 2011–2012 election cycle, with conservative ones leading the way. They have become the favored vehicles of very rich individuals who are not worried about their identities being known. In 2012, Karl Rove, George W. Bush's former chief strategist, formed a super PAC called "American Crossroads," which spent nearly $105 million opposing Democratic candidates.

**DOES MONEY TALK?** Money matters a great deal in the presidential nomination process—aspirants for party nominations who cannot raise sizable funds always drop out of the race—but not so much during the post-convention run for the White House.[54] Some reports of the 2012 Romney campaign suggest it did not have enough money, especially during the summer when the Obama campaign began running attack ads that went unanswered in many states.[55] Generally, both candidates have about the same resources, especially when accounting for party organizations, money from interest groups, 527s, 501s, super PACS and free publicity from news organizations.

Money may talk at a later stage, however. It is widely believed, although difficult to prove, that contributors of money often get something back.[56] The point is not that presidential, House, and Senate candidates take outright bribes in exchange for policy favors. Indeed, exchanges between politicians and money-givers are complex and varied, sometimes yielding little benefit to contributors. Undeniably, however, cozy relationships do tend to develop between politicians and major money-givers. Contributors gain access to, and a friendly hearing from, those whom they help to win office. And, groups that spend lavishly on issue campaigns often influence the policy agenda in Washington. Though this influence is indirect rather than direct, it is surely considerable.

It is clear that money-givers are different from average citizens. They have special interests of their own. As we have indicated, a large amount of campaign money comes from large corporations, investment banking firms, wealthy families, labor unions, professional associations (e.g., doctors, lawyers, or realtors), and issue-oriented groups such as the National Rifle Association, Focus on the Family, and the National Abortion Rights Action League. The big contributors generally do not represent ordinary workers, consumers, or taxpayers, let alone minorities or the poor. Surveys show that the individuals who give money tend to have much higher incomes and more conservative views on economic issues than the average American.[57] This is true as well for those who contribute by way of the Internet.[58]

The result is political inequality. Those who are well organized or have a lot of money to spend on politics have a better chance of influencing policy than ordinary citizens do, and they tend to influence it in directions different from what the public wants.[59] People seem to recognize this; surveys show that a large majority of Americans disagree with the *Citizens United* decision. The role of money in nomination and election campaigns is a major problem for the working of democracy in the United States.

# Election Outcomes

**10.6**  Assess how presidential elections are decided

fter the parties and candidates have presented their campaigns, the voters decide. Exactly how people make their voting decisions affects how well or how poorly elections contribute to the democratic control of government.

10.1

10.2

10.3

10.4

10.5

10.6

## ☐ How Voters Decide

Years of scholarly research have made it clear that feelings about the parties, the candidates, and the issues, as well as their own social characteristics, have substantial effects on how people vote.[60]

**SOCIAL CHARACTERISTICS** People's socioeconomic status, place of residence, religion, ethnic backgrounds, gender, and age are related to how they vote (see Figure 10.5). Minorities, especially African Americans, women, lower-income citizens, and residents living in urban areas tend to vote Democratic, while rural, religious, and white voters tend to vote Republican. Much of this stayed the same in 2012, but some things changed as well.

**PARTY LOYALTIES** To a great extent, these social patterns of voting work through long-term attachments to, or identification with, political parties. As indicated

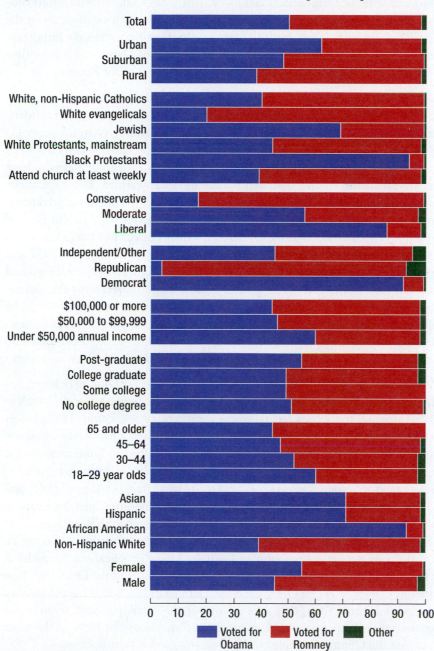

**FIGURE 10.5** PRESIDENTIAL VOTE IN 2012, BY SOCIAL GROUP

Racial and ethnic minorities, urbanites, young people, liberals, people with post-graduate degrees, and women voted strongly for Democrat Barack Obama in the 2012 election, while white Catholics and Protestants, regular church-goers, and evangelicals rural people, conservatives, older people, and men favored Republican Mitt Romney.

*Source:* The Election Day Polls, Edison Research, November 6, 2012; and the Pew Research Center, November 7, 2012.

10.1

10.2

10.3

10.4

10.5

10.6

earlier, a majority of Americans still say they consider themselves Republicans or Democrats, especially if we include so-called "leaners." Party loyalties vary among different groups of the population, often because of past or present differences between the parties on policy issues, especially economic and social issues. For this reason, when people use their party identification as a shortcut for choosing a candidate, they are likely choosing a candidate who is close to them on the issues. The ability of party identification to serve as a useful tool for people to choose candidates that are close to them on the issues is further enhanced by the close linkages between the parties and ideologies, with Democrats generally more liberal (including party identifiers, activists, and candidates) and Republicans generally more conservative.

Again, as we pointed out earlier, party loyalties are very good predictors of how people will vote.[61] Those who say they consider themselves Republicans tend to vote for Republican candidates in one election after another, and those who consider themselves Democrats vote for Democratic candidates. This is especially true in congressional elections and in state and local races, where most voters know little more about the candidates than their party labels, but the party loyalty factor is extremely important in presidential elections as well. Thus, in 2012, 92 percent of Democratic identifiers voted for Obama, and 93 percent of Republican identifiers voted for Romney.

**CANDIDATES** Presidential election outcomes have not simply reflected the party balance in the country; if that were true, Democrats would have won most presidential elections during the post–World War II period given their persistent party ID advantage over Republicans. Voters also pay a lot of attention to their perceptions of the personal characteristics of candidates. They vote heavily for candidates who have experience, appear strong and decisive, and convey personal warmth. The Republican candidate in 1952 and 1956, Dwight D. Eisenhower, had a tremendous advantage in these respects over his Democratic opponent, Adlai Stevenson;[62] so did Ronald Reagan over Walter Mondale in 1984, George H. W. Bush over Michael Dukakis in 1988, and George W. Bush over John Kerry in 2004. In elections between 1952 and 1972, the contrast between Republican and Democratic candidates typically gained the Republicans four or five percentage points—just enough to overcome the Democrats' advantage in what political scientists call the *normal vote*: how votes would be cast if only party identification determined voters' choices for president. Democrats have won when they have managed to add attractive candidates to augment their lead in party identification; Clinton in 1996 and Obama in 2008 and 2012 are examples.

**ISSUES** Voters also pay attention to issues. Sometimes this means choosing between different policy proposals for the future (as in the responsible party voting model), such as Reagan's 1980 promises to cut back federal government activity or Clinton's 1992 pledges of jobs and a middle-class tax cut. Most often, however, issue voting has meant retrospective voting (the electoral reward and punishment model), making judgments about the past, especially on major questions about the state of the economy and war and peace.

The voters tend to reward the incumbent party for what they see as good times and to punish it for what they see as bad times. In especially bad economic times, for example, Americans tend to vote the incumbent party out of office, as they did the Republicans during the Great Depression in 1932. In 1992 the electorate punished Republican George H. W. Bush for the poor state of the economy and punished the Republicans in the midst of the Great Recession in 2008 when Obama handily beat McCain and the Democrats won big majorities in Congress. When Obama and the Democrats failed to bring the country out of bad economic times when they were in control, the voters punished them in the 2010 congressional elections, and gave big gains to the Republicans. In 1996, on the other hand, it rewarded Bill Clinton for being president during good economic times.

Foreign policy can be important as well, especially when war and peace are at issue. Bitter disillusionment over the Korean War hurt the Democrats in 1952, just as the Vietnam War cost them in 1968, and unhappiness about American hostages in Iran and the Soviet intervention in Afghanistan hurt Jimmy Carter in 1980. During nearly all of the past half-century, in fact, Republican candidates have been seen as better at providing foreign policy strength and at keeping us out of war. The bloody, expensive, and drawn-out war in Iraq undermined traditional GOP advantages in this area in 2006 and 2008, however. In most elections, though, foreign policy concerns take a back seat to domestic ones for most voters. Even in 2008, in the midst of war, economic troubles triggered by the sub-prime mortgage and credit crunch disasters trumped foreign policy issues for a majority of voters.

## ☐ The Electoral College

Determining the winner of House and Senate elections is straightforward: the candidate with the most votes in a statewide contest for the Senate and the candidate with the most votes in a House district is elected. It's different for presidential elections. In contrast, the outcome of presidential elections is determined not by the number of popular votes cast for each candidate but by the candidate who wins a majority in the Electoral College.

When Americans vote for a presidential candidate whose name appears on the ballot, they are actually voting for a slate of **electors** in their state—equal to the number of the state's U.S. senators and representatives—who have promised to support a party's presidential candidate. (Very rarely have electors reneged on their promises and cast ballots for someone else; there was one so-called "faithless elector" in 2000.) Nearly all states now have winner-take-all systems in which the winner of the popular vote wins the state's entire allotment of electoral votes; Maine and Nebraska, in slight variations, choose electors on a winner-take-all basis for each congressional district.

The "college" of electors from the different states never actually meets together; instead, the electors meet in their respective states and send lists of how they have voted to Washington, D.C. (see the Twelfth Amendment to the Constitution). The candidate who receives a majority of all the electoral votes in the country is elected president. Not since 1824 has it been necessary to resort to the odd constitutional provisions that apply when no one gets a majority of electoral votes: the House of Representatives chooses among the top three candidates, by majority vote of state delegations. Each state in this procedure has one vote.

Most of the time, this peculiar Electoral College system works about the same way as if Americans chose their presidents by direct popular vote, but it has certain features that are politically consequential.

- *It magnifies the popular support of winners.* A candidate who wins in many states, by a narrow margin in each, can win a "landslide" in the Electoral College. In 1996, for example, Bill Clinton's 49 percent of the popular vote translated into 379 electoral votes, or 70 percent of the total. Ordinarily, this magnification simply adds legitimacy to the democratic choice, especially when the winner has only a plurality of the popular vote, that is, more than anybody else but less than a majority of all votes. Many of our presidents have been elected by only a plurality and not a majority of votes cast—most recently, Clinton (1992 and 1996), Richard Nixon (1968), John Kennedy (1960), and Harry Truman (1948). (See Table 10.2.)

- *It may let the less popular candidate win.* A president can be elected who had *fewer* votes than an opponent, if those votes happened to produce narrow margins in many states. Such a result has occurred three times: in 1876, when Rutherford Hayes defeated Samuel Tilden; in 1888, when Benjamin Harrison beat the more popular Grover Cleveland; and in 2000, when George W. Bush defeated Al Gore. (Gore beat Bush by more than a half million votes nationally.) Several early-nineteenth-century presidents were probably chosen with only small fractions of the popular vote, although we cannot be sure because some of the statistics are unreliable. Most notably, in 1824, John Quincy Adams defeated the very popular Andrew Jackson in the House of Representatives after an election when no candidate won a majority of electoral votes.

- *It discourages third parties.* Our constitutional arrangements for a single president and single-member congressional districts (rather than proportional representation) already discourage third parties; if candidates cannot win a plurality, they get nothing. The Electoral College adds significantly to this disadvantage: a third party with substantial support may get no electoral votes at all if its support is scattered among many states. In 1992, for example, Ross Perot's impressive

**electors**
Representatives who are elected in the states to formally choose the U.S. president.

10.1
10.2
10.3
10.4
10.5
10.6

10.1

10.2

10.3

10.4

10.5

10.6

**TABLE 10.2** ELECTION RESULTS, 1980–2012

| Year | Candidate | Party | Percentage of Popular Votes | Percentage of Electoral Votes |
|------|-----------|-------|-----------------------------|-------------------------------|
| 1980 | Ronald Reagan | Republican | 51% | 91% |
|      | Jimmy Carter | Democratic | 41% | 9% |
|      | John Anderson | Independent | 7% | 0% |
| 1984 | Ronald Reagan | Republican | 59% | 98% |
|      | Walter Mondale | Democratic | 41% | 2% |
| 1988 | George H. W. Bush | Republican | 53% | 79% |
|      | Michael Dukakis | Democratic | 46% | 21% |
| 1992 | William Clinton | Republican | 43% | 69% |
|      | George H. W. Bush | Democratic | 37% | 31% |
|      | H. Ross Perot | Independent | 19% | 0% |
| 1996 | William Clinton | Democratic | 49% | 70% |
|      | Robert Dole | Republican | 41% | 30% |
|      | H. Ross Perot | Reform Party | 8% | 0% |
| 2000 | George W. Bush | Republican | 48% | 60.5% |
|      | Albert Gore | Democratic | 48% | 49.5% |
|      | Ralph Nader | Green Party | 3% | 0% |
| 2004 | George W. Bush | Republican | 51% | 53% |
|      | John Kerry | Democratic | 48% | 47% |
| 2008 | Barack Obama | Democratic | 53% | 68% |
|      | John McCain | Republican | 46% | 32% |
| 2012 | Barack Obama | Democratic | 50% | 62% |
|      | Mitt Romney | Republican | 48% | 38% |

*Sources:* Data from the Federal Election Commission and Harold Stanley and Richard C. Niemi, *Vital Statistics in American Politics 2011–2012* (Washington, D.C.: CQ Press, 2012) authors' calculations for 2012.

19 percent of the popular vote translated into zero electoral votes because he failed to win a plurality in any single state.

There have been many calls over the years to change the Electoral College system of electing the president.[63] Majorities of Americans have told pollsters repeatedly that they want a system based on direct popular vote. Simply count up the votes nationally, and the candidate with the most votes wins the presidency. Simple.

But perhaps it's not so simple. What if three, four, or five candidates run and the plurality winner only receives, let us say, 30 percent of the vote? Would Americans be comfortable with a president elected by so few people? One way to solve this, as they do in France, among other places, is to have a second-round run-off election between the top two candidates so that the person elected comes to office with majority support.

Another idea that has been floated around is to retain the Electoral College but to remove the "winner-take-all" feature whereby the winner of a state receives all of the state's Electoral College votes even if the win is by the slimmest of margins. Various methods for apportioning a state's electoral votes in a way that approximates the division in the popular vote in the state have been suggested.

One way to get to such a system would be for each of the states to act on its own. The Constitution leaves it up to the states to choose how they determine the distribution of their Electoral College votes. The problem here, of course, is that unless all states acted at the same time, the first movers would be disadvantaged. If a state were to divide up its electoral votes to approximate the popular vote division, it would no longer be such a prize for the candidates compared to those states that were still operating on a "winner-take-all" basis. First-movers would lose influence in national elections, and there would be no assurance that other states would live up to their reform promises down the road. So, a change in the Electoral College along these lines would require national action, perhaps even a constitutional amendment.

Additionally, some benefit from the current system and do not want to change it. Small states, for example, have more influence than they would have in a direct popular election system because the number of electoral votes a state has is determined by adding up its number of representatives (based on population) and senators (two for each state). Thus, small states have more weight in presidential elections than

# Mapping American Politics

## Ad Buys and Battleground States

10.1
10.2
10.3
10.4
10.5
10.6

### Introduction

As you have seen, presidents are selected not by the people directly, but by votes in the Electoral College. The winner is that candidate who wins a majority of electoral votes. Campaigns are conducted on a state-by-state basis in a bid to put together a majority of electoral votes. With the exception of Nebraska and Maine, states use winner-take-all systems in which the candidate with the most votes (not necessarily a majority) wins all the state's electoral votes. Knowing this, campaign managers and their candidates focus on a relative handful of states where the contest is too close to call and where winning might affect the outcome of the presidential contest. They virtually ignore states that are not "in play," where the outcome is a foregone conclusion. In the 2012 election, for example, Democrats were in such a commanding position in California and New York that neither Democrats nor Republicans thought it wise to use scarce funds to campaign there. As well, Republicans were so far ahead in Texas, Utah, and Alabama that neither party thought it worthwhile to campaign there.

### Mapping Ad Buys

The cartogram below, with the size of the states reflecting the number of electoral votes, highlights the states where the parties and campaign organizations bought the greatest number of television ads urging votes for their candidate in the month or so before the 2004 election. You can see that significant television ad buys occurred in only 10 states, but those 10 accounted for 88 percent of all such ads bought across the entire country. The focus of the campaign on battleground states is very evident. Note that several of the very largest Electoral College states were not among those 10, including California, Illinois, New Jersey, and New York (reliably Democratic) and Texas and the Deep South (reliably Republican), not including Florida. Ad buys occurred overwhelmingly in states where party and campaign professionals believed either party's presidential candidate had a chance to win. The cartogram below shows the final electoral vote outcome.

### What Do You Think?

Taking a look at how the vote turned out in the battleground states, whose campaign seems to have done a better job of using ad buys effectively? Referring to the chapter-opening story, who did a better job in the battleground states in 2012? If you lived in a nonbattleground state, did it seem that there was very little campaign advertising on television? If you lived in a battleground state, did it seem that there was too much advertising? Is there any way to convince parties and presidential campaigns to wage the presidential battle on a nationwide basis so long as we use the Electoral College system for selecting presidents?

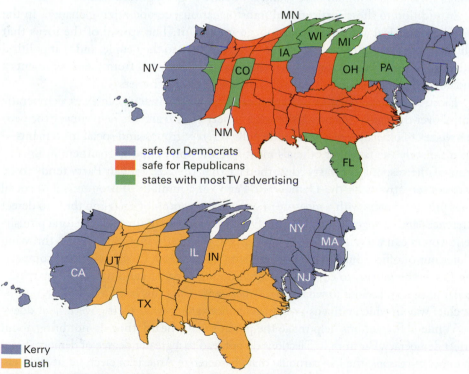

safe for Democrats
safe for Republicans
states with most TV advertising

Kerry
Bush

States Sized by Electoral Vote Totals, Colored by Election Outcomes, 2004

*Source:* © 2006 M. D. Ward. Source for top left cartogram: "Presidential TV Advertising Battle Narrows to Just Ten Battleground States," Nielsen Monitor-Plus and the University of Wisconsin Advertising Project (press release, October 12, 2004).

Standard US Map

**Note:** In cartograms, Alaska is not shown (although information is included in calculations), and Hawaii is moved closer to the mainland.

**Source for top left cartogram:** "Presidential TV Advertising Battle Narrows to Just Ten Battleground States," Nielsen Monitor-Plus and the University of Wisconsin Advertising Project (press release, October 12, 2004).

10.1

10.2

10.3

10.4

10.5

10.6

they would have if electoral votes were tied to the number of its seats in the House. Politicians and activists in battleground states also tend to like the Electoral College system because they gain attention—including visits, ad campaigns, and the like—from candidates and parties in close elections where a bloc of electoral votes might make the difference in the outcome of a national election. And, because a constitutional amendment requires ratification by three-fourths of the states, it would be very hard to make a change that small states and battleground states such as Ohio, Missouri, Florida, and Colorado, among others, are likely to oppose.

# Using the DEMOCRACY STANDARD

## Do voting and elections make government leaders listen to the people?

Elections and citizen political participation in the United States have been substantially democratized over the years, altering some of the constitutional rules introduced by the framers. For example, the Seventeenth Amendment, adopted in 1913, transformed the Senate into an institution whose members are elected directly by voters rather than by state legislatures. The manner of electing the president is completely different from what the framers thought they had created: an independent body for presidential selection. By custom or by law, virtually all electors today are pledged to a particular candidate before the presidential election, so that, for all intents and purposes, the president is directly elected by the people (although disparities between the electoral and popular vote occasionally happen, as in 2000). Equally important, the franchise has been so broadened—to include previously excluded racial minorities and women—that today almost all Americans 18 years and older are eligible to vote, something that few of the framers envisioned or would have found conducive to good government.

In addition to these institutional transformations, democratizing changes in the prevailing political culture have also been important. The spread of the ideas that political leaders ought to be responsible and responsive to the people, and that political leaders ought to pay attention to what the mass public wanted from them, represents a fundamental change from the prevailing view among the framers.

Elections are the most important means by which citizens can exert democratic control over their government. Although a variety of instruments help convey the people's wishes to officials—public opinion polls, interest groups, and social movements—it is ultimately the fact that officials must face the voters that keeps them in line. In terms of the responsible party idea, the fact that the Republican Party tends to be more conservative than the Democratic Party on a number of economic and social issues provides voters with a measure of democratic control by enabling them to detect differences and make choices about the future. Alternatively, through electoral punishment, voters can exercise control by reelecting successful incumbents and throwing failures out of office, thus making incumbents think ahead. Finally, electoral competition forces the parties to compete by nominating centrist candidates and by taking similar issue stands close to what most Americans want. This last force, in fact, may be the chief way in which citizens' policy preferences affect what their government does.

While U.S. elections help make the public's voice heard, they do not bring about perfect democracy. Far from it. Elections do not lead to a greater degree of democracy for a number of reasons: the low turnouts that characterize American elections at all levels, the educational and income biases in participation rates, and the role of interest groups and well-off contributors in campaign finance. Uneven participation and the influence of money on campaigns undermine political equality by giving some people much more political clout than others. Ever fiercer partisanship, moreover, increasingly is keeping candidates from choosing policies that reflect the wishes of the median voter in the electoral competition model, making this democracy-enhancing electoral mechanism less effective. So, notwithstanding the spread of democracy beyond the imaginings of the framers, those who support the democratic idea think we have some distance yet to travel.

# Review the Chapter

## Elections and Democracy

**10.1** Evaluate three models of how elections can lead to popular control, p. 279

In theory, at least, elections are the most important means by which citizens can exert democratic control over their government by forcing elected officials to pay attention to the wishes of voters.

Three theoretical models of voting are at play in making elections a potentially democratic instrument of the people: responsible parties/prospective voting; reward and punishment/retrospective voting; and the electoral competition/median voter model. Elections matter not only when there is a clear choice but also when electoral reward or punishment occurs or when electoral competition forces both parties to take similar popular stands.

## The Unique Nature of American Elections

**10.2** Distinguish American elections from those in other countries, p. 282

There are more elections here than in other democratic countries. They are on a fixed date and the offices voted upon have a fixed term. Elections almost always are of the winner-take-all, first-past-the-post variety, encouraging a two-party system. And, elections are administered by state and local governments rather than the national government.

## Voting in the United States

**10.3** Analyze the importance of political participation in elections, p. 285

The right to vote, originally quite limited, was expanded in various historical surges to include nearly all adults and to apply to most major offices. The changes came about because of changes in American society and the struggle for democracy waged by various groups of Americans.

## Who Votes?

**10.4** Identify demographic factors that increase the likelihood of voting, p. 291

The higher the income and the higher the education a person has, the more likely that person is to vote. When education and income are accounted for, the long-time differentiation between white and black turnout disappears.

Women now vote at a slightly higher rate than men.

## Campaigning for Office

**10.5** Outline the process of campaigns for the presidency and Congress, p. 295

Candidates for the party nomination for president start by testing the waters, raising money, and forming campaign organizations; in a series of state primaries and caucuses, they seek delegates to the national nominating conventions, which generally choose a clear front-runner or the incumbent president.

Candidates who cannot raise money or have money raised for them by others do not become serious contenders in the party nomination contests. Money differences between the candidates in the presidential contest in the general election are less important in determining the outcome because of public financing, party spending, interest and advocacy group spending, and intense and costless press coverage of the election.

The goal of presidential candidates in the fall campaign is to rally the party base and win over a substantial proportion of independent and moderate voters. Campaign activity and spending focus on battleground states.

## Election Outcomes

**10.6** Assess how presidential elections are decided, p. 308

Voters' decisions depend heavily on party loyalties, the personal characteristics of the candidates, and the issues, especially the state of the economy.

The president is selected not by direct popular vote but by a majority in the Electoral College vote.

# Learn the Terms

# Test Yourself

Answer key begins on page T-1.

**10.1** Evaluate three models of how elections can lead to popular control

1. In the electoral competition voting model of democratic elections, unified parties compete for votes by taking:
   a. The least popular position
   b. The middle-of-the-road position
   c. The most popular position
   d. The most controversial position
   e. The least controversial position

**10.2** Distinguish American elections from those in other countries

2. Which of the following is a distinguishing feature of elections in the United States?
   a. Elections are infrequent
   b. Elections are all conducted around the same time
   c. Elected positions do not have fixed terms of office
   d. Inconsistent election procedures and vote-counting
   e. Elections are not held on a fixed date

**10.3** Analyze the importance of political participation in elections

3. Most delegates to the Republican and Democratic national conventions are selected when party supporters and activists hold neighborhood and area-wide meetings to select delegates. These are called:
   a. State elections
   b. Party caucuses
   c. Primary elections
   d. Party conventions
   e. Local elections

**10.4** Identify demographic factors that increase the likelihood of voting

4. What factor does NOT generally influence the likelihood of a person voting?
   a. Age
   b. Income
   c. Gender
   d. Race
   e. Location

**10.5** Outline the process of campaigns for the presidency and Congress

5. Refers to contributions and spending that fall under the jurisdiction of the Federal Election Commission:
   a. Hard money
   b. Soft money
   c. Voter contribution
   d. Federal support
   e. Public funding

**10.6** Assess how presidential elections are decided

6. When a candidate has more votes than any other candidate, but less than a majority of all votes cast, this is called:
   a. Majority vote
   b. Minority vote
   c. Plurality
   d. Majority election
   e. Landslide

# Explore Further

## INTERNET SOURCES

Democratic National Committee **www.democrats.org**
Official site of the Democratic Party, with information on party
positions and candidates, how to work as a volunteer or
contribute money, and more.

The Federal Election Commission **www.fec.gov**
Rules and data on campaign fund-raising and spending in federal
elections.

The National Archives Electoral College Site **www.archives.gov/
federal_register/electoral_college/index.html**
Everything there is to know about the law and practices of the
Electoral College and the process by which it elects the
president.

Voting America: United States Politics **www.americanpast.org/
voting/**
A comprehensive collection of interactive maps detailing elections
from 1840–2008. This site also has discussions by scholars on
past elections and U.S. voting.

Open Secrets at the Center for Responsive Politics **www
.opensecrets.org**
An especially good site for following the money trail—how
campaign money is gathered and spent.

Project Vote Smart **www.votesmart.org**
A political portal loaded with links to information about
candidates, parties, election rules, and issues.

Intrade **www.intrade.com**
A futures market focusing on elections and public opinion about
issues; extraordinarily accurate in predicting election outcomes.

Republican National Committee **www.gop.com**
Official site of the Republican Party, with information on party
positions and candidates, how to work as a volunteer or
contribute money, and more.

A Plain Blog About Politics **plainblogaboutpolitics.blogspot.com**

Follow contemporary politics on this site through the eyes of
practicing political scientists who bring disciplinary perspectives
to bear on tough questions about democracy and governance.

## SUGGESTIONS FOR FURTHER READING

Kamarck, Elaine C. *Primary Politics: How Presidential Candidates
Have Shaped the Modern Nominating System.* Washington, D.C.:
Brookings Institution Press, 2009.
A history of the changing presidential nominating process and how
candidates take advantage of existing primary and caucus rules
and try to change rules to their advantage.

Maisel, Sandy L. *American Political Parties: A Very Short
Introduction.* New York: Oxford University Press, 2007.
The best brief book on American voting and elections; surprisingly
insightful for such a short book.

Polsby, Nelson W., Steven E. Schier, and David A. Hopkins.
*Presidential Elections*, 13th ed. Lanham, MD: Rowman &
Littlefield, 2011.
A comprehensive textbook on the presidential nominating process,
the general election, and voting.

Shea, Daniel M. *Let's Vote: The Essentials of the American Electoral
Process.* New York: Pearson, 2013.
A lively and accessible account of the American electoral system,
what is enduring about it, and what is changing.

Verba, Sidney, Kay Lehman Schlozman, and Henry E. Brady. *Voice
and Equality: Civic Volunteerism in American Politics.* Cambridge,
MA: Harvard University Press, 1995.
A comprehensive analysis of inequalities in political participation and
their meaning for the quality of democracy in the United States.

Wattenberg, Martin P. *Where Have All the Voters Gone?* Cambridge,
MA: Harvard University Press, 2002.
A clear-headed and accessible look at this perennial and complex
question.

# 11

# Congress

## A DYSFUNCTIONAL CONGRESS?

**M**any observers considered the first year of the 113th Congress, 2013, to be Congress at its worst. That year, deep divisions between Senate Democrats and House Republicans led to a crisis over the debt ceiling and caused the government to shut down for sixteen days. At one point, the institution's approval rating sank below 10 percent, making Congress less popular than jury duty, witches, and the IRS.[1] Despite attempts by President Obama to pressure members into action on a variety of policy issues, Congress accomplished very little, and the year ended without any major legislative action on important issues such as tax reform, immigration reform, and assistance for the weak economy.

In many ways, the difficulty Congress had in 2013 is a direct result of the framers' design. Congress is made up of two distinct chambers, each with different rules, different constitutional functions, and different members. Representatives and senators must not only cooperate with each other, they must also compromise with the other chamber and the president. After all, our separated system requires a bill to pass with a majority vote (or supermajority, in many cases) in both the House and the Senate, even before it can be sent to the president for signature or veto. And, despite the power of the president, there is virtually nothing he can do to force Congress to act.

When this separated system is combined with intense ideological divisions and political polarization, as we have today, legislative inaction or gridlock becomes commonplace. Public anger is a natural result of lawmaking failures, but are members of Congress really to blame? Their job is to represent their constituents, the various individuals who live within a congressional district or a state. Today, however, the policy preferences of voters in, say, inner-city Chicago are substantially different from those of voters in rural Texas. Members of Congress are caught between advocating for the interests of the voters who sent them to Washington and the greater interests of the country as a whole.

This tension has rarely been more evident in our history than it is now, and it calls into question the very design of our lawmaking branch. Put simply, many worry whether Congress is up to the task of dealing with complex national problems in a divided country. Americans increasingly

| **11.1** | **11.2** | **11.3** | **11.4** | **11.5** |
|---|---|---|---|---|
| Identify the ways in which the Constitution shapes Congress, p. 321 | Assess how and to what extent the members of Congress represent their constituents, p. 323 | Describe what leaders, political parties, and committees do in Congress, p. 336 | Outline the process by which a bill becomes a law, p. 349 | Explain why Congress is doing less oversight than in the past, p. 352 |

**DIVIDED WE STAND**  Just three days after resounding Republican victories in the 2014 mid-term elections, President Obama invited (from left) Speaker of the House John Boehner, Democratic Leader Harry Reid, and new Senate Majority Leader Mitch McConnell to the White House for lunch to discuss issues on which the two sides may reach compromises in the 114th Congress.

look at our democratic counterparts in parliamentary systems—systems in which it is much easier for the majority party to accomplish its policy goals—as a better institutional model.

It also seems as if legislative gridlock is likely to become worse in 2015 and 2016. Though most predicted Republican gains in both the House and in the Senate, the size of the Republican victory in the 2014 mid-term elections was surprising. Not only did a number of Republican challengers defeat incumbent Democrats but a contingent of seemingly unpopular Republican senators and representatives also managed to fend off competitors. In fact, Republicans gained enough seats in the Senate to take control of the body for the first time since 2006 and added around 15 more seats to their already sizable majority in the House.[2] For the first time during his term in office, President Obama will face a unified Congress controlled by the Republican Party.

The 2014 election results were driven by a few factors. First, despite a slowly improving economy, economic gains, by and large, had yet to be felt by average Americans. For example, median household incomes and weekly wages still had not increased substantially since the end of the recession, leaving many workers feeling pessimistic despite strong job growth. Largely as a consequence of continuing economic weakness, the president remained relatively unpopular. In polls taken immediately before the election, the president's approval rating was only about 41 percent, and low support for the president tends to hurt members of his party during mid-term elections. Second, a number of Senate Democrats who lost their reelection bids ran in states that traditionally vote Republican, including North Carolina, Arkansas, and Alaska. Other states that held Senate elections were in swing states, such as Colorado and Iowa, or in right-leaning states such as Georgia, West Virginia, and South Dakota. Because of the dramatic wins by Democrats in 2008, few pickups were available in Democratic states, resulting in an electoral map that did Democrats no favors. Finally, preliminary estimates of turnout indicate that it was very low, with only 36 percent of eligible voters casting a ballot. Low-turnout elections tend to favor the GOP because the most reliable voters tend to be older, white, and economically better off, all demographic groups that typically vote Republican. It seems that Democratic constituencies, including young people, minorities, and poorer voters, were not motivated enough to show up at the polls in large numbers in 2014.

Whatever the reason for the Republicans' sweeping victories in 2014, the party's congressional leaders will feel that the public supports Republican policy positions and, as a result, are likely to put additional pressure on President Obama. Divided government will force the two sides to find areas of compromise if any significant legislation is to be passed. More likely, polarization and partisan bickering may prove to be the defining characteristic of the 114th congressional session, leading to further erosion of public confidence in the institution of Congress.

## Thinking Critically About This Chapter

In this chapter, we turn our attention to the Congress of the United States, examining how Congress works as both a representative and governing institution.

## Using the Framework

In this chapter you will learn how the way in which Congress works is affected by other government actors and institutions; political linkage level factors such as interest groups, public opinion, the media, and elections; and structural factors, such as constitutional rules and economic and social change.

## Using the Democracy Standard

Using the concept of democracy used in this book, you will be able to evaluate how well Congress acts as a democratic institution. You will see that the story of Congress and democracy is a mixed one: Congress is, at times and under certain circumstances, highly responsive to the American public; at other times and under other circumstances, it is most responsive to special interest groups and large contributors.

# Constitutional Foundations of the Modern Congress

**11.1** Identify the ways in which the Constitution shapes Congress

11.1
11.2
11.3
11.4
11.5

**enumerated powers**
Powers of the federal government specifically mentioned in the Constitution.

**elastic clause**
Article I, Section 8, of the Constitution, also called *the necessary and proper clause*; gives Congress the authority to make whatever laws are necessary and proper to carry out its enumerated powers and other of its powers vested in the Constitution.

**bicameral**
As applied to a legislative body, consisting of two houses or chambers.

T he framers of the Constitution recognized the legislature, Congress, as potentially the most dangerous to individual freedom. Yet, they tried to balance their worries of government tyranny with their desire to create a legislature that was both energetic and capable enough to deal with national problems. These multiple and conflicting objectives are reflected in the constitutional design of Congress.

## Empowering Congress

The framers began by empowering Congress, making the legislative branch the center of lawmaking in the federal government. In Article I, Section 1, of the Constitution, they gave Congress the power to make the laws: "All legislative power herein granted shall be vested in a Congress of the United States." For the framers, Congress was the main bearer of federal governmental powers. In listing its powers and responsibilities in Article I, Section 8—the **enumerated powers**—they were largely defining the powers and responsibilities of the national government itself.[3] The framers enhanced the enumerated powers by adding the **elastic clause**, granting broad power to Congress to pass whatever legislation was necessary to carry out its enumerated powers and other responsibilities vested in it from other sections of the Constitution.

## Constraining Congress

Worried that too strong a legislative branch would lead to tyranny, the framers also limited congressional power. They made Congress a **bicameral** body—divided into two chambers—so that legislation could occur only after patient deliberation. Single-house legislative bodies, they believed, would be prone to rash action. They then added provisions—Article I, Section 9—specifically to prohibit certain kinds of actions: bills of attainder, ex post facto laws, the granting of titles of nobility, and the suspension of the right of habeas corpus. In the 1st Congress, additional constraints on congressional action were added in the form of the Bill of Rights. Note that the First Amendment, perhaps the most important constitutional provision protecting political liberty, begins with the words "Congress shall make no law . . ."

We also learned in the chapter on the Constitution that the national government was organized on the basis of a "separation of powers" and "checks and balances" so that "ambition might check ambition" and protect the country from tyranny. This means that although the framers envisioned the legislative branch as the vital center of a vigorous national government, they wanted to make sure that Congress would be surrounded by competing centers of government power. We will see that this fragmentation of governmental power in the United States affects how Congress works and often makes it difficult for it to fashion coherent and effective public policies. In this regard, we will see in this chapter and the chapter on the presidency how separation of powers invites conflict between the president and Congress, especially when divided party government exists.

## Bicameralism and Representation

Congress is organized into two legislative chambers, each with its own principles of representation and constitutional responsibilities. While we often use the word "Congress" and think of it as a single institution, it is worth remembering that the House and Senate are very different from one another and are "virtually autonomous chambers."[4] Here are the most important things in the constitutional design of Congress that make the two chambers different from one another.

In what came to be known as the Great Compromise, the framers decided to apportion the House of Representatives on the basis of population and the Senate on the basis of equal representation of the states. Equal representation in the Senate of states that are highly unequal in terms of population, we will see, has important negative impacts on democracy in the United States.[5] The terms of office of the members of the House of Representatives were set at two years. The terms of the members of the Senate were set at six years, with only one-third of the seats up for election in each two-year election cycle. We learn in this chapter how these differences affect the legislative process.

The Constitution called for the election of senators by state legislatures, not by the people. The objective was to insulate one house of Congress from popular pressures and to make it a seat of deliberation and reflection. As James Madison put it, "The use of the Senate is to consist in its proceeding with more coolness . . . and with more wisdom than the popular branch."[6] The election of senators by the state legislatures could not survive the democratizing tendencies in the country, however. The Seventeenth Amendment, passed in 1913 after years of agitation for reform pressed by labor and farm groups and progressive reformers, gave the people the power to elect senators directly.

In addition to its general grants of power to Congress, the Constitution assigns particular responsibilities to each of the legislative chambers (see Table 11.1). For example, the House of Representatives has the power to impeach the president for "high crimes and misdemeanors," which it did in the case of Bill Clinton arising out of the Monica Lewinsky affair; the Senate has the power to conduct the trial of the president and remove him from office, if the impeachment charges are proved to its satisfaction (which they were not for Clinton).

## ◻ Federalism

Congress is also greatly affected by the federal design of the Constitution. In our federal system, some powers and responsibilities are granted to the national government, some are shared between the national government and the states, and some are reserved for the states. It is inevitable in such a system that conflicts will occur between state governments and the national government, but the general trend over time has been an increase in congressional power, frequently justified through the commerce clause. Historically, the Supreme Court has been willing to grant Congress broad leeway in dealing with issues through its commerce clause powers, though this remains controversial and even today, the policy-making roles of Congress and the states frequently conflict. For example, in 2012, though the Court upheld the individual mandate in the Affordable Care Act, which requires all individuals to obtain health insurance, it rejected the commerce clause justification offered by Congress.

**TABLE 11.1** CONSTITUTIONAL DIFFERENCES BETWEEN THE HOUSE AND THE SENATE

| | Senate | House of Representatives |
|---|---|---|
| Term | 6 years | 2 years |
| Elections | One-third elected in November of even-numbered years | Entire membership elected in November of even-numbered years |
| Number per state | 2 | Varies by size of state's population (minimum of 1 per state) |
| Total membership | 100 | 435 (determined by Congress; at present size since 1910) |
| Minimum age for membership | 30 years | 25 years |
| Unique powers | Advice and consent for judicial and upper-level executive branch appointments | Origination of revenue bills |
| | Trial of impeachment cases | Bringing of impeachment charges |
| | Advice and consent for treaties | |

Instead, because the government imposes a fine if an individual does not have health insurance, the Supreme Court said the individual mandate was constitutional under Congress's power to tax. By doing so, the Court signalled that it was anxious to further cut back the powers of the national government relative to the states.

Federalism also infuses "localism" into congressional affairs.[7] Although Congress is charged with making national policies, we should remember that the members of the Senate and the House come to Washington as the representatives of states and districts. They are elected by and are beholden ultimately to the voters and interest groups at home and have voters' and important groups' interests and opinions in mind even as they struggle with weighty issues of national importance. This remains true even as rising partisanship and the increasing influence of ideologically oriented advocacy groups have forced representatives and senators to be more sensitive to issues beyond their electoral districts and states.

# Representation and Democracy

**11.2** Assess how and to what extent the members of Congress represent their constituents

**M**embers of Congress serve as our legislative representatives. But do they carry out this representative responsibility in a way that can be considered democratic?[8] To answer this question, we need to look at several aspects of representation: styles of representation, how closely the demographics of members of Congress match the demographics of the population in general, and the electoral process.

## ☐ Styles of Representation

In a letter to his constituents written in 1774, English politician and philosopher Edmund Burke described two principal styles of representation. As a **delegate**, the representative tries to mirror perfectly the views of his or her constituents. As a **trustee**, the representative acts independently, trusting to his or her own judgment of how to best serve the public interest. Burke preferred the trustee approach: "Your representative owes you, not his industry only, but his judgment; and he betrays you, instead of serving you, if he sacrifices it to your opinion."[9]

Campaigning for Congress in Illinois several decades later, Abraham Lincoln argued otherwise: "While acting as [your] representative, I shall be governed by [your] will, on all subjects upon which I have the means of knowing what [your] will is."[10] (If only he had access to public opinion polls!)

Every member of the House and Senate chooses between these two styles of representation. Their choice usually has less to do with their personal tastes than it has to do with the relative safety of their seats and how often they must face the electorate. Senators with six-year terms face the electorate less often than members of the House, so they are generally freer than representatives to assume the trustee style. As they get closer to the end of their terms and the prospect of facing the voters for reelection, however, senators edge toward the delegate style.[11] Because members of the House must run for reelection every two years, and tend to be in campaign mode at all times, they are pushed almost inexorably toward the delegate style.[12]

## ☐ Race, Gender, and Occupation in Congress

Representation also implies that elected officials are like us in important ways—that they represent us because they are similar to us. Which raises the question: is the makeup of Congress in a demographic sense similar to that of the nation as a whole? This is often called **descriptive representation**. From the point of view of descriptive representation, the views of significant groups—let us say, women and African Americans—will only be taken into account in policymaking if members of these

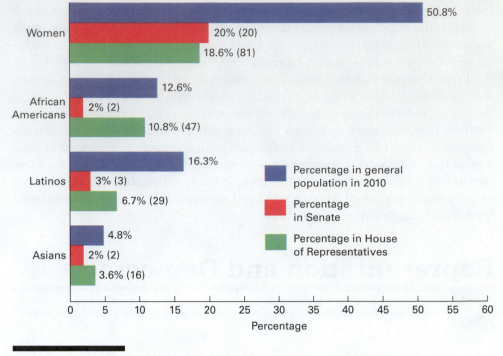

**FIGURE 11.1** WOMEN AND MINORITIES IN THE CONGRESS, 2015–2016 (estimate)

Although their numbers in Congress have increased in recent years, women and racial minorities are still substantially underrepresented compared with their proportion in the American population. This graph compares the percentage of women and racial minorities in each house of the 114th Congress with their percentages in the population in the 2010 census.

*Note:* Data not adjusted to reflect races undecided as of November 11, 2014, four of which involve women.

*Sources:* U.S. Bureau of the Census; the website of the U.S. Senate at www.senate.gov; the website of the House of Representatives at www.house.gov.

groups hold seats in a legislative body in rough proportion to their size in the population. From this perspective, a perfectly representative legislative body would be similar to the general population in terms of race, sex, ethnicity, occupation, religion, age, and the like. In this sense, the U.S. Congress is highly *unrepresentative.*[13]

**GENDER AND RACE**  Both women and racial minorities are significantly underrepresented in Congress, particularly in the Senate, despite important recent gains. We can see this in Figure 11.1 which compares the distribution of women and minorities in the 114th Congress (2015–2016) with their distribution in the country as a whole.

Black representation reached its peak during the post–Civil War Reconstruction period, when blacks played an important political role in several southern states. African Americans disappeared from Congress for many years after the reimposition of white supremacy and the creation of Jim Crow laws in the South at the end of the nineteenth century. Although a handful of black representatives from northern cities served during the first half of the twentieth century—Oscar De Priest from Chicago's predominantly black South Side and Adam Clayton Powell from New York City's Harlem, for example—very few African Americans were elected to Congress until the late 1960s. While there has been some improvement in representation of African Americans in the House of Representatives—from 26 to 47 between the 102nd (1991–1992) and 114th Congresses—their numbers are still well below what might be expected, given the proportion of African Americans in the population. Currently two African American senators, the most ever at one time, serve in the U.S. Senate: Tim Scott (SC-R) and Corey Booker (NJ-D). In fact, since 1900, there have been only seven African American senators, five of them Democrats. The trend of increased diversity continued in 2014, and the 114th Congress will have the largest number of Hispanics and women serving in American history. And, for the first time ever, the Republican Party elected a female African American to Congress—Mia Love, of Utah.

Hispanics are even more poorly represented than African Americans relative to their proportion of the population, but the increase in their number in recent years has given the Hispanic caucus a greater voice in legislative affairs than in the past. Interestingly, while Hispanics have now replaced African Americans as the largest minority group in the population, they are less well represented than African Americans in Congress. In the 113th Congress there were thirty-seven Hispanics in the House and three in the Senate (a record number for both chambers). Other minority groups are represented in the House, including thirteen Asian Americans and two Native Americans.

The first woman to sit in Congress was Jeannette Rankin of Montana, a suffragist and pacifist, elected in 1916. The number of women in Congress increased during the 1990s, with a big gain coming in the 1992 elections (often called the "year of the woman"), which sent 48 women to the House and 7 to the Senate in the 103rd Congress (compared with only 29 and 2, respectively, in the 102nd Congress). There are a record number of women in Congress in the 113th, with 20 in the Senate and 81 in the House. Proportionally, however, female representation in Congress is quite low, compared either to the percentage of women in the American population (slightly more than one-half) or to the percentage of women in national legislative bodies in countries globally. On the latter point, as of late 2010, the United States ranked only 71st on the world list.[14] Leadership posts in Congress are overwhelmingly held by men, but a few women have gained important party and institutional leadership posts. Most notable is Nancy Pelosi (D–CA), who became the first female Speaker of the House in American history after the Democrats won the House in 2006. When Republicans regained control of the House in the 2010 elections she lost the speakership, but retained her position as Democratic leader.

**SEXUAL ORIENTATION** As acceptance of homosexuals has become more common, so too have openly gay members of Congress, another important trend in congressional demographics. In 2012, Tammy Baldwin became the first openly gay member of the Senate. Barney Frank, a Democratic member from Massachusetts, became the first openly gay House member in 1987, but today there are seven openly gay members in the House.

**INCOME AND OCCUPATION** Members of Congress are far better educated than the rest of the population. They also are quite wealthy, having been born into high-income families, or earning it before entering Congress or even while serving in Congress (until 2012, members of Congress had not bound themselves with "insider trader" rules as they had bound Wall Street). Significantly, three-quarters of senators are millionaires, as are almost one-half of members of the House, though only about 2 percent of the American population makes more than $250,000 a year.[15] By occupational background, members lean heavily toward the law or business occupations, though many have been career politicians. In recent Congresses, only about 15 percent came from working-class backgrounds, whether of the blue-collar or white-collar service variety, and there was no one who had been a farm laborer.[16]

Most members of Congress, however, did not step into their current posts directly from a profession or occupation. Before putting themselves up for election, representatives and senators, for the most part, had been career politicians or in some other form of public service. Strikingly, many of the members of Congress are former staffers. More than a few representatives and senators came from the military, while senators included former governors and cabinet secretaries in previous administrations.

Does it matter that descriptive representation is so low in Congress, that its members are so demographically unrepresentative of the American people? Some political scientists and close observers of Congress think not. They suggest that the need to face the electorate forces lawmakers to be attentive to all significant groups

**11.1**

**11.2**

**11.3**

**11.4**

**11.5**

**constituency**
The district of a legislator.

**constituent**
A citizen who lives in the district of an elected official.

**RELAXING ON THE LINKS**

Like many leading members of Congress, House Speaker John Boehner, here playing a round of golf with President Obama as they tried (without success) to tone down the partisan rancor that too often paralyzes Congress, is a wealthy man with a background in business.

in their **constituency**. A representative from a farm district tends to listen to farm **constituents**, for example, even if that representative is not a farmer.[17]

Nevertheless, many who feel they are not well represented—women, African Americans, Asian Americans, Hispanics, blue-collar workers, gays and lesbians, those with disabilities, and the poor—often believe that their interests would get a much better hearing if their numbers were substantially increased in Congress. There is significant evidence supporting this view: women members of the House introduce more bills related to women's and children's issues than do their male colleagues.[18] The same has been found to be true for African American legislators and issues considered to be important to African Americans in the country.[19] As members of the upper 1 percent of income earners—senators' and representatives' salaries of roughly $175,000 and the considerable investments most of them have, place them solidly in that group—they don't have much in common, one would suspect, with the daily concerns of middle- or low-income households. The demographic disparity between the American population and the makeup of Congress, then, suggests a violation of the norm of political equality, an important element of democracy.

## ☐ The Electoral Connection

As a result of the Great Compromise, members of the House represent relatively small districts of equal population, while senators represent states with varying population. Unlike the Senate, House districts must occasionally be redistributed across states and redrawn within states to ensure equal population of House districts. These processes, which are two of the most controversial aspects of American politics today, have an enormous influence on political representation.

**THE STATE AS THE SENATE'S ELECTORAL UNIT** Each state elects two senators for six-year terms (though not at the same time). This has important implications for politics in the United States, as well as the quality of democratic representation here. Equal representation gives extraordinary power in the Senate to states with small populations. Wyoming, our least-populous state, for example, has exactly the same number of senators as California, but it has less than one-seventieth of California's population; two senators in Wyoming in 2010, for example, represented only about 560,000 people, while the two senators from California represented just over 37 million. This means that a coalition of 51 senators from the 26 smallest-population states, representing a mere 18 percent of the American population, can pass a bill in the Senate. You will see later in this chapter that the Senate's rules and procedures give even more power in the body to a small minority of the population, magnifying the antimajoritarian qualities produced by the Constitution.

**THE DISTRICT AS THE HOUSE'S ELECTORAL UNIT** Each member of the House of Representatives is elected from a single-member geographical district (a 1967 law prohibits multimember districts). The number of representatives each state is entitled to in the House is determined by a state's population, with the proviso that each state must have at least one congressional district; the low-population states Alaska, Delaware, Montana, North Dakota, South Dakota, Vermont, and Wyoming fall into this category. The House of Representatives decided that, beginning in 1910, its upper limit would be 435 members (the House can change this number at any time, although it is highly unlikely).

*Reapportionment* Because the American population is constantly growing in size and changing where it lives, the 435 House representatives must be periodically redistributed among the states. **Reapportionment**, the technical name for this redistribution, occurs every 10 years, after the national census (see Figure 11.2 for the most recent changes). Based on the official census, some states keep the same number of seats; others gain or lose them depending on their relative population gains or losses. The big winner following the 2010 census count was Texas, which gained four additional seats in the House. Florida gained two seats, followed by Arizona, Georgia, Nevada, South Carolina, Utah, and Washington with one additional seat. The biggest losers were New Jersey, New York, and Ohio, which lost two seats each; Illinois, Louisiana, Massachusetts, Michigan, Missouri, and Pennsylvania each lost one seat. These patterns reflect the general trend of the last 50 years with fewer Americans living in the upper Midwest and Northeast, and more living in the South and Southwest. Those states that lose representatives subsequently have less influence in Congress on issues like securing federal funds for the state.

*Redistricting* Except for states with only a single representative whose House district is the entire state, those states gaining or losing seats must redraw the boundary lines of their congressional districts so that they are of roughly equal population size.[20] Redrawing district lines within a state is known as **redistricting** and is done primarily by state legislatures, although the courts have been playing a more active role lately in cases which legislatures are unable to decide (redistricting is the job of a nonpartisan commission in 13 states). Very often in the past, because it was then legal to do so, legislatures created congressional districts of vastly different population sizes—in New York in the 1930s, some congressional districts had 10 times the population of others—and significantly overrepresented rural populations. The Supreme Court ruled in *Wesberry v. Sanders* (1964), however, that the principle of one person, one vote applies to congressional districts, meaning that congressional districts within a state must be of roughly equal population size. Because the distribution of the population changes in many states over the course of 10 years—some people moving from the cities to the suburbs; some people moving from rural areas to cities—many congressional district boundaries must be redrawn even in those states that have neither gained nor lost congressional seats due to reapportionment, because of the Supreme Court's ruling that districts within states must be roughly equal in population size.

**reapportionment**
The reallocation of House seats among the states, done after each national census, to ensure that seats are held by the states in proportion to the size of their populations.

**redistricting**
The redrawing of congressional district lines within a state to ensure roughly equal populations within each district.

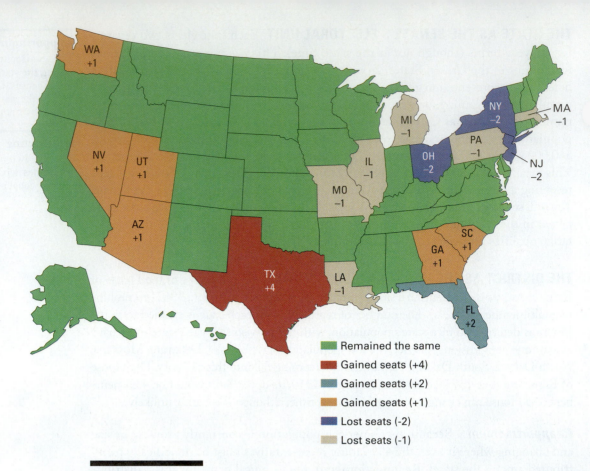

**FIGURE 11.2** STATES GAINING AND LOSING CONGRESSIONAL SEATS FOLLOWING THE 2010 CENSUS

The number of representatives for each state in the House of Representatives is based on the size of its population. Because the relative sizes of the states' populations change over time while the number of representatives in the House is fixed, the number of representatives from each state is recalculated after each census. This process is called reapportionment. This map shows which states gained and lost seats after the 2010 census.

*Source:* "U.S. Census Population Estimates for 2011," press release, U.S. Census Bureau, December 2011 and January 2012.

**partisan**

A committed member of a party; also, seeing issues from the point of view of the interests of a single party.

**gerrymandering**

Redrawing electoral district lines in an extreme and unlikely manner to give an advantage to a particular party or candidate.

Although congressional districts must hold approximately equal numbers of citizens, state legislatures are relatively free to draw district lines where they choose. The party that controls the state legislature and governorship usually tries to draw the lines in a way that will help its candidates win elections.[21] The results are often strange indeed. Rather than creating compact and coherent districts, neighborhoods, towns, and counties can be strung together in odd-looking ways in order to take full **partisan** advantage of the redistricting process. Taken to an extreme, the process is known as **gerrymandering**, after Governor Elbridge Gerry of Massachusetts, who signed a bill in 1811 that created a district that looked like a salamander.

The tradition lives on. Recently, 2012 was a banner year for gerrymandering. In Illinois, four Republicans lost after a Democratic gerrymander. In Pennsylvania, Republicans won thirteen of eighteen House seats, despite receiving fewer votes than Democrats statewide. Texas gained four additional House seats after the 2010 census, mostly because of the increase of its Hispanic population. The Republican-controlled state legislature in 2011 created a redistricting plan that added one supermajority Hispanic district that would likely elect a Democrat, then created three other districts with so few Hispanics in them that they would likely elect Republicans. Because Texas has had a long history of using redistricting to dilute the influence of minorities, it was forced under terms of the Voting Rights Act to submit its plan to the Justice Department for approval. Justice refused to accept it and a federal court in Washington ordered the Texas Court to come up with a new plan.

Though the Supreme Court sometimes has tried to prevent the most flagrant abuses, especially when some identifiable group of voters is disadvantaged—for example, a racial or ethnic group such as Hispanics in Texas as described above—it has turned a blind eye to partisan redistricting in which parties try to draw district lines to their own advantage. The Court, along with most politicians, seems to accept the notion that "to the victor belongs the spoils." Partisan redistricting happens when the same party controls both houses of the state legislature and the governor's office, although even here there are sometimes conflicts if one or another of the party's incumbent House members feels that he or she has been hurt by the redrawn district lines. This situation of unified party control existed in 42 states when the states began to redistrict after the 2010 census, with Republicans in control of 24 of them. Parties in unified control of a state where the legislature draws district lines follow several strategies to gain seats on the rival party. One is to **crack** a district where the party enjoys too big a margin. Too large a majority wastes votes in a district where the party would win anyway, so legislators can spread its party voters across two or more districts in hopes of winning additional seats in a state's congressional delegation. On the flip side of the coin, a party that controls the redistricting machinery can **pack** voters for its rival party into fewer districts, giving the rival party bigger margins of victory in them, leading them to waste their strength.

Gerrymandering is highly controversial and seems to violate our notions of fairness. Through the redistricting process, politicians are able to ensure that one party wins the seat, which also reduces the number of competitive elections nationwide. As two political scientists put it, "politicians select voters rather than voters electing politicians."[22] One proposal to stop gerrymandering is to use independent or bipartisan commissions made up of citizens, rather than politicians, to draw the lines. A number of states, including California, Arizona, New Jersey, and Iowa, have adopted redistricting commissions. The idea is that they will draw more fair and competitive districts, rather than simply favoring one party. The evidence is mixed so far on whether independent commissions work.[23] In many states, they have simply not been around long enough to determine their effect. Many political scientists believe that residential patterns—where different types of people live—are more important than the effects of gerrymandering. Democrats tend to cluster in urban areas, while Republicans tend to cluster in rural areas, making it hard to draw competitive districts, regardless of who is in charge of the redistricting process.

Whatever the cause, the decline in the number of competitive districts in House elections means that the vast majority of districts in the United States are safely Republican or safely Democratic where candidates need not appeal to the general constituency but only to members of their own party, contributing to the ever-deepening partisan divide in Congress.

*Majority-Minority Districts*   Amendments to the 1965 Voting Rights Act passed in 1982 encouraged the states to create House districts in which racial minorities would be in the majority. Sponsors of the legislation hoped that this would lead to an increase in the number of members of racial minority groups elected to the House. The result was the formation of 24 new **majority-minority districts**, 15 with African American majorities and 9 with Hispanic American majorities.[24] The creation of some of these districts has taken great imagination. North Carolina's Twelfth District, for instance, created after the 1990 census, linked a narrow strip of predominantly African American communities along 160 miles of Interstate 85 connecting Durham and Charlotte. After going back and forth on the issue, the Court accepted a slightly redrawn North Carolina Twelfth District map in *Hunt v. Cromartie* (2001), ruling that race can be a significant factor in drawing district lines "so long as it is not the dominant and controlling one." Of course, determining whether a district meets these criteria is difficult, resulting in controversy and numerous legal challenges every ten years when new majority-minority districts are drawn. (For more insight into how district lines are drawn, see the "By the Numbers" feature).

The creation of majority-minority districts has been successful in increasing the number of racial minorities in the House as these districts nearly always elect a member of the racial group the district is intended to empower. Ironically, however, the creation of such districts has undermined Democratic Party strength in other districts by taking traditionally Democratic-oriented minority group voters away from previously Democratic-dominated districts in order to form majority-minority ones. (One political scientist reports that after 1991 Republicans

**crack**
The act of dividing a district where the opposing party has a large majority, rendering it a minority in both parts of the redrawn districts.

**pack**
The process of concentrating voters for the other party into fewer districts in order to weaken them elsewhere.

**majority-minority districts**
Districts drawn to ensure that a racial minority makes up the majority of voters.

# By the Numbers

## Can congressional districts be drawn in different ways to include equal numbers of voters yet favor one party over the other?

Here is a headline that might have appeared in any city newspaper in late 2011 or early 2012: "Legislature fails to reach agreement on congressional district lines; Issue to be decided by the state courts." What's going on? How difficult can it be to count people and draw congressional district lines? Actually, it is difficult and the issues are important.

### Why It Matters

How congressional district lines are drawn has a lot to do with which political party will control the House of Representatives, at least until the next census.

### Behind Redistricting

In the House of Representatives, seats are apportioned to each state based on the state's population. Thus, after a new census is taken, a state may gain or lose seats based on the current count of people residing there. To gain a seat means that a new congressional district must be carved out of the state; to lose a seat means that lines must be redrawn to fill in the gap. Even in states where the size of its congressional delegation has not changed, lines must always be redrawn because of population shifts within state boundaries (e.g., more people moving to the suburbs) and the Court's ruling that each congressional district within a state must be of roughly the same population size.

### How District Lines Are Drawn

In theory, as long as district lines create congressional districts of roughly equal size, and as long as district lines do not unduly disadvantage racial and ethnic groups, congressional district lines can be drawn in any way that politicians choose. The politicians can be very imaginative in doing so, as they try to ensure that their own party and favored members of Congress are advantaged by the outcome.

Where the district lines are drawn is extremely important in determining the composition of the congressional delegation from each state. Note the following hypothetical example, which shows how easily district lines can be used to effect different outcomes. Let "D" stand for 100,000 Democratic voters; let "R" stand for 100,000 Republican voters; and let "A" stand for 100,000 African Americans, most of whom vote for Democrats. Taking the same number and locations of voters, district lines can be drawn one way to yield three Democratic seats and no Republican seats (the hypothetical map on the left) and another way to yield two Republican seats and one Democratic seat (the hypothetical map on the right).

### Comment on the Process for Drawing District Lines

These alternative outcomes are somewhat exaggerated in order to make a point about how politicians strive for maximum flexibility in the redistricting process. In real life, the Court has also demanded that district lines not deviate too much from their historical patterns and that they be relatively compact, putting people who live near each other in the same district. The federal courts also have

CONGRESSIONAL DISTRICTS

Bay Area
8,9,12
13,14

Los Angeles–
Orange County
24,26,27,28
29,30,31,32
33,34,35,36
37,38,39,41
45,46,47,48

Congressional Districts

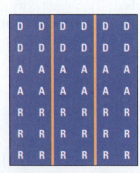

**Result:** districts equal in size (1.4 million each); three Democratic seats, zero Republican seats.

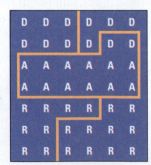

**Result:** districts equal in size (1.4 million each); one Democratic seat carved out to create a position for an African American and two Republican seats.

D = 100,000 white Democrats    R = 100,000 white Republicans
A = 100,000 African Americans, mostly Democrats

Different Congressional District Lines, Different Party Outcomes

*Source:* State of California.

*(Continued)*

rejected districting maps that disadvantage protected minorities such as African Americans and Hispanics.

### What to Watch For

Redistricting is one of the most important things that goes on in our political system, yet it is virtually invisible to the general public. Pay attention to the debates over redistricting in your state and determine what political alliances appear and what political bargains are being struck.

### What Do You Think?

What might be a nonpartisan, scientific method to draw district lines that would avoid the sometimes unseemly process of reshaping congressional districts to suit political parties and interested groups? If there was such a method, do you think it would be better than our current system? Why or why not?

won and held every congressional seat in which redistricting had reduced the African American population by 10 percentage points or more.[25]) Naturally, Republicans have been eager to support minority group efforts to form their own districts. Concentrating black voters in homogeneous districts—packing them, as it were—has tipped the balance to Republicans in many congressional districts in the South. One result was that policies favored by African Americans were less likely to be enacted when Republicans were in the majority because of the decreased strength of Democrats in the House, this despite an increase in the number of African American representatives.[26]

**open-seat election**

An election in which there is no incumbent officeholder.

**MONEY AND CONGRESSIONAL ELECTIONS**  Running for the House or the Senate is a very expensive proposition, and the costs keep growing. In 2012, the average cost of winning a House seat was about $1.5 million, while a Senate seat cost the winner more than $10 million.[27] House and Senate candidate campaigns do not receive public funding and, by virtue of that fact, face no limits on what they can spend in the general election. To fill their campaign coffers, they rely on contributions from individuals (who are limited in what they can contribute), PACs, and political party committees. In 2010, 59 percent of contributions to House campaigns came from individual contributors (including the candidates themselves), 38 percent was from PACs, and 3 percent from party committees. The numbers for the Senate were 77 percent from individuals, 15 percent from PACs, and 8 percent from party committees.[28] More than a few rich individuals self-fund a portion

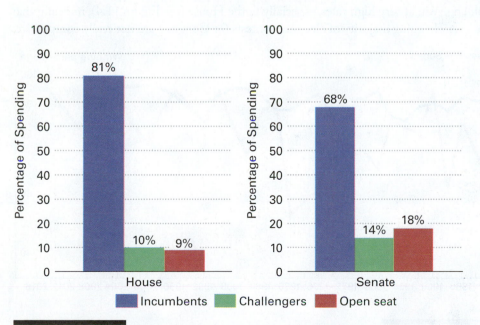

**FIGURE 11.3**  CAMPAIGN MONEY RAISED BY INCUMBENTS, CHALLENGERS, AND OPEN-SEAT CANDIDATES, 2013–2014 ELECTION CYCLE

Because campaign contributors want access to important decision-makers in Congress, contributors tend to give a disproportionate share of campaign contributions to incumbents and to those open-seat candidates who have a good chance to win their elections.

*Source:* Federal Election Commission.

*Note:* At this writing, the Federal Election Commission has not reported on campaign money raised in the 2014 congressional elections.

of their campaign expenses. Democrat John Corzine set the record in 2000 with contributions of $62 million to his campaign, which he won narrowly. Many congressional candidates also receive campaign contributions from PACs associated with congressional party leaders such as House Speaker John Boehner (R–OH) and Senate Majority Leader Harry Reid (D–NV). Similar to presidential campaigns, contributions to PACs are dominated by business corporations and trade associations, while individual contributors to congressional campaigns come primarily from top income earners and wealth holders.

Not to be overlooked, parties, committees, interest groups, corporations, unions, and advocacy organizations spend lavishly on issue and candidate ad campaigns and get-out-the-vote efforts that are extremely helpful to congressional candidates. In the 2011–2012 cycle, following the groundbreaking *Citizen's United* decision, corporations and unions—especially the former—increased their spending in direct support of or in opposition to particular Senate and House candidates. Super-wealthy individuals did the same by way of large contributions to Super PACs.

Incumbents, especially in the House, have an easier time raising money than their challengers and spend more (see Figure 11.3). The reasons are fairly obvious: those who give want access to senators and representatives and, because incumbents are reelected at very high rates, the smart play is to donate to those in power and likely to remain in power. **Open-seat election** races, in which no incumbent is involved, also attract and use lots of money, especially in the Senate, because the stakes are so high for each of the parties and allied interest and advocacy groups, with control of Congress hanging in the balance at nearly every election. For example, in the 2009–2010 cycle, the average open-seat candidate in House and Senate races raised 46 percent more than challengers to incumbents.[29] Moreover, being a member of the majority party in Congress serves as a magnet for money because contributors generally want to be able to have access to those in power.[30] These money sources are for what is called "hard" or "regulated" money that goes into the treasuries of the official campaign committees of House and Senate candidates. It is but the tip of a very large iceberg, however, as you have seen. Much more money is spent independently on issue ads and get-out-the-vote campaigns by interest and advocacy groups and by 501 and 527 organizations and Super PACs that indirectly pump up the resources that support congressional candidate campaigns.

**THE INCUMBENCY FACTOR** As we have seen, incumbents in Congress—current office holders—win at very high rates, especially in the House (see Figure 11.4), meaning that the overwhelming majority of electoral contests for Congress are not really competitive;

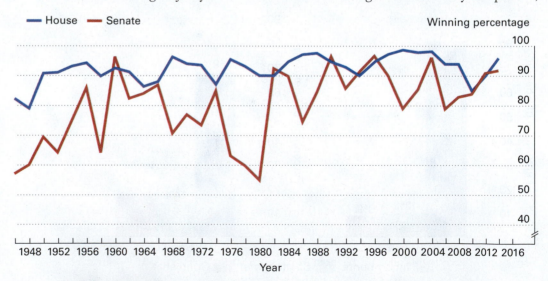

**FIGURE 11.4** RATES OF INCUMBENT REELECTION IN CONGRESS

The probability that incumbents will be reelected remains at historic highs. This does not mean, however, that the membership of Congress is stagnant. Turnover in membership is substantial because of retirements and the defeat of incumbents in primary elections.

*Note:* Senate rate for 2014 does not include one undecided contest scheduled for runoff in early 2015.

*Sources:* Congressional Quarterly Weekly Reports (November and December 2008); "Norm Colman Concedes," Associated Press (June 30, 2009); and "Incumbent reelection over the years," Center for Responsive Politics," (www.opensecrets.org), November 10, 2012.

**IN THE HOME DISTRICT**
Members of Congress must spend considerable time staying in personal touch with their constituents, even when Congress is in session. Here Connecticut representative Jim Himes talks with a constituent at a VFW gathering in his home district. Should representatives spend less time staying in touch and more time legislating, or is this an important role for representatives in a democracy?

for the most part, seats in the House today are considered "safe," with the incumbent facing little serious challenge from the opposition party candidate. Since the end of World War II, in fact, on average, 93 percent of House incumbents have been reelected and 80 percent of Senate incumbents have done the same. Incumbents won at very high rates even in big party swing elections as in 1994, 2006, 2008, and 2010. In 1994 and 2010, when Republicans took over control of Congress, incumbent losses were concentrated in Democratic districts and states; in 2006 and 2008, when the Democrats won many seats, most incumbent losses were among Republicans. To be sure, there is still substantial turnover in the House and Senate. Many members retire, especially if they believe they are likely to lose in the next election; others lose to challengers in their party's primary; still others take other positions. Some members leave only upon their deaths. But most of those who choose to stay and run do win their seats.

There are several reasons incumbents almost always win when they seek reelection. The most important, of course, is that the redistricting process in many states in recent years—reviewed earlier in this chapter—has been fashioned to protect incumbents in each of the parties. On the face of it, this process has been very effective.

Incumbents also have the advantage of attracting and spending much more campaign money than their rivals. Many contributors look at campaign contributions as an "investment" in access to key members of Congress.[31] To contribute to a challenger is to jeopardize access if the challenger loses, which is most often the case.

Incumbents also use the congressional machinery to help their reelection chances.[32] Already well known to voters because they garner so much free media coverage, members of Congress have many ways to advertise their accomplishments and keep their names before the public. For example, the **franking privilege** allows them to mail

**franking privilege**
Public subsidization of mail from the members of Congress to their constituents.

# Using the FRAMEWORK

## Why can't our government seem to solve our most pressing national problems?

**Background:** During the last several years, Congress and the president have, as the saying goes, "kicked the can down the road" on nearly every important national issue. We have failed to address the rising costs of health care, already the highest in the world. We have shied away from short-term stimulus measures that might address unemployment. We have backtracked on market-based approaches to cutting down on carbon emissions. And we cannot seem to agree on the mix of government program cuts and additional taxes that are required to cut into the national debt. Things are so bad that major business groups such as the World Economic Forum and the World Bank recently have downgraded the United States on the quality of its governance. Why has this happened? Taking a broad look at how structural, political linkage, and governmental factors affect what government does will help explain the situation.

### Government Action

Late and short-term fixes with no long-term solutions to big national problems: program cuts but none on Medicare or defense, and no tax increases on the wealthy to deal with national debt; no economic stimulus or other job-creation actions; no action on climate change; no action on cost containment in health care.

### Government

Senators and representatives of both parties pay disproportionate attention to their most well-off constituents and those who fund their campaigns. → Business and trade association groups help write legislative bills and have an important presence in committee hearings and bill markups. → Divided government in 2011 and 2012, with the anti-tax, anti-regulation Tea Party caucus dominating the House GOP, and a Democratic president (Obama) in office who seems willing to trade away taxes on upper income groups for the sake of compromise. → Speaker Boehner cannot carry through on bargains he has negotiated with the Senate and the president because of Tea Party resistance.

### Political Linkage

Decline of labor union density weakens voice of working and middle classes in politics. → Political influence of corporations and upper income groups increases. → 501 and 527 groups, regular PACs, and super PACs representing entrenched interests, dominate campaign finance. → Bitter partisanship increases, with the GOP less and less inclined to nominate candidates for any office who would consider new government regulations or increasing taxes, especially on thewealthy. → Media buys into the "deficit is the problem" narrative, with little attention to other problems, especially jobs.

### Structure

Income and wealth inequality soars. → Default positions of American political culture are anti-government and pro-market.

Productivity-enhancing technological change puts pressure on jobs. → Global outsourcing puts pressure on jobs. → Declining manufacturing sector undermines middle-class lifestyles. → Rise of financial sector and CEO compensation funnels much of national income to the top.

newsletters, legislative updates, surveys, and other self-promoting literature free of charge. The House and the Senate also provide travel budgets for lawmakers to make periodic visits to their states or districts. Because members believe that time spent in their districts helps their electoral chances, they spend lots of time back home.[33] Some manage to spend three or four days a week in their districts or states, meeting constituents, giving speeches, raising money, and keeping in the public eye. The congressional leadership helps by scheduling important legislative business only during the Tuesday-to-Thursday period and cutting down the number of hours Congress is in session.

Incumbents also use their offices to "service the district." One way is through **casework**, helping constituents cut through the red tape of the federal bureaucracy, whether it be by speeding up the arrival of a late Social Security check or expediting the issuance of a permit for grazing on public land.[34] Generous budgets for establishing and staffing offices in the constituency help representatives and senators do casework. Another way to service the district is to provide **pork**—federal dollars for various projects in the district or state. In 2005, for example, Congress passed a massive $286 billion highway and mass transit bill that poured federal construction money into the constituencies of senators and representatives for highway and bridge projects, rail and bus improvements, urban bike paths, and more. Pork is controversial because many view it as wasteful spending, but it is also enormously important to local areas that depend on federal money to finance a project. For example, money spent in a district creating a new park, building a new highway bridge, or funding a hospital research lab benefits all members of the community.

## ☐ How Representative?

There are several respects in which Congress may not be broadly representative of the American people. For one thing, as we have seen, women and members of minority racial and ethnic groups are vastly underrepresented in the ranks of House and Senate members compared with their proportions in the population. We have learned, as well, that senators and representatives by a very wide margin are more financially well off than the average American. For another thing, we have seen that people in very small states have much more voice than people in large states in the U.S. Senate because of the constitutional provision mandating two senators for each state. This feature of the Constitution means that the 12 smallest states, with only about 7 percent of the American population, elect almost one-fourth of all senators.[35] Elections and attentiveness to public opinion on the part of lawmakers help rectify some of this, but imperfectly.

But representatives and senators pay a great deal of attention to the interests and the preferences of the people in their districts and states. Because they are worried about being reelected—even popular incumbents tend to run scared, perhaps afraid of being the exception that proves the rule. (Consider Eric Cantor, who was the number two Republican in the House and a potential candidate for Speaker until he lost to an unknown challenger in his 2014 primary.) As a result, members of Congress undertake a wide variety of activities to ensure they can win reelection. These activities give them an advantage to be sure, as incumbents can raise more money, perform services for their constituents, and use the powers of their office to raise their profile.

Is it possible members of Congress are so successful at winning reelection because they represent their districts well? There is some support for this argument. It is almost always the case that the overall ideology of the member closely reflects the views of voters in his or her district. Conservative representatives almost always come from conservative districts, while liberal members reflect their districts. Occasionally, a conservative candidate manages to win in a liberal district (or vice versa), but typically a member who is not well matched to the district will not last long. Other members are famous for their ability to bring home pork (though Congress has recently tried to limit the use of pork, with mixed success) or help with casework, and these practices make them popular with their voters; members who are not seen as accessible or who do not make frequent visits back home often lose their reelection races. All of these

**casework**
Services performed by members of Congress for constituents.

**pork**
Also called *pork barrel*; federally funded projects designed to bring to the constituency jobs and public money for which the members of Congress can claim credit.

patterns seem to confirm the notion that most of the time, individual members do a fairly good job of representing their states or districts, though there is ample room, given the complexity and near-invisibility of many issues before the Congress, to accommodate powerful interest groups as well.

In a substantial number of cases, moreover, Congress does *not* follow public opinion, even on highly visible issues. If members of Congress follow public opinion two-thirds of the time on important bills, that still leaves one-third of the time that they go their own way. Moreover, on many issues of high complexity or low visibility, such as securities and telecommunications regulation, the public may have no well-formed opinions at all. It is in these areas that we can most fully see the influence of money and interest groups at work.

One of the reasons members of Congress have some latitude in representing public opinion in their districts—indeed, in the nation—is that, as we have shown, most come to Congress from relatively "safe" districts where being turned out by the voters is not common. Consequently, House elections do not adequately fulfill the role assigned to elections in democratic theory: as the principle instrument for keeping elected leaders responsive and responsible.[36] A case could be made, however, that despite these shortcomings, Congress has done a great deal to make voting and citizenship more inclusive (see the "Can Government Do Anything Well?" feature).

# How Congress Works

**11.3**   Describe what leaders, political parties, and committees do in Congress

**C**ongress is a vital center of decision making and policymaking in our national government. It is not a place where the executive's bills are simply rubber-stamped, as it is in legislative bodies in many parliamentary systems. By all accounts, Congress is the most influential and independent legislative body among the Western democratic nations. In this section, we turn our attention to how Congress is organized and how it functions as a working legislative body.[37]

There are a number of very important things to keep in mind as we examine how Congress is organized and operates. First, while they are alike in many ways, the House and Senate are very different institutions. They differ in size, the nature of the constituencies they represent, the terms of office of their members, and their constitutional responsibilities; together, these differences give each chamber a distinctive character.

Second, both the House and Senate have had a tendency over the years to succumb to centrifugal forces, always seemingly on the verge of flying apart, with each representative and senator tempted to go his or her own way. The task of running each body has been likened to "herding cats." The reasons are fairly obvious: representatives and senators in some sense are like independent contractors. Congressional leaders lack the normal tools of organizational leadership to force compliance with their wishes; they cannot order members about, they cannot hire or fire them (this is the role of voters), nor can they control the size of their paychecks or benefits. Moreover, in our candidate-centered form of politics, congressional leaders traditionally have had little control over the reelection of representatives and senators who run their own campaigns.

Between 1995 and 2006, however, Republicans used party resources and leadership positions to gain a great deal of control over legislative affairs, especially in the House of Representatives. Republicans not only granted more formal powers to the office of the Speaker but learned to channel campaign money from their own PACs, party campaign committees, and conservative groups and individuals to maintain discipline among members who might be tempted to stray too far from where legislative party leaders want them to be on important matters. The process of centralization of leadership in the Senate did not advance as far as in the House but, given leadership influence over the flow of campaign money from diverse sources, some centralization occurred there as well.[38]

# Can Government Do Anything Well?

## How Congress made voting and citizenship in America more inclusive

The framers had a fairly narrow definition of who might be best suited to vote and hold public office. For the most part, they left the question of voting eligibility to the states, with full knowledge that the states did not allow access to women, Native Americans, slaves, free blacks, or young people. Many required a poll tax or evidence of property ownership. A few even required people to belong to an established church. A majority of people residing in the United States when the Constitution was ratified in 1788 were not eligible to vote in American federal elections.

Over the broad course of American history, the suffrage has expanded to include virtually every excluded group. These democratizing actions took place first at the state level, where poll taxes were gradually eliminated (later reinstituted for African Americans in the South during the Jim Crow period), as were property qualifications and religious tests. By the late 1820s, white male suffrage was universal in the United States. Then, a series of constitutional amendments gradually incorporated other excluded groups. First, male former slaves were granted the right to vote, then women, and finally 18- to 21-year-olds. In all of this, the Congress of the United States played a central role, as it must in the process of amending the Constitution.

*Support for the claim that Congress has played the central role in making voting and citizenship in America more inclusive:*

■ For a few years after the end of the Civil War, Congress was controlled by radical Republicans who were committed to refashioning the slave system of the South, with the protection of former slaves and their enfranchisement as full citizens among their primary goals. To ensure that the Emancipation Proclamation was not regarded as a temporary war measure, Congress passed the Thirteenth Amendment in 1864 abolishing slavery, sending it to the states for ratification, which happened in 1865. When it became clear that many Southern states were instituting harsh measures of near servitude to control their African American population—called Black Codes—Republicans in Congress passed the Fourteenth Amendment making all persons born or naturalized in the United States full citizens of the nation and of the states where they live, with the full rights and obligations of all other citizens, with rights to due process and equal protection (meaning the right to equal treatment by government). The Amendment was ratified in 1868. The Fifteenth Amendment, passed by Congress and ratified in 1870, was the third and last of the so-called "Reconstruction Amendments" and the one of most interest to us in this feature on making voting more inclusive. In it, Congress specified that the vote could not be denied on the basis of race, color, or previous condition of servitude. With passage of the Fourteenth and Fifteen Amendments, Congress and the states effectively overruled the *Dred Scott* (1857) case in which the Supreme Court said that African Americans, whether free or slave, had no rights that others were obliged to respect.

■ In 1920, the House and Senate passed the Nineteenth Amendment, stating that neither state governments nor the federal government could deny a citizen the right to vote based on that citizen's sex. The Amendment was passed during a special session of Congress called specifically to consider it, and was ratified by the requisite number of states that same year.

■ The Twenty-Sixth Amendment, passed by Congress and ratified by the states in 1971, set the minimum voting age in the United States at 18, and stipulated that no state government nor the federal government could deny the vote to anyone 18 years or older strictly on the account of his or her age. The measure passed during the Vietnam War, in which most of the fighting was being done by people who could not vote in U.S. elections.

■ A Democratic-controlled Congress passed and President Bill Clinton signed the National Voter Registration Act in 1993. Also known as the "Motor Voter" act, the law required that the states allow people to register to vote when they were applying for their driver's license or social services such as food stamps or welfare benefits. The new law had been pushed by civil rights organizations and organized labor and was enacted after Democrats regained unified control of the federal government in the 1992 national elections.

*Rejection of the claim that Congress has played the central role in making voting and citizenship in America more inclusive:*

■ There is no denying that Congress played an important role in passage of each of the voting inclusion initiatives described above. In some sense it could not be otherwise; when it comes to amending the Constitution, Congress necessarily is involved because the main alternative route to changing our founding document—an Amendment proposed by a national constitutional convention called by two-thirds of the states then ratified by the state legislatures of three-fourths of the states—is so fraught with difficulties that it has only been used once. The question of Congress's "centrality," however, is another matter. And so too is the degree to which Congress stopped short of what it might have done better or acted only after a very long period of time, pressed hard by social movements and voters to finally move ahead.

(Continued)

11.1

11.2

11.3

11.4

11.5

- With respect to the Fifteenth Amendment, Congress failed to include under its protection at least one-half of former slaves, namely women. This was no oversight. Though women and women's suffrage organizations had been prominent in the abolitionist movement to end slavery, many among them had allowed themselves to be convinced by congressional leaders that granting the right to vote to former slaves and to women at the same time would be too radical a step and would endanger suffrage for African Americans.

- Again, with respect to the Fifteenth Amendment, Congress did little for almost a century to put federal muscle behind African Americans' right to vote in the South. It would take the Voting Rights Act of 1965 to make the promise of the Fifteenth Amendment real.

- With respect to women's right to vote, Congress had rejected proposals similar to that of the Nineteenth Amendment in 1887, 1914, 1915, 1918, and 1919. It was finally enacted after pressure was brought to bear by a militant women's suffrage movement, the coming to power in Washington of a political class born in the progressive movement (with Woodrow Wilson as president), and an agreement by suffragettes to cease their disruptions during World War I and to actively support the war effort in trade for a constitutional amendment.

- The Twenty-Sixth Amendment was passed not only in the midst of the Vietnam War, perhaps recognizing the sacrifice and service of many 18- to 21-year-olds fighting in Southeast Asia, but also at the height of the antiwar movement that was disrupting cities and campuses across the country. Support for it began to build after a model amendment was crafted by students and faculty at Dartmouth College with the express purpose of moving young people from the streets into the voting booth. It was seen as a way to have young people's voices heard and to fashion a more viable democracy in the midst of an unpopular war. Congress passed the proposed Amendment, to be sure, but the initiative and energy behind it was from elsewhere.

- Republicans have accused Democrats of passing the Motor Voter Act as a way to enhance its chances in local, state, and national elections by allowing more people from its electoral base to register to vote, namely young people (at motor vehicle departments), racial and ethnic minorities, and the poor in particular. Partly to counter this, Republicans later began to champion efforts for voter ID laws and other restrictions at the state level, claiming that such laws would stymie vote fraud. Democrats rightly or wrongly have interpreted such proposed statutes as a device to decrease the voting participation of people likely to vote Democratic.

## WHAT DO YOU THINK?

What do you think about the past, present, and future role of Congress in making voting and citizenship more inclusive? Which of the following positions is closest to your own?

- Congress has played an admirable role in making voting and citizenship more inclusive and should continue to look for ways to improve matters further.
- Congress has played an admirable role in making voting and citizenship more inclusive, but only at the bequest of voters and activists; further progress can only come if such people continue to press Congress.
- Congress has played an admirable role in making voting and citizenship more inclusive, but there is not much more to be done.
- Congress has been late to the party and has not done as much as it might to make voting and citizenship more inclusive. We really cannot count on it.

How would you defend this position to a fellow student? What would be your main line of argument? What evidence do you believe best supports your position? For help in developing your argument, please refer to the sources listed in the "Can Government Do Anything Well?" feature in Chapter 2 on p. 45.

Additional sources for this feature: James MacGregor Burns and Stewart Burns, *A People's Charter: The Pursuit of Rights in America* (New York: Knopf, 1991).

When they regained control of Congress after the 2006 elections, Democrats tried with some success to become more centralized and coordinated as well, using the political party and congressional leadership positions as its main tools. But the game remains one of "herding cats," typified by Majority Leader Harry Reid's months-long effort to put together the 60 Democratic votes he needed to break a Republican filibuster and pass a health insurance reform bill on the morning of Christmas Eve, 2009. Gaining the votes of Ben Nelson (D–NE) and Joe Lieberman (I–CT) didn't happen until a few days before the final vote and required big leadership concessions to them. For Lieberman, it meant removing the "public option" from the bill.

Republicans retook the House in the 2010 elections. But the large new crop of Tea Party-backed freshman refused to toe the leadership line. On several occasions, as in the debt ceiling and payroll tax cut extension, they embarrassed House Speaker John Boehner by refusing to support the compromise agreements he had reached with Senate Democratic leaders and President Obama.

## ☐ Political Parties in Congress

Political parties have a very strong presence in Congress. Its members come to Washington, D.C., as elected candidates of a political party. At the start of each session, they organize their legislative business along political party lines. At the start of each new Congress, each **party conference**—all the members of a political party in the House or the Senate (although House Democrats use the term **caucus** rather than conference)—meets to select its leaders; approve committee assignments, including committee and subcommittee chairs; and reach agreement on legislative objectives for the session. The majority party in the House selects the Speaker of the House, while the majority party in the Senate selects the president pro tempore (usually its most senior member) and the majority leader. The minority party in each chamber also selects its leaders. Political parties, as we shall see, also are influential in what policies representatives and senators support and how they cast their votes on important bills. So, political parties are at the very core of legislative business in the United States and are becoming ever more important as the partisan divide between Democratic and Republican voters, activists, advocacy groups, and elected officials gets steadily wider.[39]

**PARTY VOTING IN CONGRESS** The political parties provide important glue for the decentralized fragments of Congress and the legislative process. Party labels are important cues for members of Congress as they decide how to vote on issues before the

**party conference**
An organization of the members of a political party in the House or Senate.

**caucus**
A regional, ethnic, racial, or economic subgroup within the House or Senate. Also used to describe the party in the House and Senate, as in Republican caucus.

11.1

11.2

11.3

11.4

11.5

**PARTY DIVISION**

Democratic administrative and congressional leaders applaud the president during his State of the Union address to the nation in January, while Republicans "sit on their hands." This graphically illustrates how Congress operated in the first years of the Obama administration: Democrats largely supported major legislation while Republicans were nearly unanimous in saying no. In spite of this, President Obama and the Democrats produced a historic legislative record: an economic stimulus, health care reform, and financial industry regulation, among other things. Is this development of party government a good thing or something to be worried about? Why?

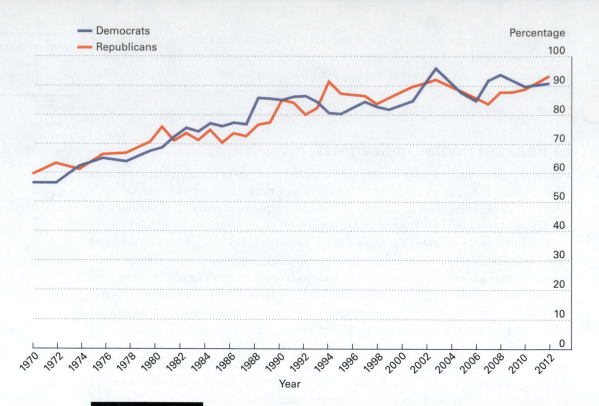

**FIGURE 11.5** PARTY VOTING IN CONGRESS

Partisanship has been growing in Congress. One indicator is the increase in the percentage of times the average Democrat and Republican in the House and Senate sided with his/her party on partisan votes—those votes when a majority of Democrats voted against a majority of Republicans.

*Source:* Davidson, Roger H., Walter J. Oleszek, and Frances E. Lee. Congress and Its Meembers, 13th ed. Washington, D.C.: CQ Press, 2012; Brookings Institution, "Historical House Ideology and Party Unity, 35th-112th Congress (1857-2012)," interactive, November 25, 2013.

committees and on the floor of the House and the Senate. Indeed, it has been shown that party affiliation is the best predictor of the voting behavior of members of the Congress and that it is becoming ever more important. In the words of several leading congressional scholars, following what party leaders and other party legislators want is the default position of most senators and representatives.[40]

One way to track partisanship is a statistic showing how often the average Democrat and Republican voted with his or her party in partisan votes in Congress (see Figure 11.5). You can see that partisanship has been rising steadily since the early 1970s and is evident today in about 9 out of 10 votes. In 2009, for example, Democratic leaders were only able to muster only three Republican votes in the Senate for President Obama's emergency economic stimulus package and none at all for the final health care bill in 2010.

One result is that reaching bipartisan agreements is becoming more difficult. Then-Maine Republican Senator Olympia Snowe observed, "The whole Congress has become far more polarized and partisan so it makes it difficult to reach bipartisan agreements. The more significant the issue, the more partisan it becomes."[41]

**WHY PARTY-LINE VOTING IN CONGRESS HAS INCREASED** A number of reasons explain increasing partisanship,[42] including the changing regional bases of the parties, particularly the historic transformation of the Deep South at the congressional level from solidly Democratic to solidly Republican.[43] This trend continued after the 2014 elections. Both Mark Pryor (AR) and Kay Hagan (NC) lost their reelection bids to Republicans. A number of Democratic House members also lost, including Nick Rahall (WV), who had served 19 terms until his 2014 defeat.

Another reason that partisanship is on the rise in Congress is that partisan conflict has been on the rise nationally, especially among party activists and party-associated advocacy groups. Members of Congress are afraid of losing in primary elections in which activists are the crucial voters, and they need the money and time enthusiastic activists donate to candidates. The inevitable result is that members of Congress have been facing an ever-more partisan-divided electorate and interest group environment.

It is not entirely clear whether party voting differences are caused directly by party affiliation or indirectly by the character of constituencies or by the preexisting ideological commitments of members of Congress. Some scholars have found strong independent party effects regardless of constituency or ideology. Others argue that the tendency of people in the same party to vote together is simply a reflection of the fact that Democratic lawmakers tend to come from districts and states that are similar to one another and that Republican lawmakers come from places that are different from the constituencies of Democrats. For example, compared to Democrats, Republicans generally come from districts where more people go to church on a regular basis. Democratic districts, in turn, tend to contain more union members and racial minorities or large university campuses.[44] The result is that while it appears members of Congress are voting with their party, their behavior is instead driven by highly polarized constituents and one-party-dominated districts.

Increasingly, however, internal party unity and conflict between the parties seem attributable to ideology. Both in the electorate and among the members of Congress and other political elites, Democrats have become somewhat more liberal, while Republicans have become much more consistently conservative.[45] Political scientist and former Democratic representative from Oklahoma Mickey Edwards observes the following about the ideological tendencies of members of Congress: "Most people who run for office have . . . [strong] feelings not only about specific issues but about general philosophical concepts, such as the proper role of government, the impact of taxation on investment and savings, and the reasons for crime and poverty."[46]

Even now, there are some important instances when members stray from the party line. Recent fights between Republicans in the House have demonstrated how hard it can be to convince members to vote for the party's preferred position, and members of Congress have to weigh many competing concerns when casting a roll-call vote. Nonetheless, members of each party in each chamber stick closely to one another.

## ◻ Congressional Leadership

The political parties work through the leadership structure of Congress because the leaders of the majority political party are, at the same time, the leaders of the House and the Senate.[47] As Congress becomes more partisan, party becomes ever more important in shaping the actions of House and Senate leaders.[48]

**LEADERSHIP IN THE HOUSE**   The leader in the House of Representatives is the Speaker of the House. This position is recognized in the Constitution and stands second in the line of succession to the presidency, immediately after the vice president.

Until 1910, the Speaker exercised great power over the House legislative process. The bases of his power were his right to appoint committees and their chairs and his position as chair of the powerful Rules Committee, which controls the flow of legislation in the House. The revolt of the rank and file against Speaker "Uncle Joe" Cannon in 1910 resulted in the Speaker's removal from the Rules Committee and the elimination of the Speaker's power to appoint committees and their chairs. From 1910 until the early 1970s, the weakened Speaker competed with a handful of powerful committee chairs for leadership of the House.

The Democratic caucus staged a revolt against the committee system after 1974 and restored some of the powers of the Speaker, especially in making committee assignments. Many liberal Democrats felt that older, southern, conservative committee chairs were blocking their progressive legislation and sought to give the Speaker more power to bypass them. The Democratic caucus gave the Speaker more power to refer bills to committee, control the House agenda, appoint members to select committees, and direct floor debate. This change gave Speakers Tip O'Neill, Jim Wright, and Tom Foley considerable leadership resources.

**whip**

A political party member in Congress charged with keeping members informed of the plans of the party leadership, counting votes before action on important issues, and rounding up party members for votes on bills.

In 1995, the Republican caucus gave even more power to control the House legislative process to their first Speaker since 1954, Newt Gingrich. Some scholars suggest that Gingrich's speakership was the most powerful one since Cannon's.[49] Unexpected losses of Republican House seats in the 1998 elections, after a failed attempt to impeach the president, and a personal scandal of his own led to Gingrich's power waning and his subsequent resignation from the speakership and from the House.

Democrat Nancy Pelosi (D–CA) exercised a strong hand as Speaker of the House from 2007 through 2010, when the Republicans took over. To advance the Democratic agenda, she pushed through several important rule changes in 2009, which made it difficult for minority members to obstruct legislation.[50] She is generally credited with convincing the president, several of his advisers, and other Democratic congressional leaders to make a final push for health care reform when they were wavering—and eventually prevailed.[51] When the Republicans regained their majority in the House in the 2010 elections, John Boehner (R–OH) became Speaker.

Boehner's speakership has been a more difficult one and demonstrates that the power of the Speaker is not absolute. The House Republicans are divided between extremely conservative Tea Party members and other House Republicans (who are still very conservative). On several occasions in 2011 and 2012, the members of the Tea Party caucus in the Republican Party refused to support compromises that Boehner had negotiated with the Senate and the president. In 2013, largely driven by Tea Party members in the House and Senate, Republicans forced a government shutdown, a politically disastrous move for Republicans and one that the Speaker and most of the party leadership was opposed to.

No matter which party is the majority, the Speaker has more power and influence in the legislative branch than any other representative or senator. This power and influence has come about because of House rules and political party rules that have evolved since the 1970s that give the Speaker important powers and prerogatives in determining the flow of legislative business. The Speaker names conference committee members, appoints members to the powerful Rules Committee, and exercises strong influence over the appointment of the chairs of other committees and referral of bills to committees for hearings and review. The Speaker appoints the leaders of the majority party's organizations, including the campaign finance committee and the party caucus. The Speaker also has the power to recognize (or not recognize) people to speak during floor debates and is in charge of the House's schedule, which can be used to encourage favored bills and stop others.[52] The ability to allow certain bills to be reported out of committee and to control the schedule are the Speaker's most important powers.

The majority party in the House also selects a majority leader to help the Speaker plan strategy and manage the legislative business of the House, and a majority **whip**. Neither House nor party rules spell out their precise responsibilities. The nature of these jobs depends very much on what the Speaker wants, on the majority leader's talents and energy, and on what the Speaker and majority leader want the whip to do. In general, however, the Speaker may be likened to the chairman of the board in a business corporation, while the majority leader may be likened to the chief executive officer, responsible for the day-to-day operations of the enterprise.[53] The whip is the majority leader's deputy, carrying out many of the tasks of getting bills passed, including counting votes and twisting arms. Lest one think that this arrangement runs like a well-oiled machine, personality and ideological differences, and conflicting ambitions—the majority leader may think that he would make a better Speaker than the incumbent—sometimes get in the way. During many of the tense negotiations between President Obama and Speaker Boehner to increase the debt ceiling and avoid default on the nation's debt in 2011, for example, Majority Leader Eric Cantor (R–VA), second in the leadership hierarchy to Boehner, was noticeably cool to the initial compromise and failed to support it in the Republican caucus.

The minority party elects a minority leader, who acts as the chief spokesperson and legislative strategist for the opposition. The minority leader not only tries to keep the forces together but also seeks out members of the majority party who might be willing to vote against the House leadership on key issues, although this is getting more difficult to do because of rising partisanship.

**LEADERSHIP IN THE SENATE** Leadership in the Senate is less visible. Senators with formal leadership titles, such as the president pro tempore, exercise little influence. The Senate majority leader is as close as one comes to a leader in this body, but the powers of the office pale before those of the Speaker of the House. The Senate majority leader has some influence in committee assignments, office space designation, and control of access to the floor of the Senate. The majority leader is also important in the scheduling of the business of the Senate and has the right of first recognition, meaning he or she is able to speak on a bill before other members do. This gives the majority leader the power to propose his or her amendments first. The degree of actual influence is based less on formal powers, however, than on skills of personal persuasion, the respect of colleagues, visibility in the media as majority party spokesperson, and a role at the center of many of the various communication networks. In addition, campaign contributors often take the advice of the majority leader in how they allocate money for incumbents seeking reelection, giving the majority leader additional influence.

The power of the position is personal and not institutional; it cannot be passed on to the next leader. The Senate remains a body of independent, relatively equal members loosely tied together by threads of party loyalty, ideology, and mutual concern about the next election. It is not an environment conducive to decisive leadership, although a few, such as Lyndon Johnson, managed to transcend the limits of the office. And, with partisanship on the rise in the Senate, it is increasingly difficult for any majority leader to push the majority party's agenda, because important bills now require 60 votes to pass due to the increasing use of the filibuster requirement and the willingness of minority party members to ignore the majority leader's requests on items such as unanimous consent agreements.

The minority leader in the Senate has even less power than the majority leader but still plays an important role. The minority leader is expected to represent the party in the media and during debates on bills. The minority leader also negotiates directly with the majority leader on committee assignments, schedules, unanimous consent requests, and other items, and party members expect the minority leader to look out for their best interests.

## ☐ Congressional Committees

Much of the work of Congress takes place in its many committees and subcommittees. Committees are where many of the details of legislation are hammered out and where much of the oversight of the executive branch takes place. As recently as the 1960s and 1970s, committees and their chairs were relatively autonomous, exercising great power over the course of legislation, because parties were not unified and House and Senate leaders had little power. As partisanship rose in the country and Congress, however, Republicans and Democrats decided, as we have seen, to give much more power to the Speaker and some additional powers to the majority leader in the Senate, especially over committee appointments and most especially to appointments to the most important committees. The result is a dramatic decline in the power of committees and of committee chairs in the legislative process and an increase in the influence of the parties and their leaders.[54] Sometimes, and most especially in the House, leaders will completely bypass the committee process, creating special party task forces to consider important bills or bringing bills to the floor directly by the leadership team. This direct leadership-to-floor consideration of legislation happened with the pay equity bill passed early in 2009, for example.

**WHY CONGRESS HAS COMMITTEES** Committees serve several useful purposes. For one thing, they allow Congress to process the huge flow of business that comes before it. The committees serve as screening devices, allowing only a small percentage of the bills put forward to take up the time of the House and the Senate.

Committees are also islands of specialization, where members and staff develop the expertise to handle complex issues and to meet executive branch experts on equal terms. The Ways and Means Committee of the House can go toe-to-toe with the

**standing committees**
Relatively permanent congressional committees that address specific areas of legislation.

**hearings**
The taking of testimony by a congressional committee or subcommittee.

**markup**
The process of revising a bill in committee.

**select committees**
Temporary committees in Congress created to conduct studies or investigations; they have no power to report bills.

**joint committees**
Congressional committees with members from both the House and the Senate.

**conference committees**
Ad hoc committees, made up of members of both the Senate and the House of Representatives, set up to reconcile differences in the provisions of bills.

**seniority**
The principle that one attains a position on the basis of length of service.

**ranking minority member**
The highest-ranking member of the minority party on a congressional committee.

Treasury Department, for instance, on issues related to taxation. Committee expertise is one of the reasons Congress remains a vital lawmaking body.

Members of Congress also use their committee positions to enhance their chances for reelection. Rational lawmakers usually try to secure committee assignments that will allow them to channel benefits to their constituents or to advance an ideological agenda popular in their district or state.

**TYPES OF COMMITTEES IN CONGRESS** There are several kinds of committee, each of which serves a special function in the legislative process.

**Standing committees** are set up permanently, as specified in the House and Senate rules. These committees are the first stop for potential new laws. In both chambers, the party membership of the committees are appointed in proportion to the size of their party in Congress—if 55 percent of the House membership is Republican, then roughly speaking, about 55 percent of each committee will also be Republican. The majority party naturally enjoys a majority on each of the committees and controls the chair, as well as a substantial majority on the most important committees, such as the Budget and Finance Committee in the Senate and the Rules Committee and the Ways and Means Committee in the House. Not surprisingly, the ratio of Democrats and Republicans on committees is a point of considerable contention between the two parties, especially when they are evenly divided.

The avalanche of legislative business cannot be managed and given the necessary specialized attention in the full House and Senate standing committees. For most bills, **hearings**, negotiations, and **markup** take place in subcommittees. It is in the subcommittees, moreover, that most oversight of the executive branch takes place.

**Select committees** are usually temporary committees created by congressional leaders to conduct studies or investigations. Their distinguishing feature is that they have no power to send bills to the House or Senate floor. They exist to resolve matters that standing committees cannot or do not wish to handle. Often the issues before select committees are highly visible and gain a great deal of public attention for their members. Select committees investigated the Watergate scandal, the Iran-Contra affair, and intelligence failures regarding the 9/11 attacks and the run-up to the war in Iraq.

**Joint committees**, with members from both houses, are organized to facilitate the flow of legislation. The Joint Budget Committee, for instance, helps speed up the normally slow legislative process of considering the annual federal budget.

Before a bill can go to the president for signature, it must pass in identical form in each chamber. Most often, the committee that irons out the differences between House and Senate versions is called a **conference committee**. A conference committee is created as needed for each piece of major legislation. Members are selected by the Speaker of the House and the Senate majority leader in consultation with the chairs of the committees that originally considered the bills in each chamber and sometimes with the leaders of the minority party. Although they are supposed to reconcile versions of bills coming out of the House and the Senate, conference committees sometimes add, subtract, or amend provisions that are of great consequence. Much of the power of conference committees comes from the fact that bills reported by them to the House and Senate must be voted up or down; no new amendments are allowed. Like most other things in Congress, conference committees have become more partisan and divisive, resulting in less frequent use.[55] During the early and mid-2000s, Republican leaders often excluded their Democratic counterparts from conference committees, making the conference a place to work out differences among House and Senate Republicans. Given the unanimous and near-unanimous opposition of Senate and House Republicans to the Affordable Care Act, Democrats did not include GOP members on the conference committee for this legislation in 2010.

**COMMITTEE CHAIRS AND RANKING MEMBERS** For most of the twentieth century before the 1970s, appointment by **seniority** was an unbreakable rule. The most senior committee member of the majority party automatically became chair of the committee; the most senior member of the minority party automatically became the **ranking minority member**. After 1974, however, both Republicans and Democrats in the House instituted the secret ballot among party members for the election of chairs, and seniority was occasionally ignored. Seniority became even less important in the 1990s when Speaker Newt Gingrich began to bypass the most senior committee members in favor of members who would support his conservative legislative program. Appointment of committee chairs in the House remains firmly in the hands of majority party leaders today. Speaker Nancy Pelosi followed suit when the Democrats took over the House in 2007. In the Senate, however, seniority continues to be an important criterion for appointment to a chairmanship position although, even there, party leaders and members increasingly are demanding more ideological and policy conformity as a condition of appointment.

Not long ago, chairs of committees were the absolute masters of all they surveyed. From the early twentieth century to the early 1970s, the heads of congressional committees went virtually unchallenged. They hired and assigned staff, controlled the budget, created or abolished subcommittees at will, controlled the agenda, scheduled meetings, and reported (or refused to report) bills to the floor. Things are different today. As we have shown, much of the power of committee chairs over legislation has migrated to the party leadership in each house. The upshot is that decisions that were entirely the province of the chair in the past have now been greatly diminished and are shared with others.[56] Committee chairs and ranking minority members—oftentimes in the past, mavericks opposed to their own parties who were protected by seniority— now must be attentive to the party caucus and party leaders or risk losing their positions.[57] Still, committee chairs remain the most influential and active members within their committees, being at the center of all of the lines of communication, retaining the power to schedule meetings and organize the staff, having an important say on the committee's agenda and appointments to conference committees, and often winning deference as the most experienced members of their committees.

**POWER COMMITTEE MINUS 2?**

The ranking member of Senate's powerful Armed Services Committee, Carl Levin (D-MI), who has announced that he will retire at the end of his term in 2015, may soon be joined by the chairman of the committee, John McCain (R-AZ). McCain has hinted that he may leave the Senate in 2016 at the end of his term, no doubt leaving many ambitious senators wondering about their odds of obtaining one seat or the other. Not only are important national security issues on the committee's agenda, garnering senators much appreciated attention and giving them influence on important policy matters, but the size of the defense budget and the needs of the Defense Department afford ample opportunity for senators to shape the flow of defense contracts to their states.

**reciprocity**
Deferral by members of Congress to the judgment of subject-matter specialists, mainly on minor technical bills.

**unanimous consent**
Legislative action taken "without objection" as a way to expedite business; used to conduct much of the business of the Senate.

**hold**
A tactic by which a single senator can prevent action on a bill or nomination; based on an implied threat of refusing to agree to unanimous consent on other Senate matters or willingness to filibuster the bill or nomination.

## ☐ Rules and Norms in the House and Senate

Like all organizations, Congress is guided by both formal rules and informal norms of behavior.[58] Rules specify precisely how things should be done and what is not allowed. Norms are generally accepted expectations about how people ought to behave and how business ought to proceed.

Traditionally, members of the House have been expected to become specialists in some area or areas of policy and to defer to the judgment of other specialists on most bills. This mutual deference is known as **reciprocity**. While reciprocity is still common, deference to specialists—usually chairs or ranking members of committees—is declining in favor of deference to the wishes of party leaders. In the Senate, the norm of reciprocity was always less prevalent than it was in the House. Because there are fewer members in the Senate, because senators are elected on a statewide basis, and because the Senate has been the breeding ground for many presidential candidacies, a senator has more prestige, visibility, and power than a member of the House. As a result, senators are generally unwilling to sit quietly for a term or two, waiting their turn. It is not unusual for a first-term senator to introduce major bills and make important speeches. In the House, such a thing was very unusual in the past. There the old rule held sway: "To get along, go along."

Legislative life is much more rule-bound in the House of Representatives, because of its large size, than in the Senate; it tends to be more organized and hierarchical (see Table 11.2). Leaders in the House have more power, the majority party exercises more control over legislative affairs, the procedures are more structured, and the individual members have a harder time making their mark. It is geared toward majority rule, with the minority playing a lesser role. The Senate tends to be a more open and fluid place, and it lodges less power in its leaders than the House does. Each senator is more of an independent operator than his or her House colleagues. The Senate is a much more relaxed place, one that accommodates mavericks (though less so than in the past), tolerates the foibles of its members, and pays more attention to members of the minority party. It is a place where the minority and individual senators play important roles in the legislative process.

Differences between the House and the Senate are especially apparent in floor debate. Bills are scheduled for floor debate in the Senate, for instance, not by a powerful committee but by **unanimous consent**, meaning that business can be blocked by a single dissenter. Outgoing Senator Jim Bunning (R–KY) blocked Senate consideration of an unemployment insurance extension for a whole week in early 2010 by responding "no" to the majority leader Harry Reid's request for unanimous consent to bring the bill to the floor. In the Senate, moreover, each senator has the power to place a **hold** on a bill or nomination to delay consideration by the whole body. While holds cannot be found

**TABLE 11.2** DIFFERENCES BETWEEN HOUSE AND SENATE RULES AND NORMS

| Senate | House |
|---|---|
| Informal, open, nonhierarchical | Rule-bound, hierarchical |
| Leaders have only a few formal powers | Leaders have many formal powers |
| Members may serve on two or more major committees | Members restricted to one major committee |
| Less specialized | More specialized |
| Unrestricted floor debate | Restricted floor debate |
| Unlimited amendments possible | Only limited amendments possible |
| Amendments need not be germane | Amendments must be germane |
| Unlimited time for debate unless shortened by unanimous consent or halted by invocation of cloture | Limited time for debate |
| More prestige for each member | Less prestige for each member |
| More reliance on staff | Less reliance on staff |
| Minority party plays a larger role; hard to put majority rule into effect | Minority party plays a smaller role; majority rule drives legislative process |

in the formal rules of the Senate, they have become part of the many informal customs of the body. Their use is regulated only by the majority leader, who may decide on whether to grant holds and how long they can be in effect, but only by using complex and time-consuming procedural mechanisms. In 2009, Senator Jim DeMint (R–SC) held up President Obama's nominee to head the Transportation Safety Administration (TSA) for months in an effort to block TSA employees from joining a union. Later that same year, Senator Richard Shelby of Alabama blocked consideration of 70 nominees submitted by the president, using the hold as a tool to force the Obama administration to put a new FBI lab in his state and to award a military tanker contract to a firm in Alabama. Unlike the House, moreover, where debate on a bill is strictly regulated regarding the number and kinds of amendments as well as time limits for debate (determined by the Rules Committee with the agreement of the Speaker), the Senate's tradition allows for unlimited numbers of amendments—that need not be germane to the bill under consideration—and unlimited debate.

Senators in the minority have increasingly used this tolerance of unlimited amendments and debate to good effect. Because limiting debate is so difficult in the Senate, the opponents of a bill can tie up legislative business by refusing to stop debating its merits. This practice is known as the **filibuster**. In the past, senators engaged in a filibuster had to be on the floor of the Senate addressing the body. Senators trying to hold up a bill often talked for hours through night and day, working together in shifts. Under Senate rules, filibustering senators did not even have to talk about the bill itself; some read from novels or quoted verse, others told stories about their children, and still others quoted long lists of sports statistics. The purpose was serious, however: to force the majority to give up the fight and move on to other business. This tactic was highly successful but used only occasionally because it was so hard to pull off; filibustering senators had to hold the floor for hours and days, fending off challenges to end debate. And, it held up all other business in the Senate.

Today, it is much easier to filibuster because a group of senators can simply announce a filibuster—not actually engage in the act of filibustering, that is to say—and a bill is stopped in its tracks unless 60 votes to end the filibuster can be mustered (Senate Rule XXII). Needless to say, the motion to end debate, known as **cloture**, is very hard to pass in an evenly divided Senate, where a party with a small majority must attract several members of the minority party to reach the 60-vote threshold. Or, in the rare case when the majority party has 60 or more votes—which the Democrats had in 2009 and 2010—cloture is possible only if the leadership can prevent defections from its side. This gives enormous power to a handful of senators who can threaten defection.

Not surprisingly, given the power that the filibuster gives to the minority party and to a handful of senators in the majority party, the number of filibusters and the number of cloture votes to end them have multiplied dramatically. Political scientist Barbara Sinclair has shown that "extended debate" tactics—filibusters threatened or used—affected 8 percent of important bills during the 1960s, 27 percent during the 1980s, and a staggering 70 percent after the Democrats took control of the Senate in 2007.[59]

Senators' positions on the filibuster depend somewhat on whether one's party is in the majority or the minority. In 2005, after Democratic senators blocked a number of President Bush's federal court judge nominees, the Republican majority threatened to change the rules through a procedural tactic requiring only a majority vote to end debate, rather than 60 votes. In response, the Democrats threatened to begin objecting to *all* unanimous consent agreements, which would have effectively slowed Senate business to a crawl. A compromise was eventually reached and the Senate avoided what is sometimes called "the nuclear option." However, Democrats, frustrated by Senate filibusters of President Obama's nominees in 2013, changed the rules to require only 51 votes to invoke cloture on all non–Supreme Court judicial nominees and on bureaucratic appointees. The Democrats were tired of what they perceived as Republican abuse of the filibuster, which they used to block judicial nominees to federal appeals courts, not because the nominees weren't qualified, but because the Republicans objected to their politics. Republicans claimed that they had done nothing different than what Senate

**filibuster**
A parliamentary device used in the Senate to prevent a bill from coming to a vote by "talking it to death," made possible by the norm of unlimited debate.

**cloture**
A vote to end a filibuster; requires the votes of three-fifths of the membership of the Senate.

# Mapping American Politics

## Majorities, Minorities, and Senate Filibusters

### Introduction

Unlimited debate is a tradition in the U.S. Senate. Senate rules make it very difficult to end debate on a proposed bill and bring it to a vote if a number of senators wish to continue deliberations. Increasingly, senators try to kill a bill by "filibustering"—talking it to death, if you will—by not allowing other business to be taken up on the floor of the Senate. Filibusters can only be ended by passage of a cloture motion, which requires 60 votes, so the votes of only 41 senators can keep a filibuster going. The filibuster is often defended as an important instrument of deliberative democracy, because it allows the minority in the Senate to have an important say in legislative matters and not be steamrolled by the majority. Critics of the filibuster, whether Democrats or Republicans, liberals or conservatives, usually claim that filibusters are contrary to the principle of majority rule. Who is right?

### Different Maps; Different Stories

Both are right and wrong. The filibuster can be considered to serve the minority or the majority, depending on who we think the senators represent. Sustaining a filibuster, while requiring the votes of only 41 of 100 senators, may involve senators representing a large majority of the American population, a small minority, or anything in between. A filibuster sustained by a coalition of 41 senators from the most populous states would represent about 78 percent of Americans (red states on the cartogram), but a filibuster sustained by a coalition of 41 senators from the least populous states would represent only about 11 percent of Americans (green states). The cartogram, with states drawn to reflect the sizes of their populations, shows this very clearly.*

Today, of course, the filibuster usually is the tool of the minority party. In the first year of the 112th Congresss, for example, 40 GOP senators forced cloture votes on nearly every major piece of legislation. These 40 senators represented about 36 percent of the American population.

### What Do You Think?

When they were a majority in the Senate, Republicans wanted to change the filibuster rule, especially on votes that involve judicial and executive branch appointments on which the Senate has constitutional "advise and consent" responsibilities. Their argument was that a minority should not be able to block this important constitutional role. Concurring with this view, majority Democrats in 2013 ended the filibuster for all judicial and executive branch appointments save for the Supreme Court. What do you think about this change? Should the filibuster on presidential appointments still be allowed if filibustering senators represent states with a majority of the U.S. population?

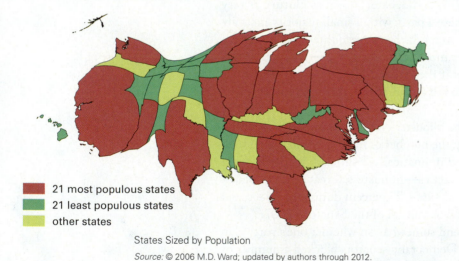

- 🟥 21 most populous states
- 🟩 21 least populous states
- 🟨 other states

States Sized by Population

*Source:* © 2006 M.D. Ward; updated by authors through 2012.

Standard US Map

*41 senators represent 20½ states, but there is no way reasonably to draw one-half of a state. In this cartogram, the large-state bloc and the small-state block each is composed of 21 states.

Democrats did during the Bush administration. In a sense, Republicans are correct that Democrats also used the tactic, but the sheer number of filibusters used by Republicans against nominees increased dramatically during the Obama presidency.[60] For more on the status of the majority and the minority in filibusters and cloture, see the "Mapping American Politics" feature.

# Legislative Responsibilities: How a Bill Becomes a Law

**11.4**   Outline the process by which a bill becomes a law

W e can put much of what we have learned to work by seeing how a bill moves through the legislative labyrinth to become a law. The path by which a bill becomes a law is so strewn with obstacles that few bills survive; in fact, only about 6 percent of all bills that are introduced are enacted. To make law is exceedingly difficult; to block bills from becoming laws is relatively easy. At each step along the way (see Figure 11.6), a "no" decision can stop the passage of a bill in its tracks. As one account points out, members of the House or the Senate have "two principal functions: to make laws and to keep laws from being

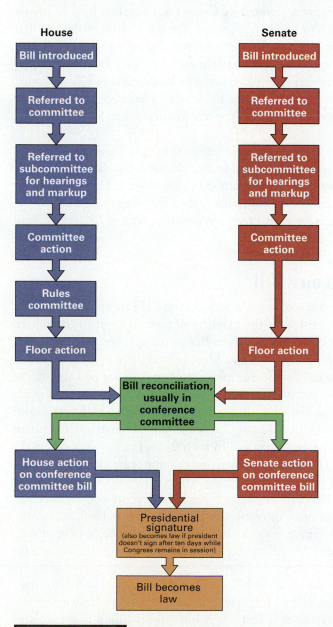

**FIGURE 11.6** HOW A BILL BECOMES A LAW

This diagram shows the path by which major bills introduced in Congress become law. As explained in the text, the road that bills must travel is complex and difficult, and few bills survive it. A bill can be derailed at any stop in its passage. A subcommittee can refuse to report a bill; a bill may be defeated on the floor of each chamber; a conference committee may fail to reach an agreement on a compromise; the conference bill may be defeated in either chamber; or the president may veto the bill.

**hopper**
The box in the House of Representatives in which proposed bills are placed.

**discharge petition**
A petition signed by 218 House members to force a bill that has been before a committee for at least 30 days while the House is in session out of the committee and onto the floor for consideration.

made. The first of these [they] perform only with sweat, patience, and a remarkable skill in the handling of creaking machinery; but the second they perform daily, with ease and infinite variety."[61]

What follows describes how major bills become law most of the time. Minor bills are often considered in each house under special rules that allow shortcuts.[62] Thus, in the House, the "suspension calendar" and the "corrections calendar" set aside certain times for consideration of minor matters. It is also worth noting that bills involving the federal budget—authorization and appropriations bills—have several unique aspects to them, which need not concern us here. And, more importantly, on some major bills, House and Senate leaders have made changes in bills coming out of committee on their way to floor action, or made important changes to bills in conference committees. Some observers claim that these "unorthodox" routes for lawmaking are becoming more and more common.[63]

## ☐ Introducing a Bill

A bill can be introduced only by a member of Congress. In reality, bills are often written in the executive branch or by interest groups. The initial draft of the bill that became the Tax Reform Act of 1986, for instance, was fashioned in the Treasury Department by a committee headed by the department's secretary, James Baker. Industry trade groups, to take another example, wrote substantial parts of bills designed to roll back timber and mining regulations in 1995, while pharmaceutical industry trade group representatives wrote key portions of the Medicare drug benefit bill that went into effect in 2006.

With the exception of tax bills (which must originate in the House), a bill may be introduced in either the House or the Senate. In the House, a member introduces a bill by putting it into the **hopper** (a box watched over by one of the House clerks). In the Senate, a member must announce a bill to the body after being recognized by the presiding officer. The bill is then assigned a number, with the prefix *H.R.* in the House or *S.* in the Senate.

## ☐ Committee Action on a Bill

The presiding officer in the Senate or the Speaker in the House refers the bill to the appropriate standing committee. In the majority of cases, referral to committee is routine; the subject matter of the bill clearly indicates the appropriate committee. Revenue bills go automatically to the Ways and Means Committee in the House and to the Finance Committee in the Senate, for instance. In a small but still significant number of cases, however, the relevant committee is not so obvious because of overlapping committee jurisdictions. For example, the House Committee on International Relations is in charge of "international policy," whereas the Commerce Committee is in charge of "foreign commerce generally." In such cases, the Speaker can make multiple referrals, that is, send a bill to more than one committee for consideration. In the Senate, bills must go to a single committee, regardless of any ambiguity that may exist about its exact content. Needless to say, the more bills there are without an obvious committee destination, the more discretionary power there is in the hands of the Speaker of the House and the Senate majority leader. Where they decide to send such bills often determines whether bills will survive the legislative process and what form they will take in the end.

Committee chairs normally pass the bill on to the appropriate subcommittee for hearings. Many a bill dies at this stage, when either the subcommittee or the full committee declines to consider it further. A bill quietly killed in committee can reach the floor only by a device called a **discharge petition**, which is rarely successful.

If a bill is accepted for consideration, the subcommittee generally holds hearings, taking testimony from people for and against it. Subcommittee staff not only help prepare representatives and senators for the questioning but also often take part in the questioning themselves. The subcommittee may then forward the bill as rewritten by the staff and subcommittee members to the full committee, or it can decide to allow the bill to go no further.

Rewriting the bill in committee is called the *markup* (discussed earlier), which usually occurs amid very intense bargaining and deal making, with an eye toward fashioning a bill that will muster majority support in the full committee and on the floors of the House and the Senate and that will gain the support of the president. The staff plays a central role in the markup.

The subcommittee reports its action to the full committee. The committee chair, in consultation with other important members of his or her committee, may opt for the committee to hold its own hearings and markup sessions, may decide to kill the bill outright, or may simply accept the action of the subcommittee. If the subcommittee has done its job well and has consulted with the most important players on the full committee (especially the chair), the committee will simply rubber-stamp the bill and move it along for floor action.

**FLOOR ACTION ON A BILL** If a bill is favorably reported from committee, congressional leaders schedule it for floor debate. In the House, major bills must first go to the Rules Committee, which decides where bills will appear on the legislative calendar and the terms under which bills will be debated by the House. A rule specifies such things as the amount of time for debate and the number (if any) and nature of amendments allowed. The Rules Committee may choose not to issue a rule at all or to drag its feet, as it did with civil rights bills until the mid-1960s. This has happened less often in recent years because both Democratic and Republican Speakers have had more power over Rules Committee appointments. The committee can also grant a "closed rule," allowing only a yes or no vote without amendments, as it generally does with tax bills.

**PUBLIC WHIPPING**

John Mack, chairman of Morgan Stanley, tries to explain to members of the Senate Finance Committee why the financial collapse happened, why industry profits were soaring, and why bonuses were being paid, even as loan money for small businesses and homeowners was scarce. The chief executives of other leading financial firms wait their turns to testify. What role in our political system do congressional hearings play? Do they lead to substantive changes in regulations and laws, or are they more often opportunities to play to the anger or frustration of the public?

**11.1**

**veto**

Presidential disapproval of a bill that has been passed by both houses of Congress. The president's veto can be overridden by a two-thirds vote in each house.

**11.2**

**11.3**

**pocket veto**

Rejection of a bill if the president takes no action on it for 10 days and Congress has adjourned during that period.

**11.4**

**oversight**

Congressional responsibility for monitoring the actions of executive branch agencies and personnel to ensure conformity to federal statutes and congressional intent.

**11.5**

Floor debate in the Senate, where rules do not limit debate as in the House, is much more freewheeling. Floor debate is also more important in the Senate in determining the final form a bill will take because Senate committees are less influential than House committees. Senators are also less likely to defer to committee judgments. Also, the threat of a hold or a filibuster means that the minority in the Senate plays an important role in determining the final shape of legislation.

After floor debate, the entire membership of the chamber votes on the bill, either as reported by the committee or (more often) after amendments have been added. If the bill receives a favorable vote, it then goes through the same obstacle course in the other chamber or awaits action by the other house if the bill was introduced there at the same time.

**CONFERENCE COMMITTEE** Even if the bill makes it through both houses, its journey is not yet over. Bills passed by the House and the Senate almost always differ from one another, sometimes in minor ways and sometimes in quite substantial ways. Before the bill goes to the president, its conflicting versions must be rewritten so that a single bill gains the approval of both chambers of Congress. This compromise bill usually is fashioned in a conference committee made up of members from both the House and the Senate appointed by the Speaker and the Senate majority leader, customarily from the relevant committees but not always. Increasingly, House and Senate leaders appoint people who will write a final bill that will be acceptable to them and to their party. Sometimes a conference committee is not used; separate House and Senate versions of a bill can be reconciled by the two trading amendments until they are similar, for example, or one chamber can simply defer to the other and accept that version of a bill.

A bill from a conference committee must be voted up or down on the floors of the House and the Senate; no amendments or further changes are allowed. If, and only if, both houses approve it, the bill is forwarded to the president for consideration.

**PRESIDENTIAL ACTION** Because the president plays an important constitutional role in turning a bill into a law, he or his assistants and advisers are usually consulted throughout the legislative process, especially if the president is of the same party that controls Congress. If the president approves the bill, he signs it and it becomes law. If he is not particularly favorable but does not want to block the bill, it becomes law after 10 days if he takes no action. He can also **veto** the bill and return it to Congress. A bill can still become law by a two-thirds vote of each house, which will override the president's veto. A president can also kill a bill at the end of a congressional session if he takes no action and Congress adjourns before 10 days pass. This is known as a **pocket veto**.

# Legislative Oversight of the Executive Branch

**11.5** Explain why Congress is doing less oversight than in the past

versight is another important responsibility of Congress. Oversight involves keeping an eye on how the executive branch carries out the provisions of the laws that Congress has passed and on possible abuses of power by executive branch officials, including the president.

Oversight is primarily the province of the committees and subcommittees of Congress, and it is among Congress's most visible and dramatic roles, guided by the wishes of House and Senate leaders and the majority party caucus in each. High-profile examples of legislative probes of alleged administrative malfeasance and incompetence include Watergate, the Iran-Contra affair, the federal response to the Hurricane Katrina disaster in New Orleans, the death of diplomats at the American embassy in Benghazi, Libya, the NSA spying scandal, and the sub-prime mortgage meltdown. In many cases, investigations have led to resignations, new legislation, and even criminal charges.

In these highly partisan times, whether oversight hearings take place and the relative vigor with which they are carried out depend increasingly on which party controls which branch of government. In the years 2003 through 2006, when Republicans controlled both houses of Congress and Republican George W. Bush was president, Congress did not probe very deeply into a number of troublesome areas, including failed prewar intelligence on weapons of mass destruction in Iraq or warrantless searches and eavesdropping on American citizens. Asked why not much oversight took place during these years, representative Chris Shays (R–CT) remarked that fellow Republicans asked him, "Why do we want to embarrass the administration?"[64] After the 2006 elections, when Democrats won majorities in both chambers, oversight hearings ratcheted up on a wide range of issues, including the alleged use of harsh interrogation methods like waterboarding on detainees and access to the courts for terrorism detainees being held at Guantanamo Bay. Democrats, apparently, were not as concerned as Republicans about embarrassing a Republican administration. After Barack Obama came to office, Democrats in Congress were less aggressive in their use of the oversight tools, though they held hearings in 2009 on bank bailouts and approval of lucrative bonuses to many of their executives, in 2010 on the TSA's and the Department of Homeland Security's failure to detect a suicide bomber (whose bomb failed to detonate) on a flight from Europe to the United States, and on BP's oil blowout in the Gulf of Mexico.

Overall, however, the number of committee hearings has declined dramatically since 1980, with only slightly more than half the number of hearings in the 2011 as there were then. This is probably because committee chairs have less power now, with less independence from the leadership on what they may do in committee.[65] Members also spend more time raising money for their reelection campaigns.[66] Still, hearings are an important part of the oversight process. Testimony is taken from agency officials, outside experts, and congressional investigatory institutions such as the Government Accounting Office and the Office of Technology Assessment. The hearings are not simply information-gathering exercises, however. As often as not, they are designed to send signals from committee members to the relevant part of the bureaucracy. Hearings that focus on the overly aggressive efforts of Internal Revenue Service agents to collect taxes, for example, are a clear signal to IRS officials that they had better rein in their agents before the next round of hearings on the budget.

Congress's final instrument of oversight of the executive branch is **impeachment** (responsibility of the House) and trial and removal from office (responsibility of the Senate) of high executive officials, including the president. While the Constitution gives the power of impeachment and removal to Congress, it has only been used once against a bureaucratic official (in 1876, against Secretary of War William W. Belknap, who was not removed from office), and only rarely against judges. No president has ever been convicted and removed from office, but the impeachment processes in the House of presidents Andrew Johnson, Nixon, and Clinton were deeply divisive, so Congress treads very cautiously in this area.

**impeachment**
House action bringing formal charges against a member of the executive branch or the federal judiciary that may or may not lead to removal from office by the Senate.

# Using the DEMOCRACY STANDARD

## Is Congress out of touch with the American people?

Although Congress was significantly democratized by passage of the Seventeenth Amendment in 1913, which transferred the election of senators from state legislatures to voters, the institution is still significantly shaped by the antimajoritarian constitutional design of the framers. Most important in this regard is its bicameral nature, the equal representation of the states in the Senate, Senate rules on the filibuster and cloture, and its immersion in a system of checks and balances.

The framers settled on bicameralism for two reasons. First, it was the only way to break the deadlock between large and small states at the constitutional convention. Had the Connecticut Compromise not been agreed to, the convention would most likely have adjourned without completing its historic task. Second, bicameralism conformed to the framers' belief that the legislative branch—the center of policymaking for government—ought to be a place where the public's business is deliberated carefully and slowly, free from the pressure of fickle public opinion. As any observer of our national legislature can report, this part of the vision was fulfilled; Congress is a place where the legislative process grinds slowly, with only a few pieces of major legislation produced in each Congress and most bills never seeing the light of day. The need for legislation to pass through two powerful chambers—one upper and one lower, each organized in different ways and each tuned to different election cycles and constituencies—is the central reason for the slow pace of this process.

As noted earlier, equal representation of the states in the Senate violates the democratic principle of political equality. Small-population states such as Wyoming, Nevada, and North Dakota have the same number of senators as large-population states such as California, New York, Texas, and Florida, meaning that the people in each of the states are unequally represented. This characteristic affects much of what the Senate does and does not do. For example, a coalition of 41 senators from the smallest population states, representing a mere 11 percent of the American population, can block any bill in the Senate (because 60 votes are needed to override a filibuster). To say that the Senate enshrines unequal representation is no exaggeration.

We must not forget, moreover, the antimajoritarian effects of the system of checks and balances within which Congress operates. Designed by the framers as the most "popular" branch—and not very "popular" at that in its original design—Congress finds itself continually hemmed in by the other two branches. Even on those rare occasions when it acts vigorously in response to public opinion, it may not always have the support it needs from the president and the courts. Further, the balance against democracy in Congress is even more disproportionate once one takes into account the important role played by interest groups and campaign contributors in its affairs.

It appears, then, that Congress has not drifted very far from what the framers had envisioned. To be sure, senators are now elected directly by the people. Also, senators and members of the House are more prone than in the past to pay attention to public opinion. Nevertheless, it remains an institution that the framers would recognize as their own creation.

# Review the Chapter

## Constitutional Foundations of the Modern Congress

**11.1** Identify the ways in which the Constitution shapes Congress, p. 321

The framers of the Constitution granted Congress legislative power, gave it an existence independent of the executive branch, enumerated an impressive range of powers, and gave it elastic powers sufficient to carry out its enumerated ones. However, they also gave the other branches powers to check legislative excesses, created a bicameral body, and strictly denied certain powers to Congress.

## Representation and Democracy

**11.2** Assess how and to what extent the members of Congress represent their constituents, p. 323

Congress is a representative institution but not necessarily fully democratic; its members are constantly balancing the preferences of the people in their constituencies and important interest groups and contributors as well as their own conceptions of the public interest.

Because elections are the most important mechanism for representation, and because they are the way in which members attain office, elections dominate the time and energy of lawmakers and shape how Congress organizes itself and goes about its business.

## How Congress Works

**11.3** Describe what leaders, political parties, and committees do in Congress, p. 336

Nearly every aspect of congressional organization and operations are defined by political parties. Leadership in each of the chambers, committee leadership and membership, and the agenda are determined by the majority party.

The House invests great powers in its leaders, with the Speaker of the House acting very much like a leader in a parliamentary system. Leadership in the Senate is much more elusive; each senator has a great deal of independent power and must be persuaded to side with party leaders.

Most of the business of the House and Senate takes place in committees and their subcommittees. Here hearings are held on bills, negotiations on bills take place, and members of Congress can bring their subject matter expertise to bear.

Over the past several decades, however, each of the political parties has given its leaders more powers, reducing that of committees and their chairs.

To conduct its business, Congress depends on an elaborate set of norms and rules and a web of committees and subcommittees, political parties, legislative leaders, and an extensive staff.

## Legislative Responsibilities: How a Bill Becomes a Law

**11.4** Outline the process by which a bill becomes a law, p. 349

After they are introduced, bills are referred to committee. Only a few make it out of committee for consideration by the entire membership of the House or Senate. In the House, the Rules Committee must issue a rule for a bill to reach the floor for debate.

If related bills pass each chamber, but in different forms, differences must be resolved in a conference committee. The report of the conference committee cannot be amended and must be voted up or down in the House and the Senate. If a bill makes it this far, it goes to the president for his signature or veto.

A bill becomes law if the president signs it, or absent his signature, if 10 days pass while Congress is in session, or if both the House and the Senate vote by a two-thirds majority to override a veto.

## Legislative Oversight of the Executive Branch

**11.5** Explain why Congress is doing less oversight than in the past, p. 352

Oversight is a way for members of Congress to bring attention to issues and to turn the spotlight on the performance of executive branch agencies. Oversight is done through committee or subcommittee hearings.

When there is unified government, Congress is reluctant to embarrass a president of its own party.

When there is divided government in today's partisan charged atmosphere, most other political actors and the media know that hearings are more about gamesmanship than about serious oversight of the executive.

# Learn the Terms

enumerated powers, p. 321
elastic clause, p. 321
bicameral, p. 321
delegate, p. 323
trustee, p. 323
descriptive representation, p. 323
constituency, p. 326
constituent, p. 326
reapportionment, p. 327
redistricting, p. 327
partisan, p. 328
gerrymandering, p. 328
crack, p. 329
pack, p. 329

majority-minority districts, p. 329
open-seat election, p. 331
franking privilege, p. 333
casework, p. 335
pork, p. 335
party conference, p. 339
caucus, p. 339
whip, p. 342
standing committees, p. 344
hearings, p. 344
markup, p. 344
select committees, p. 344
joint committees, p. 344
conference committees, p. 344

seniority, p. 344
ranking minority member, p. 344
reciprocity, p. 346
unanimous consent, p. 346
hold, p. 346
filibuster, p. 347
cloture, p. 347
hopper, p. 350
discharge petition, p. 350
veto, p. 352
pocket veto, p. 352
oversight, p. 352
impeachment, p. 353

# Test Yourself

Answer key begins on page T-1.

## 11.1  Identify the ways in which the Constitution shapes Congress

1. Congress is organized into

   **a.** One legislative chamber.
   **b.** Two legislative chambers.
   **c.** Three legislative chambers.
   **d.** Four legislative chambers.
   **e.** Five legislative chambers.

## 11.2  Assess how and to what extent the members of Congress represent their constituents

2. This happens when the same party controls both houses of the state legislature and the governor's office.

   **a.** Packing
   **b.** Partisan redistricting
   **c.** Gerrymandering
   **d.** Reapportionment
   **e.** Partisan advantage

## 11.3  Describe what leaders, political parties, and committees do in Congress

3. These types of committees are usually temporary, and created by congressional leaders to conduct studies or investigations.

   **a.** Hearing committees
   **b.** Joint committees
   **c.** Conference committees
   **d.** Select committees
   **e.** Standing committees

## 11.4  Outline the process by which a bill becomes a law

4. A bill quietly killed in committee can reach the floor only by a device called

   **a.** Discharge petition.
   **b.** Hopper petition.
   **c.** Favorable vote.
   **d.** Oversight.
   **e.** Presidential action.

## 11.5  Explain why Congress is doing less oversight than in the past.

5. Why do members of Congress spend less time than in the past questioning members of the executive branch about their activities and practices?

   **a.** They are of a generation that does not like to work very hard at their jobs.
   **b.** They find that agencies such as the GAO can do a better job.
   **c.** They spend more time than in the past raising money for their reelection campaigns.
   **d.** They are more interested in national defense policies than in domestic policies.
   **e.** Under a unified government, members of Congress do not want to embarrass their president.

# Explore Further

## INTERNET SOURCES

CongressLink at the Dirksen Center **www.congresslink.org**
Designed for teachers of American government, history, and civics, this is a very rich information site on Congress. Features include access to information on pending legislation, legislative schedules, caucuses, committees, rules, histories of the House and Senate, ways to contact members of Congress, and much more.

National Atlas **nationalatlas.gov/printable/congress.html**
Maps of all House districts.

Congress.org by CQ Roll Call **www.congress.org**
Congressional news, legislation, issues, personalities, and more, as well as information on how to have your voice heard on Capitol Hill.

Political MoneyLine by CQ Roll Call **www.politicalmoneyline. com/**
Information on campaign finance for presidential and congressional elections.

Office of the Clerk **houselive.gov**
Streaming video from the floor proceedings since the 111th Congress.

Congress.gov **www.congress.gov/**
Expansive repository of information on the House of Representatives, including the full text and progress of bills, the Congressional Record, legislative procedures and rules, committee actions, and more.

U.S. House of Representatives home page **www.house.gov**
House schedule, House organization and procedures, links to House committees, information on contacting representatives, and historical documents on the House of Representatives.

U.S. Senate Home Page **www.senate.gov**
Similar to the House of Representatives home page, focused on the Senate. One exciting new feature is a virtual tour of the Capitol.

## SUGGESTIONS FOR FURTHER READING

Caro, Robert. *The Years of Lyndon Johnson.* New York: Knopf, 1982.
This classic and award-winning biography of Lyndon Baines Johnson of Texas reveals more about how Congress worked in the "old days" than virtually any academic treatise.

Davidson, Roger H., Walter J. Oleszek, and Frances E. Lee. *Congress and Its Members*, 15th ed. Washington, D.C.: CQ Press, 2015.
The classic textbook on Congress, now in its 15th edition.

Oleszek, Walter J. *Congressional Procedures and the Policy Process*, 9th ed. Washington, D.C.: CQ Press, 2014.
The most comprehensive compilation yet published of the rules and operations of the legislative process in Congress, written by a scholar who served as the policy director of the Joint Committee on the Organization of Congress.

Quirk, Paul J., and Sarah A. Binder. *The Legislative Branch.* New York: Oxford University Press and the Annenberg Foundation Trust, 2005.
A very accessible compendium of essays by leading scholars on every aspect of Congress and the legislative process.

Sinclair, Barbara. *Unorthodox Lawmaking: New Legislative Processes in the U.S. Congress*, 4th ed. Washington, D.C.: CQ Press, 2011.
Argues that the traditional textbook rendition of "how a bill becomes a law" has dramatically changed over the past two decades.

Specialized newspapers and journals: *The Hill*, *Roll Call*, *Congressional Quarterly*, *National Journal*.
Valuable sources for up-to-the-minute, in-depth coverage of what is happening in Congress.

Swers, Michele L. *Women in the Club: Gender and Policy Making in the Senate.* Chicago: University of Chicago Press, 2013.
Analysis and insight about the role and impact of women in the U.S. Senate.

# 12

# The Presidency

## PRESIDENT OBAMA USES HIS UNITARY POWERS

**W**ith Democratic majorities in the House and Senate, President Barack Obama won significant legislative victories during his first two years in office. Most notable were a big economic stimulus bill to help the country get out of the Great Recession, new legislation to regulate many of the dangerous practices that led to the 2008 financial collapse, a budget that included middle-class tax cuts, and passage of the Affordable Care Act, often referred to as Obamacare. Things got much tougher for the president after the midterm 2010 elections when Republicans made big gains, winning control of the House and diminishing the Democratic majority in the Senate from sixty seats to fifty-three. Though Democrats won some seats back in the 2012 elections, the GOP retained control of the House, with Tea Party members more numerous in Republican ranks and remained powerful in the Senate, where all major bills require sixty votes to pass because of the filibuster rule, a number Democrats cannot reach on their own. Faced with this new math, President Obama's legislative agenda ground to a halt. After 2010, presidential-congressional relations were marked by bitter partisan combat, legislative gridlock, and brinksmanship on matters such as the debt ceiling fight in 2011, which closed the federal government for a time and almost led to default on the national debt.

Like most presidents before him who have faced a recalcitrant Congress, Obama has used his unitary powers to advance important parts of his agenda. As discussed in earlier chapters, given our constitutional system of separated powers and checks and balances, passing multiple bills that transform major elements of American public policy is very difficult at any time. Our system is better geared to stopping big policy changes than to encouraging them. Making big policy

| 12.1 | 12.2 | 12.3 | 12.4 | 12.5 |
|---|---|---|---|---|
| Trace the expansion of presidential responsibilities and power, p. 361 | Identify the many roles presidents play, p. 367 | Outline the functions filled by the president's many advisers and helpers, p. 376 | Analyze the conflict between presidents and Congress, p. 379 | Assess how democratic the presidency is and whether presidents respond to the public, p. 382 |

**THANKS FOR GETTING BIN LADEN** President Obama can act more decisively in foreign and military affairs than he can on domestic matters. Here he thanks Vice Admiral William McRaven, the operational commander of the SEAL raid into Pakistan that killed Osama Bin Laden. Obama had ordered the secret operation.

changes in a bitterly partisan environment is even more difficult. When divided government is thrown into the mix, the degree of difficulty increases.

Facing this reality, Obama made liberal use of the unitary powers of the presidency to move public policies in a direction he favored. For example, as commander in chief, he shifted the attention of the military from Iraq to Afghanistan and the Pakistan border area without needing to ask Congress. He not only increased troop levels there, but he dramatically increased the number of drone attacks on Al Qaeda sites in the region and authorized special forces actions against radical jihadist groups in Somalia and Yemen. He also authorized the raid in which Navy Seals killed Osama Bin Laden. Later he moved additional military and intelligence assets to various locations in Asia to counter the rise of China and signal a new national defense posture for the United States. (However, spillovers from the brutal civil war in Syria—a refugee crisis in the countries bordering Syria, ISIS's invasion of Iraq, and the involvement of Shia Iran and Sunni Saudi Arabia in the conflict—quashed the president's hope for a shift of U.S. foreign policy attention away from the Middle East.)

As chief executive—that is, the administrative head of the executive branch of government—he issued a string of executive orders to various bureaucratic agencies, reversing Bush administration policies on stem-cell research, climate change, and the use of torture in the interrogation of enemy combatants; ordered the Department of Transportation to allow states to impose emissions requirements that exceed those of the federal government; and overturned the ban on government contributions to international organizations that offer family planning services that include abortion. He supported the Environmental Protection Agency (EPA) when it issued rules increasing gas mileage requirements on cars, and in 2011 he issued an executive order formalizing a negotiated agreement between the EPA, the Department of Transportation, and the auto companies to dramatically increase gas mileage requirements on cars, SUVs, and trucks by 2025. In 2014, acting on his authority under the Clean Air Act, he worked with the EPA to issue a rule ordering power plants to cut carbon emissions by 30 percent from their 2005 levels by 2030, with coal-powered plants the main target. He ordered the Department of Education to make it easier for states to receive waivers from the requirements of the "No Child Left Behind" law. During the troubled rollout of Obamacare in late 2013 and early 2014, he ordered the Department of Health and Human Services to extend deadlines for people to sign up for insurance on health care exchanges. (Notably, in spite of his vigorous use of executive orders, he issued fewer of them through the first six years of his presidency than did George W. Bush during his first six years in office. His use of executive orders increased, however, after Republicans won majorities in the House and Senate in the 2014 elections.)

\* \* \* \* \*

Presidents must gain the cooperation of Congress on many matters if they are to achieve the major elements of their policy agendas and fulfill the promises made during their campaigns for office, in their inauguration speeches, and in their State of the Union addresses. What many people fail to appreciate, however, is the degree to which presidents can act on their own, without Congress, on many important matters. These unitary powers encompass a broad range of tools, including executive orders, executive agreements, signing statements, presidential proclamations, national security directives, and regulatory review, as well as authority over the armed forces and American foreign policy.[1] In this chapter we will examine the key features of the modern presidency, including the broad range of the office's unitary powers and the rise of the office to a position of preeminence in American government and why it happened.

## Thinking Critically About This Chapter

This chapter is about the American presidency, how it has evolved, and what role it plays in American politics and government.

## Using the Framework

You will see in this chapter how the presidential office has changed substantially from how the framers envisioned it, primarily because of changes in America's international situation, the nature of its economy, and popular expectations. You will also see how presidents interact with other governmental institutions (such as Congress and the Court) and with political linkage–level actors (such as political parties, public opinion, the mass media, and interest groups), and how these interactions influence what presidents do.

## Using the Democracy Standard

You will see in this chapter how the presidential office, although not envisioned by the framers to be a democratic one, has become more directly connected to and responsive to the American people. On the other hand, you will be asked to think about whether presidents' growing ability to influence the thinking of the public and shape their perceptions of public events undermines democracy.

# The Expanding Presidency

**12.1** Trace the expansion of presidential responsibilities and power

T he American presidency has grown and changed considerably since our nation's beginning. Substantial growth and changes have occurred in presidential responsibilities, burdens, power, and impact. The transformation of the office has been so considerable that two leading scholars have said that "the Constitution's framers would have great trouble recognizing today's presidency."[2]

When George Washington took office as the first president, he had a total budget (for 1789–1792) of just over $4 million and only a handful of federal employees. Even by 1801, only about 300 federal office-holders were in the capital. Washington's cabinet had only secretaries of state, war, and the treasury; a postmaster general; and an attorney general (who acted as the president's personal attorney, not as head of a full-fledged Justice Department). The entire Department of State consisted of one secretary, one chief clerk, six minor clerks, and one messenger. In 1790, only about 700 Americans were in uniform. Federal government functions were few. The entire United States occupied but 864,746 square miles; the population was only about 4 million persons, most living on small farms.[3]

When Barack Obama was first sworn into office 220 years later, he presided over a federal budget with more than $2.7 trillion in annual expenditures and a federal bureaucracy with approximately 2.7 million civilian employees (postal workers accounted for 656,000 employees). He was commander in chief of the armed forces, with about 1.5 million men and women in active-duty service; hundreds of military bases at home and scattered throughout the world; and about 10,000 nuclear warheads, 2,600 of which are operational, enough to obliterate every medium-sized or large city in the world many times over.[4] The United States in early 2009 had a population of almost 307 million diverse people; a gross domestic product of more than $14 trillion; and a land area of some 3.8 million square miles, stretching from Alaska to Florida and from Hawaii to Maine.[5]

## ☐ The Framers' Conception of the Presidency

The Founders certainly had in mind a presidency more like Washington's than Obama's. Article II of the Constitution provided for a single executive who would be strong, compared with his role under the Congress-dominated Articles of Confederation, but

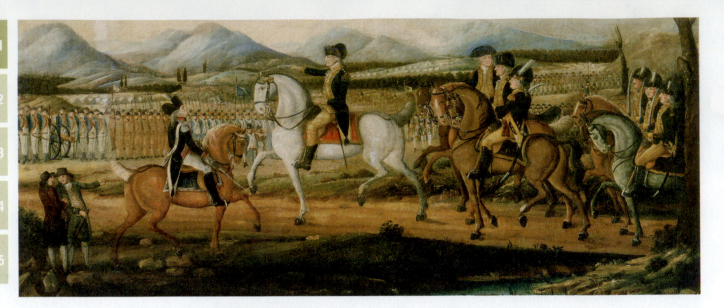

**WASHINGTON REVIEWS THE TROOPS**

The presidency has grown in scale and responsibility. As commander in chief of the armed forces, George Washington, here reviewing his troops during his first year as president, commanded an army of just over 700 soldiers and had little to do with affairs outside the United States. Today, the president commands a force of about 1.4 million active duty personnel stationed all over the world. How has this change in the role of the president affected the relative balance of power among the three branches of government?

the Constitution's sparse language declaring that "The executive power shall be vested in a President of the United States," barely hinted at the range of things twentieth- and twenty-first-century presidents would do.[6] The Constitution made the president "commander in chief" of the armed forces, for example, without any suggestion that there would be a vast standing army that presidents could send abroad to fight in places such as Bosnia and Somalia without a declaration of war. It empowered presidents to appoint and to "require the opinion in writing" of executive department heads without indicating that a huge federal bureaucracy would evolve. The Constitution provided that presidents could from time to time "recommend . . . measures" to Congress without specifying that these proposals would very often come to dominate Congress's agenda. Still, the vague language of the Constitution proved flexible enough to encompass the great expansion of the presidency.

## ☐ The Dormant Presidency

From the time of George Washington's inauguration at Federal Hall in New York City to the end of the nineteenth century, the presidency, for the most part, conformed to the designs of the Founders. The presidency did not, by and large, dominate the political life of the nation. Presidents saw their responsibility as primarily involving the execution of policies decided by Congress. Congress was a fully equal branch of government, or perhaps more than equal. But the office changed after that.

**STRUCTURAL FACTORS** Why does the early presidency seem so weak in comparison with the contemporary presidency? Surely it is not because early presidents were less intelligent, vigorous, or ambitious; indeed, this era produced some of our greatest presidents—as well as some who are largely forgotten. A more reasonable answer is that the nation did not often require a very strong presidency before the twentieth century, particularly in the key areas of foreign policy and military leadership. Only in the twentieth century did the United States develop into a world power, involved in military, diplomatic, and economic activities around the globe. With that *structural* development came a simultaneous increase in the power and responsibility of the president.

It was not until the late nineteenth century, moreover, that the economy of the United States was transformed from a simple free market economy of farmers and small firms to a corporate-dominated economy, with units so large and interconnected that their every action had social consequences for all Americans. The emergence of big banks and Wall Street finance added to the broad and consequential reach of a handful of large and interconnected firms. This transformation eventually led to demands for more government supervision of the American economic system. As this role of government grew, so did the president's role as chief executive of the federal government.

Although the presidency was largely dormant until the end of the nineteenth century, events and the actions of several presidents during the early period anticipated what was to happen to the office in our own time. Presidential actions created precedents for their successors; what the public and political elites expected of presidents changed; and new laws were passed that gradually enhanced presidential responsibilities and powers.

**IMPORTANT EARLY PRESIDENTS** The war hero George Washington solidified the prestige of the presidency at a time when executive leadership was mistrusted.[7] Washington also affirmed the primacy of the president in foreign affairs and set a precedent for fashioning a domestic legislative program. Thomas Jefferson, although initially hostile to the idea of a vigorous central government, boldly concluded the Louisiana Purchase with France, which roughly doubled the size of the United States and opened the continent for American settlement. Andrew Jackson, elected with broader popular participation than ever before, helped transform the presidency into a popular institution, as symbolized by his vigorous opposition to the Bank of the United States (which was seen by many ordinary Americans as a tool of the wealthy).

James Polk energetically exercised his powers as commander in chief of the armed forces, provoking a war with Mexico and acquiring most of what is now the southwestern United States and California. Abraham Lincoln, in order to win the Civil War, invoked emergency powers based on his broad reading of the Constitution: he raised and spent money and deployed troops on his own initiative, with Congress acquiescing only afterward; he temporarily suspended the right of *habeas corpus* and allowed civilians to be tried in military courts; and he unilaterally freed the slaves in the Confederate states by issuing the Emancipation Proclamation justifying it as a war measure under his commander-in-chief powers.

## ☐ The Twentieth-Century Transformation

More enduring changes in the presidency came only in the twentieth century, when new structural conditions made an expanded presidency both possible and necessary. Theodore Roosevelt vigorously pushed the prerogatives and enhanced the powers of the office as no president had done since Lincoln. Roosevelt was happiest when he was deploying the troops as commander in chief or serving as the nation's chief diplomat to protect American economic and political interests. On the domestic front, Roosevelt pushed for regulation of the new and powerful business corporations, especially by breaking up trusts, and he established many national parks. (See the "Can Government Do Anything Well?" feature.) In Theodore Roosevelt, we see the coming together of an energetic and ambitious political leader and a new set of structural factors in the United States, particularly the nation's emergence as a world power and an industrialized economy. The interplay of these three factors expanded the power and responsibilities of the presidency.

Woodrow Wilson's presidency marked further important steps in the expansion of the federal government and the presidency. Wilson's "New Freedom" domestic program built on the Progressive Era measures of Theodore Roosevelt, including further regulation of the economy by establishment of the Federal Reserve Board (1913) and the Federal Trade Commission (1914). Under Wilson, World War I brought an enormous increase in activity: a huge mobilization of military personnel and a large, new civilian bureaucracy to oversee the production and distribution of food, fuel, and armaments by the American "arsenal of democracy."

It was Franklin D. Roosevelt, however, who presided over the most significant expansion of presidential functions and activities in American history and changed American expectations about the office. In response to the Great Depression, Roosevelt and the Democratic majority in Congress pushed into law a series of measures for

*habeas corpus*
The legal doctrine that a person who is arrested must have a timely hearing before a judge.

# Can Government Do Anything Well?

## The National Park System

Taking a break from a presidential tour of the country during April 1903 in which he was to deliver two hundred speeches (presumably the same speech at each stop in this time before radio, television, and the Internet), President Theodore Roosevelt wanted some time alone. In the vicinity of Yellowstone National Park, TR left his entourage and protectors behind and spent a day riding through the wilderness with the army officer in charge of the park (the army was given this task since there was no state government). On the same trip, he visited the Grand Canyon, not yet a national park. A month after his stay in Yellowstone, he camped in Yosemite National Park for three nights with conservationist John Muir, who wanted Roosevelt to add the beautiful Yosemite Valley to the park.

Roosevelt was no neophyte in the wilderness. He spent much of his youth watching and categorizing birds, writing a major book on the subject before he entered Harvard. He spent years during his teen and adult life working in and around wilderness areas, switching off between being a cowboy, a big-game hunter, and a rancher, and even put in a stint as a marshal chasing outlaws through the badlands of North Dakota. He loved the wilderness and thrived in its solitude. He was moved and saddened when Muir described how much of the natural world was fast disappearing as the country was filling up. Convinced by Muir that action was required before a point of no return was reached, Roosevelt acted boldly on his return to Washington. From then until the end of his presidency in 1909, Roosevelt signed bills creating 5 new national parks; issued executive orders under the Antiquities Act creating 18 new national monuments, including the Grand Canyon, Muir Woods, the Devil's Tower, and Chaco Canyon; and set aside over 100 million acres of public land as national forests.

The National Park System, now numbering 59 parks with almost 84 million acres, and administered since 1916 by the National Park Service, is among the most appreciated accomplishments of the national government. The parks are heavily used—some say too heavily used—by Americans and visitors from other countries, with more than 281 million visits in 2012.

*Support for the claim that the federal government has been successful in creating and managing a system of national parks:*

- Consistently positive evaluations by the public in surveys, the number of annual visitors to the park system, and the degree to which the U.S. system has been copied around the world suggest that the national parks are a significant achievement.

- The creation of national parks was part and parcel of a larger conservation movement that helped preserve tens of millions of acres of national forests and wilderness, making the natural world accessible to America's people.

- The National Park Service employs just over 20,000 people to administer the parks, but 10 times that many volunteers pitch in, making the operation more cost effective.

- The park service has taken on the difficult task of restoring ecosystems and has made much progress in projects such as the South Florida Restoration Initiative that are beyond the means of state and local governments.

*Rejection of the claim that the federal government has been successful in creating and managing a system of national parks:*

**Rejection of the concept of wilderness protection in principle (from the Cato Institute)**

- A free country needs a wide diffusion of private property; the government already holds and manages too much land, so there should be no further expansion of the national parks or wilderness areas in general. Private ownership is the most efficient way to manage land use and the best way to preserve our freedom.

- Restricted access to the energy and mineral wealth in the parks lessens GDP growth and hurts the standard of living of Americans.

**The private sector would be better at park administration**

- The NPS often does a poor job maintaining and protecting national parks and national monuments. For example, the Organ Pipe Cactus National Monument in Arizona has been so degraded that it has lost its "wilderness" character.

- Given budget constraints, the park service cannot keep up with maintenance and upgrading needs as well as the other obligations Congress has assigned to it, even though its budget has been gradually increasing.

- Private enterprise is the best solution to resource and management problems; more extensive public–private partnerships would do much to improve the state of the parks, which are finding it increasingly difficult to maintain and improve visitor facilities and amenities.

**WHAT DO YOU THINK?**

What do you think about the past, present, and future role of the federal government in creating and managing the national park system?

- The federal government (i.e., the National Park Service) has been very successful in its administration and protection of national parks throughout the United States and no private intervention is necessary.
- The federal government (i.e., the National Park Service) has been successful in its administration and protection of national parks throughout the United States, but because of budget problems, some private sector involvement would be helpful.
- The federal government (i.e., the National Park Service) has not been successful in its administration and protection of national parks throughout the United States and should rely substantially on the private sector to rectify the current problems.

How would you defend your position to a fellow student? What would be your main line of argument? What evidence do you believe best supports your position? For help in developing your argument, please refer to the sources listed in the "Can Government Do Anything Well" feature in Chapter 2 on p. 45.

economic relief that grew into vast programs of conservation and public works, farm credit, business loans, and relief payments to the destitute. Roosevelt's New Deal also established a number of independent commissions to regulate aspects of business (the stock market, telephones, utilities, airlines) and enacted programs such as Social Security, which provided income support for retired Americans, and the Wagner Act, which helped workers join unions and bargain collectively with their employers. As Congress created these and many other new agencies in the executive branch, the role of the presidency grew because of his constitutional powers as chief executive.

Even bigger changes, however, resulted from World War II, when the government mobilized the entire population and the whole economy for the war effort. With the end of World War II, the United States was established as a military superpower. Since the time of Franklin Roosevelt, all U.S. presidents have administered a huge national security state with large standing armed forces, nuclear weapons, and bases all around the world.

Although he accomplished little on the legislative front during his brief time in office—he did introduce the 1964 Civil Rights Act, passed after his death—John F. Kennedy was the first president to appreciate the importance of television as both a campaign tool and as an instrument for influencing the public and political actors in Washington, the states, and other countries. His televised speeches and press conferences, where his charm, intelligence, and sense of humor were clearly evident, became one of his most effective governing tools. Presidents after him tried to follow his lead, but only Ronald Reagan, Bill Clinton, and Barack Obama matched Kennedy's mastery of the medium.

In the 1980s, Ronald Reagan managed to bring many of the main items of the conservative agenda to fruition: a massive tax cut to stimulate the economy, cutbacks in the number of regulations that affect business, cuts in a wide range of domestic social programs, and a substantial buildup of U.S. armed forces. Perhaps more importantly, he showed the American people and others around the world that a vigorous and popular presidency was still possible after the failed presidency of Richard Nixon, and the relatively weak presidencies of Gerald Ford and Jimmy Carter.

After the 9/11 terrorist attacks on the United States, George W. Bush pushed what many consider to be among the most expansive readings of presidential power in American history. In order to protect the United States against future terrorist attacks, President Bush felt it both necessary and constitutionally permissible, for example, to advise the armed forces and the CIA to ignore the Geneva Convention on the treatment of detainees captured in the war on terrorism. He claimed the right, moreover, to keep detainees indefinitely without trial or hearings, even if they were American citizens. He also authorized warrantless surveillance of American citizens by the National Security Agency, which the agency is forbidden to do without the permission of a special court.[8]

In addition to being the nation's first African American president, Barack Obama will likely be remembered for the passage of the Affordable Care Act (ACA), which was designed to extend medical insurance coverage to those who were previously uninsured and to bring health care spending under control. Only time will tell whether the ACA has transformed the delivery of health care in the United States and met its ambitious goals.

**REAGAN AND GORBACHEV IN RED SQUARE**

Whether rightly or wrongly, Ronald Reagan—whose foreign policies included a dramatic arms buildup followed by proposals to refashion the basic relationship between the two superpowers—is often given credit for ending the Cold War and nurturing the collapse of the Soviet Union. Here, President Reagan and Soviet leader Mikhail Gorbachev enjoy the sun and meet people in Red Square. How do world events shape the president's popularity in the United States?

## ☐ How Important Are Individual Presidents?

We cannot be sure to what extent presidents themselves caused this great expansion of the scope of their office. Clearly, they played a part. Lincoln, Wilson, and Franklin Roosevelt, for example, not only reacted vigorously to events but also helped create events; each had something to do with the coming of the wars that were so crucial in adding to their activities and powers. Yet these great presidents were also the product of great times; they stepped into situations that had deep historical roots and dynamics of their own.

Lincoln found a nation in bitter conflict over the relative economic and political power of North and South and focused on the question of slavery in the western territories; war was a likely, if not inevitable, outcome. Wilson and Franklin Roosevelt each faced a world in which German expansion threatened the perceived economic and cultural interests of the United States and in which U.S. industrial power permitted a strong response. The Great Depression fairly cried out for a new kind of presidential activism. Kennedy faced an international system in which the Soviet Union had become especially strident and menacing. George W. Bush was president when the 9/11 terrorist attacks on the United States occurred, allowing him to make the broadest claims possible concerning the president's powers to defend the nation. Thus, the great upsurges in presidential power and activity were, at least in part, a result of forces at the *structural* level, stimulated by events and developments in the economy, American society, and the international system.

We see, then, that it is this mixture of a president's personal qualities (personality and character) and deeper structural factors (such as the existence of military, foreign policy, or economic crises) that determines which presidents transform the office.

**THE WAR LEADER**

President George W. Bush imposed a strong national defense orientation on nearly every aspect of American foreign policy in the wake of the 9/11 terrorist attacks. As foreign policy leader and commander-in-chief, the president had sufficient tools to move the United States in this direction. Secretary of Defense Donald Rumsfeld (left) and Vice President Richard Cheney (center) were strong and able advocates of such an orientation in foreign affairs.

Most of these big presidential transformations become part of the presidency as an institution. Presidents want and need the powers accumulated by their predecessors, and use the precedents set by them. The American people have tended to support—and in crisis situations, demand—strong presidential leadership. Congress has passed laws over the years in response to new challenges that directly or indirectly increase presidential responsibilities and power. And the courts, with some notable exceptions to be mentioned elsewhere in this book, generally have accepted the development path the presidency has taken as it became the preeminent office in American government.

# The Powers and Roles of the President

**12.2**     Identify the many roles presidents play

The American presidency has assumed powers and taken on roles unimaginable to the Founders. Each touches on the daily lives of everyone in the United States and affects tens of millions of people around the world as well. In this section, we examine the many roles of the president and see how each role has a set of responsibilities associated with it as well as a set of powers that have become more expansive over the years.

**State of the Union**
Annual report to the nation by the president, now delivered before a joint session of Congress, on the state of the nation and his legislative proposals for addressing national problems.

## ☐ Chief of State

The president is both the chief executive of the United States—responsible for the executive branch of the federal government—and the chief of state, a symbol of national authority and unity. In contrast to European parliamentary democracies such as Britain or Norway, where a monarch acts as chief of state while a prime minister serves as head of the government, in the United States the two functions are combined. It is the president who performs many ceremonial duties (attending funerals of important people, proclaiming official days, lighting the national Christmas tree, honoring heroes, celebrating national holidays) that are carried out by members of royal families in other nations. As one journalist once put it, "The office of President is such a bastardized thing, half royalty and half democracy, that nobody knows whether to genuflect or spit."[9] Because it adds to their prestige and standing with other government officials and the public, presidents have always found the chief of state role to be a useful tool in their political arsenal, enabling them to get their way on many important issues. Especially in times of armed conflict, criticism of the president seems to many Americans to amount to criticism of the country itself and the troops who are in harm's way, something skilled presidents can and do use to maximize support for their policies.

## ☐ Domestic Policy Leader

The president has taken on important responsibilities on the domestic front that were probably not anticipated by the framers. These include his role as the nation's legislative leader and manager of the economy.[10]

**LEGISLATIVE LEADER**  While the Constitution seems to give primary responsibility for the legislative agenda of the United States to Congress, over time, the initiative for proposing big policy changes and new programs has shifted significantly to the president and the executive branch. The bases of this change may be found in the Constitution, statutes passed by Congress, and the changing expectations of the American people. The Constitution, for example, specifies that the president must, ". . . from time to time give the Congress information on the state of the union, and recommend to their consideration such measures as he shall judge necessary and expedient." Until Woodrow Wilson's presidency, the "**State of the Union**" took the form of a written report sent every year or every two years to Congress for its consideration. These reports often gathered dust in the House and Senate clerks' offices. Wilson, a strong believer in the role of the president as chief legislative leader similar to the prime minister in a parliamentary system, began the practice of delivering the State of the Union to Congress in an address to a joint session of the House and Senate, in which the president sets out his agenda for congressional legislation. Wilson correctly sensed that the American people were in the mood for vigorous legislative leadership from the president, given the enormous technological, economic, and social changes that were happening in the United States and the problems that were being generated by these changes.

In modern times, the State of the Union address has become one of the most important tools by which presidents gain the attention of the public and other public officials for what they want to accomplish. The State of the Union is now a very dramatic and visible event, delivered before a joint session of Congress, with members of the Supreme Court, the president's cabinet, and the military joint chiefs in attendance, and a national television audience. In the State of the Union, presidents, much as Wilson did, set out what issues they hope Congress will address, with a promise that detailed proposals for legislation will be forthcoming.

The president's legislative role also was enhanced by the Budget Act of 1921, which requires the president to submit an annual federal government budget to Congress for its consideration, accompanied by a budget message setting out the president's rationale and justifications. Prior to the Act, the budget of the United States was prepared initially in Congress. This change in the location of where initial decisions were to be made about proposed spending for government programs and agencies from the legislative to the executive branch represented a formidable enhancement in both the responsibilities and power of the president.

Although the House and Senate often take action on their own with regard to the nation's legislative agenda, what is striking is the degree to which Congress waits for and acts in response to presidential State of the Union addresses, budgets, and legislative proposals to meet various national problems. Indeed, the twentieth century is dotted with presidential labels on broad legislative programs: Wilson's New Freedom, Roosevelt's New Deal, Truman's Fair Deal, Kennedy's New Frontier, and Johnson's Great Society. On the other hand, presidents invite trouble when they fail to lead on major pieces of legislation about which they care deeply. Barack Obama, for example, left it almost entirely to Congress to fashion the Affordable Care Act. The result was a bitter year-and-a-half-long struggle in Congress that dismayed the public and undermined presidential and congressional popularity, and produced a bill which the president signed that satisfied few, even its supporters.[11]

**MANAGER OF THE ECONOMY** We now expect presidents to "do something" about the economy when things are going badly. The Great Depression taught most Americans that the federal government has a role to play in fighting economic downturns, and the example of Franklin Roosevelt convinced many that the main actor in this drama ought to be the president. Congress recognized this in 1946 when it passed the Employment Act, requiring the president to produce an annual report on the state of the economy, assisted by a new Council of Economic Advisers, with a set of recommendations for congressional action to maintain the health of the American economy. The role is now so well established that even conservative presidents like Ronald Reagan and George W. Bush felt compelled to involve the federal government in the prevention of bank failures, the stimulation of economic growth, and the promotion of exports abroad. George W. Bush, for example, supported an economic stimulus package in 2008 to fight a growing recession and the collapse of the real estate market. He also authorized the Treasury Department to work with the Federal Reserve to reorganize investment banks, provide bailouts to big commercial banks, and take over failing mortgage giants Freddie Mac and Fannie Mae. Though he came to office in the midst of a recession, President Obama's popularity was damaged badly as his actions failed to visibly change the situation for average Americans by the end of his first two years in office, leading to massive losses to the Republicans in the 2010 national elections. A similar dynamic played out in the 2014 elections.

## Chief Executive

Although he shares influence over the executive branch of the federal government with Congress and the courts, the president is the chief executive of the United States, charged by the Constitution and expected by the American people to ensure that the nation's laws are efficiently and effectively carried out by bureaucratic agencies such as the Justice, Interior, and Commerce Departments; the National Aeronautics and Space Administration (NASA); and the National Weather Service. When an agency fails, as the Federal Emergency Management Agency (FEMA) did spectacularly in the aftermath of the Katrina disaster, the president invariably takes the heat. In addition to their power to nominate and appoint the topmost leaders of federal departments and agencies, presidents exercise influence over the bureaucracy mainly by the use of **executive orders**—formal directives to executive branch departments and agencies that have the force of law.[12] These orders take many specific forms, including presidential proclamations, decision memoranda, signing statements, and national security directives. The problem is that presidents have something less than full control over the federal bureaucracy, so they cannot be certain that agency leaders and personnel will do what presidents want them to do.[13] Nevertheless, presidents exercise more influence over executive branch agencies than any other government actor or set of actors.

Presidents have various tools to shape the behavior of executive branch agencies. Sometimes presidents try to get federal bureaucrats to act by issuing executive orders— formal directives to executive branch departments and agencies that have the force of law. These orders take many forms, including presidential proclamations, decision memoranda, and national security directives. The legitimacy of such orders is based sometimes

**executive order**
A rule or regulation issued by the president that has the force of law, based either on the constitutional powers of the presidency as chief executive or commander in chief or on congressional statutes.

12.1

12.2

12.3

12.4

12.5

**unitary executive**
Constitutional doctrine that proposes that the executive branch is under the direct control of the president, who has all authority necessary to control the actions of federal bureaucracy personnel and units without interference from the other federal branches.

on the constitutional positions of the president as chief executive and commander in chief, sometimes on discretionary authority granted to the president by Congress in statutes, and often on precedents set by past presidents. Executive orders are not only about minor administrative matters; many have been issued by presidents to institute important federal policies and programs.[14] Thomas Jefferson executed the Louisiana Purchase by proclamation (though he needed money appropriated by Congress to complete the agreement with France), and Abraham Lincoln did the same when he ordered the emancipation of slaves held in states that were in revolt against the United States during the Civil War. Franklin Roosevelt ordered the internment of Japanese Americans during World War II. His successor, Harry Truman, ordered the end of racial segregation in the armed forces. Bill Clinton issued orders to set aside millions of acres of land as national monuments off-limits to logging and roads. President George W. Bush issued executive orders to, among other things, establish the White House Office of Faith-Based and Community Initiatives and restrict stem-cell research supported by federal funds. President Obama issued executive orders increasing fuel mileage requirements on cars and trucks and allowing children of illegal immigrants brought to this country at a young age to stay in the country. Some scholars worry that the use of executive orders has become so important in fashioning government policies that it amounts to unilateral presidential rule, legislating, as it were, without need of Congress or public support.[15]

Believing that the presidency had been crippled by too much congressional and judicial interference in recent decades, members of George W. Bush's administration and many conservatives revived and gave a very expansive reading to a long-dormant constitutional theory known as the **unitary executive** in an attempt to "unstymie" the office. The concept is based on Article II's "vesting" ("The executive Power shall be vested in a President of the United States of America.") and "take care" clauses ("The President shall take care that the laws be faithfully executed . . .") to suggest that the office is free to exercise command and authority over the executive branch in all respects. Presidential adviser and Justice Department official John Yoo proposed early in the Bush administration that the Constitution created a unified and hierarchical executive branch under the direct control of the president, who has all authority necessary to control the actions of federal bureaucracy personnel and units without interference from the other federal branches, including the courts.[16]

Under this doctrine, the president has the sole authority, for example, to direct the actions of agencies such as the Central Intelligence Agency (CIA) and, the National Security Agency (NSA). He alone can interpret, in his signing statements, the meaning of laws passed by Congress for executive branch personnel and units. He alone can determine the degree to which departmental and agency personnel cooperate with Congress, in terms of the release of documents or testimony before congressional committees, for example. And, he can order the review of all regulations issued by regular and independent regulatory agencies for their consistency with the law as interpreted by the president. The doctrine of the unitary executive is, to say the least, controversial, and it is not broadly accepted among constitutional scholars or by the courts.

The reality of politics on the ground, however, is that the president cannot entirely control what the executive branch does. In the day-to-day operations of the federal bureaucracy, direct command is seldom feasible. Too much is going on in hundreds of agencies. Presidents cannot keep track personally of each one of the millions of government officials and employees. Most of the time, the president can only issue general guidelines and pass them down the chain of subordinates, hoping that his wishes will be followed faithfully. But lower-level officials, protected by civil service status from being fired, may have their own interests, their own institutional norms and practices, that lead them to do something different. President Kennedy was painfully reminded of this during the Cuban Missile Crisis of 1962, when Soviet Premier Khrushchev demanded that U.S. missiles be removed from Turkey in return for the removal of Soviet missiles from Cuba: Kennedy was surprised to learn that the missiles had not already been taken out of Turkey, because he had ordered them removed a year earlier. The people responsible for carrying out this directive had not followed through.[17]

**CLOSE CALL**

The American destroyer USS *Vesole* escorts a Soviet cargo ship carrying nuclear missiles away from Cuba after President Kennedy and Soviet Premier Nikita Khrushchev reached an agreement to end what came to be known as the Cuban Missile Crisis 1962. The two nuclear powers came very close to war, but the two leaders managed to pull back from the brink despite a number of advisors on each side urging military action.

To a significant extent, a president cannot simply order things to be done to accomplish his goals but must also *persuade* executive branch officials and personnel to do things. He must bargain, compromise, and convince others that what he wants is in the country's best interest and in their own interest as well. One prominent presidential scholar has said, "Presidential power is the power to persuade."[18] Of course, presidents can do many things besides persuade: appoint top officials to executive branch departments and agencies who share the president's goals; put White House observers in second-level department positions; reshuffle, reorganize, or even—with the consent of Congress—abolish agencies that are not responsive; influence agency budgets and programs through Office of Management and Budget review; and generate pressure on agencies by Congress and the public.[19]

> **treaty**
> A formal international agreement between two or more countries; in the United States, requires the "advice and consent" of the Senate.

## ☐ Foreign Policy and Military Leader

Although the framers gave a role to Congress in fashioning foreign and military policies—note congressional control of the federal purse strings, its role in declaring war, and the Senate's "advice and consent" responsibilities with respect to treaties and appointment of ambassadors—they wanted the president to be the major player in these areas. What they could not have anticipated was that the United States would develop into the world's superpower, with global responsibilities and commitments, a development that enormously expanded the power of the presidency in the federal government.

**FOREIGN POLICY LEADER** In a case decided in 1936, the Supreme Court confirmed the president's position as the nation's preeminent foreign policy maker, saying: ". . . the president is the sole organ of the federal government in the field of international relations."[20] The president's role as foreign policy leader is rooted in the diplomatic and treaty powers sections of Article II of the Constitution, as well as in his role as commander in chief of the armed forces.[21]

The Constitution specifies that the president shall have the power to appoint and receive ambassadors and to make **treaties**. Although these formal constitutional powers may seem minor at first glance, they confer on the president the main

**executive agreement**

An agreement with another country signed by the president that has the force of law, like a treaty; does not require Senate approval; originally used for minor technical matters, now an important tool of presidential power in foreign affairs.

## OUTREACH TO THE MUSLIM WORLD

President Obama made reaching out to the world's 1.5 billion Muslims one of the main priorities of his foreign policy agenda. When he visited Cairo in June 2009, he gave a historic and widely televised speech before Egypt's parliament to assert that the United States and Muslims were not enemies. But presidents cannot always control events. Since Cairo, a democratically elected regime in Egypt has been upended by a military coup d'état that imposed a repressive regime that has stifled dissent and jailed the opposition. We continue to give military aid to Egypt given our need for that country's cooperation regarding terrorism, but such aid has not encouraged the development of democracy there. So what should our foreign policy objectives in Egypt be?

responsibility for fashioning American foreign policy. Take the power to appoint and receive ambassadors. From the very beginning of the American republic, presidents have used this provision as a tool for recognizing or refusing to recognize foreign governments. In 1793, for example, George Washington refused to accept the credentials of the French ambassador, Citizen Edmond Genet, signaling that the United States did not recognize the legitimacy of the French revolutionary government. In the twentieth century, presidents Wilson, Harding, Coolidge, and Hoover refused to recognize the revolutionary communist government of the Soviet Union, a policy that was reversed by Franklin D. Roosevelt in 1933. The Chinese communist government went unrecognized by the United States for 23 years after it came to power, a policy that was eventually reversed by Richard Nixon. The president's sole power to proclaim U.S. policy in this area is suggested by the following: neither Franklin D. Roosevelt nor Richard Nixon required the permission of any other government institution or public official—whether Congress or the courts or state legislatures, for example—to change American policy with respect to the Soviet Union or Communist China. The decision was the president's alone to make.

The power to initiate the treaty-making process is also a powerful tool of presidential diplomacy and foreign policymaking. By virtue of this power, the president and the foreign policy officials in the State, Treasury, Commerce, and Defense departments that report to him consult, negotiate, and reach agreements with other countries. Sometimes the agreements with other countries take the form of treaties—the Paris Treaty ending the Revolutionary War is an example, as are the various arms control, human rights, trade, and environmental treaties to which the United States is a party. More often, however, international agreements take the form of **executive agreements** entered into by the president and one or more foreign governments. Executive agreements appeal to presidents because they do not require the "advice and consent" of the Senate yet are understood to be lawful and binding just like treaties.[22] Originally about minor details associated with a treaty, executive agreements eventually began to be used for very important matters. In 2002 President Bush made an executive agreement with Russia that committed both to reducing the size of their nuclear stockpiles.[23]

**A TOAST TO A NEW ERA**
President Richard Nixon reestablished diplomatic relations with China in 1972. The two countries had been estranged since the Communists came to power in China in 1949 after defeating a long-time ally of the United States. The president did not require any action by Congress, the courts, or the American people to make this momentous change in policy, though most eventually welcomed it. Here he joins a toast to the new era with Chinese foreign minister Zhou Enlai.

**COMMANDER IN CHIEF** Article II, Section 2, of the Constitution specifies that the president is the commander in chief—without saying anything at all about what this actually means. On the other hand, Article I, Section 8, specifies that Congress has the power to declare war. Clearly the framers meant the president to be in charge of troops once American forces became engaged in hostilities. But they also seem to have had in mind a distinction regarding who decides whether to wage defensive war and who decides whether to wage offensive war, with the president the primary decision maker with respect to the former and Congress preeminent with respect to the latter. Thus, the president was given the power to use American forces to protect the United States against external invasions and internal insurrections; Congress was given the power to declare war against another country. As president, George Washington adhered to this distinction. As he put it in 1792, "The Constitution vests the power of declaring war with Congress; therefore no offensive expedition of importance can be undertaken until after they shall have deliberated upon the subject, and authorized such a measure."[24] Over the years, this distinction between offensive and defensive war disappeared; American forces are now sent into hostilities abroad, deployed by presidents without a formal declaration of war by Congress, in the name of defending the United States. In fact, though the United States has been involved in many military conflicts since then, Congress last declared war—against Japan and the various Axis powers—in the months following the attack on Pearl Harbor in December 1941 that brought us into World War II. Here is what seems to have been going on: as the United States became a global power, presidents, other American leaders, and the public came to believe that defending the United States required more than simply defending against cross-border invasions from other countries. Other threats seemed to many to be equally dangerous, including communism, nationalist threats to American economic interests, drug trafficking, and, most recently, terrorism.

Here is a sampling of how presidents have used American military power abroad since the Second World War. In the early 1950s, Harry Truman fought a bitter war in Korea against North Korean and Chinese forces, without a declaration of war from Congress, in the name of halting communist aggression. Presidents Eisenhower, Kennedy, Johnson, and Nixon did the same in Vietnam. Ronald Reagan used American forces in Grenada and Nicaragua to fight communism and launched an air attack against Libya to punish it for its involvement in terrorism. George H. W. Bush launched an invasion of Panama to capture its president and drug lord Manuel Noriega, and in 1991 used more than 500,000 U.S. troops in Operation Desert Storm to push Iraq out of Kuwait. President Bill Clinton sent several thousand American troops as peacekeepers to Bosnia in 1995, Haiti in 1996, and Kosovo in 1999 and waged an air war against Serbia to try to prevent further "ethnic

# Using the FRAMEWORK

## How was President Obama able to wage a war of drone strikes against jihadist targets in the Afghanistan–Pakistan border areas?

**Background:** The strategy of the United States to root out the Taliban from Afghanistan and to help install a stable government in Kabul in the wake of the 9/11 attacks on America was long frustrated by the Taliban's (and Al Qaeda's) use of the Afghanistan–Pakistan tribal areas as bases to launch attacks. Because Pakistan has been a quasi-ally of the United States during the Afghanistan operation, direct ground attacks on Taliban base areas were out of the question because it would have embarrassed the Pakistan military and roused anti-American feelings among that nation's public. Attacking by drone proved to be an attractive alternative for a while (the Pakistani public and government eventually turned against drone attacks). But how is it that President Obama was able to have the armed forces wage such a military campaign inside an allied country without authorization from Congress or oversight of the operation? We can better understand how by looking at structural, political linkage, and governmental factors that were at play.

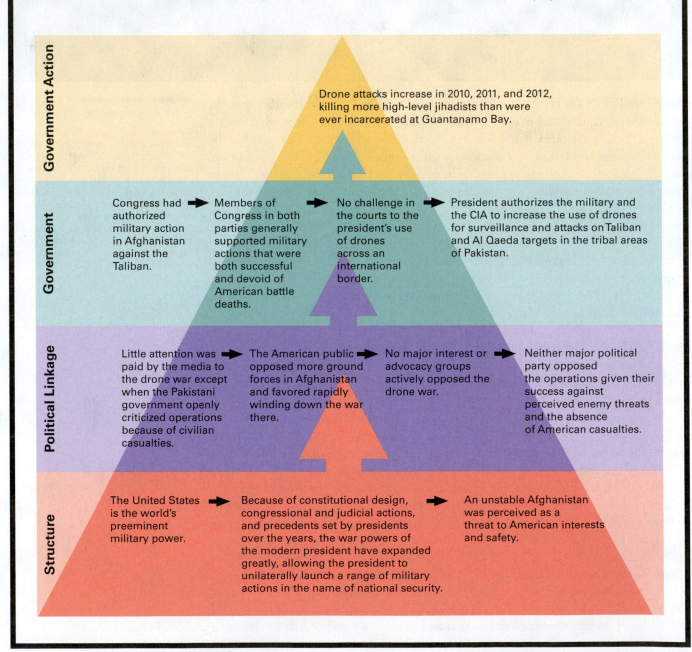

**Government Action**

Drone attacks increase in 2010, 2011, and 2012, killing more high-level jihadists than were ever incarcerated at Guantanamo Bay.

**Government**

Congress had authorized military action in Afghanistan against the Taliban. → Members of Congress in both parties generally supported military actions that were both successful and devoid of American battle deaths. → No challenge in the courts to the president's use of drones across an international border. → President authorizes the military and the CIA to increase the use of drones for surveillance and attacks on Taliban and Al Qaeda targets in the tribal areas of Pakistan.

**Political Linkage**

Little attention was paid by the media to the drone war except when the Pakistani government openly criticized operations because of civilian casualties. → The American public opposed more ground forces in Afghanistan and favored rapidly winding down the war there. → No major interest or advocacy groups actively opposed the drone war. → Neither major political party opposed the operations given their success against perceived enemy threats and the absence of American casualties.

**Structure**

The United States is the world's preeminent military power. → Because of constitutional design, congressional and judicial actions, and precedents set by presidents over the years, the war powers of the modern president have expanded greatly, allowing the president to unilaterally launch a range of military actions in the name of national security. → An unstable Afghanistan was perceived as a threat to American interests and safety.

cleansing" in its province of Kosovo. After the September 11, 2001, attacks on the United States, George W. Bush launched a military campaign against the Taliban regime and the Al Qaeda terrorist network in Afghanistan, then invaded and occupied Iraq in 2003 to protect the country against the Iraqi regime's purported weapons of mass destruction program and ties to the 9/11 terrorists (both claims proved, in the end, to be untrue). President Barack Obama, as we have seen, increased the number of troops in Afghanistan, upped the number of drone attacks on terrorist targets along the Pakistani border, and used special forces in operations in Somalia and Yemen. In none of these or related cases was Congress called upon to pass a formal declaration of war nor were they notified under terms of the War Powers Act that the United States was engaged in hostilities. (To explore how President Obama was able to wage a drone war without much public or congressional oversight, see the framework on the previous page.) In 2013, when President Obama asked Congress for permission to use force in Syria to protect civilians against attacks from the Assad regime, many commentators were aghast, believing that going to Congress in this way weakened the presidency and America's national defense capabilities.[25]

To be sure, when presidents choose to use American military power, they ordinarily consult widely with members of Congress and other government and opinion leaders. They do everything they can, moreover, to enlist the support of the public. They may even at times ask that Congress pass a resolution of support authorizing presidential use of the armed forces to defend the national security of the United States, although they are not legally bound to do so. Thus, President George H. W. Bush asked Congress to pass a resolution supporting Desert Storm in 1991, which it did. Likewise, in 2002, his son, President George W. Bush, asked Congress for a resolution supporting military action against Saddam Hussein's Iraq, which it did. Tellingly, each of the Bush presidents let it be known that military action would be forthcoming no matter the outcome of congressional deliberations.

Some presidents also have claimed that the office's commander in chief powers allow them to take extraordinary actions on the home front that seemingly violate civil liberties of some Americans, if such actions are required to defend the nation. Thus, Abraham Lincoln used military tribunals to try a number of southern sympathizers during the Civil War, Woodrow Wilson censored the press during World War I, Franklin Roosevelt ordered placement of Japanese Americans into internment camps during World War II, and George W. Bush detained without trial American citizens he defined as "enemy combatants" and authorized domestic eavesdropping by the National Security Agency to find terrorists. The Supreme Court ruled in each of these cases that the president had gone beyond his constitutional authority, but the rulings were not issued until years after they had begun.

## ☐ Head of His Political Party

One of the great difficulties all presidents face is the seeming contradiction between their role as president of all the people—as commander in chief, chief diplomat, and chief executive, for example—and their role as the leader of their political party seeking partisan advantage as well as the public good.[26] Much of the apparent contradiction has been eased by the fact that presidents, like all political leaders, generally see the public good and commitment to party principles and programs as one and the same. Thus, Ronald Reagan, as leader of the Republican party and as president, believed that the public good and his own party's prospects in upcoming elections were well served by his successful efforts to increase defense spending, deregulate the economy, and decrease domestic spending. For his part,

**institutional presidency**
The permanent bureaucracy associated with the presidency, designed to help the incumbent of the office carry out his responsibilities.

**chief of staff**
A top adviser to the president who also manages the White House staff.

**national security adviser**
A top foreign policy and defense adviser to the president who heads the National Security Council.

12.1
12.2
12.3
12.4
12.5

Lyndon Johnson, as the leader of the Democratic Party and as president, believed that the public and his party would benefit from programs to end racial discrimination and reduce poverty. Sometimes, however, the public reacts negatively when a president plays his party leader role too vigorously, seeing it as perhaps unpresidential. In 1938, in an oft-cited example, Franklin Roosevelt's effort to campaign for Democratic congressional candidates was not well received and his party won fewer seats than expected. George W. Bush's campaign involvement in the 2006 congressional elections did not prevent Democrats from winning control of both houses of Congress, nor did Obama's do much for the Democrats in 2010.

# The President's Support System

**12.3** Outline the functions filled by the president's many advisers and helpers

 **E**ach of the president's functions is demanding; together, they are overwhelming. Of course, presidents do not face their burdens alone; they have gradually acquired many advisers and helpers. The number and responsibilities of these advisers and helpers have become so extensive, and the functions they perform so essential, that they have come to form what some call the **institutional presidency**.[27]

## ☐ The White House Staff

The White House staff, for example, which is specially shaped to fit the particular needs of each president, includes a number of close advisers.

One top adviser, usually designated **chief of staff**, tends to serve as the president's right hand, supervising other staff members and organizing much of what the president does. Presidents use their chiefs of staff in different ways. Franklin Roosevelt kept a tight rein on things himself, granting equal but limited power and access to several close advisers in a *competitive* system. Dwight Eisenhower, on the other hand, used to the *hierarchical* army staff system, gave overall responsibility to his chief of staff, Sherman Adams.

Another important staff member in most presidencies is the **national security adviser**, who is also head of the president's National Security Council, operating out of the White House. The national security adviser generally meets with the president every day to brief him on the latest events that might affect the nation's security and offer advice on what to do. Several national security advisers, including Henry Kissinger (under Nixon) and Zbigniew Brzezinski (under Carter), have been strong foreign policy managers and active, world-hopping diplomats who sometimes clashed with the secretaries of state and defense. Most recent presidents, however, have appointed team players who have closely reflected the president's wishes and quietly coordinated policy among the various executive departments. This was true of President Obama's first national security advisor, former Marine Corps commandant James Jones.

Most presidents also have a top domestic policy adviser who coordinates plans for new domestic laws, regulations, and spending, although this role is often subordinate to that of the chief of staff and is not usually very visible. Close political advisers, often old comrades of the president from past campaigns, may be found in a number of White House or other government posts (e.g., James Baker served as George H. W. Bush's secretary of state, while Karen Hughes served as White House counselor to the younger Bush during his first term) or may have no official position at all (such as consultant Dick Morris, who crafted Clinton's 1996 reelection strategy). Prominent in every administration is the press secretary, who holds press conferences, briefs the media, and serves as the voice of the administration. All have a legal counsel. There are also one or more special assistants who act as a liaison with Congress, deal with interest groups, handle political matters, and consult on intergovernmental relations. Facing a deep recession and continuing financial crisis when he came to office, President Obama appointed a team of economic advisers, led by Larry Summers, to try to keep him abreast of daily developments.

However, the exact shape of the White House staff changes greatly from one presidency to another, depending on the preferences and style of the president. What was particularly striking about President George W. Bush's management style was his penchant for setting overall goals and policies but giving his staffers a great deal of freedom and latitude in getting the job done.[28] Presidents Clinton and Obama were more closely involved in the day-to-day work of their staffs.

## ☐ The Executive Office of the President

One step removed from the presidential staff, and mostly housed in the Executive Office Building next door to the White House, is a set of organizations with more than 1,800 employees that forms the **Executive Office of the President (EOP)**.

Most important of these organizations is the **Office of Management and Budget (OMB)**. The OMB advises the president on how much the administration should propose to spend for each government program and where the money will come from. The OMB also exercises legislative clearance; that is, it examines the budgetary implications of any proposed bills that will be sent to Congress and sometimes kills proposals it deems too expensive or inconsistent with the president's philosophy or goals. The OMB director often is a very powerful player in the White House and in Washington politics; good examples include David Stockman and Peter Orszag, the one serving Ronald Reagan, the other Barack Obama.

The **Council of Economic Advisers (CEA)** advises the president on economic policy. Occasionally, the head of the council exercises great influence, as Walter Heller did during the Kennedy administration. However, Obama economic czar Lawrence Summers and Treasury Secretary Tim Geithner, skilled bureaucratic infighters, made sure that CEA head Christina Romer was not much of a factor in the administration's response to the Great Recession because they disagreed with her on the size of the stimulus necessary to revive the economy (she wanted a much bigger one).[29]

The Executive Office of the President also includes the **National Security Council (NSC)**, a body of leading officials from the Departments of State and Defense, the Central Intelligence Agency (CIA), the military, and elsewhere who

**12.1**

**12.2**

**12.3**

**12.4**

**12.5**

**Executive Office of the President (EOP)**

A group of organizations that advise the president on a wide range of issues; includes, among others, the Office of Management and Budget, the National Security Council, and the Council of Economic Advisers.

**Office of Management and Budget (OMB)**

An organization within the Executive Office of the President that advises on the federal budget, domestic legislation, and regulations.

**Council of Economic Advisers (CEA)**

An organization in the Executive Office of the President made up of a small group of economists who advise on economic policy.

**National Security Council (NSC)**

An organization in the Executive Office of the President made up of officials from the State and Defense Departments, the CIA, and the military, who advise on foreign and security affairs.

**A UNIQUELY POWERFUL VICE PRESIDENT**

Richard Cheney is generally acknowledged to be the most engaged and influential vice president in American history, playing especially prominent roles in the development of doctrines and policies ranging from the use of American military power to the treatment of prisoners detained in the "war on terrorism" and the particulars of national energy policy. Is it important to the nation and presidents that vice presidents play a central role in fashioning administration policies, or should they stay more in the background?

**Intelligence Advisory Board**
An organization in the Executive Office of the President that provides information and assessments to the president's director of national intelligence and to the president directly.

advise the president on foreign affairs. The NSC has been particularly active in crisis situations and covert operations. The NSC staff, charged with various analytical and coordinating tasks, is headed by the president's national security adviser.

Increasingly important in the effort to protect the United States against terrorist attacks is the **Intelligence Advisory Board**, which provides information and assessments to the president's director of national intelligence and to the president directly. This agency was criticized for failing to "connect the dots" that allowed Nigerian national Umar Farouk Abdulmutallab to carry explosives onto a Delta Air Lines flight from London to Detroit on Christmas Day 2009.

## ☐ The Vice Presidency

In 1804, the Twelfth Amendment fixed the flaw in the original Constitution in which the person with the second most electoral votes became the vice president. Under the old rules, Aaron Burr, Thomas Jefferson's running mate in 1800, had tied Jefferson in electoral votes and tried, in the House of Representatives, to grab the presidency for himself. Since then, vice presidents have been elected specifically to that office on a party ticket with their presidents. But now there is also another way to become vice president. The Twenty-Fifth Amendment (ratified in 1967) provides for succession in case of the temporary or permanent inability of a president to discharge his office. It also states that if the vice presidency becomes vacant, the president can nominate a new vice president, who takes office on confirmation by both houses of Congress. This is how Gerald Ford became vice president in 1973 when Spiro Agnew was forced to resign because of a scandal, and how Nelson Rockefeller became vice president in 1974, when Ford replaced Richard Nixon as president.

Until quite recently, the vice presidency has not been a highly regarded office. John Nance Garner, Franklin Roosevelt's first vice president, has been quoted as saying in his earthy Texan way that the office was "not worth a pitcher of warm piss."[30] Within administrations, vice presidents were considered to be fifth wheels, not fully trusted (because they could not be fired) and not personally or politically close to the president. Vice presidents used to spend much of their time running minor errands of state, attending funerals of foreign leaders not important enough to demand presidential attention, or carrying out limited diplomatic missions. Some vice presidents were virtually frozen out of the policymaking process. For example, while vice president, Harry Truman was never informed of the existence of the Manhattan Project, which built the atomic bomb. He learned of the bomb only months before he was obligated to make a decision on using it to end the war against Japan, soon after he became president on the death of Franklin D. Roosevelt.

Recent presidents, however, have involved their vice presidents more.[31] Bill Clinton gave Al Gore important responsibilities, including the formulation of environmental policy, coping with Ross Perot's opposition to NAFTA, and the ambitious effort to "reinvent government." Barack Obama's vice president, Joe Biden, for many years a prominent senator, played a particularly important role in foreign policy, meeting with many foreign leaders, and in the several difficult budget negotiations with Congress during the period of divided government in 2011 and 2012. More than any other vice president in American history, however, Dick Cheney was at the center of the policymaking process in the White House, serving (by all accounts) as President George W. Bush's principal adviser on both domestic and foreign policy, the key player within the administration on long-range policy planning and selection of Supreme Court justices, the main liaison to Republicans in Congress,[32] an important consumer of information from the intelligence community,[33] the chief advocate for a war against Iraq, and the leading advocate of a muscular interpretation of presidential war powers.[34]

## ☐ The Cabinet

The president's cabinet is not mentioned in the Constitution. No legislation designates the composition of the cabinet, its duties, or its rules of operation. Nevertheless, all presidents since George Washington have had one. It was Washington who established the practice of meeting with his top executive officials as a group to discuss policy matters. Later presidents continued the practice, some meeting with the cabinet as often as twice a week, and others paying it less attention or none at all. Today, the cabinet usually consists of the heads of the major executive departments, plus the vice president, and whichever other officials the president deems appropriate, including the Director of National Intelligence and the White House Chief of Staff.

Presidents do not rely on the cabinet as a decision-making body. Not only is there no constitutional warrant for such a body to make policies, presidents know that they alone will be held responsible for decisions, and they alone keep the power to make them. According to legend, when Abraham Lincoln once disagreed with the entire cabinet, he declared, "Eight votes for and one against; the nays have it!"

Most recent presidents have convened the cabinet infrequently and have done serious business with it only rarely. Ronald Reagan held only a few cabinet meetings each year, and those were so dull and unimportant that Reagan was said to doze off from time to time. Bill Clinton, with his "policy wonk" mastery of details, thoroughly dominated cabinet discussions. Barack Obama hardly ever met with his full cabinet, preferring instead to consult with advisers and department secretaries only when he needed their specific expertise.

One reason for the weakness of the cabinet, especially in recent years, is simply that government has grown large and specialized. Most department heads are experts in their own areas, with little to contribute elsewhere. It could be a waste of everyone's time to engage the secretary of Health and Human Services in discussions of military strategy. Another reason is that cabinet members occupy an ambiguous position: they are advisers to the president but also represent their own constituencies, including the permanent civil servants in their departments and the organized interests that their departments serve. They may have substantial political stature of their own—consider Hillary Clinton, Obama's secretary of state—somewhat independent of the president's.

**PRESSING AMERICAN INTERESTS**

Then-Secretary of State Hillary Clinton meets with her Saudi counterpart in 2010 to gain Saudi Arabian cooperation with imposing new U.N. sanctions on Iran for the development of its nuclear weapons program. Clinton's considerable impact as secretary of state came not only because she was an appointee of the president and a member of his cabinet, but because of the considerable stature she brought to the office as a former senator and contender for the Democratic Party's presidential nomination. How might foreign leaders be affected by dealing with secretaries of state who have their own independent standing in politics?

# The President and Congress: Perpetual Tug-of-War

Analyze the conflict between presidents and Congress

he president and Congress are often at odds. This is a *structural* fact of American politics, deliberately intended by the authors of the Constitution.[35]

## □ Conflict by Constitutional Design

The Founders created a system of separation of powers and checks and balances between Congress and the president, setting "ambition to counter ambition" in order to prevent tyranny. Because virtually all constitutional powers are shared, there is a potential for conflict over virtually all aspects of government policy; our system is quite exceptional in this regard. In parliamentary systems such as Great Britain, Germany, Sweden, and Japan, there is no separation of powers between the executive and legislative branches. Recall that in such systems the prime minister and cabinet—who together make up the government, what we would call the executive branch—are themselves parliamentarians selected by the majority party or a majority coalition of parties in parliament. The executive and legislative functions thus are fused in such systems, not separated. The government—the prime minister and the cabinet—serves at the behest and will of parliament and can be dissolved by it. So checks and balances between the executive and legislative powers do not exist because the executive and the legislative are one and the same. Not so in the United States; separated powers and mutual checks are real and consequential for what government does; even though presidents have, as we have seen, dramatically expanded their powers by increasing their use of signing statements, executive orders, and executive agreements, and interpreting their war powers quite expansively.

**divided government**
Control of the executive and the legislative branches by different political parties.

**SHARED POWERS** Under the Constitution, presidents may propose legislation and can sign or veto bills passed by Congress, but both houses of Congress must pass any laws and can (and sometimes do) override presidential vetoes. Presidents can appoint ambassadors and high officials and make treaties with foreign countries, but the Senate must approve them. Presidents nominate federal judges, including U.S. Supreme Court justices, but the Senate must approve the nominations. Presidents administer the executive branch, but Congress appropriates funds for it to operate, writes the legislation that defines what it is to do, and oversees its activities.

Presidents cannot always count on the members of Congress to agree with them. The potential conflict written into the Constitution becomes real because the president and Congress often disagree about national goals, especially when there is **divided government**, that is, when the president and the majority in the House and/or the Senate belong to different parties. Bill Clinton was impeached by the Republican-controlled House of Representatives in late 1998, for example, while George W. Bush's Iraq War policies were bitterly opposed by a Democratic-dominated Congress in the last two years of his presidency. The Republican House's opposition to Barack Obama's budget plans and priorities in 2011 was so strident that it almost led to the United States defaulting on the national debt, courting financial disaster for the country and the global economy. It is not uncommon, however, for presidents to clash with members of Congress even if they are of the same party. George W. Bush ran into trouble with co-partisans on a number of issues during his second term, especially on the issue of a path to citizenship for undocumented immigrants (Bush favored such a path).

**SEPARATE ELECTIONS** In other countries' parliamentary systems, the national legislatures choose the chief executives so that unified party control is ensured. But in the United States, there are separate elections for the president and the members of Congress. Moreover, our elections do not all come at the same time. In presidential election years, two-thirds of the senators do not have to run and are insulated from new political forces that may affect the choice of a president. In nonpresidential, "off" years, all members of the House and one-third of the senators face the voters, who sometimes elect a Congress with views quite different from those of the president chosen two years earlier. In 1986, for example, halfway through Reagan's second term, the Democrats recaptured control of the Senate and caused Reagan great difficulty with Supreme Court appointments and other matters. The Republicans did the same thing to Clinton in 1994 after they gained control of Congress. Obama ran into trouble with his programs in Congress after the 2010 election, when Republicans gained control of the House and reduced the Democrat's majority in the Senate.

**OUTCOMES** In all these ways, our constitutional structure ensures that what the president can do is limited and influenced by Congress, which in turn reflects various political forces that may differ from those that affect the president. At its most extreme, Congress may even be controlled by the opposing party. This divided government situation always constrains what presidents can do and may sometimes lead to a condition called "gridlock," in which a president and Congress are locked in battle, neither able to make much headway. This is hardly surprising; a president is not only the chief executive and commander in chief of the United States but the leader of his party, so members of the opposition are not inclined to give him what he wants on the chance that it will benefit his election prospects or those of his party in Congress. Right after the 2010 Republican landslide victory, then–Senate Minority Leader Mitch McConnell, explaining his party's strategy, said his goal was to ensure that Barack Obama would be a one-term president. This hardly offered the promise of compromise on important legislative issues.

## ☐ What Makes a President Successful with Congress?

A number of political scientists have studied presidents' successes and failures in getting measures that they favor enacted into law by Congress and have suggested reasons some presidents on some issues do much better than others.[36]

**PARTY AND IDEOLOGY** The most important factor is a simple one: when the president's party controls both houses of Congress, he is much more likely than at other times to find that he gets his way in terms of legislation, approval of his appointments, and more gentle handling of executive branch problems by congressional oversight committees.[37] The president's success under this condition of unified control does not come from the president ordering party members around. Rather, the president and the members of his party in Congress tend to be like-minded on a wide range of issues, sharing values and policy preferences and a common interest in reelection. For these reasons, members of Congress tend to go along most of the time with a president of their own party.[38]

Because the parties have become so ideologically cohesive since the mid-1990s, presidents can get their way with Congress even when they have only a very slim party majority in the House and a small but somewhat larger majority in the Senate—where 60 votes are needed to get past the filibuster barrier. Between 2001 and 2006, for example, George W. Bush enjoyed many legislative successes though Republican majorities in the House and Senate were paper-thin. He was able to do this because the highly cohesive and disciplined Republican Party in the Senate was joined by a handful of moderate Democrats on many bills, making Democratic filibusters rare events. Because Barack Obama enjoyed bigger party majorities in Congress than did George W. Bush during his first two years in office—with a 60–40 margin in the Senate (counting two independents who caucused with the Democrats)—and because the Democratic Party stayed cohesive when it came to decisive votes in Congress, he was able to put together a very substantial legislative record in his first two years. According to the *Congressional Quarterly (CQ)*, Obama forged the highest presidential success score with Congress since *CQ* began keeping score in 1953.[39] The result was victory for the president on a wide range of matters, including a massive economic stimulus bill, a historic overhaul of health insurance in the United States, and wide-ranging regulation of the financial services industry. After the GOP gained seats in the Senate and gained control of the House in the 2010 elections, Obama's success with Congress sank dramatically in 2011 and 2012. Though he was reelected in 2012, congressional elections that year did not change the party balance of power in the House and Senate, so Obama remained stymied in 2013 and 2014. Obama-favored legislation died in the legislative branch, as did a record number of presidential appointments to the federal courts and to the executive branch until Senate Democrats pushed through a new rule in 2013 ending filibusters for judicial (excluding the Supreme Court) and executive branch nominations. His prospects grew bleaker in the wake of the GOP takeover of Congress after the 2014 elections.

**FOREIGN POLICY AND NATIONAL SECURITY ISSUES** Presidents tend to do better with Congress on foreign policy issues than on domestic ones, mainly because Americans want to appear united when dealing with other countries and because members' constituents pay less attention to events abroad than to what is going on in the United States. Political scientist Aaron Wildavsky went so far as to refer to "two presidencies," domestic and foreign, with the latter presidency much more dominant.[40]

This difference between domestic and foreign policy success by the president has decreased since the Vietnam War, but it remains significant. Although there was significant dissent, Congress voted in January 1991, despite many misgivings, to authorize President George H. W. Bush to use force against Iraq, once again illustrating presidential primacy in foreign affairs. Congress eventually supported Clinton's decision to send U.S. forces to Haiti, Bosnia, and Kosovo as part of multinational peacekeeping operations, despite considerable initial grumbling.

It is also the case, as you saw in the section on presidential war powers, that Congress may not be able to alter or stop presidential actions when it involves national security threats, real or perceived, even when it may want to do so. Presidents can simply act unilaterally when it comes to the deployment and use of U.S. armed forces, particularly when the public supports the overall mission.

With the rise of partisanship, the House and Senate are more willing than in the past to criticize and oppose the president on foreign and military policies, especially when one or both chambers are controlled by the party other than the president's. Democrats used House and Senate hearings to air grievances about President Bush's military actions in Iraq. During the 2012 presidential campaign, House Republicans used hearings on the terrorist attacks on the American diplomatic compound in Benghazi to attack President Obama and Secretary of State Hillary Clinton.

**VETOES**[41] When the issue is a presidential veto of legislation, the president is again very likely to prevail.[42] Vetoes have not been used often, except by certain "veto-happy" presidents, such as Franklin Roosevelt, Truman, and Ford. But when vetoes have been used, they have seldom been overridden—only 5 percent of the time for Truman and only 1.5 percent for Roosevelt. Bill Clinton did not use the veto at all during his first two years in office, when he had a Democratic majority in Congress, but he used it 11 times in 1995 alone during his budget battles with the Republican-controlled 104th Congress. Because Republicans committed to the president's agenda controlled the House from 2001 through 2006 and the Senate between 2003 and 2006, George W. Bush did not resort to the veto at all during this period. However, he used the veto several times in 2007 and 2008, most especially on bills from the Democratic-controlled Congress setting a timetable for withdrawal of American forces from Iraq and for expanding the number of children covered by the Children's Health Insurance Program (CHIP). With his party in control of Congress, Barack Obama did not use the veto in 2009 and vetoed only two minor bills in 2010. With Republicans in control of the House, nothing emerged from Congress in 2011, 2012, or 2013 that generated a veto.[43]

**POPULARITY** Most scholars and observers of Washington politics, as well as elected officials and political operatives, agree that presidential effectiveness with Congress is significantly affected by how popular a president is with the American people.[44] The reasons are not hard to fathom. Voting against proposals from a very popular president may encourage quality challengers in the next election, for example, or slow the flow of campaign funds to one's war chest, whether the president is of one's party or not. Voting with a popular president, on the other hand, can offer protective cover for a member of Congress who favors the proposal but whose constituents may not ("This is a vote for the president").[45] When a president's popular approval collapses—as George W. Bush's did after 2004—even members of his own party are loath to follow executive leadership. Bush was unable to win his own party's approval in Congress, for example, for policies he favored on immigration, Social Security reform, and the bank bailout bill.

# The President and the People: An Evolving Relationship

**12.5** Assess how democratic the presidency is and whether presidents respond to the public

The special relationship between the president and the general public has evolved over many years to make the presidency a more democratic and powerful office. Let's look at several aspects of this relationship.

## ☐ Getting Closer to the People

The Founders thought of the president as an elite leader, relatively distant from the people, interacting with Congress often but with the people only rarely. Most nineteenth-century presidents and presidential candidates thought the same. They seldom made speeches directly to the public, for example, generally averaging no more than 10 such speeches per year.[46] In the earliest years of the American Republic, presidents were not even chosen directly by the voters but by electors chosen by state legislators or, in case no one got an electoral college majority, by the House of Representatives. The Constitution thus envisioned very indirect democratic control of the presidency.

As we have also seen, however, this system quickly evolved into one in which the people played a more direct part. The two-party system developed, with parties nominating candidates and running pledged electors and the state legislators allowing ordinary citizens to vote on the electors. Presidential candidates began to win clear-cut victories in the Electoral College, taking the House of Representatives out of the process. Voting rights were broadened as well. Property and religious qualifications were dropped early in the nineteenth century. Later, slaves were freed and male former slaves were granted the right to vote; still later, women, Native Americans, and 18-year-olds won the franchise.

By the beginning of the twentieth century, presidents began to speak directly to the public. Theodore Roosevelt embarked on a series of speech-making tours in order to win passage of legislation to regulate the railroads. Woodrow Wilson made appeals to the public a central part of his presidency, articulating a new theory of the office that highlighted the close connections between the president and the public. Wilson saw the desires of the public as the wellspring of democratic government: "As is the majority, so ought the government to be."[47] He argued that presidents are unique because only they are chosen by the entire nation. Presidents, he said, should help educate the citizens about government, interpret their true will, and faithfully respond to it.

Wilson's theory of the presidency has been followed more and more fully in twentieth- and twenty-first-century thought and practice. All presidents, especially since Franklin Roosevelt, have attempted to both shape and respond to public opinion; all, to one degree or another, have attempted to speak directly to the people about policy.[48]

More and more frequently, presidents go public, using television and the Internet to bypass the print media and speak to the public directly about policy. They have held fewer news conferences with White House correspondents (where awkward questions cannot be excluded).[49] Richard Nixon pioneered prime-time television addresses, at which Ronald Reagan later excelled. Bill Clinton was more interactive with citizens, appearing on radio and TV talk shows and holding informal but televised "town hall meetings." George W. Bush liked to appear before carefully screened audiences of supporters. Barack Obama was most comfortable doing speeches and town hall–style meetings, but he also depended upon the same Internet-based technologies, especially social media, that he used so successfully in his 2008 campaign to get his message to the public, unfiltered by the news media.

## ☐ Leading Public Opinion

Especially since the rise of television, modern presidents have enhanced their power to shape public opinion. Some studies have indicated that when a popular president takes a stand in favor of a particular policy, the public's support for that policy tends to rise.[50] But there are many cases where presidents have tried but failed to move public opinion in a favorable direction, despite strong efforts to build public support for favored programs.[51] Barack Obama gave a televised address from the Oval Office to build support for his approach to the BP oil crisis in the Gulf in June 2010, but he was unable to improve his own flagging job ratings or build much enthusiasm or political support for his program of alternative energy development or a proposed "cap-and-trade" system to fight global warming.

Although not as likely to happen as is often believed, the power to lead the public also implies a power to *manipulate* public opinion if a president is so inclined—that is, to deceive or mislead the public so that it will approve policies that it might oppose if it were fully informed.[52] It is useful to remember that every modern White House has had communications specialists adept at getting out the administration's views, whether through formal channels—such as press releases, the daily briefing for reporters, and materials posted on the White House website—or informal ones, including leaks to favored journalists and in-house-written but anonymous news stories and commentaries for use in newspapers, television news broadcasts, and weblogs.[53] Especially in foreign affairs, presidents can sometimes control what information the public gets, at least in the short run.

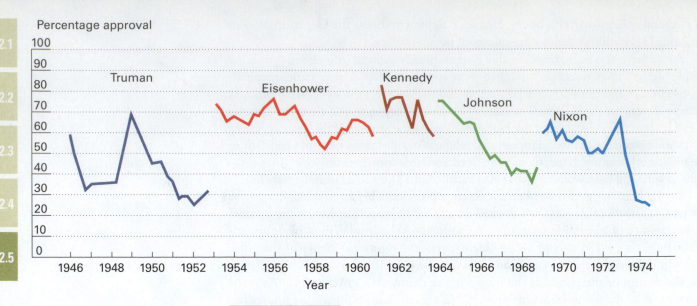

Percentage approval

Truman    Eisenhower    Kennedy    Johnson    Nixon

**FIGURE 12.1** TRENDS IN PRESIDENTIAL JOB APPROVAL, 1946–2014

Ratings of how well presidents are doing their jobs rise and fall in response to political, social, and economic events.

*Source:* Gallup surveys (graph based on average job approval for each year through October 2014).

**presidential job approval**

The percentage of Americans who believe the president is doing a good job.

## ☐ Responding to the Public

Besides trying to lead the people, presidents definitely tend to respond to public opinion. Electoral competition produces presidents who tend to share the public's policy preferences. Moreover, most presidents want to be reelected or to win a favorable place in history, and they know that they are unlikely to do so if they defy public opinion on many major issues. Usually, they try to anticipate what the public will want in order to win electoral reward and avoid electoral punishment.

There is plenty of evidence that presidents pay attention to what the public is thinking. At least since the Kennedy administration, presidents and their staffs have carefully read the available public opinion surveys and now have full-blown polling operations of their own.[54] Although such polling is often deplored, it helps presidents choose policies that the American public favors and change or discard those that are unpopular. It is worth considering another view about the role of presidential polling, however: that its purpose is to uncover not what the public wants but what words and symbols can be used by a president to sell a program.[55]

## ☐ Presidential Popularity

**Presidential job approval** affects how influential a president is with Congress, the judicial branch, and elected officials at the state and local level. Since the 1930s, Gallup and other poll takers have regularly asked Americans whether they approve or disapprove of "the president's handling of the job." The percentage of people who approve varies from month to month and year to year, and as time passes, these varying percentages can be graphed in a sort of fever chart of how the public has thought the president was doing (see Figure 12.1). A number of factors seem to be especially important in determining presidential popularity, including the stage in the president's term of office, the state of the economy, and foreign policy crises.[56]

Historically, most presidents have begun their terms of office with a majority of Americans—usually 60 percent or more—approving of how they are handling their job. Most presidents have tended to lose popularity as time passes. But this loss of popularity does not represent an inexorable working of time: Eisenhower, Reagan, and Clinton actually gained popularity during their second terms. Those who lose popularity do so in response to bad news. Good news generally makes presidents more popular.[57]

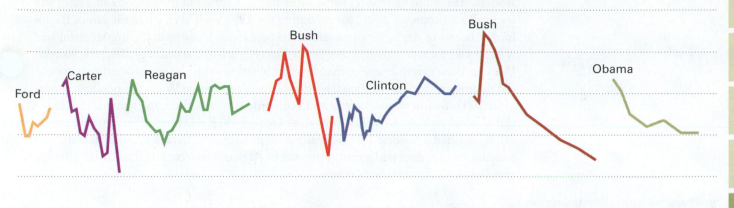

Ford

Carter

Reagan

Bush

Clinton

Bush

Obama

1976 1978 1980 1982 1984 1986 1988 1990 1992 1994 1996 1998 2000 2002 2004 2006 2008 2010 2012 2014*

Year

One of the most serious kinds of bad news involves economic recession. When the economy goes sour, fewer Americans approve of the job the president is doing. This happened to George H. W. Bush in mid-1991, as the economy faltered. Barack Obama, too, after initial support from the public, felt the sting of the public's disapproval when unemployment stayed high and disposable income stagnated, even though he had inherited a deep recession and financial crisis when he became president.

**BAD ECONOMY, POOR PRESIDENTIAL JOB APPROVAL**

Here, a woman in New York City shops for bargains before yet another retail store closes. The scene could have been repeated in cities and towns across the country as the nation suffered through a deep recession and jobless recovery from late 2007 through 2012. As is almost always the case, a bad economy, especially joblessness and declining disposable income, led to blows to public approval of the president and his party. Is this fair? Should we judge presidents mainly on the state of the economy, or are there other matters that are equally as important?

Successful military actions may sometimes add to presidential popularity, as Ronald Reagan happily discovered after the U.S. invasion of Grenada in 1982. The senior Bush's approval rating soared during the 1991 Gulf War, while the junior Bush's initial success in Afghanistan sustained his popularity. Conversely, an unsuccessful war is bad news for a president, as president Harry Truman learned regarding the Korean War. Bad news from Iraq—perhaps in combination with the administration's apparent failures in the Katrina disaster—steadily eroded George W. Bush's public approval after 2003. Bad news on the war and economic fronts at the same time can be especially lethal to a president's approval, as George W. Bush learned in 2008 when his rating reached a historic low in presidential polling, and Barack Obama did in 2010 as economic troubles and a sputtering war in Afghanistan combined to undermine his standing with the American public.

# Using the DEMOCRACY STANDARD

## Presidents and the American People

When considering the role of the chief executive, the framers never intended that it be a democratic office. In creating the Electoral College, for example, they imagined an independent body whose members (or electors) would be chosen in a manner decided by state legislatures. For the most part, they understood that state legislatures would leave the responsibility of selecting electors to themselves rather than the people. The electors from the states would then meet to elect the president from among the nation's leading citizens, free from the pressures of public opinion. As Alexander Hamilton put it in *The Federalist Papers*, No. 68, "The immediate election [of the president] should be made by men most capable of analyzing the qualities adapted to the station, and acting under circumstances favorable to deliberation, and to a judicious combination of all the reasons and inducements which were proper to govern their best choice." Because a president chosen in such a manner would not be beholden to the people for his election or reelection, he would not be overly concerned with or unduly influenced by the views of the mass public.

In addition, when designating the powers and responsibilities of the president in Article II of the Constitution, the framers evidently envisioned an office somewhat detached from national policymaking, something like a constitutional monarchy, in which the office holder would symbolize the nation but not do much in the way of running it. Although they gave the president important powers for conducting foreign affairs and defending the nation against civil unrest and invasion by foreign powers, they placed most national policymaking powers in Congress.

More than any other of the three branches of government in the Constitution created by the framers, the presidency has been democratized, with the changes so dramatic that the office would be hardly recognizable to them. As we have described this situation at various places in this chapter, the presidency has become a popular office, tied to the American people in a variety of important ways. Although the Electoral College remains in place—and can still have antimajoritarian democratic outcomes, as in the 2000 election—for all intents and purposes, presidents are elected directly by the American people as a whole, the only national office (other than the vice president) carrying this distinction. As such, modern presidents are prone to claim the mandate of the people when governing, and the American people are prone, for their part, to see the president as the center of governance and the locus for their hopes and aspirations for the nation. Presidents have used these ties to the people as the foundation for expanding presidential powers in the course of responding to national problems and emergencies.

We also know that modern presidents pay close attention to what the public wants, following public opinion polls closely and commissioning their own. To be sure, presidents sometimes manipulate the public, especially in foreign and military affairs, where presidential constitutional powers are considerable and public scrutiny is lower, but in the end, presidents cannot succeed unless they enjoy strong public support.

# Review the Chapter

## The Expanding Presidency

**12.1** Trace the expansion of presidential responsibilities and power, p. 361

The American presidency began small; only a few nineteenth-century presidents (among them Jefferson, Jackson, Polk, and Lincoln) made much of a mark.

In the twentieth century, however, as a result of the problems of industrialization, two world wars and the Cold War, and the Great Depression, presidential powers and resources expanded greatly. The presidency attained much of its modern shape during Franklin Roosevelt's presidency.

The constitutional bases of the expansion of presidential responsibilities and power lie in the president's roles as chief executive, commander in chief, and chief diplomat.

Additional sources of presidential expansion come from public expectations, legislative grants of power, and the office's role as de facto legislative leader of the nation.

## The Powers and Roles of the President

**12.2** Identify the many roles presidents play, p. 367

Presidents play many roles, including that of chief of state, chief executive, domestic policymaking leader, foreign policy and military leader, and head of their political party.

Some of the president's roles are formally inscribed in the Constitution, but others have evolved through precedent, public expectations, and congressional actions.

## The President's Support System

**12.3** Outline the functions filled by the president's many advisers and helpers, p. 376

The job of the president has become so complex and the range of the office's responsibilities so broad that the occupant needs a great deal of help carrying out his duties. The staff and agencies in the White House and the Executive Office Building that help him carry out his duties have grown to such an extent that they have come to be called the institutional presidency.

White House staff members are numerous and do such things as advise the president on domestic and national security policies, maintain relationships with Congress, convey the president's views to the media and the public, and help fashion legislation.

The main agencies in the Executive Office of the President advise and help the president carry out policies regarding the economy, the federal budget, and national security.

## The President and Congress: Perpetual Tug-of-War

**12.4** Analyze the conflict between presidents and Congress, p. 379

The tug-of-war between the president and Congress is an inherent part of the constitutional design of our government as embodied in the separation of powers and checks and balances.

Presidents also have different constituencies than members of the House and Senate, the president being the only nationally elected office.

Representatives and senators often are elected at times when the president is not a candidate, so they may come to office propelled by a different public mood than that which prevailed when the president was elected.

Conflict is exacerbated when there is divided government and high levels of partisanship.

## The President and the People: An Evolving Relationship

**12.5** Assess how democratic the presidency is and whether presidents respond to the public, p. 382

The presidency has become a far more democratic office than the framers envisioned: the people play a more important role in the election of the president, and research shows that presidents listen to public opinion and respond to it most of the time (though they sometimes do not).

# Learn the Terms

# Test Yourself

Answer key begins on page T-1.

**12.1** Trace the expansion of presidential responsibilities and power

1. This president provoked a war with Mexico, thus acquiring most of the southwestern United States and California.

   **a.** Thomas Jefferson
   **b.** Andrew Jackson
   **c.** George Washington
   **d.** Abraham Lincoln
   **e.** James Polk

**12.2** Identify the many roles presidents play

2. Presidents have used American military power abroad on many occasions without congressional declarations of war. Against which country did Congress last declare war?

   **a.** China
   **b.** Iraq
   **c.** Japan
   **d.** North Korea
   **e.** Vietnam

**12.3** Outline the functions filled by the president's many advisers and helpers

3. This organization advises the president on how much the administration should propose to spend on each government program and where the money will come from.

   **a.** Office of Management and Budget
   **b.** Council of Economic Advisers
   **c.** Intelligence Advisory Board
   **d.** Executive Office of the President
   **e.** National Security Council

**12.4** Analyze the conflict between presidents and Congress

4. What factors have the ability to make a president successful with Congress?

   **a.** Party, foreign policy, religious background
   **b.** Foreign policy, party, popularity
   **c.** Party, leadership style, religious background
   **d.** Party, effective speeches, charisma
   **e.** Leadership style, foreign policy, effective speeches

**12.5** Assess how democratic the presidency is and whether presidents respond to the public

5. This president thought that a president should help educate the citizens about government, interpret their true will, and faithfully respond to it.

   **a.** George Washington
   **b.** Theodore Roosevelt
   **c.** Franklin Roosevelt
   **d.** Woodrow Wilson
   **e.** Abraham Lincoln

# Explore Further

## INTERNET SOURCES

Executive Orders **www.archives.gov/federal-register/executive-orders/disposition.html**

A complete list with full text of presidential executive orders from the National Archives, from Herbert Hoover through Barack Obama.

Miller Center's "American President" website **www.millercenter.virginia.edu/academic/americanpresident**

A site full of historical documents, current developments, and descriptions of how the role of the president has changed.

POTUS **www.potus.com**

Biographies and other information about every American president.

National Archives Presidential Libraries **www.archives.gov/presidential_libraries/addresses/addresses.html**

Access to presidential addresses, libraries, and other information about the office.

Office of the Clerk **artandhistory.house.gov/house_history/vetoes.aspx**

Information and concise tables showing the number of vetoes, as well as the type, used by all the presidents of the United States.

PollingReport.com **www.pollingreport.com**

Collection of all major presidential job performance and popularity polls.

White House **www.whitehouse.gov**

Information on the first family, recent presidential addresses and orders, text from news conferences, official presidential documents, and ways to contact the White House.

PBS's American Experience: the Presidents **www.pbs.org/wgbh/americanexperience/collections/presidents**

Online streaming of first-rate documentary films on the lives and works of selected presidents.

## SUGGESTIONS FOR FURTHER READING

Crenson, Matthew, and Benjamin Ginsberg. *Presidential Power, Unchecked and Unbalanced.* New York: Norton, 2007.

The authors submit that the American system has been sliding toward "presidentialism," a system in which presidents are no longer checked by the other branches of government, the press, or the public.

Edwards III, George C., and Stephen J. Wayne. *Presidential Leadership: Politics and Policy Making.* Belmont, CA: Wadsworth, 2012.

A comprehensive textbook on the American presidency by two of the leading scholars of the office.

Fisher, Louis. *Defending Congress and the Constitution.* Lawrence: University of Kansas Press, 2011.

A rigorous yet passionate defense of Congress's central role in the decision to go to war and how and why modern presidents have illegitimately bypassed Congress.

Howell, William G. *Power Without Persuasion: The Politics of Direct Presidential Action.* Princeton, NJ: Princeton University Press, 2003.

Rejecting the common view among political scientists that presidential power is based primarily on the president's ability to persuade, Howell suggests instead that presidents have many tools for taking unilateral action to get their way.

Pfiffner, James, and Roger H. Davidson, eds. *Understanding the Presidency*, 7th ed. New York: Pearson Publishers, 2012.

A comprehensive anthology of recent scholarship on all aspects of the presidency and its place in the American political system.

Suskind, Ron. *Confidence Men.* New York: Harper, 2011.

An inside and devastating look at the first two years of the Obama presidency with a focus on the role of influential staff in shaping a presidency (not always for the best).

Wills, Gary. *Bomb Power: The Modern Presidency and the National Security State.* New York: Penguin Press, 2010.

Traces the rise in presidential powers to the rise of the national security state associated with nuclear weapons and the secrecy surrounding them, suggesting that these developments are dangerous to democracy and liberty, and unconstitutional.

Yoo, John. *The Powers of War and Peace: The Constitution and Foreign Affairs After 9/11.* Chicago: University of Chicago Press, 2005.

An argument for expansive and unitary presidential powers in the post–9/11 world by one of the architects of Bush administration policies on the treatment of detainees during war.

# 13

# The Executive Branch

## CUTTING FAT OR CUTTING BONE?

**B**ending to harsh criticism from the news media, consumer groups, and members of Congress for its lax oversight, and to specific regulatory requests from companies like Mattel and Walmart, the Consumer Product Safety Commission (CPSC) in June 2007 issued recalls for " . . . 68,000 folding chairs, 2,300 toy barbecue grills, 12,000 space heaters, 5,300 earrings, 1.5 million 'Thomas the Tank Engine' toy trains and 19,000 children's necklaces" imported from China because of defects in manufacturing or the use of dangerous materials such as lead paint that might harm the American public.[1] American companies had been losing sales because scared consumers were refusing to buy goods made in China even when they carried American brand names, and they wanted action. So, too, did consumer groups. The Consumer Product Safety Commission had been slow to do its own research on the safety of many of these products and had not been thorough in its efforts. Agency leaders were reluctant to take regulatory action until public, business, and political pressure mounted. But, it's hard to blame CPSC's career employees for all of this, given the size of the agency, their limited resources, and the antiregulatory atmosphere in Washington during the George W. Bush years, all coupled with the explosion of imports from China.

To ensure the safety of the public in using some 15,000 consumer products sold in the United States—20 percent of which were imported from China in 2007—the CPSC had only about 400 employees in 2007, down from about 1,000 in 1980; its budget for inspections and compliance had shrunk in real terms over the same period. In 2007, the agency had one person—yes, one person—assigned to test all domestic- and foreign-produced toys. Another

| 13.1 | 13.2 | 13.3 | 13.4 | 13.5 | 13.6 |
|------|------|------|------|------|------|
| Compare and contrast our executive branch bureaucracy with those in other countries, p. 393 | Outline the structure of the executive branch, p. 396 | Identify the kinds of activities bureaucrats perform, p. 400 | Determine how demographically representative bureaucrats are, p. 405 | Isolate various influences on executive branch decision making, p. 408 | Assess what's wrong and what's right with the federal bureaucracy, p. 415 |

**CONTAINER SECURITY** A federal inspector examines freight containers at the Port of Long Beach in California, where cargo shipments can be checked only randomly when budget cuts compel workforce reductions.

person was assigned to test the flammability of consumer products using techniques and technologies that are at least three decades old. In that year, the agency had only 81 field investigators, all working out of their homes, rather than the 133 who had worked out of a national network of field offices as recently as 2002. In the Los Angeles–Long Beach port area, which transfers 15 million semi-truck–sized shipping containers a year and where most Chinese imports enter the country, the agency had assigned a lone inspector, working two or three days a week. In the gigantic harbor of New York, goods-laden shipping containers were mostly inspected by customs agents looking for counterfeit goods, with an inspector or two from CPSC occasionally showing up. When asked in September 2007 when he had last seen a CPSC inspector, one customs inspector supervisor reported, "It was around December."[2]

Oddly enough, in the midst of the recalls and news about dangerous imported consumer products, Nancy Nord, the acting head of the agency and formerly an official of the staunchly anti-regulatory U.S. Chamber of Commerce, told Congress that her agency did not need more employees, a bigger budget, or expanded enforcement powers. She suggested that her agency was already doing a top-flight job and that, more importantly, voluntary compliance and cooperation from industry and reliance on the free market was the best strategy for protecting consumers and helping companies stay profitable.

Anti–big government and deregulatory rhetoric has been part of the standard stump speech of virtually every aspiring politician in the country for many years. Although pushed especially hard by Republicans, Democrats have played a role as well, with Bill Clinton famously saying in a State of the Union address that "the era of big government is over." Every president since Reagan has come into office with plans to cut the number of federal employees.

The result is that various executive branch departments and agencies, responsible for seeing that laws are carried out and regulations complied with, have less capacity and capability than in the past, with resources perhaps below what is minimally acceptable, according to many observers. We saw the Federal Emergency Management Agency (FEMA) fail miserably in the aftermath of Hurricane Katrina, for example. Also, tainted meat and produce have recently made their way through the thinning inspection net at the Department of Agriculture. Lax regulation by distracted and under-staffed agencies such as the Securities and Exchange Commission and the Federal Deposit Insurance Corporation was a big part of the story in the collapse of the financial industry in 2008 that plunged the country into the deepest recession since the Great Depression.

Have we managed over the past three decades or so to not only cut out the fat from the federal government, but also cut into the bone of very important agencies, making them less effective than they might be in serving the public interest? The question of whether to increase or decrease the responsibilities of federal bureaucratic agencies is an enduring one in American politics and will remain an important one in our politics for many years to come, because it is a matter that fires partisan passions.

## Thinking Critically About This Chapter

This chapter is about the executive branch of the federal government—often called the federal bureaucracy—responsible for carrying out programs and policies fashioned by Congress, the federal courts, and the president. We focus on how the executive branch is organized, what it does, and what effects its actions have on public policies and American democracy.

## Using the Framework

You will see in this chapter how the federal bureaucracy has grown over the years, primarily as a result of structural transformations in the economy and international position of the United States, but also because of the influence of political linkage level actors and institutions, including voters, public opinion, and interest groups. Primary responsibility for many of the enduring features of the federal bureaucracy will be shown to be associated with our political culture and the Constitution.

## Using the Democracy Standard

You will see in this chapter that the federal bureaucracy in general, despite much speculation to the contrary, is fairly responsive to the American people, reacting in the long run to pressures brought to bear on it by the elected branches, the president, and Congress. On the other hand, bureaucrats in specific agencies, in specific circumstances, can be relatively immune from public opinion, at least in the short and medium run. You will be asked to think about what this means in terms of our democratic evaluative standard.

**federal bureaucracy**
The totality of the departments and agencies of the executive branch of the national government.

**bureaucracy**
A large, complex organization characterized by a hierarchical set of offices, each with a specific task, controlled through a clear chain of command, and where appointment and advancement of personnel is based on merit.

**bureaucrat**
A person who works in a bureaucratic organization.

13.1
13.2
13.3
13.4
13.5
13.6

# The American Bureaucracy: How Exceptional?

**13.1** Compare and contrast our executive branch bureaucracy with those in other countries

The **federal bureaucracy** in America—that is, the executive branch of the national government—is different from government bureaucracies in other democratic nations. Structural influences such as the American political culture and the constitutional rules of the game have a great deal to do with these differences. Before looking at how we are different, however, it is important that we are clear about the term *bureaucracy*.

Bureaucracy has always been a dirty word in American politics, implying red tape, inefficiency, and non-responsiveness. To social scientists, however, **bureaucracy** and **bureaucrat** are neutral terms describing a type of social organization and the people who work in it. Bureaucracies are large organizations in which many people with specialized knowledge are organized into a clearly defined hierarchy of bureaus or offices, each of which has a specified mission. There is a clear chain of command and a set of formal rules to guide behavior. Appointment and advancement, moreover, are based on merit rather than inheritance, power, or election. This is, of course, a model or "ideal type" traceable back to the German sociologist Max Weber;[3] in the real world, there are many variations.

Bureaucracy exists in a wide range of sectors including government, private business (as in most large corporations), and the nonprofit sector, including big organizations like the Red Cross and the Girl Scouts of America. The fact that it is so common suggests that bureaucracy serves important purposes even if the popular mantra in business circles these days is to flatten hierarchies and to be more nimble. One advantage of bureaucracy

**13.1**

**13.2**

**13.3**

**13.4**

**13.5**

**13.6**

**civil servants**
Government workers employed under the merit system; not political appointees.

**civil service**
Federal government jobs held by civilian employees, excluding political appointees.

is its ability to organize large tasks like delivering Social Security checks, churning out automobiles from factories, delivering overnight packages, or fighting wars. Hierarchical organizations with clear chains of command are able to mobilize and coordinate the activities of thousands of people. Another advantage of bureaucracies is the concentration of specialized talent that is found in them. When Apple wants to bring a new product to market, it has thousands of software engineers, product design specialists, and marketing experts on hand to do the necessary work, though it may, at times, subcontract work to other firms, many of which are themselves bureaucratic organizations. When a pandemic threatens, the federal government is able to mobilize an impressively talented group of doctors and scientists at the National Institutes of Health and at the Centers for Disease Control and Prevention to find a solution and put it into effect.

Despite the complaints and jokes about federal bureaucrats, then, bureaucracies have certain advantages as a form of organization both in the private sector and the public sector. This is not to say, of course, that bureaucracy is unproblematic; it is to say that the American rhetorical distaste for bureaucracy tends to hide some of its benefits. In this chapter, we look at the large and complex bureaucracy that is the executive branch of the federal government. In this section, we focus on how our government bureaucracy is different from those in other rich democratic countries.

## ☐ Hostile Political Culture

Americans generally do not trust their government and government leaders, nor do they have much confidence that government can accomplish most of the tasks assigned to it. They believe, on the whole, that the private sector can usually do a better job and, most of the time, want responsibilities lodged there rather than with government. Figure 13.1 shows how poorly the federal government was regarded by the American public in 2013 compared to various private sector industries. At the same time, when difficulties or emergencies occur—whether economic recessions, natural disasters, or terrorist attacks—they want the federal government to be ready and able to respond.

This generally hostile environment influences the American bureaucracy in several important ways that, paradoxically, make it more difficult for it to respond when needed. For one thing, our public bureaucracy is surrounded by more legal restrictions and is subject to more intense legislative oversight than bureaucracies in other countries.[4] Because **civil servants** have so little prestige, moreover, many of the most talented people in our society do not aspire to work in government. In many other democratic countries, by way of contrast, civil service is highly respected and attracts talented people. In France, Britain, and Germany, for example, the higher **civil service** positions are filled by the top graduates of the countries' elite universities on the basis of rigorous examinations and are accorded enormous prestige. In France, the main feeder institution for higher positions in the government, the Ecole Nationale d'Administration, accepted only 80 students out of 1,352 in 2009.[5] Not surprisingly, given the elite educations that are required for these posts and the prestige accorded to civil servants, people of decidedly upper-class and aristocratic backgrounds fill the top civil service posts in France, Great Britain, and Germany; in the United States, the civil service looks much more like the general American population in terms of family background, race, gender, and the like.[6] Finally, the highest policymaking positions in the U.S. executive branch are closed to civil servants; they are reserved for presidential political appointees. This is not true in other democracies.

## ☐ Incoherent Organization

Our bureaucracy is an organizational hodgepodge. It does not take the standard pyramidal form, as bureaucracies elsewhere do. There are few clear lines of control, responsibility, or accountability. Some executive branch units have no relationship at all to other agencies and departments. As one of the leading students of the federal bureaucracy once put it, other societies have "a more orderly and symmetrical, a more prudent, a more cohesive and more powerful bureaucracy," whereas we have "a more

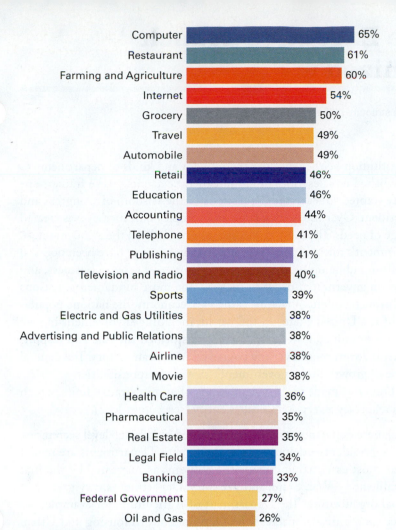

13.1

13.2

13.3

13.4

13.5

13.6

**FIGURE 13.1** PUBLIC PERCEPTION OF DIFFERENT INDUSTRIES (PERCENTAGE WITH POSITIVE VIEWS)

Americans do not think much of the federal government. In 2013, only a little more than one in four Americans thought favorably of it, trailed only by the long-reviled oil and gas industry.

*Source:* Jeffery M. Jones, "U.S. Images of Banking, Real Estate Making Comeback," Gallup, August 23, 2013.

internally competitive, a more experimental, a noisier and less coherent, a less powerful bureaucracy."[7] Our bureaucracy was built piece by piece over the years in a political system without a strong central government. Bureaucracies in other democratic nations were often created at a single point in time by powerful political leaders, such as Frederick the Great in Prussia and Napoleon in France.[8]

## ☐ Divided Control

Adding to the organizational incoherence of our federal bureaucracy is the fact that it has two bosses—the president and Congress—who are constantly vying with one another for control. In addition, the federal courts keep an eye on it. This situation is created by the separation of powers and checks and balances in our Constitution, which give each branch a role in the principal activities and responsibilities of the other branches.[9] To be sure, the president is the chief executive and has significant influence over agencies in the executive branch, but Congress plays a very large role in the creation of executive branch units, determining their annual budgets and exercising oversight of their many activities, and the courts make their presence felt as well. No other democratic nation has opted for this arrangement. Civil servants in parliamentary democracies are accountable to a single boss, a cabinet minister appointed by the prime minister, and to the parliamentary majority elected by the people.[10]

**departments**

Generally the largest units in the executive branch, each headed by a cabinet secretary.

**13.2**

**bureau**

Generally, a subunit of a cabinet department.

**13.3**

**agency**

A general name used for a subunit of a cabinet department.

**13.4**

**13.5**

**13.6**

**13.1**

# How the Executive Branch Is Organized

**13.2**   Outline the structure of the executive branch

he Constitution neither specifies the number and kinds of departments to be established nor describes other bureaucratic agencies. The framers apparently wanted to leave these questions to the wisdom of Congress and the president. Over the years, a large and complex bureaucracy was created to meet a wide range of needs. The most immediate reasons behind the transformation of the federal government's role and the growth of the bureaucracy have been political sector pressures—from public opinion, voters, parties, interest groups, business, and social movements—on government decision makers. The more fundamental reasons have been changes in such structural factors as the U.S. economy, the nation's population, and the role of the United States in the world, including involvement in war. Earlier in the text, we examined how these things transformed the role and responsibilities of the federal government over the course of American history. The general picture has been one of growth in the government's size and responsibilities.

The executive branch is made up of several kinds of administrative units, which make the federal bureaucracy a very complicated entity (see Figure 13.2):[11]

- The most familiar are **departments**, which are headed by cabinet-level secretaries, appointed by the president and approved by the Senate. Departments are meant to carry out the most essential government functions, as suggested by the first three to be established—War, State, and Treasury. Departments vary greatly in size and internal organization. The Department of Agriculture, for example, has almost 50 offices and bureaus, whereas the Department of Housing and Urban Development has only a few operating agencies. And they range in size from the Department of Defense, with about 764,000 employees (civilian) in 2012—not counting military contractors—to the Department of Education, with about 4,300 employees. Over the years, departments (and employees) were added as the need arose, as powerful groups demanded them, or as presidents and members of Congress wished to signal a new national need or to cement political alliances with important constituencies. The timeline in Figure 13.3 shows when each department was established. The newest department, Homeland Security, was created in the wake of the 9/11 terrorist attacks on the United States.

- Subdivisions within cabinet departments are **bureaus** and **agencies**. Departmental bureaus and agencies are not only numerous but varied in their relative autonomy. In some departments, such as the Department of Defense, bureaus and agencies are closely controlled by the department leadership, and the entire department works very much like a textbook hierarchical model. In other cases, where the bureaus or agencies have fashioned their own relationships with interest groups and powerful congressional committees, the departments are little more than holding companies for powerful bureaucratic subunits.[12] During the long reign of J. Edgar Hoover, for example, the FBI did virtually as it pleased, even though it was (and remains) a unit within the Justice Department. Some departments have so many diverse responsibilities that central coordination is almost impossible to achieve. The Department of Homeland Security, for example, has bureaus and agencies responsible for border control; immigration and citizenship; disaster relief and recovery; transportation security; and emergency preparedness against terrorist use of nuclear, biological, and other weapons. It also houses the U.S. Secret Service, for protection of the president and other high-profile public officials, and the U.S. Coast Guard, for protection and assistance for public and private maritime activities.[13]

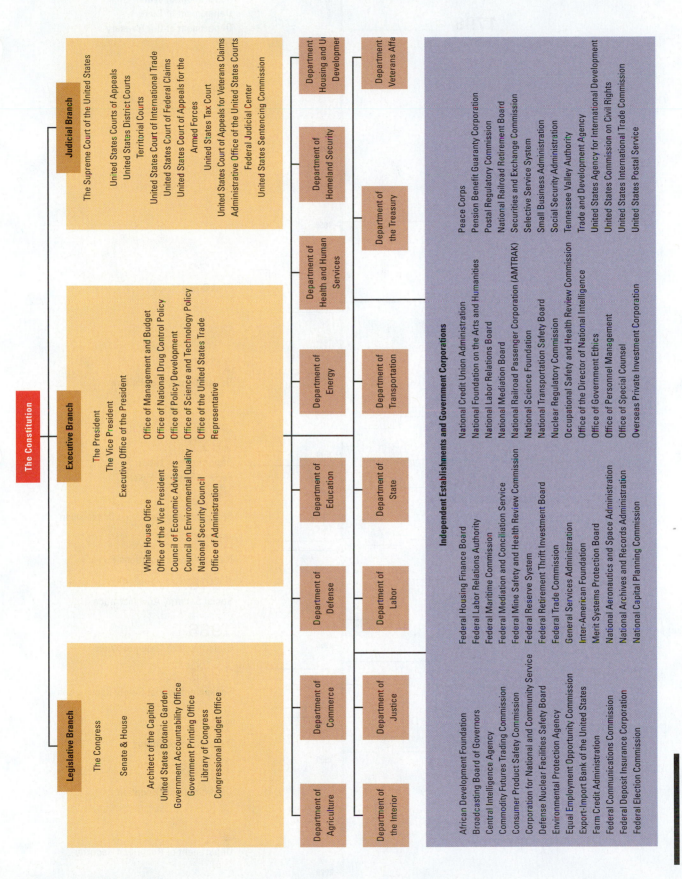

**FIGURE 13.2** THE EXECUTIVE BRANCH OF GOVERNMENT

*Source:* U.S. Government Organization Manual.

13.1
13.2
13.3
13.4
13.5
13.6

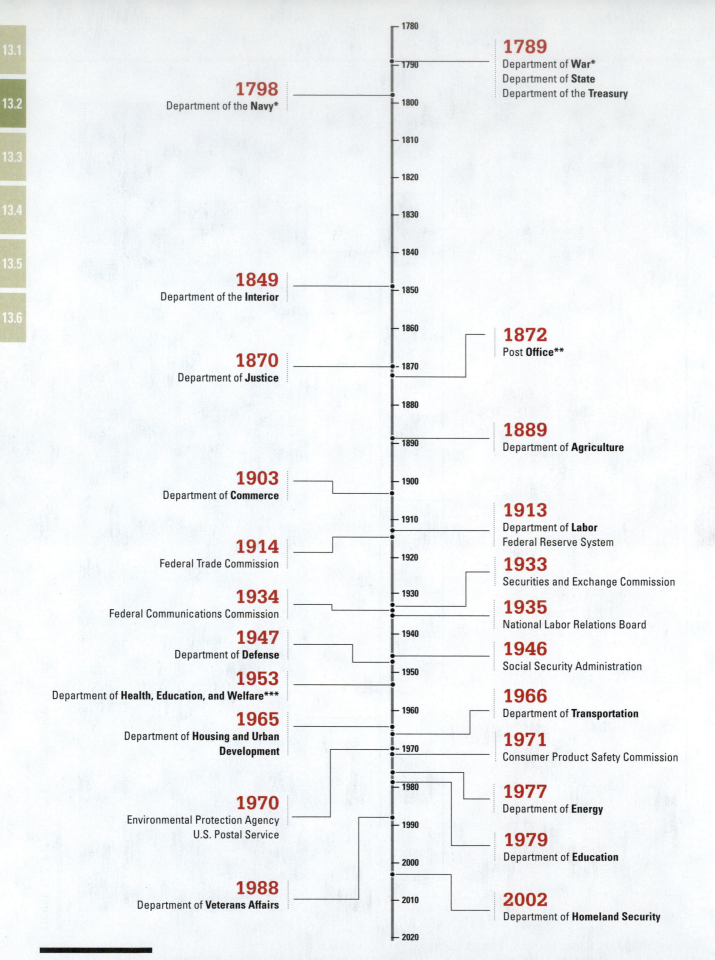

13.1

13.2

13.3

13.4

13.5

13.6

**1780**

**1789**
Department of **War***
Department of **State**
Department of the **Treasury**

**1790**

**1798**
Department of the **Navy***

**1800**

**1810**

**1820**

**1830**

**1840**

**1849**
Department of the **Interior**

**1850**

**1860**

**1872**
Post **Office****

**1870**
Department of **Justice**

**1870**

**1880**

**1889**
Department of **Agriculture**

**1890**

**1903**
Department of **Commerce**

**1900**

**1913**
Department of **Labor**
Federal Reserve System

**1910**

**1914**
Federal Trade Commission

**1920**

**1933**
Securities and Exchange Commission

**1930**

**1934**
Federal Communications Commission

**1935**
National Labor Relations Board

**1940**

**1947**
Department of **Defense**

**1946**
Social Security Administration

**1950**

**1953**
Department of **Health, Education, and Welfare*****

**1966**
Department of **Transportation**

**1960**

**1965**
Department of **Housing and Urban Development**

**1971**
Consumer Product Safety Commission

**1970**

**1977**
Department of **Energy**

**1980**

**1970**
Environmental Protection Agency
U.S. Postal Service

**1990**

**1979**
Department of **Education**

**2000**

**1988**
Department of **Veterans Affairs**

**2002**
Department of **Homeland Security**

**2010**

**2020**

**FIGURE 13.3** TIMELINE: CREATION OF EXECUTIVE BRANCH DEPARTMENTS AND SELECTED AGENCIES, INDEPENDENT COMMISSIONS, AND CORPORATIONS

*Became part of newly formed Department of Defense in 1947.
**Transformed into U.S. Postal Service, an independent agency, in 1970.
***Later split into Department of Education and Department of Health and Human Services.

13.1
13.2
13.3
13.4
13.5
13.6

| ☎ Telephones | ↑ ✈ Gates 11 to 21 | ↑ 🚫 Security Check |
| 🧳 Baggage Claim | | → ☎ Telephones |

**AIRPORT SECURITY**

New national problems often bring new federal agencies to address them. The Transportation Security Agency (TSA) was created in the wake of the 9/11 terrorist attacks on the United States (in which airplanes were used to attack the World Trade Center and the Pentagon) to screen airline passengers. Many critics believe the airport screening process is too expensive, intrusive, and ineffective. If this is true—it may not be, of course—how might we design bureaucratic agencies such as the TSA to be more nimble in meeting changing problems?

- **Independent regulatory commissions**, such as the Securities and Exchange Commission and the Consumer Product Safety Commission, are responsible for regulating sectors of the economy in which it is judged that the free market does not work properly to protect the public interest. The commissions are "independent" in the sense that they stand outside the departmental structure and are protected against direct presidential or congressional control. A commission is run by commissioners with long, staggered, and overlapping terms, and many require a balance between Republicans and Democrats.

- **Independent executive agencies** report directly to the president rather than to a department- or cabinet-level secretary. They are usually created to give the president greater control in carrying out some executive function, or to highlight some particular public problem or issue that policymakers wish to address. The Environmental Protection Agency, for example, was given independent status to focus government and public attention on environmental issues and to give the federal government more flexibility in solving environmental problems.

- **Government corporations** are agencies that operate very much like private companies. They can sell stock, retain and reinvest earnings, and borrow money, for instance. They are usually created to perform some crucial economic activity that private investors are unwilling or unable to perform. The Tennessee Valley Authority, for example, was created during the Great Depression to bring electricity to most of the upper South; today it provides about 6 percent of all U.S. electrical power.[14] The U.S. Postal Service was transformed from an executive department to a government corporation in 1970 in the hope of increasing efficiency.

**independent regulatory commission**

An entity in the executive branch that is outside the immediate control of the president and Congress that issues rules and regulations to protect the public.

**independent executive agency**

A unit of the executive branch outside the control of executive departments.

**government corporation**

A unit in the executive branch that operates like a private business but provides some public service.

**13.1**

**13.2**

**13.3**

**13.4**

**13.5**

**13.6**

**quasi-governmental organization**

An organization that has governmental powers and responsibilities but has substantial private sector control over its activities.

**foundation**

An entity of the executive branch that supports the arts or sciences and is designed to be somewhat insulated from political interference.

- **Quasi-governmental organizations** are hybrids of public and private organizations. They allow the federal government to be involved in a particular area of activity without directly controlling it. They are distinguished from government corporations by the fact that a portion of the boards of directors are appointed by the private sector. The Federal Reserve Board, responsible for setting the nation's monetary policy, and increasingly a key player in restructuring the financial system and saving it from collapse, is owned by 12 regional banks but run by a Board of Governors and a Chairman (all of whom serve overlapping, staggered terms) appointed by the president. The Corporation for Public Broadcasting fits into this category, as did the mortgage institutions Fannie Mae (the Federal National Mortgage Association) and Freddie Mac (the Federal Home Mortgage Corporation), until they were taken over by the government in the wake of the financial collapse in 2008.

- **Foundations** are units that are separated from the rest of government to protect them from political interference with science and the arts. Most prominent are the National Foundation on the Arts and the Humanities and the National Science Foundation. Over the years, members of Congress and presidential administrations have tried on various occasions to redirect the activities of these foundations—for example, to deny grants for the support of controversial art projects or for certain areas of scientific inquiry—but such efforts, while not unimportant, have not undermined the autonomy of government foundations to the extent many critics have feared.

# What Do Bureaucrats Do?

**13.3**  Identify the kinds of activities bureaucrats perform

ureaucrats engage in a wide range of activities that are relevant to the quality of democracy in the United States and affect how laws and regulations work. Let's look at the more prominent and significant of these activities.

## ☐ Executing Programs and Policies

The term *executive branch* suggests the branch of the federal government that executes or carries out the law. This is sometimes called implementation. The framers of the Constitution assumed that Congress would be the principal national policymaker and stipulated that the president and his appointees to administrative positions in the executive branch "shall take care that the laws be faithfully executed" (Article II, Section 2). For the most part, this responsibility is carried out routinely; mail is delivered, troops are trained, Social Security checks are mailed on time, and foreign intelligence is collected.

Sometimes, executing the law is not so easy, however, because it is not always clear what the law means. Often, Congress passes laws that are vague about goals and short on procedural guidelines. It may do so because its members believe that something should be done about a particular social problem but are unclear on specifics about how to solve it or disagree among themselves. This, perhaps, is why Congress gave so much discretionary power to Bush's Treasury Secretary Henry Paulson to respond to the credit freeze and stock market collapse in fall 2008 when it passed the $700 billion Troubled Asset Relief Program (TARP). Later, the Dodd–Frank Wall Street Reform and Consumer Protection Act gave power to the head of the new Office of Complex Financial Institutions to dismantle any of the 22 largest banks if they ran into trouble as a way to avoid having to bail out banks that are "too big to fail." Vaguely written statutes and directives, then, leave a great deal of discretion to bureaucrats (see the

# Using the FRAMEWORK

## How is it that unelected bureaucrats can make important rulings that affect people's lives?

**Background:** One of the emerging conflicts that will be playing itself out over the next few years, both in the United States and in the global economy, concerns the safety of genetically engineered food and the rules that will apply for protecting the public from its possible harmful effects. In the United States, unless Congress chooses to act in its own right, the rules will be made by the Food and Drug Administration. We can better understand why the FDA can make rules on genetically engineered foods by using a broad perspective that takes into account structural, political linkage, and governmental level factors.

**Government Action**

The FDA issues rules (1) for testing genetically engineered food for safety and (2) for labeling of food with ingredients derived through bioengineering.

**Government**

The FDA scientific staff has pressed the FDA's leadership to become more active in rulemaking for genetically engineered food. → No laws specifically addressing genetically engineered food have been enacted, leaving rulemaking in this area to the FDA.

The Court has allowed bureaucratic agencies to make rules within the boundaries set by Congress. → Congress created the Food and Drug Administration, defined its overall mission, but left room for the FDA to make rules in its areas of responsibility.

**Political Linkage**

Public opinion polls show that some Americans are very worried about genetically engineered food and want some action. → Interest groups, for and against genetically engineered food, have pressed their positions on public officials, using both "inside" and "outside" forms of lobbying.

**Structure**

The Constitution says little about the organization and operations of the Executive Branch and leaves the details to be filled in by Congress. → Scientific researchers have made dramatic breakthroughs in plant and animal genetics, causing some segments of society to call for regulations. → Global agribusiness corporations are always looking for the most efficient forms of production, and genetically engineered products help them do this.

13.1
13.2
13.3
13.4
13.5
13.6

13.1

13.2

13.3

13.4

13.5

13.6

**cost-benefit analysis**
A method of evaluating rules and regulations by weighing their potential costs against their potential benefits to society.

"Mapping American Politics" feature later in this chapter on discretionary leeway at the Department of Homeland Security).

Rising partisanship also can make executing the law an action fraught with danger for executive branch officials. Under the Voting Rights Act, states with a history of using subtle legal devices to deny the vote to racial and other protected class groups must gain the approval of the Justice Department for changes in their electoral laws that seem to make it more difficult for members of such groups to vote. Believing that the intention of more stringent voter identification laws in many Republican-controlled states was to depress the votes of Democratic-leaning groups such as African Americans, the poor, and the young, then–Attorney General Eric Holder blocked South Carolina's voter ID law in 2012 and challenged Texas's in federal court. This brought a storm of criticism from Republicans who claimed that the new laws enacted in 34 states were designed to cut down on voter fraud rather than a device to hold down the Democratic vote; Holder spent much of 2012 and 2013 in front of several hostile committees defending his actions in the Republican-run House of Representatives.

## ☐ Regulating

Congress often gives bureaucratic agencies the power to write specific rules. Because of the complexity of the problems that government must face, Congress tends to create agencies and to specify the job or mission that it wants done and then charges the agency with using its expertise to do the job. Congress created the Environmental Protection Agency (EPA), for instance, and gave it a mission—to help coordinate the cleanup of the nation's air and water—but it left to the EPA the power to set the specific standards that communities and businesses must meet. The standards set by the EPA have the force of law unless they are rescinded by Congress or overruled by the courts. The Food and Drug Administration (FDA) writes rules about the introduction of new drugs that researchers and pharmaceutical companies are obliged to follow. (See the "Using the Framework" feature for more on the FDA.)

Some critics believe that Congress delegates entirely too much lawmaking to the executive branch,[15] but it is difficult to see what alternative Congress has. It cannot micromanage every issue; Congress lacks the time, resources, and expertise. (See the "Can Government Do Anything Well?" feature to learn more about an agency with a particular kind of expertise.) And in the end, Congress retains control; it can change the rules written by bureaucrats if they drift too far from congressional intent or constituent desires.

Other critics believe there simply are too many rules and regulations. When candidates promise to "get government off our backs," they usually are referring to regulatory burdens, though taxes are a target as well. Several attempts have been made to roll back executive branch rule-making. Under Ronald Reagan, **cost-benefit analysis** was introduced as a way to slow the rule-making process, for example, and the result was a decline in the number of rules issued. After a period of growth in federal regulations during the presidencies of George H. W. Bush and Bill Clinton, the second President Bush managed to cap further growth, consistent with his conservative philosophy (see Figure 13.4). Bush issued an executive order in 2007 mandating that prior to issuing a new rule, agencies must first determine and report why market forces are unable to address a problem the new rule is designed to solve. He then ordered that each agency appoint a presidentially approved regulatory policy officer to review all proposed rules to see if they fit the administration's priorities. Clearly this was an effort to slow the pace of rule-making by federal agencies by a president who opposed a too active government in domestic affairs. Barack Obama, more supportive of an active government, rescinded both rules within the first 10 days of his new administration.[16]

13.1

13.2

13.3

13.4

13.5

13.6

# Can Government Do Anything Well?

## The Centers for Disease Control (CDC)

The Colorado Department of Public Health reported to the CDC on September 2, 2011 that it had uncovered seven cases of listeria—a deadly form of food poisoning caused by a bacterium in the food supply—among ill Coloradans. Until the source of the infection could be identified, rapid spread of the illness was inevitable. In a mere four days, however, CDC investigators were able to trace the source of the bacteria to cantaloupes from Jensen Farms in Colorado and announced the finding to the public, warning them against eating cantaloupe. By September 12, a mere 10 days from the outbreak of listeria, the CDC had traced the exact cause of the bacterial infection to specific food handling processes at Jensen Farms, tracked where Jensen Farm cantaloupes had been distributed within the U.S. food supply chain, issued nationwide warnings about the infected cantaloupes, and reached an agreement with Jensen Farms for a voluntary national recall of their product. Though 29 people in Colorado and other states died as a result of listeria—this was the deadliest foodborne disease outbreak in the country in 26 years—the outcome could have been much worse had the Colorado Department of Health not had the CDC to turn to.

The CDC has a long list of responsibilities—prevention of the spread of infectious diseases, prevention of chronic health problems, diminution of workplace and household injuries, improvements in environmental health, and more—but it is the first of these that has garnered the agency the most attention. In its early days, it was credited with creating a system for tracking and aggressively vaccinating against smallpox in Central and West Africa that the World Health Organization eventually expanded, leading to the eradication of this epidemic killer by 1977. CDC scientists were responsible for identifying the AIDS virus, Legionnaires' disease, and Ebola fever; the CDC was also instrumental in educating the public about the H1N1 (swine flu) outbreak in 2009. After 9/11, the CDC turned much more of its attention to surveillance and tracking of bioterrorism, and, in the process, enhanced its ability to track infectious and foodborne diseases, although it was slow to respond to the threat of Ebola from west Africa in 2014.

*Support for the claim that the Centers for Disease Control is indispensable for protecting the public against the spread of infectious diseases and foodborne illnesses:*

- The CDC has become an important center of scientific and medical research and surveillance that has not and, perhaps, cannot be matched by state governments.
- The CDC's partnerships with major research universities enhances its already formidable capabilities in this area.
- The CDC's partnerships with other federal agencies—the FDA, for example, when it comes to the food supply as well as the creation of vaccines for infectious diseases—further enhance its capabilities to protect the nation's public health.
- No private sector firm has an economic interest or the resources to look out for the public health and safety of Americans as its first order of business; the private sector cannot be counted upon to do the "public good" jobs that the CDC does—doing what is in the general interest without regard to its own interests as a firm.

*Rejection of the claim that the Centers for Disease Control is indispensable for protecting the public against the spread of infectious diseases and foodborne illnesses:*

**Here are some arguments that focus on poor performance by the CDC in the past, suggesting that a very different sort of agency with more oversight might be in order:**

- The CDC, or rather the agency that eventually became the CDC, was responsible for conducting the infamous Tuskegee study of syphilis in which many African American men were infected with the disease but denied the penicillin that would have cured them.
- In 1976, the vaccine it helped develop to battle swine flu—this form of flu killed between 10 and 20 million people worldwide right after the end of World War I—triggered Guillain-Barré Syndrome among many people (the vaccination campaign was stopped when this became known).
- The CDC, working with the FBI, was never able to definitively identify the source of the anthrax attack on public officials that occurred a few months after the 9/11 attacks on the United States.

**Here is an argument that focuses on the public–private balance in the provision of essential services for the American people:**

- As with any government-run program that involves a large bureaucracy, there is waste and inefficiency in the system and a lack of transparency; some activities of the CDC should be spun off to the private sector entirely or become part of public–private partnerships.

13.1

13.2

13.3

13.4

13.5

13.6

(Continued)

## WHAT DO YOU THINK?

What do you think about the past, present, and future role of the federal government—particularly by the CDC—in protecting the public against the spread of infectious diseases and foodborne illnesses?

- The federal government has not been perfect in this area, but on balance, this is one of its indispensable responsibilities. We should spend more to enhance the capabilities of the CDC because of the increasingly global sourcing of our food supply and the threat of bioterrorism.
- The federal government has not been perfect in this area, but on balance, it is an important responsibility of government that the CDC does well. We should maintain its present level of funding.
- The federal government has failed in this responsibility more than a few times, and its chronic inefficiencies suggest that the private sector should be more engaged in doing what the CDC has been responsible for over the years. We certainly should not increase its budget.

How would you defend your position to a fellow student? What would be your main line of argument? What evidence do you believe best supports your position? For help in developing your argument, you can refer to www.cdc.gov.

## ☐ Adjudicating

Congress has given some executive branch agencies the power to conduct quasi-judicial proceedings in which disputes are resolved. Much as in a court of law, the decisions of an administrative law judge have the force of law, unless appealed to a higher panel. The National Labor Relations Board (the NLRB), for instance, adjudicates disputes between labor and management on matters concerning federal labor laws. Disputes may involve claims of unfair labor practices, for example—firing a labor

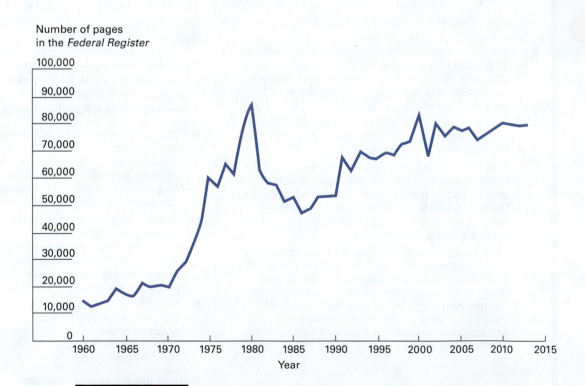

**FIGURE 13.4** GROWTH IN FEDERAL AGENCY RULES AND REGULATIONS

This graph shows the annual number of pages in the *Federal Register,* which is published daily and contains all new rules and changes to existing rules proposed by each and every executive branch agency. While not perfect, tracking its growth is an interesting way, widely used by scholars and journalists, to chart the course and scale of bureaucratic regulation in the United States. The graph shows the dramatic rise in regulations during the 1970s, the decline during the Reagan years, the slow increase in rule writing during the first Bush and Clinton presidencies, and a leveling out during George W. Bush's tenure in office. Rule writing increased slightly again under Barack Obama.

*Source:* Tutorials, History, and Statistics, Federal Register Pages Published, 1936–2013, Office of the *Federal Register,* 2014.

organizer falls into this category—or disagreements about whether proper procedures were followed in filing for a union certification election. Often these disputes can be quite contentious, spilling over into the broader political arena. In 2011, for example, the NLRB ruled that Boeing had violated labor laws when it decided, as a way to punish the Machinists Union that had recently struck the company in its Puget Sound plants, to open an assembly line for its new 787 Dreamliner airliner in non-union South Carolina. It ordered the company to move the work back to the state of Washington. Needless to say, political and business leaders, as well as many ordinary South Carolinians, were furious at the decision and demanded that Congress clip the wings of the NLRB. Congressional Republicans tried to do so, but to little effect. The NLRB later removed its complaint when Boeing and the Machinists Union reached an agreement to move additional 787 (and 737) work back to Washington while keeping a production line in South Carolina as well.

## ☐ Discretion and Democracy

It is quite clear, then, that bureaucrats exercise a great deal of discretion. They do not simply follow a set of orders from Congress or the president, but find many opportunities to exercise their own judgment. In 2011, for example, the Department of Transportation and the EPA reached a voluntary agreement with U.S.-based automakers to dramatically increase over time the average fuel mileage of their fleets of cars and trucks. Because bureaucrats make important decisions that have consequences for many other people, groups, and organizations, we can say that they are policymakers. And, because they make the overwhelming majority of public policy decisions in the United States,[17] we can say they are important policymakers. They are *unelected* policymakers, however, and this fact should immediately alert us to some potential problems with regard to the practice of democracy.

# Who Are the Bureaucrats?

**13.4**   Determine how demographically representative bureaucrats are

**B**ecause bureaucrats exercise substantial discretion as policymakers, we want to know who they are. How representative are they of the American people? In a democracy, we would probably want to see a pretty close correspondence between the people and bureaucrats. In the sections that follow, we'll take a look at each of the different personnel systems in the executive branch and consider how well the American people are represented in their ranks.

## ☐ The Merit Services

Merit services choose employees on the basis of examinations, educational credentials, and demonstrable skills. These services have evolved in size and complexity, in tandem with the federal bureaucracy, and are of three general types.[18]

**COMPETITIVE CIVIL SERVICE**   From the election of Andrew Jackson in 1828 until the late nineteenth century, the executive branch was staffed through what is commonly called the **spoils system**. It was generally accepted that the "spoils of victory" belonged to the winning party. Winners were expected to clear out people who were loyal to the previous administration and to replace them with their own people. Also known as **patronage**, this system of appointment caused no great alarm in the beginning because of the small and relatively unimportant role of the federal government in American society. The shortcomings of the War Department and other bureaucratic agencies during the Civil War, however, convinced many people that reform of the

13.1

13.2

13.3

13.4

13.5

13.6

13.1

13.2

13.3

13.4

13.5

13.6

federal personnel system was required. Rampant corruption and favoritism in the government service during the years after the Civil War gave an additional boost to the reform effort, as did the realization that the growing role of the federal government required more skilled and less partisan personnel. The final catalyst for change was the assassination in 1881 of President James Garfield by a person who, it is said, badly wanted a government job but could not get one.

The Civil Service Act of 1883, also known as the Pendleton Act, created a bipartisan Civil Service Commission to oversee a system of appointments to certain executive branch posts on the basis of merit. Competitive examinations were to be used to determine merit. In the beginning, the competitive civil service system included only about 10 percent of federal positions. Congress gradually extended the reach of the career civil service; today, it covers about 60 percent of the roughly 2 million federal civilian employees (total federal employees does not include postal workers). In 1978, Congress abolished the Civil Service Commission and replaced it with two separate agencies, the Office of Personnel Management (OPM) and the Merit Systems Protection Board. The former administers the civil service laws, advertises positions, writes examinations, and acts as a clearinghouse for agencies that are looking for workers. The latter settles disputes concerning employee rights and obligations, hears employee grievances, and orders corrective action when needed.

**AGENCY MERIT SERVICES** Many federal agencies require personnel with particular kinds of training and experience appropriate to their special missions. For such agencies, Congress has established separate merit systems administered by each agency itself. The Public Health Service, for instance, recruits its own doctors and biomedical researchers. The Department of State has its own examinations and procedures for recruiting foreign service officers. The National Aeronautics and Space Administration (NASA) recruits scientists and engineers without the help of the Office of Personnel Management. About 35 percent of all federal civilian employees fall under these agency-specific merit systems.

**EXCEPTED SERVICES** There are other variations on how civil servants are hired.[19] Positions in the federal government are classified by a schedule system that determines specific requirements for filling each job. Schedule A allows various departments and agencies to hire attorneys and accountants who are tested and certified by professional associations. Schedule B appointments are used to hire people with skills that are needed and in short supply, as determined by the agencies themselves, in consultation with the OPM. Schedule C is used to hire people in what are called "policy-sensitive" positions, such as personal assistants and drivers. Other excepted authorities allow hiring for short assignments in areas of special service to the country, such as the Peace Corps.

**SENIOR EXECUTIVE SERVICE** Created in 1978, these 9,000 or so positions were meant to be a sort of super–civil service, somewhat akin to the top civil service posts in France filled by *grandes ecoles* graduates, requiring high-level skills and education. Individuals in these positions are granted broad responsibilities and autonomy, with promotions, salary increases, and termination determined by rigorous performance reviews. The original idea was that they would serve as a corps of highly skilled people who could be deployed to various agencies as need appeared for their services, serving as a bridge between political appointees at the tops of the agencies and the career civil service. Things have not worked out that way, however; members of the senior executive service have not been entirely trusted by political appointees, and most have stayed put within their agencies throughout their careers.[20]

**HOW DIFFERENT ARE CIVIL SERVANTS?** Civil servants are similar to other Americans.[21] Their educational levels and regional origins are close to those of other Americans, for example, although they tend to be a little bit older (40 percent are over the age of 50)[22] and a little better paid (though higher-level civil servants still seriously lag behind their counterparts in the private sector), and they have better job security, retirement plans, and health insurance than most. Civil servants' political beliefs and opinions also are pretty close to those of the general American public, although they tend to favor the Democrats a bit more than the general public and are slightly more liberal on social issues than the national average.[23] Women and minorities are very well represented (the latter are actually overrepresented), with women holding 43 percent of all non-postal jobs and racial and ethnic minorities about 33 percent.[24] It is worth noting, however, that women and minorities are overrepresented in the very lowest civil service grades and are underrepresented in the highest. They also are far less evident in the special-agency merit systems (such as the Foreign Service and the FBI) and in the professional categories (scientists at the National Institutes of Health; doctors in the Public Health Service).[25]

## Political Appointees

The highest policymaking positions in the federal bureaucracy (e.g., department secretaries, assistants to the president, leading officials in the agencies), about 4,000 in number, enter government service not by way of competitive merit examinations but by presidential appointment. About one-quarter of them—designated Executive Schedule appointees—require Senate confirmation.[26] These patronage positions, in theory at least, allow the president to translate his electoral mandate into public policy by permitting him to put his people in place in key policymaking jobs. Top appointees who have the confidence of the president tend to become important policymakers and public figures in their own right. Treasury Secretary Timothy Geithner and Budget Director Peter Orszag, because of the central roles they played in President Barack Obama's economic recovery plans, achieved this status.

Most presidents use patronage not only to build support for their programs but also to firm up their political coalition by being sensitive to the needs of important party factions and interest groups. Ronald Reagan used his appointments to advance a conservative agenda for America and made conservative beliefs a prerequisite for high bureaucratic appointments.[27] President Clinton, by contrast, promised to make government "look more like America" and did so by appointing many women and minorities to top posts in his administration. Presidents also reserve important appointments for people they trust and who bring expertise and experience. John F. Kennedy appointed his brother and political confidant Robert ("Bobby") to the post of attorney general. George W. Bush was particularly eager to fill cabinet posts and his inner circle with people who had a great deal of experience in the upper reaches of the federal government: Donald Rumsfeld (secretary of defense), Colin Powell (secretary of state in his first administration), and Condoleezza Rice (national security advisor).

Presidents also want to find appointments for people who played important roles in their election, even if they are not particularly able.[28] The idea is to put them where they will be out of harm's way, in places not critical to advancing the president's agenda. In Republican administrations, political cronies are likely to end up in Housing and Urban Development, although the inexperienced Michael Brown was made head of FEMA for no apparent reason—his only executive experience was as the director of the Arabian Horse Association—with disastrous results for New Orleans and the Gulf Coast following Katrina. Democratic administrations tend to use the Department of Commerce and the Small Business Administration to reward their campaign workers and contributors.

In these highly partisan times, the Senate often sits on presidential nominations for executive branch positions (and judicial nominations as well) as a way to extract policy concessions from the president as the price for bringing a nomination to a vote on the floor. To get around this gridlock and to fill important leadership posts, presidents have made so-called **recess appointments** after Congress adjourns for the year in December and before it reconvenes again in mid-January or otherwise takes long breaks.[29] In 2014, the Supreme Court severely restricted the president's power to make recess appointments, saying that President Obama had unconstitutionally appointed members to the National Labor Relations Board when the House insisted, although most of its members were gone, that it was still in session.

Recent presidents have broadened their definition of "recess" to include any period when Congress is not in session, including long weekends and the traditional August

13.1

13.2

13.3

13.4

13.5

13.6

**recess appointments**
Presidential action to temporarily fill executive branch positions without the consent of the Senate; done when Congress is adjourned.

13.1

13.2

13.3

13.4

13.5

13.6

vacation break. Such appointments now are usually made not because it is difficult for senators to come back to Washington to vote on important matters—the reason why the framers put it in the Constitution—but because it gives presidents a way to bypass an intransigent Congress. When Democrats controlled the Senate in 2005, Republican George W. Bush used a recess appointment to make the extremely conservative and anti-United Nations advocate John Bolton UN ambassador. President Obama, frustrated by Republicans' energetic use of the filibuster to block his nominees, filled many important positions as recess appointments, including Richard Cordray to head the Consumer Protection Bureau created by the Dodd-Frank Wall Street and Consumer Protection Act (Republicans said they would block the nomination unless and until the president agreed to radically scale back the powers of the bureau) and two pro-union Democrats to vacant seats on the NLRB.

Recess appointments of this sort will not be a big factor in the future for two reasons. First, in 2013, Senate Democrats passed a rule that a filibuster cannot be used when considering presidential executive branch and judicial nominees (with the exception of those to the Supreme Court), thus making it likely that presidents will get their way more often on nominations and will not need to resort to desperate measures. Second, the Supreme Court ruled in 2014 that recess appointments can only be made in the period between sessions of Congress when it has officially adjourned.

At any rate, top political appointees do not last very long. On average, they stay in office only 22 months; political scientist Hugh Heclo called them "birds of passage."[30] They leave for many reasons. Most are accomplished people who see government service as only a short-term commitment. Most make financial sacrifices. Many don't find the public notoriety appealing. Some find themselves the target of partisan campaigns that leave them with damaged reputations. Many become frustrated by how difficult it is to change and implement policy. Finally, recess appointees must vacate their positions within a year of their appointments (unless the Senate relents and proceeds to confirm their nominations, but that is rare when there is divided government).

# Political and Governmental Influences on Bureaucratic Behavior

**13.5**  Isolate various influences on executive branch decision making

R ather than there being a single chain of command with clear lines of authority, the bureaucracy in general (and bureaucrats in particular) must heed several important voices. The president is the most important, but Congress, the courts, the public (including interest groups), and the press play a significant role in influencing what agencies do. Figure 13.5 gives an overview of these several influences on bureaucratic behavior.

**FIGURE 13.5** POPULAR CONTROL OF THE BUREAUCRACY: IMPERFECT POPULAR SOVEREIGNTY

Popular control of the federal bureaucracy is complex, indirect, and only partially effective. The public does not elect government bureaucrats, and public opinion has little direct effect on their behavior. However, members of Congress and the president, both of whom are answerable to the electorate and attentive to public opinion, exercise an important influence on bureaucratic behavior. So, too, do federal judges. Because elected officials and judges often send mixed signals, however, some of the effectiveness of such controls is diminished.

*Source*: Federal Registry

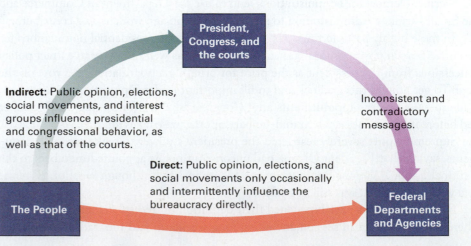

**President, Congress, and the courts**

**Indirect:** Public opinion, elections, social movements, and interest groups influence presidential and congressional behavior, as well as that of the courts.

Inconsistent and contradictory messages.

**Direct:** Public opinion, elections, and social movements only occasionally and intermittently influence the bureaucracy directly.

**The People**

**Federal Departments and Agencies**

# The President and the Bureaucracy

Being the nation's chief executive, the president is the formal head of the executive branch. But, the president's ability to control the executive branch is not unlimited. In fact, virtually every modern president has been perplexed by the discovery that he cannot assume that bureaucrats will do what he wants them to do.[31] Richard Nixon was so frustrated by his inability to move the federal bureaucracy that he came to think of it as an alien institution filled with Democratic Party enemies. His strategy was to intimidate bureaucrats or bypass them. He created the notorious "plumbers" unit in the White House to act as his personal domestic surveillance and espionage unit. Revelation of its activities was one of the factors leading the House Judiciary Committee to recommend approval of three articles of impeachment in the Watergate scandal.

**WHY PRESIDENTS OFTEN FEEL STYMIED BY THE BUREAUCRACY** The sheer size and complexity of the executive branch is one reason presidents are frustrated by it. There is so much going on, in so many agencies, involving the activity of tens of thousands of people, that simply keeping abreast of it all is no easy task even with a large White House staff to help. Moreover, because of civil service regulations, presidents have no say about the tenure or salary of most federal bureaucrats beyond those they have appointed. When presidents want something to happen, they are unlikely to get instantaneous acquiescence from bureaucrats, who do not fear their nominal boss as they would fear a private employer. Bureaucratic agencies also are heavily insulated against presidential efforts to control them because of agency alliances with powerful interest groups and various House and Senate committees. Above all, presidents find that they are not the only ones with the authority to influence how officials and civil servants in the executive branch behave; they find that they share this authority with Congress and often with the courts.

**TOOLS OF PRESIDENTIAL LEADERSHIP** Presidents hardly are helpless, of course; they have a number of ways to encourage bureaucratic compliance.[32] Occasionally, because of a crisis or a widely shared national commitment, decisive bureaucratic action is possible, as during Roosevelt's New Deal era, Lyndon Johnson's first years as president, Ronald Reagan's first administration, and George W. Bush's war on terrorism.

Even during ordinary times, however, the president has important management tools. First, although it is difficult to measure precisely, the president's prestige as our only nationally elected political leader makes his wishes hard to ignore. When Theodore Roosevelt called the presidency a "bully pulpit," he meant that only the president can speak for the nation, set the tone for the government, and call the American people to some great national purpose. A popular president, willing and able to play this role, is hard to resist. Bureaucrats are citizens and respond like other Americans to presidential leadership. When a president chooses to become directly involved in some bureaucratic matter—for example, with a phone call to a reluctant agency head or a comment about some bureaucratic shortcoming during a press conference—most bureaucrats respond. Research done over many years in many agencies demonstrates, in fact, that career civil servants will generally go along with the president, regardless of whether they share his party or ideology.[33]

The power of appointment is also an important tool of presidential leadership.[34] If a president is very careful to fill the top administrative posts with people who support him and his programs, he greatly increases his ability to have his way. The Senate must advise on and consent to most of his top choices, and the process of approving the president's appointees has become much more contentious and drawn out than in the past, as you have seen. It is not unusual for important posts to be empty for a long time or to be filled with recess appointments. For example, Republican resistance meant that the position of head of the Transportation Security Administration (TSA) was not filled for more than a full year after Barack Obama's swearing in as president.

13.1

13.2

13.3

13.4

13.5

13.6

**unitary executive**

Constitutional doctrine that proposes that the executive branch is under the direct control of the president, who has all authority necessary to control the actions of federal bureaucracy personnel and units without interference from the other federal branches.

The president's power as chief budget officer of the federal government is also a formidable tool of the administration. No agency of the federal bureaucracy, for instance, can make its own budget request directly to Congress; its budget must be submitted to Congress as part of the president's overall budget for the U.S. government formulated by the Office of Management and Budget (OMB), whose director reports directly to the president. The OMB also has the statutory authority to block proposed legislation coming from any executive branch agency if it deems it contrary to the president's budget or program. But Congress can and usually does go its own way on executive branch budgets, especially when there is divided government.

And finally, presidents have broad unitary powers to help in controlling executive branch agencies, including regulatory review and executive orders. To repeat a point made earlier in Chapter 12:

> [George W. Bush and Vice President Dick Cheney] revived and gave a very expansive reading to a long-dormant constitutional theory known as the **unitary executive** in an attempt to "unstymie" the office. The concept is based on Article II's "vesting" ("The executive Power shall be vested in a President of the United States of America.") and "take care" clauses ("The President shall take care that the laws be faithfully executed . . .") to suggest that the [president] is free to exercise command and authority over the executive branch in all respects. Presidential adviser and Justice Department official John Yoo proposed early in the Bush administration that the Constitution created a unified and hierarchical executive branch under the direct control of the president, who has all authority necessary to control the actions of federal bureaucracy personnel and units without interference from the other federal branches.

What this meant in practice was the aggressive use by President Bush of powers all presidents have used, including signing statements, executive orders, and regulatory review.[35] Though President Bush tried to exercise this form of tight control over executive agencies and personnel, in the end it proved too difficult to achieve. For example, though his staffers and agency appointees tried to edit and change the conclusion of several reports from government scientists on global warming, the information still found its way to the public through leaks to the news media and the appropriate people in Congress. But presidents, including Barack Obama, increasingly have tried to centralize more power over the far-flung bureaucracy in the White House.[36] The White House staff has grown steadily larger and presidents, paritcularly Barack Obama, have become ever more enamored of so-called "czars"—as in "energy czar" or "anti-drug czar"—to oversee important policy areas that involve several departments, bureaus, and agencies. President Obama appointed Elizabeth Warren as the czar (actually, he appointed her as a special advisor) to oversee the creation of the new Consumer Protection Bureau in 2011 as a way to bypass Senate Republican opposition to her.

## ☐ Congress and the Bureaucracy

Congress exercises considerable influence over the federal bureaucracy by legislating agency organization and mission, confirming or refusing to confirm presidential appointments, controlling the agency budget, holding oversight hearings, and using inspectors general.

**LEGISLATING AGENCY ORGANIZATION AND MISSION** The president and Congress share control over the executive branch. The congressional tools of control, in fact, are at least as formidable as those of the president.[37] Congress legislates the mission of bureaucratic agencies and the details of their organization and can change either one, and alter agency policy as well. In 1999, for example, Congress passed a bill requiring the Census Bureau to do the 2000 census by direct count, disallowing the use of statistical sampling, which the technical staff at the Bureau wanted to use. Congress also can and does create new departments, such as the Department of Homeland Security. The new department was created by Congress in 2002 after members of both parties in the House and Senate determined that the president's approach—an Office of Homeland Security in the White House Office—would not

# Mapping American Politics

## Tracking Where Homeland Security Dollars First Ended Up

13.1

13.2

13.3

13.4

13.5

13.6

### Introduction

The Department of Homeland Security (DHS) was established in 2002 to coordinate federal, state, and local efforts to defend the nation against terrorist attacks and deal with their aftermath and recovery. The establishment of the new executive branch department was triggered, of course, by the 9/11 terrorist attacks on the World Trade Center in New York City and on the Pentagon near Washington, D.C. The terrorists selected targets that were not only of great symbolic importance—the plane that crashed in Pennsylvania seems to have been headed toward a major target in the nation's capital as well—but also critical to the operations of American government and economy. One would assume, then, that the Department of Homeland Security would have distributed its funds to states and communities in some rough proportion to their vulnerability to attack and their centrality to the health and survival of the nation. In fact, as with other executive agencies, the distribution depended not just on assessments by professionals and leaders at Homeland Security, but also on the wishes of representatives and senators ever anxious to bring federal dollars to their districts and states. But just how far did the initial spending by the DHS deviate from the nation's security and recovery needs when DHS first got started?

### Mapping Importance and Spending

There is no commonly agreed upon metric to say how important different targets might be for potential terrorists, no sure way to gauge symbolic importance and economic impact. As a rough measure, we use the total size of each state's economy, shown in the cartogram on the top. This assumes that the size of a state's economy indicates its importance in the overall economic life of the nation and that serious damage to targets in the most economically important states would have the most negative effects on the entire country. The cartogram on the bottom shows states drawn in terms of per-capita DHS spending. If spending were going to where it was needed, and if the size of a state's economy is a reasonable indicator of its importance as a possible terrorist target, the two cartograms should look very similar. It is clear that they do not. Note how much money from the DHS's first distribution of funds in 2004 went to less economically important states, including Idaho, Wyoming, the Dakotas, New Hampshire, Vermont, Rhode Island, and Maine. Note, as well, how little went to California, Texas, New York, and Florida.

### What Do You Think?

How do you assess DHS initial spending in terms of national needs? What might be a better measure of a state or city's symbolic and economic importance than the total size of the state's economy, what we used here? Finally, if you believe there is a serious and troubling mismatch between needs and spending, how do you think we might improve matters? Should the influence of individual members of Congress influence how executive departments and agencies spend their appropriated budget, or should the advice of professionals carry more weight?

Gross State Products: States Drawn to Size of Their Economy
*Source:* © 2006 M. D. Ward

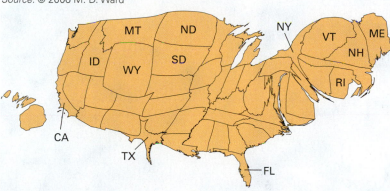

Homeland Security Department: Spending per Capita by State
*Source:* © 2006 M. D. Ward

Standard US Map

**MAP NOTE:** Alaska is not shown, although information about Alaska is included in calculations where relevant, and Hawaii is moved closer to the mainland.

**SOURCES:** (for gross state product for 2004): Bureau of Economic Analysis (www.bea.gov/bea/regional/data.htm); the U.S. Bureau of the Census, *Statistical Abstract of the United States*, 2006, Table 17. (for HSD spending in 2004): V. de Rugy, "What Does Homeland Security Spending Buy?" (Washington, D.C.: The American Enterprise Institute, 2005).

13.1

13.2

13.3

13.4

13.5

13.6

have the necessary authority and resources to coordinate the government's antiterrorism activities. After initial resistance, the president agreed and signed legislation creating the new cabinet-level department.

**CONFIRMING PRESIDENTIAL APPOINTMENTS** Top-level executive branch posts are filled through presidential nomination and Senate confirmation. In the past, the Senate almost always approved presidential nominations to these posts, but presidential success on these appointments, as you have seen, has decreased as divided government has become more common. Past or present, however, the Senate often uses the "advice and consent" process to shape policies in bureaucratic departments and agencies, not confirming the appointment until the nominee or the president promises policy changes, for example. Senator Shelby (R–AL) held up scores of appointments until he could be assured that a new FBI facility would be placed in his state and that more defense contracts would go to companies in his state. The Senate on occasion may even turn down presidential nominations, as it did in the case of George H. W. Bush's nominee for the post of defense secretary, John Tower. Defeat of nominees and the longest delays are most likely to happen during periods of divided government.[38] Delays caused by threats of filibustering nominees decreased, however, after the Democratic-run Senate ended, in 2013, the use of the filibuster to hold up or prevent executive branch presidential nominations.

**CONTROLLING THE AGENCY BUDGET** Congress can also use its control over agency budgets to influence agency behavior. (One common result is the seemingly irrational distribution of agency funds as you can see in the "Mapping American Politics" feature.) In theory, Congress uses the budget process to assess the performance of each agency every year, closely scrutinizing its activities before determining

**SIGNS OF THE TIMES**

The bursting of the "housing bubble" and the subsequent wave of foreclosures led many Americans to wonder if Congress could do something to help. In a series of oversight committee hearings in 2009 and 2010, prominent representatives and senators pressed Fed and Treasury officials to give direct assistance to troubled homeowners from the previously passed TARP rescue package, which they did on a limited basis. In what other circumstances might it make sense for the government to intervene in private markets, or should it avoid doing this at all?

13.1

13.2

13.3

13.4

13.5

13.6

**BUDGET BLUDGEON**

Republicans in the House in 2011, in a bid to role back the power of labor unions in the airline industry, refused for a time to reauthorize the budget of the Federal Aviation Administration. This delayed scores of airport improvement projects across the country, including this near-completed airport expansion in Oakland, California. Is controlling the budget of an agency the correct way for Congress to shape policies of executive branch agencies, or are there better ways to do so?

its next **appropriation**, the legal authority for the agency to spend money. Congress actually has neither the time nor the resources to do such a thing and usually gives each agency some small increment over what it had in the previous year.[39] Of course, if a particular agency displeases Congress, its budget may be cut; if a new set of responsibilities is given to an agency, its budget is usually increased. Sometimes these agency budget actions are taken with the full concurrence of the president; often they are not. Congress sometimes lends a sympathetic ear and increases the budgets of agencies that are not favored by the president. In the 1980s, Congress consistently gave more money than President Reagan wanted given to the EPA, the National Institutes of Health, and the National Science Foundation. In 2011, in a bid to roll back airline workers' right to form labor unions, House Republicans temporarily blocked the reauthorization of the Federal Aviation Administration, halting airport improvement projects around the country, furloughing over 4,000 FAA employees, and preventing the collection of over $300 million in airport fees from the airlines.[40]

**appropriation**
Legal authority for a federal agency to spend money from the U.S. Treasury.

**HOLDING OVERSIGHT HEARINGS** Oversight hearings are an important instrument for gathering information about the policies and performance of executive branch departments and agencies and a handy forum for conveying the views of the members of Congress to bureaucrats. There is a great deal of evidence that agency heads listen when the message is delivered clearly.[41] For example, after the Senate Finance Committee held hearings on purported Internal Revenue Service harassment of taxpayers in 1999, the head of the IRS responded by apologizing to taxpayers and promising changes in his agency's behavior and policies.

Congress does not always speak with a single voice, however. Congress is a highly fragmented and decentralized institution, and its power is dispersed among scores of

13.1

13.2

13.3

13.4

13.5

13.6

subcommittees. Often the activities of a particular bureaucratic agency are the province of more than a single committee or subcommittee, and the probability of receiving mixed signals from them is very high. A skilled administrator can often play these competing forces off of each other and gain a degree of autonomy for his or her agency.

**USING INSPECTORS GENERAL**  In 1978, Congress mandated that an office of inspector general be established in nearly every executive branch department and agency. These inspectors general report directly to Congress and are charged with keeping an eye out for waste, fraud, and bureaucratic abuses of power. The inspectors general in the Department of Education, for example, recently reported widespread fraud in several department grant and loan programs. Inspectors general issue periodic formal reports to the relevant congressional committees, and many meet with congressional staffers on a regular basis, giving Congress a good handle on what is going on in the bureaucracy.

## ☐ The Courts and the Bureaucracy

In our system of separation of powers and checks and balances, the federal judiciary also has a say in what bureaucratic agencies do.[42] It does so in a less direct manner than the president and Congress, to be sure, because the judiciary must wait for cases to reach it and cannot initiate action on its own. Nevertheless, the courts affect federal agencies on a wide range of issues. For example, executive branch agencies cannot violate the constitutional protections afforded to citizens by the Bill of Rights, so citizens who feel their rights have been violated have turned to the courts for relief on a variety of issues, including illegal searches, detentions without trials, denial of access to an attorney, harsh treatment by federal authorities, and National Security Agency (NSA) surveillance of telecommunications. Executive branch agencies are also obligated to treat citizens equally, that is, on a nondiscriminatory basis, and turn to the courts for relief when they feel that discriminatory practices have occurred. The Small Business Administration cannot deny loans to women or racial minorities, for example, nor can federal highway funds be denied to minority contractors.

The Administrative Procedure Act of 1946, amended several times since, puts forth a set of procedures on how executive branch agencies must make their decisions.[43] Basically, the Act attempts to make sure that agencies are bound by the due process guarantees in the Fifth and Fourteenth Amendments; which means, in the end, that they cannot act capriciously or arbitrarily when carrying out their missions, whether distributing benefits, overseeing federal programs, enforcing regulations, or formulating new regulatory rules. The amended Act requires, among other things, that agencies give adequate notice of their actions, solicit comments from all interested parties, and act without bias or favoritism. Citizens, advocacy groups, and interest groups pay attention to decisions and rules from agencies that directly affect them, and it is quite common for them to turn to the courts when they feel that agencies have acted improperly.

## ☐ The Public and the Press

Most Americans pay little attention to bureaucratic agencies as such. The public focuses mainly on the *content* of public policies rather than on the bureaucratic agencies or the bureaucrats who carry them out. Americans have opinions about Social Security—level of benefits, eligibility, taxes, and so on—but do not concern themselves much with the Social Security Administration per se. In general, then, the public does not directly know or think much about bureaucratic agencies.

There are exceptions to this generalization, however. Some agencies are constantly in the public eye and occasion the development of opinions. Because taxes are a constant irritant for most people, Americans tend to have opinions about the Internal Revenue Service. Foul-ups can often focus public attention on an agency, as well. The FBI and the CIA came under fire in 2005, for example, for intelligence failures relating to 9/11 and Iraq's purported weapons of mass destruction. Later in the same year, the Army Corps of Engineers and FEMA were strongly criticized during and

13.1

13.2

13.3

13.4

13.5

13.6

after the Hurricane Katrina disaster, the first for its failed levee system in and around New Orleans, the second for its painfully slow and incomplete rescue and recovery operations. The Fed and Treasury were the brunt of widespread discontent in 2009 and 2010 because of a public perception that they were more interested in bailing out and helping financial firms than in helping consumers. The NSA was widely criticized when private contractor Edward Snowden leaked details in 2013 of massive data gathering on American citizens and foreign leaders (even of close allies).

Needless to say, bureaucratic failures are pointed out to the public by the various news media and information sources. Scandals and disasters, we learned, are particularly attractive to the news media, so information about them gets to the public in short order through a variety of outlets, from television news broadcasts blogs and social media. The news media are also more likely to report goings-on in bureaucratic agencies when there is controversy—for example, the debate over the FBI's use of the USA Patriot Act to conduct surveillance on American citizens. The news media are less likely, perhaps, to report on the routine activities of reasonably effective agencies, whether the Agriculture Extension Service or the National Archives.

## ☐ Interest Groups

Because bureaucratic agencies make important decisions that affect many people, interest and advocacy groups pay lots of attention to what they do and use a variety of lobbying tools to influence these decisions. Groups lobby Congress, for example, to shape the missions of executive branch departments and agencies, as environmental organizations did to give the EPA authority over development in wetland areas. Groups also lobby bureaucratic agencies directly, as when they appear before them to offer testimony on proposed rules. (Public comment is required in many agencies before binding rules can be issued.) Although various environmental, labor, and consumer advocacy associations regularly offer formal comment on rules, this process is dominated by associations that represent business and the professions, who often get their way.[44] There is a strong body of evidence that business interest groups are deeply involved in the actual process of rule-writing itself.[45] It is hardly surprising, then, to learn that for years livestock producers have been able to prevent the Department of Agriculture from imposing stringent rules for tracking cattle products despite several outbreaks of "mad cow" disease in recent years.

# Reforming the Federal Bureaucracy

**13.6** Assess what's wrong and what's right with the federal bureaucracy

**H**ow can we improve the federal bureaucracy? The answer depends on what a person thinks is wrong with it and what needs improving. Let's look at some possibilities.

## ☐ Scaling Back Its Size

If the problem with the federal bureaucracy is perceived to be its size, there are two ways to trim government activities: slimming them down and transferring activities to others, usually states and private sector contractors. Each solution has its own set of problems.

**CUTTING THE FAT** For observers who worry that the federal bureaucracy is simply too big and costly, mainly due to bloat and waste, the preferred strategy is what might be called the "meat ax" approach. Virtually every presidential candidate today promises to "cut the fat" if elected. Bill Clinton made such a promise during the 1992 presidential campaign, and he carried through after his election. In the early weeks of his

**13.1**

**13.2**

**13.3**

**13.4**

**13.5**

**13.6**

**privatizing**
Turning over certain government functions to the private sector.

administration, he ordered that 100,000 federal jobs be eliminated within four years, that freezes be placed on the salaries of government workers, that cost-of-living pay adjustments be reduced, and that the use of government vehicles and planes be sharply restricted. Needless to say, this approach probably doesn't do much to enhance the morale of federal government employees, who receive the clear message in these sorts of actions that they are held in low regard by political leaders and the public.

To some extent this effort to cut the size and cost of the bureaucracy has worked; the number of federal employees has diminished steadily since the early 1990s and even more dramatically since the Ford administration when considered in relationship to the U.S population (see Figure 13.6). The cuts have taken place even as the government has initiated new programs. One way this has been done is to off-load many activities and their costs to the states; the No Child Left Behind testing requirement, for example, has forced them to hire more people in order to comply with federal law, without providing enough federal money to fully compensate the states.

As we saw in the chapter-opening story, furthermore, "cutting the fat" sometimes goes too far and cuts into the bone of programs. This often results in decreases in important services and protections for the public. Fewer campgrounds may be available in national parks, the Food and Drug Administration may take longer to examine and approve new drugs, and the Army Corps of Engineers may slow the pace of repairing levees along important waterways.

**PRIVATIZING** A much-discussed strategy for scaling back the federal bureaucracy is to contract out some of its functions and responsibilities to the private sector.[46] This **privatization** approach is based on two beliefs:

- Private business can almost always do things better than government.
- Competitive pressure from the private sector will force government agencies to be more efficient.

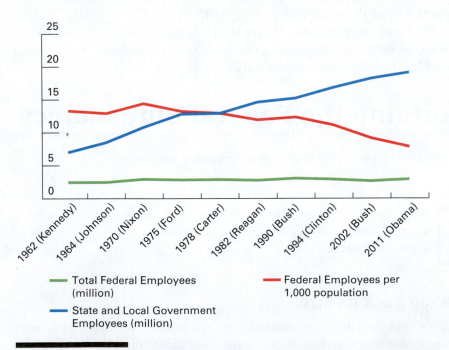

**FIGURE 13.6** NEW GOVERNMENT EMPLOYEES AT THE FEDERAL, STATE, AND LOCAL LEVEL

While the absolute number of federal employees has been fairly constant for a long time and has actually declined as a proportion of the U.S. population, the number of state and local government employees has grown substantially. This may be one reason why such a concerted effort was made by Republican-controlled state governments to cut back the number of public employees after their anti-big government party's substantial victories across the country in the 2010 elections.

*Source:* U.S. Census Bureau. The numbers for federal employees include those in the Postal Service.

13.1
13.2
13.3
13.4
13.5
13.6

**RIDING SHOTGUN**

Private contractors, such as this U.S. Army veteran riding in an SUV providing convoy protection in Kabul, Afghanistan, now serve roles in combat theatres formerly carried out by the U.S. armed forces. Often they operate under different rules than regular soldiers. How might this sometimes create problems for American foreign policy?

Privatization has actually been happening for many years. For example, the Defense Department does not produce its own weapons systems but uses an elaborate contracting system to design, build, and purchase fighter planes, submarines, and missiles from private corporations. In Iraq, moreover, the Defense Department depended on private contractors, including companies such as Halliburton and its subsidiary Kellogg Brown and Root, to feed and house soldiers, fight oil field fires and rebuild oil pipelines, build telephone networks, maintain the military's high-tech weapons, make gasoline deliveries to Iraqi consumers, train local police, protect dignitaries, and interrogate detainees.[47] The Corps of Engineers uses private contractors to build and maintain levees and clear waterways. Homeland Security has contracted with Boeing to build a high-tech security system along the U.S.-Mexican border. The rollout of the Obamacare website was troubled because multiple private contractors carried out portions of the job with no one in government or in the private sector closely monitoring and coordinating their activities. To fix the website's problems, the administration turned to private contractors.

While it is evident to all observers that the contracting out has been expanding dramatically, the exact number of people working on a contract basis for the federal government is hard to determine. But expanded it has; money in the federal budget for private contracts rose 37 percent between 2005 and 2010 to reach $538 billion,[48] though the total fell back to $460 billion in 2013 as Washington turned its attention to shrinking how much government spends. That is still a considerable amount of money for government work carried out by private-sector firms and employees. Figuring out how many such employees there are is more complicated, but some good estimates exist. According to Paul Light, the leading expert in this area, the number of private contractor jobs done for departments and agencies of the executive branch stood at around 7.5 million in 2007, about four times more than the total of federal civilian employees.[49]

Advocates of privatizing simply want to expand the process, turning over to private companies functions such as the postal system, the federal prisons, and air traffic control. Critics worry that privatizing government carries significant costs.[50]

• Some matters seem so central to the national security and well-being that citizens and officials are unwilling to risk that the private sector will necessarily do the job well or at all. A good example is the transfer of the responsibility for screening

13.1

13.2

13.3

13.4

13.5

13.6

**red tape**
Overbearing bureaucratic rules and procedures.

airline passengers and baggage from the airlines to a new government agency, the Transportation Security Administration after 9/11.

- Private business firms might not be willing to provide services that are unprofitable. Delivering mail to remote locations is a service the U.S. Postal Service provides, for instance, but that a private company might determine is too costly, and eliminate.

- A private business under government contract is several steps removed from political control, and the normal instruments of democratic accountability, however imperfect, might not be as effective in controlling private business as they are in controlling government agencies. The voice of the public, expressed in public opinion polls or elections, might not be heard with much clarity by private companies, particularly if they are the only supplier of some essential service.

- Private contractors may not be bound by many of the regulations and statutes that apply to other executive branch employees. For example, the military apparently has depended a great deal on private contractors to interrogate detainees in Afghanistan, Iraq, and Guantanamo Bay, believing, perhaps, that contractors could use methods not sanctioned for use by active service military personnel. After abuses were uncovered involving security personnel working in Iraq for Blackwater Security Consulting International, the Pentagon said it was tightening the rules under which its contractors worked.

- Citizens are not customers, and privatization tends to serve the latter. A citizen in a democracy usually requires not only satisfaction with a product or service like a customer; but also equity, transparency, and accountability as required by our constitutional rules.

- Many public services and the agencies that provide them were created because of what are called "market failures," activities that are necessary but that private firms either cannot provide or cannot be trusted to provide. One of the things that led to the collapse of the financial industry, for example, was that private rating agencies like Moody's and Standard and Poor's, hired by investment banks to rate their securities, gave AAA and AA ratings to mortgage-backed securities built on a weak foundation of sub-prime loans.[51]

## ☐ Becoming More Businesslike

If the problem with the federal bureaucracy is perceived to be the inefficiencies of its operations and excessive **red tape**, then the key to reform might be to reinvent governmental bureaucracy along businesslike lines. President Clinton turned over the responsibility for "reinventing government" to Vice President Al Gore at the beginning of his administration. The term "reinventing government" comes from a popular and influential book by that name written by David Osborne and Ted Gaebler,[52] although the ideas for these reforms come from advocates of what is called "the new public management."[53] "Reinventing" advocates propose transforming the federal bureaucracy not only by cutting the fat and privatizing (as discussed in the preceding section), but also by introducing business principles into the executive branch. They believe that government agencies will provide better public services if they are run like private businesses: using pay-for-performance to determine salaries, for example, or focusing more on customer needs. Most observers have not been impressed by either the scale or effectiveness of efforts to make government more "businesslike."[54]

## ☐ Protecting Against Bureaucratic Abuses of Power

Many people believe that the problem with a bureaucracy the size, shape, and power of our present one is that it is potentially unresponsive to the public and a dangerous threat to individual liberty. The preferred solution has been closer control over the bureaucracy by elected political bodies and by clear legislative constraints. Accordingly, many legislative enactments have tried to keep bureaucratic activity within narrow boundaries. The Freedom of Information Act of 1966 was designed to enhance the ability of the press and private citizens to obtain information about bureaucratic policies and activities. The Ethics in Government Act of 1978 strengthened requirements of financial disclosure by officials and prohibitions against conflicts of interest. Some reformers would like to see greater protection provided for **whistle-blowers**—bureaucrats who report corruption, financial mismanagement, abuses of power, or other official malfeasance.

A potentially important innovation has been the rapid growth in what has been called e-government (and sometimes, "Google your government"), a reform based on a statute passed in 2006, which requires the OMB to make more information available online in a user-friendly database for public inspection of bureaucratic activities and expenditures. People could go, for example, to stimulus.gov to track where their economic stimulus dollars were being spent after Congress passed the bill in 2009. Data.gov is a rich source for all things related to keeping tabs on what government is doing and how well it is doing it. Then there are, of course, a legion of government employees and contractors like Edward Snowden who release information to media organizations and to online sites such as WikiLeaks.

## ☐ Increasing Presidential Control

One suggestion for reform of the federal bureaucracy is to have it more closely controlled by elected representatives of the people. This suggestion follows directly from the principle of popular sovereignty, which requires that the elected representatives of the people closely control the bureaucracy. Popular sovereignty implies that administrative discretion should be narrowed as much as possible and that elected officials should communicate clear directions and unambiguous policies to bureaucratic agencies. (Note that this goal is very different from the one envisioned by the advocates of privatization and reinventing government.) Some advocates of popular sovereignty have argued that the president is the only public official who has an interest in seeing that the bureaucracy *as a whole* is well run and coherently organized. Accordingly, one suggestion for reform is to increase the powers of the president so that he can be the chief executive, in fact and not just in name. This is the view of the president and the bureaucracy shared by many liberals who admire the leadership of Franklin Roosevelt during the Great Depression and the Second World War, and many conservatives who advocated so strongly for the concept of the unitary executive during George W. Bush's two terms.

## Using the DEMOCRACY STANDARD

### Does the bureaucracy advance or retard democracy?

The framers of the Constitution would no doubt be surprised by the great expansion in the responsibilities of the national government and the growth in the size of the bureaucracy required to carry out these responsibilities. Although they believed they had put in place constitutional provisions to restrain the size and reach of the national government—federalism, separation of powers, and checks and balances—they failed to account for the substantial democratization of the American republic or for structural changes demanding increased government involvement: urbanization, scientific and technological innovations, economic crises, the emergence of the United States as a superpower, and the need to provide national security in an interconnected world.

But as it has grown in size and reach, the federal bureaucracy has also grown more democratic in many ways. For one thing, most of what government bureaucrats do is carry out the missions defined for them by elected public officials, namely, Congress and the president, who are quite attentive to public opinion. And for the most part,

**whistle-blowers**
People who bring official misconduct in their agencies to public attention.

13.1

13.2

13.3

13.4

13.5

13.6

13.1

13.2

13.3

13.4

13.5

13.6

civil servants are very much like other Americans, both in their demographic makeup and in what they think the government should be doing.

On the other hand, there are many ways in which the bureaucracy falls short in terms of democracy. Bureaucrats enjoy substantial discretion in carrying out their missions—much of what they do in the federal bureaucracy goes largely unnoticed, making popular control difficult. For one thing, there are so many decisions being made and rules being issued that no one could possibly keep track of them all. Moreover, many of the rules issued by bureaucrats and decisions made by them are highly technical in nature, with only specialists and experts paying very close attention. Agency capture, iron triangles, and business involvement in rule-making and administration surely is cause for concern from a democratic point of view. Finally, the elite and big business backgrounds of most high-level presidential appointees must cause some concern for those who care strongly about democratic responsiveness.

While democratic theorists may not be comfortable with every aspect of bureaucratic growth, the expansion of the role of government in American life, and the creation of the bureaucratic machinery associated with this expansion, is testament to the impact of democratic forces in American politics. Government has taken on new responsibilities in large part because of the demands of the people over many years that it do so. The bureaucracy that emerged to carry out these new government responsibilities has sometimes seemed inefficient and at cross purposes; probably best explained by the separation of powers and checks and balances designed by the framers.

# Review the Chapter

## The American Bureaucracy: How Exceptional?

**13.1** Compare and contrast our executive branch bureaucracy with those in other countries, p. 393

Compared to public bureaucracies in other rich democracies, ours in the United States operates in a more hostile political/culture environment where anti–big government attitudes are widespread, it is less coherently organized, and it has several masters in addition to the chief executive (the president).

## How the Executive Branch Is Organized

**13.2** Outline the structure of the executive branch, p. 396

The federal bureaucracy is comprised of cabinet departments, agencies and bureaus within departments, independent agencies, government corporations and foundations, independent regulatory commissions, and quasi-governmental organizations such as the Federal Reserve Board.

The executive branch has grown in size and responsibility over the course of our history. This growth is a consequence of a transformation in the conception of the proper role of government because of economic and social structural changes.

## What Do Bureaucrats Do?

**13.3** Identify the kinds of activities bureaucrats perform, p. 400

Bureaucrats are involved in three major kinds of activities: executing the law, regulating, and adjudicating disputes. In each of these, they exercise a great deal of discretion.

Although bureaucracy is not a popular concept in the American political tradition, we have created a sizable one. The reason is partly that bureaucratic organizations have certain strengths that make them attractive for accomplishing large-scale tasks like preparing for war and delivering retirement checks.

## Who Are the Bureaucrats?

**13.4** Determine how demographically representative bureaucrats are, p. 405

Bureaucrats in the merit services are very much like other Americans in terms of demographic characteristics and attitudes. Political appointees (the most important bureaucratic decision makers) are very different from their fellow citizens, coming from more elite backgrounds.

Because they are unelected policymakers, democratic theory demands that we be concerned about who the bureaucrats are.

## Political and Governmental Influences on Bureaucratic Behavior

**13.5** Isolate various influences on executive branch decision making, p. 408

Though bureaucrats are technically independent of influences beyond the bureaucratic chain of command and the rules and regulations that define their agency missions and operations, bureaucrats are in fact influenced by other political and governmental actors and institutions, including the president, Congress, and the courts, as well as public opinion and interest groups.

## Reforming the Federal Bureaucracy

**13.6** Assess what's wrong and what's right with the federal bureaucracy, p. 415

Proposals to reform the executive branch are related to what reformers believe is wrong with the federal bureaucracy. Those who worry most about size and inefficiency propose budget and personnel cuts, privatization, and the introduction of business principles into government. Those who want to make democracy more of a reality propose giving more control over the bureaucracy to the president and diminishing the role of interest groups.

Problems with the bureaucracy, while real, are either exaggerated or the result of forces outside the bureaucracy itself: the constitutional rules and the struggle between the president and Congress.

# Learn the Terms

federal bureaucracy, p. 393
bureaucrat, p. 393
bureaucracy, p. 393
civil servants, p. 394
civil service, p. 394
departments, p. 396
bureau, p. 396
agency, p. 396

independent regulatory commission, p. 399
independent executive agency, p. 399
government corporation, p. 399
quasi-governmental organization, p. 400
foundation, p. 400
cost-benefit analysis, p. 402

spoils system, p. 405
patronage, p. 405
recess appointments, p. 407
unitary executive, p. 410
appropriation, p. 413
privatizing, p. 416
red tape, p. 418
whistle-blowers, p. 419

# Test Yourself

Answer key begins on page T-1.

**13.1** Compare and contrast our executive branch bureaucracy with those in other countries

1. Civil servants in parliamentary democracies are accountable to:

   a. The president
   b. Congress
   c. The prime minister
   d. A cabinet minister
   e. Parliament

**13.2** Outline the structure of the executive branch

2. Independent executive agencies report directly to:

   a. The president
   b. A department
   c. A cabinet-level secretary
   d. The Speaker of the House
   e. The vice president

**13.3** Identify the kinds of activities bureaucrats perform

3. Congress often gives bureaucratic agencies the power to:

   a. Control small business
   b. Regulate the law
   c. Write specific rules
   d. Pass bills into laws
   e. Regulate spending

**13.4** Determine how demographically representative bureaucrats are

4. These appointments are used to hire people with skills that are needed and in short supply.

   a. Schedule A
   b. Schedule B
   c. Schedule C
   d. Schedule D
   e. Schedule E

**13.5** Isolate various influences on executive branch decision making

5. The Administrative Procedure Act of 1946 attempts to make sure that agencies:

   a. Follow the orders of Congress
   b. File their budgets on time
   c. Comply with the Better Business Bureau
   d. Stay out of the public eye
   e. Are bound by due process guarantees

**13.6** Assess what's wrong and what's right with the federal bureaucracy

6. This implies that administrative discretion should be narrowed as much as possible and that elected officials should communicate clear directions to bureaucratic agencies.

   a. Cutting the fat
   b. Popular sovereignty
   c. Privatization
   d. The Ethics in Government Act
   e. E-government

# Explore Further

## INTERNET SOURCES

Data.gov **www.data.gov**
A rich source of information about what the federal government
is doing.

The Federal Register **www.archives.gov/federal_register**
All rules issued by federal agencies can be found here.

FedWorld **fedworld.ntis.gov/**
The gateway to the federal government's numerous websites;
connections to virtually every federal department, bureau,
commission, and foundation, as well as access to government
statistics and reports.

Government Is Good **www.governmentisgood.com**
A site replete with information about what government does well.

The President's Cabinet **www.whitehouse.gov/government/
cabinet.html**
A site listing all cabinet members, as well as links to each
department's website.

Office of Personnel Management **www.opm.gov**
The best site to find statistics and other information about federal
government employees.

The Cato Institute **www.cato.org**
The conservative institute's home page, featuring defenses of
small government and proposals to solve social and economic
problems without creating a bigger government.

## SUGGESTIONS FOR FURTHER READING

Aberbach, Joel D., and Mark A. Peterson, eds. *The Executive Branch*
New York: Oxford University Press, 2005.
A highly accessible collection of essays on diverse aspects of
the federal executive branch by leading scholars and
practitioners.

Durant, Robert F. *The Oxford Handbook of American Bureaucracy.*
New York: Oxford University Press, 2012.
An indispensable reference book; a collection of essays by leading
scholars on all aspects of the executive branch of government.

Goodsell, Charles T. *The New Case for Bureaucracy,* Washington,
DC: CQ Press, 2014.
A well-written polemic that suggests that most criticisms of
bureaucracy are not well founded.

Gormley, William T., and Steven J. Balla. *Bureaucracy and
Democracy: Accountability and Performance.* Washington, DC:
CQ Press, 2012.
Examination of how well government bureaucracies perform and
how accountable they are to the public.

Kerwin, Cornelius M. *Rulemaking: How Government Agencies
Write Law and Make Policy.* Washington, D.C.: CQ Press,
2010.
A comprehensive treatment of rule-making by executive branch
agencies.

Light, Paul C. *A Government Ill Executed: The Decline of the Federal
Service and How to Reverse It.* Cambridge, MA: Harvard
University Press, 2009.
A thorough examination of what has gone wrong with the
executive branch's ability to execute the law and serious
proposals on what to do about it by America's leading scholar
on the federal bureaucracy.

*The National Journal.*
Comprehensive coverage of Congress, the presidency, and the
executive branch, with a strong focus on the analysis of federal
policies.

*The 9/11 Commission Report: Final Report of the National
Commission on Terrorist Attacks Upon the United States.* New
York: W. W. Norton, 2004.
An exhaustive study of how 9/11 happened and a set of
recommendations—including reorganization of the executive
branch—for better homeland defense and security.

*Washington Monthly.*
Washington's leading journal of "bureaucracy bashing"; filled with
outrageous and (sometimes) illuminating stories.

# 14

# The Courts

## THE BATTLE FOR THE COURTS

Tension filled the hearing room as Samuel Alito, President Bush's strongly conservative nominee for a position on the U.S. Supreme Court, began testifying before the Senate Judiciary Committee on January 9, 2006. Knowing that federal courts were deciding cases having to do with the most contentious issues of the day—including presidential powers in times of war, affirmative action, gay rights, the relationship between church and state, the role of the federal government in relationship to the states, and more—Republican and Democratic partisans and conservative and liberal advocacy groups were mobilized to fight over Alito's nomination. Lurking in the background was the Democrats' threat to filibuster the nomination, meaning that Alito's confirmation would need 60 votes, not a simple majority of 51. Republicans claimed the filibuster could not be properly used when the Senate was exercising its constitutional duty to "advise and consent" on judicial nominations. Most Democrats believed it was the only way to prevent the accession of judges to the federal bench who would threaten hard-won rights and protections, particularly a woman's right to terminate her pregnancy.

Partisan tensions over the judicial filibuster had been festering for years. Republicans fell seven votes short of the 60 votes needed to end Democratic filibusters blocking Senate votes on several very conservative Bush federal judicial nominees, including Priscilla Owen for the Fifth Circuit. Republicans were furious, saying they were ready to proceed with the so-called nuclear option ending filibusters on judicial nominations.[1] Democrats pointed out, in response, that Republicans had blocked many Clinton nominees during the 1990s but had not needed the filibuster because, as the majority, they could stop nominations in the Judiciary Committee, never allowing them to reach the floor for a vote, refusing to hold hearings for several Clinton nominees and delaying hearings for others for up to 18 months.

**CHANGING THE BALANCE OF THE COURT** When strong conservative Samuel Alito joined the Court in 2006, replacing moderate conservative Sandra Day O'Conner, it changed the ideological balance of the Court on a wide range of issues. Because the stakes were so high, the battle in the Senate over his confirmation was contentious and attracted a large audience to his televised testimony before the Judiciary Committee.

The issue was revived when President Bush renominated Priscilla Owen in early 2005. When Democrats announced they would again use the filibuster to block the nomination, Republican Majority Leader Bill Frist (R–TN) warned that he would begin the process of outlawing the filibuster for judicial confirmation votes. Democrats countered that they would tie up the business of the Senate for the foreseeable future if Republicans imposed the nuclear option. Partisans on both sides in the Senate and the country were itching for a fight on this issue because they believed the stakes had never been higher. A train wreck loomed.

Into the fray stepped the so-called gang of 14, a group of Republican and Democratic moderates who worked out a compromise. Wielding enormous power because their 14 votes would be decisive on any vote related to this issue, they agreed that the judicial filibuster could be used only in undefined "extraordinary circumstances." Under the agreement, the Senate confirmed the long-delayed nominations of Priscilla Owen and two other nominees, but took no action on two other nominees who presumably fit the "extraordinary circumstances" requirement that would allow Democrats to use the filibuster. (In 2013, the Democratic majority in the Senate outlawed filibusters on judicial nominations, with the exception of those to the Supreme Court.)

The temporary truce held, even when conservative jurist John Roberts was nominated for the post of Chief Justice after the death of Chief Justice William Rehnquist in late 2005, perhaps because he was a conservative jurist replacing another conservative on the Court. Samuel Alito was another matter entirely, however, because he was to replace the retiring Sandra Day O'Connor, a relatively moderate voice and swing vote on the Court who played an important role in protecting abortion rights and affirming the use, under certain circumstances, of affirmative action in higher education admissions. In the end, however, the Democrats were unable to mount much of a challenge to Alito, and calls for a filibuster by a few Democratic senators failed to gain traction. His nomination was confirmed on January 31, 2006.

As predicted by almost everyone, Alito's ascension to the Court swung it sharply in a conservative direction on issues ranging from affirmative action and voting rights, to abortion, business regulation, unions, religion in public life, and campaign finance,[2] matters to be examined in greater detail later in this and later chapters. The fundamental balance on the Court was not affected much when Obama nominee Sonia Sotomayor joined the Court in 2009, because she was a liberal replacing a liberal, David Souter, who retired. The same thing was true regarding the appointment of Elena Kagan in 2010; she was a liberal replacing a liberal stalwart, John Paul Stevens, so the balance on the Court was unaffected. The key appointment in determining the balance of power on the Court remained that of Alito replacing O'Connor in 2006, which created a solid conservative 5-4 majority under the able leadership of Chief Justice Roberts that still endures.[3]

In the system of separated powers and federalism created by the framers, the judicial branch, most especially the Supreme Court, assesses, in cases that come before it, the legitimacy of actions taken by the other two branches and by the states in light of the Constitution. Although the Supreme Court does not legislate or regulate on its own, its decisions strongly influence the overall shape of federal and state policies in a number of important areas. As such, the Supreme Court is a key national policymaker, and an important political actor in Washington, every bit as much a part of the governing process as the president and Congress.[4]

## Thinking Critically About This Chapter

This chapter is about the judicial branch of the federal government, with a special focus on the Supreme Court. We examine how the federal judiciary and Supreme Court are organized, what they do in the American political and government systems, and what effects their actions have on public policies and American democracy.

## Using the Framework

You will see in this chapter that the Court is embedded in a rich governmental, political linkage, and structural environment that shapes its behavior. The other branches of government impinge on and influence its composition, deliberations, and rulings; political linkage institutions such as elections, interest groups, and social movements matter; and structural factors such as economic and social change influence its agenda and decisions.

## Using the Democracy Standard

You will see in this chapter that an unelected Court makes important decisions about public policies, raising questions about the degree to which popular sovereignty and majority rule prevail in our system. You will also see that the Court often turns its attention to cases that involve issues of political equality and liberty, so essential to the existence of a healthy representative democracy.

**judicial review**
The power of the Supreme Court to declare actions of the other branches and levels of government unconstitutional.

14.1
14.2
14.3
14.4
14.5
14.6

# The Foundations of Judicial Power

**14.1**   Trace the evolution of judicial power in the United States

*The judicial Power of the United States shall be vested in one supreme Court, and in such inferior Courts as the Congress may from time to time ordain and establish.*

—U.S. Constitution, Article III, Section 1

*We are under a Constitution, but the Constitution is what the judges say it is, and the judiciary is the safeguard of our liberty and our property under the Constitution.*

—Chief Justice Charles Evans Hughes (1907)

## ☐ Constitutional Design

The Constitution speaks only briefly about the judicial branch and doesn't provide much guidance about what it is supposed to do or how it is supposed to go about its job. The document says little about the powers of the judicial branch in relationship to the other two federal branches or about its responsibilities in the area of constitutional interpretation. Article III is considerably shorter than Articles I and II, which focus on Congress and the president. It creates a federal judicial branch, it creates the office of "chief justice of the United States," it states that judges shall serve life terms, it specifies the categories of cases the Court may or must hear (to be explained later), and it grants Congress the power to create additional federal courts as needed. Article III of the Constitution is virtually devoid of detail.[5]

## ☐ Judicial Review

Extremely interesting is the Constitution's silence about **judicial review**, the long-established power of the Supreme Court to declare state and federal laws and actions null and void when they conflict with the Constitution. Debate has raged for many years over the question of whether the framers intended that the Court should have this power.[6]

14.1

14.2

14.3

14.4

14.5

14.6

The framers surely believed that the Constitution ought to prevail when other laws were in conflict with it. But did they expect the Supreme Court to make the decisions in this matter? Jefferson and Madison thought that Congress and the president were capable of rendering their own judgments about the constitutionality of their actions. Alexander Hamilton, however, believed that the power of judicial review was inherent in the notion of the separation of powers and was essential to balanced government. As he put it in *The Federalist*, No. 78 (see the Appendix), the very purpose of constitutions is to place limitations on the powers of government, and it is only the Court that can ensure such limits in the United States. The legislative branch, in particular, is unlikely to restrain itself without the helping hand of the judiciary.

There is reason to believe that Hamilton's view was the prevailing one for a majority of the framers.[7] They were firm believers, for instance, in the idea that there was a "higher law" to which governments and nations must conform. Their enthusiasm for written constitutions was based on their belief that governments must be limited in what they could do in the service of some higher or more fundamental law, such as that pertaining to individual rights. The attitudes of the time, then, strongly supported the idea that judges, conversant with the legal tradition and free from popular pressures, were best able to decide when statutory and administrative laws were in conflict with fundamental law.[8]

**MARBURY v. MADISON** Chief Justice John Marshall boldly claimed the power of judicial review for the U.S. Supreme Court in the case of *Marbury v. Madison* in 1803.[9] The case began with a flurry of judicial appointments by President John Adams in the final days of his presidency, after his Federalist Party had suffered a resounding defeat in the election of 1800. The apparent aim of these so-called midnight appointments was to establish the federal courts as an outpost of Federalist Party power (federal judges are appointed for life) in the midst of rising Jeffersonian sentiment. After the 1800 election, control of the presidency and the Congress was firmly in Republican hands.

William Marbury was one of the midnight appointments, but he was less lucky than most. His judgeship commission was signed and sealed, but it had not been delivered to him before the new administration took office. Jefferson, knowing what Adams and the Federalists were up to, ordered Secretary of State James Madison not to deliver the commission. Marbury sued Madison, claiming that the secretary of state was obligated to deliver the commission, and asked the Supreme Court to issue a *writ of mandamus* to force Madison to do so.

Marshall faced a quandary. If the Court decided in favor of Marbury, Madison would almost surely refuse to obey, opening the Court to ridicule for its weakness. The fact that Marshall was a prominent Federalist political figure might even provoke the

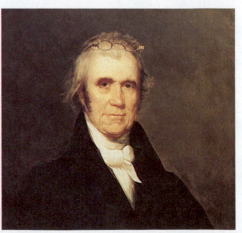

**ADVOCATES OF JUDICIAL REVIEW**

Although the Constitution is silent on the issue of judicial review, many of the Founders probably agreed with Alexander Hamilton (left), who argued that the Supreme Court's power to interpret the Constitution and declare state and federal laws and actions unconstitutional is inherent in the notion of the separation of powers. However, it was not until the Supreme Court's 1803 *Marbury v. Madison* decision that Chief Justice John Marshall (right) affirmed the Court's power of judicial review. How might a lack of the power of judicial review hinder the classic American system of checks and balances?

Jeffersonians to take more extreme measures against the Court. But if the Court ruled in favor of Madison, it would suggest that an executive official could defy without penalty the clear provisions of the law.

Marshall's solution was worthy of Solomon. The Court ruled that William Marbury was entitled to his commission and that James Madison had broken the law in failing to deliver it. By this ruling, the Court rebuked Madison. However, the Court said it could not compel Madison to comply with the law because the section of the Judiciary Act of 1789 that granted the Court the power to issue writs of mandamus was unconstitutional. It was unconstitutional, he said, because it expanded the **original jurisdiction** of the Supreme Court as defined in Article III, which could not be done except by constitutional amendment.

On the surface, the decision was an act of great modesty. It suggested that the Court could not force the action of an executive branch official. It suggested that Congress had erred in the Judiciary Act of 1789 by trying to give the Supreme Court too much power. Beneath the surface, however, was a less modest act: the claim that judicial review was the province of the judicial branch alone. In Marshall's words in his written opinion, "It is emphatically the province and duty of the judicial department to say what the law is." In making this claim, he was following closely Hamilton's argument in *The Federalist*, No. 78.

Until quite recently, the Supreme Court used the power of judicial review with great restraint, perhaps recognizing that its regular use would invite retaliation by the other branches. Judicial review of a congressional act was not exercised again until 54 years after *Marbury* and was used to declare acts of Congress unconstitutional only about 230 times from then until 2007. However, the Court has been much less constrained about overruling the laws of the states and localities; it did so more than 1,100 times during this same period.[10] During the 1990s and early 2000s, the Rehnquist Court was much more inclined to review and overturn congressional actions, especially in cases involving federalism and the powers of Congress under the commerce clause, trimming back the power of the federal government relative to the states. Indeed, it

**original jurisdiction**
The authority of a court to be the first to hear a particular kind of case.

14.1

14.2

14.3

14.4

14.5

14.6

**DETENTION**
Though the Supreme Court ruled at first in favor of greater access of suspected terrorism detainees to the American judicial system, it has increasingly deferred to the president, military authorities, and Congress on how such detainees should be treated and how long they can be held in custody. Here a detainee is escorted to his cell at Guantanamo Bay, Cuba by military police.

14.1

14.2

14.3

14.4

14.5

14.6

invalidated congressional actions at a rate double that of the Warren Court of the 1960s, considered by many to be the most "activist" Court since the early 1930s.[11]

The Court has been less inclined to exercise judicial review on presidential actions, though some important ones have occurred during our history.[12] Between 2004 and 2008, however, the Court four times invalidated presidential actions pertaining to the treatment of detainees designated as enemy combatants.[13] It also ruled in 2014 that President Obama had abused his power to make recess appointments to the executive branch, a topic addressed in the chapters on the presidency and the federal bureaucracy.

**JUDICIAL REVIEW AND DEMOCRACY**  Judicial review involves the right of a body shielded from direct accountability to the people—federal judges are appointed, not elected, and serve for life (barring impeachment for unseemly, unethical, or illegal behavior)—to set aside the actions of government bodies whose members are elected. Many believe that judicial review has no place in a democratic society. One prominent democratic theorist has described the issue this way:

> But the authority of a high court to declare unconstitutional legislation that has been properly enacted by the coordinate constitutional bodies— . . . in our system, the Congress and the president—is far more controversial . . . The contradiction remains between imbuing an unelected body—or in the American case, five out of nine justices on the Supreme Court—with the power to make policy decisions that affect the lives and welfare of millions of Americans. How, if at all, can judicial review be justified in a democratic order?[14]

Political scientists and legal scholars use the phrase the "counter-majoritarian difficulty," coined by Alexander Bickel in 1962, to describe this enduring problem in the American political system; Bickel described judicial review as a "deviant institution in American democracy."[15] On the other hand, some observers believe that judicial review is the only way to protect the rights of political and racial minorities, to check the potential excesses of the other two government branches and the states, and to preserve the rules of the democratic process. Many political scientists believe that the problem of democratic accountability of a nonelected judiciary with life tenure is less dire than it seems on the surface because the Supreme Court and other federal courts are influenced directly and indirectly by elected officials, public opinion, and other important actors in American society.[16] We come back to this issue later in this chapter.

# The U.S. Court System: Organization and Jurisdiction

**14.2**  Outline the organization of the U.S. court system

Our country has one judicial system for the national government (the federal courts) and another in each of the states. In each state, courts adjudicate cases on the basis of the state's own constitution, statutes, and administrative rules.[17] In total, the great bulk of laws, legal disputes, and court decisions (roughly 99 percent) are located in the states. Most important political and constitutional issues, however, eventually reach the federal courts. In this chapter, our focus is on these federal courts. In the following sections, we'll look at the source of the power of the federal courts, their jurisdiction, and the organization of the federal court system.

## ☐ Constitutional Provisions

The only court specifically mentioned in the Constitution's Article III is the U.S. Supreme Court. The framers left to Congress the tasks of designing the details of the Supreme Court and establishing "such inferior courts as the Congress may from time to time ordain and establish." Beginning with the Judiciary Act of 1789, Congress has periodically reorganized the federal court system. The end result is a three-tiered pyramidal system (see Figure 14.1), with a handful of offshoots. At the bottom are 94 U.S. federal district courts, with at least one district in each state. In the middle are 13 courts of appeal. At the top of the pyramid is the Supreme Court. These courts are called **constitutional courts** because they were created by Congress under Article III, which discusses the judicial branch. Congress has also created a number of courts to adjudicate cases in highly specialized areas of concern, such as taxes, patents, and maritime law. These were established under Article I, which specifies the duties and powers of Congress, and are called **legislative courts**.

Article III does not offer many guidelines for the federal court system, but the few requirements that are stated are very important. The Constitution requires, for instance, that federal judges serve "during good behavior," which means, in practice, until they retire or die in office, as Chief Justice William Rehnquist did in 2005 at the age of 81. Because impeachment by Congress is the only way to remove federal judges, the decision about who will be a judge is an important one because they are likely to serve for a very long time. Article III also states that Congress cannot reduce the salaries of judges once they are in office. This provision was designed to maintain the independence of the judiciary by protecting it from legislative intimidation.

The jurisdiction of the federal judiciary—that is, the kinds of cases they have the authority to hear and make rulings about—include the following:

- *Disputes about the Constitution* (e.g., the meaning or scope of the commerce clause)
- *Disputes about federal statutes* (e.g., the meaning of a law, such as the extent to which the EPA can require MPH standards for cars)
- *Disputes about ambassadors and diplomats* (e.g., the meaning and extent of diplomatic immunity)
- *Disputes about treaties* (e.g., the extent to which states must follow the provisions of a treaty signed with a foreign government)
- *Disputes involving admiralty and maritime issues* (involving commerce on the high seas)
- *Disputes in which the U.S. government is a party* (e.g., for a perceived violation of a fundamental freedom, such as speech, by a government agency)
- *Disputes between states* (e.g., the proper location of borders or the split of sales taxes)
- *Disputes between a state and a citizen of another state* (e.g., recognition of same-sex marriages)
- *Disputes between a state (or citizen of a state) and foreign states or citizen* (e.g., claims of copyright or patent infringement)

## ◻ Federal District Courts

Most cases in the federal court system are first heard in one of the 94 district courts. District courts are courts of original jurisdiction, that is, courts where cases are first heard; they do not hear appeals from other courts. They are also trial courts; some

14.1

14.2

14.3

14.4

14.5

14.6

**constitutional courts**
Federal courts created by Congress under the authority of Article III of the Constitution.

**legislative courts**
Highly specialized federal courts created by Congress under the authority of Article I of the Constitution.

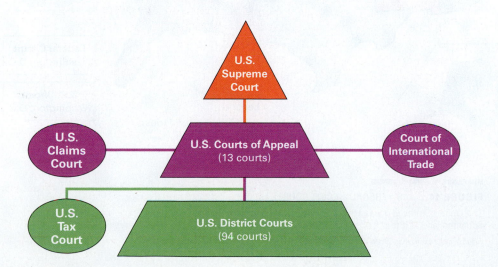

**FIGURE 14.1** THE U.S. FEDERAL COURT SYSTEM

The federal court system is a three-tiered pyramidal system, with the Supreme Court at the top. Below it are 13 federal courts of appeal and 94 district courts, with at least one district in each state. Additional courts exist to hear cases in highly specialized areas, such as taxes, international trade, and financial claims against the U.S. government.

*Source:* Administrative Office of the U.S. Courts.

**431**

**grand juries**
Groups of citizens who decide whether there is sufficient evidence to bring an indictment against accused persons.

**petit (trial) juries**
Juries that hear evidence and sit in judgment on charges brought in civil or criminal cases.

**circuit courts**
The 12 geographical jurisdictions and one special court that hear appeals from the federal district courts.

use juries—either **grand juries**, which bring indictments, or **petit (trial) juries**, which decide cases—and in some, cases are heard only by a judge.

Most of the business of the federal courts takes place at this level. In 2011, about 379,000 cases were filed; roughly 76 percent of them were civil cases, and 24 percent were criminal cases.[18] Civil cases include everything from antitrust cases brought by the federal government, to copyright infringement suits (as when Apple sued Amazon for its use of the term "Appstore" on the Amazon website), and commercial and contract disputes between citizens (or businesses) of two or more states. Criminal cases include violations of federal criminal laws, such as bank robbery, interstate drug trafficking, and kidnapping.

Most civil and criminal cases are concluded at this level. In a relatively small number of disputes, however, one of the parties to the case may feel that a mistake has been made in trial procedure or in the law that was brought to bear in the trial, or one of the parties may feel that a legal or constitutional issue is at stake that was not taken into account at the trial stage or was wrongly interpreted. In such cases, one of the parties may appeal to a higher court—a Court of Appeals.

## U.S. Courts of Appeal

The United States is divided into 12 geographic **circuit courts** (see the map in Figure 14.2) that hear appeals from federal district courts. The one for Washington, D.C., not only hears appeals from the federal district court there but also is charged with hearing cases arising from rule-making by federal agencies like the Securities and Exchange Commission and the National Labor Relations Board. A 13th circuit court, also located in Washington, D.C., called the U.S. Court of Appeals for the Federal Circuit, hears appeals from U.S. district courts from all over the nation on patents and government contracts. In 2013, almost 58,000 cases were filed in the federal appeals

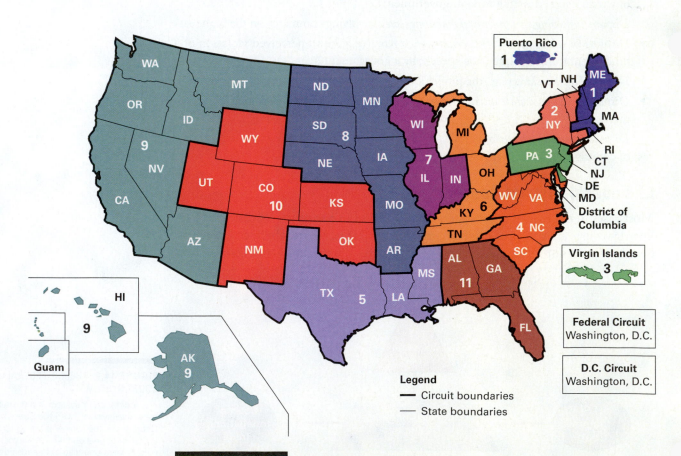

**FIGURE 14.2** U.S. FEDERAL CIRCUIT COURTS

The United States is divided into 12 geographic regions, each housing one U.S. court of appeals. One additional circuit, the U.S. Court of Appeals for the Federal Circuit, is located in Washington, D.C.

*Source:* Administrative Office of the U.S. Courts.

courts, although only about 8,000 reached the formal hearing stage (most of these end in negotiated settlements without going to trial).[19] Cases cannot originate in these courts but must come to them from district courts. Because they exist only to hear appeals, they are referred to as **appellate courts**. New factual evidence cannot be introduced before such courts; no witnesses are called or cross-examined. At the appellate level, lawyers do not examine witnesses or introduce new evidence; instead, they submit **briefs**, which set out the legal issues at stake. Judges usually convene as panels of three (on important cases, there are more—sometimes seven members) to hear oral arguments from the lawyers on each side of the case and to cross-examine them on points of law. Weeks or even months later, after considerable study, writing, and discussion among the judges, the panel issues a ruling. In important cases, the ruling is usually accompanied by an **opinion** that sets forth the majority side's reasoning for the decision.

Once appellate decisions are published, they become **precedents** that guide the decisions of other judges in the same circuit. Although judges do not slavishly follow precedents, they tend to move away from them only when necessary and only in very small steps. This doctrine of closely following precedents as the basis for legal reasoning is known as **stare decisis**.

It is important to know that the decisions of the 12 geographic circuit courts determine the meaning of laws for the people who live in the states covered by each circuit. They have become more important as they have ruled on ever more cases recently, without review by the Supreme Court, which decides fewer than 80 cases each year.

Sometimes particular circuits play a more important role than others in changing constitutional interpretation. For example, the Fourth Circuit Court, based in Richmond, Virginia, has been a leader in the trend toward reasserting the power of the states in the federal system.[20] The Ninth Circuit Court, which sits in San Francisco, on the other hand, is known to be especially liberal on civil rights and civil liberties cases. Because the Supreme Court considers only a relative handful of cases from the appeals courts each term, the rulings of the Fourth Circuit are binding for almost 24 million people in the southeastern United States, while the rulings of the Ninth Circuit Court of Appeals hold for roughly 61 million people in the western United States, including California. Although it has had several of its rulings reversed in recent years by the more conservative U.S. Supreme Court, the Ninth Circuit's rulings, nevertheless, cover about 20 percent of the American population.

## The Supreme Court

Congress decides how many judges sit on the Supreme Court. The first Court had six members. The Federalists, however, reduced the number to five in 1801 to prevent newly elected president Thomas Jefferson from filling a vacancy. In 1869, Congress set the number at its present nine members (eight associate justices and the chief justice). It has remained this way ever since, weathering the failed effort by President Franklin Roosevelt to "pack" the Court with more politically congenial justices by expanding its size to 15.

The Supreme Court is both a court of original jurisdiction and an appellate court. That is, some cases are first heard in the Supreme Court though most heard there are on appeal. Disputes involving ambassadors and other diplomatic personnel, as well as disputes between two or more states, must start in the Supreme Court rather than in some other court, though the Court is not obliged to hear such cases.[21]

The Supreme Court also, in its most important role, serves as an appellate court for the federal appeals courts and for the highest courts of each of the states. Cases in which a state or federal law has been declared unconstitutional can be heard by the Supreme Court, as can cases in which the highest state court has denied a claim that a state law violates federal law or the Constitution (see Figure 14.3). It also takes appeals that involve the interpretation of the meaning of federal statutes and regulations.

This last point is worth emphasizing. There is a popular misconception that the Supreme Court only takes cases having to do with constitutional questions. This is not correct. The Court takes both constitutional and statutory cases; it can rule on issues related

14.1
14.2
14.3
14.4
14.5
14.6

**appellate courts**
Courts that hear cases on appeal from other courts.

**briefs**
Documents setting out the arguments in legal cases, prepared by attorneys and presented to courts.

**opinion**
The explanation of the majority's and the minority's reasoning that accompanies a court decision.

**precedents**
Past rulings by courts which guide judicial reasoning in subsequent cases.

**stare decisis**
The legal doctrine that says precedent should guide judicial decision making.

14.1

14.2

14.3

14.4

14.5

14.6

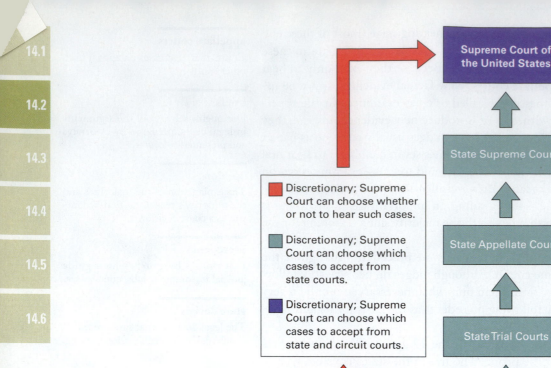
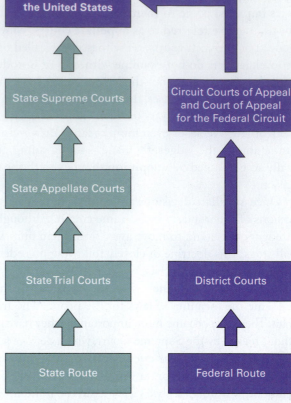

**FIGURE 14.3** HOW CASES GET TO THE SUPREME COURT

The vast majority of cases that reach the Supreme Court (over 65 percent) come to it from the federal court system. Most of the others (over 30 percent) come on appeal from the highest state courts. A handful of cases (about 2 percent) originate in the Supreme Court itself.

*Source:* based on from Storm Center: The Supreme Court in American Politics, Seventh Edition, by David M. O'Brien. Copyright © 2005, 2003, 2000, 1996, 1993, 1990, 1986 by David O'Brien. Used by permission of W. W. Norton & Company, Inc.

to the constitutionality of actions by federal, state, and local governments, but it can also rule on disputes centered on the meaning of statutes and regulations.[22] For example, in *Grove City College v. Bell* (1984), the Court ruled that Title IX of the Federal Education Act did not mean that institutions of higher education receiving federal funds would lose all federal funding if they practiced gender discrimination (as Congress clearly intended). Rather, it ruled that only the discriminating program or department would lose funding, say the athletic department or the physics department. Congress cannot ignore a constitutional ruling about a law it has passed. It can and does amend statutes to satisfy the concerns of the Court—or to get around the Court—when the meaning of a law to the Court is not consistent with Congress's understanding.

Congress determines much of the appellate jurisdiction of the Court. In 1869, following the Civil War, a Congress controlled by radical Republicans removed the Court's power to review cases falling under the Reconstruction program for the South. In 1995, responding to a plea from Chief Justice Rehnquist to lighten the Court's caseload, Congress dropped the requirement that the Supreme Court *must* hear cases in which a state court declares a federal statute unconstitutional. It can choose, but is not obligated, to do so.

Because it is the highest appellate court in the federal court system, the decisions and opinions of the Supreme Court become the main precedents on federal and constitutional questions for courts at all other levels of jurisdiction. It is for this reason that Supreme Court decisions receive so much attention from other political actors, the media, and the public.

# Appointment to the Federal Bench

**B**ecause federal judges are appointed for life and make important decisions, it matters in a democratic society who they are and how they get to the bench. If they are isolated from popular influence, democracy is at risk. If they are too responsive, they ignore their judicial role to act as neutral arbiters of the meaning of the Constitution in political and government affairs.

## ☐ Who Are the Appointees?

The Constitution offers no advice on what qualifications a federal judge should have. By custom and tradition, appointees to the federal bench must be lawyers, but until quite recently, they did not have to have judicial experience. Indeed, almost one-half of all Supreme Court justices during the twentieth century had no prior experience as judges. Among the ranks of the "inexperienced" are some of the most prominent and influential justices in our history, including John Marshall, Louis Brandeis, Harlan Stone, Charles Evans Hughes, Felix Frankfurter, and Earl Warren.[23] Former Chief Justice William Rehnquist also came to the bench without judicial experience, as did the most recently appointed justice, Elena Kagan, who served in the Clinton White House in the late 1990s after years in private practice and law school teaching.

As the federal courts—particularly the circuit courts and the Supreme Court—have become more important in determining American public policies, and as partisan and ideological conflicts have become more pronounced in the country, having judicial experience has become more important in the nomination and confirmation process. Because the stakes seem so high to many people—whether *Roe v. Wade* (1973) will be overturned, let us say, or what constitutional limits can be placed on the president during a war—they want to know the judicial philosophies and general ideological outlooks of the people who will become Supreme Court and appeals court judges. One way to know this is to examine the rulings and written opinions of nominees who have been judges. The new, though unwritten, rules about prior judicial experience became apparent in the firestorm that erupted within Republican and conservative circles after President Bush nominated Harriet Miers in late 2005 to fill the Sandra Day O'Connor vacancy. Many people who were normally Bush supporters were upset by the fact that Miers was an unknown in terms of constitutional law, having never served as a judge. They could not be sure they could trust her on the central issues of the day. They were much more comfortable with Bush nominees John Roberts and Samuel Alito, who had established extensive conservative records on the federal bench.[24]

Like most lawyers, federal judges tend to come from privileged backgrounds. Moreover, federal judges, and particularly Supreme Court justices, come from the most elite parts of the legal profession. For most of our history, they have been white male Protestants from upper-income or upper-middle-class backgrounds, who attended the most selective and expensive undergraduate and graduate institutions.[25] The current Supreme Court has moved entirely away from the almost exclusive Protestant membership that marked its history—indeed three current members, Ginsburg, Breyer, and Kagan, are Jewish and six, Scalia, Thomas, Kennedy, Roberts,

14.1

14.2

14.3

14.4

14.5

14.6

14.1

14.2

14.3

14.4

14.5

14.6

**senatorial courtesy**
The tradition that a judicial nomination for a federal district court seat be approved by the senior senator of the president's party from the state where a district court is located before the nominee is considered by the Senate Judiciary Committee.

Alito, and Sotomayor, are Catholic—and is more diverse in terms of race and gender than at any time in its history. On the current Supreme Court, there is one African American (Clarence Thomas), one Hispanic (Sotomayor), and three women (Ginsburg, Sotomayor, and Kagan). The racial and gender representativeness of judicial appointees at the circuit and district court levels is better, and improving rapidly, but it is still a long way from reflecting the composition of the legal profession, much less the American people as a whole.

## ☐ The Appointment Process

Federal judges assume office after they have been nominated by the president and confirmed by the Senate in a process that has become ever more contentious as national politicians have become more partisan.[26] Presidents pay special attention to judicial appointments, because they are a way for presidents to affect public policy long after their presidential term is up.[27]

Presidents take many things into consideration besides merit.[28] No president wants a nomination rejected by the Senate, for example, so the president and presidential advisers consult with key senators, especially those on the Judiciary Committee, before nominations are forwarded. Nominations for district court judgeships are subject to what is called **senatorial courtesy**, the practice of allowing the senior senator from the president's party to approve nominees from the state where the district court is located. Senatorial courtesy does not operate, however, in appointments to the circuit courts, whose jurisdictions span more than a single state, or to the Supreme Court, whose jurisdiction is the entire nation. There is also the *blue slip*, the informal Senate practice in which the Judiciary Committee solicits opinions on the nominee from the two senators from the state where the nominee resides. *Holds*—an informal practice in which a member of the majority party can inform the majority leader that he or she wishes to keep a judicial nomination from coming to the floor for a vote—are also widely used. So, presidents must be extremely mindful of the views of key senators, even those in the opposing party when the opposing party controls the Senate.

On occasion, despite presidential efforts to placate it, the Senate has refused to give its consent. Of the 143 nominees for the Supreme Court since the founding of the Republic, the Senate has refused to approve 28 of them, although only five of these

**BORK REJECTED**
The Democratic Senate's rejection in 1987 of conservative legal scholar Robert Bork, President Reagan's nominee for a vacant seat on the Supreme Court, helped trigger the long ideological and partisan battle over the composition of the Supreme Court that persists to the present day. Here Bork explains his judicial philosophy to members of the Senate Judiciary Committee.

refusals have occurred since 1900. Rejection of nominees has usually happened when the president was weak or when the other party was in control of the Senate. The defeat of Ronald Reagan's nominee, Robert Bork, was the product of deep ideological differences between a Republican president and a Democratic-controlled Senate. There have also been several near defeats. George H. W. Bush's nominee, Clarence Thomas, was confirmed by a margin of only four votes after questions were raised about his legal qualifications and about sexual harassment charges brought by law professor Anita Hill.

As the chapter-opening story shows, Senate confirmations of judicial nominees, especially for the federal circuit court and the Supreme Court, have become very contentious. Battles over presidential judicial nominees raged during the Clinton presidency and during the Bush presidency, culminating in the Democrats' use of the filibuster on several judicial nominations, and Republican threats to use the nuclear option to end judicial filibusters. In 2013, frustrated by the record low rate of confirmation of President Obama's judicial (and executive branch) nominees despite a Democratic majority in the Senate, Democrats finally exercised the nuclear option by outlawing the use of the filibuster on nominations for federal district and circuit court judgeships (the filibuster can still be used for Supreme Court nominations).

Although presidents must be concerned about the merit of their candidates and their acceptability to the Senate, they also try by their appointments to make their mark on the future. Presidents go about this in different ways.

For the most part, presidents are interested in nominating judges who share their ideological and program commitments.[29] John Adams nominated John Marshall and a number of other judges to protect Federalist principles during the ascendancy of the Jeffersonians. Franklin Roosevelt tried to fill the courts with judges who favored the New Deal. Ronald Reagan favored conservatives who were committed to rolling back affirmative action and other civil rights claims, abortion rights, protections for criminal defendants, and broad claims of **standing** in environmental cases. Both Bushes carried on the Reagan tradition of nominating conservative judges to the federal courts.

Bill Clinton, eager to avoid a bitter ideological fight in the Senate, where he was trying to forge a bipartisan coalition to support the North American Free Trade Agreement and a national crime bill, nominated two judges with reputations as moderates for the high court—Ruth Bader Ginsburg and Stephen Breyer—in the first years of his administration. The Ginsburg nomination was also indicative of Clinton's apparent commitment to diversifying the federal court system. (More than one-half of federal court nominees during his presidency were women and minorities.)

Diversity was also important to President Barack Obama. During his first year in office, he nominated 12 people for federal circuit court positions. Of these 12, nine were women and/or minorities. He also was anxious to appoint the first Hispanic to the Supreme Court, and did so in 2009, choosing Sonia Sotomayor.[30] He added another woman to the Court when he nominated Elena Kagan in 2010.

Presidents are often disappointed in how their nominees behave once they reach the Court. Dwight Eisenhower was dumbfounded when his friend and nominee, Earl Warren, led the Court in a liberal direction by transforming constitutional law regarding civil rights and criminal procedure. Richard Nixon was stunned when Chief Justice Warren Burger voted with a unanimous Court to override the president's claim of **executive privilege** and forced him to give up the documents that would seal his fate in the Watergate affair. He and other Court observers were also surprised by the odyssey of his nominee Harry Blackmun, who, despite a conservative judicial record before joining the Court, had become one of its most liberal justices by the time of his retirement in 1994 (he wrote the majority opinion in *Roe v. Wade* [1973]). The elder George Bush no doubt was surprised when his nominee, David Souter, refused to vote for the overturn of *Roe* in *Planned Parenthood v. Casey* (1992). Despite these dramatic examples, the past political and ideological positions of federal court nominees are a fairly reliable guide to their later behavior on the bench.[31] No one was surprised that the Court moved in a very conservative direction after Bush nominees Roberts and Alito joined the Court, given the record of their past political activities and judicial opinions.

14.1

14.2

14.3

14.4

14.5

14.6

**standing**
Authority to bring legal action because one is directly affected by the issues at hand.

**executive privilege**
A presidential claim that certain communications with subordinates may be withheld from Congress and the courts.

14.1

14.2

14.3

14.4

14.5

14.6

**separate but equal doctrine**
The principle articulated in *Plessy v. Ferguson* (1896) that laws prescribing separate public facilities and services for nonwhite Americans are permissible if the facilities and services are equal to those provided for whites.

**superprecedents**
Landmark rulings that have been reaffirmed by the Court over the course of many years and whose reasoning has become part of the fabric of American law.

# The Supreme Court in Action

**14.4**   Outline how the Supreme Court decides cases

he Supreme Court meets from the first Monday in October until late June or early July, depending on the press of business. Let's see how it goes about accepting, processing, and deciding cases.[32]

## ☐ Norms of Operation

A set of unwritten but clearly understood rules of behavior—called *norms*—shapes how the Court does things. One norm is *secrecy,* which keeps the conflicts between justices out of the public eye and elevates the stature of the Court as an institution. Justices do not grant interviews very often, though several recently have authored books. Reporters are not allowed to stalk the corridors for a story. Law clerks are expected to keep all memos, draft opinions, and conversations with the justices they work for confidential. Justices are not commonly seen on the frantic Washington, D.C., cocktail party circuit. When meeting in conference to argue and decide cases, the justices meet alone, without secretaries or clerks. Breaches of secrecy have occurred only occasionally. As a result, we know less about the inner workings of the Court than about any other branch of government.

*Seniority* is another important norm. Seniority determines the assignment of office space, the seating arrangements in open court (the most junior are at the ends), and the order of speaking in conference (the chief justice, then the most senior, and so on down the line). Speaking first allows the senior members to set the tone for discussion.

Finally, the justices are expected to stick closely to *precedent* when they decide cases. When the Court departs from a precedent, it is essentially overruling its own past actions, in effect, exercising judicial review of itself. In most cases, departures from precedent come in only very small steps over many years. For example, several decisions chipped away at the **separate but equal doctrine** of *Plessy v. Ferguson* (1896) before it was decisively reversed in *Brown v. Board of Education of Topeka* (1954) to end state and local laws requiring racial segregation. Times may be changing, however, as the Court has become more sharply divided along ideological lines. When it came to its *Citizens United* ruling in 2010 allowing corporations to spend unlimited money in funding issue advertising during election campaigns, for example, the Roberts Court showed no inclination to move slowly; it simply over-ruled a series of its previous rulings, one being but three years old.

Some legal theorists, both conservative and liberal, have begun to talk of **superprecedents** or super–*stare decisis* landmark rulings, that have been reaffirmed by the Court over the course of many years and whose reasoning has become part of the fabric of American law, making them especially difficult to reverse. Senator Arlen Specter, chair of the Senate Judicial Committee at the time, asked Chief Justice nominee John Roberts during his confirmation hearings in 2005 where he stood on this issue. While Roberts agreed that such fundamental rulings exist, he was unwilling to say whether *Roe v. Wade* (1973) was one of them, leaving observers unsure how he would eventually stand on the abortion issue. Other legal thinkers and jurists, however, are not impressed with this idea of superprecedents; cases that are wrongly decided, they say, should not be protected against reversal, no matter how many times they have been affirmed in the past by the Court.[33]

## ☐ Controlling the Agenda

The Court has a number of screening mechanisms to control what cases it will hear so that it can focus on cases that involve important federal or constitutional questions.[34]

Several technical rules help keep the numbers down. Cases must be *real* and *adverse;* that is, they must involve a real dispute between two parties. The disputants in a case must have *standing;* that is, they must have a real and direct interest in the issues that are raised. The Court sometimes changes the definition of *standing* to make access for **plaintiffs** easier or more difficult. The Warren Court (1956–1969) favored an expansive definition; the Rehnquist Court (1986–2005), a restricted one. Cases must also be *ripe;* that is, all other avenues of appeal must have been exhausted, and the injury must already have taken place (the Court will not accept hypothetical cases). Appeals must also be filed within a specified time limit, the paperwork must be correct and complete, and a filing fee of $300 must be paid. The fee may be waived if a petitioner is poor and files an affidavit *in forma pauperis* ("in the manner of a pauper"). One of the most famous cases in American history, *Gideon v. Wainwright* (1963), which established the right of all defendants to have lawyers in criminal cases, was submitted *in forma pauperis* on a few pieces of lined paper by a Florida State Penitentiary inmate named Clarence Earl Gideon.

The most powerful tool that the Court has for controlling its own agenda is the power to grant or not to grant a **writ of certiorari**. A grant of "cert" is a decision of the Court that an appellate case raises an important federal or constitutional issue that it is prepared to consider.[35] Under the **rule of four**, petitions are granted cert if at least four justices vote in favor. There are several reasons a petition may not command four votes, even if the case involves important constitutional issues: it may involve a particularly controversial issue that the Court would like to avoid, or the Court may not yet have developed a solid majority and may wish to avoid a split decision. Few petitions survive all of these hurdles. Of the 10,000 or so cases that are filed in each session, the Court today grants cert for fewer than 80 (this number varies a bit year to year), down from the 150 that was typical in the 1970s and 1980s. In cases denied cert, the decision of the federal appeals court or the highest state court stands.

**plaintiff**
One who brings suit in a court.

*in forma pauperis*
Describing a process by which indigents may file a suit with the Supreme Court free of charge.

**writ of certiorari**
An announcement that the Supreme Court will hear a case on appeal from a lower court; its issuance requires the vote of four of the nine justices.

**rule of four**
An *unwritten* practice that requires at least four justices of the Supreme Court to agree that a case warrants review by the Court before it will hear the case.

14.1

14.2

14.3

14.4

14.5

14.6

**CLERKING FOR JUSTICE THOMAS**
Law clerks play an extremely important role at the Supreme Court, with each justice selecting his or her own from among graduates of the nation's leading law schools. Here, Justice Clarence Thomas relaxes with three of his clerks after a long day. What is the importance of clerks to the effectiveness of the justices?

14.1

14.2

14.3

14.4

14.5

14.6

*amicus curiae*
Latin for "a friend of the court"; describes a brief in which individuals not party to a suit may have their views heard.

Deciding how freely to grant cert is a tricky business for the Court. Granted too often, it threatens to inundate the Court with cases. Granted too sparingly, it leaves in place the decisions of 13 different federal appeals courts on substantial federal and constitutional questions, as well as the decisions of state supreme courts, which often leads to inconsistent constitutional interpretations across the country. Because the Court now takes so few cases, more influence than ever is being exercised by the 13 federal circuit courts. For many important cases, the federal circuit courts have become the judicial forum of last resort. When the Supreme Court wants to reach out and settle differences in decisions in lower federal courts or among the states, however, it is entirely free to do so; it controls its own agenda. In 2011, it granted cert to appeals involving several very controversial issues, including state laws trying to control illegal immigration.

## □ Deciding Cases

Almost all cases granted cert are scheduled for oral argument (about 10 to 15 are decided without oral argument, depending on the session). Lawyers on each side are alerted to the key issues that the justices wish to consider, and new briefs are invited. Briefs are also submitted on most important cases by other parties who may be interested in the disputes. These "friend of the court," or *amicus curiae*, briefs may be submitted by individuals, interest groups, or some agency of the federal government, including the Justice Department or even the president.

Each case is argued for one hour, with 30 minutes given to each side in the dispute. Oral argument is not so much a presentation of arguments, however, as it is a give-and-take between the lawyers and the justices and among the justices themselves. When the federal government is a party to the case, the solicitor general or one of his or her deputies presents the oral arguments. Some justices—Antonin Scalia and Chief Justice John Roberts, for example—are famous for their relentless grilling of lawyers. Ruth Bader Ginsburg often asks that lawyers skip abstract legal fine points and put the issues in terms of their effect on ordinary people.

After hearing oral arguments and reading the briefs in the case, the justices meet in conference to reach a preliminary decision. The custom is for each justice to state his or her position, starting with the chief justice and moving through the ranks in order of seniority. Chief justices of great stature and intellect, such as John Marshall and Charles Evans Hughes, used the opportunity to speak first as a way of structuring the case and of swaying votes. Those who did not command much respect from the other justices (e.g., Warren Burger) were less able to shape the decision process.[36]

Political scientists have tried to determine what factors are most important in predicting how the justices will vote.[37] One approach looks at the ideological predilections of the justices and manages to explain a great deal about their voting behavior that way.[38] Another approach looks at the strategic behavior of judges, using the diaries and personal papers of retired justices to show that a great deal of negotiating and "horse trading" goes on, with justices trading votes on different cases and joining opinions they do not like so that they can have a hand in modifying them.[39] Another approach tries to link voting behavior to social background, types of previous judicial experience, and the political environment of family upbringing.[40] Still another believes that justices often vote to maintain the influence and standing of the Court in American society even if it means departing from their own ideological preferences.[41] None of these approaches has been totally successful in explaining decision making by justices, though the ideological model seems to do the best job in explaining judicial behavior over the long term.[42]

About all one can say is that the justices tend to form relatively stable voting blocs over time, with ideology increasingly the most important factor.[43] For example, during the 1990s and early 2000s, the Rehnquist Court, on many cases involving federalism and the rights of criminal defendants, divided into two blocs, a five-member conservative one (Justices Scalia, Thomas, Rehnquist, Kennedy, and O'Connor) and a four-member liberal one (Justices Stevens, Breyer, Ginsburg, and Souter). The Roberts

Court is dominated by a solid conservative majority, as has been shown, even though the Chief Justice surprisingly sided with his liberal colleagues in upholding the Affordable Care Act in 2012.

The vote in conference is not final, however. As Justice John Harlan once explained, "The books on voting are never closed until the decision finally comes down."[44] The justices have an opportunity to change their votes in response to the opinion supporting the majority decision. Some conservative commentators have reported that Chief Justice Roberts initially voted in favor of declaring the Affordable Care Act unconstitutional in 2012 before switching sides.[45] He then wrote the ruling opinion in the case that upheld Obamacare.

An opinion is a statement of the legal reasoning that supports the decision of the Court. There are three kinds of opinions. The **opinion of the Court** is the written opinion of the majority. A **concurring opinion** is the opinion of a justice who supports the majority decision but has different legal reasons for doing so. A **dissenting opinion** presents the reasoning of the minority. Dissenting opinions sometimes become the basis for future Court majorities.

If he votes with the majority in conference, the chief justice assigns the writing of the opinion. He can assign it to any justice in the majority; chief justices often write majority opinions themselves. Some jurists and scholars believe that this power to assign is the most important role of the chief justice, and it is guarded jealously. Warren Burger was so eager to play a role in opinion assignments that, much to the distress of his colleagues, he would often delay announcing his vote so that he could place himself with the majority. Justice William Douglas angrily charged that Burger voted with the majority in *Roe* only so that he could assign the case to a justice who was closer to the minority view.[46] If the chief justice's opinion is with the minority, the opinion is assigned by the most senior member of the majority.

The justice assigned to write the opinion does not work in isolation. He or she is assisted by law clerks and other justices, who helpfully provide memoranda suggesting wording and reasoning. Justices also consider the legal reasoning presented to the Court in *amicus curiae* briefs.[47] Most opinions go through numerous revisions and are subject to a considerable amount of bargaining among the justices.

Only when an opinion is completed is a final vote taken in conference. The justices are free to change their earlier votes: they may join the majority if they are now persuaded by its reasoning, or a concurring opinion may be so compelling that the majority may decide to replace the original majority opinion with it.

# The Supreme Court as a National Policymaker

**14.5** Evaluate the Supreme Court as a national policymaker

People often say that the Court should settle disputes and not make policy. But because the disputes it settles involve contentious public issues (such as abortion rights and affirmative action) and fundamental questions about the meaning of our constitutional rules (such as the extent of presidential powers in wartime), the Court cannot help but make public policy.

It seems likely that the Court recognizes and cultivates its policymaking role. In the main, the Court does not see itself as a court of last resort, simply righting routine errors in the lower courts or settling minor private disputes. It sees itself, instead, as the "highest judicial tribunal for settling policy conflicts" and constitutional issues and chooses its cases accordingly.[48] The fact that decisions are not simply handed down but come with an opinion attached for the purpose of guiding the actions of other courts, litigants, and public officials is another demonstration that the Court recognizes its policymaking role. Let's look at judicial policymaking—which takes the form of the

**opinion of the Court**
The majority opinion that accompanies a Supreme Court decision.

14.1

**concurring opinion**
The opinion of one or more judges who vote with the majority on a case but wish to set out different reasons for their decision.

14.2

14.3

**dissenting opinion**
The opinion of the judge or judges who are in the minority on a particular case before the Supreme Court.

14.4

14.5

14.6

14.1

14.2

14.3

14.4

14.5

14.6

**laissez-faire**
The political-economic doctrine that holds that government ought not interfere with the operations of the free market.

Court's constitutional interpretations as revealed in its decisions—and see how it has evolved over time.

## ☐ Structural Change and Constitutional Interpretation

Scholars generally identify three periods in the history of constitutional interpretation by the Supreme Court in the United States, one stretching from the early 1800s to the Civil War, the next from the end of the Civil War to the Great Depression, and the last from World War II to the mid-1980s.[49] We would add a fourth, covering the years from 1991 to the present (see Figure 14.4). We will see how changes in constitutional law have been influenced by structural factors, particularly economic change.

**PERIOD 1: NATIONAL POWER AND PROPERTY RIGHTS** The United States experienced significant growth and change during the first 75 years of its existence. This growth was accompanied by changes in constitutional law. Chief Justice John Marshall, who presided over the Supreme Court from 1801 to 1835, was the key judicial figure during this important period in our history.[50] Marshall was a follower of the doctrines of Alexander Hamilton, who believed that American greatness depended on a strong national government, a partnership between government and business in which industry and commerce were encouraged, and a national market economy free of the regulatory restraints of state and local governments. In a string of opinions that have shaped the fundamentals of American constitutional law—especially important are *Fletcher v. Peck* (1810), *Dartmouth College v. Woodward* (1819), *McCulloch v. Maryland* (1819), and *Gibbons v. Ogden* (1824), discussed elsewhere in this text— Marshall interpreted the Constitution to mean "maximum protection to property rights and maximum support for the idea of nationalism over states' rights."[51]

**PERIOD 2: GOVERNMENT AND THE ECONOMY** The Industrial Revolution and the Civil War triggered the development of a mass-production industrial economy dominated by the business corporation. Determining the role to be played by government in such an economy was a central theme of American political life in the late nineteenth and early twentieth centuries. The courts were involved deeply in this rethinking. At the beginning of this period, the Supreme Court took the position that the corporation was to be protected against regulation by both the state and federal governments; by the end, it was more sympathetic to the desire of the people and the political branches for the expansion of government regulation and management of the economy during the crisis of the Great Depression.

The main protection for the corporation against regulation came from the Fourteenth Amendment. This amendment was passed in the wake of the Civil War to guarantee the citizenship rights of freed slaves. The operative phrase was from Section 1: "Nor shall any state deprive any person of life, liberty, or property without due process of law"—on its face, hardly relevant to the world of the corporation. But in one of the great ironies of American history, the Court took up this expanded federal power over the states to protect rights and translated it to mean that corporations (considered "persons" under the law) and other forms of business should have increased protection from state regulation.

This reading of **laissez-faire** economic theory into constitutional law made the Supreme Court the principal ally of business in the late nineteenth and early twentieth centuries.[52] Keeping the government out of the economy in general, the Court overturned efforts by both the state and federal governments to provide welfare for the poor; to regulate manufacturing monopolies; to initiate an income tax; to regulate interstate railroad rates; to provide scholarships to students; to regulate wages, hours, and working conditions; and to protect consumers against unsafe or unhealthy products. The Court also supported the use of judicial injunctions to halt strikes by labor unions.

The business–Supreme Court alliance lasted until the Great Depression. Roosevelt's New Deal reflected a new national consensus on the need for a greatly expanded federal government with a new set of responsibilities: to manage the economy;

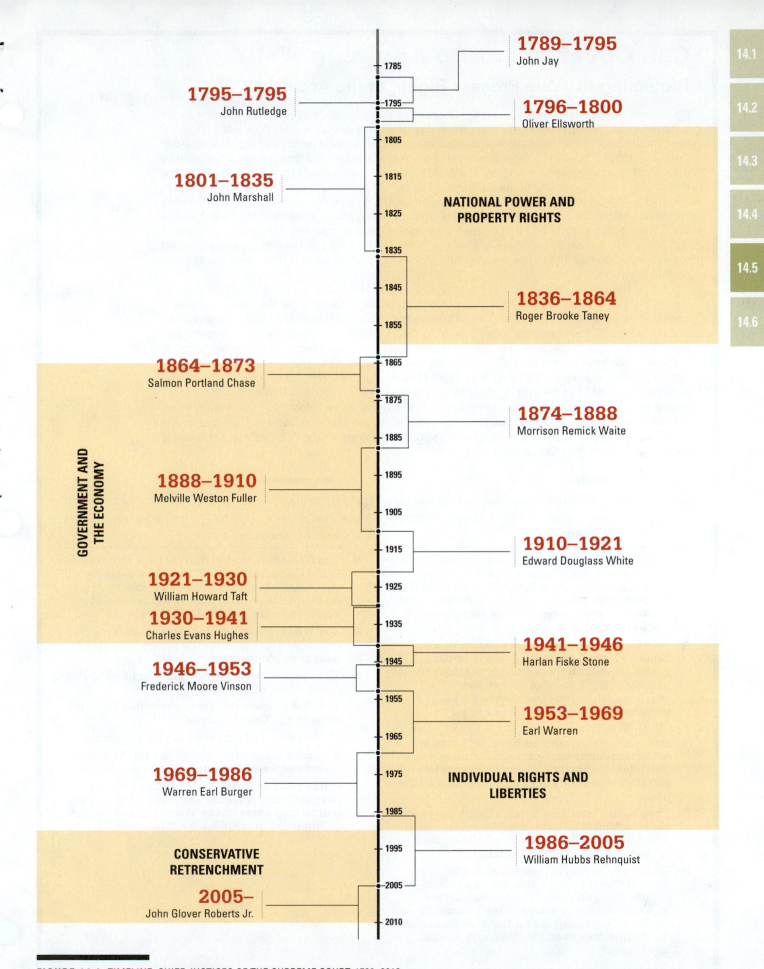

14.1

14.2

14.3

14.4

14.5

14.6

**1789–1795**
John Jay

**1795–1795**
John Rutledge

**1796–1800**
Oliver Ellsworth

**1801–1835**
John Marshall

**NATIONAL POWER AND PROPERTY RIGHTS**

**1836–1864**
Roger Brooke Taney

**1864–1873**
Salmon Portland Chase

**GOVERNMENT AND THE ECONOMY**

**1874–1888**
Morrison Remick Waite

**1888–1910**
Melville Weston Fuller

**1910–1921**
Edward Douglass White

**1921–1930**
William Howard Taft

**1930–1941**
Charles Evans Hughes

**1941–1946**
Harlan Fiske Stone

**1946–1953**
Frederick Moore Vinson

**1953–1969**
Earl Warren

**1969–1986**
Warren Earl Burger

**INDIVIDUAL RIGHTS AND LIBERTIES**

**CONSERVATIVE RETRENCHMENT**

**1986–2005**
William Hubbs Rehnquist

**2005–**
John Glover Roberts Jr.

**FIGURE 14.4** TIMELINE: CHIEF JUSTICES OF THE SUPREME COURT, 1789–2013

*Source:* United States Supreme Court.

14.1
14.2
14.3
14.4
14.5
14.6

# Can Government Do Anything Well?

## Protecting the Due Process Rights of the Accused

By the mid-1960s, billboards screaming "Impeach Earl Warren" dotted the highways of the American South. Though most of the anger there was generated by Warren Court decisions declaring much of the South's elaborate system of segregation unconstitutional (especially *Brown v. Board of Education* [1954]), additional anger there and in much of the rest of the country was generated by a series of Court decisions broadening the protections for those suspected or accused of a felony crime. The Court, for example, ruled that police could not coerce confessions from the accused and that evidence gathered by illegal searches and seizures was not admissible in court. Police would henceforth be bound by the requirement of obtaining a search warrant from a judge. The Court ruled that the accused must be read their rights upon being taken into custody—the list of rights is widely known as the Miranda warnings—including the right to remain silent and the right to have legal counsel. The indigent were to be provided with an attorney if they could not hire one on their own.

"Law and order" advocates sharply criticized the Warren Court, saying that rulings expanding the rights of those suspected or accused of a crime were handcuffing the police and would undermine civic order. Police echoed these complaints, though they complied with the new order in most cases. Even dissenting members of the Court on the *Miranda* decision were outraged; Byron White wrote in his dissenting opinion that "the decision would return a killer, rapist, or other criminal to the streets to repeat his crime whenever it pleases him." The novelist Truman Capote (*In Cold Blood*) wondered, "Why do they seem to totally ignore the rights of the victims and the potential victims?" For his part, Richard Nixon made the decline of "law and order" the central theme of his winning presidential campaign in 1968, drawing away from the Democrats many working-class whites upset by urban riots and escalating violent crime rates in their cities. This drift of non–college-educated whites, as well as southern whites, to the Republican column would eventually reshape American politics.

*Support for the claim that government has protected the due process rights of the accused without endangering the rights of others:*

- The framers believed that due process rights were among the most important liberties they aimed to protect in the Constitution; due process protections are found in Article I and in five of the ten amendments that comprise the Bill of Rights.
- Police departments in every region of the United States had been regularly forcing confessions from the accused, violating the privacy of the homes of people suspected of crimes, and detaining people for long periods of time without access to an attorney.
- Police are not hampered by adhering to a set of standards that protect all persons suspected or accused of a felony crime; these standards protect the innocent as well as the guilty.
- Even in the rare case when a guilty party is set free, this is a better outcome than one in which an innocent is falsely punished for a crime he or she did not commit.
- While crime rates increased after the Warren Court rulings, this was a product of crowded and poverty-stricken ghettos in American cities. Crime rates eventually declined beginning in the 1990s as economic conditions improved for racial and ethnic minorities.

*Rejection of the claim that government has protected the due process rights of the accused without endangering the rights of others:*

- The framers intended due process protections in the Constitution to be confined to those suspected of and accused of a crime by federal authorities; the framers did not bind the states to these specific standards.
- The Warren Court wrongly used the 14th Amendment to restrict the states (and localities) in fighting crime.
- The Warren Court rulings paid no heed to the rights of victims of crimes.
- The due process rulings undermined law and order in the United States.
  - Police were hampered in crime-fighting.
  - Crime rates soared after the rights of the accused were expanded.
- Crime rates only declined later as first the Burger Court, then the Rehnquist Court, began to chip away at the Warren Court rulings, giving some powers back to the police.

14.1

14.2

14.3

14.4

14.5

14.6

*(Continued)*

## WHAT DO YOU THINK?

What do you think about the past, present, and future role of the government in protecting the due process rights of those suspected or accused of a crime?

- Government should protect the due process rights of those suspected or accused of a crime as one of its top priorities.
- Government should protect the due process rights of those suspected or accused of a crime, though this should be balanced against other priorities like maintaining law and order.
- Government has gone much too far in protecting the due process rights of those suspected or accused of a crime, which has made the United States a much less safe society. Many of these rights are due to judicial over-interpretation and should be rolled back.

How would you defend your position to a fellow student? What would be your main line of argument? What evidence do you believe best supports your position? For help in developing your argument, please refer to the sources listed in the "Can Government Do Anything Well?" feature in Chapter 2 on p. 45.

Additional sources for this feature: Rick Perlstein, *Nixonland: The Rise of a President and the Fracturing of America* (New York: Scribner, 2008).

to provide a safety net for the poor, the unemployed, and the elderly; to protect workers' rights to form labor unions; and to regulate business in the public interest. The Supreme Court, however, filled with justices born in the nineteenth century and committed to the unshakable link between the Constitution and laissez-faire economic doctrine, was opposed to the national consensus and in 1935 and 1936 declared unconstitutional several laws that were part of the foundation of the New Deal. In an extraordinary turn of events, however, the Supreme Court reversed itself in 1937, finding the Social Security Act, the Labor Relations Act, and state minimum wage laws acceptable. It is not entirely clear why the so-called switch-in-time-that-saved-nine occurred, but surely Roosevelt's landslide reelection in 1936, the heightening of public hostility toward the Court, and Roosevelt's threat to expand and "pack the Court" all played a role. Whatever the reason, the Court abandoned its effort to prevent the government from playing a central role in the management of the economy and the regulation of business, and it came to defer to the political linkage branches of government on such issues by the end of the 1930s. In doing so, it brought another constitutional era to a close.

**PERIOD 3: INDIVIDUAL RIGHTS AND LIBERTIES**  Three fundamental issues of American constitutional law—the relationship of the states to the nation, the nature and extent of private property rights, and the role of government in the management of the economy—were essentially settled by the time World War II broke out. From then until the mid- to late 1980s, the Court turned its main attention to the relationship between the individual and government.[53]

Later chapters tell the story on civil liberties and civil rights. For now, it is sufficient to point out that the Court, especially during the tenure of Chief Justice Earl Warren, decided cases that expanded protections for free expression and association, religious expression, fair trials, and civil rights for minorities. (For more about the role of the Supreme Court in protecting the due process rights of those accused of a crime, see the "Can Government Do Anything Well?" feature). In another series of cases dealing with the apportionment of electoral districts, the Court declared for political equality, based on the principle of "one person, one vote." In many of its landmark decisions, the Court applied the Bill of Rights to the states. Although the Court's record was not without blemishes during and after World War II—see the "Using the Framework" feature on *Korematsu v. United States* (1944)—it made significant strides in expanding the realm of individual freedom.

**PERIOD 4: CONSERVATIVE RETRENCHMENT**  A new conservative majority emerged on the Supreme Court in the early 1990s, fashioned by the judicial nominations of Presidents Ronald Reagan and George H. W. Bush, and the patient efforts of

14.1
14.2
14.3
14.4
14.5
14.6

# Using the FRAMEWORK

## If the Supreme Court exists to protect individual rights, why did it allow the military to keep Japanese Americans in internment camps during World War II?

**Background:** On the advice of the U.S. military, President Franklin Roosevelt signed a series of executive orders in early 1942 authorizing the relocation of 112,000 Japanese Americans living on the West Coast, 70,000 of whom were citizens, into internment camps. In 1944, the Supreme Court in *Korematsu v. United States* upheld the legality of the exclusion and confinement orders. In *Total War and the Constitution* (Alfred A. Knopf, 1947), constitutional scholar Edward Corwin described the internment and the Court's action as "the most drastic invasion of the rights of citizens of the United States by their own government" in modern American history. Taking a broad overview of structural, political linkage, and governmental factors that influenced the Supreme Court's decision will help explain this situation.

### Government Action

The Supreme Court, in *Korematsu* v. *United States* (1944), upholds the legality of internment.

### Government

President Franklin Roosevelt, troubled by the action, but fully aware of the feelings of the public and the wishes of military leaders in wartime, signed the necessary executive orders.

→ The Supreme Court, unwilling to act against opinion of military leaders that Japanese Americans living on the West Coast posed a national security threat, supported the exclusion order in a case brought by Fred Korematsu.

Military authorities believed that Japanese Americans living on the West Coast posed a national security threat to the United States; asked the president to authorize curfews, relocation, and confinement.

→ Congress passed supporting legislation making relocation and internment possible.

### Political Linkage

Anti-Japanese attitudes were widespread among the public, particularly in the West Coast states, whose populations feared a Japanese invasion.

→ Public opinion strongly supported the war against Japan and whatever military policies were necessary to win it.

→ The media whipped up hysteria about a possible Japanese invasion.

### Structure

Japanese immigrants to the United States in the late nineteenth and early twentieth centuries settled mainly in the West Coast states.

→ The Japanese attack on Pearl Harbor on December 7, 1941, plunged the United States into World War II.

→ The Constitution vests enormous powers in the president as commander-in-chief during wartime.

conservative Chief Justice William Rehnquist. This new majority—with O'Connor and Kennedy usually, but not always, joining the three most consistently conservative justices, Scalia, Thomas, and Rehnquist—moved the Court to reconsider many of its long-established doctrines in the areas of rights and liberties and the relationship between the national and state governments. Its reconsideration of federalism in favor of "states' rights" was particularly noteworthy.

In a string of landmark cases, the Court curtailed national authority in favor of the states, overturning several federal statutes that were based, in its view, on an overly expansive reading by Congress of its powers under the interstate commerce clause. In 1995, for example, the Court overturned a federal statute that banned guns from the area immediately around public schools, saying that the statute was unrelated to interstate commerce. Using the same reasoning, it overturned legislation requiring background checks for gun buyers. In 2000, the Court used such reasoning to strike down parts of the Violence Against Women Act and the federal law barring age discrimination in employment.

However, for a brief time spanning the years 2002 through 2005, the Supreme Court became more moderate in a significant number of areas—especially on affirmative action, gay rights, the right of individuals to sue states for violations of federal civil rights laws, and the rights of terrorism detainees—with the now-retired Sandra Day O'Connor casting the decisive swing vote in most of the notable cases. Although O'Connor usually voted with the conservatives during her years on the Court—note especially her vote with the majority in 2000 in *Bush v. Gore* that settled the disputed vote in Florida in favor of Bush and determined the outcome of the presidential election—she surprised many people in 2003 when she joined the majority in the Michigan Law School case that upheld the use of race in law school admissions, and the Texas case that banned states from forbidding private gay sexual behavior. In 2004 she wrote the majority opinion in the decision on the rights of citizens held as enemy combatants, pointing out that "a state of war is not a blank check for the president when it comes to the rights of the nation's citizens."[54]

After O'Connor retired and Alito joined the Court, and with the strong leadership of Chief Justice Roberts, an even more consistently conservative majority emerged.[55] In 2006, for example, the Court approved state measures giving police greater power to execute a search warrant without "knocking and announcing." In 2007, the Court ruled that school districts could not use racial criteria to promote school integration. It also upheld federal restrictions on late-term abortions (called "partial birth abortions" by abortion opponents). In 2008, the Court for the first time ruled that Americans have a constitutional right to own guns for their personal use; the Court later ruled in 2010 that state and local regulations that effectively banned guns were unconstitutional. In 2009, it ruled in favor of a group of New Haven firefighters in a reverse discrimination case that bodes ill for the constitutional acceptability of state and local affirmative action programs. In 2013, in a case involving the University of Texas, it made the standard for using race in college admissions so stringent that few college affirmative action programs are likely to survive. That same year, the Court's conservative majority struck down a key provision of the 1965 Voting Rights Act, which has been instrumental in protecting the equal citizenship of African Americans. In 2014, the same 5-4 majority ruled that privately held companies whose owners object on religious grounds to health insurance coverage for contraceptives for their employees, as required by the Affordable Care Act, need not comply.

The Roberts Court has been especially friendly to business interests and large corporations. In a stunningly broad ruling in 2010, the Court said that Congress could not restrict the campaign activities of corporations as specified by the McCain–Feingold reforms of 2002—*Citizens United v. FEC*—in the process overturning three of its own past rulings (precedents) on the same issue in which it had upheld restrictions on corporation campaign activity in the statutes of 21 states. It ruled in another case that Exxon was not fully financially liable to communities damaged by the *Exxon Valdez* oil spill. In another case it said a woman paid less than her male colleagues for many years

14.1

14.2

14.3

14.4

14.5

14.6

14.1

14.2

14.3

14.4

14.5

14.6

**REDUCED DAMAGES**
The Exxon Valdez oil spill in Prince William Sound in Alaska caused substantial environmental damage and hurt the area's fishing- and tourist-based economy. After a long legal battle, the Roberts Court in 2008 dramatically reduced the money Exxon owed in punitive damages for negligence, overturning the actions of lower federal courts.

**judicial activism**
Actions by the courts that purportedly go beyond the role of the judiciary as interpreter of the law and adjudicator of disputes.

could not sue because she had failed to file a suit within 180 days of the first violation, though she didn't learn about it for years. In a 2011 case involving Walmart, the Court issued a ruling making it more difficult for consumers and employees to bring class action lawsuits against businesses. In 2012, it made a ruling making it more difficult for public sector unions to raise money to use in political campaigns. In a series of cases in 2013, the Court made it more difficult to bring class action suits against large corporations. Perhaps the best indicator of the ideological leaning of the Roberts Court is the following: of the many cases supported by the U.S. Chamber of Commerce, the Court came down on the Chamber's side 68 percent of the time in the 2006–2010 time period, up from 56 percent in the 1994–2005 span.[56] The trend has continued; two leading researchers on the Supreme Court show that the tilt toward business has grown even more pronounced since 2010.[57]

## ☐ The Debate over Judicial Activism

Has the Court become too involved in national policymaking? Many people think so; others think not. Let us examine several of the ways in which what is called **judicial activism** is expressed.[58]

**JUDICIAL REVIEW** We have already seen how the Court under John Marshall's leadership claimed the right of judicial review in the case of *Marbury v. Madison* (1803). Still, the power was not exercised by the Court to any great extent until the late nineteenth century. The use of judicial review increased during the twentieth century, however, with most of the Court's adverse attention being paid to the states. As described earlier, however, the Rehnquist Court was fairly aggressive in overturning federal statutes, averaging almost six per term in the years from 1994 to 2005, compared with one every two years from the end of the Civil War to the early 1990s.[59] Oddly, given the tendency of conservative activists and organizations to be the most vociferously concerned about an overly activist judiciary, it was the most conservative members of the Court who most frequently voted to overturn congressional statutes during these years.[60] The Roberts Court seems to be even more aggressively moving in this direction with the conservative majority most often ruling against the actions of the political bodies, Congress and the president.[61] These trends in the use of judicial review suggest that the Court over time has become more willing to monitor the activities of other governmental entities.

The aggressive use of judicial review in recent years, as well as the fairly broad claims in several of its opinions that it and it alone has the final say on the meaning of the Constitution, has prompted talk among many legal scholars about "judicial imperialism" and "judicial supremacy."[62] Ironically, perhaps, it is now mainly liberal scholars who worry that the Court, dominated by a solid conservative majority, is too frequently reversing the actions of popularly elected bodies—Congress and state legislatures—a position once held mostly by conservatives.[63] Liberals worry that the Court will exercise judicial review on matters such as federal, state, and local governments' affirmative action programs as a violation of the "equal protection" clause of the Fourteenth Amendment.

**REVERSING THE DECISIONS OF PAST SUPREME COURTS** Despite the norm of precedent (*stare decisis*) that guides judicial decision making, the Warren, Burger, Rehnquist, and Roberts Courts overturned all previous Court decisions. The most dramatic instance was the reversal by the Warren Court of *Plessy v. Ferguson* (1896), which had endorsed legal segregation in the South, by *Brown v. Board of Education* (1954), which removed segregation's legal underpinnings. The Rehnquist Court overturned a number of previous Court decisions that had expanded the rights of criminal defendants and that had supported the extension of federal government power, reviewed earlier. When the Roberts Court upheld the federal Partial-Birth Abortion Ban Act, it reversed its own position on an identical Nebraska law it had declared unconstitutional in 2000. In *Citizens United v. Federal Election Commission* (2010), the Court overturned three of its own precedents, including cases from 1990, 2003, and 2007. In his dissent in this case, read from the bench as a sign of his deep displeasure with the majority, Justice John Paul Stevens lamented what he took to be the overly broad and ambitious reach of the majority, saying "essentially, five justices were unhappy with the limited nature of the case before us, so they changed the case to give themselves an opportunity to change the law."

**DECIDING "POLITICAL" ISSUES** Critics claim that the Court is taking on too many matters that are best left to the elected branches of government. An oft-cited example is the Court's willingness to become increasingly involved in the process of drawing congressional electoral district boundaries in the states. Defenders of the Court argue that when such basic constitutional rights as equality of citizenship are at peril, the Court is obligated to protect these rights, no matter what other government bodies may choose to do. The Court's intervention in the 2000 presidential election generated widespread criticism for its meddling in politics, although its many defenders insist that the Court's decision in *Bush v. Gore* saved the nation from a constitutional crisis.

**REMEDIES** The most criticized aspect of judicial activism is the tendency for federal judges to impose broad remedies on states and localities. A **remedy** is what a court determines must be done to rectify a wrong. Since the 1960s, the Court has been more willing than in the past to impose remedies that require other governmental bodies to take action. Some of the most controversial of these remedies include court orders requiring states to build more prison space and mandating that school districts bus students to achieve racial balance. Such remedies often require that governments spend public funds for things they do not necessarily want to do. Critics claim that the federal judiciary's legitimate role is to prevent government actions that threaten rights and liberties, not to compel government to take action to meet some policy goal.

**ORIGINAL INTENT** Much of the debate about the role of the Court centers on the issue of the original intent of the framers.[64] Advocates of **original intent** believe that the Court must be guided by the original intent of the framers and the exact words

**remedy**
An action that a court determines must be taken to rectify a wrong done by government.

**original intent**
The doctrine that the courts must interpret the Constitution in ways consistent with the intentions of the framers rather than in light of contemporary conditions and needs.

14.1

14.2

14.3

14.4

14.5

14.6

**449**

14.1
14.2
14.3
14.4
14.5
14.6

**strict construction**
The doctrine that the provisions of the Constitution have a clear meaning and that judges must stick closely to this meaning when rendering decisions.

**DECIDING THE 2000 PRESIDENTIAL ELECTION**
The outcome of the closely fought 2000 presidential election was not finally decided until the Supreme Court stopped the recount in Florida, giving the state's electoral votes to George W. Bush. Here, passionate supporters of Bush and Al Gore demonstrate in front of the Supreme Court building while awaiting its decision. Do you think the Court's intervention was in the nation's best interests?

found in the Constitution, using **strict construction** as a way to stay close to its true meaning. Originalists believe that the expansion of rights that has occurred since the mid-1960s—such as the new right to privacy that formed the basis of the *Roe v. Wade* decision and rights for criminal defendants—is illegitimate, having no foundation in the framers' intentions or the text of the Constitution. Justices Antonin Scalia and Clarence Thomas are the strongest originalists on today's Court.

Critics of original intent and strict construction believe that the intentions of the framers are not only impossible to determine but also unduly constricting. As to the first assertion,[65] critics point out that original intent cannot be known, mostly because the only record of the debates at the constitutional convention are Madison's notes, which incorporated only about 10 percent of what was said, according to scholars. Moreover, it is not entirely clear how to define the framers. Is it all who attended the convention? All who signed the document? And what about the ratification conventions in the states? Do we include them among what we might call the Founders, knowing that there were several states that voted against the Constitution and many who dissented from the majority in those state conventions which voted to ratify? As to the second, critics suggest that sticking to a very narrow understanding of what the framers and Founders intended is unduly constricting in light of the great transformations that have occurred in American society in the years since ratification. What seems more reasonable, in this view, is to have jurists try to reconcile the fundamental principles of the Constitution with changing conditions in the United States and the democratic aspirations of the American people.[66]

Clearly, the modern Supreme Court is more activist than it was in the past; most justices today hold a more expansive view of the role of the Court in forging national policy than did their predecessors. And because the Court is likely to remain activist under Chief Justice John Roberts, the debate about judicial activism is likely to remain important in American politics.

# Outside Influences on the Court

14.1

14.2

14.3

14.4

14.5

14.6

**14.6** Assess the factors and players that influence Supreme Court decisions

T he Supreme Court makes public policy when it issues its rulings and will continue to do so, but it does not do so in splendid isolation; many other governmental and political linkage actors and institutions influence what it does. Indeed, many scholars suggest that what the Supreme Court does reflects the prevailing politics and opinion of the day. Justices, after all, are nominated by presidents and confirmed by senators whose views are known to the public and who are elected by them. As new coalitions come to power in American politics, they make appointments to the federal courts in general and the Supreme Court in particular that are in tune with the electoral coalition supporting the president and a majority of the Senate. A highly politicized judiciary, whose decisions become entangled in and engaged with the prevailing issues of the day and whose decisions reflect the views of the winners, in this view, is not to be lamented but celebrated as a reflection of democratic politics. Aggressive use of judicial review by the Supreme Court, in the view of several leading scholars, is simply a way for the new majority in the country to clear the way for its own policies.[67] Critics of this view would point out, however, that the courts might be out of touch with the mood of the country for long periods of time because judges on federal district and circuit courts and justices on the Supreme Court serve life terms and are slow to be replaced (see Table 14.1).

Government and political influences on the Court come not only during times of partisan realignment and the appearance of new electoral coalitions but on an everyday basis. Here are important ways this happens.

## ☐ Governmental Influences

The Supreme Court must coexist with other governmental bodies that have their own powers, interests, constituencies, and visions of the public good.[68] Recognizing this, the Court usually tries to stay somewhere near the boundaries of what is acceptable to other political actors. Being without "purse or sword," as Hamilton put it in *The Federalist*, No. 78, the Court cannot force others to obey its decisions. It can only hope that respect for the law and the Court will cause government officials to do what it has mandated in a decision. If the Court fails to gain voluntary compliance, it risks a serious erosion of its influence, for it then appears weak and ineffectual.

**THE PRESIDENT** The president, as chief executive, is supposed to carry out the Court's decrees. However, presidents who have opposed particular decisions or been lukewarm to them have dragged their feet, as President Eisenhower did on school desegregation after the Court's *Brown* decision in 1954.

**TABLE 14.1** SUPREME COURT JUSTICES, 2012

| Justice | Born | Sworn In | Appointed By |
|---|---|---|---|
| Chief Justice John Roberts | 1955 | 2005 | George W. Bush |
| Antonin Scalia | 1936 | 1986 | Ronald Reagan |
| Anthony M. Kennedy | 1936 | 1988 | Ronald Reagan |
| Clarence Thomas | 1948 | 1991 | George H. W. Bush |
| Ruth Bader Ginsburg | 1933 | 1993 | Bill Clinton |
| Stephen G. Breyer | 1938 | 1994 | Bill Clinton |
| Samuel A. Alito Jr. | 1950 | 2006 | George W. Bush |
| Sonia Sotomayor | 1954 | 2009 | Barack Obama |
| Elena Kagan | 1960 | 2010 | Barack Obama |

14.1

14.2

14.3

14.4

14.5

14.6

**test case**
A case brought to force a ruling on the constitutionality of some law or executive action.

**class-action suit**
A suit brought on behalf of a group of people who are in a situation similar to that of the plaintiffs.

The president has constitutional powers that give him some degree of influence over the Court. In addition to the Court's dependence on the president to carry out its decisions (when the parties to a dispute do not do it voluntarily), for example, the president influences the direction of the Court by his power to nominate judges when there are vacancies. He can also file suits through the Justice Department, argue cases before the Court, or introduce legislation to alter the Court's organization or jurisdiction (as Franklin Roosevelt did with his Court-packing proposal).

**CONGRESS** Although Congress can alter the size, organization, and appellate jurisdiction of the federal courts, including the Supreme Court, it rarely does so.[69] The size of the Court, for example, has not changed since 1860. Nor, since that time, has Congress changed its jurisdiction as a reaction to its decisions, despite the introduction of many bills over the years to do so. In 2003, for example, a bill was introduced by Republicans in the House to take away the Court's jurisdiction to hear cases challenging the inclusion of the phrase "under God" in the Pledge of Allegiance. In 2004 a resolution was introduced in the House decrying the citation of the opinions of foreign and international courts and international law in U.S. judicial pronouncements—something Justice Kennedy had done in his majority opinion in a case overturning the state of Texas's antisodomy statute in *Lawrence v. Texas* (2003)—and threatening impeachment for any federal judge doing so. (Neither bill passed.) Congress is more likely to bring pressure to bear on the courts by being unsympathetic to pleas from the justices for pay increases or for a suitable budget for clerks or office space. The Senate also plays a role in the appointment process, as we have learned, and can convey its views to the Court during the course of confirmation hearings. Finally, Congress can change statutes or pass new laws that specifically challenge Supreme Court decisions, as it did when it legislated the Civil Rights Act of 1991 to make it easier for people to file employment discrimination suits.[70] All of this matters. There is evidence that throughout American history, the Supreme Court exercises a great deal of restraint in its judicial review of congressional actions when Congress is clearly hostile to the Court.[71]

## ☐ Political Linkage Influences

The Supreme Court is influenced not only by other government officials and institutions, but also by what we have termed political linkage factors.

**GROUPS AND MOVEMENTS** Interest groups, social movements, and the public not only influence the Court indirectly through the president and Congress but often do so directly. An important political tactic of interest groups and social movements is the **test case**. A test case is an action brought by a group that is designed to challenge the constitutionality of a law or an action by government. Groups wishing to force a court determination on an issue that is important to them will try to find a plaintiff on whose behalf they can bring a suit. When Thurgood Marshall was chief counsel for the NAACP in the 1950s, he spent a long time searching for the right plaintiff to bring a suit that would drive the last nail into the coffin of the *Plessy* separate-but-equal doctrine that was the legal basis for southern segregation. He settled on a fifth-grade girl named Linda Brown who was attending a segregated school in Topeka, Kansas. Several years later, he won the landmark case *Brown v. Board of Education of Topeka* (1954).

Many test cases take the form of **class-action suits**. These are suits brought by an individual on behalf of a class of people who are in a similar situation. A suit to prevent the dumping of toxic wastes in public waterways, for example, may be brought by an individual in the name of all the people living in the area who are adversely affected by the resulting pollution. Class-action suits were invited by the Warren Court's expansion of the definition of *standing* in the 1960s. The Rehnquist Court later narrowed the definition of *standing*, making it harder to bring class-action suits. As you learned above, the Roberts Court further limited the ability of similarly situated people to bring such suits.

Interest groups often get involved in suits brought by others by filing *amicus curiae* briefs.[72] Pro-abortion and anti-abortion groups submitted 78 such briefs in *Webster v. Reproductive Health Services* (1989), a decision that allowed states to regulate and limit abortion availability.[73] These briefs set out the group's position on the constitutional issues or talk about some of the most important consequences of deciding the case one way or the other. In a sense, this activity is a form of lobbying. Some scholars believe that the Court finds such briefs to be a way to keep track of public and group opinion on the issues before it, which is helpful to its work.[74]

Remember that business power in politics is substantial, ranging across a wide range of political activities, from campaign advertising to lobbying Congress and regulatory agencies in Washington. It is also large corporations within the business sector that have the means—money, subject matter specialists, outside lawyers, and in-house lawyers—to bring suits in state and federal courts against government attempts to regulate their activities. As we saw above, they have enjoyed considerable success before the Supreme Court.

**LEADERS** The Supreme Court does not usually stray very far from the opinions of public and private sector leaders when a consensus exists among them.[75] Social and economic leaders use their influence in a number of ways. As we learned in earlier chapters, their influence is substantial in the media, the interest group system, party politics, and elections at all levels. It follows, then, that elites play a substantial role in the thinking of presidents and the members of Congress as they, in turn, deal with the Court.

In addition to this powerful but indirect influence, the Court is also shaped by developments on issues and doctrine within the legal profession as these are expressed by bar associations, law journals, and law schools. To take but one example, Justice O'Connor, in her opinion in the 2004 Michigan Law School affirmative action case, justified her vote by pointing out that the use of race as one criterion among many in law school admission decisions was now widely accepted in the university and legal communities, as was the legitimacy of the goal of "diversity" in higher education.

**PUBLIC OPINION** We might think that the Supreme Court is immune from public opinion, because the justices are appointed for life and do not need to face the electorate. There is reason to believe, however, that what the Court does and what the public wants—at least as expressed in public opinion polls—are highly correlated; a substantial body of research shows that Court rulings and public opinion are consistent with one another about two-thirds of the time, about the same level of consistency with the public as the president and Congress.[76] There does not seem to be a yawning gap, then, between the public and the Supreme Court. We cannot say for sure, however, that public opinion causes the Court to act in particular ways when making decisions.[77] Indeed, it is just as likely that third factors—such as major events, political developments, and cultural changes conveyed in the media—shape the perceptions of judges and citizens alike. Nevertheless, the close association between Court decisions and public opinion is good news in a society that aspires to be democratic.

Having said that, it also is important to point out that there have been times during our history when the Court was so influenced by other political actors that it set aside, if only for a short while, its responsibility to protect the rights and liberties of all citizens. Although the Court has played an important role in advancing rights and liberties in the United States, it has not been entirely immune from pressure brought to bear by the public, other government officials, and private sector leaders to punish suspect groups. For example, the Court went along with local, state, and federal actions to punish dissident voices during the McCarthy era's anti-Communist hysteria of the 1950s. It also approved the forced relocation and internment of Japanese Americans during World War II, as discussed earlier in the "Using the Framework" feature.

**CIVIL RIGHTS CHAMPION**
Social movements often use test cases to challenge the constitutionality of laws and government actions. After a long search, NAACP attorney Thurgood Marshall—shown here in front of the Supreme Court, where he would later sit as a justice—selected Linda Brown, a fifth-grader from Topeka, Kansas, who was not permitted to attend the school closest to her house because it was reserved for whites, as the principal plaintiff in *Brown v. Board of Education of Topeka*, the historic case that successfully challenged school segregation. How else has the Court been a vehicle for social change?

14.1
14.2
14.3
14.4
14.5
14.6

## Using the DEMOCRACY STANDARD

14.1
14.2
14.3
14.4
14.5
14.6

### Does the Supreme Court enhance American democracy?

The framers designed the Supreme Court as an institution that would serve as a check on the other branches, most especially on Congress, the only semi-democratic institution of the lot in their original design. They also structured the Court to be the least democratic of the branches in the new federal government, with justices appointed rather than elected and serving for life rather than for a fixed term of office. The framers wanted the judiciary to function as a referee who stands above the fray, preserving the rules, overseeing the orderly changing of some rules when the situation demands it, protecting minorities against the potentially tyrannical behavior of the majority, and protecting individuals in the exercise of their constitutionally guaranteed rights. From the perspective of democratic theory, however, it is unacceptable that one of the three main branches of the federal government in the United States—with the power to override the decisions of presidents, Congress, and state legislatures and to make binding decisions for the nation as a whole—is staffed with members who never face the judgment of the voters.

Although designed as an antimajoritarian institution, the Supreme Court is much more responsive to majoritarian political actors and to the public than the framers ever imagined would be the case. For example, we have seen that the Supreme Court does not often stray very far from what is acceptable to the president and Congress or to private elites; we have seen, also, that the Court acts consistently with public opinion about as often as Congress and the president do. Moreover, the chapters on civil rights and civil liberties show that the Court plays an important and positive role in the protection of minority rights and liberties in the United States, although it has often been inconsistent and slow in doing so.

The overall view suggests that, whatever the intention of the framers, the Court has not acted consistently as an antimajoritarian institution, though it has sometimes done so. In fact, it has often protected popular democracy.

# Review the Chapter

## The Foundations of Judicial Power

**14.1** Trace the evolution of judicial power in the United States, p. 427

Despite the fact that Article III of the Constitution is quite vague about the powers and responsibilities of the U.S. Supreme Court, the Court has fashioned a powerful position for itself in American politics, coequal with the executive and legislative branches.

Under Justice John Marshall in the early nineteenth century, the Court first claimed its right to rule on the constitutionality of state and federal legislation. The Court exercised its power of judicial review in the nineteenth century primarily over state actions, with particular regard to preventing regulation of business.

The Court became much more aggressive in overturning federal legislation during the New Deal and vigorously used the Fourteenth Amendment's due process and equal protection clauses starting in the 1960s to overrule state practices that restricted civil liberties and civil rights.

The Rehnquist and Roberts Courts regularly overruled Congress and the president in the 1990s and 2000s.

## The U.S. Court System: Organization and Jurisdiction

**14.2** Outline the organization of the U.S. court system, p. 430

The federal court system is made up of three parts. At the bottom are 94 federal district courts, in which most cases originate. In the middle are 13 appeals courts. At the top is the Supreme Court, with both original and appellate jurisdiction. Only a relative handful of the thousands of cases filed in the federal district courts make it to the Supreme Court.

## Appointment to the Federal Bench

**14.3** Describe the background of appointees to the federal bench and the process by which they are appointed, p. 435

Until quite recently, the federal judiciary was dominated by white Protestant men from top law firms and law schools or government service.

Today, many more women and racial and ethnic minorities serve in the federal judiciary, with two women, one African American, and one Hispanic woman on the Supreme Court. A majority on today's high court is Catholic.

The appointment process is highly political and increasingly contentious, with presidents trying to leave their mark in the Courts, the political parties bringing ideological views to the process, and interest and advocacy groups fully engaged.

## The Supreme Court in Action

**14.4** Outline how the Supreme Court decides cases, p. 438

The Supreme Court operates on the basis of several widely shared norms: secrecy, seniority, and adherence to precedent. The Court controls its agenda by granting or not granting a writ of certiorari to cases filed with it.

Cases before the Court wend their way through the process in the following way: submission of briefs, oral argument, initial consideration in conference, opinion writing, and final conference consideration by the justices.

Published opinions serve as precedents for other federal courts and future Supreme Court decisions.

## The Supreme Court as a National Policymaker

**14.5** Evaluate the Supreme Court as a national policymaker, p. 441

The Supreme Court is a national policymaker of considerable importance. Its rulings not only settle disputes between political actors on critical matters and help define the meaning of the Constitution for others in the political system, but the Court is also quite active in pushing its own policy agenda.

The Court often serves as the referee of the democratic process and the rights of minorities, although it has sometimes failed to do this.

## Outside Influences on the Court

**14.6** Assess the factors and players that influence Supreme Court decisions, p. 451

The decisions of the Court are influenced not only by the judicial philosophies of the justices themselves, but also by the actions and preferences of other political actors such as the president and Congress, as well as by interest groups and public and elite opinion.

Increasingly the ideological predispositions of the justices are determinative. The Supreme Court is now dominated by a conservative majority.

# Learn the Terms

# Test Yourself

Answer key begins on page T-1.

**14.1**  Trace the evolution of judicial power in the United States

1. From 1803 to 2007 judicial review of a congressional act was only used about:

   **a.** 2 times
   **b.** 150 times
   **c.** 230 times
   **d.** 1,100 times
   **e.** 2,000 times

**14.2**  Outline the organization of the U.S. court system

2. Which of these is NOT a subject matter solely the province of the federal courts?

   **a.** Maritime issues
   **b.** The Constitution
   **c.** Disputes between the states
   **d.** Disputes between citizens
   **e.** Federal statutes and treaties

**14.3**  Describe the background of appointees to the federal bench and the process by which they are appointed

3. During President Barack Obama's first year in office he nominated 12 people for federal court positions, of which this number were women and/or minorities:

   **a.** 3
   **b.** 4
   **c.** 9
   **d.** 11
   **e.** 12

**14.4**  Outline how the Supreme Court decides cases

4. Which of the following are the norms, or the clearly understood rules of behavior, that shape how the Court does things?

   **a.** Seniority, standing, and secrecy
   **b.** Precedent, record, and standing
   **c.** Secrecy, precedent, and record
   **d.** Secrecy, seniority, and precedent
   **e.** Standing, merit, and seniority

**14.5**  Evaluate the Supreme Court as a national policymaker

5. The most criticized aspect of judicial activism is the tendency for federal judges to:

   **a.** Impose remedies
   **b.** Decide political issues
   **c.** Reverse past Supreme Court decisions
   **d.** Impose judicial review
   **e.** Use strict construction

**14.6**  Assess the factors and players that influence Supreme Court decisions

6. An action brought by a group that is designed to challenge the constitutionality of a law or an action by government is called a:

   **a.** Class-action suit
   **b.** Public opinion ruling
   **c.** Leader designation
   **d.** Constitution test
   **e.** Test case

# Explore Further

## INTERNET SOURCES

Federal Courts Home Page **www.uscourts.gov**
Information and statistics about the activities of U.S. district courts, circuit courts of appeal, and the Supreme Court.

Legal Information Institute, Cornell University Law School **www.law.cornell.edu**
The gateway to a world of information and links to associated law and court sites on the Web. Among its sections you will find the following: the Supreme Court calendar; biographies and opinions of the justices; directories of law firms, law schools, and legal associations; constitutions and codes, including U.S. statutes, regulations, and judicial rules of procedure; and court opinions, including those of state supreme courts.

The Oyez Project **www.oyez.org/oyez/frontpage**
A website that archives multimedia material concerning the U.S. Supreme Court (including recordings of oral arguments).

C-SPAN Judicial and Legal Resources **http://series.c-span.org/ Resources/Supreme-Court-Judiciary/**
A treasure trove of links to sites having to do with the law and the courts.

Senate Judiciary Committee **judiciary.senate.gov/nominations/**
Track the status of federal judicial nominations and confirmations.

Scotus Blog **www.scotusblog.com**
A blog on the inner workings of the Supreme Court administered by one of the nation's most experienced Supreme Court attorneys.

The Supreme Court **www.supremecourtus.gov/**
The official website of the Supreme Court, with a wealth of information about the Court's docket and decisions.

## SUGGESTIONS FOR FURTHER READING

Barnett, Randy E. *Restoring the Lost Constitution: The Presumption of Liberty*. Princeton, NJ: Princeton University Press, 2013.
A conservative case for understanding the Constitution as a legal framework for the protection of individual rights.

Breyer, Stephen. *Active Liberty: Interpreting Our Democratic Constitution*. New York: Knopf, 2005.
The Justice's attempt to define a coherent doctrine of a "Living Constitution."

Collins, Paul M., and Lori A. Ringhand, *Supreme Court Confirmation Hearings and Constitutional Change*. New York: Cambridge University Press, 2014.
An empirical and theoretical examination of the judicial confirmation process and how it contributes to democratic deliberation in the United States.

Greenburg, Jan Crawford. *Supreme Conflict: The Inside Story of the Struggle for Control of the United States Supreme Court*. New York: Penguin, 2008.
A fascinating account of the politics behind the conservative transformation of the Supreme Court.

McCloskey, Robert G. *The American Supreme Court*, 5th ed. Chicago: University of Chicago Press, 2010.
First published 45 years ago, and revised for the 2005 and 2010 editions by noted legal scholar Sanford Levinson, this remains the classic interpretation of the Supreme Court's role in shaping the meaning of the Constitution.

Schwartz, Bernard. *Decision: How the Supreme Court Decides Cases.* New York: Oxford University Press, 2005.
A revealing behind-the-scenes look at how the Supreme Court considers and decides the cases before it.

Steven, John Paul. *Five Chiefs: A Supreme Court Memoir*. New York: Little Brown, 2011.
An unusually candid and insightful look inside the Supreme Court by one of its most influential justices.

Wittington, Keith E. *Political Foundations of Judicial Supremacy: The Presidency, the Supreme Court, and Constitutional Leadership in U.S. History*. Princeton, NJ: Princeton University Press, 2007.
A provocative book that suggests that the Supreme Court has not so much taken power over the course of U.S. history but has had power thrust upon it by presidents and senators as a way to advance their own political interests and agendas.

# 15

# Civil Liberties: The Struggle for Freedom

## ELECTRONIC SURVEILLANCE AND THE WAR ON TERROR

n June 13, 2013, the British newspaper the *Guardian* revealed that it had obtained documents exposing a secret spy program operated by the National Security Agency (NSA), an intelligence bureau within the U.S. Department of Defense. The source of the leaks was later discovered to be Edward Snowden, a former computer technician who worked for a private contractor with access to NSA computers. Snowden's revelations led the U.S. government to charge him with espionage, but others called him a hero for exposing massive (and unprecedented) government-authorized monitoring of ordinary citizens.[1] PRISM, the most prominent information-gathering program exposed by Snowden, seems to have scooped up millions of phone records, e-mails, and other information on Internet usage through sophisticated technologies, all with the cooperation of the largest telecommunications firms in the country, including Verizon, AT&T, and Sprint.

In the wake of the terrorist attacks of September 11 and the subsequent war on terror, the U.S. government sought new ways to gather electronic data for the purposes of surveillance. Changes to existing laws passed by Congress in 2001, 2007, and 2008 apparently authorized the use of PRISM and other intelligence-gathering programs. The sheer size and scope of PRISM was controversial when first exposed to the American public, but the outrage spawned by additional details revealed since has forced Congress to reassess. For example, leaked documents demonstrate

| 15.1 | 15.2 | 15.3 | 15.4 |
|---|---|---|---|
| Identify civil liberties protections in the Constitution, p. 461 | Trace the evolution of civil liberties in the nineteenth century, p. 461 | Outline the liberties guaranteed by the Bill of Rights and their gradual application to the states by the Supreme Court, p. 465 | Analyze how concerns about terrorism may affect civil liberties, p. 486 |

**WHERE IS MY PRIVACY?** Although most government officials describe Edward Snowden as a traitor, civil liberties advocates view him as a hero for revealing government surveillance practices that they see as violations of citizens' freedom from government interference.

that the NSA collected information about phone numbers called by American citizens and about the length of those calls, though not what was actually said. This data was then used to map people's social networks, allowing the NSA to spot the friends and frequent contacts of potential targets. Further, the NSA tapped the personal cell phones of foreign leaders, including German Chancellor Angela Merkel, and listened to private conversations held in foreign embassies, tactics typically implemented only against hostile governments, not important European allies.

Despite denials from the NSA, the *Guardian* also reported that the agency tapped fiber optic cables, which carry Internet data, and stored associated metadata on Internet usage, metadata that the *Guardian* described as "a record of almost anything a user does online, from browsing history to account details, e-mail activity, and even some account passwords."[2] Various newspapers have since reported that the NSA can't even keep track of the data it collects and frequently violates its own rules about data collection. The *Wall Street Journal* chronicled, for instance, that NSA officers sometimes used its technologies to spy on their love interests.[3]

Proponents of the NSA's intelligence-gathering programs say they are necessary to root out terrorists and thwart future attacks. There is some truth to this claim, and many people believe that there is an inherent tradeoff between individual liberty and the power of government to locate, investigate, and prevent destructive acts. One of the primary and explicit goals of government is to protect its citizens from harm. But, as the framers were assuredly aware, governments frequently use their police powers to tyrannize individuals and groups. To counter the power of government, the framers enshrined civil liberties into the Constitution, especially through the Bill of Rights. Civil liberties are freedoms granted to citizens that protect them from certain types of government interference and that prevent government from becoming too powerful.

Although the liberties outlined in the Constitution seem relatively simple, changes in technology and in society as a whole leave us struggling to interpret the boundaries between government actions and our rights. Certainly the framers never could have imagined spying programs as sophisticated as those implemented by the NSA, but we must still use the Constitution as the standard against which to assess whether issues such as the storage of private e-mails violate an individual's civil liberties. There is no clear way of determining the limits of government action, as the Constitution provides only the vaguest of outlines of our liberties. Appropriate uses of government power are determined through the Supreme Court, through the lawmaking process, and through the public's changing perceptions of what civil liberties mean.

## Thinking Critically About This Chapter

This chapter is about civil liberties in the United States, with special attention on how historical developments, politics, and government policies have influenced the degree to which Americans can and do exercise their freedoms.

### Using the Framework

You will see in this chapter how structural, political linkage, and governmental factors influence the meaning and practice of civic freedoms. Although the decisions of the Supreme Court are particularly important in determining the status of civil liberties at any particular moment in American history, you will learn how they are also the product of influences from a wide range of actors, institutions, and social processes.

### Using the Democracy Standard

You will see in this chapter how the expansion of the enjoyment of civil liberties in the United States has been a product of the struggle for democracy and how civil liberties are fundamental to the democratic process itself.

# Civil Liberties in the Constitution

**15.1** Identify civil liberties protections in the Constitution

15.1

**civil liberties**
Freedoms found primarily in the Bill of Rights, the enjoyment of which are protected from government interference.

15.2

**habeas corpus**
The legal doctrine that a person who is arrested must have a timely hearing before a judge.

15.3

**bill of attainder**
A governmental decree that a person is guilty of a crime that carries the death penalty, rendered without benefit of a trial.

15.4

**ex post facto law**
A law that retroactively declares some action illegal.

**economic liberty**
The right to own and use property free from unreasonable government interference.

The framers were particularly concerned about establishing a society in which liberty might flourish. While government was necessary to protect liberty from the threat of anarchy, the framers believed that government might threaten liberty if it became too powerful. **Civil liberties** are freedoms protected by constitutional provisions, laws, and practices from certain types of government interference. As embodied in the Bill of Rights, civil liberties are protected by prohibitions against government actions that threaten the enjoyment of freedom. These liberties fall into two major groups: first, those associated with freedoms of expression, belief, and association; and second, those involving protections for people accused of committing a crime.

In the Preamble to the Constitution, the framers wrote that they aimed to "secure the Blessings of Liberty to ourselves and our Posterity." But in the original Constitution, they protected few liberties from the national government they were creating and almost none from state governments. To safeguard against tyranny, the framers preferred to give the national government little power with which to attack individual liberties. Rather than listing specific prohibitions against certain kinds of actions, then, they believed that a republican constitutional design that fragmented government power and that included separation of powers, checks and balances, and federalism would best protect liberty. Still, the framers singled out certain freedoms as too crucial to be left unmentioned. For example, the Constitution prohibits Congress and the states from suspending the writ of **habeas corpus**, except when public safety demands it because of rebellion or invasion, and from passing **bills of attainder** or **ex post facto laws** (see Table 15.1 for an enumeration).

Many citizens found the proposed Constitution too stingy in its listing of liberties, so that the Federalists were led to promise a "bill of rights" as a condition for passing the Constitution. The Bill of Rights was passed by the 1st Congress in 1789 and was ratified by the required number of states by 1791. Passage of the Bill of Rights made the Constitution more democratic by specifying protections of political liberty and by guaranteeing a context of free political expression that makes popular sovereignty possible.

Reading the Constitution and its amendments, however, reveals how few of our most cherished liberties are to be found in this document. Decisions by government officials and changes brought about by political leaders, interest groups, social movements, and individuals remade the Constitution in the long run; hence many of the freedoms we expect today are not specifically mentioned there. Some extensions of protected liberties were introduced by judges and other officials. Others have evolved as the culture has grown to accept novel and even once-threatening ideas. Still other liberties have secured a place in the Republic through partisan and ideological combat. The key to understanding civil liberties in the United States, then, is to follow their evolution over the course of our nation's history.

# Rights and Liberties in the Nineteenth Century

**15.2** Trace the evolution of civil liberties in the nineteenth century

During the nineteenth century, the range of protected civil liberties in the United States was somewhat different from their range today. Especially noteworthy were the special place of **economic liberty** and the understanding that the Bill of Rights did not apply to state governments.

**TABLE 15.1** CIVIL LIBERTIES IN THE U.S. CONSTITUTION

The exact meaning and extent of civil liberties in the Constitution are matters of debate, but here are some freedoms spelled out in the text of the Constitution and its amendments, or clarified by early court decisions.

**Constitution**

*Article I, Section 9*

Congress may not suspend habeas corpus.

Congress may not pass bills of attainder or ex post facto laws.

*Article I, Section 10*

States may not pass bills of attainder or ex post facto laws.

States may not impair obligation of contracts.

*Article III, Section 2*

Criminal trials in national courts must be jury trials in the state in which the defendant is alleged to have committed the crime.

*Article III, Section 3*

No one may be convicted of treason unless there is a confession in open court or testimony of two witnesses to the same overt act.

*Article IV, Section 2*

Citizens of each state are entitled to all privileges and immunities of citizens in the several states.

**The Bill of Rights**

*First Amendment*

Congress may not make any law with respect to the establishment of religion.

Congress may not abridge the free exercise of religion.

Congress may not abridge freedom of speech or of the press.

Congress may not abridge the right to assemble or to petition the government.

*Second Amendment*

Congress may not infringe the right to keep and bear arms.

*Third Amendment*

Congress may not station soldiers in houses against the owner's will, except in times of war.

*Fourth Amendment*

Citizens are to be free from unreasonable searches and seizures.

Federal courts may issue search warrants based only on probable cause and specifically describing the objects of search.

*Fifth Amendment*

Citizens are protected against double jeopardy (being prosecuted more than once for the same crime) and self-incrimination.

Citizens are guaranteed against deprivation of life, liberty, or property without due process of law.

Citizens are guaranteed just compensation for public use of their private property.

*Sixth Amendment*

Citizens have the right to a speedy and public trial before an impartial jury.

Citizens have the right to face their accuser and to cross-examine witnesses.

*Eighth Amendment*

Excessive bail and fines are prohibited.

Cruel and unusual punishments are prohibited.

## ☐ Economic Liberty in the Early Republic

Liberty may be understood as protection against government interference in certain kinds of private activities. Among the few such protections mentioned in the original Constitution was one that concerned the use and enjoyment of private property. This is hardly surprising; recall that the constitutional convention was convened, in part, because many of the new nation's leading citizens by the mid-1780s were growing ever more alarmed by threats to their holdings represented by passage of stay laws and the production of cheap paper money in several states, and insurrections like Shays' Rebellion. Property rights protections are stated most directly in the Constitution in the language of contracts (i.e., the freedom to enter into binding private agreements about many things, including the use of one's property): "No State shall . . . pass any . . . Law impairing the Obligation of Contracts" (Article I,

Section 10).[4] The framers protected private property in a number of other constitutional provisions as well, including provisions that created a system for recognizing intellectual property (patents and copyrights) and for safeguarding property in the form of slaves by requiring Americans to return runaway slaves to their owners. The **full faith and credit** clause (Article IV, Section 1), moreover, obligated each state to recognize contracts and other legal obligations entered into by its citizens with citizens or legal bodies in other states. The so-called takings clause of the Fifth Amendment—ratified in 1791 with other amendments that constitute the Bill of Rights—declares that "private property [shall not] be taken for public use, without just compensation." The importance of property rights as a fundamental liberty in the body of the Constitution and its Amendments was reinforced by more than a century of judicial interpretation.[5]

15.1
15.2
15.3
15.4

**full faith and credit**
The provision in Article IV, Section 1 of the Constitution which provides that states must respect the public acts, laws, and judicial rulings of other states.

**contract clause**
The portion of Article I, Section 10 of the Constitution that prohibits states from passing any law "impairing the obligations of contracts."

**THE MARSHALL COURT (1801–1835)** Although the Supreme Court ruled (in *Barron v. Baltimore,* 1833) that the Bill of Rights did not apply to the states, it ruled on several occasions that the **contract clause** in the Constitution directly applied against unwarranted state action. In the hands of Chief Justice John Marshall, the clause became an important defense of property rights against interference by the states. In *Fletcher v. Peck* (1810), for example, the Marshall Court upheld a sale of public land, even though almost all of the legislators who had voted for the land sale had been bribed by the prospective purchasers. Chief Justice Marshall wrote in his majority opinion that even a fraudulent sale created a contract among private individuals that the state could not void. In *Dartmouth College v. Woodward* (1819), Marshall argued in his majority opinion that New Hampshire could not modify the charter of Dartmouth College because the original charter constituted a binding contract, the terms of which could not be changed without impairing the obligations in the original contract. The framers' attempt to protect the contractual agreements of private parties ballooned in the hands of the Marshall Court to bar virtually any and all changes by the states of established property relations.[6] This expansion of property rights protections under the contract clause made it very difficult for states to regulate business activities because any such regulation could be interpreted as interfering with those binding contracts by which businesses were established and operated.

**HISTORIC RULING**
An important Supreme Court ruling solidifying property rights under the Constitution involved Dartmouth College, shown here in a drawing from 1819, the same year *Dartmouth College v. Woodward* was decided. Why did the framers and the Supreme Court place such importance on property rights?

**due process clause**
The section of the Fourteenth Amendment that prohibits states from depriving anyone of life, liberty, or property "without due process of law," a guarantee against arbitrary or unfair government action.

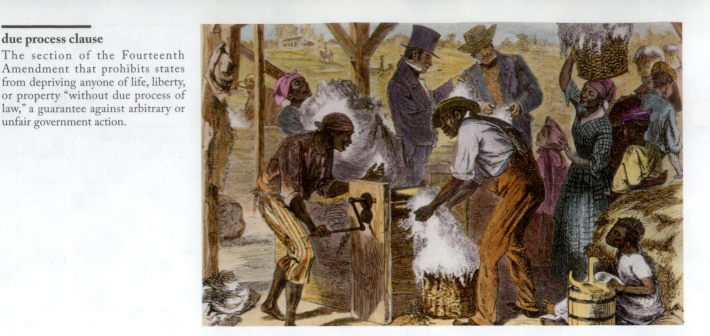

**SLAVES BRINGING IN THE COTTON CROP**

Prior to passage of the Thirteenth and Fourteenth Amendments after the Civil War, African American slaves were considered to be nothing more or less than the private property of their owners. How did the framers make the Constitution amenable to the practice of slavery?

**THE TANEY COURT (1836–1864)** Under the leadership of Chief Justice Roger Taney, the Court began to make a distinction between private property used in ways that encouraged economic growth and private property used for simple enjoyment. In landmark cases, the Taney Court issued rulings favoring the former when the two concepts of property conflicted.[7] In *Charles River Bridge v. Warren Bridge* (1837), investors who had secured a contract from the Massachusetts legislature for the construction of the Charles River Bridge charged that the state had violated its contract by chartering the construction of a competing bridge less than a decade later. In the majority opinion, Chief Justice Taney argued that the original charter for the Charles River Bridge did not imply a monopoly that closed off competitors. He ruled that Massachusetts could charter the rival Warren Bridge because the states should encourage economic competition and technological advances. It did not matter that the second bridge would result in financial losses for stockholders in the Charles River Bridge. Taney argued that the "creative destruction" of established but idle property in a dynamic market economy is the price of economic and social progress.

The Court's defense of property rights was especially and tragically strong when it came to slavery. Until the Civil War, courts in the North and the South consistently upheld the right of slaveholders to recapture fugitive slaves. In his opinion in *Dred Scott v. Sandford* (1857)—a case that helped bring on the Civil War because it declared that Congress could not regulate slavery in any way, voiding the "Missouri Compromise" that had balanced the interests of free states and slave states as the country expanded westward—Chief Justice Taney declared that slaves who traveled to free states (nonslave) with their masters could not sue for their freedom because that would mean depriving slave owners of their property. Slaves, in this view, like land and tools, were nothing more nor less than private property belonging to their owners, not people in a legal sense.

## ☐ Economic Liberty After the Civil War

The Fourteenth Amendment, passed after the Civil War, was designed to guarantee the citizenship rights of the newly freed slaves. It included a clause—the **due process clause**—stating that no state "may deprive a person of life, liberty, or property, without due process of law." Strangely, the Supreme Court in the late nineteenth century began to interpret this clause as a protection for businesses against the regulatory efforts of the national government and the states. In the view of the Court in *Santa Clara County v. Southern Pacific Railroad* (1886), corporations were "persons" in the eyes of the law and were subject to the same protections provided by the Fourteenth Amendment for any other "persons" in the United States.

The Court's most famous decision in this regard was *Lochner v. New York* (1905). Lochner ran a bakery in Utica, New York. He was convicted of requiring an employee to work more than 60 hours per week, contrary to a New York State maximum-hours statute. But Justice Rufus Peckham wrote for a 5–4 Supreme Court majority that the right of employer and employee to negotiate hours of work was part of the "liberty" of which, under the Fourteenth Amendment, no person could be deprived without due process of law. In other words, New York State had no right to regulate the hours of labor.

The nineteenth century was an era in which the rights of property were expanded, refined, and altered to become consistent with an emerging, dynamic industrial economy. The twentieth century would bring new approaches to property rights and to political liberties in general. These new approaches would be triggered by structural transformations in the economy and culture, the efforts of new political groups and movements, and the actions of government officials, all of which we will examine in greater detail.

**selective incorporation**
The gradual and piecemeal spread of the protections of the Bill of Rights to the states by the U.S. Supreme Court.

# Nationalization of the Bill of Rights

**15.3**  Outline the liberties guaranteed by the Bill of Rights and their gradual application to the states by the Supreme Court

**A**mericans rightly understand the Bill of Rights to be a foundation of American freedom. Until the twentieth century, however, the protections of the Bill of Rights did not apply to the states, only to the national government. The Supreme Court only gradually applied the Bill of Rights to the states through a process known as **selective incorporation**.[8]

The framers were worried more about national government intrusions on individual freedom than about state government intrusions. Most of the states, after all, had bills of rights in their own constitutions, and, being closer to the people, state governments would be less likely to intrude on the people's freedom, or so the framers believed. This reading of the Bill of Rights as a prohibition of certain actions by the national government seems explicit in the language of many of the first 10 amendments. The first, for instance, starts with the words "*Congress shall make no law. . . .*" This understanding of the Bill of Rights as a set of prohibitions against certain actions by the national government and not the states was confirmed by Chief Justice John Marshall in *Barron v. Baltimore* (1833). As he put it:

> The Constitution was ordained and established by the people of the United States for themselves, for their own government, and not for the government of the individual states.

After the Civil War, the majority in Congress very clearly wanted to change the reach of the Bill of Rights, extending it to the states. It did so by approving the Fourteenth Amendment in 1866, which was ratified by the states by 1868. After declaring that "all persons born or naturalized in the United States are citizens of both the United States and the states in which they reside," the Amendment's three key clauses specify that the states cannot violate the rights and liberties of the people living in them:

**15.1**

**15.2**

**15.3**

**15.4**

**privileges and immunities clause**
The portion of Article IV, Section 2 of the Constitution that says that citizens from out of state have the same legal rights as local citizens in any state.

**equal protection clause**
The section of the Fourteenth Amendment which guarantees that everyone will be treated equally by government.

**nationalizing**
The process by which provisions of the Bill of Rights become incorporated. See *incorporation*.

**incorporation**
The process by which the Supreme Court has made most of the provisions of the Bill of Rights binding on the states. See *nationalizing*.

**ordinary scrutiny**
The assumption that the actions of elected bodies and officials are legal under the Constitution.

**strict scrutiny**
The assumption that actions by elected bodies or officials violate constitutional rights.

- The **privileges and immunities clause** specifies that no *state* "shall make or enforce any law which shall abridge the privileges or immunities of citizens of the United States."

- The due process clause specifies that no *state* shall "deprive any person of life, liberty, or property, without due process of law."

- The **equal protection clause** requires states to provide equal treatment for all persons within their boundaries.

Although Congress wrote the Fourteenth Amendment to guarantee that states would protect all of U.S. citizens' rights and liberties, including those found in the Bill of Rights, the Supreme Court was very slow in **nationalizing** or **incorporating** the Bill of Rights, making it binding on the state governments. Indeed, the Supreme Court has not yet fully incorporated or nationalized the Bill of Rights. Rather, it has practiced selective incorporation, only slowly adding, step by step, even traditional civil liberties to the constitutional obligations of the states. Several Amendments have not been incorporated, including the Third on quartering troops, the Fifth on a right to a grand jury hearing, the Seventh on a right to a jury trial in civil suits, and the Eighth's prohibition against excessive bail and fines.

The Second Amendment's right of gun ownership was declared a fundamental individual right by the Court in 2008 in *District of Columbia v. Heller* and was incorporated—that is, made incumbent upon the states to not unreasonably restrict the enjoyment of this right—soon after in *McDonald v. Chicago* (2010). The prevailing view in the courts until then had been that the wording of the Second Amendment protects a collective right to form militias rather than an individual right to have guns. Gun advocates such as the National Rifle Association and libertarian organizations like the Cato Institute, on the other hand, had long held that the Amendment is not a collective right but a fundamental individual right, which the Court affirmed in *Heller*. The issue of gun rights is not entirely settled, however; just how much state and local regulation of gun ownership the Court will allow remains an open question.

How does the Supreme Court decide whether to incorporate some portion of the Bill of Rights? That is, what standard does the Court use to protect a liberty specified in the Bill of Rights from violation by a state government? The answer is quite simple and is spelled out, strange as it may seem, in footnote 4 of the opinion of the Court in *United States v. Carolene Products Company* (1938), written by Justice Harlan Fiske Stone, where he set out the legal standards the Court had been using in this area of constitutional interpretation, which he hoped and expected future justices would follow. Stone suggested in his footnote that most legislative enactments by states would fall under what he called **ordinary scrutiny**, meaning that the Court would assume, unless convinced otherwise, that its actions were constitutional. However, the footnote declares, three types of state actions would automatically be presumed unconstitutional, the burden being on the states to prove otherwise. When state actions are presumed to be unconstitutional, the Court is said to be exercising **strict scrutiny**. The three types of suspect state actions that bring strict scrutiny are the following:

- Those that seem to contradict specific prohibitions in the Constitution, including those in the Bill of Rights.

- Those that seem to restrict the democratic process.

- Those that seem to discriminate against racial, ethnic, or religious minorities.

The first of these is the subject matter of this chapter. The second has been addressed at several points in the text; for example in the cases establishing "one person, one vote." In the remainder of this chapter, we focus on specific civil liberties, clarifying their present status in both constitutional law and political practice.

It is important to note in the course of these discussions that the freedoms guaranteed in the Bill of Rights and in other sections of the Constitution hold and have always held with respect to actions of the national government; incorporation is about the process of extending these protections against government violations of freedom on the part of state and local governments. When the Supreme Court exercises strict scrutiny with respect to some law or statute or regulation, it can focus its displeasure at the federal level—for example, bills passed by Congress and signed into law by the president—or at state and local governments—for example, actions by governors, legislators, mayors, and police departments.

## ☐ Freedom of Speech

*Congress shall make no Law . . . abridging the freedom of speech.*

—First Amendment to the U.S. Constitution

Speech can take many forms. The Court has had to consider which forms of speech are protected under the Constitution. (See Figure 15.1 for a timeline on milestones in free expression, of which speech is a key component.)

**POLITICAL SPEECH** For many people, the right to speak one's mind is the first principle of a free and democratic society. Democratic theorists have argued, by and large, that a democratic society is based not only on popular sovereignty, but on the existence of a range of freedoms that allow free and open conversations among the people about the kind of government that is best for them and the sorts of public policies they consider most appropriate. Central among these freedoms is speech, the idea being that public conversations about government and politics depend on the ability and willingness of people to express their views, even if it means saying unpopular, even inflammatory things. Justice Oliver Wendell Holmes described the centrality of this "marketplace of ideas" in a free society in his famous and influential dissenting opinion in *Abrams v. United States* (1919).

Given the centrality of free speech to democracy, it is perhaps odd that free speech was not incorporated (made applicable to state governments) by the Supreme Court until 1925 in *Gitlow v. New York* (1925). Benjamin Gitlow had published *The Left Wing Manifesto*, which embraced a militant, revolutionary socialism to mobilize the proletariat to destroy the existing order in favor of communism. Gitlow did not advocate specific action to break the law, but he was nonetheless convicted of a felony under the New York Criminal Anarchy Law (1902).

The Supreme Court majority held that New York State was bound by the First Amendment—thus incorporating the First Amendment, making it binding on all states—but then argued that even the First Amendment did not prohibit New York from incarcerating Gitlow for his publishing and distributing his pamphlet because it represented a danger to peace and order for which, said Justice Edward Sanford, "A single revolutionary spark may kindle a fire that, smoldering for a time, may burst into a sweeping and destructive conflagration. It cannot be said that the State is acting . . . unreasonably when . . . it seeks to extinguish the spark without waiting until it has enkindled the flame or blazed into the conflagration." In his famous dissent, Justice Oliver Wendell Holmes said, "Every idea is an incitement. . . . Eloquence may set fire to reason. But whatever may be thought of the redundant discourse before us, it had no chance of starting a present conflagration."

Freedom of speech has grown in the ensuing years so that far more speech is protected than is not. In general, no U.S. government today—whether federal, state,

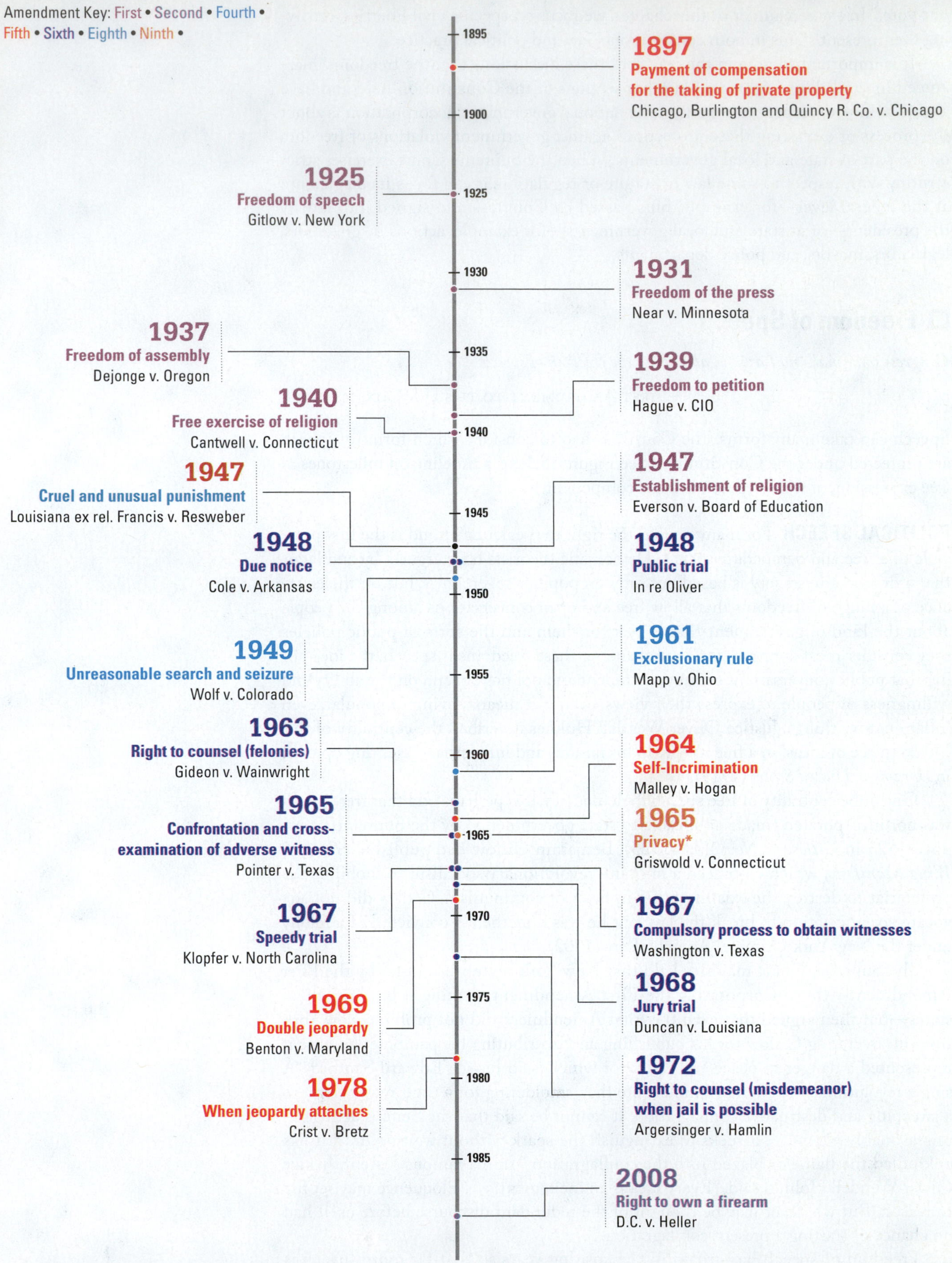

Amendment Key: First • Second • Fourth •
Fifth • Sixth • Eighth • Ninth •

**1895**

**1897**
**Payment of compensation
for the taking of private property**
Chicago, Burlington and Quincy R. Co. v. Chicago

**1900**

**1925**
**Freedom of speech**
Gitlow v. New York

**1925**

**1930**

**1931**
**Freedom of the press**
Near v. Minnesota

**1937**
**Freedom of assembly**
Dejonge v. Oregon

**1935**

**1939**
**Freedom to petition**
Hague v. CIO

**1940**
**Free exercise of religion**
Cantwell v. Connecticut

**1940**

**1947**
**Cruel and unusual punishment**
Louisiana ex rel. Francis v. Resweber

**1947**
**Establishment of religion**
Everson v. Board of Education

**1945**

**1948**
**Due notice**
Cole v. Arkansas

**1948**
**Public trial**
In re Oliver

**1950**

**1949**
**Unreasonable search and seizure**
Wolf v. Colorado

**1961**
**Exclusionary rule**
Mapp v. Ohio

**1955**

**1963**
**Right to counsel (felonies)**
Gideon v. Wainwright

**1964**
**Self-Incrimination**
Malley v. Hogan

**1960**

**1965**
**Confrontation and cross-
examination of adverse witness**
Pointer v. Texas

**1965**

**1965**
**Privacy***
Griswold v. Connecticut

**1967**
**Speedy trial**
Klopfer v. North Carolina

**1970**

**1967**
**Compulsory process to obtain witnesses**
Washington v. Texas

**1968**
**Jury trial**
Duncan v. Louisiana

**1975**

**1969**
**Double jeopardy**
Benton v. Maryland

**1980**

**1972**
**Right to counsel (misdemeanor)
when jail is possible**
Argersinger v. Hamlin

**1978**
**When jeopardy attaches**
Crist v. Bretz

**1985**

**2008**
**Right to own a firearm**
D.C. v. Heller

**FIGURE 15.1** TIMELINE: MILESTONES IN INCORPORATION OF THE BILL OF RIGHTS

a"Privacy" does not appear in the Ninth Amendment, only reference to "other rights retained by the people."

*Source:* United States Supreme Court

or local—can regulate or interfere with the content of speech without a compelling reason. In 1919, Justice Holmes argued that the government could restrict only speech that poses a "clear and present danger." The meaning of this standard was debated in the years that followed, with Holmes arguing that justices in later cases interpreted the meaning of the standard too broadly. The Supreme Court established a new "imminent lawless action" standard in *Brandenburg v. Ohio* (1969)—a case involving an appeal of the conviction of a leader of the Ku Klux Klan under Ohio's criminal syndicalism law. In that case the Court ruled that "the constitutional guarantees of free speech . . . do not permit a State to forbid or proscribe advocacy of the use of force or of law violation except where such advocacy is directed to incitement or producing imminent lawless action and is likely to incite or produce such action." This "imminent lawless action" test protects abstract advocacy of ideas, even if these ideas are considered dangerous by police, politicians, or popular majorities, unless it meets both conditions: substantiality and directness.

In the name of free speech the Court has also been gradually taking apart legislative efforts to restrict campaign spending in federal elections. In *Buckley v. Valeo* (1976) it invalidated parts of the Federal Election Campaign Act, most significantly, a restriction on how much money a candidate for federal office might put into his or her own campaign. Other important cases struck down various other laws limiting the ability of corporations and unions to collect and spend money on elections, giving rise to super PACs (see Chapter 10 on campaigns and elections). The foundation for the Supreme Court's decisions in *Wisconsin* (2007) and *Citizens United* (2010) was that money spent in campaigns expressing political ideas is speech that must be protected and that corporations and unions are "persons" under the Constitution with the same liberties as you and I have.[9]

Not all political speech is protected against government restriction. The Supreme Court has allowed governments to restrain and punish speakers whose words can be shown to lead or to have led directly to acts of violence or vandalism, interfered with the constitutional rights of others (e.g., blocking access to an abortion clinic), disrupted a legitimate government function (e.g., a sit-in demonstration in the House chambers), talked to others of information contained in classified documents, or trespassed on private or public property, whether people's businesses and homes or a secured defense installation. The Court has also allowed some restrictions on speech during time of war. But over the years, the Court has been careful to keep the leash tight on government officials who have tried to quiet the voice of citizens. Any attempt to restrict political speech must be content neutral (i.e., it cannot favor some views over others), serve a legitimate government purpose, be narrowly tailored to address a specific problem (i.e., it cannot be vague), and not have a chilling effect on other people's willingness to exercise their free speech rights. All in all, then, freedom of speech has gained powerful legal foundations over the years and is an important component of democracy in the United States.[10]

**ACTIONS AND SYMBOLIC SPEECH** Difficult questions about free expression persist, of course. Speech mixed with *conduct* may be restricted if the restrictions are narrowly and carefully tailored to curb the conduct while leaving the speech unmolested. Symbolic expressions (such as wearing armbands or picketing) may also receive less protection from the Court. The use of profanity or words that are likely to cause violence ("fighting words") may be regulated in some cases, as may symbolic actions that prevent others from carrying out legitimate activities. Still, freedom of speech throughout the United States has grown to the point at which contenders wrestle with relatively peripheral issues, leaving a large sphere of expressive freedom. *Texas v. Johnson* (1989) shows just how far the protection of free speech has expanded. In this case, Gregory Johnson challenged a Texas state law against flag desecration under which he had been convicted for burning an American flag as part of a demonstration at the 1984 Republican convention. Although dominated by a conservative majority, the Rehnquist Court overturned the Texas law, saying that flag burning falls under the free expression protections of the Constitution unless imminent incitement or violence is likely. In response, some members of Congress have tried on several occasions, without success, to pass an anti–flag desecration constitutional amendment for consideration by the states.

**SUPPRESSION OF FREE EXPRESSION**  A major exception to the expansion of freedom of expression has been the periodic concern among the authorities about internal security and national defense.[11] Fearing a rise of radicalism inflamed by the French Revolution, Congress passed the Sedition Act of 1798 to forbid criticism of the government and its leaders. The Civil War saw some restrictions on speech by the states, although the national government remained surprisingly lenient on this score (the Lincoln administration did, however, jail some rebel sympathizers without trial and used military tribunals to try civilians accused of actively helping the southern cause). Censorship of dissent and protests occurred during and after World War I; 32 states enacted laws to suppress dangerous ideas and talk, and local, state, and national officials led raids on the offices of "radicals." Hoping to become president, Attorney General A. Mitchell Palmer conducted raids on the headquarters of suspect organizations in 1919 and 1920, sending the young J. Edgar Hoover out to collect information on suspected anarchists and communists.

A similar period of hysteria followed World War II. Its foundations were laid when the Democrat-controlled House of Representatives created the House Un-American Activities Committee (generally referred to as the HUAC). When the Republicans won control of the Congress in 1952, they professed to see security risks in the Truman administration, labor unions, and Hollywood. Soon Democrats and Republicans alike were exploiting the "Red scare" for political gain. The greatest gain (and, subsequently, the hardest fall) was for Senator Joseph McCarthy (R–WI). McCarthy brandished lists of purported communists and denounced all who opposed him as traitors.[12]

**SOUNDING THE ALARM ON THE COMMUNIST THREAT**

Senator Joseph McCarthy made his reputation and career sounding the alarm bell about communists and communist sympathizers in every nook and cranny of the federal government. Though he was almost always wrong in his assertions, and ruined the lives and careers of many, he did not stir the wrath of other elites until he took on the Army in 1954. Army counsel Joseph Welch listens in disbelief as the junior senator from Wisconsin points out the location of the latest threats during a committee hearing.

More recently, many observers worry about the possible chilling effect on free speech and privacy violations stemming from new laws passed to combat terrorism. Most important is the USA PATRIOT Act—passed in 2001 and renewed in 2006 with a few small changes to allow for a little more judicial oversight—granting the federal government access to Americans' private and business records. Revelations that the FBI and the NSA had been conducting secret and warrantless searches of phone conversations (land lines and cell phones), financial transactions, and Internet communications ever since 9/11 led to intense press scrutiny, public condemnation, and congressional probes in early 2006, but the opposition was unable to block renewal of the PATRIOT Act. In 2007, in a revelation that came too late to affect congressional deliberations on renewal, FBI director Robert Mueller reported to Congress that, since 2001, his agents had improperly and sometimes illegally obtained personal information on thousands of American citizens by overzealously using tools provided by the Act.[13] To the disappointment of many of his supporters, President Barack Obama continued many of the policies instituted during the Bush years, including searching business records and roving wiretaps, something we explore in a later section of this chapter.

## ☐ Freedom of the Press

*Congress shall make no law . . . abridging the freedom . . . of the press.*

—First Amendment to the U.S. Constitution

In an aside in the opinion of the Court in *Gitlow v. New York* (1925), the Supreme Court included freedom of the press as a freedom guaranteed against state interference by the Fourteenth Amendment. Incorporation of this aspect of the Bill of Rights seems reasonable in light of the importance of the free flow of information in a society that aspires to freedom and democracy.

**PRIOR RESTRAINT**  In *Near v. Minnesota* (1931), the Court made good on the promise of *Gitlow* by invalidating the Minnesota Public Nuisance Law as a violation of freedom of the press.[14] Jay Near published the *Saturday Press,* a scandal sheet that attacked local crime, public officials, and a few other groups that he disliked: Jews, Catholics, blacks, and unions, for example. Near and his associates were ordered by a state court not to publish, sell, or possess the *Saturday Press.* This sort of state action is called **prior restraint** because it prevents publication before it has occurred. Freedom of the press is not necessarily infringed if publishers are sued or punished for harming others after they have published, but Minnesota was trying to keep Near and his associates from publishing in the future.

The prohibition of prior restraint on publication remains the core of freedom of the press.[15] Freedom of the press and freedom of speech tend to be considered together as freedom of expression, so the general principles applicable to free speech apply to freedom of the press as well. Thus, the Court will allow the repression of publication only if the state can show some "clear and present danger" that publication poses, similar to its position on free speech. In *New York Times v. United States* (1971), the Court ruled that the U.S. government could not prevent newspapers from publishing portions of the Pentagon Papers, secret government documents revealing the sordid story of how the United States had become involved in the Vietnam War. A major expansion of freedom of the press in *New York Times v. Sullivan* (1964) protects newspapers against punishment for trivial or incidental errors when they are reporting on public persons. This limits the use or threat of libel prosecutions by officials because officials can recover damages only by showing that the medium has purposely reported untruths or has made no effort to find out if what is being reported is true.

**PROTECTING SOURCES**  Many reporters and executives in news organizations believe that reporters must be able to protect their sources if they are to have access

**prior restraint**
The government's power to prevent publication, as opposed to punishment afterward.

**obscenity**

As defined by the Supreme Court, the representation of sexually explicit material in a manner that violates community standards and is without redeeming social importance or value.

to insider information that the public needs to know. Without protection of sources, newspeople suggest, the stream of information that the public requires in a democracy will flow more slowly. This is the argument that *New York Times* reporter Judith Miller made when she went to jail for 85 days in 2005 for refusing to testify about her source in the administration who had revealed the identity of CIA operative Valerie Plame, who happened to be the wife of a vocal critic of President Bush's reasons for going to war in Iraq. Although most states have shield laws allowing reporters to protect their sources, there is no such federal law, and the Supreme Court has rejected the argument that constitutional doctrines on freedom of the press give reporters immunity from testifying when they have been issued a subpoena by a court (see *Branzburg v. Hayes*, 1972).

**OFFENSIVE MEDIA** *Pornography* is a nonlegal term for offensive sexual materials; the legal term is **obscenity**. Although the courts have held that *obscenity* is not protected by the First Amendment, the definition of obscenity has provoked constitutional struggles for half a century. Early disputes concerned the importation and mailing of works that we regard today as classics: James Joyce's *Ulysses* and D. H. Lawrence's *Lady Chatterley's Lover,* for example.[16] Although the justices admitted that principled distinctions sometimes eluded them (Justice Potter Stewart once famously said that he did not know how to define hard-core pornography but that he knew it when he saw it), a reasonably clear three-part test emerged from *Miller v. California* (1973):

1. The average person, applying contemporary community standards, must find that the work as a whole appeals to the prurient interest (lust).

2. The state law must specifically define what depictions of sexual conduct are obscene.

3. The work as a whole must lack serious literary, artistic, political, or scientific value.

If the work survives even one part of this test, it is not legally obscene and is protected by the First Amendment. Community standards, applied by juries, are used to judge whether the work appeals to lust and whether the work is clearly offensive. However, literary, artistic, political, and scientific value (called the *LAPS test,* after the first letter of each of the four values) is *not* judged by community standards but by the jury's assessment of the testimony of expert witnesses. If, and only if, all three standards are met, the Supreme Court will allow local communities to regulate the sale of obscene materials. Because these tests are not easily met in practice, the *Miller* ruling has done little to stem the tide of sexually explicit material in American popular culture.[17] The Court has ruled, however, in *New York v. Ferber* (1982) that states can prohibit the production, distribution, and sale of child pornography.

Recently, many Americans have begun to worry about the availability to minors of sexually offensive material on the Internet. Responding to this concern, Congress and President Clinton cooperated in 1996 to pass the Communications Decency Act, which made it a crime to transmit over the Internet or to allow the transmission of indecent materials to which minors might have access. The Supreme Court, in *Reno, Attorney General of the United States v. American Civil Liberties Union* (1997), ruled unanimously that the legislation was an unconstitutional violation of the First Amendment, being overly broad and vague and violative of the free speech rights of adults to receive and send information (the Court reaffirmed this ruling in 2004). The strong and unambiguous words of the opinion of the Court make it clear that government efforts to regulate the content of the Internet, as well as cable television, will not get very far. Because the government licenses a limited number of airwaves (there are only so many frequencies available at any one time) and they are considered public property, broadcast television falls under different rules. Thus, the Court has allowed the Federal Communications Commission to ban cursing and nudity on broadcast TV, something it cannot do with respect to other electronic or print media or cable television. The Court went further in affirming new media press freedoms in 2011 when it ruled that efforts by governments to ban violent video games are constitutionally

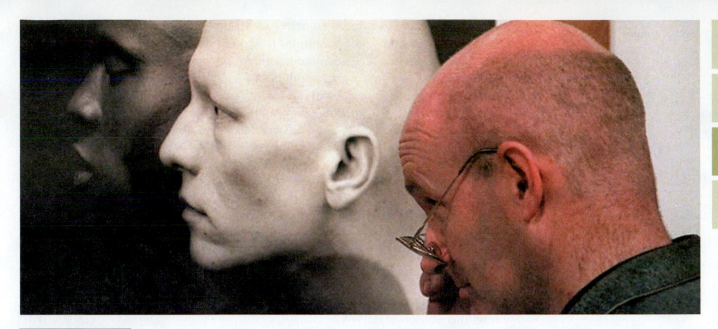

**CONTROVERSIAL ART**

The distinction between art and obscenity can be very difficult to establish, and battles over the banning of controversial works, such as Robert Mapplethorpe's homoerotic photographs, are quite common in American communities. How does the Court decide what constitutes obscenity?

unacceptable. As Justice Scalia wrote in *Brown v. Entertainment Merchants Association* (2011), "Like the protected books, plays and movies that preceded them, video games communicate ideas—and even social messages—through familiar literary devices (such as characters, dialogue, plot and music) and through features distinctive to the medium (such as the player's interaction with the virtual world). That suffices to confer First Amendment protection."

## ☐ Religious Freedom

For much of our history, Congress did not impede the exercise of religion because it did not legislate much on the subject. Because the states were not covered by the First Amendment, the free exercise of religion was protected by state constitutions or not at all. The Supreme Court was content to defer to the states on issues of religious freedom.

As late as 1940, in *Minersville School District v. Gobitis*, the Supreme Court upheld the expulsion of two schoolchildren who refused to salute the flag because it violated their faith as Jehovah's Witnesses. Justice Harlan Stone wrote a stinging dissent:

> The Constitution expresses more than the conviction of the people that democratic processes must be preserved at all costs. It is also an expression of faith and a command that freedom of mind and spirit must be preserved, which government must obey, if it is to adhere to that justice and moderation without which no free government can exist.

Stone's dissent, as well as a series of decisions deferring to state restrictions on Jehovah's Witnesses in 1941 and 1942, eventually moved other justices to Stone's side. In *West Virginia v. Barnette* (1943), the Court reversed *Gobitis* and firmly established free exercise of religion as protected against infringement by the states.

### FREE EXERCISE OF RELIGION

*Congress shall make no law . . . prohibiting the free exercise [of religion].*

—First Amendment to the U.S. Constitution

The core of the **free exercise clause** today is that neither the federal government nor state governments may interfere with religious *beliefs*. This is one of the few absolutes in U.S. constitutional law. Religious *actions*, however, are not absolutely protected.

**free exercise clause**
That portion of the First Amendment to the Constitution that prohibits Congress from impeding religious observance or impinging upon religious beliefs.

**establishment clause**
The part of the First Amendment to the Constitution that prohibits Congress from establishing an official religion; the basis for the doctrine of the separation of church and state.

In general, people in the United States are free to practice their religious beliefs as they wish. However, some exceptions to the free exercise of religion are enforced where they may violate general statutes that serve a compelling public purpose. For example, state and federal laws prohibit the ritualistic use of some drugs, and local public health ordinances ban such worship practices as animal sacrifice in most locales. The Court has upheld state laws, for instance, outlawing the use of peyote (an illegal hallucinogen) in Native American religious ceremonies. The passage of the Affordable Care Act (ACA), known colloquially as Obamacare, has given rise to a thorny question about the free exercise of religion, because the act requires that employer-provided health insurance policies cover basic preventive care, including contraceptive care. Explicitly religious employers like churches opposed to birth control are excluded from this provision of the law, but some non-faith-based employers who oppose birth control for religious reasons argue that the government should not be permitted to force them, in effect, to pay for their employees' contraceptives. This portion of the law was challenged in *Burwell v. Hobby Lobby Stores, Inc.* The Court ruled that closely held corporations like Hobby Lobby—a company that is owned by members of a single family who share similar religious beliefs—must also be exempt from this portion of the law.

## ESTABLISHMENT OF RELIGION

*Congress shall make no law respecting an establishment of religion.*

—First Amendment to the U.S. Constitution

Many countries in the world have an official state religion. Sometimes this means that religious law trumps secular law in almost every instance, as in Saudi Arabia and Iran. Sometimes this means that religious law takes precedence in a narrow range of matters, usually involving family matters like marriage and divorce, as in Israel. Often, a state church will exist but not affect everyday life, playing more of a symbolic role. In most Western European democracies that have monarchies, for example, the king or queen must be a member in good standing of the state church. For example, monarchs in Great Britain must be members of the Church of England.

There is no state church in the United States but many churches (and mosques and synagogues and temples) and many religious people. What allows them to peacefully coexist, in the view of many, is not only the broad freedom to worship or not worship as one pleases under the terms of the "free exercise" clause of the First Amendment, but keeping religion and government at arm's length from one another. Freedom of conscience, it is often argued, requires that government not favor one religion over another by granting it special favors, privileges, or status, or interfering in the affairs of religious institutions. It requires, in Jefferson's famous terms, "a wall of separation between church and state." The framers were mindful of the violent history in Europe and Great Britain over whether Catholicism or Protestantism would be supreme in the state. The Thirty Years' War, the Inquisition, the struggle over the British crown following the reign of Henry VIII, and conflicts within Protestantism that contributed to the English Civil War were the sad results. Many people who settled in the New World were fleeing these religious conflicts.[18]

Nevertheless, despite general support for the doctrine of "separation of church and state," incorporation of the **establishment clause** by the Court proved to be a particularly messy matter. In *Everson v. Board of Education* (1947), Justice Hugo Black for the Supreme Court determined that no state could use revenues to support an institution that taught religion, thus incorporating the First Amendment ban into the Fourteenth Amendment. But the majority in that case upheld the New Jersey program that reimbursed parents for bus transportation to parochial schools. A year later, Justice Black wrote another opinion incorporating the establishment clause in *McCollum v. Board of Education* (1948). This time, a program for teaching religion in public schools was found unconstitutional. In *Zorach v. Clauson* (1952), however, the Court upheld a similar program that let students leave school premises early for

**NO SEPARATION OF CHURCH AND STATE**

This young woman was sentenced to death by stoning for having committed adultery by a Sharia Islamic court in Nigeria. The man in the adulterous relationship was not charged with a crime. Her sentence was overturned by Nigerian authorities after the case sparked international outrage and censure. What might our country look like if the majority's religious preferences became the basis for constitutional law and statutes?

religious instruction. The establishment clause had been incorporated, but the justices long have had difficulty determining what "separation of church and state" means in practice.

**THE *LEMON* TEST** The Warren Court (1953–1969) brought together a solid church–state separationist contingent whose decisions the early Burger Court (1969–1973) distilled into the major doctrine of the establishment clause: the "*Lemon* test." In *Lemon v. Kurtzman* (1971), Chief Justice Warren Burger specified three conditions that every law must meet to avoid "establishing" religion:

1. The law must have a secular *purpose*. That secular purpose need not be the only or primary purpose behind the law. The Court requires merely some plausible non-religious reason for the law.

2. The *primary effect* of the law must be neither to advance nor to retard religion. The Court will assess the probable effect of a governmental action for religious neutrality.

3. Government must never foster *excessive entanglements* between the state and religion.

While the *Lemon* test would seem to have erected substantial walls that bar mixing church and state, the Court has not been entirely consistent over time in applying it.[19] In *Rosenberger v. University of Virginia* (1995), it ruled that the university (a state-supported institution) must provide the same financial subsidy to a student religious publication that it provides to other student publications. In other cases, the Court ruled that public monies can go to parochial schools if they are for programs that are similar to ones in public schools and not used to advance religious instruction. This would include things such as funds to purchase science books or support drug education programs.[20] However, the Court has been unwilling to depart too far from the principle of separation of church and state; in 2004, for example, the Court ruled that the state of Washington had done no constitutional harm when it denied a state-funded scholarship to a student studying for the ministry.

With regard to religious displays in courthouses and other public buildings, the Rehnquist Court seemingly adopted Justice Sandra Day O'Connor's somewhat vague proposition that the establishment clause does not forbid religious displays in courthouses and other public buildings unless a "reasonable observer would view them as endorsing religious beliefs or practices."[21] The Court seems to have decided that it will need to look at such things as religious displays—lights, manger scenes, and the like—at public buildings on a case-by-case basis. In 2005, it ruled in one instance that hanging framed copies of the Ten Commandments in a courthouse in Kentucky went too far in promoting a particular set of religious beliefs (*McCreary County, Kentucky, et al. v. ACLU*). As Justice David Souter put it in his majority opinion, "The reasonable observer could only think that the counties meant to emphasize and celebrate the religious message. . . . The display's unstinting focus was on religious passages [posted with the Commandments], showing that the counties posted the Commandments precisely because of their sectarian content." In another ruling handed down the same day (*Van Orden v. Perry*), the Court allowed a display of a six-foot-high monument of the Ten Commandments in front of the state capitol in Austin because it was one of 40 monuments and historical markers that, in the words of Justice Stephen Breyer, ". . . [served] a mixed but primarily nonreligious purpose." Similarly, in *Town of Greece v. Galloway* (2014), the Court considered whether a town council's practice of beginning meetings with a prayer was unconstitutional. Although the prayers were neither exclusively nor overtly Christian, the town residents who challenged the practice argued that most prayers were "uniquely Christian" and often referred explicitly to Jesus. The Court found that this practice did not violate the establishment clause because the practice of opening government meetings with prayer was long-standing and because the town neither prevented non-Christians from offering a prayer nor forced attendees to participate.

In 2012, in *Hosanna-Tabor Church v. Equal Employment Opportunity Commission*, the Court ruled unanimously that employees of religious organizations who carry out some religious duties—leading services, teaching bible classes, and the like—cannot bring job discrimination suits under federal law. Arguing for a "ministerial exception" to federal employment laws, the justices said their enforcement would be an unconstitutional intrusion of government into the affairs of religious institutions, breaking the wall of separation between church and state. Religious organizations from virtually all denominations in the United States hailed the decision, though worries were expressed by many others that this might mean that teachers of theology in religious-affiliated colleges, let us say, might not be able to bring suits under federal law for age discrimination or sexual harassment at work.[22] Such issues no doubt will be litigated in the years ahead.

Waiting in the wings are a range of issues involving the separation of church and state that the Court will eventually consider, given the number of cases that are working their way up from state courts and federal district courts. These include the legitimacy of the words "one nation under God" in the Pledge of Allegiance, and the acceptability of the nondenominational prayers that open the daily sessions in Congress. The point here is fairly straightforward: the debate over where to draw the line that separates church and state is a continuing one in America and is unlikely to ever be resolved once and for all.

**RELIGION IN PUBLIC SCHOOLS** One of the most controversial aspects of constitutional law regarding the establishment of religion concerns school prayer. Although a majority of Americans support allowing a nondenominational prayer or a period of silent prayer in the schools, the Court has consistently ruled against such practices since the early 1960s, perhaps believing that children in school settings, as opposed to adults in other areas of life, are more likely to feel pressure from those conveying religious messages. In *Engel v. Vitale* (1962), the Court ordered the state of New York to suspend its requirement that all students in public schools recite a nondenominational prayer at the start of each school day. In *Stone v. Graham* (1980), the Court ruled against posting the Ten Commandments in public school classrooms. In *Lee v. Weisman* (1992), it ruled against allowing school-sponsored prayer at graduation ceremonies. In *Santa Fe Independent School District v. Doe* (2000), the Court ruled that student-led prayers at school-sponsored events such as football games are not constitutionally permissible because they have the "improper effect of coercing those present to participate in an act of religious worship." In these and other cases the Court has consistently ruled against officially sponsored prayer in public schools as a violation of the separation of church and state.

Returning prayer to the public schools and making schools less secular are very high on the agenda of religious conservatives. Bills supporting voluntary classroom prayer (such as a moment of silent contemplation) are constantly being introduced into Congress and state legislatures, with little success so far. Christian conservatives have also tried without success to pass a school prayer constitutional amendment. In several very religious communities, school officials have simply ignored the Supreme Court and continue to allow prayer in public classrooms.

An important battle about religion in the schools concerns attempts by some committed believers to either exclude Darwinian evolutionary biology from the school curriculum or to balance it with alternative interpretations such as "creationism" (the idea that God created the earth as described in the Bible) or "intelligent design" (the idea that the natural world is so complex that it could not have evolved as scientists propose and that a higher being must have designed it). Because courts at all levels have rejected the teaching of "creationism" in the science curriculum as an improper intrusion of religion into public education, many religious activists have pushed "intelligent design" as an alternative approach that might pass court muster. The Dover, Pennsylvania, school board tried this strategy but lost in federal court. As Judge John Jones put it in his opinion in *Kitzmiller v. Dover Area School District* (2005), ". . . we conclude that the religious nature of ID [intelligent design] would be readily apparent to an objective observer, adult, or child. . . . The overwhelming evidence at trial established that ID is a religious view, a mere relabeling of creationism, and not a scientific theory."

**PRAY AND PLAY**

Here, a high school coach leads his team in prayer before a game. This practice, quite common across America, raises important questions about the "establishment" clause, especially the degree to which local school authorities in many communities are willing to comply with the doctrine of "separation of church and state." Should the federal government take a harder line against such practices, or should they be left alone as long as no one complains?

With no sign that the tide of religious feeling is about to recede in the United States, debates over school prayer, religious displays in school, and the teaching of evolution will continue for the foreseeable future. The main reason these issues will linger is that neither the courts nor the American people are entirely certain where the line between church and state should be drawn.

## ☐ Privacy

The freedoms addressed so far—speech, press, and religion—are listed in the First Amendment. The freedom to be left alone in our private lives—what is usually referred to as the *right to privacy*—is not mentioned in the First Amendment nor in any of the other amendments that make up the Bill of Rights. Nevertheless, most Americans consider the right to privacy to be one of our most precious freedoms. Americans believe, in most cases, that citizens should be able to make their own personal decisions regarding their own health and welfare, for example, and should be free from too much government monitoring of what they say and do in their everyday lives. Many (though not all) constitutional scholars believe, moreover, that a right to privacy is inherent in the Bill of Rights, even if it is not explicitly stated. Examples abound in the Constitution of an implied right to privacy, including prohibitions against illegal searches and seizures and against quartering of troops in our homes, as well as the right to free expression and conscience. Such scholars also point to the Ninth Amendment as evidence that the framers believed in the existence of liberties not specifically mentioned in the Bill of Rights: "The enumeration in the Constitution of certain rights, shall not be construed to deny or disparage others retained by the people."

Most jurists and legal scholars have come to accept that a fundamental right to privacy exists, though a group of "original intent" conservatives like Justice Clarence Thomas do not agree. Even among those who accept the fundamental right to privacy, there is disagreement about how far this right extends. Of course, we aren't free to do what we want at all times because the government frequently has a compelling interest in protecting individuals and society from dangerous actions. Drawing the line on the right to privacy has implications for many of the most controversial issues in American society, including abortion, gay and lesbian rights, the right to die, and the security of interpersonal communications during wartime.

The Supreme Court's first important right to privacy case was *Griswold v. Connecticut* (1965), in which it ruled that a law banning the sale of contraceptives by the state of Connecticut was unconstitutional. The Supreme Court said that the right to privacy is included in the penumbra of other rights found in the Constitution, meaning it exists in the shadows or emanations of other rights. Specifically, the Court pointed to the rights outlined in the First, Third, Fourth, Fifth, Ninth, and Fourteenth Amendments as all implying a right to privacy.

**ABORTION** *Griswold*'s right to privacy doctrine became the basis for Justice Harry Blackmun's majority opinion in the landmark case *Roe v. Wade* (1973), in which the Court ruled in favor of a woman's right to terminate her pregnancy. The ruling transformed abortion from a legislative issue into a constitutional issue, from a matter of policy into a matter of rights. It remains one of the most contentious issues in American politics.

According to the Court, the right to an abortion is constitutionally protected and states cannot interfere with a woman's decision to have an abortion in the first two trimesters of her pregnancy. The Court's decision hardly resolved matters. Many states began to place restrictions on abortion, ranging from parental notification to waiting periods, counseling about alternatives to abortion, and prohibitions on the use of public money for the procedure. In *Webster v. Reproductive*

*Health Services* (1989), the Court seemed to invite these restrictions. A few years later, however, in *Planned Parenthood v. Casey* (1992), the Court ruled that these restrictions cannot go so far as to make abortion virtually impossible to obtain. In the words of Justice Sandra Day O'Connor, while some restrictions are acceptable, none could "place an undue burden" on a woman's fundamental right to terminate a pregnancy.

*Casey* involved regulations established by the state of Pennsylvania that included a 24-hour waiting period and a requirement that women notify their husbands. The notification requirement was the only part of the Pennsylvania law that failed the "undue burden" test.

As a result of *Casey*, many states have become more aggressive in passing new laws restricting access to abortion and new regulations that have the intended effect of making it much more difficult for women to obtain abortions. In 2013, Texas passed a very restrictive abortion law that required, among other things, that doctors performing abortions have admitting privileges at a hospital within 30 miles of their clinic, a requirement many rural doctors are unable to meet. In fact, much of the current controversy over abortion is over limitations imposed by states that are meant to impede access to the procedure.

**PRIVATE SEXUAL ACTIVITY**  The Supreme Court had ruled as recently as 1986 in *Bowers v. Hardwick* that private sexual activity between consenting adults was not a protected right under the constitution. States could, in its view, continue to outlaw certain sexual acts, particularly those involving homosexuals, as the state of Georgia continued to do after winning *Bowers*. Things changed after privacy was recognized as a fundamental right in *Griswold*. In *Lawrence v. Texas* (2003) the Court ruled that state anti-sodomy laws prohibiting consensual gay and lesbian sexual relations are unconstitutional. "Private lives in matters pertaining to sex," declared Justice Anthony Kennedy in his majority opinion, "are a protected liberty." This reversal of its own ruling in so short a period of time is unusual in the history of the Court; though, as we saw in this chapter's section on free speech, it did so recently in the campaign finance case, *Citizens United v. Federal Election Commission* (2010).

**THE RIGHT TO DIE**  Though the topic has not received as much attention recently as issues like gay marriage and abortion, controversy over the right of a terminally ill individual to commit suicide has been ongoing since the 1990s and led to Oregon enacting the first law legalizing the "right to die" in 1997. The law allows doctors to provide lethal doses of medication to terminally ill patients—patients who say they prefer to die "with dignity" rather than undergo a long, slow, and painful death.

By 2013, five states had laws allowing terminally ill patients to end their lives, and in January 2014, a state judge in New Mexico ruled that there exists a constitutionally protected right to die.

It is relatively unclear yet whether the courts will support a privacy-based "right to die." So far the Supreme Court has refused to endorse or reject the existence of such a right, though it upheld, in 2004, Oregon's assisted suicide law. Should a patient who might be saved by a risky, painful, and dangerous procedure be allowed to forgo the procedure and instead end their life?[23] These questions are not easily answered, but support for the right to die is growing. A 2013 Gallup Poll found that 70 percent of Americans thought doctors should be allowed to help a patient die.[24] In the absence of a clear Supreme Court ruling, right to die laws are in the hands of the states unless Congress chooses to legislate on the issue.

**PRIVATE COMMUNICATIONS**  Finally, there are issues relating to government intrusion on private communications. Many of these issues are closely related to the Fourth Amendment's prohibition against unreasonable searches and seizures, but

**exclusionary rule**
A standard promulgated by the Supreme Court that prevents police and prosecutors from using evidence against a defendant that was obtained in an illegal search.

policies instituted to combat terrorism have raised broader questions about privacy. The USA PATRIOT Act (passed in 2001, with reauthorizations in 2006 and 2011), as previously mentioned, grants the federal government access to the private records of citizens and businesses. Revelations that the FBI and the NSA have conducted secret and warrantless searches of phone conversations, financial transactions, and Internet communications ever since 9/11 has led to intense press scrutiny, public condemnation, and congressional probes. In 2007, in a disclosure that came too late to affect congressional deliberations on renewal in 2006, FBI director Robert Mueller reported to Congress that his agents had improperly and sometimes illegally obtained personal information on thousands of American citizens.[25] Disappointing many supporters, Barack Obama has continued many of the security policies instituted during the Bush years, including searching business records and roving wiretaps.

## ☐ Rights of the Accused

The framers were so concerned about protections for individuals suspected, accused, or convicted of a crime that they included important protections in the main body of the Constitution. Article I, as you have learned, prohibits Congress, and by implication, the federal government, from issuing bills of attainder, passing ex post facto laws, or suspending the right of habeas corpus (an important issue now because of the types of hearings used for terrorism detainees, something we will look at later in the chapter). As further indication of their concern for the rights of those accused of a crime, consider that 5 of the 10 amendments that make up the Bill of Rights are about providing such protections. The framers were worried about the ability of the new government to accuse and imprison individuals it did not like, so the Bill of Rights offers significant protections for individuals. Most Americans today treasure the constitutional rights and liberties that protect innocent individuals—what are generally termed *due process* protections—from wrongful prosecution and imprisonment. But most Americans also want to control crime as much as possible. Balancing these two needs is an issue that the Supreme Court and society continually struggle with. Still, the rise of "tough on crime" measures has significantly increased the number of people in American jails; although the United States accounts for a little less than 5 percent of the world's population, it has almost one-fourth of the world's total prison population.[26]

As with most other civil liberties, the Court has alternately expanded and narrowed the rights of those accused of crimes. The more liberal Warren Court (1953–1969) greatly expanded protections, Burger Court rulings (1969–1986) trimmed protections for defendants, and the Rehnquist Court (1987–2004) quickened the pace of favoring prosecutors. It remains too early to predict the direction of the Roberts Court, though the strongly unified conservative majority and the addition to the Court of Obama nominee and former prosecutor Sonia Sotomayor suggests that further movement away from the Warren Court on protections for those accused of a crime may be coming.

**UNREASONABLE SEARCHES AND SEIZURES** The Fourth Amendment secures the right of all persons against unreasonable searches and seizures and allows the granting of search warrants only if the police can specify evidence of serious lawbreaking that they reasonably expect to find. Until the Warren Court compelled the states to abide by the Fourth Amendment in 1961, they had frequently used searches and seizures that the federal courts would consider "unreasonable" in an effort to control crime. In *Mapp v. Ohio* (1961), the Supreme Court said that evidence that had been gathered through a warrantless and unreasonable search may not be used at trial, even if the evidence is incriminating. The so-called **exclusionary rule** now applies to states, and the justices hoped that it would force the police to play by constitutional rules while conducting their investigations. Generally, the Warren Court required police to obtain a warrant whenever a person subjected to a search had a "reasonable expectation of privacy."[27]

Since this ruling, the Supreme Court has been asked to clarify exceptions to a number of issues that have been the basis of later rulings. The Supreme Court has often dealt with clarifying exceptions to the exclusionary rule and standards under which searches are legal without a warrant (1) due to **probable cause** or (2) in places where privacy could not reasonably be expected. On this first point, the Burger Court authorized a "good-faith" exception to the exclusionary rule, under which prosecutors may introduce evidence obtained illegally if they can show that the police had relied on a warrant that appeared valid but later proved to be invalid.[28] The Court allowed another exception for illegally gathered evidence that would have been discovered eventually without the illegal search.[29] The Rehnquist Court (1986–2005) further narrowed the exclusionary rule when it held in *Wyoming v. Houghton* (1999) that police who have probable cause to search an automobile for illegal substances may also search personal possessions (in this case, a purse) of passengers in the car. On the other hand, the Roberts Court ruled that police need not knock or announce their presence when entering a house with a search warrant.

However, the Court has stopped short of taking the exclusionary rule back to pre–Warren Court days. It ruled, for example, that police could not search every driver or car involved in petty traffic offenses. Thus, a bag of marijuana discovered in a search incident to a speeding ticket in *Knowles v. Iowa* (1998) was excluded as the product of an illegal search. Moreover, the Court ruled in *Kyllo v. United States* (2001) that police could not use high-technology thermal devices to search through the walls of a house to check for the presence of high-intensity lights used for growing marijuana. Justice Scalia was especially incensed, saying in his opinion that to allow such searches "would leave the homeowner at the mercy of advancing technology . . ." Finally, in 2013, the Court also ruled in *Florida v. Jardines* that bringing drug-sniffing dogs to the front door of a house was an unreasonable search as there was no probable cause to justify the search. In general, the Court has generally been more willing to protect individuals from searches inside their homes than inside their cars or in public places where the Court has consistently ruled there is a lower expectation of privacy.

**SELF-INCRIMINATION** The Warren Court was instrumental in incorporating Fifth Amendment protections against self-incrimination. It determined, for example, that the privilege not to be forced to incriminate oneself was useless at trial if the police coerced confessions long before the trial took place. To forestall "third-degree" tactics in the station house, the Court detailed a stringent set of procedural guarantees: the famous rights established in *Miranda v. Arizona* (1966). Once detained by authorities, all persons had to be informed of their rights to remain silent and to consult with an attorney. Although the Burger Court upheld *Miranda,* it allowed exceptions: it allowed the use of information obtained without "Mirandizing" suspects if the suspects took the stand in their own defense. It also allowed the use of information obtained without *Miranda* warnings if some immediate threat to public safety had justified immediate questioning and postponing warnings.[30] The Rehnquist Court went beyond these exceptions when it held that a coerced confession may be "harmless error" that does not constitute self-incrimination.[31] The Roberts Court has imposed a few new restrictions on Miranda rights. In 2010 the Court ruled that suspects have the burden of invoking their Miranda rights, and in 2013 it ruled that pre-arrest silence could be used to convict a suspect. In that case, the suspect answered some questions but not others prior to being arrested, and thus, according to the Court, his silence on a question about the murder weapon was not constitutionally protected.

**probable cause**
Legal doctrine that refers to a reasonable belief that a crime has been committed.

**"YOU HAVE THE RIGHT TO REMAIN SILENT"**

An Occupy Wall Street demonstrator in 2012 is arrested and read his rights as defined by the landmark Supreme Court ruling *Miranda v. Arizona* (1966). Though the requirement that arrestees be notified of their rights has been challenged by police departments ever since the ruling, Miranda remains solidly in place. How have police adjusted to the restrictions on their actions required by Miranda?

**capital crime**

Any crime for which death is a possible penalty.

**THE RIGHT TO COUNSEL** The Sixth Amendment's right to counsel was incorporated in two landmark cases. In *Powell v. Alabama* (1932)—the famed Scottsboro Boys prosecution—the Court ruled that legal counsel must be supplied to all indigent defendants accused of a **capital crime** (any crime in which the death penalty can be imposed). Before this decision, many poor people in the southern states, especially African Americans, had been tried for and convicted of capital crimes without the benefit of an attorney. Thirty-one years later, in *Gideon v. Wainwright* (1963), the Court ruled that defendants accused of any felony in state jurisdictions are entitled to a lawyer and that the states must supply a lawyer when a defendant cannot afford to do so. Justice Black wrote the following for a unanimous Court:

> Not only . . . precedents but also reason and reflection require us to recognize that in our adversary system of criminal justice, any person hauled into court, who is too poor to hire a lawyer, cannot be assured of a fair trial unless counsel is provided for him. This seems to be an obvious truth.

By incorporating the Sixth Amendment's guarantee of legal counsel, the Court has ensured that every criminal defendant in the United States can, at least in theory, mount a defense regardless of socioeconomic status.

**CAPITAL PUNISHMENT** The Eighth Amendment's ban on "cruel and unusual punishment" has implications for the death penalty in the United States. In *Furman v. Georgia* (1972), a split Burger Court found that the death penalty, as used in the states, constituted "cruel and unusual punishment" because the procedures by which states were sentencing people to death sentence were, in its words, "capricious and arbitrary." Responding to the Court's criticisms, Congress and 35 states passed new authorizations of the death penalty aimed at rectifying procedural problems identified by the Court. The Burger Court held in *Gregg v. Georgia* (1976), after states had changed their sentencing procedures, that capital punishment was not inherently cruel or unusual so long as procedures were nonarbitrary and nondiscriminatory. However, the Court tended to create an "obstacle course" of standards that the states had to meet if they wanted to use the death penalty. Basically, the Court insisted that defendants be given every opportunity to show mitigating circumstances so that as few convicts as possible would be killed.

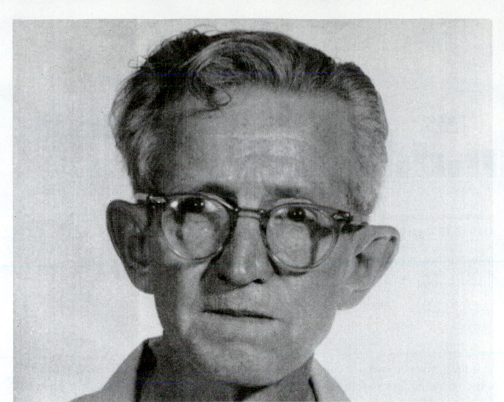

**GIDEON'S PETITION**
Clarence Gideon, who had been convicted of burglary, took the extraordinary step of writing his own appeal to the Supreme Court from his Florida prison cell using pencil and paper. He argued that his rights had been violated because he was tried without the assistance of counsel. When he was retried—this time with the help of a defense lawyer—Gideon was acquitted. Before Gideon won his case before the Supreme Court in 1963, states did not have to provide attorneys for people accused of a felony. The Court agreed with Gideon, thus incorporating this part of the Sixth Amendment. How did the Court support its decision?

The Rehnquist Court later expedited the use of the death penalty. (Some of the reasons are examined in the "Using the Framework" feature.) In *McCleskey v. Kemp* (1987), the Court said that statistical evidence that blacks who kill whites are four times more likely to be sentenced to death than whites who kill blacks is not sufficient to prove racism in death penalty cases; individual defendants, it ruled, must show that racism played a role in their specific cases. In *Penry v. Lynaugh* (1989), the Court allowed the execution of a convicted murderer who had the intelligence of a seven-year-old. In *Stanford v. Kentucky* (1989), it allowed the execution of a minor who had been convicted of murder. The Rehnquist Court also limited avenues of appeal and delay in death penalty cases. In *McCleskey v. Zant* (1991), it made delays much less likely by eliminating many means of challenging capital convictions. In *Keeney v. Tamayo-Reyes* (1992), the Court limited the ability of "death row" inmates convicted in state courts to appeal to the Supreme Court.

Part of the reason for the Court's decisions on the death penalty has to do with the political environment in the country from the middle of the 1960s to the late 1990s. During this period, urban decay increased along with the crime rate, and political leaders, driven by public opinion, were only too happy to get "tough on crime" through strict sentencing laws and increased use of the death penalty. In this environment, the Court removed most of the obstacles to its use. It is hardly surprising, then, that the number of people executed in the United States in 1999 reached its highest level (98) since 1976, when the Court reinstated the death penalty, with Texas accounting for more than one-third of the total (see Figure 15.2).[32]

Much to the surprise of seasoned observers, the Rehnquist Court began in 2002 to pull back from its unstinting support for the death penalty. In *Atkins v. Virginia* (2002), the Court followed the lead of 18 states in banning the use of the death penalty for mentally retarded defendants, saying, in Justice John Paul Stevens's majority opinion, that "a national consensus now rejects such executions as excessive and inappropriate" and that "society views mentally retarded offenders as categorically less culpable than the average criminal." In *Ring v. Arizona* (2002), the Court overruled the death sentences of more than 160 convicted killers, declaring that only juries, and not judges, can decide on the use of the death penalty for those convicted of capital crimes. In 2005, the Supreme Court struck down death penalty convictions in cases

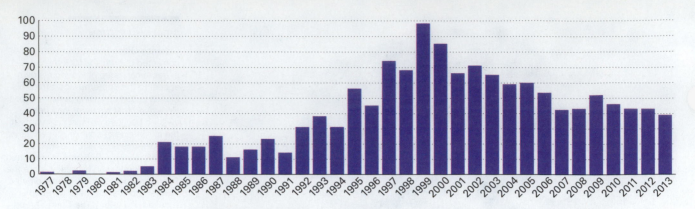

**FIGURE 15.2** EXECUTIONS IN THE UNITED STATES, 1977–2013

Fueled by fear of violent crime, executions in the United States increased dramatically from the early 1980s to the late 1990s but declined significantly after that as public concerns rose about how fairly the death penalty is used. Also, the crime rate began to drop in the mid-1990s (and has continued to drop), leading to diminished support for the death penalty.

*Source:* Bureau of Justice Statistics, "Prisoners Executed under Civil Authority in the United States, by Year, Region, and Jurisdiction, 1977–2013."

in which it was convinced that a defendant had inadequate legal defense, another in which a defendant was brought to a death penalty sentencing hearing in shackles (terming it "inherently prejudicial"), and yet another in which the defendant was under the age of 18.

The Roberts Court has sent mixed signals about how it views the death penalty. Two prominent trends in American society will likely have an effect on the Court's future decisions. The first is the continued decline in crime and the public's declining support for the death penalty.[33] The second trend is the more frequent use of DNA testing to exonerate those wrongly convicted. In 2011, Illinois banned the use of the death penalty after 13 inmates on death row were found to have been wrongly convicted, joining 17 other states (6 of which have abolished capital punishment only since 2000).[34] According to the Innocence Project, an organization that advocates for prisoners, there have been 312 convictions overturned since 1989, 18 of which were exonerations of persons on death row.[35] These results have led to a rethinking about the death penalty, based on concerns about the quality of legal defense for those accused and the fairness of the judicial system toward racial minorities.

In 2009, the Roberts Court ruled that the states and the federal government should determine the circumstances under which a prisoner can view DNA tests, though the Court did not make it entirely clear whether or not there is a constitutional right to DNA testing. In 2011, in a very narrow ruling, the Supreme Court seemed to allow those convicted of crimes slightly greater access to DNA testing.[36] Although the issue is far from settled, the Court's rulings have thus far served only to complicate matters. As a result, future rulings in this area are likely.

Other death penalty rulings illustrate the Court's efforts to strike a balance between prisoners' rights and the ability of the state to execute inmates. In 2008, the Roberts Court ruled in a case involving the state of Kentucky that the most widely used method of execution by lethal injection was constitutionally permissible, rejecting the argument that it caused unacceptable pain, as many medical professionals have claimed. In 2006, the Court ruled unanimously that states cannot deny the introduction of evidence in capital cases that suggests a person other than the defendant had committed the crime. In 2007, however, it made it easier than it had been for prosecutors to exclude from juries people who were unsure about the appropriateness and morality of the death penalty.

Even Americans who favor the death penalty in principle say they support life sentences without the possibility of parole as an alternative.[37] President George W. Bush asked Congress to look at this alternative to the death penalty in federal cases in his 2005 State of the Union message. By 2005, 28 of 37 death penalty states, including Texas, had legislated life without parole as a sentence that

# Mapping American Politics

## Violent Crime and the Death Penalty

### Introduction

It is well known that the United States has more prisoners on death row and executes more prisoners annually than any other rich democratic country. (The death penalty has been abolished in virtually all of them; in fact, abolition is a condition of membership in the European Union and the Council of Europe.) However, the use of the death penalty is not distributed uniformly across the United States. State-by-state variations are extraordinarily high. Why this is the case is not entirely obvious. One reason could be that the frequency of violent crime—including murder—varies substantially among the states. Or it could be that violent crime does not vary much, but that the responses to it by the public, prosecutors, and juries vary a great deal. Some states, that is to say, may be more inclined than others to use the ultimate penalty in response to crime. We examine the two explanations in these cartograms.

### Crime and Punishment Maps

The cartogram on top shows the rate of violent crime for each state per 100,000 people. States are expanded or diminished from their normal size by incidence of violent crime. If the violent crime rates were relatively uniform across the country, the cartogram would appear undistorted, similar to a standard map. We can see that the cartogram is only slightly distorted. To be sure, Oklahoma, Louisiana, Florida, South Carolina, Tennessee, Maryland, and Delaware are enlarged a bit because they suffer from more violent crime than other states, and California, Texas, and New York are smaller because their crime rates are lower than those of other states. Nevertheless, the variation among the states is not great. In the cartogram on the bottom, in contrast, each state is expanded or diminished by how many prisoners it has on death row per 100,000 people (the number of annual executions in the

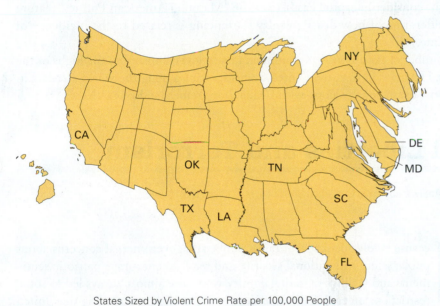

States Sized by Violent Crime Rate per 100,000 People

Standard US Map

States Sized by Prisoners on Death Row per 100,000 People

*(Continued)*

United States is not high enough to allow for statistical analysis of the sort being used here). This cartogram suggests that the imposition of capital sentences has little to do with levels of violent crime and much more to do with state-by-state differences in political cultures, legal codes, prosecutorial practices, and jury behaviors. States that are especially prone to impose death penalty sentences include many states of the Deep South (Texas, Mississippi, Arkansas, Alabama, South Carolina, and Georgia), as well as Nevada, Missouri, Oregon, Rhode Island, Connecticut, Maryland, and Delaware. Relative to their violent crime rates, Minnesota, Wisconsin, Maine, and Vermont have few people on death row, and Washington and California are quite low as well.

**What Do You Think?**

Why is it acceptable, or unacceptable, that the penalty for a crime in one state might be different from that in another state? What kinds of federal statutes or guidelines would ensure national uniformity in sentencing for felony crimes, including the imposition of the death penalty? Or should the people in each state be free, as they are now, to treat crime in a way that seems most appropriate to them? How about your state? Does it have a relatively high death row population or a low one? Why do you think that might be the case?

**SOURCES:** U.S. Bureau of the Census, *Statistical Abstract of the United States, 2010*, Table 297 (violent crime); and Bureau of Justice Statistics, "Prisoners under Sentence of Death, by Region, Jurisdiction, and Race, 2007 and 2008."

---

juries might consider in capital cases. (See the "Mapping American Politics" feature for a consideration of how death penalty sentencing is related to the incidence of violent crime.)

The number of executions has continued to stay low compared to the highs of the late 1990s. Having said that, the United States remains among the world's leaders in the use of the death penalty along with China, Iran, Yemen, and North Korea.[38]

# Civil Liberties and Terrorism

**15.4** Analyze how concerns about terrorism may affect civil liberties

Because involvement in war raises public and governmental concerns about public safety and national security and tends to encourage patriotic sentiments and feelings of national unity, wars have almost always led to some restrictions on civil liberties in democratic countries, including the United States, particularly for those who vocally dissent from the war effort and those who seem to be associated with the enemy in one way or another.[39] Note, for example, the Sedition Act of 1798, which made criticism of government officials and their policies off limits, the use of military tribunals for civilians during the Civil War, the Red Scare following World War I, the forced internment of Japanese Americans during World War II, and the McCarthy anticommunist hysteria in the early years of the Cold War with the Soviet Union.[40]

## ☐ Bush Administration Policies

Actions by President Bush to fight what he and others called the war on terrorism produced significant restrictions on civil liberties in the United States. Many Americans believed that what had been done was a reasonable price to pay in perilous times.[41] Civil libertarians worried and continue to worry that these restrictions represent a serious long-term danger for American freedom. Some of the controversial policies adopted under President Bush as part of efforts to combat and prevent terrorism include:

• The USA PATRIOT Act, passed soon after the 9/11 attacks on the United States, gave the federal government expanded powers to use wiretapping and electronic surveillance, impose stricter penalties for harboring or financing terrorists,

# Using the FRAMEWORK

## Why did executions in the United States peak in the 1990s, then decline?

**Background:** Between the reinstatement of the death penalty by the Supreme Court in 1976 and the end of 2001, 737 inmates were executed in the United States. Of the total, 619 (84 percent) took place in the 1990s. In 1999, 98 executions were carried out, the highest total since 1951, with Texas, Virginia, and Florida leading the way. During the first decade of the twenty-first century, however, the number of executions declined. By 2013, the number had fallen to 39. We can understand better why this is so by looking broadly at how structural, political linkage, and governmental factors have influenced the death penalty issue.

**Government Action**

Illinois, New Jersey, and New York join 12 existing non-death-penalty states by the mid-2000s. → Fewer inmates on death row. → The number of executions declines from its high point in 1999.

**Government**

Between 1976 and 2002, Supreme Court supports most state efforts to reinstate the death penalty. → After that, Supreme Court tightens some rules on the use of the death penalty. → Juries increasingly choose "life without parole" as alternative to death penalty when available as an option. → Prosecutors after mid-2000s less willing to ask for imposition of the death penalty. → Many state governments in financial difficulties because of the Great Recession begin to rethink death penalty given high costs of death rows.

**Political Linkage**

Long history of public support of death penalty; increases as crime wave hits. → Political candidates, in response, run on "get tough on crime" platform. → Some advocacy and religious groups come out against death penalty as number of executions increases in 1990s. → A number of death row inmates are exonerated by DNA evidence, leading many to worry about fairness of capital punishment sentencing.

**Structure**

For the most part, states are responsible for criminal statute writing, prosecution, and punishment of law-breakers. → Though the Constitution prohibits "cruel and unusual punishment," there is little evidence that the framers considered the death penalty to be such. → Violent crime increased in 1970s and 1980s, but decreases thereafter. → Advances made in the science of DNA. → Increasing numbers of countries ban death penalty.

monitor the bank accounts and e-mail of suspect individuals and organizations, turn away from our borders anyone who endorses terrorism, and detain without a hearing any noncitizens living in the United States whom the attorney general deemed to be a threat to national security.

- By executive order, the president expanded the use of a little-known and little-used law created in the 1970s to give the FBI secret authorization to access personal information about U.S. citizens, including phone and financial records and information from businesses' customer databases. Between 2002 and 2005, almost 150,000 such "national security letters" were issued.[42] Under terms of the law, people were given no notice of the request, firms were obligated to comply, and no one was permitted to make public the fact that such requests had been made. Issuance of these letters required approval by the Office of Intelligence Policy and Review in the Justice Department; there was no judicial oversight.[43]

- The president authorized the indefinite detention without hearings of American citizens discovered to have been fighting against U.S. troops in Afghanistan or aiding Al Qaeda, designating them "enemy combatants."

- The administration instituted secret deportation hearings for detainees held on immigration violations and indefinite detention without a hearing for people designated "material witnesses" in terrorism cases.

- The president authorized a vast eavesdropping and data-mining operation by the National Security Agency on the electronic and wire communications of American citizens. Under terms of the Foreign Intelligence Surveillance Act, NSA eavesdropping on American citizens requires a warrant granted by a special court. When it was revealed in late 2005 that the NSA had been doing this without warrants, the president claimed he had the power to do so as the commander in chief charged with protecting the country. He also pointed to congressional legislation authorizing the president to "use all necessary and appropriate force" to pursue those involved in 9/11 and to prevent future attacks.

Despite strong criticism of the USA PATRIOT Act by civil libertarians, it was renewed by Congress in 2006, with only minor changes in its original provisions. In 2008, Congress passed a bill proposed by President Bush to allow more latitude in the use of wiretaps and to immunize phone companies against lawsuits for their cooperation with the government. That the USA PATRIOT Act was renewed with so few changes and that a Democratic Congress gave a Republican president more authority to use wiretaps are probably testament to the public's strong support for government actions that prevent terrorist attacks. By a 40–36 margin in 2009, Americans said they are more concerned that the government has not gone far enough in protecting the country as compared with not going far enough to protect civil liberties.[44]

## ☐ Obama Administration Policies

Though Barack Obama campaigned against many of these Bush-era policies and made some stabs at improving the civil liberties climate—he released some documents related to the treatment of detainees, dropped the designation "enemy combatants" for people held without trial, drastically cut back the use of national security letters to gather information, and ended the use of most harsh interrogation techniques—he ended up continuing many of the policies bequeathed to him by the Bush administration. Congressional Republicans blocked his efforts to close the prison at Guantanamo and to try 9/11 conspirators in civilian courts. But he also fought efforts to reveal information about secret NSA wiretapping, and he asked Congress to reauthorize the PATRIOT Act, perhaps thinking that it had proved effective in preventing terrorist attacks (see the "Can Government Do Anything Well?" feature on this issue). His administration also successfully pressed the courts to prevent terrorism suspects at U.S. bases abroad from having access to American federal courts to review their confinement. In 2011, he signed a defense appropriations bill that had Republican-sponsored riders attached to it stripping the FBI, federal prosecutors, and the federal courts of powers to arrest and prosecute suspected terrorists, handing these off to the military.

# Can Government Do Anything Well?

## The USA PATRIOT Act and protecting citizens against terrorist attacks

There has been no major terrorist attack on American soil since 9/11. There have been several close calls, to be sure. There was, for example, the Nigerian man on a flight from Amsterdam to Detroit who tried to explode a bomb over Detroit in late 2009. In 2010, a car bomb placed near Times Square by Faisal Shahzad ignited but failed to detonate. In that same year, large plastic explosives placed by Al Qaeda operatives were discovered on two cargo planes bound for the United States. There also have been others that managed to kill or came close to killing several people in the name of religion, though no links to terrorist organizations have been discovered regarding them. In 2009, a Muslim Army psychiatrist, likely mentally unstable, gunned down 13 soldiers at Ft. Hood in Texas. A Muslim convert claiming he was trying to stop a war by the United States against Islam shot two soldiers at a military recruiting station in Little Rock, Arkansas. Also in 2010, a pipe bomb exploded in a mosque in Jacksonville, Florida, but no one was hurt.

All in all, this seems to represent a solid record of achievement on the part of the federal government in protecting the American people since 9/11 against jihadist organizations that say they want to do great harm on American soil. As of this writing in 2014, with the exception of the Boston Marathon bombing in 2013 that killed 3 people, this has not happened. Why this record? Those who credit federal government efforts point to a variety of things. There is the stepped-up intelligence capacities of the NSA, the CIA, and the uniformed services. There are the operations by Special Forces and unmanned drone aircraft that capture or kill leaders of jihadist organizations in Pakistan, Afghanistan, Yemen, and Somalia. There was the preventive detention and harsh interrogation of suspects at Guantanamo and other prisons. And, there is the PATRIOT Act, which allows security agencies of the government to track potential terrorist threats by gaining access to the financial, telecommunications, business, library, and other records of American citizens who may be plotting or be in contact with others plotting attacks. Much of this, to say the least, has been highly controversial, with widespread concern that these initiatives are damaging our liberties. We focus here on the PATRIOT Act (described in more detail in this chapter).

*Support for the claim that the government's use of the PATRIOT Act has been effective without undermining the civil liberties of Americans:*

- The world remains a dangerous place and intelligence and police agencies need tools to stay ahead of those trying to do harm to the country.

- In war—which this is—there is always some trade-off between civil liberties and security.

- Compared to the civil liberties trade-offs of the Alien and Sedition period, the Civil War, World War I, and World War II, the current retreat of some civil liberties is mild, affecting few Americans.

- The Act simply gives counterintelligence agencies the same powers that police have in investigating criminal cases.

- The Act specifies that Americans cannot be investigated for exercising their First Amendment rights.

*Rejection of the claim that the government's use of the PATRIOT Act has been effective without undermining the civil liberties of Americans:*

- The operating presumption of federal authorities today is that purported terrorists are guilty until proven innocent; people are detained under "material witness" claims or deported by immigration authorities on the slimmest of evidence of terrorist involvement.

- There is no real judicial oversight of federal agency requests for bank and library records; the Foreign Intelligence Surveillance Court routinely grants requests, which are overused.

- A 2007 report from the inspector general of the Justice Department said that the FBI used tools of the PATRIOT Act against many people who had no evident association with terrorism.

- People can be and have been prosecuted for "material support" of terrorist organizations when giving speeches or writing articles in support of such organizations, violating many peoples' conception of free speech.

- Terrorists only need to succeed once; the American people cannot be assured that they will be protected against future attacks because of the PATRIOT Act.

(Continued)

What do you think about the past, present, and future role of the government in preventing terrorist attacks on the United States?

- The government has done an excellent job of protecting Americans without undermining their liberties.
- The government has done an excellent job of protecting Americans, though there has been a necessary price to pay in diminished liberty.
- The government has done an excellent job of protecting Americans, but the cost in undermining our liberty has been too high.
- There is no way of knowing how effective the government will be in protecting Americans against a terrorist attack.

How would you defend your position to a fellow student? What would be your main line of argument? What evidence do you believe best supports your position? For help in developing your argument, please refer to Geoffrey R. Stone, *Perilous Times: Free Speech in Wartime* (New York: W. W. Norton, 2004).

## ☐ The Court Responds

Naturally, the courts have been wrestling with the issue of the proper balance between national security and civil liberties at a time when people feel legitimately threatened by terrorism. For the most part, they have supported government national security concerns, but they have, at the same time, rejected overly broad claims of presidential war powers. In a stunning blow to the Bush administration's claim of extraordinary executive power in wartime, for example, the Supreme Court ruled in 2004 (*Hamdi v. Rumsfeld*) that both foreigners and American citizens detained as "enemy combatants" have a right to a hearing to contest the basis of their detentions. In her opinion in the case, Justice Sandra Day O'Connor reminded everyone, "We have long since made clear that a state of war is not a blank check for the president when it comes to the rights of the nation's citizens." In 2007, the Ninth Circuit Court ruled that enemy combatants could not be held indefinitely in military detention in the United States.

The Roberts Court has also been troubled by the legal treatment of foreign detainees. In 2006, the Court ruled that all detainees held at Guantanamo Bay and elsewhere are entitled to protections guaranteed under the Geneva Convention. It also ruled that the military tribunal-style hearings used at Guantanamo were unacceptable because they had not been authorized by Congress. In response, Congress passed the Military Commissions Act of 2006, which set up a system of tribunals but, almost provocatively, added language to the effect that no court would be allowed to consider habeas corpus petitions from foreigners held as enemy combatants. Perhaps seeing this "habeas" provision as a direct challenge by the legislative branch to the independent powers of the judicial branch, the Court rejected this in 2008 when it ruled that foreign detainees held at Guantanamo have a constitutional right to take their cases to the federal courts to challenge their detention.

With the exception of those instances when the executive branch seems to be challenging the authority and legitimacy of the judicial branch, the Court has granted broad leeway to the government in fighting terrorism. In the first test of the constitutionality of the PATRIOT Act's "material support" provision, for example, the Court ruled in 2010 that the government has very broad authority and can prosecute people for seemingly benign activities—for example, providing legal services and expert advice to government-designated terrorist organizations seeking to overturn their designation.

The direction that civil liberties will take as a result of the effort to protect the United States against terrorism is hard to predict. Challenges to many policies are making their way through the court system. For example, a Colorado man is currently mounting a legal challenge to the NSA's warrantless surveillance program, but even if his case reaches the Supreme Court it is unclear how the justices will rule.[45] Ultimately it is likely that some civil liberties restrictions will exist for the duration of the campaign to contain terrorism, and that the severity of these restrictions will be directly related to the degree to which the American people feel afraid that further attacks will occur and their judgment about how much freedom they are willing to trade for security. So far, we have not taken as harsh a line as several other rich democracies, including Australia, Canada, and Great Britain, which have instituted the practice of preventive detention—incarceration of terrorism suspects who are citizens or otherwise legally in the country without charges or hearings—and placed strict limits on subversive speech.[46] Americans' attitudes about these matters appear to shift in response to world events. In the wake of highly publicized revelations that the NSA was gathering data on millions of citizens, a nationwide poll conducted early in 2014 found that 44 percent of the public said the government had gone too far in restricting the average person's civil liberties compared with 39 percent who said that the government had not gone far enough. In the wake of the sudden rise of the Islamic State in the Middle East, however, these numbers have reversed. In September 2014, 50 percent of Americans said that the government had not gone far enough to protect the country.[47]

# Using the DEMOCRACY STANDARD

## Has the state of American freedom improved?

Both the framers and more recent democratic theorists are committed to civil liberties, but each has taken a somewhat different approach concerning how civil liberties might be enjoyed by Americans. Recall that the framers focused their attention on the potential for violations of liberty by the national government and paid little attention to the states, believing that freedom in the states was well protected. Note as well that many of the framers and most political leaders who followed during the long course of the nineteenth century seemed most concerned about protecting property rights, or economic liberty. Civil liberties, broadly understood, became widely available to Americans only in the twentieth century in response to the spread of democratic aspirations in politics and of democratic ideas in the culture, the efforts of individuals and groups to struggle for liberty, and a federal judiciary that finally agreed to nationalize most of the protections of the Bill of Rights.

There has been an enormous expansion of freedom in the United States; the freedoms of speech, association, press, conscience, and religion, as well as the rights of those accused of a crime, are far more extensively developed and protected in the United States today than they were in the past. However, we must also recognize a serious flaw in the current status of civil liberties. While civil liberties today are fairly well protected against intrusions by government, not all people have the capacities and resources to use their liberties effectively. Substantial income and wealth inequality often creates political inequality. Thus, only a privileged few can make substantial campaign contributions; form political lobbying organizations; and run ads for their favorite candidates, parties, and issues.

We cannot say with total confidence, moreover, that freedom cannot and will not be violated by government at some point in the future. In the past, waves of hysteria among political leaders and the public have led to the violation of civil liberties. Given the right conditions—war, civil unrest, economic depression—the same might happen again. Many worry, with some justification, that the war on terrorism may represent just such a setting for the suppression of civil liberties. What makes the possibility especially troubling is the indeterminate time period of such a war. One can imagine it stretching on into the indefinite future. We can only hope that such a suppression of civil liberties will not happen and that people will struggle for democracy if it does.

# Review the Chapter

## Civil Liberties in the Constitution

**15.1** Identify civil liberties protections in the Constitution, p. 461

The formal foundation of American liberties is found in the Constitution and its amendments, particularly the Bill of Rights and the Fourteenth Amendment, but the degree to which civil liberties have been enjoyed in practice during our history has depended upon the actions of courts, the behavior of government officials, and the struggle for democracy by the American people.

## Rights and Liberties in the Nineteenth Century

**15.2** Trace the evolution of civil liberties in the nineteenth century, p. 461

During the nineteenth century, the Supreme Court concerned itself mainly with protecting property rights. Somewhat belatedly, it used the Fourteenth Amendment to make the protections in the Constitution and the Bill of Rights apply to state and local governments. This considerably expanded Americans' enjoyment of the familiar liberties of expression, association, press, and religion.

The Court's changing interpretation of the meaning of liberty was influenced by changing attitudes among the public and elected officials, as well as by the nation's leading law journals.

## Nationalization of the Bill of Rights

**15.3** Outline the liberties guaranteed by the Bill of Rights and their gradual application to the states by the Supreme Court, p. 465

American history has witnessed an expansion of the boundaries of liberties, with the Supreme Court gradually incorporating the Bill of Rights based on the Fourteenth Amendment under terms described in a footnote in the *Carolene* case. This footnote suggested that the Court would apply "strict scrutiny" to government actions that seemed to violate democracy, failed to offer equal protection to minorities, or prevented the enjoyment of liberties spelled out in the Bill of Rights.

The broadest expansion of due process protections and equal protection came during the Warren and Burger Court years.

The expansion of the rights of the accused was always a hotly disputed political issue, and the conservative orientation of the Rehnquist and Roberts Courts has resulted in the reversal of many of the due process innovations of the Warren and Burger Courts. The Roberts Court has also ruled against a number of government efforts to expand civil rights protections to racial minorities.

## Civil Liberties and Terrorism

**15.4** Analyze how concerns about terrorism may affect civil liberties, p. 486

The fight against terrorism has resulted in the widespread surveillance of American citizens and restrictions of the civil liberties of noncitizens living legally in the United States. How long these restrictions remain in place will depend on the severity of terrorist threats and public perceptions about these threats.

# Learn the Terms

civil liberties, p. 461
habeas corpus, p. 461
bill of attainder, p. 461
ex post facto law, p. 461
economic liberty, p. 461
full faith and credit, p. 463
contract clause, p. 463
due process clause, p. 464

selective incorporation, p. 465
privileges and immunities clause, p. 466
equal protection clause, p. 466
nationalizing, p. 466
incorporation, p. 466
ordinary scrutiny, p. 466
strict scrutiny, p. 466

prior restraint, p. 471
obscenity, p. 472
free exercise clause, p. 473
establishment clause, p. 474
exclusionary rule, p. 480
probable cause, p. 481
capital crime, p. 482

# Test Yourself

Answer key begins on page T-1.

**15.1** Identify civil liberties protections in the Constitution

1. In this amendment, citizens are protected from double jeopardy, or being prosecuted more than once for the same crime.

   a. Second Amendment
   b. Third Amendment
   c. Fourth Amendment
   d. Fifth Amendment
   e. Sixth Amendment

**15.2** Trace the evolution of civil liberties in the nineteenth century

2. This clause obligated each state to recognize contracts and other legal obligations entered into by its citizens with citizens or legal bodies in other states.

   a. Takings clause
   b. Full faith and credit clause
   c. Fundamental liberty clause
   d. Rebellion clause
   e. Contract clause

**15.3** Outline the liberties guaranteed by the Bill of Rights and their gradual application to the states by the Supreme Court

3. The right to privacy is covered in this amendment:

   a. The First Amendment
   b. The Second Amendment
   c. The First and Second Amendment
   d. It is not covered in the Bill of Rights
   e. It is implied in almost every Amendment

**15.4** Analyze how concerns about terrorism may affect civil liberties

4. Congress passed this act that set up a system of tribunals for foreign detainees, but added in that no court would be allowed to consider habeas corpus petitions from foreigners held as enemy combatants.

   a. Military Commissions Act of 2006
   b. Roberts–Guantanamo Act of 2006
   c. National Citizens Act of 2007
   d. The USA PATRIOT Act
   e. Civil Liberties and Terrorism Act of 2006

# Explore Further

## INTERNET SOURCES

The American Civil Liberties Union **www.aclu.org**
Website of the long-time defender of civil liberties in the United States.

Bureau of Justice Statistics **www.bjs.gov**
Official statistics on crimes, trials, incarceration rates, and executions are available at this site.

The Cato Institute **www.cato.org**
A comprehensive site covering civil liberties issues from the conservative libertarian point of view.

The Death Penalty Information Center **www.deathpenaltyinfo.org**
Information on the death penalty around the world.

Findlaw Supreme Court Opinions **www.findlaw.com/casecode/ supreme.html**
Find historical and contemporary Supreme Court decisions and opinions on civil liberties at this site.

First Amendment Center **www.firstamendmentcenter.org**
Rich source of history and recent developments related to First Amendment freedoms.

Financial Crimes Enforcement Network **www.fincen.gov/ statutes_regs/patriot/index.html**
This site contains the official wording and full text of the USA PATRIOT Act.

The Bill of Rights **billofrightsinstitute.org/founding-documents/ bill-of-rights/**
A site dedicated to the Bill of Rights and the Constitution, along with full text of both of these documents.

## SUGGESTIONS FOR FURTHER READING

Abraham, Henry J., and Barbara A. Perry. *Freedom and the Court,* 8th ed. Lawrence: University of Kansas Press, 2003.
A trusted introduction to the study of civil rights and liberties for more than 30 years.

Barker, Lucius J., Twiley W. Barker Jr., Michael W. Combs, Kevin L. Lyles, and H. W. Perry Jr. *Civil Liberties and the Constitution: Cases and Commentaries.* New York: Longman, 2011.
Encyclopedic overview of American civil liberties presented in an engaging style.

Epstein, Lee, and Thomas G. Walker. *Rights, Liberties, and Justice.* Washington, DC: CQ Press, 2010.
An exhaustive and compelling examination of the rulings that have shaped the status of civil liberties in the United States.

Fallon, Richard. *The Dynamic Constitution: An Introduction to American Constitutional Law.* New York: Cambridge University Press, 2005.
An accessible introduction to all aspects of American constitutional law.

Lewis, Anthony. *Freedom for the Thought We Hate: A Biography of the First Amendment.* New York: Basic Books, 2007.
A celebration of the expansion of First Amendment freedoms and the story of how it happened.

Stone, Geoffrey R. *Perilous Times: Free Speech in Wartime.* New York: W. W. Norton, 2004.
A history of the tension between free speech and national security during American conflicts.

Zimring, Franklin. *The Contradictions of American Capital Punishment.* New York: Oxford University Press, 2003.
Examines the question of why Americans so strongly support the death penalty compared with people in other rich democracies.

# 16

# Civil Rights: The Struggle for Political Equality

## THE RETURN OF SEGREGATED SCHOOLS

**"I** don't know why they left," said one fourth-grader at Reid Park Elementary School in Charlotte, North Carolina. "Maybe they didn't like it here."[1] She was referring to the virtual disappearance of white children at her school where, only one year earlier, about one-third of her schoolmates had been white. What was happening at Reid Park Elementary was happening all over the South at the turn of the new century. Fifty years after the Supreme Court had ruled in *Brown v. Board of Education* (1954) that "separate but equal" was unconstitutional, schools were becoming more segregated. By 2003, only 29 percent of black children in the South were in schools that were majority white, a decrease from 44 percent as recently as 1988, and it has stayed that way ever since.[2]

For those Americans committed to a racially integrated society, there was much to be proud of in the record of desegregation of public education in the United States after the *Brown* decision, especially in the South where school segregation was official policy from the early twentieth century until the Court's 1954 decision. After a slow start for a few years following *Brown*, school integration took off in the mid-1960s and gained steadily until it reached its peak in the late 1980s. By 1988, only one in four black children in the South were in schools

**SCHOOL RESEGREGATION** Resegregation has occurred in many schools in the South where cort-ordered integration plans have been lifted. During the 1970s and 1980s, under court-ordered plans, the South had more thoroughly integrated its schools than any other region of the country. Is this a problem that requires federal action or is it a matter best addressed by the states and localities?

that were 90 to 100 percent black, a far cry from the pre-*Brown* years when virtually all black children were in such schools. During the 1990s, however, the trend reversed all over the South, with more black children going to school where there were few whites or none at all and where white children had less contact with African American children than in many years.[3]

As troubling as the picture might be, the South does better on the school integration front than other parts of the country. In the Northeast, for example, more than one-half of all African American children are in schools that are 90 to 100 percent black, closely followed by the states in the Midwest. In addition, black children are least exposed to white children in public schools in New York, Illinois, Michigan, California, Maryland, and New Jersey and are most exposed to their white counterparts in the South and the border states. And, as in the South, school segregation in every region of the nation has become more pronounced.[4] By 2010, a typical black student in a public school in the United States went to a school that was 29.2 percent white, down from 36.2 percent in 1981.

So why did the trend in the South toward a more integrated public school system first level off, then recede during the 1990s and 2000s? The answer is fairly straightforward: The federal courts, following the lead of the Supreme Court in *Dowell v. Oklahoma City* (1991)—which ruled that school districts that had made lengthy good-faith efforts to end the effects of previously legal school segregation in their jurisdictions had fulfilled their constitutional obligations for equal protection of the races in education—began to lift court-ordered desegregation plans that required busing and other methods to integrate schools across local jurisdictions. About 40 school districts over the past 20 years have been relieved of such orders, and it is precisely in these districts where the reversals in school integration trends are most evident.

But that still leaves the question of why lifting federal court orders would lead to such a development. Again, the answer is fairly straightforward: when most whites and most blacks live in racially homogeneous neighborhoods, local neighborhood schools, absent busing or other student assignment strategies designed to foster integration, will also be racially homogeneous.[5]

It remains to be seen what the outcomes of these changes will be. Many whites and African Americans believe that integrated schooling, whether achieved voluntarily or under court order, is important for children's educational achievement and for teaching tolerance in a racially diverse society. However, other whites and African Americans believe that integration by itself does little to increase academic achievement, and that court-ordered busing mainly leads to intergroup tensions and wasted tax money. Many African Americans who think this way have become attracted to the idea of school vouchers that allow children to use public funds to go to either a public or private school as a way to improve schools in predominantly black neighborhoods. Many others are being attracted to charter schools as an alternative within public schools. The thinking here is that competition for students between public and private schools, as well as competition between different kinds of public schools, will force schools to offer a better educational product.

Civil rights are government guarantees of equality for people in the United States regarding judicial proceedings, the exercise of political rights, treatment by public officials, and access to and enjoyment of the benefits of government programs. (The terms *equal citizenship* and *civil rights* often are used interchangeably, which is our practice in this textbook.) The expansion of civil rights protections for African Americans as well as for other racial, ethnic, and religious minorities and for women, gays, and lesbians is one of the great achievements of American history. These changes on the civil rights front have not come easily or quickly; it took the struggle of millions of Americans to force change from political leaders and government institutions. The result has been a significant democratization of the republican constitutional system of the framers. As this opening story suggests, however, the expansion of civil rights protection in the United States is neither complete nor free of problems and controversy. And, there continue to be setbacks.

## Thinking Critically About This Chapter

This chapter is about civil rights in the United States and how politics and public policies have affected the status of equal protection and equal treatment for all Americans.

## Using the Framework

In this chapter, you will see that the meaning of civil rights has changed over the course of American history, and you will learn how structural, political linkage, and governmental factors, taken together, explain that change.

## Using the Democracy Standard

In this chapter, you will learn how civil rights are at the very center of our understanding of democracy in the United States. You will see how the struggle for democracy helped expand civil rights protections. You also will see how the expansion of civil rights has enhanced formal political equality in the United States, one of the basic foundations of a democratic political order.

**civil rights**
Guarantees of equal treatment by government officials regarding political rights, the judicial system, and public programs.

16.1

16.2

16.3

16.4

# Civil Rights Before the Twentieth Century

**16.1** Trace the evolution of civil rights protections for racial minorities and women to the twentieth century

**C**ivil rights for racial minorities and women were a comparatively late development in the United States, and most major advances were not evident until well into the twentieth century. In this section, we look at the period before the expansion of civil rights.

## ☐ An Initial Absence of Civil Rights

Neither the original Constitution nor the Bill of Rights said anything about equality beyond insisting that all Americans are equally entitled to due process in the courts.[6] Indeed, the word *equality* does not appear in the Constitution at all. Nor did state constitutions offer much in the way of guaranteeing equality other than equality before the law. Americans in the late eighteenth and early nineteenth centuries seemed more interested in protecting individuals against government than in guaranteeing certain political rights through government.[7] For most racial or ethnic minorities and women, equality eluded constitutional protection until the twentieth century, although the groundwork was laid earlier.

   The inequality of African Americans and women before the Civil War is quite striking. In the South, African Americans lived in slavery, with no rights at all. Outside the South, although a few states allowed African Americans to vote, the number of states doing so actually declined as the Civil War approached, even as universal white male suffrage was spreading. In many places outside the slave South, African Americans were denied entry into certain occupations, required to post bonds guaranteeing their good behavior, denied the right to sit on juries, and occasionally threatened and harassed by mobs when they tried to vote or to petition the government. Chief Justice Roger Taney, in *Dred Scott v. Sandford* (1857), went so far as to claim that the Founders believed that blacks had no rights that whites or government were bound to honor or respect. As for women, no state allowed them to vote, few allowed them to sit on juries, and a handful even denied them the right to own property or enter into contracts.

Many African Americans and women refused to play a passive political role, however, even though the pre–Civil War period was not conducive to their participation in politics. African Americans, for instance, voted in elections where they were allowed, helped organize the Underground Railroad to smuggle slaves out of the South, and were prominent in the abolitionist movement against slavery. Both black and white women played an important role in the abolitionist movement—the antislavery speaking tours of Angelina and Sarah Grimké caused something of a scandal in the 1840s when women's participation in public affairs was considered improper—and a few began to write extensively on the need for women's emancipation and legal and political equality. In 1848, Elizabeth Cady Stanton issued her call for a convention on women's rights to be held at the village of Seneca Falls, New York. The Declaration of Sentiments and Resolutions issued by the delegates to the convention stands as one of the landmarks in women's struggle for political equality in the United States:

> *All men and women are created equal . . . but the history of mankind is a history of repeated injuries and usurpations on the part of man toward woman, having in direct object the establishment of a direct tyranny over her. . . . [We demand] that women have immediate admission to all the rights and privileges which belong to them as citizens of the United States.*

## ☐ The Civil War Amendments

In the years following the Civil War, Congress passed a number of constitutional amendments that essentially created the foundations for civil rights as we understand them today.

**ADVOCATING FOR WOMEN'S RIGHTS**

In 1848, Elizabeth Cady Stanton helped organize the Seneca Falls Convention on women's rights. The resulting Declaration of Sentiments and Resolutions was patterned after the Declaration of Independence, stating that "all men and women are created equal," and included a list of the injustices of men against women. Stanton remained an activist for many years, helping to found the National Women's Suffrage Association in 1896 to press for the vote for women, and became the first president of the National American Woman Suffrage Association in 1890. Why did it take so many years of such outspoken activism for women to finally be granted the right to vote?

- The Thirteenth Amendment to the Constitution, ratified in 1865, outlawed slavery throughout the United States, settling once and for all the most divisive issue of our early history as a nation.

- The Fourteenth Amendment (1868) reversed *Dred Scott* by making all people who are born or naturalized in the United States, black or white, citizens both of the United States and of the states in which they reside. To secure the rights and liberties of recently freed slaves, Article I of the amendment further provided that "no State shall make or enforce any law which shall abridge the privileges or immunities of citizens of the United States" (the **privileges and immunities clause**); "nor shall any State deprive any person of life, liberty, or property, without due process of law" (the **due process clause**); "nor deny to any person within its jurisdiction the equal protection of the laws" (the **equal protection clause**). As imposing as this constitutional language sounds, the Supreme Court would soon transform it into protections, not for the civil rights of African Americans, women, or Native Americans, but for business firms.

- The Fifteenth Amendment (1870) said states could not prevent people from voting on the grounds of "race, color, or previous condition of servitude" (former slaves).

**UNDERMINING THE CIVIL WAR AMENDMENTS** In the two decades following their passage, the Supreme Court blocked the promise of equal citizenship for African Americans found in the Civil War amendments. During this time, when many Americans in the northern states had grown weary of efforts to reconstruct the South and uplift and protect former slaves, white supremacists were regaining control in many areas of the South, and racist attitudes were widespread across the nation, the Supreme Court struck against key provisions of the amendments. For example, the *Slaughterhouse Cases* (1873) rendered the privileges and immunities clause virtually meaningless. Writing for the Court, Justice Samuel Miller found that the clause did not guarantee citizenship rights against violations by state governments, only against violations by the federal government. The Court ruled that it was powerless to protect African Americans against abuses by state governments, including barriers to voting and office holding. Within five years of its passage, then, this section of the Fourteenth Amendment was seriously compromised by the Court, foiling the attempt by the post–Civil War radical Republican Congress to amend the Constitution in favor of equality.

Though the equal protection clause of the Fourteenth Amendment survived the *Slaughterhouse Cases,* it soon lost all practical meaning as a guarantor of equality for African Americans. First, the Court ruled in the *Civil Rights Cases* (1883) that the Fourteenth Amendment gave Congress no power to prohibit discrimination unless it was practiced by state government. "Equal protection of the laws" did not, therefore, preclude race discrimination by private owners or managers of restaurants, theaters, hotels, and other public accommodations. Then the Court made even government-sponsored discrimination constitutional in *Plessy v. Ferguson* (1896). The Court said that the states could separate the races in intrastate railways if they provided "equal" facilities for the races. This ruling gave the doctrine of "separate but equal" full constitutional status and legitimacy, and provided the legal underpinnings for the segregation of the races in nearly every area of life throughout the South. This system of racial segregation—usually referred to as **Jim Crow**—would remain in force until *Plessy was* overturned in *Brown v. Board of Education of Topeka* (1954) more than half a century later.

The Fifteenth Amendment's voting guarantees were also rendered ineffectual—this time by a variety of devices invented to prevent African Americans from voting in the former states of the Confederacy. The **poll tax** was a tax required of all voters in many states, and it kept many African Americans away from the polls, given their desperate economic situation in the South in the late nineteenth and early twentieth centuries. Several states required voters to pass a **literacy test** devised

16.1

16.2

16.3

16.4

**privileges and immunities clause**
The portion of Article IV, Section 2 of the Constitution which states which citizens from out of state have the same legal rights as local citizens in any state; also in the Fourteenth Amendment assuring national citizenship.

**due process clause**
The section of the Fourteenth Amendment that prohibits states from depriving anyone of life, liberty, or property "without due process of law," a guarantee against arbitrary or unfair government action.

**equal protection clause**
The section of the Fourteenth Amendment requiring states to provide equal treatment to all people within their boundaries.

**Jim Crow**
Popular term for the system of state-sanctioned racial segregation that existed in the American South until the middle of the twentieth century.

**poll tax**
A tax to be paid as a condition of voting; used in the South to keep African Americans away from the polls.

**literacy test**
A device used by the southern states to prevent African Americans from voting before the passage of the Voting Rights Act of 1965, which banned its use; usually involved interpretation of a section of a state's constitution.

**JIM CROW**

For more than half a century, until the Court's 1954 *Brown* decision, the civil rights movement, and the 1964 Civil Rights Act ended it, the Jim Crow system of racial segregation of public facilities was virtually universal in the southern states. Should states have been left alone to address how to change this system or was federal intervention essential?

**grandfather clause**
A device that allowed whites who had failed the literacy test to vote anyway by extending the franchise to anyone whose ancestors had voted prior to 1867.

and administered by local officials (see Table 16.1). The evaluation of test results was entirely up to local officials, who rarely passed blacks, even those with a college education or a PhD. If white voters failed the literacy test, many states allowed them to vote anyway under the **grandfather clause**, which provided that anyone whose ancestors had voted prior to 1867 could vote as well. Because the ancestors

**TABLE 16.1** SELECTED ITEMS FROM THE ALABAMA LITERACY TEST

These 10 questions, part of the 68-question Alabama Literacy Test, still in use in the 1950s and early 1960s, were used to decide on the eligibility of voters in that state. The test and others like it were declared illegal by the 1965 Voting Rights Act. Most white voters who were unable to pass this or similar tests in the states of the Deep South were protected by a "grandfather clause" allowing people to vote whose grandfathers had done so.

1. A person appointed to the U.S. Supreme Court is appointed for a term of _____.

2. If a person is indicted for a crime, name two rights which he has.

3. Cases tried before a court of law are of what two types: civil and _____.

4. If no candidate for president receives a majority of the electoral vote, who decides who will become president?

5. If no person receives a majority of the electoral vote, the vice president is chosen by the Senate. True or False?

6. If an effort to impeach the President of the United States is made, who presides at the trial?

7. If the two houses of Congress do not agree to adjournment, who sets the time?

8. A president elected in November takes office the following year on what date?

9. Of the original 13 states, the one with the largest representation in the first Congress was _____.

10. The Constitution limits the size of the District of Columbia _____.

**Answers:** (1) good behavior; life; (2) jury trial, protection against self incrimination, right to counsel, speedy trial, protection against excessive bail; (3) criminal; (4) the House of Representatives; (5) true; (6) although not stipulated in the Constitution, the House has always turned to its Judiciary Committee to manage the impeachment process; (7) the president; (8) January 20; (9) Virginia; (10) not to exceed 10 miles square.

of African Americans in the South had been slaves, the grandfather clause was no help to them at all.

Several states instituted **white primaries** that excluded African Americans from the process of nominating candidates for local, state, and national offices. The states argued that excluding blacks from primaries was acceptable because political parties were private associations that could define their own membership requirements, including skin color. In the one-party (Democratic) South at the time, the actual election of public officials happened in the state Democratic primaries, leaving those few African Americans who voted in the November general elections without any voice at all. And, for those African Americans who might try to vote anyway in the face of the poll tax, the literacy test, and the white primary, there was always the use of terror as a deterrent: night riding, bombings, and lynchings were used with regularity, especially during times when blacks showed signs of assertiveness.

The statutory devices for keeping African Americans away from the polls were consistently supported by state and federal courts until well into the twentieth century. Terror as a means of preventing voting remained a factor until the 1960s, when the civil rights movement and federal intervention finally put an end to it.

**WOMEN AND THE FIFTEENTH AND NINETEENTH AMENDMENTS** Politically active women were stung by their exclusion from the Fifteenth Amendment's extension of the right to vote, as the amendment said only that no state could exclude people on the grounds of "race, color, or previous condition of servitude." Thus, they quickly turned their attention to winning the vote for women. Once the Supreme Court had decided, in *Minor v. Happersett* (1874), that women's suffrage was not a right inherent in the national citizenship guarantees of the Fourteenth Amendment, many women abandoned legal challenges and turned to more direct forms of political agitation: petitions, marches, and protests. After years of struggle, the efforts of the women's suffrage movement bore fruit in the Nineteenth Amendment, ratified in 1920: "The right of citizens of the United States to vote shall not be denied or abridged by the United States or by any State on account of sex."

# The Contemporary Status of Civil Rights for Racial and Ethnic Minorities

**16.2**  Assess the present status of civil rights protections for racial minorities

T he Supreme Court, using the guidelines written by Justice Harlan Fiske Stone in *United States v. Carolene Products Company* (1938), gradually extended the protections of the Bill of Rights to the states, based on the Fourteenth Amendment. Recall that among the actions by the states that would trigger **strict scrutiny** under the *Carolene* guidelines were those that either "restricted the democratic process" or "discriminated against racial, ethnic, or religious minorities." This reading of the Fourteenth Amendment, particularly the equal protection clause, lent judicial support to the gradual advance of civil rights guarantees for African Americans and other minorities and eventually (although less so) for women. In the following sections, we look at the extension of the civil rights of racial and ethnic minorities, women, and other groups, including gays and lesbians. Here we concentrate mainly (although not exclusively) on Supreme Court decisions,[8] the actions of other branches of government regarding civil rights, and the standing of these groups in American politics. As you consider these materials, recall the important role that protest and social

**white primaries**
Primary elections open only to whites in the one-party South where the only elections that mattered were the Democratic Party's primaries; this effectively disenfranchised blacks.

**strict scrutiny**
The assumption that actions by elected bodies or officials violate the Constitution.

**suspect classification**
The invidious, arbitrary, or irrational designation of a group for special treatment by government, whether positive or negative; historically, a discriminated against, visible minority without the power to protect itself.

movements played in improving the civil rights of a broad range of Americans. Without these movements and the pressures they brought to bear on public opinion, elected officials, and the courts, many of the changes we now take for granted would surely not have happened.

Two basic issues have dominated the story of the extension of civil rights for African Americans since the mid-1960s:

- The ending of legally sanctioned discrimination, separation, and exclusion from citizenship.

- The debate over what actions to take that would remedy the past wrongs done to African Americans.

We examine both in this section.

## Ending Government-Sponsored Separation and Discrimination

We reviewed earlier how the Constitution was long interpreted to condone slavery and segregation. In the twentieth century, however, the legal and political battles waged by the civil rights movement eventually pushed the Supreme Court, the president, and Congress to take seriously the equal protection clause of the Fourteenth Amendment. The "Can Government Do Anything Well?" feature looks closely at the role of the federal government in this story.

In 1944, amid World War II (a war aimed in great part at bringing down the racist regime of Adolf Hitler) and the NAACP's campaign to rid the nation of segregation, the Supreme Court finally declared that race was a **suspect classification** that demanded strict judicial scrutiny. This meant that any local ordinance, or state

**GRUDGING INTEGRATION**

The erosion of official segregation in education came slowly and reluctantly in many parts of the nation. When ordered by a federal court in 1948 to admit a qualified black applicant, the University of Oklahoma law school did so but forced the lone student to sit separated from other students. Did the ruling truly allow for the university to so blatantly discriminate against minority students, or did the university follow the law by just admitting them?

# Can Government Do Anything Well?

## Making "equal protection" a reality

It required federal government intervention and oversight of the states of the former Confederacy to fulfill the promise of the "equal protection" clause of the Fourteenth Amendment for African Americans. Passed in the wake of the Civil War, the Fourteenth Amendment was intended to make former slaves (in effect, males only, since the states did not allow women to vote) full citizens of the United States and of the states in which they lived, with all the rights and privileges of other citizens. Beginning in 1877 when the federal government withdrew its troops from the South marking the end of Reconstruction, the Southern states imposed a system of racial separation and subordination, called Jim Crow, that was similar to the apartheid system of South Africa. Under this system, African Americans were barred from "white only" establishments (restaurants, taverns, hotels, boarding houses, and the like), had separate sections to which they were confined on public conveyances such as trains and buses, had separate and inferior schools, were denied access to certain occupations, enjoyed few protections from the police, and were denied the right to vote and to hold public office.

By the 1960s, national leaders became persuaded that Jim Crow would have to end and that the South would not or could not do it on its own. There are many reasons why they reached this conclusion. They were embarrassed by the existence of racial segregation when we were in a Cold War struggle with the Soviet Union for the "hearts and minds" of people in the Third World, most of whom had dark skin. There was the fact, as well, that African Americans outside the South had the right to vote and used it effectively, especially in states where they lived that had lots of electoral votes (Illinois, New York, Pennsylvania, and California, among others), something to which elected leaders paid attention. The civil rights movement gained strength in the 1950s and reached full fruition in the 1960s, bringing moral pressure on national leaders to end Jim Crow, but also the political muscle of organized labor. So here is a partial list of what the national government did to end Jim Crow. In 1954, the Supreme Court ruled in *Brown v. Board of Education* that "separate but equal" in schools, and by implication other areas of social life, was constitutionally unacceptable. In follow-up cases, the Court pressed the southern states to end segregated schools "with all deliberate speed" and, when they violently resisted in some instances, presidents sent in troops to carry out court orders—President Eisenhower sent the 101st Airborne to Little Rock, Arkansas, in 1957, and President Kennedy sent troops to Oxford, Mississippi, in 1962. President Johnson used the FBI to infiltrate and disrupt the KKK in the mid-1960s. In 1964, Congress and the president passed the Civil Rights Act to end segregation in public accommodations. In 1965, the Voting Rights Act declared illegal the various devices used by the southern states to keep African Americans from the polls, provided for federal officials to take over the voting registration process, and forced the states in the South that had done the most to keep African Americans from voting to seek approval from the Justice Department when they legislated anything to do with the voting process.

*Support for the claim that the federal government has been necessary for the provision of "equal protection" for African Americans:*

- All citizens are guaranteed equal protection by the Constitution. The Fourteenth Amendment requires states to do this, but the southern states failed to do this for their African American citizens for three-quarters of a century after its adoption. It is the responsibility of the federal government to enforce the Constitution and court orders related to it.
- Southern states, especially in the Deep South, showed no signs of ending segregation on their own, even into the 1960s.
- After 1965, African Americans began to vote in the South, electing African Americans across all levels of government, from representatives in Congress, to members of state legislatures, city council members, and county sheriffs.
- By the end of the 1960s, de jure segregation of the races in restaurants, taverns, theaters, buses, trains, and hotels had disappeared.

*Rejection of the claim that the federal government has been necessary for the provision of "equal protection" for African Americans:*

- The various actions described above are a violation of states' rights under our federal Constitution; a solution to the equal protection problem should have been left to the states.
- The Supreme Court failed to practice stare decisis in their *Brown* decision, overturning historic precedents preserving states' rights in the area of race relations.
- Presidents and Congresses, in passing the Civil Rights Act and the Voting Rights Act, were practicing social engineering, and brought unwanted change to an entire region of the United States.
- Rapid changes in race relations wrought by federal government action led to social tensions, violent street protests, and more crime.
- As often happens when the federal government gets involved, the push for equal protection went too far, morphing into affirmative action and racial quotas to redress past discrimination and bring more diversity.

503

*(Continued)*

## WHAT DO YOU THINK?

What do you think about the past, present, and future role of the federal government in providing equal protection for African Americans and other minorities?

- The federal government needed to take actions to force states to provide equal protection and must continue to do so as some states seek ways to limit the participation of African Americans in the voting process.
- The federal government needed to take actions to force states to provide equal protection but no further action is needed as African Americans are now fully integrated into American life and politics.
- The federal government was never needed to force states to provide equal protection for its African American citizens and it violated the letter and spirit of federalism in doing so. It certainly is no longer needed as African Americans are now fully integrated into American life and politics.

How would you defend your position to a fellow student? What would be your main line of argument? What evidence do you believe best supports your position? For help in developing your argument, please refer to the sources listed in the "Can Government Do Anything Well" feature in Chapter 2 on p. 45.

Additional sources for this feature: James MacGregor Burns and Stewart Burns, *A People's Charter* (New York: Knopf, 1991).

or national statute, using racial criteria was presumed to be unconstitutional unless it could be shown that such an ordinance or statute was both necessary and compelling. Pressed by the legal efforts of the NAACP, the Court gradually chipped away at the *Plessy* "separate but equal" doctrine and the edifice of segregation it helped create. In *Smith v. Allwright* (1944), the Court declared that the practice of excluding nonwhites from political-party primary elections was unconstitutional. Then the Court ruled that the states' practice of providing separate all-white and all-black law schools was unacceptable. Many of the key cases before the Supreme Court that eroded the official structure of segregation were argued by Thurgood Marshall—later a justice of the Supreme Court—for the NAACP.[9]

The great legal breakthrough for racial equality came in *Brown v. Board of Education of Topeka* (1954), also argued on the plaintiffs' side by Thurgood Marshall. The Court declared that "separate but equal" was inherently contradictory and that segregation imposed by state and local laws was constitutionally unacceptable in public schools because it violated guarantees of equal protection. Chief Justice Earl Warren, speaking for a unanimous Court, said that education was "perhaps the most important function of state and local governments" and that segregation in education communicated the message that blacks were inferior and deserving of unequal treatment. "In the field of education [in Warren's words] the doctrine of 'separate but equal' has no place."[10] *Brown* was a constitutional revolution, destined to transform racial relations law and practices in the United States, because it struck down the foundations of segregation and discrimination.[11]

The white South did not react violently at first, but it did not desegregate either. Once recognition spread that the Court was going to enforce civil rights, however, massive resistance to racial integration gripped the South. Citizens Councils (white) committed to imposing economic sanctions and boycotts on anybody who supported desegregation had over 250,000 members by 1956. Membership in the KKK increased dramatically, along with beatings, cross-burnings, and killing of blacks and their white supporters.[12] This resistance was what Dr. Martin Luther King Jr. and others had to work (and die) to overcome. The Court—even with many follow-up cases—was able to accomplish little before the president and Congress backed up the justices with the 1964 Civil Rights Act and the 1965 Voting Rights Act. The civil rights movement and supportive changes in American public opinion in favor of protections for blacks helped spur these legislative and judicial actions.

The drive to protect the rights of racial minorities has occupied the nation ever since. The prevailing legal doctrine on racial discrimination is straightforward: Any use

**THE MARCH ON WASHINGTON**
Dr. Martin Luther King Jr. waves to a crowd of an estimated half-million people at the March on Washington at the Lincoln Memorial after delivering his "I Have a Dream" speech on August 28, 1963. This event, one of the high points of the civil rights movement, helped convince Congress to pass the Civil Rights Act of 1964.

of race in law or government regulations to discriminate—sometimes called **de jure discrimination**—will trigger strict scrutiny (a presumption of unconstitutionality) by the courts. Recall from our earlier discussion that a state or the federal government can defend its acts under strict scrutiny only if it can produce a *compelling* government interest for which the act in question is a *necessary* means. Almost no law survives this challenge; laws that discriminate on the basis of race are dead from the moment of passage. In *Loving v. Virginia* (1967), for example, the Court ruled that Virginia's law against interracial marriage served no compelling government purpose that would justify unequal treatment of the races. Needless to say, other racial minority groups in addition to African Americans—Latinos, Asian Americans, and Native Americans—have benefited from the constitutional revolution that has occurred.[13]

To say that racial discrimination in the law is no longer constitutionally acceptable does not mean that discrimination against racial minorities has disappeared from the United States. **De facto discrimination**—unequal treatment of racial or ethnic minority groups based on practices rather than statutes or regulations mandating discrimination (as in Jim Crow laws)—remains a fact of life, although its exact extent is hard to measure accurately. For example, in 2013, 35 percent of African Americans and 20 percent of Hispanics said that in the previous year they had been treated unfairly in stores and restaurants because of their race or ethnicity (for whites, it was 10 percent). Complaints from African Americans and other minorities about discriminatory treatment by public officials abound as well. Seventy percent of African Americans report feeling that police treat them less well than they treat others, and 68 percent say the same about the courts. For Hispanics, the numbers are 51 percent and 40 percent, respectively.[14] Young black and Hispanic men are especially likely to experience negative contact with police.

States and localities have instituted many laws and practices that can have discriminatory effects without any explicit reference to race or ethnicity. The self-described "toughest sheriff in America," Joe Arpaio of Maricopa County, Arizona, claimed that his policy of stopping suspicious automobiles was aimed only at stopping illegal immigration and was not targeted at Hispanics, although they were 4 to 9 times more likely than whites to be stopped. Several states, including Arizona, require that police

**de jure discrimination**
Unequal treatment based on government laws and regulations.

**de facto discrimination**
Unequal treatment of racial or ethnic minority groups based on practices rather than on statutes and regulations mandating discrimination.

**affirmative action**
Programs of private and public institutions favoring minorities and women in hiring and contracting, and in admissions to colleges and universities, in an attempt to compensate for past discrimination or to create more diversity.

ask about the immigration status of anyone during routine stops if there is a "reasonable suspicion" that a person stopped may be undocumented. The Supreme Court ruled in 2013 that states could require police to make such inquiries, but they would need to do so on a nondiscriminatory basis. In New York City, during the tenure of Mayor Michael Bloomberg, police depended heavily on "stop and frisk" tactics to find illegal weapons, get dangerous felons off the streets, and decrease gang violence. In 2012, the practice resulted in more than 200,000 stop and frisks, with 53 percent of those stopped being African American and 34 percent Hispanic[15] (a federal judge ruled in 2013 that the practice was discriminatory and must cease in its present form).

New voter identification laws in dozens of states, purportedly aimed at ending voter fraud, may have the effect, without mentioning race or ethnicity, of keeping poorer African Americans and Latinos from the polls, because they are least likely to have government-issued ID cards. The spread of such laws became especially popular in states controlled by Republicans—African Americans and Hispanics vote overwhelmingly for Democrats—after the Supreme Court overturned a key section of the 1965 Voting Rights Act in 2013 (*Shelby County v. Holder*) that had compelled states with a history of voting discrimination (named in the law) to have the Justice Department "pre-clear" any changes in their election rules before they could go into effect. Despite this setback, the Justice Department has brought suit against several states over voter ID laws and other new laws that might diminish the votes of minority groups, such as curtailing early voting, and several state courts have ruled that such statutes violated their own state constitutions. It remains to be seen how all this will be sorted out and what the future may hold for continuing de facto discrimination in the private and public sectors.

## ☐ Affirmative Action

Despite these examples of real or perceived mistreatment by governments, it is now widely accepted that the Constitution protects racial minorities against any discrimination or disadvantage that is sanctioned or protected by law or government action. The issues are not as clear-cut, however, in the area of government actions that *favor* racial and ethnic minorities (and women) in **affirmative action** programs designed to rectify past wrongs.[16]

**ORIGINS OF AFFIRMATIVE ACTION** The main goal of the civil rights movement of the 1950s and 1960s was to remove barriers to equal citizenship for black Americans. This goal was largely accomplished by Court decisions, passage of the 1964 Civil Rights Act and the Voting Rights Act of 1965 and by broad changes in public attitudes about race. But even with these important changes, the economic and social situations of African Americans did not seem to be improving much. It seemed to an increasing number of people that ending discrimination was a start, but that more proactive government actions would be required if African Americans were to escape the conditions that years of discrimination had put them in. President Lyndon Johnson, Robert Kennedy, and Martin Luther King Jr., among others, eventually came to believe that the advancement of black Americans could happen only if there was a broad societal effort to eradicate poverty by equipping the poor, black and white, with the tools for success. This led to the founding of the Johnson administration's Great Society and War on Poverty and programs such as Head Start.

After Martin Luther King's assassination, however, and the urban riots that followed, many people in government, the media, higher education, and the major foundations began to support the notion that progress for African Americans would happen only if government encouraged proactive efforts to increase the levels of black representation in private and public sector jobs and contracting, and in colleges and universities.[17] Somewhat surprisingly, it was Richard Nixon, not generally thought of as a booster of civil rights, who took the most important step, requiring in his 1969 Philadelphia Plan that construction companies with federal contracts and the associated construction trade unions hire enough blacks and other minorities to achieve "racial balance" (a proportion roughly equal to the racial distribution in the community).

Although initially skeptical of racial preferences, Justices William Brennan, Byron White, Thurgood Marshall, and Harry Blackmun supported temporary programs to remedy the effects of past discrimination. Joined by Justice Lewis Powell, they formed the majority in *Regents v. Bakke* (1978), in which the Court authorized a compromise on affirmative action programs. The Constitution and federal law prohibited employers and admissions committees from using strictly racial quotas, the Court said, but it saw no problem with the use of race as one factor among several in hiring or college admissions.

Since *Bakke,* government and higher education racial outreach programs, which were preferred at that time, have become relatively permanent rather than temporary, and their aim has shifted from providing remedies for past discrimination to enhancing diversity. The proliferation of diversity programs, diversity training, and diversity offices has become commonplace in colleges and universities, in government, and in the corporate world but now they are in great jeopardy.

**WHY AFFIRMATIVE ACTION?**[18]  For the most part, according to proponents, affirmative action programs that promote diversity are needed for the following reasons:

- The effects of past discrimination disadvantage, to one degree or another, all members of discriminated-against groups, so simply removing barriers to advancement is insufficient. When government policies themselves have had profound and lasting effects—slavery being the most obvious, but also state-sanctioned segregation, and racial discrimination in major benefit programs such as the post–World War II GI Bill[19]—the proper remedy is to prefer members of such groups in hiring, contracts, and education until such time as they reach parity with the majority. For example, despite big gains since passage of the Civil Rights Act in 1964, African Americans are a long way from reaching economic parity with whites, lagging significantly in educational attainment, annual income, and wealth (net worth for white households was 17 times that of African American households in 2012).[20]

- In a diverse society such as the United States, tolerance and a sense of community can develop only if we work together in educational, workplace, and government institutions that are diverse.

- People from disadvantaged and discriminated-against groups will improve themselves only if they have experience with successful role models.

Critics of affirmative action are not convinced by these arguments. They believe:

- Affirmative action violates basic American principles: that people be judged, rewarded, and punished as individuals, not because they are members of one group or another.

- Affirmative action benefits those within each preferred group who are already advantaged and need little help. Thus, the main beneficiaries of affirmative action in higher education have been middle-class African Americans, not the poor.

- Affirmative action seeks to remedy the effects of past discrimination by discriminating against others today—most notably, white males—simply because they belong to nonpreferred groups.

- Affirmative action increases intergroup and interracial tension by heightening the saliency of group membership. That is, social friction is increased by encouraging people to think of themselves and others as members of groups and to seek group advantages in a zero-sum game in which one group's gain is another group's loss.

**PUBLIC OPINION ON AFFIRMATIVE ACTION**  In survey after survey, a vast majority of Americans say they approve of the diversity goals of affirmative action—special programs to help those who have been discriminated against get ahead; outreach programs to hire minority workers and find minority students—but disapprove of racial preferences in hiring, awarding of government contracts, and admission to colleges.[21] Not surprisingly, perhaps, racial differences on the issue of preferential treatment are

**AFFIRMATIVE ACTION AT MICHIGAN**

These two University of Michigan room mates expressed their surprise to journalists that the Supreme Court had ruled the university's undergraduate admissions process unconstitutional because of its overt and mechanical use of race in the admitting decision in the landmark case *Gratz v. Bollinger* (2003). Should some form of affirmative action continue so long as deep racial disparities in higher education continue or should other methods be found for overcoming such disparities?

wide; in 2013, 66 percent of African Americans and 59 percent of Latinos supported racial preferences compared to only 22 percent of whites.[22]

American discomfort with affirmative action programs can perhaps be best seen in actions in several of the states. For example, referenda banning affirmative action in any state and local government activity were passed in California (1996), Washington (1997), and Michigan (2006)—three very liberal states—and other states have severely restricted affirmative action by executive order of their governors.[23] In 2008, Nebraska voters approved a measure that bans government use of affirmative action; Colorado voters narrowly rejected a ban, the first time affirmative action bans at the state level had failed at the polls.

**THE SUPREME COURT ON AFFIRMATIVE ACTION** The Supreme Court has been grappling for years with the issue of which forms of affirmative action, if any, are constitutionally permissible. Recall that the prevailing constitutional doctrine on matters of race holds that any mention of race in a government statute, ordinance, or rule is subject to strict scrutiny—that is, unconstitutional—unless the government can show some compelling and necessary reason for it. Historically, of course, there is good reason for the Court to take this position, given the fact that laws mentioning race were usually designed to deny equal protection to African Americans and other racial and religious minorities. But what about government actions meant to compensate African Americans and others for past discriminatory actions? Or initiatives to increase diversity in a broad range of institutions such as police departments and universities?

Since the mid-1980s, the Supreme Court has been moving gradually toward the position that laws and other government actions that are not colorblind should be subject to strict scrutiny. State and local statutes that use racial preferences to increase diversity have been ruled constitutionally unacceptable in government hiring and contracting, and their use in higher education admissions has been substantially restricted. With this history in mind, civil rights organizations and advocates were braced for a decision by the Supreme Court in 2003 involving the University of Michigan that would have rendered affirmative action admissions policies in higher education unconstitutional once and for all. Liberals and conservatives alike were stunned when the Court ruled, by a 5-4 vote, that universities could take race into consideration when considering applications for admission, so long as the consideration of race was not done in a mechanically quantitative manner or used as part of a racial and ethnic quota system, reaffirming, as it were, its position in the 1978 *Bakke* decision. (See the "Using the Framework" feature for more on why this happened.) In its twin decisions, the Court rejected the University of Michigan's undergraduate admissions affirmative action program—because it automatically assigned extra points to each minority applicant— but accepted the law school's—whose admissions process uses race as but one among several factors in a holistic examination of each applicant's file. What surprised observers the most, perhaps, was not the decision itself, but the broad language that Justice Sandra Day O'Connor used in her majority opinion, in which she stressed that achieving diversity in universities, and especially in its elite law schools, was indeed a compelling reason for not applying strict scrutiny by the Court:

> In order to cultivate a set of leaders with legitimacy in the eyes of the citizenry, it is nec-essary that the path to leadership be visibly open to the talented and qualified individu-als of every race and ethnicity. . . . Access to legal education (and thus the legal profession) must be inclusive of talented and qualified individuals of every race and ethnicity so that all members of our heterogeneous society may participate in the educational institutions that provide the training and education necessary to succeed in America. . . . Cross-racial understanding helps to break down racial stereotypes and better prepares graduates for the working world. . . . The law school's educational judgment that such diversity is essential to its educational mission is one to which we defer.[24]

Remember that the balance on the Court swung dramatically in a conservative direc-tion after Samuel Alito replaced the retiring Sandra Day O'Connor, who favored affir-mative action in higher education under certain not-too-difficult-to-achieve conditions. With Alito anchoring a 5-4 conservative majority, the Court refused to allow race to be used in a number of important cases.[25] Finally, in *Fisher v. Texas* (2013), the Court set out standards for universities to meet that are so stringent that the use of racial preferences in higher education admissions will become much less common. The Court said that such admissions programs would be subject to strict scrutiny and could only be justified if all other possible non-race-based methods had been used to try to achieve diversity and if a college or university could show that a critical mass of minority students had not already been achieved. The Court gave no guidance on what constitutes a critical mass.

The Roberts Court also weighed in on the use of race in assigning students to public schools, again coming down against a broad reading of affirmative action. In 2007 it ruled that race-based systems for making primary and secondary school assignments in Seattle and Louisville were unconstitutional.[26] Although the Chief Justice and three of his col-leagues wanted to exercise strict scrutiny in both—as Roberts put it, "The way to stop discrimination on the basis of race is to stop discriminating on the basis of race"—Justice Anthony Kennedy, who cast the deciding votes on these cases, refused to go this far. He simply stated in his majority opinions that the Seattle and Louisville systems were not sufficiently tailored to remedy past discrimination in these particular school districts.

Outside of education, the Roberts Court edged very close in *Ricci v. DeStefano* (2009) to ending the use of race at all in government programs except in manifest cases of overt discrimination. The case was brought by 18 New Haven firefighters (1 Hispanic, 17 white) who claimed they were denied the opportunity for promotion when the city threw out promotion examination results because no African American was in the top group. The city decided not to promote anyone. The Supreme Court agreed with the firefighters that the city of New Haven had practiced reverse discrimination in throw-ing out the examination results, overturning New Haven's victories at the district and appeals court levels. Significantly, the Court based its ruling on narrow grounds, rather than on broad constitutional ones, saying that New Haven was guilty of "disparate treat-ment based on race," which was contrary to the Civil Rights Act. Justice Antonin Scalia was not happy, saying in his concurring opinion that the Court was simply postponing the inevitable day when race-based laws and programs would be deemed unconstitu-tional under the "equal protection" clause of the Fourteenth Amendment.[27]

So, here is where affirmative action programs stand after the *Fisher* ruling, taking into account all of the Court's rulings on racial preferences since *Bakke*:

- Any program by a government entity that uses race to define who receives or does not receive benefits or services is subject to strict scrutiny—that is, considered unconstitutional unless compelling and necessary reasons for the policies are proved. This holds whether or not such policies are designed to discriminate against or favor racial minorities.

- With respect to the award of government contracts and government hiring—whether federal, state, or local—affirmative action programs are acceptable only if they are narrowly tailored to rectify past discriminatory actions by that particular government agency. In the view of the Court, rectifying past racist actions by a particular government agency is a compelling reason. Such programs, however, must be temporary efforts to transcend past practices and not a permanent feature of hiring and contracting. Affirmative action in hiring and contracting is not valid if it is designed simply to increase diversity or to decrease racism in society.

- With respect to admission to educational institutions—into undergraduate and graduate programs, law schools, and medical schools—actions to rectify past discriminatory admissions policies by a particular higher education institution are compelling and necessary, and are permitted.

- With respect to higher education admissions, the goal of achieving a diverse student body is a compelling reason to have affirmative action programs. However, race can only be used if it is one among several factors in a holistic consideration of each applicant's file, if other non-race-based methods to increase diversity have been tried, and if the college or university has not already achieved a critical mass of minority students.

Affirmative action programs in the United States have been designed to help not only African Americans, of course, but other racial and ethnic minorities as well, including Latinos, Asian Americans, and Native Americans. Most of the programs also have included women as beneficiaries. The present Supreme Court guidelines on affirmative action described here apply to all of these groups, not only African Americans. So the extreme narrowing of the acceptability by the Court of affirmative action affects each of these groups.

# The Contemporary Status of Civil Rights for Women

**16.3** Assess the present status of civil rights protections for women

**A**fter years of struggle, the efforts of the women's suffrage movement bore fruit when the Nineteenth Amendment, which gave women the vote, was ratified in 1920: "The right of citizens of the United States to vote shall not be denied or abridged by the United States or by any State on account of sex." At first, women did not vote in the same proportion in elections as men. But they gradually caught up. Indeed, women now vote at higher rates than do men in U.S. elections. As their turnout increased over the years, not only did male elected officials need to pay more attention to the interests of women, but women increasingly became officeholders themselves.

Voting was not the only avenue to advance equality, however. As the civil rights movement helped put the issue of equality for African Americans on the nation's political agenda, so did several women's rights movements advance civil rights protections for women. Fifty years later, the women's movement of the 1970s and 1980s helped win civil rights protections for women and broaden the participation of women in all

# Using the FRAMEWORK

## Why did the Supreme Court dramatically narrow the scope of affirmative action programs?

**Background:** During the 1990s, the Supreme Court rendered a number of decisions that narrowed the use of racial preferences in the areas of government hiring and contracting, congressional redistricting, and university admissions. It therefore came as a great surprise to both proponents and critics of affirmative action when the Supreme Court ruled by a 5–4 vote in a pair of cases involving the University of Michigan in 2003 that affirmative action of a certain kind—one that uses race as only one among several factors in a holistic consideration of each individual's file—is permissible in university admissions. The ruling was made possible by the emergence in the late 1990s of a new Court majority, on civil rights issues, led by Sandra Day O'Connor. After she was replaced by Samuel Alito in 2006, the Court veered sharply again against affirmative action.

### Government Action

The Roberts Court ruled in *Ricci* that "reverse discrimination" is illegal under the Civil Rights Act.  *In Fisher v. University of Texas* (2013), the Court issued guidelines making it difficult though not impossible for affirmative action in college admissions to continue.

The Supreme Court rejected diversity as a compelling state interest in programs involving government jobs and contracting, and in congressional districting.  The Rehnquist Court ruled in 2003 that the use of race in university admissions is permissible if it is not used as part of a mechanical, quantitative formula.

### Government

A slim new majority, led by Sandra Day O'Connor, that supported affirmative action in important institutions to increase diversity had emerged by the late 1990s. O'Connor retired in 2006 and was replaced by committed conservative Samuel Alito.

Republican presidents Reagan and Bush nominated conservatives to the Court. ➡ The Senate approved the nominees. ➡ A narrow but firm conservative majority under the leadership of Chief Justice William Rehnquist controlled the Court on many issues during the early 1990s.

### Political Linkage

Anti-government conservatives gained political influence in the 1980s. ➡ Republicans, whose platform rejects affirmative action, reached parity with Democrats in national elections. ➡ Republicans won control of the Senate from 1981–1986 and from 1995 to 2000.

The political influence of civil rights organizations declined in the 1980s and 1990s. ➡ The majority white population reported in polls that it believed the goals of the civil rights movement had been met. ➡ A substantial majority of Americans reported support for nondiscrimination laws but distaste for laws that give minorities and women special advantages in college admissions, jobs, and government contracts.

### Structure

The Fourteenth Amendment's promise of "equal protection" bars government discrimination against groups of citizens but is unclear about the need for remedies for past discrimination. ➡ The political culture honors individual rather than group rights and responsibilities. ➡ The white middle and working classes suffered economic reverses during the 1980s and early 1990s, creating a climate that was generally hostile to affirmative action programs.

# Mapping American Politics

## Gender Equality

### Introduction

Despite the many advances in gender equality in the United States over the past several decades—increased representation in the government at all levels, in the professions, and in many corporations; rising incomes among educated women; and more household role-sharing among married men and women—America does not fare very well in international comparisons. Of course, the nation's relative standing depends on the types of measures used.

### Mapping Gender Equality

This cartogram shows the relative position of the United States compared with other countries based on the United Nation's index of gender inequality. The index is a composite measure that combines assessments of women's positions in society in the areas of reproductive health, empowerment, and the labor market. More specifically, the index is an additive measure based on the following statistics: maternal mortality rate (number of women who die in childbirth per 100,000 births), the adolescent birth rate (number of births to females ages 15 to 19 per 100,000 females of the same age), the female share of seats in the national parliament (in Congress, in our case), the percentage of adult females with some secondary school education compared with males, and the female workforce participation rate, again compared with males.

In the cartogram, each country is resized according to its index score. Those with the highest scores on gender equality are proportionally bigger than they appear on a normal geographical map of the world; those with the lowest scores are proportionally smaller. The sharp reader will see that the cartogram measures gender equality rather than gender inequality. It uses the reciprocal of the gender inequality index number so that countries with more gender equality are bigger (and darker in tone) than those with less gender equality, which are smaller and lighter in tone.

Three conclusions are immediately evident. First, the countries with the greatest gender equality are found in Europe, including not only western European countries such as Germany, France, and Sweden, but central and eastern European countries, including Slovenia, Lithuania, the Czech Republic, and Estonia. Second, India and China, otherwise impressively economically developing giants, do very poorly on gender equality. Third, and most important for our purposes, the United States does not score very well on gender equality issues when compared with other countries. This seems to fly in the face of the seemingly steady advance of women's position in American society, the economy, and politics noted above.

We can see what is going on by looking at the particular measures calculated in the UN index. The low position of the United States—we rank forty-seventh on the index—is accounted for by three index measures. First, we have substantially higher maternal mortality than other economically advanced countries. Second, we have a very high adolescent birth rate compared with other economically advanced countries. Third, and despite recent advances on this front, female representation in the U.S. national legislature (Congress) is the lowest by far among rich democratic countries and quite poor in relation to middle-income countries.

### What Do You Think?

Do you believe the UN index to be a fair measure of gender equality? Do you believe the indicators used to construct the index are the best ones to use in terms of assessing how the United States fares on gender equality compared with other countries? If so, which ones would you remove from the index? What new ones would you add? Would women's standing in the culture, for example, be a useful addition? Perhaps the percent of best-selling authors and artists who are female might be useful, or the percentage of women in executive and legislative positions in state and local government.

If you believe the index is a fair measure, what policies would you propose to decrease maternal mortality and the number of births to adolescent mothers and increase female representation in the House and Senate? What roles would you assign to the public sector and to the private sector to improve matters?

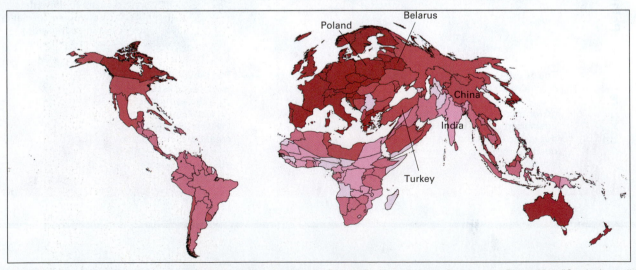

**SOURCE:** United Nations, "Sustaining Human Progress: Reducing Vulnerabilities and Building Resilience," Human Development Report 2014: "Gender Inequality," Table 4," http://hdr.undp.org/en/content/human-development-report-2014. Cartogram produced in ArcMap using Tom Gross's Cartogram Geoprocessing Tool (v2). The tool uses the Newman-Gastner method [see details in Michael T. Gastner and Mark E. J. Newman, "Diffusion-Based Method for Producing Density-Equalizing Maps," *Proceedings of the National Academy of Sciences* 101 (2004): 7499-7504].

aspects of American society, economy, and politics. Although the movement did not win one of its main objectives—passage of the Equal Rights Amendment (ERA) to the U.S. Constitution—the broad advance of women in gaining equal treatment and respect on virtually all fronts in the United States attests to its overall effectiveness.[28] Issues such as pay equity, family leave, sexual harassment, and attention to women's health problems in medical research are now a part of the American political agenda. Women have made important gains economically and are becoming more numerous in the professions, corporate managerial offices (although there is evidence that a glass ceiling remains blocking many women from the most senior posts in corporations; in 2013, only 23 CEOs of *Fortune* 500 companies were women),[29] and political office. (See the "Mapping American Politics" feature for more about how women's standing in the private sector in the United States compares with their standing in other countries.) Having said that, it remains the case that a wage gap still exists between men and women, and that the poverty rate for women is considerably higher than it is for men.

In terms of constitutional law, however, the expansion of civil rights protections for women has taken a path that differs decidedly from that for African Americans.[30]

## ☐ Intermediate Scrutiny

By 1976 the proposed Equal Rights Amendment (ERA) to the Constitution to guarantee full legal equality for women had stalled, falling short of the required three-fourths of the states. Moreover, the Supreme Court did not have the necessary votes for a strict scrutiny interpretation of gender classification. There was support, however, for the new doctrine that came to be called **intermediate scrutiny.** In *Craig v. Boren* (1976), six justices supported Justice William Brennan's compromise, which created a more rigorous scrutiny of gender as a *somewhat* suspect classification. In the view of the justices, the use of strict scrutiny would endanger traditional sex roles, while the use of ordinary scrutiny would allow blatant sex discrimination to survive. The Burger Court defined a test that it believed to be "just right." Under intermediate scrutiny, government enactments that relied on gender would be constitutional if the use of gender were *substantially related* to an *important government interest.*[31] The test in *Craig* was refined in *United States v. Virginia* (1996), when the Court ruled that a male-only admissions policy at the state-supported Virginia Military Institute was unacceptable in that it discriminated against women. In this case, the standard to be met when men and women are treated differently in statutes and state government practices became "an exceedingly persuasive justification." Intermediate scrutiny defines a legal test, then, somewhere between strict and lax. Thus, for example, certain laws protecting pregnant women from dangerous chemicals in the workplace have passed this test. Unlike race, then, *gender* is not considered a suspect classification by which laws and government practices are reviewed under the strict scrutiny standard, but only a semi-suspect classification, less likely to be declared unconstitutional. The improvement of women's rights under the doctrine of intermediate scrutiny is less than what many in the women's movement have wanted.

Thus, women's rights have not followed the path of other rights and liberties. The nation has not restructured civil rights for women based on the courts' expansive reading of the equal protection clause of the Fourteenth Amendment. Rather, advances have come by virtue of changing societal attitudes about the role of women in society, increased involvement of women in politics (see Figure 16.1), and new statutes designed to equalize women's opportunities. In the private sector, women have made important advances in the corporate world and in the professions. Women now outnumber men among law school and medical school students, and more women than men go to college and graduate. However, significant wage disparities still exist between men and women in every occupation, at every level of education, and in every area of the country, though the gap has narrowed somewhat for college graduates between the ages of 25 and 34.[32]

**intermediate scrutiny**
A legal test falling between ordinary and strict scrutiny relevant to issues of gender; under this test, the Supreme Court will allow gender classifications in laws if they are *substantially* related to an *important* government objective.

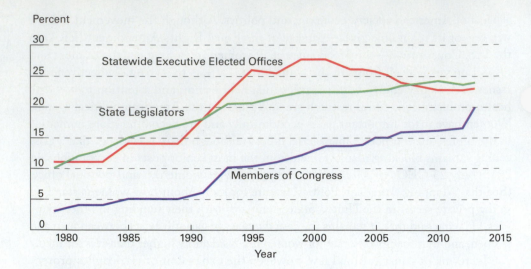

**Percent**

*Statewide Executive Elected Offices*

*State Legislators*

*Members of Congress*

Year

FIGURE 16.1  PERCENTAGE OF ELECTIVE OFFICES HELD BY WOMEN, 1979–2013

Although accounting for more than one-half the American population, women hold a much smaller proportion of elected federal, state, and local offices across the nation than men. However, the percentage of offices held by women has been increasing steadily since the 1970s. Given rising education and incomes among women, as well as changing social attitudes toward women's role in society, the proportion of elected offices held by women is likely to continue to increase.

*Source:* Center for American Women and Politics, Rutgers University.

Women have also successfully pushed for laws that compensate for past injustices. One example of such a law is Title IX of the Civil Rights Act of 1964, which prohibits discrimination against women at federally funded institutions, including universities. Title IX is generally credited with enhancing funding for women's sports programs in colleges and dramatically improving the quality of women's athletics in the United States. Another example is the Lilly Ledbetter Fair Pay Restoration Act, signed into law by President Barack Obama in January 2009 only days after his inauguration, which makes it easier for women and others to sue their companies over pay discrimination and may serve to narrow the pay gap between men and women. The new law was designed to override the Supreme Court's ruling in *Ledbetter v. Goodyear Tire & Rubber Co.* (2007), which made pay discrimination lawsuits exceedingly difficult to mount.

## ☐ Abortion Rights

For many women (and men), the right of women to abort an unwanted pregnancy is a central element of the civil rights agenda falling under the equal protection clause of the Fourteenth Amendment. (To be sure, many others are against abortion on religious grounds.) That may well be, but the Supreme Court, in a number of important cases beginning with *Roe v. Wade* (1973), has based a woman's right to terminate a pregnancy on privacy grounds rather than equal protection grounds. It is for this reason that we have addressed the abortion issue, with its contentious politics and string of Court rulings revising and refining *Roe,* in the previous chapter. Please refer to that section to see more on the politics and law of the struggle over abortion in the United States.

## ☐ Sexual Harassment and Hostile Environment

Another issue of concern to many women (and many men) is sexual harassment in the workplace. One poll reported that 20 percent of women say they have experienced sexual harassment of one kind or another at work:[33] In a speech in early 2014, President Obama said that the same percentage run into it on college campuses. Many have filed complaints with the Equal Employment Opportunity Commission (EEOC), which reported that more than 11,000 complaints for sexual harassment (16 percent of them from men) were filed with the agency in fiscal year 2012.

People disagree, of course, about what kinds of behavior constitute sexual harassment, although the courts, regulatory agencies, and legislative bodies are gradually

**VICE PRESIDENTIAL CANDIDATE SARAH PALIN**

Sarah Palin was the first women vice presidential candidate in the Republican Party, nominated to join presidential candidate John McCain on the 2008 ticket. In the years since her ticket lost the presidential race, she has remained a prominent voice in the conservative movement and an advocate for Tea Party candidates in Republican primaries.

defining the law in this area. In 1980, the EEOC ruled that making sexual activity a condition of employment or promotion violates the 1964 Civil Rights Act, a ruling upheld by the Supreme Court. The EEOC also ruled that creating "an intimidating, hostile, or offensive working environment" is contrary to the law. The U.S. Supreme Court took a major step in defining sexual harassment when it ruled unanimously, in *Harris v. Forklift Systems Inc.* (1993), that workers do not have to prove that offensive actions make them unable to do their jobs or cause them psychological harm, only that the work environment is hostile or abusive. In a pair of rulings in June 1998, the Court broadened the definition of sexual harassment by saying that companies were liable for the behavior of supervisors even if top managers were unaware of harassing behavior. However, companies were offered a measure of protection by the Court when it ruled that companies with solid and well-communicated harassment policies could not be held liable if victims failed to report harassment in a reasonable period of time.

An increase in public awareness about sexual harassment has triggered an increase in lawmaking by state legislatures to erase sexual harassment in the workplace. Moreover, most major corporations and state and local government entities (including public colleges and universities) have sexual harassment and hostile environment prohibitions in place and require their employees to participate in training programs to lessen their incidence.

# Broadening the Civil Rights Umbrella

**16.4** | Analyze the expansion of civil rights protections to the elderly, the disabled, and gays and lesbians

T he expansion of civil rights protections for women and racial minorities encouraged other groups to press for expanded rights protections.

**civil union**

A legal status in which same-sex couples have the same rights, benefits, and protections as married couples.

## ☐ The Elderly and the Disabled

Interest groups for the elderly have pressed for laws barring age discrimination and have enjoyed some success in recent years. Several federal and state laws, for instance, now bar mandatory retirement. And, the Age Discrimination in Employment Act passed in 1967 prohibits employers from discriminating against employees over the age of 40 in pay, benefits, promotions, and working conditions. The courts also have begun to strike down hiring practices based on age unless a compelling reason for such age requirements can be demonstrated. But problems persist; downsizing companies often lay off older workers first because the pay and benefits of older workers are almost always higher than those of younger workers. And, because people are living longer and worried about the size of their pensions and the rising costs of medical care (even with Medicare), many more Americans say they want to work, at least part time, beyond the normal retirement age.

Disabled Americans have also pushed for civil rights and other protections and have won some notable victories, including passage of the Americans with Disabilities Act (ADA) of 1990. The act prohibits employment discrimination against the disabled and requires that reasonable efforts be made to make places of employment and public facilities (such as concert halls, restaurants, retail shops, schools, and government offices) accessible to them. The proliferation of wheelchair ramps and wheelchair-accessible toilet facilities is a sign that the legislation is having an important effect. Several advocates for the disabled, however, claim that the act depends too much on voluntary compliance.

In 2001, the Supreme Court dramatically narrowed the reach of the ADA, saying that state employees could not sue states for damages arising from violations of the act, as provided for in the legislation. Advocates for the rights of the disabled worried that this judicial ruling expanding the scope of state immunity from congressional actions means that other sections of the ADA act are doomed, including the requirement that state governments make their services and offices accessible to people with disabilities. Others worried that a wide range of civil rights laws that require nondiscriminatory behavior by state agencies—schools and hospitals, for example—may be at risk, as well, because the basis of the Court's decision was that Congress had gone beyond its authority in telling the states what to do under the interstate commerce clause.[34] If the states are immune from the requirements of the Americans with Disabilities Act, the reasoning goes, why should they not be immune from the provisions of other civil rights laws passed by Congress? The Supreme Court, perhaps concerned about the backlash from its 2001 decision, ruled in *Tennessee v. Lane* (2004) that those with disabilities could sue a state for money damages in federal court if the state fails to make its courts fully accessible. Congress pushed back against the Court's 2001 ruling even more in 2008 when it renewed and amended the ADA, extending antidiscrimination protections to those with a disability to a wider range of private and public settings.

## ☐ Gays and Lesbians

The gay and lesbian civil rights movement began in earnest following the 1969 "Stonewall rebellion"—three days of rioting set off by police harassment of the patrons of a popular gay bar in Greenwich Village, New York. The movement picked up steam as the gay community reacted to the powerful inroads of AIDS and in response to the Supreme Court's decision in *Bowers v. Hardwick* (1986) upholding Georgia's ban against homosexual sexual relations. The movement was also inspired by and borrowed many of the tactics of the civil rights and women's movements. The goal was to gain the same civil rights protections under the law enjoyed by African Americans and other minority groups and women and to gain respect from the public. The tactics have ranged from patient lobbying and voting to mass demonstrations and direct action. While substantial gains have been made, often in close partnership with groups representing bisexual and transgendered people (thus the common designator LGBT), its open advocacy for antidiscrimination legislation targeting employment and housing, the right to adopt children, civil unions, and same-sex marriage has triggered strong counterattacks by conservative religious groups, such as the American Family Association, Concerned Women for America, and Focus on the Family.

Not surprisingly, given the advances made in the arts and entertainment by LGBT actors and entertainers, public attitudes about gays and lesbians are growing steadily more tolerant. Sympathetic gay and lesbian characters appear regularly on television, in movies, and on stage. Today, fewer Americans think that gay and lesbian relationships are wrong; indeed, the percentage has dropped dramatically and rapidly, from 77 percent thinking they are wrong in 1991 to 46 percent in 2012.[35] Substantial majorities favor ending discrimination against gays and lesbians in jobs, housing, and education and favor passing hate-crime legislation. Fully 53 percent of Americans believe that same-sex couples should be allowed to marry, up from 27 percent in 1996, a remarkable change in public attitudes in so short a time. Among the 18-34 age group, fully 73 percent favor extending equality of marriage rights to same-sex couples.[36] In addition, 92 percent of members of the LBGT community in 2013 agreed with the statement that "compared with 10 years ago, society is now more accepting of people who are LBGT." Only 5 percent of respondents reported "being treated unfairly by an employer in the past year" because of their sexual orientation or gender identity or "receiving poor service in a restaurant, hotel, or place of business in the past year."[37]

Successes on the public policy front for gay and lesbian equality came slowly at first and are not yet fully realized. In the 1990s, Congress passed several bills that denied equal treatment for gays and lesbians. In 1993—responding to decisions by several major universities to bar military recruiters from campus because the military would not allow openly practicing homosexuals to serve—Congress passed the Solomon Amendment to the defense appropriations act; the amendment barred federal money to colleges and universities that deny military recruiters the same campus access as other private and public employers. In 1996, in response to the decision of Hawaii's Supreme Court in 1991 that denying same-sex couples the right to marry violated the state's constitution, Congress passed the Defense of Marriage Act (referred to as DOMA). This act defined marriage as a union of a man and a woman and declared that states are under no legal obligation to recognize same-sex marriages performed in other states. It also barred same-sex couples in civil unions or marriages from receiving federal benefits like Social Security in the same way as heterosexual couples. Former president Bill Clinton, who had signed DOMA, later renounced his action and called for its repeal. In 2011, with many challenges to DOMA making their way forward in the federal courts, President Obama issued an executive order directing the Justice Department to stop defending DOMA. Finally, the Supreme Court ruled DOMA unconstitutional in 2013.

It took time, but progress on equal treatment for gays and lesbians in the military has also happened. For most of the twentieth century, openly gay people were not allowed to serve in the military. Discovery of one's homosexual orientation was grounds for a dishonorable discharge, with loss of all veterans' benefits. Under pressure from LBGT activists and organizations, which generally supported Democrats, candidate Bill Clinton promised during his presidential campaign in 1992 to lift the ban on gays and lesbians in the military. Because of the hostile reaction from Congress and from the top brass in the armed services, he introduced a compromise measure called "don't ask, don't tell, don't pursue," a policy that pleased few people but stayed in place through George W. Bush's presidency. True to his campaign promise, President Barack Obama persuaded Congress in late 2010 to repeal the policy, allowing gays and lesbians to openly serve in the military. After considerable Pentagon study and preparation, the new policy went into effect in September 2011.

Much of the action on same-sex marriage has taken place in various states. The story there has been mixed. At this writing in early 2014, seventeen states allow same-sex marriage, twenty-nine have passed constitutional amendments defining marriage as a union between a man and a woman, and four allow civil unions that have most of the legal obligations and rights of marriage. Some of the states allowing same-sex marriage did so through the action of their highest state court (Massachusetts, Connecticut, New Mexico, and California are examples), many more by actions of their state legislature (Hawaii, Illinois, Vermont, and New York are examples), and one state by public initiative (Maine). In 2014, about one in three Americans lived in states that allow same-sex marriage.

Until 2012 same-sex marriage faired poorly with voters. Only Colorado and Minnesota voters have rejected bans on same-sex marriage. And thirteen states in 2004, eight in 2006, and three more in 2008 passed voter initiatives banning same-sex marriage. Even voters in states considered to be liberal on social issues have surprised same-sex marriage advocates. In California, for example, voters passed Proposition 8 in 2008 overturning the California Supreme Court's decision allowing such marriages (since overturned by the U.S. Supreme Court). This mixed record at the state level probably can be explained by two factors. First, public opinion in favor of such unions has been growing rapidly, and, in several states, measures to allow same-sex marriage or civil unions would probably now pass voter muster, though we cannot know for sure until such time as the issue returns to the ballot. Second, there is still strong opposition to same-sex marriage, particularly among conservatives and religiously committed people. To the extent that these groups are mobilized and participate in politics, and to the extent that these groups remain influential in a broad swath of states, legalization of same-sex unions will remain a patchwork for the foreseeable future unless the Supreme Court rules otherwise.

Gays and lesbians also have won important Supreme Court cases in recent years. This may seem surprising given the conservative majority on the Court for the whole of this period. Whatever the reason may be, long-time conservative justice Anthony Kennedy has become the leading voice on the Court in favor of equal treatment for gays and lesbians, joining the four liberal justices on major rulings. He wrote the opinion of the Court on each of its three most important rulings in this area of the law. In *Romer v. Evans* (1996), for example, the Court

**GAYS IN THE MILITARY**

After a long period when homosexuals were not allowed to serve in the military at all, then an almost two-decade long period of "don't ask, don't tell, don't pursue" during which gays and lesbians could serve so long as their sexual orientation stayed hidden, President Obama and Congress agreed on a bill in late 2010 that allowed homosexuals to openly serve their country. Here two active-duty sailors demonstrate their feelings during a Gay Pride parade in San Diego in 2011.

ruled that state laws designed to deny basic civil rights to gays and lesbians are unconstitutional. In this case, the Court looked at Colorado's provision (known as Amendment 2) prohibiting local communities from passing gay antidiscrimination ordinances. The Court ruled that the law was constitutionally unacceptable because not only was there was no rational basis for the law but, as Justice Anthony Kennedy declared in his opinion, "a state cannot so deem a class of persons [gays and lesbians] a stranger to its laws." In a stunning and highly unexpected decision in 2003, the Supreme Court overturned its own *Bowers* decision from 1986 and ruled in *Lawrence v. Texas* that state antisodomy laws designed to make homosexual sexual relations illegal were unconstitutional. Justice Kennedy again gave the ruling a very expansive reading, declaring that gay people "were entitled to freedom, dignity, and respect for their private lives." In *United States v. Windsor* (2013), which overturned DOMA, Kennedy declared in his opinion that "the federal statute is invalid, for no legitimate purpose overcomes the purpose and effect [of DOMA] to disparage and injure those whom the state, by its marriage laws, sought to protect in personhood and dignity. . . . By seeking to displace this protection and treating those persons as living in marriages less respected than others, the federal statute is in violation of the Fifth Amendment."

Note that the Court did not base its ruling on the "equal protection" clause of the Fourteenth Amendment. It did not declare lesbians and gays (or bisexuals and transvestites) a protected class like racial minorities, requiring "strict scrutiny," nor did it declare them to be a semi-protected class, like women, requiring "intermediate scrutiny." Instead, Kennedy said in his opinion that overturning DOMA was based on the "deprivation of equal liberty of persons protected by the Fifth Amendment," a foundation for advancing equality that has rarely been used and a justification that Justice Scalia, writing for the minority, found utterly mystifying.

*Windsor* had a number of important early effects. President Obama moved quickly to make federal programs consistent with the overturn of DOMA and with his support for same-sex marriage. Under his direction, for example, the Veterans Administration began to distribute benefits to gay married couples (though only to those living in states allowing same-sex marriages because of congressional language in the authorization of veterans' benefits programs that deferred to the states). The Social Security Administration announced that it would treat partners in same-sex marriages the same way that it treats spouses in opposite-sex marriages when distributing Social Security checks, no matter where the same-sex couple might reside. The IRS acted similarly, stating that beginning with the 2013 tax year, people in same-sex marriages could no longer file their tax returns as two single individuals.

The *Windsor* decision also had an immediate effect on the federal courts. Beginning in late 2013 federal judges used the reasoning in that ruling to, among other things, overturn bans on same-sex marriage in several states, told the state of Ohio that it must recognize same-sex marriages performed in other states, and set aside bans on jury service based on sexual orientation. It will surprise no one that cases on same-sex marriage soon will work their way up to the Supreme Court for a decision about whether such marriages are a matter for each of the states or a right that must be protected on a national basis.

Whatever transpires, it is evident that the struggle over gay and lesbian civil rights will remain an important part of the American political agenda for a long time to come. Feelings on both sides of the issue are strong and the stakes are high.

## Using the DEMOCRACY STANDARD

### Is equal citizenship a reality in the United States?

It is with respect to civil rights—guarantees of equality for people in the United States with regard to judicial proceedings, the exercise of political rights, treatment by public officials, and access to and enjoyment of the benefits of government programs—that the differences between the ideas of the framers and the demands of democracy theory are most evident. It is with respect to civil rights, moreover, that democratic aspirations and the struggle for democracy have most altered the original Constitution of the United States. Recall that the framers not only paid scant attention to guarantees of equality, but they also included a number of provisions in the Constitution that accepted and sustained the institution of slavery as well as the noncitizen status of Native Americans. Further, in leaving voting and office-holding requirements largely to the states, the framers implicitly accepted prevailing practices in the states, including the exclusion of women from political life, but also property qualifications and religious tests for voting and office holding. For the framers, civil rights guarantees—other than equality in the courts—were not among the first principles of good government. In fact, the framers worried a great deal about "leveling tendencies" in society that might lead to too much equality and a system of governance in which people of virtue, character, and education would not be in control. In democratic theory, on the other hand, equal citizenship—another way of saying civil rights—is the very essence of good government, one of the three essential pillars of democracy, joining popular sovereignty and liberty. Absent equal citizenship, democracy cannot be said to exist.

The glaring absence of a strong constitutional foundation for the principle of equal citizenship—buttressed for much of U.S. history by a popular culture that favored broad political inclusion for white males but not for other groups—meant that the spread of civil rights protections has been slow and uneven. Thus, women were denied the vote well into the twentieth century. Most African Americans were slaves until passage of the Thirteenth Amendment after the Civil War and were not admitted into full citizenship across the nation until at least 1965, after passage of the Civil Rights and Voting Rights Acts. Even today, women, racial and ethnic minorities, and gays and lesbians fail to play a role in the political process commensurate with their numbers in the population.

Having said that, it is undeniably true that civil rights dramatically increased in the United States during the second half of the twentieth century as guarantees of equal citizenship were extended—unevenly to be sure—to women, African Americans, other racial and ethnic minorities, and partially to gays and lesbians. These developments were a product of the struggle for democracy by previously excluded groups who insisted on their right to full citizenship, the emergence of a more egalitarian society and culture in the United States, the rational behavior of elected public officials responding legislatively to a public increasingly supportive of civil rights, and changes in the judicial interpretation of equal citizenship in a country turned more favorable to claims of equality.

This advance of civil rights protections since the end of World War II has enriched American democracy because it has made political equality more of a reality in the United States. This is not to say that racial and ethnic minorities and women have attained full social or material equality; many areas of American life, from wealth holding to representation in the professions and in Congress, remain unequal and unrepresentative. Nor is this to say that all civil rights issues are settled; note the continuing disagreements over same-sex marriages and affirmative action. Nevertheless, the attainment of formal political equality is real and something about which many Americans take a great deal of pride.

# Review the Chapter

## Civil Rights Before the Twentieth Century

**16.1** Trace the evolution of civil rights protections for racial minorities and women to the twentieth century, p. 497

The original Constitution and the Bill of Rights were relatively silent on equality other than providing for equality before the law.

The Fourteenth Amendment that was adopted after the Civil War was a foundation for later civil rights advances.

Although the Court paid little attention to civil rights during the nineteenth century, structural changes in society, the transformation of attitudes about race and gender, and the political efforts of racial and ethnic minority group members and women of all races finally prompted the Court to begin to pay attention by the middle of the twentieth century. These contributed to important civil rights gains for racial and religious minorities and women.

## The Contemporary Status of Civil Rights for Racial and Ethnic Minorities

**16.2** Assess the present status of civil rights protections for racial minorities, p. 501

It is now settled law that discrimination of any kind against racial minorities in the statutes and administrative practices of federal, state, or local government is unconstitutional. It is also settled law that governments may use affirmative action to rectify the past discriminatory practices of a particular public entity such as a fire department in its hiring practices or county government in letting road-building contracts. The status of affirmative action programs meant to achieve general societal progress for minorities (or women) or to enhance diversity, however, remains unsettled, though the Court is leaning strongly against such efforts.

## The Contemporary Status of Civil Rights for Women

**16.3** Assess the present status of civil rights protections for women, p. 510

The Court has taken the position that laws mentioning gender fall under the doctrine of "intermediate scrutiny," signaling that it will allow more latitude than it does to race to federal, state, and local governments that wish to give gender special attention.

Recent political, social, and economic gains by women are the result of changes in social attitudes, the political efforts of women, and the changing occupational needs of the American economy, rather than the product of a series of favorable Court rulings about gender equality.

## Broadening the Civil Rights Umbrella

**16.4** Analyze the expansion of civil rights protections to the elderly, the disabled, and gays and lesbians, p. 515

The civil rights movement gave impetus not only to the women's movement but also to a range of other groups of Americans who felt they were discriminated against, including the elderly, the disabled, and gays and lesbians. Statutes have been passed at all levels of government addressed to the equal protection needs of the elderly and the disabled, though compliance has been very uneven.

The question of whether lesbians and gay men can be discriminated against in housing, employment, and education has been largely settled in law and increasingly in social practice. Gays and lesbians can now openly serve in the military. However, the issue of same-sex marriage remains the subject of considerable political debate and legal disputation.

# Learn the Terms

civil rights, p. 497

privileges and immunities clause, p. 499

due process clause, p. 499

equal protection clause, p. 499

Jim Crow, p. 499

poll tax, p. 499

literacy test, p. 499

grandfather clause, p. 500

white primaries, p. 501

strict scrutiny, p. 501

suspect classification, p. 502

de jure discrimination, p. 505

de facto discrimination, p. 505

affirmative action, p. 506

intermediate scrutiny, p. 513

civil union, p. 516

# Test Yourself

Answer key begins on page T-1.

**16.1** Trace the evolution of civil rights protections for racial minorities and women to the twentieth century

1. This amendment reversed the *Dred Scott* case by making all those born in the United States both citizens of the United States and of the states they live in.

   a. First Amendment
   b. Fourth Amendment
   c. Fourteenth Amendment
   d. Fifteenth Amendment
   e. Sixteenth Amendment

**16.2** Assess the present status of civil rights protections for racial minorities

2. Which of the following is NOT a reason affirmative action programs are needed:

   a. Past discrimination
   b. Current discrimination
   c. A need for a diverse environment in work and school
   d. A need for tolerance and a sense of community
   e. A need to educate the less wealthy

**16.3** Assess the present status of civil rights protections for women

3. The U.S. Supreme Court ruled in *Harris v. Forklift Systems Inc.* that workers do not have to prove that offensive actions make them unable to do their jobs, only that the work environment:

   a. Is hostile and abusive
   b. Causes psychological harm
   c. Is uncomfortable
   d. Is unprofessional
   e. Causes unneeded stress

**16.4** Analyze the expansion of civil rights protections to the elderly, the disabled, and gays and lesbians

4. Which of these states does NOT permit same sex marriage?

   a. New York
   b. Massachusetts
   c. Alabama
   d. Iowa
   e. Vermont

# Explore Further

## INTERNET SOURCES

Civil Rights Project **www.civilrightsproject.ucla.edu**
Cutting-edge research on race in America.

Infoplease Civil Rights Timeline: Milestones in the Modern Civil Rights Movement **www.infoplease.com/spot/civilrightstimeline1.html**
A richly detailed timeline of the African American civil rights movement.

Cornell Legal Information Institute **www.law.cornell.edu**
Links to the Constitution, landmark and recent Supreme Court civil rights decisions, international treaties on human rights, the Civil Rights Division of the Justice Department, and more.

Equal Employment Opportunity Commission **www.eeoc.gov**
Statistics and reports about and rulings on employment discrimination.

Issues: Gay Rights **www.politics1.com/issues-gay.htm**
Links to organizations in favor of and opposed to advancing gay and lesbian civil rights.

Martin Luther King Jr. and the Civil Rights Movement **seattletimes.nwsource.com/mlk**
Created by the *Seattle Times*, the site includes study guides on King and the civil rights movement, interactive exercises,

audios of King speeches, and links to other King and civil rights websites.

Yahoo/Civil Rights **http://www.yahoo.com/Society_and_Culture/ Issues_and_Causes/Civil_Rights/**

Links to a vast compendium of information on civil rights and to organizations devoted to the protection and expansion of domestic and international rights.

United States Department of Labor: Affirmative Action **http:// www.dol.gov/dol/topic/hiring/affirmativeact.htm**

Links to official laws and information regarding affirmative action and hiring people with disabilities.

The Woman's Rights Movement **utc.iath.virginia.edu/abolitn/ wmhp.html**

A site focusing on the link between the woman's rights movement and abolitionism with multiple links to valuable texts on the subject.

## SUGGESTIONS FOR FURTHER READING

Baer, A. Judith, and Leslie Friedman Goldstein. *The Constitutional and Legal Rights of Women.* Belmont, CA: Roxbury Publishing, 2006.

A rich blend of judicial politics, the women's movement, and constitutional interpretation.

Barry, Brian. *Culture and Equality.* Cambridge, MA: Harvard University Press, 2001.

An assault on multiculturalism in the name of liberal egalitarianism by a distinguished political philosopher.

Bowen, William G., and Derek C. Bok. *The Shape of the River: Long-Term Consequences of Considering Race in College and University Admissions.* Princeton, NJ: Princeton University Press, 1998.

Based on surveys of more than 60,000 white and African American students at highly selective colleges and universities, Bowen and Bok argue that affirmative action in college and university admissions has had substantial and widespread positive effects on American society.

Branch, Taylor. *At Canaan's Edge: America in the King Years, 1965–1968.* New York: Simon and Schuster, 2006.

The third volume in Taylor Branch's brilliant and award-winning biographies of Martin Luther King; focuses not only on King in this volume but on the transformation of race relations and American politics during this decisive period.

Gates, Henry Louis, Jr. *Live Upon These Shores: Looking at African American History, 1513-2008.* New York: Knopf, 2011.

A history of Americans of African descent, informed by the best scholarship on the subject, but lively and richly illustrated.

Katznelson, Ira. *When Affirmative Action Was White: An Untold History of Racial Inequality in Twentieth-Century America.* New York: W. W. Norton, 2005.

An eye-opening look at how a long list of federal government programs, beginning in the New Deal, favored whites over blacks.

O'Brien, David M. *Constitutional Law and Politics: Civil Rights and Civil Liberties.* New York: W. W. Norton, 2014.

The 9th edition of a leading textbook on civil liberties and civil rights, mixing cases with revealing commentaries about the cases and their impact on American society and politics.

# 17

# Domestic Policies

## ECONOMIC CRISIS AND THE EXPANSION OF THE FEDERAL GOVERNMENT

**T**he 2008 economic collapse in the United States was, by all accounts, both the worst economic event in U.S. history since the Great Depression and the worst economic downturn that most living Americans had ever experienced.[1] While the **recession** officially began in the fourth quarter of 2007, matters came to a head in the fall of 2008 when several major investment banks realized they were taking huge losses on their investments in the collapsing housing market. Major investment banks went out of business and others teetered on the edge of ruin. The collapse of the financial system had a domino effect across the economy. Banks stopped lending money, and without access to credit, consumers cut back on their purchases, devastating big and small companies as sales plummeted. Companies put off plans to expand, cut orders to their suppliers, and laid off employees. The effects of these difficulties were reflected in all the major economic indicators. The stock market lost more than half of its value, taking a toll on public pensions and individual retirement funds. Millions lost their homes to foreclosure, with Sunbelt states such as Florida, Arizona, and California hit especially hard. In each month between November 2008 and April 2009, about 645,000 Americans lost their jobs. Unemployment surpassed 10 percent in October 2009, with more than one-third of those without jobs unemployed for more than twenty-seven weeks, a post–World War II record. By the spring of 2010, about 8.4 million jobs had been lost in the downturn.

The recession had a major impact on American domestic policy. The response from the federal government has now spanned two presidencies. The recession technically ended in mid-2009, but the country still faces what some have termed a "jobless recovery": While the economy is growing, many people still cannot find work.[2] These lingering effects continue to drive the policy agendas and political posturing of President Obama and members of Congress.

| **17.1** | **17.2** | **17.3** | **17.4** | **17.5** | **17.6** | **17.7** | **17.8** | **17.9** |
|---|---|---|---|---|---|---|---|---|
| Assess why governments are so involved in economic and social affairs, p. 528 | Analyze economic policymaking in terms of goals, players, and tools, p. 529 | Identify the components of the federal budget and analyze the problem of the national debt, p. 534 | Explain the reasons for government regulation and predict the future of regulation, p. 540 | Differentiate among types of safety net programs in the United States, p. 542 | Describe the main social insurance programs in the United States and assess their effectiveness, p. 544 | Describe the main means-tested programs in the United States and assess their effectiveness, p. 548 | Explain how the Affordable Care Act changes health care, p. 554 | Compare and contrast the American system of social safety nets with those in other rich democracies, p. 557 |

**GREAT DEALS TO BE HAD** The real estate bubble collapse that began in the middle of 2007 led directly to the financial collapse the following September and the deepest recession since the Great Depression of the 1930s, causing great harm to millions of Americans. The deregulation of many previously regulated real estate and financial investment products was partly to blame for this sequence of developments and triggered a strong federal government response to prevent even deeper economic troubles. Would the country have been better off if the government had not responded at all, leaving economic outcomes to the free play of market forces?

**recession**

Two quarters or more of declining gross domestic product.

We can think of the federal policy response to the economic crisis as coming in four phases. In the first phase, the government was responding to a new crisis with decisive action. President George W. Bush has written in his memoirs that he feared that the only way to avoid another Great Depression was with legislation, and in February 2008 he and the Democratic Congress passed a $152 billion economic stimulus package that primarily featured tax rebates aimed at providing the American people with more spending money. The Federal Reserve (the Fed), headed by Chairman Ben Bernanke, aggressively cut short-term interest rates to stimulate economic activity and stepped up its lending to banks in an attempt to head off troubles in the financial system. The Fed also took the surprising step of arranging and partially paying for J. P. Morgan's purchase of the failing investment bank Bear Stearns as well as for Bank of America's absorption of troubled Merrill Lynch. The Treasury Department, led by then-Secretary Hank Paulson, and the Federal Reserve together bailed out Fannie Mae and Freddie Mac, the two firms that guarantee most home loans, to the tune of $25 billion.

In the second phase, the federal government sought to shore up the troubled financial system. Worried that these first steps were not enough to prevent a financial collapse, Bernanke and Paulson convinced President Bush and Congress to pass a massive $700 billion rescue package directed primarily at the nation's largest financial institutions (the Troubled Asset Relief Program, or TARP). The idea was to buy up the nearly worthless assets of the nation's major financial institutions and infuse new money into the banking system, freeing banks up to begin lending again to individuals and companies. In a remarkable step, Bernanke and Paulson decided to use a portion of TARP to inject money into the financial system by buying ownership shares in banks and other financial institutions—in effect, partially nationalizing them until they could buy back the shares. In doing this, these two Bush appointees moved a considerable distance from the free-market philosophy that had dominated Washington policies since the beginning of the Reagan administration in 1981.

The third phase, which came quickly after the election of President Barack Obama in 2008, was focused on reinvigorating America's sagging economy. On the heels of their big election victories, President Obama and Democratic congressional leaders facilitated the passage of a $787 billion stimulus bill less than thirty days from the date of his inauguration. The stimulus package was a combination of tax cuts, unemployment benefit extensions, and, perhaps most important, new expenditures on programs that funded research and development in alternative energy sources, school construction, and increased spending on infrastructure (roads, bridges, canals, etc.). This government spending, which provoked the ire of small-government Republicans and was deemed too modest by many more liberal Democrats, was aimed at injecting the economy with the money and jobs necessary to carry it through the difficult economic times. It is very difficult to know how well these stimulus efforts worked, but many leading economists think that these government actions at least prevented the economy from further decline.[3]

The fourth phase came in July 2010 when Congress and President Obama sought to revise the regulatory system that allowed the collapse to happen in the first place. The Dodd–Frank Wall Street Reform and Consumer Protection Act was a far-reaching reform of the financial industry. Among other things, Dodd–Frank instituted new transparency rules, put limits on executive salaries, limited some of the risks that investment banks can take, and increased oversight of financial institutions with the creation of a new Consumer Financial Protection Bureau. Such increases in regulation would have been unlikely had Republicans controlled either Congress or the presidency at the time—indeed, such reforms are almost unimaginable in today's Congress, with its bitter partisan division.[4] Since the implementation of Dodd–Frank, there has been steady Republican resistance to it. For example, Senate Republicans blocked the confirmation of an official director for the Consumer Financial Protection Bureau until 2013 as a way of limiting the new agency's effectiveness and authority.

While the financial sector appears at present to be stable and GDP and the stock market have been growing, the economy has not returned to its pre-recession luster—a reality that continues to have an impact on our politics. Many Americans are worried about stagnant wages and the number of long-term unemployed; more than a few are disquieted by the increase in the national debt caused by addressing the economic crisis and chronic needs; and many are simply concerned that government is getting too big and intrusive. As of May 2013, 54 percent of Americans believed that government has too much power.[5]

In this chapter we explore the major American economic and social welfare policies with an eye toward developing a better understanding of how the government came to have such a vast array of responsibilities. In particular, we consider the role the American government has in managing the economy and ensuring minimum living standards for all citizens.

## Thinking Critically About This Chapter

### Using the Framework
You will see in this chapter how the framework can be used to explain why government does what it does in the areas of economic, budget, and safety net policies. You will use what you learned in previous chapters about structural, political linkage, and government factors to better understand what government does in terms of spending, taxing, regulating, subsidizing, and providing income and medical support for the elderly and the poor.

### Using the Democracy Standard
In previous chapters, you used the democracy standard to examine the extent to which American political and government institutions have enhanced popular sovereignty, political equality, and liberty. You will use the democracy standard in this chapter to ask whether the American people get the sorts of policies and performance they want from government.

17.1

17.2

17.3

17.4

17.5

17.6

17.7

17.8

17.9

**inflation**
A condition of rising prices and reduced purchasing power.

**depression**
A severe and persistent drop in economic activity.

# Why Does the Federal Government Do So Much?

**17.1** Assess why governments are so involved in economic and social affairs

I t is hard to imagine any activity in our daily lives that is not touched in one way or another by what the government does regarding the food supply, energy, health care, transportation, education, public safety, environmental quality, and the economy. Why does it do so many things in a country long committed to the idea of limited government? One must start, of course, with the Constitution itself, which gives the federal government a number of broad areas of responsibility, including the charges that it "establish Justice, insure Domestic tranquility . . . promote the general Welfare, and secure the blessings of Liberty. . . ." More specifically, the Constitution empowers the government to regulate interstate commerce, coin money, establish post offices and post roads, create a system to protect intellectual property (patents), borrow money and collect taxes to meet its many responsibilities, and more.

Though one must start with the Constitution, one cannot end there. While the Constitution provides broad grants of responsibility and power, it has been the American people, using the political tools available to them in a democracy, who have pressed elected officials over the course of American history to institute a broad range of policies and programs to improve and protect their safety and well-being. The American people, as well as business leaders on a number of occasions, have asked government to do more because of profound economic and social changes that have affected their lives, often creating problems that have not been easily solved by individuals or the private market (see below). One of the enduring themes in our recent politics is the question of whether we have gone too far in expanding the role of government even though there were good reasons why the expansion took place.

Governments in all rich democracies play a substantial role in managing economic affairs and providing a range of safety nets for their citizens. Let's see why this is so.

## ☐ Managing the Economy

No government today would dare leave problems such as stagnant economic growth, unemployment, international trade imbalances, inflation or financial collapse to work themselves out "naturally," though that is what free-market purists here and abroad insist we should be doing today. Citizens and political leaders in the rich democracies have learned that free market economies, left to themselves, are subject to periodic bouts of **inflation**, financial bubbles which inevitably burst, and occasional sustained periods of deep unemployment and declining economic output (called **depressions**). The worldwide trauma of the Great Depression in the 1930s was the event that etched this lesson into the minds of virtually everyone and changed the role of government in economic affairs in all the rich democracies.

Government responsibility for the state of the national economy is now so widely accepted that national elections are often decided by the voters' judgment of how well the party in power is carrying out this responsibility. When times are good, the party or president in power is very likely to be reelected; when times are bad, those in power have an uphill battle staying in office.[6] This is what happened to Jimmy Carter in 1980, George H. W. Bush in 1992, John McCain (a Republican running on the record of Republican president George W. Bush) in 2008. A weakened economy also dogged Barack Obama's re-election bid in 2012 (see the chapter-opening story in Chapter 10).

## □ Providing Safety Nets

All rich democracies have programs that protect the minimum standards of living against loss of income due to economic instability, old age, illness and disability, and family disintegration.[7] These are sometimes called safety net programs, the terminology we use here. All rich democracies provide safety nets, and the reason is simple: Their citizens have demanded it. They have apparently recognized that market economies, even when working at peak efficiency, do not guarantee a minimum decency of living for all or offer protection against economic dislocations even for people making their best efforts.[8] A range of studies, for example, show that bouts of long-term unemployment for people who have been regularly employed contributes to serious physical and mental illness, shortened life spans, family tensions including higher rates of divorce, and educational under-achievement for their children.[9]

# Economic Policies

| 17.2 | Analyze economic policymaking in terms of goals, players, and tools |

**G**overnment economic policies have a number of goals, including stimulating economic growth, preventing inflation and trade imbalances, providing infrastructure for economic activities, and compensating for or controlling negative externalities like air and water pollution. This section considers these goals in detail and then explores the fiscal and monetary tools American government has at its disposal to try and achieve these goals.

## □ The Goals of Economic Policy

Although economic policy goals sometimes conflict and involve important trade-offs,[10] they are consistently driven by six key concerns, which we will explore next.

**ENCOURAGE ECONOMIC GROWTH** The quintessential goal of economic policymakers is sustained economic growth—defined here as an annual increase in the **gross domestic product (GDP)**.[11] (GDP is a measure of the total value of goods and services produced in a nation on an annual basis.) A growing economy means more jobs, more products, and higher incomes, so most Americans support this goal. Economic growth is also the basis for increased profits, so business tends to support it as well. For political leaders, economic growth, accompanied by rising standards of living, brings public popularity and heightened prospects for reelection, as well as more revenues for government programs.

**CONTROL INFLATION** When inflation occurs, the purchasing power of money declines. When inflation rises, people's wages, salaries, savings accounts, and retirement pensions diminish in value. So, too, do the holdings of banks and the value of their loans. To nobody's surprise, political leaders seek to enact policy solutions that dampen inflation and that keep prices stable, usually through management of interest rates. In the United States, the **Federal Reserve**—the Fed—uses interest rates to control the supply of money in circulation and have an impact on inflation rates.

Government leaders face a classic trade-off problem, however, in trying to have both economic growth and low rates of inflation. The problem is that addressing one goal often gets in the way of achieving the other goal. For example, one way to combat inflation is to slow down the economy by having the Fed raise interest rates. This slows down the economy because higher interest rates make it harder and more expensive for consumers to borrow for the purchase of a car or a house and for businesses to raise money to fund expansion. Conversely, when the economy is stagnant or declining, one strategy is to pump more money into the hands of consumers and businesses by either lowering interest rates or increasing government spending (or both, as the government did in 2008 and 2009, as described in the chapter-opening story). A little too much stimulus, however, can generate inflation as too many dollars chase too few goods and services.

**gross domestic product (GDP)**
Monetary value of all goods and services produced in a nation each year.

**Federal Reserve Board (Fed)**
The body responsible for deciding the monetary policies of the United States.

17.1

17.2

17.3

17.4

17.5

17.6

17.7

17.8

17.9

17.1
17.2
17.3
17.4
17.5
17.6
17.7
17.8
17.9

**balance of payments**
The annual difference between payments and receipts between a country and its trading partners.

**ELECTED IN TOUGH TIMES**

Tough economic times have political consequences. Both Bill Clinton and Barack Obama were elected, in part, because the parties they were running against in their first presidential election campaigns were in power when the nation's economy turned sour. President Obama's Democrats suffered big election losses in the 2010 congressional elections because of ongoing high unemployment and slow recovery from the Great Recession. Are voters acting rationally when they focus on the state of the economy, or should other factors play an equally important role?

**AVOID BALANCE OF PAYMENTS PROBLEMS** All nations, including the United States, strive to keep their **balance of payments** in positive territory, that is, to export more goods and services—things such as insurance, banking, accounting, and advertising, for example—than they import. They do so because sustained negative trade balances—where more money leaves the country than is brought in—can lead to a decline in the value of a nation's currency in international markets. In this situation, businesses and consumers find that their dollars buy less, and they must either do without or borrow to make up the difference. The United States has run substantial balance-of-payments deficits for most of the past two decades.

**MAINTAIN BUDGETARY DISCIPLINE** All nations try—or at least claim they try—to keep their government budgets in rough balance between revenues (taxes and fees) and expenditures on things like national defense and pensions for retirees. Most of the time since the end of World War II, budgets in the rich democracies have tilted slightly toward the deficit side of things, with spending outpacing revenues by a few percentage points. A small deficit helps spur economic growth if it is spent on things that improve long-range economic prospects: infrastructure, like roads and harbors, and human capital, like education, training, and research and development (R&D). A big deficit is trouble, however, because it can only be funded by borrowing from people

17.1
17.2
17.3
17.4
17.5
17.6
17.7
17.8
17.9

**CHINA RISING**

One of the most important developments in the global economy is the emergence of China as a major player—something that is reflected in this scene of Shanghai's rapidly rising skyline. China is the destination for many U.S. exports, while the United States is the destination for many Chinese exports. Unfortunately, the trade is heavily unbalanced in favor of China. Addressing this trade imbalance is a continuing concern of American policymakers, though little progress has been made to date. To what extent are policymakers correct in worrying about trade imbalances?

here and abroad and from foreign governments through their purchase of U.S. government bonds and Treasury notes. (Deficits grew dramatically in 2009 and 2010 in the United States and in Europe when spending increased for stimulus purposes and tax revenues plummeted because of the recession.[12])

**externalities**
The positive and negative effects of economic activities on third parties.

**AVOID EXTERNALITIES** Most people also want to avoid negative **externalities,** the bad side effects that often accompany normal economic activity. A growing manufacturing economy, for example, often produces things such as air and water pollution, toxic waste, and workplace injuries and health hazards. High demand for oil and the decline of easily drilled areas on and near shore have driven companies such as British Petroleum to drill in very deep waters, increasing the risk of blowouts and environmental catastrophes. In response to these negative externalities, the public has pressed the government to take actions that compensate those who have been negatively impacted and, hopefully, prevent future problems. After British Petroleum's Deep Water Horizon oil rig exploded in 2010, the company wound up paying billions of dollars in damages to compensate those whose lives and businesses were hurt by the resulting oil spill.[13]

**PROVIDE FIRM FOUNDATIONS FOR A VIBRANT ECONOMY** Finally, there are economic activities that are essential for the health of the national economy but which are unlikely to be provided by private firms. For example, the United States and all European countries subsidize farmers, who are vital to the nation's food supply. Also, the federal government encourages business activity in America's inner cities by using enterprise zone tax incentives; and supports the defense industry by directly purchasing weapons systems and subsidizing research. In the aftermath of the Great Recession and the long jobless recovery from it, the government intervened to save the American auto industry, bailing out, taking temporary ownership, and encouraging the reorganization of General Motors (which reported record profits in 2011, just three years

**macroeconomic policy**
Policy that has to do with the performance of the economy as a whole.

**fiscal policy**
Government efforts to affect overall output and incomes in the economy through spending and taxing policies.

**monetary policy**
Government efforts to affect the supply of money and the level of interest rates in the economy.

after the bailout).[14] Economic growth also requires good roads, airports, and harbors, something the private sector normally does not provide on its own. Governments in the rich democracies have stepped into the breach and provided support for such vital activities and services, usually by providing subsidies and tax breaks, but sometimes by direct public ownership (as in the case of the interstate highway system).

## ☐ The Government's Macroeconomic Policy Tools

The government's main tools for dealing with inflation, unemployment, and national output are fiscal policy and monetary policy. However, government action is complicated by the considerable disagreement that exists about which tool works best for solving particular economic problems. The multidimensional phenomenon of globalization also increasingly intensifies the complexity of national policymaking choices as policies enacted abroad impact the economy at home (and vice versa).[15]

Government efforts to encourage economic growth, low unemployment, and stable prices, and to rescue the economy after a disastrous collapse like our recent one, fall under the heading of **macroeconomic policy,** or policy that affects the performance of the economy as a whole. The main tools of macroeconomic policy are fiscal policy and monetary policy.

**FISCAL POLICY** **Fiscal policy,** all government actions having to do with spending and taxes, is in theory a flexible tool for stimulating the economy when it is underperforming and for slowing down the economy when it is getting too hot—that is, growing so fast that it triggers inflation. The president and Congress can increase government spending or decrease taxes when economic stimulation is required, thus getting more money into circulation; they can cut spending or increase taxes when the economy needs a cooling-off period.

Fiscal tools are not easy to use, however. Decisions about how much government should spend or what level and kinds of taxes ought to be levied are not made simply on the basis of their potential effects on economic stability and growth. The elderly want Social Security and Medicare benefits to keep pace with inflation, for example, regardless of their effect on the overall economy. Similarly, auto companies want subsidies when faced with collapse, no matter the more general consequences. Timing also is a problem. When the country needs massive deficit spending to stimulate an economy in deep recession, as was the case in 2008 and 2009, it is easy enough to do, but knowing when to put on the brakes is difficult. Too soon, and economic recovery can stall; too late, and public debt mounts rapidly.

Perhaps the greatest challenge to a nimble fiscal policy, however, is America's own ideological politics. As we learned in previous chapters, Congress is anything but efficient and often debilitated by deep partisan divisions. Democrats tend to back a fiscal policy that favors increased spending and taxes while Republicans tend to favor one marked by reduced spending and taxes. Regardless of the state of the economy, these partisan divisions often stand in the way of fiscal reforms—even those reached by way of compromise.

**MONETARY POLICY** **Monetary policy** refers to Fed policies that affect how much money is available to businesses and individuals from banks and how much it costs. The more money that is available and the lower the interest rates at which money can be borrowed, the higher overall consumer and business spending are likely to be. For example, if the Fed wants to increase total spending in the economy, it increases the money supply by buying government securities from the private sector. When it does this, paying from its reserve funds, it puts more money into circulation. It can also lower the discount rate, which lowers the cost member banks pay to borrow money from the Fed—which they can then lend at lower rates to consumers and firms.

The Fed's influence on interest rates and the availability of credit is not unlimited. Interest rates, for example, are also affected by such things as the value of the dollar and the willingness of foreign investors to put their money into American firms, properties, and government bonds. Also, the Fed has very little impact on many factors that affect long-term economic performance, such as productivity growth or the price of commodities like oil.[16]

**DEBATES ABOUT THE BEST USE OF THE GOVERNMENT'S ECONOMIC TOOLS** People may agree that government has a role to play in the management of the economy, but they disagree about how it should be done.[17] **Keynesians**—who trace their roots to English economist John Maynard Keynes's classic work, *The General Theory of Employment, Interest, and Money*—have one view. They believe that in an economy where the tools of production (labor, equipment, factories, and the like) are not being used to full capacity, government must stimulate economic activity by increasing government spending or by cutting taxes (or both). Most Keynesians would prefer to see increased spending rather than lower taxes, and they are associated with an activist conception of the role of government most favored by liberal Democrats. Keynesians went out of fashion with the election of Ronald Reagan in 1980 and the ascendancy of the Chicago school of free market economics associated with Milton Friedman. But, in the midst of the Great Recession, the governments of many countries, including the United States, Germany, China, and Japan, stimulated their economies by increasing spending and reducing taxes. The results of these efforts have been mostly positive as these countries continue on a track of steady (if sometimes lackluster) economic recovery. Alternatively, harsh austerity budgets—with deep cuts in spending—as in Greece, Spain, and the UK appear to have led to higher unemployment and continued economic stagnation as Keynesians predicted.[18] Keynes is once again in vogue among many policy experts.[19] However, the popularity of the Tea Party (whose adherents want to cut spending and taxes dramatically) and the focus of elected officials of all stripes (here and in Europe) on balancing budgets shows that Keynes's thinking is still not ingrained in everyday politics and policymaking.

**Monetarists,** such as the late Nobel Prize–winning economist Milton Friedman, believe that government (e.g., the Federal Reserve in the United States or the European Central Bank in the case of the European Union) should confine

**Keynesians**
Advocates of government programs to stimulate economic activity through tax cuts and government spending.

**monetarists**
Advocates of a minimal government role in the economy, limited to managing the growth of the money supply.

17.1
17.2
17.3
17.4
17.5
17.6
17.7
17.8
17.9

**STIMULATING SOLAR POWER**
President Obama's massive stimulus package, passed in early 2009, included generous tax credits for people who chose to improve the insulation of their homes, buy energy-saving appliances, and install alternative energy devices such as solar power. Here, a construction worker installs solar panels on a roof of a home in San Ramon, California. Are tax credits the best way to encourage energy savings? If not, what other strategies might work better?

17.1

17.2

17.3

17.4

17.5

17.6

17.7

17.8

17.9

**Office of Management and Budget (OMB)**

Part of the Executive Office of the President charged with helping the president prepare the annual budget request to Congress; also performs oversight of rule-making by executive branch agencies.

its activity to managing the growth in the supply of money and credit so that it closely tracks the growth in productivity in the economy as a whole. In the monetarist view, this will stimulate private investment, which in turn will allow slow but steady economic growth without inflation. Balanced federal budgets are essential in the monetarist position because unbalanced budgets, in their view, make it difficult for central banks to control the money supply properly. Monetarism is the economic policy, then, of those who believe in a minimal federal government and the virtues of the free market most associated with conservatives and Republicans.

Monetarists are closely associated with "efficient market" economists who believe that markets tend toward efficiency and the rational allocation of resources if left alone, reducing the need for regulation by government.[20] These economists have dominated their discipline for several decades now and have influenced public policies on regulation, including the financial and energy industries.

# Fashioning the Federal Budget

**17.3**  Identify the components of the federal budget and analyze the problem of the national debt

**A**merica's fiscal policy is the outcome of decisions made by the president and Congress on spending and taxes. These matters are settled in the budget and in separate tax and spending bills.[21]

The federal budget has a number of interesting characteristics.[21] First, it is an executive budget, meaning that it is prepared by the president and his staff (and the **Office of Management and Budget,** or the **OMB**); considered, amended, and passed by Congress; then put into effect by the president and the executive branch. Second, the budget is an annual one—that is, a new one is prepared and legislated each year. And third, the budget takes the form of line items, with funds allocated for specific activities of federal programs such as salaries, supplies, travel, and the like, rather than a lump sum given to an agency or department that might be used more flexibly.

From start to finish, preparation of the annual budget takes longer than a year.[22] It is a complex and often harrowing process. As we saw in the Chapter 9 opening story, failure to fund the government leads to a government shutdown.[23]

**THE PRESIDENT AND THE OMB**  In the spring, the president and his staff prepare a broad budget outline that is sent to all federal departments and agencies through the Office of Management and Budget, proposing total government spending, the revenues that will be available to fund this spending, and the spending limits that will apply to each department and agency. A process of negotiation then begins among executive branch departments and agencies, the OMB, and presidential staffers about these proposals. Because economic conditions and the business climate will affect how the budget works out in practice—for example, the level of government receipts that flow into government coffers from taxes will depend on how fast the economy is growing or contracting—the Council of Economic Advisers and the Treasury Department are active participants in the discussions surrounding these guidelines and the more formal budget that later gets put together.

**THE EXECUTIVE BRANCH**  Like most organizations, executive branch agencies try to gain more money and personnel to fulfill their missions,[24] although they generally try not to be too unreasonable, given the competing demands of other agencies and the president's concern with staying under the federal government's planned budget ceiling. These requests are filtered through the OMB, whose job it is to examine department and agency requests (usually holding hearings in October and November as part of this process), negotiate changes, and package the requests into a final budget proposal that fits the president's priorities. The director of the OMB then reviews the budgets for each department and agency and passes them on to the White House for its consideration. After some adjustments are made to accommodate new needs, changing economic forecasts, pleas from some departments and agencies, and the political agenda of the president, a final budget is prepared in the White House for presentation to Congress within 15 days from when it first convenes in January.

**CONGRESS** After receiving the budget request from the president, both the House and the Senate pass concurrent resolutions. With technical advice from the Congressional Budget Office (Congress's counterpart to the OMB), the resolutions specify broad budget boundaries, such as total spending and deficit or surplus targets. The budget that Congress eventually passes, however, does not guarantee that agencies or programs will be funded at requested levels. The budget is not a law. Rather, it serves as a blueprint for Congress as it makes its official funding decisions throughout the remainder of the year.

The process by which the government officially funds federal departments, agencies, and programs is called the appropriations process. Decisions about funding levels are first the responsibility of House and Senate **appropriations committees**, with subcommittees generally focusing on appropriations for individual departments, such as the Department of Defense. Subcommittees hold hearings, taking testimony from department and agency officials as well as friends and (sometimes) critics of particular programs. Each chamber then considers the appropriations committees' spending bills—which hopefully have been written with the budget in mind—and, like any other bill, these must be signed by the president.

The thirteen or fourteen appropriations bills that make their way to the floor of each chamber must be enacted by September 15. One complication is that appropriations cannot be made until standing committees pass funding authority bills, which create and maintain the programs that government spends on. Some programs must be authorized annually; others are authorized every few years (or longer). A final process—budget reconciliation—allows the House and Senate to pass a law by September 25 that brings the already passed funding levels into closer alignment with the annual budget. The executive branch operates within the new budget on October 1, the start of the federal government's new fiscal year. Budget making in Congress is never easy, even when revenues are plentiful, when economic prospects are good, and when Republicans and Democrats are willing to settle differences amicably through compromise. Absent these conditions, the processes by which annual appropriations bills work their way through Congress can be a torturous, conflict-laden, blame-apportioning business, especially as new tax legislation must sometimes be considered alongside a specific spending allotment. In recent years, as partisanship has increased, the budget process has become fraught with difficulties, delays, and debt-ceiling crises.

In 2011 Congress passed a special law that made automatic, dramatic cuts to hallowed domestic and defense programs if a broader agreement on a more balanced approach to reducing spending could not be found. Congress failed to meet that broader agreement, leading to nearly $1 trillion in across-the-board cuts. Then, in 2013, a failure to pass the necessary appropriations bills led to a seventeen-day government shutdown—the first shutdown since the Clinton administration. Needless to say, these outcomes make it exceedingly difficult for agencies to plan and execute policy on a rational and consistent basis.

**FEDERAL GOVERNMENT SPENDING** The federal government spent almost $3.8 trillion in 2013, just under 25 percent of GDP, a big jump from only a few years earlier. Figure 17.1 shows the change over time in federal outlays as a percentage of GDP. Several things are immediately apparent.

First, the most dramatic increases in federal government spending are associated with involvement in major wars; note the big spike in the graph for the years

17.1

17.2

17.3

17.4

17.5

17.6

17.7

17.8

17.9

**appropriations committees**
The committees in the House and Senate that set specific spending levels in the budget for federal programs and agencies.

17.1
17.2
17.3
17.4
17.5
17.6
17.7
17.8
17.9

**discretionary spending**
That part of the federal budget that is not tied to a formula that automatically provides money to some program or purpose.

**payroll tax**
Tax levied on salaries and wages for Social Security and Medicare.

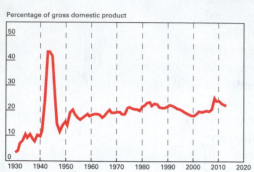

Percentage of gross domestic product

**FIGURE 17.1** FEDERAL GOVERNMENT SPENDING AS A PERCENTAGE OF GDP, 1930–2013

This graph shows the scale of federal government spending relative to the size of the U.S. economy. We see that the increase in the relative size of the federal government is a phenomenon related to depressions, recessions, and wars.

*Note:* Data for 2013 is estimated.

*Source:* Office of Management and Budget, *Budget of the United States, Fiscal Year 2014.*

associated with World War II. Second, the relative spending level of the federal government increased steadily from the early 1930s to the early 1980s, then leveled off and declined after that. This decrease was caused, in large part, by a substantial decrease in the relative size of the national defense budget after the end of the Cold War. Third, the wars in Afghanistan and Iraq, the Medicare prescription drug program, and stimulus and bailout spending to fight the Great Recession again increased federal government spending as a percentage of the economy in the 2000s.

The largest portion of the federal budget—65 percent in 2013—is for mandatory spending, over which Congress and the president exercise little real control.[25] Mandatory expenditures are automatic, unless the program legislation is changed or language is changed in the budget authority bills, for programs such as Social Security retirement benefits or Medicare spending, which distribute benefits by formula. Medicare benefits go automatically to Americans over age 65, for example. Medicaid is distributed to the states according to a formula based on the number of poor people in each state. Expenditures on these programs happen outside the annual appropriations process and are triggered by changes in, for example, the number of elderly or poor people. Almost 6 percent of the federal budget for 2013 was for payment of interest on the national debt; such payments are required, as well. The upshot is that only 34 percent of the 2013 budget was discretionary, open to changes in funding through the annual appropriations process. And because the costs of mandatory programs are increasing rapidly—particularly Social Security and Medicare—elected leaders have less and less discretion over spending decisions.[26]

Moreover, much of the **discretionary spending** budget—over half, in fact—was taken up by national defense, which totaled $666 billion in 2013, representing about 18 percent of the total federal budget. Another $48 billion went to homeland security. Taking defense, homeland security, interest on the national debt, and mandatory programs together, only about 17 percent was left in the budget for all other federal programs and activities. Only about $600 billion of the total budget of $3.7 trillion was left for education, scientific and medical research, transportation, energy, agriculture, housing, national parks, the administration of justice, environmental protection, international affairs, the space program, public works projects, the arts and humanities, and everything else.

## ☐ Federal Revenues

Government can spend money, of course, only if it has a stream of revenues coming in. Such revenues are raised by various kinds of taxes.[27] Although the American system of taxation shares some features with those of other countries, it is unique in a number of ways.

First, although Americans from all walks of life report feeling squeezed by taxes, the total of all taxes levied by all government jurisdictions in the United States as a proportion of GDP is relatively low when compared with the tax bite in the other rich democracies (see Figure 17.2). Second, the relative size of the tax bite in the United States has been getting smaller. Federal taxes as a share of GDP were 15.8 percent in 2012—since 2009, taxes as a share of GDP have been a bit lower than in previous decades going back to the 1950s.[28] And, on average, what individual Americans pay in taxes as a percentage of their incomes has stayed about the same for the past 30 years.[29] Third, being a federal system, states and localities levy their own taxes, which take forms that are different from those at the federal level. The national government depends primarily on individual income taxes (personal and corporate) and **payroll taxes** to fund its activities. The states get most of their revenues from sales taxes, although many have income taxes as well. Local governments depend most heavily on property taxes.

Also, the American tax system is uniquely complex. The U.S. Tax Code is a voluminous document, filled with endless exceptions to the rules and special treatment

17.1

17.2

17.3

17.4

17.5

17.6

17.7

17.8

17.9

**FIGURE 17.2** TOTAL TAX BURDEN AS A PERCENTAGE OF GDP IN THE UNITED STATES AND OTHER RICH DEMOCRACIES, 2012

The total tax burden of the United States is lighter than that of the other rich democracies.

*Source:* The Organization for Economic Cooperation and Development, 2012.

*Note:* The data for Japan is from 2011.

for individuals, companies, and communities, usually the product of political influence of one kind or another. Thus hedge fund and private equity managers and partners make the bulk of their money from hefty fees that, for some reason, are taxed not as normal income but at the capital gains rate of only 15 percent. Few people besides accountants and tax attorneys fully understand the Code, and their services are available mainly to those who can afford them.

On the surface the federal income tax looks quite **progressive**—a system in which tax rates increase as income and wealth increase—but in actuality it is only mildly progressive. In 2010, the average American paid a tax rate of 18.1 percent, with the top fifth of earners paying about 24 percent and the middle fifth paying about 11.5 percent.[30] However, high-income individuals, particularly the very wealthy, pay only a slightly higher percentage of their income than others do, after all deductions, exclusions, credits, and tax shelters are taken into account. Other federal taxes, such as Social Security and Medicare taxes and excise taxes on alcohol and cigarettes, are **regressive**—that is, they take a higher proportion of income in taxes from those lower on the income scale. The result is an overall federal tax system that is relatively flat, meaning that most people in the United States pay about the same percentage of their income in taxes regardless of their earnings.[31]

The 2001 and 2003 Bush tax cuts, which favored high-income earners and reduced the estate tax, made the **effective tax rate** on the wealthy even lower. The struggle between Republicans and Democrats on whether and how to extend these cuts has been part of our politics ever since. The Bush tax cuts, which expired in 2013, were reinstated for all but the highest earners. In 2013, the highest marginal individual tax rate (for income over $400,000) was 39.6 percent.

## ☐ Budget Deficits and the National Debt

In early 2001, federal officials and private economists issued confident predictions that the government's budget would be in the black by more than $230 billion in 2002 and that total cumulative surpluses through 2012 would be about $5.6 trillion. This changed dramatically in 2002. The Bush White House announced that the federal budget was going to be at least $106 billion in the red for 2002 and would remain in deficit for years. The **Congressional Budget Office (CBO)** estimated that the 10-year accumulated deficit would be $1.6 trillion. The change from an estimated surplus of

**progressive taxation**

A tax system in which higher-income individuals are taxed at a higher rate than those who make less.

**regressive taxation**

A tax system in which lower-income individuals are taxed at a higher rate than those who make more.

**effective tax rate**

The actual amount a person pays in taxes as a percentage of his or her total income.

**Congressional Budget Office (CBO)**

An agency of the U.S. Congress that provides technical support and research services on budget issues for its members and committees.

**17.1**

**17.2**

**17.3**

**17.4**

**17.5**

**17.6**

**17.7**

**17.8**

**17.9**

**budget deficit**
The amount by which annual government expenditures exceed revenues.

**national debt**
The total outstanding debt of the federal government; the sum total of all annual budget deficits and surpluses.

$5.6 trillion to a deficit of $1.6 trillion represented the most dramatic reversal of the fiscal health of the nation in more than 50 years.

That proved to be an optimistic forecast, however. When President Bush submitted his last budget to Congress (fiscal year 2009), the CBO had increased its estimate for cumulative deficits for the years 2002–2012 to $2.75 trillion, all of which would be added to the national debt. In his fiscal 2013 budget, President Obama reported a deficit of $1.3 trillion in 2012. These are stunning numbers, to say the least.

Though the deficit shrunk considerably in 2013 and 2014 due to reduced spending by the federal government, a 2014 report from the CBO indicates that deficits are expected to rise considerably again over the next decade because of rising entitlement costs.[32]

Why the turnaround in the deficit picture? The simple answer is that we have been taking in dramatically less revenue and spending more money. On each side of the equation, there are long-term and short-term factors at work. Regarding revenues, there is much less coming in both because we have been cutting tax rates (long term), particularly for the wealthy, and because the Great Recession and its aftermath meant less economic activity by firms and individuals to tax. Regarding expenditures, at the same time we tried to stimulate economic activity to quit the Great Recession (short term), we also have been increasing our long-term obligations for things such as Medicare, Social Security, and Medicaid, the first two because Americans are living longer, the latter because more people are eligible.

Like any other person, organization, or institution that spends more than it makes—when it runs an annual **budget deficit**—the federal government must borrow from others to cover the shortfall and must pay interest to those from whom it borrows. The **national debt** is the total of what the government owes in the form of Treasury bonds, bills, and notes to American citizens and institutions (financial institutions, insurance companies, corporations, etc.), foreign individuals and institutions (including foreign governments and banks), and even to itself (i.e., to units such as the Social Security Trust Fund).

Are annual deficits necessarily bad? Is having a national debt a bad thing? It depends. Economists generally agree that running a budget deficit in a slow economy is a good thing because it helps stimulate economic activity. It puts money into the economy when individuals and firms have cut back on their own spending leaving government to fill the gap. They also agree that a national debt that grows larger

Percentage of gross domestic product

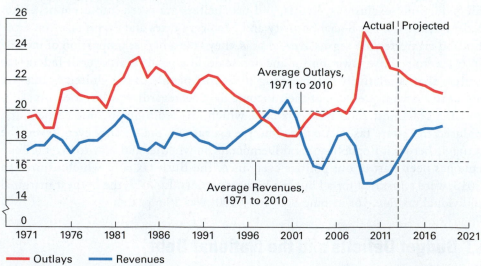

**FIGURE 17.3** FEDERAL GOVERNMENT SPENDING (OUTLAYS) AND REVENUES AS A PERCENTAGE OF GDP, 1971–2018

Figure 17.3 shows annual federal spending (outlays) and revenues as a percentage of GDP. When outlays are greater than revenues, the federal government is running a deficit and accumulating debt.

*Note*: Data for 2013–2018 are estimated and averages are computed from data going back to 1930 and through the 2018 projections.

*Source*: "Long-Term Budget Outlook," (Washington, D.C.: the Congressional Budget Office, 2012).

to meet emergencies—such as waging a war or fighting a recession—is unavoidable and that borrowing to make investments that will have positive long-term effects on society and the economy—such as building schools and roads, modernizing ports and airports, and funding research and development—is a good thing. However, borrowing to pay current operating costs is dangerous, something akin to living on one's credit card to buy groceries and pay the mortgage. Most economists believe that running annual deficits of this sort weakens the dollar and hurts purchasing power.

The budget will be in deficit territory for years to come, so the national debt will continue to grow, though perhaps more slowly as the economy recovers and grows. Equally troubling to many is that annual deficits and the national debt are increasing not because of investments that will bring long-term returns in better economic performance in the future but because of decreased tax revenues and increased entitlement spending. Spending by the United States on research and development and infrastructure as a percentage of GDP has been steadily declining for the past three decades.[33] Figure 17.4 shows the U.S. national debt as a percentage of GDP. As you can see, in recent years the Great Recession has caused the size of debt relative to the economy to increase but it still remains below the historic highs of World War II. Eminent economists such as Paul Krugman have consistently maintained that the country is able to handle a fairly high level of debt without a problem—particularly during recessionary times,[34] although more conservatively oriented economists disagree.

As a math problem, solving the deficit and debt problems is a simple matter: increase revenues and decrease expenditures. But this is unlikely, at least in the short-term, for a number of reasons. First, Americans do not agree among themselves about what they want or are willing to tolerate by way of sacrifice. Hardly anyone wants his or her taxes increased. Nor do recipients of government program dollars want fewer coming in, whether they are farmers receiving agricultural subsidy payments or older Americans receiving Medicare benefits.

Additionally, one of the central obstacles to solving the long-term debt problem is the extreme partisanship that exists in Washington and across the country. Pushed by

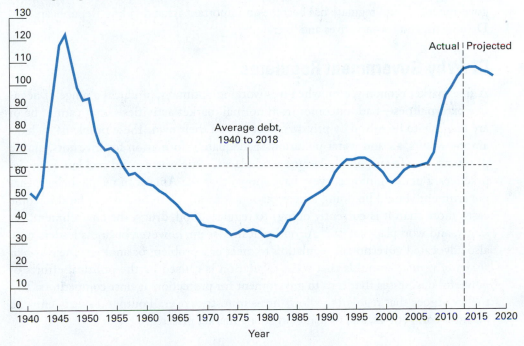

Percentage of gross domestic product

**FIGURE 17.4  THE NATIONAL DEBT AS A PERCENTAGE OF GDP, 1940–2018**

After a long period of decline, the relative national debt—that is, the size of the debt compared with the total size of the American economy (GDP)—grew considerably during the 1980s and up to the late 1990s when a booming economy helped to drive the debt down. The relative debt began to grow dramatically again as the Great Recession economy took hold and government spending increased. Even so, recent highs are lower than the historic high points reached during World War II.

*Source:* Office of Management and Budget, *Budget of the United States, Fiscal Year 2014.*

**539**

17.1

17.2

17.3

17.4

17.5

17.6

17.7

17.8

17.9

**regulation**
The issuing of rules by government agencies with the aim of reducing the scale of negative externalities produced by private firms.

their base, including the Tea Party movement, Republicans now stand firmly against tax increases of any sort, even as they oppose cuts in spending for national defense and the military, and for subsidies for the energy industry and farmers. Democrats, while willing to raise taxes, also have pushed for increased government spending on a range of existing and new programs, and strongly support stimulus spending during recessions to try to generate economic growth. When President Obama asked Congress to create a bipartisan commission to make recommendations on how to tackle the debt problem, Republicans blocked the measure. Seven Republican senators who had originally cosponsored the bill eventually voted against it. President Obama then issued an executive order in February 2010 creating a commission and appointed moderate Republican Alan Simpson and moderate Democrat Erskine Bowles to head it.[35] After it made its report in December 2011, President Obama ignored its recommendations.

It is not clear at this writing whether American political leaders of either political party will be willing and able to do what must be done to solve the long-term debt problem. Not only is partisanship a roadblock, but so is the mixed message coming from the American people: Americans are "in favor of Medicare, Social Security, good schools, wide highways, a strong military—and low taxes."[36]

# Regulation

**17.4** Explain the reasons for government regulation and predict the future of regulation

**R**egulation is one of the most visible and important activities of the federal government. For example, federal agencies issue rules that private businesses must follow. These rules may involve how a company treats its toxic wastes, what hiring procedures it practices, how much reporting it must do to inform its investors, or how it reports its profits and losses. The question of how much government should regulate has become an important issue dividing Republicans and Democrats, and conservatives and liberals.

## ☐ Why Government Regulates

A free market economy, even when it is working optimally, produces a range of negative externalities—bad outcomes from normal market activities—that cannot be or are unlikely to be solved by private businesses on their own. These problems include, among others, air and water pollution, inadequate information for investors, unsafe products, unsafe and unwholesome workplaces, toxic wastes, and reckless financial practices. Public opinion surveys have shown that the American people believe that government should be doing at least as much as it is currently doing (and in some cases more than it is currently doing) to regulate food, drugs, the environment, car safety, and workplace safety.[37] As odd as it may seem, however, business leaders have also advocated government regulation to meet one problem or another. The *economic theory of regulation* holds that most regulation is caused by the political efforts of powerful businesses that turn to government for protection against competitors. This theory argues that regulation allows firms to restrict overall output, to deny entry to business competitors, and to maintain above-market prices.[38]

## ☐ A History of American Regulation

A brief review of the history of regulation illustrates how the interaction of democratic and nondemocratic factors has produced today's regulatory agencies and policies.[39]

Between 1900 and World War I, laws were passed to regulate activities of powerful new corporations. These progressive era reforms were pushed by labor unions, the Populists, and middle-class Americans anxious about the conditions reported by muckraking journalists. Landmark regulatory measures included the Federal Trade Commission Act, the Meat Inspection Act, the Pure Food and Drug Act, and the Federal Reserve Act. These measures dealt with problems such as monopolies, unstable financial institutions, unwholesome products, and unsafe working conditions.

Some scholars believe, however, that large corporations were major players in the conception, formulation, and enactment of regulatory legislation.[40] Seen in this light, the Federal Reserve Act, which created the Federal Reserve System of banks and the Federal Reserve Board that is responsible for U.S. monetary policy, was primarily a government response to the entreaties of the American Bankers Association, which worried that financial panics would destroy its business.

Franklin Roosevelt's New Deal in the 1930s focused on speculative and unsafe practices in the banking and securities industries that had contributed to the onset of the Great Depression. The goal was to restore stability to financial markets and important industries. Legislation focused on such issues as federal bank inspection, federal deposit insurance, the prohibition of speculative investments by banks, and the creation of the Securities and Exchange Commission to regulate stock market operations. Again, the political sources of New Deal regulation were mixed. Some came from popular pressures,[41] but some also came from the business community, seeking stability in its various industries.[42]

The successes of the consumer, environmental, and civil rights movements of the late 1960s to the late 1970s resulted in a substantial increase in the federal government's regulation of business. The aim of these regulatory efforts was to protect against health and environmental hazards, to provide equal opportunity, and to allow more public access to regulatory rule-making. Under the authority of new laws, agencies such as the Environmental Protection Agency, the Equal Opportunity Employment Commission, and the Food and Drug Administration issued numerous rules that affected business operations and decisions. It was one of the only times in our history when business was almost entirely on the defensive, unable to halt the imposition of laws and regulations to which it was strongly opposed.[43]

By the end of the 1970s, the mood of opinion leaders had turned against regulation in the name of economic efficiency. Many blamed excessive regulation for forcing inefficient practices on American companies, contributing to sluggish economic growth, low productivity, and disappointing competitiveness in the global economy. And many found fault with the government for imposing uniform national standards, strict deadlines for compliance with regulations, and detailed instructions.[44] The deregulatory mood was spurred by a business–political offensive that funded think tanks, foundations favorable to the business point of view, and electoral campaigns of sympathetic candidates.[45] From then until 2008, when the housing and credit crises caused political and business leaders and the public to rethink the issue, the watchword was **deregulation,** the attempt to loosen the hand of government in a variety of economic sectors including banking and finance, transportation, and telecommunications.

The rollback in federal regulation has been a bipartisan affair. Early reforms such as the deregulation of the airline and trucking industries occurred at the end of the Carter administration and were followed by the deregulation of the financial and oil industries during the Reagan administration—Reagan was perhaps deregulation's most stalwart advocate. In 1999, Bill Clinton signed the Gramm-Leach-Bliley Act, which allowed commercial banks, insurance companies, and investment banks to compete in the same markets and innovate new products (such as highly risky mortgage-backed securities and credit default swaps, among other things) relatively free from government oversight. During George W. Bush's administration, the SEC allowed Wall Street investment banks to regulate themselves and to dramatically lower the amount of money they had to keep on hand to back up the new securities they were inventing and marketing (called the "net capital rule"), with predictable results. In a speech in early 2010, Fed Chairman Ben Bernanke placed responsibility for the financial collapse in the United States on weak government regulation of the industry's underwriting and risk management practices, as well as on the lax ratings standards on the quality and safety of mortgage-backed securities and derivatives given by private agencies such as Standard and Poor's, Moody's, and Fitch.[46]

**deregulation**
The process of diminishing regulatory requirements for business.

17.1
17.2
17.3
17.4
17.5
17.6
17.7
17.8
17.9

17.1

17.2

17.3

17.4

17.5

17.6

17.7

17.8

17.9

## ☐ The Future of Regulation

For years, pollsters have reported that while Americans generally want a smaller and less expensive government in the abstract they also want government to protect them against the bad practices of firms and other externalities. As economic activity and technological change generate new problems, and when firms take advantage of their market power, people demand that government intervene. Thus, when people become ill from tainted beef, the public demands higher standards of meat inspection and tracking. When companies such as Enron collapse, taking with them the retirement savings of their employees, or when accounting firms allow companies such as World-Com to mislead investors, Americans demand that government protect them against similar behavior by other companies. When American companies import dangerous products from abroad—children's toys, for example—people demand closer scrutiny of manufacturing practices abroad and testing of imported products. When an unregulated, little understood, and highly leveraged "shadow banking" system[47] collapses and triggers a deep and long-lasting recession, as it did in 2008, the public, leaders of other industries, and elected officials push for increased regulation to diminish dangerous financial practices. The Dodd–Frank Wall Street Reform and Consumer Protection bill that passed in 2010 imposes a range of new requirements on financial institutions—including greater transparency in their operations, higher reserve requirements, and clearer language for consumers on mortgage loans and credit cards—and new powers to regulatory agencies to enforce them.

Importantly, American firms are affected not only by the regulatory activities of the U.S. government but by those of other governments and international agencies. Increasingly, for example, American firms are voluntarily conforming to tougher European standards on food additives possible carcinogens in cosmetics, and mercury in electronic devices. They are doing so not only because they wish to sell in the huge European Union market but because they want access to the markets of fast-developing countries such as India, Brazil, and China that are slowly adopting the European regulatory standards on a wide range of products.[48]

This dynamic of the appearance of new problems, public pressures to regulate firms and activities related to these new problems, and industry push back—in 2011, affected companies tried to prevent the Consumer Product Safety Commission from putting online a searchable database of injury reports on cribs and strollers[49]—is typical of American politics. Some periods see a wave of new regulatory initiatives; some periods experience a rollback of government regulation. Yet the need for regulation over a wide range of activities is evident to the public, political leaders, and many business leaders, and new technologies and a dynamic and changing economy cannot help but generate new regulatory demands. Government's regulatory role is here to stay, as is the contentious political debate that surrounds the question of how extensive this role should be.

# Safety Net Programs

**"S**afety nets" refers to a broad range of programs that protect the minimum standards of living of families and individuals against some of life's unavoidable circumstances: unemployment, income loss and poverty, physical and mental illness and disability, family disintegration, and old age. Such programs come in a variety of forms and account for the largest share of the annual federal budget.

## Types of Safety Net Programs

Social safety nets in the United States are made up of a fairly complex mix of programs, but we can distinguish two basic kinds. The first is **social insurance**, typified by Social Security and Medicare, in which individuals contribute to an insurance trust fund—in reality, a set of federal government bonds—by way of a payroll tax on their earnings and receive benefits based on their lifetime contributions. The second kind is **means-tested**, meaning that benefits are distributed on the basis of need to those who can prove that their income is low enough to qualify. The food stamp program is an example, as are federal grants-in-aid to the states to help pay to support the very poor served by the **Temporary Assistance for Needy Families (TANF)** program.

Some safety net programs are administered directly from Washington, while others are jointly administered by federal and state governments. Social Security is an example of a program run from the nation's capital. Payroll taxes for Social Security are levied directly on wages and salaries by the federal government, and benefit checks are issued to the elderly and the disabled by the Social Security Administration. By contrast, **Medicaid** is jointly funded and administered by state and federal governments, as is the unemployment compensation system. This means that each state has its own Medicaid and its own unemployment compensation system with wide variation in benefit levels across the states.

Some safety net programs are **entitlement** programs; that is, payments are made automatically to people who meet certain eligibility requirements. For example, citizens whose income is under a certain level are entitled to food stamps and Medicaid. People over the age of 65 are entitled to Medicare benefits. Because payments are made automatically, these expenditures are locked into the federal budget, and Congress can only tinker around the margins of the budget unless it changes the underlying statutes or passes revised program authorizations, which is hard to do, given the way the legislative process works. In passing the so-called "Ryan budget," House Republicans tried in 2011 and 2012 to change the entitlement status of Medicare and Medicaid. The efforts died in the Democratic-controlled Senate.

## The Costs of Safety Net Programs

We spend a substantial amount of money on what is designated in the annual federal budget as human resources (this includes means-tested and social insurance programs, but also spending for student loan programs, job training, medical research, and military pensions). In 2013, total federal expenditure for this category was $2.5 trillion, amounting to about two-thirds of total federal government outlays. This considerably outstrips spending in any other area of federal government responsibility, including national defense and homeland security.[50]

Social insurance represents the largest single portion of the federal budget. Social Security and Medicare, taken together, account for almost one-third of the federal budget. Moreover, Social Security and Medicare have been growing steadily as a share of federal expenditures. Means-tested programs (including Medicaid and TANF block grants to the states), on the other hand, represent a substantially smaller portion of the federal budget (see Figure 17.5) but have also been growing in size (as a portion of GDP) since the 1970s.[51] In addition, with the passage of the Affordable Care Act (ACA), many states are using new federal allotments to expand Medicaid, to insure more of America's poor, and to expand federal subsidies to help middle-income Americans afford private insurance.

Several things are immediately evident from the pattern of expenditures shown in Figure 17.5. First, the non-poor rather than the poor are the main beneficiaries of the American welfare state, because social insurance programs are the largest programs and go mainly to those who have been employed the longest, had the highest incomes, and paid the

**social insurance**
Government programs that provide services or income support in proportion to the amount of mandatory contributions made by individuals to a government trust fund.

**means-tested**
Meeting the criterion of demonstrable need.

**Temporary Assistance for Needy Families (TANF)**
Program that provides income and services to many poor families; has benefit time limits and a work requirement.

**Medicaid**
Program administered by the states that pays for health care services for the poor; jointly funded by the federal government and the states.

**entitlements**
Government benefits that are distributed automatically to citizens who qualify on the basis of a set of guidelines set by law; for example, Americans over the age of 65 are entitled to Medicare coverage.

17.1
17.2
17.3
17.4
17.5
17.6
17.7
17.8
17.9

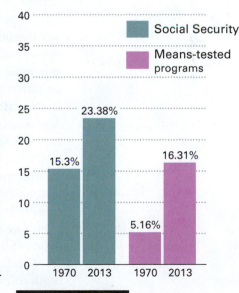

Spending as a percentage of government outlays

- Social Security
- Means-tested programs

1970: 15.3%
2013: 23.38%
1970: 5.16%
2013: 16.31%

**FIGURE 17.5** COMPARING SOCIAL INSURANCE AND MEANS-TESTED PROGRAMS

This graph compares the percentage of federal spending that goes to Social Security with the percentage that goes to means-tested programs in both 1970 and 2013. Social insurance programs (such as Social Security and Medicare) receive more federal funding than means-tested programs (such as public assistance, food stamps, and Medicaid).

*Source:* Office of Management and Budget, Budget of the United States, 2013.

maximum level of payroll taxes. Second, because Social Security and Medicare benefits go to those who are over 65, the elderly fare much better in the American welfare state than the young. One result has been a significant decline over the years in the poverty rate among the elderly and continuing high poverty among children.

In the next several sections, we examine America's main safety net programs. We start with social insurance programs.

# Social Insurance

**17.6** Describe the main social insurance programs in the United States and assess their effectiveness

T he main social insurance programs in the United States are **Social Security** and **Medicare**. Social Security was created in 1935 in the midst of the **Great Depression** to provide income to the elderly. Within a year, however, benefits were added for survivors (popularly referred to as the "widows-and-orphans" program). Coverage for those with disabilities was added in 1956. Today, almost all employed Americans are covered by Social Security, the main exception being the employees of state and local governments that have Social Security–like programs of their own. Medicare was created in 1965 just after Lyndon Johnson's landslide election in 1964 and the Democrats' win of near-historic proportions in that year's congressional elections. In the following sections on social insurance, because of their importance for the federal budget and their broad impact on American society, we focus on the old age pensions in the Social Security program and Medicare. It is worth noting, however, that almost one-third of total benefits from the Social Security program go to survivors and those with disabilities.[52]

## ☐ Social Security

Retirement income support for the elderly accounts for about two-thirds of Social Security expenditures; the other third goes to cover benefit payments for the disabled and survivors of deceased workers. The system is funded by a payroll tax on employees and employers under the Federal Insurance Contributions Act (the familiar FICA on your weekly or monthly pay stub). Because the program is paid for to a substantial degree by those who are currently working, the net effect is to redistribute income across generations.

Social Security pensions were never meant to pay the full cost of retirement for Americans. Planners had always assumed that the program was part of a three-legged stool for income in old age that included private pensions from people's employers and individual savings. Unfortunately, most people do not make enough to save a substantial amount of money on their own, and company pensions, particularly of the "defined benefit" variety once common for employees of large companies, are less generous today and fewer in number than they once were. Survey research in 2011 found that more than half of all retired Americans rely on Social Security as their primary source of income.[53]

Many Americans worry that Social Security funds will run out before they can begin collecting benefits. In large part, this is the result of years of commentary about the system's coming insolvency from conservative think tanks, political leaders, and radio and cable television talk-show hosts who have never been entirely friendly to the idea of government-mandated social insurance.[54] Alarm bells have also been raised by some economists about the long-term viability of the Social Security trust fund under current laws. Presently, with the exception of the post–Great Recession years of 2010 and 2011 when the fund suffered deficits, Social Security takes in much more in payroll taxes than it pays out in benefits each year, so its trust fund shows a strong positive balance and is growing. However, because the population is aging—meaning there will be fewer working people paying taxes to pay the benefits for additional elderly

17.1

17.2

17.3

17.4

17.5

17.6

17.7

17.8

17.9

**ARCHITECTS OF SOCIAL SECURITY**

This telegram from Labor Secretary Francis Perkins, now displayed at the Wisconsin Historical Society, congratulates economics professor A. J. Altmeyer on the passage of the Social Security Act of 1935, a centerpiece of Franklin Roosevelt's New Deal. Altmeyer and fellow University of Wisconsin economist Edwin Witte were major architects of the legislation. Is Social Security still a viable program?

recipients—a time will come when the fund will be paying out at a faster clip than it is being replenished. Especially troublesome to many is the sizable baby-boom generation, whose first members reached retirement age in 2010.

Current projections indicate that the trust fund will move into the red between 2033 and 2041, but the well will not run completely dry. Given a continued inflow of payroll taxes even after the fund goes into deficit, the current system will be able to pay about 75 percent of full benefits until at least 2087.[55] The system may also stay viable for a longer period of time if trends continue in which healthier and more active seniors choose not to retire at 65. Indeed, Americans appear to have caught on to this looming problem as nearly two-thirds of those who are not yet retired indicate that Social Security will not be their primary source of income when they do retire.[56]

Of course, well before Social Security runs dry, Americans could decide to solve the long-term trust fund problem. We could do so in any number of ways.[57]

- raising the payroll tax rate. One study shows that raising the payroll tax by 2 percent of earnings would solve the system's fiscal shortfall.[58]

- raising the ceiling on taxable income subject to the payroll tax ($110,100 in 2012).

- taxing all income rather than only income from wages and salaries, the current practice.

- cutting back recipient benefits. Cutting benefits by 13 percent would fully fund the system, for example.[59]

- taxing the benefits of the wealthy at higher rates.

- raising the retirement age.

None of these changes would be politically popular or easy to achieve, to be sure—Democrats generally oppose raising the retirement age, for example, and Republicans

17.1

17.2

17.3

17.4

17.5

17.6

17.7

17.8

17.9

say they will oppose tax increases of any kind—but adapting one or more would leave years of Social Security surpluses. The problem, of course, is that older Americans approaching retirement would be unlikely to appreciate having to wait longer to retire. Because older Americans vote at high rates compared to others and support powerful groups like the AARP to represent their interests, elected leaders are likely to listen to them. And younger Americans are unlikely to be enthusiastic about the prospect of paying more payroll taxes or having to retire later.

The deep partisan divide also makes change difficult, though not impossible. Generally, Democrats think the system is in reasonably good health and requires only some tinkering to solve emerging problems. Many Republicans, on the other hand, believe the system is seriously flawed and that the only way to save it is with major overhauls, including using a portion of the payroll tax to set up individual private accounts for retirement.[60] While many (particularly younger) Americans seem to support the private accounts idea in principle, it has not fared well as a policy proposal.[61] President George W. Bush emphasized it after his reelection in 2004 but it gained little traction and it is probably off the table for the foreseeable future in the wake of the financial collapse.[62]

## □ Medicare

Franklin Roosevelt wanted to include comprehensive health insurance for all Americans as part of Social Security when it was introduced to Congress in 1935. The proposal met fierce opposition from the American Medical Association (AMA), and the provision was dropped for fear of endangering prospects for passing Social Security. President Harry Truman tried to introduce a similar plan after the end of the Second World War, but the AMA and others were able to label the proposal "socialized medicine"—a very effective tool to block a new program during this time in American history when anticommunist sentiment was strong. Finally, with mounting evidence that health care costs were a leading cause of poverty, and buttressed with an electoral mandate and huge Democratic majorities in Congress after the 1964 elections, President Lyndon Johnson was able to create the Medicare insurance program for the elderly and a means-tested Medicaid program for the poor in 1965. (We consider Medicaid later in this chapter.) These programs fell well short of covering all Americans, but they were a highly significant step toward guaranteeing health care for those who were most in danger of becoming sick and least equipped to afford it.

Medicare dramatically transformed access to health care for the elderly in the United States. Millions of people who at one time would have been priced out of the health care market now have quality care available to them. In 2013, it is estimated that about 52 million people were enrolled in Medicare.[63] Everyone 65 and over is automatically enrolled in Medicare Part A, which pays for a portion of the bill for hospital stays and short-term skilled nursing after hospitalization. But people need to buy additional insurance (Medicare Part B) for coverage to help pay for doctors, durable medical equipment, tests, and X rays, if they choose to do so. And, because there are many gaps in coverage and significant co-pays under Parts A and B, many over the age of 65 choose as well to buy so-called *Medicare Advantage* (Part C) insurance that fills in these holes with added coverage. Medicare Part D went into effect in 2006 and pays a substantial portion of prescription drug costs for the elderly.

There is no question that the Medicare program has been extremely successful. People over the age of 65 have more access to health care services today than at any time in American history and it shows; people are living longer and healthier lives.[64] But there are widespread concerns about the program's costs. Paying for Medicare over the long term is a problem. First, the American population is getting older, meaning that the number of people on Medicare is growing and the number in the workforce paying payroll taxes supporting the program is shrinking in a relative sense. Second,

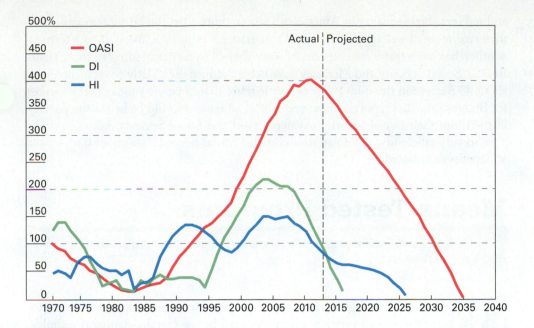

**FIGURE 17.6** MEDICARE AND SOCIAL SECURITY TRUST FUND BALANCES (ASSETS AS A PERCENTAGE OF ANNUAL COST)

Though much of the political and public discussion of social insurance financing (OASI in the graph) tends to be on the long-term problems of funding retirement, a much bigger and more pressing problem concerns the financing of Medicare. Funding for the two main parts of Medicare, the hospital trust fund (HI) and the supplemental trust fund for paying for doctors and tests (DI), runs into the negative territory where outlays exceed receipts much earlier than is the case for Social Security. (When the lines drop below 100 percent, the trust fund lacks the money to fulfill its obligations.)

*Source: Annual Report,* 2013, Social Security and Medicare Trustees.

health care costs—doctors, hospitals, tests, and prescription drugs—have been rising much faster than the payroll taxes that support Medicare Part A and general tax revenues that fund (in addition to premiums paid by beneficiaries) Parts B, C (Medicare Advantage plans), and D. The Medicare program is growing so fast that it will pass Social Security as the federal government's most expensive endeavor somewhere around the year 2030. One can see the scale of the problem in Figure 17.6, which shows the status of social insurance trust funds. It is clear that Medicare is in more serious short-term fiscal trouble than Social Security. The Affordable Care Act passed in 2010 aimed to contain some of these costs, but, unfortunately, it won't be able to do much to "bend the cost curve." Paul Ryan's budget plan passed in the House several times in 2011 and 2012 proposed that Medicare be turned into a voucher system in which seniors would use government-funded vouchers to shop for health insurance in the private market.

Whatever its problems, Medicare is here to stay (as a member of the GOP ticket in 2012, Ryan spoke infrequently about his voucher plan.) People use it, depend on it, and support it. Even at anti–big government rallies supported by the Tea Party, it is not uncommon to see signs that read "keep government out of my Medicare."

## Do Social Insurance Programs Work?

In an era when it is fashionable to deride the ability of government to do anything well, it is important to recognize how successful America's social insurance programs have been. There is no doubt that Social Security and Medicare work beyond the wildest dreams of their founders. Although the benefits do not allow people to live luxuriously, they provide an income floor for the retired and pay for costly medical services that, before 1965, were as likely as not to impoverish those who had serious illnesses and long hospital stays.

The effectiveness of Social Security and Medicare was shown in a 1989 Census Bureau study on the effects of all federal government taxing and spending programs on income inequality and poverty. The principal finding was that Social Security (including Medicare) "is the Federal government's most effective weapon against poverty

17.1

17.2

17.3

17.4

17.5

17.6

17.7

17.8

17.9

**Aid to Families with Dependent Children (AFDC)**
The federal entitlement program that provided income support for poor families until it was replaced by TANF in 1996.

and reduces the inequality of Americans' income more than the tax system and more than recent social welfare [means-tested] programs."[65] This conclusion, in one form or another, has been reaffirmed repeatedly since then.[66] In fact, according to the Census Bureau, Social Security and Medicare have helped reduce the elderly poverty rate from about 48 percent in the mid-1950s to a little more than 9 percent today.[67] The Center for Budget Priorities reports almost one-half of all seniors would be below the poverty line without their Social Security payments. And, the Social Security Administration does so very efficiently; administrative costs for Social Security are about 0.6 percent of benefits distributed.[68]

# Means-Tested Programs

**17.7** Describe the main means-tested programs in the United States and assess their effectiveness

**M**eans-tested programs are designed to provide income support and services for those with very low means who fall below certain income thresholds. One scholar suggests that these programs might more accurately be called "absence of means" programs.[69] Rather than being paid by payroll taxes, money for means-tested programs come from government's general revenues. While accounting for a much smaller portion of the federal budget than social insurance programs (see Figure 17.5), means-tested programs have traditionally attracted more criticism than virtually anything else government does. While Social Security and Medicare enjoy widespread support, welfare (a popular term for means-tested programs) has long been the object of scorn.

Most Americans say they want government to help the poor,[70] but almost everyone disliked the longest-lasting but now defunct public assistance program: **Aid to Families with Dependent Children (AFDC)**. A consensus long existed that something was wrong with AFDC.[71] For most Americans, AFDC and other means-tested programs seemed to contradict such cherished cultural values as independence, hard work, stable families, and responsibility for one's own actions. Public opinion polls consistently showed that Americans believed that welfare kept people dependent; didn't do a good job of helping people stand on their own two feet; and encouraged divorce, family disintegration, and out-of-wedlock births.[72] Although AFDC has now been replaced by the Temporary Assistance for Needy Families program (TANF), much of the thinking about means-tested programs and public assistance recipients remains unchanged. (See the "By the Numbers" feature to learn more about how the number of poor people in the United States is calculated.)

The federal government has several means-tested programs to assist poor Americans. Let us look at the five most important ones.

## ☐ Temporary Assistance for Needy Families

The Temporary Assistance for Needy Families (TANF) Act, passed in 1996, replaced AFDC with an entirely new system of public assistance, and "ended welfare as we know it," as President Bill Clinton put it. (See the "Using the Framework" feature on why the change happened.) Its major features were:

- The status of welfare assistance as a federal entitlement was ended. The families of poor children are no longer guaranteed assistance by the federal government.

- The design and administration of welfare programs have been turned over to the states, meaning there are 50 different welfare programs in the United States.

- States receive block grants from the federal government to help them finance the welfare systems they devise. States add their own money in varying amounts, with some states, such as New York, much more generous than others.

**THE POOR ARE AMONG US**
However poverty is measured, it is clear that the percentage of the population living in poverty in the United States is higher than in any other rich democracy. Although the United States arguably has the least generous set of safety nets among these countries, families like this one can usually depend on food stamps, some income support, and Medicaid to maintain a minimum standard of living. Why are so many people in the United States living at or below the poverty line?

- States use these combined funds to give both direct cash assistance to families—usually, a monthly welfare check—and money for child care, education and training, and other services to encourage recipients to enter paid employment. Recently, the proportion going to cash benefits has fallen dramatically.[73]

- The head of every family receiving welfare is required to work within two years of receiving benefits and is limited to a total of five years of benefits. States are allowed to impose even more stringent time requirements. States are also allowed to use their own funds (not federal block grant money) to extend the two-year and five-year limits. Many are not willing to do so.

- Unmarried teenage parents can receive welfare benefits only if they stay in school and live with an adult.

- States must provide Medicaid and CHIP (described in a later section) health care benefits to all who qualify under current law.

Proponents of welfare reform believed the new welfare system would end welfare dependency, reestablish the primacy of the family in poor communities, improve the income situation of the poor as they enter the job market, and help balance the federal budget. Opponents of welfare reform believed the legislation would lead to more poverty, homelessness, and hunger—especially among children—once recipients reached their five-year time limit. Here is what the research shows to date about the effects of the reform. Welfare rolls across the country dramatically dropped after the new law was passed; many people trained for jobs and entered the paid workforce, and many raised their incomes, especially during the latter part of the 1990s and from 2004 until the financial collapse in 2008.[74] However, because pay levels for entry-level

17.1
17.2
17.3
17.4
17.5
17.6
17.7
17.8
17.9

549

17.1

17.2

17.3

17.4

17.5

17.6

17.7

17.8

17.9

**poverty line**
The federal government's calculation of the amount of income families of various sizes need to stay out of poverty.

jobs are so low—about half take minimum-wage jobs—only a small percentage of former welfare recipients were able to cross the official **poverty-line** threshold in the first years of the program. And, while the poverty rate decreased among former welfare recipients between 1996 and 2000, it slowly increased after that.[75] Even at its highest level of usage, moreover, only about one-quarter of families living below the poverty line receive TANF benefits, either because of the stigma of being on welfare, the complexities of signing up and determining eligibility, or reaching the program's time limits.[76] So the vast majority of poor families in the United States do not receive TANF benefits. With states in dire economic straits today, moreover, many of them have been making it harder for people to get back on the welfare rolls even when they are technically eligible for more benefits.[77]

## ☐ Food Stamps

This program, funded from the budget of the Department of Agriculture and called the Supplemental Nutrition Assistance Program (SNAP) since 2008, helps poor Americans falling below a certain income to buy food for themselves and their families. Although other nutritional assistance programs exist to help the poor—the free or reduced-price school lunch program and the Women, Infants, and Children nutrition program are examples—the food stamp program does the most. About 47 million people (roughly 1 in 7 Americans) received food stamps in 2013. About 50 percent of food stamp recipients are children; about 75 percent of recipients are poor families with children. Food stamp benefit levels are set by the individual states under general federal guidelines, and states vary substantially in their generosity. Stamps can be used only for food; they cannot be used for alcohol, cigarettes, beauty care products, or gambling, despite rumors to the contrary. The program seems to have made a significant dent in the prevalence of malnutrition in the United States, even though the average benefit was only $1.48 per meal in 2012.[78]

**WELFARE TO WORK**
Like others covered by TANF, these aid recipients in Georgia are required to work or be in training for jobs as a condition for receiving assistance. Here a young mother searches job listings for a suitable position. What are some advantages of the TANF program? Disadvantages?

# By the Numbers

## How many Americans are poor?

Although the Bible says, "For you will have the poor with you always," it does not tell us how many of the poor will be with us at any given time.

### Why It Matters

Knowing how many poor there are, and being relatively confident in the validity and reliability of that number, is extremely important for a number of reasons:

- Comparing the number who are poor in the United States over time gives us an indication of how well we are doing as a society.

- Comparing the number who are poor in the United States over time lets us know the dimensions of a serious social problem that may require government action, or the mobilization of private charities, or both.

- The number of people living in poverty helps determine the size (and thus the cost) of many government programs, including food stamps, Medicaid, rent supplements, and the Earned Income Tax Credit.

Interestingly, if the numbers are to be believed, we made good progress during the 1990s—the poverty rate fell to 11.3 in 2000, its lowest point in 21 years—but increased again as the United States went through a recession and a recovery that added jobs later than usual in such recoveries. According to the Census Bureau, by 2010, at the height of the Great Recession, 15.3 percent of Americans—over 46 million people—were living below the poverty line.

### The Story Behind the Poverty Measure

But what is poverty and how can we measure it? Most would probably agree that poverty involves living in dire circumstances; that is, being poorly housed, underfed, and without adequate medical care. But we might have a harder time agreeing on the exact dividing line between adequate and inadequate living standards. To get around this, government statisticians use *income* as a proxy for calculating poverty. Rather than collect information about how people live—what their homes and apartments are like, for example—the Census Bureau collects information about how much money they earn. The assumption, of course, is that in an economy such as ours, what one earns is directly related to how one lives and consumes.

### Calculating the Poverty Line

The poverty line was first calculated in 1964 by Census Bureau statisticians. They started with the Department of Agriculture's determination of what it would cost a family of four to buy enough food to survive (called the "emergency food budget"). Then, because it had been determined that the average American family in 1964 spent one-third of its after-tax income on food, the statisticians multiplied the Agricultural Department's emergency food budget figure by three to determine the official government poverty line. They then adjusted this income number for family size, creating poverty line numbers for single persons living alone, two-person families, and so on.

This 1964 baseline figure is used to the present day. Starting in 1965, and every year since then, the poverty line from the previous year is adjusted for inflation, taking into account different family sizes. The accompanying table shows the official poverty line thresholds for 2012. To be under the line is to be officially poor.

### Criticisms of the Poverty Line Measure

As with most official statistics, the poverty line calculation has its critics:

- Because the typical American household today spends a much lower proportion of its income on food than in 1964, the "emergency food budget" figure from the Agriculture Department should be multiplied not by three, as it has been since the beginning, but by five or six, to calculate the poverty threshold, say some critics. This would result in a substantial increase in the number of people officially designated to be poor.

- If poverty is really about lifestyles and consumption patterns, argue conservatives, then household income calculations should include the income equivalents of noncash government benefits such as public housing, rent supplements, Medicaid support, and food stamps. Doing this would reduce the number of people officially living in poverty.

- By calculating a single, national poverty threshold, the Census Bureau fails to take into account the substantial differences in the cost of living that exist across states and communities. A family of four earning $17,000, for example, could no doubt stretch its dollars further in rural Alabama than in San Francisco.

### What to Watch For

All government statistics are built on a set of assumptions, some of which are sensible and some of which defy common sense. Be aware of such assumptions when you use official statistics. Luckily, every government agency describes in detail how it collects and calculates statistics, so you can figure it out once you read the documentation. You might also want to look at alternative measures. The Census Bureau, for example, is trying out a new Supplemental Poverty Measure that takes account of the criticisms of the standard measure discussed above. It shows that 16 percent of Americans are poor.

### What Do You Think?

With all its problems, why do we continue to depend on the Census Bureau's poverty line calculation? Do the virtues of simplicity, consistency, and historical comparability of the present way of calculating poverty trump its several problems? How else could poverty rates be calculated? What do you think should be included and excluded from such a calculation?

17.1
17.2
17.3
17.4
17.5
17.6
17.7
17.8
17.9

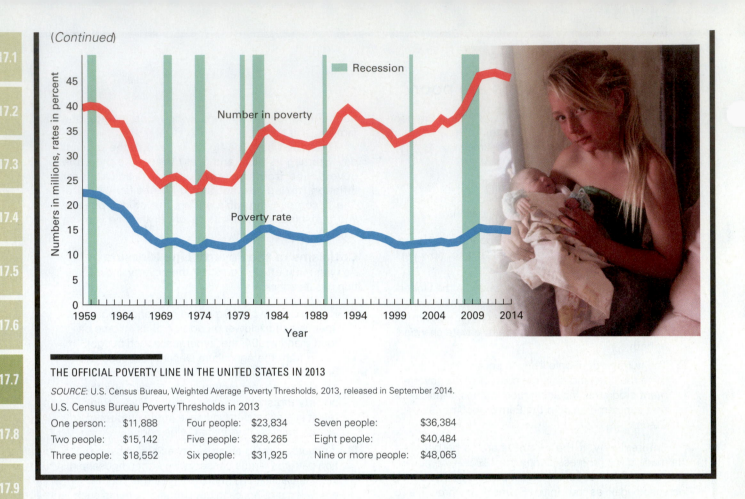

(Continued)

Number in poverty

Poverty rate

Recession

**THE OFFICIAL POVERTY LINE IN THE UNITED STATES IN 2013**

*SOURCE*: U.S. Census Bureau, Weighted Average Poverty Thresholds, 2013, released in September 2014.

U.S. Census Bureau Poverty Thresholds in 2013

| One person: | $11,888 | Four people: | $23,834 | Seven people: | $36,384 |
| Two people: | $15,142 | Five people: | $28,265 | Eight people: | $40,484 |
| Three people: | $18,552 | Six people: | $31,925 | Nine or more people: | $48,065 |

**Children's Health Insurance Program (CHIP)**

Program that pays for health care services for children in households above the poverty line but below 133 percent to 400 percent of the poverty line, depending on the state.

## ☐ Medicaid and Health Insurance for Poor Children

The federal government allocates money to the states to help them pay for medical services for many of their indigent adult citizens and children in two big and rapidly growing programs: Medicaid and **CHIP (the Children's Health Insurance Program)**. Medicaid is now the nation's second largest public assistance program. According to a May 2014 report, more than 20 percent of Americans are enrolled in Medicaid and CHIP and that percentage will continue to grow as the health care reform law is implemented.[79] When state expenditures for Medicaid are added to the federal contribution, Medicaid is almost as big as Medicare. The program is funded by both the states and the federal government; states receive from 50 to 83 percent of the cost of their state-designed and -administered Medicaid programs from Washington, with the poorest states receiving the highest percentage of reimbursements. Funding Medicaid has become one of the most difficult fiscal problems for the states, especially during tough economic times when state tax revenues decline and the need for Medicaid assistance increases. A large, mandatory increase in Medicaid coverage is one of the reason why so many Republican-controlled states joined the suit against the Affordable Care Act. The Supreme Court, while upholding the other provisions of the Act in 2012, overturned the Medicaid increase, deciding that Congress's interpretation of federal powers under the commerce clause was too broad. Cutting Medicaid by changing it from an entitlement program to one funded by smaller block grants to the states was an important part of the Republican platform during the 2012 national elections.

Medicaid is quite complicated and varies a great deal by state; it is difficult to describe in simple terms. All one can say with assurance is that if a state chooses to participate in the program, it is required to provide a specific range of medical services for people who are defined as "medically indigent"—defined under the new health care reform legislation as anyone falling at or under 138 percent of the poverty line (an increase over pre-ACA levels in order to help more people meet the insurance mandate). Medicaid pays for hospital, physician, and nursing services; home health care;

# Using the FRAMEWORK

## Why did our welfare system change so drastically in 1996?

**Background:** America's traditional welfare system, created in 1935 almost as an afterthought to Social Security, had grown to the point that it provided cash payments to families of one in nine children in the United States by 1995. Although it did not pay very much to individual families and represented but a tiny portion of the federal government's budget, the program was never very popular with the public, grew even less popular in the 1980s and the 1990s, and was replaced by a radically new program in 1996. Examining structural, political linkage, and governmental factors that contributed to a dramatic change in welfare policy will make the story clearer.

17.1
17.2
17.3
17.4
17.5
17.6
17.7
17.8
17.9

**Government Action**

The Temporary Assistance for Needy Families Act became law in 1996.

**Government**

The Republican controlled Congress delivered on its promise in the Republican Contract with America to pass a bill to radically transform welfare.

President Clinton, a believer in welfare reform (he had promised to "end welfare as we know it"), signed the bill into law near the beginning of the 1996 presidential campaign.

**Political Linkage**

Conservative intellectuals and think tanks attacked the AFDC welfare system during the 1980s on the grounds that it killed individual initiative and created dependency, destroyed families, and rewarded immorality.

Public opinion became more critical of welfare in the 1980s.

The Republican Party used the "welfare mess" issue with great effect in election campaigns, winning the presidency in 1980, 1984, and 1988 and the Senate for much of the 1980s.

The Democratic Party lost from its electoral base a substantial number of blue-collar, unionized workers, concerned about "wasteful spending" on welfare.

Moderate Democrats of the Democratic Leadership Council (DLC) also embraced welfare reform.

Republican conservatives won control of the House and Senate in the 1994 elections.

**Structure**

The American political culture celebrates competitive individualism, small government, and self-reliance, and denigrates handouts to the "undeserving" poor.

Competitive pressures from the global economy in the 1990s pushed governments in all of the rich democracies to make their welfare states more efficient.

The fall of communism and the post–Cold War boom in the United States enhanced the attractiveness of conservative ideas in America.

Federalism allowed states to experiment with alternative modes of welfare delivery.

diagnostic screenings and tests; as well as nursing home costs—provided that recipients do not exceed the income ceilings for the program. Some states also provide prescription drug coverage. In addition to providing medical services for the very poor, Medicaid has become increasingly used to pay for nursing home care for those who have exhausted their savings, including many people who had been long-time members of the middle class. Indeed, about 70 percent of nursing home residents in the United States receive aid from the program to pay for their housing and care. States have some latitude in determining who receives benefits and who does not—federal statutes identify around 50 categories of people potentially eligible for Medicaid benefits—and how much service providers receive in compensation, so benefits vary widely across the states.[80]

Despite the size of the program and the seemingly broad eligibility, simply being poor does not necessarily mean that one receives benefits. In fact, less than one-half of the people who fall below the government's poverty line are covered by Medicaid in any given year.[81]

CHIP is a program that pays for medical care for poor children not covered by Medicaid. The program, first enacted in 1997, is funded jointly by the states and the federal government, with states having significant discretion in determining benefit levels and covered services. In terms of coverage, CHIP has been an unqualified success. Between 1997 and 2010, for example, the number of medically uninsured poor and near-poor children in the United States dropped by more than a third, down to 15.4 percent among poor children.[82] A congressionally mandated study demonstrated that virtually all children in CHIP would not have any health insurance at all if not for the program.[83] President Obama signed a bill in early 2009 expanding the program, bringing in an additional 4 million children. (For arguments on how well government has done in providing nutritional well-being among poor children see the "Can Government Do Anything Well?" feature.)

There is no question that Medicaid and CHIP have been very successful in terms of allowing many poor and disadvantaged people to gain access to needed medical services. But many people are worried about the rising costs to the federal government and to the states of these programs. Others worry less about the costs than about the fact that people of limited means remain uninsured, eligible neither for Medicaid nor CHIP, and not old enough for Medicare.

## ◻ The Earned Income Tax Credit

The working poor benefit greatly from a provision in the U.S. Tax Code that allows low-income individuals with at least one child to claim a credit against taxes owed or, for some, to receive a direct cash transfer from the IRS. The Earned Income Tax Credit (EITC) benefits more than 28 million low-income families without much bureaucratic fuss.[84]

# The Affordable Care Act (ACA)

**17.8** Explain how the Affordable Care Act changes health care

On March 23, 2010, President Barack Obama signed the Affordable Care Act into law, the most far-reaching reform of the nation's health care system since passage of Medicare in 1965. Although the law is long and complex, it does a number of fairly straightforward things. First, the ACA extends health insurance coverage to a substantial share of 46 million previously uninsured Americans. It mandates that every American have health insurance either through their workplaces or on their own. Those who elect not to purchase health care pay a penalty. Those who can't afford to do so get government subsidies or, in many states, access to Medicaid. Under the ACA, the federal government helps states increase access to Medicaid by providing them with most of the funds necessary to expand it. The ACA also encourages small businesses to offer coverage to their employees by enabling them to shop for the best programs with

# Can Government Do Anything Well?

## Enhancing the nutritional well-being of poor children

The federal government plays a very large role in providing nutritious food for poor children in the United States who would otherwise be hard pressed to find a proper meal. The federal food stamp program—now the Supplemental Nutrition Assistance Program (SNAP)—helps 46 million Americans gain access to nutritious food by allowing families to shop for groceries (but not alcohol or cigarettes). More than one-half of beneficiaries of the program are children. College students, people on strike, and undocumented immigrants are not eligible for the program. The Department of Agriculture's Child and Adult Care Food Program provides meals for 2.6 million children in day care, many of whose parents are working but in low-wage jobs, and to children in homeless shelters and poor children in after-school programs. The WIC program—the nutritional program for poor women, infants, and children up to the age of 5 who are nutritionally at risk—provides recipients with the means to buy healthy food to supplement the diets of poor children.

*Support for the claim that the federal government has done a good job in enhancing the nutritional well-being of poor children and their families:*

- SNAP helps only the very poor; 93 percent in 2012 went to households that were below the poverty line.

- The program helps the households of the long-term unemployed, whose numbers rose dramatically during the Great Recession; the program is one of the few benefits remaining for the households of the long-term unemployed who are at or near the poverty line.

- Three-quarters of SNAP benefits go to households in which adults are working, though in low-wage jobs.

- Studies have shown that oversight of the program is rigorous, with no more than 2 percent going to households that are not technically eligible; though it does not affect children directly, about one-third of seniors who are eligible do not take part in SNAP or other nutrition programs.

- SNAP and other government nutrition programs have almost entirely eliminated malnutrition in the United States, which for long stretches of our history was a not-uncommon problem. Because about one in five children live in poverty, it would be fair to say that malnutrition or food deprivation among the poor would be much more common in the United States absent these government programs.

- Private charity spends only about one-tenth what the federal government spends on aid to the poor; private charity would unlikely be able to fill the gap if the federal role were drastically cut back.

*Rejection of the claim that the federal government has done a good job in enhancing the nutritional well-being of poor children and their families:*

- Federal food assistance programs are simply too expensive; they depend on taxes, which individuals and firms could otherwise use for productive economic activities that would help the economy grow.

- The food assistance programs are poorly administered and there are many bureaucratic obstacles for potential beneficiaries to get past in order to qualify.

- Many people and households who are not eligible get food assistance.

- Being closer to the problem, states could run nutrition programs better than the federal government; states would need block grants to be able to do this.

- People and households receive nutrition assistance for too long a time, fostering dependence; young people in such households do not learn self-sufficiency.

## WHAT DO YOU THINK?

What do you think about the past, present, and future role of the government in food programs for poor children and their families?

- The federal government has done an excellent job in meeting the nutritional needs of the poor, but needs to do much more given the increase in poverty.
- The federal government has done a good job in meeting the nutritional needs of the poor, but our current budget problems mean that we can't do more than we are doing now. We may even have to cut back a bit.
- The federal government's food programs suffer the same problems of all large bureaucracies centered in Washington. We should transfer responsibility for such programs to the states.

17.1
17.2
17.3
17.4
17.5
17.6
17.7
17.8
17.9

17.1

17.2

17.3

17.4

17.5

17.6

17.7

17.8

17.9

- Like any welfare program, food assistance from the government, whether federal, state, or local, fosters dependency and should be eliminated.

How would you defend your position to a fellow student? What would be your main line of argument? What evidence do you believe best supports your position? For help in developing your argument, please refer to the sources listed in the "Can Government Do Anything Well" feature in Chapter 2 on p. 45.

Additional sources for this feature: The Center on Budget and Policy Priorities at www.cbpp.org.

the lowest rates in state insurance pools. Likewise, it has set up state insurance marketplaces (or "exchanges") that allow people who do not get insurance through the government or an employer to compare and purchase plans. Second, it sets rules for insurance companies to keep people covered in a variety of circumstances in which they would have lost coverage in the past (i.e., it forbids insurance companies from rejecting people for preexisting conditions or from placing annual or lifetime limits on benefits). It also allows young people to stay on their parents' policies through age 26. And third, it sets baseline standards for what health care plans must cover (including emergency services, maternity and newborn care, mental health care, and wellness services among others).

The new law does not set up a "single-payer" system in which the government essentially provides health insurance to everyone (as in Canada and under Medicare). Nor does it include a government-run plan ("public option") to compete with private insurance companies within state insurance pools. In the end, the ACA—with its mandates, subsidies, and changes in regulations—*continues* a system in which health care is provided by private practitioners and most insurance is provided by private companies.

The ACA is expensive, with the nonpartisan Congressional Budget Office (CBO) estimating that the program will cost the federal government $710 billion between 2014 and 2019.[85] To pay for this, Medicare taxes are now collected on investment income (previously these taxes were levied only on wages and salaries). Additional funding will come from a new tax on high-end insurance policies available from some employers. Finally, the ACA mandates a $500 billion cut over ten years in federal government reimbursements to health care providers under Medicare and Medicaid. While this is aimed at increasing efficiency, many doctors are not happy about it. When the dust settles, the CBO projects that the ACA will improve federal budget balances by about $138 billion over ten years. This remains to be seen.

The implementation of the ACA got off to rocky start. Most notably, the federal government failed to successfully launch its insurance exchange website on October 1, 2013—a public relations catastrophe for the Obama administration and a black mark on the government's ability to administer the complex ACA. Healthcare.gov, which allows people in states that elected not to set up their own exchanges to compare and purchase their plans, is now working and sign-ups have met federal goals.[86] The implementation of ACA has also been marked by lawsuits and controversies over state Medicaid obligations (see the Federalism chapter) and the essential services that all health insurance plans must cover. In particular, some religious organizations (primarily the Catholic Church) and companies have taken exception to a rule that all plans cover certain forms of contraception. The Obama administration has stood fast in its belief that all plans should cover contraception as a matter of public health and so it instituted an alternative for religious organizations that allows them to "opt out" of the requirement and have insurance companies cover the cost of contraception for them. However, even this "opt-out" alternative is being disputed by some as de facto support for contraception. In *Burwell v. Hobby Lobby* (2014) the Supreme Court ruled that the federal government cannot force private companies to cover services that they object to on religious grounds. The precise consequences of the *Hobby Lobby* decision for health insurance coverage will play out over the ensuing months and years. While experts expect that most companies will continue to cover contraception, the *Hobby Lobby* decision was a blow to both ACA supporters and women's rights advocates.

Bumps in the road are to be expected in the implementation of a major new law like the ACA. Over the coming years we will develop a better sense of how effective the ACA is at getting more Americans covered and reducing the costs of health care.

# Differences in the American System of Safety Nets

17.1

17.2

17.3

17.4

17.5

17.6

17.7

17.8

17.9

**17.9** Compare and contrast the American system of social safety nets with those in other rich democracies

 he American safety net system is quite exceptional compared with those found in most other rich democracies.[87]

## How Exceptional?

Here are the main ways the United States is different:[88]

- *The American system is much less costly.* Despite complaints about its overall cost, ours is among the least costly.[89] Among the rich democracies, only Japan and Australia spend relatively less than we do on social safety nets.

- *The American system covers fewer people than systems in other rich democracies.* Most of the Western European nations blanket their entire populations with benefits. Family allowances in places such as Austria, the Netherlands, Norway, and Sweden, for instance, go to all citizens who have children. In the United States, in contrast, safety net provision is a patchwork, and many citizens are not protected or covered at all.

- *The American system favors the elderly, while others distribute benefits more evenly across age groups.* Medicare and Social Security, aimed at people 65 and older, make up the largest parts of the federal government's social safety net spending, far larger than programs whose benefits go to the nonelderly poor, especially children. In most other systems, family allowances and universal health care coverage keep benefit distributions more balanced.

- *The American system is less redistributive.* The degree of income equality in the Organization for Economic Cooperation and Development (OECD) nations (with the exception of Japan) is a function of the amount of money they spend on safety net programs and the degree to which program coverage is universal. The United States ranks very low on both, so our safety net state does not make much of a dent in the degree of income and wealth inequality in comparison with those of other nations.[90]

- *The American system requires less of private employers.* All Western European countries require that employers help employees with their parenting obligations. For example, all require employers to offer maternity and parenting leaves (three months of unpaid leave now required for workers in firms with 50 or more employees in the United States under the Family and Medical Leave Act) with pay (not required here), and all require that work schedules be adjusted for parenting needs. German mothers receive six weeks' paid leave before giving birth and eight weeks' paid leave after.

- *The American system lacks universal health insurance coverage.* The American system has not included health insurance coverage for most Americans until now, and it may not get there for a long time or ever given the Court's decision to disallow federally-mandated expansion of Medicaid and the partisan gridlock in Washington that makes big domestic initiatives unlikely for a while. The OECD countries either provide health services directly to their populations (the National Health Service in Great Britain is an example), offer universal health insurance coverage (e.g., the Canadian system), or use some combination of the two. In the United States, the health care delivery and insurance systems have been extremely complex, with spotty and incomplete coverage for the population and with Medicare providing health insurance coverage for the elderly and a limited but important prescription drug benefit, Medicaid and CHIP providing coverage for many of the poor, and the Veterans Administration covering

17.1
17.2
17.3
17.4
17.5
17.6
17.7
17.8
17.9

costs for veterans of the military and their dependents. Other Americans have depended on company-provided health insurance, purchased their own private insurance, paid out-of-pocket for their health care, or have done without. Until passage of the Affordable Care Act in 2010, more than 46 million people in the United States had no health insurance coverage at all. The new health care insurance system that will gradually go into effect from now until 2020 will provide health care access to about one-half to three-quarters of the previously uninsured (depending on how states respond to the opportunity to expand their Medicaid programs), fill many of the holes in coverage for the poor and the elderly, and keep insurance companies from denying coverage to people with preexisting conditions. These changes will not happen, however, if Republicans, as promised, manage to repeal what they call "Obamacare."

## Factors That Influence the Shape of the American Safety Net System

How to explain the special character of American safety nets? Here we identify structural and political linkage factors that influence the kind of safety net programs we have.

**CONSTITUTIONAL RULES** Federalism is one reason safety net programs were introduced here so late when compared to other rich democracies. Until the 1930s, it was not clear where the main responsibility for social safety nets was constitutionally lodged. In fact, it was not generally accepted that the national government had any authority at all on these matters until the U.S. Supreme Court belatedly relented and accepted the New Deal. Federalism is also responsible for the incredible administrative complexity of our system and for the great unevenness in program coverage.

**ENTITLED TO A HELPING HAND**
The Swedish universal health care system not only pays for almost all the costs of doctors, hospitals, and drugs, but it provides a wide range of services, including home helpers for those recovering from an illness or accident and for those with a permanent disability. Would such universal care be attractive to Americans? What difficulties might such a system pose?

17.1

17.2

17.3

17.4

17.5

17.6

17.7

17.8

17.9

Because of federalism, that is, our system takes into account the needs and interests of each state. The result is great variation among the states in benefits, eligibility requirements, and rules. The only large-scale programs that are universal in the European sense (uniform, comprehensive, and administered and funded by the national government) are Social Security and Medicare.

**RACIAL DIVISIONS** It is often argued that Europe's greater propensity toward welfare states with universal coverage is a result of the ethnic and racial homogeneity in their societies when they first created them. In homogeneous societies, the argument goes, voters are willing to support generous welfare programs because they believe recipients are very much like themselves—neighbors, down on their luck.[91]

Whether or not this argument is valid—the growing diversity within European countries, especially their large and growing Muslim populations, will eventually make it possible to test this idea—it is apparent that racial tensions influenced the shape of the American safety net system.[92] Some of the hostility toward AFDC, for instance, was probably related to the fact that African Americans made up a disproportionately large share of AFDC recipients (although less than a majority of all recipients) and that media stories about welfare recipients focused almost entirely on African Americans.[93] In fact, research conducted in the mid-1990s found that racial attitudes are the most important driver of how white Americans view welfare.[94]

**POLITICAL CULTURE** Almost every aspect of the American political culture works against a generous and comprehensive safety net system. The belief in competitive individualism is especially important. Voters who believe that people should stand on their own two feet and take responsibility for their lives are not likely to be sympathetic to appeals for helping able-bodied, working-age people.[95] Antigovernment themes in the political culture also play a role. Generous and comprehensive safety nets, such as those in Europe, are almost always large and centralized states supported by high taxes, and many Americans are deeply suspicious of politicians and centralized government, and resistant to high taxes.

**BUSINESS POWER** Business plays a powerful role in American politics. Almost without exception, the business community has been a voice for low taxes and limited benefits and for voluntary efforts over government responsibility. Given the many veto points created in the design of our goverment—checks and balances, federalism, separation of powers, and the like—in which it is easy to block legislation on many fronts, business is quite effective at stopping government actions that might correct for the outcomes of market operations. And, business has almost free rein to use its considerable resources in political affairs. Most scholars generally believe that business is not nearly as powerful in the politics of the other rich democracies.[96]

**WEAK LABOR UNIONS** Countries where workers are organized and exercise significant political power have extensive and generous social safety net systems; countries where this is not the case have less extensive and generous ones.[97] American labor unions have never been as strong or influential as labor unions in most of the other rich democracies, partly because the proportion of American workers who belong to labor unions has always been and remains smaller than in comparable countries. Today, union membership is at historically low levels with only about 11.3 percent of employed workers in unions (compared to its peak of 28.3 percent in 1954).[98]

## ☐ Final Thoughts on American Domestic Policies

The federal government is engaged in a wide range of programs and activities that affect the well-being of the American people, including management of the overall economy, regulation of a wide range of business activities, provision of income support and medical assistance for the elderly, and a safety net for the poor and disabled. Though not discussed in this chapter, the federal government is also engaged in programs affecting education, transportation, scientific research, agriculture, environmental protection, and more. Americans disagree how well the federal government carries out these activities, whether it sufficiently addresses many of the most important problems facing society, and whether it is properly financing the programs for the problems it does address. So there is much disagreement about the federal government's role, something we try to address throughout this book in the "Can Government Do Anything Well?" feature. What is clear is that what the federal government does is a product of America's constitutional rules, changes in the nature of society and economy over the long course of American history, and the interplay of political forces involving a broad range of individuals, groups, and firms, as well as elected and unelected public officials.

## Using the DEMOCRACY STANDARD

### Do Americans get the economic policies and safety net policies they want from government?

It is difficult to draw firm conclusions about the relative weight democracy has in determining what sorts of economic policies exist in the United States, partly because the government does so many different things in this area of activity. Economic policies that encompass spending and taxing, control of the money supply, and regulation are more often than not the result of the combined influences of popular pressures on elected political leaders and business and interest group influence. Business regulation is a good example of a set of policies that resulted from this joint influence.

The American public gets at least part of what it wants in terms of economic policies from government. For example, people tell pollsters that they distrust big government and don't want to pay high taxes—which they don't, compared with other rich democracies. And, they want government to control and help clean up some of the bad effects of economic activity like air and water pollution—which it has done with varying degrees of enthusiasm and success over the years.

The American people get the sorts of economic policies they want. But it is also the case that the hand of special interests can be found in abundance in the details of many of our economic policies. First, this is the case for spending where commitments to specific priorities and projects, from weapons systems procurement to direct business subsidies, are hammered out in a legislative process dominated by special interests. Second, this is the case for taxation, where the detailed provisions of the Tax Code come from the efforts of special interests—who are also the main beneficiaries.[99] Third, this is the case in regulatory policy, where far too many regulatory agencies remain "captured" or heavily influenced by those they are charged with regulating and where too many companies—especially financial firms—have escaped regulation almost entirely.

It also is difficult to determine if Americans get the kinds of safety net programs they want from government. On the one hand, we might easily argue that the size and types of programs fit what Americans say they want. For example, surveys show that strong majorities support Social Security and Medicare—achievements that were brought about by democratic struggles during the Great Depression (for the former) and the 1960s (for the latter), a fact confirmed on numerous occasions by voters' punishment of candidates who have dared to threaten either program. The public's desire

560

for government to do something about lessening or eliminating poverty has borne some fruit, as programs such as the Earned Income Tax Credit, food stamps, CHIP, and Medicaid have helped to halve the poverty rate over the past five decades—although the poverty rate in the United States remains among the highest of the rich democracies.

The most obvious hole in America's safety net has been the absence of universal health insurance coverage. Americans told pollsters for years that they wanted better coverage—though there was a great deal of disagreement among people about what type of program would be best—and they had not gotten it, though it had been on the reform agenda of several Democratic and Republican presidents since the end of World War II. For the most part, these efforts were undermined by powerful interest groups—mainly doctors' and hospital associations, insurance companies, and pharmaceutical companies—that elected officials were loath to cross. To make health reform happen, these powerful interests had to be brought on board by accommodating their needs, perhaps undermining the objective of bringing overall health care costs under control. Whether a majority of the American public will eventually embrace the new health care system remains to be seen.

One of the greatest challenges facing contemporary domestic policy—social and economic—is rising income inequality. A 2014 poll by the Pew Research Center for the People & the Press found that more than two-thirds of Americans believe that the gap between the rich and poor has increased in the last decade, and even more believe that government should be doing something to reduce this gap.[100] And their perception is right: Income inequality is at its highest levels since 1928.[101] But there is also partisan division on what exactly should be done: Democrats tend to support increased taxes and increased programs for the poor, and Republicans tend to support decreased taxes aimed at spurring growth. Interestingly, there does seem to be bipartisan consensus for raising the minimum wage. The same Pew poll found that 73 percent of Americans support an increase in the federal minimum wage from the current $7.25 per hour to $10.10 per hour.[102]

The issue of income inequality also appears to be catching on with our elected officials. In his 2014 State of the Union address, President Obama remarked, "Today, after four years of economic growth, corporate profits and stock prices have rarely been higher, and those at the top have never done better. But average wages have barely budged. Inequality has deepened. Upward mobility has stalled. The cold, hard fact is that even in the midst of recovery, too many Americans are working more than ever just to get by—let alone get ahead. And too many still aren't working at all."[103] We will all have to stay tuned to see whether the public continues to be concerned about income inequality and, if so, whether Washington acts.

17.1

17.2

17.3

17.4

17.5

17.6

17.7

17.8

17.9

# Review the Chapter

## Why Does the Federal Government Do So Much?

**17.1** Assess why governments are so involved in economic and social affairs, p. 528

The Constitution provides that the government is responsible for providing for "the general welfare."

The normal operations of a market economy produce abundance but a range of diseconomies and dislocations that people want addressed.

## Economic Policies

**17.2** Analyze economic policymaking in terms of goals, players, and tools, p. 529

Policymakers try to achieve a number of objectives, including stimulating economic growth, preventing inflation and trade imbalances, providing infrastructure for economic activities, and compensating for or controlling negative externalities like air and water pollution.

Fiscal policy refers to the overall spending and taxing impact of the federal government. Policymakers can use spending and taxing to stimulate economic activity—by increasing spending and/or cutting taxes—or slow it down—by cutting spending and/or increasing taxes. Fiscal policy, however, is not very flexible.

Monetary policy refers to Federal Reserve policies that influence the availability and cost of credit in the overall economy. The Fed uses these tools to expand credit when the economy is stalled or in decline and to shrink credit when inflation becomes a problem.

## Fashioning the Federal Budget

**17.3** Identify the components of the federal budget and analyze the problem of the national debt, p. 534

The federal budget is the detailed accounting of how government plans to spend taxpayer money, and the total and types of receipts (taxes of one kind or another) that have come in or will come in to pay for government programs.

Federal government outlays cover a very broad range of programs, including national defense, social insurance such as Social Security and Medicare, safety nets for the poor such as Medicaid and food stamps, subsidies to various businesses such as agriculture and oil and natural gas, scientific research and higher education, food and drug safety regulation, and more. Government receipts mainly come from income, payroll, corporate, and excise taxes.

The deficit is the difference each year between government outlays and government receipts. Annual deficits have grown dramatically in recent years.

The national debt is the total of what the U.S. government owes to individuals, firms, and governments to pay for the sum total of annual deficits. The national debt has grown most dramatically during war and economic crises, including the recent Great Recession.

## Regulation

**17.4** Explain the reasons for government regulation and predict the future of regulation, p. 540

The federal government plays an important regulatory role where markets do not operate to protect the public; these include things like food, drug, and product safety; the many unsafe and exploitative practices of financial institutions; air and water pollution; deep water oil drilling; and regulation of utility rates where companies have monopoly power.

The deregulation fervor of the 1980s and 1990s has been doused by the reaction to the flood of unsafe products from abroad, the collapse of the financial system because of the unregulated practices of many of its leading firms, and the oil spill disaster in the Gulf of Mexico, and the demand that government do more to protect the public. The regulatory responsibilities of the federal government are likely to remain substantial, and even increase.

## Safety Net Programs

**17.5** Differentiate among types of safety net programs in the United States, p. 542

The major distinction among safety net programs is between programs that are based on insurance principles (Social Security and Medicare), and means-tested programs (food stamps and Medicaid).

Programs can also be distinguished by whether they are funded and run out of Washington, joint programs of state and federal governments, or federal mandates to the states.

Finally, programs may or may not be entitlements in which everyone who fits a particular description—age 65 or over for Medicare benefits, for example, or below a certain income level—is automatically covered.

## Social Insurance

**17.6** Describe the main social insurance programs in the United States and assess their effectiveness, p. 544

Social insurance programs like Social Security, Medicare, and unemployment compensation, are funded by a payroll tax on the earnings of individuals who may receive benefits; such benefits are based on their lifetime contributions.

Social Security and Medicare have proven very successful and are highly popular. Both programs primarily benefit older Americans, as well as their dependents, survivors, and the disabled.

## Means-Tested Programs

**17.7** Describe the main means-tested programs in the United States and assess their effectiveness, p. 548

Means-tested programs distribute benefits on the basis of need to those who can prove that their income is low enough to qualify. These programs are funded by general income tax revenues.

TANF has been successful in shrinking the welfare rolls, but the degree to which it has helped lift former recipients out of poverty has not been impressive.

Public assistance has grown more slowly than social insurance programs and accounts for a much smaller portion of the federal government's safety net budget.

## The Affordable Care Act (ACA)

**17.8** Explain how the Affordable Care Act changes health care, p. 554

People are required to buy health insurance or pay a penalty if they fail to do so.

The new system subsidizes individuals and small businesses who cannot afford to buy private health insurance.

Insurance companies are no longer allowed to deny coverage to people with pre-existing conditions or to place lifetime limits on benefits.

A substantial portion of the previously uninsured will be covered by health insurance though the total is unknown because of uncertainties on how the states will respond to incentives to expand their Medicaid coverage.

## Differences in the American System of Safety Nets

**17.9** Compare and contrast the American system of social safety nets with those in other rich democracies, p. 557

The American welfare state is very different from others. Ours is smaller, less comprehensive, less redistributive, and more tilted toward the benefit of the elderly.

Structural and political linkage factors explain most of the differences. Federalism and the decentralization of power in our constitutional system are important in this story, as is the prevailing political culture that celebrates individualism and is uncomfortable with big government. The power of business and the weakness of organized labor are important as well.

# Learn the Terms

# Test Yourself

Answer key begins on page T-1.

**17.1** Assess why governments are so involved in economic and social affairs

1. All rich democracies have programs that protect the minimum standards of living against loss of income due to economic instability, old age, and illness and disability. These programs are often called:

   a. Inflation programs
   b. Depression programs
   c. Regression programs
   d. Standard operations programs
   e. Safety net programs

**17.2** Analyze economic policymaking in terms of goals, players, and tools

2. Refers to Fed policies that affect how much money is available to businesses and individuals from banks and how much it costs:

   a. Budgetary policy
   b. Macroeconomic policy
   c. Fiscal policy
   d. Monetary policy
   e. Economic policy

**17.3** Identify the components of the federal budget and analyze the problem of the national debt

3. The amount by which annual government expenditures exceed revenue is called:

   a. Congressional budget
   b. National debt
   c. Budget deficit
   d. Progressive debt
   e. Regressive deficit

**17.4** Explain the reasons for government regulation and predict the future of regulation

4. Progressive era reforms were pushed for by:

   a. The Populists, the Reformists, and upper-class Americans
   b. Labor unions, the Populists, and middle-class Americans
   c. Labor unions, high-ranking officials, and the president
   d. The president, the Reformists, and journalists
   e. Middle-class Americans, the Populists, and high-ranking officials

**17.5** Differentiate among types of safety net programs in the United States

5. Two basic kinds of social safety nets in the United States are:

   a. Social insurance and means-tested
   b. Means-tested and Social Security
   c. Social Security and Medicaid
   d. TANF and Medicaid
   e. Social insurance and TANF

**17.6** Describe the main social insurance programs in the United States and assess their effectiveness

6. Retirement income support for the elderly accounts for this amount of Social Security expenditures:

   a. 50%
   b. 80%
   c. 20%
   d. One-third
   e. Two-thirds

**17.7** Describe the main means-tested programs in the United States and assess their effectiveness

7. Medicaid is the nation's second largest public assistance program, with benefits going to:

   a. 1 in 2 Americans
   b. 1 in 3 Americans
   c. 1 in 5 Americans
   d. 1 in 10 Americans
   e. 1 in 16 Americans

**17.8** Explain how the Affordable Care Act changes health care

8. The Affordable Care Act:

   a. Sets up a single-payer system
   b. Includes a public option plan
   c. Allows young people to stay on their parents' insurance policies through age 26
   d. Requires every person over 30 to buy insurance
   e. Will be relatively inexpensive for the government

**17.9** Compare and contrast the American system of social safety nets with those in other rich democracies

9. Which of these is NOT a way in which the American safety net system is different from other rich democracies?

   a. The American system covers fewer people
   b. The American system is less redistributive
   c. The American system requires less of private employers
   d. The American system is more expensive
   e. The American system favors the elderly

# Explore Further

## INTERNET SOURCES

American Enterprise Institute **www.aei.org**
A prominent conservative think tank with information about economic and social policies.

The Brookings Institution **www.brookings.org**
A left-center think tank with a wide-ranging agenda that includes many aspects of economic policy.

Budget of the United States **www.whitehouse.gov/omb/budget/index.html**
The budget of the United States, with numbers, documentation, and analyses.

Fedstats **www.fedstats.gov**
Links to statistics and data from a broad range of federal government agencies, including those most relevant for economic policy in the United States. These include the Federal Reserve Board, the Bureau of Labor Statistics, the Bureau of the Census, and the Bureau of Economic Analysis.

The Peterson Institute for International Economics **www.iie.com/**
A nonpartisan research center that focuses on international economic policies that affect the United States and other countries with a focus on trade, intellectual property rights, foreign investment, and currencies.

Center on Budget and Policy Priorities **www.cbpp.org**
Descriptions of and studies on trends and outcomes for every federal social safety net program in the United States.

The Kaiser Family Foundation **www.kff.org**
A rich and unbiased source of information and analyses of virtually every aspect of America's health care system.

Public Agenda **www.publicagenda.org**
A nonpartisan site with comprehensive information about government policies, alternative proposals to solve societal problems, and what the public thinks about existing and alternative policies.

Health Care **www.healthcare.gov**
A government website with information on health care, insurance plans, and a full text of the Affordable Care Act.

Social Security and Medicare **www.ssa.gov/pgm/medicare.htm**
The official website of the Social Security Administration.

## SUGGESTIONS FOR FURTHER READING

Bartlett, Bruce. *The Benefit and the Burden.* New York: Simon and Schuster, 2012.
The best popular treatment of the U.S. Tax Code and why it should be changed, by a leading conservative economist.

Baumol, William J., Robert E. Litan, and Carl J. Schramm. *Good Capitalism, Bad Capitalism.* New Haven, CT: Yale University Press, 2007.
The authors argue that Americans must encourage an economy of entrepreneurship and innovation if the nation is to compete globally; they suggest a limited menu of tax and regulatory policies to accomplish this.

Cassidy, John. *How Markets Fail.* New York: Farrar, Straus and Giroux, 2009.
The author discusses two things: first, he shows how and why market failures are inescapable and require government to fix them; second, he shows how the economics profession went off track and forgot this lesson and thus contributed to the current economic crisis.

Giles, Martin. *Affluence and Influence: Economic Inequality and Political Power in America.* Princeton University Press, 2012.
A rich empirical analysis that reveals the powerful impact that the wealthy have on government policymaking.

Hacker, Jacob S. *The Great Risk Shift.* New York: Oxford University Press, 2006.
Suggests that American social policies are moving away from public and shared provision of safety nets, leaving individuals increasingly to fend for themselves.

Howard, Christopher. *The Hidden Welfare State.* Princeton, NJ: Princeton University Press, 2001.
Argues that the American welfare state is every bit as big and comprehensive as those of Western Europe, but that they take a different form: public–private partnerships, indirect subsidies, loan guarantees, and the like.

Peters, Guy B. *American Public Policy: Promise and Performance,* 8th ed. Washington, DC: CQ Press, 2010.
A comprehensive examination of the formation and content of American public policies.

Piketty, Thomas. *Capital in the Twenty-First Century.* Belknap Press, 2014.
An expansive work on the history of income inequality in Europe and the United States.

Stiglitz, Joseph E. *Freefall: America, Free Markets and the Sinking of the World Economy.* New York: W. W. Norton, 2010.
A detailed and lively analysis by the Nobel Prize–winning economist on the causes of the financial collapse and the Great Recession and how it is affecting the long-term well-being of the country and its standing in the world.

# 18

# Foreign Policy and National Defense

## THE PRESIDENT MEETS WITH ONE OF AMERICA'S BANKERS

**W**hen President Barack Obama visited China for the first time in November 2009 for three days of talks with its president Hu Jintao, he brought along with him not only the usual officials responsible for military, diplomatic, and trade affairs, but also Peter Orszag, the director of the Office of Management and Budget. The budget director's job, as the title implies, is to help the president put together the annual budget of the United States, keep track of how executive branch agencies are sticking to budget targets, and plan future budgets with agency heads and top presidential aides. So why was he in China? According to reports of the meetings, Chinese officials were concerned about the Affordable Care Act then being considered by Congress. They were not, of course, much concerned about the details of the bill, but they were concerned about the likely long-term impact of the bill on American deficit spending. And the reason they wanted to know more is because China is the United States's biggest foreign lender, and it is likely to carry even more American loans on its books in the future. The Chinese government, in the form of its sovereign wealth fund (a government-owned investment fund), as well as its banks and private citizens, fund that debt mostly by buying U.S. Treasury securities. President Obama was in China, it soon became apparent, not only to talk with Chinese officials about pressing issues such as nuclear proliferation in North Korea and Iran, the problems in U.S.–China relations tied to human rights,

---

**18.1**

Assess the extent to which foreign policymaking can be democratic, p. 569

**18.2**

Explain why the United States is a superpower and analyze the policy choices and challenges it has in playing this role, p. 570

**18.3**

Evaluate problems facing the post–Cold War world, p. 581

**18.4**

Identify the main American foreign and national security policymakers, p. 592

**WELCOME TO CHINA, MR. PRESIDENT** A magazine cover welcomes President Obama to China in 2009 for important talks about the two countries' relations. Though the two countries have close economic ties, their national interests do not always coincide, leading to some tension in their bi-lateral relationship. What factors will likely influence the extent to which China's rise as a world economic, political, and military power will increase or decrease these tensions?

the status of Tibet, the future of Taiwan, and cyber attacks on American companies and military contractors, but also to reassure one of its most important lenders that the United States would be able to pay its debts.[1]

A few years later, in 2013, when Republicans and Democrats deadlocked on a bill to extend the debt ceiling, an action that would have made it impossible for the Treasury to pay its domestic and international creditors for debts already incurred by the United States, the Chinese government issued a blistering indictment of America's global financial leadership in the form of an editorial in the office news agency Xinhau, expressing its concern and a warning:

> The cyclical stagnation in Washington for a viable bipartisan solution over a federal budget and an approval for raising debt ceiling has again left many nations' tremendous dollar assets in jeopardy and the international community highly agonized. . . . the pernicious impasse [should lead to efforts to create a] "de-Americanized world."[2]

For the time being, nothing has come of this because Republicans finally relented and agreed to raise the debt ceiling in time to avoid a default. In addition, the leading financial powers, firms, and investors see no alternative to the dollar as the world's reserve currency, nor do they trust China to be a steward of the global economic system.

These stories are tied to China's remarkable rise as an economic power in the world since 1979, when market-oriented reforms were introduced by Deng Xiaoping to change the communist, centrally planned economy, and China opened itself to investment from abroad. Over the past quarter century, China's rate of GDP growth has been unprecedented, far higher than that of Great Britain, the United States, and Japan during their comparable periods of industrialization and "economic take-off." Over the past three decades, China grew by about 10 percent a year, allowing more people to leave the ranks of the poor over a shorter period of time than in any other place and in any other time in recorded history. By 2009, it had passed Germany as the world's biggest exporter and today is the destination of the largest pool of direct investment in the world. By then it was also the world's leading customer for commodities such as oil, iron ore, and phosphate ores. If present trends continue, the size of the Chinese economy measured by GDP likely will surpass that of the United States between 2016 and 2027, depending on which GDP measure is used.[3] (China has almost five times as many people, however, so it will lag behind the United States for a very long time in terms of GDP per person; the standard of living of the average Chinese will not match that of the average American or European for some time to come.)[4]

The United States has gained a great deal from the rise of China, including a growing market for American manufacturers and farmers and a source of cheap consumer goods for American shoppers that contributes, for the most part, to higher standards of living here (though many jobs have migrated from here to there as well). And the willingness of the Chinese to buy up American debt and to accept very low rates of return on their investment has allowed us to expand public programs (including national defense) without fully taxing ourselves to pay for them. So in many ways, China and the United States are partners and allies. But our interests and those of China do not always coincide, and we continue to have deep disagreements on a wide range of issues. In the years ahead, China will have the means and perhaps the inclination to challenge the United States on a number of fronts internationally, because economic, political, and military power in the world tend to go together. While the United States remains by orders of magnitude the world's most imposing military superpower, continues to have the world's largest and most innovative economy, and retains a cultural influence that is unrivaled,[5] China is bound to have more say in the world's economic and diplomatic affairs in the years ahead, and its military capabilities are sure to improve. Figuring out how to deal with this rising power, how to make room for it, is certain to be a central concern of American presidents and policymakers for a long time to come.

In this chapter, we examine American foreign and national security goals and policies, the nation's resources for achieving them, what constraints on America's freedom of action exist, and how policies in these areas are made. As always, we remain interested in whether the processes of making and carrying out these policies arise from democratic processes and whether Americans get the sorts of policies they want.

national interest
What is of benefit to the
nation as a whole.

18.1

18.2

18.3

18.4

## Thinking Critically About This Chapter

This chapter is about American foreign and military policies, how these policies are made, and how they affect Americans and others.

## Using the Framework

You will see in this chapter how foreign and military policies are the product of the interaction of structural factors (such as American economic and military power, and globalization), political linkage factors (such as the choices the media make about foreign news coverage, public opinion about what the U.S. role in the world ought to be, and what various interest groups want the government to do), and governmental factors (such as the objectives and actions of presidents, members of Congress, and important executive branch agencies such as the Central Intelligence Agency and the Joint Chiefs of Staff).

## Using the Democracy Standard

Using the evaluative tools you learned in Chapter 1, you will see that foreign policy is not always made with the public as fully informed or as involved as they are in domestic affairs. You will see why this is so, ask whether policies would be better if they were made more democratically, and investigate how the public might play a larger role.

# Foreign Policy and Democracy: A Contradiction in Terms?

**18.1** Assess the extent to which foreign policymaking can be democratic

Unlike domestic policymaking, presidents and the executive branch tend to play a much more important part in foreign and defense policy formulation and implementation than does Congress, primarily because the Constitution lodges most responsibilities and powers for foreign and military affairs there. The Constitution makes the president commander in chief of the nation's armed forces as well as its chief diplomat. Consequently, in the perpetual tug-of-war between presidents and Congress, presidents usually prevail in national defense and foreign policy matters, especially during crises.

Groups and actors such as interest groups and the public are sometimes set aside in favor of the **national interest** as defined by a small number of national security advisors, intelligence officials, military leaders, other executive branch officials, and, most especially, the president. While public opinion can have an important influence on foreign and national defense policy matters, in the short run and medium run, it often is simply ignored. In crisis situations, citizens, whose opinions are sometimes reshaped by government leaders,[6] often "rally 'round the flag," similarly accepting a president's actions, at least as long as the results seem good and little dissent is heard. When things go wrong or seem to be going wrong in the foreign and defense policy sphere, domestic politics can return with a vengeance to the national stage, as when, in the cases of both the Vietnam and the Iraq wars, public support eventually dwindled.

Involvement by ordinary citizens in foreign and defense policy is also diminished by the sheer complexity of international matters, their remoteness from day-to-day life, and the unpredictability of other countries' actions. Also, much of foreign policy

**superpower**
A nation with the military, economic, and political resources to project force anywhere in the world.

18.1

18.2

18.3

18.4

is influenced by fundamental factors that are continually in flux, such as the relative power and resources of the United States and its economic interests abroad. All of these aspects of foreign and defense policy, taken together, tend to make the public's convictions about foreign and military affairs less certain and more subject to revision. In military matters, in particular, the need for speed, unity, and secrecy in decision making often argue for the exclusion of the public.

At the same time, however, the exclusion of the public from foreign and defense policy is far from total. The American public has probably always played a larger part in the making of foreign policy than some observers have imagined, and its role has become increasingly important in the areas of trade, economic crisis management, immigration, and global environmental protection, where government actions have noticeable impacts on Americans' economic well-being. When the International Monetary Fund (IMF) asked its most important members, including the United States, to increase contributions to a rescue fund to fight the European debt crisis in 2011 and 2012, President Obama declined, knowing full well that the American public, which was suffering through its own economic troubles, would be disinclined.

# The United States as a Superpower

**18.2** Explain why the United States is a superpower and analyze the policy choices and challenges it has in playing this role

I n the autumn of 1990, the United States sent more than half a million troops, 1,200 warplanes, and six aircraft carriers to the Persian Gulf region to roll back Iraq's invasion of Kuwait. In 1999, the United States supplied almost all the pilots, airplanes, ordnance, supplies, and intelligence for the NATO (North Atlantic Treaty Organization) bombing campaign to force the Serb military out of Kosovo province. American armed forces were again called into action in Afghanistan in very short order following 9/11. In 2003, the United States invaded Iraq and in less than four weeks had routed Iraq's regular army and its Republican Guard; gained nominal control of all its major cities, including Baghdad; and removed the Saddam Hussein regime from power. In 2011, while still fighting in Iraq and Afghanistan—where initial victories turned into long counterinsurgency wars—the United States supplied intelligence, mid-air refueling, missiles and other munitions, and air support for the NATO "no-fly zone" and "civilian protection" missions that supported the successful rebellion in Libya against Muammar Gaddafi. The United States, as the world's reigning **superpower**, is the only nation strong enough militarily and economically to project its power into any area of the globe. (American armed forces have been used abroad with a frequency that might surprise most Americans; see the timeline in Figure 18.1.) In this section, we examine the foundations of this superpower status and how these foundations are beginning to erode.

## ☐ The American Superpower: Structural Foundations

A nation's place in the international system is largely determined by its *relative* economic, military, and cultural power. Since the end of the Second World War in 1945, the United States has enjoyed strong advantages over other countries in all three areas, although U.S. advantages have diminished somewhat in recent years.[7] Still, the combination of economic, military, and cultural advantages the United States enjoys makes it the world's only superpower, although not as preeminent as it used to be. At the height of our power in the 1990s and early 2000s, there was widespread talk in the United States and Europe, some approving, some disapproving, of the emergence of a new American empire,[8] though the talk died out as the United States got bogged down in Iraq and Afghanistan, its financial system collapsed in 2008, and the so-called

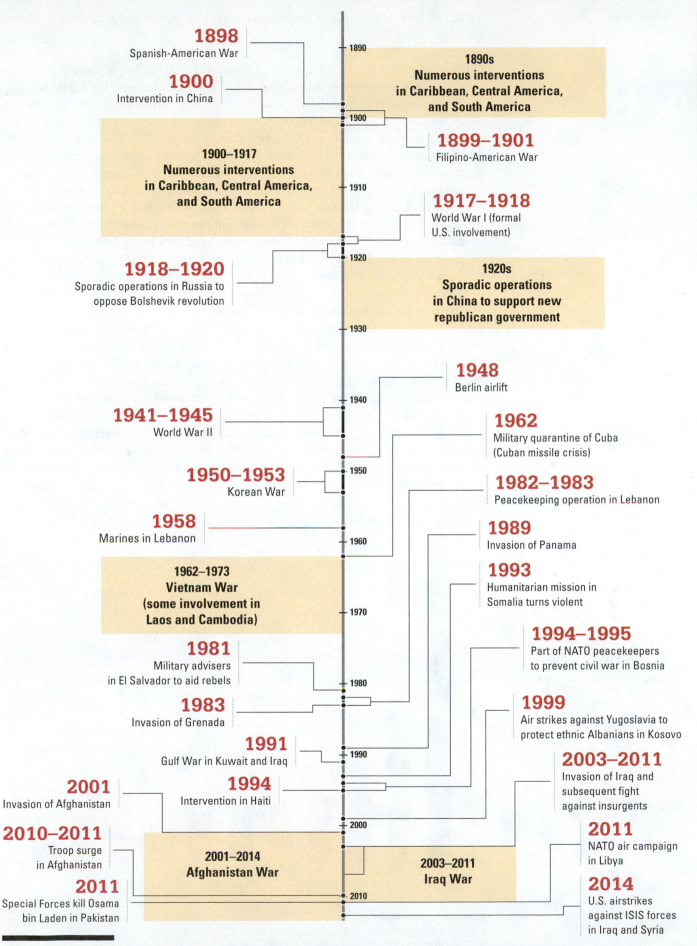

**1898**
Spanish-American War

**1900**
Intervention in China

**1890**

**1890s
Numerous interventions
in Caribbean, Central America,
and South America**

**1900**

**1899–1901**
Filipino-American War

**1900–1917
Numerous interventions
in Caribbean, Central America,
and South America**

**1910**

**1917–1918**
World War I (formal
U.S. involvement)

**1918–1920**
Sporadic operations in Russia to
oppose Bolshevik revolution

**1920**

**1920s
Sporadic operations
in China to support new
republican government**

**1930**

**1948**
Berlin airlift

**1940**

**1941–1945**
World War II

**1962**
Military quarantine of Cuba
(Cuban missile crisis)

**1950**

**1950–1953**
Korean War

**1982–1983**
Peacekeeping operation in Lebanon

**1958**
Marines in Lebanon

**1989**
Invasion of Panama

**1960**

**1962–1973
Vietnam War
(some involvement in
Laos and Cambodia)**

**1993**
Humanitarian mission in
Somalia turns violent

**1970**

**1994–1995**
Part of NATO peacekeepers
to prevent civil war in Bosnia

**1981**
Military advisers
in El Salvador to aid rebels

**1980**

**1983**
Invasion of Grenada

**1999**
Air strikes against Yugoslavia to
protect ethnic Albanians in Kosovo

**1991**
Gulf War in Kuwait and Iraq

**1990**

**2003–2011**
Invasion of Iraq and
subsequent fight
against insurgents

**2001**
Invasion of Afghanistan

**1994**
Intervention in Haiti

**2010–2011**
Troop surge
in Afghanistan

**2000**

**2011**
NATO air campaign
in Libya

**2001–2014
Afghanistan War**

**2003–2011
Iraq War**

**2011**
Special Forces kill Osama
bin Laden in Pakistan

**2010**

**2014**
U.S. airstrikes
against ISIS forces
in Iraq and Syria

**FIGURE 18.1** TIMELINE: SIGNIFICANT AMERICAN FOREIGN MILITARY OPERATIONS AND CONFLICTS, POST–CIVIL WAR

*Note:* Timeline does not include foreign interventions by agencies, such as the CIA, that have not involved the armed services of the United States.

*Source:* In part, from Pearson Education, publishing on Infoplease.com.

BRICs (Brazil, Russia, India, and China) began to play a much larger role in the global economy.

**ECONOMIC POWER** In 2013, the United States had a population of about 320 million people—considerably fewer than China's 1.4 billion or India's roughly 1.2 billion, but enough to support the world's largest economy, with an annual gross domestic product (GDP) of about $16.2 trillion. This was just a little less than the next three largest economies of the world, combined: China, Japan, and Germany. The United States's GDP, moreover, about two times larger than that of fast-rising China (but about six times larger on a per-capita basis[9]—see Figure 18.2). China will have a larger GDP than the United States sometime between 2016 and 2027 depending on what assumptions one makes about U.S. and Chinese growth rates in the coming years.[10] Between 2001 and 2011, China's GDP growth averaged 10.6 percent per year as compared to America's 1.8 percent, so it is catching up quickly (it has since dipped well below 10 percent).[11]

Starting in the 1990s, U.S.-headquartered companies established preeminence in the economic sectors that count the most in the new global economy: telecommunications, mass entertainment, biotechnology, software, finance, e-commerce, business services, transportation, and computer chips. Despite the financial sector's 2008 disaster and the Great Recession associated with it, many U.S.-headquartered companies have continued to prosper globally—without necessarily creating jobs in the United States, to be sure—even as European-, Russian-, Chinese-, Brazilian-, and Indian-based companies have improved their competitive positions. Still, American corporations lead the pack, with eight of the world's top ten "best brands" headquartered in the United States.[12]

The fact that major American corporations are increasingly global affects U.S. foreign policy. For the largest of them, a substantial portion of their revenues comes from sales abroad, much of their manufacturing takes place in other countries, and many of the parts for items manufactured domestically are imported. And in industries such as oil and petrochemicals, many of the sources of raw materials are outside our borders

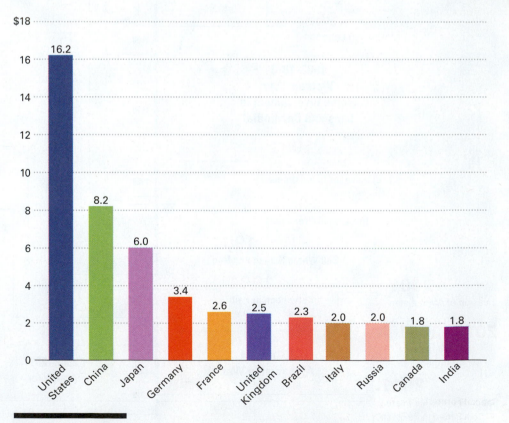

**FIGURE 18.2** ECONOMIC LEADERS IN 2012: COUNTRIES RANKED BY GDP (IN TRILLIONS, MEASURED BY EXCHANGE RATES)

*Source:* The International Monetary Fund, 2013

*Note:* China is much closer to the United States when GDP is measured using purchasing power parities rather than exchange rates.

(though the natural gas boom and new oil recovery methods are turning the United States into a net exporter of these primary products). Because American businesses can be found almost anywhere, American national interests can be said to exist almost anywhere, as well. It follows that American officials are attentive to potential trouble spots around the globe. Today, they are attentive to a wide range of potential threats that the government must deal with on a global scale. One is **terrorism** (whether the threat is to embassies and consulates, or to private American companies and their employees). But threats also include actions of other governments that challenge U.S. access to resources and markets or that violate the intellectual property rights of American companies. Alone or in combination, fines levied by the European Union on American producers, cyber spying on the plans of U.S. firms, and the counterfeit production of American movies, software, and pharmaceuticals—often tainted—in China have the potential to damage American economic interests.

**terrorism**
The use of deadly violence against civilians to further some political goal.

18.1

18.2

18.3

18.4

**MILITARY POWER**   This enormous economic strength enables the United States to field the most powerful armed forces in the world. The scale of American military superiority, as well as the nation's ability to deploy and use these resources, is orders of magnitude beyond any existing or potential rival. Indicators of the disproportionality of U.S. military power[13] are numerous and convincing:

- The United States's defense budget exceeded those of all other NATO countries (including the United Kingdom, France, Germany, Italy, and others), Russia, China, Japan, Saudi Arabia, and India combined (see Figure 18.3). Indeed, the defense budget of the United States is more than that of the next 11 nations combined.[14] Announced increases in China's defense budget in 2012 and 2013 did not change this overall picture, nor did some cuts in the U.S. defense budget caused by federal budget problems.

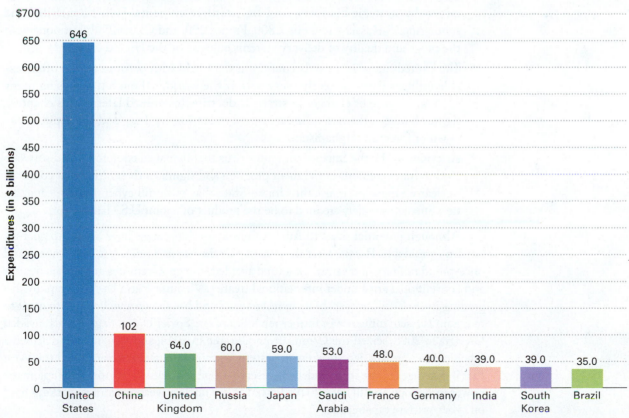

**FIGURE 18.3** EXPENDITURES FOR NATIONAL DEFENSE, 2012 (NOT INCLUDING THE COST OF COMBAT OPERATIONS IN IRAQ OR AFGHANISTAN)

The national defense budget of the United States is higher than those of friends and potential foes alike. There is no reason to suspect this will change, although China is rapidly modernizing its military forces.

*Source:* The Center for Arms Control and Non-Proliferation, 2013.

- The United States's naval power is unrivaled. It has 10 super carrier battle groups in operation; no other country has even one super carrier vessel—ships that displace at least 70,000 tons—let alone full battle groups (though the UK, France, and China are each building one and more are in China's pipeline; China will have its second by 2018). The U.S. has more modern submarines than the rest of the world combined, including the stealthy Seawolf-class, nuclear-powered submarine.

- The United States's air power is unrivaled. It has more advanced fighter aircraft and bombers, many of the stealth variety, than the rest of the world combined. Its aerial tanker fleet allows these aircraft to reach any target in the world. These aircraft also have the advantage of carrying a varied arsenal of "smart" munitions. Moreover, the United States leads the world in the number, variety, and lethalness of unmanned drone aircraft, first used extensively in the Pakistan border regions during the Afghanistan War.

- The United States's ground warfare capabilities are unrivaled. While China has a large standing army, it is not as well armed as U.S. ground forces and lacks many of the logistical and technological capabilities of American forces, though it is being modernized rapidly. In addition, no other nation comes close to matching America's armored forces, which include approximately 9,000 M1 Abrams tanks firing smart munitions.

- The United States's electronic warfare capabilities are unmatched. These capabilities include, among other things, global positioning systems to guide smart weapons to their targets, self-guided anti-tank missiles that seek out enemy tanks, sophisticated jamming systems to confuse anti-aircraft guns and missiles, and underwater sensing systems to track submarines.

- The United States's strategic nuclear arsenal is unrivaled, with approximately 2,150 active and deployed nuclear warheads in 2013 that can be delivered to their targets by strategic bombers, land-based intercontinental ballistic missiles, and submarines.[15] Russia has about 1,800, France 290, and China 250[16] but none with the range and quality of delivery systems enjoyed by the United States.

- The United States is the only country in the world with permanent and often sizable military bases in nearly every part of the world,[17] though it is closing many of them because of changes in strategic doctrine (examined later in this chapter), tighter budgets, the end of most ground operations in Iraq, and the rapid drawdown of forces in Afghanistan.

- As evidenced by the Stuxnet computer virus that damaged equipment and software used in Iran's uranium-enrichment program and significantly set back that country's nuclear weapons program, the United States has powerful cyber-warfare capabilities; Stuxnet is widely credited to be the product of a joint U.S.–Israel effort.

Although potential rivals to American military dominance have a ways to go, they remain formidable. Russia, after the breakup of the Soviet Union left its economy and once-proud military in disarray, for a time avoided foreign adventures and cut its nuclear and conventional arms under international treaties. Vladimir Putin has been rapidly upgrading Russia's military capability in recent years and has shown a willingness to use it to maintain Russian influence in former republics of the Soviet Union (e.g., Russia invaded Georgia in 2008, seized the Crimea from Ukraine in 2014, and fomented and armed a rebellion among Russian speakers in eastern Ukraine). Russia also reminded the West that it was eager to use its considerable reserves of oil and natural gas to wield diplomatic power in Europe and the world. And it has many nuclear weapons and is working hard on cyber-warfare capabilities.

The richest countries of Europe (the United Kingdom, Germany, France, and Italy) together have relatively small military establishments and a relatively small number of nuclear weapons. These countries do, however, produce, deploy, and operate very sophisticated military technologies, usually under the umbrella of NATO, in which the United States plays the leading role.

Commensurate with its rapidly growing economy and wishing, no doubt, to wield more influence in its region, China is rapidly upgrading its capabilities. Though by most estimates it remains far behind the United States, China is investing heavily in national defense, with a particular focus on aircraft carriers (five or six being the goal), submarines armed with cruise missiles, anti-submarine detection and munitions targeting systems, anti-ship missile systems, anti-spy satellite missiles, unmanned armed drone aircraft, and offensive and defensive cyber-war capacities.[18] In a rare public statement in 2013, the U.S. government identified a unit of the Chinese Liberation Army as the source of cyber attacks and cyber snooping on American military contractors and the Department of Defense.[19]

The data presented here on national defense spending does not include the considerable amount of money the United States spends on medical care for its veterans. We explore that in the "Can Government Do Anything Well?" feature.

As much as the United States spends on national defense, and as numerous and sophisticated its weaponry, its armed forces found themselves clearly overstretched after 2003, fighting wars in Iraq—where close to 1 million eventually served—and Afghanistan; mounting operations against suspected terrorists in Yemen, Somalia, the Pakistani border areas, and elsewhere; protecting the world's shipping lanes and oil supply with naval forces; and supplying intelligence, logistics, supplies, and airstrikes for the NATO operation in Libya. Matters were not helped by the shrinking size of the military during George W. Bush's first term when then-Secretary of Defense Donald Rumsfeld pushed for a lighter, more mobile, and technologically advanced force. As a result of these changes, active-duty troop totals dropped from about 2 million in the early 1990s to about 1.4 million by 2006, then grew again to 1.6 million by 2009. Given that "boots on the ground" were still necessary in Iraq and then Afghanistan— something Rumsfeld did not plan for—repeated and long tours of duty for active-duty troops and shorter rest periods between deployments as well as unprecedented dependence on National Guard and reserve forces became the norm.

Even with its considerable military power, the United States is not omnipotent. For example, conventional and strategic military power may not be terribly useful in rooting out terrorists. A terrorist enemy is not a country, but loosely organized shadow cells that may best be uprooted by police investigations, intelligence-gathering operations in cooperation with other countries, and perhaps special forces operations like the one that killed Osama bin Laden in Pakistan in 2011. America's military might, moreover, has not enabled it to control events in important oil-producing nations— including Venezuela, Nigeria, Russia, and Iran—where direct intervention would adversely affect oil supplies and prices. It has not been of much use in leading Israel and the Palestinians to a peace agreement. And, perhaps most importantly, we have seen that resourceful enemies, using what has been called **asymmetric warfare** tactics and weapons—roadside bombs, rocket-propelled grenades, sniper rifles, and AK-47 assault rifles—can inflict tremendous damage on U.S. and allied conventional forces, as happened in Iraq and Afghanistan. Iran has threatened on several occasions to take on American naval forces in the Persian Gulf with swarms of rocket-firing speedboats. Worse yet, an overwhelming military response to these tactics against those who hide among the civilian population has proved extremely problematic in terms of civilian casualties, as Israel has learned in waging war against Hamas in heavily populated Gaza.

It seems as if the American military has gotten the message. Early in 2008, for example, the Army issued a new operations manual that not only emphasizes its traditional mission of defeating the adversary in the field, but gives equal footing to stabilizing war-torn nations and fighting counterinsurgencies against foes using asymmetric tactics from among vulnerable civilian populations.[20] (The Marines similarly changed their operations manual.) The idea is that the Army will emphasize these multiple missions in its training and operations, as well as in its procurement policies. The new manual was shaped by General David Petraeus's influential counterinsurgency manual written several years earlier (and ignored by then-Defense Secretary Donald Rumsfeld), parts of which were put into effect when he led the "surge" in Iraq in 2007 and 2008. Both General Stanley McChrystal, then David Petraeus who replaced him, employed similar counterinsurgency tactics in the Afghanistan surge in 2010, drastically reducing

**asymmetric warfare**
Unconventional tactics used by a combatant against an enemy with superior conventional military capabilities.

# Can Government Do Anything Well?

## Providing Health Care for Veterans

The United States has been the world's dominant military power since the end of the Second World War and has used that considerable power more frequently than most people generally recognize. Since the end of the World War II, we have fought the Korean War, the Vietnam War, the Gulf War, and the wars in Iraq and Afghanistan. We have also used our military in armed conflicts at various times in Somalia, Lebanon, Nicaragua, El Salvador, Grenada, Panama, Libya, Serbia-Kosovo, and Syria. Special forces have been used in a wide range of actions in Pakistan, Yemen, Somalia, and other undisclosed locations. Veterans of these conflicts with injuries and conditions related to their military service, as well as those from World War II (there are no living veterans from World War I), can get help from the Veterans Administration for their health care if they so choose.

Every year, the Veterans Administration treats over five and a half million veterans. They do this in 151 hospitals, 850 outpatient clinics, 126 nursing homes, and veterans' own homes and apartments. The federal government spends about $57 billion providing services and medications to veterans. A mix of over 125,000 military and civilian personnel work in these various facilities and in the Home Based Primary Care Program providing care for those who have served their country. Because of recent conflicts in Iraq and Afghanistan, both the number of veterans in the VA's health care system and overall costs of care have risen dramatically, resulting in delays in treatment for many veterans and a big buildup in the backlog of benefit claims. This became widely known after stories surfaced about officials at a number of VA hospitals covering up or falsifying statistics about denied or delayed coverage for veterans. In August 2014, Congress and President Obama agreed to a bill that infused an additional $16.3 billion into the VA health care system.

*Support for the claim that the VA system has been successful in providing health care to veterans and should continue to be supported by the government:*

- Long criticized for its inefficiency and poor health care delivery, a growing number of studies suggests that the VA is now among the leading health care organizations, public or private. Since major reforms got underway in the late 1990s, the VA has cut personnel, trimmed costs, and improved health outcomes and patient satisfaction.

- Research reported in the *New England Journal of Medicine* shows high ratings on quality of care throughout the VA health care system, exceeding in most cases the quality of care provided by fee-for-service–supported and private doctor–provided health care under Medicare.

- The VA has become a leader in home-based primary care health care delivery for the elderly.

- The VA has become a leader in the use of electronic health care records.

- The VA has become a leader in developing measurements for assessing the quality of health care delivery, focusing on health outcomes and patient satisfaction.

- The VA outperforms other public and private community health care providers in the delivery of preventive care.

- Health care in VA hospitals has moved towards team-based service in which doctors and nurses from various specialties share responsibility for coordinated patient care.

- Because doctors in the system are salaried, they have no cause to order unnecessary tests in the course of practicing defensive medicine.

*Refutation of the claim that the VA system has been successful in providing health care to veterans and should continue to be supported by the government:*

**Criticism of the VA takes two basic forms, first, that it falls short in providing quality health care, and second, that it is expensive and inefficient.**

**The VA provides poor care**

- The Cato Institute claims that the VA health care system provides lower quality care than the private sector and veterans would do better if they were simply integrated into the mainstream health care system.

- Cato claims that veterans often wait hours and sometimes months to receive medical treatment. (This has proved to be true.)

- Even wounded vets from Iraq and Afghanistan are "being buffeted by a VA disability system clogged by delays, lost paperwork, redundant exams, denial of claims, and inconsistent diagnoses."

- "About 90 percent of eligible veterans choose private alternatives over the VA for their health care needs."

**The VA is too expensive and inefficient**

- The VA health care budget represents a significant share of the annual federal budget and much of the spending is wasted or used less efficiently than it would be in the private sector.

- Some vets with serious conditions must prove that their conditions are serious enough for higher medical coverage, and wait for months as the VA bureaucracy processes their paperwork.

- The VA is accountable for medical malpractice claims filed against its doctors and nurses.

## WHAT DO YOU THINK?

What do you think about the past, present, and future role of the government in providing health care for veterans?

- The Veterans Administration is a government success story, which provides high levels of health care at reasonable cost to veterans.
- The Veterans Administration has been somewhat successful, providing respectable levels of health care at reasonable cost to veterans, but significant remaining problems with health care quality and cost effectiveness require fixing.
- While the Veterans Administration has provided valuable health care services for veterans, it is inferior to the private health care system. Veterans' health care should be integrated into the system used by most other Americans.

How would you defend your position to a fellow student? What would be your main line of argument? What evidence do you believe best supports your position? For help in developing your argument, please refer to the sources listed in the "Can Government Do Anything Well" feature in Chapter 2 on p. 45.

Additional sources for this feature: Baker Spring, "Saving the American Dream," the Heritage Foundation website, November 17, 2011 (www.heritage.org/research/reports/2011/11/saving-the-american-dream-improving-health-care-and-retirement-for-military-service-members); Phillip Longman, "The Best Care Anywhere," *The Washington Monthly* (January/February 2005), pp. 12–14; "The VA's Health Care Program," CBS News MoneyWatch, December 8, 2006 (www.cbsnews.com/video/watch/?id=2243672n&tag=mncol;lst;5); James W. Holsinger Jr., "Veterans Health Care Program Could Be Model for Medicare," *Roll Call Online*, November 8, 2011 (www.rollcall.com/issues/57_55); Abby Goodnough, "Many Veterans Praise Care, but All Hate the Wait," *New York Times*, May 31, 2014.

---

airstrikes in heavily populated areas, for example, unless U.S. forces were in imminent danger (though drone strikes against Al Qaeda and the Taliban in Pakistan and Afghanistan increased during this time under President Obama).

In 2012, President Obama and then-Defense Secretary Panetta announced a major restructuring of the U.S. force structure and its deployment. It replaced the 60-year-old principle that the United States should be prepared to fight two major land conflicts at the same time with a new concept called "Air-Sea Battle" that proposes the ability to fight one major land war while projecting and extending the reach of our military power globally by enhancing and integrating naval and air power.[21] The new arrangement lowers the number of active-duty troops (one major land war requires fewer troops than two major land wars) and big bases (especially in Europe), in favor of more high technology to integrate and improve the response times of U.S. air and naval assets, and an enhanced capacity to cover a larger geographical area. Counterinsurgency, under the new arrangement, is left mainly to special forces and armed drone aircraft. Budget problems and concerns about China's rising power in the Pacific region seem to have driven the change in thinking. To dramatize the change in orientation, President Obama announced in 2012 that some U.S. troops stationed in Germany would be brought back to the United States and that 2,500 marines would be assigned to Australia, the first increase in troop levels in the Pacific since the end of the Vietnam War.[22] Disastrous developments in the Middle East—the sectarian civil wars in Syria and Iraq, the rise of ISIS, and Israel's war with Hamas in Gaza—show that such a major shift in doctrine and resources may be more difficult to achieve than anticipated.

**soft power**
Influence in world affairs that derives from the attractiveness to others of a nation's culture, products, and way of life.

**"SOFT POWER"** In assessing superpower status and capabilities, we should not underestimate the influence of what some have called America's **soft power**: the attractiveness of its culture, ideology, and way of life for many people living in other countries.[23] As political scientist Joseph Nye has pointed out, it is important for the U.S. position in the world that more than a half million foreign students study in American colleges and universities; that people in other countries flock to American entertainment and cultural products; that English has become the language of the Internet, business, science, and technology; and that the openness and opportunity of American society are admired by many people around the world.[24] If this very openness and opportunity place the United States in the best position to prosper in the new global, information-based economy—which many believe to be the case—then the United States's soft power enhances its harder economic and military powers.[25]

Soft power is no easy thing to measure, though *Monocle Magazine* in the United Kingdom, using a panel of experts from a variety of fields, rates countries on fifty indicators—everything from the effectiveness and openness of its governance and the standard of living of its population to the appeal of its cuisine, popular culture, architecture, companies, and attractiveness as a tourist destination. In its 2013 Soft Power Index[26] ranking, the United States was third in the world, a very high mark indeed, and substantially higher than any of its diplomatic or military rivals.

Though considerable, U.S. soft power has taken some hits over the past fifteen years. Anti-Americanism rose dramatically after we invaded Iraq in the spring of 2003. Although this was most pronounced in the Arab and Muslim worlds, it also intensified in Western Europe, Latin America, and Russia.[27] The Pew Research Center reported the following grim news in 2005, based on its annual surveys in countries around the world: ". . . anti-Americanism is deeper and broader now than at any time in modern history. It is most acute in the Muslim world, but it spans the globe—from Europe to Asia, from South America to Africa."[28] (See the drop in U.S. favorability between 1999 and 2007 in Figure 18.4.) The reasons for the drop were reasonably straightforward. First, the invasion was extremely unpopular outside the United States even in countries allied at the time with the United States, including the United Kingdom, Italy, and Spain.[29] Second, revelations of torture of prisoners at Abu Ghraib in Iraq and at Guantanamo further undermined America's standing. Third and finally, both foreign publics and leaders expressed concern at the unilateralist tendencies of the United States under President George W. Bush, especially his renunciation of several international treaties and the proclamation of the right of the United States to take preemptive/preventive military action when the president considered it appropriate.

President Barack Obama made restoring America's image and standing in the world a top priority. Both his popularity abroad[30] and changes in presidential language about America's place in the world—more negotiations with adversaries and increased collaboration with allies and international bodies—gave a big boost to U.S. favorability around much of the world compared to the George W. Bush years. But favorable views of the United States dropped a few percentage points with revelations of the NSA's widespread surveillance of foreign populations and governments and the heavy use of drone strikes to kill militants in Pakistan, Afghanistan, Yemen, and Somalia.[31] (See Figure 18.4 for the percentages of the populations in select countries with favorable views of the United States and China.)

America's soft power advantages as a responsible and trusted leader of the world's trade and financial system also took hits. Most important were the financial collapse in 2008, which most political and economic leaders around the world blamed on the

PATROLLING THE HIGH SEAS
Here a few ships from the carrier-group John C. Stennis patrols in the Pacific off Guam. The United States has eleven such groups and remains the only nation with fully deployed carrier battle groups.

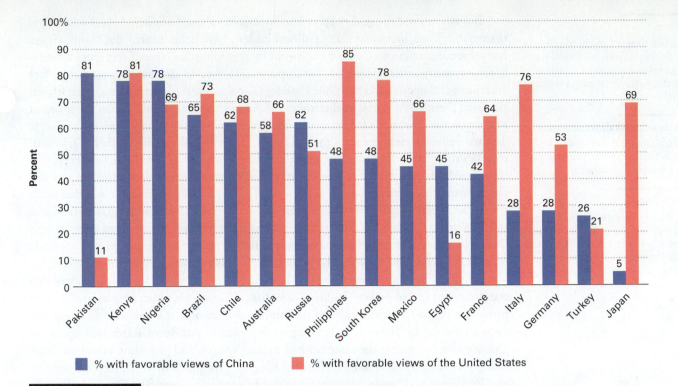

**FIGURE 18.4** FAVORABLE VIEWS OF THE UNITED STATES AND CHINA, 2013

With the exception of many Muslim countries—see Pakistan, Turkey, and Egypt as examples—the United States remains broadly popular around the world. Increasingly, however, China is challenging U.S. standing, especially in countries in Africa and Latin America that are strong trading partners of China's.

*Source:* "Global Indicators Database," Pew Research Center, January 2014.

reckless behavior of U.S. financial firms. America's poor economic performance, the inability of its leaders (locked in partisan combat) to agree on a way forward, and the continued rapid growth of China increased the global appeal of China's state capitalism model (a society in which the economy is guided by the state with widespread government ownership of firms) compared to the free market or free enterprise capitalism model of the American and British variety.[32] As Figure 18.4 shows, the United States remains deeply unpopular in Muslim countries, even in those who are our nominal allies, and China is popular in countries that provide raw materials for China's economic growth.

Despite these blows to America's standing among the world's population, it nevertheless remains the case that the United States ranks among the highest in whichever ways one chooses to measure soft power. The United States remains a very attractive place for many people around the world and for many global leaders in politics, business, and culture. This combination of soft and hard power is what makes the United States unique in world affairs and as yet an unmatched superpower.

## ☐ The American Superpower: Strategic Alternatives

The United States must make a number of decisions about how to use its considerable power.

**GOALS** Like the leaders of any other country in the international system, foreign and military policymakers, most especially the president, take as one of their primary duties the defense of the nation against real or potential attacks. This goes almost without saying. Like the leaders of any other country in the international system, moreover, American leaders try to first define and then advance and protect the national interest. Components of the national interest are hard to clearly define, to be sure, and people disagree about what they might be, but at a minimum they include such things as protecting American citizens when they are living or traveling abroad and ensuring that American firms are treated fairly when operating in other countries, that vital raw materials are available to consumers and firms, and that markets remain open to American goods and services.

**hegemon**

Term used to refer to the dominant power during various historical periods that takes on responsibilities for maintaining and protecting a regional or global system.

**weapons of mass destruction**

Nuclear, biological, or chemical weapons with the potential to cause vast harm to human populations.

**unilateralists**

Those who believe the United States should vigorously use its military and diplomatic power to pursue American national interests in the world, but on a "go it alone" basis.

But what about the goal of spreading American values? Whether rightly or wrongly, many Americans, including many political leaders, have believed that the United States has a special mission to improve the world by spreading liberty and representative democracy; many others have said that improving the world also involves spreading free enterprise and open markets. While President George W. Bush perhaps more clearly articulated these goals as essential elements of American foreign policy than other recent presidents, his aspirations for American foreign policy would not have been unfamiliar to Thomas Jefferson (who referred to the United States as "the empire of liberty"), Woodrow Wilson ("the world must be made safe for democracy"), Franklin Roosevelt (the "four freedoms"), or John F. Kennedy (whose inaugural address pledged to "oppose any foe to assure the survival and success of liberty"). One scholar suggests, in fact, that while President Bush's rhetoric may have been different, "the U.S. quest for an international order based on freedom, self-determination, and open markets has changed astonishingly little."[33] President Barack Obama expressed more modest goals, bringing accusations from Republican politicians that he wanted to diminish America's place in the world.

Finally, it has long been argued by foreign policy experts and political leaders that the dominant global power—political scientists call such countries **hegemons**[34]—must provide a range of services to the international system if the world is to enjoy any degree of stability. These include using one's power to put down states that upset the global order, protecting the international trading system, and providing economic leadership. This role was played by the United Kingdom for much of the nineteenth century and by France and Spain before then in the European context. The Ottoman Empire played a similar role in the sixteenth century for large swatches of the known world. Until quite recently, many believed that it was the turn of the United States to play the role of hegemon.[35] It must not only protect itself from attack and pursue its own interests, but use its power to prevent the outbreak of regional wars (India and Pakistan, perhaps), stop the spread of **weapons of mass destruction**, coordinate the effort to prevent pandemics, provide protection for a wide range of countries important for the world economy (e.g., European countries and Japan), protect and maintain the international trading and financial systems (i.e., patrol key shipping lanes, provide the world's reserve currency, act as the world's banker—for the most part, through the World Bank and the International Monetary Fund), and help make and enforce trade rules.

Do Americans and their leaders believe that U.S. foreign policy goals should include more than national defense and a strict focus on defending national interests? It is not clear that either leaders or citizens support such goals, nor is it certain that they want to assume the responsibility for and shoulder the costs in lives and dollars of spreading American values and acting as the global hegemon. Nor is it clear that rising global powers such as China, Turkey, Indonesia, Brazil, Russia, and India want the United States to fill the role of hegemon or believe it is capable of doing so. Nevertheless, most scholars believe that the stability of the global system requires a hegemon and that the hegemon—in this case, the United States and its citizens—derive substantial benefits from playing this role.[36]

**APPROACHES TO USING AMERICA'S POWER** American leaders and citizens must decide not only what goals to pursue as a superpower, but how best to go about using America's power. Debate about this has been organized for many years around two poles: How to use American power separates into the opposing viewpoints of unilateralists versus multilateralists.

- **Unilateralists** would have the United States pursue American national interests in the world on a "go it alone" basis, if necessary. While it might often act in concert with others, unilateralists would have the United States act on the international stage on its own terms, without asking the permission of others, binding itself to restrictive international agreements, or following the lead of international organizations such as the United Nations. The existence of this theme in American foreign policy may explain, for example, the United States's unwillingness to sign treaties to establish an international criminal court and ban land mines. Unilateralists are also interested in using American power unilaterally, if it comes to that, to spread American values such as liberty, free enterprise, and democracy, believing these values to be universally valid and appealing. Unilateralists do not see a contradiction between power and principle. Indeed, they believe that they are inextricable.[37]

For most of his presidency, George W. Bush was a strong advocate of unilateralism. By the end of the Bush years, the cost—in lives, treasure, and global favorability—of war and occupation in Iraq and the continuing struggle in Afghanistan had dampened much of the enthusiasm for unilateralism, though Republican Mitt Romney articulated the need for a more muscular American foreign policy during the 2012 presidential campaign.

Today, unilateralism is closely tied to the position that the United States has the capacity to maintain its position as the world's leading superpower, to continue its economic, military, and soft-power lead over emerging rivals, and need not accommodate them if it is not in our national interest to do so. People holding such views suggest that the United States remains the essential nation in the world, whose strength and leadership has and will continue to benefit the global system as well as itself. We must, in this view, reject the idea that America is a declining superpower and take measures to keep our military and economy preeminent in the world.[38]

- **Multilateralists** believe that American interests are compatible with the interests of others in the world and that protecting these interests requires cooperation and collaboration with other nations and international organizations. Although the United States is undeniably the most powerful nation in the world, the thinking goes, it cannot solve all important problems on its own. Problems such as **global climate change**, pollution, the wider availability of the means to make weapons of mass destruction, the spread of Ebola and other infectious diseases, and terrorism threaten virtually every country in the world, and solving these problems, insist multilateralists, will require broad cooperation and collaboration by many countries and international organizations.[39] Barack Obama often articulated this position in his public addresses, though he intensified fighting in Afghanistan in 2010 despite unhappiness among and a drawdown of forces by some NATO allies,[40] and waged a drone war against Al Qaeda and Taliban targets in Pakistan and elsewhere.

The multilateralist view is consistent with the idea that the needs and interests of rising powers in the developing world—for example, those of China, India, Turkey, Brazil, and Indonesia—must be taken into consideration and accommodated on a wide range of issues. In a world characterized by what commentator Fareed Zakaria calls "the rise of the others," the United States, the argument goes, cannot and should not go it alone.[41] The others have the capacity to resist American pressures at any rate, in this view, so cooperation and collaboration seem the more sensible options.

# Problems of the Post–Cold War World

**18.3**  Evaluate problems facing the post–Cold War world

With the end of the **Cold War**, the main concerns of that era—the possibility of global thermonuclear war, a land war in Europe against the Soviet Union, and communist takeovers of Third World countries—have disappeared from the list of foreign policy problems that concern Americans and their leaders. But a host of problems remain and new ones have arisen. We review these in the next several sections, keeping in mind that the debate among unilateralists and multilateralists will help shape our response to each one.

## ☐ Security Issues

Although the security threat represented by the Soviet Union has disappeared, many potential threats to American security remain.

**SPECIAL OPS**

The United States has no rival in the number and quality of its special operations forces and its ability to deploy them to places around the globe where they are needed. Here special ops troops do fast-rope training in Jordan in 2012.

**nuclear proliferation**
The spread of nuclear weapons to additional countries or to terrorist groups.

**TERRORISM**  The issue of terrorism moved front and center on the American political agenda after the September 11, 2001, attacks on the World Trade Center and the Pentagon. The retaliatory U.S. attacks on the Taliban regime and Al Qaeda in Afghanistan were the first among many steps that have been taken and will be taken in terms of a military response to terrorist attacks and threats. These include a wide range of overt and covert activities, some undertaken in cooperation with others, some undertaken unilaterally. At a minimum, American policymakers will try to improve intelligence gathering, create rapid-strike armed forces to attack terrorist cells and kill their leaders, and increase the use of drone aircraft surveillance and missile strikes as President Obama did in Yemen and the Afghanistan–Pakistan border area.

Other nations are more skeptical of a military response to the threat of terrorism, believing that solid policing and intelligence operations offer better protection. Military responses, moreover, are unlikely to improve America's security against large-scale cyber attacks on the nation's economic, military, energy, or communications infrastructure. Policing and intelligence gathering would seem to be the only way to address a possible increase in the number of homegrown terrorists. In the long run, then, it is likely that military, policing, and intelligence methods to counter terrorism will all be necessary, the choice of methods depending on circumstances.

**WEAPONS OF MASS DESTRUCTION**  A high priority task for American foreign policymakers since the presidency of John F. Kennedy has been to slow the arms race between the Soviet Union and the United States and to prevent **nuclear proliferation,** the spread of nuclear weapons throughout the world, including terrorist organizations. The first goal has been achieved. In a series of agreements reached first with the Soviet Union and then with its successor Russia, the two powers' stockpiles of deployed nuclear weapons has shrunk from about seventy-five thousand at their peak in the early 1980s to about four thousand today.[42]

Nuclear proliferation results are more mixed. France, Great Britain, and China also have nuclear weapons but are members of the Nuclear Non-Proliferation Treaty that commits these countries to measures that prevent the further spread of those weapons (the United States and Russia are also signatories to the treaty). India, Israel, and Pakistan also are nuclear powers but have not signed the Nuclear Non-Proliferation Treaty. After the breakup of the Soviet Union in 1991, Belarus, Kazakhstan, and Ukraine, formerly included in the Soviet Union but independent countries after the breakup, agreed to give up their nuclear arsenals. In 2003, Libya agreed to destroy its nuclear weapons.

In his 2002 State of the Union address, President Bush designated Iraq, Iran, and North Korea as the "axis of evil," nations both capable of creating weapons of mass destruction—chemical, biological, and/or nuclear—and using them against neighbors, American allies, or the United States. We know now that Iraq did not have a credible nuclear weapons program—the original reason given for the invasion in 2003—but that North Korea has one and that Iran is well on its way to producing one.

With respect to North Korea and Iran, some mix of diplomatic pressure, multilateral organized sanctions, International Atomic Energy Agency inspections, and threats of force have all been used. North Korea's program probably cannot be closed down and its existing weapons-grade plutonium stockpile destroyed, given how far it has developed, how committed its leader Kim Jong Un is to the program, and how little the Chinese, Un's principle ally, seem willing to do to put the brakes on. A combination of tight sanctions, close surveillance of North Korean imports and exports, and a change in attitude by the Chinese regime might slow the growth, however, and keep North Korea from weaponizing its plutonium stockpile, miniaturizing its warheads, and advancing its intercontinental missiles.[43]

With respect to Iran, there is a possibility that negotiations with the regime, backed by strong sanctions supported by most of the world community, including Russia and China, and the threat of a military strike by the United States and/or Israel

**TERROR AT HOME**

One of the continuing challenges faced by the United States is how to prevent terrorist attacks on home soil, such as the Boston Marathon bombing of April 15, 2013. Especially troubling are attacks by American citizens who have connections to terrorist organizations abroad, seemingly the case for the Boston bombers, one of whom, Tamerlan Tsarnaev, had close ties to radical Islamic groups in Chechnya.

if negotiations fail, might keep Iran from crossing the line from enriching uranium to making a bomb. Many commentators fear that development of a nuclear weapon by Shiite-led Iran might lead to a nuclear arms race that would include the Sunni-led regimes of Egypt and Saudi Arabia.

For many in the U.S. defense establishment, however, Pakistan represents the most significant proliferation threat, given its history and the turmoil that exists in the country. For one thing, Pakistani scientist A.Q. Khan, probably with help from parts of the state security services, was responsible for helping develop nuclear weapons programs in North Korea, Iran, and Libya. For another, Pakistan is itself a nuclear power, has regions under the control of jihadists, and has a state security service riddled with people who have long-term ties to the Taliban and terrorists operating in Kashmir.

One major advance in controlling chemical weapons was achieved in Syria in the midst of its terrible and seemingly endless civil war. In 2013 and 2014, under almost universal censure for its use of chemical weapons to fight insurgents and worried about air attacks by NATO and the United States on its chemical weapons facilities—which inevitably would have helped the insurgents as well—Bashar al-Assad agreed to dismantle his weapons and have the international community monitor the process and destroy the deadly chemicals and the equipment used in their manufacture.

**CHINA** With its huge population, fast-growing economy, and modernizing military, China someday may pose a security threat to the United States in the Asia-Pacific region or even globally. Some Americans have warned of a great "clash of civilizations" between the West and "Confucian" China.[44] This seems a bit overblown given the strong economic ties between China and the United States, but tensions do exist. Disputes over trade, intellectual property rights protections (on software, movies, and so on), Taiwan, Tibet, and human rights periodically cloud U.S.–Chinese relations, for example. China also has been reluctant to help in reining in nuclear programs in North Korea, and has made strong diplomatic efforts to enhance its ties to oil- and other resource-rich countries in Africa and Latin America, joining with some of them (as in Sudan and Venezuela) to oppose U.S. policies in their regions. China (along with Russia) is the key player, according to the U.S. Office of National Counter-Intelligence, in cyber attacks on American firms, including defense contractors, in an attempt to gain access to technology that will aid its economic and military rise.[45] Moreover, China has been pressing its claims over territories in its region that are rich in oil and natural gas reserves, as well as fishing grounds, creating disputes with American allies including Vietnam, Taiwan, Indonesia, South Korea, and Japan. These countries as well as India have become increasingly worried about rising Chinese economic and military power in the region and the aggressiveness with which it has pressed its territorial claims and have forged closer relationships with the United States.[46] (China unsettled them further in 2014 when it unilaterally extended into international waters its so-called Air Defense Identification Zone, requiring all commercial aircraft to ask China's permission to enter the zone.)

Concern about China has affected U.S. military planning. President Obama announced in 2012 a "pivot to Asia" in America's foreign policy priorities, though the president said he did not want to prevent China's "peaceful rise."[47] The shift initially involved a buildup in the number of American troops in Australia and a redeployment of some naval assets to the Asia-Pacific theater. Then-Defense Secretary Leon Panetta said that 60 percent of naval vessels would be in that area by 2020, including six supercarriers. Also, as mentioned earlier, the Pentagon has been developing contingency plans for what it calls Air-Sea Battle, which visualizes deep strikes by stealthy bombers and submarine-launched missiles into China to take out command-and-control and cyber capabilities as a prelude to any military conflict with China.[48]

Despite these many friction points, China and the United States are strong trading and manufacturing partners and their financial systems are deeply entwined, making them economically dependent on one another. The U.S.–Chinese relationship is a complicated one, both rival and partner, with China becoming more economically and militarily significant with each passing year. Inescapably, among the most important

**CHINA GLOBALIZING**

A worker among tobacco plants on a large Chinese-owned farm in Zimbabwe. China has been investing heavily in agriculture and extractive industries in Africa to support its rapidly growing economies. How might such a growing economic presence affect China's political influence on the affairs of various African countries?

questions for American foreign policymakers in the years ahead will be how to respond to China's rise. Will we try to resist it or try to accommodate it in some way?

**THE MIDDLE EAST AND THE PERSIAN GULF** Although some countries there have huge oil wealth, the Middle East is home to some of the least developed nations in the world in terms of economic development, democracy and freedom, women's rights, and education.[49] It is also a veritable tinderbox, with a number of conflicts festering. There is the one between Shiite and Sunni, intensified by the war in Iraq, civil war in Syria, and the actions of ISIS extremists, but tied in the long run to Shiite Iran's growing power and regional ambitions and discomfort with these developments among the Sunni governments of Saudi Arabia, Jordan, Egypt, and the Persian Gulf states.

There is, as well, the long conflict between Turkey and the Kurds, with Turkey conducting cross-border incursions into Iraq to battle anti-Turkish PKK (the Kurdish Workers Party) guerillas and other elements yearning for an independent Kurdistan (which would include portions of Turkey). In this conflict, the United States is caught in the middle. Turkey is a NATO ally and has a long-standing military alliance with the United States, but over the years a vibrant Kurdistan has emerged in the north of Iraq with the full support of the United States.

Then there is the seemingly unending conflict between Israel and the Palestinians, which stirs passions in the Arab and Muslim worlds and feeds anti-Americanism. What to do about this conflict is a matter of intense debate. Although groups such as Hamas and Hezbollah are committed to the destruction of Israel, most of the Arab states in the region support some sort of two-state solution in which Israel and Palestine live side by side as independent countries, though the popular passions loosed by the Arab Spring may move countries. The United States and the European Union are committed to this outcome, though it is not entirely clear whether a majority of the Israeli and Palestinian publics still believe that such an outcome is attractive or possible.[50]

The Arab Middle East has been a region where people long were saddled with unelected and corrupt governments, near-useless educational systems, stagnant economies, and mass unemployment. The popular and largely peaceful uprising known as the Arab Spring toppled autocratic governments in Tunisia and Egypt and brought elected governments to power, generating great hope at first among people in the Middle East and forcing rulers in other places—Morocco, Jordan, and even Saudi Arabia—to pay more attention to popular aspirations. However, in other places the Arab Spring was brutally crushed (in Libya, before Muammar Gaddafi was killed, and in Saudi-backed Bahrain). In Egypt, elections brought to power the Muslim Brotherhood, which ruled for only about a year before a military coup removed it from power and put its leaders and activists in prison. In Syria in 2011, Arab Spring-like reformers took to the streets to demand that Assad step down. The largely peaceful movement was violently put down by the regime, and a terrible civil war unfolded, gradually taking on the form of a conflict between Sunnis and Shias, with secular reformers caught in the middle. Its regional ambitions, which worry its Sunni neighbors, and its efforts to develop a nuclear weapons capability have made Iran even more salient to those who fashion American foreign and military policies.

American policymakers are caught in a series of conundrums in the region. Rule by autocratic governments is a dead end in terms of Arab development and the improvement in the well-being of the Arab peoples, yet open elections in Tunisia and Egypt brought Islamists hostile to the United States and its ally Israel to power. Our longtime partner Saudi Arabia, a major oil supplier to the West, is also largely responsible for the spread of radical and intolerant forms of Sunni Islam. In Syria, American policymakers desire to remove the Assad regime from power—and weaken its partners Iran and Hezbollah by doing so—but problems in getting assistance to anti-Assad insurgents without it falling into the hands of ISIS and Al Qaeda–affiliated groups are rife. Our relationship with Israel, a cornerstone of American foreign policy, puts the United States at odds with most of Sunni, Shia, or secular people of the region and fuels anti-Americanism. Efforts to negotiate a deal that will allow Iran to use and develop nuclear energy, not nuclear weapons, has met strong resistance from Israel, conservative forces in Iran, and Republicans and many Democrats in Congress. It is no wonder that the Obama administration has talked about a "pivot to Asia" and, by implication, away from the Middle East. It may be that the U.S. oil and natural gas boom and its slow but steady progress toward energy efficiency will make the country less dependent on the region's energy.[51] It is far too early to tell.

The current Iranian regime poses many problems for its neighbors, the United States, and its own people. Iran's nuclear ambitions seem to be part of a larger ambition to become the leading regional power in the Gulf. For years it tried with some success to wield power in the struggle against Israel, funneling funds and weapons to Syria and through Syria to Hezbollah in Lebanon and Hamas in Gaza. It was and continues to be an active player in Iraq, where the Shiite-dominated government and the Sunni majority and Kurdish minority are locked in a struggle over the future of the country. It has a strong military presence on the Strait of Hormuz, the narrow passage through which the abundant oil from the Persian Gulf is shipped. Not to be forgotten, the regime brutally suppressed the mostly peaceful movement for democracy each time that it rose, late in 2009 and again in 2011. For those making American foreign policy, Iran long has been on the front burner, as the expression goes, primarily because of its inescapable role in the oil economy of the Persian Gulf.

**THE INDIAN SUBCONTINENT** U.S. policymakers also must be concerned about the possible outbreak of war between India and Pakistan, each armed with nuclear weapons. The issues between the two will not be easily resolved, given the history of enmity between them, past military conflicts, and the struggle over the fate of the future of Muslim-majority Kashmir. Indeed, the two countries mobilized for war in late 2001 and 2002, and each implied that it would use nuclear weapons if necessary. The situation is complicated for the United States by the fact that Pakistan is deemed crucial in the fight against the Taliban and Al Qaeda, yet elements of its security and military forces openly aid and protect its leadership in Pakistan itself. When Navy Seals killed Osama bin Laden, he was living in a compound not far from Pakistan's elite military training academy. At the same time, the United States is forming a stronger strategic alliance with India, partly as a counter to the rising power of China, partly because of the increasing ties between the American and Indian economies, and partly because of sympathy with India as a target of terrorist attacks widely thought to be encouraged by Pakistan.

**RUSSIA**  If China can be considered a rising power, Russia is the opposite, a dangerous declining power trying to maintain its position, increasingly willing to use military force and its control of much of Europe's natural gas supplies to influence events. When the Soviet Union splintered in 1991, Russia became but a shell of its former self. For a period after the fall of the Soviet Union and during the years of Boris Yeltsin's presidency, relations between Russia and the United States were surprisingly cordial, given the long Cold War that existed between them after World War II. Under Vladimir Putin, however, Russia began, quite naturally, to try to act again as a great power with its own national interests.

At home, Putin took control of the Russian media, parliament, and large portions of the economy. Dissidents went to prison, troublesome journalists were attacked, and a law was passed making so-called homosexual propaganda a crime. Abroad, Putin was most concerned about keeping what Russians call the "near abroad"—now independent countries such as Belarus and Ukraine that were once part of the old Soviet Union—under Russian economic and political control. He was especially upset about NATO and European expansion to the east and the incorporation into them of former Soviet republics. Quoted as saying that the breakup of the Soviet Union was the greatest tragedy of the twentieth century, Putin's objective has been to try to pull it back together in some fashion, if not in a formal sense, then in a de facto sense.

Putin has used surprisingly harsh rhetoric in making it clear that he fundamentally opposes American foreign and military policies across a broad front. In one speech in 2007, he likened America's use of its power to that of Nazi Germany. In that same year, he threatened to pull Russia out of a treaty limiting intermediate-range missiles in Europe and later proclaimed that the use of military force by anyone in the oil-rich Caspian Sea region (which includes Iran) was unacceptable. Putin also publicly and vocally opposed the United States, the United Nations, and the European Union on Kosovo independence (Russia is a traditional ally of Serbia), which happened in 2008. Later that year, he invaded Georgia on Russia's border. A close and longtime ally of Syria, Putin continued to be, along with Iran, the main military supplier to the Assad

**RUSSIA'S BAD BREAKUP**

Russian President Vladimir Putin, here watching a military exercise at sea, has made it his goal to rebuild and modernize Russian military capabilities and to reassert Russian influence over the now-independent states of the former Soviet Union, such as Georgia and Ukraine. Putin, who once characterized the breakup of the Soviet Union as the greatest tragedy of the twentieth century, has made no secret of his desire to reverse this event.

regime during its long civil war. His efforts to pull Ukraine back into close association with Russia included funding anti-Western and pro-Russian parties and media there, seizing Crimea and incorporating it into Russia, and arming pro-Russian separatists in eastern Ukraine.

How to ease relations with this major continental power and gain greater cooperation on pressing global problems are important issues for American policymakers. There are signs that, in spite of the tensions between the United States and Russia, deals can be struck when the interests of the two sides coincide. Beginning in 2011, for example, the two voted together at the United Nations on several occasions for new sanctions against Iran and its nuclear program. They worked closely together as well in dismantling Syria's chemical weapons program in 2013 and 2014. And the United States and Russia have acted in concert to reduce their own stockpiles of nuclear weapons and to prevent nuclear proliferation. In the long run, however, with the U.S. "pivot to Asia," the European Union may become the key Western player in shaping relations with Russia, given its proximity to and its important trade relationships with Russia.

## ☐ Economic and Social Issues

In addition to national security concerns, a number of other international issues have drawn the attention of American policymakers and the public. **Globalization** is particularly important in this regard. Recall that globalization is the integration of much of the world into a single market and production system in which the United States plays a leading role. It raises a number of new issues for American policymakers and citizens to address in addition to those raised about globalization's impact on the strategic behavior of American-based corporations and financial institutions and how their actions have affected jobs and prospects for the American middle class.

**TRADE** Counting total imports and exports together, the United States is the world's largest trading nation—though second to the European Union (27 nations), and with China closing fast—and the leading player in the design and management of the global trading system. Since the end of World War II, the United States has been the leading advocate for the freer and more open trading system that has evolved. In 1948, under American leadership, the most important trading nations adopted the **General Agreement on Tariffs and Trade (GATT)**, an agreement designed to lower, then eliminate, tariffs on most traded goods and to end nontariff trade restrictions as well. Periodically, members of GATT enter into talks (called rounds) and reach new agreements designed to refine and expand the system. The Uruguay Round in 1994 agreed to replace GATT with the **World Trade Organization (WTO)**, which came into being the following year. U.S. negotiators hoped that the new agreement eventually would open more markets to American agricultural products and services and halt the piracy of patented and copyrighted goods such as software and films. The failure of the Doha Round of negotiations in 2008 signals, perhaps, that the lowering of trade barriers has gone about as far as it's likely to go. Indeed, the financial collapse and recession in 2008–2009 pushed more than a few countries to raise trade barriers again—though not to previous levels—in an effort to protect jobs and keep stimulus spending within national boundaries.

Most economists believe that trade is generally good for all countries involved, whether rich or poor,[52] though not all agree.[53] Many Americans believe that the loss of manufacturing jobs can be traced to free trade and trade agreements such as the **North American Free Trade Agreement (NAFTA)** with Canada and Mexico, because goods manufactured abroad using cheap labor and by firms that have few labor protections or environmental requirements can enter the United States tariff-free. Most economists, however, believe the majority of manufacturing job loss can be linked to technological change and rising productivity. Organized labor passionately believes free trade costs American jobs. Others worry that a flood of cheap, yet high-quality, goods and services threatens firms that are important for the health of the American economy and point to the decline of the American auto, steel, and consumer electronics industries as examples. Still others believe that the threat of trade sanctions—a violation of free trade agreements—should be used to improve environmental standards, human rights practices, and religious toleration in other countries. Trade, then, is likely to remain an important political issue for a long time to come.

**GLOBAL ECONOMIC INSTABILITY** The United States has been the leading player in the global economy since the end of World War II, and its leaders have been involved in trying to ensure the health and vitality of the overall global economy. In addition to encouraging trade, American leaders have been concerned with stabilizing global financial markets when necessary and in rescuing countries on the verge of economic collapse. They do so because our own economy is closely tied to the global economy. A strong American role is guaranteed by our leadership of and large financial contributions to the International Monetary Fund (IMF; charged with rectifying and preventing currency collapses) and the World Bank (charged with financing projects to assist economic development and poverty reduction). Ironically, perhaps, given its traditional financial leadership role, the United States's housing bubble, credit crunch, investment bank collapse, and stock market decline in 2008 imperiled the world's financial system. With its own economy in a stall, its reputation hurt by the financial collapse, the Great Recession, and political gridlock on the national budget, the United States increasingly is being forced to share global financial and economic leadership with others, particularly with China and Germany.

**INTELLECTUAL PROPERTY RIGHTS** How strongly should our foreign policy attempt to protect the intellectual property rights—patents and copyrights—of American-based companies and citizens? The issue is fairly straightforward when it comes to the "piracy" of movies, music CDs, and software in places such as China; Americans and U.S.-based firms generally support policies aimed at ending these practices. Protection of patents for life-saving drugs is another matter—antimalarial and anti-AIDS medications, for example. Many Americans believe companies ought to provide such drugs at low prices or allow poor countries to find or produce generic

**GLOBAL PRODUCTION AND SALES**

In a globalized economy, many products consumed by Americans are manufactured abroad. Here, a consumer in a Costco store in California evaluates a Japanese flat-screen television manufactured in China. How difficult is it to buy products that are made entirely in the United States? Why does it matter where products are made that American consumers use?

**Millennium Challenge Account**
A Bush administration initiative to distribute development aid on the basis of a country's degree of improvement in areas such as the rule of law, women's rights, protection of property rights, anticorruption measures, and political and civil rights.

substitutes despite the patent protections of Western pharmaceutical companies. There has been some movement on this front. For example, the U.S. government signed an agreement in 2003 to suspend the normal trade rules of the WTO and allow the production and use of certain critical generic drugs. Global firms have lowered prices on a range of drugs—Bristol-Myers Squibb announced in 2006, for example, that it would allow companies in India and South Africa to produce generic versions of its two most powerful AIDS drugs. In early 2008, GlaxoSmithKline announced its fifth cut in the prices of HIV/AIDS drugs. In 2010, the World Health Organization (WHO) announced plans to form a public–private patent pool to lower the cost of the most expensive HIV treatments; the program is up and running but it is too early to reach a firm conclusion about its success.

**FOREIGN AID** Rich nations, whether for humanitarian or security reasons, have given assistance to extremely poor countries for many years in an effort to improve living standards. There have been some successes—such as the conquest of river blindness, a disease that once affected tens of millions of Africans. But dreadful poverty persists in places such as Bangladesh and sub-Saharan Africa. Mean household income in sub-Saharan Africa is lower now than it was in the 1960s, but GDP has been growing at a healthy pace over the past few years, especially in those countries enjoying large sales of commodities like oil, coal, and phosphate ores to China. Although the United States contributes to World Bank developmental loans for poor countries and has programs such as Food for Peace, the Peace Corps, and technical and educational assistance programs, U.S. government spending for foreign aid is low. Spending for foreign aid in 2013 was 1.0 percent of the federal budget.[54] Although we spend more dollars on foreign assistance than any other country, relative to the size of our economy we spend the least (see Figure 18.5). It is worth noting, however, that Americans give a great deal of aid through private philanthropy, with the Bill and Melinda Gates Foundation leading the way in assistance to poor countries. Between its founding in 2000 and the end of 2010, for example, the foundation gave about $14.4 billion to support global health initiatives, considerably more than the WHO spent for its activities during the same period.[55]

President George W. Bush promised a big boost for development assistance and a new approach to foreign aid in his **Millennium Challenge Account**—a dramatically different form of aid in which across-the-board payments to countries have been replaced by a system in which money to poor countries became tied to a range of performance indicators for things like the rule of law, women's rights, protection of property rights, anticorruption measures, political rights, governmental effectiveness, and the like—but appropriated totals have fallen far short of promises because of deep cuts in the discretionary part of the federal budget in the last few years. (In 2012, President Obama asked Congress for about $1.2 billion for the Challenge Account.) The new approach was partly a product of a growing sense among many in the development community, scholars, and think tanks that not much development has occurred as a result of aid from rich governments and international organizations. Most of the aid, the argument goes, has gone to big projects that have had little development impact or has been siphoned off to government leaders and their followers and cronies.[56] Far better, critics of traditional foreign aid suggest, would be policies to encourage real economic development as in India, China, and Brazil. How to make economic development happen, of course, remains a much-debated question. (See the "By the Numbers" feature for a better way to measure development assistance.)

**THE GLOBAL ENVIRONMENT** Increasingly, Americans realize that environmental problems cross national borders. Thus, the United States and Canada have worked out a joint approach to reduce acid rain, and the United States has signed on to agreements on the prevention and cleanup of oil spills, the use of Antarctica, the protection of fish species, and the protection of the ozone layer. The United States is also a signatory to the biodiversity treaty. Global climate change is a different story, however. Although the Clinton administration was involved in hammering out the details of the Kyoto Protocol to limit greenhouse gases, Clinton, fearing rejection, never submitted

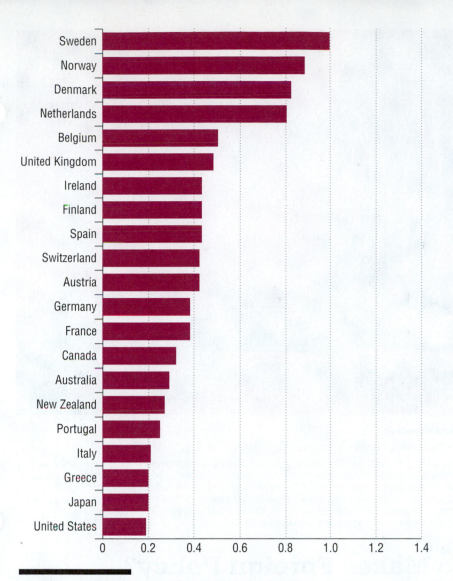

**FIGURE 18.5** FOREIGN AID AS A PERCENTAGE OF GDP, 2013

Although Americans often complain about how much aid we give to other countries, a comparison with other donor countries shows that we give very little compared to other countries as a percentage of GDP.

*Source:* World Bank, 2014.

the treaty to the Senate for its "advice and consent." In 2001, George W. Bush pulled out of the treaty entirely, citing his concern that strict controls on developed countries coupled with no controls on large, fast-growing economies in developing countries, such as China and India, would do irreparable harm to the American economy. President Obama professed a strong interest in bringing the United States into a new international agreement with mandatory targets for greenhouse gas reductions, with China, India, and Brazil included, but no agreement could be worked out at the Copenhagen climate summit in late 2009. China's reluctance to agree to mandatory measures and lack of confidence in Obama's ability to deliver a "cap and trade" climate bill in Congress were major issues in the Copenhagen failure. Conferees were correct in their predictions; a "cap and trade" bill died in the U.S. Senate in 2010.

Awareness of the threat of global climate change is high among Americans, although there is a deep divide, mostly along partisan lines, about how seriously to take the threat, whether human actions are responsible for global warming, and what to do about it.[57] Among the handful of conservative Republicans who think climate change is a real phenomenon, the inclination is to see the trend as part of a natural cycle and oppose government policies to diminish carbon production; liberal Democrats are more likely to blame human activity for climate change and want governments to take action to diminish emissions.

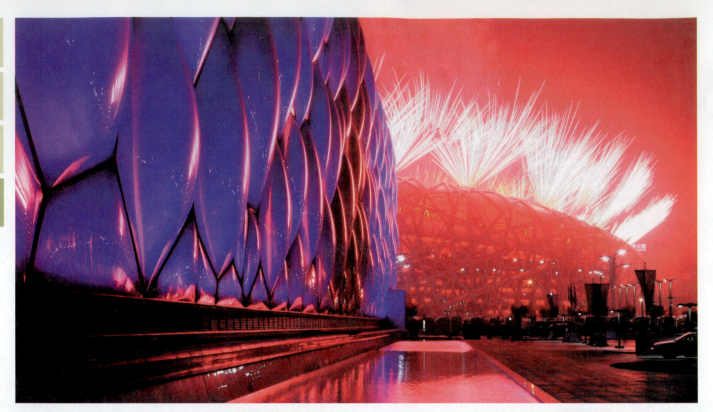

**CELEBRATING CHINA'S POWER**

The Chinese leadership used the 2008 Beijing Olympic Games to announce the emergence of China as a power on the world stage. Although the government squelched domestic and foreign dissidents, many of whom were protesting Chinese actions in Tibet and Sudan, the games had the intended effect. The spectacular opening and closing ceremonies were held in the stunning "bird's nest" stadium pictured here. Did the grandeur of the opening and closing ceremonies and the excitement of the games work to make people forget the controversy and outcry leading up to them?

# Who Makes Foreign Policy?

**18.4** Identify the main American foreign and national security policymakers

**W**e pointed out at the beginning of this chapter that the president is the key player in making foreign and national security policies and is especially powerful during international crises and in times of war—recently in Afghanistan and Iraq and in the war on terrorism. (The "Using the Framework" feature applies the analytical framework to the U.S. decision to invade Iraq in 2003 and demonstrates that, while the president is central to fashioning matters of war and peace, many other factors, actors, and institutions play important roles as well.) But Congress has always been involved, especially in decisions about international trade, foreign aid, military spending, immigration, and other matters that clearly and directly touch constituents' local interests, but also when presidential policies on foreign and national security issues fail. Public opinion, the mass media, the parties, and interest and advocacy groups (e.g., corporations, unions, nongovernmental organizations, and religious organizations) affect what both Congress and the executive branch do.

## ☐ The President and the Executive Branch

Presidents have broad discretion and sometimes exercise extraordinary powers in foreign and national security matters derived from their status as commander in chief and from constitutionally assigned diplomatic powers. Over the years, broad deference has been given to presidents in the vigorous use of these powers by the public, Congress, and the courts.[58] Thus it was Kennedy who made the decision to impose a

# By the Numbers

## How much do rich countries help poor countries develop?

There is a great deal of talk in the United States and other rich democracies about helping poor countries develop so they can provide a better standard of living for their people. Hollywood stars and other celebrities raise money for refugees, religious organizations of various denominations provide charity and education, and foundations address issues of clean water and public health. But what are rich-country governments doing to close the yawning gap between the rich and the poor in the world?

### Why It Matters

For many Americans and for many who live in the other rich democracies, the great inequalities in well-being and life prospects that exist between themselves and people in poor countries are morally wrong and must be rectified. For many others, particularly political and economic leaders, the existence of desperately poor countries represents a threat to global stability and security. Such places are more likely than others to become "failed states," where important resource supplies may be imperiled, terrorism may breed, and from which desperate refugees often stream to neighboring countries, destabilizing them as well.

### What Governments Do

People are most familiar with foreign aid in which rich-country governments give money to poor-country governments. But rich governments do many more things that affect poor-country development. For example, they have a lot to say about whether farmers and firms in poor countries have access to rich-country markets to sell their products. They can encourage large companies to invest in countries that need it by, let us say, providing insurance for building new production facilities in poor countries where people want work. They can encourage or discourage migration to their own countries and make it more or less difficult for migrants to send remittances back home. Rich countries can help or hinder the security situation in poor countries—which affects whether investors are willing to be there—with some selling arms to one side or another in a civil war, and others providing peacekeepers. And rich countries will differ in their policies on intellectual property rights: some allowing substantial technology transfers to poor-country companies by their home-based companies, and others restricting transfers.

### Measuring Commitment to Development

The Center for Global Development has created a measure it calls the Commitment to Development Index (CDI) that seeks to capture the multidimensional nature of development assistance that rich countries can offer poor ones. In it, the center uses a panel of judges to rate the following things:

- The quantity of foreign aid relative to GDP and whether it is targeted to projects that encourage economic growth.

- The degree to which trade policies encourage poor-country imports.
- The degree to which investments in poor countries are encouraged.
- The relative contribution the country makes to peace and security in poor countries.
- The degree of openness to migrants from poor countries.
- The relative openness or restrictiveness of technology transfer to poor countries.
- The relative contribution to global climate change (based on the presumption that global climate change hurts people in poor countries more than in rich ones).

The graph on the following page shows the Commitment to Development Index for the year 2013. In the array of rich countries, the United States does quite poorly, ranking 19th out of a total of 26 countries. Examination of the individual components of the final score at the Center for Global Development's website (www.cgdev.org) shows that the principal U.S. contribution to development comes mainly from three components of the measure: the security its military has provided for the global system, including fighting pirates and keeping major sea lanes open to merchant shipping and humanitarian interventions in developing countries; and our openness to imports from poor countries.

### Should We Rely on This Index?

The index is very useful for alerting us to the fact that rich-country governments do lots of things, in addition to providing foreign aid, that might affect the prospects for economic development in poor countries. But critics point to a number of problems with the CDI. First, it relies entirely on the evaluations of judges—academics, think tank scholars, and CGD staffers—giving quantitative form to what are highly qualitative judgments. How does one weigh, for example, the relative contribution to security and insecurity of arms sales as compared to a manpower contribution to a peacekeeping mission? Second, it includes components in the index that not everyone would agree are essential for the economic development of poor countries. The tie between global climate change and the economic development of such countries is not entirely self-evident, nor, for that matter, is openness to immigration. Third and finally, some critics might reject the entire premise, namely, that economic development in poor countries is primarily the product of the policies of rich-country governments. The examples of India and China would suggest that policies internal to poor countries may be much more important for economic development in the long run.

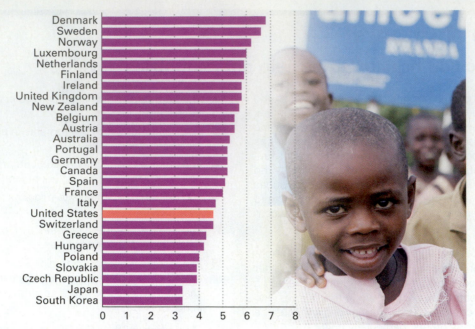

Source: Center for Global Development, Commitment to Development Index, 2013.

**What Do You Think?**

Do you think the United States can and should do more to help poor countries develop economically? If you think we should do more, would you like to see more put into foreign aid, or do you think there are other things we could do that might be more effective? What are some arguments for leaving countries alone to find their own paths to development? On the other hand, why might this tactic be detrimental to the United States?

naval blockade on Cuba that brought the United States and the Soviet Union to the brink of nuclear war. It was Nixon who decided to expand the Vietnam conflict into neighboring Cambodia. George H. W. Bush made the decision to invade Panama to capture its president and drug lord Manuel Noriega. Clinton made the decision to wage an air war against Serbia to halt ethnic cleansing in Kosovo. It was Obama who decided to increase the use of drone attacks inside Pakistan and authorized cyber attacks on Iran's nuclear weapons program.

Though they have the final word in foreign and military policy decisions, presidents rely on many people and several agencies to assist and advise them. By most accounts, during George W. Bush's presidency and with his backing, Vice President Cheney was the key architect of the invasion of Iraq and policies on the harsh treatment of enemy combatants and detainees. The secret and widespread surveillance of American citizens and others also stemmed from Cheney's influence, though some of this was authorized by the USA Patriot Act passed by Congress. Secretary of Defense Rumsfeld was influential until his failure to anticipate the insurgency in Iraq. His decision not to put "boots on the ground" to quell Iraqi insurrectionists led to his resignation and dealt the GOP a blow in the 2006 congressional elections. Robert Gates, who succeeded Rumsfeld and who continued as defense secretary under Obama, was instrumental in convincing Bush to increase troop levels in Iraq and convincing Obama to do the same in Afghanistan.

The national security adviser plays a prominent role in every administration, informing the president daily on foreign and national security matters. The Department of State, headed by the secretary of state, is the president's chief arm for carrying out diplomatic affairs. Some secretaries of state have been extremely important in helping the president make foreign policy—Henry Kissinger in the Nixon and Ford administrations comes to mind, as does Hillary Clinton in the Obama administration—although others have not been among the key players in

**MINGLING WITH THE TROOPS**

Presidents have broad powers to deploy and use American armed forces. President George W. Bush mingles here with troops from Fort Benning, Georgia, whom he has ordered deployed to Iraq. Should presidents have such broad powers? If not, how might these powers be constrained without undermining national security?

the inner circle around the president. It was widely reported that Colin Powell was less influential with President Bush than were Cheney and Rumsfeld, for example. The department itself is organized along both functional lines—economic affairs, human rights, counterterrorism, and refugees—and geographic lines, with "country desks" devoted to each nation of the world. The State Department has nearly 300 embassies, consulates, and missions around the world that carry out policy and advise the department on new developments. Attached to the State Department are the Arms Control and Disarmament Agency, the U.S. Information Agency, and the Agency for International Development, which oversees foreign economic aid. As issues of trade, U.S. corporate investment in other countries, and protection of intellectual property rights (patents and copyrights) become more important in the global economy, both the Department of Commerce, another cabinet department, and the Office of the U.S. Trade Representative, part of the Executive Office of the President, have become more important in foreign policymaking.

The Department of Defense (DOD) is particularly influential in shaping foreign and military policies. The DOD is headed by a civilian secretary of defense, who has authority over the entire department and reports directly to the president. Strong defense secretaries who enjoy the confidence of the president, such as Robert McNamara under Presidents Kennedy and Johnson and Donald Rumsfeld under President George W. Bush, often impose policies about which the military services are not keen. Several Army leaders insisted that the light and technologically advanced fighting forces favored by Rumsfeld, ignored the fact that holding and exploiting battlefield gains in places like Iraq and Afghanistan would require a larger military than Rumsfeld had planned for. Civilian secretaries are also in charge of the Departments of the Army, Navy, and Air Force and report to the secretary of defense. Each service also has a military command structure headed by people in uniform: the Army and Air Force chiefs of staff, the chief of naval operations, the commandant of the Marine

**Joint Chiefs of Staff (JCS)**
The military officers in charge of each of the armed services.

Corps, and their subordinates. The uniformed chiefs of each branch serve together in the **Joint Chiefs of Staff (JCS)**, headed by the chairman of the Joint Chiefs, who reports not only to the secretary of defense but also directly to the president.

A large intelligence community is also involved in fashioning and implementing of foreign and military policy. This community is made up of a number of specific agencies. The National Security Agency (NSA) is responsible for intercepting and monitoring electronic messages from around the world, including, as we know from the massive leaks by Edward Snowden, American citizens, citizens of foreign countries, and the leaders of friendly allies. The National Reconnaissance Office (NRO) is responsible for satellite reconnaissance. Each of the armed services also has a separate tactical intelligence unit. The Central Intelligence Agency (CIA) was established in 1947 to advise the National Security Council, to coordinate all U.S. intelligence agencies, to gather and evaluate intelligence information, and to carry out such additional functions as the NSC directs. Congress, the press, and the public subjected the CIA to intense scrutiny in 2004 because of its failure to alert the nation to the September 11, 2001, terrorist attacks, and its misreading of the existence of weapons of mass destruction in Iraq prior to the U.S. invasion. In 2005, a presidential commission excoriated the CIA for these failures. In response to these failures, Congress and President Bush established a new cabinet-level post of Director of National Intelligence (DNI) to coordinate the intelligence-gathering and interpretation activities of 15 scattered agencies, thus taking over some important responsibilities from the CIA. It remains to be seen how effective this change will be, though the failure to "connect the dots" regarding a Nigerian terrorist planning to blow up a Delta flight from Amsterdam to Detroit in 2009 and the Boston Marathon bombers did not fill Americans with confidence.

## ☐ Congress

Congress has generally played a less active role in foreign and military policy than in domestic policy. Members of Congress not only recognize the strong constitutional foundations of the president's preeminence in these areas, but generally believe that their constituents care more about policies that are close to home than they do about those that are far away. Of course, the exception is when wars go badly, not meeting public expectations, as in Vietnam and Iraq; then Congress becomes more assertive.

In national defense emergencies, Congress tends to take a back seat to the president. This was the case in the immediate aftermath of the terrorist attacks on the United States in 2001. No congressional leader or political party was about to take on George W. Bush's broad assertion of powers, given the crisis situation and the president's extraordinary popularity at the time. However, as the occupation of Iraq dragged on and the president's popularity plummeted, and after Democrats gained control of the House and Senate after the 2006 elections, Congress reasserted itself, focusing most especially on the decision to invade Iraq and management of the aftermath by the president and his team. However, because Democrats did not have enough votes to break Republican filibusters in the Senate, Congress failed on several occasions in 2007 and 2008 to pass legislation setting a date for withdrawal of troops from Iraq. It may not have mattered that much because President Bush had already announced plans for an end to combat missions in Iraq. President Obama moved the withdrawal of combat troops to an earlier date, though not early enough to satisfy the antiwar elements in the Democratic Party.

The Constitution gives Congress the power to declare war—which it has not been asked to do since the beginning of World War II—and to decide about any spending of money. It also gives the Senate the power to approve or disapprove treaties and the appointment of ambassadors. At times, Congress has used its treaty or spending powers to challenge the president on important issues, such as when Congress tried to force an end to the Vietnam War, resisted the Reagan administration's aid to the Nicaraguan Contras, and barely acquiesced to military and peacekeeping operations in Bosnia and Kosovo.

# Using the FRAMEWORK

## Why did we invade Iraq in 2003?

**Background:** Operation "Iraqi Freedom" began on March 20, 2003, when American and British forces, supported by very small contingents from other countries in the so-called "coalition of the willing," launched aerial bombardments across Iraq with initial strikes aimed at air defenses and command and control facilities. The stated goal was to shut down Iraq's weapons of mass destruction program, which was later shown not to have existed at the time. After the initial air strikes, American and British ground forces struck from the south through Kuwait. Baghdad fell on April 9. Rather than the short war that the Bush administration had promised, however, U.S. forces stayed in Iraq for an additional ten years, sustaining thousands of casualties as it fought a fierce insurgency.

### Government Action

President Bush orders the attack on Iraq.

### Government

Vice President Cheney and his aides push hard for invasion of Iraq, as does Defense Secretary Rumsfeld. →

Intelligence agencies support WMD story; unclear whether they truly believe this or feel pressured to be "on board." →

President Bush believes WMD program exists in Iraq; believes downfall of Iraq will be good for Middle East. →

Mostly reluctant Democrats join Republicans in late 2002 to vote for joint congressional resolution authorizing use of force.

### Political Linkage

Conservative and neo-conservative think tanks issue reports on the danger of Iraq's WMDs and how democratizing Iraq will start democratizing the Middle East. →

News media fail to examine WMD story line persuaded, perhaps, by the fact that most western intelligence agencies believed WMD threat to be real. →

In the crisis atmosphere of post-9/11 period, the public is willing to give president broad latitude to protect the country. →

Mass demonstrations in United States and around the world fail to stop the momentum toward war. →

Democrats offer little resistance to the buildup for fear of being labeled weak on national defense. →

Some critics are disarmed by Secretary of State Powell's presentation of WMD evidence before the U.N. Security Council.

### Structure

The United States is the world's only superpower in 2003, able and willing to project military power. →

America's Constitution and the development of its constitutional rules over time give enormous powers to the president in the area of national security. →

The know-how for making WMDs is broadly available in the world.

Congress has probably exerted its greatest foreign and military policy influence on issues that involve spending money, all of which must pass through the regular congressional appropriations process. It has tended to resist calls to increase foreign aid and to support requests for increased defense spending and procurement of new weapons systems. Military contracts are a special focus of attention because each has powerful interest group backers and a great economic effect on many congressional districts. Recently, however, many Americans have worried about the size of the federal budget, which has led Congress to implement a modest cutback in defense appropriations.

# Using the DEMOCRACY STANDARD

## What role do the people play in foreign and defense policymaking?

Democracy is less evident in the process of making military and foreign policies than in making domestic policies. For one thing, Americans generally care more about what is going on in the United States and how it affects them directly than they do about issues and developments in distant places. They also know more about what is going on in the United States—whether it be health care, living standards, or the environment—than they do about what is happening elsewhere, particularly in the poor countries that get very little media news coverage. Additionally, to be effective, many foreign and military policies must be made in secret, so citizens often do not have the information necessary to be politically effective. And political leaders have sometimes misled or ignored the public.[59] Given this, Americans are clearly more competent as citizens when faced with domestic matters than with military and foreign affairs and are more interested in playing a role in shaping domestic policies. The result is that Americans give political, diplomatic, and military leaders a relatively free hand in making foreign and military policy. This is very much what the framers had in mind when they fashioned the Constitution.

Americans are not powerless in the foreign and military policy arenas, however. Although they give their leaders a great deal of latitude in this area, the leaders are ultimately answerable to the people, and they know it. Presidents and members of Congress pay very close attention to public opinion and worry about the next election, so they are careful to avoid actions that may eventually prove unpopular.

Furthermore, Americans seem to be becoming more informed about other places in the world—whether through the mass media or the Internet—and are coming to recognize the interconnectedness of our fate with the fates of others. Globalization, perhaps, has forced Americans to be more attentive to how they are connected to other parts of the world, whether the issues are trade, outsourcing, climate change, human rights violations, or disasters like the earthquake, tsunami, and nuclear plant meltdown in Japan, which adversely affected the U.S. economy. So it may well be that Americans are increasing their capacities to be attentive and effective citizens when it comes to foreign and military affairs.

Nonetheless, it is still the case that the framers put the major responsibility for foreign and military affairs in the hands of the president and, by extension, the executive branch. Although Congress has control over the budget and the constitutional power to declare war against other nations, it is usually at a great disadvantage relative to the president in these areas, primarily because of the president's "war powers." The war powers represent a broad grant of constitutional power that presidents have used over the years to expand their responsibilities for national security, a concept that now involves a wide range of potential threats to the United States and its interests, ranging from direct military attacks on the nation (nuclear, conventional, terrorist), to attacks on U.S. citizens and business firms abroad.

Moreover, in the president's treaty powers and in his responsibility for naming and receiving ambassadors, the Constitution gives the president working control over most other aspects of foreign policymaking. In crisis situations, such as existed after the 1941 attack on Pearl Harbor, and in 2001 after the attacks on the World Trade Center and the Pentagon, the president fashions foreign and military policies without much interference from Congress or the public. In such cases, the Constitution, historical precedents of strong leadership in crisis times by the chief executive, and public opinion all contribute to the broad powers and responsibilities of the president, with little scope, however, for conventional democratic processes.

# Review the Chapter

## Foreign Policy and Democracy: A Contradiction in Terms?

**18.1** Assess the extent to which foreign policymaking can be democratic, p. 569

Democratic theorists tend not to make distinctions between domestic policy and foreign and national security policies, believing that democratic processes are relevant to each; the people can and should be sovereign in all areas, it is argued.

In reality, however, democracy plays a less central role in foreign and national security policymaking. The reasons are varied: the public, for the most part, knows and cares more about domestic policies; foreign and national security policymaking often require secrecy and speed and are less amenable to full deliberation; and the constitutional powers of the president to act independently are considerable.

## The United States as a Superpower

**18.2** Explain why the United States is a superpower and analyze the policy choices and challenges it has in playing this role, p. 570

The superpower status of the United States rests on three pillars: its large and innovative economy, the world's most powerful military, and widespread admiration for its national culture and way of life.

The United States is the world's military superpower. The United States's advantages in high-tech and smart weapons, aerial reconnaissance, and the ability to deploy large forces to world trouble spots are particularly important.

The United States also possesses a good deal of soft power, as American culture and ideology wield a fair amount of influence around the world. But the war in Iraq, the 2008 financial collapse, the Great Recession, and budget gridlock have taken a toll on our soft power advantage.

The United States's policies during its superpower era have combined unilateralist and multilateralist tendencies. In certain periods, it has tilted toward unilateralism. At other periods, it has tilted toward a less "go it alone" stance, depending more on cooperation with allies, negotiations with antagonists, and collaboration with international institutions. Each administration faces the choice of what stance it will take toward the world in its foreign and national security policies.

American policymakers also must decide on what goals to pursue. At the two extremes are policies to extend and protect a set of values or an ideology, and policies that are more pragmatic, such as providing for the material well-being and safety of the nation's people.

The United States's superpower preeminence will likely be challenged at some point by the rise of China as an economic and military power.

## Problems of the Post–Cold War World

**18.3** Evaluate problems facing the post–Cold War world, p. 581

The collapse of the Soviet Union in the early 1990s changed the nature of American foreign and national security policy, which had been focused on fighting communism for more than 40 years.

National security has expanded to include not only the threat of direct attack by large-scale forces on American territory—the main concern during the Cold War years—but other threats including terrorism, global economic and financial instability, the rapid spread of infectious diseases, poverty in less developed countries, global climate change, and cyber attacks on the government and private firms.

Traditional concerns like possible proliferation of weapons of mass destruction, and regional and interethnic conflicts that might lead to global instability, remain important elements on the agenda of policymakers.

China is both an important economic partner of the United States and a potential rival whose interests are not always aligned with America's. Knowing how to balance these opposite tendencies will remain an important problem for American policymakers.

## Who Makes Foreign Policy?

**18.4** Identify the main American foreign and national security policymakers, p. 592

Foreign policy has traditionally been made mostly in the executive branch, where the president is assisted by a large national security bureaucracy, including the National Security Council, the Department of Defense, the Department of State, and various intelligence agencies.

Congress has been little involved in crises or covert actions and has generally gone along with major decisions on defense policy; it has asserted itself chiefly on matters of foreign trade and aid, military bases, and procurement contracts.

Public opinion affects policymakers, perhaps increasingly so, but this influence is limited by the executive branch's centralization of decision making, secrecy, and control of information. How large a part interest groups play is disputed, but is probably substantial in limited areas.

# Learn the Terms

national interest, p. 569
superpower, p. 570
terrorism, p. 573
asymmetric warfare, p. 575
soft power, p. 577
hegemon, p. 580
weapons of mass destruction,
p. 580

unilateralists, p. 580
multilateralists, p. 581
global climate change, p. 581
Cold War, p. 581
nuclear proliferation, p. 582
globalization, p. 588
General Agreement on Tariffs and
Trade (GATT), p. 588

World Trade Organization (WTO),
p. 588
North American Free Trade
Agreement (NAFTA),
p. 588
Millennium Challenge Account,
p. 590
Joint Chiefs of Staff (JCS), p. 596

# Test Yourself

Answer key begins on page T-1.

**18.1** Assess the extent to which foreign policymaking can be democratic

1. In matters of foreign policy, ordinary political factors, such as public opinion and interest groups, are sometimes set aside in favor of considerations of:

   a. Foreign policy
   b. Domestic policy
   c. The national debt
   d. The national interest
   e. War

**18.2** Explain why the United States is a superpower and analyze the policy choices and challenges it has in playing this role

2. This group believes that American national interests should be pursued throughout the world, even without the support of other countries.

   a. Democrats
   b. Republicans
   c. Unilateralists
   d. Multilateralists
   e. Conservatives

**18.3** Evaluate problems facing the post–Cold War world

3. The United States has been forming a stronger strategic alliance with this country, partially as a counter to the rising power of China, and partially for economic reasons.

   a. Pakistan
   b. Russia
   c. Japan
   d. North Korea
   e. India

**18.4** Identify the main American foreign and national security policymakers

4. The military officers in charge of the armed services act as:

   a. The Department of Defense
   b. Joint Chiefs of Staff
   c. The National Security Agency
   d. Security Council
   e. Executive Council

# Explore Further

## INTERNET SOURCES

Amnesty International **www.amnesty.org**
Reports and documents from the international human rights organization.
World Bank **www.worldbank.org**
The website for one of the most important actors in the distribution of aid to poor countries.
The State Department **www.state.gov**

The website for the department responsible for U.S. diplomacy; the site contains a wealth of information relating to countries around the world and the United States's relations with them.
The U.N. Millennium Project **www.unmillenniumproject.org**
The website for the United Nations' formal effort to reduce poverty in the Third World.
International Herald Tribune Online **www.iht.com**

Complete international news with a much broader perspective than that found in most U.S. newspapers and other media outlets.

National Security and Defense Website **www.heritage.org/issues/national-security-and-defense**

Essays and news about foreign and military policy, sponsored by the Heritage Foundation, from a conservative point of view.

Organization for Economic Cooperation and Development **www.oecd.org**

Its statistical section is loaded with information about the economic performance of its member states and how much each spends on programs, including national defense, foreign assistance, and development aid.

United Nations **www.un.org**

Home page of the United Nations; links to a wealth of statistics, documents and reports, U.N. departments and conferences, and information on reaching U.N. officials.

U.S. Department of Defense **www.defense.gov**

The website for the Department of Defense.

The National Security Agency **www.nsa.gov**

The official site for the National Security Agency.

The Central Intelligence Agency **www.cia.gov**

The official site for the CIA, as well as a link to *The World Factbook*.

The Joint Chiefs of Staff **www.jcs.mil**

The official site for the Joint Chiefs of Staff, containing information on both leadership and membership.

## SUGGESTIONS FOR FURTHER READING

Gries, Peter. *The Politics of American Foreign Policy*. Stanford: Stanford University Press, 2014.

An examination of how the liberal-conservative divide in American politics has come to shape ideological divisions about America's role in the world.

Jacques, Martin. *When China Rules the World: The End of the Western World and the Birth of a New Global Order*. New York: Penguin Group, 2009.

A somewhat breathless but still highly informative and detailed account of the rise of China and what it might mean for the United States and the world.

Kagan, Robert. *The World America Made*. New York: Knopf, 2012.

A passionate defense of the notion that the United States is and will long remain the world's superpower and that the world is better off because of it.

Nye, Joseph. *The Paradox of American Power: Why the World's Only Superpower Can't Go It Alone*. Oxford, UK: Oxford University Press, 2002.

A passionate argument for a multilateral rather than a unilateral foreign policy.

Osnos, Evan. *Age of Ambition: Chasing Fortune, Truth, and Faith in the New China*. New York: Farrar, Straus, and Giroux, 2014.

A close-up look at everyday life in China and what its people expect from themselves, their government, and the world, written by the long-time China correspondent of the *New Yorker*.

Sen, Amartya Kumar. *Development as Freedom*. New York: Knopf, 1999.

The Nobel Prize winner in economics argues that freedom is the basis for the development of poor countries, a fact that should inform the foreign policies of the rich countries.

Shapiro, Ian. *Containment: Rebuilding a Strategy Against Global Terror*. Princeton, NJ: Princeton University Press, 2008.

The author suggests that the classic containment policy used to counter the Soviet Union offers a model for how to counter global terrorism while maintaining American values and legitimacy.

*U.S. Army/Marine Corps Counterinsurgency Field Manual*. Chicago: University of Chicago Press, 2007.

Authored by a team assembled by General David Petraeus, the manual lays out a strategy for fighting counterinsurgencies involving not only rooting out the enemy but protecting the lives and well-being of the civilian population.

Zakaria, Fareed. *The Post-American World*. New York: W. W. Norton, 2008.

This provocative book suggests that America's relative power has declined in the world because of the rise of the "others," namely, China, India, Brazil, Russia, and the European Union.

# APPENDIX

THE DECLARATION OF INDEPENDENCE

THE CONSTITUTION OF THE UNITED STATES

*THE FEDERALIST PAPERS,* NOS. 10, 51, AND 78

PRESIDENTS AND CONGRESSES, 1789–2015

# The Declaration of Independence

When in the Course of human events, it becomes necessary for one people to dissolve the political bands which have connected them with another, and to assume among the Powers of the earth, the separate and equal station to which the Laws of Nature and of Nature's God entitle them, a decent respect to the opinions of mankind requires that they should declare the causes which impel them to the separation.

We hold these truths to be self-evident, that all men are created equal, that they are endowed by their Creator with certain unalienable Rights, that among these are Life, Liberty and the pursuit of Happiness. That to secure these rights, Governments are instituted among Men, deriving their just powers from the consent of the governed, That whenever any Form of Government becomes destructive of these ends, it is the Right of the People to alter or to abolish it, and to institute new Government, laying its foundation on such principles and organizing its powers in such form, as to them shall seem most likely to effect their Safety and Happiness. Prudence, indeed, will dictate that Governments long established should not be changed for light and transient causes; and accordingly all experience hath shown, that mankind are more disposed to suffer, while evils are sufferable, than to right themselves by abolishing the forms to which they are accustomed. But when a long train of abuses and usurpations, pursuing invariably the same Object evinces a design to reduce them under absolute Despotism, it is their right, it is their duty, to throw off such Government, and to provide new Guards for their future security.—Such has been the patient sufferance of these Colonies; and such is now the necessity which constrains them to alter their former Systems of Government. The history of the present King of Great Britain is a history of repeated injuries and usurpations, all having in direct object the establishment of an absolute Tyranny over these States. To prove this, let Facts be submitted to a candid world.

He has refused his Assent to Laws, the most wholesome and necessary for the public good.

He has forbidden his Governors to pass Laws of immediate and pressing importance, unless suspended in their operation till his Assent should be obtained; and when so suspended, he has utterly neglected to attend to them.

He has refused to pass other Laws for the accommodation of large districts of people, unless those people would relinquish the right of Representation in the Legislature, a right inestimable to them and formidable to tyrants only.

He has called together legislative bodies at places unusual, uncomfortable, and distant from the depository of their Public Records, for the sole purpose of fatiguing them into compliance with his measures.

He has dissolved Representative Houses repeatedly, for opposing with manly firmness his invasions on the rights of the people.

He has refused for a long time, after such dissolutions, to cause others to be elected; whereby the Legislative Powers, incapable of Annihilation, have returned to the People at large for their exercise; the State remaining in the mean time exposed to all the dangers of invasion from without, and convulsions within.

He has endeavoured to prevent the population of these States; for that purpose obstructing the Laws of Naturalization of Foreigners; refusing to pass others to encourage their migration hither, and raising the conditions of new Appropriations of Lands.

He has obstructed the Administration of Justice, by refusing his Assent to Laws for establishing Judiciary Powers.

He has made Judges dependent on his Will alone, for the tenure of their offices, and the amount and payment of their salaries.

He has erected a multitude of New Offices, and sent hither swarms of Officers to harass our People, and eat out their substance.

He has kept among us, in times of peace, Standing Armies without the Consent of our legislature.

He has affected to render the Military independent of and superior to the Civil Power.

He has combined with others to subject us to a jurisdiction foreign to our constitution, and unacknowledged by our laws; giving his Assent to their acts of pretended legislation:

For quartering large bodies of armed troops among us:

For protecting them, by a mock Trial, from Punishment for any Murders which they should commit on the Inhabitants of these States:

For cutting off our Trade with all parts of the world:

For imposing taxes on us without our Consent:

For depriving us in many cases, of the benefits of Trial by Jury:

For transporting us beyond Seas to be tried for pretended offences:

For abolishing the free System of English Laws in a neighbouring Province, establishing therein an Arbitrary government, and enlarging its Boundaries so as to render it at once an example and fit instrument for introducing the same absolute rule into these Colonies:

For taking away our Charters, abolishing our most valuable Laws, and altering fundamentally the Forms of our Governments:

For suspending our own Legislature, and declaring themselves invested with Power to legislate for us in all cases whatsoever.

He has abdicated Government here, by declaring us out of his Protection and waging War against us.

He has plundered our seas, ravaged our Coasts, burnt our towns, and destroyed the lives of our people.

He is at this time transporting large armies of foreign mercenaries to compleat the works of death, desolation and tyranny, already begun with circumstances of Cruelty & perfidy scarcely paralleled in the most barbarous ages, and totally unworthy the Head of a civilized nation.

He has constrained our fellow Citizens taken Captive on the high Seas to bear Arms against their Country, to become the executioners of their friends and Brethren, or to fall themselves by their Hands.

He has excited domestic insurrections amongst us, and has endeavoured to bring on the inhabitants of our frontiers, the merciless Indian Savages, whose known rule of warfare, is an undistinguished destruction of all ages, sexes and conditions.

In every stage of these Oppressions We have Petitioned for Redress in the most humble terms: Our repeated Petitions have been answered only by repeated injury. A Prince, whose character is thus marked by every act which may define a Tyrant, is unfit to be the ruler of a free People.

Nor have We been wanting in attention to our British brethren. We have warned them from time to time of attempts by their legislature to extend an unwarrantable jurisdiction over us. We have reminded them of the circumstances of our emigration and settlement here. We have appealed to their native justice and magnanimity, and we have conjured them by the ties of our common kindred to disavow these usurpations, which, would inevitably interrupt our connections and correspondence. They too have been deaf to the voice of justice and of consanguinity. We must, therefore, acquiesce in the necessity, which denounces our Separation, and hold them, as we hold the rest of mankind, Enemies in War, in Peace Friends.

We, therefore, the Representatives of the united States of America, in General Congress, Assembled, appealing to the Supreme Judge of the world for the rectitude of our intentions, do, in the Name, and by Authority of the good People of these Colonies, solemnly publish and declare, That these United Colonies are, and of Right ought to be Free and Independent States; that they are Absolved from all Allegiance to the British Crown, and that all political connection between them and the State of Great Britain, is and ought to be totally dissolved; and that as Free and Independent States, they have full Power to levy War, conclude Peace, contract Alliances, establish Commerce, and to do all other Acts and Things which Independent States may of right do. And for the support of this Declaration, with a firm reliance of the Protection of Divine Providence, we mutually pledge to each other our Lives, our Fortunes and our sacred Honor.

John Hancock,
Josiah Bartlett, Wm Whipple, Saml Adams, John Adams, Robt Treat Paine, Elbridge Gerry, Steph. Hopkins, William Ellery, Roger Sherman, Samel Huntington, Wm Williams, Oliver Wolcott, Matthew Thornton, Wm Floyd, Phil Livingston, Frans Lewis, Lewis Morris, Richd Stockton, Jno Witherspoon, Fras Hopkinson, John Hart, Abra Clark, Robt Morris, Benjamin Rush, Benja Franklin, John Morton, Geo Clymer, Jas Smith, Geo. Taylor, James Wilson, Geo. Ross, Caesar Rodney, Geo Read, Thos M:Kean, Samuel Chase, Wm Paca, Thos Stone, Charles Carroll of Carrollton, George Wythe, Richard Henry Lee, Th. Jefferson, Benja Harrison, Thos Nelson, Jr., Francis Lightfoot Lee, Carter Braxton, Wm Hooper, Joseph Hewes, John Penn, Edward Rutledge, Thos Heyward, Junr., Thomas Lynch, Junor., Arthur Middleton, Button Gwinnett, Lyman Hall, Geo Walton.

# The Constitution of the United States

We the people of the United States, in Order to form a more perfect Union, establish Justice, insure domestic Tranquility, provide for the common defence, promote the general Welfare, and secure the Blessings of Liberty to ourselves and our Posterity, do ordain and establish this constitution for the United States of America.

## ☐ Article I

**SECTION 1** All legislative Powers herein granted shall be vested in a Congress of the United States, which shall consist of a Senate and House of Representatives.

**SECTION 2** The House of Representatives shall be composed of Members chosen every second Year by the People of the several States, and the Electors in each State shall have the Qualifications requisite for Electors of the most numerous Branch of the State Legislature.

No person shall be a Representative who shall not have attained to the Age of twenty-five Years, and been seven Years a Citizen of the United States, and who shall not, when elected, be an Inhabitant of that State in which he shall be chosen.

Representatives and direct Taxes shall be apportioned among the several States which may be included within this Union, according to their respective Numbers, which shall be determined by adding to the whole Number of free Persons, including those bound to Service for a Term of Years, and excluding Indians not taxed, three fifths of all other Persons. The actual Enumeration shall be made within three Years after the first Meeting of the Congress of the United States, and within every subsequent Term of ten Years, in such Manner as they shall by Law direct. The Number of Representatives shall not exceed one for every thirty Thousand, but each State shall have at Least one Representative; and until such enumeration shall be made, the State of New Hampshire shall be entitled to chuse three, Massachusetts eight, Rhode-Island and Providence Plantations one, Connecticut five, New-York six, New Jersey four, Pennsylvania eight, Delaware one, Maryland six, Virginia ten, North Carolina five, South Carolina five, and Georgia three.

When vacancies happen in the Representation from any State, the Executive Authority thereof shall issue Writs of Election to fill such Vacancies.

The House of Representatives shall chuse their Speaker and other Officers; and shall have the sole Power of Impeachment.

**SECTION 3** The Senate of the United States shall be composed of two Senators from each State, chosen by the Legislature thereof, for six Years; and each Senator shall have one Vote.

Immediately after they shall be assembled in Consequence of the first Election, they shall be divided as equally as may be into three Classes. The Seats of the Senators of the first Class shall be vacated at the Expiration of the second Year, of the second Class at the Expiration of the fourth Year, and of the third Class at the Expiration of the sixth Year, so that one-third may be chosen every second Year; and if Vacancies happen by Resignation, or otherwise, during the Recess of the Legislature of any State, the Executive thereof may make temporary Appointments until the next Meeting of the Legislature, which shall then fill such Vacancies.

No Person shall be a Senator who shall not have attained to the Age of thirty Years, and been nine Years a Citizen of the United States, and who shall not, when elected, be an Inhabitant of that State in which he shall be chosen.

The Vice President of the United States shall be President of the Senate, but shall have no vote, unless they be equally divided.

The Senate shall chuse their other Officers, and also a President pro tempore, in the absence of the Vice President, or when he shall exercise the Office of the President of the United States.

The Senate shall have the sole Power to try all Impeachments. When sitting for that purpose, they shall be on Oath or Affirmation. When the President of the United States is tried, the Chief Justice shall preside: And no person shall be convicted without the Concurrence of two thirds of the Members present.

Judgment in Cases of Impeachment shall not extend further than to removal from Office, and disqualification to hold and enjoy any Office of honor, Trust, or Profit under the United States: but the Party convicted shall nevertheless be liable and subject to Indictment, Trial, Judgment, and Punishment, according to Law.

**SECTION 4** The Times, Places and Manner of holding Elections for Senators and Representatives, shall be prescribed in each state by the Legislature thereof; but the Congress may at any time by Law make or alter such Regulations, except as to the Places of Chusing Senators.

The Congress shall assemble at least once in every Year, and such Meeting shall be on the first Monday in December, unless they shall by Law appoint a different Day.

**SECTION 5** Each House shall be the Judge of the Elections, Returns and Qualifications of its own Members, and a Majority of each shall constitute a Quorum to do Business; but a smaller number may adjourn from day to day, and may be authorized to compel the Attendance of absent Members, in such Manner, and under such Penalties, as each House may provide.

Each House may determine the Rules of its Proceedings, punish its Members for disorderly Behavior, and, with the Concurrence of two thirds, expel a Member.

Each House shall keep a Journal of its Proceedings, and from time to time publish the same, excepting such Parts as may in their Judgment require Secrecy; and the Yeas and Nays of the Members of either House on any question shall, at the Desire of one fifth of those Present, be entered on the Journal.

Neither House, during the Session of Congress, shall, without the Consent of the other, adjourn for more than three days, nor to any other Place than that in which the two Houses shall be sitting.

**SECTION 6** The Senators and Representatives shall receive a Compensation for their Services, to be ascertained by Law, and paid out of the Treasury of the United States. They shall in all Cases, except Treason, Felony, and Breach of the Peace, be privileged from arrest during their Attendance at the Session of their respective Houses, and in going to and returning from the same; and for any Speech or Debate in either House, they shall not be questioned in any other Place.

No Senator or Representative shall, during the Time for which he was elected, be appointed to any civil Office under the Authority of the United States, which shall have been created, or the Emoluments whereof shall have been increased, during such time; and no Person holding any Office under the United States shall be a Member of either House during his continuance in Office.

**SECTION 7** All Bills for raising Revenue shall originate in the House of Representatives; but the Senate may propose or concur with Amendments as on other bills.

Every Bill which shall have passed the House of Representatives and the Senate, shall, before it become a Law, be presented to the President of the United States; If he approve he shall sign it, but if not he shall return it, with his Objections, to that House in which it shall have originated, who shall enter the Objections at large on their Journal, and proceed to reconsider it. If after such Reconsideration two thirds of that House shall agree to pass the bill, it shall be sent, together with the objections, to the other House, by which it shall likewise be reconsidered, and if approved by two thirds of that House, it shall become a Law. But in all such Cases the Votes of both Houses shall be determined by Yeas and Nays, and the Names of the Persons voting for and against the Bill shall be entered on the Journal of each House respectively. If any Bill shall not be returned by the President within ten Days (Sundays excepted) after it shall have been presented to him, the Same shall be a Law, in like Manner as if he had signed it, unless the Congress by their Adjournment prevent its Return, in which Case it shall not be a Law.

Every Order, Resolution, or Vote to which the Concurrence of the Senate and House of Representatives may be necessary (except on a question of Adjournment) shall be presented to the President of the United States; and before the Same shall take Effect, shall be approved by him, or being disapproved by him, shall be repassed by two thirds of the Senate and House of Representatives, according to the Rules and Limitations prescribed in the Case of a Bill.

**SECTION 8** The Congress shall have Power

To lay and collect Taxes, Duties, Imposts and Excises, to pay the Debts and provide for the common Defence and general Welfare of the United States; but all Duties, Imposts and Excises shall be uniform throughout the United States;

To borrow money on the credit of the United States;

To regulate Commerce with foreign Nations, and among the several States, and with the Indian Tribes;

To establish a uniform Rule of Naturalization, and uniform Laws on the subject of Bankruptcies throughout the United States;

To coin Money, regulate the Value thereof, and of foreign Coin, and fix the Standard of Weights and Measures;

To provide for the Punishment of counterfeiting the Securities and current Coin of the United States;

To establish Post offices and post Roads;

To promote the Progress of Science and useful Arts, by securing for limited Times to Authors and Inventors the exclusive Right to their respective Writings and Discoveries;

To constitute Tribunals inferior to the Supreme Court;

To define and punish Piracies and Felonies committed on the high Seas, and Offences against the Law of Nations;

To declare War, grant Letters of Marque and Reprisal, and make Rules concerning Captures on Land and Water;

To raise and support Armies, but no Appropriation of Money to that Use shall be for a longer Term than two Years;

To provide and maintain a Navy;

To make Rules for the Government and Regulation of the land and naval forces;

To provide for calling forth the Militia to execute the Laws of the Union, suppress Insurrections and repel Invasions;

To provide for organizing, arming, and disciplining the Militia, and for governing such Part of them as may be employed in the Service of the United States, reserving to the States respectively, the Appointment of the Officers, and the Authority of training the Militia according to the discipline prescribed by Congress;

To exercise exclusive Legislation in all Cases whatsoever, over such District (not exceeding ten Miles square) as may, by Cession of particular States, and the acceptance of Congress, become the Seat of Government of the United States, and to exercise like Authority over all Places purchased by the Consent of the Legislature of the State in which the Same shall be, for the Erection of Forts, Magazines, Arsenals, dock-Yards, and other needful Buildings;—And

To make all Laws which shall be necessary and proper for carrying into Execution the foregoing Powers, and all other Powers vested by this Constitution in the government of the United States, or in any Department or Officer thereof.

**SECTION 9** The Migration or Importation of such Persons as any of the States now existing shall think proper to admit, shall not be prohibited by the Congress prior to the Year one thousand eight hundred and eight, but a tax or duty may be imposed on such Importation, not exceeding ten dollars for each Person.

The privilege of the Writ of Habeas Corpus shall not be suspended, unless when in Cases of Rebellion or Invasion the public Safety may require it.

No Bill of Attainder or ex post facto Law shall be passed.

No capitation, or other direct, Tax shall be laid unless in Proportion to the Census or Enumeration herein before directed to be taken.

No Tax or Duty shall be laid on Articles exported from any State.

No Preference shall be given by any Regulation of Revenue to the Ports of one State over those of another: nor shall Vessels bound to, or from, one state, be obliged to enter, clear, or pay Duties in another.

No Money shall be drawn from the Treasury, but in Consequence of Appropriations made by Law; and a regular Statement and Account of the Receipts and Expenditures of all public Money shall be published from time to time.

No Title of Nobility shall be granted by the United States: And no Person holding any Office of Profit or Trust under them, shall, without the Consent of the Congress, accept of any present, Emolument, Office, or Title, of any kind whatever, from any King, Prince, or Foreign State.

**SECTION 10**  No state shall enter into any Treaty, Alliance, or Confederation; grant Letters of Marque and Reprisal; coin Money; emit Bills of Credit; make any Thing but gold and silver Coin a Tender in Payment of Debts; pass any Bill of Attainder, ex post facto Law, or Law impairing the Obligation of Contracts, or grant any Title of Nobility.

No State shall, without the Consent of the Congress, lay any Imposts or Duties on Imports or Exports, except what may be absolutely necessary for executing its inspection Laws: and the net Produce of all Duties and Imposts, laid by any State on Imports or Exports, shall be for the Use of the Treasury of the United States; and all such Laws shall be subject to the Revision and Control of the Congress.

No State shall, without the Consent of Congress, lay any duty of Tonnage, keep Troops, or Ships of War in time of Peace, enter into any Agreement or Compact with another State, or with a foreign Power, or engage in War, unless actually invaded, or in such imminent Danger as will not admit of delay.

## ☐ Article II

**SECTION 1**  The executive Power shall be vested in a President of the United States of America. He shall hold his Office during the Term of four years, and, together with the Vice President, chosen for the same Term, be elected, as follows:

Each State shall appoint, in such Manner as the Legislature thereof may direct, a Number of Electors, equal to the whole Number of Senators and Representatives to which the State may be entitled in the Congress; but no Senator or Representative, or Person holding an Office of Trust or Profit under the United States, shall be appointed an Elector.

The Electors shall meet in their respective States, and vote by Ballot for two persons, of whom one at least shall not be an Inhabitant of the same State with themselves. And they shall make a List of all the Persons voted for, and of the Number of Votes for each; which List they shall sign and certify, and transmit sealed to the Seat of the Government of the United States, directed to the President of the Senate. The President of the Senate shall, in the Presence of the Senate and House of Representatives, open all the Certificates, and the Votes shall then be counted. The Person having the greatest Number of Votes shall be the President, if such Number be a Majority of the whole Number of Electors appointed; and if there be more than one who have such Majority, and have an equal Number of Votes, then the House of Representatives shall immediately chuse by Ballot one of them for President; and if no Person have a Majority, then from the five highest on the List the said House shall in like Manner chuse the President. But in chusing the President, the votes shall be taken by States, the Representation from each State having one Vote; a quorum for this Purpose shall consist of a Member or Members from two-thirds of the States, and a Majority of all the States shall be necessary to a Choice. In every Case, after the Choice of the President, the Person having the greatest Number of Votes of the Electors shall be the Vice President. But if there should remain two or more who have equal votes, the Senate shall chuse from them by Ballot the Vice President.

The Congress may determine the time of chusing the Electors, and the Day on which they shall give their Votes; which Day shall be the same throughout the United States.

No person except a natural-born Citizen, or a Citizen of the United States, at the time of the Adoption of this Constitution, shall be eligible to the Office of President; neither shall any Person be eligible to that Office who shall not have attained to the Age of thirty-five years, and been fourteen Years a Resident within the United States.

In Case of the Removal of the President from Office, or of his Death, Resignation, or Inability to discharge the Powers and Duties of the said Office, the same shall devolve on the Vice President, and the Congress may by Law provide for the Case of Removal, Death, Resignation, or Inability, both of the President and Vice President, declaring what Officer shall then act as President, and such Officer shall act accordingly, until the disability be removed, or a President shall be elected.

The President shall, at stated Times, receive for his Services a Compensation, which shall neither be increased nor diminished during the Period for which he shall have been elected, and he shall not receive within that Period any other Emolument from the United States, or any of them.

Before he enter on the execution of his Office, he shall take the following Oath or Affirmation:—"I do solemnly swear (or affirm) that I will faithfully execute the Office of President of the United States, and will, to the best of my Ability, preserve, protect, and defend the Constitution of the United States."

**SECTION 2**  The President shall be Commander in Chief of the Army and Navy of the United States, and of the Militia of the several States, when called into the actual Service of the United States; he may require the Opinion, in writing, of the principal Officer in each of the executive Departments, upon any subject relating to the Duties of their respective Offices, and he shall have Power to Grant Reprieves and Pardons for Offences against the United States, except in Cases of Impeachment.

He shall have Power, by and with the Advice and Consent of the Senate, to make Treaties, provided two thirds of the Senators present concur; and he shall nominate, and by and with the Advice and Consent of the Senate, shall appoint Ambassadors, other public Ministers and Consuls, Judges of the supreme Court, and all other Officers of the United States, whose Appointments are not herein otherwise provided for, and which shall be established by Law: but the Congress may by Law vest the Appointment of such inferior Officers, as they think proper, in the President alone, in the Courts of Law, or in the Heads of Departments.

The President shall have Power to fill up all Vacancies that may happen during the Recess of the Senate, by granting Commissions which shall expire at the End of their next Session.

**SECTION 3** He shall from time to time give to the Congress Information of the State of the Union, and recommend to their Consideration such Measures as he shall judge necessary and expedient; he may, on extraordinary occasions, convene both Houses, or either of them, and in Case of Disagreement between them, with respect to the Time of Adjournment, he may adjourn them to such Time as he shall think proper; he shall receive Ambassadors and other public Ministers; he shall take Care that the Laws be faithfully executed, and shall Commission all the Officers of the United States.

**SECTION 4** The President, Vice President and all civil Officers of the United States, shall be removed from Office on Impeachment for, and Conviction of, Treason, Bribery, or other high Crimes and Misdemeanors.

## ☐ Article III

**SECTION 1** The judicial Power of the United States, shall be vested in one supreme Court, and in such inferior Courts as the Congress may from time to time ordain and establish. The Judges, both of the supreme and inferior Courts, shall hold their Offices during good Behaviour, and shall, at stated Times, receive for their Services, a Compensation, which shall not be diminished during their Continuance in Office.

**SECTION 2** The judicial Power shall extend to all Cases, in Law and Equity, arising under this Constitution, the Laws of the United States, and treaties made, or which shall be made, under their Authority;—to all Cases affecting ambassadors, other public ministers and consuls;—to all cases of admiralty and maritime Jurisdiction;—to Controversies to which the United States shall be a Party;—to Controversies between two or more States;—between a State and Citizens of another State;—between Citizens of different States,—between Citizens of the same State claiming Lands under Grants of different States, and between a State, or the Citizens thereof, and foreign States, Citizens or Subjects.

In all Cases affecting Ambassadors, other public Ministers and Consuls, and those in which a State shall be Party, the supreme Court shall have original Jurisdiction. In all the other Cases before mentioned, the supreme Court shall have appellate Jurisdiction, both as to Law and Fact, with such Exceptions, and under such Regulations as the Congress shall make.

The trial of all Crimes, except in Cases of Impeachment, shall be by Jury; and such Trial shall be held in the State where the said Crimes shall have been committed; but when not committed within any State, the Trial shall be at such Place or Places as the Congress may by Law have directed.

**SECTION 3** Treason against the United States, shall consist only in levying War against them, or in adhering to their Enemies, giving them Aid and Comfort. No Person shall be convicted of Treason unless on the testimony of two Witnesses to the same overt Act, or on Confession in open Court.

The Congress shall have power to declare the Punishment of Treason, but no Attainder of Treason shall work Corruption of Blood, or Forfeiture except during the Life of the Person attained.

## ☐ Article IV

**SECTION 1** Full Faith and Credit shall be given in each State to the public Acts, Records, and judicial Proceedings of every other State. And the Congress may by general Laws prescribe the Manner in which such Acts, Records and Proceedings shall be proved, and the Effect thereof.

**SECTION 2** The Citizens of each State shall be entitled to all Privileges and Immunities of Citizens in the several States.

A Person charged in any State with Treason, Felony, or other Crime, who shall flee from Justice, and be found in another State, shall on demand of the executive Authority of the State from which he fled, be delivered up, to be removed to the State having Jurisdiction of the crime.

No Person held to Service or Labour in one State, under the Laws thereof, escaping into another, shall, in Consequence of any Law or Regulation therein, be discharged from such Service or Labour, but shall be delivered up on Claim of the Party to whom such Service or Labour may be due.

**SECTION 3** New States may be admitted by the Congress into this Union; but no new State shall be formed or erected within the Jurisdiction of any other State; nor any State be formed by the Junction of two or more States, or parts of States, without the Consent of the Legislatures of the States concerned as well as of the Congress.

The Congress shall have Power to dispose of and make all needful Rules and Regulations respecting the

Territory or other Property belonging to the United States; and nothing in this Constitution shall be so construed as to Prejudice any Claims of the United States, or of any particular State.

**SECTION 4** The United States shall guarantee to every State in this Union a Republican Form of Government, and shall protect each of them against Invasion; and on Application of the Legislature, or the Executive (when the Legislature cannot be convened) against domestic Violence.

## ☐ Article V

The Congress, whenever two-thirds of both Houses shall deem it necessary, shall propose Amendments to this Constitution, or, on the Application of the Legislatures of two-thirds of the several States, shall call a Convention for proposing Amendments, which, in either Case, shall be valid to all Intents and Purposes, as part of this Constitution, when ratified by the Legislatures of three-fourths of the several States, or by Conventions in three-fourths thereof, as the one or the other Mode of Ratification may be proposed by the Congress; Provided that no Amendment which may be made prior to the Year One thousand eight hundred and eight shall in any Manner affect the first and fourth Clauses in the Ninth Section of the first Article; and that no State, without its Consent, shall be deprived of its equal Suffrage in the Senate.

## ☐ Article VI

All Debts contracted and Engagements entered into, before the Adoption of this Constitution, shall be as valid against the United States under this Constitution, as under the Confederation.

This Constitution, and the Laws of the United States which shall be made in Pursuance thereof; and all Treaties made, or which shall be made, under the Authority of the United States, shall be the supreme Law of the Land; and the Judges in every State shall be bound thereby, any Thing in the Constitution or Laws of any State to the Contrary notwithstanding.

The Senators and Representatives before mentioned, and the Members of the several State Legislatures and all executive and judicial Officers, both of the United States and of the several States, shall be bound by Oath or Affirmation to support this Constitution; but no religious Test shall ever be required as a qualification to any Office or public Trust under the United States.

## ☐ Article VII

The Ratification of the Conventions of nine States shall be sufficient for the Establishment of this Constitution between the States so ratifying the same.

Done in Convention by the Unanimous Consent of the States present the Seventeenth Day of September in the Year of our Lord one thousand seven hundred and Eighty seven, and of the Independence of the United States of America the Twelfth. In Witness whereof We have here-unto subscribed our Names.

Go. Washington, President and deputy from Virginia; Attest William Jackson, Secretary; Delaware: Geo. Read,* Gunning Bedford, Jr., John Dickinson, Richard Basset, Jaco. Broom; Maryland: James McHenry, Daniel of St. Thomas' Jenifer, Danl. Carroll; Virginia: John Blair, James Madison, Jr.; North Carolina: Wm. Blount, Richd. Dobbs Spaight, Hu Williamson; South Carolina: J. Rutledge, Charles Cotesworth Pinckney, Charles Pinckney, Pierce Butler; Georgia: William Few, Abr. Baldwin; New Hampshire: John Langdon, Nicholas Gilman; Massachusetts: Nathaniel Gorham, Rufus King; Connecticut: Wm. Saml. Johnson, Roger Sherman,* New York: Alexander Hamilton; New Jersey: Wil. Livingston, David Brearley, Wm. Paterson, Jona. Dayton; Pennsylvania: B. Franklin,* Thomas Mifflin, Robt. Morris,* Geo. Clymer,* Thos. FitzSimons, Jared Ingersoll, James Wilson, Gouv. Morris.

Articles in Addition to, and Amendment of, the Constitution of the United States of America, Proposed by Congress, and Ratified by the Legislatures of the Several States, Pursuant to the Fifth Article of the Original Constitution.

## ☐ Amendment I [1791]

Congress shall make no law respecting an establishment of religion, or prohibiting the free exercise thereof; or abridging the freedom of speech, or of the press; or the right of the people peaceably to assemble, and to petition the Government for a redress of grievances.

## ☐ Amendment II [1791]

A well regulated Militia, being necessary to the security of a free State, the right of the people to keep and bear Arms shall not be infringed.

## ☐ Amendment III [1791]

No Soldier shall, in time of peace, be quartered in any house, without the consent of the Owner, nor in time of war, but in a manner to be prescribed by law.

## ☐ Amendment IV [1791]

The right of the people to be secure in their persons, houses, papers, and effects, against unreasonable searches and seizures, shall not be violated, and no Warrants shall issue, but upon probable cause, supported by Oath or affirmation, and particularly describing the place to be searched, and the persons or things to be seized.

## ☐ Amendment V [1791]

No person shall be held to answer for a capital or otherwise infamous crime, unless on a presentment or indictment of a Grand Jury, except in cases arising in the land or naval forces, or in the Militia, when in actual service in time of War or public danger; nor shall any person be subject for the same offence to be twice put in jeopardy of life or limb; nor shall be compelled in any criminal case to be a witness against himself, nor be deprived of life, liberty, or property, without due process of law; nor shall private property be taken for public use, without just compensation.

## ☐ Amendment VI [1791]

In all criminal prosecutions, the accused shall enjoy the right to a speedy and public trial, by an impartial jury of the State and district wherein the crime shall have been committed, which district shall have been previously ascertained by law, and to be informed of the nature and cause of the accusation; to be confronted with the witnesses against him; to have compulsory process for obtaining witnesses in his favor, and to have the Assistance of Counsel for his defence.

## ☐ Amendment VII [1791]

In suits at common law, where the value in controversy shall exceed twenty dollars, the right of trial by jury shall be preserved, and no fact tried by a jury, shall be otherwise reexamined in any Court of the United States, than according to the rules of the common law.

## ☐ Amendment VIII [1791]

Excessive bail shall not be required, nor excessive fines imposed, nor cruel and unusual punishments inflicted.

## ☐ Amendment IX [1791]

The enumeration in the Constitution, of certain rights, shall not be construed to deny or disparage others retained by the people.

## ☐ Amendment X [1791]

The powers not delegated to the United States by the Constitution, nor prohibited by it to the States, are reserved to the States respectively, or to the people.

## ☐ Amendment XI [1798]

The Judicial power of the United States shall not be construed to extend to any suit in law or equity, commenced or prosecuted against one of the United States by Citizens of another State, or by Citizens or Subjects of any Foreign State.

## ☐ Amendment XII [1804]

The Electors shall meet in their respective States and vote by ballot for President and Vice President, one of whom, at least, shall not be an inhabitant of the same State with themselves; they shall name in their ballots the person voted for as President, and in distinct ballots the person voted for as Vice President, and they shall make distinct lists of all persons voted for as President, and of all persons voted for as Vice President, and of the number of votes for each, which lists they shall sign and certify, and transmit sealed to the seat of the government of the United States, directed to the President of the Senate;—The President of the Senate shall, in the presence of the Senate and House of Representatives, open all the certificates and the votes shall then be counted;—The person having the greatest number of votes for President, shall be the President, if such number be a majority of the whole number of Electors appointed; and if no person have such majority, then from the persons having the highest numbers not exceeding three on the list of those voted for as President, the House of Representatives shall choose immediately, by ballot, the President. But in choosing the President, the votes shall be taken by states, the representation from each state having one vote; a quorum for this purpose shall consist of a member or members from two-thirds of the states, and a majority of all the states shall be necessary to a choice. And if the House of Representatives shall not choose a President whenever the right of choice shall devolve upon them, before the fourth day of March next following, then the Vice President shall act as President, as in the case of the death or other constitutional disability of the President.—The person having the greatest number of votes as Vice President, shall be the Vice President, if such number be a majority of the whole number of Electors appointed, and if no person have a majority, then from the two highest numbers on the list, the Senate shall choose the Vice President; a quorum for the purpose shall consist of two-thirds of the whole number of Senators, and a majority of the whole number shall be necessary to a choice. But no person constitutionally ineligible to the office of President shall be eligible to that of Vice President of the United States.

## ☐ Amendment XIII [1865]

**SECTION 1** Neither slavery nor involuntary servitude, except as a punishment for crime whereof the party shall have been duly convicted, shall exist within the United States, or any place subject to their jurisdiction.

**SECTION 2** Congress shall have power to enforce this article by appropriate legislation.

## ☐ Amendment XIV [1868]

**SECTION 1** All persons born or naturalized in the United States, and subject to the jurisdiction thereof, are citizens of the United States and of the State wherein they reside. No State shall make or enforce any law which shall abridge the privileges or immunities of citizens of the United States; nor shall any State deprive any person of life, liberty, or property, without due process of law; nor deny to any person within its jurisdiction the equal protection of the laws.

**SECTION 2** Representatives shall be apportioned among the several States according to their respective numbers, counting the whole number of persons in each State, excluding Indians not taxed. But when the right to vote at any election for the choice of electors for President and Vice President of the United States, Representatives in Congress, the Executive and Judicial officers of a State, or the members of the Legislature thereof, is denied to any of the male inhabitants of such State, being twenty-one years of age, and citizens of the United States or in any way abridged, except for participation in rebellion, or other crime, the basis of representation therein shall be reduced in the proportion which the number of such male citizens shall bear to the whole number of male citizens twenty-one years of age in such State.

**SECTION 3** No person shall be a Senator or Representative in Congress, or elector of President and Vice President, or hold any office, civil or military, under the United States, or under any State, who, having previously taken an oath, as a member of Congress, or as an officer of the United States, or as a member of any State legislature, or as an executive or judicial officer of any State, to support the Constitution of the United States, shall have engaged in insurrection or rebellion against the same, or given aid or comfort to the enemies thereof. But Congress may by a vote of two-thirds of each House, remove such disability.

**SECTION 4** The validity of the public debt of the United States, authorized by law, including debts incurred for payment of pensions and bounties for services in suppressing insurrection or rebellion, shall not be questioned. But neither the United States nor any State shall assume or pay any debt or obligation incurred in aid of insurrection or rebellion against the United States, or any claim for the loss or emancipation of any slave; but all such debts, obligations, and claims shall be held illegal and void.

**SECTION 5** The Congress shall have the power to enforce, by appropriate legislation, the provisions of this article.

## ☐ Amendment XV [1870]

**SECTION 1** The right of citizens of the United States to vote shall not be denied or abridged by the United States or by any State on account of race, color, or previous condition of servitude.

**SECTION 2** The Congress shall have power to enforce this article by appropriate legislation.

## ☐ Amendment XVI [1913]

The Congress shall have power to lay and collect taxes on incomes, from whatever source derived, without apportionment among the several States, and without regard to any census or enumeration.

## ☐ Amendment XVII [1913]

The Senate of the United States shall be composed of two Senators from each State, elected by the people thereof, for six years; and each Senator shall have one vote. The electors in each State shall have the qualifications requisite for electors of the most numerous branch of the State legislatures.

When vacancies happen in the representation of any State in the Senate, the executive authority of such State shall issue writs of election to fill such vacancies: Provided, That the legislature of any State may empower the executive thereof to make temporary appointments until the people fill the vacancies by election as the legislature may direct. This amendment shall not be so construed as to affect the election or term of any Senator chosen before it becomes valid as part of the Constitution.

## ☐ Amendment XVIII [1919]

**SECTION 1** After one year from the ratification of this article the manufacture, sale, or transportation of intoxicating liquors within, the importation thereof into, or the exportation thereof from the United States and all territory subject to the jurisdiction thereof for beverage purposes is hereby prohibited.

**SECTION 2** The Congress and the several States shall have concurrent power to enforce this article by appropriate legislation.

**SECTION 3** This article shall be inoperative unless it shall have been ratified as an amendment to the Constitution by the legislatures of the several States, as provided in the Constitution, within seven years from the date of the submission hereof to the States by the Congress.

## ☐ Amendment XIX [1920]

The right of citizens of the United States to vote shall not be denied or abridged by the United States or by any State on account of sex.

Congress shall have power to enforce this article by appropriate legislation.

## Amendment XX [1933]

**SECTION 1** The terms of the President and Vice President shall end at noon on the 20th day of January, and the terms of Senators and Representatives at noon on the 3d day of January, of the years in which such terms would have ended if this article had not been ratified; and the terms of their successors shall then begin.

**SECTION 2** The Congress shall assemble at least once in every year, and such meeting shall begin at noon on the 3d day of January, unless they shall by law appoint a different day.

**SECTION 3** If, at the time fixed for the beginning of the term of the President, the President elect shall have died, the Vice President elect shall become President. If a President shall not have been chosen before the time fixed for the beginning of his term, or if the President elect shall have failed to qualify, then the Vice President elect shall act as President until a President shall have qualified; and the Congress may by law provide for the case wherein neither a President elect nor a Vice President elect shall have qualified, declaring who shall then act as President, or the manner in which one who is to act shall be selected, and such person shall act accordingly until a President or Vice President shall have qualified.

**SECTION 4** The Congress may by law provide for the case of the death of any of the persons from whom the House of Representatives may choose a President whenever the right of choice shall have devolved upon them, and for the case of the death of any of the persons from whom the Senate may choose a Vice President whenever the right of choice shall have devolved upon them.

**SECTION 5** Sections 1 and 2 shall take effect on the 15th day of October following the ratification of this article.

**SECTION 6** This article shall be inoperative unless it shall have been ratified as an amendment to the Constitution by the legislatures of three-fourths of the several States within seven years from the date of its submission.

## Amendment XXI [1933]

**SECTION 1** The eighteenth article of amendment to the Constitution of the United States is hereby repealed.

**SECTION 2** The transportation or importation into any State, Territory, or possession of the United States for delivery or use therein of intoxicating liquors, in violation of the laws thereof, is hereby prohibited.

**SECTION 3** This article shall be inoperative unless it shall have been ratified as an amendment to the Constitution by conventions in the several States, as provided in the Constitution, within seven years from the date of the submission hereof to the States by the Congress.

## Amendment XXII [1951]

No person shall be elected to the office of the President more than twice, and no person who has held the office of President, or acted as President, for more than two years of a term to which some other person was elected President shall be elected to the office of the President more than once.

But this Article shall not apply to any person holding the office of President when this Article was proposed by the Congress, and shall not prevent any person who may be holding the office of President or acting as President, during the term within which this Article becomes operative from holding the office of President or acting as President during the remainder of such term.

## Amendment XXIII [1961]

**SECTION 1** The District constituting the seat of Government of the United States shall appoint in such manner as the Congress may direct:

A number of electors of President and Vice President equal to the whole number of Senators and Representatives in Congress to which the District would be entitled if it were a State, but in no event more than the least populous State; they shall be in addition to those appointed by the States, but they shall be considered, for the purposes of the election of President and Vice President, to be electors appointed by a State; and they shall meet in the District and perform such duties as provided by the twelfth article of amendment.

**SECTION 2** The Congress shall have power to enforce this article by appropriate legislation.

## Amendment XXIV [1964]

**SECTION 1** The right of citizens of the United States to vote in any primary or other election for President or Vice President, for electors for President or Vice President, or for Senator or Representative in Congress, shall not be denied or abridged by the United States or any State by reason of failure to pay any poll tax or other tax.

**SECTION 2** The Congress shall have the power to enforce this article by appropriate legislation.

## Amendment XXV [1967]

**SECTION 1** In case of the removal of the President from office or his death or resignation, the Vice President shall become President.

**SECTION 2** Whenever there is a vacancy in the office of the Vice President, the President shall nominate a Vice President who shall take the office upon confirmation by a majority vote of both houses of Congress.

**SECTION 3** Whenever the President transmits to the President pro tempore of the Senate and the Speaker of the House of Representatives his written declaration that he is unable to discharge the powers and duties of his office, and until he transmits to them a written declaration to the contrary, such powers and duties shall be discharged by the Vice President as Acting President.

**SECTION 4** Whenever the Vice President and a majority of either the principal officers of the executive departments, or of such other body as Congress may by law provide, transmit to the President pro tempore of the Senate and the Speaker of the House of Representatives their written declaration that the President is unable to discharge the powers and duties of his office, the Vice President shall immediately assume the powers and duties of the office as Acting President.

Thereafter, when the President transmits to the President pro tempore of the Senate and the Speaker of the House of Representatives his written declaration that no inability exists, he shall resume the powers and duties of his office unless the Vice President and a majority of either the principal officers of the executive departments, or of such other body as Congress may by law provide, transmit within four days to the President pro tempore of the Senate and the Speaker of the House of Representatives their written declaration that the President is unable to discharge the powers and duties of his office. Thereupon Congress shall decide the issue, assembling within 48 hours for that purpose if not in session. If the Congress, within 21 days after receipt of the latter written declaration, or, if Congress is not in session, within 21 days after Congress is required to assemble, determines by two-thirds vote of both houses that the President is unable to discharge the powers and duties of his office, the Vice President shall continue to discharge the same as Acting President; otherwise, the President shall resume the powers and duties of his office.

## ☐ Amendment XXVI [1971]

**SECTION 1** The right of citizens of the United States, who are 18 years of age or older, to vote shall not be denied or abridged by the United States or any state on account of age.

**SECTION 2** The Congress shall have the power to enforce this article by appropriate legislation.

## ☐ Amendment XXVII [1992]

No law varying the compensation for the service of Senators and Representatives shall take effect until an election of Representatives shall have intervened.

# The Federalist Papers

*The Federalist Papers* is a collection of 85 essays written by Alexander Hamilton, John Jay, and James Madison under the pen name Publius. They were published in New York newspapers in 1787 and 1788 to support ratification of the Constitution. *Federalist* Nos. 10, 51, and 78 are reprinted here.

## James Madison: *Federalist* No. 10

Among the numerous advantages promised by a well constructed Union, none deserves to be more accurately developed than its tendency to break and control the violence of faction. The friend of popular governments never finds himself so much alarmed for their character and fate as when he contemplates their propensity to this dangerous vice. He will not fail, therefore, to set a due value on any plan which, without violating the principles to which he is attached, provides a proper cure for it. The instability, injustice, and confusion, introduced into the public councils, have, in truth been the mortal diseases under which popular governments have everywhere perished; as they continue to be the favorite and fruitful topics from which the adversaries to liberty derive their most specious declamations. The valuable improvements made by the American constitutions on the popular models, both ancient and modern, cannot certainly be too much admired; but it would be an unwarrantable partiality, to contend that they have as effectually obviated the danger on this side, as was wished and expected. Complaints are everywhere heard from our most considerate and virtuous citizens, equally the friends of public and private faith, and of public and personal liberty, that our governments are too unstable; that the public good is disregarded in the conflicts of rival parties; and that measures are too often decided, not according to the rules of justice, and the rights of the minor party, but by the superior force of an interested and overbearing majority. However anxiously we may wish that these complaints had no foundation, the evidence of known facts will not permit us to deny that they are in some degree true. It will be found, indeed, on a candid review of our situation, that some of the distresses under which we labor, have been erroneously charged on the operation of our governments; but it will be found, at the same time, that other causes will not alone account for many of our heaviest misfortunes; and, particularly, for the prevailing and increasing distrust of public engagements, and alarm for private rights, which are echoed from one end of the continent to the other. These must be chiefly, if not wholly, effects of the unsteadiness and injustice, with which a factious spirit has tainted our public administrations.

By a faction, I understand a number of citizens, whether amounting to a majority or minority of the whole, who are united and actuated by some common impulse of passion, or of interest, adverse to the rights of other citizens, or to the permanent and aggregate interests of the community.

There are two methods of curing the mischiefs of faction: The one, by removing its causes; the other, by controlling its effects.

There are again two methods of removing the causes of faction: the one, by destroying the liberty which is essential to its existence; the other, by giving to every citizen the same opinions, the same passions, and the same interests.

It could never be more truly said, than of the first remedy, that it was worse than the disease. Liberty is to faction what air is to fire, an aliment, without which it instantly expires. But it could not be a less folly to abolish liberty, which is essential to political life because it nourishes faction, than it would be to wish the annihilation of air, which is essential to animal life, because it imparts to fire its destructive agency.

The second expedient is as impracticable, as the first would be unwise. As long as the reason of man continues fallible, and he is at liberty to exercise it, different opinions will be formed. As long as the connection subsists between his reason and his self-love, his opinions and his passions will have a reciprocal influence on each other; and the former will be objects to which the latter will attach themselves. The diversity in the faculties of men, from which the rights of property originate, is not less an insuperable obstacle to a uniformity of interests. The protection of those faculties is the first object of government. From the protection of different and unequal faculties of acquiring property, the possession of different degrees and kinds of property immediately results; and from the influence of these on the sentiments and views of the respective proprietors, ensues a division of the society into different interests and parties.

The latent causes of faction are thus sown in the nature of man; and we see them everywhere brought into different degrees of activity, according to the different circumstances of civil society. A zeal for different opinions concerning religion, concerning government, and many other points, as well of speculation as of practice;

an attachment to different leaders, ambitiously contending for preeminence and power; or to persons of other descriptions, whose fortunes have been interesting to the human passions, have, in turn, divided mankind into parties, inflamed them with mutual animosity, and rendered them much more disposed to vex and oppress each other, than to cooperate for their common good. So strong is this propensity of mankind, to fall into mutual animosities, that where no substantial occasion presents itself, the most frivolous and fanciful distinctions have been sufficient to kindle their unfriendly passions, and excite their most violent conflicts. But the most common and durable source of factions has been the various and unequal distribution of property. Those who hold, and those who are without property, have ever formed distinct interests in society. Those who are creditors, and those who are debtors, fall under a like discrimination. A landed interest, a manufacturing interest, a mercantile interest, a moneyed interest, with many lesser interests, grow up of necessity in civilized nations, and divide them into different classes, actuated by different sentiments and views. The regulation of these various and interfering interests forms the principle task of modern legislation, and involves the spirit of party and faction in the necessary and ordinary operations of government.

No man is allowed to be a judge in his own cause; because his interest will certainly bias his judgment, and, not improbably, corrupt his integrity. With equal, nay, with greater reason, a body of men are unfit to be both judges and parties at the same time; yet what are many of the most important acts of legislation, but so many judicial determinations, not indeed concerning the rights of single persons, but concerning the rights of large bodies of citizens? And what are the different classes of legislators, but advocates and parties to the cause which they determine? Is a law proposed concerning private debts? It is a question to which the creditors are parties on one side, and the debtors on the other. Justice ought to hold the balance between them. Yet the parties are, and must be, themselves the judges; and the most numerous party, or, in other words, the most powerful faction, must be expected to prevail. Shall domestic manufactures be encouraged, and in what degree, by restrictions on foreign manufactures? are questions which would be differently decided by the landed and the manufacturing classes; and probably by neither with a sole regard to justice and the public good. . . .

It is in vain to say, that enlightened statesmen will be able to adjust these clashing interests, and render them all subservient to the public good. Enlightened statesmen will not always be at the helm; nor, in many cases, can such an adjustment be made at all, without taking into view indirect and remote considerations, which will rarely prevail over the immediate interest which one party may find in disregarding the rights of another, or the good of the whole.

The inference to which we are brought is, that the causes of faction cannot be removed; and that relief is only to be sought in the means of controlling its effects.

If a faction consists of less than a majority, relief is supplied by the republican principle, which enables the majority to defeat its sinister views, by regular vote. It may clog the administration, it may convulse the society; but it will be unable to execute and mask its violence under the forms of the constitution. When a majority is included in a faction, the form of popular government, on the other hand, enables it to sacrifice to its ruling passion or interest, both the public good and the rights of other citizens. To secure the public good, and private rights, against the danger of such a faction, and at the same time to preserve the spirit and the form of popular government, is then the great object to which our inquiries are directed. Let me add, that it is the great desideratum, by which alone this form of government can be rescued from the opprobrium under which it has so long labored, and be recommended to the esteem and adoption of mankind.

By what means is this object attainable? Evidently by one of two only. Either the existence of the same passion or interest in a majority, at the same time must be prevented; or the majority, having such coexistent passion or interest, must be rendered, by their number and local situation, unable to concert and carry into effect schemes of oppression. If the impulse and the opportunity be suffered to coincide, we well know, that neither moral nor religious motives can be relied on as an adequate control. They are not found to be such on the injustice and violence of individuals, and lose their efficacy in proportion to the number combined together; that is in proportion as their efficacy becomes needful.

From this view of the subject, it may be concluded, that a pure democracy, by which I mean a society consisting of a small number of citizens, who assemble and administer the government in person, can admit of no cure from the mischiefs of faction. A common passion or interest will, in almost every case, be felt by a majority of the whole; a communication and concert, results from the form of government itself; and there is nothing to check the inducements to sacrifice the weaker party, or an obnoxious individual. Hence it is, that such democracies have ever been spectacles of turbulence and contention; have ever been found incompatible with personal security, or the rights of property; and have, in general been as short in their lives, as they have been violent in their deaths. Theoretic politicians, who have patronized this species of government, have erroneously supposed that by reducing mankind to a perfect equality in their political rights, they would, at the same time, be perfectly equalized and assimilated in their possessions, their opinions, and their passions.

A republic, by which I mean a government in which the scheme of representation takes place, opens a different prospect, and promises the cure for which we are seeking. Let us examine the points in which it varies from pure democracy, and we shall comprehend both the nature of the cure and the efficacy which it must derive from the union.

The two great points of difference, between a democracy and a republic, are, first, the delegation of the government, in the latter, to a small number of citizens elected by the rest; secondly, the greater number of citizens, and greater sphere of country, over which the latter may be extended.

The effect of the first difference is on the one hand, to refine and enlarge the public views, by passing them through the medium of a chosen body of citizens, whose wisdom may best discern the true interest in their country, and whose patriotism and love of justice, will be least likely to sacrifice it to temporary or partial considerations. Under such a regulation, it may well happen, that the public voice, pronounced by the representatives of the people, will be more consonant to the public good, than if pronounced by the people themselves, convened for the purpose. On the other hand, the effect may be inverted. Men of factious tempers, of local prejudices, or of sinister designs, may by intrigue, by corruption, or by other means, first obtain the suffrages, and then betray the interests, of the people. The question resulting is, whether small or extensive republics are most favorable to the election of proper guardians of the public weal; and it is clearly decided in favor of the latter by two obvious considerations.

In the first place, it is to be remarked, that however small the republic may be, the representatives must be raised to a certain number, in order to guard against the cabals of a few; and that however large it may be, they must be limited to a certain number, in order to guard against the confusion of a multitude. Hence, the number of representatives in the two cases not being in proportion to that of the constituents, and being proportionally greatest in the small republic, it follows that if the proportion of fit characters be not less in the large than in the small republic, the former will present a greater option, and consequently a greater probability of a fit choice.

In the next place, as each representative will be chosen by a greater number of citizens in the large than in the small republic, it will be more difficult for unworthy candidates to practice with success the vicious arts, by which elections are too often carried; and the suffrages of the people being more free, will be more likely to center in men who possess the most attractive merit, and the most diffusive and established characters. . . .

The other point of difference is, the greater number of citizens, and extent of territory, which may be brought within the compass of republican, than of democratic government; and it is this circumstance principally which renders factious combinations less to be dreaded in the former, than in the latter. The smaller the society, the fewer probably will be the distinct parties and interests composing it; the fewer the distinct parties and interests, the more frequently will a majority be found of the same party; and the smaller the number of individuals composing a majority, and the smaller the compass within which they are placed, the more easily they will concert and execute their plans of oppression. Extend the sphere, and you take in a greater variety of parties and interests; you make it less probable that a majority of the whole will have a common motive to invade the rights of other citizens; or if such a common motive exists, it will be more difficult for all who feel it to discover their own strength, and to act in unison with each other . . . .

Hence, it clearly appears, that the same advantage, which a republic has over a democracy, in controlling the effects of faction, is enjoyed by a large over a small republic—is enjoyed by the union over the states composing it. Does this advantage consist in the substitution of representatives, whose enlightened views and virtuous sentiments render them superior to local prejudices, and to schemes of injustice? It will not be denied, that the representation of the union will be most likely to possess these requisite endowments. Does it consist in the greater security afforded by a greater variety of parties, against the event of any one party being able to outnumber and oppress the rest? In an equal degree does the increased variety of parties, comprised within the union, increase this security? Does it, in fine, consist in the greater obstacles opposed to the concert and accomplishment of the secret wishes of an unjust and interested majority? Here, again, the extent of the union gives it the most palpable advantage. The influence of factious leaders may kindle a flame within their particular states, but will be unable to spread a general conflagration through the other states; a religious sect may degenerate into a political faction in a part of the confederacy; but the variety of sects dispersed over the entire face of it, must secure the national councils against any danger from that source; a rage for paper money, for an abolition of debts, for an equal division of property, or for any other improper or wicked project, will be less apt to pervade the whole body of the union, than a particular member of it; in the same proportion as such a malady is more likely to taint a particular country or district, than an entire state.

In the extent and proper structure of the union, therefore, we behold a republican remedy for the diseases most incident to republican government. And according to the degree of pleasure and pride we feel in being republicans, ought to be our zeal in cherishing the spirit, and supporting the character of Federalists.

## James Madison: *Federalist* No. 51

To what expedient then shall we finally resort, for maintaining in practice the necessary partition of power among the several departments, as laid down in the constitution? The only answer that can be given is, that as all these exterior provisions are found to be inadequate, the defect must be supplied, by so contriving the interior structure of the government, as that its several constituent parts may, by

their mutual relations, be the means of keeping each other in their proper places . . . .

In order to lay a due foundation for that separate and distinct exercise of the different powers of government, which, to a certain extent, is admitted on all hands to be essential to the preservation of liberty, it is evident that each department should have a will of its own; and consequently should be so constituted, that the members of each should have as little agency as possible in the appointment of the members of the others . . . .

It is equally evident, that the members of each department should be as little dependent as possible on those of the others, for the emoluments annexed to their offices. Were the executive magistrate, or the judges, not independent of the legislature in this particular, their independence in every other would be merely nominal.

But the great security against a gradual concentration of the several powers in the same department, consists in giving to those who administer each department, the necessary constitutional means, and personal motives, to resist encroachments of the others. The provision for defense must in this, as in all other cases, be made commensurate to the danger of attack. Ambition must be made to counteract ambition. The interest of the man must be connected with the constitutional rights of the place. It may be a reflection on human nature, that such devices should be necessary to control the abuses of government. But what is government itself, but the greatest of all reflections on human nature? If men were angels, no government would be necessary. If angels were to govern men, neither external nor internal controls on government would be necessary. In framing a government, which is to be administered by men over men, the great difficulty lies in this: You must first enable the government to control the governed; and in the next place, oblige it to control itself. A dependence on the people is, no doubt, the primary control on the government; but experience has taught mankind the necessity of auxiliary precautions.

This policy of supplying by opposite and rival interests, the defect of better motives, might be traced through the whole system of human affairs, private as well as public. We see it particularly displayed in all the subordinate distributions of power; where the constant aim is, to divide and arrange the several offices in such a manner, as that each may be a check on the other; that the private interest of every individual, may be a sentinel over the public rights. These interventions of prudence cannot be less requisite to the distribution of the supreme powers of the state.

But it is not possible to give to each department an equal power of self-defense. In republican government, the legislative authority necessarily predominates. The remedy for this inconvenience is, to divide the legislature into different branches; and to render them by different modes of election, and different principles of action, as little connected with each other, as the nature of their common functions, and their common dependence on the society will admit. It may even be necessary to guard against dangerous encroachments, by still further precautions. As the weight of the legislative authority requires that it should be thus divided, the weakness of the executive may require, on the other hand, that it should be fortified. An absolute negative on the legislature, appears, at first view, to be the natural defense with which the executive magistrate should be armed. But perhaps it would be neither altogether safe, nor alone sufficient. On ordinary occasions, it might not be exerted with the requisite firmness; and on extraordinary occasions, it might be perfidiously abused. May not this defect of an absolute negative be supplied by some qualified connection between this weaker department, and the weaker branch of the stronger department, by which the latter may be led to support the constitutional rights of the former, without being too much detached from the rights of its own department?

There are, moreover, two considerations particularly applicable to the federal system of America, which place that system in a very interesting point of view.

**FIRST.** In a single republic, all the power surrendered by the people is submitted to the administration of a single government, and the usurpations are guarded against by a division of the government into distinct and separate departments. In the compound republic of America, the power surrendered by the people is first divided between two distinct governments, and then the portion allotted to each subdivided among distinct and separate departments. Hence a double security arises to the rights of the people. The different governments will control each other, at the same time that each will be controlled by itself.

**SECOND.** It is of great importance in a republic not only to guard the society against the oppression of its rulers, but to guard one part of the society against the injustice of the other part. Different interests necessarily exist in different classes of citizens. If a majority be united by a common interest, the rights of the minority will be insecure. There are but two methods of providing against this evil: the one by creating a will in the community independent of the majority—that is, of the society itself; the other, by comprehending in the society so many separate descriptions of citizens as will render an unjust combination of a majority of the whole very probable, if not impracticable. The first method prevails in all governments possessing an hereditary or self-appointed authority. This, at best, is but a precarious security; because a power independent of the society may as well espouse the unjust views of the major, as the rightful interests of the minor party, and may possibly be turned against both parties. The second method will be exemplified in the federal republic of the United States. Whilst all authority in it will be derived from and dependent on the society, the society itself will be broken into so many parts, interests and classes of citizens, that the rights of individuals, or of the minority, will be in little danger from interested combinations of the majority. In a free government the security for civil rights must be the same as that for religious rights. It consists in the one case in the multiplicity of interests, and in the other in the multiplicity of sects. The degree of security in both cases will depend on the number of interests and sects; and this may be presumed to depend on the extent of country and number of people comprehended under the same government. This view of the subject must particularly recommend a proper federal system to all the sincere and considerate friends of republican government, since it shows that in exact proportion as the territory of the Union may be formed into more circumscribed Confederacies, or States, oppressive combinations of a majority will be facilitated; the best security, under the republican forms, for the rights of every class of citizens, will be diminished; and consequently the stability and independence of some member of the government, the only other security, must be proportionately increased. Justice is the end of the government. It is the end of civil society. It ever has been and ever will be pursued until it be obtained, or until liberty be lost in the pursuit. In a society under the forms of which the stronger faction can readily unite and oppress the weaker, anarchy may as truly be said to reign as in a state of nature, where the weaker individual is not secured against the violence of the stronger; and as, in the latter state, even the stronger individuals are prompted, by the uncertainty of their condition, to submit to a government which may protect the weak as well as themselves; so, in the former state, will the more powerful factions or parties be gradually induced, by a like motive, to wish for a government which will protect all parties, the weaker as well as the more powerful. It can be little doubted that if the State of Rhode Island was separated from the Confederacy and left to itself, the insecurity of rights under the popular form of government within such narrow limits would be displayed by such reiterated oppressions of factious majorities that some power altogether independent of the people would soon be called for by the voice of the very factions whose misrule had proved the necessity of it. In the extended republic of the United States, and among the great variety of interests, parties, and sects which it embraces, a coalition of a majority of the whole society could seldom take place on any other principles than those of justice and the general good; whilst there being thus less danger to a minor from the will of a major party, there must be less pretext, also, to provide for the security of the former, by introducing into the government a will not dependent on the latter, or, in other words, a will independent of the society itself. It is no less certain than it is important, notwithstanding the contrary opinions which have been entertained, that the larger the society, provided it lie within a practical sphere, the more duly capable it will be of self-government. And happily for the republican cause, the practicable sphere may be carried to a very great extent, by a judicious modification and mixture of the federal principle.

## Alexander Hamilton: *Federalist* No. 78

We proceed now to an examination of the judiciary department of the proposed government.

In unfolding the defects of the existing confederation, the utility and necessity of a federal judicature have been clearly pointed out. It is the less necessary to recapitulate the considerations there urged; as the propriety of the institution in the abstract is not disputed; the only questions which have been raised being relative to the manner of constituting it, and to its extent. To these points, therefore, our observations shall be confined.

The manner of constituting it seems to embrace these several objects: 1st. The mode of appointing the judges; 2nd. The tenure by which they are to hold their places; 3rd. The partition of the judiciary authority between courts, and their relations to each other.

**FIRST.** As to the mode of appointing the judges: This is the same with that of appointing the officers of the union in general, and has been so fully discussed . . . that nothing can be said here which would not be useless repetition.

**SECOND.** As to the tenure by which the judges are to hold their places: This chiefly concerns their duration in office; the provisions for their support; the precautions for their responsibility.

According to the plan of the convention, all the judges who may be appointed by the United States are to hold their offices during good behavior; which is conformable to the most approved of the state constitutions. . . . The standard of good behavior for the continuance in office of the judicial magistracy is certainly one of the most valuable of the modern improvements in the practice of government. In a monarchy, it is an excellent barrier to the despotism of the prince; in a republic, it is a no less excellent barrier to the encroachments and oppressions of the representative body. And it is the best expedient which can be devised in any government, to secure a steady, upright, and impartial administration of the laws.

Whoever attentively considers the different departments of power must perceive, that, in a government in which they are separated from each other, the judiciary, from the nature of its functions, will always be the least dangerous to the political rights of the constitution; because it will be at least in a capacity to annoy or injure them. The executive not only dispenses the honors, but holds the sword of the community. The legislature not only commands the purse, but prescribes the rules by which the duties and rights of every citizen are to be regulated. The judiciary, on the contrary, has no influence over either the sword or the purse; no direction either of the strength or of the wealth of the society; and can take no active resolution whatever. It may truly be said to have neither force nor will, but merely judgment; and must ultimately depend upon the aid of the executive arm for the efficacious exercise even of this faculty.

This simple view of the matter suggests several important consequences: It proves incontestably, that the judiciary is beyond comparison, the weakest of the three departments of power, that it can never attack with success either of the other two: and that all possible care is requisite to enable it to defend itself against their attacks. It equally proves, that, though individual oppression may now and then proceed from the courts of justice, the general liberty of the people can never be endangered from that quarter; I mean so long as the judiciary remains truly distinct from both the legislature and executive. For I agree, that "there is no liberty, if the power of judging be not separated from the legislative and executive powers." It proves, in the last place, that as liberty can have nothing to fear from the judiciary alone, but would have everything to fear from its union with either of the other departments; that, as all the effects of such a union must ensue from a dependence of the former on the latter, notwithstanding a nominal and apparent separation; that as, from the natural feebleness of the judiciary, it is in continual jeopardy of being overpowered, awed or influenced by its coordinate branches; that, as nothing can contribute so much to its firmness and independence as permanency in office, this quality may therefore be justly regarded as an indispensable ingredient in its constitution; and, in a great measure, as the citadel of the public justice and the public security.

The complete independence of the courts of justice is peculiarly essential in a limited constitution. By a limited constitution, I understand one which contains certain specified exceptions to the legislative authority; such, for instance, as that it shall pass no bills of attainder, no ex post facto laws, and the like. Limitations of this kind can be preserved in practice no other way than through the medium of the courts of justice, whose duty it must be to declare all acts contrary to the manifest tenor of the constitution void. Without this, all the reservations of particular rights or privileges would amount to nothing.

Some perplexity respecting the right of the courts to pronounce legislative acts void, because contrary to the constitution, has arisen from an imagination that the doctrine would imply a superiority of the judiciary to the legislative power. It is urged that the authority which can declare the acts of another void, must necessarily be superior to the one whose acts may be declared void. As this doctrine is of great importance in all the American constitutions, a brief discussion of the grounds on which it rests cannot be unacceptable.

There is no position which depends on clearer principles than that every act of a delegated authority, contrary to the tenor of the commission under which it is exercised, is void. No legislative act, therefore, contrary to the constitution, can be valid. To deny this would be to affirm, that the deputy is greater then his principal; that the servant is above his master; that the representatives of the people are superior to the people themselves; that men, acting by virtue of powers, may do not only what their powers do not authorize, but what they forbid.

If it be said that the legislative body are themselves the constitutional judges of their own powers, and that the construction they put upon them is conclusive upon the other departments, it may be answered, that this cannot be the natural presumption, where it is not to be collected from any particular provisions in the constitution. It is not otherwise to be supposed that the constitution could intend to enable the representatives of the people to substitute their will to that of their constituents. It is far more rational to suppose that the courts were designed to be an intermediate body between the people and the legislature, in order, among other things, to keep the latter within the limits assigned to their authority. The interpretation of the laws is the proper and peculiar province of the courts. A constitution is, in fact, and must be, regarded by the judges as a fundamental law. It must therefore belong to them to ascertain its meaning, as well as the meaning of any particular act proceeding from the legislative body. If there should happen to be an irreconcilable variance between the two, that which has the superior obligation and validity ought, of course, to be preferred; in other words, the constitution ought to be preferred to the statute, the intention of the people to the intention of their agents.

Nor does this conclusion by any means suppose a superiority of the judicial to the legislative power. It only supposes that the power of the people is superior to both; and that where the will of the legislature declared in its statutes, stands in opposition to that of the people declared in the constitution, the judges ought to be governed by the latter, rather than the former. They ought to regulate their decisions by the fundamental laws, rather than by those which are not fundamental. . . .

It can be of no weight to say, that the courts, on the pretense of a repugnancy, may substitute their own pleasure to the constitutional intentions of the legislature. This might as well happen in the case of two contradictory statutes; or it might as well happen in every adjudication upon any single statute. The courts must declare the sense of the law; and if they should be disposed to exercise will instead of judgment, the consequence would equally be the substitution of their pleasure to that of the legislative body. The observation, if it proved anything, would prove that there ought to be no judges distinct from the body.

If then the courts of justice are to be considered as the bulwarks of a limited constitution, against legislative encroachments, this consideration will afford a strong argument for the permanent tenure of judicial officers, since nothing will contribute so much as this to that independent spirit in the judges, which must be essential to the faithful performance of so arduous a duty.

This independence of the judges is equally requisite to guard the constitution and the rights of individuals, from the effects of those ill-humors which are the arts of designing men, or the influence of particular conjunctures, sometimes disseminate among the people themselves, and which, though they speedily give place to better information, and more deliberate reflection, have a tendency, in the meantime, to occasion dangerous innovations in the government, and serious oppressions of the minor party in the community. . . . Until the people have, by some solemn and authoritative act, annulled or changed the established form, it is binding upon themselves collectively, as well as individually; and no presumption, or even knowledge of their sentiments, can warrant their representatives in a departure from it, prior to such an act. But it is easy to see, that it would require an uncommon portion of fortitude in the judges to do their duty as faithful guardians of the constitution, where legislative invasions of it had been instigated by the major voice of the community.

But it is not with a view to infractions of the constitution only, that the independence of the judges may be an essential safeguard against the effects of occasional ill-humors in the society. These sometimes extend no farther than to the injury of the private rights of particular classes of citizens, by unjust and partial laws. Here also the firmness of the judicial magistracy is of vast importance in mitigating the severity, and confining the operation of such laws. It not only serves to moderate the immediate mischiefs of those which may have been passed, but it operates as a check upon the legislative body in passing them; who, perceiving that obstacles to the success of an iniquitous intention are to be expected from the scruples of the courts, are in a manner compelled by the very motives of the injustice they meditate, to qualify their attempts . . . .

That inflexible and uniform adherence to the rights of the constitution, and of individuals, which we perceive to be indispensable in the courts of justice, can certainly not be expected from judges who hold their offices by a temporary commission. Periodical appointments, however regulated, or by whomsoever made, would, in some way or other, be fatal to their necessary independence. If the power of making them was committed either to the executive or legislature, there would be danger of an improper compliance to the branch which possessed it; if to both, there would be an unwillingness to hazard the displeasure of either; if to the people, or to persons chosen by them for the special purpose, there would be too great a disposition to consult popularity to justify a reliance that nothing would be consulted but the constitution and the laws.

There is yet a further and a weighty reason for the permanency of judicial offices, which is deducible from the nature of the qualifications they require. It has been frequently remarked, with great propriety, that a voluminous code of laws is one of the inconveniences necessarily connected with the advantages of a free government. To avoid an arbitrary discretion in the courts, it is indispensable that they should be bound down by strict rules and precedents, which serve to define and point out their duty in every particular case that comes before them; and it will readily be conceived, from the variety of controversies which grow out of the folly and wickedness of mankind, that the records of those precedents must unavoidably swell to a very considerable bulk, and must demand long and laborious study to acquire a competent knowledge of them. Hence it is, that there can be but few men in the society, who will have sufficient skill in the laws to qualify them for the stations of judges. And making the proper deductions for the ordinary depravity of human nature, the number must be still smaller, of those who unite the requisite integrity with the requisite knowledge . . .

# Presidents and Congresses, 1789–2013

| Year | President and Vice President | Party of President | Congress | Majority Party | |
|---|---|---|---|---|---|
| | | | | House | Senate |
| 1789–1797 | **George Washington** | None | 1st | Admin. Supporters | Admin. Supporters |
| | John Adams | | 2nd | Federalist | Federalist |
| | | | 3rd | Democratic-Republican | Federalist |
| | | | 4th | Federalist | Federalist |
| 1797–1801 | **John Adams** | Federalist | 5th | Federalist | Federalist |
| | Thomas Jefferson | | 6th | Federalist | Federalist |
| 1801–1809 | **Thomas Jefferson** | | 7th | Democratic-Republican | Democratic-Republican |
| | Aaron Burr (to 1805) | | 8th | Democratic-Republican | Democratic-Republican |
| | George Clinton (to 1809) | | 9th | Democratic-Republican | Democratic-Republican |
| | | | 10th | Democratic-Republican | Democratic-Republican |
| 1809–1817 | **James Madison** | Democratic-Republican | 11th | Democratic-Republican | Democratic-Republican |
| | George Clinton (to 1813) | | 12th | Democratic-Republican | Democratic-Republican |
| | Elbridge Gerry (to 1817) | | 13th | Democratic-Republican | Democratic-Republican |
| | | | 14th | Democratic-Republican | Democratic-Republican |
| 1817–1825 | **James Monroe** | Democratic-Republican | 15th | Democratic-Republican | Democratic-Republican |
| | Daniel D. Tompkins | | 16th | Democratic-Republican | Democratic-Republican |
| | | | 17th | Democratic-Republican | Democratic-Republican |
| | | | 18th | Democratic-Republican | Democratic-Republican |
| 1825–1829 | **John Quincy Adams** | National-Republican | 19th | Admin. Supporters | Admin. Supporters |
| | John C. Calhoun | | 20th | Jacksonian Democrats | Jacksonian Democrats |
| 1829–1837 | **Andrew Jackson** | Democratic | 21st | Democratic | Democratic |
| | John C. Calhoun (to 1833) | | 22nd | Democratic | Democratic |
| | Martin Van Buren (to 1837) | | 23rd | Democratic | Democratic |
| | | | 24th | Democratic | Democratic |
| 1837–1841 | **Martin Van Buren** | Democratic | 25th | Democratic | Democratic |
| | Richard M. Johnson | | 26th | Democratic | Democratic |
| 1841 | **William H. Harrison** (died a month after inauguration) | Whig | | | |
| | John Tyler | | | | |
| 1841–1845 | **John Tyler** | Whig | 27th | Whig | Whig |
| | (VP vacant) | | 28th | Democratic | Whig |
| 1845–1849 | **James K. Polk** | Democratic | 29th | Democratic | Democratic |
| | George M. Dallas | | 30th | Whig | Democratic |
| 1849–1850 | **Zachary Taylor** (died in office) | Whig | 31st | Democratic | Democratic |
| | Millard Fillmore | | | | |
| 1850–1853 | **Millard Fillmore** | Whig | 32nd | Democratic | Democratic |
| | (VP vacant) | | | | |
| 1853–1857 | **Franklin Pierce** | Democratic | 33rd | Democratic | Democratic |
| | William R. King | | 34th | Republican | Democratic |

| Year | President and Vice President | Party of President | Congress | Majority Party | |
|------|------|------|------|------|------|
| | | | | **House** | **Senate** |
| 1857–1861 | **James Buchanan** | Democratic | 35th | Democratic | Democratic |
| | John C. Breckinridge | | 36th | Republican | Democratic |
| 1861–1865 | **Abraham Lincoln** (died in office) | Republican | 37th | Republican | Republican |
| | Hannibal Hamlin (to 1865) | | 38th | Republican | Republican |
| | Andrew Johnson (1865) | | | | |
| 1865–1869 | **Andrew Johnson** | Republican | 39th | Unionist | Unionist |
| | (VP vacant) | | 40th | Republican | Republican |
| 1869–1877 | **Ulysses S. Grant** | Republican | 41st | Republican | Republican |
| | Schuyler Colfax (to 1873) | | 42nd | Republican | Republican |
| | Henry Wilson (to 1877) | | 43rd | Republican | Republican |
| | | | 44th | Democratic | Republican |
| 1877–1881 | **Rutherford B. Hayes** | Republican | 45th | Democratic | Republican |
| | William A. Wheeler | | 46th | Democratic | Democratic |
| 1881 | **James A. Garfield** (died in office) | Republican | 47th | Republican | Republican |
| | Chester A. Arthur | | | | |
| 1881–1885 | **Chester A. Arthur** (VP vacant) | Republican | 48th | Democratic | Republican |
| 1885–1889 | **Grover Cleveland** | Democratic | 49th | Democratic | Republican |
| | Thomas A. Hendricks | | 50th | Democratic | Republican |
| 1889–1893 | **Benjamin Harrison** | Republican | 51st | Republican | Republican |
| | Levi P. Morton | | 52nd | Democratic | Republican |
| 1893–1897 | **Grover Cleveland** | Democratic | 53rd | Democratic | Democratic |
| | Adlai E. Stevenson | | 54th | Republican | Republican |
| 1897–1901 | **William McKinley** (died in office) | Republican | 55th | Republican | Republican |
| | Garret A. Hobart (to 1901) | | 56th | Republican | Republican |
| | Theodore Roosevelt (1901) | | | | |
| 1901–1909 | **Theodore Roosevelt** | Republican | 57th | Republican | Republican |
| | (VP vacant, 1901–1905) | | 58th | Republican | Republican |
| | Charles W. Fairbanks (1905–1909) | | 59th | Republican | Republican |
| | | | 60th | Republican | Republican |
| 1909–1913 | **William Howard Taft** | Republican | 61st | Republican | Republican |
| | James S. Sherman | | 62nd | Democratic | Republican |
| 1913–1921 | **Woodrow Wilson** | Democratic | 63rd | Democratic | Democratic |
| | Thomas R. Marshall | | 64th | Democratic | Democratic |
| | | | 65th | Democratic | Democratic |
| | | | 66th | Republican | Republican |
| 1921–1923 | **Warren G. Harding** (died in office) | Republican | 67th | Republican | Republican |
| | Calvin Coolidge | | | | |
| 1923–1929 | **Calvin Coolidge** (VP vacant, 1923–1925) | Republican | 68th | Republican | Republican |
| | | | 69th | Republican | Republican |
| | Charles G. Dawes (1925–1929) | | 70th | Republican | Republican |
| 1929–1933 | **Herbert Hoover** | Republican | 71st | Republican | Republican |
| | Charles Curtis | | 72nd | Democratic | Republican |
| 1933–1945 | **Franklin D. Roosevelt** (died in office) | Democratic | 73rd | Democratic | Democratic |
| | | | 74th | Democratic | Democratic |
| | John N. Garner (1933–1941) | | 75th | Democratic | Democratic |

| Year | President and Vice President | Party of President | Congress | Majority Party | |
|------|------------------------------|--------------------|----------|-------|--------|
| | | | | **House** | **Senate** |
| | Henry A. Wallace (1941–1945) | | 76th | Democratic | Democratic |
| | Harry S Truman (1945) 77th | Democratic | 77th 78th | Democratic Democratic | Democratic Democratic |
| 1945–1953 | **Harry S Truman** | Democratic | 79th | Democratic | Democratic |
| | (VP vacant, 1945–1949) | | 80th | Republican | Republican |
| | Alben W. Barkley (1949–1953) | | 81st | Democratic | Democratic |
| | | | 82nd | Democratic | Democratic |
| 1953–1961 | **Dwight D. Eisenhower** | Republican | 83rd | Republican | Republican |
| | Richard M. Nixon | | 84th | Democratic | Democratic |
| | | | 85th | Democratic | Democratic |
| | | | 86th | Democratic | Democratic |
| 1961–1963 | **John F. Kennedy** (died in office) | Democratic | 87th | Democratic | Democratic |
| | Lyndon B. Johnson | | | | |
| 1963–1969 | **Lyndon B. Johnson** | Democratic | 88th | Democratic | Democratic |
| | (VP vacant, 1963–1965) | | 89th | Democratic | Democratic |
| | Hubert H. Humphrey (1965–1969) | | 90th | Democratic | Democratic |
| 1969–1974 | **Richard M. Nixon** (resigned office) | Republican | 91st | Democratic | Democratic |
| | | | 92nd | Democratic | Democratic |
| | Spiro T. Agnew (resigned office) | | | | |
| | Gerald R. Ford (appointed vice president) | | | | |
| 1974–1977 | **Gerald R. Ford** | Republican | 93rd | Democratic | Democratic |
| | Nelson A. Rockefeller (appointed vice president) | | 94th | Democratic | Democratic |
| 1977–1981 | **Jimmy Carter** | Democratic | 95th | Democratic | Democratic |
| | Walter Mondale | | 96th | Democratic | Democratic |
| 1981–1989 | **Ronald Reagan** | Republican | 97th | Democratic | Republican |
| | George H. W. Bush | | 98th | Democratic | Republican |
| | | | 99th | Democratic | Republican |
| | | | 100th | Democratic | Democratic |
| 1989–1993 | **George H. W. Bush** | Republican | 101st | Democratic | Democratic |
| | J. Danforth Quayle | | 102nd | Democratic | Democratic |
| 1993–2001 | **Bill Clinton** | Democratic | 103rd | Democratic | Democratic |
| | Albert Gore Jr. | | 104th | Republican | Republican |
| | | | 105th | Republican | Republican |
| | | | 106th | Republican | Republican |
| 2001–2009 | **George W. Bush** | Republican | 107th | Republican | Democratic |
| | Richard Cheney | | 108th | Republican | Republican |
| | | | 109th | Republican | Republican |
| | | | 110th | Democratic | Democratic |
| 2009–2017 | **Barack Obama** | Democratic | 111th | Democratic | Democratic |
| | Joseph Biden | | 112th | Republican | Democratic |
| | | | 113th | Republican | Democratic |
| | | | 114th | Republican | Republican |

**Notes**

1. During the entire administration of George Washington and part of the administration of John Quincy Adams, Congress was not organized in terms of parties. This table shows that during these periods the supporters of the respective administrations maintained control of Congress.

2. This table shows only the two dominant parties in Congress. Independents, members of minor parties, and vacancies have been omitted.

# GLOSSARY

## A

**active partisans**   People who identify with a party, vote in elections, and participate in additional party and party-candidate activities.

**advocacy group**   An interest group organized to support a cause or ideology.

**advocacy groups**   Interest groups, also known as *public interests*, organized to support a cause or ideology.

**affirmative action**   Programs of private and public institutions favoring minorities and women in hiring and contracting, and in admissions to colleges and universities, in an attempt to compensate for past discrimination or to create more diversity.

**agency**   A general name used for a subunit of a cabinet department.

**agenda setting**   Influencing people's opinions about what is important.

**agents of socialization**   Those institutions and individuals that shape the core beliefs and attitudes of people.

**Aid to Families with Dependent Children (AFDC)**   The federal entitlement program that provided income support for poor families until it was replaced by TANF in 1996.

*amicus curiae*   Latin for "a friend of the court"; describes a brief in which individuals not party to a suit may have their views heard.

**Anti-Federalists**   Opponents of the Constitution during the fight over ratification.

**appellate courts**   Courts that hear cases on appeal from other courts.

**appropriation**   Legal authority for a federal agency to spend money from the U.S. Treasury.

**appropriations committees**   The committees in the House and Senate that set specific spending levels in the budget for federal programs and agencies.

**Articles of Confederation**   The first constitution of the United States, adopted during the last stages of the Revolutionary War, created a system of government with most power lodged in the states and little in the central government.

**asymmetric warfare**   Unconventional tactics used by a combatant against an enemy with superior conventional military capabilities.

**autocracy**   General term that describes all forms of government characterized by rule by a single person or by a group with total power, whether a monarchy, a military tyranny, or a theocracy.

## B

**balance of payments**   The annual difference between payments and receipts between a country and its trading partners.

**beat**   The assigned location where a reporter regularly gathers news stories.

**bias**   Deviation from ideal standards such as representativeness or objectivity.

**bicameral**   As applied to a legislative body, consisting of two houses or chambers.

**bill of attainder**   A governmental decree that a person is guilty of a crime that carries the death penalty, rendered without benefit of a trial.

**Bill of Rights**   The first 10 amendments to the U.S. Constitution, concerned with the protection of basic liberties.

**block grants**   Federal grants to the states to be used for general activities.

**briefs**   Documents setting out the arguments in legal cases, prepared by attorneys and presented to courts.

**budget deficit**   The amount by which annual government expenditures exceed revenues.

**bureau**   Generally, a subunit of a cabinet department.

**bureaucracy**   A large, complex organization characterized by a hierarchical set of offices, each with a specific task, controlled through a clear chain of command, and where appointment and advancement of personnel is based on merit.

**bureaucrat**   A person who works in a bureaucratic organization.

## C

**capital crime**   Any crime for which death is a possible penalty.

**capitalism**   An economic system characterized by private ownership of productive assets where most decisions about how to use these assets are made by individuals and firms operating in a market rather than by government.

**casework**   Services performed by members of Congress for constituents.

**categorical grants**   Federal aid to states and localities clearly specifying what the money can be used for.

**caucus**   A regional, ethnic, racial, or economic subgroup within the House or Senate. Also used to describe the party in the House and Senate, as in Republican caucus.

**checks and balances**   The constitutional principle that each of the separate branches of government has the power to hinder the unilateral actions of the other branches as a way to restrain an overreaching government and prevent tyranny.

**chief of staff**   A top adviser to the president who also manages the White House staff.

**Children's Health Insurance Program (CHIP)** Program that pays for health care services for children in households above the poverty line but below 133 percent to 400 percent of the poverty line, depending on the state.

**circuit courts** The 12 geographical jurisdictions and one special court that hear appeals from the federal district courts.

**civil disobedience** Intentionally breaking a law and accepting the consequences as a way to publicize the unjustness of the law.

**civil liberties** Freedoms found primarily in the Bill of Rights, the enjoyment of which are protected from government interference.

**civil rights** Guarantees by government of equal citizenship to all social groups.

**civil servants** Government workers employed under the merit system; not political appointees.

**civil service** Federal government jobs held by civilian employees, excluding political appointees.

**civil union** A legal status in which same-sex couples have the same rights, benefits, and protections as married couples.

**Civil War Amendments** The Thirteenth, Fourteenth, and Fifteenth Amendments to the Constitution, adopted immediately after the Civil War, each of which represented the imposition of a national claim over that of the states.

**class-action suit** A suit brought on behalf of a group of people who are in a situation similar to that of the plaintiffs.

**cloture** A vote to end a filibuster; requires the votes of three-fifths of the membership of the Senate.

**Cold War** The period of tense relations between the United States and the Soviet Union from the late 1940s to the late 1980s.

**collective public opinion** The political attitudes of the public as a whole, expressed as averages, percentages, or other summaries of many individuals' opinions.

**concurrent powers** Powers under the Constitution that are shared by the federal government and the states.

**concurring opinion** The opinion of one or more judges who vote with the majority on a case but wish to set out different reasons for their decision.

**conditional grants** Federal grants with provisions requiring that state and local governments follow certain policies in order to obtain funds.

**confederation** A loose association of states or territorial divisions in which very little power or no power at all is lodged in a central government.

**conference committees** Ad hoc committees, made up of members of both the Senate and the House of Representatives, set up to reconcile differences in the provisions of bills.

**Congressional Budget Office (CBO)** An agency of the U.S. Congress that provides technical support and research services on budget issues for its members and committees.

**Connecticut Compromise** Also called the *Great Compromise*; the compromise between the New Jersey and Virginia plans formulated by the Connecticut delegates at the Constitutional Convention; called for a lower legislative house based on population size and an upper house based on equal representation of the states.

**consciousness-raising groups** Meetings of small groups of women designed to raise awareness of discrimination against women and to encourage involvement in movement activities.

**conservative** The political position, combining both economic and social dimensions, that holds that the federal government ought to play a very small role in economic regulation, social welfare, and overcoming racial inequality, that abortion should be illegal, and that family values and law and order should guide public policies.

**constituency** The district of a legislator.

**constituent** A citizen who lives in the district of an elected official.

**constitution** The basic framework of law for a nation that prescribes how government is to be organized, how decisions are to be made, and what powers and responsibilities government shall have.

**constitutional courts** Federal courts created by Congress under the authority of Article III of the Constitution.

**contract clause** The portion of Article I, Section 10 of the Constitution that prohibits states from passing any law "impairing the obligations of contracts."

**cooperative federalism** Federalism in which the powers and responsibilities of the states and the national government are intertwined and in which they work together to solve common problems; said to have characterized the 1960s and 1970s.

**core beliefs (political)** Individuals' views about the fundamental nature of human beings, society, the economy, and the role of government; taken together, they comprise the political culture.

**core beliefs** The most fundamental beliefs in a national population about human nature, the country, government, and the economy.

**cost-benefit analysis** A method of evaluating rules and regulations by weighing their potential costs against their potential benefits to society.

**Council of Economic Advisers (CEA)** An organization in the Executive Office of the President made up of a small group of economists who advise on economic policy.

**crack** The act of dividing a district where the opposing party has a large majority, rendering it a minority in both parts of the redrawn districts.

# D

**dealignment** A gradual reduction in the dominance of one political party without another party supplanting it.

**de facto discrimination** Unequal treatment of racial or ethnic minority groups based on practices rather than on statutes and regulations mandating discrimination.

**de jure discrimination** Unequal treatment based on government laws and regulations.

**delegate** According to the doctrine articulated by Edmund Burke, an elected representative who acts in perfect accord with the wishes of his or her constituents.

**democracy**   A system of government in which the people rule; rule by the many.

**demographic**   Pertaining to the statistical study and description of a population.

**departments**   Generally the largest units in the executive branch, each headed by a cabinet secretary.

**depression**   A severe and persistent drop in economic activity.

**deregulation**   The process of diminishing regulatory requirements for business.

**descriptive representation**   Sometimes called *statistical representation*; the degree to which the composition of a representative body reflects the demographic composition of the population as a whole.

**devolution**   The delegation of power over and responsibilities for federal programs to state and/or local governments.

**direct democracy**   A form of political decision making in which policies are decided by the people themselves, rather than by their representatives, acting either in small face-to-face assemblies or through the electoral process as in initiatives and referenda in the American states.

**discharge petition**   A petition signed by 218 House members to force a bill that has been before a committee for at least 30 days while the House is in session out of the committee and onto the floor for consideration.

**discretionary spending**   That part of the federal budget that is not tied to a formula that automatically provides money to some program or purpose.

**dissenting opinion**   The opinion of the judge or judges who are in the minority on a particular case before the Supreme Court.

**disturbance theory**   A theory positing that interest groups originate with changes in the economic, social, or political environment that threaten the well-being of some segment of the population.

**divided government**   Control of the executive and the legislative branches by different political parties.

**dual federalism**   An interpretation of federalism in which the states and the national government have separate jurisdictions and responsibilities.

**due process clause**   The section of the Fourteenth Amendment that prohibits states from depriving anyone of life, liberty, or property "without due process of law," a guarantee against arbitrary government action.

**due process clause**   The section of the Fourteenth Amendment that prohibits states from depriving anyone of life, liberty, or property "without due process of law," a guarantee against arbitrary or unfair government action.

# E

**earmarks**   Provisions written into congressional legislation that appropriate money for specific pet projects of members of Congress, usually done at the behest of lobbyists, and added to bills at the last minute with little opportunity for deliberation.

**economic conservatives**   People who favor private enterprise and oppose government regulation of business.

**economic liberals**   People who favor government regulation of business to protect the public from harm, and government spending for social programs.

**economic liberty**   The right to own and use property free from unreasonable government interference.

**effective tax rate**   The actual amount a person pays in taxes as a percentage of his or her total income.

**elastic clause**   Article I, Section 8, of the Constitution, also called *the necessary and proper clause*; gives Congress the authority to make whatever laws are necessary and proper to carry out its enumerated powers and other of its powers vested in the Constitution.

**elastic clause**   Article I, Section 8 of the Constitution, also called the *necessary and proper clause*; gives Congress the authority to make whatever laws are necessary and proper to carry out its enumerated responsibilities.

**Electoral College**   Elected representatives of the states chosen during the November presidential election, a majority of whose votes cast at a later date formally elect the president of the United States. The number of electors in each state is equal to the total number of its senators and representatives. In all but two states, the candidate who wins a plurality of the popular vote wins all of a state's electoral votes.

**Electoral College**   Representatives selected in each of the states, their numbers based on each state's total number of its senators and representatives; a majority of Electoral College votes elects the president.

**electoral competition voting model**   A form of election in which parties seeking votes move toward the median voter or the center of the political spectrum.

**electors**   Representatives who are elected in the states to formally choose the U.S. president.

**entitlements**   Government benefits that are distributed automatically to citizens who qualify on the basis of a set of guidelines set by law; for example, Americans over the age of 65 are entitled to Medicare coverage.

**enumerated powers**   Powers of the federal government specifically mentioned in the Constitution.

**equal protection clause**   The section of the Fourteenth Amendment requiring states to provide equal treatment to all people within their boundaries.

**equal protection clause**   The section of the Fourteenth Amendment that provides for equal treatment by government of people residing within the United States and each of its states.

**equal protection clause**   The section of the Fourteenth Amendment which guarantees that everyone will be treated equally by government.

**Equal Rights Amendment (ERA)**   Proposed amendment to the U.S. Constitution stating that equality of rights shall not be abridged or denied on account of a person's gender; it failed to win the approval of the necessary number of states.

**establishment clause**   The part of the First Amendment to the Constitution that prohibits Congress from establishing an official religion; the basis for the doctrine of the separation of church and state.

**exclusionary rule**   A standard promulgated by the Supreme Court that prevents police and prosecutors from using evidence against a defendant that was obtained in an illegal search.

**executive agreement**   An agreement with another country signed by the president that has the force of law, like a treaty; does not require Senate approval; originally used for minor technical matters, now an important tool of presidential power in foreign affairs.

**Executive Office of the President (EOP)**   A group of organizations that advise the president on a wide range of issues; includes, among others, the Office of Management and Budget, the National Security Council, and the Council of Economic Advisers.

**executive order**   A rule or regulation issued by the president that has the force of law, based either on the constitutional powers of the presidency as chief executive or commander in chief or on congressional statutes.

**executive privilege**   A presidential claim that certain communications with subordinates may be withheld from Congress and the courts.

**ex post facto law**   A law that retroactively declares some action illegal.

**externalities**   The positive and negative effects of economic activities on third parties.

# F

**factions**   Madison's term for groups or parties that try to advance their own interests at the expense of the public good.

**federal**   Describing a system in which significant governmental powers are divided between a central government and smaller territorial units, such as states.

**federal bureaucracy**   The totality of the departments and agencies of the executive branch of the national government.

**federalism**   A system in which governmental powers are divided between a central government and smaller units, such as states.

**Federalists**   Proponents of the Constitution during the ratification fight; also the political party of Hamilton, Washington, and Adams.

**Federal Reserve Board (Fed)**   The body responsible for deciding the monetary policies of the United States.

**filibuster**   A parliamentary device used in the Senate to prevent a bill from coming to a vote by "talking it to death," made possible by the norm of unlimited debate.

**fiscal federalism**   That aspect of federalism having to do with federal grants to the states.

**fiscal policy**   Government efforts to affect overall output and incomes in the economy through spending and taxing policies.

**foundation**   An entity of the executive branch that supports the arts or sciences and is designed to be somewhat insulated from political interference.

**framing**   Providing a context for interpretation.

**franchise**   The legal right to vote; see suffrage.

**franking privilege**   Public subsidization of mail from the members of Congress to their constituents.

**free enterprise**   An economic system characterized by competitive markets and private ownership of a society's productive assets; a form of capitalism.

**free exercise clause**   That portion of the First Amendment to the Constitution that prohibits Congress from impeding religious observance or impinging upon religious beliefs.

**full faith and credit**   The provision in Article IV, Section 1 of the Constitution which provides that states must respect the public acts, laws, and judicial rulings of other states.

# G

**General Agreement on Tariffs and Trade (GATT)**   An international agreement that requires the lowering of tariffs and other barriers to free trade.

**general revenue sharing**   Federal aid to the states without any conditions on how the money is to be spent.

**gerrymandering**   Redrawing electoral district lines in an extreme and unlikely manner to give an advantage to a particular party or candidate.

**global climate change**   The upset of historical climate patterns, with rising temperatures and more extreme climate events, tied to the increase in atmospheric carbon whether caused by human activities or naturally occurring cycles.

**globalization**   The increasing tendency of information, products, and financial capital to flow across national borders, with the effect of more tightly integrating the global economy.

**government corporation**   A unit in the executive branch that operates like a private business but provides some public service.

**grandfather clause**   A device that allowed whites who had failed the literacy test to vote anyway by extending the franchise to anyone whose ancestors had voted prior to 1867.

**grand juries**   Groups of citizens who decide whether there is sufficient evidence to bring an indictment against accused persons.

**grants-in-aid**   Funds from the national government to state and local governments to help pay for programs created by the national government.

**grassroots lobbying**   The effort by interest groups to mobilize local constituencies, shape public opinion to support the group's goals, and bring that pressure to bear on elected officials.

**Great Depression**   The period of global economic crisis that lasted in the United States from the stock market crash of 1929 to America's entry into World War II.

**gridlock**   A situation in which things cannot get done in Washington, usually because of divided government.

**gross domestic product (GDP)**   Monetary value of all goods and services produced in a nation each year, excluding income residents earn abroad.

# H

***habeas corpus***   The legal doctrine that a person who is arrested must have a timely hearing before a judge.

**hearings**   The taking of testimony by a congressional committee or subcommittee.

**hegemon**   Term used to refer to the dominant power during various historical periods that takes on responsibilities for maintaining and protecting a regional or global system.

**hold**   A tactic by which a single senator can prevent action on a bill or nomination; based on an implied threat of refusing to agree to unanimous consent on other Senate matters or willingness to filibuster the bill or nomination.

**hopper**   The box in the House of Representatives in which proposed bills are placed.

**horizontal federalism**   Term used to refer to relationships among the states.

# I

**impeachment**   House action bringing formal charges against a member of the executive branch or the federal judiciary that may or may not lead to removal from office by the Senate.

**incorporation**   The process by which the Supreme Court has made most of the provisions of the Bill of Rights binding on the states. See *nationalizing*.

**independent executive agency**   A unit of the executive branch outside the control of executive departments.

**independent regulatory commission**   An entity in the executive branch that is outside the immediate control of the president and Congress that issues rules and regulations to protect the public.

**industrialization**   The transformation of a society's economy from one dominated by agricultural pursuits to one dominated by manufacturing.

**inflation**   A condition of rising prices and reduced purchasing power.

*in forma pauperis*   Describing a process by which indigents may file a suit with the Supreme Court free of charge.

**infotainment**   The merging of hard news and entertainment in news presentations.

**initiatives**   Procedures available in some states for citizens to put proposed laws and constitutional amendments on the ballot for voter approval or rejection.

**institutional presidency**   The permanent bureaucracy associated with the presidency, designed to help the incumbent of the office carry out his responsibilities.

**integration**   Policies encouraging the interaction between different races in schools or public facilities.

**Intelligence Advisory Board**   An organization in the Executive Office of the President that provides information and assessments to the president's director of national intelligence and to the president directly.

**interest groups**   A private organization or voluntary association that seeks to influence public policy as a way to protect or advance its interests.

**intermediate scrutiny**   A legal test falling between ordinary and strict scrutiny relevant to issues of gender; under this test, the Supreme Court will allow gender classifications in laws if they are *substantially* related to an *important* government objective.

**interstate compacts**   Agreements among states to cooperate on solving mutual problems; requires approval by Congress.

**iron triangles**   An enduring alliance of common interest among an interest group, a congressional committee, and a bureaucratic agency.

**isolationism**   The policy of avoiding undue involvement in the affairs of other countries and multilateral institutions.

**issue networks**   Broad coalitions of public and private interest groups, policy experts, and public officials that form around particular policy issues; said to be more visible to the public and more inclusive.

# J

**Jim Crow**   Popular term for the system of legally sanctioned racial segregation that existed in the American South until the middle of the twentieth century.

**Joint Chiefs of Staff (JCS)**   The military officers in charge of each of the armed services.

**joint committees**   Congressional committees with members from both the House and the Senate.

**judicial activism**   Actions by the courts that purportedly go beyond the role of the judiciary as interpreter of the law and adjudicator of disputes.

**judicial review**   The power of the Supreme Court to declare actions of the other branches and levels of government unconstitutional.

# K

**Keynesians**   Advocates of government programs to stimulate economic activity through tax cuts and government spending.

# L

**laissez-faire**   The political-economic doctrine that holds that government ought not interfere with the operations of the free market.

**leak**   Inside or secret information given to a journalist or media outlet by a government official.

**leaners**   People who claim to be independents but consistently favor one party over another.

**legislative courts**   Highly specialized federal courts created by Congress under the authority of Article I of the Constitution.

**liberal**   The political position, combining both economic and social dimensions, that holds that the federal government has a substantial role to play in providing economic justice and opportunity, regulating business in the public interest, overcoming racial discrimination, protecting abortion rights, and ensuring the equal treatment of gays and lesbians.

**liberal democracy**   Representative democracy characterized by popular sovereignty, liberty, and political equality.

**literacy test**   A device used by the southern states to prevent African Americans from voting before the passage of the Voting Rights Act of 1965, which banned its use; usually involved interpretation of a section of a state's constitution.

**lobbying**   Effort by an interest or advocacy group to influence the behavior of a public official.

**lobbyists**   A person who attempts to influence the behavior of public officials on behalf of an interest group.

# M

**macroeconomic policy**   Policy that has to do with the performance of the economy as a whole.

**majority-minority districts**   Districts drawn to ensure that a racial minority makes up the majority of voters.

**majority rule**   The form of political decision making in which policies are decided on the basis of what a majority of the people want.

**majority tyranny**   Suppression of the rights and liberties of a minority by the majority.

**mandate**   A formal order from the national government that the states carry out certain policies.

**markup**   The process of revising a bill in committee.

**mass mobilization**   The process of involving large numbers of people in a social movement.

**means-tested**   Meeting the criterion of demonstrable need.

**media monopoly**   Term used to suggest that media corporations are so large, powerful, and interconnected that the less economically and politically powerful cannot have their views aired.

**median household income**   The midpoint of all households ranked by income.

**median voter**   The voter who is, ideologically, at the center of the political issue spectrum.

**Medicaid**   Program administered by the states that pays for health care services for the poor; jointly funded by the federal government and the states.

**Medicare**   Federal health insurance program for the elderly and the disabled.

**Millennium Challenge Account**   A Bush administration initiative to distribute development aid on the basis of a country's degree of improvement in areas such as the rule of law, women's rights, protection of property rights, anticorruption measures, and political and civil rights.

**monarchy**   Rule by the one, such as where power rests in the hands of a king or queen.

**monetarists**   Advocates of a minimal government role in the economy, limited to managing the growth of the money supply.

**monetary policy**   Government efforts to affect the supply of money and the level of interest rates in the economy.

**multilateralists**   Those who believe the United States should use its military and diplomatic power in the world in cooperation with other nations and international organizations.

**multiparty system**   A political system in which three or more viable parties compete to lead the government; because a majority winner is not always possible, multiparty systems often have coalition governments where governing power is shared among two or more parties.

# N

**national debt**   The total outstanding debt of the federal government; the sum total of all annual budget deficits and surpluses.

**national interest**   What is of benefit to the nation as a whole.

**nationalist position**   The view of American federalism that holds that the Constitution created a system in which the national government is supreme, relative to the states, and that it granted that government a broad range of powers and responsibilities.

**nationalizing**   The process by which provisions of the Bill of Rights become incorporated. See *incorporation*.

**national security adviser**   A top foreign policy and defense adviser to the president who heads the National Security Council.

**National Security Council (NSC)**   An organization in the Executive Office of the President made up of officials from the State and Defense Departments, the CIA, and the military, who advise on foreign and security affairs.

**nativist**   Antiforeign; applied to political movements active in the nineteenth century in the United States.

**necessary and proper clause**   Article I, Section 8, of the Constitution, also known as the *elastic clause*; gives Congress the authority to make whatever laws are necessary and proper to carry out its enumerated powers and the responsibilities mentioned in the Constitution's preamble.

**New Deal coalition**   The informal electoral alliance of working-class ethnic groups, Catholics, Jews, urban dwellers, racial minorities, and the South that was the basis of the Democratic party dominance of American politics from the New Deal to the early 1970s.

**New Deal**   The programs of the administration of President Franklin D. Roosevelt.

**New Jersey Plan**   Proposal of the smaller states at the Constitutional Convention to create a government with slightly more power in a central government than under the Articles, with the states equally represented in a unicameral national legislature.

**news management**   The attempt by those in political power to put the presentation of news about them and their policies in a favorable light.

**newsworthy**   Worth printing or broadcasting as news, according to editors' judgments.

**North American Free Trade Agreement (NAFTA)**   An agreement among the United States, Canada, and Mexico to eliminate nearly all barriers to trade and investment among the three countries.

**nuclear proliferation**   The spread of nuclear weapons to additional countries or to terrorist groups.

**nullification**   An attempt by states to declare national laws or actions null and void.

# O

**objective journalism**   News reported with no evaluative language and with opinions quoted or attributed to a specific source.

**obscenity** As defined by the Supreme Court, the representation of sexually explicit material in a manner that violates community standards and is without redeeming social importance or value.

**Office of Management and Budget (OMB)** An organization within the Executive Office of the President that advises on the federal budget, domestic legislation, and regulations.

**oligarchy** Rule by the few, where a minority holds power over a majority, as in an aristocracy or a clerical establishment.

**open-seat election** An election in which there is no incumbent officeholder.

**opinion** The explanation of the majority's and the minority's reasoning that accompanies a court decision.

**opinion of the Court** The majority opinion that accompanies a Supreme Court decision.

**ordinary scrutiny** The assumption that the actions of elected bodies and officials are legal under the Constitution.

**original intent** The doctrine that the courts must interpret the Constitution in ways consistent with the intentions of the framers rather than in light of contemporary conditions and needs.

**original jurisdiction** The authority of a court to be the first to hear a particular kind of case.

**oversight** Congressional responsibility for monitoring the actions of executive branch agencies and personnel to ensure conformity to federal statutes and congressional intent.

## P

**pack** The process of concentrating voters for the other party into fewer districts in order to weaken them elsewhere.

**party caucuses** The process for selecting delegates to the national party conventions characterized by neighborhood and area-wide meetings of party supporters and activists.

**party conference** An organization of the members of a political party in the House or Senate.

**party convention** A gathering of delegates who nominate a party's presidential candidate.

**party identification** The sense of belonging to one or another political party.

**party platform** A party's statement of its positions on the issues of the day passed at the quadrennial national convention.

**patronage** The practice of distributing government offices and contracts to the supporters of the winning party; also called the *spoils system*.

**payroll tax** Tax levied on salaries and wages for Social Security and Medicare.

**petit (trial) juries** Juries that hear evidence and sit in judgment on charges brought in civil or criminal cases.

**plaintiff** One who brings suit in a court.

**pluralism** The political science position that American democracy is best understood in terms of the interaction, conflict, and bargaining of groups.

**plurality** More votes than any other candidate but less than a majority of all votes cast.

**pocket veto** Rejection of a bill if the president takes no action on it for 10 days and Congress has adjourned during that period.

**policy preferences** Citizens' ideas about what policies they want government to pursue.

**political action committees (PACs)** An entity created by an interest group whose purpose is to collect money and make contributions to candidates in federal elections.

**political attitudes** Individuals' views and preferences about public policies, political parties, candidates, government institutions, and public officials.

**political culture** The set of core beliefs in a country that help shape how people behave politically and what they believe government should do.

**political efficacy** The sense that an individual can affect what government does.

**political equality** The principle that each person carries equal weight in the conduct of the public business.

**political ideology** A system of interrelated and coherently organized political beliefs and attitudes.

**political liberty** The principle that citizens in a democracy are protected from government interference in the exercise of a range of basic freedoms, such as the freedoms of speech, association, and conscience.

**political party** An organization that tries to win control of government by electing people to office who carry the party label.

**political socialization** The process by which individuals come to have certain core beliefs and political attitudes.

**poll tax** A tax to be paid as a condition of voting; used in the South to keep African Americans away from the polls.

**popular sovereignty** The basic principle of democracy that the people are the ultimate source of government authority and of the policies that government leaders make.

**populism** The belief that the common person is every bit as good as those with wealth and power.

**pork** Also called *pork barrel*; federally funded projects designed to bring to the constituency jobs and public money for which the members of Congress can claim credit.

**poverty line** The federal government's calculation of the amount of income families of various sizes need to stay out of poverty.

**precedents** Past rulings by courts which guide judicial reasoning in subsequent cases.

**preemption** Exclusion of the states from actions that might interfere with federal authority or statutes.

**presidential job approval** The percentage of Americans who believe the president is doing a good job.

**presidential job approval rating** A president's standing with the public, indicated by the percentage of Americans who tell survey interviewers that they approve a president's "handling of his job."

**primary election** Statewide elections in which voters choose delegates to the national party conventions.

**prior restraint** The government's power to prevent publication, as opposed to punishment afterward.

**private interests**   Interest groups that seek to protect or advance the material interests of its members.

**privatizing**   Turning over certain government functions to the private sector.

**privileges and immunities clause**   The portion of Article IV, Section 2 of the Constitution that says that citizens from out of state have the same legal rights as local citizens in any state.

**probable cause**   Legal doctrine that refers to a reasonable belief that a crime has been committed.

**progressive taxation**   A tax system in which higher-income individuals are taxed at a higher rate than those who make less.

**proportional representation**   The awarding of legislative seats to political parties to reflect the proportion of the popular vote each party receives.

**prospective voting model**   A theory of democratic elections in which voters decide what government will do in the near future by choosing one or another responsible party.

**provisional ballot**   A vote that is cast but not counted until determination is made that the voter is properly registered.

**public interests**   Interest groups, also known as *advocacy groups*, that work to gain protections or benefits for society at large.

**public opinion**   The aggregated political attitudes of ordinary people as revealed by surveys.

**pundits**   Somewhat derisive term for print, broadcast, and radio commentators on the political news.

# Q

**quasi-governmental organization**   An organization that has governmental powers and responsibilities but has substantial private sector control over its activities.

# R

**random sampling**   The selection of survey respondents by chance, with equal probability of being selected, to ensure their representativeness of the whole population.

**ranking minority member**   The highest-ranking member of the minority party on a congressional committee.

**rational public**   The notion that collective public opinion is rational in the sense that it is generally stable and consistent and that when it changes it does so as an understandable response to events, to changing circumstances, and to new information.

**realignment**   The process by which one party supplants another as the dominant party in a two-party political system.

**reapportionment**   The reallocation of House seats among the states, done after each national census, to ensure that seats are held by the states in proportion to the size of their populations.

**recess appointments**   Presidential action to temporarily fill executive branch positions without the consent of the Senate; done when Congress is adjourned.

**recession**   Two quarters or more of declining gross domestic product.

**reciprocity**   Deferral by members of Congress to the judgment of subject-matter specialists, mainly on minor technical bills.

**redistricting**   The redrawing of congressional district lines within a state to ensure roughly equal populations within each district.

**red tape**   Overbearing bureaucratic rules and procedures.

**referenda**   Procedures available in some states by which state laws or constitutional amendments proposed by the legislature are submitted to the voters for approval or rejection.

**regressive taxation**   A tax system in which lower-income individuals are taxed at a higher rate than those who make more.

**regulation**   The issuing of rules by government agencies with the aim of reducing the scale of negative externalities produced by private firms.

**remedy**   An action that a court determines must be taken to rectify a wrong done by government.

**representative democracy**   Indirect democracy, in which the people rule through elected representatives.

**republicanism**   A political doctrine advocating limited government based on popular consent, protected against majority tyranny.

**reservation clause**   Part of the Tenth Amendment to the Constitution that says powers not given to Congress are reserved to the states or to the people.

**responsible party**   The notion that a political party will take clear and distinct stands on the issues and enact them as policy once elected to office.

**retrospective voting model (or electoral reward and punishment model)**   A theory of democratic elections in which voters look back at the performance of a party in power and cast ballots on the basis of how well it did in office.

**revolving door**   The common practice in which former government officials become lobbyists for interests with whom they formerly dealt in their official capacity.

**rule of four**   An *unwritten* practice that requires at least four justices of the Supreme Court to agree that a case warrants review by the Court before it will hear the case.

# S

**sample survey**   An interview study asking questions of a set of people who are chosen as representative of the whole population.

**sampling error**   Statistical uncertainty in estimates associated with the fact that surveys do not interview every individual in a population of interest.

**scope of conflict**   Refers to the number of groups involved in a political conflict; a narrow scope of conflict involves a small number of groups, and a wide scope of conflict involves many.

**secularization**   The spread of nonreligious values and outlooks.

**select committees**   Temporary committees in Congress created to conduct studies or investigations; they have no power to report bills.

**selective incorporation** The gradual and piecemeal spread of the protections of the Bill of Rights to the states by the U.S. Supreme Court.

**senatorial courtesy** The tradition that a judicial nomination for a federal district court seat be approved by the senior senator of the president's party from the state where a district court is located before the nominee is considered by the Senate Judiciary Committee.

**seniority** The principle that one attains a position on the basis of length of service.

**separate but equal doctrine** The principle articulated in *Plessy v. Ferguson* (1896) that laws prescribing separate public facilities and services for nonwhite Americans are permissible if the facilities and services are equal to those provided for whites.

**separation of powers** The distribution of government legislative, executive, and judicial powers to separate branches of government.

**signing statement** A document sometimes issued by the president in connection with the signing of a bill from Congress that sets out the president's understanding of the new law and how executive branch officials should carry it out.

**sit-down strike** A form of labor action in which workers stop production but do not leave their job site.

**social contract** The idea that government is the result of an agreement among people to form one, and that people have the right to create an entirely new government if the terms of the contract have been violated by the existing one.

**social insurance** Government programs that provide services or income support in proportion to the amount of mandatory contributions made by individuals to a government trust fund.

**social (lifestyle) conservatives** People who favor traditional social values; they tend to support strong law-and-order measures and oppose abortion and gay rights.

**social (lifestyle) liberals** People who favor civil liberties, abortion rights, and alternative lifestyles.

**social movement** A loosely organized group that uses unconventional and often disruptive tactics to have their grievances heard by the public, the news media, and government leaders.

**Social Security** Social insurance program that provides income support for the elderly, those with disabilities, and family survivors of working Americans.

**soft power** Influence in world affairs that derives from the attractiveness to others of a nation's culture, products, and way of life.

**spin** The attempt by public officials to have a story reported in terms that favor them and their policies; see news management.

**spoils system** The practice of distributing government offices and contracts to the supporters of the winning party; also called *patronage*.

**standing** Authority to bring legal action because one is directly affected by the issues at hand.

**standing committees** Relatively permanent congressional committees that address specific areas of legislation.

**stare decisis** The legal doctrine that says precedent should guide judicial decision making.

**State of the Union** Annual report to the nation by the president, now delivered before a joint session of Congress, on the state of the nation and his legislative proposals for addressing national problems.

**states' rights position** The view of American federalism that holds that the Constitution created a system of dual sovereignty in which the national government and the state governments are sovereign in their own spheres.

**stay acts** Laws forbidding farm foreclosures for nonpayment of debts.

**strict construction** The doctrine that the provisions of the Constitution have a clear meaning and that judges must stick closely to this meaning when rendering decisions.

**strict scrutiny** The assumption that actions by elected bodies or officials violate constitutional rights.

**strict scrutiny** The assumption that actions by elected bodies or officials violate the Constitution.

**sub-governments** Another name for an iron triangle.

**suffrage** The legal right to vote; see franchise.

**Sun Belt** States of the Lower South, Southwest, and West, where sunny weather and conservative politics have often prevailed.

**superdelegates** Elected officials from all levels of government who are appointed by party committees to be delegates to the national convention of the Democratic Party; not selected in primary elections or caucuses.

**superpower** A nation with the military, economic, and political resources to project force anywhere in the world.

**superprecedents** Landmark rulings that have been reaffirmed by the Court over the course of many years and whose reasoning has become part of the fabric of American law.

**supremacy clause** The provision in Article VI of the Constitution which states that the Constitution and the laws and treaties of the United States are the supreme law of the land, taking precedence over state laws and constitutions.

**suspect classification** The invidious, arbitrary, or irrational designation of a group for special treatment by government, whether positive or negative; historically, a discriminated against, visible minority without the power to protect itself.

# T

**Temporary Assistance to Needy Families (TANF)** Program that provides income and services to many poor families; has benefit time limits and a work requirement.

**Tenth Amendment** Part of the Bill of Rights, the Amendment says that those powers not given to the federal government and not prohibited to the states by the Constitution are reserved for the states and the people.

**terrorism** The use of deadly violence against civilians to further some political goal.

**test case** A case brought to force a ruling on the constitutionality of some law or executive action.

**The Great Depression** The period of economic crisis in the United States that lasted from the stock market crash of 1929 to America's entry into World War II.

**treaty** A formal international agreement between two or more countries; in the United States, requires the "advice and consent" of the Senate.

**trustee** An elected representative who believes that his or her own best judgment, rather than instructions from constituents, should be used in making legislative decisions.

**turnout** The proportion of either eligible or all voting-age Americans who actually vote in a given election; the two ways of counting turnout yield different results.

**two-party system** A political system in which two parties vie on relatively equal terms to win national elections and in which each party governs at one time or another.

**tyranny** The abuse of the inalienable rights of citizens by government.

# U

**unanimous consent** Legislative action taken "without objection" as a way to expedite business; used to conduct much of the business of the Senate.

**unicameral** A legislative body with a single chamber.

**unified government** Control of the executive and legislative branches by the same political party.

**unilateralists** Those who believe the United States should vigorously use its military and diplomatic power to pursue American national interests in the world, but on a "go it alone" basis.

**unitary executive** Constitutional doctrine that proposes that the executive branch is under the direct control of the president, who has all authority necessary to control the actions of federal bureaucracy personnel and units without interference from the other federal branches.

**unitary executive** Constitutional doctrine that proposes that the executive branch is under the direct control of the president, who has all authority necessary to control the actions of federal bureaucracy personnel and units without interference from the other federal branches.

**unitary system** A system in which a central government has complete power over its constituent units or states.

**urbanization** The movement of people from rural areas to cities.

# V

**veto** Presidential disapproval of a bill that has been passed by both houses of Congress. The president's veto can be overridden by a two-thirds vote in each house.

**Virginia Plan** Proposal by the large states at the Constitutional Convention to create a strong central government with power in the government apportioned to the states on the basis of population.

# W

**watchdog** The role of the media in scrutinizing the actions of government officials.

**weapons of mass destruction** Nuclear, biological, or chemical weapons with the potential to cause vast harm to human populations.

**whip** A political party member in Congress charged with keeping members informed of the plans of the party leadership, counting votes before action on important issues, and rounding up party members for votes on bills.

**whistle-blowers** People who bring official misconduct in their agencies to public attention.

**white primaries** Primary elections open only to whites in the one-party South where the only elections that mattered were the Democratic Party's primaries; this effectively disenfranchised blacks.

**wire services** Organizations such as the Associated Press and Reuters that gather and disseminate news to other news organizations.

**World Trade Organization (WTO)** An agency designed to enforce the provisions of the General Agreement on Tariffs and Trade and to resolve trade disputes between nations.

**writ of certiorari** An announcement that the Supreme Court will hear a case on appeal from a lower court; its issuance requires the vote of four of the nine justices.

# NOTES

## 1

1. William H. Chafe, *The Unfinished Journey: America Since World War II* (New York: Oxford University Press, 1986), p. 304; Howard Zinn, *SNCC: The New Abolitionists* (Boston: Beacon Press, 1964), p. 64.

2. Chafe, *Unfinished Journey,* p. 305

3. Pei-te Lien, Dianne M. Pinderhughes, Carol Hardy-Fanta, and Christine M. Sierra, "The Voting Rights Act and the Election of Non-white Officials," *PS: Political Science and Politics 40, no. 3* (July 2007), pp. 489–494.

4. Michael Coppedge and John Gerring, "Conceptualizing and Measuring Democracy," *Perspectives on Politics* 9, no. 2 (June 2011), pp. 247–267.

5. See a summary of polls at Latinobarómetro, http://www.latinobarometro.org/; AsiaBarometer, https://www.asiabarometer.org; and the PEW Center for the People and the Press, http://www.pewresearch.org/.

6. See the Freedom House report, *Freedom in the World, 2014* (Washington, DC: Freedom House, 2014), http://www.freedomhouse.org.

7. James Surowiecki, *The Wisdom of Crowds* (New York: Doubleday, 2004).

8. For a fuller treatment of the claims in this paragraph, as well as supporting evidence, see Robert A. Dahl, *Democracy and Its Critics* (New Haven, CT: Yale University Press, 1989), and Robert A. Dahl, *On Democracy* (New Haven, CT: Yale University Press, 1998). Also see Benjamin Radcliff, "Politics, Markets, and Life Satisfaction: The Political Economy of Human Happiness," *American Political Science Review* 95 (December 2001), pp. 939–952.

9. Robert A. Dahl, "James Madison: Republican or Democrat?," *Perspectives on Politics* 3, no. 3 (September 2005), pp. 439–448.

10. John Dewey, *The Public and Its Problems* (New York: Holt, 1927).

11. Charles Tilly, *Democracy* (Cambridge, UK: Cambridge University Press, 2007), p. 59.

12. Tilly, *Democracy,* pp. 26–28. Also see Josiah Ober, "What the Ancient Greeks Can Tell Us About Democracy," *Annual Review of Political Science* 11 (2008), pp. 67–91.

13. Dahl, *Democracy and Its Critics,* p. 13.

14. See Robert A. Dahl, *After the Revolution: Authority in the Good Society* (New Haven, CT: Yale University Press, 1970); Dahl, *Democracy and Its Critics*; and Jane Mansbridge, *Beyond Adversary Democracy* (New York: Basic Books, 1980). Also see Kevin O'Leary, *Saving Democracy* (Stanford, CA: Stanford University Press, 2006), ch. 1.

15. See Benjamin Barber, *Strong Democracy: Participatory Democracy for a New Age* (Berkeley, CA: University of California Press, 1984); Peter Bachrach, *The Theory of Democratic Elitism* (Boston: Little, Brown, 1967); Robert A. Dahl, *A Preface to Economic Democracy* (Berkeley, CA: University of California Press, 1985); Edward S. Greenberg, "Spillovers from Cooperative and Democratic Workplaces," in Brandon Sullivan and John Sullivan, eds., *Cooperation as the Basis of Individual and Group Functioning* (Minneapolis, MN: University of Minnesota Press, 2006); Edward S. Greenberg, *Workplace Democracy: The Political Effects of Participation* (Ithaca, NY: Cornell University Press, 1986); C. B. MacPherson, *Democratic Theory: Essays in Retrieval* (Oxford, UK: Clarendon Press, 1973); Carole Pateman, *Participation and Democratic Theory* (London: Cambridge University Press, 1970).

16. Esther Dyson, *Release 2.0* (New York: Broadway Books, 1997); Lawrence K. Grossman, *The Electronic Republic: Reshaping Democracy in the Information Age* (New York: Viking Press, 1995); Jerome Armstrong and Markos M. Zuniga, *Crashing the Gate: Netroots, Grassroots, and the Rule of People-Powered Politics* (White River Junction, VT: Chelsea Green Publishing Co., 2006).

17. For the very mixed evidence on the degree to which the Internet and digital communications have enhanced democracy, see Michael Margolis and Gerson Moreno-Riano, *The Prospect of Internet Democracy* (London: Ashgate Publishing, 2009).

18. Christian Welzel and Ronald Inglehart, "The Role of Ordinary People in Democratization," *Journal of Democracy* 19, no. 1 (2008), p. 126.

19. On deliberation and democracy, see Jason Barabas, "How Deliberation Affects Policy Opinions," *American Political Science Review* 98 (2004), pp. 687–701; Seyla Benhabib, "Toward a Deliberative Model of Democratic Legitimacy," in *Democracy and Difference, ed.* Seyla Benhabib (Princeton, NJ: Princeton University Press, 1996); John Dryzek, *Discursive Democracy* (Cambridge, UK: Cambridge University Press, 1990); Nancy Fraser, "Rethinking the Public Sphere," in *Habermas and the Public Sphere, ed.* Craig Calhoun (New Brunswick, NJ: Rutgers University Press, 1992), pp. 109–142; Amy Guttman and Dennis Thompson, *Democracy and Disagreement* (Cambridge, UK: Belknap Press, 1996); and Jurgen Habermas, *The Structural Transformation of the Public Sphere* (Cambridge, MA: MIT Press, 1989).

20. Kenneth May, "A Set of Independent, Necessary, and Sufficient Conditions for Simple Majority Decision," *Econometrical* 20 (1952), pp. 680–684, shows that only majority rule can guarantee popular sovereignty, political equality, and neutrality among policy alternatives. See also Douglas W. Rae, "Decision Rules and Individual Values in Constitutional Choice," *American Political Science Review* 63 (1969), pp. 40–53; and Phillip D. Straffin Jr., "Majority Rule and General Decision Rules," *Theory and Decision* 8 (1977), pp. 351–360. On the other hand, Hans Gersbach argues in *Designing Democracy* (New York: Springer Publishers, 2005) that larger majorities ought to be required for more important decisions.

21. Mark Warren, "Democracy and the State," in *The Oxford Handbook of Political Theory,* ed. John S. Dryzek, Bonnie Honig, and Ann Phillips (Oxford, UK: Oxford University Press, 2006), pp. 385–386; and Gordon S. Wood, *The Idea of America: Reflections on the Birth of the United States* (New York: Penguin Press, 2011), pp. 189–212.

22. For a review of contemporary research on this issue, see Larry M. Bartels, *Unequal Democracy: The Political Economy of the New Gilded Age* (New York: Russell Sage Foundation, 2008); Seymour Martin Lipset and Jason M. Lakin, *The Democratic Century* (Norman, OK: University of Oklahoma Press, 2004); and Tilly, *Democracy.*

23. Dahl, *A Preface to Economic Democracy,* p. 68.

24. U.S. Congress, Congressional Budget Office, *Trends in the Distribution of Household Income Between 1979 and 2007* (Washington, DC: Author, October 2011).

25. Robert A. Dahl, "On Removing Certain Impediments to Democracy in the United States," *Political Science Quarterly* 92, no. 1 (Spring 1977), p. 14; Elaine Spitz, *Majority Rule* (Chatham, NJ: Chatham House, 1984), p. 83; Dahl, *Democracy and Its Critics,* p. 170.

26. See Marc Plattner, "Liberalism and Democracy," *Foreign Affairs* (March–April 1998), pp. 171–180. On the inevitability of tension between and the necessity of balancing the claims of liberty and majority rule, see Adam Przeworski, "Self-Government in Our Times," *Annual Review of Political Science* 12 (2009), pp. 88–90; and Coppedge and Gerring, "Conceptualizing."

27. David Caute, *The Great Fear* (New York: Simon & Schuster, 1978); Victor Navasky, *Naming Names* (New York: Viking, 1980); and Michael Rogin, *The Intellectuals and McCarthy* (Cambridge, MA: MIT Press, 1967).

28. Fareed Zakaria, *The Future of Freedom: Illiberal Democracy at Home and Abroad* (New York: Norton, 2004).

29. See Bartels, *Unequal Democracy*; Bernard R. Berelson, Paul F. Lazarsfeld, and William N. McPhee, *Voting* (Chicago: The University of Chicago Press, 1954); V. O. Key Jr., *Public Opinion and American Democracy* (New York: Knopf, 1961); Herbert McClosky and Alida Brill, *Dimensions of Tolerance: What Americans Believe About Civil Liberties* (New York: Russell Sage Foundation, 1983); Robert Weissberg, *Polling, Policy, and Public Opinion: The Case Against Heeding the Voice of the People* (New York: Palgrave Press, 2003); Robert Weissberg, "Politicized Pseudo Science," *PS: Political Science and Politics 39, no. 1* (January 2006), pp. 39–42; and Alan Wolfe, *Does American Democracy Still Work?* (New Haven, CT: Yale University Press, 2006). But see, in rebuttal, James L. Gibson, "Political Intolerance and Political Repression during the McCarthy Red Scare," *American Political Science Review* 82 (1988), pp. 511–529; and Benjamin I. Page and Robert Y. Shapiro, *The Rational Public: Fifty Years of Trends in Americans' Policy Preferences* (Chicago: The University of Chicago Press, 1992).

30. Katherine Brandt, "Madisonian Majority Tyranny, Minority Rights, and American Democracy: A New Defense of the Electoral College" (paper presented at the annual meeting of the Midwest Political Science Association, Chicago, IL, April 2004); Dahl, *A Preface to Democratic Theory*; and Desmond S. King and Rogers M. Smith, *Still a House Divided: Race and Politics in Obama's America* (Princeton, NJ: Princeton University Press, 2011).

31. Dahl, *Democracy and Its Critics*, p. 161.

32. Thanks to Professor Larry Martinez of the California State University, Long Beach, for this insight.

33. Philip A. Klinkner with Rogers M. Smith, *The Unsteady March: The Rise and Decline of Racial Equality in America* (Chicago: The University of Chicago Press, 1999).

# 2

1. "In U.S., 65% Support Drone Attacks on Terrorists Abroad," Gallup Poll, May 25, 2013, http://www.gallup.com/poll/161474/support-drone-attacks-terrorists-abroad.aspx.

2. "Letter to Governor William Moultrie, August 28, 1793," in *The Writings of George Washington*, vol. 33 (Charlottesville, VA: University of Virginia On-line Library, Washington Collection), accessed April 1, 2014, http://etext.lib.virginia.edu/washington.

3. On the president's unitary powers, especially the office's war powers, see Kenneth R. Mayer, "The Presidential Power of Unilateral Action," and Richard W. Waterman, "Assessing the Unilateral Presidency," in *The Oxford Handbook of the American Presidency*, ed. George C. Edwards III and William G. Howell (Oxford: Oxford University Press, 2010); and William G. Howell, *Power Without Persuasion: The Politics of Direct Presidential Action* (Princeton: Princeton University Press, 2003). On the drone program specifically, see Daniel Klaidman, "The Case for Killing Americans," *Newsweek*, January 23, 2012, http://www.newsweek.com/obama-team-break-silence-al-awlaki-killing-64257; Scott Shane, "Targeted Killing Comes to Define War on Terror," *New York Times*, April 7, 2013; and

Peter W. Singer, "Do Drones Undermine Democracy, *New York Times*, January 12, 2012.

4. Richard Bushman, "Revolution," in *The Reader's Companion to American History*, ed. Eric Foner and John A. Garraty (Boston: Houghton Mifflin, 1991), p. 936; and Gordon S. Wood, *The Creation of the American Republic* (New York: Norton, 1972), p. 12.

5. Joseph J. Ellis, *Founding Brothers: The Revolutionary Generation* (New York: Alfred A. Knopf, 2001), pp. 212–213; and Roger Wilkins, *Jacob's Pillow: The Founding Fathers and the Dilemma of Black Patriotism* (Boston: Beacon Press, 2002).

6. Sarah M. Evans, *Born for Liberty: A History of Women in America* (New York: Free Press, 1997); and John Hope Franklin and Alfred A. Moss Jr., *From Slavery to Freedom* (New York: Knopf, 1967).

7. See Hannah Arendt, *On Revolution* (New York: Viking, 1965).

8. Page Smith, *The Shaping of America: A People's History of the Young Republic*, vol. 3 (New York: McGraw-Hill, 1980).

9. Richard Hofstadter, *The American Political Tradition* (New York: Vintage Books, 1948), p. 4.

10. For a review of thinking about relevance of republicanism in our own time, see Frank Lovett and Philip Pettit, "Neorepublicanism: A Normative and Institutional Research Program," *Annual Review of Political Science* 12 (2009), pp. 11–29.

11. Kevin O'Leary, *Saving Democracy* (Stanford, CA: Stanford University Press, 2006), ch. 3; and Gordon S. Wood, *The Idea of America: Reflections on the Birth of the United States* (New York: Penguin Press, 2011), ch. 4.

12. Alexander Hamilton, James Madison, and John Jay, *The Federalist Papers*, ed. Clinton Rossiter (New York: New American Library, 1961; originally published 1787–1788), No. 10.

13. See Gordon S. Wood, *The Radicalism of the American Revolution* (New York: Knopf, 1992).

14. Wood, *Creation of the American Republic*, pp. 311–318.

15. Ibid., ch. 8.

16. Samuel Eliot Morison, *The Oxford History of the American People* (New York: Oxford University Press, 1965), p. 274.

17. See Wood, *Creation of the American Republic*, p. 400.

18. Smith, *Shaping of America*, pp. 24–26.

19. Quoted in Jackson Turner Main, *The Anti-Federalists* (Chapel Hill: University of North Carolina Press, 1961), p. 62.

20. David Brian Robertson, "Madison's Opponents and Constitutional Design," *American Political Science Review* 99 (May 2006), pp. 225–243.

21. Melvin I. Urofsky, *A March of Liberty* (New York: Knopf, 1988), p. 89.

22. Al Kamen, "Marshall Blasts Celebration of Constitution Bicentennial; Justice Calls Document 'Defective From Start,' " *Washington Post*, May 7, 1987. See also Lee Epstein and Thomas G. Walker, *Constitutional Law for a Changing America* (Washington, DC: CQ Press, 2000), p. 6.

23. Charles Beard, *An Economic Interpretation of the Constitution* (New York: Macmillan, 1913). For a more recent work broadly supporting Beard's interpretation, see Robert A. McGuire, *To Form a More Perfect Union: A New Economic Interpretation of the United States Constitution* (New York: Oxford University Press, 2003).

24. See Robert Brown, *Charles Beard and the Constitution* (Princeton, NJ: Princeton University Press, 1956); Hofstadter, *American Political Tradition*; Leonard Levy, *Constitutional Opinions* (New York: Oxford University Press, 1986); Robert A. McGuire and Robert L. Ohsfeldt, "An Economic Model of Voting Behavior over Specific Issues at the Constitutional Convention of 1787," *Journal of Economic History* 66 (March 1986), pp. 79–111; James A. Morone, *The Democratic Wish* (New York: Basic Books, 1990); Forrest McDonald, *We the People: The Economic Origins of the Constitution* (Chicago: The University of Chicago Press, 1958); Gordon S. Wood, *The Convention and the Constitution* (New York: St. Martin's Press, 1965); and Wood, *Creation of the American Republic*.

25. Wood, *Idea of America*, p. 131.

26. Quoted in Wood, *Creation of the American Republic*, p. 473.

27. Ibid., p. 432.

28. Charles Stewart, "Congress and the Constitutional System," in *The Legislative Branch*, ed. Paul J. Quirk and Sarah A. Binder (New York: Oxford University Press, 2005).

29. See Robertson, "Madison's Opponents and Constitutional Design," for more information on how the Great Compromise shaped the Constitution as a whole.

30. Ellis, *Founding Brothers*, p. 110.

31. Max Farrand, *The Records of the Federal Convention of 1787* (New Haven, CT: Yale University Press, 1937).

32. Hamilton, Madison, and Jay, *The Federalist Papers*, No. 10.

33. "The Invention of Centralized Federalism," in *The Development of Centralized Federalism*, ed. William H. Riker (Boston: Kluwer Academic, 1987).

34. Robert A. Dahl, "On Removing the Impediments to Democracy in the United States," *Political Science Quarterly* 92 (Spring 1977), p. 5.

35. Akhil Reed Amar, *America's Constitution: A Biography* (New York: Random House, 2005), p. 14.

36. Hamilton, Madison, and Jay, *The Federalist Papers*, No. 51.

37. Thomas Jefferson, *Notes on the State of Virginia*, ed. Thomas Perkins Abernathy (New York: Harper & Row, 1964), p. 120.

38. Jefferson wrote this in a letter to James Madison dated November 18, 1788, quoted in *The Life and Selected Writings of Thomas Jefferson*, ed. Adrienne Koch and William Peden (New York: Random House/The Modern Library, 1944), p. 452.

39. See Main, *Anti-Federalists*; Wood, *Creation of the American Republic*; Smith, *Shaping of America*, p. 99; Herbert Storing, *What the Anti-Federalists Were For* (Chicago: The University of Chicago Press, 1981), p. 71; and Robertson, "Madison's Opponents and Constitutional Design."

40. See Cass R. Sunstein, *A Constitution of Many Minds: Why the Founding Document Doesn't Mean What It Meant Before* (Princeton, NJ: Princeton University Press, 2009), for a particularly compelling statement of this idea.

41. On the undemocratic Constitution, see Sanford Levinson, *Our Undemocratic Constitution: Where the Constitution Goes Wrong* (New York: Oxford University Press, 2006).

**3**

1. James B. Stewart, "In Obama's Victory, a Loss for Congress," *New York Times*, June 29, 2012.

2. Sources for this chapter-opening story include Jonathan H. Adler, "Silver Linings in the Health Care Decision," *The Volokh Conspiracy* (blog), July 12, 2012, http://www.volokh.com/2012/07/12/silver-linings-in-the-health-care-decision/; Paul M. Barrett, "John Roberts, CEO," *Bloomberg/BusinessWeek*, July 3, 2012, p. 23; Pamela S. Karlan, "No Respite for Liberals," *New York Times*, June 30, 2012; David Kopel, "Online Symposium: The Bar Review Version of *NFIB v. Sebelius*," *SCOTUSblog*, July 6, 2012, http://www.scotusblog.com/2012/07/online-symposium-the-bar-review-version-of-nfib-v-sebelius/; and The Henry J. Kaiser Family Foundation, "The Coverage Gap: Uninsured Poor Adults in States that Do Not Expand Medicaid," *Health Reform*, October 23, 2013, http:// http://kff.org/health-reform/issue-brief/the-coverage-gap-uninsured-poor-adults-in-states-that-do-not-expand-medicaid/.

3. William H. Riker, *The Development of American Federalism* (Boston: Kluwer Academic, 1987), pp. 56–60.

4. Gabriel A. Almond, G. Bingham Powell Jr., Russell J. Dalton, and Kaare Strom, *Comparative Politics Today: A World View*, updated 9th ed. (New York: Pearson Longman, 2010), p. 108.

5. Mark Rush, "Voting Power in *Federal Systems: Spain as a Case Study*," PS: Political

6. Rodney Hero, *Faces of Inequality: Social Diversity in American Politics* (New York: Oxford University Press, 1998). See also Regina P. Branton and Bradford S. Jones, "Reexamining Racial Attitudes: The Conditional Relationship Between Diversity and Socioeconomic Environment," *American Journal of Political Science* 49, no. 2 (April 2005), pp. 359–372.

7. Dale Krane, "The Middle Tier in American Federalism: State Government Policy Activism During the Bush Presidency," *Publius: Journal of Federalism* 37, no. 3 (Summer 2007), pp. 453–477.

8. J. Schwartz, "After New York, New Look at Defense of Marriage Act," *New York Times*, Jun 27, 2011; S. Sullivan, "The Battle Over Gay Marriage in Three Maps," *Washington Post*, Mar 27, 2013; F. Santos, "New Mexico Becomes 17th State to Allow Gay Marriage," *New York Times*, Dec 19, 2013; A. Liptak, "Supreme Court Delivers Tacit Win to Gay Marriage," *New York Times*, Oct 6 2014.

9. Stephen Wermiel, "SCOTUS for Law Students: The Defense of Marriage Act and the Constitution (sponsored by Bloomberg Law)," *SCOTUSblog*, March 23, 2013, http://www.scotusblog.com/2012/03/scotus-for-law-students-the-defense-of-marriage-act-and-the-constitution-sponsored-by-bloomberg-law/.

10. The study of the complex constitutional, legal, fiscal, and political links between states and the national government is often called the study of *intergovernmental relations* (the ever-changing constitutional, legal, fiscal, and political linkages among the states and the national government). For more on this, see B. Guy Peters and Jon Pierre, "Developments in Intergovernmental Relations: Towards Multi-Level Governance," *Policy and Politics* 29, no. 2 (April 2001), pp. 131–141; Robert B. Albritton, "American Federalism and Intergovernmental Relations," in *Developments in American Politics, ed.* Gillian Peele, Christopher J. Bailey, Bruce Cain, and B. Guy Peters (New York: Palgrave, 2008).

11. Thomas Gais and James Fossett, "Federalism and the Executive Branch," in *The Executive Branch, ed.* Joel D. Aberbach and Mark A. Peterson (New York: Oxford University Press, 2005), pp. 486–524.

12. Hero, *Faces of Inequality*, pp. 31–34.

13. Robert G. McCloskey, *The American Supreme Court, 5th ed., ed. Sanford Levinson* (Chicago: The University of Chicago Press, 2010), pp. 49–51.

14. See "Symposium: Congress, Preemption, and Federalism," in *PS: Political Science and Politics* 38, no. 3 (July 2005), pp. 359–378.

15. McCloskey, *American Supreme Court*, pp. 104–107, 118–119.

16. Pew Research Center for the People & the Press, "A Partisan Public Agenda: Opinion of Clinton and Congress Improves," January 16, 1997, http://www.people-press.org/1997/01/16/a-partisan-public-agenda/; Pew Research Center for the People & the Press, "How Americans View Government: Deconstructing Distrust" Pew Research Center, March 10, 1998, http://www.people-press.org/1998/03/10/how-americans-view-government/; "National Omnibus Survey" (Cambridge, MA: Cambridge Reports/Research International, 1982).

17. Tim Conlan and John Dinan, "Federalism, the Bush Administration, and the Transformation of American Conservatism," *Publius: The Journal of Federalism* 37, no. 3 (Summer 2007), pp. 279–303.

18. Krane, "Middle Tier in American Federalism."

19. Shama Gamkhar and J. Mitchell Pickerill, "The State of American Federalism, 2010–2011: The Economy, Healthcare Reform and Midterm Elections Shape the Intergovernmental Agenda," *Publius: The Journal of Federalism* 41, no. 3 (Summer 2011), pp. 361–394.

20. Michael Cooper, "More U.S. Rail Funds for 13 States as 2 Reject Aid," *New York Times*, December 9, 2010; Timothy Williams, "Florida's Governor Rejects High-Speed Rail Line,

Fearing Cost to Taxpayers," *New York Times,* February 16, 2011.

21. For example, in *Bond v. United States (2013),* the Court ruled that individuals can sue the federal government when Congress goes too far in creating statutes that intrude on the legitimate authority of the states. In *Sossamon v. Texas (2011),* it ruled that states do not give up their sovereign immunity against monetary lawsuits from their own citizens for violating a federal law when states accept federal funds under that law.

22. Ann O'M. Bowman and George A. Krause, "Power Shift: Measuring Policy Centralization in U.S. Intergovernmental Relations, 1947–1998," *American Politics Research* 31, no. 3 (May 2003), pp. 301–313; B. Guy Peters, *American Public Policy: Promise and Performance* (Washington, DC: CQ Press, 2009), pp. 24–29; Robert Nagel, *The Implosion of American Federalism* (New York: Oxford University Press, 2002).

23. Morton Grodzins, *The American System* (New Brunswick, NJ: Transaction Books, 1983), p.8.

24. Riker, *Development of American Federalism, pp. 157-190;* David B. Walker, *Toward a Functioning Federalism* (Cambridge, MA: Winthrop, 1981), pp. 60–63.

25. Paul E. Peterson, Barry G. Rabe, and Kenneth Wong, *When Federalism Works* (Washington, DC: Brookings Institution Press, 1986), p. 2.

26. Gamkhar and Pickerill, "State of American Federalism," p. 363.

27. Timothy Conlan, *From New Federalism to Devolution: Twenty-Five Years of Intergovernmental Reform* (Washington, DC: Brookings Institution Press, 1998), p. 71.

28. Ed Gillespie and Bob Schellhas, eds., *Contract with America: The Bold Plan by Rep. Newt Gingrich, Rep. Dick Armey and the House Republicans to Change the Nation* (New York: Random House, 1994), p. 125.

29. Brady Dennis, "Obama Administration Will Not Block State Marijuana Laws, If Distribution Is Regulated," *Washington Post,* August 29, 2013.

30. William H. Riker, *Federalism: Origin, Operation, Significance* (Boston: Little, Brown, 1964), ch. 6.

31. Paul E. Peterson, *City Limits* (Chicago: The University of Chicago Press, 1981), pp. 17-38; Paul E. Peterson, *The Price of Federalism* (Washington, DC: Brookings Institution Press, 1995), pp. 16-49.

**4**

1. The title of this opening story comes from a remark made by a member of Local 751, as quoted in Roger Bybee, "Boeing Holds Jobs Hostage in Two-Pronged Fight with State Government and Machinists," *In These Times,* November 25, 2013, http://inthesetimes.com/working/entry/15922/boeing_holds _jobs_hostage_in_two_pronged_fight_with_state_government _and_ma. See also Timothy Egan, "Under My Thumb," *New York Times,* November 14, 2013, http://www.nytimes .com/2013/11/15/opinion/egan-under-my-thumb.html?_r=0; Dominic Gates, "Boeing picks 15 potential sites nationwide to build 777X," *Seattle Times,* November 23, 2013, http:// seattletimes.com/html/businesstechnology/2022318847 _boeing777xrfpxml.html; and Edward S. Greenberg, Leon Grunberg, Sarah Moore, and Pat Sikora, *Turbulence: Boeing and the State of American Workers and Managers* (New Haven, CT: Yale University Press, 2010).

2. However, the United States fell slightly below replacement level during the Great Recession. See "Births: Final Data for 2010," *National Vital Statistics Reports* 61, no. 1 (Washington, DC: U.S. Department of Health and Human Services, August 28, 2012).

3. For a history of immigration and government policies regarding immigration, see Aristide R. Zolberg, *A Nation by Design:*

*Immigration Policy in the Fashioning of America* (Cambridge, MA: Harvard University Press, 2006).

4. Drew DeSilver, "World's Muslim population more widespread than you might think," *Fact Tank* (blog), Pew Research Center, June 7, 2013, http://www.pewresearch.org/fact-tank/2013 /06/07/worlds-muslim-population-more-widespread-than -you-might-think/.

5. U.S. Department of Homeland Security, *Yearbook of Immigration Statistics* (Washington, DC: U.S. Government Printing Office, 2012).

6. U.S. Census Bureau, "USAQuickFacts," http://quickfacts.census .gov/qfd/states/00000.html.

7. Ibid.

8. U.S. Census Bureau, Newsroom, news release, May 15, 2012.

9. U.S. Census Bureau, 2012 National Population Projections: Summary Tables, Table 6, Percent Distribution of the Projected Population by Race, and Hispanic Origin for the United States: 2015 to 2060, http://www.census.gov/population/projections /data/national/2012/summarytables.html.

10. Paul Taylor and D'Vera Cohn, "A Milestone En Route to a Majority Minority Nation," Pew Rew Research Center, September 24, 2013, http://www.pewsocialtrends.org /2012/11/07/a-milestone-en-route-to-a-majority-minority -nation/.

11. "Most Say Illegal Immigrants Should Be Allowed to Stay, But Citizenship Is More Diverse," Pew Research Center, March 28, 2013, http://www.people-press.org/2013/03/28 /most-say-illegal-immigrants-should-be-allowed-to-stay-but -citizenship-is-more-divisive/

12. Ibid.

13. Daniel J. Tichenor, *Dividing Lines: The Politics of Immigration Control in the United States* (Princeton, NJ: Princeton University Press, 2002), p. 284; and Mark Hugo Lopez, "The Latino Electorate in 2010: More Voters, More Non-Voters," Pew Research Hispanic Trends Project, Pew Research Center, April 26, 2011, http://www.pewhispanic.org/2011/04/26/the -latino-electorate-in-2010-more-voters-more-non-voters/.

14. "Low Marks for the 2012 Election," Pew Research Center, November 15, 2012, http://www.people-press.org/2012/11/15 /low-marks-for-the-2012-election/.

15. "The Census: Minority Report," *The Economist* (April 2, 2011), p. 25; and "The 2010 Census Data," Washington, D.C.: Census Bureau, 2012).

16. Lindsay M. Howden and Julie A. Meyer, "Age and Sex Composition, 2010," *2010 Census Briefs* (Washington, DC: U.S. Census Bureau, May 2011), http://www.census.gov/prod /cen2010/briefs/c2010br-03.pdf.

17. Pew Research Social & Demographic Trends, "Recession Turns a Graying Office Grayer," Pew Research Center, September 3, 2009, http://www.pewsocialtrends.org/2009/09/03 /recession-turns-a-graying-office-grayer/.

18. "World Population Ageing: 1950-2050," United Nations, Population Division, http://www.un.org/esa/population/publications /worldageing19502050/.

19. Based on purchasing power.

20. *Human Development Report, 2012* (New York: United Nations, 2013).

21. All income data are from Carmen DeNavas-Walt, Bernadette D. Proctor, and Jessica C. Smith, *Income, Poverty, and Health Insurance Coverage in the United States: 2012* (Washington, DC: U.S. Census Bureau, September 2013), https://www .census.gov/prod/2013pubs/p60-245.pdf.

22. See the article by Brenda Cronin reporting statistics from Sentier Research based on Census Bureau data, "Slow Recovery Feels Like Recession," *The Wall Street Journal,* October 31, 2011, p. 1.

23. Ianthe Jeanne Dugan, "Returning Workers Face Steep Pay Cuts," *The Wall Street Journal* (November 12, 2009), p. 1.; and Shobhana Chandra and Steve Matthews, "Having A Job Ain't

What It Used to Be," *Bloomberg/Businessweek* (October 17–October 23, 2011), pp. 19–20.

24. U.S. Census Bureau, reported in Conor Dougherty, "Income Slides to 1996 Levels," *Wall Street Journal*, September 14, 2011.

25. Steven Greenhouse, "Our Economic Pickle," *New York Times*, January 12, 2013.

26. Stanley B. Greenberg, *Middle-Class Dreams* (New York: Times Books, 1995); and Susan J. Tolchin, *The Angry American* (Boulder, CO: Westview Press, 1999). On the more general relationship between income growth and political mood, see Benjamin M. Friedman, *The Moral Consequences of Economic Growth* (New York: Knopf, 2005).

27. David Leonhardt and Marjorie Connelly, "81 Percent in Poll Say Nation Is on the Wrong Track," *New York Times*, April 4, 2008. Also see Brian Blackstone, "Economy Sheds Jobs in March, Fueling Fears of Recession," *Wall Street Journal*, April 4, 2008.

28. Carmen DeNavas-Walt, Bernadette D. Proctor, and Jessica C. Smith, *Income, Poverty, and Health Insurance Coverage in the United States: 2012* (Washington, DC: U.S. Census Bureau, September 2013).

29. DeNavas-Walt, Proctor, and Smith, *Income, Poverty, and Health Insurance Coverage.*

30. Ibid.

31. William Julius Wilson, *When Work Disappears: The World of the New Urban Poor* (New York: Vintage, 1997).

32. Florence Jaumotte, Subir Lall, and Chris Papageorgiou, "Rising Income Inequality: Technology, or Trade and Financial Globalization" (working paper, International Monetary Fund, July 2008); "As you were: special report on the world economy," *Economist*, October 13, 2012, pp. 24–33.

33. Emmanuel Saez, "Striking It Richer: The Evolution of Top Incomes in the United States" (working paper, updated with 2012 preliminary estimates, University of California–Berkeley, September 3, 2013).

34. "CEO Pay Sinks Along with Profits," *The Wall Street Journal* (April 3, 2009), p. A1.

35. "CEO Pay Rebounds," *Bloomberg/Businessweek* (September 12, 2011), p. 35.

36. Natasha Singer, "In Executive Pay, a Rich Game of Thrones," *The New York Times* (April 7, 2012), p. 1.

37. Edward N. Wolff, "The Asset Price Meltdown and the Wealth of the Middle Class" (working paper, New York University, 2013). Also see Larry M. Bartels, *Unequal Democracy: The Political Economy of the New Gilded Age* (New York and Princeton, NJ: The Russell Sage Foundation and Princeton University Press, 2008), ch. 1. Thomas Piketty in *Capital in the Twenty-First Century* shows that wealth distribution in capitalist countries is always more unequally distributed than income and tends to remain so unless the property position of the wealthy is undermined by extreme events such as economic depression (The Great Depression) and war (the First and Second World Wars in particular).

38. DeNavas-Walt, Proctor, and Smith, *Income, Poverty, and Health Insurance Coverage in the United States: 2012.*

39. The research is summarized and discussed in Jacob S. Hacker and Paul Pierson, *Winner-Take-All Politics* (New York: Simon and Schuster, 2010); and Robert B. Reich, *Aftershock: The Next Economy and America's Future* (New York: Knopf, 2010), ch. 7.

40. Raymond Boudon and Francois Bourricaud, *A Critical Dictionary of Sociology* (Chicago: The University of Chicago Press, 1989), pp. 340–346.

41. DeNavas-Walt, Proctor, and Smith, *Income, Poverty, and Health Insurance Coverage in the United States: 2012.*

42. See the research cited and summarized in Hacker and Pierson, *Winner-Take-All Politics*, ch. 1; Jacob S. Hacker, *The Great Risk Shift* (New York: Oxford University Press, 2006); and Reich, *Aftershock.*

43. Gerald F. Seib, "Populist Movements Rooted in Same Soil," *Wall Street Journal*, November 15, 2011.

44. Reich, *Aftershock*, Part II, "Backlash."

45. David Coen, Wyn Grant, and Graham Wilson, "Perspectives on Business and Government (Political Science)," in *The Oxford Handbook of Business and Government*, ed. David Coen, Wyn Grant, and Graham Wilson (New York: Oxford University Press, 2010).

46. Thomas Piketty, *Capital in the Twenty-First Century* (Cambridge, MA: Harvard University Press, 2014).

47. On the different forms of capitalism in the modern world, see William J. Baumol, Robert E. Litan, and Carl J. Schramm, *Good Capitalism, Bad Capitalism and the Economics of Growth and Prosperity* (New Haven, CT: Yale University Press, 2007); Gosta Esping-Andersen, "The Three Political Economies of the Welfare State," *Canadian Review of Sociology and Anthropology* 26 (1989), pp. 10–36; Bob Hancke, "Varieties of Capitalism and Business," in Coen, Grant, and Wilson, *Oxford Handbook of Capitalism and Business*; Jonas Pontusson, "The American Welfare State in Comparative Perspective," *Perspectives on Politics* 4, no. 2 (June 2006); pp. 315–326. Harold L. Wilensky, *Rich Democracies: Political Economy, Public Policy, and Performance* (Berkeley, CA: University of California Press, 2002).

48. U.S. Department of Commerce, *International Direct Investment* (Washington, DC. U.S. Government Printing Office, 1984), p. 1.

49. For entertaining yet highly informative critiques of extreme pro-globalization advocates and extreme anti-globalization advocates, see Michael Veseth, *Selling Globalization: The Myth of the Global Economy* (Boulder, CO: Lynne Rienner, 1998); and Michael Veseth, *Globaloney: Unraveling the Myths of Globalization* (Lanham, MD: Rowman & Littlefield, 2005).

50. Robert B. Reich, *Supercapitalism: The Transformation of Business, Democracy, and Everyday Life* (New York: Alfred A. Knopf, 2007).

51. See John Markoff, "Google Puts Money on Robots, Using Man Behind Android," *New York Times*, December 4, 2013.

52. Louis Uchitelle, "Is Manufacturing Falling Off the Radar?," *New York Times*, September 10, 2011; Anton Troianovski, "Wireless Jobs Vanish," *Wall Street Journal*, July 18, 2011; and "The Age of Smart Machines," *Economist*, May 25, 2013, pp. 22–24.

53. Shobhana Chandra and Steve Matthews, "Having a Job Ain't All It's Cracked Up to Be," *BloombergBusinessWeek*, October 12, 2011.

54. Andrew Kohut, "A Popular Obama Heads to G20," Pew Research Center, September 3, 2013, http://www.pewresearch.org/2013/09/03/obama-shines-on-world-stage.

55. Pew Center for the People & the Press, "Public Sees U.S. Power Declining as Support for Global Engagement Slips," Pew Research Center, December 3, 2013, http://www.people-press.org/2013/12/03/public-sees-u-s-power-declining-as-support-for-global-engagement-slips/.

56. See Seymour Martin Lipset, *American Exceptionalism: A Double-Edged Sword* (New York: Norton, 1996); Jennifer L. Hochschild, *Facing Up to the American Dream* (Princeton, NJ: Princeton University Press, 1995), ch. 1; and John Micklethwait and Adrian Wooldridge, *The Right Nation: Conservative Power in America* (New York: Penguin Press, 2004), part IV. For a contrary view—namely, that America is divided into distinct political cultural traditions—see Rogers M. Smith, *Civic Ideals: Conflicting Visions of Citizenship in U.S. History* (New Haven, CT: Yale University Press, 1997). For an answer to Smith that defends the idea that the American political culture is of a single large cloth, see Marc Stears, "The Liberal Tradition and the Politics of Exclusion," *Annual Review of Political Science* 10 (2007), pp. 85–101.

57. For a contrary view of the place of individualism in American life, see Desmond King, *The Liberty of Strangers: Making the American Nation* (New York: Oxford University Press, 2004).

58. See Jennifer L. Hochschild, *What's Fair? American Beliefs about Distributive Justice* (Cambridge, MA: Harvard University Press, 1981); Herbert McClosky and John R. Zaller, *The American Ethos: Public Attitudes Toward Capitalism and Democracy* (Cambridge, MA: Harvard University Press, 1984); and Sidney Verba and Gary R. Orren, *Equality in America* (Cambridge, MA: Harvard University Press, 1985). However, see Benjamin I. Page and Lawrence R. Jacobs, *Class War: What Americans Really Feel About Inequality* (Chicago: The University of Chicago Press, 2009), which shows that public support exists for programs to lessen inequality.

59. See Joel F. Handler and Yeheskel Hasenfeld, *Blame Welfare, Ignore Poverty and Inequality* (Cambridge, UK: Cambridge University Press, 2007). For arguments suggesting that Americans are uncomfortable with income inequality and are willing to let government do something about making it less extreme, see Page and Jacobs, *Class War*.

60. Verba and Orren, *Equality in America,* p. 255.

61. Page and Jacobs, *Class War*, pp. 96–97.

62. Frank Newport, "Americans' Views on Bank Takeovers Appear Fluid," Gallup Poll, February 24, 2009, http://www.gallup.com/poll/116065/americans-views-bank-takeovers-appear-fluid.aspx.

63. Pew Research Center for the People & the Press, "Support for Health Care Principles, Opposition to Package," news release, October 8, 2009, http://www.people-press.org/files/legacy-pdf/551.pdf.

64. John Judis, "Anti-Statism in America," *New Republic,* November 11, 2009, p. 2.

65. Russell Hanson, *The Democratic Imagination in America* (Princeton, NJ: Princeton University Press, 1985).

66. McClosky and Zaller, *American Ethos*, p. 18; Pew Research Center for the People & the Press, "Views of a Changing World 2003," Pew Research Center, June 3, 2003, http://www.people-press.org/2003/06/03/views-of-a-changing-world-2003/.

67. Alan Wolfe, *Does American Democracy Still Work?* (New Haven, CT: Yale University Press, 2006).

68. Gary Wills, *Under God: Religion and American Politics* (New York: Simon and Schuster, 1991); Micklethwait and Wooldridge, *Right Nation;* and Kevin Phillips, *American Theocracy: The Peril and Politics of Radical Religion, Oil, and Borrowed Money in the 21st Century* (New York: Viking, 2006).

69. Pew Research Center for the People & the Press, "Views of a Changing World 2003."

70. Micklethwait and Wooldridge, *Right Nation.*

# 5

1. Joseph C. Goulden, *Truth Is the First Casualty: The Gulf of Tonkin Affair—Illusion and Reality* (Chicago: Rand McNally, 1969). Also see Scott Stane, "Vietnam War Intelligence Deliberately Skewed, Secret Study Says," *The New York Times* (December 2, 2005), p. A1.

2. All public opinion polls cited in this chapter-opening story are from John E. Mueller, *War, Presidents and Public Opinion* (New York: Wiley, 1973).

3. U.S. Department of Defense, OASD (Comptroller), *Selected Manpower Statistics* (Washington, D.C.: Government Publications, June 1976), pp. 59–60.

4. Alexander Hamilton, James Madison, and John Jay, *The Federalist Papers,* ed. Clinton Rossiter (New York: New American Library, 1961; originally published 1787–1788). See Benjamin I. Page and Robert Y. Shapiro, *The Rational Public: Fifty Years of Trends in Americans' Policy Preferences* (Chicago: University of Chicago Press, 1992), chs. 1 and 2.

5. Walter Lippmann, *Public Opinion* (New York: Macmillan, 1922), p. 127.

6. Philip E. Converse, "The Nature of Belief Systems in Mass Publics," in David Apter, ed., *Ideology and Discontent* (New York: Free Press, 1964), pp. 206–261; Philip E. Converse, "Attitudes and Non-Attitudes: Continuation of a Dialogue," in Edward R. Tufte, ed., *The Quantitative Analysis of Social Problems* (Reading, MA: Addison-Wesley, 1970), pp. 168–189. Also see Larry M. Bartels, *Unequal Democracy: The Political Economy of the Gilded Age* (New York and Princeton, NJ: Russell Sage Foundation and Princeton University Press, 2008), for an argument that people find it hard to understand whether public policies are consistent with their values and wishes.

7. Bartels, *Unequal Democracy.*

8. Bryan Caplan, *The Myth of the Rational Voter: Why Democracies Choose Bad Policies* (Princeton, NJ: Princeton University Press, 2007).

9. Robert S. Erikson and Kent L. Tedin, *American Public Opinion: Its Origins, Content, and Impact,* 8th ed. (New York: Pearson Longman, 2011), Table 2.1. This book offers an excellent introduction to how surveys are done.

10. Erikson and Tedin, *American Public Opinion,* p. 42.

11. George F. Bishop, *The Illusion of Public Opinion: Fact and Artifact in American Public Opinion Polls* (Lanham, MD: Rowman & Littlefield, 2004).

12. For a review of the research literature on political socialization, see Erikson and Tedin, *American Public Opinion,* ch. 5.

13. M. Kent Jennings, "Political Socialization," in *The Oxford Handbook of Political Behavior,* ed. Russell Dalton and Hans-Dieter Klingman (Oxford, UK: Oxford University Press, 2004); M. Kent Jennings, Laura Stoker, and Jake Bowers, "Politics Across Generations: Family Transmission Reexamined," *Journal of Politics* 71, no. 3 (July 2009), pp. 782–799; and Laura Stoker and Jackie Bass, "Political Socialization," in *The Oxford Handbook of Public Opinion and the Media, ed.* Robert Shapiro and Lawrence R. Jacobs (Oxford, UK: Oxford University Press, 2011).

14. Doris A. Graber, *Mass Media and American Politics,* 8th ed. (Washington, DC: CQ Press, 2010), pp. 161–166.

15. For data on how the economic prospects of young people have changed for the worse and on how their political attitudes differ from other age cohorts, see Richard Fry, D'Vera Cohn, Gretchen Livingston, and Paul Taylor, "The Rising Age Gap in Economic Well-Being," Pew Research Social & Demographic Trends, Pew Research Center, November 7, 2011, http://www.pewsocialtrends.org/2011/11/07/the-rising-age-gap-in-economic-well-being/; and Pew Research Center for the People & the Press, "The Generation Gap and the 2012 Election," Pew Research Center, November 3, 2011, http://www.people-press.org/2011/11/03/the-generation-gap-and-the-2012-election-3/.

16. For articulations on how we are divided, see Henry E. Brady, "The Art of Political Science: Spatial Diagrams as Iconic and Revelatory," *Perspectives on Politics 9, no. 2* (June 2011), pp. 311–331; and Desmond S. King and Rogers M. Smith, *Still a House Divided: Race and Politics in Obama's America* (Princeton: Princeton University Press, 2011).

17. Paul Sniderman and Thomas Piazza, *Black Pride and Black Prejudice* (Princeton, NJ: Princeton University Press, 2002), pp. 175–179; and Erikson and Tedin, *American Public Opinion,* pp. 199–200.

18. Pew Research Center for the People & the Press, "Trends in Political Values and Core Attitudes: 1987–2009," news release, May 21, 2009, http://www.people-press.org/files/legacy-pdf/517.pdf; and Laura R. Olson and John C. Green, *Beyond Red State, Blue State: Electoral Gaps in the Twenty-First Century American Electorate* (New York: Pearson Prentice-Hall, 2009).

19. Pew Research Center for the People & the Press, "Trends," pp. 78–79.

20. This and the votes of other groups reported in this section are from the American National Election Study (2012).

21. Fredrick C. Harris, "The Contours of Black Public Opinion," in Shapiro and Jacobs, *Oxford Handbook of American Public Opinion and the Media.*

22. Pew Research Center for the People & the Press, "Trends."

23. Ibid., sec. 9; and Erikson and Tedin, *American Public Opinion,* pp. 200–201.

24. Jeffrey M. Jones, "In U.S., Most Reject Considering Race in College Admissions," Gallup Poll, July 24, 2013, http://www.gallup.com/poll/163655/reject-considering-race-college-admissions.aspx.

25. Paul Taylor, Mark Hugo Lopez, Jessica Martínez, and Gabriel Velasco, "When Labels Don't Fit: Hispanics and Their Views of Identity," Pew Research Hispanic Trends Project, Pew Research Center, April 4, 2012, http://www.pewhispanic.org/2012/04/04/when-labels-dont-fit-hispanics-and-their-views-of-identity/. Hispanic Protestants, however, are more consistently conservative on social issues, according to research reported by Rodolfo O. de la Garza and Seung-Jin Jang, "Latino Public Opinion," in Shapiro and Jacobs, *The Oxford Handbook of American Public Opinion and the Media.*

26. S. K. Ramakrishnan, J. S. Wong, T. Lee, and J. Junn, "Race-Based Considerations and the Obama Vote: Evidence from the 2008 National Asian American Survey," *Du Bois Review* 6, no. 1 (2009), 219–238.

27. Rich Morin, "Rising Share of Americans See Conflicts Between Rich and Poor," Pew Research Social & Demographic Trends, Pew Research Center, January 11, 2012, http://www.pewsocialtrends.org/2012/01/11/rising-share-of-americans-see-conflict-between-rich-and-poor/.

28. Nolan McCarty, Keith T. Poole, and Howard Rosenthal, *Polarized America: The Dance of Ideology and Unequal Riches* (Cambridge, MA: MIT Press, 2006), p. 107; and Larry M. Bartels, *Unequal Democracy: The Political Economy of the New Gilded Age* (New York: Russel Sage Foundation, 2008).

29. See Pew Research Center for the People & the Press, "Trends," p. 24. For pre-2009 data, see Erikson and Tedin, *American Public Opinion,* pp. 191–199, using overtime reports from the National Election Study surveys; and McCarty, Poole, and Rosenthal, *Polarized America.*

30. Pew Research Center for the People & the Press, "Trends," sec. 2.

31. Leslie McCall and Jeff Manza, "Class Differences in Social and Political Attitudes in the United States," in Shapiro and Jacobs, *Oxford Handbook of American Public Opinion and the Media.*

32. Earl Black and Merle Black, *The Rise of Southern Republicans* (Cambridge, MA: Harvard University Press, 2002); and Earl Black and Merle Black, *Divided America: The Ferocious Power Struggle in American Politics* (New York: Simon and Schuster, 2007).

33. General Social Survey, 2008.

34. Ibid.

35. Larry J. Sabato, *Pendulum Swing* (New York: Pearson Education, 2011).

36. General Social Survey, 2008; and Erikson and Tedin, *American Public Opinion,* pp. 213–218.

37. Morris P. Fiorina, *Culture War: The Myth of a Polarized America* (New York: Pearson Longman, 2005); and Morris P. Fiorina and Samuel J. Abrams, "Political Polarization in the American Public," *Annual Review of Political Science* 11 (2008), pp. 563–588; and Erikson and Tedin, *American Public Opinion,* pp. 214–215.

38. Erikson and Tedin, *American Public Opinion,* p. 195.

39. Ibid., pp. 196–197.

40. Pew Research Center for the People & the Press, "Trends," p. 21. See also Julie Dolan, Melissa Deckman, and Michele L. Swers, *Women and Politics: Paths to Power and Influence* (New York: Longman, 2011), pp. 59–62.

41. Data on voting behavior and partisanship drawn from the American National Election Study 2012; Fiorina, *Culture War,* pp. 34–35, 66–76; and Karen M. Kaufman, "The Gender Gap," *PS: Political Science and Politics* 39, no. 3 (2006), pp. 447–453. For a contrary view, see Janet M. Box-Steffensmeier, Suzanna De Boef, and Tse-Min Lin, "The Dynamics of the Partisan Gender Gap," *American Political Science Review* 98, no. 3 (August 2004), pp. 515–528.

42. Mark Schlesinger and Caroline Heldman, "Gender Gap or Gender Gaps?" *Journal of Politics* 63, no. 1 (February 2001), pp. 59–92; Erikson and Tedin, *American Public Opinion,* pp. 219–223; General Social Survey, 2008; and Leonie Huddy and Erin Cassese, "On the Complex and Varied Political Effects of Gender," in Shapiro and Jacobs, *Oxford Handbook of American Public Opinion and the Media.*

43. Fiorina, *Culture War,* pp. 66–69.

44. Pew Research Center for the People & the Press, "Trends."

45. ABC News/*Washington Post* poll, March 2011.

46. Pew Research Center for the People & the Press, "Trends," sec. 4; and Nicholas L. Danigelis, Melissa Hardy, and Stephen J. Cutler, "Population Aging, Intracohort Aging, and Sociopolitical Attitudes," *American Sociological Review* 72 (2007), pp. 812–830.

47. For detailed information on the size, beliefs, and political attitudes of various religious denominations in the United States, see Pew Research Religion & Public Life Project, "U.S. Religious Landscape Survey," Pew Research Center, November 9, 2009. All of the survey data in this section, unless otherwise noted, comes from this source.

48. Black and Black, *Divided America.*

49. Pew, "The U.S. Religious Landscape Survey."

50. Toni Johnson, "Muslims in the United States," (New York: The Council on Foreign Relations, September 19, 2011).

51. The data in this section is from *Trends, 2005* (Washington, DC: Pew Research Center, 2005), http://www.pewresearch.org/files/old-assets/trends/trends2005.pdf.

52. Fiorina, *Culture War*; Fiorina and Abrams, "Political Polarization."

53. King and Smith, *Still a House Divided.*

54. Erikson and Tedin, *American Public Opinion,* pp. 83–84.

55. Michael X. Delli Carpini and Scott Keeter, *What Americans Know About Politics and Why It Matters* (New Haven, CT: Yale University Press, 1996); and Alan Wolfe, *Does American Democracy Still Work?* (New Haven, CT: Yale University Press, 2006).

56. For full details, see Erikson and Tedin, *American Public Opinion,* Table 3.1. See also Page and Shapiro, *Rational Public,* pp. 9–14; Wolfe, *Does American Democracy Still Work?,* pp. 24–30.

57. Pew Research Center for the People & the Press, Omnibus Final Topline Survey, September 25-28, 2014, p. 8, http://www.people-press.org/files/2014/09/Knowledge-topline-for-release.pdf.

58. Jacob S. Hacker and Paul Pierson, *Winner–Take–All Politics* (New York: Simon and Schuster, 2010), pp. 154–155; and Bartels, *Unequal Democracy.*

59. Suzanne Mettler, *The Submerged State: How Invisible Government Policies Undermine American Democracy* (Chicago: The University of Chicago Press, 2011).

60. Ibid.

61. Pew Research Center for the People & the Press, "Public Knowledge of Current Affairs: Little Changed by News and Information Revolutions," Pew Research Center, April 15, 2007, http://www.people-press.org/2007/04/15/public-knowledge-of-current-affairs-little-changed-by-news-and-information-revolutions/.

62. Paul M. Sniderman, Richard A. Brody, and Philip E. Tetlock, *Reasoning and Choice: Explorations in Political Psychology* (New York: Cambridge University Press, 1991). See also Carpini and Keeter, *What Americans Know About Politics*; and Samuel Popkin, *The Reasoning Voter* (Chicago: The University of

Chicago Press, 1991). For the view that it matters a great deal that Americans don't know many of the details about what is going on in Washington, see Bartels, *Unequal Democracy*; Bryan Caplan, *The Myth of the Rational Voter: Why Democracies Choose Bad Policies (Princeton, NJ: Princeton University Press, 2008)*; and Wolfe, *Does American Democracy Still Work?*.

63. Robert E. Lane, *Political Ideology: Why the American Common Man Believes What He Does* (New York: Free Press, 1962); Jennifer L. Hochschild, *What's Fair? American Beliefs about Distributive Justice* (Cambridge, MA: Harvard University Press, 1986); and Carroll J. Glynn, Susan Herbst, Garrett O'Keefe, and Robert Y. Shapiro, *Public Opinion* (Boulder, CO: Westview Press, 1999), ch. 8.

64. Binyamin Appelbaum and Robert Gebeloff, "Even Critics of Safety Net Increasingly Depend on It," *New York Times*, February 11, 2012.

65. Page and Shapiro, *Rational Public*. See also Doris A. Graber, "Re-Measuring the Civic IQ: Decline, Stability, or Advance?" (paper prepared for presentation at the annual meeting of the American Political Science Association, Boston, August 28–31, 2008); Taeku Lee, *Mobilizing Public Opinion: Black Insurgency and Racial Attitudes in the Civil Rights Era* (Chicago: The University of Chicago Press, 2002); and Erikson and Tedin, *American Public Opinion*, pp. 93–94. This view is strongly rejected by Caplan, *Myth of the Rational Voter*, who believes that, at least on issues related to economic policies, errors by the public are systematic rather than random, so they do not balance out.

66. Robert Y. Shapiro and Lawrence R. Jacobs, "The Democratic Paradox," in Shapiro and Jacobs, *Oxford Handbook of American Public Opinion and the Media*, pp. 720–722.

67. Frank Newport, "Most in U.S. Still Proud to Be an American," Gallup Poll, July 4, 2013, http://www.gallup.com/poll/163361/proud-american.aspx.

68. Harris Poll, June 2004.

69. Pew Research Global Attitudes Project, "The American-Western European Values Gap," Pew Research Center, November 17, 2011, updated February 29, 2011, http://www.pewglobal.org/2011/11/17/the-american-western-european-values-gap/.

70. Pew Research Center for the People & the Press, "Trends," p. 78.

71. Pew Research Center for the People & the Press, "Public Trust in Government: 1958–2013," Pew Research Center, October 18, 2013, http://www.people-press.org/2013/10/18/trust-in-government-interactive/.

72. Gallup Poll, March 6–9, 2014.

73. Gallup Poll, December 2013.

74. "Congress Less Popular Than Cockroaches, Traffic Jams," Public Policy Polling, January 8, 2013, http://www.publicpolicypolling.com/main/2013/01/congress-less-popular-than-cockroaches-traffic-jams.html.

75. "Gallup Daily: Obama Job Approval," Gallup Poll, http://www.gallup.com/poll/124922/presidential-approval-center.aspx

76. Vanessa Williamson, Theda Skocpol, and John Coggin, "The Tea Party and the Remaking of Republican Conservatism," *Perspectives on Politics 9, no. 1* (2011), pp. 25–43.

77. Steven Kull, *Americans and Foreign Aid: A Study of American Public Attitudes* (Washington, DC: Program on International Policy Attitudes, 1995).

78. Pew Research Center for the People & the Press, "Trust."

79. Pew Research Center poll, February12–26, 2014 (N=3,338 adults nationwide, margin of error ± 2); Bloomberg National poll, conducted by Selzer & Company, March 7-10, 2014 (N=1,001 adults nationwide, margin of error ± 3.1.)

80. Pew Research Center for the People & the Press, "Broad Approval for New Arizona Immigration Law," Pew Research Center, May 12, 2010, http://www.people-press.org/2010/05/12/broad-approval-for-new-arizona-immigration-law/.

81. Scott Bittle, Jonathan Rochkind, with Amber Ott, "Confidence in U.S. Foreign Policy Index," PublicAgenda.org *and Foreign Affairs* 7 (Spring 2010), http://www.publicagenda.org/pages/foreign-policy-index-2010.

82. William Caspary, "The 'Mood Theory': A Study of Public Opinion and Foreign Policy," *American Political Science Review* 64 (1970), pp. 536–547; John E. Reilly, ed., *American Public Opinion and U.S. Foreign Policy, 1995* (Chicago: Chicago Council on Foreign Relations, 1995), p. 13; Lydia Saad, "Growing Minority Wants Minimal U.S. Role in World Affairs" The Gallup Poll, February 21, 2011, http://www.gallup.com/poll/146240/growing-minority-wants-minimal-role-world-affairs.aspx. See also Pew Research Center for the People & the Press, "Trends," sec. 6.

83. Survey by Time, Cable News Network. Methodology: Conducted by Yankelovich Partners on April 21, 1994 and based on 600 telephone interviews. Sample: National adult.

84. Survey by Cable News Network, USA Today. Methodology: Conducted by Gallup Organization, September 21–September 22, 2001 and based on 1,005 telephone interviews. Sample: National adult.

85. Gallup Poll, August 5–8, 2010.

86. NBC News/Wall Street Journal poll conducted by Hart Research Associates (D) and Public Opinion Strategies (R), June 11-15, 2014.

87. Summary of polls on American foreign policy reported at PublicAgenda.org, http://www.publicagenda.org/; and Benjamin I. Page with Marshall M. Bouton, *The Foreign Policy Disconnect: What Americans Want from Our Leaders But Don't Get* (Chicago: The University of Chicago Press, 2006).

88. This seems to be the case in foreign and national defense issues as well. See John H. Aldrich, Christopher Gelpi, Peter Feaver, Jason Reifler, and Kristin Tompson Sharp, "Foreign Policy and the Electoral Connection," *Annual Review of Political Science* 9 (2006), pp. 477–502.

89. For a summary of the evidence, see Erikson and Tedin, *American Public Opinion*, pp. 305–312.

90. Alan D. Monroe, "Consistency Between Public Preferences and National Policy Decisions," *American Politics Quarterly* 7 (January 1979), pp. 3–19; and Benjamin I. Page and Robert Y. Shapiro, "Effects of Public Opinion on Policy," *American Political Science Review* 77 (1983), pp. 175–190.

91. James A. Stimson, *Public Opinion in America: Moods, Cycles and Swings* (Boulder, CO: Westview Press, 1991).

92. Paul Burstein, "The Impact of Public Opinion on Public Policy: A Review and an Agenda," *Political Research Quarterly* 56, no. 1 (March 2003). See also Vincent L. Hutchings, *Public Opinion and Democratic Accountability: How Citizens Learn About Politics* (Princeton, NJ: Princeton University Press, 2003).

93. The various arguments for this are summarized in Benjamin I. Page, "The Semi-Sovereign Public," in *Navigating Public Opinion: Polls, Policy, and the Future of American Democracy*, ed. Jeff Manza, Fay Lomax Cook, and Benjamin I. Page (New York: Oxford University Press, 2002); and in Shapiro and Jacobs, "The Democratic Paradox," in Shapiro and Jacobs, *Oxford Handbook of American Public Opinion and the Media*.

94. For the argument that public opinion is largely a media creation, see W. Lance Bennett, "News Polls: Constructing an Engaged Public," in Shapiro and Jacobs, *Oxford Handbook of American Public Opinion and the Media*.

95. Lawrence R. Jacobs and Robert Y. Shapiro, *Politicians Don't Pander: Political Manipulation and the Loss of Democratic Responsiveness* (Chicago: The University of Chicago Press, 2000); Shapiro and Jacobs, "The Democratic Paradox," in Shapiro and Jacobs, *Oxford Handbook of American Public Opinion and the Media*; John Zaller, *The Nature and Origins of Mass Opinion* (New York: Cambridge University Press, 1992); and Wolfe, *Does American Democracy Still Work?*

96. W. Lance Bennett, Regina G. Lawrence, and Steven Livingston, *When the Press Fails: Political Power and the News*

*Media from Iraq to Katrina* (Chicago: The University of Chicago Press, 2007), ch. 5.

97. Page and Bouton, *The Foreign Policy Disconnect.* Also see Lawrence R. Jacobs and Benjamin I. Page, "Who Influences Foreign Policy," *American Political Science Review* 99, no. 1 (February 2005), pp. 107–124. On the elite–mass public disconnect also see Daniel W. Drezner, "The Realist Tradition in American Public Opinion," *Perspectives on Politics* 6, no. 1 (March 2008), pp. 51–70.

98. Bartels, *Unequal Democracy.*

99. Public opinion scholar Larry Bartels suggests that the 2001 tax cut (the largest in two decades, with tax relief going overwhelmingly to upper-income people) was supported by the public out of sheer ignorance and confusion about the impact of changes in the Tax Code. See Larry M. Bartels, "Homer Gets a Tax Cut: Inequality and Public Policy in the American Mind," *Perspectives on Politics* 3, no. 1 (March 2005), pp. 15–29. In the same issue (pp. 33–53), Jacob Hacker and Paul Pierson disagree; in their article "Abandoning the Middle: The Bush Tax Cuts and the Limits of Democratic Control," they suggest that manipulation and deception were prominent in the successful effort to raise public support for the 2001 tax cuts.

# 6

1. Material for this chapter opener is from W. Lance Bennett, Regina G. Lawrence, and Steven Livingston, *When the Press Fails: Political Power and the News Media from Iraq to Katrina* (Chicago: University of Chicago Press, 2007), pp. 13–45.

2. Adam Schiffer, "Blogswarms and Press Norms: News Coverage of the Downing Street Memos" (Washington, D.C.: paper presented at annual meetings of the American Political Science Association, August 31–September 3, 2006).

3. Bennett, Lawrence, and Livingston, *When the Press Fails*, p. 27.

4. Dana Milbank, "Democrats Play House to Rally Against the War," *The Washington Post* (June 6, 2005), p. 17.

5. Doris Graber, *Mass Media and American Politics*, 8th ed. (Washington, D.C.: Congressional Quarterly Press, 2010), pp. 16–19.

6. Joseph Cappella and Kathleen Hall Jamieson, *Spiral of Cynicism: The Press and the Public Good* (New York: Oxford University Press, 1997); Larry J. Sabato, Mark Stencel, and S. Robert Lichter, *Peepshow: Media and Politics in an Age of Scandal* (Boulder, CO: Rowman & Littlefield Publishers, 2000).

7. *The State of the News Media, 2008* (Washington, D.C.: Pew Research Center, Project for Excellence in Journalism, 2008).

8. For a description and a review of a group of thinkers celebrating the birth of a new journalism see Dean Starkman, "Confidence Game: the Limited Vision of the News Gurus," *Columbia Journalism Review* (November 9, 2011), at www.cjr.org, accessed February 20, 2012.

9. *The State of the News Media, 2014* (Washington, D.C.: Pew Research Center, Project for Excellence in Journalism, 2014). http://www.journalism.org/2014/03/26/state-of-the-news-media-2014-overview/; http://www.journalism.org/media-indicators/where-americans-get-news/.

10. For a description and a review of a group of thinkers celebrating the birth of a new journalism see Dean Starkman, "Confidence Game: the Limited Vision of the News Gurus," *Columbia Journalism Review* (November 9, 2011), at www.cjr.org, accessed February 20, 2012.

11. Andrew Kohut, *Internet's Broader Role in Campaign 2008* (Washington, D.C.: Pew Research Center, 2008).

12. Jordan Weissmann, "The Decline of Newspapers Hits a Stunning Milestone," *Slate*, April 28, 2014, http://www.slate.com/blogs/moneybox/2014/04/28/decline_of_newspapers_hits_a_milestone_print_revenue_is_lowest_since_1950.html.

13. Alex S. Jones, *Losing the News: The Future of the News That Feeds Democracy* (New York: Oxford University Press, 2009), pp. 180–181.

14. Rosenstiel and Mitchell, "Overview," *The State of the Media 2011;*" Pew Research Center, http://stateofthemedia.org/2011/overview-2/, and the Pew Research Center poll, release date February 7, 2012.

15. Bennett, Lawrence, and Livingston, *When the Press Fails*, pp. 57–59.

16. Matthew Hindman, *The Myth of Digital Democracy* (Princeton, NJ: Princeton University Press, 2009), ch. 6.

17. Rosenstiel and Mitchell, "Overview," *The State of the Media 2011.*

18. Graber, *Mass Media and American Politics,* pp. 36–37.

19. "Who Owns the News Media," *The State of the Media 2011,*" Pew Research Center.

20. "Who Owns What," *Columbia Journalism Review Online,* the Media," http://www.cjr.org/resources/ (updated and accessed, June 18, 2010).

21. "Read All About It," *The New Yorker* (August 13, 2007), p. 21.

22. W. Lance Bennett, *News: The Politics of Illusion* (New York: Pearson Longman, 2011), pp. 231–246, reviews the debate. The term *media monopoly* is from University of California–Berkeley journalism professor Ben Bagkikian's book, *Media Monopoly,* 5th ed. (Boston: Beacon Press, 1997).

23. Bennett, *News,* pp. 242–244.

24. Ibid., p. 241.

25. Jones, *Losing the News,* p. 7.

26. Doug Underwood, "Market Research and the Audience for Political News," in Doris Graber, Denis McQuail, and Pippa Norris, eds., *The Politics of News: The News of Politics* (Washington, D.C.: CQ Press, 1998), p. 171; also see Bennett, *News,* ch. 7.

27. Graber, *Mass Media and American Politics,* pp. 87–91.

28. Leon V. Sigal, *Reporters and Officials: The Organization and Politics of News Reporting* (Lexington, MA: Heath, 1973), p. 124.

29. Bennett, *News,* pp. 112–114; Steven Livingston and W. Lance Bennett, "Gatekeeping, Indexing, and Live Event News," *Political Communication,* 20, no. 4 (October–December 2003), pp. 363–380; Graber, *Mass Media and American Politics,* pp. 79–82.

30. Bennett, *News*, pp. 164–167.

31. Ibid., pp.127–134.

32. Mark Hertsgaard, *On Bended Knee* (New York: Farrar, Straus & Giroux, 1988), p. 5.

33. Anne E. Kornblut, "Administration Is Warned About Its News Videos," *The New York Times* (January 19, 2005), p. A9; Anne E. Kornblut, "Third Journalist Was Paid to Promote Bush Policies," *The New York Times* (January 29, 2005), p. A13; Charlie Savage and Alan Wirzbicki, "White House-Friendly Reporter Under Scrutiny," *The Boston Globe* (February 2, 2005), p. A1; "Source Watch," *Center for Media and Democracy* (http://www.prwatch.org/cmd/index.html), February 2005.

34. The Audit, "Learning Journalism Lessons of the Past," *Columbia Journalism Review* (posted June 5, 2009 at http://www.cjr.org/the_audit/learning_journalism_lessons_of.php).

35. David Murray, Joel Schwartz, and S. Robert Lichter, *It Ain't Necessarily So: How Media Make and Unmake the Scientific Picture of Reality* (Lanham, MD: Rowman & Littlefield Publishers, 2001), pp. 29–30.

36. Journalism.org (accessed, November 30, 2011).

37. Graber, *Mass Media and American Politics,* ch. 11. 42.

38. For the best analysis of why and how this happens and its unfortunate impact on the democratic process, see Bennett, Lawrence, and Livingston, *When the Press Fails.*

39. Matthew Gentzkow and Jesse M. Shapiro "What Drives Media Slant? Evidence from U.S. Daily Newspapers." *Econometrica* 78 (2010): 35–71.

40. Neal Hickey, "Is Fox News Fair?" *Columbia Journalism Review*, 31 (March/April 1998), pp. 30–35; David Weaver and G. Cleveland Wilhoit, *The American Journalist* (Mahwah, NJ: Lawrence Erlbaum, 1996); Graber, *Mass Media and American Politics*, pp. 86–89; and Erikson and Tedin, *American Public Opinion*, pp. 233–234.

41. Bennett, *News*, pp. 34–35; Graber, *Mass Media and American Politics*, pp. 76–77; Thomas E. Patterson and Wolfgang Donsbach, "News Decisions: Journalists as Partisan Actors," *Political Communications* 13 (October–December 1996), pp. 455–468.

42. Erikson and Tedin, *American Public Opinion*, pp. 238–239.

43. Matthew Gentzkow and Jesse M. Shapiro, "Media Bias and Reputation." *Journal of Political Economy* 114 (2006): 280-316; Gentzkow and Shapiro, "What Drives Media Slant?"

44. Lydia Saad, "TV Is Americans' Main Source of News," Gallup Poll, July 8, 2013, http://www.gallup.com/poll/163412 /americans-main-source-news.aspx

45. Carmen M. Reinhart and Kenneth Rogoff, *This Time Is Different: Eight Centuries of Financial Folly* (Princeton, NJ: Princeton University Press, 2009); John Cassidy, *How Markets Fail* (New York: Farrar, Straus, and Giroux, 2009).

46. John Zaller, *A Theory of Media Politics* (Chicago: University of Chicago Press, 2004).

47. Bennett, *News*, pp. 238–241; Graber, *Mass Media and American Politics*, pp. 97–100; Jones, *Losing the News*, p. 51; and James Fallows, "Learning to Love the (Shallow, Divisive, Unreliable) New Media," *The Atlantic Monthly* (April, 2011).

48. "Coverage of Jackson's Death Seen as Excessive" (Washington, D.C.: Pew Research Center, July 1, 2009).

49. Bennett, *News*, pp. 238–240.

50. Alan Wolfe, *Does American Democracy Still Work?* (New Haven, CT: Yale University Press, 2006), pp. 108–110.

51. Joseph N. Cappella and Kathleen Hall Jamieson, *Spiral of Cynicism: The Press and the Public Good* (Oxford University Press, 1997).

52. For a review of the literature on the subject, see Samuel L. Popkin, "Changing Media, Changing Politics," *Perspectives on Politics* (June 2006), pp. 327–341; Wolfe, *Does American Democracy Still Work?* ch. 5.

53. David L. Paletz, "The Media and Public Policy," in Doris Graber, Denis McQuail, and Pippa Norris, eds., *The Politics of News: The News of Politics* (Washington, D.C.: CQ Press, 1998).

54. Shanto Iyengar and Donald R. Kinder, *News That Matters* (Chicago: University of Chicago Press, 1987); also see Erikson and Tedin, *American Public Opinion*, pp. 247–248, for a review of the research on news media agenda setting.

55. W. Lance Bennett, "News Polls: Constructing an Engaged Public," in Robert Y. Shapiro and Lawrence R. Jacobs, eds., *The Oxford Handbook of American Public Opinion and the Media* (Oxford: Oxford University Press, 2011).

56. G. Ray Funkhauser, "The Issues of the Sixties: An Exploratory Study in the Dynamics of Public Opinion," *Public Opinion Quarterly* 37 (Spring 1973), pp. 62–75.

57. George C. Edwards, "Who Influences Whom? The President, Congress and the Media," *The American Political Science Review* 93 (June 1999), pp. 327–344.

58. Bennett, Lawrence, and Livingston, *When the Press Fails*.

59. On framing, see Thomas E. Nelson, "Issue Framing," in Shapiro and Jacobs, *The Oxford Handbook of American Public Opinion and the Media*.

60. Shanto Iyengar, *Is Anyone Responsible? How Television News Frames Political Issues* (Chicago: University of Chicago Press, 1991); Kathleen Hall Jamieson and Paul Waldman, *The Press Effect* (Washington, D.C.: CQ Press, 2002).

61. Paul M. Kellstedt, *The Mass Media and the Dynamics of American Racial Attitudes* (Cambridge, UK: Cambridge University Press, 2003).

62. Benjamin I. Page, Robert Y. Shapiro, and Glenn R. Dempsey, "What Moves Public Opinion?" *American Political Science Review* 81 (1987), pp. 23–43.

63. Joseph Cappella and Kathleen Jamieson, *Spiral of Cynicism: The Press and the Public Good* (New York: Oxford University Press, 1997); Stephen C. Craig, ed., *Broken Contract: Changing Relations Between Americans and Their Government* (Boulder, CO: Westview Press, 1996); Mark J. Hetherington, "Declining Trust and Shrinking Policy Agenda," in Robert Hart and Daron R. Shaw, eds., *Communications in U.S. Elections* (Lanham, MD: Rowman & Littlefield, 2001); Bennett, *News*; Thomas E. Patterson, "Bad News, Period," *PS* (March 1996), pp. 17–20.

64. John A. Ferejohn and James H. Kuklinski, eds., *Information and Democratic Processes* (Urbana, IL: University of Illinois Press, 1990); Benjamin I. Page, *Who Deliberates? Mass Media in Modern Democracy* (Chicago: University of Chicago Press, 1996).

## 7

1. Information for this story is from the following sources: David Barstow, Laura Dodd, James Glanz, Stephanie Sauo, and Ian Urbina, "Regulators Failed to Address Risks in Oil Rig Fail-Safe Device," *The New York Times* (June 20, 2010), p. 1; Ian Urbina, "Inspector General's Inquiry Faults Regulators," *The New York Times* (May 24, 2010), p. 1; "The Oil Well and the Damage Done," *The Economist Online* (June 17, 2010). www .economist.com/node/16381032; "How Did This Happen and Who Is to Blame," *Bloomberg/Businessweek* (June 14–20, 2010), pp. 60–64.

2. On the most recent deregulation movement in American politics and the thinking behind it, see Richard Harris and Sidney Milkis, *The Politics of Regulatory Change* (New York: Oxford University Press, 1989); John Cassidy, *How Markets Fail* (New York: Farrar, Straus and Giroux, 2009). Also see Marver Bernstein, *Regulation by Independent Commission* (Princeton, NJ: Princeton University Press, 1955); Grant McConnell, *Private Power and American Democracy* (New York: Vintage Books, 1966); James Buchanan and Gordon Tullock, "Polluters, Profits and Political Responses: Direct Control versus Taxes," *American Economic Review* 65 (1975), pp. 139–147; Murray Weidenbaum, *The Costs of Government Regulation of Business* (Washington, D.C.: Joint Economic Committee of Congress, 1978); Kevin P. Phillips, *The Politics of Rich and Poor: Wealth and the American Electorate in the Reagan Aftermath* (New York: Random House, 1990).

3. David Brooks, "Strengthen the Presidency," *New York Times*, December 12, 2013, http://www.nytimes.com/2013/12/13 /opinion/brooks-strengthen-the-presidency.html?_r=0. For other books on the growth and dominance of interest groups and how their effect on the governing process and the distribution of political power, see Francis Fukuyama, "The Decay of American Political Institutions," *American Interest*, December 8, 2013, http://www.the-american-interest.com /articles/2013/12/08/the-decay-of-american-political -institutions/; Jacob S. Hacker and Paul Pierson, *Winner -Take-All Politics* (New York: Simon and Schuster, 2010); and Hedrick Smith, *Who Stole the American Dream* (New York: Random House, 2012).

4. Jeffrey M. Berry and Clyde Wilcox, *The Interest Group Society*, 5th ed. (New York: Pearson Longman, 2009), pp. 4–6.

5. Alexander Hamilton, James Madison, and John Jay, *The Federalist Papers*, ed. Clinton Rossiter (New York: New American Library, 1961; originally published 1787–1788), No. 10.

6. The classics of the pluralist tradition include Arthur F. Bentley, *The Process of Government* (Chicago: The University of Chicago Press, 1908); David Truman, *The Governmental Process* (New York: Knopf, 1951); V. O. Key Jr., *Politics, Parties, and Pressure Groups* (New York: A. Crowell, 1952); Robert A.

Dahl, *A Preface to Democratic Theory* (Chicago: The University of Chicago Press, 1956); and Robert A. Dahl, *Who Governs?* (New Haven, CT: Yale University Press, 1961). For a summary treatment of the pluralist tradition and its thinking about interest groups, see Berry and Wilcox, *Interest Group Society,* ch. 1.

7. E. E. Schattschneider, *The Semi-Sovereign People* (New York: Holt, Rinehart & Winston, 1960).

8. John S. Ahlquist and Margaret Levi, *In the Interest of Others: Organizations and Social Activism* (Princeton, NJ: Princeton University Press, 2013); Michael Goldfield, *The Decline of Organized Labor in the United States* (Chicago: The University of Chicago Press, 1987); Edward S. Greenberg, Leon Grunberg, Sarah Moore, and Patricia B. Sikora, *Turbulence: Boeing and the State of American Workers and Managers* (New Haven, CT: Yale University Press, 2010); Robert B. Reich, *Supercapitalism: The Transformation of Business, Democracy, and Everyday Life* (New York: Knopf, 2007), pp. 80–86; Jake Rosenfeld, *What Unions No Longer Do* (Cambridge, MA: Harvard University Press, 2014), and David Vogel, *Fluctuating Fortunes: The Political Power of Business in America* (New York: Basic Books, 1989), ch. 8.

9. U.S. Department of Labor, Bureau of Labor Statistics, "Union Members Summary," news release, January 24, 2014, http://www.bls.gov/news.release/union2.nr0.htm.

10. Reich, *Supercapitalism.* A country's institutional and legal structure also matter. The proportion of workers in labor unions actually increased over the past several decades in the Scandinavian countries. See Lyle Scruggs and Peter Lange, "Where Have All the Workers Gone? Globalization, Institutions, and Union Density," *Journal of Politics* 64, no. 1 (February 2002), pp. 126–153.

11. Kenneth McLennan, "What Do Unions Do? A Management Perspective," in *What Do Unions Do? A Twenty-Year Perspective, ed.* James T. Bennett and Bruce E. Kaufman (New Brunswick, NJ: Transaction Publishers, 2007).

12. For the broader context in which the assault on labor unions has taken place, see Michael Goldfield and Amy Bromsen, "The Changing Landscape of US Unions in Historical and Theoretical Perspective," *Annual Review of Political Science* 16 (May 2013), pp. 231–257; and Rosenfeld, *What Unions No Longer Do.*

13. Jeffrey M. Berry, *Lobbying for the People* (Princeton, NJ: Princeton University Press, 1977), p. 7; Berry and Wilcox, *Interest Group Society,* pp. 24–26; and Berry, *New Liberalism,* p. 2.

14. Ronald Brownstein, *The Second Civil War: How Extreme Partisanship Has Paralyzed Washington and Polarized America* (New York: The Penguin Press, 2007), pp. 106–112; Berry, *Lobbying for the People;* David Broder, *Changing the Guard* (New York: Simon & Schuster, 1980); Hugh Heclo, "Issue Networks and the Executive Establishment," in *The New American Political System,* ed. Anthony King (Washington, DC: American Enterprise Institute, 1978); Kay Lehman Schlozman and John A. Tierney, *Organized Interests and American Democracy* (New York: Harper and Row, 1986); Jack L. Walker Jr., "The Origins and Maintenance of Interest Groups in America," *American Political Science Review* 77 (1983), pp. 390–406; and Theda Skocpol, *Diminished Democracy: From Membership to Management in American Civil Life* (Norman, OK: University of Oklahoma Press, 2003).

15. Skocpol, *Diminished Democracy;* Theda Skocpol, "Associations Without Members," *American Prospect* 10, no. 4 (July/August 1999), pp. 66–73; Theda Skocpol, "Voice and Inequality: The Transformation of American Civil Democracy," *Perspectives on Politics* 2, no. 1 (March 2004), pp. 3–20.

16. The numbers above are from Roger H. Davidson, Walter J. Oleszek, and Francis E. Lee, *Congress and Its Members,* 13th ed. (Washington, DC: CQ Press, 2014), p. 369.

17. Ibid., p. 370; and The Center for Responsive Politics, "Lobbying Database," OpenSecrets.org, 2013, http://www.opensecrets.org/lobby/, which is based on required reports to the House and Senate.

18. David Coen, Wyn Grant, and Graham Wilson, "Political Science Perspectives on Business and Government," in *The Oxford Handbook of Business and Government, ed.* David Coen, Wyn Grant, and Graham Wilson (Oxford, UK: Oxford University Press, 2010).

19. Reich, *Supercapitalism,* pp. 143–148; and Ken Auletta, "The Search Party," *New Yorker,* January 14, 2008, pp. 30–37.

20. Gary J. Andres, *Lobbying Reconsidered* (New York: Pearson Longman, 2009), ch. 4.

21. Reich, *Supercapitalism,* pp. 144–146.

22. Joseph E. Stiglitz, *The Price of Inequality: How Today's Divided Society Endangers Our Future* (New York: Norton, 2012), p. 196.

23. Truman, *Governmental Process.*

24. Jack L. Walker Jr., *Mobilizing Interest Groups in America* (Ann Arbor, MI: University of Michigan Press, 1991).

25. Jacob S. Hacker and Paul Pierson, "Winner-Take-All Politics: Public Policy, Political Organization, and the Precipitous Rise of Top Incomes in the United States," *Politics & Society vol. 38, no. 2* (2010), p. 172.

26. "Pork and Scandals," *The Economist* (January 28, 2006), p. 29.

27. From the watchdog group Public Citizen, reported in a news release dated April 19, 2010. Also see the Center for Public Integrity, "Annual Lobbying Reports," at www.publicintegrity.org.

28. Frank Rich, "The Rabbit Ragu Democrats," *New York Times,* October 3, 2009, http://www.nytimes.com/2009/10/04/opinion/04rich.html.

29. Mark A. Smith, *Business and Political Power: Public Opinion, Elections and Democracy* (Chicago: The University of Chicago Press, 2000). Also see Pepper D. Culpepper, *Quiet Politics and Business Power* (New York: Cambridge University Press, 2011), ch. 1.

30. Schattschneider, *Semi-Sovereign People.*

31. Robert Draper, "Inside the Power of the N.R.A.," *New York Times Magazine,* December 12, 2013, at http://www.nytimes.com/2013/12/15/magazine/inside-the-power-of-the-nra.html.

32. Frank R. Baumgartner, Jeffrey M. Berry, Marie Hojnacki, David C. Kimball, and Beth L. Leech, *Lobbying and Policy Change: Who Wins, Who Loses, and Why* (Chicago: The University of Chicago Press, 2009), pp. 150–155; and Davidson, Oleszek, and Lee, *Congress and Its Members,* pp. 377–386.

33. Berry and Wilcox, *Interest Group Society,* p. 138.

34. Peter Katel, "The Lobbying Boom," *CQ Researcher,* July 22, 2005, p. 1.

35. Berry and Wilcox, *Interest Group Society,* pp. 142–145.

36. Baumgartner et al., *Lobbying and Policy Change,* pp. 155–157.

37. Berry and Wilcox, *Interest Group Society,* pp. 118–120.

38. Schattschneider, *Semi-Sovereign People.*

39. Berry, *New Liberalism.*

40. Schlozman and Tierney, *Organized Interests,* p. 175.

41. Bruce Bimber, *Information and American Democracy* (New York: Cambridge University Press, 2003).

42. For a comprehensive examination of interest group involvement in campaigns, see Michael M. Franz, *Choices and Changes: Interest Groups in the Electoral Process* (Philadelphia: Temple University Press, 2008).

43. Schattschneider, *Semi-Sovereign People, p.* 2.

44. Timothy Werner and Graham Wilson, "Business Representation in Washington," in Coen, Grant, and Wilson, *Oxford Handbook of Business and Government.*

45. Berry, *Lobbying for the People;* Skocpol, "Voice and Inequality"; Dara Strolovitch, "Do Interest Groups Represent the Disadvantaged? Advocacy at the Intersections of Race, Class, and Gender," *Journal of Politics* 68, no. 4 (November 2006),

pp. 894–910; and Hacker and Pierson, "Winner-Take-All Politics," pp. 180–181.

46. Werner and Wilson, "Business Representation"; and Hacker and Pierson, *Winner-Take-All Politics*.

47. Jim Drinkard, "Drugmakers Go Further to Sway Congress," *USA Today,* April 26, 2005; and Leslie Wayne and Melody Petersen, "A Muscular Lobby Rolls Up Its Sleeves," *New York Times,* November 4, 2001.

48. Eric Dash and Nelson D. Schwartz, "As Reform Takes Shape, Some Relief on Wall St.," *New York Times,* May 23, 2010.

49. Adam Liptak, "Justices, 5–4, Reject Corporate Spending Limit," *New York Times,* January 21, 2010; "Unbound: The Supreme Court Undermines Convoluted Campaign Finance Rules," *Economist,* January 30, 2010.

50. For elaboration of the points made here and the supporting scholarly evidence, see Gregory C. Shaffer, "Law and Business," in Coen, Grant, and Wilson, *Oxford Handbook of Business and Government*, pp. 66–70.

51. Davidson, Oleszek, and Lee, *Congress and Its Members*, pp. 383–386.

52. "Money Talks, Congress Listens," *Boston Globe,* December 12, 1982.

53. Russ Choma, "The 2012 Election: Our Price Tag (Finally) for the Whole Ball of Wax," *OpenSecretsblog,* The Center for Responsive Politics, March 13, 2013, http://www.opensecrets.org/news/2013/03/the-2012-election-our-price-tag-fin.html.

54. "The Trillion-Dollar Tax Holiday," *Bloomberg Businessweek,* October 3–9, 2011, pp. 66–67.

55. The term "issue networks" is from Heclo, "Issue Networks." For a review and evaluation of the scholarly debate over sub-governments and issue networks, see Baumgartner et al., *Lobbying and Policy Change*, pp. 57–67. See also Berry and Wilcox, *Interest Group Society*, pp. 163–165; Berry, *New Liberalism*; Scott H. Ainsworth, *Analyzing Interest Groups: Group Influence on People and Policies (New York: Norton, 2002);* Allan J. Cigler, "Interest Groups," *Political Science: Looking to the Future,* ed. William Crotty, vol. 4 (Evanston, IL: Northwestern University Press, 1991); Robert H. Salisbury, John P. Heinz, Edward O. Laumann, and Robert L. Nelson, "Triangles, Networks, and Hollow Cores," and Mark P. Petracca, "The Rediscovery of Interest Group Politics," both in *The Politics of Interests: Interest Groups Transform,* ed. Mark P. Petracca (Boulder, CO: Westview Press, 1992); and Robert M. Stein and Kenneth Bickers, *Perpetuating the Pork Barrel: Policy Subsystems and American Democracy* (Cambridge, UK: Cambridge University Press, 1995).

56. Shaffer, "Law and Business," pp. 66–67.

57. Charles Lindblom, *Politics and Markets* (New York: Basic Books, 1977), p. 356.

58. Neil J. Mitchell, *The Conspicuous Corporation: Business, Public Policy and Representative Democracy* (Ann Arbor, MI: University of Michigan Press, 1997), p. 167.

59. Dan Clawson, Alan Neustadt, and Mark Weller, *Dollars and Votes* (Philadelphia: Temple University Press, 1998), pp. 26–28, 64–71, 97–99; and Berry and Wilcox, *Interest Group Society*, pp. 184–185.

60. Jeffrey A. Winters and Benjamin I. Page, "Oligarchy in the United States?," *Perspectives on Politics* 7, no. 4 (December 2009), pp. 731–751.

61. The full story of what has happened is told in Hacker and Pierson, "Winner-Take-All Politics."

62. Government Accounting Office, 2013.

63. Vogel, *Fluctuating Fortunes*, p. 291.

64. Coen, Grant, and Wilson, "Political Science: Perspectives on Business and Government," and Werner and Wilson, "Business Representation in Washington, D.C.," both in Coen, Grant, and Wilson, *Oxford Handbook of Business and Government*.

65. See, especially, Martin Gilens, *Affluence and Influence: Economic Inequality and Political Power in America* (New York

and Princeton, NJ: Russell Sage Foundation and Princeton University Press, 2012); and Martin Gilens and Benjamin I. Page, "Testing Theories of American Politics: Elites, Interest Groups, and Average Citizens," *Perspectives on Politics* (September 2014), Volume 12, number 3, in press.

66. Hacker and Pierson, *Winner-Take-All Politics*.

67. For a comparison of U.S. lobbying rules with those of other democracies, see Raj Chari, Gary Murphy, and John Hogan, "Regulating Lobbyists: A Comparative Analysis of the United States, Canada, Germany, and the European Union," *Political Quarterly* 78, no. 3 (July–September 2007), pp. 422–438.

# 8

1. James MacGregor Burns and Stewart Burns, *A People's Charter: The Pursuit of Rights in America* (New York: Knopf, 1991), ch. 5; E. McGlen and Karen O'Connor, *Women's Rights* (New York: Praeger, 1983), ch. 3; and Sarah M. Evans, *Born for Liberty: A History of Women in America* (New York: Free Press, 1997).

2. Woodrow Wilson, "Declaration of War Message to Congress, April 2, 1917," Records of the United States Senate, Record Group 46, National Archives, http://www.ourdocuments.gov/doc.php?flash=true&doc=61.

3. Sidney Tarrow, *Power in Movement* (New York: Cambridge University Press, 1998); David S. Meyer and Sidney Tarrow, eds., *The Social Movement Society* (Lanham, MD: Rowman & Littlefield Publishers, 1997); Doug McAdam, John D. McCarthy, and Mayer N. Zald, "Social Movements," in *Handbook of Sociology,* ed. Neil J. Smelser (Newbury Park, CA: Sage, 1994); Doug McAdam, *Political Process and the Development of Black Insurgency* (Chicago: The University of Chicago Press, 1982); and Doug McAdam, Sidney Tarrow, and Charles Tilly, *Dynamics of Contention* (Cambridge, UK: Cambridge University Press, 2001).

4. Sidney Tarrow, "Social Movements as Contentious Politics," *American Political Science Review* 90 (1996), pp. 853–866; Ronald R. Aminzade, Jack A. Goldstone, Doug McAdam, Elizabeth J. Perry, William H. Sewell Jr., and Sidney Tarrow, eds., *Silence and Voice in the Study of Contentious Politics* (New York: Cambridge University Press, 2001).

5. Our focus is on social movements in politics and their impact on public policies. For a review of the scholarly literature on social movements more broadly considered, see Edwin Amenta, Neal Caren, Elizabeth Chiarello, and Yang Su, "The Political Consequences of Social Movements," *Annual Review of Sociology* 36 (2010), pp. 287–307; Elizabeth A. Armstrong and Mary Bernstein, "Culture, Power, and Institutions: A Multi-Institutional Approach to Social Movements," *Sociological Theory* 26, no. 1 (March 2008), pp. 74–99.

6. Malcolm X was a complex and compelling character who changed political course during his active political lifetime. See Manning Marable, *Malcolm X: A Life of Redefinition* (New York: Viking Press, 2011).

7. CBS News telecast, February 16, 2003.

8. Jackie Smith, "Globalizing Resistance: The Battle of Seattle and the Future of Social Movements," *Mobilization: An International Journal* 6, no. 1 (2000), pp. 1–19.

9. Mark Penn, *Microtrends: The Small Forces Behind Tomorrow's Big Changes* (New York: Twelve, 2007), pp. 43–52.

10. Pew Research Center for the People & the Press, "Public Divided Over Occupy Wall Street," Pew Research Center poll, October 24, 2011, http://www.people-press.org/2011/10/24/public-divided-over-occupy-wall-street-movement/.

11. E. E. Schattschneider, *The Semi-Sovereign People* (New York: Holt, Rinehart & Winston, 1960), p. 142.

12. Richard Polenberg, *One Nation Divisible* (New York: Penguin Press, 1980), p. 268; and Craig A. Rimmerman, *From Identity*

to Politics: The Lesbian and Gay Movements in the United States (Philadelphia, PA: Temple University Press, 2002), ch. 1.

13. Frances Fox Piven, *When Movements Matter: How Ordinary People Change America* (Lanham, MD: Rowman & Littlefield, 2006).

14. Theodore J. Lowi, *The Politics of Disorder* (New York: Basic Books, 1971), p. 54.

15. Piven, *When Movements Matter*.

16. Aminzade et al., *Silence and Voice;* Meyer and Tarrow, *Social Movement Society;* McAdam, McCarthy, and Zald, "Social Movements"; and Sidney Tarrow, *Social Movements, Collective Action, and Politics* (New York: Cambridge University Press, 1994).

17. Neil J. Smelser, *Theory of Collective Behavior* (New York: Free Press, 1962); and Elaine Walker and Heather J. Smith, *Relative Deprivation: Specification, Development, and Integration* (Cambridge, UK: Cambridge University Press, 2001).

18. Barbara Sinclair Deckard, *The Women's Movement* (New York: Harper & Row, 1983); and Ethel Klein, *Gender Politics: From Consciousness to Mass Politics* (Cambridge, MA: Harvard University Press, 1984), ch. 2.

19. Donald P. Haider-Markel, "Creating Change—Holding the Line," in Ellen D. B. Riggle and Barry L. Tadlock, eds., *Gays and Lesbians in the Political Process* (New York: Columbia University Press, 1999).

20. Rimmerman, *From Identity to Politics*.

21. Jo Freeman, *The Politics of Women's Liberation* (New York: McKay, 1975); and Nancy Burns, "Gender: Public Opinion and Political Action," in *Political Science: The State of the Discipline,* ed. Ira Katznelson and Helen V. Milner (New York: Norton, 2002), pp. 472–476.

22. William Gamson, *The Strategy of Social Protest* (Homewood, IL: Dorsey, 1975); and John D. McCarthy and Mayer N. Zald, "Resource Mobilization and Social Movements: A Partial Theory," *American Journal of Sociology* 82 (1977), pp. 1212–1241.

23. Bruce Bimber, *Information and American Democracy: Technology and the Evolution of Political Power* (New York: Cambridge University Press, 2003), chs. 3 and 5.

24. Amenta, Caren, Chiarello, and Su, "Political Consequences," p. 299; McAdam, *Political Process;* Tarrow, *Social Movements;* and Peter K. Eisenger, "The Conditions of Protest Behavior in American Cities," *American Political Science Review* 67 (1973), pp. 11–28.

25. Frances Fox Piven and Richard A. Cloward, *Poor People's Movements: Why They Succeed, How They Fail* (New York: Vintage, 1979), ch. 3.

26. Klein, *Gender Politics*, pp. 90–91.

27. Pew Research Center for the People & the Press, "In Gay Marriage Debate, Both Supporters and Opponents See Legal Recognition as 'Inevitable,'" Pew Research Center, June 6, 2013, http://www.people-press.org/2013/06/06/in-gay -marriage-debate-both-supporters-and-opponents-see-legal -recognition-as-inevitable/.

28. Pew Research Center for the People & the Press, *"Trends in Political Values and Core Attitudes: 1987–2009,"* news release, May 21, 2009, http://www.people-press.org/files/legacy -pdf/517.pdf.

29. Pew Charitable Trust, Economic Mobility Project, 2011, http://www.pewstates.org/projects/economic-mobility -project-328061.

30. G. William Domhoff, *The Higher Circles* (New York: Random House, 1970); Edward S. Greenberg, *Capitalism and the American Political Ideal* (Armonk, NY: Sharpe, 1985); Gabriel Kolko, *The Triumph of Conservatism* (Chicago: Quadrangle, 1967); and James Weinstein, *The Corporate Ideal in the Liberal State* (Boston: Beacon Press, 1968).

31. Rimmerman, *From Identity to Politics*.

32. Piven, *When Movements Matter*.

33. Taylor Branch, *Parting the Waters: America in the King Years* (New York: Simon and Schuster, 1986); and William H. Chafe, *The Unfinished Journey: America Since World War II* (New York: Oxford University Press, 2003).

34. Amenta, Caren, Chiarello, and Su, "Political Consequences," pp. 294–298.

35. Jane Mansbridge, *Why We Lost the ERA* (Chicago: The University of Chicago Press, 1986).

36. Christian Davenport, Hank Johnson, and Carol Mueller, eds., *Mobilization and Repression* (Minneapolis: University of Minnesota Press, 2005).

37. See David Caute, *The Great Fear* (New York: Simon & Schuster, 1978); Robert Justin Goldstein, *Political Repression in Modern America* (Cambridge, MA: Schenkman, 1978); and Alan Wolfe, *The Seamy Side of Democracy* (New York: McKay, 1978).

38. Greenberg, *Capitalism and the American Political Ideal*.

39. *National Roster of Black Elected Officials, Fact Sheet* (Washington, DC: Joint Center for Political and Economic Studies, 2013), p. 1.

40. Desmond S. King and Rogers M. Smith, *Still a House Divided: Race and Politics in Obama's America* (Princeton, NJ: Princeton University Press, 2011), pp. 268–280; and "A Dream Examined," *New York Times*, August 23, 2013, http:// www.nytimes.com/interactive/2013/08/24/us/a-dream -examined.html?action=click&module=Search&region=search Results%230&version=&url=http%3A%2F%2Fquery.nytimes .com%2Fsearch%2Fsitesearch%2F%23%2FDream%2Bexamined %2F&_r=0.

41. Chafe, *Unfinished Journey*, pp. 430–468; Deckard, *Women's Movement*; Klein, *Gender Politics*, ch. 2; Freeman, *Politics of Women's Liberation*. See also debates on the relative progress of women in the United States collected in Dorothy McBride Stetson, *Women's Rights in the United States: Policy Debates and Gender Roles* (London: Routledge, 2004).

42. "By the Numbers," Catalyst.org, 2013, www.catalyst.org /knowledge/by-the-numbers.

# 9

1. Andrew Austin, "The Debt Limit: History and Recent Increases (RL31967)," CRS Report for Congress (Washington, DC: Congressional Research Service, April 29, 2008); and James Surowiecki, "Smash the Ceiling," *New Yorker,* August 1, 2011.

2. Matt Bai, "Obama v. Boehner: Who Killed the Debt Deal?" *New York Times Magazine,* March 28, 2012; and Carl Hulse and Helene Cooper, "Obama and Leaders Reach Debt Deal," *New York Times,* July 31, 2011.

3. "American Idiocy," *Economist,* August 13, 2011, p. 38.

4. "Special Report: How Washington Took the U.S. to the Brink," Reuters, August 4, 2011.

5. Jonathan Weisman and Ashley Parker, "Republicans Back Down, Ending Crisis over Shutdown and Debt Limit," *New York Times,* October 16, 2013.

6. Ronald Brownstein, *The Second Civil War: How Extreme Partisanship Has Paralyzed Washington and Polarized America* (New York: Penguin Press, 2007); Nicol C. Rae, "Be Careful What You Wish For: The Rise of Responsible Parties in American National Politics," *Annual Reviews, Political Science* 10 (2007), pp. 169–191; and Thomas E. Mann and Norman J. Ornstein, *It's Even Worse Than It Looks: How the American Constitutional System Collided with the New Politics of Extremism,* (New York: Basic Books, 2012).

7. Geoffrey C. Layman, Thomas M. Carsey, and Juliana Menasce Horowitz, "Party Polarization in American Politics: Characteristics, Causes, and Consequences," *Annual Review*

*of Political Science* 9 (2006): 83–110; and Sean M. Theriault, *Party Polarization in Congress* (New York: Cambridge University Press, 2008).

8. E. E. Schattschneider, *Party Government* (New York: Holt, Rinehart & Winston, 1942), p. 208.

9. Marjorie Randon Hershey, *Party Politics in America*, 14th ed. (New York: Pearson Longman, 2011), p. 7.

10. Robert A. Dahl, *On Democracy* (New Haven, CT: Yale University Press, 1998); Hershey, *Party Politics*, pp. 1–2; and E. E. Schattschneider, *Party Government* (Portsmouth, NH: Praeger, 1977), p. 208. See also Jonathan White and Lea Ypi, "On Partisan Political Justification," *American Political Science Review* 105, no. 2 (May 2011).

11. Schattschneider, *Party Government*, p. 208. See also White and Ypi, "On Partisan Political Justification."

12. See Hershey, *Party Politics*, ch. 1; and A. James Reichley, *The Life of the Parties: A History of American Political Parties* (Lanham, MD: Rowman & Littlefield, 2002), ch. 1.

13. Steven J. Rosenstone and John Mark Hansen, *Mobilization, Participation, and Democracy in America* (New York: Macmillan, 1993).

14. E. E. Schattschneider, *The Semi-Sovereign People* (New York: Holt, Rinehart & Winston, 1960).

15. John H. Aldrich and John D. Griffin, "Parties, Elections, and Democratic Politics," in *The Oxford Handbook of American Elections and Political Behavior,* ed. Jan E. Leighley (Oxford, UK: Oxford University Press, 2010). See also John H. Aldrich, *Why Parties? A Second Look* (Chicago: The University of Chicago Press, 2011).

16. The classic statement on electoral rules is from Maurice Duverger, *Political Parties* (New York: Wiley, 1954).

17. Ibid.

18. Marjorie Randon Hershey, "Like a Bee: Election Law and the Survival of Third Parties," in *Election Law and Electoral Politics,* ed. Matthew J. Streb (Boulder, CO: Lynn Rienner, 2004); and Hershey, *Party Politics*, pp. 37–38.

19. Much of this discussion is drawn from Steven J. Rosenstone, Roy L. Behr, and Edward H. Lazarus, *Third Parties in America*, 2nd ed. (Princeton, NJ: Princeton University Press, 1996). See also Paul S. Herrnson and John C. Green, *Multiparty Politics in America* (Lanham, MD: Rowman & Littlefield, 2002); Hershey, *Party Politics,* pp. 37–40; John F. Bibby and L. Sandy Maisel, *Two Parties or More?* (Boulder, CO: Westview Press, 2003); and Shigeo Hirano and James M. Snyder Jr., "The Decline of Third-Party Voting in the United States, *Journal of Politics* 69, no. 1 (February 2007), pp. 1–16.

20. Ibid.

21. On realignment, see Walter Dean Burnham, *Critical Elections and the Mainsprings of American Politics* (New York: Norton, 1970); Jerome Clubb, William H. Flanigan, and Nancy H. Zingale, *Partisan Realignment* (Newbury Park, CA: Sage, 1980); V. O. Key Jr., "A Theory of Critical Elections," *Journal of Politics* 17 (1955), pp. 3–18; Hershey, *Party Politics*, ch. 7; James L. Sundquist, *Dynamics of the Party System* (Washington, DC: Brookings Institution Press, 1973); and Samuel Merrill, Bernard Grofman, and Thomas L. Brunell, "Cycles in American National Electoral Politics, 1854–2006," *American Political Science Review* 102, no. 1 (February 2008), pp. 1–17. For the special place that war has played in altering parties and party systems, see David R. Mayhew, "Wars and American Politics," *Perspectives on Politics* 3, no. 3 (September 2005), pp. 473–493.

22. John Aldrich and Richard Niemi, "The Sixth American Party System," in *Broken Contract: Changing Relationships Between Americans and Their Government, ed.* Stephen C. Craig (Boulder, CO: Westview Press, 1996); and Walter J. Stone and Ronald B. Rapoport, "It's Perot Stupid! The Legacy of the 1992 Perot Movement in the Major-Party System, 1994–2000," *PS: Political Science and Politics* XXXIV, no. 1 (March 2001), pp. 49–56.

23. Larry M. Bartels, *Unequal Democracy: The Political Economy of the Guided Age* (New York and Princeton, NJ: Russell Sage Foundation and Princeton University Press, 2008); Thomas Byrne Edsall and Mary D. Edsall, *Chain Reaction: The Impact of Race, Rights and Taxes on American Politics* (New York: Norton, 1991); Stanley B. Greenberg, *Middle Class Dreams: The Politics and Power of the New American Majority* (New Haven, CT: Yale University Press, 1996); and Desmond S. King and Rogers M. Smith, *Still a House Divided: Race and Politics in Obama's America* (Princeton, NJ: Princeton University Press, 2011).

24. Brownstein, *Second Civil War*, pp. 93–136.

25. Larry Sabato, *The Party's Just Begun* (Glenview, IL: Scott, Foresman, 1988); Sundquist, *Dynamics of the Party System;* Martin P. Wattenberg, *The Decline of American Political Parties* (Cambridge, MA: Harvard University Press, 1994); Greenberg, *Middle Class Dreams;* and Everett C. Ladd, "The 1994 Congressional Elections," *Political Science Quarterly* 110 (1995), pp. 1–23.

26. Earl Black and Merle Black, *Divided America: The Ferocious Power Struggle in American Politics* (New York: Simon & Schuster, 2007); Stanley B. Greenberg, *The Two Americas: Our Current Political Deadlock and How to Break It* (New York: Thomas Dunn Books, 2004); Geoffrey C. Layman, Thomas M. Carsey, and Juliana Menasce Horowitz, "Party Polarization in American Politics: Characteristics, Causes, and Consequences," *Annual Reviews: Political Science* 9 (2006), pp. 83–110; and Brownstein, *Second Civil War*, pp. 137–174.

27. Morris P. Fiorina, *Disconnect: The Breakdown of Representation in American Politics* (Norman: University of Oklahoma Press, 2009). Alan Abramowitz disagrees with Fiorina, arguing that the politically attentive mass public is deeply polarized. See his *The Disappearing Center: Engaged Citizens, Polarization, and American Democracy* (New Haven, CT: Yale University Press, 2010). Bill Bishop joins Abramowitz's position in his book *The Big Sort: Why the Clustering of Like-Minded Americans Is Tearing Us Apart* (New York: Houghton Mifflin, 2008).

28. Alan I. Abramowitz and Kyle L. Saunders, "Is Polarization a Myth?" *Journal of Politics* 70, no. 2 (2008), pp. 542–555.

29. Hershey, *Party Politics*, ch. 6.

30. On the "great sorting out" of groups and regions along party lines in the United States, see Brownstein, *Second Civil War*, ch. 6.

31. R. Florida, *The Rise of the Creative Class* (New York: Basic Books, 2002); R. Florida, *The Flight of the Creative Class* (New York: Harper Business, 2005); and D. Chinni and J. Gimpel, *Our Patchwork Nation* (New York: Penguin, 2011).

32. Hershey, *Party Politics,* ch. 4.

33. L. Sandy Maisel, *American Political Parties and Elections: A Very Short Introduction* (New York: Oxford University Press, 2007), pp. 66–68.

34. Hershey, *Party Politics*, pp. 115–116.

35. J. A. Schlesinger, "The New American Political Party," *American Political Science Review* 79 (1985), pp. 1152–1169; and Aldrich, *Why Parties?*

36. David Menefee-Libey, *The Triumph of Campaign-Centered Politics* (New York: Chatham House Publishers, 2000); and Hershey, *Party Politics*, pp. 75–78.

37. Stephen Doyle, "The Very, Very Personal Is the Political," *New York Times Magazine*, February 15, 2004, pp. 42–47.

38. Maisel, *American Political Parties*, pp. 63–64.

39. Ibid., pp. 65–67.

40. Roger H. Davidson, Walter J. Oleszek, and Frances E. Lee, *Congress and Its Members*, 13th ed. (Washington, DC: CQ Press, 2012), pp. 59, 168.

41. Norman Schofield and Gary Miller, "Elections and Activist Coalitions in the United States," *American Journal of Political Science* 51, no. 3 (July 2007), pp. 518–531.

42. Nicholas Confessore, "Outside Groups Eclipsing G.O.P. as Hub of Campaigns," *New York Times,* November 1, 2011.

43. Hershey, *Party Politics*, p. 289.

44. Data Trend, Party Identification, Pew Research Center, http://www.pewresearch.org/data-trend/political-attitudes/party-identification/.

45. Greenberg, *Two Americas*; Morris P. Fiorina, "Parties, Participation, and Representation in America," in *Political Science: The State of the Discipline,* ed. Ira Katznelson and Helen V. Milner (New York: Norton, 2002); Morris P. Fiorina, *Culture War? The Myth of a Polarized America* (New York: Pearson Longman, 2005), ch. 8; Hershey, *Party Politics*, ch. 15; Marc J. Hetherington, "Resurgent Mass Partisanship: The Role of Elite Polarization," *American Political Science Review* 95, no. 1 (September 2001), pp. 619–632; and Gerald Pomper, "Parliamentary Government in the United States," in *The State of the Parties,* ed. J. C. Green and D. M. Shea (Lanham, MD: Rowman & Littlefield, 1999).

46. Brownstein, *Second Civil War*, p. 12.

47. Lewis L. Gould, *Grand Old Party: A History of the Republicans* (New York: Random House, 2003); "When American Politics Turned European," *Economist,* October 25, 2005, p. 74; Nils Gilman, "What the Rise of the Republicans as America's First Ideological Party Means for the Democrats," *Forum* 2, no. 1 (2004), pp. 1–4; Brownstein, *Second Civil War*; and Layman, Carsey, and Horowitz, "Party Polarization."

48. American National Election Studies, 2013, Preliminary Release of the ANES 2012 Time Series Study, http://electionstudies.org/studypages/anes_timeseries_2012/anes2012TS_codebook.pdf.

49. American National Election Studies, 2008.

50. Ibid.

51. Pew Center for the People & the Press, "Trends in Political Values and Core Attitudes: 1987–2012, Section 9: Trends in Party Affiliation." Note that Pew reports percentages as a portion of the total population, but the text reports them as a percentage of independents.

52. Pew Research Center for the People & the Press, "Trends in Political Values and Core Attitudes: 1987–2009," news release, May 21, 2009, http://www.people-press.org/files/legacy-pdf/517.pdf.

53. Alan D. Monroe, "American Party Platforms and Public Opinion," *American Journal of Political Science* 27 (February 1983), p. 35; Layman, Carsey, and Horowitz, "Party Polarization"; and Maisel, *American Political Parties*, pp. 73–76.

54. *New York Times*/CBS News, "Republican Convention Delegate Poll," news release, July 18, 2004, and *New York Times*/CBS News, "Democratic Convention Delegate Poll," news release, August 24, 2004.

55. Hershey, *Party Politics*, pp. 289–293.

56. Ron Suskind, *Confidence Men: Wall Street, Washington, and the Education of a President* (New York: HarperCollins, 2011).

57. James MacGregor Burns, *Deadlock of Democracy* (Englewood Cliffs, NJ: Prentice Hall, 1967).

58. On the pernicious effects of divided government, see Benjamin Ginsberg and Martin Shefter, *Politics by Other Means: The Declining Significance of Elections in America* (New York: Basic Books, 1990). For the contrary view, see Morris P. Fiorina, *Divided Government* (New York: Macmillan, 1992); Gary Jacobson, *The Electoral Origins of Divided Government: Competition in U.S. House Elections* (Boulder, CO: Westview Press, 1990); David R. Mayhew, *Divided We Govern: Party Control, Lawmaking, and Investigations, 1946–1990* (New Haven, CT: Yale University Press, 1991); and Layman, Carsey, and Horowitz, "Party Polarization," pp. 88–101.

59. Jason M. Roberts and Steven S. Smith, "Procedural Contexts, Party Strategy, and Conditional Party Voting in the U.S. House of Representatives," *American Journal of Political Science* 47 (2003), pp. 305–317; Douglas Hibbs, *The American Political Economy* (Cambridge, MA: Harvard University Press, 1987); Dennis P. Quinn and Robert Shapiro, "Business Political Power: The Case of Taxation," *American Political Science*

*Review* 85 (1991), pp. 851–874; and Kenneth N. Bickers and Robert M. Stein, "The Congressional Pork Barrel in a Republican Era," *Journal of Politics* 62, no. 4 (November 2000), pp. 1070–1086.

60. Donald Green, Bradley Palmquist, and Eric Schickler, *Partisan Hearts and Minds: Political Parties and the Social Identity of Voters* (New Haven, CT: Yale University Press, 2002); Robert S. Erikson and Kent L. Tedin, *American Public Opinion* (New York: Pearson Longman, 2011), pp. 85–89; Hershey, *Party Politics*, pp. 118–136; and Pew Research Center for the People & the Press, "Trends," pp. 97–110.

61. Data are from 2004, reported in Alan Abramowitz and Kyle Saunders, "Culture War in America: Myth or Reality," *Forum* 3, no. 2 (2005), pp. 1–22.

62. Bruce E. Keith, David B. Magleby, Candice J. Nelson, Elizabeth Orr, Mark C. Westlye, and Raymond E. Wolfinger, *The Myth of the Independent Voter* (Berkeley, CA: University of California Press, 1992). See also Hershey, *Party Politics*, pp. 113–115.

63. "Trends in Political Values and Core Attitudes: 1987–2009," p. 11.

64. Brownstein, *Second Civil War*; Rae, "Be Careful What You Wish For"; and Layman, Carsey, and Horowitz, "Party Polarization."

# 10

1. For a summary of a wide range of polls on matters related to the 2012 presidential election, access http://www.pollingreport.com. On the superiority of polls to the assertions of pundits of various political stripes, see Michael Cooper, "Election Result Proves a Victory for Pollsters and Other Data Devotees," *New York Times,* November 7, 2012. For consideration of the many factors that may have affected the 2012 presidential election, see Maggie Haberman, "9 takeaways from the 2012 election," Politico, November 6, 2012, http://www.politico.com/news/stories/1112/83370.html; Maggie Haberman, "The Takeaways," *Burns & Haberman* (blog), Politico, November 7, 2012, http://www.politico.com/blogs/burns-haberman/2012/11/the-takeaways-148829.html; Peter Hamby, "Analysis: Why Romney Lost," CNN Politics, CNN, November 7, 2012, http://www.cnn.com/2012/11/07/politics/why-romney-lost/; Adam Liptak, "The Vanishing Battleground," *New York Times,* November 3, 2012; and Paul Taylor and D'Vera Cohn, "A Milestone En Route to a Majority Minority Nation," Pew Research Social & Demographic Trends, Pew Research Center, November 7, 2012, http://www.pewsocialtrends.org/2012/11/07/a-milestone-en-route-to-a-majority-minority-nation/.

2. For further discussion, see Benjamin I. Page, *Choices and Echoes in Presidential Elections: Rational Man and Electoral Democracy* (Chicago: The University of Chicago Press, 1978), ch. 2; Robert A. Dahl, *Democracy and Its Critics* (New Haven, CT: Yale University Press, 1989); Robert A. Dahl, *On Democracy* (New Haven, CT: Yale University Press, 1998); and Hans Gersbach, *Designing Democracy* (New York: Springer Publishers, 2005).

3. See Russell Muirhead, "A Defense of Party Spirit," *Perspectives on Politics* 4, no. 4 (December 2006), pp. 713–727; Austin Ranney, *The Doctrine of Responsible Party Government: Its Origins and Present State* (Urbana: University of Illinois Press, 1962); E. E. Schattschneider, *Party Government* (New York: Holt, Rinehart & Winston, 1942); and Jonathan White and Lea Ypi, "On Partisan Political Justification," *American Political Science Review* 105, no. 2 (May 2011), pp. 381–396.

4. Marjorie Randon Hershey, *Party Politics in America*, 14th ed. (New York: Pearson Longman, 2011), pp. 263–269.

5. Nicol C. Rae, "Be Careful What You Wish For: The Rise of Responsible Parties in American National Politics," *Annual Reviews, Political Science* 10 (2007), pp. 169–191

6. Keith Poole and Howard Rosenthal, *Congress: A Political-Economic History of Roll Call Voting* (New York: Oxford University Press, 1997).

7. Anthony Downs, *An Economic Theory of Democracy* (New York: Harper & Row, 1957); and Otto Davis, Melvin Hinich, and Peter Ordeshook, "An Expository Development of a Mathematical Model of the Electoral Process," *American Political Science Review* 64 (1970), pp. 426–448.

8. See V. O. Key Jr., *Public Opinion and American Democracy* (New York: Knopf, 1961); and Morris P. Fiorina, *Retrospective Voting in American National Elections* (Cambridge, MA: Harvard University Press, 1981).

9. Gary C. Jacobson, "The 2008 Presidential and Congressional Elections," *Political Science Quarterly* 124, no. 1 (Spring 2009), pp. 1–30.

10. David Stout, "Study Finds Ballot Problems Are More Likely for Poor," *New York Times,* July 9, 2001; and Katharine Q. Seelye, "Study Says 2000 Election Missed Millions of Votes," *New York Times,* August, 10, 2001.

11. L. Sandy Maisel, *American Political Parties and Elections: A Very Short Introduction* (New York: Oxford University Press, 2007), p. 5.

12. Mary Fitzgerald, "Greater Convenience but Not Greater Turnout: The Impact of Alternative Voting Methods on Electoral Participation in the United States," *American Politics Research* 33, no. 6 (November 2005), pp. 842–867.

13. Chilton Williamson, *American Suffrage* (Princeton, NJ: Princeton University Press, 1960), pp. 223, 241, 260; and Gordon S. Wood, *The Idea of America* (New York: Penguin Press, 2011), ch. 6. See also Hershey, *Party Politics,* pp. 140–144, and Maisel, *American Political Parties,* pp. 47–51.

14. See John Hope Franklin, *From Slavery to Freedom* (New York: Knopf, 1967); Leon Litwack, *North of Slavery* (Chicago: The University of Chicago Press, 1961); Alexander Keyssar, *The Right to Vote: The Contested History of Democracy in the United States* (New York: Basic Books, 2001); and Wood, *Idea of America,* pp. 209–210.

15. Walter Dean Burnham, "The Turnout Problem," in A. James Reichley, ed., *Elections, American Style* (Washington, D.C.: Brookings Institution, 1987), pp. 113–114.

16. For a brief but excellent discussion of the scholarly literature on the cause of low voting turnout, see Daniel M. Shea, *Let's Vote: The Essentials of the American Electoral Process* (New York: Longman, 2013), pp. 169–178; Kay Lehman Schlozman, "Citizen Participation in America: What Do We Know? Why Do We Care?," in *Political Science: The State of the Discipline,* ed. Ira Katznelson and Helen V. Milner (New York: Norton, 2002), pp. 439–443; Martin P. Wattenberg, *Where Have All the Voters Gone?* (Cambridge, MA: Harvard University Press, 2002); and André Blais, "What Affects Turnout?," *Annual Review of Political Science* 9 (2006), pp. 111–125.

17. Robert D. Brown, "Voter Registration," in *The Oxford Handbook of American Elections and Political Behavior,* ed. Jan E. Leighley (Oxford, UK: Oxford University Press, 2010).

18. Peverill Squire, Raymond E. Wolfinger, and David P. Glass, "Residential Mobility and Voter Turnout," *American Political Science Review* 81 (1987), pp. 45–65.

19. U.S. Census Bureau, 2007; and Hershey, *Party Politics,* p. 140.

20. 17. Robert D. Brown, "Voter Registration."

21. Ari Berman, "The GOP War on Voting," *Rolling Stone,* August 30, 2011, http://www.rollingstone.com/politics/news/the-gop-war-on-voting-20110830; and Wendy R. Weiser and Lawrence Norden, *Voting Law Changes in 2012* (New York: The Brennan Center, New York University School of Law, 2011).

22. Wattenberg, *Where Have All the Voters Gone?,* ch. 6.

23. Ronald Brownstein, *The Second Civil War: How Extreme Partisanship Has Paralyzed Washington and Polarized America* (New York: Penguin, 2007), ch. 6; Roger H. Davidson, Walter J. Oleszek, and Frances E. Lee, *Congress and Its Members,*

11th ed. (Washington, D.C.: CQ Press, 2008), pp. 62–65, 108–110; Maisel, *American Political Parties and Elections,* pp. 126–130; Steven S. Smith, Jason M. Roberts, and Ryan J. Vander Wielen, *The American Congress,* 5th ed. (New York: Cambridge University Press, 2007), pp. 68–78; Alan Wolfe, *Does Democracy Still Work?* (New Haven, CT: Yale University Press, 2006), pp. 50–56.

24. "House Members Who Won with 55 Percent or Less in 2008," The Cook Political Report, http://www.cookpolitical.com/sites/default/files/55andunder_0.pdf, November 10, 2008.

25. Steven J. Rosenstone and John Mark Hansen, *Mobilization, Participation, and Democracy in America* (New York: Macmillan, 1993).

26. Alan S. Gerber and Donald M. Green, "The Effects of Canvassing, Telephone Calls, and Direct Mail on Voter Turnout," *American Political Science Review* 94 (2000), pp. 653–663.

27. Shea, *Let's Vote,* pp. 169–178 for a summary of the research on voter turnout.

28. Sidney Verba, Kay Lehman Schlozman, and Henry E. Brady, *Voice and Equality: Civic Volunteerism in American Politics* (Cambridge, MA: Harvard University Press, 1995); Sidney Verba and Norman H. Nie, *Participation in America* (New York: Harper & Row, 1972); and Hershey, *Party Politics,* pp. 150–153.

29. Thom File, *The Diversifying Electorate—Voting Rates by Race and Hispanic Origin in 2012 (and Other Recent Elections)* (Washington, DC: U.S. Census Bureau, May 2013), http://www.census.gov/prod/2013pubs/p20-568.pdf.

30. John A. Garcia, "Latinos and Political Behavior," in Leighley, *Oxford Handbook of American Elections and Political Behavior.*

31. Adam Nagourney, "Latino Growth Not Fully Felt at Voting Booth," *New York Times* (June 9, 2012), p. 1.

32. John B. Judis and Ruy Teixeira, *The Emerging Democratic Majority* (New York: Scribner's, 2004).

33. Mark Hugo Lopez and Paul Taylor, "Dissecting the 2008 Electorate: Most Diverse in U.S. History," Pew Research Hispanic Trends Project, Pew Research Center, April 30, 2009, p. 6.

34. Susan A. MacManus, *Young v. Old* (Boulder, CO: Westview Press, 1996), ch. 2; and Martin P. Wattenberg, *Is Voting for Young People?* (New York: Pearson, 2012).

35. Margaret M. Conway, *Political Participation in the United States,* 3rd ed. (Washington, DC: CQ Press, 2000), p. 37; and Julie Dolan, Melissa Deckman, and Michele L. Swers, *Women and Politics: Paths to Power and Political Influence* (New York: Pearson Longman, 2011), pp. 55–72.

36. E. J. Dionne, "If Nonvoters Had Voted: Same Winner, but Bigger," *New York Times,* November 21, 1988.

37. Sidney Verba, Kay Lehman Schlozman, Henry E. Brady, and Norman H. Nie, "Citizen Activity: Who Participates? What Do They Say?," *American Political Science Review* 87 (1993), pp. 303–318; Robert S. Erikson and Kent L. Tedin, *American Public Opinion* (New York: Pearson Longman, 2007), ch. 7; and Eric Shiraev and Richard Sobel, *People and Their Opinions* (New York: Pearson Longman, 2006), chs. 7–9.

38. Wattenberg, *Is Voting for Young People?.*

39. Martin Gilens, "Preference Gaps and Inequality in Representation," *PS* (April 2009), pp. 331–335; Lawrence R. Jacobs and Theda Skocpol, eds., *Inequality and American Democracy: What We Know and What We Need to Learn* (New York: Russell Sage Foundation, 2005); Larry M. Bartels, Hugh Heclo, Rodney E. Hero, and Lawrence R. Jacobs, "Inequality and American Governance," *Perspectives on Politics* 2, no. 4 (December 2004), pp. 651–668; and Larry M. Bartels, *Unequal Democracy: The Political Economy of the Gilded Age* (New York and Princeton, NJ: The Russell Sage Foundation and Princeton University Press, 2008).

40. Jacob Hacker and Paul Pierson, *Off Center* (New Haven, CT: Yale University Press, 2005); Larry M. Bartels, "Is the Water

Rising?: Reflections on Inequality and American Democracy," *PS* (January 2006), pp. 39–42; and Kay Lehman Schlozman, "On Inequality and Political Voice," *PS* (January 2006), pp. 55–57.

41. David D. Kirkpatrick, "Wealth Is a Common Factor Among 2008 Hopefuls," *New York Times,* May 17, 2007.

42. Nelson W. Polsby and Aaron Wildavsky, *Presidential Elections*, 12th ed. (Lanham, MD: Rowman & Littlefield, 2007), pp. 53–55, 57.

43. Hershey, *Party Politics*, pp. 181–182.

44. Stephen J. Wayne, *The Road to the White House* (Belmont, CA: Wadsworth, 2007); and Hershey, *Party Politics in America*, p. 181.

45. Larry Bartels, *Presidential Primaries and the Dynamics of Public Choice* (Princeton, NJ: Princeton University Press, 1988); John H. Aldrich, *Before the Convention* (Chicago: The University of Chicago Press, 1980); and Stephen J. Wayne, *The Road to the White House.*

46. Jeremy W. Peters, "Campaigns Blitz 9 Swing States in a Battle of Ads," *New York Times,* June 8, 2012.

47. Polsby and Wildavsky, *Presidential Elections*, pp. 143–147.

48. John G. Geer, *In Defense of Negativity* (Chicago: The University of Chicago Press, 2006); Ken Goldstein and Paul Freedman, "Campaign Advertising and Voter Turnout: New Evidence for a Stimulation Effect," *Journal of Politics* 64 (2002), pp. 721–740; and Caterina Gennaioli, "Go Divisive or Not: How Political Campaigns Affect Turnout" (Working Paper 3298, London School of Economics and Political Science, London, UK, December 30, 2010).

49. Anna Greenberg, "Targeting and Electoral Gaps," in *Beyond Red State, Blue State: Electoral Gaps in the Twenty-First Century American Electorate,* ed. Laura R. Olson and John C. Green (Upper Saddle River, NJ: Pearson Prentice Hall, 2009); David B. Magleby, "How Barack Obama Changed Presidential Campaigns," in *Obama: Year One,* ed. Thomas R. Dye, George C. Edwards, Morris P. Fiorina, Edward S. Greenberg, Paul C. Light, David B. Magleby, and Martin P. Wattenberg (New York: Pearson, 2010). See also D. Sunshine Hillygus and Todd G. Shields, *The Persuadable Voter: Wedge Issues in Presidential Campaigns* (Princeton, NJ: Princeton University Press, 2008).

50. Federal Election Commission, 2009.

51. Jonathan D. Salant, "Why the 2012 Election Will Cost $6 Billion," *Bloomberg Businessweek,* September 29, 2011, pp. 32–34.

52. Federal Election Commission, 2011; the Center for Responsive Politics, 2012.

53. Ibid.

54. Polsby and Wildavsky, *Presidential Elections*, pp. 62–67.

55. Mark Halperin and John Heilemann, *Double Down: Game Change 201* (New York: Penguin Press, 2013).

56. On this research, see Thomas E. Mann, "Linking Knowledge and Action: Political Science and Campaign Finance Reform," *Perspectives on Politics* 1, no. 1 (2003), pp. 69–83.

57. See Verba, Schlozman, and Brady, *Voice and Equality.*

58. Matthew Hindman, *The Myth of Digital Democracy* (Princeton, NJ: Princeton University Press, 2009).

59. Benjamin I. Page, Larry M. Bartels, and Jason Seawright, "Democracy and the Policy Preferences of Wealthy Americans," *Perspectives on Politics* 11, no. 1 (2013), pp. 51–73.

60. Efforts to sort out their relative contributions include Benjamin I. Page and Calvin Jones, "Reciprocal Effects of Policy Preferences, Party Loyalties, and the Vote," *American Political Science Review* 73 (1979), pp. 1071–1089; Gregory B. Markus and Philip E. Converse, "A Dynamic Simultaneous Equation Model of Public Choice," *American Political Science Review* 73 (1979), pp. 1066–1070; and William G. Jacoby, "The American Voter," in Leighley, *Oxford Handbook of American Elections and Political Behavior.*

61. Larry M. Bartels, "Partisanship and Voting Behavior, 1952–1996," *American Journal of Political Science* 44 (January 2000),

pp. 35–50; Hershey, *Party Politics*, pp. 108–111; D. Sunshine Hillygus and Simon Jackman, "Voter Decision Making in Election 2000: Campaign Effects, Partisan Activation, and the Clinton Legacy," *American Journal of Political Science* 47 (2003), pp. 583–596; Stephen A. Jessee, "Spatial Voting in the 2004 Presidential Election," *American Political Science Review* 103, no. 1 (February 2009), pp. 59–81; and Jacoby, "American Voter," in Leighley, *Oxford Handbook of American Elections and Political Behavior*, pp. 263–265.

62. Donald E. Stokes, "Some Dynamic Elements of Contests for the Presidency," *American Political Science Review* 60 (1966), pp. 19–28.

63. Maisel, *American Political Parties,* pp. 107–112.

# 11

1. "Americans Like Witches, the IRS, even Hemorrhoids Better than Congress," Public Policy Polling, October 8, 2013, http://www.publicpolicypolling.com/main/2013/10/americans-like-witches-the-irs-and-even-hemorrhoids-better-than-congress.html.

2. Exact totals were not known as of press time. Not all votes had been counted and certified in a few very close races and the Louisiana Senate race went to a run-off election.

3. Roger H. Davidson, Walter J. Oleszek, and Frances E. Lee, *Congress and Its Members*, 13th ed. (Washington, DC: CQ Press, 2012), pp. 19–28.

4. Ibid., pp. 27–28. See also Walter J. Oleszek, *Congressional Procedures and the Policy Process*, 8th ed. (Washington, DC: CQ Press, 2010), pp. 23–28.

5. Sanford Levinson, *Our Undemocratic Constitution: Where the Constitution Goes Wrong* (New York: Oxford University Press, 2006); and Robert A. Dahl, *How Democratic Is the American Constitution?* (New Haven, CT: Yale University Press, 2001).

6. Quoted in Charles Warren, *The Supreme Court in U.S. History* (Boston: Little, Brown, 1919), p. 195.

7. Oleszek, *Congressional Procedures and the Policy Process*, p. 5.

8. On this general question, see Jane Mansbridge, "Rethinking Representation," *American Political Science Review* 97, no. 4 (November 2003), pp. 515–528; and Nadia Urbinati and Mark E. Warren, "The Concept of Representation in Contemporary Democratic Theory," *Annual Review of Political Science* 11 (2008), pp. 387–412. See also Davidson, Oleszek, and Lee, *Congress and Its Members*, pp. 140–141.

9. Quoted in Charles Henning, *The Wit and Wisdom of Politics* (Golden, CO: Fulcrum, 1989), p. 235.

10. Abraham Lincoln, announcement in the New Salem, Illinois, *Sagamo Journal,* June 13, 1836.

11. Kenneth A. Shepsle, Robert P. Van Houweling, Samuel J. Abrams, and Peter C. Hanson, "The Senate Electoral Cycle and Bicameral Appropriations Politics," *American Journal of Political Science* 53, no. 2 (April 2009), pp. 343–359.

12. Davidson, Oleszek, and Lee, *Congress and Its Members*, pp. 122–124. For a dissenting view—one that suggests that senators, facing much more competitive elections than representatives do, are just as likely as House members to lean toward the delegate style throughout their six-year term of office—see Charles Stewart III, "Congress and the Constitutional System," in *The Legislative Branch,* ed. Paul J. Quirk and Sarah A. Binder (New York: Oxford University Press, 2005).

13. Davidson, Oleszek, and Lee, *Congress and Its Members,* pp. 110–115.

14. "Women in National Parliaments," The Inter-Parliamentary Union, February 1, 2014, http://www.ipu.org/wmn-e/world.htm.

15. Andrew Ross Sorkin, "Rich and Sort of Rich," *New York Times,* May 14, 2011.

16. Davidson, Oleszek, and Lee, *Congress and Its Members*, pp. 127–128.

17. The distinction between descriptive and substantive representation—the latter meaning that legislators act in the interests of their constituents irrespective of the demographic makeup of the constituency—is made by Hanna Pitkin in her classic work *The Concept of Representation* (Berkeley, CA: University of California Press, 1967).

18. Arturo Vega and Juanita Firestone, "The Effects of Gender on Congressional Behavior and the Substantive Representation of Women," *Legislative Studies Quarterly* 20 (May 1995), pp. 213–222. See also Michele L. Swers, *The Difference Women Make: The Policy Impact of Women in Congress* (Chicago: The University of Chicago Press, 2002), and the collection of research on women's impact on the legislative process in Cindy Simon Rosenthal, ed., *Women Transforming Congress* (Norman, OK: University of Oklahoma Press, 2002).

19. Katrina L. Gamble, "Black Political Representation: An Examination of Legislative Activity within U.S. House Committees," *Legislative Studies Quarterly* 32, no. 3 (August 2007), pp. 421–448.

20. For a review of research on the political impacts of redistricting, see Raymond La Raja, "Redistricting: Reading Between the Lines," *Annual Review of Political Science* 12 (2009), pp. 202–223.

21. Gary W. Cox and Jonathan N. Katz, "The Reapportionment Revolution and Bias in U.S. Congressional Elections," *American Journal of Political Science* 43, no. 3 (1999), pp. 812–841; Davidson, Oleszek, and Lee, *Congress and Its Members*, pp. 48–58; and Steven S. Smith, Jason M. Roberts, and Ryan J. Vander Wielen, *The American Congress*, 7th ed. (New York: Cambridge University Press, 2011), pp. 62–64.

22. Michael McDonald and Micah Altman, "Pulling Back the Curtain on Redistricting," *Washington Post*, July 9, 2010.

23. For more information about the effects of independent commissions, see Josh M. Ryan and Jeffrey Lyons, "The Effect of Redistricting Commissions on District Partisanship and Member Ideology," *Journal of Elections, Public Opinion, and Parties* 24 (2014).

24. Davidson, Oleszek, and Lee, *Congress and Its Members*, pp. 53–58.

25. Charles S. Bulloch, "Affirmative Action Districts: In Whose Face Will They Blow Up?," *Campaigns and Elections* (April 1995), p. 22.

26. Charles Cameron, David Epstein, and Sharyn O'Halloran, "Do Majority-Minority Districts Maximize Black Representation in Congress?," *American Political Science Review* 90 (December 1996), pp. 794–812; David Epstein and Sharyn O'Halloran, "A Social Science Approach to Race, Districting and Representation," *American Political Science Review* 93 (March 1999), pp. 187–191; David Lublin, *The Paradox of Representation: Racial Gerrymandering and Minority Interests* (Princeton, NJ: Princeton University Press, 1997); and David T. Canon, "Representing Racial and Ethnic Minorities," in Quirk and Binder, *Legislative Branch*, pp. 185–186.

27. The Campaign Finance Institute, "The Cost of Winning an Election," 2012.

28. Federal Election Commission, 2011.

29. Davidson, Oleszek, and Lee, *Congress and Its Members*, pp. 75–77.

30. Gary W. Cox and Eric Magar, "How Much Is Majority Status in the U.S. Congress Worth?," *American Political Science Review* 93, no. 2 (June 1999), pp. 299–309.

31. Richard Hall and Frank W. Wayman, "Buying Time: Moneyed Interests and the Mobilization of Bias in Congressional Committees," *American Political Science Review* 84 (1990), pp. 797–820.

32. See the classic work on this subject, David R. Mayhew, *Congress: The Electoral Connection* (New Haven, CT: Yale University Press, 1974). See also Davidson, Oleszek, and Lee, *Congress and Its Members*, ch. 4; and Smith, Roberts, and Vander Wielen, *American Congress*, pp. 97–104.

33. Richard F. Fenno Jr., *Home Style: House Members and Their Districts* (New York: Pearson Longman, 2003); and Richard F. Fenno Jr., *Senators on the Home Trail* (Norman: University of Oklahoma Press, 1996).

34. Bruce Cain, John A. Ferejohn, and Morris P. Fiorina, *The Personal Vote: Constituency Service and Electoral Independence* (Cambridge, MA: Harvard University Press, 1987); Glenn Parker, *Homeward Bound: Explaining Change in Congressional Behavior* (Pittsburgh: University of Pittsburgh Press, 1986); and Fenno, *Home Style*.

35. Levinson, *Our Undemocratic Constitution*, p. 51. Calculations by authors for 2011.

36. Alan Wolfe, *Does American Democracy Still Work?* (New Haven, CT: Yale University Press, 2006), ch. 3.

37. Walter J. Oleszek, *Congressional Procedures and the Policy Process*, 9th ed. (Washington, DC: CQ Press, 2013), ch. 1.

38. Jacob Hacker and Paul Pierson, *Off Center* (New Haven, CT: Yale University Press, 2005).

39. Hershey, *Party Politics*, pp. 243–244; Davidson, Oleszek, and Lee, *Congress and Its Members*, ch. 6; Gary W. Cox and Keith T. Poole, "On Measuring Partisanship in Roll-Call Voting," *American Journal of Political Science* 46, no. 3 (July 2002), pp. 477–489; Keith T. Poole and Howard Rosenthal, "On Party Polarization in Congress," *Daedalus* 136, no. 3 (2007), pp. 104–107; Gerald D. Wright and Brian F. Schaffner, "The Influence of Party: Evidence from the State Legislatures," *American Political Science Review* 96, no. 2 (June 2002), pp. 367–379; and Smith, Roberts, and Vander Wielen, *American Congress*, pp. 23–24.

40. Davidson, Oleszek, and Lee, *Congress and Its Members*, pp. 266–267.

41. Ibid., p. 193.

42. For the fullest review of the scholarly literature, see Geoffrey C. Layman, Thomas M. Carsey, and Juliana Menasce Horowitz, "Party Polarization in American Politics: Characteristics, Causes, and Consequences," *Annual Review of Political Science* 9 (2006), pp. 83–110.

43. On the transformation of the South in American politics and how it has affected Congress, see Nelson W. Polsby, *How Congress Evolves: Social Bases of Institutional Change* (New York: New York University Press, 2004); Earl Black and Merle Black, *The Rise of Southern Republicans* (Cambridge, MA: Harvard University and Belknap Press, 2003); Earl Black and Merle Black, *Divided America: The Ferocious Power Struggle in American Politics* (New York: Simon and Schuster, 2007); and Stanley B. Greenberg, *The Two Americas* (New York: St. Martin's Griffin, 2005).

44. Dante Chinni and James Gimpel, *Our Patchwork Nation* (New York: Penguin, Gotham Publishers, 2010).

45. Alan I. Abramowitz and Kyle L. Saunders, "Ideological Realignment in the U.S. Electorate," *Journal of Politics* 60 (1998), pp. 634–652; Nolan McCarty, Keith T. Poole, and Howard Rosenthal, *Polarized America: The Dance of Ideology and Unequal Riches* (Cambridge, MA: MIT Press, 2006); *Evenly Divided and Increasingly Polarized: The 2004 Political Landscape* (Washington, DC: Pew Research Center, 2003); Pew Research Center for the People & the Press, "Trends in Political Values and Core Attitudes: 1987–2007," Pew Research Center, March 22, 2007; http://www.people-press.org/2007/03/22/trends-in-political-values-and-core-attitudes-1987-2007/; Pew Research Center for the People & the Press, "Trends in Political Values and Core Attitudes: 1987–2009," news release, May 21, 2009, http://www.people-press.org/files/legacy-pdf/517.pdf; and Nils Gilman, "What the Rise of the Republicans as America's First Ideological Party Means for the Democrats," *The Forum* 2, no. 1 (2004), pp. 1–4.

46. Mickey Edwards, "Political Science and Political Practice," *Perspectives on Politics* 1, no. 2 (June 2003), p. 352.

47. See John J. Kornacki, ed., *Leading Congress: New Styles, New Strategies* (Washington, DC: CQ Press, 1990); David W. Rohde, *Parties and Leaders in the Postreform Congress* (Chicago: The University of Chicago Press, 1991); Randall Strahan, *Leading Representatives: The Agency of Leaders in the Politics of the U.S. House* (Baltimore: Johns Hopkins University Press, 2007); and Marjorie Randon Hershey, *Party Politics in America,* 14th ed. (New York: Pearson Longman, 2011), pp. 244–249.

48. Alan A. Abramowitz, "'Mr. Mayhew, Meet Mr. DeLay,' or the Electoral Connection in the Post-Reform Congress," *PS* 34, no. 2 (June 2001), pp. 257–258; Layman, Carsey, and Horowitz, "Party Polarization in American Politics," pp. 88–90.

49. Oleszek, *Congressional Procedures,* pp. 160–161.

50. Davidson, Oleszek, and Lee, *Congress and Its Members,* pp. 157–159.

51. Sheryl Gay Stolberg, Jeff Zeleny, and Carl Hulse, "Health Vote Caps a Journey Back from the Brink," *New York Times,* March 20, 2010.

52. Smith, Roberts, and Vander Wielen, *American Congress,* p. 137.

53. This analogy is that of Congressman Tom DeLay reported in Jonathan Kaplan, "Hastert, DeLay: Political Pros Get Along to Go Along," *The Hill,* July 22, 2003, p. 8.

54. Davidson, Oleszek, and Lee, *Congress and Its Members,* pp. 210–211; Smith, Roberts, and Vander Wielen, *American Congress,* pp. 163–164; Ronald Brownstein, *The Second Civil War: How Extreme Partisanship Has Paralyzed Washington and Polarized America* (New York: Penguin Press, 2007), pp. 124–127.

55. Josh M. Ryan, "The Disappearing Conference Committee: The Use of Procedures by Minority Coalitions to Prevent Conferencing," *Congress & the Presidency* 38, no. 1 (2011), pp. 101–125.

56. Jonathan Allen, "The Legacy of the Class of '94," *CQ Weekly,* September 4, 2004.

57. Brownstein, *Second Civil War,* p. 158.

58. Davidson, Oleszek, and Lee, *Congress and Its Members,* ch. 8; and Donald R. Matthews, *U.S. Senators and Their World* (Chapel Hill, NC: University of North Carolina Press, 1960).

59. Ezra Klein, "The Rise of the Filibuster: An Interview with Barbara Sinclair," *Washington Post,* December 26, 2009, http://voices.washingtonpost.com/ezra-klein/2009/12/the_right_of_the_filibuster_an.html.

60. "The Filibuster's Power to Block Nominees," *New York Times,* November 21, 2013, http://www.nytimes.com/interactive/2013/11/21/us/politics/senate-filibusters.html?_r=0.

61. Robert Bendiner, *Obstacle Course on Capitol Hill* (New York: McGraw-Hill, 1964), p. 15.

62. Walter J. Oleszek, *Congressional Procedures and the Policy Process,* 9th ed. (Washington, DC: CQ Press, 2013), ch. 1.

63. Barbara Sinclair, *Unorthodox Lawmaking: New Legislative Processes in the U.S. Congress* (Washington, DC: CQ Press, 2007).

64. Brownstein, *Second Civil War,* p. 277.

65. Suzy Khimm, "The Decline of Congressional Oversight, in One Chart," *Washington Post,* November 29, 2011, http://www.washingtonpost.com/blogs/wonkblog/post/the-decline-of-congressional-oversight-in-one-chart/2011/11/29/gIQAwq078N_blog.html.

66. Lawrence Lessig, *Republic, Lost: How Money Corrupts Congress—and a Plan to Stop It* (New York: Twelve, 2011).

## 12

1. On the president's unitary powers, their origins, development, and implications, see Kenneth R. Mayer, "The Presidential Power of Unilateral Action," and Richard W. Waterman, "Assessing the Unilateral Presidency," in George C. Edwards III and William G. Howell, eds., *The Oxford Handbook of the American Presidency* (Oxford: Oxford University Press, 2010); and William G. Howell, *Power Without Persuasion: The Politics of Direct Presidential Action* (Princeton, NJ: Princeton University Press, 2003). For an overview of presidential scholarship on the powers of the presidency, see Louis Fisher, "Teaching the Presidency: Idealizing a Constitutional Office," *PS: Political Science* (January 2012), pp. 17–31.

2. Lee Epstein and Thomas G. Walker, *Constitutional Law for a Changing America: Institutional Powers and Constraints* (Los Angeles and Washington, DC: Sage Publications and CQ Press, 2014), p. 183.

3. U.S. Department of Commerce, *Historical Statistics of the United States, Colonial Times to 1970* (Washington, DC: U.S. Government Printing Office, 1971), pp. 8 and 1143.

4. Federation of American Scientists, "Status of World Nuclear Forces, 2009," http://www.fas.org/programs/ssp/nukes/nuclearweapons/nukestatus.html. (The current page shows numbers for 2013.)

5. U.S. Census Bureau.

6. George C. Edwards III and Stephen J. Wayne, *Presidential Leadership: Politics and Policy Making* (Belmont, CA: Cengage Wadsworth, 2009), pp. 2–9; and James P. Pfiffner and Roger H. Davidson, eds., *Understanding the Presidency* (New York: Pearson, 2011), pp. 1–6.

7. On the contributions of particular presidents in shaping today's presidency, see Scott C. James, "The Evolution of the Presidency," in *The Executive Branch,* ed. Joel D. Aberbach and Mark A. Peterson (New York: Oxford University Press, 2005).

8. James P. Pfiffner, "Constraining Executive Power: George W. Bush and the Constitution," and Andrew Rudalevige, "A New Imperial Presidency?," both in *Understanding the Presidency,* ed. James P. Pfiffner and Roger H. Davidson (New York: Pearson Longman, 2013).

9. Jimmie Breslin, quoted in Laurence J. Peter, *Peter's Quotations* (New York: Morrow, 1977), p. 405.

10. See Edwards and Wayne, *Presidential Leadership,* ch. 12.

11. Ron Suskind, *Confidence Men: Wall Street, Washington, and the Education of a President* (New York: HarperCollins, 2011).

12. Roger H. Davidson, Walter J. Oleszek, Frances E. Lee, and Eric Schickler, *Congress and Its Members,* 14th ed. (Washington, DC: CQ Press, 2014), pp. 288–291 and 295–297.

13. Richard E. Neustadt, *Presidential Power and the Modern Presidents: The Politics of Leadership from Roosevelt to Reagan* (New York: Free Press, 1990); and David E. Lewis and Terry M. Moe, "The Presidency and the Bureaucracy: The Levers of Presidential Control," in *The Presidency and the Political System,* ed. Michael Nelson (Washington, DC: CQ Press, 2010).

14. Howell, *Power Without Persuasion;* Phillip J. Cooper, *By Order of the President: The Use and Abuse of Executive Direct Action* (Lawrence: University of Kansas Press, 2002); Adam L. Warber, *Executive Orders and the Modern Presidency* (Boulder, CO: Lynne Rienner Publishers, 2006); and Andrew Rudalevige, "The Presidency and Unilateral Power: A Taxonomy," in Nelson, *Presidency and the Political System.*

15. Matthew Crenson and Benjamin Ginsberg, *Presidential Power, Unchecked and Unbalanced* (New York: Norton, 2007); Pfiffner, "Constraining Executive Power: George W. Bush and the Constitution," Rudalevige, "A New Imperial Presidency?," and Richard Pious, "Prerogative Power and the War on Terrorism," all in Pfiffner and Davidson, *Understanding the Presidency.*

16. See John Yoo, *The Powers of War and Peace: The Constitution and Foreign Affairs After 9/11* (Chicago: The University of Chicago Press, 2005). In contrast, see Crenson and Ginsberg, *Presidential Power,* and Waterman, "Assessing the Unilateral Presidency."

17. Graham T. Allison, *Essence of Decision: Explaining the Cuban Missile Crisis* (Boston: Little, Brown, 1971), pp. 141–142.

18. Neustadt, *Presidential Power,* ch. 2.

19. Michael Nelson, "Neustadt's *Presidential Power* at 50," *Chronicle of Higher Education*, March 28, 2010.

20. *United States v. Curtiss-Wright* (1936). For more on judicial interpretations of presidential powers in foreign policy and war, see R. Shep Melnick, "The Courts, Jurisprudence, and the Executive Branch," in Aberbach and Peterson, *Executive Branch*; Richard A. Brisbin Jr., "The Judiciary and the Separation of Powers," in *The Judicial Branch*, ed. Kermit L. Hall and Kevin T. McGuire (New York: Oxford University Press, 2005).

21. Melnick, "Courts, Jurisprudence, and the Executive Branch."

22. Epstein and Walker, *Constitutional Law*, pp. 255–256.

23. Edwards and Wayne, *Presidential Leadership*, p. 480.

24. Arthur Schlesinger Jr., *The Imperial Presidency* (New York: Popular Library, Atlantic Monthly Press, 1973).

25. David Nather and Anna Palmer, "Bushies Fear Obama Weakening Presidency," Politico, September 1, 2013, http://www.politico.com/story/2013/09/bushies-fear-obama-weakening-presidency-96143.html.

26. Marjorie Randon Hershey, *Party Politics in America* (New York: Pearson, 2012), pp. 266–272; and Sidney M. Milkis and Jesse H. Rhodes, "George W. Bush, the Republican Party, and the New American Party System," *Perspectives on Politics* 5, no. 3 (September 2007), pp. 461–488.

27. James P. Pfiffner, *The Modern Presidency* (New York: St. Martin's Press, 1998), ch. 4. See also Edwards and Wayne, *Presidential Leadership*, ch. 6; Pfiffner and Davidson, *Understanding the Presidency*, pp. 222–252.

28. Edwards and Wayne, *Presidential Leadership*, p. 209.

29. Suskind, *Confidence Men*.

30. Nathan Miller, *FDR: An Intimate History* (Lanham, MD: Madison Books, 1983), p. 276.

31. Thomas E. Cronin and Michael A. Genovese, *The Paradoxes of the American Presidency* (New York: Oxford University Press, 2004), ch. 10; and Joseph A. Pika, "The Vice Presidency: Dick Cheney, Joe Biden, and the New Vice Presidency," in Nelson, *Presidency and the Political System*.

32. Edwards and Wayne, *Presidential Leadership*, p. 216.

33. Elisabeth Bumiller and Eric Schmitt, "In Indictment's Wake, a Focus on Cheney's Powerful Role in the White House," *New York Times*, October 20, 2005.

34. Stephen F. Hayes, *Cheney: The Untold Story of the Nation's Most Powerful and Controversial Vice President* (New York: HarperCollins, 2007); and Barton Gellman, *Angler: The Cheney Vice Presidency* (New York: Penguin Press, 2008).

35. Charles O. Jones, *Separate but Equal: Congress and the Presidency* (New York: Chatham House, 1999); Davidson, Oleszek, Lee, and Schickler, *Congress and Its Members*, pp. 302–307; and Roger H. Davidson, "Presidential Relations with Congress," in Pfiffner and Davidson, *Understanding the Presidency*.

36. Andrew Rudalevige, "The Executive Branch and the Legislative Process," in Aberbach and Peterson, *Executive Branch*, pp. 432–445; and Davidson, Oleszek, Lee, and Schickler, *Congress and Its Members*, ch. 10.

37. Edwards and Wayne, *Presidential Leadership*, pp. 336–348; Jon R. Bond and Richard Fleisher, eds., *Polarized Politics: Congress and the President in a Partisan Era* (Washington, DC: CQ Press, 2000); and Glen Biglaiser, David J. Jackson, and Jeffrey S. Peake, "Back on Track: Support for Presidential Trade Authority in the House of Representatives," *American Politics Research* 32 (November 2004), pp. 679–697.

38. Terry Sullivan, "Headcounts, Expectations and Presidential Coalitions in Congress," *American Journal of Political Science* 32 (1988), pp. 657–689; Davidson, Oleszek, Lee, and Schickler, *Congress and Its Members*, pp. 301–302; and Hershey, *Party Politics*, pp. 266–270.

39. "2009 Was the Most Partisan Year Ever," *Congressional Quarterly Weekly Report*, January 11, 2010.

40. Aaron Wildavsky, "The Two Presidencies," in *Perspectives on the Presidency*, ed. Aaron Wildavsky (Boston: Little, Brown, 1975), pp. 448–461.

41. For a review of the leading scholarship on the various uses and consequences of the presidential veto, see Charles M. Cameron, "The Presidential Veto," in Edwards and Howell, *Oxford Handbook of the American Presidency*.

42. Roger H. Davidson, "Presidential Relations with Congress," in Pfiffner and Davidson, *Understanding the Presidency*.

43. Gerhard Peters, "Presidential Vetoes," *The American Presidency Project*, ed. John T. Woolley and Gerhard Peters (Santa Barbara, CA: University of California, 1999–2014), http://www.presidency.ucsb.edu/data/vetoes.php.

44. For the most sophisticated analysis of the effects of presidential approval on a president's success with Congress, see George C. Edwards III, "Presidential Approval as a Source of Influence in Congress," in Edwards and Howell, *Oxford Handbook of the American Presidency*. See also Richard Brody, *Assessing the President: The Media, Elite Opinion, and Public Support* (Stanford, CA: Stanford University Press, 1991); George C. Edwards III, *At the Margins: Presidential Leadership of Congress* (New Haven, CT: Yale University Press, 1989); and George C. Edwards III, "Aligning Tests with Theory: Presidential Approval as a Source of Influence in Congress," *Congress and the Presidency* 24 (Fall 1997), pp. 113–130.

45. Edwards and Wayne, *Presidential Leadership*, pp. 348–350.

46. Jeffrey K. Tulis, *The Rhetorical Presidency* (Princeton, NJ: Princeton University Press, 1987), chs. 2 and 3, esp. p. 64.

47. Woodrow Wilson, *Leaders of Men*, ed. T. H. Vail Motter (Princeton, NJ: Princeton University Press, 1952), p. 39; quoted in Tulis, *Rhetorical Presidency*, ch. 4, which analyzes Wilson's theory at length and expresses some skepticism about it.

48. Tulis, *Rhetorical Presidency*, pp. 138, 140.

49. Samuel Kernell, *Going Public: Strategies of Presidential Leadership*, 3rd ed. (Washington, DC: CQ Press, 1997), p. 92 and ch. 4.

50. Benjamin I. Page and Robert Y. Shapiro, "Presidents as Opinion Leaders: Some New Evidence," *Policy Studies Journal* 12 (1984), pp. 649–661; and Benjamin I. Page, Robert Y. Shapiro, and Glenn R. Dempsey, "What Moves Public Opinion," *American Political Science Review* 81 (1987), pp. 23–43; but see Donald L. Jordan, "Newspaper Effects on Policy Preferences," *Public Opinion Quarterly* 57 (1993), pp. 191–204.

51. For an examination of the complexities of the scholarly literature on the effects of presidential opinion leadership, see George C. Edwards III, "Leading the Public," in Edwards and Howell, *Oxford Handbook of the American Presidency*.

52. Lawrence R. Jacobs and Robert Y. Shapiro, *Politicians Don't Pander: Political Manipulation and the Loss of Democratic Responsiveness* (Chicago: The University of Chicago Press, 2000); and Jacob Hacker and Paul Pierson, *Off Center* (New Haven, CT: Yale University Press, 2005).

53. Doris Graber, *Mass Media and American Politics*, 8th ed. (Washington, DC: CQ Press, 2010), ch. 9; Lawrence R. Jacobs, "Communicating from the White House," in Aberbach and Peterson, *Executive Branch*, pp. 189–205.

54. Lawrence Jacobs and Robert Y. Shapiro, "The Rise of Presidential Polling: The Nixon White House in Historical Perspective," *Public Opinion Quarterly* 59 (1995), pp. 163–195; and Jacobs, "Communicating from the White House," pp. 178–189.

55. W. Lance Bennett, Regina G. Lawrence, and Steven Livingston, *When the Press Fails: Political Power and the News Media from Iraq to Katrina* (Chicago: The University of Chicago Press, 2007), ch. 5; Jacobs and Shapiro, *Politicians Don't Pander*; and James M. Druckman and Lawrence R. Jacobs, "Presidential Responsiveness to Public Opinion," in Edwards and Howell, *Oxford Handbook of the American Presidency*.

56. Edwards and Wayne, *Presidential Leadership*, pp. 112–123.

57. Brody, *Assessing the President.* Also see Edwards and Wayne, *Presidential Leadership*, pp. 112–123; John E. Mueller, "Presidential Popularity from Truman to Johnson," *American Political Science Review* 64 (1970), pp. 18–34; Samuel Kernell, "Explaining Presidential Popularity," *American Political Science Review* 72 (1978), pp. 506–522; and George C. Edwards III, *Presidential Approval* (Baltimore, MD: Johns Hopkins University Press, 1990).

# 13

1. The quote is from "The Diddle Kingdom: Tainted Chinese Goods Prompt Safety Scares around the World" *Economist*, July 5, 2007, p. 63. Other sources for this chapter-opening story include Eric Lipton, "Safety Agency Faces Scrutiny Amid Charges," *New York Times*, September 2, 2007; and Tom Lowry and Lorraine Woellert, "More Paper Tiger Than Watchdog?," *Businessweek*, September 3, 2007.

2. Lipton, "Safety Agency."

3. Max Weber, *Economy and Society*, vol. 1 (London: Owen, 1962).

4. B. Guy Peters, *American Public Policy: Policy and Performance*, 9th ed. (New York: CQ Press, 2012), p. 43.

5. "A Tough Search for Talent," *Economist*, October 31, 2011, p. 71.

6. See Charles T. Goodsell, *The Case for Bureaucracy* (Washington, DC: CQ Press, 2014), p. 85; Kenneth J. Meier, "Representative Bureaucracy: An Empirical Analysis," *American Political Science Review* 69 (June 1975), pp. 537–539; and Katherine C. Naff, "Representative Bureaucracy," *Encyclopedia of Public Administration and Public Policy*, 2nd ed. (Piscataway, NJ: Rutgers University Press, 2008).

7. Wallace Sayre, "Bureaucracies: Some Contrasts in Systems," *Indian Journal of Public Administration* 10 (1964), p. 223. For contemporary evidence in support of this claim, see Gabriel A. Almond, G. Bingham Powell Jr., Kaare Strom, and Russell J. Dalton, *Comparative Politics Today* (New York: Pearson Longman, 2010), pp. 120–124.

8. John A. Rohr, *Civil Servants and Their Constitutions* (Lawrence: University of Kansas Press, 2002); and Richard J. Stillman II, *The American Bureaucracy* (Chicago: Nelson-Hall, 1987), p. 18.

9. Rohr, *Civil Servants*, ch. 4; and David E. Lewis and Terry M. Moe, "The Presidency and the Bureaucracy: The Levers of Presidential Control," in *The Presidency and the Political System*, ed. Michael Nelson (Washington, DC: CQ Press, 2010).

10. On the problem of government accountability in our system of separated powers and checks and balances in an environment characterized by growing interest group influence and rising partisanship, see Francis Fukuyama, "The Ties That Used to Bind: The Decay of American Political Institutions," *American Interest*, December 8, 2013, http://www.the-american-interest.com/articles/2013/12/08/the-decay-of-american-political-institutions/.

11. Jay M. Shafritz, E. W. Russell, and Christopher P. Borick, *Introducing Public Administration* (New York: Pearson Longman, 2007), pp. 87–94; and Peters, *American Public Policy*, pp. 114–121.

12. Peters, *American Public Policy*, p. 116.

13. Daniel Carpenter, "The Evolution of National Bureaucracy in the United States," in *The Executive Branch*, ed. Joel D. Aberbach and Mark A. Peterson (New York: Oxford University Press, 2005), pp. 55–57.

14. Peters, *American Public Policy*, p. 118.

15. Theodore J. Lowi, *The End of Liberalism*, 2nd ed. (New York: Norton, 1979); and Christian Hunold and B. Guy Peters, "Bureaucratic Discretion and Deliberative Democracy," in *Transformation in Governance*, ed. Matti Malkia, Ari-Veikko Anttiroiko, and Reigo Savolainen, (London: Idea Group. 2004), pp. 131–149.

16. Roger H. Davidson, Walter J. Oleszek, Frances E. Lee, and Eric Schickler, *Congress and Its Members*, 14th ed. (Washington, DC: CQ Press, 2014), pp. 289–290.

17. Charles R. Shipan, "Congress and the Bureaucracy," in *The Legislative Branch*, ed. Paul J. Quirk and Sarah A. Binder (New York: Oxford University Press, 2005).

18. David Lewis, "Presidential Appointments and Personnel," *Annual Review of Political Science* 14 (2011), p. 52.

19. Patricia W. Ingraham, "The Federal Service: The People and the Challenge," in Aberbach and Peterson, *Executive Branch*, pp. 290–291.

20. Ibid., pp. 294–296.

21. See Samuel Krislov and David H. Rosenbloom, *Representative Bureaucracy and the American Political System* (New York: Praeger, 1981); Goodsell, *Case for Bureaucracy*; and Ingraham, "Federal Service."

22. Organisation for Economic Co-operation and Development (OECD), 2005, as reported on a graph in "Public Service Careers: A Tough Search for Talent," *Economist*, October 31, 2009, p. 71.

23. Goodsell, *Case for Bureaucracy*, pp. 84–90; and Stanley Rothman and S. Robert Lichter, "How Liberal Are Bureaucrats?," *Regulation* (November–December 1983), pp. 35–47.

24. Office of Personnel Management, 2012.

25. Ingraham, "Federal Service," pp. 291–294.

26. Lewis, "Presidential Appointments," p. 48.

27. Richard P. Nathan, *The Administrative Presidency* (New York: Wiley, 1983).

28. David E. Rosenbaum and Stephen Labaton, "Amid Many Fights on Qualifications, a Nomination Stalls," *New York Times*, September 24, 2005.

29. Lewis, "Presidential Appointments," p. 56.

30. Hugh Heclo, *A Government of Strangers* (Washington, DC: Brookings Institution Press, 1977), p. 103.

31. Richard E. Neustadt, *Presidential Power* (New York: Wiley, 1960); and George C. Edwards III and Stephen J. Wayne, *Presidential Leadership: Politics and Policy Making* (Wadsworth, CA: Thomson Wadsworth, 2009), ch. 9.

32. Terry M. Moe, "Control and Feedback in Economic Regulation," *American Political Science Review* 79 (1985), pp. 1094–1116; David Lewis and Terry M. Moe, "The Presidency and the Bureaucracy: The Levers of Presidential Control," in *The Presidency and the Political System*, ed. Michael Nelson (Washington, DC: CQ Press, 2010); Richard W. Waterman, *Presidential Influence and the Administrative State* (Knoxville: University of Tennessee Press, 1989); and Edwards and Wayne, *Presidential Leadership*, pp. 295–303.

33. Richard W. Waterman and Kenneth J. Meier, "Principal-Agent Models: An Expansion?," *Journal of Public Administration Research and Theory* 8 (April 1998), pp. 173–202; and Edwards and Wayne, *Presidential Leadership*, pp. 305–307.

34. For a review of research on the president's appointment powers, see Joel D. Aberbach and Bert A. Rockman, "The Appointments Process and the Administrative Presidency," *Presidential Studies Quarterly* 39, no. 1 (January 2009), pp. 38–59.

35. James P. Pfiffner, "Constraining Executive Power: George W. Bush and the Constitution," in *Understanding the Presidency*, ed. James P. Pfiffner and Roger H. Davidson (New York: Pearson Longman, 2009); and Andrew Rudalevige, "The Presidency and Unilateral Power," in Nelson, *Presidency and the Political System*.

36. Lewis, "Presidential Appointments," pp. 54–55; and Robert F. Durant and William G. Resh, "'Presidentializing' the Bureaucracy," in *The Oxford Handbook of American Bureaucracy*, ed. Robert F. Durant (New York: Oxford University Press, 2011).

37. Davidson, Oleszek, Lee, and Schickler, *Congress and Its Members*, pp. 320–338; George A. Krause, "Legislative Delegation of Authority to Bureaucratic Agencies," in Durant, *Oxford Handbook of American Bureaucracy*; and Steven S. Smith, Jason M. Roberts, and Ryan J. Vander Wielen, *The American Congress*, 5th ed. (New York: Cambridge University Press, 2007), pp. 291–301.

38. Lewis, "Presidential Appointments," pp. 55–56; and Nolan McCarty and Rose Razahgian, "Advice and Consent: Senate Responses to Executive Branch Nominations, 1885–1996," *American Journal of Political Science* 43 (October 1999), pp. 1122–1143.

39. Richard Fenno, *The Power of the Purse* (Boston: Little, Brown, 1966); Aaron Wildavsky, *The Politics of the Budgetary Process* (Boston: Little, Brown, 1964); and Davidson, Oleszek, Lee, and Schickler, *Congress and Its Members,* pp. 334–355, 412–417.

40. "Wings Clipped: A Working Example of the Effects of Congressional Stupidity," *Economist,* August 6, 2011, p. 40.

41. John A. Ferejohn and Charles R. Shipan, "Congressional Influence on Administrative Agencies: A Case Study of Telecommunications Policy," in *Congress Reconsidered*, 4th ed., ed. Lawrence C. Dodd and Bruce I. Oppenheimer (Washington, DC: CQ Press, 1989); and Davidson, Oleszek, Lee, and Schickler, *Congress and Its Members*, pp. 331–332.

42. See Jerry L. Mashaw, "Bureaucracy, Democracy, and Judicial Review," in Durant, *Oxford Handbook of American Bureaucracy*.

43. Barry R. Weingast, "Caught in the Middle: The President, Congress, and the Political-Bureaucratic System," in Aberbach and Peterson, *Executive Branch*, pp. 322–325.

44. Cornelius M. Kerwin, *Rulemaking: How Government Agencies Write Law and Make Policy* (Washington, DC: CQ Press, 2003), p. 183.

45. See especially Cornelius Kerwin, Scott Furlong, and William West, "Interest Groups, Rulemaking, and American Bureaucracy," in Durant, *Oxford Handbook of American Bureaucracy*, pp. 602–607. See Derek Bok, *The Trouble with Government* (Cambridge, MA: Harvard University Press, 2001), ch. 9.

46. Emanuel S. Savas, *Privatization: The Key to Better Government* (Chatham, NJ: Chatham House, 1987); Sheila B. Kamerman and Alfred J. Kahn, eds., *Privatization and the Welfare State* (Princeton, NJ: Princeton University Press, 1989); and Lester M. Salamon, ed., *The Tools of Government: A Guide to the New Governance* (Oxford, UK: Oxford University Press, 2002).

47. Moshe Schwartz, "Department of Defense Contractors in Iraq and Afghanistan: Background and Analysis" (Washington, DC: The Congressional Research Service, December 14, 2009).

48. John Cranford, "Job Creation: The Engine in Chief," *Roll Call,* September 29, 2011, http://www.rollcall.com/features/Outlook_Job-Creation/outlook/-209070-1.html.

49. Bernard Wysocki Jr., "Is U.S. Government Outsourcing Its Brain?" *Wall Street Journal*, March 30, 2007.

50. Bok, *Trouble with Government*, pp. 233–234; Roberta Lynch and Ann Markusen, "Can Markets Govern?" *American Prospect* (Winter 1994), pp. 125–134; and Dan Guttman, "Governance by Contract," *Public Contract Law Journal* 33 (Winter 2004), pp. 321–360.

51. John Cassidy, *How Markets Fail: The Logic of Economic Calamities* (New York: Farrar, Straus and Giroux, 2009).

52. David Osborne and Ted Gaebler, *Reinventing Government* (Reading, MA: Addison-Wesley, 1992).

53. Bok, *Trouble with Government*, pp. 234–239; Joel D. Aberbach and Bert A. Rockman, eds., *In the Web of Politics: Three Decades of the U.S. Federal Executive* (Washington, DC: Brookings Institution Press, 2000); Lester M. Salamon, "The New Governance and the Tools of Public Administration," in *The Tools of Government*, ed. Lester M. Salamon (Oxford, UK: Oxford University Press, 2002); and Steven G. Koven, "Bureaucracy, Democracy, and the New Public Management," in *Bureaucracy and Administration,* ed. Ali Farazmand (Boca Raton, FL: CRC Press, 2009); Carpenter, "Evolution," pp. 63–64; and Shafritz, Russell, and Borick, *Introducing Public Administration*, pp. 112–114.

54. Terry M. Moe, "The Politics of Bureaucratic Structure," in *Can the Government Govern?* ed. John E. Chubb and Paul E. Peterson (Washington, DC: Brookings Institution Press, 1989), p. 280; John E. Chubb and Paul E. Peterson, "American Political Institutions and the Problem of Governance," in Chubb and Peterson, *Can the Government Govern?* p. 41; and James L. Sundquist, *Constitutional Reform and Effective Government* (Washington, DC: Brookings Institution Press, 1986).

# 14

1. All quotes are from Neil A. Lewis, "Bitter Senators Divided Anew on Judgeships," *Washington Post*, November 15, 2003.

2. Jan Crawford Greenburg, *Supreme Conflict: The Inside Story of the Struggle for Control of the United States Supreme Court* (New York: Penguin Press, 2007); Jess Bravin, "Top Court Hands Conservatives Victories," *Wall Street Journal,* June 26, 2007; Linda Greenhouse, "In Steps Big and Small, Supreme Court Moves Right," *New York Times*, July 1, 2007; "Supreme Success," *Economist*, July 7, 2007, p. 36; "Conservatives Resurgent," *Economist*, April 21, 2007, p. 34; and David M. O'Brien, *Storm Center: The Supreme Court in American Politics,* 9th ed. (New York, Norton, 2011), pp. 28–29.

3. For strong empirical confirmation of the emergence of a strong conservative majority on the Court with the arrival of Samuel Alito and under the leadership of John Roberts, see Stephen A. Jessee and Alexander M. Tahk, "What Can We Learn About the Ideology of the Newest Supreme Court Justices?," *PS: Political Science and Politics* 44, no. 3 (July 2011), pp. 524–529; Linda Greenhouse, "The Real John Roberts Emerges," *New York Times,* June 28, 2013; and Adam Liptak, "Roberts Pulls the Supreme Court to the Right Step by Step," *New York Times*, June 27, 2013.

4. O'Brien, *Storm Center*, ch. 1.

5. Akhil Reed Amar, *America's Constitution: A Biography* (New York: Random House, 2005), ch. 6.

6. J. M. Sosin, *The Aristocracy of the Long Robe: The Origins of Judicial Review in America* (Westport, CT: Greenwood Press, 1989); William E. Nelson, "The Historical Foundations of the American Judiciary," Kermit L. Hall, "Judicial Independence and the Majoritarian Difficulty," and Cass R. Sunstein, "Judges and Democracy: The Changing Role of the United States Supreme Court," in *The Judicial Branch*, ed. Kermit L. Hall and Kevin T. McGuire (New York: Oxford University Press, 2005).

7. Lee Epstein and Thomas G. Walker, *Rights, Liberties, and Justice* (Washington, DC: CQ Press, 2010), pp. 47, 53; and Mark A. Graber, "Establishing Judicial Review? *Schooner Peggy* and the Early Marshall Court," *Political Research Quarterly* 51 (1998), pp. 221–239.

8. Robert G. McCloskey, *The American Supreme Court*, 4th ed. (Chicago: The University of Chicago Press, 2005), pp. 12–13.

9. On *Marbury*, see Sylvia Snowmiss, *Judicial Review and the Law of the Constitution* (New Haven, CT: Yale University Press, 1990).

10. David M. O'Brien, *Constitutional Law and Politics*, vol. 2 (New York: Norton, 2008), p. 36.

11. Linda Greenhouse, "The Imperial Presidency vs. the Imperial Judiciary," *New York Times*, March 2, 2000; and Paul Gewirtz and Chad Golder, "So Who Are the Activists?," *New York Times*, July 6, 2005.

12. See *Ex parte Milligan* (1866) and *Youngstown Sheet and Tube Co. v. Sawyer* (1952).

13. See Keith E. Whittington, "Judicial Checks on the President," in *The Oxford Handbook of the American Presidency*, ed. George C. Edwards III and William G. Howell (New York: Oxford University Press, 2009).

14. Robert A. Dahl, *How Democratic Is the American Constitution?* (New Haven, CT: Yale University Press, 2001), pp. 54–55. See also Lawrence D. Kramer, *The People Themselves: Popular Constitutionalism and Judicial Review* (New York: Oxford University Press, 2004).

15. Alexander M. Bickel, *The Least Dangerous Branch: The Supreme Court at the Bar of Politics* (Indianapolis, IN: Bobbs-Merrill, 1962), pp. 16–18.

16. Robert A. Dahl, "Decision-Making in a Democracy: The Supreme Court as a National Policy Maker," *Journal of Public Law* 6 (1957), pp. 279–295; and Mark A. Graber, "Constructing Judicial Review," *Annual Review of Political Science* 8 (2005), pp. 425–451.

17. Richard S. Randall, *American Constitutional Development* (New York: Longman, 2002), pp. 488–489.

18. Federal Court Management Statistics, 2014, http://www.uscourts.gov/Statistics/FederalCourtManagementStatistics.aspx.

19. Ibid.

20. Neil Lewis, "An Appeals Court That Always Veers to the Right," *New York Times*, May 24, 1999; and Deborah Sontag, "The Power of the Fourth," *New York Times Sunday Magazine*, March 9, 2003, pp. 38–44.

21. Lawrence Baum, *The Supreme Court* (Washington, DC: CQ Press, 2010), pp. 6–10.

22. Roger H. Davidson, Walter J. Oleszek, Frances E. Lee, and Eric Schickler, *Congress and Its Members*, 14th ed. (Washington, DC: CQ Press, 2014), pp. 347–348.

23. O'Brien, *Storm Center*, pp. 34–39. See also Joel B. Grossman, "Paths to the Bench," in Hall and McGuire, *Judicial Branch*, p. 162; and Lee Epstein, Jack Knight, and Andrew D. Martin, "The Norm of Judicial Experience," *University of California Law Review* 91 (2003), pp. 938–939.

24. Greenburg, *Supreme Conflict*.

25. Robert A. Carp and Ronald Stidham, *Judicial Process in America*, 6th ed. (Washington, DC: CQ Press, 2004), ch. 8; Grossman, "Paths to the Bench," pp. 160–161.

26. Baum, *Supreme Court*, pp. 27–50; Ronald Brownstein, *The Second Civil War: How Extreme Partisanship Has Paralyzed Washington and Polarized America* (New York: Penguin Press, 2007); Greenburg, *Supreme Conflict*; Alan Wolfe, *Does American Democracy Still Work?* (New Haven, CT: Yale University Press, 2006), ch. 5.

27. Lee Epstein and Jeffrey A. Segal, "Nominating Federal Judges and Justices," in Edwards and Howell, *Oxford Handbook of the American Presidency*.

28. Lee Epstein and Jeffrey A. Segal, *Advice and Consent: The Politics of Judicial Appointments* (New York: Oxford University Press, 2005), ch. 3; Baum, *Supreme Court*, pp. 27–50; Davidson, Oleszek, Lee, and Schickler, *Congress and Its Members*, pp. 354–364; and O'Brien, *Storm Center*, pp. 34–39.

29. Epstein and Segal, "Nominating Federal Judges," pp. 629–630 and 634–635.

30. Charlie Savage, "Obama Backers Fear Opportunities to Reshape Judiciary Are Slipping Away," *New York Times*, November 14, 2009.

31. Epstein and Segal, *Advice and Consent*, ch. 3; Epstein and Segal, "Nominating Federal Judges," pp. 634–635; Lee Epstein and Thomas G. Walker, *Constitutional Law for a Changing America: Institutional Powers and Constraints* (Los Angeles and Washington, DC: Sage and CQ Press, 2014), pp. 34–39; Baum, *Supreme Court*, pp. 123–125; Grossman, "Paths to the Bench"; Lawrence Baum, "The Supreme Court in American Politics," in *Annual Review of Political Science*, ed. Nelson W. Polsby (Palo Alto, CA: Annual Reviews, 2003), pp. 161–180; Dahl, "Decision-Making in a Democracy"; Ronald Stidham and Robert A. Carp, "Judges, Presidents, and Policy Choices,"

32. See Epstein and Walker, *Constitutional Law*, pp. 11–23; Bernard Schwartz, *Decision: How the Supreme Court Decides Cases* (New York: Oxford University Press, 2005).

33. Jeffrey Rosen, "So, Do You Believe in 'Super-Precedent'?" *New York Times*, October 30, 2005, p. IV. 1.

34. Jeffrey A. Segal, Harold J. Spaeth, and Sara C. Benesh, *The Supreme Court in the American Legal System* (New York: Cambridge University Press, 2005), ch. 11; Epstein and Walker, *Rights, Liberties, and Justice*, pp. 57–63.

35. For details, see H. W. Perry Jr., *Deciding to Decide: Agenda Setting in the United States Supreme Court* (Cambridge, MA: Harvard University Press, 2005).

36. John Paul Stevens, *Five Chiefs: A Supreme Court Memoir* (New York: Little, Brown, 2011).

37. Perry, *Deciding to Decide*. For a current review of the extensive scholarly literature, see Thomas M. Keck, "Party, Policy, or Duty: Why Does the Supreme Court Invalidate Federal Statutes?," *American Political Science Review* 101 (May 2007), pp. 321–338. Also see Epstein and Segal, *Advice and Consent*, ch. 5.

38. Segal, Spaeth, and Benesh, *Supreme Court in the American Legal System*, pp. 318–323; David Adamany, "The Supreme Court," in *The American Courts*, ed. John B. Gates and Charles A. Johnson (Washington, DC: CQ Press, 1991), pp. 111–112; Baum, "Supreme Court in American Politics," pp. 162–168; Glendon Schubert, *The Judicial Mind* (Evanston, IL: Northwestern University Press, 1965); Jeffrey A. Segal and Harold J. Spaeth, *The Supreme Court and the Attitudinal Model* (New York: Cambridge University Press, 1993); John D. Sprague, *Voting Patterns of the United States Supreme Court* (Indianapolis, IN: Bobbs-Merrill, 1968); Tom S. Clark, "Measuring Ideological Polarization on the United States Supreme Court," *Political Research Quarterly* 20, no. 10 (May 2008), pp. 1–12; and Jessee and Tahk, "What Can We Learn About the Ideology."

39. Walter Murphy, *Elements of Judicial Strategy* (Princeton, NJ: Princeton University Press, 1964); and Lee Epstein and Jack Knight, *The Choices Justices Make* (Washington, DC: CQ 39, 1997).

40. Joel B. Grossman, "Social Backgrounds and Judicial Decision-Making," *Harvard Law Review* 79 (1966), pp. 1551–1564; S. and Sidney Ulmer, "Dissent Behavior and the Social Background of Supreme Court Justices," *Journal of Politics* 32 (1970), pp. 580–589.

41. L. Epstein, J. Knight, and J. Martin, "The Supreme Court as a Strategic National Policy-Maker," *Emory Law Review* 50 (2001), pp. 583–610.

42. Epstein and Walker, *Constitutional Law for a Changing America*, pp. 23–44; Jessee and Tahk, "What Can We Learn About the Ideology"; Adam Liptak, "'Politicians in Robes?' Not Exactly, But …," *New York Times*, November 26, 2012; Segal and Spaeth, *Supreme Court and the Attitudinal Model*.

43. Nicholas Wade, "A Mathematician Crunches the Supreme Court's Numbers," *New York Times*, August 4, 2003; Segal, Spaeth, and Benesh, *Supreme Court in the American Legal System*, pp. 318–323; and Epstein and Segal, "Nominating Federal Judges," pp. 629–630 and 634–635.

44. John Harlan, "A Glimpse of the Supreme Court at Work," *University of Chicago Law School Record* 1, no. 7 (1963).

45. Linda Greenhouse, "A Justice in Chief," *Opinionator* (blog), *New York Times*, June 28, 2012, http://opinionator.blogs.nytimes.com/2012/06/28/a-justice-in-chief/.

46. Bob Woodward and Scott Armstrong, *The Brethren: Inside the Supreme Court* (New York: Simon & Schuster, 1979).

47. Lee Epstein and Jack Knight, "Mapping Out the Strategic Terrain: The Informational Role of Amici Curiae," in *Supreme Court Decision-Making*, ed. Cornell Clayton and Howard Gillman (Chicago: The University of Chicago Press, 1999);

Segal, Spaeth, and Benesh, *Supreme Court in the American Legal System*, chs. 12 and 13.

48. Herbert Jacob, *Justice in America*, 3rd ed. (Boston: Little, Brown, 1978), p. 245. See also Keith E. Whittington, "Judicial Review and Interpretation," in Hall and McGuire, *Judicial Branch*.

49. McCloskey, *American Supreme Court*. See also James H. Fowler and Sangick Jeon, "The Authority of Supreme Court Precedent" (working paper, University of California, Davis, June 29, 2005).

50. Carp and Stidham, *Judicial Process in America*, p. 28.

51. Ibid., p. 57.

52. Mark A. Graber, "From Republic to Democracy: The Judiciary and the Political Process," in Hall and McGuire, *Judicial Branch*.

53. McCloskey, *American Supreme Court*. See also H. W. Perry Jr., *The Transformation of the Supreme Court's Agenda: From the New Deal to the Reagan Administration* (Boulder, CO: Westview Press, 1991); Charles R. Epp, "The Supreme Court and the Rights Revolution," in Hall and McGuire, *Judicial Branch*; and Sunstein, "Judges and Democracy."

54. *Hamdi v. Rumsfeld* (2004).

55. Jessee and Tahk, "What Can We Learn About the Ideology."

56. "Corporations and the Court: America's Supreme Court Is the Most Business-Friendly in Decades," *Economist*, June 23, 2011, p. 17.

57. Epstein and Walker, *Constitutional Law*, Figure I-5, p. 37. See also Brent Kendall, "Supreme Court Comes to Defense of Big Business," *Wall Street Journal*, June 23, 2013; Erwin Chemerinsky, "Justice for Big Business," *New York Times*, July 1, 2013; and Adam Liptak, "Roberts Pulls Supreme Court to the Right Step by Step," *New York Times*, June 27, 2013.

58. Steven Vago, *Law and Society* (New York: Prentice Hall, 2012), pp. 166–170.

59. Gewirtz and Golder, "So Who Are the Activists?"

60. Ibid.

61. Epstein and Walker, *Constitutional Law*, p. 37.

62. Neal Devins and Louis Fischer, *The Democratic Constitution* (New York: Oxford University Press, 2004); Larry D. Kramer, *The People Themselves: Popular Constitutionalism and Judicial Review* (New York: Oxford University Press, 2004).

63. See the discussion in Allison M. Martens, "Reconsidering Judicial Supremacy: From the Counter-Majoritarian Difficulty to Constitutional Transformations," *Perspectives on Politics* 5, no. 3 (September 2007), pp. 447–459.

64. Epstein and Walker, *Rights, Liberties, and Justice*, pp. 22–28.

65. James V. Calvi and Susan Coleman, *American Law and Legal Systems* (New York: Longman, 2012), pp. 148–150.

66. Stephen Breyer, *Active Liberty: Interpreting Our Democratic Constitution* (New York: Knopf, 2005); and Cass Sunstein, *A Constitution of Many Minds: Why the Founding Document Doesn't Mean What It Meant Before* (Princeton, NJ: Princeton University Press, 2009).

67. Graber, "Constructing Judicial Review"; Thomas M. Keck, *The Most Activist Supreme Court in History: The Road to Modern Judicial Conservatism* (Chicago: The University of Chicago Press, 2004); George I. Lovell, *Legislative Deferrals: Statutory Ambiguity, Judicial Power, and American Democracy* (New York: Cambridge University Press, 2003); Kevin K. McMahon, *Reconsidering Roosevelt on Race: How the Presidency Paved the Way for Brown* (Chicago: The University of Chicago Press, 2004); and Keith E. Whittington, *Political Foundations of Judicial Supremacy: The Presidency, the Supreme Court, and Constitutional Leadership in U.S. History* (Princeton, NJ: Princeton University Press, 2007). See also Bruce Ackerman, *We the People: Transformations* (Cambridge, MA: Harvard University Press, 2000); and McCloskey, *American Supreme Court*.

68. Davidson, Oleszek, Lee, and Schickler, *Congress and Its Members*, pp. 345–354; and Epstein and Walker, *Constitutional Law*, pp 39–44.

69. Baum, "Supreme Court in American Politics," p. 167; and Davidson, Oleszek, Lee, and Schickler, *Congress and Its Members*, pp. 354–355.

70. See Davidson, Oleszek, and Lee, *Congress and Its Members*, pp. 354–358, for a discussion of legislative checks on the judiciary.

71. Tom S. Clark, "The Separation of Powers, Court Curbing, and Judicial Legitimacy," *American Journal of Political Science* 53, no. 4 (October 2009), pp. 971–989.

72. Lisa A. Solowiej and Paul M. Collins Jr., "Counteractive Lobbying in the U.S. Supreme Court," *American Politics Research* 37, no. 4 (2009), pp. 670–699.

73. Edward Lazarus, *Closed Chambers* (New York: Penguin Press, 1999), pp. 373–374.

74. Epstein and Knight, "Mapping Out the Strategic Terrain."

75. Dahl, "Decision-Making in a Democracy," pp. 279–295; Thomas R. Marshall, "Public Opinion, Representation, and the Modern Supreme Court," *American Politics Quarterly* 16 (1988), pp. 296–316; McCloskey, *American Supreme Court*, p. 22; O'Brien, *Storm Center*, p. 337; and Baum, *Supreme Court*, pp. 142–144.

76. G. Caldeira, "Courts and Public Opinion," in *The American Courts*, ed. John B. Gates and Charles A. Johnson (Washington, DC: CQ Press, 1991); Jay Casper, "The Supreme Court and National Policy Making," *American Political Science Review* 70 (1976), pp. 50–63; Marshall, "Public Opinion"; William Mishler and Reginald S. Sheehan, "The Supreme Court as a Counter-Majoritarian Institution: The Impact of Public Opinion on Supreme Court Decisions," *American Political Science Review* 87 (1993), pp. 87–101; and Benjamin I. Page and Robert Y. Shapiro, "Effects of Public Opinion on Policy," *American Political Science Review* 77 (1983), p. 183.

77. Segal, Spaeth, and Benesh, *Supreme Court in the American Legal System*, pp. 326–328; and Baum, *Supreme Court*, pp. 140–142.

## 15

1. To see a complete timeline of the NSA controversy, see Al Jazeera America at: http://america.aljazeera.com/articles/multimedia/timeline-edward-snowden-revelations.html.

2. James Ball, "NSA Stores Metadata of Millions of Web Users for Up to a Year, Secret Files Show," *Guardian*, September 30, 2013.

3. Siobhan Gorman, "NSA Officers Spy on Love Interests," *Wall Street Journal*, August 23, 2013.

4. On the "contract clause" see Lee Epstein and Thomas G. Walker, *Constitutional Law for a Changing America* (Washington, D.C.: CQ Press, 2005), ch. 9.

5. James E. Ely Jr., "Property Rights and Democracy in the American Constitutional Order," in Kermit L. Hall and Kevin T. McGuire, eds., *The Judicial Branch* (New York: Oxford University Press, 2005); Richard Fallon, *The Dynamic Constitution: An Introduction to American Constitutional Law* (New York: Cambridge University Press, 2004), ch. 3, "Protection of Economic Liberties."

6. Laurence H. Tribe, *American Constitutional Law*, 3rd ed. (New York: Foundation Press, 2000), ch. 9.

7. Morton J. Horwitz, *The Transformation of American Law, 1780–1860* (Cambridge, MA: Harvard University Press, 1977); J. Willard Hurst, *Law and the Conditions of Freedom in the Nineteenth-Century United States* (Madison: University of Wisconsin Press, 1956).

8. Lee Epstein and Thomas G. Walker, *Rights, Liberties, and Justice* (Washington, D.C.: CQ Press, 2010), pp. 67–87, 93–94.

9. Gregory C. Shaffer, "Law and Business," in Graham Wilson, Wyn Grant, and David Coen, eds., *The Oxford Handbook of Business and Government* (New York: Oxford University Press, 2010), p. 68.

10. Barker et al., *Civil Liberties and the Constitution*, pp. 32–37; Epstein and Walker, *Constitutional Law for a Changing America*, pp. 431–438; Anthony Lewis, *Freedom for the Thought That We Hate: A Biography of the First Amendment* (New York: Basic Books, 2007); John C. Domino, *Civil Rights and Liberties in the 21st Century* (New York: Pearson Longman, 2010), ch. 2.

11. See Geoffrey R. Stone, *Perilous Times: Free Speech in Wartime* (New York: W. W. Norton, 2004).

12. See Stanley I. Kutler, *The American Inquisition: Justice and Injustice in the Cold War* (New York: Hill & Wang, 1982).

13. David Stout, "FBI Head Admits Mistakes in Use of Security Act," *New York Times*, March 10, 2007, p. A1; "FBI Underreported Patriot Act Use," *Wall Street Journal*, March 9, 2007, p. 1.

14. See Fred W. Friendly, *Minnesota Rag* (New York: Vintage, 1981).

15. See Barker et al., *Civil Liberties and the Constitution*, pp. 169–178; Epstein and Walker, *Rights, Liberties, and Justice*, pp. 292–295; and Alpheus Thomas Mason and Donald Grier Stephenson Jr., *American Constitutional Law* (New York: Longman, 2012), pp. 463–467.

16. See Charles Rembar, *The End of Obscenity* (New York: Harper & Row, 1968).

17. Fallon, *The Dynamic Constitution*, p. 48.

18. Barker et al., *Civil Liberties and the Constitution*, pp. 204–205.

19. Epstein and Walker, *Rights, Liberties, and Justice*, pp. 145–192.

20. Fallon, *The Dynamic Constitution*, pp. 61–67.

21. Ibid., p. 63.

22. Adam Liptak, "Religious Groups Given 'Exception' to Work Bias Law," *New York Times*, January 11, 2012, p. 1.

23. Erik Eckholm, "'Aid in Dying' Movement Takes Hold in Some States," *New York Times*, February 7, 2014.

24. Gallup Poll, "U.S. Support for Euthanasia Hinges on How It's Described," May 29, 2013, http://www.gallup.com/poll/162815/support-euthanasia-hinges-described.aspx.

25. David Stout, "FBI Head Admits Mistakes in Use of Security Act," *New York Times* (March 10, 2007), p. 1.

26. "World Prison Brief" (London: International Center for Prison Studies, Kings College, London, press release, June 8, 2011).

27. *Katz v. United States* (1967).

28. *United States v. Leon* (1984); *Massachusetts v. Sheppard* (1984).

29. *Nix v. Williams* (1984).

30. *Harris v. New York* (1971*); New York v. Quarles* (1984).

31. *Arizona v. Fulminate* (1991).

32. Jim Yardley, "A Role Model for Executions," *New York Times*, January 9, 2000, p. A1, IV–5.

33. Gallup Poll, "Support for death penalty lowest in 40 years," 2013, http://www.gallup.com/poll/165626/death-penalty-support-lowest-years.aspx

34. See the Death Penalty Information Center at http://www.deathpenaltyinfo.org/states-and-without-death-penalty.

35. The Innocence Project, http://www.innocenceproject.org/Content/DNA_Exonerations_Nationwide.php.

36. Robert Barnes, "Supreme Court Opens Way for Prisoners to Try to Gain Access to DNA Evidence," *Washington Post*, March 7, 2011.

37. Gallup Poll, October 1–4, 2009. Mason and Stephenson Jr., *American Constitutional Law*, p. 396.

38. For all data in this paragraph, see the Fact Sheet, Death Penalty Information Center (http://www.deathpenaltyinfo.org/documents/FactSheet.pdf) accessed March 16, 2012.

39. Stone, *Perilous Times: Free Speech in Wartime*; Fallon, *The Dynamic Constitution*, ch. 12.

40. Former Chief Justice William Rehnquist believed that each successive American war involved fewer and less serious violations of civil liberties. See *All the Laws But One: Civil Liberties in Wartime* (New York: Knopf, 1998).

41. "Security Trumps Civil Liberties," a report of a poll conducted by National Public Radio, the Kennedy School of Government of Harvard University, and the Kaiser Family Fund (November 30, 2001).

42. David Stout, "FBI Head Admits Mistakes in Use of Security Act," *New York Times*, March 10, 2007, p. A1.

43. Barton Gellman, "The FBI's Secret Scrutiny," *Washington Post*, November 6, 2005, p. A1.

44. Pew Research Center, "Threat of Terrorism and Civil Liberties" (December 3, 2009).

45. Charlie Savage, "Warrantless Surveillance Challenged by Defendant," *New York Times*, (January 29, 2014).

46. Kent Roach, *The 9/11 Effect: Comparative Counter-Terrorism* (New York: Cambridge University Press, 2011); and Adam Liptak, "Civil Liberties Today," *New York Times*, September 11, 2011, p. 14.

47. Pew Research Center, "Growing Concern about Rise of Islamic Extremism at Home and Abroad," September 2014, http://www.people-press.org/files/2014/09/9-10-14-Islamic-Extremism-release.pdf.

# 16

1. Greg Winter, "Schools Resegregate, Study Finds," *New York Times*, January 21, 2003.

2. Gary Orfield, John Kucsera, and Genevieve Siegel-Hawley, *E Pluribus…Separation: Deepening Double Segregation for More Students* (Los Angeles: UCLA/The Civil Rights Project, September 19, 2012), http://civilrightsproject.ucla.edu/research/k-12-education/integration-and-diversity/mlk-national/e-pluribus…separation-deepening-double-segregation-for-more-students. The statistics in the remainder of this chapter-opening story are from this report.

3. Ibid.

4. Ibid. See also Charles T. Clotfelter, *After Brown: The Rise and Retreat of School Desegregation* (Princeton, NJ: Princeton University Press, 2004).

5. A recent study shows a decrease in the extent of white-only areas in American cities, primarily because of the influx of Latino and Asian populations. The divide between non-Hispanic whites and blacks remains relatively unchanged. See Sam Roberts, "Segregation Curtailed in U.S. Cities, Study Finds," *New York Times*, January 30, 2012.

6. Lucius J. Barker, Twiley W. Barker Jr., Michael W. Combs, Kevin L. Lyles, and H. W. Perry Jr., *Civil Liberties and the Constitution*, 9th ed. (New York: Pearson, 2011), pp. 446–447; Richard H. Fallon, *The Dynamic Constitution: An Introduction to Constitutional Law* (New York: Cambridge University Press, 2004), pp. 109–110; and John C. Domino, *Civil Rights and Liberties in the 21st Century*, 3rd ed. (New York: Pearson, 2010), pp. 2–3.

7. James MacGregor Burns and Stewart Burns, *A People's Charter: The Pursuit of Rights in America* (New York: Knopf, 1991), p. 37.

8. On why the courts were such an attractive target for people seeking to expand civil rights, see Charles R. Epp, "The Courts and the Rights Revolution," in *The Judicial Branch*, ed. Kermit L. Hall and Kevin T. McGuire (New York: Oxford University Press, 2005).

9. William H. Chafe, *The Unfinished Journey: America Since World War II* (New York: Oxford University Press, 1986), p. 149.

10. Fallon, *Dynamic Constitution*, pp. 118–120.

11. Ibid., pp. 119–122. See also Lee Epstein and Thomas G. Walker, *Rights, Liberty, and Justice* (Washington, DC: CQ Press, 2010), pp. 593–601.

12. Domino, *Civil Rights and Liberties*, p. 297; Chafe, *Unfinished Journey*, pp. 79–110.

13. Epp, "Courts and the Rights Revolution."

14. Pew Research Social & Demographic Trends, "King's Dream Remains an Elusive Goal: Many Americans See Racial Disparities," Pew Research Center, August 22, 2013, http://www.pewsocialtrends.org/2013/08/22/kings-dream-remains-an-elusive-goal-many-americans-see-racial-disparities/.

15. Federal Bureau of Investigation, "Preliminary Semiannual Uniform Crime Reports, January–June 2013," http://www.fbi.gov/about-us/cjis/ucr/crime-in-the-u.s/2013/preliminary-semiannual-uniform-crime-report-january-june-2013.

16. This section is based on Richard D. Kahlenberg, *The Remedy: Class, Race, and Affirmative Action* (New York: Basic Books, 1996); and Fallon, *Dynamic Constitution*, ch. 5.

17. Ira Katznelson, *When Affirmative Action Was White: An Untold Story of Racial Inequality in Twentieth-Century America* (New York: Norton, 2005), pp. 145–149.

18. Barker et al., *Civil Liberties and the Constitution*, pp. 514–517.

19. Katznelson, *Affirmative Action*.

20. "Black America," *Economist*, August 24, 2013, p. 27.

21. Martin Gilens, Paul M. Sniderman, and James H. Kuklinski, "Affirmative Action and the Politics of Realignment," *British Journal of Political Science* 28 (January 1998), pp. 159–184; Jack Citrin, David O. Sears, Christopher Muste, and Cara Wong, "Multiculturalism in American Public Opinion," *British Journal of Political Science* 31 (2001), pp. 247–275; and Drew DeSilver, "As Supreme Court Defers Affirmative Action Ruling, Deep Divides Persist," *Fact Tank* (blog), Pew Research Center, June 24, 2013, http://www.pewresearch.org/fact-tank/2013/06/24/as-supreme-court-defers-affirmative-action-ruling-deep-divides-persist/.

22. DeSilver, "As Supreme Court Defers Affirmative Action"; "Public Backs Affirmative Action, But Not Minority Preferences," Pew Research Center, June 2, 2009, http://www.pewresearch.org/2009/06/02/public-backs-affirmative-action-but-not-minority-preferences/; Pew Research Center for the People & the Press, "Trends in Political Values and Core Attitudes: 1987–2007," Pew Research Center, March 22, 2007; http://www.people-press.org/2007/03/22/trends-in-political-values-and-core-attitudes-1987-2007/.

23. George M. Fredrickson, "Still Separate and Unequal," *New York Review of Books*, November 17, 2005, p. 13.

24. Opinion of the Court, *Grutter v. Bollinger* (2003).

25. These cases include cases in Seattle and Louisville involving assignment of students to school districts to advance racial balance and diversity: *Meredith v. Jefferson County Board of Education* (2007) and *Parents Involved in Community Schools v. Seattle School District No. 1* (2007).

26. *Meredith v. Jefferson County Board of Education* (2007); *Parents Involved in Community Schools v. Seattle School District No. 1* (2007).

27. Epstein and Walker, *Rights, Liberties, and Justice*, pp. 686–687.

28. A. Judith Baer and Leslie Friedman Goldstein, *The Constitutional and Legal Rights of Women* (Belmont, CA: Roxbury Publishing, 2006); Chafe, *Unfinished Journey*; Barbara Sinclair Deckard, *The Women's Movement* (New York: Harper and Row, 1975); Ethel Klein, *Gender Politics* (Cambridge, MA: Harvard University Press, 1984), ch. 2; and J. Freeman, *Politics of Women's Liberation* (New York: McKay, 1975).

29. "Women CEOs of the Fortune 1000," Catalyst.org, May 1, 2014, http://www.catalyst.org/knowledge/women-ceos-fortune-1000.

30. See Epp, "Courts and the Rights Revolution"; Fallon, *Dynamic Constitution*, pp. 129–133; and Barker et al., *Civil Liberties and the Constitution*, pp. 689–691.

31. Epstein and Walker, *Rights, Liberties, and Justice*, p. 629.

32. Caitlin Peterkin, "Male-Female Pay Gap Persists and Starts Early, Study Finds," *Chronicle of Higher Education*, October, 24, 2012, http://chronicle.com/article/Male-Female-Pay-Gap-Persists/135270/. For sharply conflicting views on the seriousness of the wage gap, see Marcia Greenberger's testimony on the Paycheck Fairness Act before the House Committee on Education and Labor on September 11, 2007, and Barbara Berish Brown's testimony before the Senate Committee on Health, Labor and Pensions on April 12, 2007.

33. Harris Poll, July 2007.

34. Linda Greenhouse, "Justices Give the States Immunity from Suits by Disabled Workers," *New York Times*, February 22, 2001.

35. Seth Motel, "On Stonewall Anniversary, A Reminder of How Much Public Opinion Has Changed," *Fact Tank* (blog), Pew Research Center, June 26, 2013, http://www.pewresearch.org/fact-tank/2013/06/26/on-stonewall-anniversary-a-reminder-of-how-much-public-opinion-has-changed/.

36. CBS News Poll, March 20–24, 2013; and Dorothy Samuels, "A Long, Winding Road to Marriage Equality," *New York Times*, November 12, 2011.

37. Pew Research Social & Demographic Trends, "A Survey of LGBT Americans," Pew Research Center, June 13, 2013, http://www.pewsocialtrends.org/2013/06/13/a-survey-of-lgbt-americans/9/.

# 17

1. For general accounts, see John Cassidy, *How Markets Fail* (New York: Farrar, Straus and Giroux, 2009); Carmen M. Reinhart and Kenneth Rogoff, *This Time Is Different: Eight Centuries of Financial Folly* (Princeton, NJ: Princeton University Press, 2009); and Joseph E. Stiglitz, *Freefall: America, Free Markets and the Sinking of the World Economy* (New York: Norton, 2010).

2. Paul Krugman, "The Jobless Trap," *New York Times*, April 21, 2013.

3. Andy Sullivan, "Stimulus Added Millions of Jobs in Q2," Reuters, August 24, 2010; David Leonhardt, "Wait, Did the Stimulus Work?," *Economix* (blog), *New York Times*, June 11, 2010; Paul Krugman, "On the Inadequacy of the Stimulus," *The Conscience of a Liberal* (blog), *New York Times*, September 5, 2011; and Edward Glaeser, "What We Don't Know, and Perhaps Can't," *Economix* (blog), *New York Times*, June 1, 2010.

4. Baird Webel, *The Dodd–Frank Wall Street Reform and Consumer Protection Act: Issues and Summary*, Report 7-5700 (Washington, DC: Congressional Research Service, July 29, 2010), http://www.llsdc.org/assets/DoddFrankdocs/crs-r41350.pdf.

5. Frank Newport, "Views in U.S. That Gov't Is Too Powerful Show Little Change," GALLUP Politics, May 27, 2013, http://www.gallup.com/poll/162779/views-gov-powerful-little-changed.aspx.

6. This well-known relationship is supported by substantial research. See Robert S. Erikson and Kent L. Tedin, *American Public Opinion* (New York: Longman, 2011), pp. 121–122.

7. Fred C. Pampel, *Age, Class, Politics, and the Welfare State* (New York: Cambridge University Press, 1989), p. 16; and Harold Wilensky, *The Welfare State and Equality* (Berkeley, CA: University of California Press, 1975).

8. Robert E. Goodin, "Reasons for Welfare," in *Responsibility, Rights, and Welfare: The Theory of the Welfare State*, ed. J. Donald Moon (Boulder, CO: Westview Press, 1988); and Harold L. Wilensky, *Welfare State and Equality*. Also see Clark Kerr, John T. Dunlop, Frederick H. Harbison, and Charles A. Myers, *Industrialism and Industrial Man* (New York: Oxford University Press, 1964).

9. Dean Baker and Kevin Hassett, "The Human Disaster of Unemployment," *New York Times*, May 12, 2012.

10. This discussion is based largely on B. Guy Peters, *American Public Policy: Promise and Performance*, 8th ed. (New York: CQ Press, 2010), pp. 202–213.

11. On the benefits of economic growth, see William J. Baumol, Robert E. Litan, and Carl J. Schramm, *Good Capitalism, Bad*

*Capitalism, and the Economics of Growth and Prosperity* (New Haven, CT: Yale University Press, 2007), ch. 2; and Gregg Easterbrook, *The Progress Paradox* (New York: Random House, 2003).

12. Several Southern European countries such as Greece, Italy, Portugal, and Spain also have substantial structural deficits (meaning long-term; not tied to short-term problems like economic stimulus during down economic times) arising from an unwillingness to properly fund and/or size old age pension and health care systems.

13. Michael Kunzelman and Chevel Johnson, "Court Upholds Approval of BP Oil Spill Settlement," Associated Press, January 10, 2014.

14. Sharon Terlep, "Target at Post-Bailout GM: Earning $10 Billion a Year," *Wall Street Journal*, February 6, 2012.

15. Zachary Karabell, "Does Government Matter?," *Bloomberg Businessweek*, July 4–July 10, 2011, pp. 10–11.

16. Roger Lowenstein, "The Education of Ben Bernanke," *Sunday New York Times Magazine*, January 20, 2008, pp. 36–39, 61–68.

17. See David Coen, Wyn Grant, and Graham Wilson, "Political Science: Perspectives on Business and Government," in *The Oxford Handbook of Business and Government*, ed. David Coen, Wyn Grant, and Graham Wilson (New York: Oxford University Press, 2010), pp. 20–24.

18. Paul Krugman, "How the Case for Austerity Has Crumbled," *New York Review of Books*, June 6, 2013.

19. See "The Keynes Comeback," *Economist*, October 3, 2009, pp. 103–104; Noam Scheiber, "Market Riot," *Foreign Policy* (December 2009), pp. 45–48; and Bruce Bartlett, "Revenge of the Reality-Based Community," *American Conservative* (November 26, 2012). The theorist of financial crises, Hyman Minsky, also gained new adherents, given his near-perfect prediction, in his 1986 book *Stabilizing an Unstable Economy*, of what came to a head in 2008.

20. John Cassidy, *How Markets Fail: The Logic of Economic Calamities* (New York: Farrar, Straus and Giroux, 2009).

21. Peters, *American Public Policy*, pp. 142–144.

22. The following discussion of the budget-making process is based on Roger H. Davidson, Walter J. Oleszek, and Frances E. Lee, *Congress and Its Members*, 13th ed. (Washington, DC: CQ Press, 2012), pp. 416–434; Peters, *American Public Policy*, pp. 141–151.

23. For a detailed overview of the federal budget process, see Allen Schick, *The Federal Budget: Politics, Policy, Process* (Washington, DC: Brookings Institution Press, 2008).

24. William A. Niskanen, *Bureaucracy and Representative Government* (Chicago: Aldine, 1971).

25. Office of Management and Budget, "Table 8.5 – Outlays for Mandatory and Related Programs: 1962–2018" and "Table 8.7 – Outlays for Discretionary Programs: 1962–2018," *Budget of the United States Government, Fiscal Year 2013* (Washington, DC: Office of Management and Budget, 2013).

26. The data on the budget in these sections are from *The Budget of the United States Government, Fiscal Year 2013*, and "A People's Guide to the Federal Budget," National Priorities Project, http://nationalpriorities.org/budget-basics/peoples-guide/.

27. For a concise and stimulating discussion of forms of taxation and their effects, as well as the politics surrounding them, see B. Guy Peters, "Tax Policy," in *Handbook of Public Policy*, ed. B. Guy Peters and Jon Pierre (Thousand Oaks, CA: Sage, 2006), pp. 281–292; and Bruce Bartlett, *The Benefit and the Burden* (New York: Simon & Schuster, 2012).

28. Office of Management and Budget, *Budget of the United States Government, Fiscal Year 2013*, "Historical Tables."

29. Ibid.

30. Congressional Budget Office, *The Distribution of Household Income and Federal Taxes, 2010* (Washington, DC: Congressional Budget Office, December 4, 2013).

31. Peters, *American Public Policy*, pp. 229–231; "Effective Tax Rates," The National Bureau of Economic Research, 2010; and Seth

Hanlon, "Tax Expenditure of the Week: Capital Gains," Center for American Progress, February 23, 2011, http://www.american progress.org/issues/open-government/news/2011/02/23/9163 /tax-expenditure-of-the-week-capital-gains/.

32. Lori Montgomery, "Deficit to Dip below $600 Billion for the First Time since Recession, White House Predicts," *Washington Post,* July 11, 2014; Congressional Budget Office, 2014 Long-Term Budget Outlook, July 15, 2014.

33. Steven Rattner, "The Dangerous Notion That Debt Doesn't Matter," *New York Times*, January 20, 2012.

34. Paul Krugman, "Addicted to the Apocalypse," *New York Times,* October 24, 2013.

35. Jackie Calmes, "Party Gridlock in Washington Feeds Fear of a Debt Crisis," *New York Times*, February 17, 2010.

36. David Leonhardt, "In Greek Debt Crisis, Some See Parallels to U.S.," *New York Times*, May 12, 2010.

37. Pew Research Center for the People & the Press, "Auto Bailout Now Backed, Stimulus Divisive," February 23, 2012, Pew Research Center, http://www.people-press.org/2012/02/23 /auto-bailout-now-backed-stimulus-divisive/.

38. George J. Stigler, "The Theory of Economic Regulation," *Bell Journal* 2 (Spring 1971), pp. 3–21. See also Gabriel Kolko, *The Triumph of Conservatism* (Chicago: Quadrangle, 1967); and James Weinstein, *The Corporate Ideal in the Liberal State* (Boston: Beacon Press, 1968).

39. See Marc Allen Eisner, *Regulatory Politics in Transition* (Baltimore: Johns Hopkins University Press, 2000); Richard Harris and Sidney Milkis, *The Politics of Regulatory Change* (New York: Oxford University Press, 1989); and Michael Moran, "The Rise of the Regulatory State," in Coen, Grant, and Wilson, *Oxford Handbook of Business and Government*, pp. 383–403.

40. See G. William Domhoff, *The Higher Circles* (New York: Random House, 1970); Edward S. Greenberg, *Capitalism and the American Political Ideal* (Armonk, NY: M. E. Sharpe, 1985); Kolko, *Triumph of Conservatism*; and Weinstein, *Corporate Ideal in the Liberal State*.

41. Frances Fox Piven and Richard A. Cloward, *Poor People's Movements* (New York: Vintage, 1979).

42. Marver H. Bernstein, *Regulation by Independent Commission* (Princeton, NJ: Princeton University Press, 1955); Grant McConnell, *Private Power and American Democracy* (New York: Vintage Books, 1966); and Theodore J. Lowi, *The End of Liberalism* (New York: Norton, 1979).

43. David Vogel, *Fluctuating Fortunes: The Political Power of Business in the United States* (New York: Basic Books, 1989), pp. 59, 112.

44. James Buchanan and Gordon Tullock, "Polluters, Profits and Political Responses: Direct Control versus Taxes," *American Economic Review* 65 (1975), pp. 139–147; L. Lave, *The Strategy of Social Regulation* (Washington, DC: Brookings Institution Press, 1981); and Murray Weidenbaum, *The Costs of Government Regulation of Business* (Washington, DC: Joint Economic Committee of Congress, 1978).

45. See Thomas Byrne Edsall, *The New Politics of Inequality* (New York: Norton, 1984); Vogel, *Fluctuating Fortunes*; Kevin P. Phillips, *The Politics of Rich and Poor: Wealth and the American Electorate in the Reagan Aftermath* (New York: Random House, 1990); and Thomas Ferguson and Joel Rogers, *Right Turn: The Decline of the Democrats and the Future of American Politics* (New York: Farrar, Straus & Giroux, 1986).

46. Catherine Rampell, "Lax Oversight Caused Crisis, Bernanke Says," *New York Times*, January 6, 2001.

47. For accessible descriptions of this shadow banking system and its risky practices, see Simon Johnson and James Kwak, *13 Bankers: The Wall Street Takeover and the Next Financial Meltdown* (New York: Pantheon, 2010); Michael Lewis, *The Big Short: Inside the Doomsday Machine* (New York: Norton, 2010); and Roger Lowenstein, *The End of Wall Street* (New York: Penguin Press, 2010).

48. "How the European Union Is Becoming the World's Chief Regulator," *The Economist*, September 22, 2007, p. 66.

49. Andrew Martin, "Child-Product Makers Seek to Soften New Rules," *The New York Times*, February 21, 2011, p. 1.

50. Office of Management and Budget, "Historical Tables."

51. Congressional Budget Office, *Growth in Means-Tested Programs and Tax Credits for Low-Income Households* (Washington, DC: Congressional Budget Office, February 2013).

52. Howard Jacob Karger and David Stoesz, *American Welfare State Policy: A Pluralist Approach* (Boston: Allyn & Bacon, 2010), pp. 260–261.

53. Pew Research Center for the People & the Press, "The Generation Gap and the 2012 Election," Pew Research Center, November 3, 2011, http://www.people-press.org/2011/11/03 /the-generation-gap-and-the-2012-election-3/.

54. Jacob S. Hacker, *The Great Risk Shift* (New York: Oxford University Press, 2006), ch. 2.

55. Social Security Administration, *The 2013 OASDI Trustees Report* (Washington, DC: Social Security Administration, 2013).

56. Pew Research Center for the People & the Press, "Generation Gap."

57. Benjamin I. Page and James R. Simmons, *What Government Can Do: Dealing with Poverty and Inequality* (Chicago: The University of Chicago Press, 2000), ch. 3; Edmund L. Andrews, "4 Ways That Might Save the Government Trillions," *New York Times,* February 4, 2006; and Peters, *American Public Policy*, pp. 300–311.

58. *The Social Security Fix-It Book* (Boston: Boston College Center for Retirement Research, 2010).

59. Ibid.

60. Edward P. Lazear, "The Virtues of Personal Accounts for Social Security," *Economists' Voice* 2, no. 1 (2005), pp. 1–7.

61. Pew Research Center for the People & the Press, "Generation Gap."

62. Robert Pear, "AARP Opposed Bush Plan to Reduce Social Security with Private Accounts," *New York Times,* November 12, 2004.

63. The Henry J. Kaiser Family Foundation, "Medicare Enrollment, 1966–2013," http://kff.org/medicare/slide/medicare -enrollment-1966-2013/.

64. Diana M. DiNitto, *Social Welfare: Politics and Public Policy,* 7th ed. (New York: Pearson, 2010), pp. 310–318.

65. "U.S. Pensions Found to Lift Many of the Poor," *New York Times*, December 28, 1989. Also see Theodore R. K. Marmor, Jerry L. Mashaw, and Philip L. Harvey, *America's Misunderstood Welfare State* (New York: HarperCollins, 1990), ch. 4.

66. David S. Johnson, *2008 Income, Poverty, and Health Insurance Estimates for the Current Population Survey* (Washington, DC: U.S. Census Bureau, September 10, 2009).

67. U.S. Census Bureau, Statistical Abstracts of the United States, 2010.

68. Jason Furman, *Top Ten Facts on Social Security's 70th Anniversary* (Washington, DC: Center on Budget and Policy Priorities, 2007).

69. Peters, *American Public Policy,* p. 311.

70. Raksha Arora, "Americans Dissatisfied with Government's Efforts on Poverty," *gpns Commentary,* Gallup, October 25, 2005, http://www.gallup.com/poll/19396/americans -dissatisfied-governments-efforts-poverty.aspx; and "Majority Call Fighting Poverty a 'Top Priority,'" Zogby Poll, news release, June 4, 2007.

71. Hugh Heclo, "The Political Foundations of Anti-Poverty Policy," in *Fighting Poverty: What Works and What Doesn't?,* ed. Sheldon Danziger and Daniel Weinberg (Cambridge, MA: Harvard University Press, 1986); and Fay Lomax Cook and Edith J. Barrett, *Support for the American Welfare State: The Views of Congress and the Public* (New York: HarperCollins, 1990), ch 4.

72. Joel F. Handler and Yeheskel Hasenfeld, *Blame Welfare, Ignore Poverty and Inequality* (Cambridge, UK: Cambridge University Press, 2007); and Martin Gilens, *Why Americans Hate Welfare: Race, Media, and the Politics of Antipoverty Policy* (Chicago: The University of Chicago Press, 1999).

73. Sandra K. Danziger, "The Decline of Cash Welfare and Implications for Social Policy and Poverty," *Annual Review of Sociology* 36 (2010), pp. 523–545.

74. "From Welfare to Work," *Economist*, July 29, 2006, pp. 27–30; Lauren Etter, "Welfare Reform: Ten Years Later," *Wall Street Journal*, August 26, 2006; and Robert Pear and Erik Eckholm, "A Decade After Welfare Reform," *New York Times*, August 21, 2006.

75. Eckholm, "A Decade After Welfare Reform."

76. Karger and Stoesz, *American Social Welfare Policy*, pp. 277–280.

77. Robert Pear, "In a Tough Economy, Old Limits on Welfare," *New York Times*, April 10, 2010.

78. Number calculated by the authors from data on the SNAP Factsheet, U.S. Department of Agriculture. See also Robert Greenstein, *Dispelling Confusion on Food Stamps, Tax Rebates, and the Stimulus Package* (Washington, DC: Center on Budget and Policy Priorities, January 26, 2008); John E. Schwarz, *America's Hidden Success: A Reassessment of Public Policy from Kennedy to Reagan* (New York: Norton, 1988), p. 37; Karger and Stoesz, *American Social Welfare Policy*, pp. 453–456; and Brad Plumer, "Why Are 47 Million Americans on Food Stamps? It's the Recession—Mostly," *Washington Post,* September 23, 2013.

79. Sandhya Somashekhar and Karen Tumulty, "With New Year, Medicaid Takes on a Broader Health-care Role," *Washington Post*, December 21, 2013.

80. Ibid.

81. DiNitto, *Social Welfare*, pp. 302–310.

82. "Income, Poverty, and Health Insurance Coverage in the United States: 2010" (Washington, D.C.: U.S. Census Bureau, September 2011).

83. Center on Budget and Policy Priorities, *What Is SCHIP?* (Washington, DC: Center on Budget and Policy Priorities, 2007).

84. Center on Budget and Policy Priorities, "Policy Basics: The Earned Income Tax Credit," updated January 31, 2014, http:// www.cbpp.org/cms/?fa=view&id=2505; Peters, *American Public Policy,* p. 320; and Christopher Howard, *The Hidden Welfare State: Tax Expenditures and Social Policy in the United States* (Princeton, NJ: Princeton University Press, 1999), ch. 3.

85. Jessica Banthin and Sarah Masi, "CBO's Estimate of the Net Budgetary Impact of the Affordable Care Act's Health Insurance Coverage Provisions Has Not Changed Much Over Time," Congressional Budget Office, May 14, 2013, http:// www.cbo.gov/publication/44176.

86. John Dickerson, "System Malfunction: How Politics, Partisanship, and Spin Doomed healthcare.gov," *Slate,* November 4, 2013, http://www.slate.com/articles/news_and_politics /politics/2013/11/healthcare_gov_doomed_by_partisanship _and_spin_obamacare_s_failed_launch.html.

87. Gosta Esping-Andersen, "The Three Political Economies of the Welfare State," *Canadian Review of Sociology and Anthropology* 26 (1989), pp. 10–36; and Jonas Pontusson, "The American Welfare State in Comparative Perspective," *Perspectives on Politics* 4, no. 2 (June 2006), pp. 315–326.

88. On the state of the scholarship on this subject see Francis G. Castles, Stephan Leibfried, Jane Lewis, Herbert Obinger, and Christopher Pierson, eds., *The Oxford Handbook of the Welfare State* (Oxford: Oxford University Press, 2010).

89. See "OECD Social Indicators" at the "statistics portal" of the Organization for Economic Cooperation and Development at www.oecd.org/topicsstatsportal (February 2007). Also see Vincent A. Mahler and Claudio J. Katz, "Social Benefits in Advanced Capitalist Countries: A Cross-National Assessment," *Comparative Politics* 21 (1988), pp. 37–50; and Arnold

J. Heidenheimer, Hugh Heclo, and Carolyn Teich Adams, *Comparative Public Policy: The Politics of Social Choice in America, Europe, and Japan,* 3rd ed. (New York: St. Martin's Press, 1990).

90. Andrea Brandolini and Timothy M. Smeeding, "Patterns of Economic Inequality in Western Democracies: Some Facts on Levels and Trends," *PS* 39, no. 1 (January 2006), pp. 21–26; and Lee Kenworthy and Jonas Pontusson, "Rising Inequality and the Politics of Redistribution in Affluent Countries," *Perspectives on Politics* 3, no. 3 (September 2005), pp. 449–472.

91. Alberto Alesina and Edward L. Glaeser, *Fighting Poverty in the US and Europe: A World of Difference* (New York: Oxford University Press, 2004); and Nathan Glazer, *The Limits of Social Policy* (Cambridge, MA: Harvard University Press, 1988), pp. 187–188. Also see W. Sombart, *Why There Is No Socialism in the United States* (Armonk, NY: M. E. Sharpe, 1976).

92. Douglas S. Massey, "Globalization and Inequality: Explaining American Exceptionalism," *European Sociological Review* 25, no. 1 (2009), pp. 9–23.

93. Gilens, *Why Americans Hate Welfare*; and Jeff Manza, "Race and the Underdevelopment of the American Welfare State," *Theory and Society* 29 (2000), pp. 819–832. See also Alesina and Glaeser, *Fighting Poverty in the US and Europe*; Carol A. Horton, *Race and the Making of American Liberalism* (New York: Oxford University Press, 2005); and Desmond S. King and Rogers M. Smith, *Still a House Divided: Race and Politics in Obama's America* (Princeton, NJ: Princeton University Press, 2011).

94. Martin Gilens, "'Race Coding' and White Opposition to Welfare," *American Political Science Review* (1996), pp. 593–604.

95. Wilensky, *Welfare State and Equality;* John Micklethwait and Adrian Wooldridge, *The Right Nation: Conservative Power in America* (New York: Penguin Press, 2004); and Handler and Hasenfeld, *Blame Welfare.*

96. Koen Caminada and Megan C. Martin, "Differences in Anti-Poverty Approaches in Europe and the United States," *Poverty and Public Policy* 3, no. 2 (2011), pp. 1–14.

97. Francis G. Castles, *The Impact of Parties: Politics and Policies in Democratic Capitalist States* (Newbury Park, CA: Sage, 1982); Gosta Esping-Andersen, *Politics Against Markets* (Princeton, NJ: Princeton University Press, 1985); Walter Korpi, *The Democratic Class Struggle* (New York: Routledge, 1983); and John Stephens, *The Transition from Capitalism to Socialism* (London: Macmillan, 1979).

98. U.S. Department of Labor, Bureau of Labor Statistics, Union Affiliation Data; and Gerald Mayer, "Union Membership Trends in the United States," *CRS Report for Congress,* RL 32553, August 31, 2004.

99. David Cay Johnston, *Perfectly Legal* (New York: Portfolio, 2003).

100. Pew Research Center for the People & the Press, "Most See Inequality Growing, but Partisans Differ over Solutions," Pew Research Center, January 23, 2014, http://www.people-press.org/2014/01/23/most-see-inequality-growing-but-partisans-differ-over-solutions/2/.

101. Emmanuel Saez, "Striking it Richer: The Evolution of Top Incomes in the United States (Updated with 2012 preliminary estimates)," September 3, 2013, http://elsa.berkeley.edu/~saez/saez-UStopincomes-2012.pdf.

102. Pew Research Center for the People & the Press, "Most See Inequality Growing."

103. Barack Obama, 2014 State of the Union Address, January 28, 2014, http://www.whitehouse.gov/the-press-office/2014/01/28/president-barack-obamas-state-union-address.

## 18

1. Helene Cooper, Michael Wines, and David E. Sanger, "China's Role as Lender Alters Obama's Visit," *New York Times,* November 14, 2009.

2. Charles Riley, "World Chastises US as Debt Ceiling Looms," CNNMoney, CNN, October 14, 2013, http://money.cnn.com/2013/10/14/news/economy/debt-ceiling-world/; and Chris Isidor, "China Not Impressed by U.S. Debt Deal," CNNMoney, CNN, October 18, 2013, http://money.cnn.com/2013/10/17/news/economy/debt-ceiling-deal-china/.

3. International Monetary Fund, "World Economic Outlook, 2013," 2013.

4. John Hawksworth and Gordon Cookson, *The World in 2050—Beyond the BRICs: A Broader Look at Emerging Market Growth Prospects* (London: Pricewaterhouse Coopers, March 2008).

5. *Global Trends 2025: A Transformed World* (Washington, DC: U.S. National Intelligence Council, 2008); and Daniel W. Drezner, "… and China Isn't Beating the U.S.," *Foreign Policy* (January/February 2011), p. 67.

6. Benjamin I. Page with Marshall M. Bouton, *The Foreign Policy Disconnect: What Americans Want from Our Leaders But Don't Get* (Chicago: The University of Chicago Press, 2006).

7. For opposing views on just how much America's relative advantage has slipped or grown more pronounced, see, for the former view, Fareed Zakaria, *The Post-American World* (New York: Norton, 2008). For the latter view, see Robert Kagan, *The World America Made* (New York: Knopf, 2012).

8. Niall Ferguson, *Colossus: The Price of America's Empire* (New York: Penguin, 2004); William E. Odom and Robert Dujarric, *America's Inadvertent Empire* (New Haven, CT: Yale University Press, 2004); Chalmers Johnson, *The Sorrows of Empire* (New York: Metropolitan Books, 2004). For a thoughtful review of a shelf of relatively recent books describing, lamenting, or celebrating American empire see Emily S. Rosenberg, "Bursting America's Imperial Bubble," *The Chronicle of Higher Education* 53, no. 11 (November 3, 2006), p. B10. For an analysis that suggests that the United States is less of an imperial power than it once was, see Daniel H. Nexon and Thomas Wright, "What's at Stake in the American Empire Debate," *American Political Science Review* 101, no. 2 (May 2007), pp. 253–271.

9. We assess the relative weight of China in the world economy compared to the United States using nominal GDP, where GDP is measured in the dollar value of what goods and services are produced. We use what is called "purchasing power parity" GDP for the per capita figure to assess relative living standards because it takes into account a nation's cost of living when making comparisons.

10. "The World's Biggest Economy," *Economist,* December 18, 2010, p. 145.

11. *The Economist Intelligence Unit,* based on data from the International Monetary Fund (2012).

12. Best Global Brands, 2013, Interbrand, 2014, http://www.interbrand.com/en/best-global-brands/2013/Best-Global-Brands-2013.aspx.

13. The Center for Arms Control and Non-Proliferation, 2013, http://www.armscontrolcenter.org.

14. "Military Spending," *The Economist* (June 8, 2011) online at www.economist.com/blogs/dailychart/2011/06/military-spending.

15. Stockholm International Peace Research Institute, "Nuclear Forces Development, 2013, http://www.sipri.org/research/armaments/nbc/nuclear.

16. "Outgunned," *Economist,* November 27, 2013, http://www.economist.com/blogs/graphicdetail/2013/11/daily-chart-15.

17. Chalmers Johnson, *The Sorrows of Empire: Militarism, Secrecy, and the End of the Republic* (New York: Metropolitan Books, 2004). See also Glenn Kessler, "The Truth Behind the Rhetoric," *Fact Checker* (blog), *Washington Post,* February 9, 2012, http://www.washingtonpost.com/fact-checker.

18. "The Hobbled Hegemon," *Economist,* June 30, 2007, pp. 29–32; David Lague, "Chinese Submarine Fleet Is Growing, Analysts Say," *New York Times,* February 25, 2008; Drew

Thompson, "China's Military," *Foreign Policy* (March/April 2010), pp. 86–90; Gideon Rachman, "This Time It's for Real," *Foreign Policy* (January/February 2011), pp. 59–63; and Siobhan Gorman, "U.S. Probe Ties Chinese Cyberspying to Military," *New York Times*, December 12, 2011.

19. David E. Sanger, "U.S. Blames China's Military Directly for Cyberattacks," *New York Times,* May 6, 2013.

20. Michael R. Gordon, "U.S. Army Shifts Focus to Nation-Building," *International Herald Tribune,* February 8, 2008, p. 1.

21. U.S. Department of Defense, "Background Briefing on Air-Sea Battle," news release, November 9, 2011.

22. Laura Meckler, "U.S. to Build Up Military in Australia," *Wall Street Journal*, November 10, 2011; and Jackie Calmes, "A U.S. Marine Base for Australia Irritates China," *New York Times*, November 16, 2011.

23. For definitions of the different forms of power in international affairs, see Joseph S. Nye, "Hard, Soft and Smart Power," in *The Oxford Handbook of Modern Diplomacy,* eds. Andrew F. Cooper, Jorge Heine, and Ramesh Thakur (New York: Oxford University Press, 2013).

24. Joseph S. Nye Jr., *Soft Power: The Means to Success in World Politics* (New York: Public Affairs Press, 2005).

25. Ibid.; and Thomas L. Friedman, *The Lexus and the Olive Tree* (New York: Farrar, Straus, Giroux, 1999).

26. "Soft Power Survey 2013," *Monocle,* 2014, http://monocle .com/film/affairs/soft-power-survey-2013.

27. Pew Research Center for the People & the Press, "War with Iraq Further Divides Global Publics," Pew Research Center, June 3, 2003; Pew Research Center for the People & the Press, "A Year After Iraq War: Mistrust of America in Europe Ever Higher, Muslim Anger Persists," Pew Research Center, March 16, 2004, http://www.people-press.org/2004/03/16 /a-year-after-iraq-war/; and Pew Research Global Attitudes Project, "Global Unease with Major World Powers: Rising Environmental Concern in 47-Nation Survey," June 27, 2007, http://www.pewglobal.org/files/pdf/2007%20Pew%20 Global%20Attitudes%20Report%20-%20June%2027.pdf.

28. "Global Opinion: The Spread of Anti-Americanism," *Trends, 2005* (Washington, D.C.: Pew Research Center for the People & the Press, 2005), p. 106; "America's Image Slips, But Allies Share U.S. Concern Over Iran, Hamas," *Survey Report* (Washington, D.C.: Pew Research Center for the People & the Press, June 13, 2006); "The Great Divide: How Westerners and Muslims View Each Other," *Global Attitudes Project Report* (Washington, D.C.: Pew Research Center, June 22, 2006).

29. Pew Research Global Attitudes Project, "Global Unease," p. 20.

30. Pew Research Global Attitudes Project, "Obama More Popular Abroad Than at Home, Global Image of U.S. Continues to Benefit," Pew Research Center, June 17, 2010, http://www .pewglobal.org/2010/06/17/obama-more-popular-abroad -than-at-home/.

31. See "Global Indicators Database," Pew Research Center, January 2014, http://www.pewglobal.org/database.

32. See the special report on state capitalism in *The Economist,* January 21, 2012, pp. 90–124.

33. Melvyn P. Leffler, "Bush's Foreign Policy," *Foreign Policy* (September/October 2004), p. 23.

34. Robert O. Keohane and Joseph S. Nye Jr., *Power and Interdependence: World Politics in Transition* (Boston: Little, Brown, 1977); and Robert Gilpin, *The Political Economy of International Relations* (Princeton, NJ: Princeton University Press, 1987).

35. Michael Mandelbaum, *The Case for Goliath* (New York: Public Affairs, 2005); Niall Ferguson, *Colossus: The Rise and Fall of the American Empire* (New York: Penguin Press, 2004); and William E. Odom and Robert Dujarric, *America's Inadvertent Empire* (New Haven: Yale University Press, 2004). See also Robert Gilpin, *The Challenge of Global Capitalism: The World Economy in the 21st Century* (Princeton, NJ: Princeton University Press, 2000).

36. "American Primacy: Being in Charge Is Hard Work, But It Has Its Perks," *Economist,* November 23, 2013, p. 23.

37. John Lewis Gaddis, "A Grand Strategy," *Foreign Policy* (November/December 2002), pp. 50–57; and Ivo H. Daalder and James M. Lindsay, *America Unbound: The Bush Revolution in Foreign Policy* (Washington, DC: Brookings Institution Press, 2003).

38. Kagan, *World America Made.*

39. Zbigniew Brzezinski, *The Choice: Global Domination or Global Leadership* (New York: Basic Books, 2004); Al Gore, *The Path to Survival* (New York: Rodale Books, 2008); and Fareed Zakaria, *The Post-American World* (New York: Norton, 2008).

40. Brian Knowlton, "Gates Calls European Mood a Danger to Peace," *New York Times,* February 23, 2010.

41. Zakaria, *Post-American World.*

42. Robert S. Norris and Hans M. Kristensen, "Global Nuclear Stockpiles, 1945–2006," *Bulletin of the Atomic Scientists* 62, no. 4 (July/August 2006), pp. 64–66.

43. "Nuclear North Korea," *Economist,* October 26, 2013, pp. 27–30.

44. Samuel P. Huntington, "The Clash of Civilizations," *Foreign Affairs* 72 (1993), pp. 22–49. See also Martin Jacques, *When China Rules the World: The End of the Western World and the Birth of a New Order* (New York: Penguin Press, 2009).

45. Tabassum Zakaria, "U.S. Blames China, Russia for Cyber Espionage," *Reuters,* November 3, 2011. See also Sanger, "U.S. Directly Blames China's Military."

46. Robert D. Kaplan, "The South China Sea Is the Future of Conflict," *Foreign Policy* (February 2, 2012), pp. 34–36.

47. "America in the Asia-Pacific: America Reaches a Pivot Point in Asia," *Economist,* November 19, 2011, p. 39.

48. Greg Jaffe, "U.S. Model for Future War Fans Tensions with China and Inside the Pentagon," *Washington Post,* August 1, 2012, http://www.washingtonpost.com/world/national -security/us-model-for-a-future-war-fans-tensions-with-china -and-inside-pentagon/2012/08/01/gJQAC6F8PX_story.html.

49. *Arab Human Development Report 2009* (New York: United Nations, 2009).

50. Shibley Telhami, "The 2011 Public Opinion Poll of Jewish and Arab Citizens of Israel," Brookings Institution, March 7, 2012, http://www.brookings.edu/research/reports /2011/12/01-israel-poll-telhami; and Zogby Research Services, "ZRS Releases 2013 Israel/Palestine Poll," news release, January 30, 2014, http://www.zogbyresearchservices .com/blog/2014/1/30/israel-and-palestine-20-years-after-oslo.

51. Brad Plumer, "How the Oil Boom Could Change U.S. Foreign Policy," *Wonkblog, Washington Post,* January 16, 2014, http://www.washingtonpost.com/blogs/wonkblog /wp/2014/01/16.

52. See "Somewhere Over the Rainbow," *Economist,* January 26, 2008, pp. 27–29; "Liberty's Great Advance," *Economist,* June 28, 2003, pp. 5–9; Jagdish Bhagwati, *In Defense of Globalization* (New York: Oxford University Press, 2004); Jagdish Bhagwati and Marvin H. Kosters, eds., *Trade and Wages: Leveling Down Wages?* (Washington, DC: AEI Press, 1994); Martin Wolf, *Why Globalization Works* (New Haven, CT: Yale University Press, 2004); and Michael Veseth, *Globaloney: Unraveling the Myths of Globalization* (Lanham, MD: Rowman and Littlefield, 2005). Dani Rodrik, among others, disagrees. See his *Has Globalization Gone Too Far?* (Washington, DC: The Institute of International Economics, 1997). See also E. Stiglitz, *Globalization and Its Discontents* (New York: Norton, 2003).

53. "Economists Rethink Free Trade," *Businessweek,* February 11, 2008, pp. 32–34.

54. Office of Management and Budget, *Budget of the United States Government, Fiscal Year 2014* (Washington, DC: Office of Management and Budget, 2014).

55. Organization for Economic Cooperation and Development, "Statistical Reporting by the Bill and Melinda Gates Foundation to the OECD," April 2011.

56. For a review of the key criticism of development aid to poor countries see William J. Baumol, Robert E. Litan, and Carl J. Schramm, *Good Capitalism, Bad Capitalism, and the Economics of Growth and Prosperity* (New Haven, CT: Yale University Press, 2007), ch. 6; William Easterly, *The Elusive Quest for Growth: Economists' Adventures and Misadventures in the Tropics* (Cambridge, MA: MIT Press, 2001).

57. Pew Research Center for the People & the Press, "Deficit Reduction Declines as Policy Priority," survey report, Pew Research Center, January 2014, http://www .people-press.org/files/legacy-pdf /01-27-14%20Policy%20Priorities%20Release%202.pdf.

58. Matthew Crenson and Benjamin Ginsberg, *Presidential Power: Unchecked and Unbalanced* (New York: Norton, 2007).

59. On the gap in outlooks between American leaders and the American public on issues of foreign and national security policies, see Page with Bouton, *Foreign Policy Disconnect*.

# CREDITS

# INDEX

# C

# F

**H**

Hussein, Saddam, 116, 152, 174, 375, 570
Hyper-competition, 101–103
    lobbying efforts and, 197

# I

IBM, 103
Ideological bias, 173-174
Ideological interest groups, 191, 195
Ideological parties, 254
Ideology. *See* Political ideology
Illegal immigration, 61
    Arizona law on, 65, 143
    Tea Party and, 90
    undocumented immigrants movement, 229–230, 236
Immigrants/immigration
    nativist views toward, 90
    political importance of, 90–91
    public opinion regarding, 90
    state laws on, 77
    trends in, 88–91
    value-added, 90
    voting blocs of, 91
Impeachment
    of federal judges, 431
    of President Bill Clinton, 148, 240, 257, 267, 322, 353, 380
*In Cold Blood* (Capote), 444
Income
    Congressional membership and, 325–326
    inequality in, 95–98
    median household, 93–94
    middle class, 97
    party identification and, 124
    voter turnout and, 291–292
Incumbency factor, in congressional elections, 332–335
Incumbents, 300–301
    money in congressional elections and, 331, 332
Independent executive agencies, 399
Independent regulatory commissions, 399
Independent Television News (ITN), 164
Independent voters, 270, 271, 272–273
India
    conflict with Pakistan, 586
    income inequality in, 101
    popular rule in, 6
    population of, 87–88
    productivity in, 101
    role in global economy, 572
Indiana, right-to-work law in, 192
Indian subcontinent, 586
Individualism, 105–106
Individual rights
    majority rule and, 13–14
    Supreme Court on, 445
Individuals, campaign contributions from, 305, 306
Industrialization, 91
Inequality, 95–98
    access, 207
    income, 99–100, 101
    representational, 204–205
    resource, 205–207
Inflation, 528, 529
*In forma pauperis*, 439
Information, availability of political, 9
Infotainment, 166, 175–176
Infrastructure, government and, 530–531, 532
Initiative process, 7
Initiatives, 289
Innovation, states and, 70, 78
Inside game of lobbying, 198–201
Inspectors general, 414
Instapaper, 159

Institutional presidency, 376
Integration, of public schools, 238
Intellectual property rights, 589
Intelligence Advisory Board, 378
Intelligence agencies, 596
Intelligent design, 477
Interest groups. *See also* Political action committees (PACs); *specific groups*
    access inequality and, 207
    advocacy group, 195
    bureaucracy and, 415
    business, 190, 191
    campaigns and, 202, 204
    corporate power and, 207–212
    democracy and, 188–189, 213–214
    disturbance theory and, 197–198
    explanation of, 188, 190–195
    government entities, 191, 195, 197
    grassroots mobilization by, 201
    ideological and cause, 191, 195
    influence on public opinion, 146
    Internet sources on, 217
    labor, 191–193
    lobbying function of, 198–204 (*See also* Lobbying)
    nonprofit sector, 191, 195
    political knowledge and, 135
    politics of factions and, 188–189, 212–213
    private, 190–193
    professions, 190–191
    public, 190, 191, 195
    public opinion shaping and, 202
    reasons for, 195–198
    representational inequalities and, 204–205
    resource inequalities and, 205–207
    social movements and, 222
    Supreme Court and, 452–453
Intermediate scrutiny, 513–514
Internal Revenue Service (IRS), 307, 414
International Atomic Energy Agency inspections, 583
International Monetary Fund (IMF), 229, 570, 580, 589
Internet
    blogs, 21, 157, 161, 169
    campaign fund-raising via, 297
    global production and, 86
    government surveillance on use of, 458
    news media and, 156–160
    offensive media and, 472–473
    polling and, 121
    presidents and use of, 383
    representative democracy and, 7
    timeline of, 158
Internet sources
    on bureaucracy, 423
    on civil liberties, 493
    on civil rights, 522–523
    on Congress, 357
    on the Constitution, 51
    on corporations, 217
    on economic policy, 565
    on elections, 317
    on federalism, 83
    on foreign policy, 602
    on government and politics, 21
    on government statistics, 113
    on interest groups, 217
    on the judicial system, 457
    on news media, 182
    on political parties, 275
    on presidency, 389
    on public opinion, 150
    on safety net programs, 565
    on social movements, 245
    on voting, 317
Internment of Japanese Americans, 375, 446

# N

**689**

# T

# U

# V

## Y

## Z

# TEST YOURSELF ANSWERS

| 1 | 2 | 3 | 4 | 5 | 6 | 7 | 8 | 9 |
|---|---|---|---|---|---|---|---|---|
| 1. b | 1. d | 1. e | 1. e | 1. a | 1. d | 1. c | 1. d | 1. b |
| 2. a | 2. d | 2. d | 2. b | 2. e | 2. e | 2. e | 2. c | 2. a |
| 3. b | 3. d | 3. F | 3. d | 3. a | 3. c | 3. a | 3. c | 3. d |
|      | 4. c | 4. b | 4. b | 4. d | 4. a | 4. b | 4. b |      |
|      | 5. c | 5. c |      | 5. b |      | 5. d | 5. e |      |
|      | 6. a | 6. a |      |      |      | 6. b | 6. c |      |
|      | 7. b | 7. T |      |      |      |      |      |      |
|      |      | 8. d |      |      |      |      |      |      |
|      |      | 9. T |      |      |      |      |      |      |
|      |      | 10. a |     |      |      |      |      |      |

| 10 | 11 | 12 | 13 | 14 | 15 | 16 | 17 | 18 |
|----|----|----|----|----|----|----|----|----|
| 1. c | 1. b | 1. e | 1. d | 1. c | 1. d | 1. c | 1. e | 1. d |
| 2. d | 2. b | 2. c | 2. a | 2. d | 2. b | 2. e | 2. d | 2. c |
| 3. b | 3. d | 3. a | 3. c | 3. c | 3. d | 3. a | 3. c | 3. e |
| 4. e | 4. a | 4. b | 4. b | 4. d | 4. a | 4. c | 4. b | 4. b |
| 5. a | 5. e | 5. d | 5. e | 5. a |      |      | 5. a |      |
| 6. c |      |      | 6. b | 6. e |      |      | 6. e |      |
|      |      |      |      |      |      |      | 7. c |      |
|      |      |      |      |      |      |      | 8. c |      |
|      |      |      |      |      |      |      | 9. d |      |